UNITED STATES HISTORY

FOURTH EDITION ★ ★ ★ ★ ★

TIMOTHY KEESEE

MARK SIDWELL

bju press®

Greenville, South Carolina

Note: The fact that materials produced by other publishers may be referred to in this volume does not constitute an endorsement of the content or theological position of materials produced by such publishers. Any references and ancillary materials are listed as an aid to the student or the teacher and in an attempt to maintain the accepted academic standards of the publishing industry.

UNITED STATES HISTORY
Fourth Edition

Timothy Keesee, EdD
Mark Sidwell, PhD

Contributing Authors
    Dennis Bollinger, PhD
    Dennis Peterson, MS

Consultant
    Carl Abrams, PhD

Editors
    Manda Kalagayan
    Grace Zockoll

Bible Integration
    Brian Collins, PhD
    Bryan Smith, PhD

Cover
    Drew Fields
    Elly Kalagayan
    Dave Schuppert

Book Design
    Michael Asire

Page Layout
    Ealia Padreganda

Project Manager
    Dan Berger

Permissions
    Sylvia Gass
    Brenda Hansen
    Joyce Landis
    Holly Nelson

Illustration
    Preston Gravely, Jr.
    Del Thompson

Photograph credits appear on pages 655–58.

Excerpt from "Happy Birthday, Adam Smith!" The author, Lawrence W. Reed, was president of the Mackinac Center for Public Policy in Michigan when this article was first published by the Center in 2006. He now serves as President of the Foundation for Economic Education in Irvington, New York. Reprint permission granted by the Mackinac Center for Public Policy. (p. 4)

HAPPY DAYS ARE HERE AGAIN Words and Music by JACK YELLEN and MILTON AGER. Copyright © 1929 (Renewed) WB MUSIC CORP. All Rights Reserved. Used By Permission. (p. 462)

Handcrafted.

BJU Press employs a team of experienced writers and artists whose best work goes into every book we produce. Because of our emphasis on quality, our textbooks are the top choice in Christian education. Each book is designed to give your student a learning experience that is enjoyable, academically excellent, and biblically sound.

Features of the Book

Unit openers offer a glimpse of life during the period covered by the unit, including a timeline of major events and art objects symbolizing events or inventions from the period.

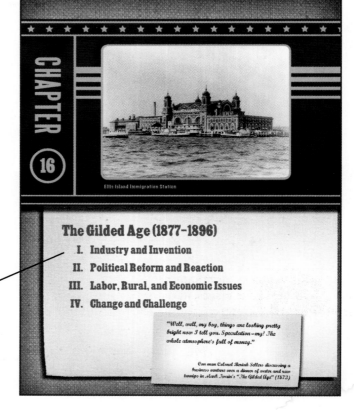

The chapter outline lists the major topics that will be covered.

Chapter 26

The bullet had stopped an inch from his heart. For the man and the times, it was one critical, providential inch. **Ronald Reagan**, looking up from the gurney into the worried faces of the physicians, smiled weakly and said, "Please tell me you're Republicans." Their faces brightened. "Mr. President, today we're all Republicans," they replied.

Reagan survived the March 1981 assassination attempt. His resilience and pluck symbolized much of the national spirit that reawakened during the succeeding decade.

The Reagan Magic

After a decade of Vietnam, Watergate, Iran, and national "malaise," Ronald Reagan revived hope, restored pride, and put new polish on patriotism. During his years in office, Reagan was a kind of commander in chief of the American spirit, marshalling national emotion with a skill that few leaders have been able to master. When Reagan came to Washington, many critics dismissed him as a has-been, B-grade actor clearly out of his element in the rough-and-tumble national scene and the world of politics. But the critics underestimated both Reagan and the American people. Someone said that Reagan was "simply saturated in the American identity." His talents were not those of an administrator nor of an economist; they were that unquantifiable quality called leadership. When Reagan left office in 1989, Americans were once again proud to be Americans, and they once again believed that America could—and would—achieve great things.

I. The Reagan Revolution

The Reagan years marked a clear shift in the nation's leadership, policies, and attitudes. Ronald Reagan projected an image of confident leadership, restoring public faith in the White House. Many Americans, tired of Carter's malaise, welcomed the new president's strong presence and inspiring rhetoric.

Yet Re... House; he... Reagan hi... ideas beca...

Confusion reigns as police and Secret Service agents respond to the attempt on Reagan's life. A Secret Service agent has just shoved Reagan to safety inside the limousine, which is about to race to the hospital.

The **Chapter Review** asks students about terms, people, places, and concepts to help them prepare for the test.

Amazing **color photographs and artwork** throughout help the students "see" the sites, people, and events discussed in the text.

People, Places, and Things to Remember

robber barons
Cornelius Vanderbilt
Andrew Carnegie
vertical integration
John D. Rockefeller
horizontal integration
trust
"New South"
John Pierpont Morgan
United States Steel Corporation
Alexander Graham Bell
Thomas Alva Edison
Roscoe Conkling
"Stalwarts"
"Half-breeds"
James A. Garfield
Chester A. Arthur
Pendleton Act
Civil Service Commission
Grover Cleveland
Interstate Commerce Act
Benjamin Harrison
Sherman Antitrust Act
McKinley Tariff
Panic of '93
Knights of Labor
American Federation of Labor
Samuel Gompers
Haymarket Riot
Homestead Strike
Eugene V. Debs
Pullman Strike
injunction
socialism
Grange
Farmers' Alliance
Populist Party
free silver
William McKinley
William Jennings Bryan
New Immigration
Charles Darwin
Darwinism
Jim Crow laws
segregation
Plessy v. Ferguson
Booker T. Washington
W.E.B. Du Bois
Mark Twain
realism
naturalism
Stephen Crane
Jack London
Horatio Alger
urban evangelism
Dwight L. Moody
Ira Sankey
Sam Jones

Chapter Review 16

Making Connections

1. With which "captain of industry" do we associate oil refining? steel production? the "New South"?

2. What crime in 1881 helped promote civil service reform by the passage of the Pendleton Act?

3. Give three reasons why many Americans opposed the "New Immigration" of the late nineteenth and early twentieth centuries.

4. What was the most widespread method of meeting the challenges of the city with the gospel?

Developing History Skills

1. Explain the difference between vertical integration and horizontal integration.

2. Review the discussions of the spoils system in Chapter 10 and in this chapter. Then list at least one advantage and one disadvantage of the spoils system. Do you think the system is good or bad?

Critical Thinking

1. Was federal regulation of the railroads, such as the Interstate Commerce Act, necessary? Why or why not?

2. Read Matthew 6:19–21, 24–34. What do those passages teach the Christian concerning his reaction to materialism?

Living as a Christian Citizen

1. Imagine that you are a Christian businessman in the late nineteenth century. Write out a series of biblical principles that will guide you in your business.

2. The opportunity for leisure time has only grown since the nineteenth century. What should a Christian think about leisure time, and how should he use it?

Section quizzes help the students remember what they have learned so far.

Margin info boxes offer intriguing bits of extra information.

Terms in bold type draw attention to important facts, ideas, people, or definitions.

In Moody's campaigns alone, millions of people heard the gospel and tens of thousands professed salvation through Christ. It is difficult to measure what impact those conversions had on American society, but it became clear in the 1890s and 1900s that the urban revivals gave at least a push to reform efforts such as Prohibition. For Moody and the urban evangelists, however, the salvation of the lost was clearly the most important result. Their motto was best summarized in the title of a gospel song—"Rescue the Perishing." As Moody said on one occasion, "I look upon this world as a wrecked vessel. God has given me a lifeboat and said to me, 'Moody, save all you can.'"

At the beginning of the nineteenth century, Methodist circuit riders and frontier camp meetings had been on the leading edge of American Christianity. By Moody's day, however, congregations had moved from brush arbors to big auditoriums. The nation now bridged two oceans, and half the country had moved to the city. As the twentieth century dawned, more change and new challenges lay ahead.

Section Quiz

1. List at least two advantages and two disadvantages of living in the city in the late 1800s.
2. What is the major difference between a traditional hymn and a gospel song?
3. Who was the most prolific hymn writer of the late nineteenth century?
★ Explain the ultimate reason for the success of the Moody campaigns.

Fanny Crosby

The most prolific hymn writer in history was Fanny Crosby. Blinded by an incompetent doctor when she was only six months old, Fanny spent most of her life in darkness. She refused to be bitter, however, and found an outlet for her talents in writing poetry.

Christian musician William Bradbury persuaded Fanny to write the words for songs. Popularized by the Moody-Sankey campaigns, her songs (including "Pass Me Not, O Gentle Saviour," "Jesus Is Calling," "Rescue the Perishing," "Blessed Assurance," "All the Way My Saviour Leads Me," "To God Be the Glory," and "Praise Him! Praise Him!") soon filled the churches of America and Great Britain.

She was so prolific that music publishers asked her to write some songs under pseudonyms so that people would not think that *all* of their songs were by her. (She used at least ninety-four pseudonyms!) Her inspiration might come from a passing thought or an overheard comment. She reportedly wrote "Pass Me Not, O Gentle Saviour," for example, after hearing someone in a rescue mission pray, "Savior, do not pass me by." Crosby's life spanned nearly a century (1820–1915), during which she wrote hundreds of verses, not for wealth or fame but from love and devotion to Christ.

distinctions. Ordering from a *Sears and Roebuck Catalog*, men and women of even modest means could dress in style.

Communications

Industrialization also created a communications revolution during the Gilded Age. The growth of businesses across the nation resulted in increased correspondence and more sophisticated record keeping. The invention of the typewriter (1867) and an improved system of shorthand (1888) met the new demands of the business world. The development of cheap paper from wood pulp and the invention of continuous action roller presses resulted in the birth of mass media. Inexpensive newspapers, magazines, and books became available for an increasingly literate and sophisticated society.

The crowning communications achievement of the time came in 1876 with the invention of the telephone by **Alexander Graham Bell**. Bell was a Scottish immigrant who arrived in the United States at the age of twenty-four to teach speech to the deaf. An innovative thinker who combined his interest in sound with his propensity for experimentation, Bell struggled for three years with the idea that he could "make iron talk." On March 10, 1876, he transmitted his first message over wire, calling an assistant in another room of his house: "Mr. Watson, come here, I want you." People have been answering phone calls ever since.

The Father of "Ma Bell"

After long and numerous legal battles to defend his patents on the telephone and various long-distance improvements, Bell and his associates formed American Telephone and Telegraph Company in 1885. By 1900, AT&T had a monopoly on the country's phone service.

Thomas Edison in his laboratory, 1888

Thought-Provoking Edison Quotations

"If we all did the things we are capable of doing, we would literally astound ourselves."

"Opportunity is missed by most people because it is dressed in overalls and looks like work."

"To invent, you need a good imagination and a pile of junk."

"We don't know a millionth of one percent about anything."

"I find my greatest pleasure, and so my reward, in the work that precedes what the world calls success."

"The three great essentials to achieve anything worthwhile are: Hard work, Stick-to-itiveness, and Common sense."

"Your worth consists in what you are and not in what you have."

"What you are will show in what you do."

"Genius is one percent inspiration and ninety-nine percent perspiration."

Electricity

America's most prolific inventor was **Thomas Alva Edison**. Although he had little formal education, Edison had a knack for new ideas and a thirst for discovery. He established an "invention factory" at Menlo Park, New Jersey, that was the forerunner of today's industrial research laboratories.

Edison was responsible for more than a thousand inventions during his lifetime, but the most influential ones were the phonograph, the motion-picture projector, and the incandescent light bulb. On September 4, 1882, after years of experimentation in developing the light bulb and the power system that could make indoor lighting practical, Edison flipped a switch that lit up New York's financial district. A new age was born in the eerie glow on Wall Street.

The contributions of George Westinghouse and Hungarian immigrant Nikola Tesla in devising alternating current generators and

American Troops in France—World War I

Key
— Armistice Line
— Front Line 1918
---- Farthest German Advance (1918)
→ American Thrusts

Maps, charts, and diagrams help the students visualize geographic locations and information.

Section Quiz

1. What German decision caused Wilson to break diplomatic relations with Germany?
2. Name two methods that Americans on the home front used to raise food and money for the war effort.
3. What conditions on the eastern front in early 1918 made the entry of the United States crucial to the Allies?
4. What World War I offensive was the largest and one of the costliest military campaigns in American history up to that time?
★ How great was the influence of U.S. troops on the outcome of the war?

Prominently waving an American flag, an exuberant crowd in Paris celebrates the Armistice.

III. Isolation

With their lines collapsing, their leadership fleeing, and their people starving, the Germans asked for an armistice, or truce, in hopes of getting the best peace terms possible—peace according to Wilson's Fourteen Points. After the Armistice, though, hopes for a favorable settlement proved empty. The German people would not be the only ones disappointed by the results of what one writer referred to as "The Great War and the Petty Peace."

Treaty of Versailles

No single treaty ended the war, although the Treaty of Versailles generally receives the most attention. For example, the Austrians signed the Treaty of St. Germain, and the Ottomans signed the Treaty of Sèvres.

Wilson as Diplomat

Just one week after the Armistice was signed, Wilson announced that he would personally lead the peace delegation to meet at Versailles near Paris. Wilson's decision drew immediate fire from his critics, who charged that by personally negotiating the treaty the president would be more susceptible to public pressures and

Treaty of Sèvres—Sowing the Seeds of Modern Islamic Terroris...

The Treaty of Sèvres b... toman Empire and fo... perhaps also beginni... ity toward the West t...

General feature boxes provide a deeper look at people, events, or concepts mentioned in the text.

Four Aces

Both sides in World War I glamorized the bravery of a new breed of warrior—the fighter pilot. "Flyboys" seemed to embody the charm, chivalry, and daring of warfare that were lacking in the muddy carnage of trench warfare. Most famous were the "aces," those who scored at least five "kills" (enemy planes shot down). Following are descriptions of the four major powers' top aces.

Manfred von Richthofen. Better known as the Red Baron because of his scarlet red triplane (a three-wing Fokker Dr 1), von Richthofen was the most successful ace in the war, scoring eighty kills. On April 8, 1918, he scored his eightieth kill. The next day, he was mortally wounded, allegedly shot by a Canadian soldier on the ground.

Paul-René Fonck. Fonck was France's premier ace, with seventy-five kills. He embodied the jaunty, cocky, almost arrogant attitude that many people associated with the aces. Fonck twice shot down six enemy planes in one day and once brought down three planes in ten seconds. Fonck survived the war and later, fittingly, became an exhibition pilot.

Edward "Mick" Mannock. The chief British ace (seventy-three kills) was "Mick" Mannock, an altogether different kind of character—moody and restless. He was blind in one eye, but he practiced his gunnery constantly to overcome his handicap. He was not a carefree "knight of the air." He took a grim delight in shooting down Germans, but he went to his quarters and wept when one of his mates was shot down. Mannock suffered from a fear of fire and was tormented by dreams of being trapped in a burning plane. Sadly, his plane was hit by antiaircraft fire in 1918, and he died in a fiery crash.

Eddie Rickenbacker. America's "ace of aces," Rickenbacker scored twenty-six kills. He was a race-car driver before the war and once held the world land-speed record. He combined his knowledge of engines with his personal bravery to become America's leading pilot. Perhaps his most famous exploit was a solo attack on seven German planes. He downed two of them and then escaped from the others unharmed. He won the Medal of Honor for his exploits.

During World War II, he was a military consultant. Once, the B-17 in which he was flying with a secret message to General McArthur crashed at sea. He took command of the situation and helped the crewmen survive against amazing odds for twenty-four days. Using Psalm 46, he encouraged them to turn to Christ. He and all but one of the crewmen were rescued. In later years, he was first president and then chairman of Eastern Airlines. He also spoke out against the "creeping socialism" he saw infesting the American government.

American ace Captain Eddie Rickenbacker

Dark Clouds Over the Peace

One of the people who felt betrayed by the truce and was still willing to fight to the death for the fatherland was a twenty-nine-year-old German corporal named Adolf Hitler. His dark mind burned with dreams of revenge. Of course, none of that was apparent on Armistice Day, only jubilation that the fighting was over.

killed in action, but the effort turned the tide. In October, the German leadership began to negotiate for peace along the lines of Wilson's Fourteen Points. By early November, the kaiser fled into exile; the German lines collapsed. On November 11, 1918—at the eleventh hour of the eleventh day of the eleventh month—the **Armistice** was signed. The Great War was over.

The French commander Ferdinand Foch (FAHSH) recalled the surrender signing ceremony: "I saw Erzberger [head of the German delegation] brandish his pen and grind his teeth. I was then glad that I had exerted my will . . . for the business was settled." Hardly. The next generation would add an enlarged second edition to the volume begun in 1914.

PRONUNCIATION GUIDE X

Unit I: Horizons

CHAPTER 1: NEW AND OLD WORLDS MEET 2

CHAPTER 2: THIRTEEN COLONIES 24

CHAPTER 3: COLONIAL LIFE 44

CHAPTER 4: RELIGION IN THE AMERICAN COLONIES 61

Unit II: Forge

CHAPTER 5: THE RISING STORM (1689-1770) 84

CHAPTER 6: INDEPENDENCE (1770-1783) 104

CHAPTER 7: THE CRITICAL PERIOD (1781-1789) 132

CHAPTER 8: THE FEDERALIST YEARS (1789-1801) 151

Unit III: Nation

CHAPTER 9: THE JEFFERSONIAN ERA (1801-1825) 170

CHAPTER 10: THE AGE OF JACKSON (1820-1840) 191

CHAPTER 11: THE GROWTH OF AMERICAN SOCIETY (1789-1861) 211

CHAPTER 12: MANIFEST DESTINY (1840-1848) 238

Unit IV: Crisis

CHAPTER 13: A HOUSE DIVIDING (1848-1861) 258

CHAPTER 14: WAR BETWEEN THE STATES (1861-1865) 280

CHAPTER 15: RECONSTRUCTION (1865-1877) 311

Unit V: Quest

CHAPTER 16: THE GILDED AGE (1877–1896) 332

CHAPTER 17: AMERICA EXPANDS (1850–1900) 361

CHAPTER 18: THE PROGRESSIVE ERA (1900–1920) 385

CHAPTER 19: THE GREAT WAR (1913–1920) 411

Unit VI: Leadership

CHAPTER 20: THE TWENTIES (1920–1929) 432

CHAPTER 21: THE THIRTIES (1929–1939) 455

CHAPTER 22: THE WORLD AT WAR (1939–1945) 481

Unit VII: Challenge

CHAPTER 23: THE POSTWAR ERA (1945–1963) 512

CHAPTER 24: THE SHATTERED SOCIETY (1963–1973) 534

CHAPTER 25: A NATION ADRIFT (1973–1980) 554

CHAPTER 26: RESURGENCE (1981–1992) 572

CHAPTER 27: NEW CHALLENGES (1993–2011) 591

APPENDIXES 612

INDEX 641

PHOTO CREDITS 655

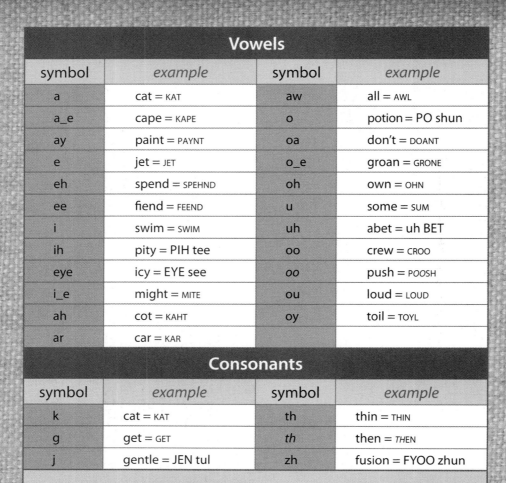

Vowels

symbol	example	symbol	example
a	cat = KAT	aw	all = AWL
a_e	cape = KAPE	o	potion = PO shun
ay	paint = PAYNT	oa	don't = DOANT
e	jet = JET	o_e	groan = GRONE
eh	spend = SPEHND	oh	own = OHN
ee	fiend = FEEND	u	some = SUM
i	swim = SWIM	uh	abet = uh BET
ih	pity = PIH tee	oo	crew = CROO
eye	icy = EYE see	*oo*	push = *POOSH*
i_e	might = MITE	ou	loud = LOUD
ah	cot = KAHT	oy	toil = TOYL
ar	car = KAR		

Consonants

symbol	example	symbol	example
k	cat = KAT	th	thin = THIN
g	get = GET	*th*	then = *THEN*
j	gentle = JEN tul	zh	fusion = FYOO zhun

The pronunciation guide used in this text is designed to give the reader a self-evident, acceptable pronunciation for a word as he reads it from the page. For more accurate pronunciations, the reader should consult a good dictionary.

Stress: Syllables with primary stress appear in LARGE CAPITAL letters. Syllables with secondary stress and one-syllable words appear in SMALL CAPITAL letters. Unstressed syllables appear in lowercase letters. Where two or more words appear together, hyphens separate the syllables within each word. For example, the pronunciation of Omar Khayyam appears as (OH-mar kie-YAHM).

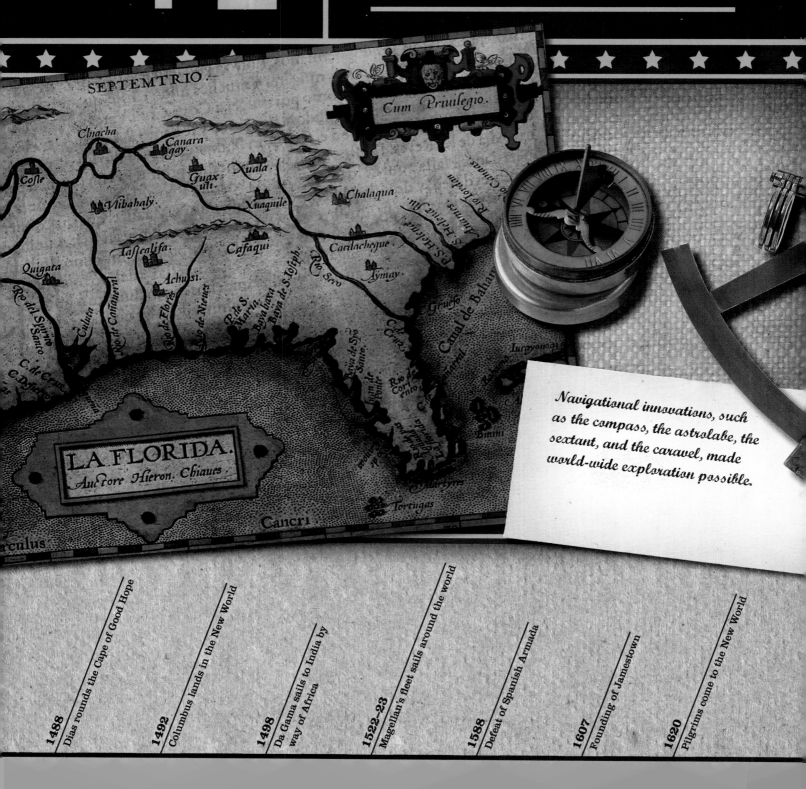

UNIT 1

HORIZONS
★
1488-1748

SEPTEMTRIO.

Cum Priuilegio.

Chiacha

Canara gay

Coſte

Guax uli.

Xuala.

Vlibahaly.

Chalaqua

Tascalifa.

Cafaqui

Carilachegue

Quigata

Achuſi.

Aymay.

Culuta

Rio del Spirito Sancto

Rio de Cañaueral

Rio de Flores

Rio de Nieues

P. de S. Maria.

Baya baya.

Baya de S.Ioſeph.

Rio Seco

Gruefo

Canal de Bahama

C. de Cruz

C. de Diente

Baya de Spo Sancto

Rio de Corriento

Bimini

LA FLORIDA.
Auctore Hieron. Chiaues.

Martyres

Tortugas

Cancri

culus

Navigational innovations, such as the compass, the astrolabe, the sextant, and the caravel, made world-wide exploration possible.

1488 Dias rounds the Cape of Good Hope

1492 Columbus lands in the New World

1498 Da Gama sails to India by way of Africa

1522-23 Magellan's fleet sails around the world

1588 Defeat of Spanish Armada

1607 Founding of Jamestown

1620 Pilgrims come to the New World

CHAPTERS

1 NEW AND OLD WORLDS MEET

2 THIRTEEN COLONIES

3 COLONIAL LIFE

4 RELIGION IN THE AMERICAN COLONIES

"The First Thanksgiving at Plymouth"
by Jennie A. Brownscombe (1914)

1630-40
Great Migration of Puritans to
Massachusetts Bay

1664
England conquers New Netherland

1689-97
King William's War

1692
Salem witch trials

1702-13
Queen Anne's War

c.1720-c.1760
The Great Awakening

1744-48
King George's War

Columbus erroneously thought he had reached the Orient when he landed on San Salvador.

New and Old Worlds Meet

I. Changes in the Old World

II. Contacts in the New World

"At two hours after midnight appeared the land. . . ."

Christopher Columbus, October 12, 1492,
Captain's Log Entry

Iron shackles clanked in the musty prison cell as huddled forms awakened. The eastern sun brightened the cell. One prisoner, gathering quill and parchments from beneath his pillow, continued his writing. In happier times he had been known as Rustichello of Pisa, a writer of romances and chivalric legends who had enjoyed modest acclaim. Now in 1296 the furies of war had cast him into prison with a living legend named **Marco Polo**.

Though a prisoner of war like Rustichello, Polo could tell the most fantastic stories. His adventures in China had spanned nearly twenty years, during which time he had been a favorite of Kublai the grand Khan of the Mongols.

Polo described mysterious Asia, a world of shimmering silks, fragrant spices, and unlimited gold. In the land of Cipango (sih PAN go; an island kingdom that would someday be called Japan), Polo had heard that gold was so common it was used for pavement.

In that prison cell, Rustichello penned the words of one of history's greatest travelers, later published under the imposing title *Description of the World*. Polo's narrative became the definitive work on the Orient for the next three centuries. Its vivid scenes enticed men to see the Orient for themselves, and this enticement prepared Europe to experience sweeping change. The Orient offered Europeans a chance to experience remarkable growth, in personal wealth as well as in the power and prestige of their homelands. Seeking this growth eventually led to the discovery of another world—a world that would make all they had known seem old.

I. Changes in the Old World

China, Innovations, and Mercantilism

Early European explorers saw China as the source of great riches and opportunities for their countries. The first peoples to take advantage of China (and the islands of South Asia called the East Indies) were the Muslims, who for decades held a virtual monopoly on all trade in the region. Soon, however, Europeans determined to get their "piece of the pie" in the Indies, and that area became the focus of exploration before the discovery of the New World.

Several innovations made it possible for the Europeans to compete with the Muslims and eventually to discover the New World. One was the development of the **compass**, which enabled sailors to know in which direction they were heading. Another invention was the **astrolabe**, which enabled them to determine their ship's latitude on the ocean.

Another important innovation was a Portuguese ship called a **caravel**. It sported two, or even three, triangular sails, making it extremely maneuverable. Armed with overwhelming cannon power and skillfully and swiftly maneuvered by their captains, the caravels enabled not only the expansion of European trade with China and the Indies but also the

The astrolabe and other new navigational instruments made it easier for explorers to sail the unknown oceans of the world more accurately.

ultimate discovery of the New World. The confrontation between Muslims and Europeans in the Indies was the second major conflict between the Muslim and the Christian European cultures. (The first confrontation was the Crusades.)

Perhaps as important as such innovations was a shift in economic thinking that occurred in Europe about the time explorations began, and it greatly spurred exploratory efforts. Monarchs in Europe were gradually shifting from the feudal, or manorial, economic thinking prevalent during the Middle Ages to a nationalistic economic system of thought known as **mercantilism**. Although that shift in thinking might have been a step *toward* free market capitalism, it most certainly was *not* capitalism or free trade.

Mercantilism was an economic system that was designed to enhance the wealth and power of a nation. It operated on two basic assumptions:

1. Mercantilists believed that a nation's wealth consisted of precious metals, especially gold. The value of a product, they thought, was determined by how much gold (or other precious metal) people were willing to give in exchange for it.

2. Mercantilists were nationalists who believed that a country could increase its wealth by increasing its surplus of gold. For one nation to increase its wealth (gold), they thought, another country had to lose it. Mercantilism saw a world of winners and losers. The monarchs' desire for gold led to numerous conflicts between and among nations, possibly accounting in large measure for the desire of France and England to separate Spain from its treasures of gold found in the New World.

Mercantilism also led to national desires to build colonial empires that would serve as both sources of riches and raw materials from which to manufacture goods and markets for those goods once they were made in the mother country. In practice, mercantilism led to the government's granting of special charters, subsidies, and bounties for some companies or individuals while it discouraged imports and encouraged exports. Mercantilists sought to achieve a "favorable balance of trade," that is, to export more than they imported, thereby collecting even more gold. It also led to the imposition of tariffs and quotas against imports, thus making foreign products more expensive than domestic products. An understanding of mercantilism is necessary for understanding both the intense competition among the major European powers and the conflict that eventually arose between the British Crown and its New World colonies.

Sugar and Spice

Marco Polo's account of China fired the imaginations of Europe's merchants and adventurers. But the overland route to China was costly and dangerous. Muslim merchants, who controlled the eastern silk and spice trade, choked the highways, prompting Western Europeans to bypass the Muslim monopoly by finding a waterway to China.

The Portuguese led the way in 1488 when **Bartolomeu Dias** (DEE ahz) sailed southward along the west coast of Africa and rounded its southern cape, which he optimistically called Good Hope. A decade later, **Vasco da Gama** (dah GAH mah) followed up Dias's discovery by sailing to India. Da Gama returned to Portugal with a cargo of spices worth sixty times the cost of his expedition.

Mercantilism in a Nutshell

"Mercantilist thinkers believed the world's wealth was a fixed pie, giving rise to endless conflict among nations. After all, if you think there's only so much and you want more, you've got to take it from someone else."

"Mercantilists were economic nationalists. They thought foreign goods were sufficiently harmful that government policy should promote exports and restrict imports. Exports were to be paid for in gold and silver, not products.

"Because they had little sympathy for self-interest, the profit motive, and the operation of prices, mercantilists wanted governments to bestow monopoly privileges on a favored few."

(The author, Lawrence W. Reed, was president of the Mackinac Center for Public Policy in Michigan when this article was first published by the Center in 2006. He now serves as President of the Foundation for Economic Education in Irvington, New York. Reprint permission granted by the Mackinac Center for Public Policy.)

Such fantastic profits signaled the end of the Muslim monopoly and the beginning of the European scramble for the spice trade. Ships laden with cinnamon, gold, ivory, and sugar would revolutionize Europe's economy, politics, and worldview.

As Portugal, Spain's neighbor, was turning the Indian Ocean into its private lake, Spaniards looked in another direction for trade with the Orient. Like most educated Europeans of the fifteenth century, the Italian-born **Christopher Columbus** believed that the world was round. Basing his calculations, or, as it turned out, his miscalculations, on the circumference estimates of the second-century Greek mathematician Ptolemy, Columbus reasoned that the shortest route to the East was west. Columbus and Ptolemy, though correct about the earth's shape, were incorrect about its size. Columbus figured that by sailing three thousand miles west, he could reach Cipango and its fabled riches. (Actually, Japan is eight thousand miles *farther* west.)

When the king of Portugal refused to underwrite a westward voyage, Columbus turned to the Spanish for help. After receiving the reluctant support of Queen Isabella, Columbus set out in early August 1492 with three ships and a fill-in-the-blank letter of greeting from the Spanish crown to the king of Cipango. The letter was to be personalized after Columbus learned the name of the distant potentate.

On the evening of October 11, Columbus wrote in his ship's log, "At ten at night the Admiral being in the stern castle, saw light . . . like a small wax candle. . . . The Admiral was certain that they were near the land." By 2:00 a.m. the light proved to be land, and though Columbus did not realize it, he had stumbled not onto an island of Cipango but onto a sliver of sand in the Bahamas. That day Columbus went ashore and named the island San Salvador (Holy Savior) in gratitude for the merciful ocean passage that God had given his expedition. Curious brown natives gathered about the strange band of pale visitors and offered gifts of parrots and raw cotton. Columbus, certain that he was on an island of the Indies in the Orient, called the people *los indios*—Indians. Many more misunderstandings between the two races would occur in the centuries to follow.

For an explorer looking for new lands, Columbus could not have been in a better location, since there are literally thousands of islands in the Caribbean archipelago. But for an explorer looking for Asian riches, Columbus could not have been in a more frustrating position. He would make three more voyages to the region in a vain search for China and Japan and would go to his grave believing he had reached the outskirts of Asia.

Other men, however, came to realize what Columbus did not—that there was a *new world* across the ocean. One of those men was **Amerigo Vespucci** (vehs POO chee), who made at least two voyages to the Caribbean and South America. One of history's interesting ironies is that in 1507 a little-known German mapmaker named Martin Waldseemüller (VAHL zee MOO ler) was so bold as to name this unnamed world not after its discoverer but *America* after Amerigo, who sailed in the wake of the great captain Columbus.

England was not idle during the race for the Orient. In 1497, the Italian explorer Giovanni Caboto—known to the English for whom he sailed as **John Cabot** (KAB uht)—reached Newfoundland in his search for a passage to China. The following year, he once again sailed west for the East, but he never returned. His fate remains a mystery; yet his initial discovery changed the course of history, for it provided the basis for England's claim to and colonization of North America.

Two continents were now added to the world map. Yet the Americas seemed more of an obstacle to sail around than a land to settle. Explorers set about finding a way to bypass it, believing riches lay just beyond the new world horizon. **Ferdinand Magellan** (muh JEHL uhn) determined that he could reach the Spice Islands of the East by sailing south around the Americas. In what would be the greatest sea voyage of all time, Magellan set out from Spain in 1519 with five ships, the largest of which was smaller than a modern tugboat. After threading his way down the coast of Brazil and Argentina, he found a passage in the wild waters of Tierra del Fuego where two oceans converge.

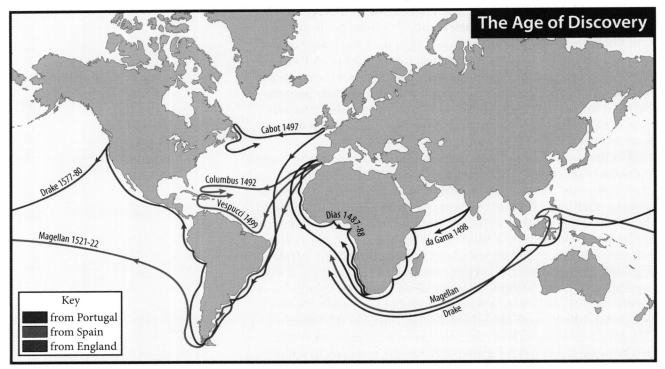

The Age of Discovery

Cabot 1497

Drake 1577-80

Columbus 1492

Vespucci 1499

Dias 1487-88

da Gama 1498

Magellan 1521-22

Magellan
Drake

Key
from Portugal
from Spain
from England

The three ships that reached the Pacific sailed through waters never before traversed by Europeans. A few years earlier, the Spanish explorer Balboa had first seen that blue expanse from a hillside in Panama, but Magellan's little fleet was now plunging through its waves. However, Asia did not lie just beyond the Americas, and as Magellan continued to pursue an ever-receding horizon, provisions ran low.

For a hundred days the crew languished on the torrid sea. The stench of foul water and death hung heavy about the ships. Gnawing hunger drove the scurvy-wracked sailors to eat leather from the ships' rigging, and rats became a prized dish. Although the ships eventually reached Guam, where the survivors were reprovisioned, it had become painfully clear that a western route to the Orient was impractical.

The ships sailed on to the Philippines, where a tribal squabble resulted in Magellan's death by poisoned arrows. Although he never lived to see it, one of his ships, the *Victoria*, reached the Spice Islands and, laden with cloves, continued the voyage westward for home. Three years after Magellan's fleet left Spain, the *Victoria* reached Seville with only eighteen of the original crew of three hundred on board. Their daring feat shook the Old World—they had sailed around the world!

Nearly five centuries later, the first circumnavigational voyage remains an incomparable achievement. Magellan had revealed the girth of the globe, yet for the time its vastness set limits on western trade routes. Increasingly, the focus would be on the Americas, a new world that offered new promise.

Religious Change

While Magellan's ships were making their global trek, a German monk named **Martin Luther** (1483-1546) was gaining the attention of all Europe. For centuries Roman Catholicism had dominated every aspect of European society. But by Luther's time the Roman Church's corruption was apparent to all. Luther stood against these corruptions, but he was different from many others who sought reform.

Luther came to realize that the root of these problems was a false view of how people could be saved from their sins. The Roman Church taught that God's grace flowed to sinners only through the Church's system of penance. Luther, however, preached that salvation was a work of God. God justified (declared to be righteous) those who trusted in Jesus' death on the cross and who called out for salvation.

Eventually, Luther and others like him formed their own churches. These churches emphasized that the Christian was free from the authority of Roman Catholicism. They also emphasized that Christians should not depend on others for their spiritual health and well being. All Christians should learn to read the Scriptures for themselves and should know how to apply God's Word to their lives.

Luther's teaching called into question the legitimacy of the Roman Church. And since the Church played a role in all aspects of European society, Luther's influence led to great changes in the culture of Europe. The movement that pressed for these changes was the **Protestant Reformation**. England, Switzerland, and parts of Germany were the places most influenced by this movement. France and Spain were the most opposed to it. As the Reformation spread across Europe, theological battle lines often became actual battle lines. Some of the rivalry between English explorers and French and Spanish explorers was motivated by a rivalry between Protestantism and Roman Catholicism. Both religious groups saw the discovery of these new lands as an opportunity to spread their influence.

As the Reformation continued, Geneva became one of its leading centers. **John Calvin** (1509-1564) was Geneva's most influential teacher. Like Luther, Calvin taught that salvation was God's work and that sinners needed simply to trust in Christ. Calvin also attempted to restructure the society of Geneva so that every part of human life experienced the renewal of the Reformation.

Believing that a solid education was the best way to produce effective leaders for church and society, Calvin and many other reformers reorganized their educational systems. They emphasized universal literacy as well as advanced education for the clergy.

Calvin and other reformers also taught that every vocation was a sacred calling. For this reason the merchant, weaver, and carpenter needed to work steadily, waste no time, and do everything in moderation. As a result, cities like Geneva enjoyed a great increase in wealth and influence. Many Protestants interpreted this growth—seen by some historians as an early success for capitalism—as God's blessing for obeying His will.

Although Calvin and other reformers emphasized that Christians should submit to their governmental leaders, Calvin did speak critically of certain kinds of government. Many reformers believed that monarchy tended toward abuse and corruption. A better form of government—one that would protect the liberty of the people—was a series of assemblies elected by the citizens. Geneva and a few other cities developed this kind of government.

Calvin's ideas proved to be very influential in Europe. In England especially, many Protestants desired not only to free themselves from the vestiges of Roman Catholicism but also to reshape their society. Geneva was seen by many as a model city—the pattern for a new world.

Section Quiz

1. Who was responsible for stirring European interest in China before the age of discovery? How did he do so?

2. How did Columbus's plan for reaching Asia differ from da Gama's?

3. What technological inventions helped sailors in their exploration and discovery of new lands?

4. What name was given to the economic system during the age of exploration and colonization whereby colonies were exploited for the benefits and wealth they could bring to the mother country?

5. What was Martin Luther's main disagreement with the Roman Catholic Church?

★ How did the teachings of men such as Luther and Calvin support the ideals of (a) freedom, (b) individualism, and (c) equality?

II. Contacts in the New World

First Peoples

While these various Europeans were discovering and exploring unknown (at least to them) oceans and lands, other non-Europeans were living in their own developed civilizations in South, Central, and North America. In South America lived the Incas. In Central America, the Mayas and the Aztecs developed civilizations. And across North America were numerous thriving groups of American Indians.

Where had they come from? In the far north, near the Arctic Circle, the massive continents of Asia and America each taper into slender fingers of land that rest just short of touching. Some historians think that sometime after the Flood, the ancestors of the American Indians entered the Western Hemisphere there. Some historians think they crossed the narrow Bering Sea in small boats or on foot over a bridge of ice. Other historians think that a land bridge, which they call **Beringia**, connected the two continents, and that the peoples perhaps simply walked over it.

The Bering Strait

However they came, those Asian immigrants moved slowly southward. Eventually, their descendants settled the entire hemisphere down to the tip of South America. When the European explorers arrived in the New World, they found it already teeming with humans living in developed civilizations. Historians estimate that as many as several million American Indians were living in North America before Columbus made his discovery.

Historians of American Indians usually group them into *tribes* (several families sharing common customs) and *culture areas* (several tribes living near each other and sharing similar customs, means of livelihood, and level of civilization). When the Europeans arrived in the New World, it was already inhabited by several major groups, each in its own culture area. For example, in the Southwest was the Pueblo civilization. In the Midwest developed first the Adena-Hopewell civilization followed by the Mississippian civilization. In the middle Atlantic region and the Northeast was the Woodlands civilization. These groups of peoples shared certain common characteristics. Yet, each of them was different from the others in many ways.

Similarities and Differences

Similarities between Indians and Europeans—Indians and Europeans shared great interest in religion, although they had very different beliefs and approaches to it. Europeans were Protestant or Catholic whereas Indian tribes practiced various animistic beliefs.

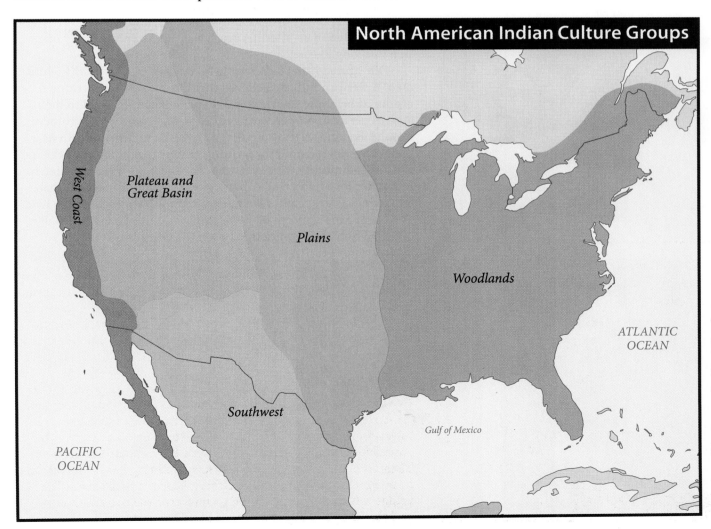

North American Indian Culture Groups

West Coast

Plateau and Great Basin

Plains

Woodlands

Southwest

PACIFIC OCEAN

ATLANTIC OCEAN

Gulf of Mexico

Indian groups differed not only from Europeans but also from each other in significant ways.

Like Europeans, many of the Indian tribes farmed, lived in villages, conducted trade with other peoples, had social organization, and fought wars among themselves. One example of the unity that these similarities produced was the fact that many whites chose to live among the Indians. Even when they could have been rescued, some whites who were captured by the Indians chose to remain with them. Also, some Indians lived with Europeans, especially if they had converted to Christianity. When the two groups lived in close proximity, certain aspects of their cultures tended to get blended.

Similarities among Indian Groups—Perhaps the most readily recognized characteristics that the various American Indian groups shared were physical. In contrast to the lighter skinned Europeans, the Indians had darker skin, hair, and eyes. Europeans categorized the natives' color as "red."

None of the Indian groups had an alphabet, so they had no written language. They passed their history and customs to the next generations by word of mouth, so storytelling skills were important to them.

They also possessed deep faith in the supernatural and shared several common beliefs about religion and life in general. All natural objects—from animals to rocks and trees—had their own spirits. Yet, the Indians believed in one "Great Spirit." They placed much emphasis on dreams and visions and actively sought them. They also had shamans, or medicine men, who they believed had supernatural powers over sickness, enemies, and harvests. They also shared a belief in an afterlife; death was not an end but only one step in a long journey.

One shared belief led directly to much conflict with the white men. American Indians believed that the land and everything it produced belonged to everyone. No person had the right to own land as personal property; therefore, no one could prevent others from using land. A tribe or village might claim certain lands as their common territory for farming or hunting, but it was held and used in community with everyone in the tribe or village. Whenever Indians from a bordering tribal region tried to encroach on that territory, warfare might result, but no one actually owned the land. The Europeans' concept of ownership was quite different, and it often led to bloody conflicts between the two groups.

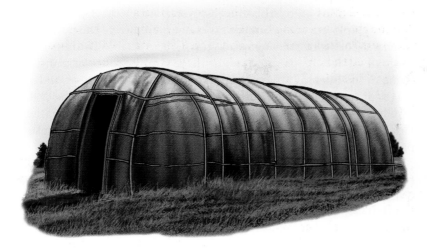

One difference among the various Indian tribes was the types of homes in which they lived.

Differences between Indians and Europeans—In addition to the obvious ethnic differences between American Indians and Europeans, there were other differences. The Europeans considered the Indians' culture primitive. Indians had minimal technology and did not use iron. Whereas the Europeans had a well-developed spoken and written language, the Indians had no written language. The architectural styles and building materials used also differed between the two groups, and Indians in North America tended to be less united than the Europeans.

Differences among Indian Groups—As alike as the American Indian groups were, they also differed in significant ways. The various American Indian groups spoke different languages. Historians estimate that as many as 2,200 different languages were being spoken by American Indians at the time whites first encountered them. Perhaps 200 or more languages were spoken in North America. About 350 languages were spoken by Mexican and Central American Indians, and more than 1,000 languages were spoken by the Caribbean and South American Indians. Communication between neighboring groups was usually accomplished by a common sign language.

Various Indian groups lived in different types of houses, depending on their geographic environment. Some lived in rectangular longhouses. Some lived in tepees. Others lived in domed wood-framed and bark- or fur-covered homes. Still others lived in baked clay, or adobe, buildings. And still others lived in caves in the sides of cliffs.

Although for some of the tribes warfare was a way of life, many tribes were peaceful, fighting only to defend themselves or their territory or to avenge attacks by enemies. Indian warfare generally involved sporadic and short-lived raids; they had few protracted battles. Perhaps the most peaceful Indians were the Hopis. More warlike tribes included the Iroquois, the Apache, and the Comanche.

The ruins at Tuzigoot National Monument in Arizona were the homes of Sinagua Indians, who lived in pueblos.

Both photos courtesy of Scott Finley.

Basic Groups of American Indians

The Pueblos—Probably the first North American Indians the Spanish explorers of the Southwest encountered were the pueblo dwellers. The word *pueblo* means "town." The **Pueblo Indians** lived in small villages made up of two or three family groups or clans. Some of the Pueblo Indians lived in caves along the rims or under ledges of canyons of the Southwest and became known as the cliff dwellers. Some of the tribes among the Pueblos were the Zuni, the Hopi, the Ute, the Paiute, the Navajo, the Apache, and the Havasupa, who lived in the bottom of the Grand Canyon.

The pueblos were independent of each other, and each town was ruled by a council of elected elders. The villages, though sometimes quite large, never developed into cities because of the scarcity of food caused by the arid conditions of the Southwest. When one of the men married, he moved in with his wife's clan, perhaps building a new room onto or above the existing adobe house. Families that had too many sons sometimes died out. Those that had many daughters grew.

Pueblo Indians were farmers, growing the "Sacred Triad"—maize (corn), squash, and beans. They also made baskets and pottery. They were basically a stationary people, but they occasionally were forced to move to ensure an adequate supply of water.

The Pueblos reached their "golden age" around AD 1000, but lack of water and frequent raids against them by the Navajos and the Apaches took a toll. A severe drought occurred from 1275 to 1310. Legend told of seven cities of gold in the area, and Spanish **conquistadores** (kohn KEES tah DOHR ays; a combination of explorer and soldier of fortune—with the emphasis on fortune) were eager to see and exploit them. But by the time Columbus made his discovery, many pueblos were falling into ruin. When Fray Marcos de Nizaq arrived in the Southwest in 1539, he found nothing but adobe villages of poor Indians. When the Spanish explorer Coronado arrived the next year, he found sixty-six pueblos. By 1700, only nineteen remained, and the population had been cut in half.

The Mound Builders—Two successive cultures developed in what is now called the Midwest—the Adena culture (1000 BC to AD 200) and the Hopewell culture (AD 500 to 1600). Their civilizations developed in villages along the Ohio River Valley and later spread eastward to the Chesapeake Bay area, New York, and New England. These peoples lived in fixed agricultural settlements where they grew squash, gourds, and sunflowers. They even grew tobacco. Their agricultural pursuits produced bountiful harvests, and that large food supply sparked population growth.

These peoples lived in large dome-shaped structures of bent saplings covered with skins or bark. They were noted for the hundreds of large burial mounds they built; hence, they were called the **Mound Builders**. In the mounds, which measured up to 30 feet high and 200 feet in circumference, they buried their dead with an elaborateness matched only by the Egyptian tombs of the pharaohs. The most famous mound visible today is the Great Serpent Mound in southern Ohio, about fifty miles east of Cincinnati. It portrays a slithering snake more than 1,300 feet long. The snake's mouth is open, apparently swallowing a small round mound. The Indians buried many artifacts in the mounds, but most of them, except for pottery and stone or iron tools, rotted in the damp soil.

Other Pueblo Indians lived under overhanging rocks, such as these at Mesa Verde, Colorado.

The Mound Builders developed an extensive, almost continent-wide trading network. They obtained copper from Indians in the Great Lakes area, seashells and shark teeth from Indians along the Atlantic and Gulf coasts, quartz and grizzly bear teeth from the Rocky Mountains, and freshwater pearls from surrounding rivers.

Eastern Woodlands Indians—Another diverse American Indian civilization developed in the Southeast and along the Atlantic coast into the Northeast. These tribes were called the **Eastern Woodlands Indians** and were probably the first Indians the English, French, Dutch, and Swedish settlers encountered in the New World. The civilization's development began around AD 700 between the areas of Memphis and St. Louis and spread quickly throughout the Southeast, especially after 1200. They tended to settle along the rich bottomlands of the Mississippi, Ohio, and Tennessee rivers and developed tight-knit agricultural communities. The women grew corn, beans, squash, and sunflowers while the men were hunters and, when necessary, warriors.

These Indians had a matriarchal society, meaning that the women held an unusual degree of power in the social structure and political decision making. They were a politically skillful people, not unorganized and uncivilized. In the Southeast, for example, the Cherokees, Chickasaws, Choctaws, Creeks, and Seminoles were known as the **Five Civilized Tribes**. Several northern tribes of Eastern Woodlands Indians (the Mohawks, Oneidas, Senecas,

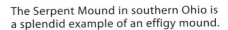

The Serpent Mound in southern Ohio is a splendid example of an effigy mound.

The Cherokees, one of the Five Civilized Tribes, lived in well-organized towns.

Frank H. McClung Museum. The University of Tennessee, Knoxville. Carlyle Urello.

Cayugas, Onondagas, and Tuscaroras) formed the League of Six Nations around 1570 when they realized, after a lot of infighting, that they would be better off cooperating rather than competing.

At various times in early American history, these tribes were either friends or enemies of the European explorers and colonists. Sometimes they helped the early settlers; other times they warred against them. Sometimes they sided with the colonists against the colonists' enemies; other times they helped those enemies. As we shall learn in later chapters, the group as a whole gradually declined over the centuries as a result of droughts, famines, European diseases (e.g., smallpox, chicken pox, and measles), infighting, wars against the colonists, enslavement, and intermarriage. The last tribes to face extinction were those in the Southeast and the Southwest, and they were instrumental in American history throughout all but the final twenty-five years of the 1800s.

Population shifts in the Southeast after the arrival of white men					
	1685	1700	1715	1730	1745
Indians	199,400	130,600	90,100	66,700	59,300
Whites	46,900	70,900	96,500	144,600	219,700
Blacks	3,300	8,700	31,400	80,600	144,600

The Spanish Century

Throughout the sixteenth century, Spain dominated the exploration and exploitation of the New World. From their Caribbean settlements on Hispaniola (begun by Christopher Columbus and his brother Bartholomew), Puerto Rico, and Cuba, the Spanish launched their conquests of the mainland. There in Mexico and Central and South America, the conquistadores discovered advanced civilizations, vast cities, and incredible treasure. Within a quarter century, the Spanish vanquished the Indian populations, amassing an empire that was virtually unrivaled in terms of both size and wealth.

Hernando Cortés was the first great conquistador. In 1519, he and his small fleet reached Mexico with strict orders from the governor of Cuba to explore the mainland coast and proceed no farther. The great Aztec king **Montezuma**, hearing of the Spanish arrival, sent emissaries offering gifts that he hoped would be picked up like door prizes by the uninvited guests on their way home. However, the enticing gleam of turquoise masks, intricate gold figurines, and massive disks of hammered gold made Cortés decide he would rather try his hand at conquest than run errands for the governor of Cuba.

To reduce the potential for mutiny against his unsanctioned mission, and knowing he would be hanged for insubordination if he were ever forced to return to Cuba, Cortés ordered his ships run aground. Proceeding inland to the Aztec capital with about four hundred soldiers, he picked up support along the way from subjugated Indian tribes who welcomed the Spaniards as deliverers from the Aztecs. Those tribes despised the Aztecs for exacting heavy tribute from them and especially for taking the best of their young warriors to offer as human sacrifices in their bloody rituals. In a daring feat of conquest, Cortés marched to the Aztec capital of Tenochtitlán (tay NAHCH tee TLAHN; modern Mexico City), where he captured Montezuma and eventually crushed the Aztec resistance.

Despite the advanced nature of a number of the Indian tribes in Central and South America, they were no match for the military superiority of the Europeans. Cortés's experiences in Mexico were indicative of the clash of cultures that would lead to European dominance in that hemisphere. At the Battle of Tlaxcala (tlah SKAHL uh) on his way to meet Montezuma, Cortés's army of four hundred was outnumbered an estimated one hundred to one; yet they were able to fight to a draw. The Tlaxcalans, equipped with spears and obsidian-bladed clubs, faced soldiers armed with muskets and artillery. Some of the Spanish soldiers were mounted on animals that the Indians had never seen—horses.

Far more devastating to the native populations than firearms were the white man's diseases, to which the Indians had little immunity. Smallpox, measles, typhus, and other contagions devastated their numbers. The Indian population dropped by an estimated 90 percent between the sixteenth and seventeenth centuries. In the West Indies, the destruction of whole Indian populations by disease created a labor shortage for the Spanish that would be forcefully remedied with the arrival of more newcomers—African slaves.

Spain did not confine its New World interests to Mexico and South America. A number of conquistadores explored the vast hinterland of North America (southeastern, southwestern, and Gulf coast regions) hoping to repeat Cortés's get-rich-quick conquest. **Francisco de Coronado**, for example, commanded an expedition that left Mexico in 1540 to explore what would later be the southwestern United States. Greedily believing the Indians' tall tales about the Seven Cities of Cibola, a fabulous land of gold and jewels, Coronado explored Arizona, New Mexico, Texas, and Kansas. That anyone in Coronado's expedition survived the four-thousand-mile trek in the extreme temperatures of the Southwest is a tribute to their courage and Coronado's leadership. His expedition did not find gold, but one of its parties did discover and explore the Grand Canyon.

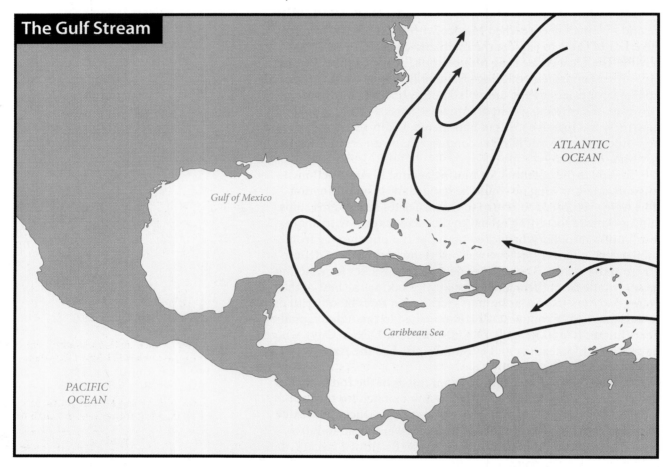

The Gulf Stream

ATLANTIC OCEAN

Gulf of Mexico

Caribbean Sea

PACIFIC OCEAN

Before the Spanish knew about what is today Florida, they had already established scores of settlements throughout the West Indies. There, and later in Central and South America, they discovered wealth, which they sent back to Spain in treasure fleets powered by the strong Gulf Stream current. Spaniards also made a number of attempts to settle the southeastern United States.

In 1513, **Juan Ponce de León** sailed northwest from Puerto Rico in search of more rumored wealth and a legendary fountain of youth. He sailed up the east coast of the Florida peninsula and landed near present-day St. Augustine, claiming the area for Spain and naming it *la Florida* ("the flowered [land]").

De León's claim went unexploited for half a century. Then, in 1565, a fleet of Spanish ships commanded by Don Pedro Menéndez sailed into the bay where the modern city of St. Augustine is located. The intention was to establish settlements in the area and drive out French Huguenots who had established a colony named

Fort Caroline near the mouth of the St. John's River to the north. Menéndez named the settlement **St. Augustine** after the Saint's Day (August 28), on which he had sighted land.

He immediately set about building a fort and amassing supplies for an assault on Fort Caroline. Before he could sail, however, French warships appeared off the coast to attack his force. But a storm suddenly arose, preventing the French ships from approaching the shore. Correctly assuming that the French had most of their fighting force from Fort Caroline aboard their warships, Menéndez marched his troops overland, surprised the small defending force, captured the fort, and executed the prisoners. Meanwhile, the storm had driven the French fleet down the coast and wrecked it.

More than one hundred years later, the Spanish began serious construction of a fort at St. Augustine. They completed it in 1695 and named it Castillo de San Marcos. For the next 105 years, it remained under Spanish control and protected the surrounding settlement of St. Augustine. Castillo measures 324 by 311 feet. Its walls are 30 feet high and are surrounded by a deep moat that is 40 feet wide. The fort helped make St. Augustine the oldest permanent settlement in North America.

In 1539, **Hernando de Soto**, a veteran of the Spanish conquest of the Inca Indians in Peru, landed at Tampa Bay, where he began a meandering trek through Florida. De Soto's journey took him as far north as modern Charlotte, North Carolina. Then, traveling through the Deep South, he eventually discovered the Mississippi River.

In later decades, the Spanish built settlements and outposts along the coast of Florida, Georgia, South Carolina, Virginia's Chesapeake Bay, and as far west as Tennessee's Great Smoky Mountains. However, disease, hunger, and hostile Indians prevented Spain from becoming firmly established in North America.

Through their exploration and settlement efforts, the Spanish claimed much of what is now the United States. But Spanish rule was not beneficial to the new land; the Spanish preferred *exploiting* the land to *developing* it. To Spain, the New World was little more than a treasure chest to be looted, not a resource to be cultivated. Also, the government that Spain brought to the New World was harsh and tyrannical. The Catholicism that the Spanish brought with them reinforced rather than reduced those authoritarian tendencies.

The Spanish and Portuguese also introduced to the New World something that would create problems that would not be resolved until the American Civil War—slavery. Not only did the Spanish enslave Indian captives, but the Spanish and the

Juan Ponce de León landed near modern St. Augustine and claimed Florida for Spain.

Castillo de San Marcos protected the oldest permanent settlement in North America.

Portuguese captured and brought African slaves to their Caribbean island settlements. Eventually, those slaves were sold to colonists in the mainland of North America. The repercussions of that slave trade would be felt for centuries afterward, as we shall see throughout our study of American history.

International Competition

By the late sixteenth century, it was clear that it was easier for Spain to claim territory than to keep it. The shiploads of gold and silver bullion that Spain was siphoning out of the New World heightened French, English, and Dutch envy of Spain and their interest in America. In addition, Spain's Catholic king **Philip II** (ruled 1556–98) was bent on crushing the Protestant menace in western Europe—and he was not altogether unsuccessful. Subsidized by Mexican gold and Peruvian silver, Philip's army was the largest, best-equipped in Europe, and thousands of Protestants were killed in its bloody wake. Bitterness over Catholic Spain's military threat made Spanish New World outposts a tempting target for Protestant sea captains, such as France's Jean Ribault (a Huguenot) and England's Sir **Francis Drake**.

Drake and his cousin Sir John Hawkins were the most famous pair in a class of mariners under Queen **Elizabeth I**. They called themselves **Sea Dogs**. Both Hawkins and Drake led attacks on Spanish shipping in the Caribbean. In 1577, Drake, commanding the *Golden Hind*, followed the course around South America that Magellan had first steered a half century earlier. Drake looted Spanish outposts on the Pacific and, failing to find a northern sea route back to the Atlantic, sailed from California westward to England. His ship laden with Spanish treasure, the circumnavigator reached Plymouth Harbor in 1580.

In 1493, to settle a dispute over who could explore and claim new lands in the Western Hemisphere, Pope Alexander VI had divided the world in half, giving Portugal rights to lands east of the "line of demarcation" and giving Spain the lands west of the line. Protestant England scorned the pope's presumption that the world was his to divide. His ruling would have shut the English out of the New World. Drake was a strong Protestant and an ardent English patriot. Sailing for the honor of England, he was determined to challenge Spain's monopoly in America. After his circumnavigation of the globe, however, Drake's concerns about Spain would be much closer to home. In 1586, Philip II began amassing a huge fleet to conquer Protestant England. In the balance lay not only the fate of the island kingdom but also the determination of who would colonize most of North America—Catholic Spain or Protestant England.

The following year, Drake led thirty ships into Spain's Cádiz harbor, where Philip's Armada lay anchored, being readied for their assault. The Sea Dogs destroyed thousands of tons of supplies, delaying the invasion by a year.

In 1588, the **Spanish Armada**, 130 ships and 30,000 men, entered the English Channel. Drake used fireships to break up the Spanish formation and sent a number of galleons to the bottom. The Spanish admiral's attempt to outrun the English guns by sailing around Ireland ended when a fierce storm, which the relieved English later called the "Protestant Wind," destroyed much of

Sir Francis Drake was the most famous of the Sea Dogs and a terror to Spanish treasure ships.

Spain's fleet. Philip's dream of conquering Protestant England lay amid the wreckage floating off the craggy Irish coast.

The defeat of the Spanish Armada was both dramatic in its scope and decisive in its results. It secured the future for Protestants in England. Clearly, God was providentially preserving His witness in that country. In addition, it spelled the end of the Spanish century and the beginning of English dominance on the seas and eventually in North America.

The English Foothold

In 1584, an English clergyman named Richard Hakluyt (HAK loot) the Younger, collaborating with Sir **Walter Raleigh**, compiled for Queen Elizabeth a list of arguments favoring the colonization of North America. Titled *A Discourse of Western Planting*, the document presented a number of advantages to settling the New World, including expanding Protestantism, boosting trade and national influence, reducing unemployment, and establishing military outposts to thwart Spanish dominance.

Evidently the queen liked what she read, for the following year she gave Raleigh permission to plant a colony in the land Raleigh called *Virginia* in honor of the virgin queen. Although Raleigh himself never came to North America, he sponsored an expedition of colonists to settle on **Roanoke Island**, located in the sound of North Carolina's Outer Banks. The colony, however, which was under the command of Sir Richard Grenville, was short-lived. After wintering on the island, the colonists encountered rough treatment from neighboring Indians and threats of a Spanish attack. As a result, the English abandoned the lonely outpost in the summer of 1586.

The determined Raleigh financed a second group to Roanoke Island in 1587 under the command of John White, a veteran of the first expedition. White's group numbered 117 and for the first time included women and children, among them White's daughter Elenor and her husband Ananias Dare. Elenor gave birth to a daughter shortly after arriving in the New World—the first English child born in America—and named her, appropriately, Virginia Dare.

Unfortunately, the colonists arrived too late in the summer to plant crops. With the prospect of a lean winter, they urged White to return to England for supplies. After he reached England, however, the war with Spain delayed his return until 1590. When Governor White returned, the little town of "Raleigh" was empty. All he found was a single word carved on a tree where the village had once stood—*Croatan*. The fate of the "**Lost Colony**" has never been determined, but it is likely that the colonists were killed or captured and carried off by Indians. (The Croatans were one tribe in the area.) When Elizabeth I died in 1603, no trace of her colonizing efforts remained in the hostile wilderness that bore her name.

New France

The British colonies were quite different from the Spanish and French settlements in the New World. Spanish America was a rigidly structured plantation society controlled directly and completely by the crown, run for its profit and the benefit of the Catholic Church. Relatively few Spaniards came to the New World to live, and fewer families migrated.

Similarly, the sparse French settlements in Canada, or **New France**, were largely dependent on the mother country for their

Sir Walter Raleigh encouraged settlers to go to the New World to establish colonies for Queen Elizabeth I.

Henry Hudson claimed what is now New York for the Dutch, and it became known as New Netherland.

(Above) Collection of the U.S. House of Representatives. *Discovery of the Hudson River*, by Albert Bierstadt, oil on canvas, 1874. Detail.

Peter Stuyvesant was the one-legged, hard-nosed, and heavy-handed ruler of New Netherland until he lost the colony to the English.

success. The French king determined colonial policies and exercised complete control over his colonial subjects. In addition, the economic realities of New France did not encourage growth and independence. The long Canadian winters reduced most farming to a subsistence level, which meant that little in the way of a cash crop could be developed as an export. And though the French fur trade was profitable, it was more suited for the frontiersman than the farmer and merchant, key participants in a mature, productive settlement.

New Netherland

The area of the North Atlantic coast of North America that is now New York was discovered and claimed for the Dutch by **Henry Hudson**, sailing the ship *Half Moon* in 1609. The area was named **New Netherland**, and its main town was named New Amsterdam. The colony became a province of the Dutch Republic in 1624. The Dutch solidified their claim by landing thirty Dutch families on what today is Governors Island.

The most famous governor of New Netherland was one-legged firebrand **Peter Stuyvesant** (STY vih sent). He took control in 1647 and sought to protect the colony from potential Indian attacks. He became very unpopular, however, for his heavy-handed though well-meaning rule and was ordered to return to the Netherlands in 1649. He refused. In 1653, Stuyvesant once again was ordered to return to Europe. Again he refused, stating that he got his authority from God and the Dutch West India Company, not from "a few ignorant subjects." In 1655, he used troops to take over the neighboring colony of New Sweden.

Typical for his time, Stuyvesant was intolerant of all religions other than Protestantism, especially Quakerism. He ordered the torture of a young Quaker preacher and then declared that not only

Quakers but also all those who harbored them were to be fined and imprisoned. The people of the town of Flushing protested, demanding freedom of religion.

In 1664, the English seized the colony, promising the citizens freedom of life, liberty, and property in return for their surrender. Stuyvesant signed the treaty ceding the colony, and it was renamed New York. The population of the area had grown from 270 in 1628 to about 9,000 (700 of which were blacks) by 1664.

New Sweden

New Sweden was the name given to a small colony along the Delaware River in parts of what today is Delaware, New Jersey, and Pennsylvania. Founded in 1638, the focal point was Fort Christina, now the city of Wilmington, Delaware.

Peter Minuit, the governor of New Sweden before it was taken over by Peter Stuyvesant and the Dutch, purchased Manhattan Island from the Indians.

The Swedes wanted to bypass the French and British merchants and started the New Sweden Company with Swedish, Dutch, and German stockholders. In 1638, six hundred Swedes and Finns sailed up the Delaware River and founded Fort Caroline on the west bank. The area where they settled was actually part of the Dutch claim, but **Peter Minuit** (MIN yoo it), the former director of New Netherland and the first governor of New Sweden, knew that the Dutch had deed to only the east bank. Minuit gathered the heads of the Delaware and Susquehannock Indian tribes in the area and convinced them to approve deeds granting the land to the Swedes. The area included what today is the city of Philadelphia. The Dutch did not press their original claim or contest the Swedish settlement.

New Sweden reached its zenith in 1654 under the leadership of governor Johan Printz. Printz extended the colony northward along both sides of the Delaware River. Although they were encroaching on Dutch claims as well as the lands of the Lenni Lenape Indians, the Swedes lived in peace with their neighbors.

Printz, however, ruled as an autocrat, and the Swedish colonists soon tired of his rule. They petitioned for reform, forcing Printz to return to Sweden in 1654. Johan Rising succeeded him as governor.

The next year, the Dutch under Peter Stuyvesant forced the surrender of Fort Christina. The Swedes came under the authority of the Dutch, but the Dutch allowed them to live with a large degree of autonomy. That situation remained the same until the English conquered the New Netherland colony in 1664.

English Dominance in North America

As we shall see in the next chapter, the English came in greater numbers than their rivals to the south and north, and by the 1620s were coming as families. They brought their English heritage with them. Their books were printed in London, their houses were styled after English architecture, and their schools were patterned after Oxford and Cambridge. They also brought their political institutions. Significantly, in Elizabeth's original charter authorizing an

American settlement, colonists and their succeeding generations were granted the full rights of English citizenship—in the words of the charter, "as if they were borne and personally residuante within our sed Realme of England."

English patterns of self-government became an early, integral part of colonial life. In 1619, the Virginia colony at Jamestown (discussed in the next chapter) established the House of Burgesses, an assembly modeled after the English Parliament. As other colonies developed, so did their political institutions. Living in relative isolation from the mother country, generations of colonists gained practical experience in self-government under a local political system that for them held more relevance than the royal government on the other side of the ocean.

Section Quiz

1. What were the three basic groups of American Indians that explorers encountered, and where were they located?

2. What European nation first dominated the exploration of the New World?

3. What great Indian empire formerly ruled Mexico? What Spaniard is responsible for conquering it?

4. Who financed the first two English attempts to settle North America? Where were these settlements located?

5. Which colonial power furthered its control over North America by promising Dutch colonists preservation of life, liberty, and property in return for their surrender?

★ Why was the defeat of the Spanish Armada in 1588 important to the history of European settlement in North America?

Chapter Review 1

Making Connections

1. For the six explorers listed below, answer the following two questions: For what country did he sail? What was his greatest accomplishment as an explorer?
   a. Vasco da Gama
   b. Christopher Columbus
   c. John Cabot
   d. Ferdinand Magellan
   e. Ponce de León
   f. Hernando de Soto

2. Why did many European states practice mercantilism?

3. How did Martin Luther differ from others who sought to reform the Roman Catholic Church?

4–6. What are three similarities that existed among the American Indian groups?

7–8. Give two reasons that the Sea Dogs made raids on Spanish shipping.

Developing History Skills

1. How do the principles of mercantilism differ from the free market system?

2. In what three ways did the English settlements in the New World differ from those of the French and the Spanish?

Thinking Critically

1. Respond to the following statement: "The defeat of the Spanish Armada had nothing to do with divine providence. We have no historical proof that God was fighting for England and Protestantism. It is true that this defeat helped Protestants, but many events in the 1500s hurt the Protestant cause. If God was fighting for Protestantism in 1588, why did He not protect the French Huguenots who were killed in the St. Bartholomew's Day massacre?"

2. Critically evaluate the exploits of Drake and the Sea Dogs. What was good in what they did? What was wrong?

Living as a Christian Citizen

1. You are Hernando Cortés. How should you deal with the native inhabitants of the Americas?

2. You are an English nobleman attempting to organize a colonizing effort in North America. You are trying to convince a group of devout Protestants to plant a colony in Virginia. Write an essay designed to persuade them to cross the ocean and establish this colony.

People, Places, and Things to Remember

Marco Polo
compass
astrolabe
caravel
mercantilism
Bartolomeu Dias
Vasco da Gama
Christopher Columbus
Amerigo Vespucci
John Cabot
Ferdinand Magellan
Martin Luther
Protestant Reformation
John Calvin
Beringia
Pueblo Indians.
conquistadores
Mound Builders
Eastern Woodlands Indians
Five Civilized Tribes
Hernando Cortés
Montezuma
Francisco de Coronado
Juan Ponce de León
St. Augustine
Hernando de Soto
Philip II
Francis Drake
Elizabeth I
Sea Dogs
Spanish Armada (1588)
Walter Raleigh
Roanoke Island
"Lost Colony"
New France
Henry Hudson
New Netherland
Peter Stuyvesant
New Sweden
Peter Minuit

Jamestown fort

Thirteen Colonies

I. **Why the English Came**

II. **English Settlements Made Permanent**

III. **The New England Colonies**

IV. **The Middle Colonies**

V. **The Southern Colonies**

"Being thus arrived in a good harbor, and brought safe to land, they fell upon their knees and blessed the God of Heaven."

William Bradford, 1650, recalling the Pilgrims' arrival in the New World

Twice the English had tried to establish colonies on the Atlantic coast of North America. First they had attempted to build a settlement on Roanoke Island, only to be discouraged by threats from the Indians and the Spanish. The next year they tried again to establish a colony there, only to have the inhabitants mysteriously disappear, leaving only the enigmatic *Croatoan* carved on a tree. By 1700, however, the east coast of North America had become a "new England," dotted with many thriving English settlements. The story of this change is a remarkable one, and it has done much to define American culture. But to understand this story, one must begin by learning something about how the English viewed the New World and the opportunities found there.

I. Why the English Came

Englishmen came to the New World for many reasons. Many of them were fortune seekers drawn by dreams of quick riches. The gold and silver never materialized, however, so the settlers took advantage of the many resources found in the New World. Tobacco, rice, lumber, pine tar, indigo, and furs became valuable exports, enriching both England and the colonies.

The English also traveled to the colonies for other reasons, including the opportunity to own land. In England, wealthy families held most of the land. Tradition kept a family from selling their land to anyone else, and only the firstborn inherited land. Younger family members and most other Englishmen had little hope of owning their own property. However, America had an abundance of available land.

Still other Englishmen desired political freedom, even though some had a limited voice in their government. The Magna Carta, a document signed by King John in 1215, had limited the power of the English monarch. It also guaranteed certain basic rights to the nobility, but most Englishmen remained unprotected from government abuse. For example, James I and Charles I tried to strengthen royal power at the cost of personal liberty. As a result, many Englishmen went to America to escape the direct rule of tyrants.

Religious freedom also became a powerful force in attracting settlers to America. However, it is important to understand that most were not interested in religious pluralism, the idea that all religious views should be treated as equal and no one should discriminate between biblical truth and error. Most understood religious liberty as the freedom to structure their society so that every part of life experienced the renewal of the Protestant Reformation.

Many of those who became settlers had been frustrated when the Church of England embraced aspects of the Reformation while continuing several Roman Catholic practices. Christians quickly discovered that the king was not interested in fully implementing the work of the Reformation. As a result, they looked on the New World as a haven where they could establish communities and complete the Reformation. This reason for settlement distinguished the colonial heritage of the United States from that of new colonies established in other regions.

One final reason some settlers came to America was a longing for adventure. However, most found hardships and great difficulty. While many of America's early settlers found plenty of adventure, the cost of life and success proved to be very high for the first settlers.

The Lure of Land

The promise of abundant land drew many colonists to America. The charter colonies in Virginia and Massachusetts began under a communal arrangement whereby individuals were to work and share alike for the good of the colony. The absence of private ownership of property robbed the colonists of incentive and productivity, so the communal system was a complete failure. The companies soon reorganized to provide for land ownership. Beginning in 1614, each Jamestown colonist received three acres of land. With a seemingly endless supply of land rolling to the west, the Virginia Company offered **headrights** (land grants) of fifty-acre tracts to those who paid for their passage or who fulfilled an **indenture** (work contract) for a specified period, usually between four and seven years. Nearly half of the arrivals to the colonies outside of New England came as indentured servants. A man who was willing to work, no matter how poor he was when he arrived, received (after fulfilling his obligation) land, tools, seed, and, above all, opportunity.

Section Quiz

1. List three reasons why the English and others came to America.

2. What political document guaranteed certain basic rights to some Englishmen?

3. Why did English believers become frustrated with the Church of England?

★ How did the English settler's view of religious liberty differ from the modern view of religious liberty?

II. English Settlements Made Permanent

Sir Walter Raleigh's Roanoke expedition was the last individual effort by an Englishman to establish a colony. Later attempts were made by companies of individuals who shared the expenses of founding a colony, with the understanding that profits would also be shared proportionately.

Joint-stock companies, whose investors shared profits without sharing liabilities, provided a means whereby enterprises could obtain large monetary resources and remain free from the government control that accompanied government-sponsored projects. These companies provided a vehicle through which individuals could work together to establish new institutions in a new land.

On April 10, 1606, King James I granted charters to two companies, the **London Company** and the **Plymouth Company**, permitting them to colonize "Virginia," a coastal region of two million square miles stretching from the Carolinas to Maine. The London Company was to colonize the land between the northern latitudes of thirty-four and forty-one degrees; the Plymouth Company, between the latitudes of thirty-eight and forty-five degrees. If either started settlements in the overlapping territory, the settlements were to be at least one hundred miles apart. The Royal Council, consisting of thirteen men appointed by the king, was to govern the companies and determine colonial policies.

Both companies, optimistic about potential riches, hurried to establish colonies. The Plymouth Company deposited forty-four men on the rocky coast of Maine in the summer of 1607 at a settlement they called St. George. After only one bitter winter, those who survived returned to England. The Plymouth Company made no further attempts at colonization and the king dismantled the company in 1609.

Jamestown

The London Company (later renamed the Virginia Company) sent 104 men to America in December 1606. After a rough ocean passage, they reached the Chesapeake Bay in May 1607, where they found a wide inlet that they cautiously entered and went ashore. The Englishmen named both the river and their little fort after their monarch. **Jamestown** became the first permanent English settlement in the New World.

Modern-day re-creation of Jamestown

The first years were bitter ones for the colony. Malaria, typhoid fever, and dysentery took a devastating toll. By the end of the first winter, half the colonists had died in this hostile land.

Indians of the Powhatan Confederacy also complicated the settlers' existence. At first, relations between the two peoples were friendly enough, but as the colonists began to clear more land, the Indian chief Wahunsonacock, or, as the Virginians called him, **Powhatan** (POW uh TAN), ordered war parties to attack the colony. Not until 1614, with the marriage of his daughter **Pocahontas** (POH kuh HAHN tus) to the Englishman John Rolfe, did a shaky peace come to the area.

Typhoid was not the only fever to wreak havoc among the colonial ranks; gold fever consumed much of the settlers' time and resources. As a result, they neglected and even scorned planting and hunting. That attitude threatened the colony with starvation. Captain **John Smith**, however, enforced the kind of discipline necessary for the survival of Jamestown. Smith improved relations with Powhatan's men, who taught the settlers how to grow maize and melons, and he enforced the biblical principle of 2 Thessalonians 3:10—that everyone should earn his livelihood through diligent work.

In 1609, the Virginia Company issued a new charter appointing a resident governor, Lord De La Warr (Delaware), to direct the colony. Detained in England by personal business, Delaware sent Thomas Gates to Jamestown as his deputy, along with five hundred "reinforcements." Gates's ship was wrecked in the Bahamas, but the other ships reached Virginia. The four hundred new arrivals,

According to legend, the intervention of Pocahontas rescued John Smith from execution by the Indians.

The Swashbuckling Career of Captain John Smith

Captain John Smith is justly famous for his role in helping establish the Virginia colony, but his adventures there were only a part of his sensational exploits. As a teenager, Smith fled the dull life of a farm laborer in England to seek adventure as a soldier of fortune. He fought for the Dutch in their war for independence against Spain and afterward traveled around Europe looking for another war and an army in need of an experienced hand.

In 1600, he joined the Austrian and Hungarian forces fighting the Turks in Hungary, where he eventually rose to the rank of captain. In one glorious but gory incident, Smith took on three Turks in separate one-on-one combats and killed and beheaded all three. He was later captured by the Turks and sold into slavery. Sent to work in the fields of what is now southern Russia, Smith

killed his Turkish master with a club used for threshing. After hiding the body, Smith donned his dead master's clothes, took his horse, and escaped into Russia. From there, he was able to make his way back to Europe, eventually ending up in England in time to join the Jamestown expedition.

As one of the leaders of the Jamestown colony, Smith had a number of close brushes with the Indians. On one occasion, he and fifteen men on a trading trip were surrounded in an Indian village by more than seven hundred Indians. Quickly, Smith seized the chief of the Indians by the hair and clapped a pistol to the chief's chest. Fearing for their leader's safety, the Indians disarmed and traded peacefully with the Englishmen.

The most famous encounter between Smith and the Indians (one which some historians still question)

involved the Indian princess Pocahontas. As Smith related the story, the Indians captured him while he was exploring. The Indian chief Powhatan had ordered his braves to club Smith to death when the chief's daughter, Pocahontas (only about thirteen years old), dashed out, cradled Smith's head in her arms, and begged that his life be spared. A somewhat indulgent father, Powhatan agreed, and Smith was spared.

Smith's adventures did not end when he left Virginia. French pirates captured him, and Smith spent several months sailing with them as they preyed on ships in the Atlantic. For the most part, however, Captain Smith spent his last years living in England, writing of his exploits, dispensing advice on colonizing to whoever would listen—and wishing that he could return at least once more to the New World for more adventure.

without their governor, were unruly and became a severe drain on the food supply. John Smith did the best he could to whip the recruits into line, but a gunpowder explosion severely injured him and forced his return to England in October 1609. The winter of 1609–10 was possibly the severest trial the Jamestown colonists ever faced. It was known as the "**starving time**" because death by starvation became a way of life. Roughly 90 percent of the colony died during that terrible winter.

In May 1610, Thomas Gates finally arrived to find only a handful of gaunt survivors. Shocked by what he saw, Gates put the pitiful remnant on ships and set out for England—which would have meant the end of Jamestown. Just as the ships reached the mouth of the James River, three relief ships under the command of Lord Delaware met them. The Englishmen returned to their desolate fort and rebuilt Jamestown. Although many more hardships awaited the settlement, the starving time was the toughest one, and they had grimly endured it. Their return was the beginning of a new era for the English in America. They were there to stay.

While the Jamestown colony got off to a shaky start, it eventually stabilized. Four events occurred in 1619 that were pivotal to the future of Virginia. First, martial law imposed by earlier governors was lifted. Strict regulations had been necessary to the survival of the fledgling colony, but now Virginia's growing pains were less severe. In addition, the need for more settlers encouraged the Virginia Company to put a happier face on a situation that had often proved grim.

The lifting of martial law and the granting of full rights to the colonists led to the formation of a representative assembly, the **House of Burgesses**. That advisory and legislative body was the first self-governing assembly in the New World. The new governor, Sir George Yeardley, organized the group of elected burgesses and held their first session in late July at the church in Jamestown. Later, the assembly would build an impressive meeting place in the new colonial capital at Williamsburg.

A month after the assemblymen undertook the business of governing the colony, the arrival of a Dutch ship at Jamestown marked the third important event of the year, although no one there could have foreseen its significance. John Rolfe simply recorded in his journal that "about the last of August twenty [Africans]" arrived. The first African slaves in British North America were treated like indentured servants, working for a period and then receiving their freedom. Gradually, though, racial distinctions were made among indentured servants, and blacks were placed in permanent bondage. Slave labor was used throughout the colonies from New England to Georgia but was particularly widespread in the agrarian South. That day in 1619, when twenty Africans were deposited by force on the banks of the James River, was the quiet beginning of tremendous social division and moral tension for succeeding generations of Americans.

Another ship's arrival in 1619 held more immediate significance for the Virginia colonists. Ninety eligible women arrived, available to be purchased as wives for the cost of their passage, which amounted to 125 pounds of tobacco (which served as currency at the time), an attractive price, and sales were brisk. The establishment of families in Virginia brought a more settled aspect and steadier growth to the colony.

"Precious Stink"

"Precious stink." That is how an early Virginian described pungent and profitable tobacco, America's first cash crop. The Spanish discovered the New World plant when they encountered Caribbean natives smoking *tabacos*—rolled leaves that they lit and inserted into both nostrils.

The Virginia settlers were the first to compete with the Spanish tobacco trade when, in 1614, John Rolfe sent a shipload of tobacco to England, where it received mixed reviews. Tobacco had reached England as early as Raleigh's first colonizing effort, but Rolfe's crop was a milder variety owing to his introduction of a sweeter strain of West Indies tobacco.

Many people believed that tobacco actually had medicinal qualities. A popular couplet of the time went "Divine Tobacco! Which gives Ease / To all our Pains and Miseries." Actually, today we know that it is the source of a great deal of pain and misery. King James I objected to the colonial crop as a "noxious weed." Yet, despite its harmful effects, the "Joviall weed" remained popular. Just five years after Rolfe's first shipment, Virginia exported forty thousand pounds of tobacco, and by the late 1630s that figure had skyrocketed to 1.5 million pounds per year.

Tobacco became so crucial to the Virginia economy that the price of goods was measured not in "shillings" or "dollars" but in pounds of tobacco. For good reason, King Charles I declared that "Virginia was founded upon Smoak."

One source of difficulty for the Virginians was Indian relations. As mentioned earlier, the initial tension between the Indians and the English eased with the marriage of Powhatan's daughter Pocahontas to John Rolfe, who was famous for introducing tobacco, which became Virginia's chief cash crop. The Indian princess converted to Christianity and even made a celebrated tour of England, which ended tragically with her death from disease (possibly smallpox or tuberculosis) on the eve of her return voyage to Virginia.

Not long afterward, Powhatan also died. His brother Opechancanough (oh PEHCH uhn KAY noh) took control of the Indian Confederation and then struck at the colonists with ferocity. On Good Friday morning, March 22, 1622, Indian warriors killed 347 colonists. The battered Virginians gathered their forces and exacted heavy revenge. Later, another Indian massacre of whites resulted in a treaty that restricted the English to the Tidewater area of Virginia. The English soon violated that treaty, and an atmosphere of animosity continued between the two groups. Because of the Indian uprising and bickering among the Virginia Company's leadership, Charles I had the company dismantled, and Virginia became a royal colony in 1624.

There were three types or categories of English colonial administration, depending on the commercial relationship of the colony to the mother country. They were charter, proprietary, and royal. Although all three types initially received a charter (a legal grant for existence), a **charter colony** was specifically one governed by a trade company (such as the Virginia Company) that received its authorization from the king. Charter colonies usually enjoyed the most independence in their government. Under the **proprietary** arrangement, the king appointed a proprietor or proprietors (ultimately responsible to the king) to govern a colony. **Royal colonies** were controlled directly by the crown, which meant that the king and his councilors appointed the governor directly. By the seventeenth century, a number of charter and proprietary colonies had become royal colonies as the king assumed increasing control over colonial affairs.

Section Quiz

1. Which Englishman tried to establish a colony on Roanoke Island?

2. What was the first permanent English settlement in the New World?

3. Who ensured the survival of that settlement by enforcing a biblical principle, and what was that principle?

4–5. Name and define the three categories of colonial government.

★ How did the trials and successes of Jamestown manifest the core values of freedom, individualism, equality, and growth? What contradictions to these values began to develop?

III. The New England Colonies

The differences and similarities of the English colonies can best be studied by arranging and examining them geographically. The four northernmost colonies were known as New England. The four colonies immediately to the south of New England were known as the middle colonies. The remaining five were called the southern colonies.

The New England Colonies

*under various claims

Massachusetts

In 1614, Captain John Smith, commissioned by the Virginia Company to explore the coast far to the north of Jamestown, found a region rich with furs and fish. Smith's account of that land, which he called **New England**, spurred the revival and reorganization of the defunct Plymouth Company into the Council for New England.

The Pilgrims

The first settlers to New England, however, did not go out under the sponsorship of the Council of New England. In November 1620, the *Mayflower*, swept off its course to Virginia by a fierce storm, anchored off Cape Cod, Massachusetts. On board were a number of Christians known as **Pilgrims**. They had left their houses and lands and crossed an ocean to worship God freely. The price they were paying in terms of hardship and sacrifice was as extraordinary as their faith.

The Pilgrims implored God's help as they set out for the New World.

To study the settling of Massachusetts by the Pilgrims and a decade later by the Puritans, one must understand the religious situation in England at that time. England was Protestant, but its official break with Roman Catholicism resulted largely from political rather than spiritual concerns. This is not to say that the Reformation failed to have a spiritual impact on England. For example, William Tyndale, before he was strangled and burned at the stake by Catholics, translated the Scriptures into English. The psalmist wrote that "the entrance of thy word giveth light" (119:130), and so it was in England. Thousands of copies of Tyndale's translation were distributed, and as the gospel was preached throughout the country, many came to trust Christ as their Savior.

However, vestiges of Roman Catholicism remained in the rituals of the Anglican Church, or Church of England, and in the conduct of its clergy. Two groups, the Puritans and the Separatists, emerged in opposition to those problems. The **Puritans** were a group of Anglicans who wanted to *purify* the state church from *within* by pushing for reforms that would rid England of Romanist influences and bring greater spiritual vitality to the nation.

The **Separatists**, though agreeing with many of the spiritual goals of the Puritans, were Independents. They believed that each local congregation should be independent of all other churches, free to worship and serve God without interference. Because of the Separatists' refusal to recognize the authority of the state church, they were harassed and many were jailed.

In 1607, one congregation of Separatists from Scrooby, England, migrated to Holland because religious tolerance there allowed them to preach and practice their faith freely. After a decade in Holland, however, the Separatists noticed that the Dutch language and habits threatened to undo their efforts to preserve their own language and culture among their children. In addition, the worldly atmosphere in Holland threatened the spiritual well-being of their children and their congregation. Because of these concerns and their desire to spread the gospel, the Pilgrims obtained a land grant from the Virginia Company to settle in the New World. Under the terms of the agreement, the Separatists would labor seven years for the company shareholders in exchange for the land deed and, most important to them, the right to worship freely.

In July 1620, **William Bradford**, leading a group of thirty-five Pilgrims, sailed from Holland in the *Speedwell*. They joined the *Mayflower* in England and together set out for America. The Speedwell, however, proved unseaworthy, forcing the expedition back to Plymouth, England, where its passengers boarded the *Mayflower*. In September, the *Mayflower* set out alone with 101 passengers. About half of the passengers were Separatists; the others were referred to as "strangers."

The ocean passage was stormy, and the little *Mayflower* was blown far north of the Virginia colony to Cape Cod, Massachusetts. From there, a second attempt to reach Virginia was also beaten back by a tempest. By then, it was November, and the scant provisions that remained were fit for only the vermin that infested them. The Pilgrims decided to settle in Massachusetts. A scouting party went ashore and chose a site that Captain John Smith had named "Plymouth" during his New England trek six years earlier.

Because they were outside the jurisdiction of the Virginia Company, the leaders drew up a contract of government to guide them until they could reorganize under the Council for New England. The agreement, known as the **Mayflower Compact**, bound the settlers into a "civill body politick" by which they agreed to submit to the laws and the duly elected leadership of the colony. That document of self-government was the first of its kind in America.

William Bradford's history of the colony, *Of Plymouth Plantation*, completed around 1650, records the spirit, courage, and faith of those stalwart Christian families:

> Being thus arrived in a good harbor, and brought safe to land, they fell upon their knees and blessed the God of Heaven who had brought them over the vast and furious ocean, and delivered them from all the perils therefore, again to set their feet on the firm and stable earth, their proper element.

William Bradford, governor and historian of Plymouth Colony

As the Pilgrims stood in the winter's chill at the edge of a hostile wilderness, Bradford recorded their plight as well as their quiet confidence in God.

> This poor people's present condition . . . no friends to welcome them, nor inns to entertain or refresh their weatherbeaten bodies, no houses. . . to repair to. . . . Whichever way they turned their eyes (save upward to the heavens) they could have little solace. . . . summer being done, all things stand upon them . . . and the whole country, full of woods and thickets, represented a wild and savage hue. If they looked behind them, there was the mighty ocean. . . . What could now sustain them but the Spirit of God and His grace?

Signing of the Mayflower Compact

Squanto and Samoset

In mid March 1621 the settlers in Plymouth received a surprise visit from an Indian named Samoset. They were probably stunned when he greeted them in broken English he had learned from contact with English fishermen. A few days later, Samoset returned to Plymouth with another Indian named **Squanto**. Squanto had been in contact with the English since 1605 and had lived in England for a few years. In 1619 he had returned to his homeland and discovered that his tribe and neighboring tribes had been wiped out by a plague.

Squanto provided the settlers with life-saving information about crop fertilization in order to increase food production. He also led them to areas where they could catch fish and eels to supplement their diet.

In addition, Squanto worked to establish peace between the settlers and the neighboring Wampanoag tribe. His efforts led to a peace that endured for nearly fifty years.

The first months at Plymouth were devastating ones. Half of the little band died before spring, including their governor, John Carver. Following that first winter, however, the colony began to prosper. Friendly Indians helped the colony raise native crops of maize (corn), pumpkins, squash, and tomatoes, and under the wise and godly leadership of their new governor, William Bradford, Plymouth gained a firm foothold.

Plymouth Colony grew steadily, though after 1630 it was surpassed in size and influence by the Puritans' Boston settlement. In 1691, Plymouth merged with the rest of Massachusetts, which by then had become a royal colony. The Plymouth Colony, however, had an influence that extended far beyond the bounds of seventeenth-century Massachusetts. As Bradford put it, "As one small candle may light a thousand, so the light here kindled hath shone to many, yea in some sort to our whole nation." The enduring legacy of our Pilgrim Fathers lies in their godly testimony, their pioneering spirit, and the way in which they defined the meaning of America—as a refuge, a land of liberty for the worship of God and the preaching of His Word.

The Puritans

In 1630, an impressive fleet of seventeen ships with a thousand Puritans on board arrived at Massachusetts Bay. Their arrival opened a new chapter in the colonization of North America. In what has been called the **Great Migration**, fifty thousand settlers sailed from England to various colonies in America and the West Indies during the 1630s. Unlike the earliest settlements that dotted the coast, the Bay Colony expedition was large, well organized, and well financed. With the flood of new arrivals, a number of

The Pilgrims and Thanksgiving Day

Faith in God sustained the members of the Plymouth Colony through their tribulations. When God delivered them from such trials, they were quick to follow Paul's command to give "thanks always for all things unto God and the Father in the name of our Lord Jesus Christ" (Eph. 5:20). After the bitter winter of 1620–21, the harvest of 1621 was a welcome relief to the colonists. In gratitude to God for His mercy, Governor William Bradford proclaimed a time of thanksgiving in the colony, celebrated in October 1621. For three days, the colony celebrated reverently but joyfully. They feasted on the bounty that God had provided for them—vegetables (such as cabbages, carrots, turnips, onions, and beets) and wild game (perhaps including turkeys, but this is not certain). Some ninety friendly Indi-

ans joined the Pilgrims, providing fresh venison as their contribution to the feast.

A day of special thanksgiving to God by His people was by no means unusual. The Israelites' Feast of Pentecost and Feast of Tabernacles, for example, were both celebrations of thanksgiving for the blessings of harvest. Moses wrote, "And thou shalt rejoice in thy feast . . . because the Lord thy God shall bless thee in all thine increase, and in all the works of thine hands" (Deut. 16:14–15). Christians throughout history have set aside special days of prayer, thanksgiving, and feasting to commemorate the blessings of God. However, the Plymouth feast—popularly regarded as "the first Thanksgiving" in America despite earlier such celebrations in Virginia—has become a part of the

nation's heritage, an almost legendary event as famous as Washington's crossing the Delaware.

Though the annual celebration of Thanksgiving Day in America owes its inspiration to the Pilgrims, the official holiday is much more recent. President George Washington proclaimed the first day of national thanksgiving on November 26, 1789. Thanksgiving became a regular annual holiday in 1863 when President Abraham Lincoln made the last Thursday in November Thanksgiving Day. This remained the standard date until 1939 when President Franklin Roosevelt moved it back one week to lengthen the Christmas shopping season. Finally in 1941 Congress officially set the fourth Thursday in November as the nation's Thanksgiving Day.

towns just north of Cape Cod quickly sprang up: Salem, Dorchester, Charlestown, and Boston, the Bay's seat of government.

The driving force behind the Puritan colony was its governor, **John Winthrop**. Cambridge-educated and a leading officer and financier in the Massachusetts Bay Company, Winthrop dreamed of establishing a "wilderness Zion" in Massachusetts, a Puritan commonwealth where the Scriptures would direct the affairs of both church and state.

Winthrop's vision for Massachusetts was set forth in a sermon he preached aboard the *Arabella* before going ashore. In his message, titled "A Modell of Christian Charity," the governor underscored the purpose of the colony: it was to be a Christian community in the most thorough sense of both of those words—*Christian* and *community*. Every member of the community—pastor and parishioner alike—would contribute to the success of the whole. It was God's purpose that "they might be all knit more nearly together in the bond of brotherly affection." Winthrop further declared that the colony represented an extraordinary opportunity and responsibility: "We shall be as a city upon a hill, the eyes of all people are upon us; so that if we shall deal falsely with our God in this work we have undertaken and so cause him to withdraw his present help from us, we shall be made a story and a by-word through the world."

At the heart of this goal of establishing a community of believers was the Puritans' belief in the **covenant**. They believed they were in a covenant (legally binding relationship) with God. They were bound to obey this covenant if they were to receive His blessings. As a result they committed to build a holy commonwealth.

The Puritans set out to apply biblical principles to every aspect of their society, including their government and educational systems. In 1636, **Harvard College** was established near Boston to train young men for the ministry. In explaining the purpose behind America's first college, one writer in 1643 also provided an interesting commentary on Puritan values in the New World:

> After God had carried us safe to New England, and wee had built our houses, provided necessaries for our livelihood, rear'd convenient places for Gods worship, and settled the Civill Government: One of the next things we longed for, and looked after was to advance Learning and perpetuate it to Posterity; dreading to leave an illiterate Ministry to the Churches, when our present Ministers shall lie in the Dust.

Capitalism and Protestantism enjoyed a close relationship in the early years. The Puritans aligned with scriptural principles that praise hard work (Prov. 12:24; 13:11; 21:25; 1 Thess. 4:11; 2 Thess. 3:10, 12). They viewed economic prosperity as God's blessing, and some even concluded that this success implied they were God's chosen people.

Sadly, many of the second and third generations did not establish a personal relationship with Christ and maintain the spiritual covenant of their fathers. Material prosperity replaced spiritual inquiry and dependence upon God. Just as Israel had done in the past, the Puritans failed to heed God's warning in Deuteronomy 6:10–15 about prosperity and the tendency to forget the Lord.

If the Bay Colony was, in Winthrop's words, "a city upon a hill," then it was a city that resembled those of Lincolnshire or Yorkshire an ocean away. In a number of cases, Puritan officials in England

John Winthrop, governor of Massachusetts Bay Colony

with their family and friends immigrated *en masse* to Massachusetts. These officials received town land grants from the Massachusetts Bay Company, which included authority to lay out the town and make property allotments. As a result, the settling of Massachusetts was more organized than that of other colonies—a fact that also meant it was more tightly controlled. Property was generally distributed in relation to social position rather than through a system of headrights. Fewer indentured servants, therefore, immigrated to New England because of the less attractive terms.

Settlers, though, continued to come to the Puritan commonwealth. As many as twenty thousand arrived in Massachusetts in the 1630s, and Boston burgeoned into the largest city on the continent. Those colonists did not all stay in Massachusetts, however. Two factors—expansion and dissension—caused Massachusetts to spawn other colonies throughout New England.

Connecticut

Not everyone wanted to live in Boston. The boundless expanse of forest laced with rivers drew settlers farther west. As early as 1633, Puritans and Plymouth Pilgrims migrated into the Connecticut River Valley and established a string of settlements.

One of the most significant migrations took place in 1636, when the Puritan minister **Thomas Hooker** moved three congregations under his leadership into the Connecticut River Valley, setting up communities at Hartford, Wethersfield, and Windsor. Since those three settlements (known collectively as the River Colony, or River Town) lay outside the jurisdiction of the Massachusetts Bay Company, each developed its own simple system of local government.

Eventually, those settlements united politically under the provisions of the **Fundamental Orders of Connecticut** (1639). This document, which has been called the first written constitution in America, established a framework for representative self-government in Connecticut. Although the Massachusetts Bay Company provided a well-organized system of self-government, Connecticut developed a more democratic order by not requiring church membership as a prerequisite for voting. Eventually, all of the Connecticut settlements, including the Puritan settlement of New Haven, were united under a royal charter obtained by John Winthrop Jr. in 1662. This charter preserved many of the self-governing practices that had been a feature of Connecticut since its founding.

The motivation behind the early political organizing among the River Towns was the need for security against the Indian threat, particularly that of the uncooperative Pequots (PEE kwots). Like the English, the Pequot Indians were newcomers to the region. Unlike the other Indians of the area, however, the Pequots did not passively accept the expansion of Massachusetts. In 1636, nine settlers in Connecticut were brutally murdered, possibly by Pequots. Colonial forces mustered out of Massachusetts and Connecticut marched on a large Pequot village on Connecticut's Mystic River. There the English demonstrated to their Indian rivals that they could beat them at brutality. The colonials reduced the village to ashes and indiscriminately murdered four hundred men, women, and children. Pequots who escaped the fire and sword were captured and sold into slavery.

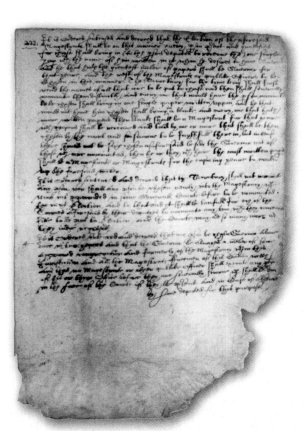

The Fundamental Orders of Connecticut have been called the first written constitution in America.

Rhode Island and New Hampshire

The natural expansion that resulted from a massive influx of settlers was not the only cause behind the new colonies coming out of Massachusetts. Dissension against the Puritan leadership in the Bay Colony contributed to the formation of Rhode Island and New Hampshire.

In 1631, **Roger Williams** arrived in Massachusetts and soon gained a reputation as a troublemaker for his novel ideas. Williams declared it a "national sinne" for England to take Indian land without just compensation, denounced his fellow Puritans for not severing all ties with the Anglican Church, and advocated complete separation of church and state. Williams did not want the state to support any church or doctrinal system. He also argued that a person's religious views should not affect his influence in society. Several of these ideas flew in the face of the Puritan ideal of a "holy commonwealth." As a result, in 1635 the General Court banished Williams. After wintering with the Narragansett Indians, Williams and some of his followers established a settlement they called Providence in the coastal region known as Rhode Island.

Williams's theology often seemed to be in a state of flux. His concept of a "pure" church became so narrow that he abandoned the institutional church. As one historian wryly observed, "Williams's belief that a true church must have no truck with the unregenerate led him eventually to the absurdity that no true church was possible, unless perhaps consisting of his wife and himself—and he may have had doubts about her."

Roger Williams was a key figure in the development of the modern conception of religious liberty. Before Williams, the state was expected to establish, maintain, and defend true Christianity from heretics who would oppose and undermine it. The Reformers and the Puritans did not seek to remove the state's role in carrying out these functions. They sought to reform the state so that it would support true religion instead of false religion. Williams's radical idea was for the state to tolerate any religious belief. This idea does not seem radical today because it has become the standard view of most Americans, secular and Christian alike. Williams's idea of religious liberty was enshrined in the Constitution, and it prepared the way for the emergence of a religiously plural United States of America.

In addition to Roger Williams, another leading dissident, **Anne Hutchinson**, fled to Rhode Island. Hutchinson was forty-five and the mother of fifteen children when she and her family followed their Puritan pastor, John Cotton, to Massachusetts in 1634. Her strong personality and way with words attracted people from the congregation to gather at her home on Mondays to discuss Cotton's Sunday sermon.

Eventually, Hutchinson went far beyond simply discussing the sermon to expounding heresy. She began to teach that outward obedience to the Scriptures was unnecessary to demonstrate an inward relationship to God (a position called **antinomianism**). Furthermore, she taught that God had given her a direct revelation that superseded the Bible.

When the leaders of the community became aware of her teachings, they followed the scriptural procedure and attempted to counsel her. She was unresponsive, however; so the court finally

Roger Williams stood for complete separation of church and state.

The Granger Collection, New York

Anne Hutchinson was banished from Massachusetts for teaching a heresy called antinomianism.

voted to banish her. Despite the sentence, she was not expelled until months later, in March 1638. Only a few of her supporters went with her to Portsmouth (PORTS muth), Rhode Island, where the group established a small settlement. Hutchinson soon grew restless and moved to New York, but the settlement at Portsmouth continued to grow. She continued to preach her radical beliefs in New York until she was killed in her home by Indians in 1643.

The antinomian controversy also contributed to the first significant settlement in New Hampshire. The earliest attempt at colonization there was short-lived. David Thomson established the first settlement in New Hampshire at Little Harbor on the Piscataqua River in 1623. He named the area after the community of Hampshire, where he had lived in England. The colony consisted of five men—not exactly a significant presence—and eventually dwindled to nothing.

The first significant settlement was not established until 1638, when John Wheelwright, along with thirty-five others, settled at Exeter. Wheelwright was an antinomian and Anne Hutchinson's brother-in-law. He left the Bay Colony during the Hutchinson controversy, and Exeter soon became a thriving settlement. However, New Hampshire did not become a separate colony until 1679, when the king of England made it a province under royal charter. Before that time, it was under the jurisdiction of Massachusetts.

Section Quiz

1. What was the difference between Puritans and Separatists?

2. Why did the English Separatists leave the Netherlands?

3. Which dissenter became so separated that he finally abandoned any institutional church?

4. What name is given to the heresy, taught by Anne Hutchinson, that outward obedience to Scripture is unnecessary to show an inward relationship to God?

★ Since the Puritans had come to the New World to worship as they saw fit, why did they not allow Roger Williams and Anne Hutchison the same freedom of worship?

IV. The Middle Colonies

No other segment of the colonies reflected the cultural diversity of British North America quite like the **middle colonies**. English, Dutch, Germans, French, Finns, Scots, and Swedes all found a niche in the stretch of land from Long Island to the Delaware Bay.

New York

As you learned already, New York began as a Dutch settlement. Henry Hudson sailed his ship the *Half Moon* into an inlet below Long Island and up the river that now bears his name, reaching as far as present-day Albany. Although he did not find the Pacific Ocean he was seeking, he claimed the land for the Dutch. Peter Minuit purchased Manhattan Island from the Indians for $24 worth of cloth and trinkets, and New Amsterdam was born. The Indian concept of ownership did not include fences or property deeds; land was a common resource that nourished all men. The Manhattans, therefore, must have thought it strange that Minuit paid them for something that they did not own.

The Middle Colonies

The Dutch of New Netherland established a unique system of settlement that became known as the **patroon** (puh TROON) **system**. A patroon was a person who transported and settled fifty families in exchange for a large tract of land in the New World. The families thus transported then had to live on the patroon's land and under his control, almost like feudal serfs on their lord's manor. The system gained the support of many investors but ultimately failed. While in place, the patroon system limited the growth of the colony because smaller landholders could not get a stake in the land and therefore had little incentive to come. Only after the abandonment of the patroon system and the growth of the colony did New York City become a major center of trade.

England was not content to have the Dutch as neighbors in the New World. However, from 1640 to 1660, civil war and political upheaval in England prevented her from dealing with the Dutch. When Charles II finally took the English throne in 1660, he granted New Netherland to his brother James, duke of York, who proceeded to conquer it in 1664. Facing the large English force, the Dutch chose to surrender rather than to resist.

Dutch influence remained, however, in prominent family names such as Roosevelt and Van Buren and in place names such as Catskill, Peekskill, Spuyten Duyvil, and Wall Street, where the Dutch had built a wall as part of their Indian defenses.

New Jersey

As you already know, New Jersey was first settled by Swedes and Dutch but came into English hands as part of the 1664 conquest of New Netherland. New Jersey was originally two colonies, East and West Jersey, and remained so during much of its colonial history. Several factors contributed to that division, one of which was the influence of settlements near what is now Philadelphia to the west and of New York City to the east. Most of the settlers near New York City were Dutch, whereas most near Philadelphia were Swedes. James II divided the region politically in 1664, when he gave the government of each area to different friends.

Strife developed when settlers who already lived in the Jerseys refused to pay rent to the new owners. The owner of West Jersey became disheartened and sold it to several Quakers. After 1676, both Jerseys were owned by Quakers, one being William Penn of Pennsylvania. Penn wrote a constitution called *Law, Concessions, and Agreements*, which provided for a self-governing assembly, full land rights, officially recorded deeds, religious freedom, and public trials by jury. This constitution contained many of the principles of civil and religious liberty that all thirteen colonies would eventually share.

In 1689, East and West Jersey united under common ownership, but they were not unified in spirit. The Jerseys continued to go their separate ways until 1702, when they were united as a royal colony by an act of the king.

Pennsylvania

More than any other colony, Pennsylvania was the product of one man's vision and labor—**William Penn**. School officials expelled Penn from Oxford for his Puritan beliefs. He later joined what was a minority group even among dissenters, the Society of Friends, or Quakers. Like the Puritans, the Quakers objected to the corruption in the Church of England. However, unlike the Puritans, the Quakers abandoned many biblical teachings. For example, the Quakers denied the Trinity. They taught that all men have a spark of grace that makes them able to achieve salvation by doing the right things. Quakers also rejected the office of pastor and the unique authority of Scripture in favor of guidance by an Inner Light. They allowed women to hold authority in their meetings, and they refused to grant governmental officials their due honor.

The English authorities were concerned about the social disruption such beliefs would bring about, and they began to suppress the Society of Friends. Officials imprisoned Penn for a time in the Tower of London for writing an anti-trinitarian tract. Following his release he continued to write and preach, emphasizing primarily the cause of religious pluralism.

William Penn arriving in Philadelphia

Penn's involvement in colonial affairs began when he served as one of the proprietors of West Jersey. In 1681, in payment for a debt owed to Penn's late father, the cash-poor King Charles II granted the Quaker leader sole proprietorship over a vast tract north of Maryland. The king appropriately named the forested area *Pennsylvania* ("Penn's Woods") in honor of William Penn's father, a naval hero. That grant was the beginning of Penn's "Holy Experiment" in America. He sought to establish a utopia of love, peace, and toleration of all.

Penn's *Frame of Government* provided religious toleration and political liberty for the colony. Penn's Quaker convictions concerning equality were reflected in his respectful treatment of the Indians, which provided a generally unheeded example for the other colonies.

The open political and religious environment and the fertile land, as well as Penn's shrewd advertising in England and Germany, attracted thousands to the colony, and Philadelphia—the "city of brotherly love"—rapidly became an important commercial center. As more and more non-Quakers moved into the colony, the Quaker ideals became diluted. The harmony that Penn hoped to achieve gave way to the hard realities of a diverse society. Even social evils such as slavery and the mistreatment of Indians began to intrude on Penn's dream of utopia.

Delaware

The king added Delaware to Penn's vast holdings; it did not become a separate colony until 1701. The little colony on the west bank of the Delaware Bay had a checkered history of ownership. Swedes first settled the area near present-day Wilmington, and Delaware was part of New Sweden. The Dutch conquered the Swedes; the English conquered the Dutch; the stubborn Dutch reconquered, only to be finally ousted by the English.

Delaware was granted to William Penn's proprietorship, but the settlers resisted being ruled by Quakers in Philadelphia. The colony was eventually granted the right to form a separate legislature, but it remained under the leadership of the Pennsylvania governor until 1776. One important Swedish contribution that came out of Delaware was the log cabin, a fixture in American society for the next two centuries.

Section Quiz

1–2. What nationality originally settled New York? Which nation eventually took control of it?

3. Why did the patroon system fail?

4. In which three of the middle colonies were the Quakers influential in government?

5. Which colony besides New York was founded by a nation other than England?

✴ Why was Pennsylvania unable to maintain the Quaker ideals that William Penn envisioned for the colony?

V. The Southern Colonies

The third of the geographical divisions of the English colonies was the South. The colonies that made up this division were Virginia, Maryland, the Carolinas, and Georgia. Since we have already examined Virginia, this section will focus on the other four **southern colonies**.

Maryland

The first group of settlers arrived in Maryland in 1634, led by Leonard and George Calvert. Their proprietor was **Cecilius Calvert**, **Lord Baltimore**. They established a settlement called St. Mary's off the north bank of the Potomac River. Charles I appropriately named the province north of the James River Maryland, in honor of his Catholic wife, Queen Henrietta Maria.

The Calverts had two motives for planting a colony in Maryland: to provide a refuge for English Catholics and to make the colony a commercial success. To give liberty to the Catholics and still attract Protestant settlers, the colony's leaders established religious toleration through the **Toleration Act of 1649**, which provided that no one professing a belief in Christ should be troubled in the free exercise of his religion. Since Protestant settlers outnumbered the Catholic leaders from the very beginning, the act was

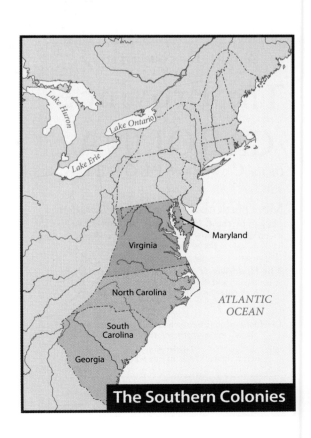

The Southern Colonies

Skull and Crossbones

"Blackbeard," whose real name was Edward Teach, was the most notorious of the pirates who plagued the settlements along the Carolina coasts. He had a long, black beard that he twisted together and tied with ribbons into little "tails." When he entered a fight, he carried a belt with "three brace of pistols" (a total of six guns) draped from one shoulder diagonally across his chest. He wore a fur hat and stuck a lighted match on each side of it to make himself look more frightful.

Advertisements such as this sought to attract settlers to the Carolinas.

indeed shrewd. By 1776, Protestants heavily outnumbered Catholics in Maryland.

The Carolinas

When Charles I dissolved the Virginia Company in 1624, he divided Virginia's vast claim, which stretched from the upper Chesapeake Bay to Spanish Florida. Being unfamiliar with humility, Charles named the region to the south of the Virginia colony Carolina (from the Latin *Carolus*, or Charles). He granted Carolina as a proprietorship to a favorite friend, Sir Robert Heath. However, Heath did nothing to colonize the area beyond paper plans.

For several decades, Carolina remained a backwater for drifters and desperados, and the many inlets of its meandering coast were favorite haunts for pirates. That began to change in 1663, when the king granted eight proprietors a new charter to develop and govern the region. From the beginning, two areas of settlement emerged: the area to the north, called Albemarle, and the area to the south at a harbor settlement named Charles Town.

Northern Carolina had fewer settlers, and its scattered farms depended largely on tobacco for income. Originally, the area was thought to be good for producing silk and wine. That assumption proved better at attracting settlers than at sustaining them in the rough coastal plain of Albemarle.

The southern Carolina settlement received more attention from the proprietors, particularly **Sir Anthony Ashley-Cooper**, the Earl of Shaftesbury. Many of the original colonists in Charles Town had been small farmers in Barbados who could no longer compete with the large sugar plantations there. Initially, the Charlestonians made a living by trading buckskins and Indian slaves. The slaves, acquired from Indian middlemen along the Savannah River, were generally sold in New England and the Caribbean. A more steady source of income came with the introduction of rice cultivation in the 1690s.

The geographic and economic division of Carolina was formalized in 1719, when South Carolina became a royal colony. Proprietors continued to rule North Carolina until 1729, when it, too, became a royal colony.

Georgia

In terms of both chronology and geography, Georgia was at the end of the line. Settlement of this southernmost colony of British North America did not begin until 1732, the year George Washington was born.

The British colonized Georgia for two purposes: to establish a military buffer against Spanish Florida and to provide a colony where debtors and vagrants, who often languished in English jails, could become productive. Emptying prison cells in England by sending their occupants to America was nothing new, but it was usually viewed as only another form of punishment, not a reprieve. In fact, John Smith observed that when English prisoners guilty of capital offenses were offered a choice between execution or banishment to the New World, "some did chuse to be hanged ere they would go thither, and were."

Georgia, however, was an exception in that its founder wanted to focus more on reforming prisoners than on punishing them. A reform-minded general named **James Oglethorpe** determined to

His Majestys Colony of Georgia in America

Savannah was the first major settlement in Georgia.

build a colony that would provide *rehabilitation* through opportunity and hard work. Each settler was given fifty acres of land and tools and seeds for the first year. Total land holdings were restricted to five hundred acres so that the small farmer was not gobbled up by land barons.

The first settlers in Georgia established Savannah in 1733, and a variety of settlers quickly followed the initial migration. Scots, Germans, Austrians, and even Portuguese Jews arrived. The colony distinguished itself by rapid growth and commercial success.

The Emerging American

America's thirteen colonies reflected their British heritage as well as their own upbringing. The vast Atlantic isolated the colonies from England, and the vast wilderness isolated them from one another. Isolation strengthened their love of freedom and encouraged their individualism. Every colony founded in America was the result of private, even individual, effort. Smith, Bradford, Winthrop, Williams, Calvert, Penn, and Oglethorpe had individual dreams of what America was to be, and they wanted to be free to live out those dreams. Of course, freedom and individualism can cause problems, as the Puritan fathers learned when Anne Hutchinson insisted that she be free to teach heresy.

A stubborn streak of independence and a firm commitment to equality also ran through the colonies. That trait is underscored by a consistent pattern of settlement. After building houses for shelter and worship, the colonists organized their own governments. Even where the crown refused to recognize the colonial legislature, as in the case of Virginia in the 1620s, the legislature continued to meet and make laws. They believed that if people in England had their Parliament, it was only right for the colonists to have their own legislatures.

Life in the colonies could be hard—even short—but there was a newness about it, a sense of hope and opportunity that attracted thousands to America's shores to build their city in the wilderness.

There were certainly risks. But many judged the opportunity to own land and increase the influence of Christ's kingdom to be worth the risks.

Yet, full equality—at least as we think of it today—was not highly valued. Political power in some colonies rested in only adult white male property owners who were church members; only they could vote or hold office. Blacks, whether free or slave, and Indians could not participate. Indentured servants did not own property, so they could not take part. Neither could women. Nonetheless, political freedoms and powers in the English colonies were open to more common people than in any other time or place.

In that and other ways, the society the colonists forged, now obscured by time, often seems to the modern reader to be as stiff and colorless as the engravings of the period. Yet, in the days when America was ruled by a distant king, daily life had its own fascinating story to tell.

Section Quiz

1. Near the bank of what river was the first settlement in Maryland established?

2. What was the religious motive in planting the Maryland colony?

3. What were the main crops of northern and southern Carolina, respectively?

4. What were the two purposes the British had in founding Georgia?

★ Using the four core values of individualism, freedom, growth, and equality, briefly describe the emerging America revealed in this chapter.

Chapter Review

Making Connections

1. What role did religious freedom play in American settlement?

2. Why did two colonies form from Massachusetts? What were those two colonies?

3. In what way were the Mayflower Compact, the Fundamental Orders of Connecticut, and William Penn's *Frame of Government* each an important step in the development of American government?

4. Which three colonies tolerated different religions from the time of their foundings?

5. Which geographic division of the thirteen colonies was the most diverse culturally?

6. Name two ways in which non-English cultures were introduced to America.

7–8. Name the colony with which each of the following men was most closely associated.

a. Peter Minuit

b. Thomas Hooker

c. James Oglethorpe

d. Roger Williams

e. Sir Anthony Ashley-Cooper, Earl of Shaftesbury

f. William Penn

g. John Winthrop

h. Cecilius Calvert, Lord Baltimore

Developing History Skills

1. Near what geographic feature did colonies tend to be established? Why?

2. Referring to Deuteronomy 6:10-15, describe how the Puritans failed to heed the warning that God gave the Israelites. How does this passage apply to your generation?

Thinking Critically

1. The Massachusetts Bay Colony and Pennsylvania took very different approaches to religious liberty. What are the benefits and liabilities of each approach?

2. Why was William Penn's dream of a utopia in the new world destined to fail? Use Scripture to justify your answer.

Living as a Christian Citizen

1. In light of what you have learned about religion and liberty, use the Bible to respond to the argument that denying homosexuals the right to marry denies them fundamental liberties that heterosexuals possess.

2. Imagine that you are the founder of a new colony. Write a constitution that will provide the rationale and form of the government.

People, Places, and Things to Remember

headrights
indenture
joint-stock companies
London Company
Plymouth Company
Jamestown
Powhatan
Pocahontas
John Smith
"starving time"
House of Burgesses
charter colony
proprietary (colony)
royal colonies
New England
Pilgrims
Puritans
Separatists
William Bradford
Mayflower Compact
Squanto
Great Migration
John Winthrop
covenant
Harvard College
Thomas Hooker
Fundamental Orders of Connecticut
Roger Williams
Anne Hutchinson
antinomianism
middle colonies
patroon system
William Penn
southern colonies
Cecilius Calvert, Lord Baltimore
Toleration Act of 1649
Sir Anthony Ashley-Cooper
James Oglethorpe

CHAPTER

3

"The Copley Family" by John Singleton Copley

Colonial Life

I. The Rhythms of Life

II. At Home

III. At Work

IV. At Play

"You would do well to advise all poor people whom you wish well to take curradge and com to this Country it will be of Benefite to ther riseing generation."

Scottish immigrant Alexander McAllister, 1750, advising his cousin in the old country to join him in North Carolina

Winston Churchill wrote, "History with its flickering lamp stumbles along the trail of the past, trying to reconstruct its scenes, to revive its echoes, and kindle with pale gleams the passion of former days."

Churchill was trying to describe the difficult but rewarding task of both the writer and reader of history. This chapter reconstructs the colorful scenes of daily life in colonial America. The colonial era, like any period past or present, is far more than the sum of its great leaders. The farmer and the merchant, the butcher, the baker, and the candlestick-maker—all of these played a role in colonial society. Looking inside their homes, meeting their wives and children, joining them for a meal, and quietly looking over their shoulder during times of leisure tells us much about them. And whether we observe these things from a delicate Chippendale settee imported from London or an oak bench as rough as the frontiersman who carved it, we should catch a glimpse of a varied and vibrant time that has been called "the morning of America."

I. The Rhythms of Life

Patchwork Population

It would not have been unusual while walking the streets of the British colonial cities of New York, Philadelphia, or Charleston to hear the chatter of German, Dutch, or French mingling with the English. Although English colonists constituted a clear majority, there was a remarkable degree of ethnic diversity in the colonies, particularly after 1700.

The two largest groups of non-English settlers were **Scots-Irish** (often erroneously called "Scotch-Irish") and Germans. The Scots-Irish were Presbyterian Scots from the Protestant colony of Ulster in Northern Ireland. Economic hard times and religious intolerance sent as many as a quarter-million Ulstermen to the colonies. Many arrived in Philadelphia, but most did not stay. Hungry for land, they migrated west and southwest, funneling down the Shenandoah Valley into the Virginia and Carolina backcountry. Their avenue through the wilderness was an old Iroquois Indian trail dubbed the "**Great Wagon Road**." The trail, as significant as any of its better-known successors, such as the National Road or the Santa Fe Trail, was the chief access to backcountry settlements from Virginia to Georgia. Tens of thousands of settlers traveled the rutted pass by foot or jostled down the rugged road in wagons built by skilled Germans from Pennsylvania's Conestoga Valley. Many of the Germans were Baptists, or "Dunkers." A string of inns along the seven-hundred-mile road grew into backcountry towns such as Frederick and Hagerstown, Maryland; Winchester, Staunton, and Fincastle, Virginia; Salisbury and Charlotte, North Carolina; Camden, South Carolina; and Augusta, Georgia.

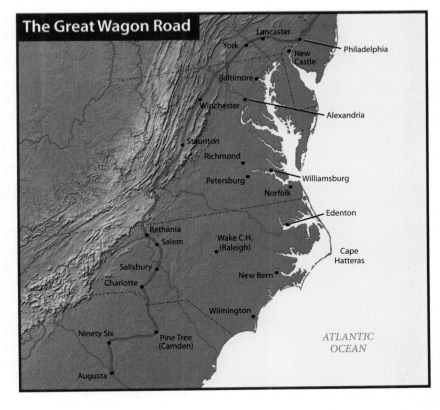

The Great Wagon Road

The German "Dunkers" were unique not only in immersing their converts but also for their "love feasts," or their commemoration of the Lord's Supper, and their practice of footwashing.

The Scots-Irish and the Germans generally occupied the vanguard of Appalachian expansion in the early eighteenth century. Some of them in their acquisition of wilderness land had little time or money for the "niceties" of land deeds and bills of sale. As squatters, they often presented their own version of a land title with lead shot.

Most of the Germans were Protestants from the Rhineland Palatinate (a region in southwestern Germany) who, tiring of the incessant raids by French Catholic armies under Louis XIV (ruled 1653–1715), came to America. Thousands of Germans arrived in Pennsylvania, attracted by the religious freedom of Penn's Quaker commonwealth and the rich farm country that was so much like their Rhine valley before the French had arrived.

A number of German immigrants remained in Pennsylvania, where they became known as **Pennsylvania Dutch**, a corruption of *Deutsch* ("German"). Others, however, followed the Scots-Irish into the Shenandoah or migrated from the Chesapeake settlements of Virginia into the Piedmont.

The rapid growth of German settlements bothered their English neighbors. To some observers, the Scots-Irish might have had strange views on religion, but at least they spoke the same language. But Germans were different. Philadelphian Benjamin Franklin lamented, "Why should the Palatine Boors be suffered to swarm into our Settlements? . . . Why should Pennsylvania, founded by the English, become a Colony of *Aliens*, who will shortly be so numerous as to Germanize us instead of Anglifying them, and will never adopt our Language or Customs?"

Despite Franklin's fears, the German and most other European immigrants quickly adapted to English ways while maintaining their own traditions. For the Rhinelander, German might have been the language with which he talked to his family and to God, but English was his language in the marketplace.

The blending of non-English cultures into the social landscape was an important influence in the development of America. A pluralistic society developed in which ethnic and religious diversity existed together. However, commercial, political, and religious bonds forged unity with diversity.

Marrying and Burying

The colonial population was not only varied but also growing. In 1700, the population stood at roughly 250,000, and it increased tenfold during the next three-quarters of the century to 2.5 million at the outset of the Revolution. Immigration was, of course, a contributing factor, but equally important was the high birthrate, which was twice that of Europe. The prolific birthrate was demonstrated in the 1790 census, which found that more than half of all Americans were under sixteen years of age.

A key reason for the increase was that colonial women married at a considerably younger age, usually around twenty. By contrast, their European counterparts married in their late twenties, if they married at all. Earlier marriages were prompted by the reversed sex ratio between the Old World and the New. In England, for example, women outnumbered men, which is a typical population feature. In the colonies, particularly in the late seventeenth-century South, men outnumbered women two or three to one. As a result, few women remained single, and earlier marriages meant more childbearing years.

Earlier marriages and large families were also favored because they provided an important labor source for the home. Fully 90 percent of the colonists depended on farming for their livelihood, and children provided helping hands and strong backs to put food on the table and in the market. Consequently, families with six to eight children were common, and even a dozen or more was not uncommon.

Unfortunately for our founding mothers, childbearing could prove fatal. Midwives of the day served to the best of their ability, but obstetrics was an unknown science. Infections and difficult deliveries sent many women to an early grave, and their babies usually followed them.

As serious as the infant death rate was in the colonies, it was dramatically lower than that experienced in Europe during the same period. The mortality rate there was grim—25 percent at birth and another 25 percent before the age of fifteen. Half the children in eighteenth-century Europe never reached adulthood. By contrast, records from late seventeenth-century Massachusetts reveal that nine out of ten children survived infancy. The scattered settlements of the New World and its productive and plentiful land inhibited the disease and famine that were prevalent in Europe's crowded conditions.

This fact offers an important clue as to why epidemics were more prevalent in eighteenth-century America than in the previous century. As cities grew, the crowded urban centers spawned contagious diseases. The problems of the Old World resurfaced in the New. Roads that emanated from the cities carried both settlers and germs to the frontier. Farmers bringing goods to the coastal market picked up not only exotic stories from the sailors they met there but also exotic diseases. Soldiers sent from crowded quarters in the cities to put down Indian attacks in the wilderness sometimes killed more settlers with their contagions than the Indians did with their weapons.

Epidemics of smallpox and infectious dysentery reduced the population in New England by as much as 10 percent during major outbreaks. The diphtheria epidemic of 1735–37 began in New Hampshire and spread southward into the middle colonies, leaving thousands dead in its wake. Children were particularly susceptible to the virus; nearly all of the victims were under twenty years of age. One interesting commentary on the commonness of childhood mortality is that homemade dolls in the colonial period sometimes came with their own coffins.

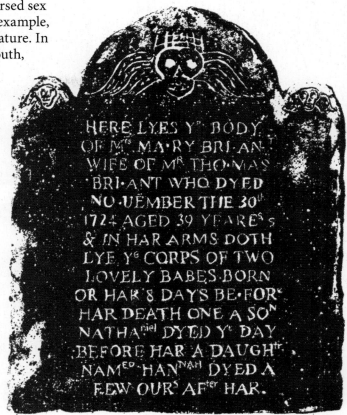

This 1724 epitaph of a Massachusetts wife tells an all too familiar story of the day.

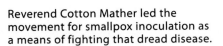

Reverend Cotton Mather led the movement for smallpox inoculation as a means of fighting that dread disease.

Despite such problems, the colonies generally flourished. The abundance of land invited expansion, and young men reaching adulthood usually married and moved on. The majority of families were isolated, independent, and largely self-sufficient. The husband, his wife, and their children shared the hardships and the rewards of carving a home out of the wilderness.

A drawing of Philadelphia in 1702 shows a bustling city where only wilderness had existed less than a hundred years before.

Fighting Smallpox

One of the first men in America to urge the use of inoculations to combat deadly smallpox was Rev. Cotton Mather, a godly Puritan pastor in Boston. Mather, a member of the British Royal Society, read that exposing a person to a mild strain of smallpox would enable him to resist the full effects of the disease. However, early inoculation attempts were risky, even fatal, and opposition to Mather's new ideas was intense. Even leading physicians of the day opposed it. Finally, Mather was put to the ultimate test when his son Samuel came down with the dreaded disease after being inoculated. In the following excerpts from his 1721 diary, Mather recorded the opposition to his pioneering efforts and his own personal struggle over the fate of his son.

[May] 26. The grievous Calamity of the *Small-Pox* has now entered the Town. The Practice of conveying and suffering the *Small-pox* by *Inoculation*, has never been used in *America*, nor indeed in our Nation. But how many Lives might be saved by it, if it were practiced? . . .

[June] 13. What shall I do? what shall I do, with regard unto *Sammy*? He comes home, when the Small-pox begins to spread in the Neighbourhood; and he is lothe to return unto *Cambridge*. I must earnestly look up to Heaven for Direction. . . .

[July] 16. At this Time, I enjoy an unspeakable Consolation. I have instructed our Physicians in the new Method used by the *Africans* and *Asiaticks*, to prevent and abate the Dangers of the *Small-pox*, and infallibly to save the Lives of those that have it wisely managed upon them. The Destroyer, being enraged at the Proposal of any Thing, that may rescue the Lives of our poor People from him, has taken a strange Possession of the People on this Occasion. They rave, they rail, they blaspheme; they talk not only like Ideots but also like *Franticks*. And not only the Physician who began the Experiment, but I also am an Object of Fury. . . .

[August] 1. Full of Distress about *Sammy*; He begs to have his Life saved, by receiving the *Small-Pox*, in the way of *Inoculation*, whereof our Neighbourhood has had no less than ten remarkable Experiments; and if he should after all die by receiving it in the common Way, how can I answer it? On the other Side, our People, who have Satan remarkably filling their Hearts and their Tongues, will go on with infinite Prejudices against me and my Ministry, if I suffer this Operation upon the Child. . . .

15. My dear *Sammy*, is now under the Operation of receiving the *Small-Pox* in the way of Transplantation. The Success of the Experiment among my Neighbours, as well as abroad in the World. . . [has] made me think, that I could not answer it unto God, if I neglected it. . . .

25. Friday. It is very critical Time with me, a Time of unspeakable Trouble and Anguish. My dear *Sammy*, has this Week had a dangerous and threatening Fever come upon him, which is beyond what the *Inoculation* for the *Small-Pox* has hitherto brought upon my Subjects of it. In this Distress, I have cried unto the Lord, and He has answered with a Measure of Restraint upon the Fever. The Eruption proceeds, and he proves pretty full, and has not the best sort, and some Degree of his Fever holds him. His Condition is very hazardous. . . .

[September] 5. *Sammy* recovering Strength. I must now earnestly putt him on considering, what he shall render to the Lord! Use exquisite Methods that he may come Gold out of the Fire. . . .

[November] 19. Certainly it becomes me and concerns me, to do something very considerable, in a way of Gratitude unto GOD my SAVIOUR, for the astonishing Deliverance, which He did the last Week bestow upon me, and upon what belong'd unto me.

When the epidemic was over, Mather was vindicated. Although the vaccine had proved fatal for 3 percent of those who received it, 15 percent of those who were not inoculated had died.

Section Quiz

1. What were the two largest groups of non-English settlers in the colonies?

2. Who were the "Pennsylvania Dutch"? Why did they settle in Pennsylvania?

3. Why did so many colonists prefer large families?

4. Why were epidemics more prevalent in eighteenth-century America than in the previous century?

★ What effect do you think the prominence of death and disease had on the colonists?

II. At Home

Housing

Styles of colonial houses changed with time, region, and the cultural heritage of their occupants. With the earliest houses, however, survival was more important than style. To weather their first wilderness winter, Plymouth settlers dug out caves and lined the walls with bark, or copied their Indian neighbors by constructing wigwams.

As a colony took on a more settled aspect, its residents built houses patterned after the styles they had known in England. Isolated by an ocean from the old country, the colonists were out of touch with the architectural "fashions" of seventeenth-century England. As a result, what we now consider "**colonial style**" or "Williamsburg style" architecture—steep gabled roofs, tall brick chimneys, brick arches over doors and windows, and interiors with exposed beam ceilings—was really the then century-old English Tudor-style construction.

The material for house exteriors depended to a large degree upon location. With rising prosperity, brick came into more common use, particularly in the tidewater regions where rich clay deposits were found. Farther inland the forest yielded a less expensive but weathertight exterior of split cedar or oak clapboard. In regions where the spring thaw produced a crop of new rocks in the field, farmers often turned stumbling stones into building blocks by using field stones to produce efficient and durable cottages.

The image of the Southern plantation as a sprawling, white mansion accented with magnolias and stately, wide verandas is largely mythical. Since a plantation was a large farm, the planter's house could best be described as a large farmhouse. Of course, there were elaborate exceptions, particularly in the early nineteenth century, but most Southern planters lived in a simple log or clapboard house. As their families and incomes grew, they added more rooms and elaborated on the structure—for example, replacing the translucent oiled paper windows with glass. Another popular addition to colonial plantation houses was the *piazza*, or roofed porch, a feature borrowed from the West Indies that provided some protection from the hot southern sun.

In the backcountry, shelters reflected the roughness of the land and its people. One observer recorded that during the first year or two, the Scots-Irish lived in "open Logg Cabbins," an open-face, three-sided log structure with a roof, crude and cold. After they were established, they generally built a cabin of notched logs, filling the chinks with moss and clay. German settlers generally squared up their logs and located the chimney in the middle of the cabin to centralize the heat source. The result was a tighter, tidier house.

Diet

The adage "you are what you eat" would certainly hold true in the colonial period, at least in terms of social standing. At a 1769 meeting of the Old Colony Club in Plymouth, Massachusetts, the menu featured nine courses: baked Indian whortleberry pudding, steaming succotash (a soup containing fowl, pork, and corned beef), a dish of clams on the half shell, a dish of oysters and codfish, roasted venison, a dish of duck, a dish of cod and eels, spicy apple pies, and a final course of succulent cranberry tarts and cheese.

Such dinners were, of course, for the wealthy. Down on the farm things were different. The standard fare for most families, particularly on the frontier, was salt pork, corn meal, Indian beans, and greens in the summer. The more settled farms often had an apple or peach orchard, a source of both food and drink. Hard cider and brandy were common beverages in the colonies; rum was more prevalent on the coast, where ports provided inlets for the West Indies liquor. Unfortunately, drunkenness was common, and its destructive force was felt throughout society. But the transforming power of the gospel proved to be a force that dried up the stills and delivered men and women from the bondage of drink.

In terms of colonial cuisine, a great deal of trading went on. The first Europeans in America discovered a new world of food. Corn, a variety of beans (such as snaps and limas), cacao (chocolate), tomatoes, squash, pumpkins, peppers, and peanuts were all Native American contributions to the colonial diet. The "Irish" potato, now a North American staple, made an interesting transatlantic trek. Spanish conquistadors first shipped white potatoes back home from Peru along with coffers of Incan gold. The unpretentious little potato would prove to be more valuable in the centuries to follow. Cultivated in Spain, Switzerland, and later the British Isles, potatoes made their way back across the Atlantic with the Scots-Irish in the 1700s, and they introduced the plant to North America.

Europeans also introduced foods to America: bananas, melons, rice, wheat, oats, and a favorite American beverage *after* the Boston Tea Party, coffee. An array of farm animals were also transplanted to America: cows, pigs, sheep, and chickens.

In what has been rightly called a "green revolution," transplanted Indian crops of corn and sweet potatoes sustained burgeoning populations across the Eurasian landmass from Beijing to Belfast. From the early days of its discovery, America was a breadbasket to the world, and clearly God's providential hand was at work in providing the blessing of food to an ever-growing world that has increased tenfold during the past three centuries. The psalmist rejoiced that the Lord "giveth food to all flesh: for his mercy endureth forever" (136:25).

Education

Whether children learned the "3 Rs" at home or attended a village school, the purpose behind the education was to provide basic skills and the ability to read the Bible. This emphasis reflected the Protestant character of America. As one historian put it, "It was the Protestant Reformation, and the Protestant insistence that every man have free access to the Word, without priestly interference, that finally broke the Church's monopoly on literacy." The completeness of the church's medieval monopoly on reading and writing is underscored by the fact that during the five hundred years from the sixth to the eleventh century, only three English kings could sign their own names.

The Reformation not only created a spiritual revolution but also triggered an educational revolution, because an obvious prerequisite for reading the Scriptures is learning to read. In England, "Puritan zeal" for the Word of God and widespread spiritual hunger produced a boom in education in the early 1600s. This fact is particularly important in understanding the educational climate in Puritan New England.

It has been estimated that there was a greater percentage of college graduates in Massachusetts during the 1630s than there is today. Despite the privations of the wilderness, the founders were determined that their children would not be deprived of an education. The home was the first schoolhouse in America.

A child's first "book," the **hornbook**, was a board shaped ominously like a paddle. On its face was a card containing the alphabet and the Lord's Prayer, and it was covered with a thin sheet of horn for durability. A child usually "graduated" from the hornbook to a primer (PRIHM er) for more thorough reading training. The ***New England Primer*** served as the standard text throughout the colonial period. It provided basic grammar and vocabulary accented with moral lessons and also included a short catechism.

Not all colonial parents were capable of or interested in teaching their children at home. Particularly in New England the concentrated pattern of village settlements contributed to the development of the village school. Such schools, open to boys and girls, were often called **dame schools** since they were generally taught by a widow or a village spinster.

Outside New England, two factors—geography and the lack of a Puritan presence with its enthusiasm for the printed page—limited the scope of colonial literacy. In the middle colonies and the South, farms were more scattered and families more isolated. As late as 1860, Virginia had 14 residents per square mile whereas Massachusetts had 127.

The majority of people living in the rugged backcountry did not have the luxury of a village school; most of them lived days from the nearest outpost. If parents were illiterate, their children would likely be as well. Many parents, however, made extraordinary efforts and sacrifices to have their children taught, even if only through infrequent contact with literate travelers, indentured servants, or missionaries. Devereaux Jarratt, born in poverty in colonial Virginia, recorded that the highest ambition of his parents "was to teach their children to read, write, and understand the fundamental rules of arithmetic." Jarratt, like others, after learning the rudiments of reading, would walk miles to borrow even a single book.

Although education in the backcountry was often hit-or-miss, those who could afford it hired private tutors for their children. A number of towns with greater resources made efforts to establish schools. Charleston, South Carolina, for example, sponsored two free schools for the education of the poor. Charleston also led the way in 1698 by establishing the first public library in America.

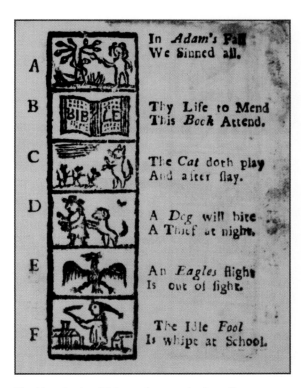

The *New England Primer*, the standard reading textbook in New England, tried to inculcate the truths of Scripture while teaching the basics of reading.

"Old Deluder Satan" Law

Leaders of the Massachusetts colony passed three laws dealing with public education in the 1640s. The most famous began with the words "ye ould deluder Satan" and explained that illiteracy enabled Satan to prevent men from direct access to God's Word. The Puritans, along with other Protestants, saw the importance of being able to read and viewed a basic education as essential to an informed and Christian-influenced society.

Other colonies passed similar laws. These laws became the foundation upon which others built compulsory public education.

Section Quiz

1. What were two of the materials used in the construction of colonial houses?

2. List at least four of the Native American foods that Europeans found in the New World.

3. Why was the literacy rate higher in New England than in the other regions?

4. According to the "Old Deluder Satan" law, what enabled Satan to prevent men from direct access to God's Word?

★ Do you think including explicitly religious instruction in the *New England Primer* was a good method of instruction? Why or why not?

III. At Work

Four fictional characters will be described to portray life in the colonies.

Louis Timothy, Rice Farmer (Edisto Island, South Carolina, 1718)

Louis Timothy felt justly proud as the carpenters put the finishing touches on the clapboards which covered his log house. His wife wanted them white-washed, but that could wait until next year. Besides the cost, it would take time away from his work in the rice fields. For the young planter, the new face on an old house was a fitting sign of the success that had marked his path in recent years.

Though successful, they had not been easy years. Louis had arrived at the Charles Town wharves as a lad with his family among a shipload of refugees. His father, the elder Louis Timothée, was a French Huguenot who had taken his family to the Carolina colony when life in France became too dangerous for Protestants. After arriving in Charles Town, the Timothée family had made their way down the coast and found a niche of cheap land on the Edisto River.

Their three-hundred-acre tract was not a pretty prospect when they arrived. Before them lay a tangle of swamp and sand covered with scrubby pines and imposing cypress trees. The elder Timothée felled the best pines, and young Louis set about squaring them up with an adze. That first year their house was no more than a two-room cabin with a roof of palmetto palms and a floor of native sand. Aside from a table, benches, and straw bedding, the house was bare of furnishings. During the first year, food, not shelter, was the priority. A man would die of starvation before he died from exposure. Subsistence crops of corn and vegetables were the first things planted to feed a hungry family. The daylight hours were spent wrestling a farm out of the wilderness.

The coastal flats had rich, productive soil, but the land had to be cleared by cutting trees and burning and digging out stumps. It was exhausting work, the merciless sun beating down on the laborers, while mosquitoes and biting sand fleas, or sand flies, usually joined them in the field—sometimes giving them killing fevers.

Louis's younger brother died during their second spring on the land. He was the family's first, but not its last, victim of malaria. The elder Timothée died of the fever in 1710 and was buried between his son and his wife beneath a moss-draped cypress. Charlotte Timothée had died in childbearing six years earlier.

Louis Timothy now stood surveying the land his father had conquered. He liked innovation. He had Anglicized his name and had moved from the subsistence farming of his youth to the cultivation of rice. The cash crop was suited to not only his land but also the needs of his growing family and his own rising expectations.

Preparing the land for growing rice had been an exhausting, back-breaking task. To undertake the work, Mr. Timothy had purchased three slaves in Charles Town, and they joined him and his eldest son in the field, along with the two slaves that he had inherited from his father. Their first task was to turn the stream that meandered through the land into an irrigation canal complete with a sluice to provide the controlled flooding needed to grow rice. The land itself had to be leveled and divided by a grid of ditches for flooding and draining. All of this labor had been done with hoes, shovels, and muscles.

In the spring, they planted the tiny rice seeds in the fresh, dark soil and then flooded the fields for a few days as the life in the seeds took hold beneath the warm cover of water. Through the summer the green shoots ripened to golden grain. By September, the rice was ready for harvest. With sickles flashing, Timothy, his son, and their slaves moved slowly through the fields cutting the rice. Sometimes the black men sang harvest songs in strange tongues of Ibo and Mandingo, the languages of their native Africa in the happier years before they fell into the hands of an enemy African chieftain, then Dutch and British middlemen, and finally, Master Timothy.

This year's harvest would amount to forty bushels to the acre. The cutting was only the beginning, however. The slaves would work until Christmas on the monotonous routine of flailing and husking the kernels. Timothy would oversee their work, as well as the cutting of timber and irrigation repairs. In late winter, he would gather his finished grain on flatboats for the Charles Town market. With money in his pocket, Louis Timothy would return with cloth, shoes, nails, tools, and a bucket of paint for his patient wife.

Debora Riedhauser, House Servant (Germantown, Pennsylvania, 1747)

As the coals glowed and fired the crackling wood, Debora could see her breath in the frosty November air. The sun was not yet up over the Pennsylvania countryside when she began to prepare breakfast. The house was quiet—though it would not be for long when the children awoke! For Debora it was her favorite time of her busy day, especially this morning because it was her sixteenth birthday.

Her mistress had remembered and promised her a pennysheet on her next trip to the market. After learning the hornbook, Debora had only dreamed of owning a book. The pennysheet was no book but was merely a page with pictures and words of wisdom from *Poor Richard's Almanack* by that witty Mr. Franklin of neighboring Philadelphia. Nonetheless, it would still be quite a treasure.

Debora's master, Josiah Hastings, had said nothing about her birthday. She figured he was probably thinking about her birthday in two years when her indenture would end. Well, Debora was thinking about that day, too—with mixed emotions. This had been her home for three years since she had arrived in Philadelphia from her native Bavaria. Debora was an orphan; her mother's death was only a vague

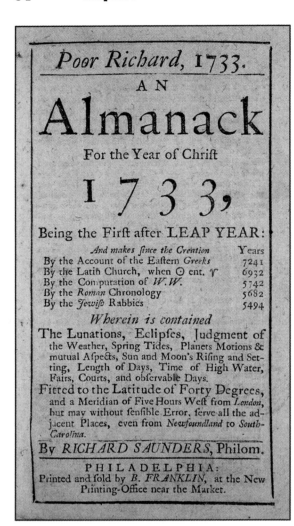

memory, and her father had been killed fighting the Austrians during one of the frequent wars that swept the German countryside. Her uncle, not wanting any more mouths to feed, had sent Debora and her two brothers to America. Their passages were paid in Philadelphia in return for five years of service. The purchasers, however, were indifferent to keeping the family together. One brother lived twenty-five miles away from Debora's Germantown home. Being a full day's journey apart, they seldom saw each other, except at Christmas. Her other brother had left with his redemptioner down the Great Wagon Road and had not been heard from since.

Master Hastings had taken on young Debora as a house servant during his wife's long and uncertain recovery from complications with pregnancy. The baby had died, and Mrs. Hastings had been left far too weak to care for her four other children.

Stirring noises upstairs shook Debora out of her thoughts. Fortunately, yesterday's coals were glowing brightly this morning, and the fire started quickly. One day last week the embers had grown cold, and no amount of coaxing could bring fire from them. Debora had had to go borrow a "chunk of fire" from the neighbor's hearth to get a fire started; breakfast was late, and Master Hastings was cross.

Debora adjusted the Dutch oven, a three-legged covered pot, and dropped a cut of 'possum fat into it. Over the sizzling grease she poured a batter of cornmeal and sour milk to make flat johnnycakes.

The table was set with seven wooden plates, seven wooden noggins, and seven wooden spoons. Pewter was only for the rich, and Debora had never even seen a China plate or a silver spoon.

The noon meal would be hearty but simple: dried apples, cold mush, and hot cider. Supper would fill the house with smells of cabbage, cheese, sausage, and maybe a stiff brew made from roasted chestnuts to warm them before the night chill set in.

Between meal preparations Debora would milk the cow, churn its milk for butter, and help her mistress weave linsey-woolsey (a

Poor Richard's Almanack

One of the most popular reading pastimes of the late colonial period was the almanac, and none surpassed Benjamin Franklin's *Poor Richard's Almanack*, which he published from 1733 to 1758. In addition to the usual astronomical and weather predictions, it was filled with witticisms that emphasized thrift, honesty, and diligence. Even today, Franklin's sayings flavor our conversation. Here are a few examples.

- Fish and visitors stink after three days.
- Well done is better than well said.

- A spoonful of honey will catch more flies than a gallon of vinegar.
- The used key is always bright.
- Little strokes fell great oaks.
- If your head is wax, don't walk in the sun.
- Beware of little expenses; a small leak will sink a great ship.
- Pay what you owe, and you'll know what is your own.
- Three may keep a secret—if two of them are dead.
- Lost time is never found again.
- Haste makes waste.

- Early to bed and early to rise makes a man healthy, wealthy, and wise.
- Keep your eyes wide open before marriage, half shut afterwards.
- Forewarned is forearmed.
- Creditors have better memories than debtors.
- Glass, china, and reputation are easily cracked and never well mended.
- If Jack's in love, he's no judge of Jill's beauty.
- Plow deep while sluggards sleep.

mixture of linen and wool) for shirt cloth. In the meantime there was old cloth that needed repairing—the sleeve of a toddler's coat, and the seat of her master's pants. Yet as little feet scampered down the stairs to breakfast, all of these things, like her life, lay ahead of her. For on her sixteenth birthday, this German orphan thought not so much about what the past had given her as what the future offered her in this new land.

Akachi, Slave
(Virginia, 1720)

Sweat pouring from his brow, Akachi heaved a barrel into the ship's hold. Only ten barrels were left, and then he could go take care of some of his own business. The New York sun was setting, and he would have to hurry if he was going to be on time to his meeting with the merchant.

Akachi was grateful to God to be where he was, but the road that he had taken to get here was one of terrible suffering. He was torn from his home in Africa as a boy by a neighboring Ibo tribesman and sold to Dutch slave traders. The "middle passage" of the journey from Africa to the New World was the worst time of Akachi's life. The slave traders kept Akachi chained and crammed in the ship's hold with many other slaves. Hunger, thirst, and the specter of death were his constant friends. Akachi watched many of his fellow slaves die before they could reach the New World. In those dark days he had wished for death, but the providence of God had preserved him for a purpose.

Once in the New World, Akachi was sold and resold to several Virginia planters, and he labored long days in the hot sun growing tobacco. Some of his masters were kind, but one master in particular was especially cruel. He demanded that Akachi change his name to the European name Henry. When Akachi refused, his master forced him to work wearing chains until Akachi submitted to the new name.

Eventually a naval officer purchased Akachi, and Akachi helped his master fight in the French and Indian War. During this time Akachi started to learn how to read, and he learned much about the navy. During this period Akachi also became a Christian. He had heard the powerful preaching of George Whitefield in Philadelphia, and the message moved Akachi to learn more of Christ. He was converted and baptized. However, because he was a slave, Akachi had to sit in the balcony of church with the other slaves and could not truly fellowship with all the Christians in the church.

After the war, a New York sea merchant, Mr. Bradfield, bought Akachi. Bradfield was a Quaker, and slavery bothered his conscience. So he allowed Akachi to do some trading on his own, and he promised to free Akachi if he could get enough money. Akachi worked hard because he could see an end to his bondage. Akachi had a hard life, but he knew that God had planned this path for him so that he could be not only physically free but also spiritually free.

Jeremy Shrimpton, Wigmaker
(Boston, Massachusetts, 1735)

The list of accounts in the large ledger brought a smile to Master Shrimpton's lips—business had been good. His decision to move his business from his native London to the colonies five years earlier had paid off handsomely. Wigmakers were as much in demand in America as they were in England and on the Continent. Ever since French royalty started wearing wigs beginning with Louis XIII a century earlier, the powdered hairpieces had remained the fashion rage for men of station. The twenty-three-year-old Louis had donned one because of his thinning hair—his ancestor Charles the Bald was called that for good reason.

Now, however, even men with thick locks were being fitted for wigs. For many it was as essential to their business attire as a coat-and-tie would be at a later day. In the eighteenth-century professional world, a wigless man might easily be taken for a witless man among the stiff upper crust of business barons. Well, such attitudes were good for business too, Shrimpton mused, and the rising merchant class in Boston was as fashion conscious as any he had fitted in London or Liverpool.

Looking up from his shop window desk, Shrimpton could see the gleaming masts of sloops and schooners anchored in Boston Harbor. Their owners were his best customers, so he always enjoyed seeing a busy harbor. A sharp rap on the door, however, interrupted his deskwork. Shrimpton opened the door to a rumpled farmer, probably in town selling produce. The wigmaker eyed his visitor coolly. He sniffed contemptuously and thought, *A backwoods bumpkin, he certainly has no use for a wig!*

In his thoughts, the gristly farmer sniffed back, *Now here's a fancy little fellow, a real dandy.*

In their own way, both men were too professional to give words to such thoughts—the visit was strictly business. "Do you buy hair?" the farmer began. "My wife's going to sell hers."

Shrimpton nodded and followed him to a wagon where a tense little woman sat. The wigmaker ran his bony fingers through her hair and held it up with an experienced hand. "Three shillings," he said to the farmer. With a nod the locks were snipped. After Shrimpton had applied his craft to these long locks, the hair would adorn the head of a merchant or minister who, unlike the farmer's wife, had more money than hair.

Jeremy Shrimpton made a variety of wig styles to suit the tastes and incomes of his clients. Common folks who wanted budget fashions could purchase a simple curled wig called a Sunday Buckle.

The wealthy had a variety to choose from, such as the Campaign Wig for traveling, the Bagwig in which the long back tresses were held in a dainty silk pouch, and the Cadogan, a foppish array of bows and curls. All of these hair pieces were large, flowing extravagances. Their owners were not called bigwigs for nothing.

Wigmaking was a careful, customized process. First, a client would arrive at Shrimpton's shop for head measurements and style selection. Next, purchased hair was cleaned, combed, rolled, and baked in rye dough to temper and strengthen the hair. Then the wigmaker drew up a pattern based on the head measurements and constructed a foundation net known as a caul into which he wove the strands of hair. He lined the caul with silk and edged it with a silk ribbon that buckled or tied in the back for a snug fit.

To that point, Shrimpton's two apprentices did most of the work. The next two steps of finishing and dressing, however, required the master's touch. In the finishing stage, he shaped the curls and added precision parts. Finally, he "dressed" the wig with powder and perfume. The powder was added for coloring, of which there were a variety of shades from white or blonde to chestnut or black.

Despite the time and talent invested in making a wig, it seemed that a wigmaker's work was never done. Not only did he have new orders to fill but also old wigs to care for. On Saturdays, Shrimpton sent his two apprentices out to make house calls to rescue drooping curls and to refragrance smelly wigs in time for Sunday worship.

Jeremy Shrimpton continued to do a brisk trade. For another generation, wigs remained essential to the well-dressed man. By the end of the century, though, neither the king's army nor his fashions dominated America, and wigs became a curious relic of a former day.

Section Quiz

1. Which of the four fictional characters in this section—Louis Timothy, Debora Riedhauser, Akachi, or Jeremy Shrimpton— had the easiest time surviving in colonial America?

2. Which of the three characters had the brightest, most promising future?

3. How did God turn Akachi's slavery into a positive outcome?

✶ How are the values of freedom and growth discussed in Chapter 2 seen in these narratives?

IV. At Play

People have several misconceptions about colonial leisure that must be dispelled before we can gain a proper understanding of it. First, leisure time existed. Naturally, in the early years of settlement along the coast, the priority was survival; virtually the only contact among pioneers, in a nonwork setting, was on Sundays at church. When life became more settled, more leisure time was possible. This pattern occurred repeatedly as the frontier moved progressively farther west. This explains some of the differences between leisure activities in the cities and in the backcountry settlements during the later colonial period.

Second, Americans *did* enjoy life during the colonial period. Modern views of the colonists (particularly the Puritans) as sour, dour sticklers with dark clothes and darker looks is at best a bad caricature. Puritans had colorful wardrobes, listened to good music, and enjoyed good literature and wholesome games. The word *pleasure* was definitely in the Puritan's vocabulary. What was also in his vocabulary was *consistency*. A godly believer did not leave off his relationship to Christ during his leisure moments; rather, he honored Christ in them. In a manner of speaking, he did not lay aside his robes of righteousness when he put on his play clothes. He believed that God was to be honored in all things, not just in the pew and the pulpit.

Children in colonial times played just as children today do, but they also worked at household chores a lot more.

Leisure activities in the urban areas and those in the backcountry definitely differed. Being closer together, city folks had more opportunities to socialize and organize clubs and activities. Their country cousins, however, were scattered and isolated by many miles and sometimes swollen rivers and dense forests. Even at the risk of being dull, survival on the frontier often meant all work and no play. Yet, the backwoodsmen, being innovators by necessity, found ways to combine the two.

Barn raisings, corn huskings, and quiltings gave opportunities for frontier families to gather and socialize while sharing the work load. At such events, adults exchanged news and children played with other children. The gatherings often culminated in a bonfire where people played music, danced, and spun tall tails.

Even worship services were social occasions in the backcountry. One Anglican missionary to the Carolinas, Charles Woodmason, complained in his journal, "No making of them sit still during Service—but they will be in and out—forward and backward the whole time (women especially) as Bees to and fro to their hives."

Such infrequent social gatherings in the isolated outback stood in sharp contrast to the other end of the geographic and economic scale. In the eastern cities of Charleston, Williamsburg, Philadelphia, New York, and Boston, wealthy planters and merchants kept a full social calendar through myriad clubs, balls, and parties. In Charleston, where wealthy planters escaped their swampy lands from May to December, a 1773 diary reveals a number of clubs that the movers and shakers could join, including the Smoking Club, Laughing Club, Beef-Steak Club, Monday-Night Club, Friday-Night Club, and the Fort Jolly Volunteers.

However, not everyone in the city was rich and famous enough for such exclusive merrymaking. Other city dwellers enjoyed bowling games on the village green, picnics, or trips to the tavern, where they could hear the news either through the usual story swapping or from a patron reading a newspaper aloud. Such newspapers, which became a part of colonial life in the second quarter of the eighteenth century, featured colonial happenings, advertisements, obituaries, and humor, as well as the latest "news" (usually several months old) from London .

Colonial newspapers were published in all the major cities; they included Boston's *New England Courant*, Philadelphia's *American Weekly Mercury* and *Pennsylvania Gazette* (published by Benjamin Franklin), and Charleston's *South Carolina Gazette*. Such newspapers liberally reprinted each others' articles. The papers filtered to outback communities by horse and rider, providing a much-needed break in the isolation of wilderness living.

The toys and games of colonial children included marbles, hoops, dolls, puzzles, hopscotch, shuffleboard, shuttlecock (badminton), "I sent a letter to my love," and whoop-and-hide (hide-and-seek). Most toys were homemade, simple, and highly prized because a child generally had very few of them. A girl, for example, usually had one doll during her childhood, often carved from a stick or made from a corncob. Swimming and fishing were popular in the summer and iceskating and sleigh rides in the winter when possible. Children of the more affluent could even take trips to the beach for swimming, or if they lacked the necessary skill, could wear a "cork jacket" which, as one 1769 New York advertisement noted, had "saved many from drowning."

Ben Franklin and His Water Tools

A little-known fact about Benjamin Franklin is that he conducted many experiments with tools for use on or in the water. An avid swimmer himself, he experimented with various flotation devices (he called them "swimmies") to help swimmers stay afloat or to rescue foundering swimmers. He also windsurfed using a kite for propulsion.

In the growing, varied leisure time of the period is an underlying fact—the colonies were maturing and prospering. Political and economic freedom leads to material prosperity and the invention of time- and labor-saving devices, which allow more leisure for the development and pursuit of the finer things of life and culture. The "starving times" seemed to be but a distant footnote as each generation built upon the foundation of their fathers. As future president John Adams explained to his wife:

> I must study politics and war, that my sons may have liberty to study mathematics and philosophy, geography, natural history and naval architecture, navigation, commerce, and agriculture, in order to give their children a right to study painting, poetry, music, architecture, statuary, tapestry, and porcelain.

Adams had a lot of politics and war to study in the late colonial period. The colonies were maturing, Britain's grip on her offspring was loosening, and Americans were gaining a greater sense of independence.

Section Quiz

1. What is the typical modern view of the Puritans? Why is that view inaccurate?
2. What are some examples of social gatherings on the frontier?
3. What are some examples of social gatherings in a colonial city?
4. List some of the toys and games of colonial children.
★ How did the Puritans reflect a Christian view of leisure?

People, Places, and Things to Remember
Scots-Irish
"Great Wagon Road"
Pennsylvania Dutch
"colonial style" architecture
hornbook
New England Primer
dame schools
Poor Richard's Almanack

Chapter Review

Making Connections

1. How did the Great Philadelphia Wagon Road aid in developing the American frontier?
2. Why was the birthrate higher in America than in Europe in the 1700s?
3. Name at least three deadly diseases that American colonists faced.
4. Why was education so important to the Puritans?
5. Where was the first public library in America established?
6. What role did colonial newspapers play in spreading news to cities and rural areas?

Developing History Skills

1. Describe a colonial style house.
2. Considering that most frontier people lived several day's journey from the nearest trading outpost, how would that affect their daily lives?

Thinking Critically

1. Considering the danger of smallpox inoculation, would you have undergone such treatment if you had lived in colonial days?
2. Was it in the best interest of the Massachusetts Bay Colony to provide public education? Is it generally good for government to provide education?

Living as a Christian Citizen

1. Choose a saying from *Poor Richard's Almanack* and write a brief paragraph telling why it would or would not be sound advice for a Christian to follow.
2. Review the quotation from John Adams and the story of Louis Timothy. What common principle can be drawn from them?

"Pilgrims Going to Church" by George Henry Boughton

Religion in the American Colonies

   I.   **Established Denominations**

   II. **Non-Established Denominations**

   III. **Colonial Worship**

   IV. **Indian Missions**

   V.   **The Great Awakening**

"And we are evidently a people blessed of the Lord! And here in this corner of the world, God dwells and manifests his glory."

Jonathan Edwards, 1736
"A Faithful Narrative of the Surprising Work of God"

The tall, lean minister stood behind the wooden pulpit and faced his audience. He began his sermon, speaking it in careful, measured tones. His words astounded his listeners. "There is nothing that keeps wicked men at any one moment out of Hell," he declared, "but the mere pleasure of God." He continued,

> O sinner, consider the fearful danger you are in! It is a great furnace of wrath, a wide and bottomless pit that you are held over in the hand of that God Whose wrath is provoked and incensed as much against you as against the damned in Hell. You hang by a slender thread, with the flames of divine wrath flashing about it and ready every moment to singe it and burn it asunder; and you have . . . nothing to lay hold of to save yourself—nothing that you have done, nothing that you can do to induce God to spare you one moment.

As the minister preached, some in the congregation cried out in fear, struck with overwhelming conviction. Others grew solemn. As the fear of divine judgment began to grip the audience, the preacher exhorted his listeners, "Therefore, let everyone that is out of Christ now awake and flee from the wrath to come."

The year was 1741, the speaker was Jonathan Edwards, and the sermon was "Sinners in the Hands of an Angry God." Next to the Pilgrims' first Thanksgiving, Edwards's preaching of this sermon is one of the most famous events in colonial American history. The sermon was a climax to religious development in colonial America. Behind "Sinners in the Hands of an Angry God" lay more than a century of diverse, complex, and intriguing religious history.

I.   Established Denominations

Denominations that enjoyed state support and protection were called established denominations. The concept of a state-supported church began with Constantine in the fourth century and continued for centuries. The established denominations included the Puritans in New England and the Anglicans in Virginia and the Carolinas. State support included financial aid from taxes and exclusive rights enforced by the state.

English Background

The heritage of the American colonies was predominantly English. Understanding the religious history of England, therefore, helps us understand the religious history of the colonies. During the 1500s, England swung back and forth like a pendulum from Catholicism to Protestantism. King Henry VIII (ruled 1509–47) broke from the Roman Catholic Church, but only because he wanted to divorce his wife, and he remained doctrinally a Catholic. Under Henry's son, Edward VI (ruled 1547–53), Protestant leaders pushed for a thorough reform, insisting on drastic and immediate changes that offended a large portion of the English people. Edward's successor, the Roman Catholic Queen Mary (ruled 1553–58), attempted to reinstate Catholicism in England by means which included burning some three hundred Protestants at the stake.

After all of this turmoil, Queen Elizabeth (ruled 1558–1603) determined to put an end to religious controversy. Elizabeth wanted a Protestant church, so the creed of the Church of England was thoroughly Protestant. At the same time, Elizabeth hoped to win over the reluctant by preserving the outward trappings of the old church—its bishops, elaborate garments for priests, and so on.

Differing reactions to this "**Elizabethan settlement**" led to the formation of three important groups within the Church of England and one outside. The **Puritans** were staunch Protestants who agreed wholeheartedly with the Anglican creed. They thought that the old ceremonies and practices, however, were too much like those of the Roman Catholic Church. The Anglican Church, they said, must be "purified" of such corruptions.

Low-church Anglicans agreed doctrinally with the Puritans but saw no problem with the church's ceremonies and structure. Such matters were unimportant, the low-church party held, as long as the church was doctrinally sound. **High-church Anglicans** held that the church's traditional practices, notably its rule by bishops, were divinely ordained. Doctrinally, the high-church Anglicans differed among themselves, but they were generally more liberal in their beliefs and less opposed to Catholicism than the Puritan and low-church parties.

Finally, the **Separatists** believed that the whole Church of England was corrupt and that true Christians must separate from it. Separatist groups included the Pilgrims and later the Baptists and the Quakers.

Puritanism in America

Although Virginia was the site of America's earliest settlement, New England was, in some respects, more influential. The Puritan views of the settlers in Massachusetts Bay and the surrounding regions affected every other colony to some extent and later shaped the religious character of the United States. In short, New England Puritanism was the most influential religious movement in colonial history.

Puritan Beliefs

Like other Protestants, the Puritans believed the basic doctrines of the Reformation: the authority of the Bible alone, justification by faith alone, and so on. The heart of Puritan theology in particular is the idea of the covenant. Puritans believed that God deals with mankind through a series of covenants, or agreements. For example, the Puritans held that in salvation the believer enters into a "covenant of grace" with God. God saves an individual and in return the believer fulfills his "covenant obligations" by obeying God's law.

The covenant idea affected every aspect of Puritan society. Like Israel in the Old Testament, the Puritans believed that as a community they had made a social covenant with God to establish a model society ruled by God's laws. The settlers hoped not only to establish a society in accordance with God's standards but also to demonstrate to England how such a godly society should operate.

The covenant idea also affected the personal lives of individual Puritans. Because each Christian is in a covenant with God, he has certain responsibilities to fulfill. Of course, the Puritans did not believe salvation resulted from good works but that good works were the natural result of salvation. Puritans agreed with Romans 12:1 that Christian dedication was simply the "reasonable service" of one who had received the "mercies of God."

Another distinguishing feature of New England Puritanism was its church polity, or system of government in the church. In **episcopal polity**, such as that in the Church of England, an authority such as a monarch appoints bishops. The bishops, in turn, appoint lower officials down to the individual churches. In **presbyterian polity** (with ascending levels of church government including the presbytery, the synod, and the General Assembly), such as that in the Church of Scotland, members of the congregation elect their ruling elders. Elders from several congregations then elect officials for the next level of authority, those officials elect the next higher level, and so on.

New England Puritans chose neither of these polities. They preferred **congregational polity**, by which each congregation elected its own officers, and each church remained independent of other churches. Other groups, notably the Baptists, also adopted congregational polity. Eventually, most of the Puritans in America came to be called simply **Congregationalists**.

EPISCOPAL POLITY
(Church of England)

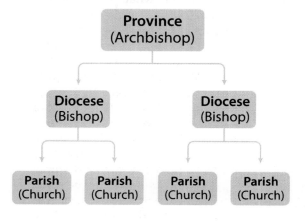

PRESBYTERIAN POLITY

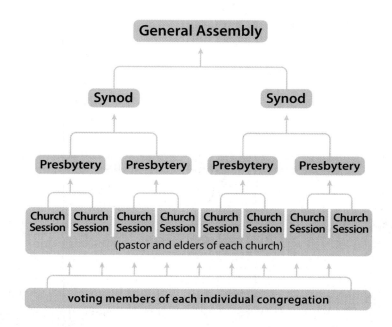

Puritan Decline

Like the children of Israel after the deaths of Joshua and the elders who outlived him (Judg. 2:7–10), the Puritans declined in religious fervor after the original generation of settlers had died. Later generations built a prosperous colony and usually remained outwardly moral, but they lacked the fervent piety of their forefathers. Materialism, the love of possessions and wealth, replaced a love for God. This decline created a serious problem in the Congregationalist churches.

During the first generation, saved adults formed the Congregationalist churches, and other adults entered upon profession of faith in Jesus Christ. The pastor baptized the children of church members as infants. These children were then considered members of the church but could not become full members and take the Lord's Supper until they "owned the covenant," declaring their personal faith in Christ. As the years passed, fewer and fewer members of the later generations owned the covenant.

The Truth About the Salem Witch Trials

In 1692 in Salem Village, Massachusetts, a group of young girls began having hysterical fits. They claimed that witches were afflicting them and began to name certain people in the village as witches. Based virtually on the testimonies of those girls alone, authorities began to arrest and then to try several astonished Salem citizens. Nineteen people were hanged; one man was pressed to death with heavy weights; an unknown number died in prison.

Ironically, only those who maintained their innocence were executed; those who confessed escaped the hangman's noose or other instruments of death. Realizing this fact, some of the accused confessed to save themselves. Others could not do so in good conscience. Mary Easty said to her judges, "I know not the least thing of witchcraft, therefore I cannot, I dare not belie my own soul. I beg your honors not to deny this my

humble petition from a poor dying innocent person." She was hanged anyway.

Several factors are ignored in the blast of accusations hurled at the Puritans. The ministers of Massachusetts, rather than being persecuting fanatics, actually counseled caution and restraint to the more zealous civil authorities. It was the opposition of some of the clergy, in fact, that helped end the witch trials. Boston pastor Cotton Mather, who is often falsely accused of urging authorities on, said, "It were better that ten suspected witches should escape than that one innocent person should be condemned."

Often forgotten too is the fact that some people in Massachusetts actually were practicing witchcraft—although it is difficult to tell whether that practice was mere superstition or real demonic activity. Even if this activity were only superstition, nearly

everyone at that time—not just the Puritans—*believed* that it was genuine witchcraft and that it must be relentlessly punished. In the century before the Salem witch trials, for example, more than three thousand accused witches were burned in the Swiss canton of Vaud alone. Salem, by contrast, was restrained.

Critics of the Puritans also ignore the repentance of Salem. Within five years the citizens of Massachusetts held a day of prayer and fasting to implore God's pardon for their actions. One of the judges in the trials, Samuel Sewall, was overcome with guilt when his son read Matthew 12:7 during the family's devotions: "But if ye had known what this meaneth, I will have mercy, and not sacrifice, ye would not have condemned the guiltless." Sewall, in remorse, went to church, confessed his guilt to the congregation, and asked for forgiveness. Anne Putnam, one of the hysterical girls, likewise stood before the congregation in Salem Village and humbly apologized for being "an instrument for the accusing of several persons of a grievous crime, whereby their lives were taken away from them, whom now I have just grounds and good reason to believe they were innocent persons."

What, exactly, happened in Salem Village? No one today can be quite sure. We do know certainly, however, that innocent people died because of fear and hysteria. We know too that the reputation of Massachusetts Puritans has been blemished. Regrettably, the worthy contributions of early American Puritanism have been obscured by the wild fanaticism of a few and by an eager willingness of later generations to believe only the worst.

The Salem witch trials were characterized by high emotions and hysteria.

The early Puritans were committed to constructing a holy commonwealth. This meant maintaining a pure church in a pure society. Though this had not been possible in England, the Puritans believed it could be a reality in New England. But as subsequent generations failed to own the covenant, the Puritans worried that the society was becoming impure, just as it was in England. They reasoned that it would be better to have non-professors filling the church pews than to exclude them and have empty pews. The leaders remained convinced that the church would be able to exercise a positive influence in society by admonishing and disciplining those whose lives became openly sinful.

The presence of unconverted church members led to another issue. Could the children of these unsaved members be baptized? Eventually, the ministers of New England devised what became known as the **Half-Way Covenant**. Church members who had not owned the covenant but whose lives were outwardly moral could present their children for baptism. Initially, neither the parents nor the children could become full members and take the Lord's Supper until they professed a personal faith in Christ. Despite its purpose of keeping people in the church and under sound preaching, the Half-Way Covenant served only to increase the number of unregenerate church members. It was a serious compromise of the principles of the original Puritans.

The Salem Witch Trials

Several factors contributed to the spiritual decline in New England. For example, in 1691 the Massachusetts colony received a new charter that required religious pluralism. This diminished the Puritan influence and encouraged a diversity that included many unbelievers. In addition, financial success lulled many Puritans into valuing material wealth over spiritual prosperity. The rapidly growing population also resulted in a large increase of unbelievers in Massachusetts. Finally, the decline of Harvard into deism and Unitarianism poisoned the spiritual and intellectual well that had produced many pastors and other leaders for the colony.

The low point in Puritan history came in 1692. Having forsaken much of the faith of their fathers, the Massachusetts colonists sank into fanaticism and hysteria. The **Salem witch trials** resulted from the claims of several young girls in Salem Village, Massachusetts, that witches were afflicting them. The authorities took the charges seriously and began to try those who were accused. Before the hysteria was over, at least twenty people were dead, and the reputation of Massachusetts suffered permanent damage. The spiritually chilling influences of the Half-Way Covenant and the reaction to the hysteria of the witch trials left New England spiritually depressed until the Great Awakening in the 1700s.

Anglicanism in America

Anglicanism came to North America in 1607 with the settlers at Jamestown, and it became, after Puritanism, the most widespread religious force in seventeenth-century America.

Beginnings

Some people have mistakenly viewed Virginia as a secular, materialistic colony in contrast to the more spiritually minded Massachusetts. In reality, some of the early settlers of Virginia were just as devout as the Puritans. For example, with the original settlers came Anglican minister Robert Hunt to serve as chaplain. One of Hunt's first acts on arriving at Jamestown was to hold services to give thanks to God for a safe arrival. He preached weekly to the settlers, holding his services under an awning made from an old sail. Hunt visited and served the many sick in the early days of the colony.

Samuel Sewall, who presided over the Salem witch trials, later apologized for the town's zealous but misguided pursuit of innocent people.

As a result of his strenuous labors, Hunt died within two years of his arrival. Captain John Smith wrote of Hunt, "He was an honest, religious, and courageous Divine; he preferred the service of God to every thought of ease at home."

The early Virginians were usually low-church Anglicans, agreeing doctrinally with the Puritans but having no objection to Anglican forms of worship. They were, therefore, less interested in establishing a new "holy commonwealth" like the Puritans than in re-creating England in America. Like the Puritans, however, the Anglicans of Virginia declined spiritually. The decline was slowed but not stopped by the ministries of James Blair and Thomas Bray.

Blair and Bray

Realizing that Anglicans in America needed guidance, church leaders in England sent **James Blair** to Virginia in 1685 and **Thomas Bray** to Maryland in 1700. Blair was most notable for attempting to secure better qualified ministers for Virginia by helping to found William and Mary College in 1693 and serving as its first president. Bray was even more important to Anglicanism in America, although he spent only about six months in America. After his brief stay in Maryland, Bray returned to England to promote missionary efforts for the colonies. Two outstanding organizations resulted from his efforts. The Society for the Promotion of Christian Knowledge (SPCK) provided Christian literature for missionary work and helped establish some forty libraries in the colonies. The Society for the Propagation of the Gospel in Foreign Parts (SPG) focused on securing ministers for the colonies. Later Bray helped found an organization aimed at evangelizing blacks in America.

Expansion

Thanks to the efforts of men such as Blair and Bray, the Anglican Church grew throughout the colonies. By the Revolution, Anglican churches existed in every colony, and Anglicanism had become the established (government supported) church in Virginia, Maryland, the Carolinas, Georgia, and parts of New York and New Jersey.

Expansion, however, did not always bring spiritual growth. Anglican churches constantly suffered from a shortage of pastors, and those they had were not always academically or spiritually qualified. (One glaring example was an Anglican minister in Georgia who abandoned his congregation to marry an already married Indian princess and who later urged an attack on the white settlers.) Growth also brought spiritual coldness as more high-church Anglican influences entered the colonies. When the Great Awakening swept the colonies in the 1700s, the Anglican Church was the least affected of the Protestant denominations.

Section Quiz

1. From what did Puritans want to "purify" the Church of England?
2. What is the "heart" of Puritan theology?
3. What are the three major kinds of church polity?
4. What were the provisions of the Half-Way Covenant?
5. How did James Blair and Thomas Bray help establish Anglicanism in America?
★ Why did the Puritan Commonwealth fail?

II. Non-Established Denominations

Several groups that grew in America were officially separate from the Church of England. These formed the non-established denominations. The Pilgrims of Plymouth were the first of those groups in America. More important ultimately, were such groups as the Baptists, the Quakers, and the Presbyterians.

Baptists

When **Roger Williams** fled from Massachusetts and founded Rhode Island, he sought to create a purer church than those in the rest of New England. In 1639, Williams and another Christian baptized each other. Williams then baptized ten others in his tiny congregation. This act marked the founding of what is generally considered the first Baptist church in America. Ironically, Roger Williams remained in the church only a few months before he left to seek an even purer church. The church, however, continued without him.

The **Baptists** grew slowly at first, and they suffered persecution from colonial authorities, particularly in Massachusetts and Virginia. Nonetheless, they succeeded in establishing churches throughout the colonies and had their largest numbers in religiously tolerant Pennsylvania.

As their name suggests, Baptists emphasize the doctrine of baptism. Like the Congregationalists, the Baptists practice congregational polity and believe that only the regenerate should be church members. Unlike the Congregationalists, who allowed baptism of infants, Baptists baptize only professing believers and then only by immersing them in water.

Quakers

The **Quakers**, or the Society of Friends, originated with the Englishman **George Fox**. Fox claimed to have received guidance by the "Inner Light," an illumination from God found in every man. Other Quakers teach that this Inner Light is some kind of "spark of divinity" and that man is saved through obeying its leading rather than through the atonement of Christ. Most (but not all) early Quakers opposed participating in war, taking oaths, or holding political office. They preferred to be called Friends rather than Quakers. The name Quaker originated from the practice of some Quakers who shook while worshipping. Those opposed to the Quaker movement assigned them this name.

The Quakers practiced an extremely plain method of worship. Believers sat in silence—often in a circle—and waited for the Inner Light to move one member to give a word of testimony or exhortation. The early Quakers did not have regular ministers or practice the church ordinances (baptism and the Lord's Supper).

Quakers did not receive a warm welcome in the colonies. The Puritans in New England quickly arrested and deported any Quaker who entered their colonies. Between 1659 and 1661, authorities in Massachusetts actually hanged four Quakers for returning to the colony after repeated warnings.

Many of the Friends lived in Rhode Island, but the center of colonial Quakerism was Pennsylvania, where William Penn established his colony as a "holy experiment" in religious pluralism. Many Quakers who did not believe in the prohibition against holding office became influential political leaders in that colony.

Presbyterians

The **Presbyterians** were the last major English Separatist group to come to America. Doctrinally, the Presbyterians were much like the Congregationalists, except that they practiced presbyterian polity. The Father of American Presbyterianism is **Francis Makemie** (mah KIM ee). Born in Northern Ireland, Makemie was converted at the age of fourteen and was later ordained in the Presbyterian Church of Northern Ireland. In 1683 he came to the New World to preach the gospel and start churches. Makemie preached with success throughout the colonies. He not only established numerous churches but also helped found the first presbytery (association of Presbyterian churches) in America.

Makemie also struck a blow for religious freedom for Presbyterians and other non-Anglican groups. In two separate court cases in Virginia and New York, Makemie persuaded colonial courts to recognize that the English Parliament's Act of Toleration (1689) applied equally to the colonies. These cases guaranteed freedom of worship for Makemie and others like him.

Reformed Groups

Reformed churches, similar in doctrine and practice to the Presbyterians, emerged in several nations in Europe during the Reformation. The **Dutch Reformed** came to the New World with the settling of New Amsterdam, but not in great numbers. The Netherlands was the most religiously tolerant nation in Europe, and few people there had religious reasons to migrate to America. The Dutch who came to the New World were often more interested in wealth than in piety.

The French Reformed, also called **Huguenots** (HYOO guh NOTS), settled throughout the colonies, especially after the French king Louis XIV took away their freedom of worship in 1685. The largest concentrations of Huguenots were in Virginia and South Carolina. In South Carolina, their political influence belied their numerical minority. They often sided with Anglicans to determine outcomes of key issues. In fact, they helped ensure the establishment of the Church of England in the colony. Generally, however, the French Reformed were rarely concentrated in any one colony and had a limited effect on religious life. Many eventually became Presbyterians.

The **German Reformed Church**, from southern Germany, also migrated to the American colonies. Unlike the French Reformed, the Germans preserved their identity by concentrating in one colony, Pennsylvania.

Lutherans

The **Lutherans**, followers of the teachings of the great German reformer Martin Luther, came to America in trickles rather than in floods. The Swedish Lutherans of New Sweden (Delaware) were among the first, and many Dutch Lutherans settled in New Amsterdam. Most American Lutherans, however, originated in Germany. Like many of the other small groups, the Lutherans flocked to Pennsylvania because of its religious freedom and abundant land. Also, like many of the other small denominations, the Lutherans suffered from disorganization. The man who molded the denomination was **Henry Mühlenberg**, often called the Father of American Lutheranism.

Francis Makemie, the Father of American Presbyterianism, by James Brooks

Born in Germany, Mühlenberg came to America in 1742 at the request of officials in Germany. Slogging through the muddy roads and deep snows of colonial America's frontier, Mühlenberg preached and prayed throughout the middle and southern colonies. Eventually, Mühlenberg was able to bring about closer cooperation among the German, Swedish, and Dutch Lutherans, thereby laying the foundation for the Lutheran denomination in America.

Anabaptist Groups

The Anabaptists arose during the Reformation in protest of what they considered the incomplete reforms of other Protestants. Anabaptists refused to have anything to do with the state; they refused to serve in the military, vote, or hold office. They also stressed the importance of a holy, simple life. The **Mennonites**, followers of the Dutch teacher Menno Simons, were the most important Anabaptist group numerically. The **Amish** were a more conservative branch of the Mennonites who practiced strict church discipline.

Persecuted by governments in Europe, many of the Mennonites and Amish fled to the New World and established farms and towns in Pennsylvania. There, by thrift and hard work, they built prosperous farms that their descendants farm even today. Both groups tried to preserve their old ways of life by rejecting modern changes and having little contact with outsiders. Some modern Mennonites and Amish still use only a horse and buggy for transportation and follow farming practices that date back to the 1700s.

Pietist Groups

In Germany in the late 1600s, an important religious movement arose known as **Pietism**. Reacting to spiritually cold churches in Europe, the Pietists, like the Puritans, emphasized the importance of conversion and the necessity of a holy life. Unlike the Puritans, however, Pietists tended to downplay doctrine. Pietism touched several denominations in Europe and America. Lutheran Henry Mühlenberg, for example, was a Pietist in much of his belief and practice.

The most important Pietist group in America was the **Moravians**, persecuted followers of the teachings of preacher John Huss of Bohemia, who was burned at the stake in 1415 for rejecting Roman Catholic teachings. In 1722 a remnant of these believers found shelter on the estate of the Lutheran nobleman Nicholas von Zinzendorf in Germany. Count von Zinzendorf was so impressed with the fervent piety of the group that he joined them and became their leader.

Evangelism was a primary concern of the Moravians. They conducted mission work among the slaves in the Caribbean and among the Indians in America. John Wesley credited his conversion in part to contact with Moravians while he was in Georgia. The Moravians built thriving communities: Nazareth, Pennsylvania; Bethlehem, Pennsylvania; and Salem (now Winston-Salem), North Carolina, to name a few. The denomination's influence

One of the Moravian settlements was Salem, North Carolina.

diminished as its membership declined and the population of the nation grew. However, as one historian noted, we still see Moravian influence in customs such as the Easter sunrise service and even more through the legacy of John Wesley and others whom they influenced.

Roman Catholics

Most Protestants in the colonies feared Roman Catholicism. Some of that feeling was simple prejudice, but much of it resulted from opposition to the unbiblical teachings of the Roman Catholic Church and from the repression of Protestantism in Catholic countries. Also, Roman Catholic Spain and France threatened the existence of the colonies, and these powers were not above using Catholic priests and missionaries to achieve their political goals.

The center of colonial Catholicism was Maryland, the colony established as a haven for Catholics. Even there, however, Catholics were still a minority. Some Catholics lived in Pennsylvania, and a few settled in New York, but virtually none were found elsewhere in the colonies. In the early 1700s, the British government took away the limited toleration that Catholics had enjoyed. The government's act placed Roman Catholics in a difficult position until the Revolution, and their numbers remained small in America until the massive Irish immigration of the 1840s.

Section Quiz

1. What are the three most important English Separatist groups to be established in the colonies?
2. Who was most responsible for the founding of American Presbyterianism? of American Lutheranism?
3. How is Pietism like Puritanism in its view of Christian living? How is it unlike Puritanism in its view of doctrine?
4. Where did the German Reformed settle?
5. Where was the center of colonial Catholicism?
* From the four core values (freedom, individualism, equality, and growth), choose two and explain how they encouraged the development of non-established denominations.

III. Colonial Worship

Generalizing about Christian worship in the colonial era is somewhat difficult. Some groups, such as the Anglicans, practiced more formal worship whereas others, such as the Quakers, were much more informal. The following section provides a broad, generalized description of how colonial Christians worshiped.

Buildings

Settlers built church buildings near the center of town to indicate the central importance of religion to the community. Structurally, many early churches resembled barns. (In fact, some of the earliest American churches were barns.) The building also served as a hall for public meetings as well as for worship services. Patrick Henry, for example, gave his famous "Liberty or Death" speech to an assembly of colonial delegates gathered in St. John's Church in Richmond, Virginia.

The WEST PARISH Meetinghouse
West Barnstable, Massachusetts   built in 1717

The interiors of early colonial churches were likewise plain. The first pews were simple benches with no padding or backs. Later, churches constructed pews paid for by gifts from members of the congregation. Those pews were then reserved for the people who had paid for them. Sometimes members reserved pews by paying an annual rental fee. In all of this was an unwritten but understood pecking order. The higher one's social standing, the nearer to the front of the church one sat. The pews were elaborate box pews, closed on three sides to reduce drafts and having a door that opened into the aisle. Families could lock their pews so that no one else could use them, regardless of whether the family was present. This practice sometimes resulted in the embarrassing situation in which some people had to stand during services while locked pews sat empty.

Pulpits also grew more elaborate as the colonies grew more settled. The early roughhewn boxes gave way to graceful pulpits. One popular style was the "wine glass" pulpit, so called because the rounded pulpit sat atop a narrow stem. Above the later pulpits was a sounding board, a wooden structure designed to bounce sound waves out so that the minister could be clearly heard.

Many colonial churches also contained a balcony. Often these balconies were three-sectioned, running along the back and both sides of the auditorium. Churches often reserved the balcony for certain groups such as servants, slaves, and free blacks. It was not uncommon for slaves to be required to enter by climbing a set of stairs or a ladder outside the church leading directly to the balcony.

Services

A drum, or later a bell, summoned the colonists to worship. Churches usually held two services on Sunday, one in the morning and one in the afternoon. Sunday school was not developed until the late 1700s, but children often attended catechism class between the two services. A **catechism** is a summary of a denomination's doctrine framed in a question-and-answer form. Children were "catechized" as they memorized and recited the answers to the questions. For example, the Westminster Shorter Catechism, the Presbyterian catechism, begins as follows:

Question: What is the chief end of man?

Answer: Man's chief end is to glorify God, and to enjoy Him forever.

The first part of the services contained a long prayer by the pastor ("bills of request" were laid on the pulpit ahead of time for the pastor's notice) and the reading of the Scripture. Puritans in particular did not simply read the Bible; they commented on it and explained its meaning as they read. Singing was, of course, an essential part of the service. At first, most colonists sang adapted versions of the psalms. One of the most famous of those was based on Psalm 100:

Make yee a joyfull sounding noyse
    unto Jehovah all the earth:
Serve yee Jehovah with gladnes:
    before his presence come with mirth.

The tune to this psalm, which came to be known as "Old Hundredth," is best known today as the tune to the Doxology ("Praise God from Whom All Blessings Flow").

In 1640, the Puritans published a book of hymns called the **Bay Psalm Book**, the first book published in America. However, not all congregations had copies of hymnals for each member. Often, a precentor (song leader) would need to "line out" a hymn for the congregation. He would call out or sing a line of the hymn, and the congregation would repeat it. They continued alternating this way until the hymn was done.

The early churches, particularly those of the Puritans, contained no instruments. Some Christians, citing passages such as Amos 5:23, believed that the Bible forbade instruments in church. Others simply could not afford to import instruments from England. By the end of the colonial period, however, organs had come into widespread use, especially in the older churches in the East.

The sermon was the centerpiece of the church service. Most Puritan and Separatist sermons lasted at least an hour. Anglican sermons varied; normally, the closer an Anglican minister was to Puritanism in his theology, the longer his sermon. An hourglass sat by the pulpit, but it did not necessarily deter the preacher from preaching at length. When the sand ran out, he simply flipped it over and continued speaking.

Ministers constructed their sermons carefully. They made detailed outlines with elaborate subpoints so that listeners could easily take notes and carry them home for further study. Sleeping or talking during the sermon was frowned upon. In the early Puritan churches, in fact, ushers walked around during the sermon looking for sleepy saints. They carried a long pole with a feather at one end for tickling the women as a warning and a knob at the other end for striking the men.

The preacher might memorize his sermon for delivery, preach with only a few notes, or write the message out completely and read it to the congregation. Reading a sermon did not necessarily lessen its impact. Jonathan Edwards might have read "Sinners in the Hands of an Angry God" to his listeners, but the sermon stirred the congregation with great conviction. Generally, despite denominational distinctives, all colonial denominations agreed in preaching the Bible as the authoritative Word of God.

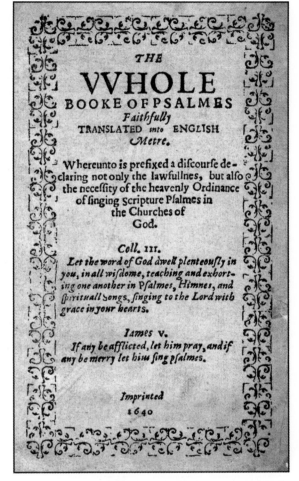

The title page of the *Bay Psalm Book,* the hymnal of the Puritans and the first book published in America

Section Quiz

1. What is a catechism?

2. What was the first book published in America?

3. Why did many colonial churches lack musical instruments?

✷ What was the central focus of the typical colonial worship service and why? Evaluate this focus.

IV. Indian Missions

Converting Native Americans to the gospel was a goal of the colonists from the very beginning. The charter for Virginia stated that the settlers aimed at "propagating [the] Christian religion to such people, as yet live in darkness and miserable ignorance of the true knowledge and worship of God." The charter of Massachusetts likewise obligated the colonists to "wynn and incite the Natives of the Country to the knowledge and obedience of the onlie true God and Savior of Mankinde, and the Christian fayth." Some historians consider these statements a cover-up to hide the ruthless exploitation of the Indians by Europeans. The evidence, however, demonstrates otherwise: many colonists were genuine in their concern. It is their success rather than their sincerity that is open to question.

Isolated Efforts

Throughout the colonial era many devout Christians attempted to reach the Indians with the gospel. Sometimes personal contact resulted in the conversion of an individual, such as Pocahontas. Ministers often preached to the Indians in addition to their other duties. Roger Williams, for example, was one of the first white men in New England to preach to the Indians. Jonathan Edwards worked with an Indian mission in the latter part of his ministry. John and Charles Wesley came to Georgia in 1736 to evangelize the Indians. (However, the Wesleys were themselves unconverted at the time, and the work was a dismal failure).

One of the most successful early efforts was that of Swedish Lutheran John Campanius, who worked among the Delaware Indians. Among his tools for the task was his translation of Luther's catechism into the Delaware language, one of the first Christian works translated into an Indian tongue. The most extensive colonial works on the whole were done by the Congregationalists and the Moravians. The Moravians ministered especially to the Cherokees of North Carolina and Georgia.

Congregationalist Efforts

While pastoring in New England, **John Eliot** became concerned about the Algonquin Indians. With the help of an Indian who knew English, Eliot learned their language and began to preach to them.

John Eliot was one of several early missionaries to the American Indians.

He translated various devotional works and finally the entire Bible into the Algonquin tongue. (The Algonquin Bible was the first Bible printed in America.) His success was remarkable; some four thousand Indians allegedly were converted under Eliot's ministry. Those converts, called "praying Indians," formed communities appropriately called "praying villages," with Indians often serving as pastors.

That effective ministry came to an end, however, during a war between the English settlers and the Indians in 1675–76. The praying Indians sided with the English, a fact that earned them the hatred of the other Indians. Nevertheless, the whites distrusted them and disbanded some of their villages. Panicky Massachusetts authorities placed many Christian Indians on an island in Boston Harbor. There, exposed to the elements, many of them sickened and died. Despite these setbacks, Eliot managed to establish the Society for the Propagation of the Gospel in New England, the main Congregationalist agency for conducting Indian mission work.

Other Congregationalists did not match Eliot's success, but several of them conducted noteworthy ministries. In the same year that Eliot started his work, Thomas Mayhew Jr. began a work among the Indians on Martha's Vineyard in Massachusetts that lasted a century. **David Brainerd**, a close friend of Jonathan Edwards and his family, conducted a brief work among the Indians before his death from tuberculosis at the age of twenty-nine. Although Brainerd's ministry was not successful numerically, his *Journal*, published after his death, inspired many other young men to enter mission work, and their efforts *were* successful. For example, Eleazar Wheelock founded a school in 1754 for training Indians as missionaries to their own people. Wheelock definitely showed foresight with that idea; he realized that any race or culture is most effectively reached with the gospel by someone else from that race or culture. Eventually, the school was opened to whites as well and became Dartmouth College.

The chief shortcoming of some Congregationalist efforts was the tendency to think that Indians had to be "civilized" before they could be converted. It is true that some Indian customs could not be reconciled with Christian morality, but some people believed that Indians needed European standards in dress and housing as much as they needed the gospel. More successful in reaching the Indians on their own terms were the Moravian missions.

Moravian Efforts

Whereas the Congregationalists performed most of their Indian mission work in New England, the Moravians conducted most of their work in the middle and southern colonies. The most successful Moravian mission was one near Bethlehem, Pennsylvania, called Gnadenhütten ("sheltered by grace") under the direction of **David Zeisberger** (ZICE berg ur). As with the Congregational ministry, however, the Moravians' efforts were undone by war. During the French and Indian War, pro-French Indians attacked Gnadenhütten, killed ten missionaries, and burned the settlement. Not trusted by the English colonists either, the Moravian Indians were forced to wander through Pennsylvania, New York, and Ohio like the children of Israel seeking the Promised Land. The Indians never found rest, however. A remnant of some ninety Moravian Indians from Gnadenhütten was massacred by American soldiers during the closing days of the War for Independence.

Despite the sad end of so many Indian missions and the prejudices of some of the missionaries, colonial Indian missions were not a failure. Thousands of Indians who had never heard the gospel were converted as a result of those efforts.

Section Quiz

1. Who was the Swedish Lutheran who ministered among the Delaware Indians?

2. List at least two ways that John Eliot ministered to the Algonquin Indians.

3. What was the name of the most successful Moravian Indian mission? What does this name mean?

★ Some have criticized missionary efforts during this period for attempting to civilize the people to whom they ministered. What are some positive and negative aspects of this attempt?

V. The Great Awakening

Religious revivals have been a recurring feature in American history. The first of those revivals, the one by which all others are judged, was the **Great Awakening**. The Awakening was not simply a revival, however; it was a powerful social, political, and religious force that permanently altered the course of American history. Some historians limit the Awakening to the years 1740–42, the years of greatest fervor and activity. Closer study, however, reveals that the whole Great Awakening and its effects cover nearly forty years, from the 1720s to the early 1760s.

Background

Religious life in the North American colonies had begun to wither by the early 1700s. Although some groups, such as the Presbyterians, were entering a period of growth (mostly the result of immigration), most people were in a spiritual lull. Secular historians in search of causes of the Great Awakening recognize the desire for security created by economic and political uncertainty of the times, and they focus on that as the primary reason for the revival. Those factors might indeed have contributed to the revival, but ultimately it was simply, in the words of Jonathan Edwards, "a surprising work of God."

The colonies needed a spiritual awakening. In New England, the Half-Way Covenant was slowly filling the Congregationalist churches with unconverted members. Some areas, such as the frontier regions of the Carolinas, had almost no religious life of any kind. Even those who attended church did so because of family traditions more than the genuine piety that had motivated their forefathers. There was no guarantee that even the ministers were converted.

Voices Crying in the Wilderness

Early Stirrings

In 1720, Dutch Reformed pastor **Theodore Frelinghuysen** (FREE ling HEY zun) came to New Jersey. Influenced by Pietism, Frelinghuysen preached to his people about practical Christian living. He emphasized personal conversion and the holiness of life that an awareness of God's holiness brings. Frelinghuysen's faithful preaching was rewarded in the 1720s by a series of revivals in his churches. The Great Awakening had begun.

A neighbor of Frelinghuysen in New Jersey, Presbyterian **Gilbert Tennent**, was another early light in the Awakening. Encouraged by Frelinghuysen, Tennent began to preach about the need for conversion and holy living. Like Frelinghuysen, Tennent saw fruit for his labor in converted souls and rededicated saints. Tennent was soon in demand by other churches. He and other preachers carried the revival throughout the colonies.

Ironically, the revival that multiplied Presbyterian membership also divided that denomination. The "**New Lights**" supported the revival wholeheartedly, whereas the "**Old Lights**" condemned the emotional displays that accompanied the Awakening. Other Old Lights complained about preachers such as Tennent who entered an area to preach without the permission of the local Presbyterian pastor. The New Lights charged the Old Lights with obstructing the work of God and accused many of the Old Light pastors of being unconverted (a charge that was sometimes true). From 1745 to 1758, the two factions divided and formed separate organizations. When the two sides reunited in 1758, the New Lights had tripled in size, whereas the Old Lights had barely held their own.

Jonathan Edwards

The greatest theologian of the Great Awakening—and perhaps of American history—was **Jonathan Edwards**. A brilliant man (having entered Yale before he was thirteen), Edwards lived with a constant sense of the presence of God. He did not simply practice an outward piety; he was consumed with love for God. As pastor of a Congregationalist church in Northampton, Massachusetts, Edwards sought to instill in his people the same passionate devotion that he felt in his own heart.

In 1734, Edwards began preaching a series of sermons on justification by faith. The sermons sparked a series of awakenings in the church that, Edwards admitted, surprised even him. Edwards soon became the leader of the Awakening in New England and its staunchest and ablest defender in print. He wrote glowingly of the revival's results and cautioned against carnal excesses and imitations.

Even in the solemn "Sinners in the Hands of an Angry God," Edwards said,

> You have now an extraordinary opportunity, a day wherein Christ has thrown the door of mercy wide open, and stands calling, crying with a loud voice to poor sinners, a day wherein many are flocking to Him, and pressing into the kingdom of God; many are daily coming from the east, west, north, and south; many . . . are now in a happy state with their hearts filled with love to Him who has loved them, and washed them from their sins in His own blood, and rejoicing in hope of the glory of God.

Edwards documented the impact of the Great Awakening in his book *A Faithful Narrative*. He also wrote *Religious Affections* to help people discern the difference between the work of the Holy Spirit reviving their love for God and mere emotionalism.

George Whitefield

If Edwards was the outstanding theologian of the Great Awakening, then **George Whitefield** (WHIT feeld) was its outstanding evangelist. Born in England, Whitefield became a friend of the Wesleys while studying at Oxford.

Like them, he was later converted and became a powerful preacher. Finding the doors of England's churches often closed to him by narrow-minded ministers, Whitefield began to preach outdoors wherever he could gather a crowd.

After seeing remarkable results from his preaching in Britain, the twenty-four-year-old Whitefield came to America for the first time in 1738. Over the next thirty years, he made seven preaching tours of the colonies. He preached in Savannah, Charleston, Philadelphia, New York, Boston, and hundreds of villages and crossroads, carrying the revival throughout the colonies. In his greatest tour, that of 1740, Whitefield preached to thousands daily, and many of those thousands were converted. Whitefield's tours also united the revivalists throughout the colonies, and he became a close friend of both Jonathan Edwards and Gilbert Tennent.

Jonathan Edwards, the outstanding theologian of the Great Awakening

The Log College

Presbyterian Gilbert Tennent graduated from an unusual college. He had no comfortable dormitory room with a private bath. The walls of his school were not covered with ivy—unless some happened to cling to the rough logs of which the building was constructed. Nor did Tennent receive instruction from a wide array of learned professors; he had only one teacher—his father, William Tennent Sr., who wanted a school to prepare his four sons for the ministry. Otherwise, they would have had to go to New England or even back to England for their education.

Tennent built a large log building near his home to house his school. He began with thirteen students—his sons and nine others who wanted to study for the ministry. Enemies derisively called the school "the Log College," but there was nothing crude about the quality of the education provided there. The students worked diligently at their studies under Tennent's direction and gained practical experience by serving in his church.

The heritage of the Log College was rich. Gilbert Tennent, his brothers, and the other graduates of the school became Spirit-empowered agents of the Great Awakening, leading hundreds—perhaps thousands—of souls to Christ. Ironically, the often-despised Log College also became an educational center. More than fifty colleges claim their descent from the ministry of the Log College and its graduates. Among those schools was the College of New Jersey (now Princeton University), which was chartered the year that William Tennent died (1746). The humble cabin college was, indeed, as George Whitefield called it, a profoundly influential "school of the prophets."

Whitefield was a gifted preacher. He had a powerful, melodious, persuasive voice. Philadelphia printer Benjamin Franklin, who published some of Whitefield's sermons in America, testified to the power of that voice. Franklin once attended one of Whitefield's meetings. Franklin determined not to give any money for the offering to support Whitefield's orphanage in Georgia. Franklin later wrote,

> I had in my Pocket a Handful of Copper Money, three or four silver Dollars, and five Pistoles in Gold. As he [Whitefield] proceeded I began to soften, and concluded to give the Coppers. Another Stroke of his Oratory made me asham' d of that, and determin' d me to give the Silver; and he finsh'd so admirably, that I empty'd my Pocket wholly into the Collector's Dish, Gold and all.

On another occasion, Franklin did an experiment during one of Whitefield's outdoor sermons. Franklin walked away from the minister as he preached and measured how far he could hear Whitefield's voice. By his reckoning, Franklin figured that Whitefield could reach a crowd of thirty thousand—and this without any modern electronic amplification equipment.

The Awakening in the South

The South was the last section to experience the Awakening, but the revival's impact there was no less profound. **Samuel Davies** carried the revival to the Presbyterians in Virginia. Second only to George Whitefield in pulpit oratory, Davies preached faithfully for some twelve years and also persuaded authorities to permit more religious liberty for non-Anglicans in the colony. He also promoted education by helping to found the school that eventually became

Washington and Lee University and by serving as president of the College of New Jersey (Princeton).

Virginia was also the scene of the early labors of Baptist **Shubal Stearns** and his brother-in-law Daniel Marshall. Stearns had trusted Christ under the preaching of Whitefield in 1745, and Whitefield had a strong spiritual influence on Marshall. Like a number of Whitefield's followers, they became Baptists—a tendency that caused the Anglican Whitefield to lament, "My chickens have turned to ducks."

After working in Virginia without much success, Stearns and Marshall traveled to North Carolina and established the Sandy Creek Baptist Church. Marshall went on to found the Kiokee Baptist Church in Georgia in 1772.

Another preacher who built on the Great Awakening in the South was **Samuel Doak**. Born in Virginia, Doak pastored a church in Abingdon, Virginia, and served as a Presbyterian circuit rider in East Tennessee. In addition, he became an early proponent of the abolition of slavery. Doak eventually settled in Tennessee, founded Salem Church, and started a school, which became Washington College in 1795.

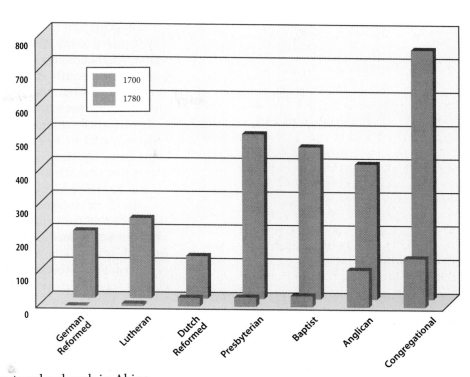

The chart shows the number of congregations each denomination had in 1700, before the Great Awakening, and in 1780, after the revival.

Results of the Awakening

The Great Awakening affected not only religious life but also social and political life. First, the effects on America's churches were dramatic. Church growth was the most visible result. The number of both churches and church members rose markedly, with Presbyterians and Baptists experiencing the greatest growth.

Second, the number of religious colleges increased. Princeton, Brown, Rutgers, and Dartmouth all grew out of the revival as training centers for the ministry. Even Yale benefited from the Awakening. However, revival fires did little to thaw cold Harvard College, which had grown increasingly liberal.

Third, the Awakening transformed the spiritual life of the churches. The Half-Way Covenant began to vanish; increasingly, churches in America required personal regeneration for membership. The revival also promoted unity among the churches. Different congregations and even different denominations overlooked their minor doctrinal differences in the interest of evangelism. This tendency toward religious unity helped to pave the way for a political uniting of the colonies in the coming break with England.

On the other hand, the Great Awakening also brought division to America's churches. Only the Presbyterians and the Dutch Reformed suffered formal splits between those who favored the revival and those who opposed it, but nearly every denomination experienced some division. Not all of the "antirevivalists" were necessarily against revivals; they were simply offended at the fanatical extremes of some people. Many of the opponents, though, were theologically opposed to the revival. They disliked the emphasis on personal experience, the attacks on unconverted pastors, and the general upsetting of "good church order."

The Anglican Church remained the denomination most generally opposed to the Awakening, despite the fact that many individual Anglicans supported the revival. The Anglican Church was powerful, especially in the southern colonies. The colonists viewed the Anglican Church as an arm of the British government, and they disliked that association, especially when the British tightened control over the colonies. That dislike intensified when the British tried to install an Anglican bishop in America. As other denominations grew, Anglican officials and their friends in colonial governments passed restrictions for licensing of preachers, building of new churches, and printing of religious material.

The Great Awakening also had political effects on the colonies. It was the first truly national movement in American history. The revival cut across sectional lines and touched every colony and nearly every class of people. The Great Awakening was not southern or northern, Presbyterian or Congregationalist, upper class or lower class; it was *American*.

The Awakening was also a breakthrough for personal liberty. By reaffirming the equality of men before God, the revival stressed the equality of all men. Also, as we have seen, the work of revivalists such as Samuel Davies resulted in greater freedom of worship for the colonists. A democratic influence swept into the churches; power moved away from traditional elites of class and education within the congregations, and all laymen began to share equally in the rule of the church. Also, by holding large meetings—often opposed by ecclesiastical authorities—Whitefield, Tennent, and others set a precedent for the constitutional rights of free speech and the freedom of assembly.

However, not all effects of the democratic influence proved to be positive. One consequence was the reduction of the pastor's authority. The proliferation of cults in the nineteenth century also resulted from this democratic influence.

Many movements that were unleashed in the Great Awakening saw their full development in the American Revolution. Foremost was an awakening of both the spirit of democracy and the spirit of religious liberty.

Section Quiz

1. What are the names of the two factions into which the Presbyterians split during the Great Awakening? Which group grew more during the revival?

2. What was the most famous sermon preached by Jonathan Edwards?

3. Who was the important theologian of the Great Awakening? the most important evangelist?

4. Give the names and denominations of three important revival leaders in the South.

★ What were the positive results of the Great Awakening? What were some of the negative results?

Chapter 4 Review

Making Connections

1. What is the difference between low-church and high-church Anglicans? between Puritans and low-church Anglicans?

2. Why was the Half-Way Covenant dangerous to the Congregationalist churches in New England?

3. List at least three distinctive beliefs of the Quakers.

4. Describe the order of a typical service in a colonial church.

5. In what ways were the mission works of John Eliot and David Zeisberger similar?

Developing History Skills

1. Why do you think Pennsylvania was the most religiously diverse colony?

2. Secular historians minimize or eliminate the supernatural from their consideration of historical events. If you were a Christian historian, how would you determine the cause or causes of the Great Awakening?

Thinking Critically

1. Had you lived in Queen Elizabeth's day, would you have been a Puritan, a low-church Anglican, a high-church Anglican, or a Separatist? Why?

2. How were the Baptists like the Congregationalists? How were they unlike them?

Living as a Christian Citizen

1. What was Eleazar Wheelock's reason for founding his school for training Indians in mission work? How can this principle be applied to modern missions?

2. Imagine a legislator in your state is proposing a bill to ban prayer before the legislative session on the grounds that such prayers are an establishment of religion. Based on what you learned in this chapter about established and non-established churches, write a letter in response to the legislator.

The Liberty Bell and the "stars and stripes" (shown being presented to General George Washington) became symbols of American freedom.

1754–63 The French and Indian War

1765 The Stamp Act

1767 The Townshend Acts

1770 The Boston Massacre

1774 The Intolerable Acts

CHAPTERS

5 THE RISING STORM (1865-1770)

6 INDEPENDENCE (1770-1783)

7 THE CRITICAL PERIOD (1781-1789)

8 THE FEDERALIST YEARS (1789-1801)

The U.S. Navy was born during the War for Independence.

In 1784, in the peace following the War for Independence, Benjamin Franklin invented bifocals.

1775–83 The American Revolution

1776 The Declaration of Independence

1783 The Treaty of Paris

1787 Constitution adopted by the convention

1791 Bill of Rights adopted

"The Death of General Wolfe" by Benjamin West

The Rising Storm (1689-1770)

I.   Frontier Feuds

II.   The French and Indian War

III.   The Growing Rift

"My lads, they will not fire."

Samuel Gray, March 5, 1770,
last words before being killed by the first
British volley during the Boston Massacre

From the 1680s to the 1760s, intermittent war raged on the American frontier. Two colonial empires—the English and the French—fought each other from the sandy beaches of Pensacola to the snowy plains of Quebec.

At the beginning, the English had been able to safely ignore their French neighbors in the New World. Settlements of New France in Canada had amounted to little more than a scattered string of outposts along the St. Lawrence River until Louis XIV took the throne in 1661. Louis, along with his chief adviser Jean Colbert, realized the untapped potential of the American heartland and determined to build an empire that would surpass that of his English adversaries.

French claims to this vast region stemmed from two important expeditions. The first was launched from Green Bay in 1673 when a trapper named **Louis Joliet** (zhoh LYAY) and a Jesuit priest named **Jacques Marquette** (mahr KEHT) canoed down the Wisconsin River in search of the "Great River" that Indians had described. The Frenchmen reached the Mississippi and journeyed as far south as its turbulent convergence with the Missouri River, where they met Indians carrying English-made muskets. The Mississippi's destination was no mystery to the Indians. The Indian men explained to the French that the "Great River" emptied into the Sea of Florida (the Gulf of Mexico). Fearful of falling captive to the Spanish and eager to tell of their discovery of an inland water route from Canada to the Caribbean, the friar and the fur trader paddled home.

Jacques Marquette preached to the Quapaw Indians in Arkansas in 1673.

For nearly ten years, Joliet and Marquette's discovery remained unexploited. Finally, in 1682, Robert de **La Salle** (lah SAL) set out to explore the length of the Mississippi. At the mouth of the river, he named the vast region **Louisiana** in honor of his sovereign Louis XIV and made a comprehensive claim of "all the nations, peoples, provinces, cities, towns, villages, mines, minerals, fisheries, streams, and rivers" as possessions of France.

The French learned, though, that it was easier to claim than to colonize. New France was never heavily populated with Frenchmen. In 1666, only 3,400 French settlers lived in Canada. Although the colony grew to 80,000 by 1750, it always had only a fraction of the number of people in British America.

The French posed a serious threat to the thirteen colonies for several reasons. First, the French had strong Indian alliances that greatly expanded their military capabilities. The prospect of well-armed Indian warriors was even more fearful to the colonists than facing French troops. However, one weak link in the French and Indian alliances was their inability to win over the powerful Iroquois. The French were aligned with the Algonquins, with whom the Iroquois had a standing blood-feud. As a result, the Iroquois became allies of the British-American forces during the colonial wars.

A second factor that worked to the advantage of the French was the nature of the frontier. The American colonies had a vaguely defined western boundary of isolated farms and villages that invited attack. In the dense wilderness, finding the enemy was difficult, and effectively defending the scattered settlements was impossible.

Settlers in New England lived in constant fear of attacks by both the Indians and the French. The Reverend Joseph Doddridge observed in the 1700s, "The Indian kills indiscriminately. His object is the total extermination of his enemies. Children are victims of his vengeance, because, if males, they may hereafter become warriors, or if females, they may become mothers. Even the fetal state is criminal in his view. It is not enough that the fetus should perish with the murdered mother, it is torn from her pregnant womb, and elevated on a stick or pole, as a trophy of victory and an object of horror to the survivors of the slain. If the Indian takes prisoners, mercy has but little concern in the transaction. He spares the lives of those who fall into his hands, for the purpose of feasting the feelings of ferocious vengeance of himself and his comrades, by the torture of his captive."

The French and Indian threats were compounded by the failure of the American colonies to present a united front. For the most part, petty jealousies and shortsightedness made the colonies divided targets for French attacks.

As bloody as the colonial wars were, the French thorn in America's side would be a key factor in changing the attitudes between England and her colonies. By the late 1770s American troops would be shouldering French muskets and wearing uniforms made in Paris. George Washington, who first made a name for himself by fighting the French, would one day depend on the French navy to defeat the British army at Yorktown.

I. Frontier Feuds

As the French expanded their claims in Canada, the Great Lakes region, and the Mississippi River basin, and as the English moved farther west, friction was inevitable. Colonial tensions were heightened by parent countries' explosive relations that often spilled over into America. Between 1689 and 1763, the four wars that erupted in Europe between England and France were also played out in the New World under "Americanized" names: **King William's War**, **Queen Anne's War**, **King George's War**, and the culminating conflict—the Seven Years' War, known in the colonies as the French and Indian War.

King William's War (1689–97)

In one of Louis XIV's many wars of expansion, the French armies crossed the Rhine and invaded the strongly Protestant German Palatinate. What Louis expected to be a quick foray turned into a nine-year war against an alliance headed by England. In Europe, the war became known as the War of the League of Augsburg, but the Americans named their frontier version after England's newly crowned king, William III.

Because of the need for men and materiel in his all-out war in Europe, Louis spared little for Canada. What French Canadians lacked in troops and finances, however, they compensated for in leadership. **Comte de Frontenac** (FRAHN tuh nak), a resourceful

---

The Indian Perspective

As the colonists spread out, they often settled on lands that Indian tribes had inhabited for generations. The Indians shared the land among their tribes and had no concept of ownership. Europeans, on the other hand, believed that whoever owned the land did not have to share it and that ownership was permanent. Sometimes the colonists paid the Indians for the lands on which they settled—often they did not. Even when the colonists did pay, the sale of Indian land resulted in the Indians having reduced access to sources of food, including deer and fish. The Indians also realized the growing threat as greater numbers of Europeans arrived and brought with them powerful weapons. Some Indian leaders sensed their diminishing power over their own people. Indians also became dependent on trade with the colonists in order to survive. Both colonists and Indians often resorted to capturing or killing members of the other group.

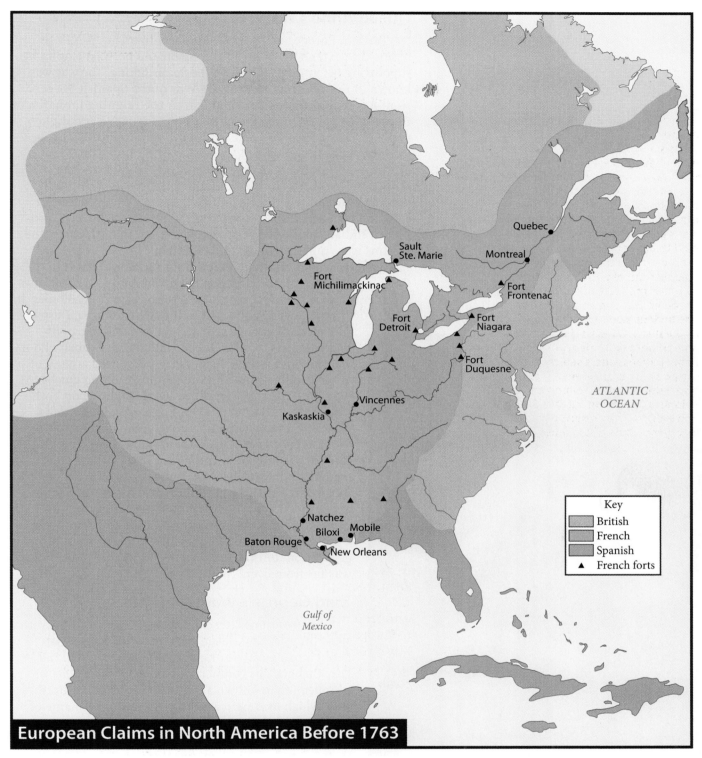

European Claims in North America Before 1763

Key
British
French
Spanish
▲ French forts

and competent leader, came to North America and, with the aid of French settlers and Indians, inflicted considerable damage and fear upon the English settlements. The English colonies had the advantage of numbers, but they did not cooperate with one another well enough to raise funds for military supplies; an intercolonial conference held in New York in 1690 failed because of a lack of unity. In Europe a peace treaty was finally signed in 1697, but all was neither forgiven nor forgotten; the mutual hatred only deepened. Meanwhile, the French continued to build forts along the Mississippi and St. Lawrence Rivers.

Queen Anne's War (1702–13)

Peace in Europe and America was short-lived. Louis XIV attempted to extend his control over Spain and her vast empire by supporting his grandson Philip to be Spanish king. The war was known in Europe, therefore, as the War of the Spanish Succession; American colonists named it after the reigning monarch of England, Queen Anne. The French king's dynastic and diplomatic expansionism was met with a military rebuff that raged for more than a decade.

In America, the war consisted mainly of sporadic but bloody fights on the frontier and along the coasts. The French and their Indian allies, for example, attacked Wells, Maine, in 1703 and massacred thirty-nine settlers; in Massachusetts, pro-French Indians murdered thirty-eight settlers. In both cases, the victims were mostly women and children.

Such treachery and the potential for territorial gains in Canada finally caught the attention of Queen Anne. In 1708, five regiments and a fleet were sent to help the beleaguered colonies. In 1710, Port Royal, Nova Scotia, fell to the British forces. Despite this success, a combined attempt by English troops and colonists to take Quebec failed disastrously. Poor weather and poorer leadership prevented a navy of about twelve thousand men from reaching Quebec.

The **Treaty of Utrecht** ended the fighting on both sides of the Atlantic in 1713. England gained title to eastern Canada while France retained control of the St. Lawrence and Great Lakes regions. England gained territory in the West Indies and even picked up strategic Gibraltar in the deal. Increasingly, the focus of European politics would include overseas holdings and a distant fight. A forgotten corner of the world could trigger war among the European nations on a global scale. Utrecht provided a shaky peace for a generation, but the feud between England and France was far from over.

King George's War (1744–48)

As a result of Utrecht, British access to the lucrative West Indies trade caused tensions with Spain that flared into a naval war known as The War of Jenkins' Ear. That curious conflict soon merged into a general European fight known as the War of Austrian Succession, which in America was fought under the name of Great Britain's King George II.

The Americans made an impressive record for themselves in 1745 when four thousand New Englanders besieged and conquered French Louisbourg, considered at the time to be the most formidable fortress in North America. A truce was declared in Europe in 1748 with the Peace of Aix-la-Chapelle. The peace, however, was a mere comma in the conflict between Britain and France. Open conflict would again erupt in 1754 and would not only settle old problems in America but also create new ones.

King George II

The Granger Collection, New York

A Redeemed Captive

The colonial wars often turned quiet backwoods settlements into the frontlines of battle, catching settlers in its savage crossfire. During Queen Anne's War, one man, Reverend John Williams, faced such a crisis with courage and faithfulness, leaving an enduring testimony to the sustaining grace of God.

Early on the morning of February 29, 1704, a war party of French soldiers and Indian warriors attacked the frontier town of Deerfield, Massachusetts. Pastor Williams and his family were still in bed when, with a flurry of axe blows, the enemy began to break open the doors and windows of their house. Williams seized his pistol and aimed it at the nearest Indian, but the gun misfired. The Indians quickly captured Williams and his family. They killed two children and a slave and then marched their captives through the winter snow back to Canada.

The French and Indians killed thirty-eight settlers and captured more than one hundred citizens of Deerfield. The number of captives dwindled as the group slogged through the frigid wilderness. Anyone who could not keep up was killed. Williams's wife, who had given birth to a child only a few weeks earlier, was one of the victims. When her strength failed, an Indian ended her life with a blow from a tomahawk. Williams suffered from the forced march as well. He recorded that each night he had to wring the blood from his socks.

When the Indians chose a Sunday to rest on the long march, they allowed Williams to preach to his flock. He spoke from Lamentations 1:18, "The Lord is righteous; for I have rebelled against his commandment: hear, I pray you, all people, and behold my sorrow: my virgins and my young men are gone into captivity."

In Montreal, the French governor took Williams and several others from the Indians. In many ways, the captives' situation improved. The French were surprisingly kind and sympathetic, caring for the captives' ills and giving them food and shelter. They faced, however, a different and subtler kind of persecution. The Jesuit priests were determined to convert the captives to Catholicism by any means possible.

Williams noted that the Indians, for all their cruelty, had allowed the captives to keep their Bibles and hymnbooks but that the priests had quickly taken them away. The Catholics worked diligently to convert Williams. They tried arguments, pleas, and even blackmail and bribery. Some captives suffered beatings for refusing to convert, but the priests seemed to realize that such treatment would not move the Massachusetts pastor. Knowing that Williams's surviving children were separated from him, the priests told Williams that he could have them back if he would convert. They also said that the governor would give him a generous pension. Williams refused. "I told them my children were dearer to me than all the world," he wrote, "but I would not deny Christ and his truths for the having of them with me; I would still put my trust in God, who could perform all things for me."

Finally, in 1706, the British rescued fifty-seven Deerfield captives and returned them to Boston. Williams and all but one of his surviving children were among them. (One daughter had become a Catholic and joined an Indian tribe; she refused to return despite her father's pleas.) Williams returned to the pastorate, and all of his sons eventually followed him into the ministry. Williams's widely read account of the ordeal, *The Redeemed Captive Returning to Zion*, first appeared in 1707. Despite his sadness for those left behind, Williams wrote, "We have reason to bless God who has wrought deliverance for so many."

Section Quiz

1. What two expeditions provided the basis for French claims to the New World?

2. What three factors increased the danger of the French threat to the thirteen colonies?

3. What were the American names for the four wars fought by Britain and France between 1689 and 1763?

★ Were the wars in this section just? Should the colonists have engaged in them?

Colonel George Washington at the time of the French and Indian War

The Granger Collection, New York.

II. The French and Indian War

Although King William's War, Queen Anne's War, and King George's War are all sometimes referred to as "French and Indian wars," the title of the **French and Indian War** is reserved for the decisive conflict fought from 1754 to 1763. In contrast to those earlier, primarily European conflicts, the French and Indian War began in the New World and spread to Europe, where it broke out "officially" in 1756 and became known as the Seven Years' War (1756–63).

The Seven Years' War eventually saw Britain and Prussia allied against Austria, Russia, France, Spain, and several other nations. With fighting on three continents among several nations (not to mention the participation of both Asian and American Indians), the war was perhaps the first "world war." The conflict began in the backwoods of western Pennsylvania with a small incident involving a twenty-two-year-old Virginian colonel named **George Washington**.

Outbreak

The Spark

In the spring of 1754, Lieutenant Colonel George Washington led his men toward the Forks of the Ohio River (the site of modern Pittsburgh). Governor Dinwiddie of Virginia had ordered Washington to clear the territory of the French who, according to the English, had illegally entered the area. On the way, Washington and his troops surprised a small group of French soldiers. In the ensuing skirmish, ten Frenchmen were killed and the rest captured— although Britain and France were officially at peace.

A much larger force of French soldiers and Indian warriors, however, was waiting at the Forks of the Ohio at the newly constructed **Fort Duquesne** (DOO KANE). Realizing that he was outnumbered, Washington retreated and hastily threw up defenses. Aptly named Fort Necessity, the structure showed Washington's inexperience. Located in a low area, the fort allowed the French to fire directly into it from nearby heights. Washington was soon forced to surrender, but the French were surprisingly gracious. They allowed the Virginians to march home after Washington naively signed a note of surrender that put the blame for the whole affair on the British. The government repudiated Washington's note, and Britain and France went to war.

The Two Sides

In the early stages of the war, the French enjoyed a friendlier relationship with their Indian allies than the British had with their Iroquois allies. The French also had an important advantage in that they understood the Indians and Indian warfare better than the British army did. The French borrowed methods of forest fighting from the Indians and practiced **guerrilla warfare**—sudden surprise attacks by small, hidden groups—against the British, whereas the British originally tried to fight in the open, ordered style used in Europe.

In the long run, however, the British enjoyed significant advantages. British colonists outnumbered French colonists by more than twenty to one. British colonists also had a subtle but significant advantage in that they had invested something material in the New World. They had roots in America—land, businesses, and families. Many of the French, by contrast, were isolated traders and trappers who took products such as furs out of the New World but put little into it. Above all, the British navy could control the waterways and thereby cut off French reinforcements and supplies.

The chief British disadvantage was the lack of unity in the colonies. The **Albany Congress** attempted to establish political unity when it met at Albany, New York, in June 1754, about the time that the war broke out. Delegates from most of the colonies north of Virginia attended the meeting. On the second day, **Benjamin Franklin** proposed his "Albany Plan" for centralized colonial rule, including a president chosen by the king and a congress chosen by the separate colonies. Representatives were to be apportioned according to the amount that each colony contributed to the central treasury. The plan was finally rejected, however, because the colonists feared that it would establish a government that was too strongly centralized. Many colonists feared centralized political control even more than they feared France.

Early in the war, in 1755, the British eliminated another potential disadvantage. The presence of some six thousand **Acadians**, French Catholics living in British-held Nova Scotia, worried the British. Fearful of rebellion, the government uprooted the Acadians and forcibly moved them to English colonies farther south. A few Acadians managed to escape and return to Nova Scotia. Many fled to French-held Louisiana, where their descendants became known as "Cajuns." Like many civilians in the midst of war, the Acadians suffered as a result of the opposing sides' fears.

This 1754 appeal by Ben Franklin for cooperation among the colonies is the earliest political cartoon in American history.

British Setbacks

Braddock's Defeat

The early years of the war were disastrous for the British in North America. The government sent General **Edward Braddock** and a thousand seasoned British troops to capture Fort Duquesne. Braddock was joined by colonial forces and by Colonel Washington, who was eager to atone for his defeat at Fort Necessity. To move his men and supplies, Braddock painstakingly cut a road through the wooded wilderness to a spot within a few miles of the French fort. Washington tried in vain to warn Braddock that the French and Indians would not fight in the open, organized fashion that the general knew in Europe.

On July 9, 1755, the French and Indians attacked. They hid in the trees and thick brush and poured deadly fire into the British ranks. The red-coated British regulars stood in close, ordered lines and braved the hail of bullets for three hours. "We would fight," one said, "if we could see anybody to fight with." Braddock, who was riding bravely about the field, overseeing the battle, was shot through the lungs. Eventually, the officers led by Colonel Washington organized a retreat. Over half of the British force was killed or wounded. Braddock died during the retreat after muttering, "Who would have thought it?"

Montcalm

The French assigned command of their American forces to the **Marquis de Montcalm** (mar-KEE deh mahnt-KAHM). Montcalm, a talented soldier and commander, engineered a series of stinging defeats on the British from 1756 to 1758. He destroyed two major British outposts, Fort Oswego on Lake Ontario and Fort

William Henry on Lake George (both located in what is now upstate New York). Montcalm also drove back a British attempt to capture the French Fort Ticonderoga. In addition, pro-French Indians raided the frontier, terrorizing the British colonists. Up to this point the British had bungled their response to the French threat.

British Successes

Pitt's Plan

The situation brightened for the British in 1757 when **William Pitt** became prime minister of Great Britain. "I am sure that I can save this country, and that nobody else can," Pitt declared. Although humility was not one of his strong points, he proved as good as his word. Pitt quickly adopted a plan to win the war. He decided to let his ally, Prussia, bear the brunt of the fighting in Europe. Meanwhile, Britain used its superb navy to isolate the French forces in America and India. Pitt also replaced old, incompetent commanders with young, energetic soldiers who would lead the army to victory. Pitt saw that British victory overseas could win an empire for Britain.

Turnaround

Among those new, energetic commanders was General **James Wolfe**. With his thin body, receding chin, and upturned nose, Wolfe did not look like an inspiring commander. His military talents, however, were tremendous. In 1758, an army under his command captured Louisbourg, still considered the most powerful fortress in North America. This victory gave Britain control of the mouth of the St. Lawrence River. The government then entrusted Wolfe with the key campaign of the war, the attack on the French Canadian capital, Quebec.

Before the Quebec campaign, the British decided to capture Fort Duquesne and secure the Forks of the Ohio. Learning from Braddock's mistakes, a larger, well-equipped force moved methodically from Philadelphia. Seeing such an overwhelming force approaching them, the French blew up their ammunition, burned their fort, and retreated. The victors renamed the site "Pittsburgh" in honor of their prime minister. Only Quebec remained as the main center of French strength.

"The Paths of Glory"

The Quebec campaign of 1759 matched the two greatest commanders of the war, Montcalm and Wolfe. Montcalm knew that Quebec, high on a cliff above the St. Lawrence River, was a natural fortress; if the French could simply hold out against the enemy, the bitter Canadian winter would force the British to retreat. A determined Wolfe, however, devised a plan to capture the city. For several days in early September, British warships sailed up and down the St. Lawrence River, confusing the French about where they would land. Then, in the early morning of September 13, a British force rowed to a point upstream from Quebec. As the boat glided across the dark waters, Wolfe relieved the tension by reciting to his officers Thomas Gray's "Elegy Written in a Country Churchyard." One line of that poem must have sounded ominous in their ears—"The paths of glory lead but to the grave."

The soldiers landed, and soon the Plains of Abraham next to Quebec swarmed with British redcoats. Deciding that he had to

William Pitt, British prime minister

hit the British before they could organize, Montcalm launched his forces at the enemy. In the brief but decisive **Battle of the Plains of Abraham**, the British routed the French. Wolfe did not live to savor the victory, however: both he and Montcalm were mortally wounded. Quebec fell, as did Montreal the following year. The war in North America was over.

Results of the War

The Treaty of Paris

The fighting in North America ended in 1760, but the war in Europe continued until 1763. The **Treaty of Paris** (1763) dramatically changed the face of North America by removing French influence as a major force in the continent. Eastern Canada and all territory east of the Mississippi River went to Britain. Spain temporarily lost Florida but in return received all of France's Louisiana Territory west of the Mississippi. (See the map below and the one on the next page.)

For the victorious British, the cost of both the war and the administration of the new possessions was high. The war alone left a debt of £140,000,000. In addition, Parliament wanted to station ten thousand troops in the colonies to protect against the Indians at a cost of £350,000 a year. Not surprisingly, the government thought the colonies should share this expense. In addition, when King **George III** came to the throne in 1760, the British government announced its intention of scrutinizing the financial and political affairs of the colonies.

The colonies, after almost a century and a half of semi-independence, resented the new attitude. Furthermore, some Americans suspected that the redcoats were intended more to enforce government policies than to guard against Indian attack. Skillful statesmen, such as William Pitt, might have been able to calm the colonies, but Pitt had resigned in 1761. The twenty-

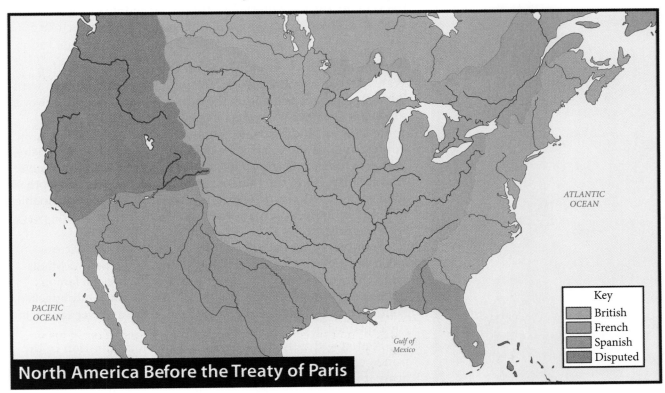

ATLANTIC OCEAN

PACIFIC OCEAN

Gulf of Mexico

Key
British
French
Spanish
Disputed

North America Before the Treaty of Paris

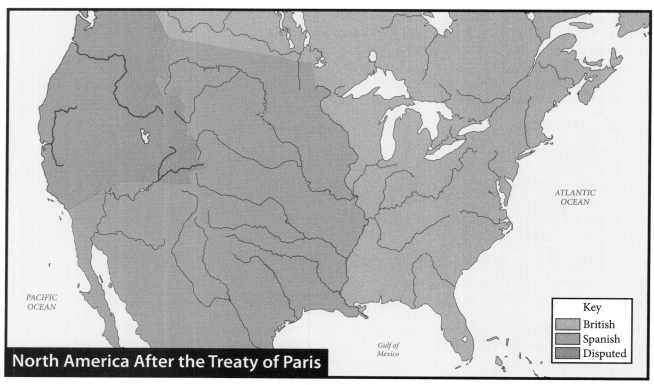

North America After the Treaty of Paris

Key
British
Spanish
Disputed

PACIFIC OCEAN

ATLANTIC OCEAN

Gulf of Mexico

Pontiac was murdered by one of his own warriors.

two-year-old king and his circle of policymakers scarcely understood the growing troubles in America and were therefore unable to resolve them.

One positive result of the French and Indian War affected the future history of North America. France in the 1700s was unbendingly and exclusively Roman Catholic. Great Britain, particularly in the colonies, was more tolerantly Protestant. A French victory could well have led to the persecution of North American Protestants. However, the British victory in the war paved the way for future American religious freedoms in which all faiths, including Roman Catholicism, would share.

Pontiac's War

One last tremor remained from the French and Indian War. After the war, the French army stopped fighting and went home, leaving the Indians on their own. As early as 1762, however, a brilliant Ottawa Indian chief named **Pontiac** had formed a confederacy of Indian tribes. Enraged by the Treaty of Paris, Pontiac and his forces waged a devastating war against British soldiers and settlers from 1763 to 1766. Eight of Britain's twelve frontier forts fell to the Indians, and hundreds of people—both soldiers and civilians—were slain. Pontiac, however, was unable to hold his confederacy together, and he eventually made peace with the British.

Four years after making peace with the Britsh, Pontiac was killed while visiting a tribe at Cahokia, Illinois (across the Mississippi River from modern St. Louis and near the site of a famous Indian temple mound). A young Indian warrior suddenly attacked Pontiac and clubbed him to death. The motive was never satisfactorily explained.

Pontiac's success, however, raised a serious question in the minds of the colonists: what was the use of the costly British army if it could not offer even basic protection? The French and Indian War settled matters between the British and the French, but it also created a host of new problems between Britain and its colonies.

Section Quiz

1. What event sparked the French and Indian War?
2. What was the chief British disadvantage in the French and Indian War?
3. Why was Braddock defeated so decisively at Fort Duquesne?
4. What was William Pitt's three-part plan to win the French and Indian War?
5. Who were the two greatest military commanders of the French and Indian War?
★ Distinguish between the "French and Indian wars" and the "French and Indian War."

III. The Growing Rift

A Sense of Nation

For a century and a half, forces were at work creating a new man in the New World—an *American*. Viewed in isolation, those forces could easily be overlooked, but their cumulative effect began to create a national consciousness in the 1760s and 1770s.

Geography was an important factor in breaking the ties with the Old World. Isolated by an ocean that could be bridged only by sail, the colonists were forced to fend for themselves. The years of settlement forged in them self-reliance, ingenuity, and independence. The mother country seemed more like a distant cousin when problems arose in the colonies. The colonies dealt with threats from Indians, pirates, the French, and the Spanish on their own. Not until King George's War in the 1740s did Britain take an active role in the defense of the colonies.

The way the land was settled also helped shape American attitudes. Private ownership of property was an attractive incentive for settlers from Europe. A man who owned property had a stake in society, and on his land he was the master of all he surveyed. This power gave him greater independence and broader horizons than he or his father had ever known in the old country. One immigrant put it thus:

> A European, when he first arrives, seems limited in his intentions, as well as in his views; but he very suddenly alters his scale; . . . he no sooner breathes our air than he forms schemes, and embarks in designs he never would have thought of in his own country.

Another factor that influenced American attitudes toward Britain was the diversity of the colonists. Not everyone was British. Although English language and institutions prevailed, many settlers had a non-English heritage. The thousands of settlers who were German, French, Dutch, Swedish, Finnish, and Scottish composed a significant portion of the population of British

King George III
The Granger Collection, New York.

North America. When tensions with Britain arose, loyalty to the crown was hardly uniform. Some non-English Americans actively supported the independence of their adopted homeland.

For example, the son of Apollos Rivoire, a French Huguenot, became a leader in the resistance movement in Boston. Apollos himself made many sacrifices for his new country, not the least of which was his name. Altering his name, as he noted, "merely on account that the bumpkins pronounce it easier," he became known as Paul Revere. His son, Paul Jr., became the famous midnight rider and a hero of the American Revolution.

A fourth factor that influenced the formation of a national consciousness was the Great Awakening. This religious revival was truly across the colonies, not merely of a local nature. And the religious unity that resulted was reflected in a cultural unity as well.

Another crucial force in the development of American nationalism was the strength of colonial self-government. Colonial governments consisted of a governor, his councilors, and an elected assembly. With few exceptions, colonial governors were not a strong political force because they usually owed their jobs to the king but their salaries to the colonial assembly.

By the beginning of the eighteenth century, the elected houses (such as the House of Burgesses in Virginia, the House of Representatives in Massachusetts, and the House of Delegates in Maryland) were clearly the most powerful forces in the governing of their respective colonies. These assemblies held the all-important **power of the purse**, which meant that salaries for royal officials, military appropriations, and taxes had to pass the scrutiny of elected officeholders. In addition, the assemblies had the power to initiate their own legislation. They were not mere rubber stamps for edicts from the royal governor.

The colonies were not unaware of their political clout. Nurtured by geographic remoteness and official neglect from Britain, generations of colonists gained experience in representative government, and the assemblies jealously guarded their power. Attempts to curb the self-governing power of the colonial legislatures were seen as threats to cherished rights and liberties.

Following the French and Indian War, the many forces that shaped America's growing sense of *nation* would be magnified by a sense of confidence and optimism. American troops had helped oust the French, clearing the way for western expansion. The Americans had also stood shoulder to shoulder with British regular troops and had come away unimpressed. The British failure at frontier fighting, Braddock's humiliating defeat, and the grating presence of troops during peacetime built up resentment. Americans came to view the redcoats less as defenders and more as invaders. The battle lines were quietly being drawn.

Taxes and Tensions

Following the French and Indian War, the relationship between Britain and the colonies changed dramatically. Although British troops had helped to eliminate the threat of French domination, the successful conclusion of the war decreased colonial dependence on Great Britain. Increasing attitudes of independence and even hostility to Britain simply reflected the heritage of self-government in the colonies.

At the same time, however, attitudes in Britain were changing toward the nation's colonial offspring. Britain had just bested France in a global war on land and sea, assembling an empire that would have made the Caesars envious. The triumph was a heady experience, and many in Britain decided that, in keeping with the Queen Mother's advice to George III to "be a king," it was time to "be an empire"—time to gain greater control over the direction and profitability of the Thirteen Colonies. In one parliamentary act after another during the 1760s and 1770s, the British pursued a policy of *coercion* instead of *cooperation*. That proved to be a costly mistake for Britain.

The Proclamation Line (1763)

In October 1763, Parliament established the **Proclamation Line**, which forbade the colonists to settle beyond the Appalachian Mountains. The British government viewed the Proclamation Line as a way to diminish conflicts with the Indians, like those that had led to Pontiac's War. American colonists, however, denounced it as an arbitrary interference with their local governments; it denied westward expansion into lands already granted by the colonial charters.

Despite the protests, expansion was continued by those who had little concern for a law laid down halfway around the world. The towns of Pittsburgh and Wheeling were established during the decade after the line was drawn. In the western land claims of Virginia and North Carolina (areas that included parts of modern West Virginia, Ohio, Kentucky, and Tennessee), the defeat of a Shawnee confederation under Chief Cornstalk and the trailblazing efforts of the intrepid Daniel Boone beckoned land-hungry settlers and speculators across the Appalachians.

The Sugar Act (1764)

In 1764, following the lead of **George Grenville**, the king's chief minister, Parliament passed the **Sugar Act**. This act placed a tariff, or tax, on certain goods imported into the colonies, such as sugar, molasses, and coffee. The stated purpose of the Sugar Act was to raise revenue "for defraying the expenses of defending, protecting, and securing" the colonies. Such external tariffs (taxes on goods imported by Americans) had been levied before, but Parliament had seldom enforced them. This time, however, the British government clearly intended to collect the duties. The colonists protested that since Parliament could now enforce such taxation with the standing army, the colonists and their legislatures were virtually powerless.

The Stamp Act (1765)

Grenville set about finding other ways to balance the imperial books. In February 1765, he proposed to Parliament a stamp tax required for newspapers, diplomas, and a variety of legal and commercial documents. The **Stamp Act** levied the first **internal tax** (a tax on goods produced and consumed entirely within the colonies) ever imposed on the colonies. For Americans, the issue was not the *amount* of the tax but that they were being taxed *without their consent* and that the traditional power of the colonial legislatures was being bypassed.

The little stamp seemed innocent enough to Parliament; only a handful of members opposed it, among them Col. Isaac Barré, a veteran of Wolfe's Quebec campaign and a man who

This stamp signified opposition to the Stamp Act.

Victorious colonists celebrated the repeal of the Stamp Act by conducting a mock funeral for it.

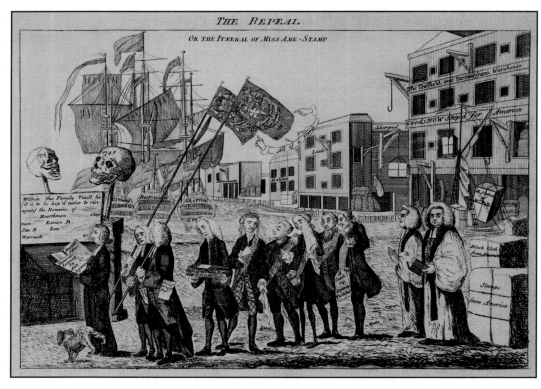

understood America. Barré stood in the House of Commons, turned his scarred face to the eager tax collectors, and declared that Britain's growing contempt for the rights of the colonists had "caused the blood of these sons of liberty to recoil within them." In America, colonists received word of Barré's speech enthusiastically. A growing body of opponents to British rule snatched Barré's phrase and proudly called themselves the **Sons of Liberty**.

The Quartering Act (1765)

Parliament passed the Stamp Act on March 22, 1765. Two days later, they passed the **Quartering Act**, which officially subjected the colonies to a standing army in peacetime and further required that the colonists help supply provisions for it. Even Prime Minister Grenville admitted that the quartering clause was "by far the most likely to create difficulties and uneasiness . . . especially as the quartering of soldiers upon the people against their will is declared by the Petition of Right to be contrary to law." The almost simultaneous passage of the Stamp Act and the Quartering Act caused the colonists to conclude that they were being oppressed by an unlawful military occupation to enforce illegal taxation.

Colonial Opposition

These parliamentary decisions, particularly the Stamp Act, sparked a firestorm of protest in America. First, on May 29, 1765, **Patrick Henry** presented resolutions to the Virginia House of Burgesses declaring that Virginians possessed all the rights and privileges of Englishmen and that to grant the right of taxation to *any* body other than the Virginia Assembly was an act of tyranny. In Henry's words, the Stamp Act was "a manifest tendency to destroy American freedom." In a blunt warning to King George III about the consequences of such tyranny, Henry told the Assembly, "Caesar had his Brutus, Charles the First his Cromwell, and George the Third . . ."

Patrick Henry became the voice of resistance to British oppression in the colonies.

"Treason! You have spoken treason!" interrupted the House Chairman in midsentence.

Henry finished his sentence—"may profit by their example! If this be treason, make the most of it."

In October 1765, in the first example of genuine colonial unity, delegates from nine colonies met in New York for the **Stamp Act Congress**, which formally denounced the Stamp Act and the usurpation of colonial rights that it represented. Elsewhere, matters became violent. In Boston, the Sons of Liberty, led by **Samuel Adams**, hanged an effigy of Andrew Oliver, the royal Stamp Distributor for Massachusetts Bay. More radical elements of the opposition ransacked Oliver's home, smashing windows and

Patrick Henry, "Voice of the Revolution"

Among the voices raised in defense of American liberty, none was as eloquent as that of Patrick Henry. After one speech, a listener said that the audience was "taken captive, and so delighted with their captivity, that they followed implicitly, whithersoever he led them; that, at his bidding their tears flowed from pity, and their cheeks flushed from indignation."

Patrick Henry must have learned some of his oratorical skills from the matchless speakers he heard as a young man. Some historians think that young Patrick might have heard George Whitefield, the great English evangelist who helped carry the Great Awakening throughout the colonies. We know for certain that Henry heard Samuel Davies, the Presbyterian leader of the Awakening in Virginia.

The effect of Davies, other ministers, and the Bible itself on Henry was profound. The Virginia statesman's speeches were filled with the rhythms and cadences of Scripture and numerous allusions to the Bible. Few speeches show that tendency more clearly than Henry's most famous speech, given in St. John's Episcopal Church in Richmond in 1775. Henry's fiery declaration that "Gentlemen may cry peace, peace—but there is no peace" echoes the prophet Jeremiah (Jer. 6:14; see also 8:11). Likewise, Henry's rhetorical question posed in the same speech a few moments later—"Why stand we here idle?"—alludes to Jesus's words in the parable of the laborers in the vineyard (Matt. 20:6).

In his early years, however, Henry showed little sign of possessing unusual talent. In fact, his first ventures into making a living proved to be dismal failures. He twice went bankrupt trying to operate a store. (Some people claim that he preferred engaging his customers in intricate debates to selling them goods.) An effort at farming proved so troublesome that Henry seemed almost relieved when his farmhouse burned and he had to seek other employment. Almost in desperation, Henry turned to law. Even then, his study was so hurried that another lawyer signed his license only after Henry solemnly promised to pursue further study as he practiced.

Henry proved far more diligent at law than at his earlier pursuits, and his natural speaking ability was a tremendous advantage in arguing cases before a jury. Henry first leaped to fame and displayed his love of American liberty in arguing against the Two-Penny Act in 1762. This law of the Virginia legislature had fixed the Anglican clergy's annual salary of sixteen thousand pounds of tobacco at a cash value of two pence per pound. Although the salary was comfortable and guaranteed, it was set below the market value. As a result, the king annulled the Two-Penny Act, and some of the parsons sued for their "back pay."

Twenty-seven-year-old Henry argued that a contract existed between the king and his people. When the king acted selfishly by striking down a law beneficial to all the people, he broke his contract, and the people were no longer obliged to obey him. Henry claimed that a king was a tyrant if he arbitrarily trampled the will of his subjects. Shouts of "Treason! Treason!" (an accusation that Henry would hear often over the next few years) filled the courtroom, but the jury agreed with the fiery orator.

After the Two-Penny Act case, Henry's career climbed dramatically. He became a prosperous, much-sought-after attorney. He was elected to Virginia's House of Burgesses and later served in both the First and Second Continental Congresses and for three terms as governor of Virginia. The greatest moment of his career came in 1775, when Virginia received word that Britain was trying to force submission from Massachusetts. Standing in St. John's Church before an assembly of the greatest leaders of Virginia, Henry raised his eloquent voice in a ringing call for the defense of liberty. Patrick Henry, like an American Joshua, stated for his countrymen the life-and-death choice before them:

Is life so dear, or peace so sweet as to be purchased at the price of chains and slavery? Forbid it, Almighty God! I know not what course others may take, but as for me, give me liberty, or give me death!

Samuel Adams led the Sons of Liberty in Boston.

John Dickinson's *Letters from a Farmer in Pennsylvania* encouraged colonists to resist the erosion of their liberties.

furniture. Although Samuel Adams distanced himself from the vandalism, he was pleased with the protest generally. Oliver resigned; Sons of Liberty organizations in other colonies took up the cause, and in March 1766 Parliament repealed the hated Stamp Act.

Townshend Acts (1767)

An uneasy calm followed the repeal of the Stamp Act, but the quiet was soon shattered by a new revenue scheme in Parliament. In 1767, Charles Townshend, the head of the British Treasury, proposed a series of taxes and enforcement measures that had far-reaching political consequences. The **Townshend Acts** proposed direct taxes on glass, paint, paper, and tea. Furthermore, the acts strengthened the writs of assistance, the general search warrants used and often abused by customs officials in their search for taxable goods. In addition, it was proposed that the revenue raised from those taxes should pay the salaries of royal officials, including the governor. This was in direct conflict with the traditional "power of the purse" that many colonial assemblies had maintained for nearly a century.

An optimistic Charles Townshend told Parliament that the colonies should submit to this unprecedented power-grab because they were "planted with so much tenderness, governed with so much affection, and established with so much care and attention." However, the crusty Colonel Barré retorted, "We did not plant the colonies. Most of them fled from oppression. They met with great difficulty and hardship, but as they fled from tyranny here they could not dread danger there. They flourished not by our care but by our neglect. They have increased while we did not attend to them. They shrink under our hand."

In America, **John Dickinson** expressed the general reaction to the Townshend Acts in his *Letters from a Farmer in Pennsylvania to the Inhabitants of the British Colonies*: "If Great Britain can order us to pay what taxes she pleases before we take [imported goods] away, or when we land them here, we are abject slaves as France or Poland can show." Dickinson urged his fellow colonists not to give up "a single iota" of their rights and liberties.

Dickinson's argument was not an economic one; it did not center on how much the taxes would cost the colonists. His emphasis, like Patrick Henry's, was the ideals of freedom and the rights of self-government.

Opposition to the Townshend Acts grew. Colonists organized **boycotts**, or refusals to buy British goods, throughout the colonies. In Boston, the hotbed of the Patriot movement, a riot broke out in 1768 when overbearing customs officials seized the *Liberty*, one of John Hancock's merchant vessels. In the fall, British troops and artillery arrived to police Boston and to quash the growing resistance.

The British Parliament, through the Sugar Act, Stamp Act, and the various Townshend measures, was moving not only to raise money—although the various taxes raised more resentment than revenue—but also to centralize authority in London.

This centralization effort came at a time of growing nationalism in the colonies. Clearly, with Britain and America headed in different directions at the same time, they were certain to butt heads along the way.

The Boston Massacre, depicted in this early drawing, was only the beginning of violence between the British and the American colonists.

First Blood

Lord North, the latest result of George III's search for a competent prime minister, told Parliament, "America must fear you before she can love you. I hope we shall never think of [repealing the Townshend Acts] till we see America prostrate at our feet." Although most of the Townshend Acts were repealed in 1770, North's words had a prophetic ring to them in ways the prime minister did not expect. In the late winter of 1770, Americans would indeed be lying at the feet of the British—cut down, not with taxes, but with lead shot in the bloody **Boston Massacre**.

With the arrival of a thousand British troops in Boston in 1768, the atmosphere in Boston had grown from tense to explosive. The sight of an occupation force and its fleet of warships eyeing a city at peace irritated Bostonians and fueled Sam Adams's Patriot network. The spark that ignited the powder keg came in late February 1770.

On a Friday afternoon, February 23, Ebenezer Richardson, a known informant for British customs officials, took it upon himself to pull down a boycott sign placed near his home by the Sons of Liberty. A small crowd gathered and began hurling stones and exchanging

The
just man shall
be in eternal
remembrance

The brave Soldier
of the Revolutionary
War 1770.

Crispus Attucks

Crispus Attucks, one of the five victims of the first clash between the colonists and British soldiers

insults with him. An angry Richardson retreated to his house, vowing revenge. When a rock smashed through his window, hitting his wife, Richardson took his musket and fired into the crowd, killing eleven-year-old Christopher Snider.

Over the weekend a blizzard struck Boston, and on Monday a huge funeral procession of Patriots made its way through the snowdrifts to bury the boy. Despite the February cold, tempers were hot.

By the end of the week, a few minor confrontations between dockworkers and redcoats brought everything to a boil. The soldiers vowed to settle the score on Monday. That evening, March 5, a band of Patriots gathered in the square outside the British barracks to demand the departure of the unwelcome soldiers. The angry crowd hurled sticks and snowballs at seven soldiers under the command of Captain Thomas Preston. One of the privates, Hugh Montgomery, was struck by a stick and slipped on the ice. While getting up, he fired his musket into the mob—whether in anger or by accident cannot be determined. With his shot, however, the other British soldiers spontaneously fired into the crowd.

As the smoke from the muskets cleared, five men lay dying in the square. This violent interaction between an angry mob and British troops became the first of many encounters that would lead to a battle for independence.

Section Quiz

1. What is "the power of the purse"?

2. Why did Parliament establish the Proclamation Line of 1763? Why did the colonists oppose it?

3. Name three of the acts of Parliament after the French and Indian War that created tension between Great Britain and its colonies.

4. What city was the site of a "massacre" in 1770?

★ Explain a possible reason for the power and eloquence of Patrick Henry's "liberty or death" speech.

Chapter 5 Review

Making Connections

1. How did wars in Europe affect events in the colonies?
2. What mistaken tactic did the British follow that led to the tragic defeat of Braddock as he marched his troops toward Fort Duquesne? What tactic did their enemy practice?
3. How did the British deal with the potential internal threat posed by the Acadians?
4. How did acts of Parliament following the French and Indian War lead to increased tensions between Britain and the colonies?

Developing History Skills

1. What factors helped establish a national consciousness, or "sense of nation," among the American colonists?
2. Explain Franklin's Albany Plan for colonial unity.

Thinking Critically

1. If you had lived at the time of the Proclamation Line of 1763, would you have viewed it as a security from Indian attacks or as interference in local government and a hindrance to expansion? Why?
2. Who was responsible for the Boston Massacre—the assembled colonists; the soldiers who fired on the crowd; or Lord North, who urged Parliament not to repeal the Townshend Acts "till we see America prostrate at our feet"? Support your answer.

Living as a Christian Citizen

1. Imagine you are a pastor in New England. Write a brief address instructing your congregation about how to respond to the conflict between the colonies and England.
2. Imagine you are a newspaper editor during the time leading up to the War for Independence. Write an article describing the man emerging from the New World: the American. Organize your article around the core values of freedom, individualism, equality, and growth.

People, Places, and Things to Remember

Louis Joliet
Jacques Marquette
La Salle
Louisiana
King William's War
Queen Anne's War
King George's War
Comte de Frontenac
Treaty of Utrecht
French and Indian War (1754–1763)
George Washington
Fort Duquesne
guerrilla warfare
Albany Congress
Benjamin Franklin
Acadians
Edward Braddock
Marquis de Montcalm
William Pitt
James Wolfe
Battle of the Plains of Abraham
Treaty of Paris (1763)
George III
Pontiac
power of the purse
Proclamation Line
George Grenville
Sugar Act
Stamp Act
internal tax
Sons of Liberty
Quartering Act
Patrick Henry
Stamp Act Congress
Samuel Adams
Townshend Acts
John Dickinson
boycotts
Boston Massacre

The harsh winter at Valley Forge tested the mettle of the Continental Army.
The Granger Collection, New York.

Independence (1770-1783)

I. The Eve of War

II. Declaring Independence

III. Early Campaigns

IV. The War in the South

"We fight, get beat, rise, and fight again."

General Nathanael Greene, 1781

"The Revolution was effected before the war commenced," John Adams, Founding Father and future president, reflected years afterward. "The Revolution was in the minds and hearts of the people. . . . This radical change in the principles, opinions, sentiments, and affections of the people was the real American Revolution."

This "Revolution in the heart" was in many ways an evolution that began on the shores of Virginia and Massachusetts more than a century earlier. Escalating events, however, gradually moved the revolution from the heart to open conflict. The question for many Americans became not whether they would submit to taxes but whether they would submit to tyranny.

One interview with an old veteran minuteman, Levi Preston, conducted more than fifty years after he fought the British, cuts to the crucial issue behind the war. The interviewer asked Preston to describe the British oppressions that led to independence. The ancient warrior replied, "What were they? Oppressions? I didn't feel them."

"What, were you not oppressed by the Stamp Act?" the reporter probed.

"I never saw one of those stamps. . . . I am certain I never paid a penny for one of them."

"Well, what then about the tea-tax?"

"Tea-tax! I never drank a drop of the stuff; the boys threw it all overboard."

"Then I suppose you had been reading Harrington or Sidney and Locke about the eternal principles of liberty."

"Never heard of 'em." the old man answered with a shrug. "We read only the Bible, the Catechism, Watts' Psalms and Hymns, and the Almanack."

The puzzled questioner demanded, "Well, then, what was the matter? and what did you mean in going to the fight?"

"Young man, what we meant in going for those redcoats was this: we always had governed ourselves, and we always meant to. They didn't mean we should."

I. The Eve of War

The Boston Massacre shocked the colonies into relative silence. The calm, however, turned out to be merely the eye of a storm. In June 1772, an armed British customs ship, the *Gaspee*, ran aground near Providence, Rhode Island. The ship's captain, who had a reputation for indiscriminate harassment around Narragansett Bay, was not welcome ashore. On the night of June 9, local citizens boarded the *Gaspee*, captured and removed its crew, and burned the ship.

This attack on one of His Majesty's ships prompted the British to establish a court of inquiry to investigate and make arrests. This was a usurpation of the power of the colonial courts. At the same time, the Massachusetts governor, Thomas Hutchinson, announced that his salary would now come from the Crown, not the colony. No longer would the legislature be able to rein in the governor or other royal officials by using the purse strings. More and more the colonists came to believe that their rights were being stripped away.

Another development in 1772 furthered this belief. In November, the Boston Town Meeting authorized the formation of a **Committee of Correspondence**. Under the guidance of Samuel Adams, the committee provided information on British threats to liberty to other areas of the colony.

The king's tax collectors often felt the brunt of the colonists' anger over British policies.

The Boston committee also encouraged, with considerable success, the formation of a network of Committees of Correspondence. Within three months, eighty new committees had sprung up in Massachusetts alone. In March 1773, the Virginia legislature voted to establish a permanent Committee of Correspondence, and other colonies quickly followed. Those committees provided not only information but also a model of intercolonial cooperation that would be an important step toward a united political and military response to British encroachments. Parliament soon gave the committees ample material to write about.

The Boston Tea Party

The Tea Act

The East India Company had been one of the most profitable business enterprises in Britain, but the company had fallen on hard times. The proof lay in warehouses along the Thames; they were stuffed with seventeen million pounds of tea. The company, verging on bankruptcy, turned to its powerful friends for a bailout. At the urging of the prime minister, Lord North, Parliament passed the **Tea Act of 1773**, which granted the East India Company a monopoly on the shipment and sale of English tea in America. The Tea Act set a very modest tax on tea in America, and the British tea was still cheaper to buy than the smuggled Dutch tea. However, far from being thankful for the low tax, the colonists were enraged. If Parliament could grant a monopoly on tea, what next? In port cities from Boston to Charleston, opposition to the tea shipments was intense. In New York and Philadelphia, for example, tea agents resigned, and sea captains returned their cargoes home to England for fear of their lives and property. Tea, like the hated stamp nearly a decade earlier, became a symbol of tyranny. Coffee replaced the British beverage on Patriot tables.

"Boston Harbor a Teapot Tonight"

When the tea arrived in Boston Harbor aboard the *Dartmouth* on November 28, 1773, Patriots made every effort to have it returned to England, but Governor Hutchinson refused to allow the *Dartmouth*'s return. The confrontation was at a stalemate. The Patriots were determined that the tea would not be unloaded in Boston; Hutchinson was determined that it would be. Since British customs law required that the tea be auctioned and the tax paid within twenty days of the cargo's arrival, time seemed to be on the governor's side.

The twenty days expired at midnight on December 16, 1773. On that evening, thousands gathered for the Boston Town Meeting in the Old South Church, not far from the waterfront. Patriot leaders made a final futile attempt to contact Governor Hutchinson. Shortly afterwards, to shouts of "Boston Harbor a teapot tonight," a group of perhaps 150 men and boys, crudely disguised as Mohawk Indians, boarded the *Dartmouth* and two other newly arrived tea ships.

The Boston Tea Party

The Bostonians had their **Tea Party** in less than three hours, 342 large cases of tea, valued at more than £10,000, were dumped into the harbor. To clarify the purpose of their protest, the raiders took great care to avoid damaging anything except the tea. Even a broken padlock was anonymously replaced the next day. Only one man was caught stealing tea, and he was promptly kicked off the ship. When the ships had been emptied of tea, the participants cleaned them and released their crews. They then lined up at attention on deck, emptied any loose tea from their boots, swept it into the harbor, and marched away singing,

> *Rally, Mohawks! Bring out your axes,*
> *And tell King George, we'll pay no taxes.*

Even pro-British colonists, or **Tories**, satirically admitted that the tea party "had been conducted as correctly as a crime could be." Across the Atlantic, however, the incident was not regarded as a mere tempest in a teapot. A law had been disregarded and property destroyed. King George III instructed Lord North that it was time for strong-arm measures against the willful colonies. "The colonists must either submit or triumph," the king declared. On this, at least, the Patriots and the king were in agreement.

Tea in Other Ports

Boston was not the only colonial port that faced an unwanted supply of tea. That city's "tea party" was copied in New York. Charleston stored its tea until the war broke out and then sold it at auction to help pay for colonial forces. Philadelphia let its tea rot in warehouses.

Political Protest by Colonial Women

One other unusual protest to the Tea Act occurred in Edenton, North Carolina, on October 25, 1774. A group of fifty-one women pledged not to drink any more tea (or buy British-made cloth and other British imports). Their action has been called the "earliest known instance of political activity on the part of American women in the American colonies."

A Heritage of Violence

Even before the Boston Tea Party, Americans made numerous violent attempts to vent their anger against perceived government abuses. Three specific groups are noteworthy.

First were the **Paxton Boys**, a large group of Scots-Irish living in the backcountry of south-central Pennsylvania near present-day Harrisburg. During Pontiac's War, they thought that Pennsylvania's colonial government was not doing enough to protect the people of the colony, especially those in the backcountry. Believing that the government would not defend them, they decided to defend themselves. They formed a vigilante group.

The nearest hostile Indians were about two hundred miles away, but the Paxton Boys took out their frustrations on the nearest Indians, the peaceful Conestogas (Susquehannocks). Many of these Indians were Christians and even lived among the settlers. But the Paxtons accused them of being spies, murdered six of them, and burned the cabin where the murders had occurred.

No one would report the murderers to authorities. Unchallenged, the Paxton Boys went after other peaceful Indians in eastern Pennsylvania. In January 1764, some of the Indians fled to Philadelphia, and 250 of the Paxtons followed. Benjamin Franklin raised a militia and negotiated with the Paxtons, thereby preventing any further bloodshed. About half of the "rescued" Indians died, however, when they contracted smallpox in the crowded city.

Another violent group was the **Regulators**. Those residents of western North Carolina were dissatisfied with the colony's wealthy, upper-class leaders, whom they considered cruel and corrupt and who imposed high taxes on the colonials. The self-styled defenders of societal order rose up in armed rebellion against the tyrants of the east. Their goal was to set up an honest government and reduce taxes. The Regulators dominated the backcountry of North Carolina from 1764 to 1771. Eventually, colonial leaders brought in the militia to suppress the rebellion. It

is worth noting that the Regulators directed their violence against local and colonial leaders, not against the British or the Crown.

A third group that turned to violent protest was the **Sons of Liberty**. They were a secret group begun in 1765 in reaction to the Stamp Act. Their actions were directed against the symbols and representatives of British authority, including the property of customs agents and Loyalists. They burned officials in effigy, tarred and feathered tax collectors, dumped the tea into Boston Harbor, and intimidated those who seemed to support the Crown's rule, policies, and agents.

The Sons of Liberty were not officially or formally organized. Their leaders tended to come from the middle and upper levels of society; the regular members came from all social levels. Almost all the colonies had some such group, but Boston's was probably the most prominent. The leader of the Boston Sons of Liberty was Samuel Adams.

The Intolerable Acts

The Boston Tea Party spurred the British government to action against Massachusetts. Beginning in March 1774, Parliament passed a series of four acts, known collectively as the **Coercive Acts**, intended to punish and subjugate the troublesome colony.

The first of the Coercive Acts, the Boston Port Act, closed the harbor effective June 1, 1774, until the value of the destroyed tea should be reimbursed. Second, in May 1774, the Massachusetts Government Act annulled the Massachusetts colonial charter. That same month, the Act for the Impartial Administration of Justice provided that British officials accused of committing crimes be tried not in Massachusetts but in another colony or in England. In June, a new Quartering Act made private homes available for the quartering of British soldiers. With the arrival of a military governor, General **Thomas Gage**, to replace Thomas Hutchinson, Bostonians knew that their city was under an army of occupation.

If colonial submission was the purpose behind the Coercive Acts, they were clearly a failure. In America these measures, called the "**Intolerable Acts**" by Patriots who refused to be coerced, hardened opposition and created an unprecedented sense of solidarity among the colonies.

In addition, in June Parliament passed the **Quebec Act**, which was directed at British Canada, not the thirteen colonies. The timing, however, could not have been worse. The Quebec Act was designed for the particular needs of French Canadians who had lived under British occupation since Quebec became a British possession in 1763. The Quebec Act set up a rigid political system, made Roman Catholicism the official religion of Quebec, and extended the territorial boundaries of Quebec southward to the Ohio River. The specter of Catholicism rising in the West under the sanction of Parliament enraged many American Protestants who had fled Catholic oppression in Europe. They also feared that the act might set a precedent for Parliament to establish Anglicanism as the state religion throughout the colonies. The Quebec Act encouraged many believers to join the growing chorus of dissent out of fear of centralized religious authority.

First Continental Congress (1774)

Sympathy for beleaguered Boston spread throughout the colonies. In the House of Burgesses in Williamsburg, a thirty-one-year-old Virginian named Thomas Jefferson called for a day of fasting and prayer as a show of support for Boston Patriots. The royal governor, upon hearing of the resolution, dissolved the House. Unperturbed, the legislators simply reconvened in the Apollo Room of the nearby Raleigh Tavern, where they adopted a resolution calling for the meeting of a **Continental Congress**. Similar calls came from Pennsylvania, New York, Rhode Island, South Carolina, and Massachusetts. The Massachusetts House of Representatives called for the Colonial Committees of Correspondence to meet in Philadelphia in September.

On September 5, representatives from all the colonies except Georgia gathered in Philadelphia's Carpenter's Hall. Far from being a gathering of rabid radicals, the delegates had been elected by their colonial assemblies or by provincial congresses and included some of the most distinguished men in America, including George

---

Philosophical Underpinnings of the War for Independence

Economic questions clearly dominated relations between the colonists and Britain leading up to the War for Independence. Colonists resisted taxation and regulation of trade by the British. This resistance led, in turn, to political debate over representation in Parliament. Also, some of Jefferson's arguments in the Declaration of Independence were political, borrowed from the Enlightenment (specifically from John Locke). Ideas such as life, liberty, pursuit of happiness (property), and natural rights reflected contemporary secular philosophy.

While Jefferson depended on philosophers like John Locke, religious Americans were influenced by the political thought of John Calvin and other reformers. Though these reformers emphasized obedience to rulers, they noted that some political systems had certain governmental officials (like the tribunes in Rome) whose job was to protect the people from tyranny. Later theologians developed the idea that the rulers and the people were bound together in a covenant. A ruler who violated the covenant lost the right to rule, and certain governmental officials should ensure that he left office. John Locke picked up on the idea of the covenant and spoke of a contract between the people and their rulers. So by the time of the War for Independence, Americans had the ideas necessary to justify their separation from England.

Washington and Patrick Henry of Virginia, John Dickinson of Pennsylvania, and John and Samuel Adams of Massachusetts.

The changing times required new thinking, and the delegates showed themselves equal to the task. The geographic and historical features that divided the eastern seaboard into thirteen colonies had to give way to united thinking. Patrick Henry declared, "The distinctions between Virginians, Pennsylvanians, and New Yorkers and New Englanders are no more. I am not a Virginian but an *American*."

A spirit of cooperation that portended good things existed among the delegates. When one member proposed that the sessions open with prayer, the idea was at first opposed on the grounds that Congregationalists, Presbyterians, Quakers, Anglicans, and Anabaptists, all represented among the delegates, could not possibly worship together. Sam Adams, who as a young man had sat under the preaching of George Whitefield, favored the prayer proposal, declaring that his faith did not prevent him from hearing anyone pray as long as the man was pious and a patriot. The other delegates conceded the point, and the next day an aged Anglican pastor, Jacob Duché, arrived. During the night, word reached the city that General Gage's troops had opened fire on civilians in Boston. With that report fresh in his ears, the old saint read Psalm 35:1–2: "Plead my cause, O Lord, with them that strive with me: fight against them that fight against me. Take hold of shield and buckler, and stand up for mine help." Then he prayed powerfully for ten minutes for the people of Boston. When he had finished, the assembly was visibly moved and many delegates wept openly.

Although the report of Boston casualties proved to be false (Gage had confiscated a stock of Patriot gunpowder, but there were no deaths), the delegates proceeded with business. Their **Declaration of American Rights** stated that the colonies must be autonomous, or self-governing, in nearly every respect. Although they maintained their allegiance to the king, they asserted that his actions had to be consistent with American rights. As self-governing states, the colonies had the right to raise militias to defend themselves.

After seven weeks of work on their declaration, the delegates agreed to reconvene the Congress in May 1775. None of them could foresee that by then the course of events would take a decidedly bloody turn.

"The Shot Heard Round the World"

When the delegates returned to their homes, they set about putting their words into action. Massachusetts led the way by establishing a popularly elected Provincial Congress in October 1774. This assembly, in addition to the usual legislative functions, prepared Massachusetts for the inevitable conflict that loomed over Boston. The Massachusetts Assembly authorized the organizing, drilling, and supplying (often at the expense of British arsenals) of Patriot militias. Special units of militiamen called **minutemen** formed a quick first line of defense in case the redcoats invaded the countryside.

Throughout the colonies, the Patriots mustered their forces militarily and politically. At a gathering of the Virginia Convention in late March 1775, the delegates discussed the issue of organizing volunteer militias. **Patrick Henry** rose to address his fellow legislators with powerful words that would soon be confirmed with blood:

Religious Changes in America

During and after the war, religious life was altered dramatically. State support for religion gave way to complete freedom of religion and the separation of church and state. The Anglican Church suffered most because of its association with England. In all the colonies where it had been the established church—with the exception of Virginia—tax support for the Anglican Church ended during the war. Even in Virginia freedom of religion was guaranteed in 1776, and tax support ended with the Virginia Statute of Religious Freedom in 1786. State support for the Congregational (Puritan) Church lingered in New England until the early 1800s. But overall it was clear that the war had made religion in America pluralistic and voluntary.

Militia vs. Regulars

Militia were "citizen soldiers," part-time fighters who left their farms and businesses to fight in emergencies. The famous "minutemen" of the War for Independence (citizens supposedly ready to fight on a minute's notice) are an example of American militia. Although militia units might serve for months or even years at a time, they remained nonprofessionals, serving only as long as the emergency lasted.

Regulars, on the other hand, were professional, full-time soldiers who made the military their career. The British army in the War for Independence consisted entirely of regulars, although some Loyalist militia units fought alongside them. The Continentals were America's regulars in the war, serving as the veteran core of Washington's army. Although militiamen often performed valiantly in battle, most generals—including Washington—preferred regulars. These seasoned professional soldiers often proved more dependable in battle.

Differences Between Revolutions

Addressing the United Nations in 1988, Soviet Premier Mikhail Gorbachev declared, "Two great revolutions, the French Revolution of 1789 and the Russian Revolution of 1917, exerted a powerful impact on the very nature of history." Gorbachev correctly considered the French and Russian Revolutions together, for they had similar causes and consequences. Yet, like most Communist leaders accustomed to censoring history for their own purposes, Gorbachev conveniently ignored the *first* modern revolution—the American War for Independence. These three events are separated by far more than time and place. The French and Russian Revolutions began with legitimate grievances but soon descended to bloody struggles for power. However, the American War for Independence was fought to obtain freedom from political and religious oppression.

In both the French and the Russian Revolutions, a narrow, ruthless minority, the Jacobins in France and the Bolsheviks in Russia, seized the reins of power in the name of the people. These fierce little factions overthrew the existing institutions of God and government and replaced them with atheistic dictatorships. Of course, this was done with the bludgeoned consent of the people. Anyone who did not like the new order could make his voice known before a guillotine or a firing squad.

The American War for Independence, however, was fundamentally different from either of the other two revolutions. The United States was settled in the early modern period and, unlike Europe, did not have the strong class divisions of feudalism. Also unlike Europe, the United States enjoyed widespread land ownership.

With these other revolutions in mind, it is easy to see why many Americans, particularly Christians, do not feel comfortable calling their War for Independence a "revolution" and thereby associating it with thuggery. The War for Independence *was* a revolution in the sense that it brought profound political and social changes to America. It was an overthrow of a recognized political power by those who had previously submitted to it. However, as a revolution it was radically different from the French and Russian versions.

France and Russia had rejected the Protestant Reformation. In stark contrast, the American colonies had been founded and populated to a large degree by Protestants who fled persecution in Europe. Enlightenment ideas influenced both France and the American colonies. However, the French accepted these ideas without the biblical restraints recognized by many American colonists. Many Russian leaders embraced humanistic concepts that denied biblical truths, including the fallen nature of man.

The French and Russian Revolutions also opposed religion and established secular states. The American colonists, however, were encouraged, supported, and often led by their Protestant religious leaders. In addition, the American colonies experienced a great spiritual awakening prior to the war and an extended period of revival during and following the war. In striking contrast, French revolutionaries exalted the goddess Reason, and Russian revolutionaries persecuted organized religion.

Alexander Hamilton, observing the Paris bloodletting in the 1790s, noted, "There is no real resemblance between what was the cause of America and what was the cause of France. The difference is no less great than that between liberty and licentiousness."

Of course, violence occurred in America. Wars *are* violent. But a distinction must be made between violence in war and violence in peace. American colonists threw off the shackles of a distant British monarch by force of arms; yet they did not destroy their local government or close their churches. In many ways, the Patriots were simply *preserving* the freedoms and rights of self-government that had been nurtured and enjoyed in America for more than a century. Popularly elected assemblies continued to govern in the states, as they had for years, and many Christians who feared the religious tyranny that comes with political tyranny felt compelled to join the Continental line.

Despite a shaky start, four years after peace was proclaimed, the Constitution—the consummation of the War for Independence—was written. This remarkable charter is now entering its third century of governance. France, on the other hand, went through three constitutions between 1789 and 1794!

To maintain their iron-fisted grip on power, revolutionary leaders in France and Russia resorted to executions rather than elections. Forty thousand Frenchmen, most of them peasants, were beheaded during their revolution. And the millions of Russians killed by Lenin and Stalin exceeded the combined death tolls of both world wars. Little wonder that the Russian revolutionaries had to bind their subjects with barbed wire and draw an iron curtain across the West, lest the people see the results of the *American* "revolution" and feel cheated.

Gentlemen may cry peace, peace—but there is no peace. The war is actually begun! The next gale that sweeps the north will bring to our ears the clash of resounding arms. Our brethren are already in the field!

In April 1775, General Gage decided to act against the growing militia strength in the Massachusetts countryside. Based on spy reports, Gage learned that a large stock of Patriot munitions was stored in Concord, a town sixteen miles west of Boston. In what he hoped would be a quiet show of force, he ordered 700 of his best troops to seize the stockpile.

On the night of April 18, 1775, about 700 grenadiers and light infantry stealthily gathered their arms and gear, rowed across the bay to Cambridge, and reassembled for the march to Concord by way of Lexington.

Having been forewarned by midnight riders **Paul Revere** and a twenty-three-year-old shoemaker named William Dawes, the Lexington minutemen were waiting on the village green when the redcoats arrived on the morning of April 19. Just as the sun was breaking through the chill morning mist, Major John Pitcairn, commanding the British advance, spotted the thin line of Patriot militia. Pitcairn ordered his troops to hold their fire and advance as he galloped forward, shouting to the Americans to disarm and disband. The minutemen's commander, Captain John Parker, had ordered them not to open fire either, only to stand in a show of defiance to the king's troops. Having accomplished this, the militia began to disperse. At that point, a shot rang out—who pulled the trigger has never been determined—but the British regulars then unleashed two volleys on the scattered band of soldier-farmers, killing eight. Most of them were shot in the back. Pitcairn, angered that his men had disobeyed orders, tongue-lashed his troops back into formation. Only one of his men had been wounded in the skirmish, and the long scarlet line proceeded to Concord.

Alerted to the British advance, hundreds of minutemen converged on the outskirts of Concord. Uncontested, the British entered the town in search of munitions. They forcibly exacted enough information to locate the stockpiles, which they proceeded to burn. The Patriots, seeing smoke rising from the village, assumed that the redcoats were torching their homes. As a result, a number of Americans advanced on the British at the North Bridge that led into Concord. Shots were exchanged with deadly effect, and the British were pushed back. Years later, poet Ralph Waldo Emerson wrote of the skirmish at Concord Bridge:

By the rude bridge that arched the flood,

Their flag to April's breeze unfurled,

Here once the embattled farmers stood,

And fired the shot heard round the world.

Paul Revere "spread the alarm to every Middlesex village and farm."

Famous Order

"Don't fire unless fired upon. But if they want to have a war, let it begin here."

—Captain John Parker at Lexington

Patriot minutemen harassed the British troops relentlessly as the British returned to Boston after having fired on the Patriots at Lexington and Concord.

For the king's men the march back to Boston was a nightmare as Patriots fired on the retreating columns from the cover of stone walls, trees, and barns. Although most of the minutemen had never had formal military training, they were used to hunting wild game, and they found the bright red uniforms of the "lobsterbacks" to be even easier targets.

Much Patriot blood was spilled in the battles of **Lexington** and **Concord**, but the Americans had clearly won the day. Forty-nine Americans had been killed and thirty-nine more wounded. But the British regulars had been hurt badly by *farmers*. Not only were 73 redcoats killed and 174 wounded, but Patriot forces now had them bottled up in Boston. The war was on.

Section Quiz

1. Why were the colonists offended by the decision to have the Crown pay Governor Hutchinson's salary?

2. Why did the colonists oppose the Tea Act of 1773 even though it provided tea at lower prices?

3. Name and briefly describe each of the four Coercive Acts. What did the colonists call these acts?

4. Why did the British army send a force to Concord?

☆ Explain why the American War for Independence was not a revolution in the sense that other wars (e.g., the French or Russian Revolutions) were.

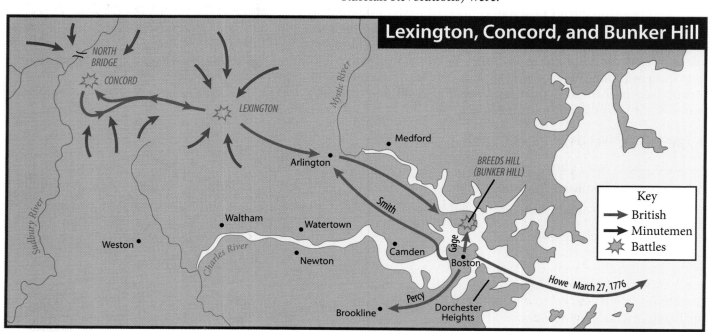

II. Declaring Independence

Divided Loyalties

The undeclared war that had erupted left the colonies deeply divided. Many colonists answered the call to arms as **Patriots**, fighting for the cause of independence. Others, however, were **Loyalists**, or Tories (named after the king's party in Parliament), because they continued to support the Crown. The division cut across regions and social classes. It tore communities and even families apart, pitting father against son (e.g., Benjamin Franklin and his son William) and brother against brother. In some areas (such as South Carolina), the War for Independence was fought almost entirely between American Patriots and American Loyalists.

It is impossible to know how many Americans supported the king during the Revolution, although they were numerous. At least one hundred thousand Loyalists left America by the end of the war. Although there clearly were many more Patriots than Tories, a sizable number of Americans refused to commit themselves to either side, waiting instead for the outcome of the war to determine their loyalty. (Some historians estimate that loyalties were divided about equally among the colonists: one-third Patriots, one-third Loyalists, and one-third apathetic or uncommitted to either side.)

Sympathy for the Patriot cause was not confined to America. When the war finally came, Englishmen were also divided over waging war against their colonial cousins. Such attitudes contributed to the Crown's need to hire thousands of German mercenaries, or **Hessians**, to fill out the ranks of the British forces in America. In addition, some of the most eloquent voices in the British Parliament were raised in opposition to the king's hard-line policies against the thirteen colonies. William Pitt, Edmund Burke, and Charles James Fox repeatedly warned their colleagues and king of the hazards of ignoring American rights. Their published speeches also fired the Sons of Liberty with words such as Pitt delivered in 1777.

> If I were an American, as I am an Englishman, while a foreign troop was landed in my country, I never would lay down my arms—never—never—never! You cannot conquer America.

Second Continental Congress

When the delegates gathered in Philadelphia on May 10, 1775, for the **Second Continental Congress**, they found themselves in an awkward situation. War in the Massachusetts countryside had erupted three weeks earlier, and thousands of New England militia had the British army pinned down in Boston. In addition, on the day of the opening session, the British-held **Fort Ticonderoga** in New York fell to Patriot forces from Vermont known as the "Green Mountain Boys" under the command of **Ethan Allen**.

The original purpose of the Continental Congress was not to make laws and supply armies but to debate and deliver cooperative resolutions concerning British colonial policies. Now, however, necessity thrust upon the shoulders of the assembly the mantle of governance.

Capture of Fort Ticonderoga

Benedict Arnold proposed a plan to capture Fort Ticonderoga, which guarded the link between Lakes George and Champlain on the La Chute River in northeast New York. Before Arnold could get approval for the campaign, however, Ethan Allen and his Green Mountain Boys were on their way to execute that very plan. Allen caught the British by surprise. Entering the fort at night, he awoke the commandant and demanded the surrender of the fort.

"By whose authority?" the commander demanded.

"In the name of the Great Jehovah and the Continental Congress!" Allen roared.

The commander surrendered the fort without a shot. Cannons from the fort were later moved to the Patriot lines surrounding Boston.

Fort Ticonderoga

Henry Knox succeeded in moving the cannons of Fort Ticonderoga to Boston, helping force the British to evacuate the city.

Title page of Thomas Paine's *Common Sense*

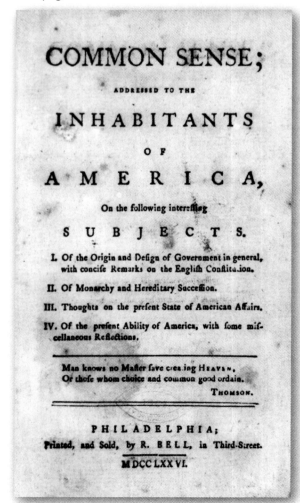

General Washington

The assembly's first priority was dealing with the military situation around Boston. The delegates appointed one of their own as commander in chief. **George Washington** had arrived in Philadelphia in uniform to offer his services in command of Virginia's militia forces. Now he was being asked to take charge of a continental army—a ragtag collection of farmers and shopkeepers facing the best-trained, best-equipped army in the world.

Washington was a natural choice for commander in chief, and as it turned out, his appointment was one of the best decisions of the Second Continental Congress. As a Southerner, the forty-three-year-old Virginian would help link the Patriot cause in New England with the rest of the country. As commander of the Virginia forces during the French and Indian War, Washington had emerged from the conflict as a local hero, though with a war record not unmixed with failure. His greatest strength, however, was not his resumé but his commanding presence, coolness under fire, and keen ability to lead and inspire—all essential to the seemingly impossible task to which the Continental Congress had unanimously elected him.

The Siege of Boston

As Washington traveled from Philadelphia to Cambridge to take charge of the army, word came of a major battle near **Bunker Hill** on the Charlestown peninsula north of Boston. On June 16, 1775, Patriot forces hastily built fortifications on Bunker Hill. The British commander Thomas Gage, with contempt for the soldier-farmers opposing him, ordered a frontal assault on the entrenched Patriots the next day. When the charge failed, he ordered a second assault; when that one failed, he ordered a third. The Patriots, having used all of their ammunition on the redcoat ranks, were then forced to retreat. The British had won a costly victory, suffering more than a thousand casualties among the two thousand soldiers sent up the slope of Breed's Hill, where most of the fighting took place. The Continental forces, by contrast, had 115 killed and 300 wounded or captured. When Washington arrived to take command of the army, the siege of Boston had returned to an uneasy standoff.

General Washington decided to break the deadlock. In December he ordered Colonel **Henry Knox** to go to Fort Ticonderoga and retrieve the captured British cannons. Knox, portly and good natured, seemed an unlikely choice to be Washington's ordnance chief, since his knowledge of artillery had come entirely from books he had read at his Boston bookstore. Nonetheless Knox was a man who got things done, even colossal things. He and his men, using oxen, sleds, and rafts, transported fifty-nine pieces of heavy artillery on a wintry, mountainous, three-hundred-mile trek.

When Knox's cannons arrived in late January 1776, Washington put them to good use. On the evening of March 4, Dorchester Heights, overlooking Boston and its harbor, was quietly fortified and the artillery wheeled into place. When the British awoke on March 5, they found themselves in an indefensible position and soon were forced to evacuate Boston. For Colonel Knox, that day had a double significance. On March 5, 1770, he had stood at the front of the crowd in a snowy Boston Square when a volley of British bullets claimed its first victims. Now, six years later, the redcoats found themselves on the muzzle-end of Knox's heavy guns.

Common Sense

Even after sending Washington off to Boston to take command of the army they had inherited, delegates of the Second Continental Congress still hoped to reconcile with Great Britain without sacrificing American rights. On July 5, 1775, the delegates drew up the **Olive Branch Petition**, which pledged loyalty to the king and requested his intervention in curbing Parliament's abusive exercise of power. The next day the Continental Congress issued a "Declaration of the Causes for Taking Up Arms," in which they pointed out that British actions had left the American people with only two choices—"unconditional submission to the tyranny of irritated ministers or resistance by force." They had chosen to fight. Yet they underscored that their purpose was to gain recognition of American rights, not to pursue any "ambitious designs of separating from Great Britain and establishing independent states."

The statements were conciliatory but unbowed. The British response? George III refused even to read the Olive Branch Petition. Instead, he issued a Proclamation of Rebellion and instructed his Boston army to treat the Americans as "open and avowed enemies." Parliament sent twenty-five thousand more troops to suppress the American cause, authorized the hiring of thousands of Hessian mercenaries, and ordered the confiscation of all American shipping. For the Patriots, the last ties of allegiance to the Crown were strained and snapping.

Public opinion was solidified against the king and for American independence in part by the 1776 publication of a pamphlet called **Common Sense**. Its author, **Thomas Paine**, was an Englishman who had lived in America little more than a year; yet he put Patriot thinking into words that fired their will. He described monarchy as a foolish form of government whose path through history was strewn with human wreckage. Paine concluded that "the blood of the slain, the weeping voice of nature cries, 'TIS TIME TO PART.'"

Sales of *Common Sense* quickly reached a half million copies. George Washington wrote in April 1776, "I find that *Common Sense* is working a powerful change in the minds of many men." Despite his support for the cause of independence, Paine opposed Christianity and advocated a radical form of democracy that John Adams thought dangerous.

"Free and Independent States"

During the spring and summer of 1776, one colony after another changed its constitution to a republican form of government. On June 7, 1776, Richard Henry Lee of Virginia presented a resolution to the Second Continental Congress calling for complete independence from Britain: "These United Colonies are, and of right ought to be, free and independent States."

Such a final and potentially fatal resolution required serious consideration, and debate dragged on through June. In the meantime a committee of five, which included **John Adams**, Benjamin Franklin, Roger Sherman, Robert Livingstone, and **Thomas Jefferson**, was appointed to draw up a declaration in support of Lee's resolution. Most of the work on the draft, however, was shouldered by the brilliant and eloquent Jefferson.

On July 2 the Congress approved the independence resolution. Two days later, July 4, 1776, Congress approved the final draft of the

---

From Common Sense

These are the times that try men's souls. The summer soldier and the sunshine patriot will, in this crisis, shrink from the service of his country; but he that stands it *now*, deserves the love and thanks of man and woman. Tyranny, like hell, is not easily conquered; yet we have this consolation with us, that the harder the conflict, the more glorious the triumph. What we obtain too cheap, we esteem too lightly; 'tis dearness only that gives everything its value. Heaven knows how to put a proper price upon its goods; and it would be strange indeed, if so celestial an article as *Freedom* should not be highly rated. . . . Panics, in some cases, have their uses; . . . their peculiar advantage is, that they are the touchstone of sincerity and hypocrisy, and bring things and men to light, which might otherwise have lain forever undiscovered.

Thomas Paine
The American Crisis (1776)

Writing the Declaration of Independence

Common Sense Realism

The Declaration of Independence is an excellent example of the spirit of Common Sense Realism, a product of the Scottish Enlightenment, as is Paine's *Common Sense*. It also was related to the philosophy of Whigs in the British Parliament, who often opposed royal authority and supported the concepts of "life, liberty, and the pursuit of happiness."

Declaration of Independence. It not only listed the grievances that Americans had against the king but also stated universal principles that would shape the character and direction of the emerging nation.

> We hold these truths to be self-evident, that all men are created equal; that they are endowed by their Creator with certain unalienable Rights; that among these are Life, Liberty, and the pursuit of Happiness. That to secure these rights, Governments are instituted among Men, deriving their just powers from the consent of the governed.

Fifty-six delegates from thirteen colonies inscribed their names on Jefferson's document. Their signing was an act of heroism unsurpassed on the battlefield. Each man knew that if the cause failed, he was signing his death warrant and could be found hanging from the liberty tree. Yet they were courageous men who found the cause worth the risk. They sealed their commitment with ink and were no less willing to seal it with their blood. Jefferson, of course, put it best: "We mutually pledge to each other our lives, our fortunes, and our sacred honor."

Section Quiz

1. What was a Hessian?
2. Why did the Continental Congress choose George Washington as commander in chief?
3. Who helped break the deadlock at Boston by bringing in artillery? From where did he bring the artillery?
4. Who was largely responsible for the original draft of the Declaration of Independence?
★ According to the above quotation from the Declaration of Independence, from whom does the government receive its power to rule? Is this a biblical view?

III. Early Campaigns

Disaster in New York

When the British army sailed from Boston to Canada, Washington's temporary relief was mixed with apprehension. Where would the British go next? When the British turned their fleet toward New York City, Washington quickly marched his army to that city and began its defense.

New York was not really defensible, however. The Americans had virtually no navy, and the city was flanked by the East and Hudson rivers and was entered by a large harbor. The British fleet could land troops at any one of numerous points on the river and march against the American forces. Although it would have been militarily wise to abandon the city, it would also have been politically disastrous. Washington and Congress both knew that the Americans could not simply give up one of their most important cities without a fight. The American people, still divided about the war, would see such an act as a sign of weakness and cowardice. Washington, therefore, prepared for the worst when in July of 1776 General **William Howe**, General Gage's replacement, landed his forces on Staten Island.

From the summer of 1776 to late fall, the British gave the Americans a painful lesson in warfare. On Long Island, Manhattan Island, and the mainland, the British won a series of apparently effortless victories. Washington's inexperience as a commanding general, the greenness of the American troops, and the superiority of the British navy combined to spell defeat for the Americans. During one typical skirmish, Washington watched in disgust as some of his infantry broke and ran from the British without firing a shot. The general hurled his hat to the ground in frustration and cried, "Are these the men with whom I am to defend America?"

A few bright spots relieved the gloom for the Continental army. After a disastrous defeat in the Battle of Long Island (August 27, 1776), Washington conducted a brilliant night retreat across the East River. While brilliant retreats would not win the war, they at least saved the army from destruction. By November, New York was in British hands, and the Continental army was in New Jersey.

Trenton and Princeton

Trenton

The onset of winter in late 1776 found the Continental army in a slough of despond. It had been driven smartly from New York, and the enlistments of many of the troops would expire at the end of the year. Most of them were unwilling to re-enlist in a losing cause. Faced with this daunting situation, Washington decided on a move as dangerous as it was daring. He would attack.

Washington's forces lay on the Pennsylvania side of the Delaware River. In **Trenton**, on the New Jersey side, lay a force of Hessians. On Christmas night of 1776, Washington led his troops across the river in the teeth of a howling storm. Snow and freezing rain pelted them as they then marched to Trenton through the midnight darkness. At least two men froze to death during the march.

> ### God's Providence
>
> The history of the War for Independence is replete with examples of the providence of God. Although Washington is often acclaimed for his military victories at Trenton, Princeton, Monmouth, and a few other battles, he also deserves credit for preventing the destruction of his army by achieving even more skillful retreats. God enabled Washington to discern the time to "call it quits," retreat from a superior force, and live to fight another day. The Patriot army escaped British forces time after time, thereby ensuring that the war would continue and wear down the enemy's will to fight. This is no less evidence of God's providence at work than is His enabling the Patriots to surprise the Hessians on Christmas Day at Trenton.

Washington crossing the Delaware

The abominable weather did give the Americans some advantages, however. The storm hid the movements of the Americans from the Hessian forces. Furthermore, the Germans were comfortably sleeping off their Christmas merry-making. They never expected that anyone would dare to attack in such weather. When Washington attacked Trenton, he caught the astonished Hessians completely off guard. After a brief and confused resistance, they surrendered. Nearly one thousand Hessians were killed or captured. Washington did not lose a single man.

Princeton

Flushed with unaccustomed success, Washington followed the brilliant stroke at Trenton with an equally daring move. When a British force under General Cornwallis camped against him at Trenton, Washington responded with a ruse. During the night, a few American soldiers stoked the campfires and made an abundance of noise while the rest of the army silently slipped away. The Americans marched toward Cornwallis's thinly defended supply base at **Princeton**.

The attack on Princeton on January 3, 1777, did not begin well. The Americans, although more numerous than the British, were disorganized. As the small but disciplined British force advanced, Washington and his officers rode into the confused American lines to restore order. General Washington himself rode in front of his lines and directed the attack. To the horror of his aides, Washington stayed between the two enemy lines and ordered the Americans to fire. One aide covered his face with his hat, fully expecting to see his commander soon lying dead on the ground. When the smoke cleared, however, Washington was completely unharmed, and the shattered British forces ran.

Trenton and Princeton were minor affairs militarily, being more like raids than battles. Their effect on American morale, however, was dramatic. After the disasters of New York, any victory would have been welcome. Such overwhelming victories only made the triumph sweeter. There was a visible result as well. Many of those soldiers whose enlistments had expired rejoined the army. The Americans had an army and hope with which to fight on.

Fight for Philadelphia

British Plans

The British launched a plan in 1777 that had the potential to win the war. A British force in Canada under General **John Burgoyne** would move south down Lake Champlain and through the wilderness of upstate New York, while General Howe would send a force north from New York City up the Hudson River to Albany. With this move, the British would cut New England off from the rest of the colonies. Fortunately for the Americans, Howe did not cooperate with the plan. Instead, he moved against the American capital, Philadelphia. Howe's action proved embarrassing to the United States initially, but in the long run it resulted in a glorious American victory.

Brandywine and Germantown

Instead of marching across New Jersey to Philadelphia, the British used their fleet to sail up the Chesapeake Bay and land in Maryland, some fifty miles from the American capital. As Howe

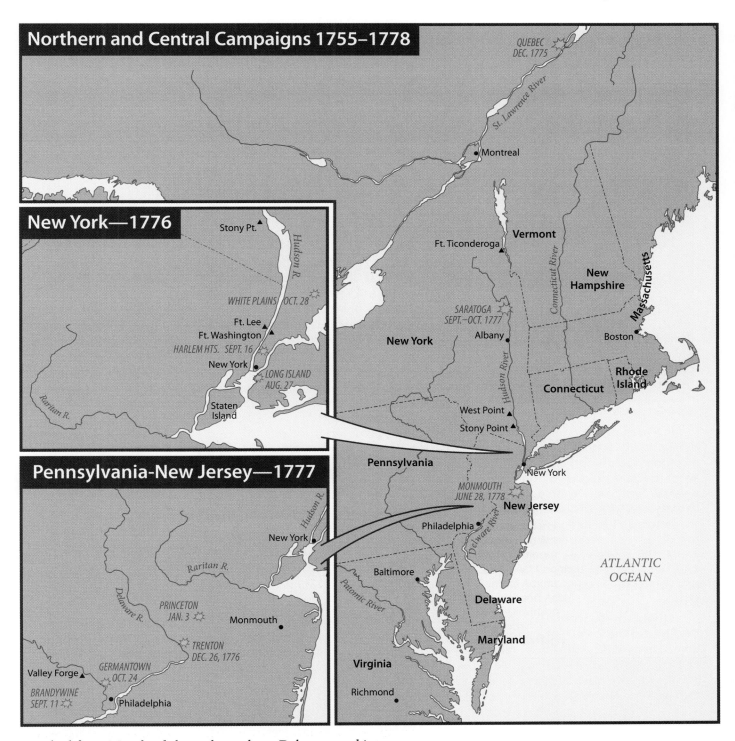

Northern and Central Campaigns 1755–1778

QUEBEC
DEC. 1775

St. Lawrence River

Montreal

Vermont

Ft. Ticonderoga

New
Hampshire

Connecticut River

Massachusetts

SARATOGA
SEPT.–OCT. 1777

Albany

Boston

New York

Hudson River

Rhode
Island

Connecticut

West Point

Stony Point

Pennsylvania

New York

MONMOUTH
JUNE 28, 1778

New Jersey

Philadelphia

Delaware River

Baltimore

ATLANTIC
OCEAN

Patomic River

Delaware

Maryland

Virginia

Richmond

New York—1776

Stony Pt.

Hudson R.

WHITE PLAINS OCT. 28

Ft. Lee
Ft. Washington
HARLEM HTS. SEPT. 16

New York

LONG ISLAND
AUG. 27

Raritan R.

Staten
Island

Pennsylvania-New Jersey—1777

Hudson R.

New York

Raritan R.

Delaware R.

PRINCETON
JAN. 3

Monmouth

TRENTON
DEC. 26, 1776

Valley Forge

GERMANTOWN
OCT. 24

BRANDYWINE
SEPT. 11

Philadelphia

marched from Maryland through northern Delaware and into Pennsylvania, Washington placed the Continental army behind Brandywine Creek, south of Philadelphia, to await the enemy. In the **Battle of Brandywine** (September 11, 1777), Howe outmaneuvered Washington. He sent a force under General Cornwallis northward to cross the Brandywine at an unprotected ford. Then the British swept down behind the Continentals, forcing them to retreat. Washington had to fall back to reorganize, and the British entered Philadelphia unopposed on September 26. On October 4 Washington made an attempt to recapture the city by attacking the British forces stationed at Germantown, north of Philadelphia. The attack failed, and the American capital remained in enemy hands.

Benedict Arnold: The American Traitor

Benedict Arnold monument, Saratoga

In a secluded spot on the site of the Battle of Saratoga stands an odd memorial. Its inscription honors "the 'most brilliant soldier' of the Continental Army" for "winning for his countrymen the Decisive Battle of the American Revolution." The sculptor dared not mention the hero's name. The soldier was Benedict Arnold, who, next to Judas Iscariot, is one of the most infamous traitors in history.

Arnold's war record was one of the finest in the Continental army. As joint commander with Ethan Allen, he had captured British-held Fort Ticonderoga in New York in one of the earliest American triumphs of the war. In an otherwise ill-fated attack on Canada in 1775, Arnold conducted a brilliant march across the winter wilderness of Maine, and he was wounded while bravely supervising a night attack on Quebec during a howling winter storm. At Saratoga, Arnold had injured his leg leading a charge that broke the British lines and turned the tide of battle.

But Arnold was dissatisfied. He was often passed over for promotion by a Continental Congress that was more interested in rewarding an officer's political connections than his bravery in battle. George Washington recognized Arnold's obvious abilities and gave him command of Philadelphia after the British retreated. But there politicians and jealous fellow officers criticized him and sought to undermine his authority.

Arnold became bitter. He seems to have felt some genuine patriotic fervor, but he also had an inordinate love of power, wealth, and glory. Dealing with an ungrateful Congress dampened his patriotism, and with opportunities for glory and wealth fading the longer he stayed in the Continental army, Arnold began to look for ways to fill his purse and feed his ego. In 1779, he secretly offered his services to the British.

Washington valued Arnold, and in 1780 he wanted to honor Arnold by giving him command of a section of the Continental army. Arnold astounded Washington by asking, instead, to be given command of West Point, an important fort on the Hudson River (now the site of the United States Military Academy). Washington was puzzled that a bold and dashing officer should request such an inactive post. Arnold pleaded that the pain from his wound at Saratoga required an undemanding command. In reality, Arnold was suffering more from wounded pride and had plotted with the British to turn the fort over to them for £20,000. Unaware of Arnold's treachery, Washington granted his request.

But Arnold's plans went disastrously wrong. Americans captured his contact, British major John André, with incriminating papers in his possession after he and Arnold had met secretly. Arnold fled to the British in New York; the unfortunate André was hanged as a spy.

Arnold traded his country for a reward and a red coat. He spent the rest of the war leading bloody but otherwise unimportant raids in Virginia and Connecticut. After the war, he returned to Britain with Cornwallis. Although financially comfortable, thanks to his treason (he received not only a reward but also a pension), Arnold was shunned by British society. He died unhappy in London in 1801, no longer known as the hero of Ticonderoga and Saratoga. Rather, Washington said, "General Arnold . . . has sullied his former glory by the blackest treason."

The Turning Point—Saratoga

While Howe was preparing his blow against Philadelphia, General Burgoyne was marching down Lake Champlain in impressive order. He easily seized Fort Ticonderoga and sent its American defenders reeling. At this point, however, the British plan began to break down. The orders to Howe from the British government were unclear, and Howe's decision to attack Philadelphia meant that only a token force would even attempt to move up the Hudson River. Another British force moving east from Lake Ontario to help Burgoyne was driven off by an American force led by General **Benedict Arnold**.

Following these indirect setbacks came several defeats inflicted directly on Burgoyne's forces. A troop of Hessians sent to Bennington, Vermont, to capture American supplies was ambushed and nearly destroyed by the Americans. Then in two separate battles south of Saratoga, New York (September 19 and October 7, 1777), the Americans dealt heavy blows to the British. The American commander, General **Horatio Gates**, received much of the glory for these victories, but the real credit belonged to Gates's subordinates, General Arnold and Colonel **Daniel Morgan**.

After the second battle, the British withdrew to Ticonderoga, but bad weather slowed their retreat. The Americans, who were more experienced woodsmen, overtook and surrounded them near Saratoga. On October 17, Burgoyne surrendered to Gates.

The **Saratoga campaign** was the turning point of the war. Not only had an entire British invasion force of more than six thousand men been killed or captured, but also France—impressed by the victory—recognized United States sovereignty and joined the war against Britain. The United States now had a powerful ally in its struggle for independence.

Benedict Arnold

A Winter of Discontent and Hope

Valley Forge

Word of the French alliance did not reach America until spring of 1778. Meanwhile, Washington and his army went through perhaps the darkest period of the war. With the British controlling Philadelphia, the American army made its headquarters for the winter of 1777–78 some twenty-five miles away at **Valley Forge**. The army had to build its camp from scratch. A "city" of wooden barracks and huts soon sprouted in Valley Forge, but its "citizens" were hungry and ill-clothed. Few men had whole uniforms, and even fewer had shoes. Washington grimly observed that "you might have tracked the army from White Marsh to Valley Forge by the blood of their feet."

Washington and Lafayette at Valley Forge

Washington could do little to relieve the suffering of his men. For one thing, the general had only the worthless paper currency of the Continental Congress to buy supplies. Farmers and merchants found it far more profitable to sell their goods to the British in Philadelphia, who paid in gold and silver. Despite the hardships, Washington's men bore up surprisingly well. Some even joked about their ragged condition. A group of officers, for example, held a party to which no one was admitted who had a whole pair of pants.

Lafayette, the Republican Aristocrat

Several European officers served with distinction in the Continental army. Among them were Baron von Steuben, the German drillmaster; Baron de Kalb, another German, who was the hero of the Battle of Camden; and Count Casimir Pulaski, veteran of a valiant but vain Polish war for independence. The most famous of these international heroes, perhaps, was the French Marquis de Lafayette (1757–1834).

Born of wealthy aristocracy in France, Lafayette seemed an unlikely candidate for honor in a republican revolution. Lafayette's father, a soldier, died in battle when his son was only two. Young Lafayette read widely, especially military books, and he too became an officer in the French army. When he was eighteen, Lafayette attended a dinner where the American War for Independence was discussed. For some reason, the American cause fired his imagination. When an American representative came to France in 1776 seeking officers for the Continental army, Lafayette enthusiastically volunteered. Because he was enormously wealthy, Lafayette declined to take a salary. He said that he would serve only for his expenses.

When Gen. Washington learned that he was receiving a nineteen-year-old major general in his command, he was cool to the idea. On meeting the young officer, however, Washington's doubts melted. Lafayette was gracious, humble, and eager both to learn and to serve. A strong affection grew between the American commander and the young French nobleman. For Washington, Lafayette became the son he had never had. For Lafayette, Washington became the father he had never known.

Lafayette served bravely with the Continental army. Of his education as a soldier, he wrote, "I read, I study, I examine, I listen, I think, and out of all that I try to form an idea into which I put as much common sense as I can." Despite his studious nature, Lafayette was no armchair soldier; he was always in the thick of the fighting. He was wounded at the Battle of Brandywine, and a small force under his command constantly harassed Cornwallis and the British in Virginia. At Yorktown, he led an attack on a major British fortification. When he returned to France after the war, Lafayette left behind him a large group of veterans who had been impressed with the young man's unflagging cheerfulness and unquestioned courage.

Back in France, Lafayette became a leader for liberal reform in his own country. He dreamed of making his native land a model of republican virtue just like his adopted nation. When the French Revolution broke out in 1789, the marquis took the lead in drawing up and adopting a new constitution for France. At one point, Lafayette was probably the most popular leader in France. The revolution turned ugly, however, and bloody violence erupted. When Lafayette tried to moderate the conflict, radicals denounced him as a traitor to the revolution. In dismay and disgust, Lafayette left France claiming American citizenship. But he was arrested and imprisoned for five years.

After his release from prison, Lafayette returned to France. He continued to fight for his republican ideals, but his battlefield was the French legislature. He made one last visit to America in 1824. To his astonishment, hordes of enthusiastic admirers and graying veterans greeted him. Hailed as a hero, Lafayette found that his efforts on behalf of the American republic were cherished and honored by a grateful people.

Drill and Discipline

In February of 1778 a colorful figure rode into the American camp. Lieutenant **Baron von Steuben** (STOY bun) came to Valley Forge in a splendid German uniform to serve as a drillmaster for the Continental army. (Actually, von Steuben was a bit of a fraud. He was not a baron, and he had never held a rank higher than major in the Prussian army.) Von Steuben knew no English, but he knew how to train men and how to instill pride and discipline. By memorizing a few English phrases, the German was able to drill the American forces. He taught them to march properly and showed them how to move and wheel in battle. Building on the experience that the Patriots had gained in past battles, von Steuben transformed the disorganized rabble that had fled from New York into a reasonably efficient fighting force. When spring brought news of the French alliance, Washington looked at his newly drilled men and thought that perhaps the time had come to strike a major blow to the British.

Monmouth—Climax in the East

The French alliance created panic in Great Britain, and the government replaced the slow-moving Howe with General Henry Clinton. Because the British had decided to focus their attention on the southern colonies (where more Loyalists lived), Clinton prepared to withdraw from Philadelphia to New York. The British move, Washington thought, would be the opportunity he had been waiting for. When the British left Philadelphia on June 18, Washington and his officers decided on a cautious plan. A segment of the American army would strike the rear of the British army on the march. If the attack went well, the rest of the Continental army could move up and join the battle. If not, the Americans could at least make things hot for the British and withdraw without risking the whole army.

Molly Pitcher at the Battle of Monmouth

Unfortunately, Washington entrusted the initial attack to Charles Lee, his second in command. Although the most experienced officer in the American army, Lee had little confidence in the quality of the American soldiers. He was completely unimpressed with von Steuben's work and claimed that the British soldiers were far superior. Furthermore, he actually opposed the attack and took command only because he feared someone else might receive the glory.

On June 28 the Americans attacked the British rear guard at Monmouth (MAHN muth) Court House in New Jersey. After a good start the American attack faltered, and Lee hurriedly ordered a retreat. As Washington rode to the front lines, he was astonished to run into his own men fleeing from the battle. Washington found Lee and asked angrily, "What is all this confusion for, and retreat?" Lee offered excuses, but Washington brushed them aside and attempted to undo the damage and save his army.

The British, seeing the American confusion, counterattacked sharply. Washington's men hurriedly fell into line to meet the attack. The temperature on the field was oppressively hot—over 100 degrees. In fact, more men may have died from the heat than from bullets. The wife of a member of an American artillery crew, Mary Hays, became a minor legend during the battle. She carried pitchers of water to the troops (earning herself the nickname "Molly Pitcher"). When her husband was wounded, she took his place and helped fire the cannon.

The **Battle of Monmouth** vindicated von Steuben's work. Despite the early disorder, the Americans quickly and professionally took their places in the battle lines and repulsed the British attacks. Clinton broke off the battle and continued his move to New York. Although the battle was a draw, it showed how far Washington's army had come since the disasters in New York.

The War in the West

While George Washington was trying to build an army that could stand up to the British regulars, a different kind of warfare was taking place on the frontier along the Ohio River. There the fighting resembled the guerrilla tactics of the French and Indian

"I Have Not Yet Begun to Fight!"

The American navy in the War for Independence was pitifully small, particularly in contrast to the mighty British fleet. Most American naval victories consisted of the capture of unarmed British merchant ships for booty. At least one triumph at sea, however, was big enough, as one historian wrote, "to set a tradition of victory" for the U.S. Navy.

Scottish-born Captain John Paul Jones was the ablest commander in the American fleet, and he needed all of his talent on September 23, 1779. Jones was commanding the *Bonhomme Richard* (named in honor of Benjamin Franklin and his *Poor Richard's Almanac*) off the coast of Great Britain when he encountered two British warships, the *Serapis* and the *Countess of Scarborough*. The *Serapis* alone outgunned the *Bonhomme Richard*, and the presence of the *Countess* only increased the odds against Jones. Nonetheless, Jones joined battle.

The three-and-a-half-hour fight started poorly for the Americans when two of their largest cannons exploded, killing several men. Jones tried to overcome the British advantage in cannons by coming close to board the *Serapis*. The British crew held off the Americans, however, and their guns tore gaping holes in the side of the American ship. At one point, an officer of the *Bonhomme Richard*, thinking that Jones was dead, called out to the British, offering to surrender. When the British captain asked, "Do you ask for quarter?" Jones rose and cried out, "I have not yet begun to fight!"

Although his ship was sinking slowly, Jones continued by sheer grit to pound at the British. Finally, the captain of the *Serapis*—his mainmast fallen—surrendered; the smaller *Countess* fled. Jones and his crew boarded the British warship and watched the shattered *Bonhomme Richard* sink beneath the waves. The Americans took their prize to the Netherlands, and Jones visited Paris, where the French greeted him with an uproarious celebration. John Paul Jones had given America its first great victory at sea.

War. Massacres, scalpings, and ambushes replaced the comparatively "civilized" battles in the East between the Continental regulars and the redcoats. A handful of British soldiers uneasily allied with fierce Indian tribes engaged in a brutal life-and-death struggle with hardy but scattered American frontiersmen. One great American leader arose out of the war in the West—**George Rogers Clark**.

Clark, a native Virginian, had come to the Ohio River Valley in 1772. As a resident of Kentucky, Clark recognized the threat that the frontier faced from the British and Indians. In 1778, the twenty-five-year-old Clark won Virginia's approval to lead an attack on British trading posts north of the Ohio River in the region then known as the Northwest. With a tiny force of some 175 men, Clark sailed down the Ohio River to what is now Illinois. From there Clark marched his men overland to the Mississippi River town of Kaskaskia (kus KAS kee uh). The town, populated mostly by French settlers who did not care for the British anyway, happily surrendered. Several other trading posts quickly fell, including the most important—**Vincennes** on the Wabash River in what is now Indiana.

The British commander at Detroit, Lt. Col. Henry Hamilton—known among Indians and American settlers as the "Hair-Buyer" for the grisly scalp trade he encouraged among his Indian allies—reacted swiftly. In December, his force of regulars, Loyalists, and Indians recaptured Vincennes. Then Hamilton settled in to wait out

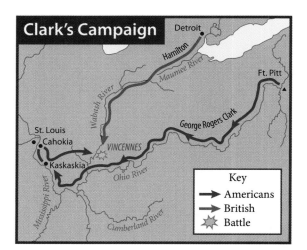

Clark's Campaign

the winter. When spring came, he thought, he would finish off the Americans farther west on the Mississippi at Kaskaskia.

Clark, however, had no intention of waiting to be attacked. Early in February 1779, he marched a small force some 150 miles from Kaskaskia to Vincennes. The weather was wet and cold. Much of the Illinois plains was flooded, and Clark's men constantly waded through waist-deep waters. Clark alternately urged, exhorted, and encouraged his men to keep them going. When those methods began to fail, he threatened to shoot them. By February 23, they were in sight of Vincennes, the last of their food having been eaten two days before.

To deceive the British about the size of his force, Clark waited until nightfall to approach the town. He ordered his men to carry a number of banners as they marched a zig-zag route to the town. When they entered the city, Clark sent his men scurrying back and forth down side streets as though they were a huge force. Hamilton thought Clark had five hundred men; the townspeople thought he had a thousand; Clark knew he had fewer than 150. Awed by Clark's imaginary army, the worried Hamilton surrendered.

Clark's victories in the Northwest were not as significant as the battles in the East in terms of numbers, but they had great strategic importance. Clark's expedition reduced Indian attacks, and his presence helped the United States lay claim to the territory north of the Ohio River. Much of the credit for securing Kentucky and the Northwest goes to the courage of George Rogers Clark.

George Rogers Clark accepting surrender of Henry Hamilton's forces at Vincennes

Section Quiz

1. What militarily indefensible city did the Continental army try to defend for reasons of politics and morale?

2. Why were the victories at Trenton and Princeton so important to the American cause?

3. Why was the Saratoga campaign the turning point of the war?

4. Who was the drillmaster of the Continental army? What battle demonstrated the success of his work?

5. Why were George Rogers Clark's victories in the Northwest strategically important?

✶ What did the winter at Valley Forge reveal about the American Patriots?

IV. The War in the South

In the early years of the war, the Southern states poured men and materiel into the military and political ranks of the Patriot cause. But the British largely ignored the region as a theater of war in favor of fighting Washington's Continentals and isolating New England. As early as 1776, though, they had tried to quell the rebellion in the South, beginning with a naval attack on Charleston, South Carolina. The British fleet, however, had been sent home roughly handled. They made no further attempts until 1778, in the wake of the British defeat at Saratoga.

On orders from London, Sir Henry Clinton sent a British transport fleet loaded with regulars, Hessians, and Loyalists for the invasion of Georgia and the drive through the southland. Clinton hoped that the presence of His Majesty's troops would awaken

Southern Campaigns

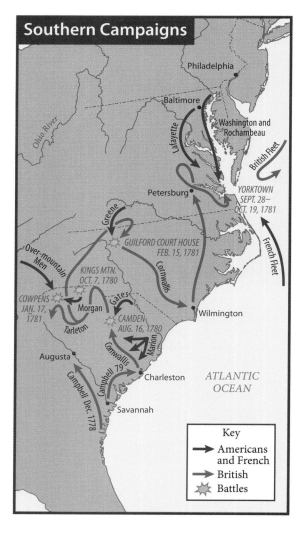

Map labels: Ohio River, Philadelphia, Baltimore, Washington and Rochambeau, Lafayette, British Fleet, Petersburg, YORKTOWN SEPT. 28—OCT. 19, 1781, Greene, French Fleet, GUILFORD COURT HOUSE FEB. 15, 1781, Cornwallis, Over-mountain Men, KINGS MTN. OCT. 7, 1780, COWPENS JAN. 17, 1781, Morgan, Gates, Tarleton, CAMDEN AUG. 16, 1780, Cornwallis, Marion, Augusta, Campbell 79, Wilmington, Charleston, ATLANTIC OCEAN, Campbell Dec. 1778, Savannah

Key
→ Americans and French
→ British
★ Battles

Francis Marion shares his meal with a British officer.

Loyalist sentiment in the backcountry, soften opposition, and sever the South from the rest of the country. His plan worked so well at first that he failed to see its flaws. The southern campaign would be Britain's last.

The British Advance

Charleston

By early 1779, all of Georgia—including Savannah, its chief city and port—had fallen into British hands. Georgia became a staging area for the more important **siege of Charleston**. If the British could conquer Charleston, they would not only capture one of the most populous and important cities in America but also gain access to the Carolina heartland through the navigable rivers that the city defended.

In late March 1780, Clinton's forces besieged Charleston. Most of the Continental forces in the South, an army of about five thousand, occupied the city. Unfortunately, the American commander, General Benjamin Lincoln, gave up the advantage of mobility and heeded the pleadings of Charlestonians to hold the city at all cost. The cost was Lincoln's entire army. With the Americans outnumbered more than two to one and their supply lines cut by the British cavalry under the ruthless Lt. Col. Banastre Tarleton, the outcome was predictable. On May 12, 1780, Lincoln surrendered his force to the British. It was America's worst defeat of the war.

Camden

With the fall of Charleston, the Carolinas lay invitingly open to the British. Before departing with a large force for New York, Clinton gave command of the Carolina conquest to General **Charles Cornwallis**. Soon scarlet columns of British troops were filing through the South Carolina low country.

The Americans sent an expedition of about three thousand Continentals and militia to meet the British advance. The Patriots were commanded by General Horatio Gates, the hero of Saratoga but a man whose reputation exceeded his abilities. When the two armies stumbled onto each other at **Camden**, South Carolina, in August 1780, the Americans were outnumbered and outgeneraled. In the heat of battle, the American militia broke and ran—led by General Gates. The American right flank, made up of troops from Maryland and Delaware and led by Baron de Kalb, bravely held. With only six hundred soldiers, they held for more than an hour against the full fury of Cornwallis's army. De Kalb was wounded eleven times before collapsing along with the Continental line. After the double disasters at Charleston and Camden, the Patriot cause looked grim.

Swamp Surprises

One small band of South Carolinians kept the war alive in the British-occupied low country of South Carolina. The group was "distinguished by small black leather caps and the wretchedness of their attire; their number did not exceed twenty men and boys, some white, some black, and all mounted, but most of them miserably equipped." The leader of this motley assortment of guerrillas was the elusive General **Francis Marion**, who soon earned the nickname "Swamp Fox."

Marion and his men would slip out of the swamps and sand flats to attack British outposts and supply lines. Such small guerrilla bands, of course, could not beat a British army in open battle. Their strategic importance lay in pressuring the enemy. Marion's successful hit-and-run operations pinned down British troops, kept them from joining the main British force, and forced Cornwallis to keep looking over his shoulder. Tarleton himself gave begrudging respect to the "Swamp Fox" when he declared that "the devil himself could not catch" Marion.

The "over-mountain men" dealt the Tories a decisive blow at the Battle of Kings Mountain.

Kings Mountain

A surprising turn of events occurred in October 1780 that gave Patriots cause for encouragement. Cornwallis sent Major Patrick Ferguson to lead an all-Tory detachment of more than a thousand men into the western foothills of South Carolina. Ferguson warned the "over-mountain men" in the backcountry settlements of the western Carolinas and in what is now Tennessee that unless they pledged their loyalty to George III, he would lay waste to their fields, burn their homes, and hang their leaders. Unfortunately for Ferguson, these grizzled frontiersmen did not respond well to threats. Led by Tennesseans Isaac Shelby and John "Nolichucky Jack" Sevier, a buckskinned force of nine hundred frontiersmen, nearly half of whom were Tennessean volunteers (hence, that state's nickname "the Volunteers"), mounted and rode to meet the blustering Briton.

The Patriot force caught Ferguson and his Tories on the wooded slopes of Kings Mountain, a peak that straddles the two Carolinas. There they killed Ferguson and destroyed 80 percent of his force. The victory at the **Battle of Kings Mountain** strengthened Patriot resolve.

Greene Turns the Tide

Cowpens

In the waning days of 1780, while the American army was in winter quarters at Charlotte, North Carolina, Congress appointed a replacement for Horatio Gates. On Washington's advice they sent the "Fighting Quaker" from Rhode Island, General **Nathanael Greene**. Greene took a small, threadbare, penniless, demoralized army and—by courage, resourcefulness, and tactical genius—made it the scourge of Cornwallis's army.

Greene's first move was to divide his outnumbered army and send a detachment south under General Daniel Morgan. Morgan, his body wracked with arthritis, rode off with six hundred Continentals, hoping that Cornwallis would also divide his force and pursue him.

The British commander sent Tarleton and his Tory legion to catch the Continentals. The Americans particularly hated Tarleton for his reputation of killing his prisoners after they had surrendered. Tarleton, however, would more than meet his match in Dan Morgan. On some rolling meadows known as the Cowpens, which in more peaceful times offered pasturage for cattle, the two armies clashed on January 17, 1781. Morgan displayed his exceptional military skill by executing the most nearly perfect victory of the war. Like Joshua at Ai, the Americans first feigned a retreat and then turned dramatically and repelled the reckless British pursuit. In less than an hour, the battle was over. The British suffered 930 casualties, the Americans only 70. The **Battle of Cowpens** was the first major step toward eventual British defeat.

Race to the Dan

After the unsettling losses at Kings Mountain and Cowpens, Cornwallis determined to crush Greene, the only serious and thus far most stubborn obstacle to a conclusive conquest of the Carolinas. Cornwallis decided to march through North Carolina to the fords of the Dan River, which snaked across its boundary with Virginia. The Dan would be Greene's best hope of escape from Cornwallis's superior force. Greene sensed Cornwallis's intentions, and in February 1781 the two armies began a **Race to the Dan**. If the Continentals won, the Dan would cut off the British pursuit. If they lost, the Americans would rein up in the face of British bayonets. After a difficult two-week march in which British and American soldiers alike fell dead in their tracks from exhaustion and starvation, Greene's army ferried across the muddy, swollen river at the site of present-day Danville, Virginia, and took all the boats with them. Greene not only had slipped out of Cornwallis's trap but also had drawn the British far from their supply bases in South Carolina.

In mid-March, the American army recrossed the Dan and advanced south to a little crossroads in North Carolina called **Guilford Court House**. To lure Cornwallis's army out to the battlefield of his choosing, Greene dispatched "Light-Horse Harry" Lee and his dragoons to strike hard and feign retreat. On March 15, Lee and his green-jacketed cavaliers shattered Tarleton's Legion and turned back to Guilford Court House with Cornwallis in hot pursuit. The two armies clashed in a fierce fight in which the British won an empty victory. Cornwallis gained possession of the field, but he lost one-fourth of his men, and Greene was still at large.

Nathanael Greene

The battered British army marched to Wilmington, North Carolina, for fresh supplies and a fresh look at what to do next. Cornwallis decided to march north to the Virginia coast. There he would have a sea route to Clinton's New York forces, and he could wreak havoc on Virginia by destroying Patriot supplies and hanging their leaders. On August 1, 1781, Cornwallis set up his headquarters at a sleepy little tobacco port on Virginia's York River. Little did he realize that **Yorktown** would be the scene of a humiliating defeat.

Victory at Yorktown

Cornwallis Cornered

By late summer of 1781, Cornwallis had amassed a force of 7,200 troops. The **Marquis de Lafayette**, commanding the outnumbered Continental forces in Virginia, watched with alarm. Although he shouldered the burdens of leadership well, the young Lafayette confided in a letter at the time, "When one is twenty-three, has an army to command and Lord Cornwallis to oppose, the time that is left is none too long for sleep."

Soon Lafayette would not be the only one losing sleep. At the end of August, the French fleet under Admiral de Grasse sailed up the Chesapeake Bay, landed three thousand French troops to join Lafayette, and then turned to defeat the British fleet. Suddenly Cornwallis found himself in trouble. Not only was he cut off by sea, but also the arrival of Washington's Continentals and a large force of French regulars meant that he was outnumbered and surrounded.

Washington had been leaking false reports that said he planned to attack Clinton in New York, all the while screening his march to Yorktown. Admiral De Grasse's victory in the Bay had been an unexpected bonus for Washington, who now caught the hapless Cornwallis in a trap.

"The World Turned Upside Down"

After desperate attempts to break the siege, Cornwallis yielded to the inevitable, asking for terms of surrender on October 17, 1781. Two days later, seven thousand redcoats marched between two half-mile lines of American and French troops to lay down their arms. The British band accompanying the redcoats, at a loss to find any dignity in the moment, struck up a rollicking nursery tune:

> *If ponies rode men,*
> *and grass ate the cow*
> *If cats should be chased*
> *into holes by the mouse . . .*

Cornwallis, who had no stomach for such a bitter occasion, was not present. A subordinate carried the general's sword to Washington, who understood the insult of Cornwallis's absence and directed that the sword be given to his subordinate, General Benjamin Lincoln.

As the sword passed hands, the band blared on with the lilting, childish tune, the words of which captured the irony of the moment.

> *. . . If summer were spring*
> *And the other way round;*
> *Then all the world would be upside down.*

Surrender of the
British at Yorktown

The Treaty of Paris, 1783

George III was shaken by the loss at Yorktown. The king at first raged that the war should be pressed further; then, sinking into depression, he offered to abdicate. Finally, he gave in to pressure from Parliament and the people to accept the war as over. Peace commissioners were appointed to meet the American negotiators—Benjamin Franklin, John Jay, and John Adams—in Paris.

Although the French alliance and the presence of Clinton's forces in New York at first complicated the settlement, the **Treaty of Paris** was finally signed on September 3, 1783. It acknowledged that the colonies were indeed independent. The United States was awarded all the land east of the Mississippi River with the exception of Florida, which returned to Spanish control.

Yorktown was not an end, however, as much as a beginning. A costly war paid in Patriot blood had secured independence; now the task of nation building lay before them. In many ways the challenges of peace would be greater than the challenges of war. Yet the generation of Americans who rallied at Lexington, weathered Valley Forge, and besieged the defenses at Yorktown would prove that they could not only win their liberty but also preserve it.

Section Quiz

1. What was the United States' worst defeat of the war?

2. Who was the leader of a band of Patriot guerrillas in South Carolina? What was his nickname?

3. Why was it so important for General Greene to reach the Dan River before the British?

4. What admiral helped trap Cornwallis at Yorktown? What nationality was he?

★ Why was the song "The World Turned Upside Down" an appropriately symbolic song for the surrender of British troops at Yorktown?

Chapter 6 Review

Making Connections

1. What did the Committees of Correspondence provide to the colonies?

2. Why were the battles of Bunker Hill and Guilford Court House empty victories for the British?

3. Why did the colonists fear the Quebec Act?

4. In what way did Howe's decision to attack Philadelphia eventually work to the advantage of the Americans?

Developing History Skills

1. Put the following acts of the Continental Congress in chronological order: Declaration of Independence, Olive Branch Petition, Declaration of American Rights, appointment of George Washington as commander in chief.

2. Since about one-third of the American colonists favored the British in the War for Independence, why was Benedict Arnold's attempted treason considered such a terrible act?

Thinking Critically

1. How did the American War for Independence differ from the French or Russian Revolutions?

2. Some historians have claimed that Britain lost the war because of the incompetence of its military commanders rather than because of any accomplishments by the Americans. Do you agree or disagree and why?

Living as a Christian Citizen

1. If you were a pastor during the era of the War for Independence, how would you counsel the political leaders who attended your church? Write an essay that summarizes your advice. Be sure to ground your counsel in Scripture.

2. Many countries today are ruled by tyrants. If you were a diplomat, how would you advise an opposition group to proceed against a military dictator? Use and evaluate the concepts from Locke and Calvin in this chapter.

People, Places, and Things to Remember

Gaspee incident
Committee of Correspondence
Tea Act of 1773
Boston Tea Party
Tories
Paxton Boys
Regulators
Sons of Liberty
Coercive Acts
Thomas Gage
Intolerable Acts
Quebec Act
First Continental Congress
Declaration of American Rights
militia
regulars
minutemen
Patrick Henry
Paul Revere
Lexington and Concord (April 19, 1775)
Patriots
Loyalists
Hessians
Second Continental Congress
Fort Ticonderoga
Ethan Allen
George Washington
Bunker Hill
Henry Knox
Olive Branch Petition
Common Sense
Thomas Paine
John Adams
Thomas Jefferson
Declaration of Independence (July 4, 1776)
William Howe
Trenton
Princeton
John Burgoyne
Battle of Brandywine
Benedict Arnold
Horatio Gates
Daniel Morgan
Saratoga campaign
Valley Forge
Baron von Steuben
Battle of Monmouth
George Rogers Clark
Vincennes
siege of Charleston
Charles Cornwallis
Camden
Francis Marion ("Swamp Fox")
Battle of Kings Mountain
Nathanael Greene
Battle of Cowpens
Race to the Dan
Guilford Court House
Yorktown
Marquis de Lafayette
Surrender at Yorktown (October 19, 1781)
Treaty of Paris (September 3, 1783)

"Scene at the Signing of the Constitution of the United States"
by Howard Chandler Christy

The Critical Period (1781-1789)

I.   Government by Confederation

II.   A New Charter

III.   The Struggle for Ratification

"This Country must be united. If persuasion does not unite it, the sword will."

Gouverneur Morris, 1787

The 1780s were arguably the most critical decade in our nation's history. From the War for Independence to the ratification of the Constitution, those years were characterized by conflict and change. At the start of the decade, for example, British troops patrolled the streets of New York City in the name of their king, George III. By the decade's end, American citizens paraded through the same streets to celebrate the inauguration of another George, President George Washington.

Americans, in fact, changed governments twice during the 1780s. They not only finally threw off British rule through success on the battlefield but also scrapped their national Confederation because of its weaknesses and set up a new form of government.

Forged by the experiences of that remarkable decade, Americans made their greatest contribution to political thought and practice: the writing of the Constitution. The Constitution capped the independence movement, providing a stable national government through which the states were united in more than name only. The new charter gave substance to the "spirit of '76."

I. Government by Confederation

On June 7, 1776—the same day that Richard Henry Lee of Virginia moved that "these colonies are, and of right ought to be, free and independent states"—the Second Continental Congress voted to draw up a charter for joining the colonies into a **confederation**, a close alliance of sovereign states. Congress entrusted the task to a committee headed by John Dickinson of Pennsylvania, and in a little more than a month, Dickinson's committee presented its work. After more than a year of debate and revision, Congress adopted these **Articles of Confederation**. By 1781, all thirteen states had approved the Articles, and they went into effect.

League of States

Dickinson originally proposed establishing a strong central government. However, the states—jealous of their power and fearing centralization—watered down his plan. The Articles of Confederation did little more than grant legitimacy to the loosely constructed Continental Congress and provide the minimum of authority needed to conduct the war. Although the states pledged themselves to "Perpetual Union," they committed themselves only to "a firm league of friendship with each other." The Articles said plainly, "Each state retains its sovereignty, freedom, and independence." In effect, the central government was only as strong as the states let it be, and that was not very strong.

The legislature was the only component of the Confederation government. The Congress of the Confederation was **unicameral** (having only one house). Each state legislature could elect two to seven representatives to attend, but each state had only one vote, regardless of how many representatives it sent. Important legislation—such as declaring war, approving treaties, and coining money—had to be approved by nine states. Amending the Articles, like ratifying them, required the unanimous consent of all thirteen states.

The chief executive, the president of Congress, was chosen by the legislature and was completely under its control. He was virtually powerless, and three officials (the superintendent of finance and the secretaries of war and foreign affairs) handled most administrative duties. A national judiciary did not exist.

Presidents Before Washington

Before George Washington took office in 1789, the United States had sixteen "presidents"—the presidents of the Continental and Confederation congresses. However, neither the men nor the office had the prestige and power of modern presidents.

Peyton Randolph (Sept. 5, 1774)

Henry Middleton (Oct. 22, 1774)

Peyton Randolph (May 10, 1775)

John Hancock (May 24, 1775)

Henry Laurens (Nov. 1, 1777)

John Jay (Dec. 10, 1778)

Samuel Huntington (Sept. 28, 1779)

Thomas McKean (July 10, 1781)

John Hanson (Nov. 5, 1781)

Elias Boudinot (Nov. 4, 1782)

Thomas Mifflin (Nov. 3, 1783)

Richard Henry Lee (Nov. 30, 1784)

John Hancock (Nov. 23, 1785)

Nathaniel Gorham (June 6, 1786)

Arthur St. Clair (Feb. 2, 1787)

Cyrus Griffin (Jan. 22, 1788)

The Articles simply formalized the status quo of thirteen states separated historically, politically, and economically. Therefore, the Articles reserved to the states every "power, jurisdiction, and right" that was not "expressly delegated" to Congress. Among the most important powers reserved to the states was the power to tax. Unable to levy taxes, Congress was forced to ask the states for money, a request that the states could—and did—ignore if they wished. The central government was reduced to scraping funds together through loans from other nations (which the government usually could not repay), the sale of public lands on the frontier, and the profits from the government-owned post office (a paltry $10,000–$15,000 a year). In its years of existence, the Confederation government barely had enough revenue to cover its expenses.

Successes of the Confederation

Despite its glaring weaknesses and ultimate failure, the Confederation achieved a few successes. Chief among these were the Treaty of Paris and the settlement of the western lands dispute.

The Treaty of Paris

The **Treaty of Paris** (see Chapter 6) was the Confederation's greatest triumph in foreign affairs. By forcing England to recognize American independence, the treaty built enormous prestige for the young nation. At the same time, enforcement of the treaty revealed several weaknesses in the Confederation and squandered much of the reputation that the United States had so carefully built up.

By the provisions of the treaty, the United States was to restore the seized property of Loyalists and allow British subjects access to American courts to recover debts owed them. The American government, however, had no means of enforcing those provisions; it could only *ask* the states to comply. When the states refused, Britain used that breach of the treaty as an excuse to keep its forts in the Great Lakes region and thus protect the profitable British fur trade. When Ambassador John Adams complained to the British about their violation of the treaty, the British calmly pointed to the United States' failure to honor its obligations. When Adams tried to argue that the states would not allow the central government to do so, the British asked pointedly whether the United States was one nation or thirteen. Other governments that dealt with the young nation soon echoed the taunt.

Benjamin West, *American Commissioners of the Treaty of Paris* (unfinished because the British commissioners refused to pose)

The Granger Collection, New York

Western Lands

Approval of the Articles of Confederation had been delayed until 1781 because Maryland refused to ratify them until the matter of the western lands had been settled. The Treaty of Paris left the United States in control of all territory east of the Mississippi River and north of Florida and Louisiana. Several states, notably Virginia and New York, claimed parts of that huge tract of land. Several other states, including Maryland, had no such claims and feared the power of the other states if they succeeded in claiming the land. Maryland, therefore, would not ratify the Articles unless the other states abandoned their claims and turned those lands over to the federal government. When Virginia and New York agreed to

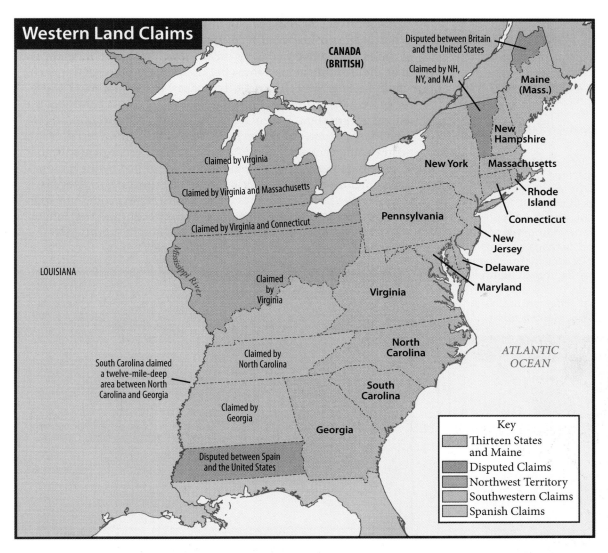

Western Land Claims

CANADA
(BRITISH)

Disputed between Britain
and the United States

Claimed by NH,
NY, and MA

Maine
(Mass.)

New
Hampshire

New York

Massachusetts

Claimed by Virginia

Claimed by Virginia and Massachusetts

Rhode
Island

Pennsylvania

Connecticut

Claimed by Virginia and Connecticut

New
Jersey

Delaware

LOUISIANA

Claimed
by
Virginia

Virginia

Maryland

Mississippi River

North
Carolina

ATLANTIC
OCEAN

Claimed by
North Carolina

South Carolina claimed
a twelve-mile-deep
area between North
Carolina and Georgia

South
Carolina

Claimed by
Georgia

Georgia

Key

Thirteen States
and Maine
Disputed Claims
Northwest Territory
Southwestern Claims
Spanish Claims

Disputed between Spain
and the United States

yield their claims to the federal government, the others eventually
followed suit, and Maryland ratified the Articles. All lands north of
the Ohio River that passed into the hands of the national government became known as the **Northwest Territory**.

The question of how to develop and govern the Northwest Territory was settled by a series of ordinances. The first and most far-
sighted was the **Ordinance of 1784**, written by Thomas Jefferson.
He proposed creating ten new states out of the territory, each of
which would be completely equal to the other states in the Union.
He also proposed banning slavery in the region and giving the land
to settlers instead of selling it.

Unfortunately, the ordinance was so far-sighted that it never
went into effect. Too many states feared the creation of ten competing states, and some states opposed the ban on slavery. The **Land
Ordinance of 1785** was far more cautious and avoided thorny
political questions. Instead, it concentrated on the settlement of the
territory. The ordinance divided the new lands into orderly town-
ships for sale and development. Each township contained thirty-six
sections, or lots, of one square mile (640 acres). Each lot was to be
sold for a dollar an acre ($640), contrary to Jefferson's hopes for free
lands for settlers. The proceeds from the sale of lot sixteen in each
township were to go toward building and maintaining schools in
the area.

Metropotamia, U.S.A.

When Thomas Jefferson drew up his 1784 ordinance for the Northwest Territory, he also proposed the names and boundaries for ten states. The following map shows the division of the territory as Jefferson envisioned it, along with the boundaries of the states that were actually created.

The other thirteen states eventually rejected Jefferson's plan. They feared sharing their power with ten new competitors. Finally, only five states (Ohio, Indiana, Michigan, Illinois, and Wisconsin), along with a portion of Minnesota, were formed from the territory. We should be relieved, perhaps, or some of us might be living in Detroit, Metropotamia; Green Bay, Michigania; Saginaw, Cherronesus; Evansville, Polypotamia; or Chicago, Assenisipia. It is obvious that Jefferson was better at governing states than at naming them.

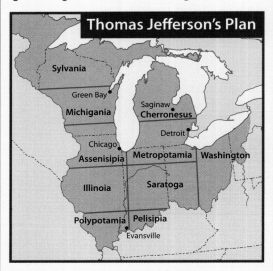

Thomas Jefferson's Plan

More sweeping was the **Northwest Ordinance of 1787.** Whereas the ordinance of 1785 concerned settlement, the ordinance of 1787 concerned government. The Northwest Territory was to be divided into at least three but no more than five states. Each would-be state went through three stages. In the first stage, the region remained almost completely under the direct control of the federal government. When a region had at least five thousand free inhabitants, it entered the second stage and became a territory. The people could then elect a legislature and send a representative to Congress. However, the governor—still appointed by the national government—could veto any act passed by the territorial legislature, and the territorial representative to Congress could not vote. In the third stage, once a territory had sixty thousand free inhabitants, it could draw up a state constitution and be admitted to the Union on an equal basis with the other states.

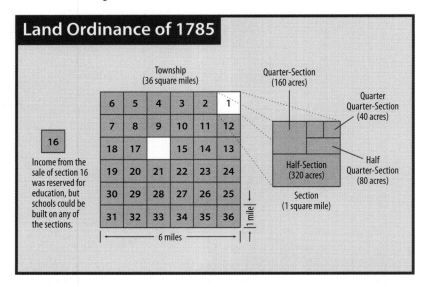

Land Ordinance of 1785

Other provisions are noteworthy. Building on the educational provisions in the Land Ordinance of 1785, the Northwest Ordinance of 1787 explicitly emphasized the importance of education: "Religion, morality, and knowledge, being necessary to good government and the happiness of mankind, schools and the means of education shall forever be encouraged." Most important, the ordinance followed Jefferson's original suggestion and prohibited slavery in the new territories. Also, most states that entered the Union afterward followed the political process set down by the Northwest Ordinance.

The Northwest Ordinances were the greatest success of the Confederation government. They allowed orderly settlement of the territory, and the land sales they permitted provided income for the government. Years later Daniel Webster said that he doubted "whether one single law of any lawgiver, ancient or modern, has produced effects of more distinct, marked, and lasting character than the ordinance of '87."

Failures of the Confederation

Financial Weakness

The financial situation of the new nation was dire, as one would expect after a six-year war on its soil. The weakness of the Articles did not help, however. The national government was almost always broke and in debt, and the individual states were not much better off. **Hard money** (silver and gold) was scarce in the United States. Paper money, the obvious answer to a lack of hard currency, presented its own difficulties. During the war, the national government had printed so much money (**"Continental dollars"**) that paper money's value plummeted, and merchants would not accept it. The expression "not worth a Continental" came to mean that something was worthless.

An example of paper money issued by a state

Compounding the problem was each state's ability to print its own currency. State currency was often as worthless as the Continental notes. Smart merchants required payment in hard currency or barter (traded goods). One Massachusetts newspaper editor announced that he would accept salt pork as payment for subscriptions.

The states dealt a final financial blow to the Congress of the Confederation. On two occasions, Congress proposed amendments to the Articles that would permit Congress to levy small tariffs for revenue (as opposed to a protective tariff). In both instances, failure to attain the required unanimous vote for an amendment killed the measure. The second failure, in particular, spurred efforts by those who desired a revision of the Articles or even a new constitution. Nothing of lasting value, it seemed, could ever be accomplished under the Articles of Confederation.

Foreign Weakness

The separate interests of the states often hampered the national government's conduct of foreign affairs. In negotiating the Treaty of Paris and in later treaty discussions, European powers such as Britain, Spain, and France learned that they could play on jealousies among the states to undercut the United States' bargaining position. Financial and military weaknesses only worsened matters. When the United States ran afoul of the Barbary pirates in northern Africa, the nation could not even pay the demanded bribes, let alone build and arm a naval squadron to protect American shipping.

Domestic Weakness

Internal weakness resulted in part from economic confusion. The existence of fourteen different currencies (one each for the national government and the thirteen states), varying tariffs, and a postwar depression weakened the financial fabric that could have bound the nation together. The most serious threat, however, was the national government's inability to keep the peace within its own borders.

In 1783, a group of officers in General Washington's headquarters in Newburgh, New York, grew frustrated by Congress's inability to pay salaries and pensions. The soldiers were backed by businessmen who feared the economic chaos that they saw looming before them. In this **Newburgh Conspiracy**, the officers intended to force Congress and the states to grant them their back pay. Some conspirators wanted more; they wanted to establish a new government under a king or a dictator. Washington was their first choice as the leader; but if he refused, they would find someone else.

Washington coldly rejected every offer to become a military ruler. When he learned that the officers planned a mass meeting in Newburgh to discuss their grievances, he came as an uninvited guest. He spoke kindly to the men, sympathizing with their needs but urging them not to destroy the nation they had fought for. At the conclusion of the speech, Washington started to reassure the men by reading a favorable letter from a congressman. Before reading it, he paused and with deliberation took out his glasses and put them on. "Gentlemen, you will permit me to put on my spectacles," the general said, "for I have not only grown gray but almost blind in the service of my country."

When Washington finished, tears filled the eyes of many of the men for reasons unrelated to the letter's contents. Before them stood the patriot who had weathered the snows of Valley Forge and faced the bullets of the British, the man whose strength of character and leadership had been the greatest weapon in the American arsenal. The Newburgh Conspiracy collapsed, but it had threatened the young and fragile government. One must wonder how a less scrupulous commander would have reacted to having a whole nation offered to him.

An even more serious problem arose in Massachusetts in 1786. Instead of simply conspiring against the government, as the ringleaders at Newburgh had done, a large body of men actually took up arms against the government. Daniel Shays, a veteran of the Revolution, led an insurrection of farmers against the courts in the western part of the state. The farmers had purchased land at inflated prices. In the depression that followed, they could not meet their obligations. When many of them were jailed, others retaliated by using force to close the courts. The insurrection climaxed with a vain attempt to seize weapons from an arsenal. Shortly thereafter, the militia crushed the uprising.

Shays's Rebellion was quelled only a few weeks before the delegates of the Constitutional Convention met at Philadelphia in 1787. The delegates, shaken by the violence, undoubtedly considered it a warning. Americans had preserved their liberty from destruction by the British; after the war, they must preserve it from destruction by themselves. The Articles of Confederation looked increasingly inadequate for that task.

A 1787 woodcut depicting Daniel Shays (left) and his lieutenant Job Shattuck (right)

Section Quiz

1. What was the greatest accomplishment in foreign affairs by the Confederation government?

2. What were the two most controversial provisions of the proposed Ordinance of 1784?

3. According to the provisions of the Northwest Ordinance of 1787, what were the three steps a region went through to become a state?

4. What were the two serious domestic threats to the government's authority under the Articles of Confederation?

★ How did the American core value of individualism cause problems in the Confederation? What is the biblical root of these problems?

II. A New Charter

The failures and weakness of the Confederation government caused thoughtful men to consider what could be done. Trade discussions gave them an opportunity to voice their ideas. Representatives from Virginia and Maryland met in 1785 at Alexandria,

Virginia, and at George Washington's home at Mount Vernon to discuss trade disputes involving the Potomac River. The Mount Vernon meeting was so profitable that the legislatures of Maryland and Virginia called for another trade convention in Annapolis, Maryland, that would include all thirteen states. The **Annapolis Convention** was not well attended; only five states bothered to send representatives. Alexander Hamilton, a delegate from New York, however, wrote a resolution calling for another convention to remedy the weaknesses of the Confederation government. Faced with growing discontent and fearful of anarchy, the Confederation Congress (which Washington described as a "half-starved limping government") reluctantly seconded the idea of a convention in Philadelphia for May 1787.

The Constitutional Convention

Heavy clouds rolled off the Delaware River and opened up as the delegates arrived for the opening session on May 25. The cool rain offered welcome relief from the already unbearably warm weather that had settled over the city. Old-timers agreed that it was the hottest summer in memory.

Drenched and mud-spattered, the delegates met at the Pennsylvania State House, where eleven years earlier the Declaration of Independence had been signed, an event which lends the old State House its present name of Independence Hall. Despite the wet weather, the delegates' spirits were high. They were eager to get down to work and enthusiastic about what could be accomplished. Virginian **James Madison**—whose many ideas justifiably earned him the title "Father of the Constitution"—declared with a little indulgence that their work would "settle forever the fate of republican government."

Thomas Jefferson, overseas at the time as minister to France, called the men who arrived for the Philadelphia Convention "an assembly of demigods"; they were indeed a remarkable gathering of talent. Numbered among the fifty-five delegates were the best political thinkers and finest lawyers in America, well read and well educated. Their talents, however, were not simply the product of book learning. They were practical men of experience, many of them as skilled with the sword as with the pen; half of them had fought in the Revolution. Thirty-nine had served in the Continental or Confederation Congresses, which gave them a broad range of practical political experience. Among these men were past, present, and future governors and two future United States presidents.

The **Constitutional Convention** was more than a gathering of talent, however; it was also a collection of regional and individual interests. Twelve independent states (Rhode Island refused to participate) were represented. These states, apart from war-time emergencies, had never been very neighborly. Diverse delegate interests, compounded by the hot Philadelphia summer, led to heated debates and threatened the survival of the convention. That these men represented their states' interests could hardly be considered a vice because they were in fact elected as *state representatives* to the convention. Happily, though, many of them had a larger, national vision of their work and were able to hammer out compromises that kept the convention and the country on track.

The first task was to elect a convention president to chair the proceedings. The delegates unanimously elected George Washington,

James Madison, "Father of the Constitution"

whose very presence gave credibility to the meeting. Interestingly, twelve years earlier in the same room in which they were meeting, Washington had been elected commander in chief of the Continental army. He likely found his war experiences beneficial in overseeing the squabbles that soon broke out at the convention.

Crucial Compromises

The most important question that the convention delegates faced initially was why they were meeting. Were they there to revise the Articles in an attempt to breathe some life into the Confederation, or were they to allow it to die and then start over? The delegates answered the question on May 30. Acting on a resolution by Delegate Gouverneur Morris, they agreed overwhelmingly that "a national government ought to be established consisting of a supreme Legislative, Executive and Judiciary."

Having quickly answered that basic question, the delegates soon saw their harmony fractured over the details of how such a government should be formed. The disputes grew largely out of regional interests and would require compromises on three major issues: representation, slavery, and trade.

Representation

How the states were to be represented was surely the most difficult question with which the delegates had to grapple. The battle lines were drawn between the large states (e.g., Virginia, Pennsylvania, and New York) and the smaller states (e.g., New Jersey, Delaware, and Maryland).

James Madison had given a great deal of thought to the composition and structure of the new Congress. His thorough study of political thought, both ancient and modern, and his careful planning resulted in a proposal known as the **Virginia Plan**, which would become the basis for much of the Constitution.

Madison's Virginia Plan, which was introduced to the convention by fellow Virginian Edmund Randolph, advocated a **bicameral**, or two-house, Congress, with the number of representatives based on state population. Members of the lower house, or House of Representatives, would be elected by direct popular vote. The lower house, in turn, would elect members of the upper house, or Senate, from nominees submitted by state legislatures.

In contrast to the powerless, penniless Confederation Congress, the legislature under the Virginia Plan would have greatly expanded powers. For example, the new Congress would be able to enforce its laws on the states and would be empowered to elect both the chief executive and the national judiciary. Those two branches, the executive and the judicial, could unite to veto congressional acts, but their veto could be overridden by a vote in both houses of Congress.

Since representation under the Virginia Plan was based on state population, it naturally favored the states with larger populations. The smaller states were quick to react to the proposal, setting forth a scheme of their own known as the **New Jersey Plan**. This small-state plan, presented by William Paterson of New Jersey, advocated a unicameral Congress, similar to the Confederation Congress, with each state having only one vote regardless of its population or the size of its delegation. Paterson's proposal was merely a throwback to the Articles presented by delegates who were suddenly nervous about where the convention was heading. John Dickinson,

representing Delaware, chided the big-state advocates, "You see the consequences of pushing things too far."

The convention deadlocked over the issue of representation. Dickinson conceded that "some of the members from the small States wish for two branches in the General Legislature and are friends to a good National Government." But he added, "We would sooner submit to a foreign power than submit to be deprived of an equality of suffrage in both branches of the Legislature, and thereby be thrown under the domination of the large states." The small states feared domination by the large states; the large states feared the diminishing of their power through lack of representation, arguing that basic democratic principles favored proportional representation. In short, the New Jersey Plan advocated a one-state, one-vote principle; the Virginia Plan advocated a one-man, one-vote principle.

The haggling went on for weeks as hot weather and hotter debates threatened the survival of the convention. The windows were raised at times in hopes of drawing a breeze, but they usually drew only unwelcome flies and fumes—sewer construction was underway in the streets outside the State House. Irritated delegates adjusted their sweaty collars but not their positions. Some threatened to go home.

Roger Sherman of Connecticut offered the embroiled assembly a solution to its dead-end debating. Sherman was a Christian with an unwavering testimony for Christ. John Adams referred to him as "that old Puritan, honest as an angel." Sherman put together a compromise that narrowly salvaged both the convention and the Constitution. The **Great Compromise** (or **Connecticut Compromise**, as it is sometimes called) proposed that representation in the lower house be based on state population, whereas representation in the Senate be equal for all states regardless of size. "A motley measure," Alexander Hamilton sniffed. But Sherman's proposal was a classic example of political compromise: both sides gave up something, and both sides got something, and the convention continued.

Slavery

The next divisive issue that confronted the delegates of the Constitutional Convention was whether slaves should be counted in determining representation for slave-holding states. Delegates from those states, of course, said yes; delegates from states that did not have slaves said no. Although slavery existed predominantly in the agrarian South, it was not confined to that region. (Pennsylvania, for example, had several thousand slaves at the time.) To settle the issue of how slaves should be counted, delegates established the **Three-Fifths Compromise**. Under this settlement, three-fifths of the total slave population of a state would be included for representation purposes in the House, but slave states would also have to pay taxes on slaves at the same rate.

Many delegates were opposed to slavery as an institution, but the issue was a thorny political question. Oliver Ellsworth of Connecticut reminded his fellow delegates that "the morality or wisdom of slavery are considerations belonging to the States themselves. . . . The States are the best judges of their particular interest." George Mason of Virginia countered, "Every master of slaves is born a petty tyrant. They bring the judgment of heaven on a Country." It would, however, be left to the children and grandchildren of the constitutional framers to resolve the slave question.

Roger Sherman

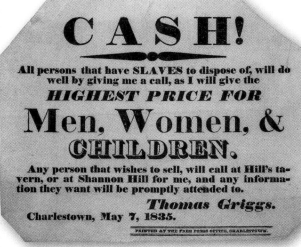

A compromise eventually eliminated slave importation.

Trade

Part of the motivation behind calling the Philadelphia Convention was the failure of the Confederation to resolve interstate trade disputes and direct international trade. Although most delegates agreed that Congress needed a role in commerce, regional interests kept them at odds over the extent of that role. The South, in particular, was concerned that the new Congress would ban the slave trade and raise revenue through export duties. Such duties would hurt the South's economy, which was dependent on the export of raw goods such as rice, cotton, timber, and tobacco.

A compromise settled the issue. By the terms of the agreement, Congress was given power over foreign and interstate commerce. However, the legislature was forbidden to impose any export taxes on the states or to interfere with the slave trade for twenty years.

Constitutional Principles

Despite disputes over details, the constitutional framers agreed on certain basic principles that they incorporated into their charter. These principles have given the Constitution and the government it outlined remarkable durability.

Many of the constitutional principles grew out of the founders' clear-eyed view of human nature. They recognized that men, both the governed and the governors, are inherently sinful. As John Adams pointed out, "Whoever would found a state, and make proper laws for the government of it, must presume that all men are bad by nature."

This is not to say that the Constitution is a "Christian" document any more than its framers were all Christians. Some were moral men, some were God-fearing men, and some were neither. But what is quite clear is that the Constitution was written in a society where biblical principles were pervasive, and the document can be best understood in that light. These principles are not spelled out in the document itself, but they plainly contribute to the fabric of the charter.

The key principles of our Constitution center on the issue of power—how to divide, balance, limit, and allot governmental power in view of man's corrupting tendencies. James Madison underscored this point when he wrote,

> What is government itself, but the greatest of all reflections on human nature. If men were angels, no government would be necessary. If angels were to govern men, neither external nor internal controls on government would be necessary. In framing a government which is to be administered by men over men, the great difficulty lies in this: you must first enable the government to control the governed; and in the next place, oblige it to control itself.

Striking a balance between liberty and order was the great challenge and triumph of the Constitutional Convention.

Republican Ideology

The Constitution established a republic, a government run by representatives chosen by and accountable to the voters. The founders opposed a monarchy or an aristocracy but also opposed a democracy, which they feared would devolve into rule by the mob.

The Constitution – A Product of its Time

When you read the Constitution it becomes obvious that the Enlightenment also played an important role in the formation of this document. In contrast with the formation of many early colonial constitutions, the framers did not refer to God in providing the reasons for the new government. Instead, they included Enlightenment concepts such as social contract, natural rights, and separation of powers.

This republican philosophy was part of the founders' thinking when they decided how various government officials would be elected: the president by the Electoral College, which through its electors represents the people of the entire nation; the House members by popular vote to represent specific local districts; and the senators by state legislators to represent state governments. Movements to change these methods and fill every position by direct popular vote (which resulted in the Seventeenth Amendment) are a move toward a pure democracy and away from the founders' original intent of a republican government.

Limited Government

The underlying theme of the Constitution is **limited government**. The nation had only recently shaken off British tyranny through a long and bloody war, so the Philadelphia delegates fully understood the consequences of unlimited government—the very definition of tyranny.

The principle of limited government is expressed by the nature of our *written* constitution, the first and oldest in continuous use. Unlike the *unwritten* British constitution, an open-ended accumulation of laws and traditions subject to Parliamentary whim, a written charter clearly defined the limits of governmental power and therefore broadened the scope of individual liberty. The principles of separation of powers and checks and balances also contribute to the limitations on governmental power.

Separation of Powers

To prevent any group or individual from gaining too much power, the founders designed the national government with the **separation of powers** in mind. That is the division of the government into three separate branches: the legislative branch (Article I of the Constitution), the executive branch (Article II), and the judicial branch (Article III). In broad terms, under our Constitution, Congress makes the laws, the president executes and enforces the laws, and the courts interpret the laws.

Although the three branches are separate, they are not fully independent. In many areas their responsibilities intersect, and a certain amount of cooperation is necessary to make the national government work effectively.

Checks and Balances

Although separation of powers is often thought to be synonymous with **checks and balances,** there is an important difference. If power were only divided, then one branch could expand its powers within its rightful sphere and come to dominate the other branches.

The principle of checks and balances thwarts such an accumulation of power by establishing a balance of power among the three branches. For example, Congress passes a bill to become law, but the president may reject, or veto, the bill if he opposes it. However, his veto may be overridden by a two-thirds vote in both houses of Congress. For its part, the Supreme Court may nullify acts of both Congress and the president if a majority of justices interprets a law as unconstitutional.

Federalism

Federalism is the division of power between national and state levels of government. The federal system, a unique contribution, was a product of American historical and political realities.

Thirteen separate, sovereign states, with often differing political and social backgrounds, had emerged from the colonial and revolutionary periods. These fiercely independent states had no intention of giving up their political power. The delegates, though representing states' regional interests, also recognized the need for the strength and order of national unity. The federal system struck a crucial balance between state and national demands. Today, federalism provides needed flexibility in a large country of varying regions by giving citizens a greater voice in their affairs at the state and local level. Many people believe that the genius of the Constitution is its ambiguity. Supporters of both limited government and a strong central government can ultimately accept it. The perpetual tension that exists between these two views actually strengthens and safeguards our freedoms.

Popular Sovereignty

Popular sovereignty, the idea that the ultimate source of governmental power lies in the people, is a constitutional principle that is evident in several areas of the Constitution. The **Preamble**, which introduced the charter with a full and flourishing sentence, reads:

> We the people of the United States, in order to form a more perfect union, establish justice, ensure domestic tranquility, provide for the common defense, promote the general welfare, and secure the blessings of liberty to ourselves and our posterity, do ordain and establish this Constitution for the United States of America.

Despite the dramatic "We the people," the Constitution was actually formed by the agreement of states, not individuals, its approval being subject to state conventions, not a national referendum.

The principle of popular sovereignty is best expressed in the Constitution through the document's provisions for representation and amendment. Representation allows the people to have a voice in their republican government through their elected officials. The constitutional framers, fearing the fickleness of public opinion, sought to limit the directness of the people's voice on the national level by providing direct election only for the House of Representatives.

The president and the senators, by contrast, were elected indirectly by the people. Senators, for example, were initially elected by their respective state legislatures rather than by a direct vote from their constituents. Likewise, the president is elected through the indirect means of the **Electoral College**. Under this constitutional provision (Article II, Section 1), each state has a number of electors equal to the state's representation in Congress. In general, all the electoral votes from a state go to the presidential candidate who receives the majority of popular votes from that state.

Constitutional **amendments**, changes to the Constitution, are also an expression of the people's sovereignty. Amendments that survive the difficult ratification process often reflect widespread popular support and always take precedence over the laws of Congress, the actions of the president, and the rulings of the courts. Chief Justice John Marshall stated, "The people made the Constitution and the people can unmake it. It is the creature of their own will, and lives only by their will."

"We the people" is an enduring declaration not only of the people's power to rule themselves but also of the people's responsibility for that rule. Self-government is no easy task. It does not occur by accident, nor is it a self-propelled machine. The members of each generation must grapple with *their* government—use its principles and cherish its freedoms to make it work for their day and the next.

Section Quiz

1. How did the Constitutional Convention reach a compromise on the issue of representation?

2. What compromise allowed the convention to settle the problem of slavery in relation to taxation and representation?

3. Between what two qualities did the Constitutional Convention seek a balance?

4. What are the six principles of government contained in the American Constitution?

★ Has the system of checks and balances been successful in preventing any one branch of government from expanding its powers? Use examples to support your answer.

★ In light of Romans 13 and Amos 1, examine and evaluate the claims of Oliver Ellsworth and George Mason regarding the Three-Fifths Compromise.

III. The Struggle for Ratification

On September 17, 1787, Washington offered the final draft of the new charter to the convention. After the delegates signed and forwarded it to the Confederation Congress, the document would pass to the states for their consent (ratification).

Eighty-one-year-old Benjamin Franklin, suffering from gout and kidney stones, gave a written address to a colleague to read in hopes of swaying undecided delegates to sign. Franklin acknowledged,

> "I confess that there are several parts of this constitution which I do not at present approve, but I am not sure I shall never approve them: For having lived long, I have experienced many instances of being obliged by better information or fuller consideration, to change opinions even on important subjects. . . . Thus I consent, Sir, to this Constitution because I expect no better, and because I am not sure, that it is not the best."

Edmund Randolph, George Mason, and Elbridge Gerry of Massachusetts objected to the expanded powers of the national government and the absence of a bill of rights. Mason adamantly declared that he "would sooner chop off his right hand than put it to the Constitution" because of the document's failure to guarantee civil liberties. Such objections foreshadowed a difficult ratification process: the approval of at least nine states was required by Article VII of the Constitution.

After the signing and a celebration supper, the delegates parted company. Their work would now be scrutinized by the nation. The greatest hurdles lay before them. The Constitution-makers had put forth a remarkable effort, but privately some of them worried about

Alexander Hamilton

George Mason

ratification because the stakes were so high. Washington wrote, "This or a dissolution of the Union awaits our choice." Yet he concluded, "The event is in the hand of God."

War of Words

Two days after the delegates went home, the text of the Constitution was first published in the *Pennsylvania Packet* of Philadelphia. For the first time, Americans learned what had been devised behind the closed doors of the Pennsylvania State House, and not everyone was pleased. The battle lines were drawn between supporters of the Constitution, called **Federalists**, and those who opposed it, whom the Federalists dubbed the **Anti-Federalists**.

Just one week after the proposed Constitution was published, a New York newspaper denounced the Constitution in an article penned under the pseudonym "**Cato.**" Cato was, in fact, New York governor George Clinton. He was soon joined by "Sidney," "Brutus," and others in a series of Anti-Federalist articles.

Alexander Hamilton, the lone New York delegate who had supported and signed the Constitution, returned home to find the political winds blowing against the Constitution. He responded to the Anti-Federalist articles by writing some Federalist articles under the pen name "**Publius.**" Hamilton also enlisted the help of James Madison and John Jay in a war of words. Together, the trio wrote eighty-five well-reasoned essays that were widely read throughout the country.

The essays were compiled and published in two volumes in May 1788 under the title *The Federalist*, or *The Federalist Papers*. This work answered Anti-Federalist objections by carefully explaining and forcefully defending constitutional provisions of power. It also predicted dangers and dismemberment for the nation if the Constitution were rejected.

The Federalist was to ratification what *Common Sense* had been to the Revolution. It was a persuasive force, particularly in those states where ratification hung in the balance. But *The Federalist* is much more than a yellowed bestseller; it is a comprehensive commentary on republican government. Jefferson praised it as "the best commentary on the principles of government which has ever been written." Clinton Rossiter perhaps best explained the universality of *The Federalist* when he wrote that the essays are

> now valued not merely as a clever defense of a particular charter, but as an exposition of certain timeless truths about constitutional government. . . . The message of *The Federalist* reads: no happiness without liberty, no liberty without self-government, no self-government without constitutionalism, no constitutionalism without morality—and none of these great goods without stability and order.

Less well known are *The Anti-Federalist Papers*, the collected writings and speeches by opponents of the new Constitution. They were the response of the Anti-Federalists to the publications of the Federalists. Although one might be tempted to view Anti-Federalists as radicals who were against free government and constitutional liberties, such is not the case at all. The Anti-Federalists included such Patriots as Patrick Henry, Edmund Randolph, James Monroe, George Mason, George Clinton, William Patterson, and others who at times shared in their positions. In addition to "Cato," "Sidney," and "Brutus," the Anti-Federalists wrote under such pseudonyms as "Centinel" and "Federal Farmer."

Thirteen Battles

Delaware led the states by giving the Constitution its unanimous consent on December 7, 1787. Within a month, four more states—Pennsylvania, New Jersey, Georgia, and Connecticut—easily ratified the Constitution with lopsided victories. The toughest battles, however, lay ahead in Massachusetts, Virginia, and New York, where the Anti-Federalists were better organized and had among their ranks leaders of considerable stature.

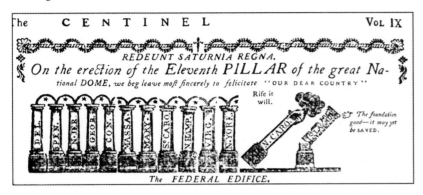

The CENTINEL Vol IX

REDEUNT SATURNIA REGNA.

On the erection of the Eleventh PILLAR of the great National DOME, we beg leave most sincerely to felicitate "OUR DEAR COUNTRY"

Rife it will.

The foundation good—it may yet be SAVED.

The FEDERAL EDIFICE.

Massachusetts approved the Constitution in a close vote in February 1788 after the Federalists gained the support of John Hancock and Samuel Adams. Three more states—Maryland, South Carolina, and New Hampshire—joined the six ratifying states to make the nine necessary for the Constitution to become law. The letter of the law, however, was not enough. Practically speaking, any hopes for a national union had to include both Virginia, which was the largest state, and New York. If New York failed to ratify, then New England would be cut off geographically from the rest of the country. If Virginia refused to join, then the South would be severed.

The Anti-Federalists of Virginia were led by the fiery orator Patrick Henry and non-signing Constitutional Convention delegates George Mason and Governor Edmund Randolph. The objections of this Anti-Federalist trio represented legitimate concerns: fear of consolidated political power in an overarching national government and the absence of guarantees of personal liberty in a bill of rights. The Federalists were not opposed to personal liberty; rather, most of them thought that a bill of rights was unnecessary or even that it was too restrictive to limit rights to a written list. The Federalists also feared that the attempt to compose a bill of rights before ratification would derail both the Constitution and the necessary precondition for such freedoms—national order. After James Madison promised to introduce amendments for a bill of rights in the first session of Congress, the Virginia Federalists won a narrow victory for ratification, 89 to 79.

Madison's concession was the tie breaker in Virginia and a catalyst for the final great state battle raging in New York. There Governor Clinton and his Anti-Federalists commanded a decisive majority against backers of the Constitution, led by Alexander Hamilton. However, news of the Anti-Federalist collapse in Virginia struck a fatal blow to Clinton's edge. By a slim margin of 30 to 27, New York ratified. North Carolina and Rhode Island held out for some time, but no one else seemed to care. Elections for the

Edmund Randolph

Baptists and the Bill of Rights

Many Protestants, including Baptists, supported the War for Independence. One reason for their support was the anticipation of religious freedom that would result. However, when the text of the Constitution became known, Baptist leaders, including Pastor John Leland, expressed serious concerns because the document contained no guarantees of religious freedom. James Madison and others argued that these guarantees were unnecessary because the federal government could likely not attain a level of power that would threaten freedom of religion. However, Pastor Leland and many others insisted that their support for the Constitution was contingent on the addition of a bill of rights. When Pastor Leland convinced Madison to offer the suggested amendments, Leland and other Baptists supported the ratification of the Constitution and helped to ensure its passage.

new Congress were set, and the opening session was scheduled for March 4, 1789, at the temporary national capital, New York City.

Ben Franklin wrote with satisfaction, "Our new Constitution is now established, and has an appearance that promises permanency; but in this world nothing can be said to be certain, except death and taxes."

A Rising Sun

The office of chief executive was one of the most significant and least controversial departures from the old Confederation government. The explanation for such smooth passage among the contentious framers of the Constitution had occupied the president's chair at the convention. George Washington—"first in war, first in peace, and first in the hearts of his countrymen"—was the natural choice for the nation's highest office.

On February 4, 1789, Washington was unanimously elected president by the Electoral College. His old Massachusetts ally, John Adams, was elected as the first vice president. Washington's triumphal journey from Mount Vernon to New York City for his inauguration was a swirl of speeches, suppers, and small-town serenades. The road to New York was lined with parents hoisting their puzzled children for a glimpse of the great man and thousands of other onlookers reaching out to touch the hero.

The modest Washington was taken aback by his welcome and privately admitted that he felt more like "a culprit who is going to his place of execution." He also felt the weight of responsibility growing as he approached his inauguration.

On April 30, 1789, on the balcony of New York's Federal Hall on Wall Street, the great Virginian placed his hand on the Bible and

Precedent Washington

"Some achieve greatness, and some have greatness thrust upon them," Shakespeare wrote. This was true of Washington and the presidency, although in his case both would be true. He had the office thrust upon him, but he made it in his own image.

Other men have had the presidency thrust upon them. Otherwise, we likely would never have heard of such presidents as Millard Fillmore or Chester Arthur. Washington, however, made the mold that he and his successors filled. Washington wanted the office to be dignified but not ostentatious, strong but not oppressive. This desire simply reflected his own character. He was also conscious that his every action would later be interpreted as a precedent. Therefore, he walked circumspectly.

He was, however, just a man. He felt aches and pains. Shortly after he was sworn in as president, he was diagnosed with a cancerous tumor on his thigh. While recovering from crude but successful surgery, the nearly toothless president was fitted with a new set of dentures made of hippopotamus tusk and pink sealing wax. He fretted as any normal person would over the myriad problems of the new government. His responsibilities included an enormous debt, a seven-hundred-man army, no navy, and the constant challenges of new nationhood. But he was no stranger to adversity.

Washington was not a perfect man, but he is an enduring example of how a man's character—what he is—shapes what he does. In his case, integrity shaped both the presidency and the direction of the nation.

promised to preserve, protect, and defend the Constitution, adding, "So help me God." With that, President Washington kissed the Bible, and the city erupted with cheers, bells, and cannons.

Washington's inauguration marked both an end and a beginning. It was the end of the long struggle for liberty and self-government begun in the 1770s, and it was a *national* beginning. While the delegates were signing the Constitution, Madison recorded that

> Dr. Franklin, looking towards the president's chair, at the back of which a rising sun happened to be painted, observed to a few members near him, that painters had found it difficult to distinguish in their art a rising from a setting sun. I have, said he, often and often during the course of the session looked at that behind the president without being able to tell whether it was rising or setting: But now at length I have the happiness to know that it is a rising not a setting sun.

Section Quiz

1. Why did Edmund Randolph, George Mason, and Elbridge Gerry oppose the Constitution?

2. Who were "Cato" and "Publius"?

3. How did James Madison win approval for the Constitution in Virginia?

★   What does Edmund Randolph, Patrick Henry, and George Mason's opposition to the Constitution say about their beliefs on human nature?

People, Places, and Things to Remember

confederation
Articles of Confederation
unicameral
Treaty of Paris
Northwest Territory
Ordinance of 1784
Land Ordinance of 1785
Northwest Ordinance of 1787
hard money
"Continental dollars"
Newburgh Conspiracy
Shays's Rebellion
Annapolis Convention
James Madison
Constitutional Convention (1787)
Virginia Plan
bicameral
New Jersey Plan
Roger Sherman
Great Compromise (Connecticut Compromise)
Three-Fifths Compromise
limited government
separation of powers
checks and balances
federalism
popular sovereignty
Preamble
Electoral College
amendments
Federalists
Anti-Federalists
"Cato"
"Publius"
The Federalist
The Anti-Federalist Papers

Chapter Review

Making Connections

1. Why was the Treaty of Paris an important foreign policy achievement for the new nation?

2. How did the Confederation encourage educational growth in the young nation?

3. How was the Northwest Territory was to be divided? Name the states that ultimately were created from it.

4. What principles was the Constitution based on?

5. What basic biblical principle concerning human nature did the framers of the Constitution recognize when writing that document?

Developing History Skills

1. What were two weaknesses of the Confederation, and how did the Constitution resolve them?

2. If there had been no Connecticut Compromise, which would have been better for the United States: the Virginia Plan or the New Jersey Plan? Why?

Thinking Critically

1. How are constitutional amendments an expression of the people's sovereignty?

2. How do you think the failure of the Articles might have contributed to the Constitution's success?

Living as a Christian Citizen

1. If you were a delegate to the Constitutional Convention, would you have voted for the compromises regarding slavery? Be careful to consider both the results these compromises had in history and the possible effects had these compromises failed to pass.

2. Divide the class into groups and have each group write its own constitution for an imagined nation. Then have each group present its constitution to the class, including an explanation for the document's provisions (especially those that are rooted in Scripture).

". . . To Execute the Laws of the Union. . ." by Donna Neary

The Federalist Years (1789–1801)

I. Launching the New Government

II. Emerging Political Parties

III. Declining Federalist Influence

"We are not to expect to be translated from despotism to liberty in a feather bed . . ."

Thomas Jefferson, 1790,
in a letter to Lafayette

Franklin's rising sun, after a rosy but brief dawn, shone across a rugged political landscape. Throughout the 1790s, the fledgling republic weathered one storm after another; some blew in from Europe, others from the backcountry, and some arose in the halls of power.

These difficulties, while not unlike those the country endured in the previous decade, had a completely different result. Rather than weakening the national government, they strengthened it. The Constitution proved to be a practical and powerful instrument. Despite the growing pains, the Federalist years were a formative era in which personal liberties were defended, national supremacy was demonstrated, and political parties were developed. The nationalist character of Federalism, so evident throughout the decade, would not grow unchecked, however. Forces for decentralization and limited government would blunt the nationalist thrust, sparking controversy and conflict.

I. Launching the New Government

Getting Started

The first order of business in 1789 was to organize the new government in accordance with the new Constitution. The key features were the cabinet, the courts, and the Congress.

The first president and his cabinet (left to right): George Washington; Henry Knox, secretary of war; Alexander Hamilton, secretary of the treasury; Thomas Jefferson, secretary of state; Edmund Randolph, attorney general

Cabinet

With congressional approval, President **George Washington** organized three departments in the executive branch—the departments of State, Treasury, and War—and appointed their secretaries, or chief officers. Washington chose **Thomas Jefferson**, recently returned from a five-year stint as minister to France, to head the Department of State. Washington chose his wartime aide, the brilliant and ambitious **Alexander Hamilton**, to be secretary of the treasury. And he tapped the three-hundred-pound Henry Knox of War for Independence fame to head the War Department. In addition, Washington appointed fellow Virginian and former governor Edmund Randolph as attorney general to provide legal counsel for his administration.

Although the term *cabinet* in the sense of an advisory body was in neither the Constitution nor Washington's vocabulary, the department heads met regularly with the president to discuss policy decisions. Eventually, these advisors took on the collective name "cabinet" and played a key role in the first and future administrations.

Courts

The constitutional blueprint directly provided for only a Supreme Court but permitted Congress to establish lower federal courts. As a result, Congress passed the **Judiciary Act of 1789**, which organized thirteen district courts (one for each of the states), established three circuit courts to handle appeals, and set the number of Supreme Court justices at six. Washington appointed John Jay to be the Court's chief justice.

Despite constitutional provisions and a working system of federal courts, the Supreme Court actually mustered little power or respect during its first few years. In fact, adding insult to injury, when the national government moved to its permanent capital of Washington, D.C. in 1800, planners forgot to provide a place for the third branch of government. The president had his executive mansion, Congress met in the Capitol, and the Supreme Court justices also met in the Capitol building—in the basement.

One significant section of the Judiciary Act of 1789 would have a powerful ramification in the future. It provided that state court decisions could be appealed to the federal court level if constitutional questions were involved. This little provision clearly declared the supremacy of the federal courts over the states and easily passed the predominantly nationalist Congress. Many of the Anti-Federalist leaders had become disgruntled after ratification losses and had not run for Congress. As a result, there was no significant bloc of states' rights advocates in the First Congress to oppose this legislation.

Congress

The First Congress accomplished more of significance than did most of its successors. During the remarkable two-year session from 1789 to 1791, it drafted the Bill of Rights, organized the executive and judicial branches, and passed a number of crucial measures to put the country on a sound financial footing. These achievements seem all the more outstanding considering that the First Congress was breaking new ground. **James Madison**, a leader in the House of Representatives at the time, observed, "We are in a wilderness without a single footstep to guide. Our successors will have an easier task."

In addition to the landmark legislation passed during the original session, the congressmen also grappled with an issue that still has a familiar ring to it: how to resolve a huge national debt without raising taxes. But they also frittered away time over issues of pomp and protocol, searching for a republican balance between respectability and regality. On what to call the president, for example, John Adams favored "His Highness, the President of the United States and Protector of Rights of the same." Fortunately, that breathtaking title was shelved in favor of a simple "Mr. President."

The First Congress members also approved a salary for themselves, a whopping six dollars a day, which raised immediate howls from constituents over congressional self-indulgence. Yet considering what these congressmen were able to accomplish so quickly, particularly in drafting what would become the first ten amendments to the Constitution, their salary was a bargain.

The Bill of Rights

Bill of Rights

In the summer of 1789, James Madison honored his pledge to his Anti-Federalist adversaries when he introduced amendments to the Constitution to protect individual rights. What emerged in 1791, after gaining the approval of three-fourths of the states, were the first ten amendments—the **Bill of Rights**.

The first and most fundamental of these amendments protects the freedoms of conscience and expression, specifically freedoms of religion, speech, press, assembly, and petition. The second, third, and fourth amendments protect the security rights of the individual by guaranteeing the right to bear arms, prohibiting the forced quartering of troops in private homes during peacetime, and protecting against unreasonable searches and seizures. The fifth, sixth, seventh, and eighth amendments guarantee fair judicial procedures for the accused. The ninth and tenth amendments place further restrictions on the extent of national power by limiting its scope to constitutional bounds and by guaranteeing that freedoms not specified in the Bill of Rights nor restricted by the states belong to the people. In the words of the Tenth Amendment:

> The powers not delegated to the United States by the Constitution, nor prohibited by it to the states, are reserved to the states respectively, or to the people.

The Bill of Rights was specifically intended to restrict the power of the *national* government and to protect individual rights. For example, the First Amendment clearly states that "Congress shall make no law respecting an establishment of religion"; yet in Massachusetts, taxes were levied to support state churches as late as 1833. Not until the twentieth century did the Supreme Court place most of the Bill of Rights' restrictions on the states, and it did so in an effort to expand national authority.

Hamilton's Plans

War debts and nearly a decade of neglect had left the country's finances in shambles. One of the greatest challenges of the 1790s was to put America's economy in order before it collapsed. Providentially, the first secretary of the treasury was a man whose ideas, imagination, and energy were equal to the challenge, although his critics accused him of trying to centralize government even further.

Alexander Hamilton's early life gave little indication of his destiny to be, as one historian put it, "the greatest administrative genius in America, and one of the greatest administrators of all time." Born out of wedlock on the Caribbean island of Nevis, Hamilton was abandoned by his father and orphaned at thirteen when his mother died. Never one to let difficulties keep him down, he managed with the help of some friends to gain admission to King's College (now Columbia University) in New York when he was seventeen. He later became Washington's chief of staff during the war and distinguished himself by his cool bravery at Yorktown.

Hamilton, having grown up in the West Indies, had none of the regional attachments that characterized many of the Founding Fathers. He viewed himself as an American first and last, not as a New Yorker or a Northerner. While his background fueled his nationalist zeal, it also made it difficult for him to appreciate the sectional differences that were such a delicate and volatile aspect of American politics.

Hamilton was a key figure in setting the course of the young republic. He had been instrumental in calling the Constitutional Convention in 1787, and his appointment as secretary of the treasury at the age of thirty-two placed him in a powerful policymaking role. In four influential reports issued to Congress in 1790 and 1791, Hamilton outlined plans for resolving the nation's debt problem, establishing a national bank and national mint, and encouraging manufacturing and economic expansion. With the ex-

---

The First Amendment and Religion

Contrary to what many people think, the First Amendment did not legislate the *absence* of religion from government or public life. Rather it prevented the establishment of a national church, such as the Anglican Church of Great Britain. Religion was, in fact, viewed as a desirable and even necessary ingredient of government, as the various inscriptions on public buildings in Washington, D.C. attest.

ception of his probusiness *Report on Manufactures*, which was too advanced for the agrarian America of that day, Hamilton's proposals were all shaped into law.

Report on Public Credit

Perhaps the most important of Hamilton's proposals was his first, the *Report on Public Credit*, which held that for the sake of national pride and future credit, government debt, both national and state, had to be paid. His ambitious plan consisted of two major aspects: **funding** and **assumption**.

Debt funding proposed that the federal government give bonds paying six percent interest to those to whom the Continental Congress owed money for goods or military services provided during the war. The bonds were to be recognized as currency, a procedure called "monetizing the debt." Despite the enormity of the debt for that day (more than $77 million), Hamilton's funding plan cleared Congress rather easily.

Assumption—the national government's takeover of all state debts—had a rougher passage through Congress. Most of the Southern states had faithfully paid off their debts whereas the New England states were delinquent, a factor that made assumption inherently unfair as well as a brewing sectional issue. Virginian James Madison, a leader in the House of Representatives, broke with his old friend Hamilton by taking a firm stand against the assumption plan. The legislative stalemate was broken only by a major compromise that still leaves its mark on the map. The site for a permanent national capital, to be known as Federal City, had not been determined. Through a mediation meeting arranged by Jefferson, Hamilton promised to get sufficient Northern votes to locate Federal City in the South, on the banks of the Potomac River, in return for Southern votes on assumption. The deal was struck, and Washington himself chose the site of the capital that would one day bear his name. The new capital was to be occupied in ten years; meanwhile, Philadelphia would serve as the temporary capital.

National Bank

Having dealt with the problem of past debts, Hamilton looked to the future in his second report. He proposed the formation of a national bank, which he saw as the centerpiece of a sound, strong economy. A national bank would issue a uniform currency, and its branches throughout the country would provide a source for business loans, a spur to economic expansion.

The bill for a national bank with a twenty-year charter cleared Congress, but by the time it reached the president's desk to be signed into law, Madison and Jefferson were challenging the constitutionality of a national bank.

This was the opening round of what would be an ongoing controversy over constitutional interpretation. The constitutional framers produced a brief document that provided a sturdy framework but left many areas open to interpretation. A detailed, lengthy Constitution would have quickly grown outdated because its writers in 1787 could not possibly anticipate the kinds of problems the nation would face in 1887, much less in the twenty-first century and beyond. They wisely chose

First Bank of the United States, Philadelphia (the first National Bank)

to draft a firm but flexible charter. *How much* flexibility was the thorny question. Those who advocated more flexibility on a given issue were called **loose constructionists**; those who held to a closer reading of the constitutional text were known as **strict constructionists**.

Congress had no specific authority to charter a national bank. Jefferson argued that "to take a single step beyond the boundaries thus specially drawn around the power of Congress is to take possession of a boundless field of power." President Washington, concerned over the questions of constitutionality raised by Jefferson and Madison, asked Hamilton to present his side of the debate.

Hamilton was surprised by this apparent Achilles' heel that Jefferson and Madison exposed in his bank bill. After several days of thought and writing, Hamilton presented the chief executive with what has become the standard justification for expanded constitutional interpretation. Hamilton wrote,

> If the end be clearly comprehended within any of the specified powers, and if the measure have an obvious relation to that end, and is not forbidden by any particular provision of the Constitution, it may safely be deemed to come within the compass of the national authority.

It is interesting that the heart of Hamilton's constitutional interpretation, that specified ends justify unspecified means, was drawn from one of the *Federalist Papers* written three years earlier by his opponent James Madison.

Washington was persuaded by Hamilton's convincing nationalist argument and signed the bill into law, creating the first **National Bank** as well as the first serious rift in his own administration.

Section Quiz

1. What three executive departments did Washington organize after taking office? Whom did he appoint to head each department?

2. Why was Massachusetts able to continue supporting an established church years after the passage of the First Amendment?

3. Name and describe the two major points of Hamilton's *Report on Public Credit*.

4. What two benefits did Alexander Hamilton believe a national bank would bring to the United States?

5. What is the difference between a "strict constructionist" and a "loose constructionist"?

★ Was it a good or a bad idea for Washington to staff his cabinet with men having such opposite views of government as Jefferson and Hamilton? Support your answer.

II. Emerging Political Parties

Political parties or factions were not unknown to the Founding Fathers, but they were unwelcome. Political parties in Europe were characterized by intrigue, conspiracy, and hostile division, and the founders feared that parties in America would rip the Union apart. They hoped rather that in free elections the best men, like cream, would rise to the top. That is why in presidential elections, before the growth of parties necessitated an amendment (the Twelfth Amendment), the candidate receiving the most electoral votes would be president and the second-place finisher, vice president. The founders assumed that leaders would act in the public, not the party, interest. Although the idea was noble, it was also unrealistic. Whereas in establishing the Constitution the founders took into consideration man's sinful nature, on the matter of elections they seemed naive about human nature.

America had always been a land of diverse interests: southerner and northerner, farmer and merchant, coastal planter and backcountry frontiersman. And in a society where the freedoms of speech, assembly, and petition enjoyed constitutional protection, the development of political parties was inevitable. In addition, the party spirit was already evident in the ratification battles in which the Constitution itself drove a wedge between Federalists and Anti-Federalists.

During the 1790s, two opposing political groups emerged: the **Federalists**, who claimed to be the true keepers of the constitutional flame, and the **Republicans**, or **Democratic-Republicans**, who viewed themselves as the last line of defense between Federalist "tyranny" and American liberty. During the early stage of party development, the labels varied considerably. Federalists might be called "Hamiltonians" or something less flattering, such as "Monarchists," if the Republicans were doing the labeling. Democratic-Republicans were called "Jeffersonians" or even "Madisonians," but they generally referred to themselves as Republicans, although they were no relation to the modern party of that name.

For his part, Washington deplored political parties. He embodied the nonpartisan attitude to public office that had been the founders' ideal. His dismay, therefore, was profound when he discovered that the political fault line that would shake up the government was in his own cabinet.

Cabinet Conflicts

James Madison led the opposition to Hamilton's treasury program in Congress. Thomas Jefferson led it within the president's cabinet. Madison was clearly the founder of the anti-Hamilton party whose members called themselves Republicans, but Hamilton's clashes with Jefferson within the administration tended to focus on Jefferson as the leader of the opposition.

Someone once said that the only thing that Hamilton and Jefferson had in common was their hatred for each other. Although that overstates the issue, the men's backgrounds and personalities almost destined them to clash. Hamilton had risen from poverty to power by his energy and intelligence. Jefferson was a Virginia planter living on an inherited estate. Hamilton was emotionally reserved, whereas Jefferson tended to wear his feelings on his sleeve, particularly in letters to Washington. Jefferson viewed Hamilton as an evil genius bent on perverting the republic into a monarchy. Hamilton viewed Jefferson as a meddler, a sower of dissent who would destroy national unity. Hamilton had intense focus; Jefferson had diverse interests. Jefferson was a man of letters; Hamilton was a man of ledgers. Both men could write well and persuasively. One historian has observed that "Hamilton feared anarchy and loved order; Jefferson feared tyranny and loved liberty."

The personality clash between Hamilton and Jefferson, however, tends to overshadow the larger issues involved in the devel-

---

Hamiltonians versus Jeffersonians

Hamiltonians:

Merchants, bankers, manufacturers, professionals from New England and Atlantic coast

Wanted British-style government run by wealthy elite

Had little confidence in common man

Favored strong central government

Had broad interpretation of Constitution

Wanted high protective tariff

Wanted national bank run by wealthy

Thought national debt was good

Wanted government spending on "internal improvements"

Jeffersonians:

Small farmers, small shopkeepers, frontier settlers, craftsmen from South and West

Wanted democratic government of the people

Suspicious of aristocrats

Had strict interpretation of Constitution

Wanted no favors from government

Wanted only a low revenue tariff

Opposed national bank

Viewed national debt as bad

Thought government spending for "internal improvements" unconstitutional

opment of a two-party system in America. Jefferson's Republican Party and Hamilton's Federalist Party had two essentially different views of America that reflected regional and economic differences. The Republican Party was the friend of the farmer, and in pre-industrial America that meant it had many friends. The Jeffersonians distrusted centralized government and feared urban growth. Cities, they believed, were centers of vice and depositories of filthy lucre that would stain the national character. Accordingly, the key to America's future was its two great resources: its land and its people—connected by a plow.

Federalists believed that America's future was in commerce and industry, and their experiences during the Confederation period taught them that economic growth occurs only under a strong national government. That does not mean that Federalists were motivated by financial gain. They believed, though, that power placed in the hands of a propertied, moneyed class would provide the country with a stable, conservative government.

The "spirit of party" growing within the government alarmed President Washington. He had hoped to retire to his beloved Mount Vernon after one term. But with the election of 1792 looming, all sides urged him to run again. Everyone in the cabinet and the Congress and, above all, across the nation knew that no one could hold the fledgling nation together like Washington. Jefferson reminded him that "North and South will hang together if they have you to hang on."

Reluctantly, the old general accepted the call for the sake of the nation and was unanimously re-elected. For Washington, the second term would be difficult, both personally and politically, but for the nation, his continuing leadership was crucial. Ill winds blowing from Europe were stirring a tempest in America, and the new nation would need a steady hand at the helm.

Foreign Feuds

The **French Revolution** broke out in 1789, just months after America inaugurated its new constitutional government. Most Americans welcomed the news from their old ally. The French, they believed, were following the path to independence that America had pioneered. By 1792, however, it was clear that there was a definite fork in the revolutionary road. The seemingly insatiable blood-thirst of the topsy-turvy French revolutionary government that led to the beheading of King Louis XVI and the Reign of Terror cooled much of the pro-French fever in America.

When France declared war on Britain in 1793, America faced its first foreign policy crisis. According to the 1778 Treaty of Alliance, America was obligated to come to the aid of France during wartime. Should the United States honor the treaty and take up the French cause against its old nemesis, Britain? Some people quickly argued that the French treaty had been made with a government and a king that the revolutionary regime had destroyed. Therefore, the United States was under no obligation to go to war for France. This was hardly the end of the issue, however.

Many Republicans favored a pro-French trade policy whereas Federalists were decidedly pro-British. Besides being America's chief trading partner, Britain controlled Canada to the north and a number of forts to the west, and her superior navy ruled the Atlantic. Pursuing a middle course, President Washington said no to both Republicans and Federalists and issued a **Proclamation of Neutrality** in April 1793. He declared that the United States would pursue a policy of friendliness and impartiality toward both nations. Challenges to American neutrality, however, would quickly arise at home and abroad.

Citizen Genêt

The already difficult neutrality policy was further complicated by the arrival of the French ambassador, Edmond Charles Édoûard Genêt, who in current French fashion rejected titles of nobility and referred to himself as simply **Citizen Genêt**. The flashy Frenchman, instead of honoring protocol by arriving at Philadelphia to present his credentials to the government, landed in Charleston, South Carolina. He made a grand tour through the country, stirring up pro-French sentiment in hopes of overturning American neutrality. Like a Parisian pied piper, Genêt gathered enthusiastic followers wherever he went, not the least of whom was Thomas Jefferson.

Genêt, however, overrated his charm with Washington. The president gave the ambassador a courteous but cold reception, reminding him that the United States was neutral and intended to stay that way. This was not what Genêt wanted to hear. Secretly, Genêt attempted to raise an army to fight Britain's ally Spain in Florida, and he authorized privateers to raid British shipping. His plottings and personal attacks on Washington, published in Republican newspapers, eventually became an embarrassment to his supporters.

When a more radical faction took over the French government, its new ambassador arrived with an arrest warrant for Genêt. His return to France would almost certainly mean his execution by guillotine. The magnanimous Washington granted the troublemaker political asylum on the condition that he keep quiet. Grateful, Genêt settled in New York, married, and took up farming.

The Genêt episode left the country deeply divided, however. At the same time, British attacks on American shipping further complicated Washington's efforts to keep the country out of a European war.

Jay's Treaty

In 1793, the British began attacking American ships trading in the French West Indies. Not only did the British seize cargoes to deprive the French of them, but they also practiced impressment, seizing American sailors and forcing them into British naval service. British violations of American neutrality particularly enraged Republicans, who were itching for a fight with England.

In 1794, Washington dispatched Chief Justice John Jay to London to settle American and British differences, including Britain's dusty promises to remove all troops from the Northwest Territory and to settle prewar debts. After difficult negotiations, Jay returned with a treaty that seemed to gain little more from Britain than an agreement to keep her promise made in the Treaty of Paris (1783). The British promised to evacuate redcoats from American territory and offered to pay compensation for the previous year of raiding carried on by the British navy against American shipping.

Given the United States' weak bargaining position (particularly because of the nation's lack of a navy), the **Jay Treaty** was the best that could be hoped for. By the narrowest of margins the treaty cleared the Senate in 1795. Republicans, though, thought that the treaty was a betrayal, and Jay grimly observed that he could travel through the country at night by the light of his burning effigies.

John Jay

Despite the howls against the "Federalist" treaty, Jay's negotiations achieved one outstanding result—they averted war with Britain.

Whiskey Rebellion

Discontent over Hamilton's economic policies had been simmering in the backcountry for some time. Hamilton had proposed raising revenue to pay the government's debt by taxing the production of liquor. Many backcountry farmers, who made their living raising corn and selling it in liquid form, hated the tax and refused to pay it. It is important to realize that this was the first time that the new government had imposed an *internal* tax (as opposed to an *external* tax, such as a tariff). Many of the farmers saw little difference between the whiskey tax and the Stamp Act. All along the frontier the "Whiskey Boys" were grumbling and looking for ways to avoid the tax and the tax collector. In western Pennsylvania, discontent turned into violence against the government.

President Washington's response was decisive. He called up thirteen thousand troops to crush the **Whiskey Rebellion** and initially took command of them personally. When the huge army reached the western counties, the rebellion collapsed. The few that were captured and convicted were pardoned by the president. Washington had made his point: the national government possessed the strength and the will to enforce the law. If citizens did not like a law, they could change it through the ballot box and the courts, not through violence. In Washington's words, Americans had to "distinguish between oppression and the necessary exercise of lawful authority."

Although the rebellion ended, discontent over the tax did not. Whiskey stills were hidden from the pursuing "revenuers," whose persistence forced the farmers to ply their illegal trade at night, giving the word "moonshine" new meaning.

The farmers' refusal to pay this tax was not limited to western Pennsylvania although historically farmers there have gotten the attention because they resorted to violence. In reality, no one in the backcountry paid the tax. Washington and Hamilton chose to make an example of the Pennsylvanians and had support among the wealthy citizens of that state to do so. One of Jefferson's first actions when he became president was to repeal Hamilton's federal excise tax program. The federal government did not attempt such taxation again until the Civil War.

Washington's Farewell

In 1796, after two terms, Washington announced his plans to retire. He left a remarkable legacy. The size of the Union by the end of his two terms had been enlarged by the admission of Vermont (1791), Kentucky (1792), and Tennessee (1796). Under Washington's presidency the country grew in strength as well as in size. Credit and commerce were stabilized, and the Constitution proved to be a practical charter.

In **Washington's Farewell Address**, however, he was looking not at the past but to the future. Issued on the ninth anniversary of the signing of the Constitution, September 17, 1796, Washington's address urged Americans to lay aside partisan divisions and encouraged the cultivation of commercial ties with Europe. But the president warned against political ties.

Daniel Boone, Kentucky Backwoodsman

In 1792, Kentucky became the fifteenth state in the Union. Its admission was the result of the pioneering efforts of many men and women, the best known of whom was frontiersman **Daniel Boone**.

Born and bred in Pennsylvania on the edge of the wilderness, Boone explored restlessly, delighting in the rugged beauty of the land. He adopted Indian ways of hunting and tracking; few men, white or Indian, could match his skills. He was a keen marksman. He called his rifle "Ticklicker" because, he boasted, it could "lick a tick" off a bear's nose at one hundred yards.

Boone began exploring Kentucky in the 1760s, supposedly to scout land for settlement. He blazed a trail called the "Wilderness Road" through the Cumberland Gap, and it became the main route of early settlers to Kentucky. He also helped establish some of the first settlements in Kentucky, one of which, Boonesborough, was named for him.

The Cherokees called Kentucky "the dark and bloody ground," and few other areas of the United States saw such fierce warfare between whites and Indians. Boone experienced that conflict firsthand. Indians captured his oldest son, James, and tortured him to death during one of Boone's first expeditions to Kentucky. Indians killed his second son, Israel, before Boone's very eyes in an ambush at the Battle of Blue Licks (1782). Indians killed and beheaded Boone's brother, Ned, while Boone was hunting a bear only a hundred yards away. Boone and an Indian were once locked in a life-and-death struggle that ended when they fell into a stream. Boone held the Indian's head underwater, drowning him. After that, the stream was called "Drowning Creek."

Always restless, Boone moved from Kentucky to Missouri in 1799, joking that someone had moved within seventy miles of him and he needed more elbow room. Actually, Boone wanted to escape the debts and lawsuits piling up in Kentucky as a result of the state's irregular settlement. In Missouri, Boone spent his time hunting, fishing, and trapping, although sometimes his rheumatism was so bad that his wife had to carry his rifle for him. In his eighties, Boone explored as far as the Yellowstone region of modern Wyoming. He died in his son's home, a legend in his own time.

Europe has a set of primary interests which to us have none or a very remote relation; Hence she must be engaged in frequent controversies, the causes of which are essentially foreign to our concerns. . . . Our detached and distant situation invites and enables us to pursue a different course. . . . It is our true policy to steer clear of permanent alliances, with any portion of the foreign world . . . [but] we may safely trust to temporary alliances for extraordinary emergencies.

Washington's influential Farewell Address outlined America's basic foreign policy until the world wars of the twentieth century.

Section Quiz

1. Who were the two most important leaders of the Republicans during Washington's administration?

2. Why was Washington's Proclamation of Neutrality in 1793 not popular with either the Federalists or the Republicans?

3. What was the most important result of Jay's Treaty?

★ Was Washington's advice about permanent alliances good or bad advice? How closely has the United States followed that advice?

III. Declining Federalist Influence

The election of 1796 marked the first real contest in presidential politics. During the first two elections, no one had the stature even to compete with Washington. With the old general's retirement, however, and the heated partisan debate between Federalists and Republicans, the stage was set for a close race. The 1796 election demonstrated two features in the political maturing of the American republic that are remarkable even today: a peaceful transfer of power and political parties competing without resorting to violence. More immediately, the close election demonstrated that the Federalist grip on power was loosening in the face of the growing Republican challenge.

The Election of 1796

The Federalists passed over their most vocal leader, Alexander Hamilton, because of his many accumulated political enemies. Instead, they gave the presidential nomination to Washington's two-term vice president, **John Adams** of Massachusetts. To balance the ticket geographically, the Federalists gave the vice-presidential slot to Thomas Pinckney of South Carolina. Republicans nominated Thomas Jefferson with Aaron Burr of New York as his running mate.

Hamilton, for personal and political reasons, opposed Adams for the presidency and secretly worked to keep him as vice president. Hamilton quietly suggested to the South Carolina electors that they should withhold their votes from Adams so that their state's favorite son, Pinckney, would win the presidency. When Massachusetts electors heard of the political intrigue, they refused to vote for Pinckney. Hamilton's attempt to engineer the election backfired.

As a result of Pinckney's loss of support, Republican Thomas Jefferson became vice president and nearly took the big prize, falling just three electoral votes short of John Adams's tally. A mixed administration of political adversaries was certainly not what the constitutional framers had in mind less than ten years earlier.

The new president, John Adams, was a man whose distinguished career stretched back to the earliest days of the independence movement when Boston was a hotbed for the Revolution. Adams was educated at Harvard, unlike his predecessor, Washington, who had less formal education than any other president in our nation's history. Despite his credentials as a lawyer, diplomat, and statesman, Adams often felt that his achievements were underrated. In 1790, for example, he complained in a letter to a friend, "The history of our Revolution will be one continued lie from one end to the other. The essence of the whole will be that Dr. Franklin's electrical rod smote the earth and out sprang George Washington."

Yet, Adams was a man of courage and conviction. Few presidents have made decisions with less concern for their own political future than he did. Such courage would prove crucial for the nation throughout Adams's troubled term.

Quasi War

During Adams's presidency the United States walked an international tightrope. To favor either France or Britain was to risk war with the other. To continue to ignore the insults of both nations toward American commerce was to irritate Americans and risk the nation's economic future.

John Adams, second president of the United States

French hostility toward the United States following the Jay Treaty was more intense than even the British raids of 1793. By 1797, the French had seized cargo on three hundred American ships and severed diplomatic ties with the United States. This "**Quasi War**" (a conflict resembling war in nearly every particular except a formal declaration) occupied much of Adams's time in office.

XYZ Affair

In 1797, French belligerence led Adams to send diplomats to negotiate with the revolutionary government in France, at that time a five-man Directory. The French foreign minister was the wily Charles Maurice Talleyrand, who hinted through three of his agents that he would negotiate with the Americans for a price—say, $250,000 for each of the Directors and a $12 million loan to the French government. The American representatives—John Marshall, C. C. Pinckney, and Elbridge Gerry—replied, "No, no, not a six-pence."

Americans of all political persuasions were incensed by France's action. When Congress later demanded to see the correspondence regarding the affair, Adams complied but substituted the letters X, Y, and Z for the names of the French agents. The episode soon became known as the **XYZ Affair**.

Retaliation

French arrogance in the XYZ Affair raised a cry in America: "Millions for defense, but not one cent for tribute." In 1798, as fear of war intensified, Congress authorized a larger army to prepare to stop a seemingly imminent French invasion. That same year, Congress formed a Department of the Navy and funded a strong shipbuilding effort. Within two years, the United States Navy had more than thirty ships in its fleet.

Many of those ships were soon tested in battle during the undeclared naval war against the French. The Federalists and a growing number of Republicans, however, wanted an all-out war effort against the French. Instead, President Adams put the interests of his country ahead of his party, a decision that probably cost him his re-election. Adams wanted to protect national honor and preserve freedom of the seas, but at the same time he believed that war would destroy the hard-earned gains of the young American republic. When the French hinted at the possibility of peace negotiations, Adams seized the opportunity.

Adams sent a peace commission to France in late 1799, even though many Federalists opposed the idea and though he knew that it would further erode his support. Napoleon Bonaparte had assumed the leadership of France and was playing the role of peacemaker at the time. Under Napoleon's favorable terms, France promised to leave American ships alone and to suspend the old Treaty of Alliance in exchange for an American promise not to seek compensation for shipping damages from the Quasi War.

Alien and Sedition Acts

Quieting the Critics

The anti-French sentiment that swept the country in the late 1790s provided the Federalists with an important political opportunity since Jefferson and his Republicans had been identified with the French cause from the beginning. In a series of four acts, known as the **Alien and Sedition Acts**, the Federalist-controlled Congress sought to silence their political opponents. Three of the acts placed restrictions on immigrants—particularly the French and Irish, ethnic groups that were predominantly Republican. The Alien Acts gave the president greatly expanded powers to expel or imprison such undesirables. The Sedition Act not only outlined penalties for antigovernment activities such as riots but also made it illegal to speak or write anything "false, scandalous and malicious . . . against the government of the United States, or the President of the United States, with intent to defame . . . or to bring them or either of them, into contempt or disrepute." Stiff penalties of fines and imprisonment awaited anyone convicted of such "treasonous" speech.

Only ten men were convicted under the Sedition Act, but the opposition Republican Party clearly got the brunt of the law. Matthew Lyon, for example, an outspoken Vermont congressman, was fined $1,000 and spent four months in jail for accusing President Adams of having an "unbounded thirst for ridiculous pomp, foolish adulation, and selfish avarice."

The Sedition Act was clearly unconstitutional—that is as clear to us today as it was to Republicans then. At the time, however, when anti-French hysteria and the fear of anarchy gripped the government, it was genuinely viewed as a means to preserve order. Many Republican newspaper editors unwittingly encouraged the act's passage by printing articles that were bitter, false, and inflammatory toward the Federalists.

This crude political cartoon scathingly satirizes clashes between factions in Congress during the late 1790s.

Kentucky and Virginia Resolutions

In November 1798, Jefferson responded to the Alien and Sedition Acts by writing the **Kentucky Resolutions**. In December, Madison further responded by writing the **Virginia Resolutions**. Both lists of resolutions opposed the Alien and Sedition Acts as a violation of the First Amendment, and both expressed the rights of the states to judge the constitutionality of a law. The resolutions held that under the Constitution the national government existed by consent of the states and, by extension, that the dissent of the states could nullify government acts that the states considered unconstitutional. The documents even suggested that the states had a right to secede when the federal government acted unconstitutionally. Neither Jefferson nor Madison wanted secession; both had worked too hard to establish the federal government. What they wanted was the repeal of the Alien and Sedition Acts. However, their nullification theory would gain importance a generation later (see Chapter 10).

The limited political persecution resulting from the Alien and Sedition Acts was short-lived. Jefferson urged his supporters to make their views known through the ballot box, not violence. The upcoming election of 1800 would give Republicans the opportunity to determine the future of the Alien and Sedition Acts as well as Federalist control of the government.

The Election of 1800

In the summer of 1800, John Adams moved to the new national capital, called Washington City in honor of the first president, who had died in 1799. His stay in the executive mansion, however, would be brief. Adams's efforts to make peace with France divided his own party, and the Alien and Sedition Acts had galvanized his opponents. The election of 1800 was one of the bitterest ever.

The Candidates

The presidential and vice-presidential candidates for both parties were very nearly repeats of the 1796 election. The Republicans chose Jefferson and Burr again, and the Federalists picked Adams and Pinckney, only this Pinckney was Charles Cotesworth, brother of Thomas.

Ridiculous accusations flew between the rival camps. Jefferson described the Federalist administration as a "reign of witches." Federalists warned the public that if Jefferson were elected the people could expect "dwellings in flames, hoary hairs bathed in blood, . . . children writhing on the pike and halberd."

The Results

The results of the election would have been comical if they had not been so serious. The Federalist electors arranged to have one of their electors not vote for Pinckney so as to distinguish between their presidential and vice-presidential candidates; Adams received 65 electoral votes and his running mate Pinckney, 64 votes. The Republicans could have learned something from their Federalist foes. The Republican electors each cast their votes for both Jefferson and Burr, giving them a tie at 73 votes apiece. As a result, the election was thrown into the House of Representatives for the Federalist-controlled Congress to decide between the lesser of two Republican evils. After a lengthy deadlock, Jefferson, considered by the reluctant kingmakers to be slightly less repugnant than Burr, was elected president on the thirty-fifth ballot. (The Republicans quickly supported a twelfth amendment to the Constitution, to avoid such a situation in the future.)

The "Midnight Appointments"

The Federalists lost control of both the executive and the legislative branches in 1800. The only branch left to them was the judicial. After the election but before Jefferson's inauguration, Adams took steps to strengthen Federalist control of the judiciary. In February 1801, he appointed the Federalist John Marshall as chief justice of the Supreme Court. Marshall, who would serve as chief justice for thirty-four years, delivering some of the court's most important decisions, was perhaps the most enduring legacy of the

Adams administration. Also, before newly elected Republican congressmen replaced the Federalists, Congress passed the **Judiciary Act of 1801**, which increased the number of federal judges. Adams, of course, filled these appointments with Federalists. He was accused of staying up until midnight the night before Jefferson's inauguration on March 4, 1801, signing commissions for the new judges. The appointments were thus called the "**midnight appointments**." Jefferson remarked begrudgingly that the wily Federalists had "retired into the judiciary as a stronghold."

A Time to Heal

When Jefferson took the oath of office, John Adams did not stay to watch what he believed was the beginning of national ruin. After thirty years of public service, the old patriot was turned out of office and returned to his home in Quincy, Massachusetts, to retire and to brood. Contrary to Federalist predictions, the nation did not disintegrate following Jefferson's inauguration. Two terms later, Jefferson also retired—to Monticello, nestled in Virginia's Blue Ridge Mountains. After a few years, the two ex-presidents started corresponding and became friends again. The lengthy letters of these presidential pen pals are more than witty commentaries on national politics; they reveal true friendship, the healing of old wounds. Even in death, the two men who at one time could not even stand each other's presence were knit together. On the fiftieth anniversary of the Declaration of Independence, the document that first brought Adams and Jefferson together in 1776, both men lay on their deathbeds. Adams's last words were about his old enemy and new friend; he whispered, "Thomas Jefferson survives." Ironically, his friend had died at Monticello a few hours earlier.

The friendship between John Adams and Thomas Jefferson illustrates much about the 1790s. The formative Federalist decade established national supremacy and enduring precedents, but it also produced deep political divisions. In time, those wounds would heal. After some maturing, the political parties brought healthy competition, not open conflict, to America. The fiery trials of the 1790s tempered the young nation, fitting it for a growing role at the dawn of a new century.

Section Quiz

1. Name the president and vice president, along with their political parties, who were elected in 1796.

2. What is the origin of the phrase "Millions for defense, but not one cent for tribute"?

3. Why was Adams's decision to pursue peace with France a politically brave act?

4. What political theory did the Virginia and Kentucky Resolutions advocate?

5. How did the Judiciary Act of 1801 allow the Federalists to continue their influence in government after the election of Jefferson in 1800?

★ The Alien and Sedition Acts were designed to silence opposition to the Federalist program. What other examples in American history involve similar attempts by one party against another?

Chapter Review

Making Connections

1. What was the most significant section of the Judiciary Act of 1789? Why?

2. What did Hamilton offer the South to win Southern support for assumption of state debts by the federal government?

3. How did the Federalist and the Republican Parties differ concerning constitutional interpretation?

4. How did the elections of 1796 and 1800 reveal flaws in the presidential election system established by the Constitution?

Developing History Skills

1. How would the application of the Alien and Sedition Acts have backfired on the Federalists if Congress had not allowed them to expire?

2. Compare and contrast the course and consequences of Shays's Rebellion and the Whiskey Rebellion.

Thinking Critically

1. Which view of constitutional interpretation do you think is better, loose or strict constructionism?

2. How was the presence of political opponents Alexander Hamilton and Thomas Jefferson in Washington's cabinet both positive and negative for the young nation?

Living as a Christian Citizen

1. Imagine that the United States Congress was sued for opening its sessions in prayer on the grounds that such prayers amount to the establishment of religion in violation of the First Amendment. You are a lawyer tasked with defending the members of Congress in court. Outline your arguments in their behalf.

2. From the biblical perspective on human nature, what dangers can be found in the Federalist emphasis on centralized government and in an Anti-Federalist push toward greater democracy?

People, Places, and Things to Remember

George Washington
Thomas Jefferson
Alexander Hamilton
cabinet
Judiciary Act of 1789
James Madison
Bill of Rights
funding
assumption
loose constructionists
strict constructionists
National Bank
Federalists
Republicans (Democratic-Republicans)
French Revolution
Proclamation of Neutrality
Citizen Genêt
Jay Treaty
Whiskey Rebellion
Daniel Boone
Washington's Farewell Address
John Adams
Quasi War
XYZ Affair
Alien and Sedition Acts
Kentucky Resolutions
Virginia Resolutions
Judiciary Act of 1801
"midnight appointments"

UNIT 3

NATION ★ 1801–1859

A DICTIONARY of the ENGLISH LANGUAGE

BY NOAH WEBSTER. L.L.D.

SPRINGFIELD, MASS.
PUBLISHED BY G. & C. MERRIAM, STATE STREET.

The first half of the nineteenth century was a time of vast advancements in knowledge, communication, transportation, and American culture.

c. 1800–c. 1825
Second Great Awakening

1803
Louisiana Purchase

1811
Battle of Tippecanoe

1812–15
War of 1812

1820
Missouri Compromise

1823
Monroe Doctrine proclaimed

CHAPTER

9 THE JEFFERSONIAN ERA (1801–1825)

10 THE AGE OF JACKSON (1820–1840)

11 THE GROWTH OF AMERICAN SOCIETY (1789–1861)

12 MANIFEST DESTINY (1840–1848)

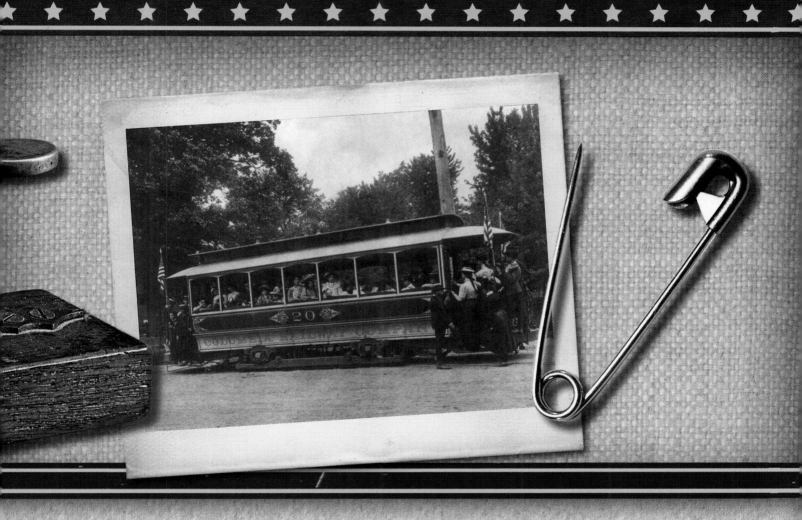

1828
"Tariffs of Abominations"

1836
Texas independence

1845
Annexation of Texas

1846
Oregon controversy settled

1846–48
Mexican War

1857–59
Prayer Meeting Revival

CHAPTER 9

"The Battle of New Orleans" by E. Percy Moran

The Jeffersonian Era (1801-1825)

I.   The Revolution of 1800

II. Jefferson's Triumphs Abroad

III. Indians and the Northwest Territory

IV. The War of 1812

V.   The Era of Good Feelings

"Our country! In her intercourse with foreign nations, may she always be in the right; but our country, right or wrong."

Stephen Decatur,
toast given at Norfolk, April 1816

In the first year of the nineteenth century, Washington, D.C., was as raw and unfinished as the nation of which it was the capital. The country's leaders trudged down muddy pathways that served as streets from the ramshackle, overcrowded boarding houses in which they lived to the half-completed buildings in which they worked. On March 4, 1801, **Thomas Jefferson** left his boarding house, strolled over to the unfinished Capitol, and took the oath of office as the third president of the United States. Then he delivered his inaugural address in a whispery, indistinct voice; much of what he said was lost on his audience. The simple ceremony would not have impressed the cultured rulers of Europe, a fact that undoubtedly pleased Jefferson.

President Thomas Jefferson

The tall, lanky president, his red hair peppered with gray, was certainly not a pretentious man. He soon offended the English ambassador by greeting him while wearing a pair of carpet slippers. On another occasion, the president astounded Washington society by taking his nephew shopping around the city to buy back-to-school items. Jefferson might not have been pretentious, but he was certainly remarkable. By 1801, his accomplishments included writing the Declaration of Independence and serving as ambassador to France, governor of Virginia, secretary of state, and vice president. He also had developed numerous inventions and architectural designs in his spare time. "Science is my passion," Jefferson once said, "politics my duty." His interests and abilities ranged from politics to art to science. In 1962, President John F. Kennedy told a gathering of Nobel Prize winners, "I think this is the most extraordinary collection of talent, of human knowledge, that has ever been gathered together at the White House, with the possible exception of when Thomas Jefferson dined alone."

The administrations of Jefferson and his handpicked successors, James Madison and James Monroe, constitute the era of **Jeffersonian Republicanism** (1801–25). The period bears Jefferson's stamp and embodies his philosophy. Through events ranging from a magnificent land purchase that doubled the size of the United States to the torching of the nation's capital by a foreign power, Jeffersonian principles endured in both prosperity and adversity. By the end of the period, Jefferson's party and philosophy stood virtually unopposed on the political landscape of America.

The unfinished U.S. Capitol as it appeared in the time of Thomas Jefferson

I. The Revolution of 1800

Jefferson called his election "the revolution of 1800," suggesting that his victory marked a transformation as dramatic as that of 1776. Although time would demonstrate that the change was not as great as Jefferson imagined, it signaled a discernible shift from the policies of the Federalist era.

Nature of Jeffersonian Republicanism

Republican ideas might best be understood in contrast to the ideas of the Federalists. The Federalists were the party of finance,

Jefferson's Religious Views

Jefferson's religious views made him an enemy of Christianity. He did admire the teachings of Jesus, calling them "a system of morals" that is "the most perfect and sublime that has ever been taught by man." However, Jefferson denied most of the scriptural teaching concerning Christ. Of the virgin birth, for example, he wrote to John Adams, "The day will come when the account of the birth of Christ as accepted in the Trinitarian churches will be classed with the fable of Minerva springing from the brain of Jupiter." He also believed that much of the New Testament writings were corruptions of Jesus' teaching.

Jefferson compiled his own version of the "true" teachings of Jesus. Using scissors, paste, and two English and two Greek New Testaments, he pieced together an account of Jesus' life and teaching that excluded every miracle and every reference to Christ as God. The result—variously called "The Philosophy of Jesus of Nazareth," "The Morals of Jesus," or "Jefferson's Bible"—limited itself almost entirely to the moral teachings of Jesus. Jefferson read from his edition nearly every night and called it "a document in proof that *I am a real Christian*, that is to say a disciple of the doctrines of Jesus."

Though Jefferson played a significant positive role in the founding of the United States, his devotion to the Enlightenment had negative consequences as well. His denial of the Scripture's teaching about human sinfulness caused him to underestimate the depravity of man. When Jefferson designed the curriculum for the University of Virginia, he placed science, rather than theology, at the center of the curriculum. Jefferson thus marks a movement toward secularism.

the great defenders of the merchant class. Jefferson's Republican Party, on the other hand, concerned itself with the interests of the farmers. Jefferson believed that liberty in the United States would be preserved only as long as the country remained predominantly a nation of independent, self-sufficient farmers. The Federalists preferred a strong central government to protect and further national interests. The Republicans operated on the principle that the less government there is, the better. Jefferson had vigorously demonstrated his adherence to the idea of states' rights against the claims of the national government in the Virginia and Kentucky Resolutions (see Chapter 8).

Despite their defense of states' rights and the farmer, the Jeffersonian Republicans were not truly a party of the "common man." Like the Federalists, the Republicans believed in rule by an elite class. The Federalists wanted rule by an elite of birth—those who came from the "best," almost aristocratic, families. The Republicans preferred the creation of an elite of talent; in each generation the most brilliant and most capable men would rise from the masses (probably through education) and take the reins of government. It is not too much to say that most Republicans took as their ideal a man much like Jefferson himself—intelligent, cultured, and accomplished.

Jefferson was right, perhaps, in seeing his election as a change, but it was no revolution. There was no wholesale repudiation of the Federalist method of governing, only an alteration of the practices that Republicans found offensive. With the benefit of hindsight, we can see that Jeffersonian Republicanism was not so much a revolution as a transition from the elitism of the Federalists to the more truly "common man" politics of Andrew Jackson that would triumph in the 1820s.

Making Changes

Jefferson undeniably made changes when he took office. The Republicans quickly repealed the offensive Judiciary Act of 1801 and allowed the Alien and Sedition Acts to expire. To guard against a repetition of the deadlocked election of 1800 (see Chapter 8), Congress and the states adopted the **Twelfth Amendment**, which enabled electors to cast separate ballots for president and vice president. The extremely formal receptions that Washington and Adams had held with political leaders gave way to Jefferson's informal discussions with congressional leaders around his dinner table. Eager to reduce the size of the national government, Jefferson ordered his secretary of the treasury, Albert Gallatin, to draw up a plan for both reducing taxes and eliminating the national debt.

Political cartoon opposing Jefferson's Embargo Act of 1807

Jefferson knew when to leave well enough alone, however. He made no attempt, for example, to destroy the National Bank. In fact, after the bank's charter expired, a Republican Congress under Jefferson's successor, James Madison, created another bank in 1816.

Another economic issue on which Jefferson seemed to depart from traditional Republican theory led to criticism from both Republicans and Federalists. In June 1807, the American frigate *Chesapeake* was fired upon by the British warship *Leopard*. Americans immediately called for retaliation for what became known as the ***Chesapeake* affair**. Jefferson ordered all British ships out of American waters. He then pushed through Congress the **Embargo Act**, which forbade trade with either Great Britain or France, with whom Britain was then at war. Furthermore, no U.S. ships could land in any foreign port without the president's express permission, and trading ships leaving U.S. ports had to post a bond equal to the value of the ship and its cargo. Subsequent acts essentially ended all exports from America. These combined actions of government devastated the U.S. economy and produced an outcry from both parties. One political cartoonist sketched a turtle-like creature called the "Ograbme" (*embargo* spelled backward) biting a merchant who is attempting to ship his cask of goods overseas. The embargo, which violated Republican ideas about free trade, was repealed days before Jefferson left office.

John Marshall, a Federalist, was the first activist chief justice.

John Marshall and the Supreme Court

One institution remained a bastion of Federalist policies—the Supreme Court. The leader of that court, and its first great chief justice, was **John Marshall**. A Virginia Federalist and cousin of Jefferson, Marshall was appointed and took office in the waning days of the Adams administration. The Supreme Court was not as honored then as it is today. The first chief justice, John Jay, resigned the office to become governor of New York, an office that he considered more prestigious. Marshall received the nomination only after two other men declined it. (Perhaps it was those refusals that caused Adams to nominate Marshall without asking him first.) After Marshall's thirty-four years on the bench, however, no one would doubt the power and prestige of the Court.

Marshall was a Federalist in the mold of George Washington. He envisioned a tremendous future for the young nation as long as the central government held the power to develop the new land's potential. In a series of landmark decisions, the Marshall Court

upheld the authority of the national government and increased the scope of the Court's authority. Marshall, and others who followed him, helped to establish the judiciary as an independent branch of government.

Marbury v. Madison

The first major case before the Marshall Court involved the infamous Judiciary Act of 1801. William Marbury had received one of Adams's "midnight appointments." However, Jefferson's secretary of state, James Madison, refused to deliver Marbury's commission, meaning that Marbury could not take office. Marbury asked the Supreme Court to issue an order forcing Madison to deliver the commission. Marshall knew that he had no means of forcing Madison to obey, and some Republicans eagerly awaited the opportunity to flout the authority of the Federalist judge.

Marshall cleverly handed down a ruling that preserved the authority of the Court without giving the Republicans an opportunity to defy the Court. Although Marbury was right in his complaint, Marshall said, the power to issue such orders was not one of the powers delegated to the Court by the Constitution. The law that permitted such orders, then, was unconstitutional and therefore invalid. Thus, in **Marbury v. Madison** the Supreme Court established the principle of **judicial review**, the right of the Court to declare a law unconstitutional. As Marshall wrote in handing down the decision, "A legislative act contrary to the Constitution is not law. . . . It is emphatically the province and duty of the judicial department to say what the law is."

Gibbons v. Ogden

Another important ruling, handed down in 1824, protected the federal government's **delegated powers**, those powers specifically given to the national government by the Constitution. This case involved Congress's right to regulate interstate commerce. New York had attempted to grant a monopoly on the use of its waterways to one steamship company, a monopoly which also limited the federal government's use of those waterways. In **Gibbons v. Ogden** the Court ruled that the delegated powers given to the national government by the Constitution could not be limited by state boundaries. Where the Constitution entrusted Congress with a power, the states had no right to interfere with that power.

McCulloch v. Maryland

Perhaps the most far-reaching decision of the Marshall Court was **McCulloch v. Maryland** (1819). The state of Maryland opposed the idea of a national bank and tried to tax the Baltimore branch of the Bank of the United States out of existence. Claiming that "the power to tax involves the power to destroy," the Court overruled the state's action. The Constitution is the supreme law of the land, Marshall said, referring to Article VI of the Constitution. Therefore, the states had no authority to interfere with Congress's ability to enact legislation that is "necessary and proper" to carry out its delegated powers (Article I, Section 8, Clause 18). (These "necessary and proper" powers that enable the government to carry out the delegated powers are called **implied powers**.) In this decision, Marshall placed the Court squarely on the side of the loose constructionists and national supremacy. The Supreme Court might have been a Federalist island in a sea of Republicanism, but John Marshall ensured that it was an island that Jeffersonians could not ignore.

Section Quiz

1. How did the Federalists and the Republicans disagree concerning the power of the central government?

2. What is judicial review? What Supreme Court decision established judicial review?

3. List the three important court cases that the Marshall Court ruled on and the important long-range principle established by each one.

★ Why is it incorrect to refer to Jefferson's administration as a "revolution"?

II. Jefferson's Triumphs Abroad

Despite his overriding concern with domestic affairs, Thomas Jefferson achieved his two greatest successes in the field of foreign affairs. Through his clash with the Barbary pirates and even more through the Louisiana Purchase, Jefferson dramatically increased the international prestige of the young nation.

To the Shores of Tripoli

As part of his plan to cut federal expenses, Jefferson wanted to reduce the size of the navy. However, several petty Muslim kingdoms in North Africa, where piracy and kidnapping were the chief sources of national income, forced the president to reconsider his budget cuts. The ships of these **Barbary states** raided Mediterranean shipping and occasionally ventured out into the Atlantic. These pirates captured unarmed merchant ships, enslaved the crews, and demanded ransom from the owners. Most nations found it cheaper and easier to pay ransom to the Barbary states than to send in their warships.

The United States was among those who paid tribute money—until Jefferson took office. Offended at the practice, Jefferson sent a squadron of warships to Tripoli to frighten the most important Barbary state with a show of force. In a brief war, the squadron bombarded Tripoli harbor, and a group of eight U.S. Marines fought alongside an army of Muslim rebels who captured the Tripolitan city of Derna. There, Lieutenant Presley O'Bannon became the first soldier to plant the American flag on foreign soil. The exploits of O'Bannon and his companions fired the pride of the young nation. O'Bannon's act later inspired a phrase in the Marine Corps' hymn—"to the shores of Tripoli."

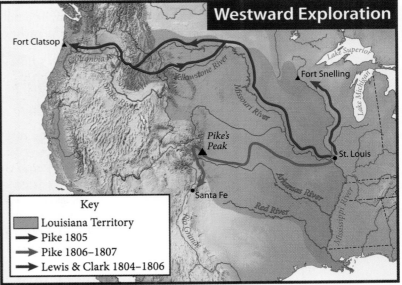

Westward Exploration

Key
- Louisiana Territory
- → Pike 1805
- → Pike 1806–1807
- → Lewis & Clark 1804–1806

The Louisiana Purchase

"A Noble Bargain"

In 1800, France and Spain secretly signed a treaty returning the Louisiana Territory to France. Word of this deal leaked out and caused panic in Washington. New Orleans was vital to American interests; the western states shipped millions of tons of American goods down the Mississippi River to New Orleans and, from there, to other markets around the world. Dealing with the relatively weak Spanish had often been troublesome. Dealing with the French under the powerful **Napoleon Bonaparte** could be potentially disastrous for the Americans.

Jefferson instructed James Monroe and Robert Livingstone, the ambassador to France, to go to Napoleon and offer him as much as $10 million for New Orleans. Napoleon's foreign minister astounded the Americans with a counteroffer: *all* of the Louisiana Territory—a region larger than the whole United States—for $15 million. The American representatives hurriedly sent word to Jefferson and urged him to accept. The offer bothered Jefferson, who was a strict constructionist. It was certainly a splendid opportunity, but the Constitution gave the government no authority to purchase land in this way. Jefferson briefly toyed with the idea of requesting a constitutional amendment to permit the purchase, but his ministers in France warned him to hurry before Napoleon changed his mind. Casting his constitutional scruples aside, Jefferson submitted the treaty to the Senate. A majority quickly approved. With the **Louisiana Purchase**, the United States more than doubled its size in one stroke.

Why did Napoleon so eagerly sell such a huge tract of land for less than three cents an acre? Although Napoleon was then at peace, he was preparing again for war with Great Britain. When war broke out, Napoleon would be pressed to defend Louisiana thousands of miles away across the Atlantic. Being land-rich and cash-poor, it made more sense to sell the territory to the United States. Napoleon would have more funds for his expected war with Britain, and he would build up favor with the United States—not a bad bargain in exchange for a territory that he probably could not keep anyway.

An important question remained: exactly what were the boundaries of Louisiana? The French foreign minister replied evasively to Livingstone that they were the same as those that France had received from Spain. Livingstone persisted. What were *those* boundaries then? The minister declined to answer but said simply, "You have made a noble bargain for yourselves, and I suppose you will make the most of it."

Meriwether Lewis

William Clark

Exploring the New Lands

To help determine what the territory was and what it contained, Jefferson asked Congress to authorize army officers **Meriwether Lewis**, the president's private secretary, and **William Clark**, brother of George Rogers Clark, to lead an expedition to explore the Louisiana Territory.

Sacajawea

Accompanying Lewis and Clark through the Pacific Northwest was a Shoshone (shoh SHOW nee) Indian woman named Sacajawea (SAC uh juh WEE uh), wife of a French fur trader. Sacajawea had been kidnapped from the Shoshones as a young girl, and she regarded the American expedition as an opportunity to see her people again. Lewis and Clark knew that they would need horses from the Shoshones to cross the Rocky Mountains. So they quickly struck a deal, and Sacajawea and her husband joined the group.

Sacajawea was already several months pregnant when she joined the expedition, and in February 1805 she gave birth to a son. Rather than being a burden to the expedition, the woman and her infant helped the explorers when they met suspicious Indians. "A woman with a party of men is a token of peace," Clark observed.

When the expedition met the Shoshones, Sacajawea interpreted for the explorers. She suddenly stopped and began to weep and ran over to the Shoshone chief, who, as it turned out, was her brother. She smoothed the way for Lewis and Clark among the Shoshones.

Contrary to popular belief, she was not a guide, although she did point out some important landmarks in Shoshone country (the Snake River area of modern Idaho).

When the expedition returned to the east, Sacajawea and her family stayed behind. Clark showed his appreciation to her by paying for the education of her son in St. Louis.

On May 14, 1804, their group of about fifty men left St. Louis. The party traveled up the Missouri River and through the Dakotas and Montana, crossed the Rocky Mountains, and by December 1805 had paddled canoes down the Columbia River to the Pacific. The explorers saw wonders of the American West previously undreamed of by white men. Raging, swirling rivers tumbled through the land, threatening to swallow any boat foolish enough to challenge them. Strange animals, such as the fierce grizzly bear and the cougar, stalked the explorers. In the mountains, shrieking winds shot pellets of ice and snow like bullets.

In addition to the dangers were breathtaking beauties. Some of the streams were fierce, but they were also sparklingly clear and fresh. The Rocky Mountains certainly held dangers, but their craggy outline and dizzying heights must have amazed those who were used to the lower, rounded peaks of the Appalachians.

The climax of the trip must have been when the explorers stood on the shores of the Pacific and gazed at an ocean that dwarfed even the mighty Atlantic. The explorers returned by way of the Yellowstone River and saw much of the awe-inspiring scenery now contained in Yellowstone National Park. The adventures finally came to an end when the party reached St. Louis again in September 1806. Few explorations in history can rival the Lewis and Clark expedition for extensive travel, spectacular sights, and fruitful discoveries.

Zebulon Pike, another army officer, directed two other important expeditions about the same time as Lewis and Clark's trip. The first (1805) went northward to the upper reaches of the Mississippi River. The second trip, in 1806 and 1807, crossed the Great Plains to the Colorado Rockies, where Pike discovered (but did not actually climb) Pikes Peak, the mountain named for him. The expedition then turned southward into Spanish-held Mexico. As a result of these and other explorations, Americans learned more about their continent and could realistically begin to envision a nation that stretched "from sea to shining sea."

Sketch of a vulture's head and notes in the Lewis and Clark journals

Aaron Burr: The Schemer Snared

Alexander Hamilton said that the driving force in Aaron Burr's life was his "inordinate ambition." For Burr, principles were merely other men's weaknesses of which he could take advantage.

Ironically, Burr had a godly heritage. He was Jonathan Edwards's grandson, and his father was a Presbyterian pastor and president of Princeton, but Burr never professed Christ.

Burr became one of the most influential men in New York. The Republicans added him to the 1800 ticket as Jefferson's running mate. In that deadlocked election, Burr denied being interested in the presidency, but rumors abounded that he was secretly hoping to win when the House of Representatives voted. Jefferson believed the rumors and never trusted his vice president again.

In 1804, Burr ran for governor of New York. Some people suspected that Burr's campaign was a plot to separate New York and New England from the Union. Thanks to Alexander Hamilton's opposition, Burr lost. Angered, Burr challenged him to a duel and shot and killed him on July 11, 1804.

With outside help, Burr began stockpiling supplies and weapons on an island in the Ohio River between Virginia and Ohio. Some people think that he intended to take over Mexico, and others think that he planned to lead the western states and territories out of the Union to form his own empire. Jefferson had Burr arrested and tried for treason. He was acquitted when Chief Justice Marshall ruled that there were not two witnesses to the alleged treason, as the Constitution required.

Section Quiz

1. What were Jefferson's two great triumphs in foreign affairs?
2. Why did Napoleon sell the Louisiana Territory to the United States?
3. Who were the three great explorers of the American West during Jefferson's administration?
★ How was Jefferson's decision to buy the Louisiana Territory a violation of his principles of limited government?

III. Indians and the Northwest Territory

The Treaty of Paris after the Revolution gave the Great Lakes region to the United States, but no one asked the Indians who lived there what they thought about the matter. If settlers were to move into the Ohio River Valley and north to the Great Lakes, they would somehow have to deal with the Indians. Unfortunately, the means of dealing with them were usually violent.

Fallen Timbers and the Opening of Ohio

As early as George Washington's administration, settlers and Indians had been locked in a bloody struggle for Ohio. Treaties existed in abundance, but the Americans did not always honor them, nor did the Indians always understand them. For example, the idea of private property belonging to a single person was strange to a people who shared all lands among tribal members. "Sell a country!" Indian chief Tecumseh once said. "Why not sell the air, the clouds, and the great sea, as well as the earth?" An old Indian once complained to William Henry Harrison that the French had been friendlier to the Indians than the Americans had been. He said,

> They [the French] never took from us our lands; indeed, they were common between us. They planted where they pleased, and they cut wood where they pleased, and so did we. But now, if a poor Indian attempts to take a little bark from a tree to cover him from rain, up comes a white man and threatens to shoot him, claiming the tree as his own.

When the Indians realized that the Americans intended to keep the lands forever—and keep the Indians *off*—they went on the warpath.

Whites, on the other hand, considered the Indians' way of living wasteful. Using the land, as the Indians did, only to raise a few crops and to hunt did not begin to tap the potential resources of the country. Many white settlers used their desire to "improve" the land as an excuse to take it from the Indians. They considered themselves better stewards of the nation's resources. These differing philosophies of whites and Indians only increased the potential for conflict.

In 1790 and 1791, the Indians inflicted two stinging and humiliating defeats on the American army. Faced with an increasingly dangerous situation, President Washington appointed Revolutionary War hero "**Mad Anthony**" **Wayne** to crush the Indians. In a careful, meticulously planned campaign, Wayne and his force marched from Fort Washington on the Ohio River (modern Cincinnati) to a site near modern Toledo. In the **Battle of Fallen Timbers**, so called because most of the fighting occurred in a maze

The signing of the Treaty of Fort Greenville, which opened Ohio to white settlement

Chicago History Museum

of tangled trees knocked down by a storm, Wayne's forces routed the Indians. In the resulting **Treaty of Fort Greenville**, the Indians surrendered all rights to the southern half of Ohio.

After Fallen Timbers, settlers began to pour into the Ohio region of the Northwest Territory. A series of land acts passed in 1796, 1800, and 1804 reduced the size of a minimum purchase to 160 acres and lowered the price from $2.00 to $1.64 an acre. In addition, these acts allowed the settler to purchase on credit with a down payment of $80. As a result, ordinary farmers and not just land speculators could buy land in the Ohio Valley. By 1799, Ohio's population had grown so much that Congress sliced it off the Northwest Territory and made it a separate territory. In 1803, Ohio was admitted to the Union as the first state from the Northwest Territory.

Harrison vs. Tecumseh

Looking over the names of the men who fought at Fallen Timbers is much like looking at a "Who's Who" of American history. Meriwether Lewis, William Clark, and Zebulon Pike, for example, all served loyally in Wayne's force. The two most important veterans of Fallen Timbers, as far as the Northwest Territory was concerned, were two young men on opposite sides—a nineteen-year-old officer named **William Henry Harrison** and an Indian scout named **Tecumseh**.

William Henry Harrison

Harrison was the son of Benjamin Harrison, governor of Virginia and signer of the Declaration of Independence. Lured by the promise of glory and adventure, Harrison joined the army, in which he served as an aide to Wayne in the Fallen Timbers campaign. In 1798, Harrison left the army and entered politics. In 1800, he was appointed governor of the Indiana Territory (modern Indiana, Illinois, Michigan, and Wisconsin), and he served in that office until 1812.

Harrison was much fairer in his dealings with the Indians than the average frontier settler—whose philosophy can be summed up in the callous statement "The only good Indian is a dead Indian." Harrison followed Jefferson in believing that Indians should receive

The Northwest Territory

Lake Superior

Lake Michigan

Lake Huron

Lake Erie

FALLEN TIMBERS 1794

Louisiana Territory

Prophetstown

Tippecanoe R.

Wabash River

TIPPECANOE 1811

Vincennes

Ohio River

Ohio

Cincinnati

Kentucky

William Henry Harrison

Shawnee chief Tecumseh

the full help and protection of the government. It genuinely distressed Harrison, for example, that he could never find a white jury that would convict a white man for killing an Indian. Harrison also approved of Jefferson's plan to encourage the Indians to give up hunting and take up farming. In that way, the Indians would lead a more settled life, and they would not need large tracts of undeveloped forests in which to hunt. As well intentioned as Jefferson, Harrison, and men like them might have been, they still insisted that the Indians give up their traditional way of life and open their lands to white settlement.

Tecumseh

Harrison's chief adversary was Tecumseh. Born around 1768 near modern Springfield, Ohio, Tecumseh led the last great Indian challenge to the United States in the Northwest Territory. As part of the Shawnee tribe, he was raised as a warrior, and because his father and two brothers were killed in battle against the whites, he retaliated with a vengeance.

Tecumseh realized that, individually, the Indian tribes could never stand against the United States. Therefore, he proposed joining all the Indian tribes into a single confederation with himself as head. When Harrison protested Tecumseh's actions, the Indian replied calmly that he was simply following the example of the United States in joining his people into one nation. Although resented by chiefs who feared him as a threat to their power, Tecumseh began building his confederation by sheer force of personality. His persuasive speeches wooed Indians to his cause. His fearlessness and code of honor won respect even among white men. (Unlike some Indians, Tecumseh never tortured prisoners or attacked women and children.)

The Prophet

Contributing to Tecumseh's success was a religious movement led by his brother, a man known as **the Prophet**. Maimed (having lost an eye in an accident with a bow and arrow), somewhat cowardly, and a virtual alcoholic, Tecumseh's brother suddenly claimed in 1805 to have received a revelation from the "Master of Life." After this experience, he quit drinking and began to preach to the tribes. Indians must reject the white man's ways, the Prophet said, especially his whiskey. All Indians must learn to treat each other fairly and to draw together against the whites, who were the offspring of an evil god.

When the Prophet began to win converts among the tribes of the Northwest, Harrison unwittingly played into his hands. The governor sent a message to the Indians, urging them to reject this so-called prophet. He said,

> Demand of him some proofs at least of his being the messenger of the Deity. . . . If he is really a prophet, ask of him to cause the sun to stand still—the moon to alter its course—or the dead to rise from their graves. If he does these things, you may then believe that he has been sent by God.

The message backfired. Somehow (perhaps through British agents in Canada), the Prophet learned of a total eclipse of the sun that was to occur in 1806. The Prophet announced to every Indian he could reach that he would indeed make the sun stand still. The

Indians were awed when the Prophet announced, "Behold! darkness has shrouded the sun," and the sun apparently did vanish. Multitudes flocked to Tecumseh and his brother. As their headquarters, the brothers built a village called Prophetstown in the Indiana Territory at the juncture of the Wabash and Tippecanoe rivers—only about a hundred and twenty miles from Harrison's territorial capital in Vincennes.

The Battle of Tippecanoe

As his warrior army grew, Tecumseh announced that no more Indian lands would be opened to the white man without the consent of all the tribes. Harrison knew full well that this demand would mean that no more land sales would be made. The governor met Tecumseh personally in 1810, but they could reach no agreement. When Harrison suggested sending Tecumseh's demands to the president, the Indian leader replied that the president "is so far off he will not be injured by the war; he may sit still in his town and drink his wine, whilst you and I will have to fight it out."

Thinking that a clash seemed inevitable, Harrison decided to act quickly. In 1811, when Tecumseh was away in the South trying to rally the tribes there to his cause, Harrison took a force of some eight hundred men up the Wabash and camped near Prophetstown on the Tippecanoe River. In his brother's absence, the Prophet ordered a night attack on the American camp, promising to charm the white man's weapons so that they would not harm the warriors. In the **Battle of Tippecanoe**, Harrison's forces drove off the Indians but took heavy losses. The Indians abandoned Prophetstown, and Harrison destroyed it. When Tecumseh returned, he found that he must begin all over again. This time, however, he had an ally. The United States and Great Britain were about to go to war.

Section Quiz

1. What battle opened the Ohio Territory to white settlement?
2. Who were the single most important white and Indian leaders, respectively, in the Northwest Territory?
3. How did Harrison's plea to the Indians to test the Prophet backfire?
* Explain the difference of viewpoint concerning private property that made conflict between the American settlers and the Indians nearly inevitable.

IV. The War of 1812

In 1808, Thomas Jefferson refused to run for a third term, but he persuaded the Republicans to nominate his secretary of state, **James Madison**, as his successor. Madison crushed Federalist Charles Cotesworth Pinckney in the election, and in 1809 he became the nation's fourth president. In spite of being a keen political philosopher (he was, after all, the Father of the Constitution) and an experienced politician, Madison was too passive as president and tended to allow Congress to dominate him. Also, he was distracted for most of his two terms as the United States rushed headlong into war with Great Britain.

Background of the War

Worsening Relations

In 1803, Great Britain and Napoleonic France went to war again. The British navy was too powerful for Napoleon to invade Great Britain, and Napoleon's army was too strong for Britain to defeat France in battle on land. As a result, each side tried to starve the other by destroying its trade. Unfortunately, the neutral United States was caught between the two. Both Britain and France seized American ships that they thought were bound for enemy ports, but Britain—with its powerful navy—seized more than the French. In addition, Britain claimed the right of **impressment**, the right to stop American ships, forcibly remove British deserters, and put them back into service. The discipline in the Royal Navy was harsh and cruel and the living conditions squalid; so it was no wonder that British seamen (many of whom had been forced into the navy in the first place) fled to American ships. As if stopping and searching American ships were not enough, British officers—in desperate need of sailors—sometimes "mistakenly" took Americans as well. Although both Britain and France oppressed American shipping, the greater number of British provocations made Britain seem more villainous to the United States.

Tension began to mount during Jefferson's second term. British and French trade restrictions merely harassed the Americans, but an incident of violence—the *Chesapeake* affair—nearly brought war in 1807.

Jefferson did not want war, however. Instead he persuaded Congress to adopt the Embargo Act, which banned all American trade with the rest of the world. In keeping needed American goods from Europe, Jefferson hoped to force Britain and France to lift their restrictions. The embargo failed miserably. France did not need American goods as much as Jefferson thought. Britain needed the goods more, but it could not risk helping Napoleon by lifting its restrictions. Those most hurt by the embargo were Americans. Shipping dropped dramatically, and economic recession threw merchants, sailors, shipbuilders, and many others out of work. Foods rotted on docks as owners could find no market for them. New England suffered the most, but all the states felt the pinch.

Just before Jefferson left office, the government admitted its failure. Congress replaced the embargo with the **Non-Intercourse Act**. This act restored some international trade (though not with Britain or France), but more importantly it offered to restore trade with either nation if either would lift its trade restrictions. Non-intercourse was no more successful than the embargo, and in 1810 Congress tried a new approach with what was known as **Macon's Bill Number Two**. This bill made the European belligerents a frank offer. It abolished the non-intercourse policy and restored all trade. The act then stated that if either country would repeal its antitrade regulations, the United States would restore trade with that side in the war and refuse to trade with the other. England and France themselves would determine which side gained the trade.

Napoleon jumped at the chance. He seemingly repealed his restrictions in 1810, and the United States resumed non-intercourse with Britain. The British correctly doubted Napoleon's honesty and rejected the offer. Despite Napoleon's continued interference with American shipping, the United States shut its eyes, took Napoleon at his word, and tried to force the British to comply. Both England and France viewed the American action as virtually bringing the United States into the war on France's side. At any rate, the action hastened America's entering into a real war against Britain.

The War Hawks

The congressional elections of 1810 nudged America closer to war. In the West and the South a number of intensely nationalistic, prowar representatives were elected to the House. These "**War Hawks**," led by **Henry Clay** of Kentucky and **John C. Calhoun** of South Carolina, pushed for war with Britain. They feared that British trade restrictions would harm western trade down the Mississippi River. They also believed that the British were supporting, and perhaps equipping, the Indians under Tecumseh in the Northwest. Some War Hawks were expansionists who wanted to seize Canada. Above all, the group saw British acts such as impressment as insults to American honor. The War Hawks quickly elected Clay to be Speaker of the House and began pressuring Madison toward war.

Declaration, Division, and Disarray

Madison did not need much pressure. On June 1, 1812, the president sent a war message to Congress. He gave the legislators five reasons for declaring war on Britain: (1) impressment of American sailors, (2) violations of American territorial waters, (3) plunderings of American goods, (4) refusal to revoke trade restrictions, and (5) incitement of the Indians to violence.

Debate over the declaration of war was bitter. Federalists, New Englanders, and easterners generally opposed the war. They depended on the sea for their livelihood and could see no advantage in making matters worse. If anything, they preferred a war against France. Many people in the South and the West, including the War Hawks, favored the war. The middle states were divided, but the prowar faction managed to build a majority in both houses. The House voted 79–49 and the Senate 19–13 for war. Ironically, only days before the declaration, Great Britain had revoked its trade restrictions. If some quick means of communicating the news had existed, the war might never have occurred.

Fighting a war is a difficult endeavor even in the best of circumstances. The United States entered the War of 1812 divided and unprepared. The New England states, in particular, resented the war and resisted giving money or men to the war effort. They called it "Mr. Madison's War," as though the whole affair had nothing to do with them. The War Hawks were eager to fight but were reluctant to pay the costs. After declaring war, they voted down an attempt to enlarge the navy. With only sixteen seagoing warships, America entered a war against the world's greatest naval power.

The United States Army was not ready either. Jefferson and the Republicans feared a large standing army as a threat to liberty. In 1812, the army numbered a mere seven thousand men, and it would take time to raise and train new recruits. The nation had thousands of state militiamen, but they often proved undependable in real fighting. As one historian noted of the militia, "Many of the troops had obviously come to see a show, not to fight a war." Most of the army's commanders were aged veterans of the War for Independence. Only the fact that Britain was tied down by the war with Napoleon gave the Americans an initial advantage.

Course of the War

Disasters in Canada

Henry Clay had bragged that "the militia of Kentucky alone" would be enough to conquer Canada. In reality, the task was far more difficult because of Canada's enormous size and pro-British population. The government assigned General William Hull to attack Canada from Detroit in the west and General Stephen Van Rensselaer to attack from New York in the east. A brilliant British

War of 1812

Lake Superior

Lake Michigan

Lake Huron

Quebec

Montreal

York (Toronto) burned by Americans Apr. 1813

BATTLE OF LAKE CHAMPLAIN

Lake Ontario

BATTLE OF THE THAMES

Ft. Niagara

Boston

Detroit

Lake Erie

Ft. Dearborn

BATTLE OF LAKE ERIE

Baltimore (Ft. McHenry)

New York

BLADENSBURG

Washington, D.C. burned by British Aug. 24, 1814

Chesapeake Bay

Mississippi Territory

ATLANTIC OCEAN

Charleston

Savannah

BATTLE OF HORSESHOE BEND

Key
★ American Victories
✷ British Victories

NEW ORLEANS

general, Isaac Brock, derailed that plan. First, his British-Indian force darted into Michigan and surrounded Hull in Detroit. By hinting that his Indian allies would be uncontrollable in an attack, Brock frightened Hull into surrendering his entire force without a fight. Thus the entire Northwest was opened to the British and the Indians. Then Brock rushed to meet Van Rensselaer's force near Niagara Falls. In the ensuing battle, Brock was killed, but the Americans were driven back into New York. The United States' opening campaign was a fiasco.

The War at Sea

The disasters in Canada were at least partly offset by early victories at sea. In engagements with single British warships, American vessels fared quite well. The **U.S.S. Constitution**, *United States*, *Hornet*, and others defeated British ships in combat. The *Constitution* was particularly effective. In battles with the British *Guerriere* and *Java*, the *Constitution* shattered the enemy with devastating broadsides. But British cannonballs often bounced off the solid oak sides of the *Constitution*, leading Americans to nickname it "**Old Ironsides**."

The British navy, however, outnumbered the American fleet in ships by at least fifty to one. As the British tightened their blockade along the coast, they forced American warships to stay in port or spend the rest of the war at sea preying on British shipping. The American victories soon ceased, but the early triumphs on the high seas had encouraged the American public.

Recovery of the Northwest

After Hull's surrender at Detroit, the government gave William Henry Harrison command of operations in the Northwest. Harrison realized that he could never secure the territory unless the United States controlled Lake Erie. American captain **Oliver Hazard Perry** rose to the challenge. Building his own ships, dragging cannons and ammunition through the wilderness to Lake Erie, and using as sailors Kentucky militiamen who had never been on anything larger than a flatboat, Perry defeated the British fleet in the **Battle of Lake Erie** (September 10, 1813). Perry sent a triumphant message to Harrison: "We have met the enemy and they are ours."

With Lake Erie secured, Harrison moved against the British army. The two armies met near the River Thames (TEMZ) some sixty miles east of Detroit on October 5, 1813. In the **Battle of the Thames**, Harrison routed the British-Indian force. Tecumseh was killed in the battle, and with him died the dream of an Indian confederation. The Northwest was never again seriously threatened by the Indians or the British.

The British Drive for Victory

Despite Harrison's victory, the American situation remained grave early in 1814. Napoleon had surrendered, allowing Britain to turn its full attention to its upstart former colonies. The British devised a threefold plan to win the war: (1) an army would descend from Canada and separate New York and New England from the rest of the states, (2) an amphibious force would attack and raid major cities on the eastern coast, and (3) another force would attack and capture New Orleans.

The first stage of the campaign ended in failure when a small American naval squadron defeated a larger British fleet on Lake Champlain on September 11, 1814. Without control of the lake, the British commander would not risk an invasion, and the force turned back.

The second stage was initially more successful. A British force landed in Maryland in August and marched toward Washington. In the **Battle of Bladensburg**, the British scattered a large force of American militia and cleared a path to the American capital. President Madison and other government leaders fled in haste, and the British army marched into the city unopposed. Madison's wife, Dolley, helped save several important items from the Executive Mansion before she fled, including one of Gilbert Stuart's famous paintings of George Washington. British officers dined in the president's mansion on a meal that the Madisons had left cooking. Soldiers soon set fire to the Capitol, the president's mansion, and several other important government buildings. British admiral Sir George Cockburn (KOH burn) personally ordered the destruction of an anti-British newspaper; he told his men particularly to destroy all the type for the letter *C* so that the paper could print no more attacks on him. Only a series of severe thunderstorms prevented the entire city from burning to the ground.

The British had no intention of holding Washington, the value of which was more symbolic than strategic, so they next turned their attention to Baltimore. That city, however, was protected by a larger, more disciplined force and by the well-designed **Fort McHenry**. The British fleet tried vainly to bombard the fort into submission. After three days of fighting, during which the British commanding general was killed, the British abandoned the task. The whole force left Chesapeake Bay and joined the effort to capture New Orleans.

The War in the South

In the South, the War of 1812 was complicated in a manner that the British never expected. As a result of Tecumseh's efforts among the southern tribes, civil war broke out among the Creek Indians in the Mississippi Territory (modern Alabama and Mississippi). The conflict between pro-American and anti-American Creeks grew sharp, and white settlers bordering Indian lands began to suffer. The government authorized Tennessee general **Andrew Jackson** to help the friendly Creeks and to defend the South against the British. Jackson was not a brilliant strategist, but he was a firm

"Don't Give Up the Ship!"

When Perry won his great victory on Lake Erie, the flag flying over his ship read, "Don't Give Up the Ship!" The quotation was by a commander who had lost his life—and his ship—in battle only a few months earlier.

On June 1, 1813, the U.S.S. *Chesapeake* (the same ship that the *Leopard* had humiliated in 1807) under Captain James Lawrence sailed out of Boston Harbor to meet the British warship *Shannon*. The two ships were relatively equal, but the crew of the British ship was more experienced and better trained. The *Shannon* manhandled the *Chesapeake* in battle. When a musket ball hit Captain Lawrence in the stomach, he said to his men, "Fight her 'till she sinks, and don't give up the ship."

But the British did capture it, and Lawrence died before the ship reached harbor. His words lived on, however. The phrase became a motto for the U.S. Navy. Perry's flag is now on display in Memorial Hall at the U.S. Naval Academy in Annapolis, Maryland.

General Andrew Jackson was the hero of the Battle of New Orleans.

"By the Dawn's Early Light"

Just before the British attack on Fort McHenry, Baltimore lawyer **Francis Scott Key** and a friend sailed out to the British fleet under a flag of truce. They asked for the release of a civilian doctor, William Beanes, who had been captured by the British. The British commander agreed to release the doctor but refused to allow them to leave because the fleet was preparing to attack Fort McHenry. The Americans had to stay aboard until the battle was over.

Key had a front-row seat as he watched the British fleet shell the fort. As the pounding continued into the night, the anxious lawyer strained to see what was happening. As dawn broke, he saw the American flag flying proudly above the fort, signaling that the bombardment had failed. Key gazed at the flag and was inspired. He began writing on the back of an envelope the first verse of a poem that came into his head. What he called "The Defense of Fort McHenry" we know today as "The Star-Spangled Banner." He wrote the other verses after he got back to shore. Set to music, the poem became one of the most popular patriotic songs in America. Eventually, in 1931, Congress officially proclaimed "The Star-Spangled Banner" the national anthem of the United States.

and unflinching leader. Jackson's men called him "Old Hickory" because he was as lean and tough as a hickory branch. Jackson knew how to handle his frontier army. When some of his militia tried to leave during the campaign, for example, Jackson laid his rifle across his horse's neck and promised to personally shoot the first man who tried to leave. Jackson's force won a series of victories against the Creeks, climaxing in the **Battle of Horseshoe Bend** (1814), in which he nearly annihilated the unfriendly Creeks.

Jackson had little time to savor his victory, however. He marched quickly to New Orleans late in 1814 to meet the British thrust there. At New Orleans Jackson stationed his troops and artillery behind fortifications made of earthworks and cotton bales. On January 8, 1815, the overconfident British, believing that their troops would make short work of the American rabble, marched directly on Jackson's lines. Old Hickory's massed artillery tore huge gaps in the British lines, and his frontier sharpshooters picked off those who managed to survive the cannons. The British lost two thousand men; the Americans lost thirteen.

The **Battle of New Orleans** was the most stunning victory of the War of 1812, but it was fought after the war was over. The **Treaty of Ghent** (signed December 24, 1814), climaxing four months of negotiations, had ended hostilities some two weeks earlier. Slow communications from Europe, however, kept that news from America for several weeks. Nonetheless, the battle made Jackson the greatest hero of the war.

Results of the War

The Treaty of Ghent was a peace without victory; conditions largely returned to what they had been in 1812. Britain and the United States simply wanted to stop fighting, and both were willing to settle their differences diplomatically later. The United States did profit from the war, however. Tecumseh's confederation was finished, and the Northwest was wide open to settlement. Also, the British blockade unintentionally spurred the growth of American industry and manufacturing (discussed in Chapter 11).

The war also brought changes in attitude. For years, the United States had tried in vain to distance itself from affairs in Europe. After the war, the nation was secure enough to retreat from the rest of the world into a shell of isolationism. Not until the Spanish-American War in 1898 would Americans again become deeply involved in foreign affairs.

Perhaps the chief result was a sense of national pride and honor. In a toast after the war, naval commander Stephen Decatur captured this spirit when he said, "Our country! In her intercourse with foreign nations, may she always be in the right; but our country, right or wrong." This surge of patriotism became an important influence in shaping the period after the war, the "Era of Good Feelings" under President James Monroe.

Section Quiz

1. By what three pieces of legislation did the United States hope to use economic pressure to avoid war with Great Britain?

2. Give at least two reasons the War Hawks offered for going to war with Britain.

3. What five reasons did President Madison give for going to war against Britain?

4. What was Britain's threefold plan for winning the War of 1812? How did each stage of the plan fare in the actual fighting?

✱ Some people have suggested that "The Star-Spangled Banner" should be replaced with a new national anthem. Do you agree or disagree? Why? If you agree, what song would you substitute as the anthem?

V. The Era of Good Feelings

The "Virginia dynasty" of presidents continued in 1816 when Secretary of State **James Monroe** was elected to succeed James Madison. Monroe maintained the dominance of the Jeffersonian philosophy into the 1820s. His quiet, modest manner pleased and impressed even the staunchest anti-Jeffersonians. So popular—or at least so unobjectionable—was Monroe that in the election for his second term he came within one electoral vote of becoming the only president besides Washington to be elected unanimously. The president's popularity, the glow of postwar triumph, and the collapse of all political opposition to the Republicans caused Monroe's two terms to be known as **the Era of Good Feelings**.

Demise of the Federalists

One cause of the Era of Good Feelings was the collapse of the Federalist Party. In 1812, the Federalists halted their decline by joining antiwar Republicans against Madison. The election of 1812 was so close in the Electoral College that the switch of Pennsylvania alone would have given the victory to Federalist-Republican DeWitt Clinton instead of Madison. Throughout the War of 1812, the Federalists led a loud chorus of protest against the progress and conduct of the war.

During the conflict's darkest days in 1814, representatives of the New England states—mostly Federalists—met in Hartford, Connecticut. The **Hartford Convention** opposed the war and hinted that New England might secede from the Union if its demands were not met. Unfortunately for the Federalists, the Treaty of Ghent and the Battle of New Orleans soon followed the Hartford Convention and removed much of the reason for its existence. If the Federalist Party was dying before the war, then it was clearly dead after it. Within a few years, the discredited party disappeared entirely.

Mending Fences with Britain

The good feelings were not necessarily limited to the United States. The Treaty of Ghent stopped the fighting with Britain, but it did not settle the problems between the two nations. The United States and Great Britain, therefore, carried out extensive negotiations to iron out their differences. One of the first and most important of these agreements was the **Rush-Bagot** (BAG ut) **Treaty** (1817), which called for disarmament in the Great Lakes. This treaty has the distinction of being one of the few disarmament treaties in history that has succeeded. Its provisions were eventually extended along the entire U.S.-Canadian border as the nations advanced westward. The United States and Canada have maintained peaceful

James Monroe was the last of the Virginia dynasty of presidents.

relations for nearly two centuries with no fortifications, barbed wire, or large armies between them. In 1818, the United States and Britain agreed to occupy the Oregon Territory on the Pacific Ocean jointly until they could decide how to divide it.

Conflict in Florida

Some members of Congress, especially the War Hawks, had hoped that the War of 1812 would result in the conquest of Florida. Although Spain exercised nominal control over the area, anarchy would be a better description of the government. Pirates, escaped slaves, and others not only lived in Florida but also used it as a haven from which to make raids across the U.S. border. When violence broke out between the Indians and settlers in Georgia, the American government authorized General Andrew Jackson to take a force into Florida and crush the Indians. In 1818, Jackson punished the Indians in a swift campaign. He also arrested two British citizens who were accused of aiding the Indians. After speedy trials, Old Hickory had one hanged and the other shot. Then, for good measure, Jackson's army captured Pensacola, the capital of Spanish Florida.

Jackson's actions exceeded his orders; the government was certainly not interested in offending the British again. But Jackson's campaign was enormously popular in the United States. Fortunately, the British were not interested in going to war over a couple of obscure Indian traders. The Spanish were understandably angry, but Secretary of State **John Quincy Adams** decided to take a hard line with the Spanish government. Jackson was only defending American lives and property, Adams argued, and the Spanish should do a better job of policing their territory. Jackson's campaign showed Spain how helpless it would be if the United States found sufficient excuse to take Florida. Rather than end up with nothing, the Spanish government decided to sell the region. Under the provisions of the **Adams-Onis Treaty**, the U.S. took possession of Florida in 1821 at a cost of $5 million. The United States now possessed all territory south of Canada and east of the Mississippi River, as well as its holdings in the Louisiana Territory.

The Monroe Doctrine

The impact of Napoleon's conquering armies and ideas was not limited to Europe. When Napoleon conquered Spain and Portugal, the Spanish and Portuguese possessions in Latin America leaped at the chance to be free. Led by revolutionary leaders **Simón Bolívar** and **José de San Martín**, most of Latin America broke from its European overlords and founded independent republics. After the fall of Napoleon, Spain began to look longingly at its former colonies, and the other powers of Europe indicated their willingness to help crush the "dangerous" revolutionary republics. One exception to this mood of reconquest was Great Britain. The British had established a profitable trade with the new nations and had no desire to see them become colonies again. So the British government asked the United States if it would join Britain in proclaiming that European powers should not intervene in the Americas.

President Monroe and Secretary of State Adams considered the offer. They decided that rather than tying America to Britain, the nation should issue its own warning. In 1823, in his annual message to Congress, President Monroe declared, "The American continents, by the free and independent condition which they have assumed and maintain, are henceforth not to be considered as subjects for future colonization by any European powers." Furthermore, he added, "In the wars of the European powers in matters relating to themselves we have never taken any part, nor does it comport with our policy so to do."

With the **Monroe Doctrine**, as Monroe's statement of policy came to be called, the United States established two principles: European nations could not intervene in the Western Hemisphere (except where they already held colonies), and the United States would not meddle in European affairs. When issued, the statement was little more than a paper pledge since the United States lacked the military might to back it up. The Monroe Doctrine, however, has become a cornerstone of American foreign policy. Since 1823, numerous presidents and statesmen have defended its principles and expanded its meaning. It affects the manner in which the United States conducts its foreign policy even today.

The Monroe Doctrine embodied one of the cherished tenets of Jeffersonianism and also solidified one result of the War of 1812—it formalized America's determination to remain isolated from Europe and its affairs. The decision to remain aloof proved to be a wise one. As Monroe's term of office and his Era of Good Feelings drew to a close, the nation confronted serious internal problems and important internal developments. The young nation had to direct all its energies toward expanding and developing the frontier, harnessing new technologies, and grappling with the problem of slavery—all of which would test the character of America's government. The Era of Good Feelings, and of Jeffersonianism in general, ended with ominous clouds of conflict on the horizon.

Section Quiz

1. Why was Monroe's time in office called the Era of Good Feelings?
2. Whose campaign in Florida motivated Spain to sell that territory to the United States?
3. What treaty settled a border dispute between the United States and Great Britain? What treaty enabled the U.S. to purchase Florida from Spain?
4. What are the two basic principles of the Monroe Doctrine?
★ Why has the Monroe Doctrine been necessary for the regions south of the United States but not for those to the north?

People, Places, and Things to Remember

Thomas Jefferson
Jeffersonian Republicanism
Twelfth Amendment
Chesapeake affair
Embargo Act
John Marshall
Marbury v. Madison
judicial review
delegated powers
Gibbons v. Ogden
McCulloch v. Maryland
implied powers
Barbary states
Napoleon Bonaparte
Louisiana Purchase
Meriwether Lewis
William Clark
Zebulon Pike
"Mad Anthony" Wayne
Battle of Fallen Timbers
Treaty of Fort Greenville
William Henry Harrison
Tecumseh
the Prophet
Battle of Tippecanoe
James Madison
impressment
Non-Intercourse Act
Macon's Bill Number Two
War Hawks
Henry Clay
John C. Calhoun
U.S.S. *Constitution* ("Old Ironsides")
Oliver Hazard Perry
Battle of Lake Erie
Battle of the Thames
Battle of Bladensburg
Fort McHenry
Andrew Jackson
Francis Scott Key
Battle of Horseshoe Bend
Battle of New Orleans
Treaty of Ghent
James Monroe
Era of Good Feelings
Hartford Convention
Rush-Bagot Treaty
John Quincy Adams
Adams-Onis Treaty
Simón Bolívar
José de San Martín
Monroe Doctrine

Chapter Review

Making Connections

1. What was the view of Thomas Jefferson and William Henry Harrison concerning American Indian policy? Why was their view unsatisfactory to the Indians?
2. Why were each of the following battles important to the overall course of the War of 1812: Lake Erie, the Thames, and Horseshoe Bend?
3. Name at least three results of the War of 1812 and explain why each was important.

Developing History Skills

1. How did Tecumseh hope to slow the advance of the Americans into the Northwest Territory?
2. Do the positive results of Jackson's invasion of Florida excuse his exceeding his orders?

Thinking Critically

1. Do you think that Thomas Jefferson's dream of a dominantly agricultural America was a realistic idea?
2. Does the principle of judicial review make the Supreme Court too powerful? Defend your answer.

Living as a Christian Citizen

1. Thomas Jefferson designed the curriculum for the University of Virginia on Enlightenment ideals. Write a paragraph outlining the core courses that a Christian university should have and how Christianity should influence the teaching of those courses.
2. Imagine that you are a pastor or a pastor's wife during the Jeffersonian era. How would you respond to the troubles in American and Indian relations?

"All Creation Going to the White House" by Robert Cruikshank

The Age of Jackson (1820-1840)

   I. Crosscurrents

  II. The Jackson Years

 III. Party Politics

"Just think, Mama! This sofa is a millionth part mine."

A young Democrat to her parents as she romped on White House furniture during Jackson's inauguration, 1829

Henry Clay proposed a broad expansion of government power through his American System.

Although the period from 1820 to 1840 is named after its hero, **Andrew Jackson**, it was actually well under way before Jackson's 1829 inauguration. Since the beginning of the century, powerful crosscurrents were roiling the political and social seas. Jackson would ride into office on its turbulent crest, but the age was shaped by forces much larger than any man. These forces were widespread currents of nationalism, sectionalism, and democratization that originated before Jackson's presidency, and they would shape America's future long after Old Hickory had gone.

I. Crosscurrents

Nationalism

The years immediately following the War of 1812 saw a growing spirit of nationalism throughout the country. The relief and the prospects that came with peace bolstered national pride and vision. The rapid expansion of the period gave the Star-Spangled Banner a larger constellation, including six more states in the West and Deep South by 1821: Louisiana (1812), Indiana (1816), Mississippi (1817), Illinois (1818), Alabama (1819), and Missouri (1821). In addition, a new breed of young, capable, and energetic leaders—men such as John Quincy Adams and Daniel Webster of New England, Henry Clay of Kentucky, and John C. Calhoun of South Carolina—were advancing the vision of a strong, burgeoning America.

At the heart of that new nationalism was a concern for the economic strength of the nation, a union of states bound by cords of commerce. **Henry Clay**, the chief advocate of this economic nationalism in Congress, dubbed it the **American System**. Clay's system consisted of three parts: protective tariffs, renewal of the National Bank, and internal improvements.

Protective Tariff

Necessity being the mother of invention, Jefferson's Embargo Act (Chapter 9) and the trade disruptions brought on by the War of 1812 had the unexpected benefit of spurring the growth of American manufacturing. This was an important step toward economic independence from Europe. Since colonial days, America had served as both a source of raw materials for Europe, particularly Britain, and a market for British finished goods. American manufacturing would shake up this longstanding arrangement. The British were quick to see the threat to their own interests posed by America's infant industry, and they determined to nip it in the bud. One member of the British Parliament even urged his country to sell goods to America well below cost "to stifle in the cradle, those rising manufactures in the United States, which war has forced into existence, contrary to the natural course of things."

A **tariff** is a tax on imported goods, and a **protective tariff** is an unusually high tariff designed to shield a nation's manufactures from potentially fatal foreign competition. The **Tariff of 1816** was America's first such protectionist legislation. The tariff, however, was a two-edged sword. Although it encouraged some economic growth, the tariff also discouraged competition, which meant higher consumer prices. In addition, regions of the country that produced raw goods, such as the agrarian South, or that depended upon shipping for their livelihood, such as New England, were hurt

Types of Tariffs

Traditionally, tariffs have been of two types. *Revenue tariffs*, relatively low taxes on imports, raise income for the operation of the government but have little effect on the average consumer or the greater economy. *Protective tariffs*, however, are designed to protect one or more industries against foreign competition. They impose such high taxes on imports that they adversely affect the entire national economy, especially the average consumer. They are aimed at the short term, not the long term. Protective tariffs generally backfire in that they lead foreign countries to retaliate with their own high tariffs on American goods, thereby stifling free trade and leading to a general economic downturn. Too often, they have also contributed to war. As one economist wisely said, "If goods don't cross borders, armies will."

by the loss of foreign trade. In the postwar nationalist euphoria, economic independence outweighed other considerations, but protective tariffs later became a sore point between the sections.

Second National Bank

The charter for the first National Bank expired in 1811, setting off an avalanche of inflationary paper money issued by a motley assortment of private banks. The financial problems created by inflation were only compounded by the war, all of which made it difficult for the national government to meet its obligations.

Interestingly, the Republicans of the 1790s were vehemently opposed to both a national bank and a protective tariff. When in power, however, they tended to set aside their constitutional qualms in favor of such "Federalist" measures. In 1816, nationalistic Republicans approved a twenty-year charter on a second Bank of the United States, patterned after Hamilton's first central bank. Such a bank would assist economic growth by providing uniform currency, a source for loans to the public and private sectors, and a depository for government revenue.

Internal Improvements

Another key element of the American System was **internal improvements**—funding for roads, canals, and harbor developments that would bolster commerce and communications. Such improvements would help link western goods with eastern markets and provide better routes for trans-Appalachian settlement.

Despite the many advantages of internal improvements and their popularity in the growing West, they were the least successful aspect of the American System. President Madison and others believed that they lacked constitutional authority to fund such projects. Why should Maine, they reasoned, be taxed to pave a road in Maryland? Roads and canals were the responsibility of the state or locality that they served. Younger Republicans complained that the president's narrow views were hindering economic growth. Calhoun, for example, protested to the president that the Constitution "was not a thesis for the logician to exercise his ingenuity on; . . . it ought to be construed with plain good sense."

Before the issue of internal improvements bogged down in the constitutional quagmire, one important step was approved: the building of the **National Road**. Begun during Jefferson's administration, the graveled road extended from Baltimore to Cumberland, Maryland, but lack of funding halted construction. After considerable debate during the Madison years, Congress appropriated additional funds to extend the route to Wheeling, Virginia (now West Virginia). Further funding in 1825 drove the road into the heart of the new western states, reaching Zanesville, Ohio, and by 1839 ending in Vandalia, Illinois. Today, motorists on Interstate 70 east of St. Louis travel basically the same route that pioneering families took in the 1830s by covered wagon or ox cart or on foot.

Sectionalism

Monroe's Era of Good Feelings turned out to be little more than that—just feelings. When hard times came to the country and tough questions were raised in Congress, the good feelings went bad and drove the sections of the country further apart. Sectional strife would have a large impact on the politics of the coming Jacksonian era.

Panic of 1819

After the War of 1812, the resumption of trade and the growth of domestic industry and western land sales brought economic good times to the country. Two unrelated events an ocean apart, however, quickly sent America's postwar prosperity tumbling, resulting in a depression, or *panic*, called the **Panic of 1819**.

In Liverpool, England, the price of cotton fell sharply, owing to higher American prices and the introduction of cheap Asian cotton from India. The collapse of cotton brought down other American goods. The financial failure was due in part to the high protectionist Tariff of 1816, and many people, particularly in the hard-hit South, were quick to point this out. The Virginia Agricultural Society told Congress in 1820 that the tariff unfairly favored a privileged class by granting them "oppressive monopolies, which are ultimately to grind both us and our children after us 'into dust and ashes.'"

The second factor contributing to the Panic of 1819 was the irresponsible action of state banks and the National Bank. The opening of western land purchases seemed to present a golden opportunity for banks to make loans to speculators and settlers. Banks, paper money, and loans all multiplied in the race for riches. When the economy soured, the Bank of the United States tried to whip the state banks into shape by tightening the money supply. As a result, many people defaulted on loans, and some people lost their lands and homes. Many people in the West and South thought that the Bank of the United States, which had been rife with fraud and scandal, was saving itself by oppressing the people. In those regions, a legacy of bitterness toward the National Bank grew.

Missouri Compromise

The routine admission of new states suddenly sparked a heated controversy, one that John Quincy Adams afterward described as a "title page to a great tragic volume."

When Missouri applied for statehood in 1818, its constitution permitted slavery (not surprising, considering that Missouri had ten thousand slaves at the time). Since there were already eleven slave states and eleven free states, the question of political balance between the South and the North lay at the heart of the debate. The South, some time before, had lost control in the House of Representatives to the more populous North; balance in the Senate, therefore, remained critical to the region's political equality.

In February 1819 Representative James Tallmadge of New York recommended that the act authorizing Missouri to become a state be amended to virtually prohibit slavery. The Tallmadge Amendment brought an outcry from the slave states because it interfered with a state's prerogatives and threatened the balance in the Senate. Voting along sectional lines, House members approved the Tallmadge Amendment despite Southern objections. On a more even playing field, however, the amendment was defeated in the Senate.

Maine's application for statehood in the summer of 1819 and Speaker of the House Henry Clay's skillful handling of the controversy helped provide a compromise solution to the statehood stalemate. The **Missouri Compromise** of 1820 proposed that Maine be admitted as a free state and Missouri as a slave state, and that in the rest of the Louisiana Territory, slavery not be permitted north of 36° 30', Missouri's southern boundary. By a narrow margin, Congress approved the Missouri Compromise and authorized Missouri to submit a constitution, the final step in the statehood process.

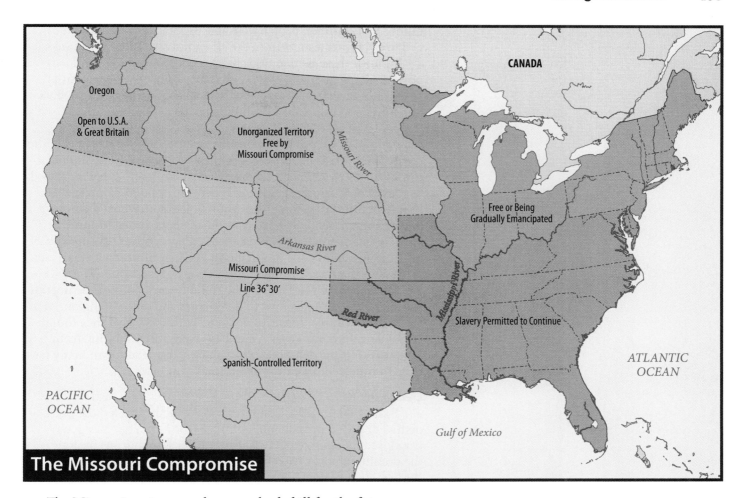

The Missouri Compromise

The Missouri controversy, however, boded ill for the future. Political lines were drawn between the sections, and with the ever-expanding westward settlement, Missouri represented a problem that would not soon go away. Former president Thomas Jefferson said of the debate, "This momentous question, like a fire bell in the night, awakened and filled me with terror. I considered it at once as the knell of the Union."

Democratization

Another growing force during the first quarter of the nineteenth century was the increasing openness of the political process. This democratization gave the average citizen a greater voice in his government. Religious changes played a role as well. In addition to the declining emphasis on God's sovereignty in salvation and the growing prominence given to human choice, men came to believe that they should have a greater voice in the political realm.

Political expansion was evident in three major changes during the period. First was the extension of voting rights to all adult white males, not just property owners. New western states entering the Union, unbound by the political customs of the older states, drafted more democratic constitutions that helped open the way for universal manhood suffrage for whites and some free blacks by the 1830s. Second, the people gained a greater voice in presidential elections. In 1800 most electors in the Electoral College were chosen by their state's legislature. After 1816, however, the majority of presidential electors were selected by popular vote, giving voters a greater influence in the choosing of their president. Even though increasing numbers of common people were able to vote, the electorate continued to elect their leaders from the elites, not from their own ranks.

In turn, these democratic changes encouraged the third important change—the fracturing of the one-party system and the emergence of a strong two-party system. Since Jefferson's 1800 victory, the Republicans had dominated national politics. In fact, with the exception of Madison's unhappy presidency, the Federalists ceased even to be a threat in presidential contests. Without genuine competition, this single-party dominance was in effect a nonpartisan system. It seemed for a time that national politics had returned to President Washington's ideal. It became popular to criticize any hint of political division. Even Andrew Jackson, who would one day be among the most partisan of presidents, urged Monroe in 1816 "to exterminate the monster called party spirit." Nonpartisan unity, however, like the Era of Good Feelings of which it was a part, proved to be a fragile thing.

Just as religion influenced the trend toward political democratization, political trends toward democracy influenced religion. Men replaced traditional forms of doctrine with those that they found reasonable. In many cases Americans were still reasoning from Scripture, but the democratic inclination also resulted in many new cults in nineteenth-century America.

Death of "King Caucus"

From 1796 to 1820, a congressional caucus selected the presidential and vice-presidential nominees for its party. (A **caucus** is a closed meeting of party leaders.) After Republicans became the dominant party, therefore, a handful of congressmen picked the president of the United States. The members of the "Virginia Dynasty"—Jefferson, Madison, and Monroe—serving a total of twenty-four years, were selected by the closed-door caucus method.

Despite those impressive presidential choices, the reign of "King Caucus" understandably came under fire as undemocratic. As early as 1800, one newspaper criticized "this factious meeting, this self appointed, self elected, self delegated club or caucus, or conspiracy," charging that about twenty-four men were deciding "for the people of the United States who should be president and vice president."

The 1824 election proved to be a political turning point in America. The caucus system of nominating candidates was completely discredited, and the divisive presidential campaign that year ended the myth of a nonpartisan government.

A "Corrupt Bargain"

Four men threw their hats into the ring as candidates for president in 1824. William H. Crawford of Georgia was the choice of the dying congressional caucus, a fact that did him more harm than good. **John Quincy Adams**, son of the former president and Monroe's secretary of state, announced his candidacy. In addition, two westerners joined the slate of candidates: the popular Speaker of the House, Kentuckian Henry Clay, and the "Hero of New Orleans," General Andrew Jackson of Tennessee.

The four-way race was not among competing parties, since all the candidates were at least in name Republicans, heirs of Mr. Jefferson. Rather, the race was between competing personalities and regions of the country. The results were predictable—no candidate received a majority of the votes. In the Electoral College tally,

John Quincy Adams

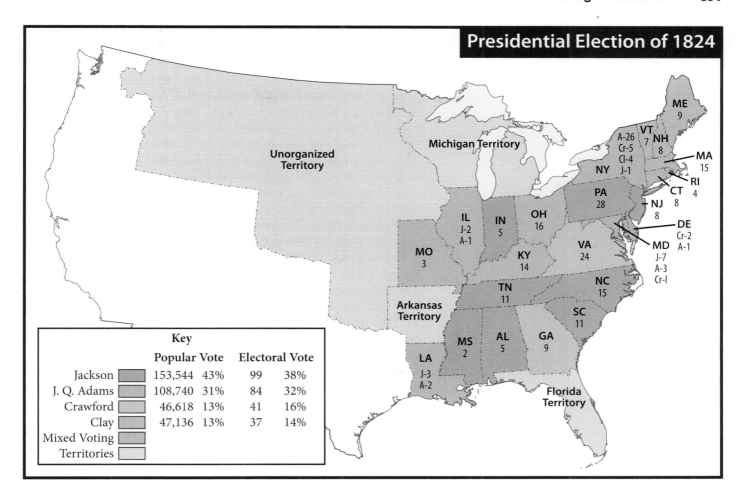

Presidential Election of 1824

Michigan Territory

Unorganized Territory

ME 9

VT 7

NH 8

MA 15

NY
A-26
Cr-5
Cl-4
J-1

RI 4

CT 8

PA 28

NJ 8

DE
Cr-2
A-1

MD
J-7
A-3
Cr-1

IL
J-2
A-1

IN 5

OH 16

VA 24

MO 3

KY 14

Arkansas Territory

TN 11

NC 15

SC 11

LA
J-3
A-2

MS 2

AL 5

GA 9

Florida Territory

Key

	Popular Vote		Electoral Vote	
Jackson	153,544	43%	99	38%
J. Q. Adams	108,740	31%	84	32%
Crawford	46,618	13%	41	16%
Clay	47,136	13%	37	14%
Mixed Voting				
Territories				

Jackson polled 99, Adams 84, Crawford 41, and Clay 37. The popular vote, which was recorded for the first time, gave (in rounded figures) Jackson 154,000, Adams 109,000, Crawford 47,000, and Clay 47,000. Since no candidate had won a majority, the Twelfth Amendment required that the election be thrown into the House of Representatives, where the president would be chosen from among the top three candidates from the Electoral College.

Clay, who did not make the cut, was placed in a unique position. He could not win the election, but as the powerful Speaker of the House, he could decide who would. Clay preferred the nationalist policies of Adams, and he considered Jackson unqualified. Clay also nursed his own ambition of being the first president from the western states. It was an easy decision for him. He guided the voting to give Adams a victory on the first ballot.

Jackson's supporters were outraged. Old Hickory had won the most electoral and the most popular votes in the general election; why then was Adams president? Adams then compounded the problem by nominating Clay as secretary of state, a position that had already produced three presidents. Jackson's supporters claimed that Adams and Clay had made a "**corrupt bargain**," an underhanded deal to give Adams the presidency in return for making Clay secretary. Although no proof of a prior deal exists, the charge stung Adams personally and impaired his administration from the start.

Adams had had a distinguished political career, having served capably in several offices. His performance as secretary of state under James Monroe—particularly his settling of differences with Britain and his negotiation of the purchase of Florida from Spain—have caused some historians to rate him as one of the greatest secretaries of state in history. He was unquestionably brilliant and morally conscientious and consistent. Nevertheless, he was an ineffective president. Like his father, Adams had little patience for the backslapping ways of politics, and he never seemed to understand the people he was asked to lead. In his first annual address to Congress, for example, Adams urged the members to support his sometimes unpopular programs, saying that the members should not fold up their arms "and proclaim to the world that we are palsied by the will of our constituents." His handling voters so ineptly strengthened the pro-Jackson forces all the more.

One of the key features of Adams's administration was its strong nationalist emphasis. Expanding on Clay's American System, Adams worked for higher protective tariffs to encourage American manufacturing and internal improvements. He even proposed federal funding for higher education and the arts.

That nationalist thrust became a distinguishing mark of Adams's wing of the party, which became known as the **National Republicans**. The Jackson wing kept the old name, Democratic-Republicans, but eventually dropped the "Republican" part, keeping the name by which the party is still called, the **Democratic Party**.

Rematch and Revenge

The candidates and perhaps the outcome of the 1828 election were probably determined four years earlier. It turned out to be an Adams-Jackson rematch. By that time, many of the former Crawford and Clay supporters had moved into the Jackson camp, including a shrewd New York senator named **Martin Van Buren**. Van Buren's skill as a politician earned the 5′6″ native of Kinderhook, New York, the name "Little Magician." He helped organize the Democratic effort and urged Jackson to avoid mentioning divisive issues, emphasizing instead a *symbolic* campaign—Old Hickory, the friend of the common man.

Jackson and his running mate, **John C. Calhoun** of South Carolina, won by a landslide, getting 56 percent of the popular vote and an electoral tally of 178 to 83. The election's two-party competition also boosted voter participation. For the first time, a million voters cast ballots for the presidency, double the number in the 1824 election.

It seemed to run in the family. John Adams had been swept from the White House in 1800 and now, nearly thirty years later, his son John Quincy Adams was suffering the same fate at the hands of the people. The people's hands, however, were damaging more than Adams's pride the day he left office. They were stripping wallpaper from the White House walls for souvenirs, scooping out globs of melting ice cream, dripping trails of it on the carpet, smashing furniture and glass, and gripping the hand of the mansion's newest occupant, Andrew Jackson, just before he slipped out a back door to leave the house to its fate. As one unamused observer grumbled, "The reign of King Mob seemed triumphant."

Although it is true that the invading army of Jackson's supporters could be blamed for being a bit raucous, they should also be credited with providing a fitting start to a new American era—the age of Jacksonian democracy, the age of the common man.

Section Quiz

1. What were the three components of Henry Clay's American System?

2. What was America's first protectionist legislation?

3. What two factors contributed to the Panic of 1819?

4. What were the three provisions of the Missouri Compromise?

5. What two men did Andrew Jackson's supporters accuse of making a "corrupt bargain" in the presidential election of 1824?

★ Evaluate the costs and benefits of the democratization of American politics and religion.

II. The Jackson Years

Old Hickory

The democratic movement that won Jackson the presidency was underway before Old Hickory became its popular hero. While it could be argued that had there not been an Andrew Jackson, it would have been necessary to invent one, Jackson's remarkable life supplied more than enough material for his hero's image. By 1828 Jackson's biography read like *A Brief History of the United States.*

Jackson was born in the Carolina backcountry in 1767. His parents were Irish-Presbyterians who had left Ulster just two years before their son was born. Frontier life then was crude and perilous. Andrew Sr. died in an accident while clearing his fields for spring planting. A few days later his grieving widow, Betty, gave birth to a third son, giving him the name of her dead husband.

Young Andrew's early life was as rough-and-tumble as the land in which he lived. At thirteen he joined Patriot forces against the invading British, serving as a messenger. In April 1781 Andrew and his brother Robert were captured by British cavalry. When one of the officers ordered Andrew to clean his boots, Jackson refused to give the redcoat so much as a bow. The enraged officer slashed the boy on his head with a saber and hacked at his raised arm. Jackson would bear the scars of his defiance for the rest of his life.

After the war Jackson studied law in Salisbury, North Carolina, and was admitted to the bar. The young lawyer soon landed a position as a public prosecutor in the Tennessee Territory. The opening West well suited the fiery, energetic Jackson. He acquired land, slaves, horses, and a taste for politics. Jackson became a state judge and in 1796 was elected to a term in Congress, where he gained some respect for his straightforward though roughshod manner.

Jackson's reputation, however, was not made in Washington; it was forged on the frontier, fighting Indians and redcoats. General Jackson drove his men hard, but he drove himself harder. His grit earned him the admiration of his ranks. "He's tough as hickory," they would say, and so he was.

As president, Andrew Jackson was not an innovator. His great success was as a symbol of what America had become. In broad strokes his life mirrored the life of the young republic. With Jackson in the White House, Jefferson's self-evident truths were indeed evident. America offered ordinary people extraordinary opportunity,

Claims to Jackson

Andrew Jackson was born in a region known as "the Waxhaws" (after the Waxhaw Indians who originally lived there). It encompassed modern-day Lancaster County, South Carolina, and Union County, North Carolina. No one knows in precisely which section Jackson was born, so both states claim him as their native son. Perhaps the greatest claim on Jackson, however, is by Tennessee, where Jackson spent most of his life and built his mansion, the Hermitage.

and this is why Jackson's tumultuous inauguration was a celebration for common folks.

The People's President

Spoils of Victory

Jackson's partisan victory for "the people" ushered in a change in the filling of government jobs. The new president believed that public service should not be a lifelong career. Up to that time bureaucratic officials such as clerks, postmasters, revenue collectors, and court officers were appointed on a fairly permanent basis. Jackson held that men who stayed in public office for too long were prone to be corrupted by their power. Accordingly, after reasonable intervals, particularly with the change of administrations, rotation in office should occur.

Jackson actually took a low-key approach to replacing officeholders. During his first year in office he turned out only 9 percent of the appointed officeholders he inherited, and less than 20 percent during his term.

The significance of Jackson's replacement of government officeholders was not so much what he did as what he started. The **spoils system**, as this patronage came to be called, would endure for half a century, taking on a highly partisan political character. While it is true that Jackson's policy did shake up an entrenched bureaucracy, it also removed some highly qualified individuals from office at times and replaced them with highly unqualified individuals. Neither did the spoils system necessarily make public servants more responsive to the public, since the bureaucrats owed their jobs to their party leaders, not to the people.

Kitchen Cabinet

Jackson's cabinet members were given their posts as political rewards for services rendered during the campaign, but they actually had little influence with the president. Jackson's real advisors were a close circle of friends that critics called his "**Kitchen Cabinet**." It included newspaper editors, prominent Democrats in Congress, and his secretary of state, Martin Van Buren—all political insiders. Increasingly the president was taking on the role of party leader.

Almost from the outset Jackson's administration was torn by infighting, particularly the jockeying for power between Martin Van Buren and Vice President Calhoun. Van Buren increasingly sought the favor of President Jackson against Calhoun. In addition, the sectional differences between the New Yorker and the South Carolinian heightened the dispute, particularly over the tariff question. Calhoun, who had been an ardent nationalist in the War of 1812, was becoming the major spokesman for the interests of the South.

Nullification Crisis

At the time of Jackson's inauguration, the tariff controversy was raging again. In 1828 Congress passed a new higher protective tariff with rates of up to 50 percent on some imports. The more industrialized North welcomed the tariff, while the South dubbed it the "**Tariff of Abominations**."

Southern leaders recognized the constitutional right of Congress to levy modest tariffs to raise revenue (Article V, Section 8, Clause 1). They declared unconstitutional, however, tariffs aimed at protecting a particular class or favoring one section of the country over another. As we have seen, the North favored a high protec-

Andrew Jackson

The Preacher and the President

Peter Cartwright, a fearless Methodist preacher during the Jackson years, was invited to speak in a Nashville-area church. The pastor of the church recognized Andrew Jackson in the crowd and, worried that Cartwright might offend the president, tugged on Cartwright's coat and warned him of the presence of the distinguished man.

"Who is General Jackson?" Cartwright roared. He then warned that if the general "don't get his soul converted," then "God will damn him" as quickly as He would any other sinner.

The next day, Cartwright ran into Jackson on the street, and Jackson said, "Mr. Cartwright, you are a man after my own heart. A minister of Jesus Christ ought to love everybody and fear no mortal man."

Cartwright later joined Jackson's Democratic Party and served as a representative in the Illinois state legislature. In 1846 Cartwright even ran for Congress but lost to an up-and-coming figure in Illinois politics—Abraham Lincoln.

John C. Calhoun   Robert Young Hayne   Daniel Webster

tive tariff to curb competing foreign imports. The South, however, depended on foreign imports in exchange for its agricultural exports. Higher tariffs meant higher prices in the South and higher sales in the North. Southerners argued that this was unfair since agricultural exports of cotton and tobacco from their region, which made up two-thirds of the country's total exports, already paid for the imports. Revenue the government received from the tariffs therefore came largely from the South but was mostly spent to fund internal improvements in the North. In short, the high tariff was a discriminatory tax.

In December 1828 the South Carolina legislature denounced the tariff as unconstitutional. It further suggested, as had Jefferson and Madison in the Kentucky and Virginia Resolutions, that any unconstitutional federal act could be nullified by the states. Georgia declared the tariff unconstitutional that same month. Mississippi and Virginia did the same two months later.

The issue of nullification was drawn from an anti-tariff pamphlet written anonymously by Vice President Calhoun. The South Carolinian proposed the doctrine of **nullification** whereby states could nullify or reject congressional acts they deemed unconstitutional. Congress then could either change the law or send it to the states as a constitutional amendment to be ratified or rejected. Nullification was Calhoun's skillful attempt to find a constitutional middle ground between submission and secession.

Nullification raised both tempers and constitutional questions in Congress. In a celebrated debate in January 1830, Senator **Robert Y. Hayne**, a gifted orator from South Carolina, rebuked New England's opposition to secession as inconsistent since it had considered secession itself in the Hartford Convention of 1815 (see Chapter 9). Hayne further denounced the Tariff of 1828 and proclaimed nullification the only hope of self-preservation for the South and the West.

Daniel Webster, a senator from Massachusetts and perhaps America's finest orator, defended New England in his response to Hayne. He insisted that the people of the United States as a whole, not as individual states, had ratified the Constitution. Webster declared, "It is . . . the people's Constitution, the people's government, made for the people, made by the people, and answerable to the people."

Therefore, he said, a state could neither secede nor nullify an act. Webster's speech climaxed with the famous phrase, "Liberty *and* Union, now and for ever, one and inseparable!" His views, however, like those of others involved in the controversy, appeared inconsistent; in 1815 he too had supported the Hartford Convention's decision to secede if Congress denied its demands. Opponents charged that Webster was seeking only what was best for his state and region. In 1815 secession had appeared best for New England; in 1830 enforcement of the tariff was best for New England.

Although nullification was discussed in 1828 and 1830, it was tested in 1832. In May 1832, John Quincy Adams, who had returned to Congress after his unsuccessful bid in 1828 for reelection to the presidency, proposed a revision to the Tariff of 1828. Congress passed the revised tariff, which was lower than that of 1828, but still higher than most Southerners wanted; Jackson signed it in July. The South Carolina legislature responded by calling for a special state convention that in turn declared the tariffs of both 1828 and 1832 unconstitutional and therefore null and void. The convention further declared that South Carolina would secede if there were any attempts to collect the tariff duties.

Senator Hayne resigned his Senate seat to head the nullification forces as governor in South Carolina. John C. Calhoun resigned as vice president to take Hayne's place on the Senate floor. Calhoun's resignation climaxed months of worsening relations between the president and vice president, a conflict that had become increasingly public. At a banquet in 1830 Jackson had pointedly looked at Calhoun as he raised a toast: "Our Union: it must be preserved." Without missing a beat, Calhoun rose and presented his own toast: "The Union: next to our liberty, most dear."

Despite Calhoun's maneuverings, only a little sympathy and no support could be found for South Carolina's action. An angry Andrew Jackson threatened to hang Calhoun and secured from Congress consideration and later passage of the **Force Bill**, which gave the president war powers against South Carolina. In his *Proclamation to the People of South Carolina*, Jackson warned,

> The laws of the United States must be executed. I have no discretionary power on the subject; my duty is emphatically pronounced in the Constitution. Those who told you that you might peaceably prevent their execution deceived you; they could not have been deceived themselves. . . . Their object is disunion. But be not deceived by names. Disunion by armed force is *treason*. Are you really ready to incur its guilt?

South Carolina declared that Jackson's constitutional views were "erroneous and dangerous," and despite its friendless position the state was prepared to "repel force by force, and . . . maintain its liberty at all hazards."

Behind these bare-knuckle pronouncements was an attempt on both sides to find a bloodless solution. At this juncture Henry Clay, "the Great Compromiser," proposed a new tariff that substantially, though gradually, reduced the Tariff of 1832, making it acceptable to South Carolina. Clay's proposed tariff, known as the **Compromise Tariff of 1833**, passed on March 1. In a parting shot to the president, though, South Carolina nullified the Force Bill.

War had been averted, but there was little to cheer about. The crisis heightened tensions between the sections, and throughout the

Nicholas Biddle

South there was a growing, uneasy sense of loss of control over the future. As one South Carolinian observed at the time of the nullification crisis, "It is useless and impracticable to disguise the fact that the South is a permanent minority, and that there is a sectional majority against it—a majority of different views and interests and little common sympathy."

Busting the Bank

The major campaign issue as Jackson faced reelection in 1832 was the future of the **Bank of the United States**. Jackson had little understanding of banking practices but had a westerner's distaste for banks nonetheless. The Panic of 1819 was still a vivid and bitter memory in the West and South, and the Bank was the culprit in the popular mind.

In the summer of 1832, the president of the National Bank, **Nicholas Biddle**, submitted the Bank's charter to Congress for a twenty-year renewal, though the existing charter did not expire until 1836. When Jackson learned that his old political rival Henry Clay had instigated the early renewal of the charter, hoping that it would help him to be elected president, Jackson growled, "The bank is trying to kill me, but I will kill it."

The Bank had such strong support in Congress that Clay believed he had a winning campaign issue. The recharter bill passed Congress; as predicted, Jackson vetoed it, claiming that it was unconstitutional. The Senate was unable to gain a two-thirds majority to override Jackson's veto; thus, the Bank was to expire in four years. Clay thought the stage was now set for him to win a great victory.

The election of 1832 introduced three political precedents. A **third party**, the **Anti-Masonic Party**, arose shortly before the election, stimulated by the questionable activities of the Masonic Lodge and other secret societies. It also opposed Catholic immigration and supported federal funding for internal improvements. The party, a precedent in itself, established two other precedents. First, it issued a **platform**, a written statement describing where the party stood on various issues. More importantly, it held a **national convention** where state delegates gathered to nominate the party's presidential and vice-presidential candidates. The major parties quickly followed its example, and nominating conventions have since become a standard part of the American political process.

The election itself was not so interesting. Clay had miscalculated badly; support in Congress for the Bank and support in the countryside turned out to be two different things. Jackson swept to victory with his old ally Van Buren as his new vice president. His reelection having convinced him more than ever that he was the choice of the people, Old Hickory again marched off to fight the Bank. His terms were unconditional surrender. Jackson claimed that withdrawing federal funds from the Bank would lessen the negative effects of the charter's expiration in 1836. After two secretaries of the treasury refused to remove the federal deposits, Jackson appointed Roger B. Taney as secretary in September 1833. The next month Taney began removing federal deposits and placing them in state banks—Jackson's "**pet banks**," as his enemies called them.

The Bank's defeat was not a victory for the common man over the wealthy financiers, as Jackson had claimed that it would be. Jackson's actions turned out to be a two-edged sword on which he inadvertently impaled the economy. The loss of federal deposits in

Both states and private banks issued paper currency during the period of "free banking."

As Genuine as a $3 Bill

Jackson's successful war against the National Bank helped open a new era in American banking from 1836 to 1864. Although state banks and branch banks had been in operation before, the absence of both a national banking system and regulations on state and private banks spawned a colorful period of "free banking."

Hundreds of banks sprang up representing towns, canal companies, insurance agencies, railroads, and factories. These diverse, largely unregulated banks issued a motley supply of money. Bills were issued in various colors, sizes, and engravings, and denominations were also varied—$1, $2, $3, $4, and $5 bills. A 1/4-cent bill was issued in Virginia, and a $9 bill was issued in Paterson, New Jersey. In contrast to the somber gallery of statesmen on our currency today, bank notes of the antebellum period were adorned with birds, bees, buffaloes, children, trains, steamboats, coal miners, cotton pickers, and timber cutters.

Twenty-five thousand varieties of notes were issued throughout the country during that period. In 1864, however, the National Bank Act imposed a uniform national currency and greater Treasury control. Most private banks died. Three-dollar bills and other oddities became only historical curiosities and collectibles.

the Bank of the United States forced it to tighten credit, which in turn hurt business expansion. At the same time, the federal funds deposited in state banks fueled wild speculation in western land sales, financed with mountains of worthless paper money that these banks issued to stay ahead of the inflation they were creating.

Jackson attempted to slow the spiraling inflation by issuing the **Specie Circular of 1836**. It ordered the prohibition of the use of anything except gold or silver coin—specie, or "hard money"—for the purchase of public land. In other words, no one could use paper money to buy land. Jackson intended the circular to restrict speculation, since there was not nearly as much specie available as there was paper money. What it did, however, was radically increase the demand for specie and thus increase the Bank's control over credit. The speculative collapse brought on a severe depression during the term of Jackson's successor, Van Buren. Unfortunately, Old Hickory handled the economy's complexities as roughly as he had the British at New Orleans and with equal effect.

Resettlement of the Indians

In his first inaugural address President Jackson promised,

> It will be my sincere and constant desire, to observe towards the Indian tribes within our limits, a just and liberal policy; and to give that humane and considerate attention to their rights and their wants, which are consistent with the habits of our government, and the feelings of our people.

The old Indian fighter, however, pursued Indian policies that were anything but "just and liberal" and that showed a remarkable lack of "humane and considerate attention to their rights and their wants."

Indian Removal

Even before Jackson took office, the United States had discussed moving all Indian tribes in the East to lands west of the Mississippi River and east of the Rockies. Such a policy seemed fair to the government, since it wanted the Indian lands and did not want the western lands—yet. The Indians were understandably less impressed with the fairness of the idea. When he took office, Jackson pursued the **Indian removal policy** zealously. Under his administration, no less than ninety-four treaties were made with the Indians, some of them forcibly. With the treaties as legal justification, the United States began moving the Indians westward and opening Indian lands in the East to white settlement.

Indian Resistance

Not all the Indians gave in meekly to this treatment. Some responded with violence. In 1832 a group of Sauk (SAHK) and Fox Indians under Chief Black Hawk crossed the Mississippi River back into northern Illinois to reclaim their land. A force of regular soldiers and Illinois militia moved to intercept the Indians. The resulting **Black Hawk War** was brief but bloody. As with most U.S.-Indian conflicts, the Indians suffered more and lost the war.

More challenging was the **Seminole War** (1835–42). The Seminoles, led by the canny Osceola (oss ee OH luh), also resisted efforts to move them west. They hid in the swamp lands and marshes of Florida as American troops tried in vain to track them down. Over 1,500 Americans and an unknown number of Indians died in the conflict. Most Seminoles were rounded up and sent west, but some

Sequoyah developed the Cherokee alphabet, enabling his tribe to read the Bible and publish a newspaper.

Sequoyah, attributed to Henry Inman, National Portrait Gallery, Smithsonian Institution held out in Florida until the government gave up and left them to live in peace.

The Cherokees, one of the "Five Civilized Tribes" (along with the Chickasaws, Seminoles, Choctaws, and Creeks) in the southeastern United States, tried a different approach. As their name suggests, the Civilized Tribes adopted many features of white civilization. They built communities with roads and schools and developed prosperous farms using European methods of agriculture. Many also converted to Christianity. A brilliant Cherokee named **Sequoyah** even developed a written Cherokee alphabet, allowing the Indians to publish newspapers and the Bible in their own language.

Believing the promises contained in their treaties with the United States that they would be left to govern themselves, the Cherokees resisted removal. Christian missionaries who worked among the Cherokees vigorously opposed the government's actions and supported the Indian opposition to forced removal. In keeping with their civilized character, the Cherokees did not go to war; they went to court. In 1832, Supreme Court Chief Justice John Marshall handed down a decision in favor of the tribe. Unfortunately, the government ignored it. Jackson is reported to have said, "John Marshall has made his decision. Now let him enforce it." The Cherokees and the other Civilized Tribes were forcibly moved west to what is today Oklahoma. The hard journey from their homes resulted in the deaths of many Indians and became known as the **Trail of Tears**.

"The Trail Where They Cried"

Perhaps the saddest event in the Indian resettlement process was the Trail of Tears, the forced removal of more than ten thousand Cherokees from North Carolina to the Indian Territory (now known as Oklahoma) from 1838 to 1839. The name comes from a Cherokee phrase describing it: *Nunna-da-ul-tsun-yi*, "the trail where they cried." Beginning in virtual prison camps in the Carolinas, the Cherokees were herded like cattle by the U.S. Army through freezing winter weather without adequate food, shelter, or even blankets. Many of them died along the way. The sick, the aged, and the very young suffered the most.

A handful of Cherokees escaped the army roundup and hid in the Smoky Mountains. They eventually emerged from hiding and were allowed to legally reclaim about fifty thousand of the seven million acres of Cherokee land the government had seized. This grant was an extremely small reparation to a people who had suffered so much and so unjustly.

Section Quiz

1. What were the three political precedents of the presidential election of 1832?

2. What did President Jackson issue to slow the inflation caused by the proliferation of paper money and to restrict land expansion?

3. How did the reactions of the Seminoles and the Cherokees to Indian removal differ? What was the result for each tribe?

★ Who was responsible for the forced removal of the Cherokees? Why?

An anti-Jackson cartoon

Martin Van Buren

III. Party Politics

A strong indication of the democratic forces at work during the Jackson years was the growing, organized, and even turbulent political competition of the era. Within a span of just a dozen years, from 1828 to 1840, two new national parties—Jackson's Democratic Party and his opposition, the Whig Party—competed effectively for the presidency and control of Congress.

Jackson and Anti-Jackson

Andrew Jackson's strong leadership at the presidential helm often made as many foes as followers. By the time of his second term, though Jackson was still popular, opposition to him was growing. His fight against the Bank of the United States and federal funds for internal improvements angered many nationalists allied with Henry Clay and John Quincy Adams. In addition, his willingness to lower the tariff to ease the pressure on the South angered New England business interests represented by Daniel Webster. Jackson's gruff treatment of South Carolina also aroused opposition throughout the South.

These anti-Jackson forces, despite their differing regions and interests, formed a political alliance in the early 1830s that became known as the **Whig Party**. The Whigs derived their name from the British party that traditionally opposed royal tyranny. Jackson's highhanded methods and the manner in which he dictated his policies to Congress and his cabinet seemed to his opponents to have the trappings of monarchy. The Whigs dubbed the so-called people's president "King Andrew I" and insisted that he did not have a monopoly on the common man's support.

Besides being anti-Jackson, the Whigs were also a nationalist party. They sought to breathe new life into Clay's American System. Whig emphasis on optimism and opportunity had a national appeal across the young republic and attracted a new crop of young leaders such as Abraham Lincoln, Horace Greeley, and William Seward. The Whig Party quickly demonstrated that it had a national organization as well as a nationalist platform when it competed in the presidential election in 1836.

Van's Victory

Having won 98 seats in the House of Representatives in 1834, the upstart Whigs devised an ambitious strategy for the 1836 election. Due to their fledgling status, their strategy was to run several candidates, each strong in his own region, who would carry enough states to prevent Van Buren from gaining a majority of the electoral votes. The election would then go to the House of Representatives, where the Whigs hoped to be strong enough to maneuver one of their men into office. Daniel Webster from Massachusetts ran in New England; William Henry Harrison, popular Indian fighter from Ohio, ran in the West; and Tennessee's Hugh White ran in the South.

On the Democratic side, Martin Van Buren had been Jackson's hand-picked successor almost from the start. In the case of Jackson and Van Buren, it seemed true that opposites do attract. Though both were born in humble circumstances, they grew up in different worlds. Jackson became a planter and an Indian fighter; Van Buren, a politician with polish. The 6'1" Jackson, with his shock of iron-gray hair, certainly contrasted with his balding, sandy-haired vice president who was seven inches shorter. Although the two men dif-

Whigs versus Democrats	
Whigs	**Democrats**
Traced their roots to Alexander Hamilton and the Federalists	Traced their roots to Thomas Jefferson and the Republican Party
Followed the ideology of Hamilton, John Quincy Adams, and the National Republicans; primary leader was Henry Clay	Followed the ideology of Jefferson and Andrew Jackson
Favored an economy dominated by commerce and manufacturing	Favored an economy dominated by agriculture
Encouraged a paternalistic national government to meet people's needs	Encouraged individual initiative and responsibility in meeting people's needs
Supported a high protective tariff and special favors (subsidies) to encourage business	Supported free trade/free markets, a minimal revenue tariff, and no special favors from government
Favored centralization of government with subservient state governments	Favored decentralization of government (wanted state and local governments to do most of the ruling)
Wanted federally funded internal improvements	Wanted any internal improvements to be done and financed by state and/or local governments
Supported a national bank	Opposed a national bank; favored state banks
Opposed territorial expansion	Supported territorial expansion
Were disinclined to violate rights of Indians	Were inclined to violate rights of Indians

fered in background, appearance, and temperament, Old Hickory owed the Little Magician a great deal for his political skills in winning elections. With general (though short-lived) prosperity at the time of the election, Jackson's endorsement was really the deciding vote in Van Buren's favor.

Even with Jackson's help Van Buren won the popular vote by only 25,000 out of the 1.5 million votes cast. Van Buren became the last incumbent vice president to be elected president until 1989, when George Bush succeeded Ronald Reagan.

Hard Times

Just weeks after Van Buren took office, the economy collapsed, pulling the country down into a deep five-year depression known as the **Panic of 1837**. Banks and businesses failed, and unemployment grew across the nation.

The economic hard times were brought on by a number of factors. Jackson's economic policies, of course, had been a financial fiasco, but his malpractice worsened—though it did not cause—all the problems of the ailing economy. Wild, irresponsible practices among the state banks, as well as a massive wheat crop failure and the collapse of cotton prices, brought the economy to its knees. As one historian put it, "By its shortsighted financial measures Jackson's administration had sown the wind. Van Buren was to reap the whirlwind." When it came to the economy, the Little Magician had run out of tricks. Blame for the depression would dog his administration throughout his term.

Van Buren had few solutions for the problems he had inherited, but he was determined at least to put the government's financial house in order. As a result Van Buren proposed an **independent treasury** to replace the state banks as a depository for federal funds. The treasury was to have only federal funds deposited in it, and only government employees were to manage it. Subtreasuries were planned for major cities throughout the nation. (Van Buren's proposal was often called the "subtreasury system.") This system would divorce private banks from federal funds so that the government's funds and credit could not be used to support speculation and credit expansion. The plan was proposed in 1837, but because of opposition, Congress did not pass it until 1840.

Log Cabin Campaign

The 1840 campaign was one of the most colorful in our nation's history, a remarkable fact considering the bland candidates that the two parties offered the country. The excitement came from the images and enthusiasm that the parties, particularly the Whigs, were able to generate.

The Democrats renominated President Van Buren and hoped to stretch General Jackson's popularity for yet another election. The Whigs realized that it would take more than the battered economy to turn the entrenched Democrats out of office. In 1840, Whigs reasoned, "If you can't beat them, learn from them." As a result they nominated an old Indian fighter, **William Henry Harrison**, the hero of the Battle of Tippecanoe nearly thirty years earlier. They added **John Tyler**, a states' rights Virginian and friend of Clay, as running mate to broaden the ticket's appeal. In the campaign to follow, the Whigs would outgeneral the general's party.

The Democrats thought bringing Harrison out of retirement was ludicrous. One Democratic newspaper in Baltimore mocked "that upon condition of his receiving a pension of $2,000 and a barrel of cider, General Harrison would no doubt consent to withdraw his pretensions, and spend his days in a log cabin on the banks of the Ohio." Unwittingly the Democrats gave the Whigs a winning theme.

The Whigs presented Harrison as a humble but heroic backwoodsman in contrast to the dainty, aristocratic Van Buren who lived in the White House, or the "Palace," as the Whigs referred to it. Actually Harrison was born into Virginia aristocracy; his father was the governor of the state and a signer of the Declaration of Independence. Van Buren, who was the son of a New York tavernkeeper, hardly grew up in the lap of luxury. But facts were never allowed to interfere with either party's campaign.

Torch-light parades, log cabin floats, and quantities of hard cider drew crowds for the Whigs. Throughout the country the Whigs were just as imaginative with their campaign slogans: "Tippecanoe and Tyler too!" and "Van, Van is a used-up man!" Songs often accented the raucous Whig parades:

Old Tip he wears a homespun coat;

He has no ruffled shirt-wirt-wirt.

But Mat has the golden plate,

And he's a little squirt-wirt-wirt.

The Whigs rode their log cabin theme all the way to the White House, with an electoral landslide of 234 to 60. The *Democratic Review* mourned, "We have taught them to conquer us!"

Harrison's inauguration was certainly anticlimactic compared to his campaign. On that dreary, drizzling day of March 4, 1841, Old Tippecanoe stood on the east steps of the Capitol and read in the rain for nearly two hours his ponderous inaugural address to a shuffling assortment of umbrellas and slickers.

The sixty-eight-year-old general was not well as it was, and in the days after he moved into the White House, he found the flood of office-seekers trying to cash in on the campaign overwhelming. Besides, his wife, Anna, was back home in Ohio. She had not been well enough to join him on the difficult journey by steamboat and stage to Washington. As a result the White House was simply not in order, and the general was not one to sit around and wait for the sun to shine—literally. In the chill spring rain, he journeyed to the fish market and the butcher shop to stock the White House cupboards. A cold that had nagged him since his inaugural speech worsened. In that speech he had pointedly declared himself to be a one-term president; ironically, he was to be a one-month president. Stricken with pneumonia on April 1, Harrison died three days later, a bare month after taking office.

The president's death stunned the nation. Harrison's larger-than-life campaign image suddenly turned mortal. The oldest president yet elected was now replaced by the youngest president yet to serve. The nation now faced its future under the leadership of Tyler, a man who it had never expected would actually govern.

Section Quiz

1. What three anti-Jackson forces came together to form the Whig Party?

2. What was the Whig strategy in the presidential election of 1836? What was the result?

3. Name two causes of the Panic of 1837.

★ What important lesson does the vice presidency of John Tyler teach us about presidential elections?

"OK"

The 1840 campaign did more than change the political landscape in America and shape the style of future campaigns; it also made an enduring contribution to our language. Van Buren's supporters rallied followers for "Old Kinderhook" (a reference to Van Buren's birthplace) by organizing O.K. Clubs. The Whigs, the masters of one-upmanship during the campaign, declared that O.K. did not stand for Old Kinderhook but rather for "Oll Korrect," a spelling the Whigs jokingly pinned on the backwoods Jackson, who was a poor speller. The Whigs then, ironically, took what began as a Democratic slogan and stamped it on their kegs of campaign cider.

The popular term "OK" has long outlived the log cabin campaign to become the nearly universal expression that H. L. Mencken called "the most successful of Americanisms." Hardly a day or hour goes by in which "OK" is not used in our conversation—a tribute to the classic, colorful contest of 1840.

People, Places, and Things to Remember

Andrew Jackson
Henry Clay
American System
tariff
protective tariff
Tariff of 1816
internal improvements
National Road
Panic of 1819
Missouri Compromise
caucus
John Quincy Adams
"corrupt bargain"
National Republicans
Democratic Party
Martin Van Buren
John C. Calhoun
spoils system
"Kitchen Cabinet"
"Tariff of Abominations"
nullification
Robert Y. Hayne
Daniel Webster
Force Bill
Compromise Tariff of 1833
Bank of the United States
Nicholas Biddle
third party
Anti-Masonic party
platform
national convention
"pet banks"
Specie Circular of 1836
Indian removal policy
Black Hawk War
Seminole War
Sequoyah
Trail of Tears
Whig Party
Panic of 1837
independent treasury
William Henry Harrison
John Tyler

Chapter Review

Making Connections

1. Why did many American leaders, such as James Madison, generally oppose federal funding of internal improvements?

2. Why did Missouri's application for statehood create controversy?

3. Why did Henry Clay favor John Quincy Adams over Andrew Jackson when the presidential election of 1824 went to the House of Representatives?

4. Why did the South oppose protective tariffs?

Developing History Skills

1. Put the following events from the nullification crisis in their proper chronological order from earliest to latest: (a) Senators Hayne and Webster debate nullification; (b) Henry Clay proposes the Compromise Tariff of 1833; (c) the Tariff of Abominations is passed; (d) President Jackson proposes the Force Bill; (e) Vice President Calhoun anonymously advocates the doctrine of nullification.

2. Why was the 1840 campaign called the "log cabin campaign"?

Thinking Critically

1. Review the toasts given by Jackson and Calhoun in 1830. With whose statement do you most agree and why?

2. Do you think the Whig approach to the election of 1840 is a proper one? Why or why not?

Living as a Christian Citizen

1. Imagine that you are a Christian missionary living with the Cherokees. Write a letter to President Jackson urging him to respect the Cherokees' legal rights. Make sure to include reasons from a Christian perspective in your letter.

2. One of the religious controversies of this period was whether the post office should be open on Sunday. Write an editorial supporting one of the views.

CHAPTER 11

"Camp-meeting" by Alexander Rider and Hugh Bridport

The Growth of American Society (1789–1861)

I. American Technology

II. American Culture

III. American Religion

"What hath God wrought!"

May 24, 1844
First telegraph message

The face of the United States changed dramatically between 1789 and 1861. Transportation improved markedly, for one thing. In 1789, George Washington traveled to his inauguration over muddy roads in a carriage; in 1861, Abraham Lincoln traveled to his on iron rails in a train. The speed of communication also increased at an incredible rate. In 1815, the United States defeated Britain at the Battle of New Orleans, unaware that the war had actually ended with the Treaty of Ghent two weeks before. With the laying of the transatlantic telegraph cable in 1858, however, the time for such communications was reduced from a matter of months to a matter of minutes. The religious face of the nation changed too. From a spiritual lull after the Revolution, the country soared to new spiritual heights through two major nationwide revivals. The era from 1789 to 1861 was one of remarkable cultural growth for the United States—technologically, intellectually, and spiritually.

I. American Technology

Manufacturing and Industry

The history of American manufacturing and industry is, basically, the history of inventions and applications of processes. But it is also the history of the people who devised the inventions and developed the processes. American industry is more than the story of machines; it is the story of the creative men and women behind the machines and the free-market economy that made those advances possible.

Textiles

In 1789, Great Britain was the world's leader in manufacturing, and the British intended to keep it that way. The British government carefully guarded not only all machinery relating to Britain's textile industry but also the blueprints for the machinery. Laws prevented skilled workers in the textile industry from emigrating. But that did not deter **Samuel Slater**. Although a successful apprentice in an English textile mill, Slater saw greater economic opportunities for himself in America. Slater carefully memorized the construction of the textile machines, disguised himself as a farm hand, and escaped to the United States in 1789.

In Providence, Rhode Island, Slater—working entirely from memory—constructed an English-style mill with the financial support of American investors. This mill proved to be the first of a series of mills that sprouted across New England. The region, with its numerous streams and rivers to drive the water wheels used to power the machinery, was a natural site for the textile industry. The factory system was critical in the establishment and growth of the fledgling American economy. It spread throughout New England and the rest of the North. An interesting example of American industry in this period is the textile mills of Lowell, Massachusetts. Textiles became America's first major industry.

Old Slater Mill, Pawtucket, Rhode Island

Interchangeable Parts

Slater's contribution in textile machinery was only one of several advances in American manufacturing. Probably the most important was **Eli Whitney's** work. Although Whitney was better known in his own day for inventing the cotton gin (discussed later), his work with **interchangeable parts** was ultimately more important. In 1798, Whitney took an order to provide ten thousand rifles for the United States government. Until that time, guns, like most machinery, were handmade by craftsmen who individually made and fitted each part. Repairs required the craftsman to make each replacement part by hand. Whitney designed a gun that was made of standardized, identical, machine-manufactured parts. When a piece broke, a new one could be easily inserted. Building on Whitney's process, every industry soon began to use standardized interchangeable parts.

Patents and Inventors

American inventors benefited from the support of the United States government, which clearly saw the importance of developing industry. The government's most important help to industry was the passage of the first national **patent** law in 1790, which allowed inventors to secure patents for new devices and processes. As long as the patent was in effect, no one else could legally copy the inventor's work, and the inventor could reap the profits from a useful invention.

Spurred by the patent law and the promise of sure profits, inventors flooded the United States with new devices. Elias Howe, for example, perfected a mechanical sewing machine. With the improvements that Howe and others made, the sewing machine permitted the quicker, cheaper manufacture of clothing and other cloth products. Samuel Colt made his mark on the firearms industry. He patented and manufactured a "six-shooter," a pistol with a revolving cylinder which allowed a user to fire six times before reloading. Colt's sales started slowly, but his weapon caught on during the Mexican War when it became the standard sidearm of the United States Army.

Heavy Industry

Americans had dabbled in coal and iron production in colonial days, but before the Revolution most iron products had to be imported from England. Much of the coal used in colonial days was bituminous, or "soft," coal, which smoked a great deal when burned and did not heat up enough to "smelt" (melt) iron ore properly so that the pure iron could be separated from waste materials. Americans soon discovered large deposits of anthracite, or "hard" coal, and iron ore in western Pennsylvania. With the cleaner-burning, higher-heating hard coal, American manufacturers could produce both more and better iron. As roads, canals, and railroads reached into the American interior, iron products soon spread throughout the nation, and western Pennsylvania became a center of American heavy industry.

Most iron went into the growing railroad industry to provide rails and engines. Smaller amounts of iron went into producing items such as tools and cooking utensils. An efficient process of producing steel from iron was developed in the 1850s in Great Britain and spread to the United States. Although steel was much stronger and more durable than iron, its production did not become important to the United States until after the Civil War.

Samuel Colt invented a pistol with a revolving cylinder that allowed the user to fire six times before he had to reload.

The Colt .45 Peacemaker was Colt's most popular revolver.

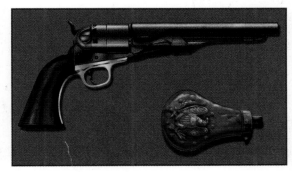

As America became more industrialized, towns grew up around the factories. Workers came from the countryside and imigrated from Europe to work in the factories. To meet the needs of these workers and their families, some entrepreneurs opened stores, inns, and other retail establishments. Others offered much-needed services, such as blacksmithing, carpentry, and saddle and harness making. Urbanization became a new way of life for many people.

Agriculture

The United States had been dominantly agricultural since its founding. The period from 1789 to 1861, however, saw important advances in agricultural technology. The applications of that technology led to an increasing division between the agricultural system of the South and that of the rest of the nation.

Agricultural Advances

As settlers streamed into the wilderness of the Northwest Territory and across the Mississippi River, they found an abundance of rich and fertile soil. The soil was so rich, in fact, that it produced more than farmers could easily harvest. The untapped potential of the frontier lands presented a challenge to the young nation.

The rich soil of the Northwest and of the plains on the west side of the Mississippi was sticky and covered with a tough sod. Several men experimented with iron plows that could cut through the sod and turn the soil over cleanly without letting it stick to the blades. Eventually, a blacksmith from Vermont named **John Deere** perfected the plow. He put an edge of steel over the iron blade of the plow, and his improved plow proved ideal for the new lands of the West. Reaping the harvest became simpler thanks to **Cyrus McCormick**. In 1834, McCormick received a patent for a reaping machine, a horse-drawn device that allowed one man to cut and stack ten to twelve acres of grain in a single day. Spurned by easterners who mocked his invention, McCormick moved his headquarters to Chicago, where his business made him a millionaire by 1860. A devout Christian, McCormick used his wealth to support Christian efforts such as seminaries and the work of Evangelist D. L. Moody.

Through these and other technical advances in agricultural machinery, American farm production grew at a tremendous rate. In 1789, farmers had generally eked out only enough to feed their own families. But by 1861, the United States was producing nearly $2 billion worth of agricultural products each year.

In the Old Northwest, farmers (most of whom had migrated from New England and Pennsylvania) soon built an agricultural empire that included the production of corn, wheat, and cattle. When one combines the migration to the Old Northwest with the migration from the coastal and mid-Atlantic states to the South, which led to the development of the cotton kingdom, more than 40 percent of Americans lived west of the Appalachian Mountains by 1840.

The Cotton Kingdom

The South differed from the North and the West in that although foodstuffs were important, the South did not produce the abundant grains of the West. Tobacco was important to some areas, particularly the states of the Upper South. A single cash crop, however, dominated the agriculture and economy of the region—cotton. "Cotton is King" was the motto of many southerners, and King Cotton placed its distinctive stamp on the culture of the South.

In 1789, cotton was a relatively unimportant crop. Most cotton grown in the South was a short-staple variety, the seeds of which clung to the cotton fibers. A slave had to work a whole day to clean just one pound of cotton. Eli Whitney changed that situation in 1793. While working as a tutor on a Georgia plantation, Whitney got the idea of making a machine to clean cotton. In just ten days,

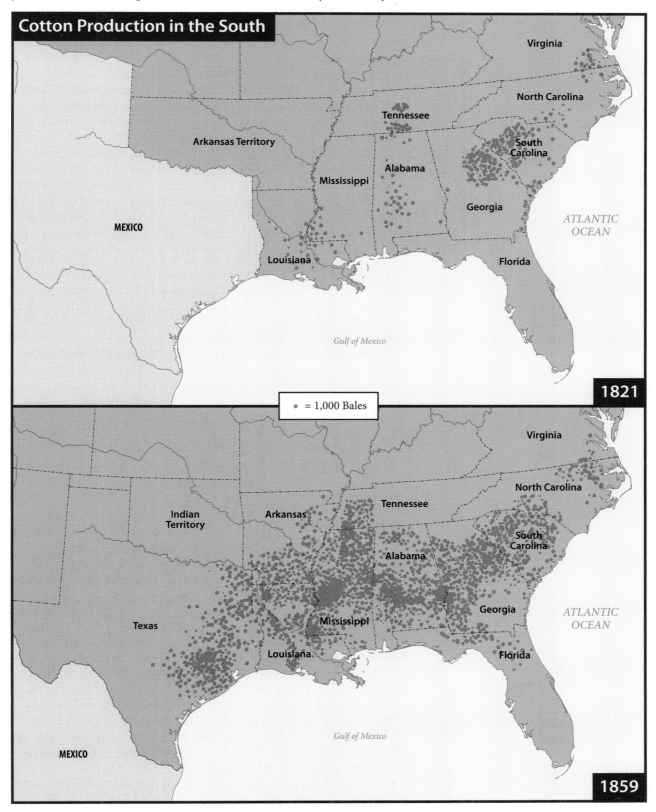

Cotton Production in the South

• = 1,000 Bales

1821

1859

Whitney devised the **cotton gin**, a machine containing a series of metal teeth mounted on rollers that separated the cotton from the troublesome seeds. The cotton gin cleaned cotton fifty times faster than slaves working by hand.

Whitney's invention transformed the Southern economy. In response to the strong demand for cotton in the textile mills of the North and Europe, farmers in the Lower South rushed to plant cotton. In 1790, the United States produced two million pounds of cotton; in 1860, the nation produced more than two *billion* pounds— seven-eighths of the cotton produced in the world. Cotton was by far the most important export of the United States.

The growth of the cotton kingdom, however, widened the gap between the South on the one hand and the North and the West on the other. Cotton growing, for one thing, revitalized slavery. In 1790, slavery had seemed an increasingly unprofitable and dying institution. With the advent of the cotton gin, however, many planters thought that slavery was necessary again. The value of field hands soon doubled, and the South became increasingly sensitive to Northern attacks on slavery. The overwhelming value of cotton also hampered Southern industrial development. Most southerners simply saw no use in developing industry and transportation networks as the North was doing. King Cotton by itself seemed sufficient to supply the region's needs.

Section Quiz

1. What was America's first major industry? In what region of the nation did it center?

2. Name three of this era's important inventors and their respective inventions.

3. Why was the discovery of anthracite coal in western Pennsylvania important?

4. How did the invention of the cotton gin increase the differences between the South and the rest of the nation?

* Which of the inventions discussed in this section do you think had the most lasting impact on American progress? Support your answer.

Transportation

Manufacturing products and growing crops was one matter; getting those products to market was another. The United States could not tame its frontier until it built a network of transportation and communication to unite the sections of the nation. The United States rose to that challenge in dramatic fashion during the period between the Revolution and the Civil War.

River Transportation

The oldest avenues in America were rivers and streams. Indians and early settlers used canoes on the numerous waterways to penetrate the dense forests. Later settlers, needing some means of moving farm products to market, used flatboats and keelboats. These were sufficient for sailing downstream but were obviously of limited use in going up. The nation needed some kind of powered water transportation.

The answer to the problem was the steamboat. Several Americans had been trying since 1763 to develop a steam-powered ship.

American Slavery

One of the most offensive features of American society between the Revolution and the Civil War was the existence of slavery. When the North American colonies were founded, slavery was already common in other regions and throughout southern Europe. Because few people opposed it initially, black slavery was introduced in all of the thirteen American colonies (although not all blacks in colonial America were slaves). By 1775, the North American colonies held five hundred thousand slaves, of whom two hundred thousand lived in Virginia and one hundred thousand in South Carolina.

But slavery was a national—not just a Southern—problem. Although fewer slaves were held in the North, regions such as New England also thrived economically as a result of slavery. Eight of the top ten names on the Newport, Rhode Island, tax rolls were traders in molasses, rum, and slaves. New York City became the hub of the slave trade, even after that trade was made illegal. Massachusetts textile mills wove cloth from cotton grown by Southern slaves. And Connecticut became a leader in the ivory trade, which often involved slave labor in Africa.

The attitudes toward slavery began to change in the last half of the 1700s. Often, the moral offense was an argument against slavery. It was difficult to reconcile the practice with the admonition to "love thy neighbour as thyself" (Matt. 22:39). It was also difficult to reconcile slavery with the principles of American government in the Declaration of Independence ("inalienable rights," including liberty).

Yet many times men discarded moral arguments in favor of economic and political motives for keeping or ending slavery. As Northern states became more mercantile and less agricultural, slavery became less desirable and was eventually abolished (though New England merchants still participated in the slave trade). In the South slavery increasingly became a vital part of the economy.

Physical treatment of the slaves varied. Some slaveholders were undeniably cruel. Others treated their slaves with care. Even so, physical mistreatment was only part of the offense of American slavery. Former slave Richard Allen noted, "Slavery is a bitter pill"—even, Allen said, when a slave had "a good master." The slave was completely under the control of his owner. Whom the slave would marry, where (and whether) he would go to church, what would happen to his children—all of these decisions belonged entirely to the slave owner. Even some of the more thoughtful slave owners often broke up slave families.

The institution of slavery had consequences that reached across society and far into the future. Slavery resulted in untold suffering. It led to the division of a nation and a bloody war to reunite it. And it brought about tension and bitterness between blacks and whites in the United States.

The idea was finally perfected by a talented, imaginative inventor from Philadelphia, **Robert Fulton**. In 1807, Fulton unveiled his steamboat, the *Clermont*, on the Hudson River. Critics called it "Fulton's Folly," but it successfully sailed upstream to Albany. The steamboat soon revolutionized river traffic. Goods and passengers could now move cheaply and easily through the interior wherever navigable rivers existed.

Roads

The rather obvious shortcoming of steamboats was that they could go only where rivers went. To link landlocked points, Americans built a system of roads across the countryside. Colonial roads, such as the Great Philadelphia Wagon Road (Chapter 3), had provided the earliest means of reaching the frontier. Braddock's Road, built for military purposes during the French and Indian War (Chapter 5), became an important commercial route. Pioneer Daniel Boone blazed the Wilderness Road, which carried travelers from southern Virginia through the Cumberland Gap and into Kentucky all the way to the Ohio River. Branches of the Wilderness Road also led to Nashville, Tennessee, and into the Carolinas.

Early roads were obviously not modern superhighways. A good road had a surface of gravel or perhaps stone. Many consisted of a

Robert Fulton revolutionized water travel by demonstrating a working steam-powered boat.

series of boards laid side by side (**plank roads**) or logs. Roads made of logs were called **corduroy roads** because of their bumpy surface. Some roads were nothing more than dirt trails—or mud in wet weather. Most roads were built by private companies that paid for them by charging tolls (fees) for their use. Such roads were called **toll roads** or **turnpikes**. (When such roads are operated by private businesses, it is free enterprise; when the government gets involved in funding, operating, and regulating them, it is *not* free enterprise.)

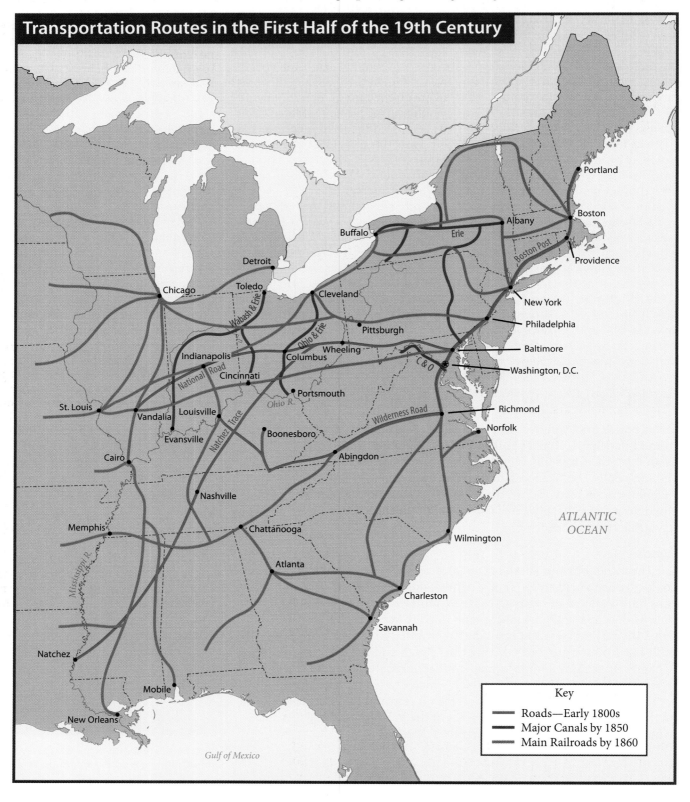

Transportation Routes in the First Half of the 19th Century

Key
— Roads—Early 1800s
— Major Canals by 1850
— Main Railroads by 1860

Maintenance of roads was almost nonexistent. By the time the National Road reached Vandalia, its eastern portions were already decaying. Nineteenth-century roads were helpful in facilitating transportation, but rapid economic expansion soon outstripped the road-making technology of the day.

Canals

The canal era began in 1817, when New York, at the urging of Governor **DeWitt Clinton**, began building a canal from Albany to Lake Erie. With the backbreaking labor required for the task, the idea of a 363-mile canal seemed, as Thomas Jefferson said, "little short of madness." At a cost of some $6 million, the canal was a gamble for the state. Critics called it "Clinton's Big Ditch." Yet the **Erie Canal** proved such a success that it had paid for itself in tolls in less than ten years. Furthermore, the cost of shipping goods plunged. Before the canal opened, it cost twenty cents a pound to ship goods from Buffalo to New York City. After the canal opened, the price dropped to less than a penny a pound. In 1827, the governor of Georgia complained that wheat from upstate New York was selling more cheaply in Savannah than wheat from central Georgia.

The success story of the Erie Canal encouraged other efforts. The Wabash and Erie Canal in Indiana and the Miami and Erie Canal in Ohio connected Lake Erie to the Ohio River. The Illinois and Michigan Canal connected Lake Michigan to the Mississippi River by way of Chicago. By the 1830s, one could travel from New York City to New Orleans completely by inland waterways.

Railroads

Nineteenth-century American transportation climaxed with the development of the railroad, which combined the flexibility of canals and roads with the dependable power of steam. The first economically successful railroad in America was the **Baltimore & Ohio** (B & O) **Railroad**. Originally, the B & O consisted of horse-drawn carriages on metal rails. Inventor Peter Cooper believed that the line could develop a steam-driven engine, like the ones British companies were using. Working mostly with scrap metal, Cooper constructed the *Tom Thumb*. This small but powerful steam engine was well designed to handle the sharp curves and steep climbs of

The National Road

The most important early American road was the **National Road** (also known as the Cumberland Road because it originally began in Cumberland, Maryland), begun in 1811. Following roughly the same route as modern Interstate 70 and U.S. Highway 40, the National Road eventually linked Baltimore to Vandalia, Illinois. The road was a major transportation route for early settlers of the Old Northwest. It was also the first federal highway; the federal government had spent some $7 million on it by the time the road was finished in 1839.

Benefits of Canals

Canals combined some of the best features of rivers and roads. Like rivers, canals permitted pioneers to use boats, a cheaper and generally faster mode of transport than wagons. A horse pulling a canal boat, for example, could pull fifty times more weight than it could pull in a wagon. Like roads but unlike rivers, a canal could be built practically wherever it was needed.

Shortcomings of Canals

Canals had their shortcomings, though. Most of them were in the North, for example, where winter freezes rendered them useless for months at a time. Also, they were expensive to build. By the 1840s, the "canal craze" was nearly over. Canals gave way to a new and better form of transportation: the railroad.

Peter Cooper's *Tom Thumb* in its famous race against a horse-drawn rail carriage

The Growth of Railroads

In 1830, the United States contained a total of 32 miles of track. By 1860, more than 30,000 miles of track fanned out across the country, and more than 20,000 miles of that had been built since 1850. Formerly unimportant cities such as Chicago and Indianapolis became major centers of rail traffic. Chicago, for example, mushroomed from a population of about 4,000 in 1840 to more than 100,000 by 1860. By the time of the Civil War, railroads had become not only the nation's most important means of transportation but also a growing economic, social, and political force.

the B & O rail line. To display the engine's capabilities, Cooper agreed to run the *Tom Thumb* in a thirteen-mile race against a horse. Although the horse won narrowly because the engine had a mechanical problem, the future of American transportation was clearly with steam power. South Carolina's Charleston-to-Hamburg line opened in 1833, and its 137-mile length made it the longest line in the world. Other lines, usually local in service, grew around major cities.

Several inventions smoothed the way for the growth of railroads. Iron rails replaced wooden ones covered with iron strips. A cowcatcher attached to the front of an engine reduced damage from collisions with animals. The perfecting of the steam engine rendered trains faster, safer, and more powerful. Most important of all, railroads, particularly in the North and West, began using a standard gauge (width) of track of 4′ 8½″. The resulting ability of trains from different companies to use the same tracks became vitally important during the Civil War in linking the war efforts of the Northeast and the West. Virtually the only drawback to railroads was that they initially cost more to build than steamboats, canals, and roads.

Sea Transportation

American sea trade on both the Atlantic and Pacific oceans boomed in the 1840s and 1850s as a result of one of the most beautiful inventions in transportation history. The **clipper ship** differed from earlier seagoing vessels. With its slender, streamlined hull and its hundreds of square feet of canvas sails, the clipper was the fastest sailing ship ever built, and those of Donald McKay of Boston were the fastest of all. McKay's *Lightning*, for example, set a record by sailing 436 miles in a single day. From 1845 to 1860, the United States carried more sea trade than any other nation.

The clipper ship eventually fell victim to another technological advance, the steamship. At first, steam power was impractical for oceangoing vessels. They could not carry enough coal to fuel their engines for a long ocean voyage. Improvements in engine design, however, soon enabled the steamship to replace the clipper. Steam gave ships a constant source of power, one not dependent on winds and currents. Also steamships were bigger and could carry more cargo. By the time of the Civil War, the British had retaken the lead in sea trade. The reign of America's clipper ships was glorious but brief.

Communication

The telegraph was the invention of **Samuel F. B. Morse**, a talented painter who studied under the famous Benjamin West in England. While he was in England, Morse's contacts with British evangelicals led to his conversion to Christ. Also while in Europe, Morse became interested in the semaphore communications system in France. The semaphore system worked by using flags to send signals from one location to another. Morse got the idea of using electricity to carry messages over wire much more quickly and over longer distances than semaphore.

Morse spent several years developing his system. A series of tests of his method impressed Congress enough to motivate members to appropriate $30,000 for constructing a model telegraph system. Stringing wire on poles from Baltimore to Washington, D.C., Morse sent the first intercity telegraph message on May 24, 1844, before a group of important political leaders in the United States Capitol. Appropriately, the first message was a Bible verse: "What hath God wrought!" (Num. 23:23). Soon telegraph lines stretched all across the United States. People living hundreds of miles apart could now communicate almost instantly. In 1858, the first successful transatlantic cable was laid between North America and the British Isles. A message between the United States and Britain would have taken weeks to deliver in 1789. Now it was a matter of minutes. Perhaps no improvement better symbolizes the rapid changes produced by technology than this linking of continents.

The Pony Express

As fast as travel became in the period between the Revolution and the Civil War, communication became even faster. One attempt to improve communication was colorful but short-lived, and it became one of the symbols of westward movement. William Russell established the **pony express** in 1860. With a stable of 500 horses and a series of 190 stations stretching from Missouri to California, Russell promised to carry mail across the continent in the shortest possible time. A series of riders working in relays carried the mail from St. Joseph, Missouri, to San Francisco in ten to twelve days. However, the company went broke in 1861, a victim of the most important communications invention of the era, the telegraph.

Section Quiz

1. Name two methods of surfacing roads in the nineteenth century.
2. What event marked the beginning of the canal era?
3. What was America's most important method of transportation by 1861?
4. What was the first economically successful railroad in America? Who designed its first steam engine?
5. What system of carrying mail across the continent began in 1860? What invention put it out of business?

☆ Why might privately developed roads, canals, or railroads be built and maintained better than government-built roads built under Clay's proposed American System?

II. American Culture

Balancing the economic and technological side of American life was the cultural side. American expansion in technology was matched by an expansion in art and thought. Americans may have thought of themselves primarily as "doers" in that era, but some were also accomplished thinkers. American achievements in art, literature, and reform were just as important as the nation's technological advances.

Reform

Paralleling American efforts to improve technology were efforts to improve society. Reform movements, attempts to eliminate evils in society, blossomed and flourished in the first half of the nineteenth century. Most of the reformers were religiously inspired; some were guided by simple humanitarian ideals. All believed that glaring evils in America should—and could—be rooted out. Many freedoms and advantages that we enjoy today resulted from the efforts of nineteenth-century reformers.

Abolition

Without doubt the most controversial reform movement in the first half of the nineteenth century was **abolitionism**, the movement to eliminate slavery. Part of the motivation for abolitionism came from evangelical Christians as a result of the Second Great

Finney, the Abolitionist

Perhaps the primary religious leader to promote abolition was Charles G. Finney (discussed in greater detail later in this chapter). In addition to his own strong antislavery preaching, Finney influenced dozens of future abolitionist preachers through his teaching at Oberlin College.

Awakening. A church in Oberlin, Ohio, was typical of many Northern churches when it resolved that "as Slavery is a Sin, no person shall be invited to preach or Minister to this church, or any Brother invited to commune who is a slaveholder." Quakers in particular had been leading advocates of abolition since colonial days.

The most important and most militant abolitionist leader, however, was **William Lloyd Garrison**. Although he looked mild and benign, Garrison was fierce and zealous in his hatred of slavery. In 1831, he launched a newspaper, the *Liberator*, dedicated to attacking the moral evil of slavery. His methods could be extreme. He once denounced the Constitution as "a league with death, and a covenant with hell" because it did not condemn slavery. On another occasion he publicly burned a copy of the Constitution. In the pages of the *Liberator*, he reported every atrocity against slaves that he could find—including a few that were not true.

Garrison enraged many southerners with his violent attacks on both slavery and those who owned slaves. He once called slaveholders the "meanest of thieves and the worst of robbers." Nor was Garrison particularly popular in the North. His uncompromising attacks on slavery offended both those who preferred gradual reform and those who cared little for any reform at all. Furthermore, some northerners disliked Garrison's linking his attacks on slavery with attacks on discrimination against free blacks in the North. The editor scathingly pointed out that blacks in some states in the North were denied access to public schools or opportunities to serve as apprentices. In short, he noted that blacks in the North were sometimes little better off than slaves in the South. Garrison also alienated many Christians and impeded their support of abolition by his firm rejection of the Bible because of its supposed proslavery sentiments.

Women also played prominent roles in the abolitionist movement. Foremost among them were the Grimké sisters, originally from a slaveholding family in Charleston, South Carolina. Sarah and Angelina were born on the same day exactly thirteen years apart. They both left the South as adults and moved to Philadelphia, where they became active with the Quakers and abolitionism—Sarah as a writer and behind-the-scenes organizer and Angelina as a speaker. Angelina was the first woman to address the Massachusetts state legislature, promoting abolition. She married fellow abolitionist Theodore Weld.

In the South, hatred of Garrison and the other abolitionists reached new heights in 1831. In August of that year, a slave and radical preacher named **Nat Turner** led a slave rebellion in Southampton County, Virginia. Some sixty whites and perhaps a hundred blacks died in the rebellion and the bloody repression that followed. Turner, along with eighteen alleged leaders, was hanged. Southerners blamed the revolt on abolitionist meddling. The economic need for slavery, the fear of revolts such as Turner's, and the resentment of abolitionist criticism made the South more determined to protect slavery.

Slavery and the Churches

American Christians differed widely on the issue of slavery. Many, almost entirely in the North, called slavery a sin and slave owners sinners. Others, almost entirely in the South, defended slavery as a "positive good" for the benefit of blacks and claimed that slavery was sanctioned by the Bible. Some, in both the North and the South, tried to straddle the issue.

The nation, however, could not avoid the issue, as several denominations discovered to their sorrow. Two of America's largest denominations—the Methodists and the Baptists—divided over slavery in 1844. In both cases, Southern members formed new denominations—the Southern Methodist Church and the Southern Baptist Convention.

However, many denominations avoided schism over the slavery issue. For example, the Congregationalists—the majority of whom were in the North, mainly New England—were both antislavery and completely unified. Other denominations that avoided division, such as the Episcopal Church, usually did so by simply avoiding the issue as much as they could.

A contemporary engraving of Nat Turner's Rebellion and its bloody aftermath

HORRID MASSACRE IN VIRGINIA.

The Scenes which the above Plate is designed to represent are—Fig. 1, a Mother intreating for the lives of her children.—2. Mr. _____, cruelly murdered by his own Slaves.—3. Mr. Barrow, who bravely defended himself until his wife escaped.—4. A comp. of mounted Dragoons in pursuit of the Blacks.

Undismayed by opposition, abolitionists pressed their cause zealously. Several former slaves helped by writing and speaking of their experiences. **Frederick Douglass** was one of the most brilliant, most eloquent, and most radical. His understandably strong hatred of slavery caused him to make statements such as: "Slaveholders not only forfeit their right to liberty but to life itself." **Harriet Tubman** not only spoke at antislavery meetings but also made some twenty trips to the South to help lead more than three hundred blacks to freedom. Despite all these efforts, however, only a major war succeeded in eliminating slavery from the American continent.

Education

Two important trends developed in the reform of American education during this period: the growth of both public education and teacher education. Most schooling since colonial days had been a private affair. Children often snatched a few months of training, usually during the winter when farm work eased, to learn the "three Rs" from someone in their church or community.

Yet despite its sporadic nature, private education was remarkably successful. The 1840 census reported that 78 percent of the entire population was able to read and write and that nine of ten whites could read and write. Despite America's having possibly the highest literacy rate in the world, a movement for change was afoot, beginning in the 1830s. Reformers argued that the states should assume a larger role in schooling their young citizens to help ensure that the rising generation of voters could make informed decisions.

One of the leading reformers in the drive for public education was **Horace Mann**. As head of the Massachusetts Board of Education, Mann brought a crusader's zeal to the task. He believed that people could find deliverance from ignorance and social problems through sound moral education. After Mann had been at his post for eleven years, every child in the state could go to school for six months out of the year, fifty new high schools had been built, and teachers' salaries increased by half. Massachusetts became a model for public education in the rest of the country.

In addition, Mann led a growing movement to train teachers. Previously, teaching was generally viewed as something a law student or seminary student did to earn money before entering his profession. But teaching as a profession itself became an important part of educational reform. Teacher colleges—called "normal schools" because they offered a uniform curriculum—developed, and more trained women began to join the profession.

Unfortunately for Horace Mann, his energetic reforms were motivated by faulty reasons. As a young man he had rejected the orthodox Christian influence of his parents and pastor and drifted to liberal Unitarianism. Mann came to believe that people could find deliverance from ignorance and social problems through sound moral education. He believed, in the words of a friend, "If we can but turn the wonderful energy of this people into right channels, what a new heaven and earth might be realized among us."

In aiming for the head, however, Mann missed the heart. As the apostle Paul reminded Titus, "Unto them that are defiled and unbelieving is nothing pure; but even their mind and conscience is defiled" (Titus 1:15). Only Christ can provide deliverance as He cleanses the heart and mind through salvation.

Another person who saw the importance of the public education movement was a Christian who also realized its potential for

Frederick Douglass

Noah Webster

One important Christian figure in early American education was Noah Webster. More than 100 million copies of his *American Spelling Book* (1782, commonly known as the "Blue-Backed Speller") were sold. He later published a self-teaching grammar book and a reader.

Webster is also known for *An American Dictionary of the English Language* (1882). In his dictionary, Webster frequently cited Bible passages to illustrate the meanings of words, and he emphasized the early American ideals of individual liberty and responsibility. His dictionary has remained the model for American dictionaries.

Although he was a lifelong churchgoer, Webster was not converted until the age of fifty, during the Second Great Awakening.

Dorothea Dix, Reformer in Mental Health

One of the most important reformers of the era was a quiet schoolteacher and writer, **Dorothea Dix**. As the head of a young women's school and author of children's books, she seemed an unlikely reformer. When she began teaching a Sunday school class in a prison in Massachusetts, however, Dix was appalled to find four mentally ill persons imprisoned there. They had been thrown into prison by officials who knew of nothing else to do with them. Secretly, she visited numerous prisons and insane asylums to get firsthand information about conditions there. Appalled by what she found, Dix wrote and lectured, attempting to inform the public about the situation. Through her efforts, legislatures in several eastern states voted to improve sanitary conditions and the treatment of inmates in asylums.

Sylvester Graham

One of the most eccentric reformers of the era was Presbyterian clergyman Sylvester Graham. Graham followed a strict vegetarian diet that excluded not only meat but also catsup and mustard (as potential causes of insanity). He set up special food stores in which only healthful "Graham foods" were available. He also recommended soaking one's head in cold water as a cure for headaches. Among those who followed his teachings were Bronson Alcott (father of Louisa May Alcott, the author of *Little Women*), Joseph Smith (founder of Mormonism), and Evangelist Charles Finney. Today, however, Graham is known only through "graham" (whole-wheat) flour and products made from such flour, notably graham crackers.

the gospel—**William H. McGuffey**. In a series of elementary reading books, McGuffey taught generations of Americans rules for living as well as rules for grammar. By the beginning of the twentieth century, 120 million copies of his *Eclectic Readers* had been sold. McGuffey believed that biblical values had a natural and necessary role for shaping character in the classroom, and his work was enormously successful.

Prohibition

Alcohol was another evil that reformers attacked. The problem of drunkenness had been long recognized, but efforts to reduce drinking had achieved only limited success. Reformers eventually replaced their call for temperance, or moderate drinking, with a call for the outright **prohibition**, or banning, of the sale and consumption of alcohol. Support for Prohibition was widespread. A growing number of Christians supported temperance or Prohibition as a moral principle. Social reformers supported Prohibition because of the suffering that drinking brought to drinkers, their families, and society generally. Employers supported Prohibition because drunkenness affected production and absence rates. The movement scored its first major victory in 1846, when Maine voted for statewide prohibition. The Prohibition movement's greatest success, however, came in the early twentieth century with the passage of the Eighteenth Amendment (see Chapter 18).

Women's Rights

As demonstrated by the work of Dorothea Dix, many of the leading advocates of reform in the first half of the nineteenth century were women. In the Prohibition and abolition movements particularly, women were both numerous and active. Some male reformers resented such "unladylike" activity. An antislavery convention in London, for example, refused to seat women delegates simply because of their sex. That rejection, combined with activism in other fields, led naturally to agitation for women's rights, notably women's suffrage (the right to vote). In 1848, a number of women reformers held a convention in Seneca Falls, New York, in which they passed resolutions calling for equal rights for women, such as the right to vote. This **Seneca Falls Convention** is now commonly regarded as the birth of the modern women's rights movement. Dramatic gains in women's rights, however, did not come until the twentieth century.

Utopian Reformers

Most reformers focused on a single major problem in society, such as prison reform or alcohol, and aimed at eliminating the problem throughout society. **Utopian reformers**, on the other hand, sought to establish small, perfect communities that would serve as models for the reform of society at large. (A utopia is an ideally perfect place. The word *utopia* means literally "nowhere," implying that there is no such thing as a true utopia on the earth.) Some of these reformers operated from religious motives. The Harmony Society, also known as the Rappites after their leader, George Rapp, founded a religiously based community in Harmonie, Indiana, in 1815. The Harmony Society established a society based on the idea of mutual helpfulness and support. (They also practiced celibacy, the abstaining from all sexual relations, a belief which limited their growth and eventually caused the group to die out.)

Other utopians operated from secular, rationalistic motives. British reformer **Robert Owen** purchased Harmonie from the Rappites in 1825. Renaming it New Harmony, Owen sought to establish a perfect society based on common ownership of property. After two years of internal fighting and a loss of $200,000, Owen abandoned the New Harmony project.

Another group that tried to develop utopian societies was the transcendentalists. They taught a liberal, unbiblical philosophy known as **transcendentalism**, which arose from Unitarianism (discussed later in this chapter). Perhaps their best-known attempt at developing a utopian society was Brook Farm, which was an experiment in communal living based on the idea that man could transcend feelings by coming into harmony with his inner being. Like all other utopian experiments, it was a failure.

Transcendentalism was primarily the creation of writer and lecturer Ralph Waldo Emerson. A graduate of Harvard, Emerson entered the Unitarian ministry but found even liberal Unitarianism too confining. He developed his own optimistic, man-centered "faith." Like Unitarianism, transcendentalism denied the miraculous, but it went even further in its teachings. Basically, it put man in the place of God. Emerson taught that man was basically good and ultimately perfectible. He rejected the Christian view of God and taught instead that everything is part of God and that God dwells within every person. Emerson denied, as he put it, a faith "*in* Christ" in favor of a faith "*like* Christ's," which Emerson said was "faith in man." Transcendentalists were never numerous, but they were influential. Among those influenced by transcendentalism were author Henry David Thoreau and poet Walt Whitman.

The utopian reformers, whether religious or secular, all ultimately failed because of their faulty view of the nature of man. Man's inherent sinfulness dooms any human attempt to build a perfect society on earth.

The Arts

Americans in the early nineteenth century did not pursue the fine arts with the same enthusiasm that they did the technological arts. Samuel F. B. Morse, for example, was an accomplished painter, but he found it far easier to put bread on the table as an inventor. However, American painters, architects, musicians, and writers produced works that displayed remarkable talent. They produced works that copied European models less and were more distinctly American in nature. This period was the real beginning of truly *American* art.

Painting and Architecture

The period from the inauguration of George Washington to that of Andrew Jackson is usually called the era of the **Federalist style** in art. The Federalist approach more or less duplicated the neoclassical style of Europe. It

Isaiah's Lips Anointed with Fire, Benjamin West, P.R.A.
From the Bob Jones University Museum & Gallery

This 1846 view of the unfinished U.S. Capitol reveals clearly the neoclassical Federalist influence on its design.

emphasized balance, emotional restraint, and a respect for the artistic styles of ancient Greece and Rome. Federalist art borrowed heavily from European models. **Benjamin West**, America's first great painter, was really more English than American, although he often painted New World subjects. He was born in Pennsylvania, but he studied in Europe and eventually settled in England. He continued to influence American painting, though, through his teaching of leading American artists.

Several of West's students came to dominate American art. One was **Gilbert Stuart**, one of the young nation's finest portrait painters. He is best known for his different portraits of George Washington, especially his "unfinished" portrait which appears on the $1 bill. Possibly the greatest of the Federalist artists was **John Trumbull**, another student of West's. Trumbull, in fact, specialized in the realistic historical paintings that West had pioneered. Among Trumbull's works are *The Battle of Bunker's Hill* and *Signing of the Declaration of Independence*.

Federalist architecture also borrowed from ancient classical civilizations. The **Greek revival**, led by architects such as **Charles Bulfinch** and **Benjamin Latrobe**, re-created the columns and porticos of ancient Greek and Roman buildings. Bulfinch was so eager to further classical styles that he even drew architectural designs free of charge to encourage people to build in the Federalist style. Both Bulfinch and Latrobe worked at different times on the design of America's most famous Federalist-style building, the United States Capitol. Ironically, Republican president and amateur architect Thomas Jefferson was a proponent of the Federalist style. Jefferson thought that Greece, the great example of ancient democracy, and Rome, the great example of ancient republicanism, provided ideal models for America's young democratic republic. Among Jefferson's designs were his home in Virginia (known as Monticello), the Virginia state capitol, and the University of Virginia rotunda.

After the rise of Jacksonian democracy, the emphasis of American art began to shift. The formal portraits of the Federalist era gave way to casual portrayals of the common man in everyday life. No one surpassed the self-described "thorough democrat" **George Caleb Bingham** in drawing the common man. His *Stump Speaking* and *The County Election*, for example, captured the boisterous, sometimes crude, but always lively activity of American politicking. Carrying the love of American beauty even further was the so-called **Hudson River school** of painters. These artists specialized in landscapes, capturing the land in its serene and majestic beauty. Post-Federalist art in general left European models and sought to celebrate the glories of American life.

Literature

America's most lasting contribution in culture in this era probably came in the field of literature. Although some American writers had achieved a degree of success in the colonial period, the first great age of American literature began with the romantic movement (1820–65). **Romanticism** rejected the balanced unemotionalism of the Federalist and neoclassical styles. Instead romanticism emphasized the emotional, the colorful, and the imaginative. Furthermore, this style placed greater stress on the love of nature and on the individual person rather than on society. (The Hudson River school of painters, for example, were romantic in their stress on portraying nature.)

The first American writer to gain fame outside America was novelist **James Fenimore Cooper**. His "Leatherstocking Tales," one of which was *The Last of the Mohicans*, created an exaggeratedly romantic view of life on the American frontier. Although Cooper's works sound dated today, his novels paved the way for later writers. **Washington Irving** rose to fame with *Knickerbocker's History of New York*, a comic fictional history of Dutch New York. Through his later stories, such as "Rip Van Winkle" and "The Legend of Sleepy Hollow," Irving helped develop the greatest American contribution to world literature, the short story.

Romanticism's central belief in the goodness—or even godhood—of man and the glory of nature, expounded by **Ralph Waldo Emerson** in his works *Nature* and *Self-Reliance*, drew both supporters and critics. Essayist **Henry David Thoreau**, author of *Walden*, and poet **Walt Whitman**, in his work *Leaves of Grass*, both celebrated the glory and nobility of man.

Other romantics attacked the idea of man's inherent goodness. **Nathaniel Hawthorne**, for example, realized the truth of man's depravity. *The Scarlet Letter*, perhaps his finest work, attempts to deal with the problem of sin and its effects, but the novel criticizes what Hawthorne considered the narrow, hypocritical views of Puritanism. **Edgar Allan Poe** delved even deeper into the dark, tortured depths of man's soul in stories such as "The Tell-Tale Heart" and poems such as "The Raven." In the process, Poe became the master short-story writer of America before the Civil War. Sadly, neither Hawthorne nor Poe recognized that the solution to man's sin is found only through the atoning work of the Lord Jesus Christ.

Music

American music from 1789 to 1861 probably represents the character of American culture better than any of the other arts. In Europe, this was the period of great classical composers such as Beethoven. America had no such musical giants. Instead, popular music dominated the United States. America's most important composer of the period was **Stephen Foster**. Foster wrote lyrical ballads such as "I Dream of Jeanie with the Light Brown Hair" (written for his wife) and spirited songs about the South such as "Camptown Races," "Oh, Susanna," and "My Old Kentucky Home" (although Foster had never even visited the South).

Another great composer of the time represented the importance of religious faith to the era. Hymnwriter **Lowell Mason** published several popular hymnbooks and composed the tunes for such hymns as "Nearer, My God, to Thee" and "My Faith Looks Up to Thee." Mason constantly sought to introduce classical European ideals into American hymn music. He arranged his tune for Isaac Watts's "When I Survey the Wondrous Cross," for example, from a medieval Gregorian chant. Mason was also a leading promoter of music education, particularly the teaching of music in public schools.

Newspapers and Magazines

The fine arts were not the only examples of American cultural growth. Rising literacy rates caused by educational improvements created a market for popular literature: newspapers and magazines.

> ### *Whitman's Romantic Beliefs*
> Whitman expressed his belief in the nobility, unity, and brotherhood of man in his "Song of Myself":
>
> I celebrate myself, and sing myself,
>
> And what I assume you shall assume,
>
> For every atom belonging to me as good belongs to you.

Stephen Foster, one of America's most beloved songwriters

Improvements in technology not only allowed printers to publish a greater number of materials but also enabled them to produce materials more quickly and more cheaply. In 1835, Americans published 1,258 newspapers; by 1860, the number had swelled to 3,343. The daily **penny newspaper** (in contrast to more expensive weekly ones) was an important means of making information widely available and more affordable. Two papers, the *New York Sun* (founded in 1833) and the *New York Tribune* (1841), represented two different approaches to journalism. The *Sun* contained sensational accounts of murders, scandals, and other lurid events to appeal to the baser tastes of readers. The *Tribune*, edited by Horace Greeley, supported reform efforts and attempted to educate and uplift its readers. The two approaches proved equally successful, and both the *Sun* and the *Tribune* attracted readers even outside of New York.

Magazines were another vehicle of popular culture. Containing short stories, serialized novels, poems, travel articles, engravings of the latest fashions from Paris, and reviews, magazines served almost as miniature libraries. *Harper's New Monthly* (founded 1850) and the *Atlantic Monthly* (1857) were two of the most popular and longest lived. Magazines aimed to reach either general audiences or some specific group. For example, *Godey's Lady's Book* (1830) was one of the first women's magazines. Magazines not only met American literary tastes but also increased them. Significantly, *Harper's* began by reprinting British material, but it soon found a wider audience for the work of American writers.

Section Quiz

1. What was the most controversial reform movement of the first half of the nineteenth century? Who was its most important leader?

2. What were the two important trends in American education in the early 1800s?

3. What is the difference between temperance and Prohibition?

4. How did utopian reformers differ from other reformers?

5. Which authors defended romanticism's idea that man is basically good? Which authors denied this idea?

6. How did the journalistic approach of the *New York Sun* differ from that of the *New York Tribune*?

★ What is at the heart of the failure of every attempted utopian society?

III. American Religion

Religious life in America also expanded from 1789 to 1861. Some of the expansion was only numerical, not spiritual; a few of the religious movements of the era were sources of spiritual darkness instead of spiritual light. Many of the movements, however, seem to have been genuine expressions of the work of the Holy Spirit. Significantly, this period in American history began and ended with a sweeping national revival.

The Second Great Awakening

Shortly after the ratification of the Constitution, America experienced its second great revival of religion. The **Second Great**

Awakening was longer and more complex in nature than the first. It touched different regions of the nation in different ways, and its effects reached even across the sea.

Background

American religion was in a sorry state after the War for Independence. **Deism** was the "faith" of several American leaders. Deists believed that reason rather than Scripture was the way men came to know God. God Himself created the world but rarely if ever became personally involved in its affairs. Deists denied the deity of Christ, the inspiration of the Bible, the reality of miracles, and any other belief that struck them as superstitious because they could not explain it by their own reason.

Besides this "intellectual religion," some Americans lacked any religion at all. For them, the pleasures of the day—drinking, gambling, and the like—were far more important than any kind of creed, Christian or otherwise. John Marshall observed sadly that the church was "too far gone ever to be revived."

The situation was not all darkness and despair, however. One of the brightest spots for Christianity was the growth of American Methodism. The **Methodists** were followers of the teachings of English minister **John Wesley**. After a long and desperate struggle with a sense of guilt and sin, Wesley had been converted. He began to travel around Great Britain, preaching the need for conversion to Christ and holy living. The Methodists remained technically part of the Church of England until Wesley's death, but afterwards they became a separate denomination.

Methodism in America grew slowly at first, partly because of its association with Anglicanism and partly because of Wesley's opposition to the War for Independence. Later, however, it proved enormously successful at reaching all classes of society with the gospel, including both free blacks and slaves. Much of the credit for the denomination's growth must go to the Father of American Methodism, **Francis Asbury**. Sent from England to America in 1772, Asbury worked for years to establish Methodist congregations. He developed the most important institution of American Methodism, **circuit riding**. The United States was too vast and its population too scattered for Asbury to establish a minister in every community. Asbury therefore divided the land into sections, or circuits. One minister, called a "circuit rider," traveled on horseback from settlement to settlement throughout his assigned circuit, ministering to Christians and preaching to the lost. Facing the challenges of an untamed wilderness, Methodist circuit riders were tough men with tender hearts. Asbury himself traveled nearly three hundred thousand miles on horseback. On the frontier in particular, Methodists became some of the most important contributors to the awakening.

Revival in the East

The Second Great Awakening began in the East. There the revivals centered in the churches and colleges, where Christian zeal had lapsed into apathy and even open sin. Yale, founded in 1701 to train ministers, was an example of how low spirituality had fallen. One minister recalled his student days at Yale in the years before the awakening:

The College was in a most ungodly state. The college church was almost extinct. Most of the students were skeptical, and

---

Deists in the Early National Period

Revolutionary War veteran Ethan Allen wrote one of the first American defenses of deism in a crude, anti-Christian work titled *Reason: The Only Oracle of Man*. Thomas Paine, author of *Common Sense*, wrote a more polished— but no more orthodox—exposition of deism, *The Age of Reason*. Other American leaders, such as Thomas Jefferson and Benjamin Franklin, also embraced deism.

Francis Asbury, Methodist circuit-riding preacher

Richard Allen

One instrument God used in reaching blacks was a former slave himself—Richard Allen. Born in Pennsylvania, Allen was converted under the preaching of a Methodist in Delaware in 1777. Shortly thereafter, Allen's master allowed the young slave to purchase his freedom.

Allen chopped wood, worked in a brick-yard, and delivered salt to make a living. He preached in the evenings and on Sundays. Allen became a circuit rider in New Jersey and Pennsylvania.

Allen enjoyed a fruitful ministry among blacks in Philadelphia. Allen and his black converts originally attended a white Methodist church in the city, but some members resented the increased numbers of blacks in their services. In 1787, Allen and the other blacks walked out and started their own church—the African Methodist Episcopal (AME) Church in Philadelphia. Bishop Francis Asbury dedicated the church in 1794, and he later ordained Allen. When several other black congregations expressed an interest in closer fellowship with Allen's church, they decided to form their own denomination, and Allen became their first bishop. Under his leadership, the denomination became one of the most effective means of reaching blacks with the gospel before the War Between the States.

rowdies were plenty. Wine and liquors were kept in many rooms; intemperance, profanity, gambling, and licentiousness were common.

Into this situation at Yale came **Timothy Dwight**, a grandson of Jonathan Edwards. Elected president of Yale in 1795, Dwight confronted the problem of a rebellious student body. He openly challenged all comers in public debates on the truths of the Christian Faith. Dwight also preached a series of sermons in chapel on basic Christian theology. The fruit of Dwight's labors was a series of revivals in which at least a third of Yale's students were converted.

Revival in the other schools and churches of the East followed the pattern of Yale. Order and restraint were the key characteristics to avoid excesses that had occurred in some instances during the First Great Awakening. The Second Great Awakening was characterized by the faithful work of local pastors and laymen rather than prominent leaders like Edwards and Whitefield. The awakening endured for sixty years and influenced the nation for several generations. The preaching was urgent in its message but calm in its tone. The spiritual fervor of the revivals in the East was deep but quiet, and the results were profound.

Revival in the West

On the frontier, the awakening appeared a little later and in a different form. The chief feature of the western revivals was the **camp meeting**, a series of religious services lasting several days and often held outdoors. Usually several preachers exhorted the crowds in simple but fiery gospel sermons. The camp meeting was originated by Presbyterian James McGready in Logan County, Kentucky. In 1800, McGready, three other Presbyterians, and a Methodist preacher held an outdoor Communion service to welcome new members into the church. During this and other services that followed, hearers began to profess a deep sense of their own sinfulness and to cry out for salvation. The results in Logan County proved so remarkable that other preachers began to hold camp meetings. Probably the most significant camp meeting was held at **Cane Ridge**, Kentucky, in 1801. Estimates of the attendance at Cane Ridge range from ten thousand to twenty-five thousand. This attendance was phenomenal, especially considering that nearby Lexington, the largest city in Kentucky at that time, had a population of only eighteen hundred people.

Camp meeting revivals contrasted markedly with the orderly and careful preaching of the revivals in the East. At an increasing number of meetings some of the hearers shook, jerked, jumped, ran, barked, and fell. While some physical responses were initially the outward manifestation of inward conviction, several preachers began to encourage these outward displays. This led to a split between those ministers who cautioned against excesses that distracted from the gospel message and those who believed that these physical responses were signs of God's favor. A number of preachers began counting how many people had fallen during the preaching in an attempt to measure God's work.

The western revivals brought about mixed results. Many people *were converted by the preaching of the gospel, and their changed* lives provided the evidence of conversion. On the other hand, the western revivals began a trend of promoting outward physical responses at the expense of true gospel preaching.

Foreign Missions

The effects of the Second Great Awakening reached beyond the shores of the United States. The first great American missions movement resulted from this revival. Among the colleges in the East that were touched by the revival was Williams College in Massachusetts. In 1806 a group of students from the college was holding an outdoor prayer meeting when a fierce thunderstorm blew in. Taking shelter under a nearby haystack, the little group began to discuss the need to carry the gospel throughout the world. One member of that group, Samuel Mills, decided to fulfill that dream and helped establish the **American Board of Commissioners for Foreign Missions (ABCFM)**, America's first foreign mission board.

The ABCFM, a Congregationalist organization, sent many missionaries throughout the world, but it was not the only American mission board for long. **Adoniram Judson** and Luther Rice went to India in 1812 under the ABCFM. On the way, however, Judson and Rice decided that their theological views were more Baptist than Congregational. Judson remained in Asia while Rice returned to the United States to raise some support among Baptists. Judson eventually moved to Burma, where his faithful translation work and preaching made him the first great hero of the American missions movement. Rice helped start a Baptist mission organization that became a major force in sending missionaries overseas. Through the efforts of men such as Mills and Rice and through the labors of missionaries such as Judson, thousands of lost souls throughout the world came to salvation in Jesus Christ.

Results of the Awakening

Like the colonial Great Awakening, the Second Great Awakening produced dramatic results. First and most important, multiplied thousands of people were converted to Christ and joined churches. American Methodists, for example, numbered 15,000 in 1785. By 1840 their numbers had grown to 850,000, and Methodism had become the largest denomination in the United States. Second, as mentioned earlier, was the birth and growth of America's foreign missions movement. Third, moral sins declined in the wake of the revival; for example, drunkenness declined. Also, the revival fueled the drive for moral reform. Many of the leaders in the Prohibition and abolition movements were zealous converts of the revival. Fourth, new methods of evangelism resulted from the revival. The Second Great Awakening touched and transformed the lives of a large segment of the American people.

Unorthodox Religion

Not all the religious movements in the first half of the nineteenth century reflected biblical teaching. In fact, several influential movements denied scriptural truth and promoted error.

Charles Finney and the "New Measures"

By the 1820s, as the first wave of revivals began to subside, **Charles Finney** tried to perpetuate the revivals with innovative methods. While practicing law in upstate New York, Finney professed conversion in 1821 during a revival. After informal study with a Presbyterian pastor, Finney began preaching in small towns across New York. Reports of numerous dramatic conversions increased Finney's reputation. By the 1830s he was preaching to huge crowds in New York City and was America's leading evangelist.

Charles Finney introduced "New Measures" to revivalism.

Finney's Methods Reflected the Society of the Time

Finney's views and the methods he used were reflective of what was occurring in politics at the same time. He allowed all, including women, to participate in his services. He encouraged women to pray publicly, to testify, and to organize and run volunteer societies, especially in urban evangelism and personal Bible studies. Similarly, Jacksonian democracy opened the doors to political participation to more people, encouraged involvement by the common man (but not yet by women), and substituted rule by "the people" for rule by an elite aristocracy.

Finney admitted his success was not due to the miraculous working of God's Spirit. Revival, according to Finney, "is a purely philosophical result of the right use of the constituted means." He developed what others dubbed "**New Measures**," new and unusual methods for conducting revivals. Finney always kept an "anxious bench" in his meetings, reserved seats for sinners who sensed a conviction of sin. He also prayed publicly by name for those known to be sinners. Finney held "protracted meetings," services held daily for up to several weeks in one location. He combined elements of both eastern and western revivals. Finney insisted on order and restraint in his meetings, like those in the East. His aggressive sermons and extended meetings, however, had the flavor of the West about them. Finney's success guaranteed that many would copy him.

Finney proved influential for American evangelists, and many evangelists and preachers today use at least some of his methods. However, he also received much-deserved criticism. Finney claimed that sinners had the responsibility and ability to change their own hearts without the gracious working of God. He also denied that all humans are born guilty sinners, that Jesus received God's wrath in the place of sinners, and that justification comes by faith alone. Still, through his hugely successful campaigns and later his influential position as professor and president of Oberlin College in Ohio, Charles Finney became one of the most dominant figures in American religion in this era.

Unitarianism

One of the most prestigious unorthodox religions is **Unitarianism**. Its name derives from its basic doctrine of the "unity" of God; that is, Unitarianism denies the Trinity and therefore the deity of Christ. Jesus, to the Unitarians, was a great religious teacher, but He was only a man, so His death provided no atonement for sin. Instead, Unitarianism teaches that people should simply live moral, upright lives to please God.

The first Unitarian church in America began in 1785, but the denomination's real growth came after 1805, when Harvard appointed its first Unitarian professor. Within twenty years, Harvard had become a center of Unitarian teaching, and many of the old Congregationalist churches in the East declined from orthodoxy to Unitarianism. The denomination's influence was even greater than its numbers, in part because many wealthy and prominent leaders of eastern society became Unitarians. The denomination initially experienced little influence outside New England, however, causing one wit to remark that Unitarian preaching was limited to "the fatherhood of God, the brotherhood of man, and the neighborhood of Boston."

Millerites

Unlike the error of many of the era's other unorthodox movements, the error of the **Millerites** was not so much wrong doctrine as wrong emphasis when they set a date for the Second Coming of Christ. William Miller was a Baptist minister in New York who began to attract attention in the 1830s. Miller was a premillennialist. He believed that Christ would return to the earth and establish the Millennium, a perfect kingdom of peace lasting a thousand years. (The word *millennium* comes from two Latin words meaning "thousand years.") However, Miller strayed from Christ's declaration in Matthew 24:36 that no man can know the day and hour of

His return. He set a date for Christ's return, sometime between March 21, 1843, and March 21, 1844. Thousands of people in the Northeast heard Miller, and perhaps as many as one hundred thousand became followers of his teaching.

The frenzied year of Miller's prediction came—and went. Mockers ridiculed Millerites, and they poured their scorn on premillennialism in general. Unproved rumors circulated of how Millerites, dressed in white "ascension robes," waited on rooftops for the great event. Miller brought reproach on the doctrine of the Second Coming by ignoring Jesus' own words about His return: "But of that day and that hour knoweth no man, no, not the angels which are in heaven, neither the Son, but the Father. Take ye heed, watch and pray: for ye know not when the time is" (Mark 13:32–33).

While Miller abandoned his efforts to predict the Lord's return, others continued to do so. Ultimately, Seventh-day Adventists developed from the Millerites.

Other Unorthodox Movements

Several other unorthodox groups developed in this era. Many of them were cults, groups that call themselves Christian but that deviate from orthodox doctrine on one or more points. One such group was the **Shakers**, who began in England in the 1700s but enjoyed their greatest growth in America in the early 1800s. Shakers took their name from the shaking or dancing that accompanied their worship. They practiced celibacy (they considered any sexual relations sinful) and owned property in common. Shakers believed that their founder, Mother Ann Lee, was an incarnation of God, just as Jesus was. The Shakers built prosperous, well-ordered farms in New England, New York, Ohio, Indiana, and Kentucky. The group won many converts in the early 1800s, but it eventually died out because of its practice of celibacy.

Probably the most significant cult to arise at this time was **Mormonism**, also known as the Church of Jesus Christ of Latter-day Saints. Mormonism was founded by **Joseph Smith** in 1830. Smith claimed that an angel showed him some golden plates inscribed with ancient writing. With the angel's help, Smith said, he translated the plates to produce the Book of Mormon, one of the holy books of Mormonism. The Mormons say that they accept the Bible as God's Word but that the Book of Mormon is "another revelation" that takes precedence. They also teach that salvation rests primarily on good works and that one who is good enough eventually becomes a god. Mormons stirred up the most controversy, however, by their practice of polygamy, the taking of more than one wife at the same time. Non-Mormons viewed that practice as a major assault on the traditional family.

Opposition drove the Mormons from New York to Ohio to Nauvoo, Illinois. In Illinois, conflicts between Mormons and local residents led to the jailing of Smith in Nauvoo. There, a lynch mob attacked the jail and killed Smith. **Brigham Young** then assumed the leadership of the group. He led the Mormons on a prolonged trek west, where they founded Salt Lake City, capital of a territory that eventually became the state of Utah. The Mormons eventually abandoned the practice of polygamy officially and built a huge temple in Salt Lake City.

Mary Baker Eddy, the founder of **Christian Science**, was reared in a strict Congregationalist home. As a child, she suffered numerous physical and emotional ailments. She married a man

Brigham Young, Mormon leader

Mary Baker Eddy, founder of Christian Science

who lived nearby, but he soon died of yellow fever, and the loss only aggravated her instability. Ten years later, she remarried, against her father's advice, but she later divorced the man. When she was in her mid-fifties, she married a third time, but her new husband also died.

Throughout that time, Mary Baker Eddy, as she was generally known, had been gathering material and ideas for a book she published titled *Science and Health with Key to the Scriptures*. It became the main document of her group, which, as someone has noted, is neither Christian nor scientific. It denies the Trinity, the inspiration of Scripture, miracles, the atonement, and other key Christian doctrines. The group also denies sickness and death. Perhaps the group's most public feature today is its national newspaper, the *Christian Science Monitor*.

The Prayer Meeting Revival

Despite the growth of false religious movements such as Mormonism, the first half of the 1800s was a time of triumph for many biblical groups. The climax of American religious life in that era came just before the Civil War in what was called by some the "third great awakening," or the **Prayer Meeting Revival** of 1857–59.

The revival began shortly after a serious financial crisis, the Panic of 1857. In September of that year in New York City, a lay evangelist named Jeremiah Lanphier began holding a weekly prayer meeting during the noon lunch hour. Attendance grew from six the first week, to twenty the next, to forty the next, and then more. Soon the group decided to meet daily, and the church building was full to overcrowding. Other churches, first in New York and then in other eastern cities, began to hold daily prayer meetings. Within months, churches and auditoriums across America were filled with men and women who met to pray for an hour. Every day in cities throughout the United States, life stood still for an hour as shopkeepers, laborers, and others paused to pray.

There was no formal organization to the prayer meetings. Each group usually met under the leadership of some Christian, often a layman. They sang a few hymns, shared requests, and listened to short devotionals, but mostly they prayed. Afterward, pastors and other Christian workers remained to help those who sought spiritual counsel.

The results of the revival were astounding. Nearly a million people were converted. Encouraged by the revival, Christians raised money to found Christian schools and support foreign missionaries. Established Christian organizations received floods of new volunteers whose lives had been transformed by the awakening. For example, the Young Men's Christian Association (YMCA), established in 1844 in Great Britain, was able to expand its ministry of providing wholesome recreation and fervent religious instruction for young people, primarily in the cities. The Prayer Meeting Revival also marked perhaps the first time that laymen had dominated the leadership of a revival. The overall impact of the revival was remarkable.

The revival came at an opportune time. Within two years of its close, the United States would go to battle against itself in the Civil War. The blessings that God so graciously shed upon the young nation in revival would help to sustain it in the fiery furnace of war.

> **One Preacher's Testimony of the Revival's Results**
>
> One Presbyterian pastor, who earlier had been skeptical of the revival, wrote to a friend, "Study I cannot, being run down by persons, many of whom I never knew, in search of counsel.... The openness of thousands to doctrine, reproof, etc., is undeniable.... You may rest assured that there is a great awakening among us."

Section Quiz

1. What system did Francis Asbury develop to solve the problem of having too few ministers to cover a large area of land?

2. Give four results of the Second Great Awakening.

3. What were the "New Measures"?

4. How did Charles Finney combine elements of both the eastern and western revivals of the Second Great Awakening?

5. Name four unorthodox religious movements of the era.

✶ In what ways did the revivalism of this era reflect the American values of liberty, equality, individualism, and growth?

People, Places, and Things to Remember

Samuel Slater
Eli Whitney
interchangeable parts
patent
John Deere
Cyrus McCormick
cotton gin
Robert Fulton
plank roads
corduroy roads
toll roads
turnpikes
National Road
DeWitt Clinton
Erie Canal
Baltimore & Ohio Railroad
clipper ship
Samuel F. B. Morse
pony express
abolitionism
William Lloyd Garrison
Nat Turner
Frederick Douglass
Harriet Tubman
Horace Mann
William H. McGuffey
Dorothea Dix
prohibition
Seneca Falls Convention
utopian reformers
Robert Owen
transcendentalism
Federalist style
Benjamin West
Gilbert Stuart
John Trumbull
Greek revival
Charles Bulfinch
Benjamin Latrobe
George Caleb Bingham
Hudson River school
romanticism
James Fenimore Cooper
Washington Irving
Ralph Waldo Emerson
Henry David Thoreau
Walt Whitman
Nathaniel Hawthorne
Edgar Allan Poe
Stephen Foster
Lowell Mason
penny newspaper
Second Great Awakening
deism
Methodists
John Wesley
Francis Asbury
circuit riding

Chapter Review

Making Connections

1. Why did western Pennsylvania become an early center of American heavy industry?

2. How did reform movements affect the American public during the first half of the nineteenth century?

3. During the Second Great Awakening, which were more emotional, the revivals in the East or the revivals in the West? In which region did the revivals center in the schools and churches?

4. Name the religious figure described by each phrase:
   a. foreign missionary to Burma
   b. originated the camp meeting
   c. founded the African Methodist Episcopal Church
   d. sparked the Prayer Meeting Revival
   e. oversaw the Yale revivals
   f. founded Mormonism
   g. Father of American Methodism
   h. taught faith in man instead of faith in Christ
   i. practiced the "New Measures"
   j. incorrectly predicted the Second Coming

Developing History Skills

1. What were at least three arguments offered by southerners in defense of slavery?

2. How would the history of America have been affected had the South developed a system of transportation and communication by 1860 as the North and West did?

Thinking Critically

1. Read Philemon 15–17 on the relationship of Paul, Philemon, and Onesimus. Although some slaveowners appealed to this passage in support of slavery, how does this passage undercut the religious arguments in support of slavery?

2. Evaluate mission work as conducted by men like Adoniram Judson and mission-support work as conducted by men like Luther Rice.

Living as a Christian Citizen

1. Perhaps you will be visiting relatives soon and your Christian education will be questioned or challenged. How will you respond? Base your answer, in part, on what you learned about Horace Mann and William H. McGuffey.

2. The Second Great Awakening was a time of expansion for the American church. Currently, the church is expanding in places such as Africa and China. What are the similarities to the Second Great Awakening, and what are the differences?

People, Places, and Things to Remember

Timothy Dwight
camp meeting
Cane Ridge
American Board of Commissioners for Foreign Missions (ABCFM)
Adoniram Judson
Charles Finney
"New Measures"
Unitarianism
Millerites
Shakers
Mormonism
Joseph Smith
Brigham Young
Mary Baker Eddy
Christian Science
Prayer Meeting Revival

"Mexican News" by Alfred Jones (detail)

Manifest Destiny (1840–1848)

I.   **Across the Wide Missouri**

II. **Politics and Protocol**

III. **War with Mexico**

"Our manifest destiny [is] to overspread and to possess the whole of the continent which Providence has given us."

John Lewis O'Sullivan, December 27, 1845
New York Morning News

According to a popular story, when Henry Clay was traveling through the Cumberland Gap in 1850, he stopped and began to concentrate as though he were listening intently to something. When a curious onlooker asked what he was doing, Clay replied, "I am listening to the tread of the coming millions."

Since the founding of the first settlements on the Atlantic coast, Americans had been courageously, stubbornly, almost irresistibly moving ever westward to settle the continent. As one pioneer wrote in her diary,

> When God made man,
> He seemed to think it best
> To make him in the East
> And let him travel west.

The 1840s saw that pattern continue with violent vigor as a burst of expansion resulted in the nation's stretching "from sea to shining sea." Supporting and motivating this growth was a philosophy that urged, even demanded, expansion. In 1845, New York journalist and Democratic operative John Louis O'Sullivan both named and described this philosophy when he wrote that

> our manifest destiny [is] to overspread and to possess the whole of the continent which Providence has given us for the development of the great experiment of liberty and federated self-government entrusted to us.

The idea of **Manifest Destiny**—that America was providentially ordained to possess the North American continent—dominated American thinking in the 1840s. The term literally means "obvious destiny." Americans asserted boldly—perhaps even arrogantly—that some "higher power" had given the whole continent to the United States. The two main factors in Manifest Destiny were land and gold. Manifest Destiny also included the seeds of a future empire beyond American borders. All that remained was for Americans to claim it.

I. Across the Wide Missouri

Expansion in the 1840s was not as sudden as it might have seemed at the time. The background of that dramatic decade lay in more than twenty years of dealings between the United States and Britain on the one hand and the United States and Mexico on the other. The basis of Manifest Destiny in the 1840s was the history of the territories of Oregon and Texas and in the development of the western trails.

Oregon

Joint Occupation

As mentioned in Chapter 9, the United States and Great Britain agreed in 1818 to occupy the Oregon Territory jointly until the two nations could decide how to divide the area. At first, Britain did more toward developing the territory. Attracted by Oregon's abundance of beaver and other animals, British fur traders and trappers flocked to the region, but they were a wandering breed, and few of them settled down to build houses and to farm. In 1840, the number of whites living in Oregon, aside from those involved in the fur

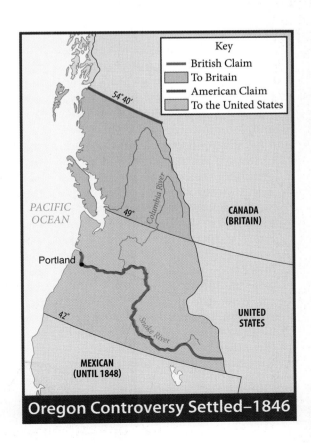

Oregon Controversy Settled—1846

trade, was only two hundred. As the 1840s proceeded, however, that situation changed rapidly.

Missions to the Northwest

One of the more positive aspects of Manifest Destiny was an increased interest in missions. In fact, the great spur to the settlement of Oregon came from American missionaries to the Indians. In 1833, an Indian convert to Christianity published an appeal for Christians to reach the Indians of the Northwest with the gospel. Many eagerly responded, the most famous of whom were two missionary couples: **Marcus Whitman** and his wife, **Narcissa**, and Henry Spalding and his wife, Eliza. The Spaldings, settling in what is today northern Idaho, enjoyed some success among the Nez Perce (NEZ PURS) Indians. They were able to establish both a church for the Nez Perces and a school for their children. Eliza handpainted visual aids, such as charts, to present the gospel pictorially to the Indians. In addition, the Spaldings attempted to help the Indians learn better methods of agriculture. Spalding said, "We point them with one hand to the Lamb of God, with the other to the hoe as the means of saving their famishing bodies."

The Whitmans had less apparent success as missionaries but had greater impact on the settlement of Oregon. The Whitmans, soon joined by other missionaries, built a mission compound near the site of modern Walla Walla, Washington, and tried to reach the fiercely independent Cayuse (kye YOOS) Indians. Although the mission featured a thriving farm, the area proved less fertile for the gospel. The suspicious Cayuses distrusted the settlers. The missionaries did not help matters by suggesting that the Indians could better please God by abandoning hunting and fishing and taking up

Narcissa and Marcus Whitman, missionaries to the Indians of the Northwest, were murdered by the very people they sought to reach for Christ.

Narcissa Whitman

Narcissa Whitman soundly refuted the argument that the Oregon country was no place for a white woman. But in many ways Narcissa was not a typical woman. A lovely and well-educated woman from New York, she penned accounts in her letters and diary that presented a vivid picture of the courage and faith of a pioneer missionary.

Several years after her conversion at the age of eleven, Narcissa became interested in the mission field, but the American Board of Commissioners for Foreign Missions refused to consider an unmarried woman missionary. When she met physician Marcus Whitman, Narcissa eagerly shared in his dream of carrying the gospel to the Indians of the Pacific Northwest. They were married, and the board approved them as missionaries.

The trip to Oregon fascinated Narcissa. She had her first encounter with buffalo meat. She also noted with amusement the westerners' figures of speech.

Like most travelers to Oregon, she had to sacrifice some of her possessions along the way. She especially hated being forced to leave her trunk in the wilderness.

Once in Oregon, the romance of mission work quickly wore off. The work of building and keeping up the mission compound/farm was heavy, and the Indians did not respond as readily as the Whitmans had hoped. Narcissa gave birth to a daughter, but the child tragically drowned in a river at the age of two. Narcissa noted that the grave of her daughter was "in sight every time [she stepped] out the door." The unvarying, unending

labor wore on Narcissa both physically and spiritually.

Through the years, though, she stayed with the task. She wrote to her parents in April 1846, "There has been considerable evidence of the movings of the Holy Spirit. . . . For ourselves, we feel that our own souls have been greatly revived, and I hope and pray that we may never again relapse into such a state of insensibility and worldly-mindedness as we many times have found ourselves in." In November 1846, she wrote home with some optimism: "We feel that God has heard prayer, for many precious souls give evidence of having passed from death to life, some among the Indians and many more among our own countrymen." About a year later, she and her husband were murdered by Indians.

farming like the whites. So the Whitmans proved more successful at recruiting settlers than reaching Indians. They sent back not only calls for more workers but also exciting descriptions of the rich, unsettled lands. Marcus Whitman even served as a scout for some parties of settlers from the East.

The increasing stream of white settlers angered the Cayuses and caused them to suspect that the white man was more interested in taking Indian land than in saving Indian souls. Marcus Whitman wrote optimistically in a letter in 1844, "The Indians are anxious about the consequences of settlers among them, but I hope there will be no acts of violence on either hand." Whitman's hopes proved vain, especially when a measles epidemic, apparently carried into Oregon by settlers, wiped out nearly half the tribe despite Whitman's efforts to treat the ill. Finally, in 1847, a party of Cayuses ambushed the mission compound, murdering Marcus, Narcissa, and twelve others.

Growing Numbers

The missionaries had unwittingly opened the door for a flood of immigrants. A thousand settlers came to Oregon in 1841; within two years the number had tripled and continued to grow. Extravagant stories of the region's beauty and wealth filtered back to the East, such as the tall tale that "the pigs are running about . . . already cooked, with knives and forks sticking in them so that you can cut off a slice whenever you are hungry." The truth about Oregon was enough to lure most settlers: abundant land, fertile soil, and a mild climate. By the mid-1840s, southern Oregon was far more American than British, and the joint occupation agreement of 1818 no longer seemed satisfactory to many Americans.

Texas

American Settlement

As part of Spain's vast North American empire, Texas remained almost unsettled until the 1820s. In 1822, **Stephen F. Austin**, with the permission of Spanish authorities, led the first of many land-hungry American settlers into Texas. Soon after arriving, Austin received the disturbing news that the Mexicans had overthrown the Spanish and gained their independence. Austin quickly secured approval for his venture by pledging allegiance to the new government of Mexico. Under the firm and diligent leadership of Austin, the transplanted Americans prospered, and others soon streamed in to take advantage of the riches of the new land. Cotton growing and cattle raising in particular became major businesses in Texas. By 1835, Americans in the area numbered between twenty and twenty-five thousand—far more than the Mexican population.

Texans grew restive as the Mexican government began to play a more active role in the territory. Mexico ended Texas's exemption from paying the equivalent of taxes commonly levied throughout the country. The Mexican government also sought to limit immigration from the United States as it became apparent that some Americans had moved to Texas with the goal of splitting the region from Mexico. When the government made these changes, Texans who had sworn allegiance to the Mexican government began to rethink this commitment. Some wanted to protest by making Texas a separate state within the Mexican federation. Stephen F. Austin led those minimalists. Another group, led by former Tennessee

The Spaldings and the Whitmans

The Spaldings and the Whitmans traveled west together, but their relations were not always cordial. Henry Spalding had been in love with Narcissa Whitman before she married Marcus, and he apparently still smarted from her rejection. The tension was partially responsible for the couples' ministering far apart. But, as when Paul and Barnabas separated over John Mark (Acts 15:36–41), the result was two missionary teams taking the gospel to different regions.

Stephen F. Austin led the first American settlers into Texas.
The State Preservation Board, Austin, Texas

Sam Houston

Sam Houston was a 6'6" giant, a soldier, statesman, and adventurer whose life was even larger than his legend.

As a teenager in East Tennessee, Houston ran off and lived with the Cherokee Indians for three years. The tribe adopted him, giving him the name "the Raven." At age twenty-three, Houston served as a lieutenant under Andrew Jackson at the Battle of Horseshoe Bend, where he received an arrow in the thigh and two bullets in the shoulder while leading a daring charge.

When Old Hickory began his rise to national power, Houston followed as Jackson's friend. He was elected as one of Tennessee's representatives to Congress. In 1827, he was elected governor of the state. Then, suddenly, his career came crashing down. In addition, his bride of only three months left him. Angry and embittered, Houston resigned as governor and—like many other Tennesseans, including Davy Crockett—moved to Texas.

In Texas, Houston became a brawling, moody loner who tried to drown his troubles in alcohol. The Indians gave him a new and more appropriate name: "Big Drunk." But the Texan War for Independence gave him new purpose and drive. His natural leadership and military talents won him the command of the Texan forces. After his decisive victory at San Jacinto, Houston was the most popular man in Texas.

Houston put his life back together and served two terms as the president of the Republic of Texas. After Texas joined the Union, he served the state as both U.S. senator and governor. He also married again in 1840 and proved to be a devoted family man, rearing eight children. He later trusted Christ and was baptized at the age of sixty-one in a Texas creek.

The final crisis of Houston's career came in 1860 when he was governor. Texas strongly favored joining the other Southern states in seceding from the Union. As loyal to the Union as he was to Texas, Houston opposed secession.

When the new Confederate government ordered all officials to take an oath of allegiance to the Confederacy, Houston refused. He resigned as governor and retired from public life. He died in 1863. The last line of the inscription on his tombstone reads, "A Consistent Christian—An Honest Man."

The tiny mission called the Alamo and the battle that occurred there stand as symbols of the Texans' determination to gain their independence.

governor **Sam Houston**, was more radical, proposing a rebellion that would lead to full independence from Mexico.

"Remember the Alamo!"

A series of revolutions in Mexico City brought to power a government that was determined to retain the loyalty of the province of Texas. In 1835, the Texans took up arms, at first to defend the Mexican constitution of 1824, which guaranteed them a degree of autonomy within Mexico. When the Mexican dictator, General **Antonio López de Santa Anna**, approached Texas with some five thousand troops, however, the Texans changed their demands to a call for outright independence from Mexico.

Santa Anna planned to drive through the heart of Texas, execute the leaders of the revolt, and expel the American pioneers. His first stop on the drive was San Antonio, which was defended by a Catholic mission turned fortress called the **Alamo**. The commander of the Texan forces, Sam Houston, ordered the tiny force holding the Alamo to destroy the fort and fall back. However, the commanders at the Alamo, Jim

Bowie and William Travis, decided to hold the post and block the Mexican advance. In February 1836, Santa Anna marched into San Antonio and laid siege to the Alamo. The Mexicans flew a blood-red flag, meaning that no mercy would be shown to the defenders. The 189 defenders—including Bowie, Travis, and the legendary Tennessee frontiersman Davy Crockett—held out for thirteen days, and they inflicted somewhere between 600 and 1,500 casualties on the Mexicans. In the end, though, the Mexicans stormed the fort and killed all the defenders.

Sam Houston did not panic. Despite the pleas of his men to attack the Mexicans and avenge the slaughter, Houston slowly fell back, forcing the Mexicans to stretch their supply lines. Santa Anna split his army into three forces to speed the crushing of the revolt. Seizing his opportunity, Houston attacked part of Santa Anna's divided army near the San Jacinto (juh SIN toh) River on April 21, 1836. In the brief but bloody **Battle of San Jacinto**, 800 enraged Texans—many shouting, "Remember the Alamo!"—routed 1,200 Mexicans. The Texans captured Santa Anna himself and forced the dictator to sign a treaty recognizing Texan independence.

(Above) Davy Crockett, "king of the wild frontier" and fallen defender of the Alamo, is a hero of both his native state of Tennessee and his adopted state of Texas. (Left) The Battle of San Jacinto forced Santa Anna to recognize Texan independence.

The Republic of Texas

Although the Mexican government quickly repudiated the treaty, Texas was in fact free from Mexico. Most Texans would have preferred to join the United States. President Andrew Jackson, however, realized that accepting Texas into the Union might spark a war with Mexico. Also, antislavery forces in the United States opposed Texan annexation because Texas would almost certainly enter as a slave state. All that Jackson would do was recognize the independence of Texas. Thus began a ten-year history of independence for the **Republic of Texas**.

Trails West

One important aspect of Manifest Destiny was simply getting to the West. Traveling to the new lands of the West in the 1800s was obviously not a matter of hopping in a car and driving down an interstate. The goal of the pioneers was the far West, and the means of getting there was the overland trails. *Trail* is an accurate term, for these routes were certainly not roads. At best, they consisted of the ruts left by preceding wagons. Packing all their belongings into sturdy ox-drawn wagons, settlers journeyed west seeking a new and better life. Often, as trails climbed into the steep passes through the Rocky Mountains, pioneers had to lighten their loads. Oak chests,

Davy Crockett

Davy Crockett, who died at the Alamo, is second in fame only to Daniel Boone among American frontiersmen. Born in Tennessee in 1786, Crockett was a farmer, hunter, and soldier. Crockett fought in the Creek campaign of 1813–14 and served in the Tennessee legislature and the U.S. House of Representatives as a Democrat.

A shrewd self-promoter and frontier humorist, Crockett enhanced his reputation as a frontiersman with outlandish tales of his achievements. For example, he explained with mock seriousness how he killed raccoons by grinning them to death. On one occasion, he said he was preparing to shoot a raccoon when it turned to him and said, "Is your name Crockett?" When Crockett admitted that it was, the animal responded, "Then you needn't take no further trouble, for I may as well come down without another word."

Because he disagreed strongly with President Jackson over Indian removal, Crockett switched to the Whig Party. Defeated for reelection to Congress in 1834, Crockett led a company of Tennessee riflemen to join the Texan War for Independence, ending up at the Alamo.

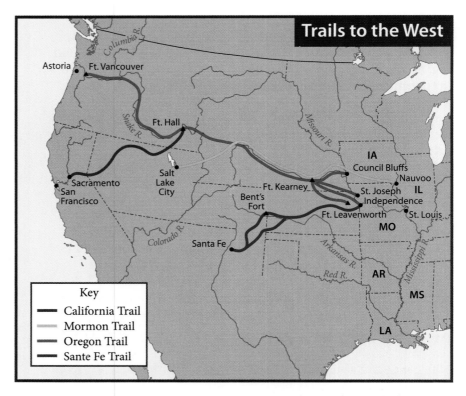

Trails to the West

Key
— California Trail
— Mormon Trail
— Oregon Trail
— Sante Fe Trail

chairs, trunks, even grandfather clocks littered the wayside, victims of the craggy heights of the Rockies. The discards could have furnished many houses—if only one had the means of carrying them.

Traveling the trails was dangerous. Indian attack, of course, was always a possibility. More mundane, but nearly as deadly, were broken axles or the death of an exhausted ox, events which could strand families in the wilderness to die.

Weather was also a factor. Storms and floods could slow the advance of a wagon train, and woe to the pioneer who did not reach his destination before winter set in. Probably the most horrible example of the dangers of the trails was the fate of the Donner Party. Heading to California in 1846, a group under the leadership of George Donner was trapped for months in the Sierra Nevada range by the winter snows. Only forty of the eighty-seven members of the party survived, and they did so by resorting to cannibalism.

Three main trails reached westward. The **Oregon Trail** was obviously the most important. Not only did the trail lead to Oregon, but it also had branches ("cutoffs") that reached into California. The **Santa Fe Trail** was also important, but it was more of a commercial route than a means of pioneer transportation. During the era of Spanish domination, American merchants began a thriving trade between Santa Fe, New Mexico, and Independence, Missouri. Even after Mexican independence, the trade flourished. Fear of growing American activity in Texas eventually caused the Mexican government to close the trail, but memories of earlier profits caused many Americans to covet New Mexico. The **Mormon Trail**, as its name indicates, was blazed by the Mormons when they fled from Nauvoo, Illinois, to Salt Lake City in 1846–47 (see Chapter 11). More Mormons followed the trail, and eventually non-Mormons found it a convenient route to California. The constant stream of pioneers along the trails began to fill the West. It also began to increase tension between the United States and both Great Britain and Mexico.

Section Quiz

1. Who first spurred American settlement of Oregon?

2. Name two characteristics of Oregon that attracted settlers to that region.

3. Why did Andrew Jackson refuse to annex Texas?

4. Name three dangers of traveling on the western trails in the first half of the nineteenth century.

5. Using both the text and the map in this section, identify the western trail (Oregon Trail, Santa Fe Trail, or Mormon Trail) described by each of the following phrases:

   a. Involved trade with the Spanish

   b. Had cutoffs that went into California

   c. The southernmost trail

   d. Blazed primarily by a religious sect

★ Explain the significance of Sam Houston, a native Tennessean, to the history of Texas.

II. Politics and Protocol

While Americans boldly settled in the West, politics in the East moved more prudently. For example, Jackson refused to annex Texas. Political developments in Washington, D.C., in the 1840s, however, profoundly affected affairs in far-off Oregon, California, and Texas. Manifest Destiny increasingly became an article of faith to American politicians. Southerners and Democrats tended to support annexation; Whigs and New Englanders opposed it.

And Tyler Too

"His Accidency"

The sudden death of President Harrison in 1841 created confusion in the Whig ranks. Party leaders had chosen Vice President **John Tyler** to win votes in the South, not to run the country. Since Harrison was the first president to die in office, some questioned Tyler's position. Was he simply "Acting President," or did he have the full powers of the presidency? At any rate, most Whig leaders in Congress and the cabinet assumed that Tyler should submit to their guidance and instruction. **Henry Clay**, the real head of the party, said, "Tyler dares not resist me. I will drive him before me."

Tyler, however, refused to be driven. He left no doubt that he was president in the full sense of the term. Rather than follow the bidding of Clay, Tyler shocked the Whigs by his policies. At heart more of an anti-Jackson Democrat than a true Whig, Tyler vetoed Clay's measures for higher tariffs, a new national bank, and internal improvements. The Whigs responded by voting Tyler out of the party, and the entire cabinet—except Secretary of State **Daniel Webster**—resigned in the fall of 1841. Embittered Whigs began to refer to Tyler as "his Accidency."

Webster-Ashburton Treaty

One reason Webster remained in the cabinet was his ongoing negotiations with Great Britain over the American-Canadian

The Whigs never expected Vice President Tyler to become president, and when he did, he caused them great consternation.

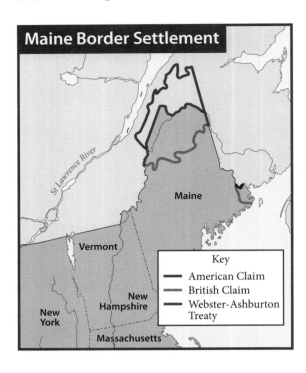

Maine Border Settlement

Key
— American Claim
— British Claim
— Webster-Ashburton Treaty

St Lawrence River

Maine

Vermont

New Hampshire

New York

Massachusetts

James K. Polk was called "Young Hickory" because of his ties to and support from Andrew "Old Hickory" Jackson.

border. The northern border of Maine was the main point of controversy. Because of ambiguities in the Treaty of Paris (1783), Britain and the United States argued over some twelve thousand square miles of territory. The conflict heightened in 1840 when lumberjacks from Maine and Canada clashed over timber claims in the disputed region. Webster and the British representative, Lord Ashburton, sought to settle the issue. After much discussion, the pair hammered out the **Webster-Ashburton Treaty** (1842). Under the treaty, the United States received seven-twelfths of the disputed area, and the British received the rest. The diplomats also clarified the border between Minnesota and Canada, so the United States received clear title to land that later was found to contain valuable deposits of iron ore.

"Who Is James K. Polk?"

Campaign of 1844

As another presidential election approached in 1844, Clay emerged as the leading Whig candidate over the discredited Tyler. The president would have liked to run for reelection on the Democratic ticket, but the Democrats were not about to trust a man who had been a Whig only four years before. The leading Democrat was, in fact, former president Martin Van Buren. Tyler tried to rally support for himself by making the annexation of Texas (which he favored) a major issue in the campaign; Clay and Van Buren tried to eliminate that issue by publishing letters stating their opposition to annexation.

A Dark Horse

Clay easily won the Whig nomination, but the Democrats surprisingly rejected Van Buren. Pushed by expansionists, the party turned to a "**dark horse**," a nominee who is not a serious candidate before the nominating convention and about whom little is usually known by the general public. In this case, the dark horse was **James K. Polk** of Tennessee. During the campaign, Whigs derisively asked, "Who is James K. Polk?"

But Polk was not a political unknown. He had served for fourteen years in the House of Representatives, including four years as Speaker of the House. He had also been the governor of Tennessee. His close association with Andrew Jackson earned him the nickname "Young Hickory." More importantly for Democratic expansionists, Polk willingly ran on a platform that called for "the reoccupation of Oregon and the reannexation of Texas."

As annexation fervor grew, Clay hedged his position. He declared that he was not necessarily opposed to annexing Texas if such an act would not result in war with Mexico. Opponents of slavery objected to Clay's shift, and many of them switched their support to James Birney, the candidate of the tiny antislavery **Liberty Party**. Polk, pledging to serve only one term and having a clear four-point agenda, won the election by a narrow margin of 38,000 out of 2.7 million votes cast and by a count of 170 to 105 in the Electoral College. Birney drew only 62,000 votes, but he might have cost Clay the election. Polk carried New York by only 5,000 votes, and Birney polled 15,000 in that state. Had Clay not lost the antislavery vote, he might have become president.

Texas Annexed

After Texas won its independence from Mexico, the new republic still faced the possibility that Santa Anna would try to reclaim Mexico's lost northernmost state. As the first president of Texas, Sam Houston sought security from both Great Britain and the United States. If either country expressed support for the new country, Mexico would be less likely to invade. Houston thought that the British might want to retain an interest in the hemisphere through Texas. He also thought that when the United States saw the potential for British influence there, U.S. lawmakers would be more willing to consider annexing Texas to prevent British influence. His problem in dealing with Britain, however, was that the British had outlawed slavery in their empire, but many Texas settlers owned slaves. The problem he had in dealing with the United States was that many U.S. lawmakers opposed annexation, especially if it might mean going to war with Mexico. Houston pleaded with Andrew Jackson to use his influence to promote annexation.

After the 1844 election, but before Polk took office, President Tyler took the election results as a mandate to push for the annexation of Texas. Tyler realized that he could not raise the two-thirds majority needed in the Senate to ratify a treaty of annexation, so he proposed to annex the region through a **joint resolution** of Congress, an action that required only a simple majority in both houses. The resolution passed, and Tyler signed it two days before leaving office. Texas became the twenty-eighth state in the Union.

Polk's Administration

A Disciplined Executive

Polk was one of the hardest-working, most self-disciplined presidents in our history. He approached each task with an almost grim determination. Eighteen-hour workdays were common for him, and he rarely took vacations. Polk paid for that unceasing labor, however. His health declined during his term, and he died within four months of leaving office.

One historian noted that Polk "knew how to get things done, which is the first necessity of government, and he knew what he wanted done, which is the second." Polk is unusual among American politicians in that he faithfully kept his campaign promises. For example, he never deviated from his pledge to serve only one term. A cabinet member recalled that on his inauguration day, Polk outlined four goals for his administration. He wanted to (1) lower the tariff, (2) restore the independent treasury system of Van Buren, (3) settle the Oregon question, and (4) acquire California from Mexico. With a Democratic majority in Congress, Polk achieved his first two goals rather easily. The last two, however, involved entering the confusing and sometimes dangerous world of international diplomacy.

The Oregon Question

The Oregon country stretched from 42° latitude in the south to 54° 40′ latitude in the north. Fired by the fervor of the 1844 presidential campaign, some expansionists began clamoring for the United States to take the whole region. Polk entered delicate negotiations with Britain while zealous members of his party were proclaiming slogans such as "Fifty-four-forty or fight!" and "All of Oregon or none!" The British, on the other hand, had long maintained that the proper boundary should be the Columbia River, a border that would have given most of the modern state of Washington to Canada.

Polk offered to extend the U.S.-Canadian border along the 49th parallel (49° latitude), the line that formed the border from Minnesota to the Rockies. Because the fur trade had declined along the Columbia River, the British had less interest in that region and were more open to compromise. In 1846, the two nations signed a treaty that settled the Oregon question by making the 49th parallel the international boundary to the Pacific, but Britain retained all of Vancouver Island, and its fur traders kept the right to travel on the Columbia. Polk did not please die-hard expansionists with that compromise, but he made what most Americans considered a fair settlement.

Section Quiz

1. Why was Tyler unpopular with the Whig Party?
2. Who received more of the disputed territory in Maine under the provisions of the Webster-Ashburton Treaty?
3. Why did Tyler annex Texas through a joint resolution of Congress rather than a treaty in the Senate?
4. What were Polk's four goals for his administration?
5. Where did extreme American expansionists want to draw the Oregon boundary? Where did Britain originally contend that it should be drawn? What became the actual boundary?
★ What made Polk unusual among politicians of his own day and would make him extremely so today?

III. War with Mexico

Polk's fourth goal, acquiring California, involved diplomatic dealings with Mexico. Affairs with that nation, however, were neither so smooth nor so amicably settled as they had been with Britain. In fact, the American desire for California coupled with difficulties over Texas plunged the United States into war with its neighbor to the south. The **Mexican War (1846–48)** was the climax and the most violent phase of Manifest Destiny.

Background of the War

Causes

The causes of the Mexican War were complex. First, and most obvious, was Mexican resentment over the annexation of Texas. Mexico had never recognized Texan independence. Second was the longing of many expansionists in the United States for California and New Mexico. Some people coveted the rich, fertile lands of California and its fine harbors; others fondly recalled the profitable trade that had existed along the Santa Fe Trail. In addition, Mexico's shaky control over these far-off regions caused some expansionists to urge that the Americans seize them before some other power, such as Britain, beat them to it. Third was a history of hostility between the two nations. Americans often looked down on the Mexicans as somehow crude and inferior. Many Texans angrily recalled the slaughter at the Alamo. Mexicans, on the other hand, resented the arrogance of the United States and feared its expansion at their expense. Mexico's unstable political situation did not help relations; the constant series of Mexican revolutions allowed little time for the two nations to work out their differences.

A fourth cause was the failure of an attempt to reach a peaceful settlement. In 1845, Polk sent an envoy to negotiate with Mexico. Polk was prepared to pay $5 million to settle the disputes about Texas and up to $30 million to purchase California and New Mexico. Mexicans considered the offer an insult to their national honor, and the Mexican government could not even discuss the offer for fear of starting another revolution among its angry populace. The Mexicans' rejection of the offer drove another wedge between the nations. Polk's envoy, furious at the treatment he had received, wrote back to his chief, "Depend on it, we can never get along with them until we have given them a good drubbing."

This photo of an American force entering Saltillo, Mexico, is one of the earliest photographs of American soldiers taken in time of war.

A fifth cause—the real spark of the conflict—was a dispute over the Texas-Mexico boundary. The Mexicans claimed that the southern border of Texas was the Nueces (noo AY sis) River; the United States claimed that it was the Rio Grande, some fifty to one hundred miles to the south. After Texas officially entered the Union, Polk sent a force under General Zachary Taylor into the disputed area between the two rivers. The Mexicans demanded that they leave immediately and posted an army on the southern bank of the Rio Grande. On April 25, 1846, Mexican troops attacked a detachment of American cavalry across the river. Polk said that "the cup of forbearance had been exhausted" and called on Congress to declare war. It did so on May 13, 1846.

Problems at Home

Although the attack in Texas enabled Polk to persuade Congress to declare war, the administration was hampered by division at home. A sizable minority of Americans considered the conflict an unjust war of conquest.

Even Southern spokesman John C. Calhoun warned, "Mexico is to us the forbidden fruit; the penalty of eating it would be to subject our institutions to political death." Young Whig congressman Abraham Lincoln of Illinois introduced a resolution that called for the administration to announce the exact spot of the Mexican attack. That way Congress could decide whether the war had actually begun on U.S. soil and was truly defensive or had been provoked. His motion, popularly known as the "Spot Resolution," was never acted upon, but it earned him the nickname "Spotty Lincoln." Nor did matters improve as the war dragged on. Less than a year after voting to declare war, the House narrowly passed a resolution stating that the conflict had been "unnecessarily and unconstitutionally begun by the President of the United States." Some opponents simply referred to it as "Mr. Polk's War."

The U.S. military had not been ready for the war. The regular army was tiny, about seven thousand men. Brave volunteers flocked in to fight, but they often proved unruly and undisciplined. The two

Poet for the Opposition

Some people thought that the war was a brazen attempt to create more slave states. New England poet James Lowell Russell wrote scathingly,

They just want this Californy
So's to lug new slave-states in
To abuse ye, an' to scorn ye,
An' to plunder ye like sin.

leading generals, Winfield Scott and Zachary Taylor, were Whigs whose every success created jealousy in the Democrats' ranks. Furthermore, neither Polk nor the army had any real overall strategy for winning the war. Typical of the president's ignorance of the situation was his suggestion that Taylor's army "live off the land" in northern Mexico, land that was mostly desert scrub. The credit for the American victory ultimately rested on the nation's clear-cut naval superiority, the valor of its troops in battle, and Mexico's similar lack of preparedness.

Campaigns of the War

The course of the Mexican War divides neatly into four campaigns: (1) Taylor's campaign in northern Mexico, (2) the New Mexico campaign, (3) the California campaign, and (4) Scott's campaign in central Mexico, which climaxed with the capture of Mexico City.

Taylor in Northern Mexico

Zachary Taylor, the commander of the troops on the Rio Grande, was a veteran of the War of 1812 and several Indian wars. Nicknamed "Old Rough and Ready" by his men, Taylor dressed sloppily and lacked the superior air that many generals carefully cultivated. New recruits often failed to recognize their slouchily dressed, rumpled-looking commander on first meeting. For example, one new lieutenant, seeing Taylor sitting behind his tent cleaning his sword, unwittingly asked him if he would take a dollar to clean the lieutenant's sword too. "Sure thing," replied the general cheerfully.

Taylor's undeniable bravery and his simple, friendly manner won him the unflinching devotion of his men. But he was not a particularly good strategist, and his battles with the Indians had given him little experience in fighting a regular army. Also, his easygoing manner did not create the most organized or disciplined of camps.

Somehow Taylor overcame his shortcomings as a commander. He began the campaign with two sharp victories, driving the Mexicans from the Rio Grande. Then, gathering his force of 6,600 men, Taylor marched to Monterrey, the main city of northern Mexico, and confronted a well-entrenched force of 7,000 Mexicans. For three days (September 21–23, 1846), the Americans assaulted the fortifications of Monterrey. After the forts fell, fierce street fighting ensued as the Americans battled house by house toward the city's central plaza. Realizing his hopeless situation, the Mexican commander finally surrendered.

Taylor had won a great victory, but several factors worked to undermine his position. Defeat at Monterrey was not enough to force the Mexican government in far-off Mexico City to make peace. Meanwhile, so many Whigs were speaking of running "Old Rough and Ready" for president that the Democratic administration resolved to give him no more opportunities for glory. A planned thrust on Mexico City was instead entrusted to Winfield Scott, Taylor's superior. Scott, to boost his own troop strength, took the best of Taylor's men and left him with only 4,500 volunteers. After Scott removed the troops, Taylor suddenly found himself facing a new army of 15,000 Mexicans under the leadership of the scourge of the Alamo, Santa Anna.

General Zachary Taylor, hero of the Mexican War

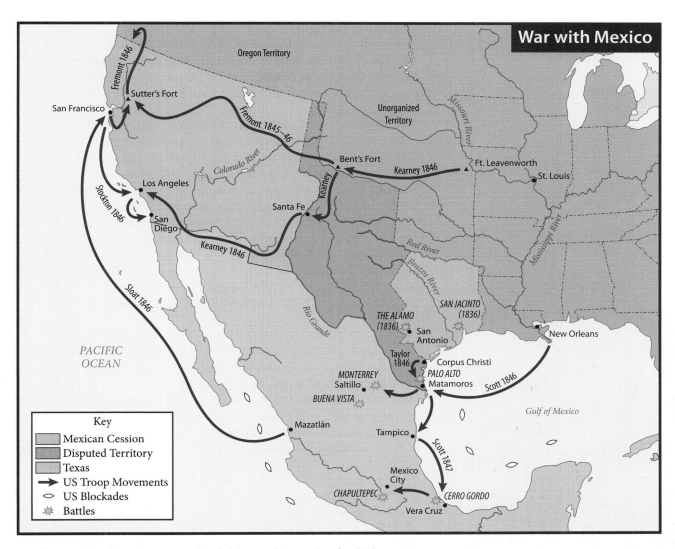

War with Mexico

Santa Anna's presence on the field was the result of a diplomatic blunder by Polk. Living in exile in Cuba when the war broke out, Santa Anna convinced the Americans that if they allowed him back into Mexico, he would arrange a peace settlement. On returning to Mexico, however, he seized power again and vowed to drive the Americans from Mexican soil. After intercepting some correspondence that revealed American plans, Santa Anna marched north to crush Taylor. In the **Battle of Buena Vista** (February 22–23, 1847), Taylor's outnumbered army held out in a desperate defensive battle that brought the Americans as close as they came to defeat during the entire war. Finally, the exhausted Mexicans broke off the fighting and began a demoralizing retreat to Mexico City to meet the next American thrust.

New Mexico Campaign

Campaign is almost too glorious a term for the capture of New Mexico; it was more a desert march than anything else. Polk appointed General **Stephen Kearny** to lead a force of 1,500 men, mostly cavalry, down the Santa Fe Trail to capture New Mexico. Kearny's army left Fort Leavenworth on June 5 and captured Santa Fe on August 18 after almost no resistance. Leaving most of his troops to occupy the newly conquered province, Kearny took part of his men west to aid in the conquest of California.

California Campaign

California proved much more difficult to capture than New Mexico. Although a number of Americans had settled in the province, the Spanish-speaking population outnumbered them ten to one. Furthermore, the Spanish Californians were suspicious of Americans.

Captain **John C. Frémont**, an explorer known as "the Pathfinder of the West," struck the next blow in California. Before the war broke out, Frémont had led a group of sixty men into California, ostensibly to explore, but Frémont's party was too numerous and too well armed to be a simple exploration team. Polk was trying to purchase California from Mexico, so he was unlikely to have sent Frémont there to stir up trouble. At any rate, Frémont found the Spanish-speaking population divided into two hostile camps and the American settlers afraid of both. When the settlers revolted from Mexico and established the **Bear Flag Republic** (because their flag featured a bear) on July 4, 1846, Frémont supported them—although as far as he knew, Mexico and the United States were still at peace.

Shortly thereafter, the American fleet arrived at California's Monterey Bay with the news that war had broken out. Relieved, Frémont joined forces with the naval commander, and they quickly subdued all of California. Initially, most Californians greeted the Americans enthusiastically. The contempt and harsh treatment that some American soldiers displayed toward the Spanish Californians, however, quickly soured relations. The Spanish revolted and recaptured Los Angeles. At this point, Kearny arrived from New Mexico with his men. With an unusual army consisting of Frémont's "explorers," armed settlers, marines from the American fleet, and Kearny's cavalry, the Americans recaptured Los Angeles and crushed the revolt. The victors treated the defeated foe generously this time, and by January 1847, California was once again quiet and firmly under U.S. control.

Scott in Central Mexico

Taylor's victories in northern Mexico and the conquest of New Mexico and California meant little if Mexico would not make peace. Finally, Polk approved an attack on Mexico City in an attempt to end the war. The administration assigned this task to General **Winfield Scott**, probably the most capable American commander. Called "Old Fuss and Feathers" because of his love for military pomp and discipline, Scott lacked the warmth of Taylor and was not as popular with the rank-and-file soldiers. But he had a better grasp of strategy, and his Mexican campaign was one of the most brilliant in American military history.

Scott planned to follow the route that the Spanish *conquistador* Cortés had followed more than three hundred years before. Scott's army landed south of the Mexican port of **Vera Cruz** early in March 1847, and he captured the city in less than three weeks. Santa Anna, recovered from his setback at Buena Vista, blocked the Americans' path. By quick movement and shrewd maneuvering, Scott drove the Mexicans back toward their capital. At least three times Scott outwitted the enemy by sending his troops over ground that Santa Anna thought impassable. In August and September, Americans and Mexicans engaged in a series of bloody battles outside Mexico City. As the Americans edged nearer, Santa Anna realized the hopelessness of his cause. With his army defeated and

General Winfield Scott, America's greatest commander during the Mexican War, later became general of all the U.S. armies.

the populace of the capital calling for his head, Santa Anna abandoned the city. Scott led the victorious Americans into Mexico City on September 14, 1847.

Results of the War

The loss of Mexico City was a final blow to Santa Anna's government. He resigned in disgrace, and a new government began negotiating with the United States. The result was the **Treaty of Guadalupe Hidalgo** (gwah-duh-LOO-pay ee-DAHL-go) in 1848. Mexico recognized American claims to Texas southward to the Rio Grande and ceded New Mexico and California to the United States. In turn, the United States paid Mexico $15 million and assumed all debts that Mexico owed American citizens.

Mexico: Dress Rehearsal for Another War

The Mexican War was the first conflict in which graduates of West Point, the United States Military Academy, played a major role. It also proved to be a training ground for many of those graduates who would see more arduous service on the battlefields of the Civil War.

Many young officers first gained distinction in Mexico. Captain Robert E. Lee was an engineer on General Scott's staff in central Mexico. While scouting the field at Cerro Gordo, Lee found a potential route for the Americans that would allow them to slip behind the Mexican position. As he scouted the route, Lee suddenly heard the voices of Mexican soldiers. Lee scrambled behind a log to hide. He lay completely still while a party of Mexican soldiers gathered and talked. Some of them even sat on the log behind which Lee was hiding. In-

sects added torment to the suspense as they crawled over the motionless American and bit him. After several hours, the Mexicans left, and Lee hurried back to Scott's headquarters. Using the information Lee supplied, the American army outflanked Santa Anna and won a smashing victory. Lee's unflinching personal discipline and his self-sacrificing character were even more evident years later when he led the Confederate Army of Northern Virginia.

Many other famous men won their first glory in Mexico. Lieutenant Ulysses "Sam" Grant showed great ingenuity under Scott in central Mexico. Sixteen years later, in the siege of Vicksburg, Grant displayed the same kind of ingenuity on a much larger scale.

Another lieutenant, Thomas J. Jackson, also won praise for his bravery with an artillery unit in the attack

on Mexico City. As bullets and shells whizzed around him, Jackson walked about in the open, calling, "There is no danger. See! I am not hit." It was that same brave determination that won Jackson the nickname "Stonewall" fourteen years later at the First Battle of Manassas (Bull Run).

However, not all the great generals of the Civil War won glory in Mexico. For example, Lieutenant William Sherman began the Mexican War as a recruiting officer in Pittsburgh and never got into the fight. In another decade, though, a different war provided more than enough action for the more than two hundred Mexican War officers who later served as generals in the War Between the States.

The Human Cost of the War

The cost of the war was high in more than dollars. About 1,700 Americans died in combat, and more than 11,000 perished from disease. In terms of the mortality rate, the war was the deadliest in American history up to that point.

In 1853, almost as a footnote to the war, the United States paid Mexico $10 million for a chunk of territory bordering the southwestern United States. The land known as the **Gadsden Purchase** was needed for the path of a transcontinental railroad. Ironically, the Mexican president who negotiated the purchase was Santa Anna, who had regained control of the government only months earlier. He was overthrown the following year in reaction to the sale. The Gadsden Purchase filled out the continental United States to its current boundaries. It was in many ways the climax of Manifest Destiny.

Section Quiz

1. List at least three causes of the Mexican War.
2. What were the four main campaigns of the Mexican War?
3. How did Santa Anna return to power in Mexico during the Mexican War?
4. What were three results of the Mexican War?
★ Why were Americans divided over going to war with Mexico?

Chapter Review

Making Connections

1. How did the Santa Fe Trail differ in purpose from the Oregon and Mormon trails?

2. Give the dates for the following steps in American expansion and then place the steps in their proper chronological order.

    a. Treaty of Guadalupe Hidalgo

    b. Annexation of Texas

    c. Maine boundary settlement

    d. Gadsden Purchase

    e. Oregon boundary settlement

3. Why did Secretary of State Daniel Webster decide not to resign with the rest of Tyler's cabinet in 1841?

4. Why did the Polk administration entrust the Mexico City campaign to Winfield Scott instead of Zachary Taylor?

Developing History Skills

1. How would you evaluate the Whitman's missionary work? What lessons can we learn from their experience?

2. How did Henry Clay's stand on Texas possibly cost him the election of 1844?

Thinking Critically

1. In his later years, Ulysses S. Grant called the Mexican War "one of the most unjust ever waged by a stronger against a weaker nation." Do you agree with that statement? Defend your answer.

Living as a Christian Citizen

1. The Whitmans' missionary work included both sharing the gospel and trying to civilize the Cayuse people. Today missions work in the third world often includes building schools, providing medical care, and doing other development work. Write a paragraph that discusses problems and benefits of such work.

2. Many Americans disapproved of the Mexican War. What are right ways for a Christian to respond when his government does wrong? What are wrong ways to respond?

UNIT 4

CRISIS
★
1848-1877

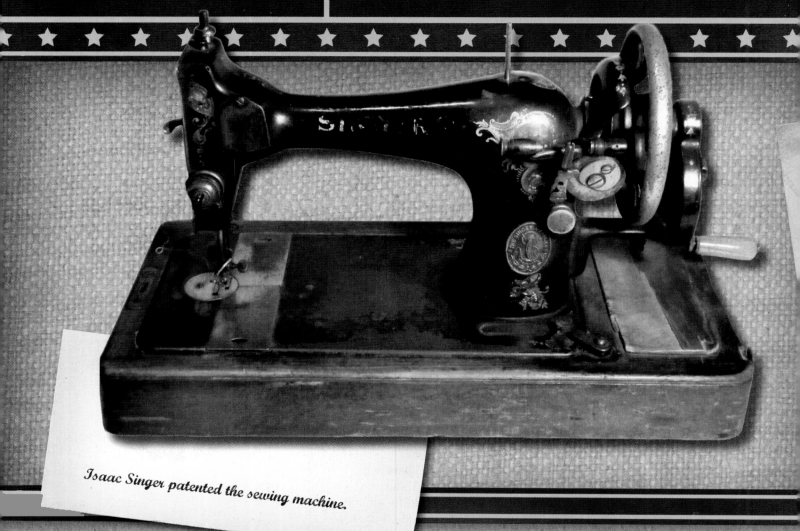

Isaac Singer patented the sewing machine.

1849 California gold rush

1850 Compromise of 1850

1854 Kansas-Nebraska Act

1857 Dred Scott Decision

1859 John Brown's raid on Harpers Ferry

1860 Election of Abraham Lincoln; South Carolina secedes

Edwin Drake drilled the first oil well in Titusville, Pennsylvania.

1861-65 The Civil War

1861 Firing on Fort Sumter

1863 Emancipation Proclamation takes effect

1866 Military Reconstruction Act

1868 Impeachment of Andrew Johnson

1877 Compromise of 1877

Members of the Kansas Free State Battery, partisans of "Bleeding Kansas"
Kansas State Historical Society, Topeka, Kansas,
www.kshs.org/research/collections/documents/photos/webuse.htm

A House Dividing (1848–1861)

I. **Controversy**

II. **Conflict**

III. **Crisis**

"And so we fool on into the black cloud ahead of us."

Mary Boykin Chesnut, April 11, 1861, diary entry from Charleston, South Carolina, the day before the firing on Fort Sumter

The 1850s was perhaps America's most *decisive* decade since nationhood, the 1860s its most *divisive*. The one decade prepared the way for the other. Although William Seward had termed the coming war an "irrepressible conflict," the 1850s actually provided many opportunities for peace and compromise. But like sand in an hourglass, they diminished with time. Americans of that day have rightly been called "the blundering generation": extremists in both the North and the South, with their ravenous rhetoric, tore at the cords of union, and most people were content to watch them.

I. Controversy

New Territories, Old Questions

As a result of the Mexican War, the United States made the largest single acquisition of territory in its history, larger even than the Louisiana Purchase. With the new lands came a revival of old problems. This time, however, the problems did not go away. They continued to fester throughout the 1850s and finally plunged the nation into war. Events seemed to vindicate the gloomy prediction by Ralph Waldo Emerson during the Mexican War: "The United States will conquer Mexico, but it will be as the man who swallows arsenic which brings him down in turn. Mexico will poison us."

Wilmot Proviso

In 1846, President Polk sent an appropriations bill to Congress for funds to pursue negotiations with Mexico even while the fighting was going on. A Democratic representative from Pennsylvania, David Wilmot, attached to the bill an amendment that became known as the **Wilmot Proviso**: that the United States prohibit slavery in any territory acquired from Mexico. The South was outraged, and Southern voting strength in the Senate kept the proviso from becoming law. Nevertheless, Wilmot's amendment became a rallying point for antislavery forces. Over the next few years, antislavery congressmen repeatedly offered the Wilmot Proviso to Congress. Several times the act passed the House only to be rejected by the Senate.

Calhoun Resolutions

Reacting to the threat of the Wilmot Proviso, many Southerners rallied to the position of Southern spokesman John C. Calhoun. In his **Calhoun Resolutions**, offered to the Senate in 1847, Calhoun set down the Southern view of the status of slavery in the territories. Territories are the common possession of the states and not of the federal government, Calhoun argued. Therefore, slave owners have the same constitutional protection of their property (including slaves) in the territories as they have in their home states. Neither Congress nor territorial legislatures, Calhoun said, had the right to limit slavery. Only when a territory became a state could it prohibit slavery. Although Congress had previously prohibited slavery in the territories under, for example, the Missouri Compromise, Calhoun claimed that such measures were extraconstitutional acts that the South had permitted simply to preserve the Union.

Seeds of Discord

One by one, the lines of communication were severed until Americans were talking past each other, then shouting past each other, then shooting at each other. The seeds of discord that had been in the soil since the founding of the republic were warmed in the 1850s by hateful rhetoric and watered with blood. They would soon yield a grim harvest.

David Wilmot

Popular Sovereignty

Between the extremes of Wilmot and Calhoun arose a compromise position known as **popular sovereignty**: the residents of a territory should decide the status of slavery in their territory. If citizens wanted slavery, they could have it; if they did not want it, they could prohibit it. The doctrine of popular sovereignty was strongest among the Democrats. Lewis Cass of Michigan and later Stephen Douglas of Illinois became its leading proponents.

Election of 1848

In the presidential election campaign of 1848, the Democrats and the Whigs sought to skirt the thorny questions raised by Wilmot and Calhoun. The Democrats nominated Lewis Cass, champion of popular sovereignty. The Whigs decided to avoid the question altogether. They nominated **Zachary Taylor**, hero of the Mexican War. Although Taylor owned slaves on his plantation in Mississippi, his political views were little known. In fact, Taylor had never even voted in a presidential election before. Copying their successful formula of 1840, the Whigs nominated a general, avoided adopting a platform, and emphasized instead the military achievements of their candidate.

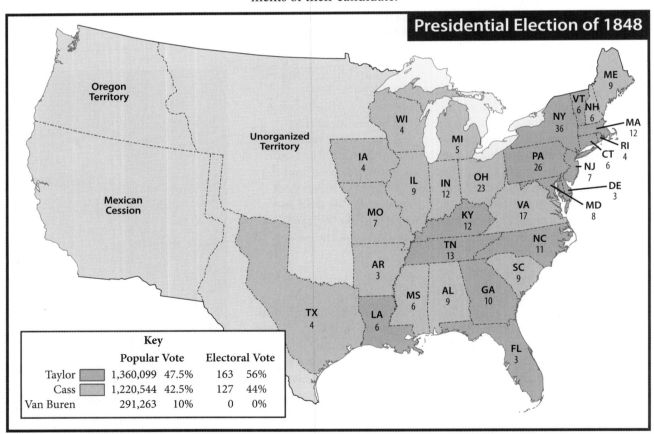

Presidential Election of 1848

Key		Popular Vote		Electoral Vote	
Taylor		1,360,099	47.5%	163	56%
Cass		1,220,544	42.5%	127	44%
Van Buren		291,263	10%	0	0%

The positions of Cass and Taylor were not likely to please either the antislavery forces or **Free-Soilers**, those who favored keeping slavery where it already existed but opposed its extension into the territories. The antislavery and Free-Soil groups joined forces to form a third party, the **Free-Soil Party**. Under the slogan "Free Soil, Free Speech, Free Labor, and Free Men," the new party warmly supported the Wilmot Proviso and nominated former president Martin Van Buren as its candidate. With Van Buren drawing off dissatisfied Democrats in the North (particularly in New York), Taylor won a narrow victory over Cass. The new president, however, faced a difficult situation. A dramatic discovery in California was about to spark a renewal of the sectional controversy.

California

Gold Rush

Swiss immigrant John Sutter arrived in California in 1839 while the region was still under Mexican control. Winning a grant of fifty thousand acres of land from the Mexican government, Sutter began building a large, self-sufficient ranch at the junction of the Sacramento and American rivers (the site of the modern city of Sacramento). The transfer of California from Mexico to the United States in 1846 did not affect Sutter—at first. He continued his construction, planning to build a sawmill to provide lumber for his extensive ranch. In 1848, during the building of the mill, one of Sutter's foremen found some glittering stones below the mill's water wheel. The stones, he soon discovered, were gold. The foreman took the gold to Sutter, who tried to keep the matter quiet.

News such as that, however, could not be kept quiet. Word spread first throughout California and then back to the eastern United States and overseas. "Gold fever" seized thousands of otherwise sensible men and drew them to California, where wealth was seemingly theirs for the taking. The **California gold rush** was on. Because the first wave of gold hunters came in 1849, they all became known as **forty-niners**. Most forty-niners followed the overland route to California, like the pioneers who had followed the Oregon Trail. A number, particularly on the East Coast, went by sea. Some sailed to Central America, crossed the narrow bridge of land by mule and canoe, and tried to find a ship on the Pacific side going to California. More took the all-water route, the long and dangerous journey around the southern tip of South America. In all, some eighty thousand men came to California in 1849, and more than four hundred thousand came in the ten years from 1848 to 1858.

Seeking gold was a gamble; only a few people were winners, and many were losers. Many gambled their savings, their occupations, and even their lives, believing that they would win. Some of those

> ### The Siren Call of Gold
> The lure of wealth irresistibly drew men to California. Whole crews deserted when their ships landed on the West Coast, leaving the hulks to rot in the harbors. (Some captains learned to take the precaution of putting their crews in chains before landing in San Francisco.) Even soldiers stationed in California began to desert to the gold fields. Lieutenant William Sherman complained bitterly, "None remain behind but we poor devils of officers who are restrained by honor."

THE WAY THEY GO TO CALIFORNIA.

This cartoon illustrates some of the fanciful ways people envisioned getting to California.

Ships rot in the harbor of San Francisco, where crews have abandoned them to hunt for gold.

who hoped to strike it rich died in shipwrecks or on the trails without ever reaching California. Those who successfully staked claims found that standing in water all day and wielding a pick and shovel was hard, discouraging work. The few who found rich ore, however—if they were not murdered or swindled out of their claims—became enviably wealthy and inspired stories that encouraged others to come.

Regardless of whether a prospector found gold, he seldom left California. The trip home was too long and the beauty of the region too appealing. Ironically, one man who did not share in the wealth was John Sutter. He lost his land to greedy gold hunters and died in Pennsylvania in 1873, never having profited from the gold rush he started.

Statehood Question

The rush of people into California resulted in governmental chaos. The military rule installed after the Mexican War proved insufficient to govern the large number of sometimes unruly forty-niners. Out of necessity, California organized a government. Encouraged by President Taylor, California decided to skip the territorial stage, write a constitution, and apply directly for statehood. Because the Californians adopted a free-state constitution, Southerners opposed the move. The admission of California would upset the balance between slave and free states in the Senate, for one thing. Also, Southerners had a tactical reason for resisting California's statehood. Even according to the Calhoun Resolutions, California had the right to determine the status of slavery within its boundaries once it became a state. Some Southern leaders would not consent, however, until Congress clarified what would be done with the other lands taken from Mexico—the Utah and New Mexico territories. The fact that President Taylor was also encouraging New Mexico to apply for direct admission as a free state further agitated Southerners. An old and bitterly divisive controversy was heating up once more.

The Great Debate

The West was driving a new wedge between the North and the South. The resulting crisis was played out on the Senate floor in what was perhaps the most extraordinary debate in congressional history. Three aging giants—Clay, Calhoun, and Webster—climbed into the political ring for the last time. The trio had begun their congressional careers in the days of Madison when they and the nation were young; now the old warriors were searching for a peaceful solution to calm the Republic's troubled waters.

Compromise of 1850

Henry Clay again took the lead, as he had in the Missouri Compromise and nullification crisis, offering the sections a compromise package. As a concession to the North, he proposed that (1) California be admitted as a free state and that (2) the slave trade—but not slavery itself—be abolished in the District of Columbia. To the proslavery forces he offered (3) a federally enforced fugitive slave act, which would put the government solidly behind the return of runaway slaves, and (4) the protection of slavery in the District of Columbia. In addition, Clay offered the two sides a joint concession, proposing that (5) the new territories of New Mexico and Utah be organized without reference to or restrictions on slavery.

Clay's proposals, collectively known as the **Compromise of 1850**, underwent intense debate from all sides. President Taylor opposed the Compromise for making concessions that might extend slavery into the territories. He thought debate on the Compromise would succeed only in deepening sectional division and delaying the admission of new territories. Despite the apparent efficiency of Taylor's direct assault on the problem, the old general quickly learned that he could not run the Senate or the country as he had his army.

The aging Calhoun came to the Senate on March 4 to present the South's position. Gaunt and wracked with pain—he would be dead within three weeks—Calhoun was too weak to speak but gave his written remarks to a fellow senator to read. Calhoun declared that the Compromise did not go far enough in protecting Southern rights. Constitutional guarantees needed to be extended so that neither section could dominate the other.

Three days later, the eloquent Daniel Webster rose to speak. His "Seventh of March" speech was the most crucial and courageous of his distinguished career. Webster declared, "I wish to speak today, not as a Massachusetts man, not as a Northern man, but as an American. . . . I speak today for the preservation of the Union. 'Hear me for my cause.'"

Webster went on to point out that the bounds of slavery were already set by the Northwest Ordinance and the Missouri Compromise, as well as by geography. The arid conditions of the new territories could not support a slave economy anyway. Therefore, the Wilmot Proviso was needless and provocative. "I would not take pains to reaffirm an ordinance of nature nor to re-enact the will of God," Webster asserted.

The silver-tongued senator then turned his arguments in favor of union and compromise against the extremists in both sections. Webster blasted the "infernal fanatics and abolitionists" in the North for their agitations and chided the hot-headed secessionists in the South: "Secession! Peaceable Secession! Sir, your eyes and mine are never destined to see that miracle." If either extreme prevailed, Webster believed, the future was a "cavern of darkness." A far brighter future for the nation lay in "liberty and union."

Abolitionists heaped every abusive adjective available upon Webster for his conciliatory speech. Despite such criticism, Webster's support of the Compromise was a critical factor in sparing the country war and disunion. Another factor in the passage of the Compromise was the sudden removal of one of its most influential critics when President Taylor died. Had he lived, the forceful pro-Union Southerner could possibly have effected a completely different outcome between the sections. But his death removed all such possibilities to the realm of speculation. The new president, Millard Fillmore, solidly backed Clay's proposals, and by September they had cleared Congress and were signed into law.

Clay addresses the Senate in the historic debate over the Compromise of 1850.

Daniel Webster

The Death of Zachary Taylor

On July 4, 1850, Zachary Taylor strolled to the unfinished Washington Monument for some Independence Day speechmaking. It was a blistering day, and when the president returned to the White House, hot and hungry, he ate some cherries and cucumbers and washed them down with milk and ice water. The President quickly grew sick and died five days later, a victim of food poisoning.

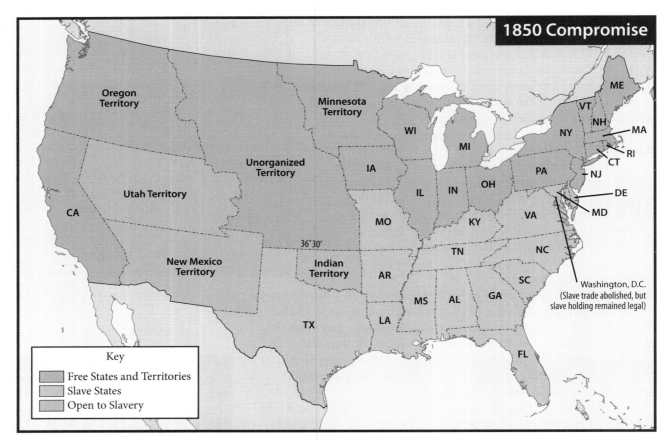

The Fugitive Slave Law gave abolitionists the opportunity to highlight the immorality of slavery to a wider public audience.

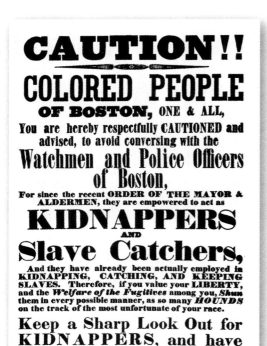

Sectional Strains

The Compromise of 1850 brought a shaky sense of relief. Tensions eased for a time even within the political parties. In 1852, the controversies over slavery expansion that had torn the Democrats apart in 1848 were laid aside. The Democrats' platform and their nominee, **Franklin Pierce** of New Hampshire, were solidly behind the Compromise. Evidently, most of the voters were too. Pierce won a lopsided electoral victory in both the South and the North over the Whigs' candidate, General Winfield Scott. The Free-Soilers, the party of Wilmot, polled only 156,000 votes of more than three million cast.

Ironically, the peace that the Compromise produced was soon shaken by the Compromise itself. One of its provisions, a concession to the South, was a new, tougher **Fugitive Slave Law.** The return of runaway slaves to bondage became a powerful emotional tool of the abolitionists in gradually turning public opinion. A number of abolitionists, such as Ralph Waldo Emerson, urged citizens to break the law on "the earliest occasion," and some states practiced a Northern version of nullification by passing "Personal Liberty" laws in defiance of the federal statute. Even some Northerners who were not abolitionists opposed the law. They feared that the lack of safeguards in the act could result in free blacks being kidnapped and sent into slavery.

By the 1850s, the abolitionist message was changing from an attack on slavery to an attack on the South as an evil empire built on the backs of black slaves. Although only 5 percent of the population owned slaves, the abolitionist attacks had a decisive effect on the Southern mind generally. In 1827, antislavery societies in the South actually outnumbered those in the North. Southerners, however, grew defensive after repeated attacks. Extremists began to promote slavery as a positive good, trying to put the best face

The Underground Railroad

The **Underground Railroad** was the escape route for fugitive slaves through the Northern states (particularly Illinois, Indiana, Ohio, and Pennsylvania). The name's origin is uncertain. Some legends credit it to a slave owner who lost track of a fugitive slave he was pursuing. According to the story, the frustrated owner grumbled that Northerners must have an "underground railroad" to spirit off slaves. In theory, and in keeping with the railroad idea, the system consisted of a series of *safe houses* (also called *stations* or *depots*), each overseen by a *conductor*. Fugitives, called *passengers*, traveled secretly from house to house until they were safe in either the far northern states or Canada. Actually, the Railroad was not as well organized as some tales might indicate.

Escaping slaves had to use their own ingenuity to reach the North. One married slave couple escaped through disguise. The light-skinned wife, who could "pass" for white, dressed herself as an ailing, elderly white planter, and her husband posed as the "planter's" devoted slave. In that disguise, the couple easily traveled north. Another slave escaped from Virginia more directly. He had a carpenter build him a large wooden crate in which he then mailed himself to Philadelphia and freedom.

Once slaves reached the North, they found more help, although some slaves escaped without ever being aware of the existence of the Underground Railroad. "Conductors" gave runaway slaves food, shelter, and further directions on the route to safety. (Despite the legends, few fugitives hid in secret rooms or scurried through secret tunnels.) The best-known conductors were white abolitionists, such as Levi Coffin, a Quaker who openly aided fugitive slaves. His work was so extensive that some people called him the "president" of the Underground Railroad.

How many slaves escaped via the Underground Railroad? Exact figures are almost impossible to determine. They certainly numbered in the thousands; how many thousands is unknown. But, in contrast to the millions of blacks who remained slaves, the number is tiny. The Underground Railroad had great symbolic value, however. For the South, it symbolized Northern refusal to keep faith and honor the fugitive slave laws. For the North, it was a protest against the injustice of slavery. For slaves, it simply meant freedom.

possible on an ugly situation. The most radical Southerners were the **"Fire-Eaters,"** extremists who advocated the South's leaving the Union as the only way to preserve the Southern way of life.

Lines of communication began to break down. Institutions that bound the regions together, such as religious denominations and political parties, fell apart along sectional lines. After 1850, the common ground of compromise would be increasingly difficult to find.

Section Quiz

1. What view of the status of slavery in the territories was expressed in the Wilmot Proviso? the Calhoun Resolutions? popular sovereignty?

2. What two sea routes did forty-niners take to California?

3. What were the five provisions of the Compromise of 1850?

4. Why did some Northerners who were not abolitionists oppose the Fugitive Slave Law?

5. What was the single most important piece of abolitionist propaganda? Who was its author?

★ Should Christians have obeyed or violated the Fugitive Slave Law? Provide biblical reasons based on Romans 13 and 1 Timothy 1:10.

Effective Abolitionist Propaganda

The most successful abolitionist literature was not William Lloyd Garrison's radical *Liberator* but a novel by Harriet Beecher Stowe—***Uncle Tom's Cabin*** (1852). The book sold three hundred thousand copies the first year and was perhaps the most influential piece of propaganda since Thomas Paine's *Common Sense*. Interestingly, Stowe never identified herself with the leading abolitionists, whom she considered fanatics. Yet *Uncle Tom's Cabin*, with its searing portrayal of the degradation of slavery, surpassed the abolitionists in capturing popular support.

Stephen Douglas

II. Conflict

Kansas-Nebraska Act

Despite the growing sectional conflicts and its own weaknesses, the Compromise of 1850 might have kept the peace for several years. The overwhelming support for the pro-Compromise Democrats in 1852 would certainly seem to indicate that most Americans wanted an end to these bitter and divisive struggles. The wounds of sectional conflict were unwittingly reopened in 1854, however, by the actions of the major Democratic leader of the 1850s, Senator **Stephen A. Douglas** of Illinois.

Douglas, like many perceptive Americans of his time, envisioned the construction of a transcontinental railroad linking the East and the far West. The United States had bought the Gadsden Purchase from Mexico, for example, as part of a potential southern route for a transcontinental line. Douglas, like any good politician, wanted his home state to benefit from the railroad by having it pass through Illinois. A transcontinental route from that state, however, would have to go through the unorganized portion of the Louisiana Purchase, which lay west of Missouri. The region would need an organized government to allow construction and maintenance of the line. Many Southerners opposed territorial organization, though, because of the still-unanswered questions about the expansion of slavery.

Douglas sought to win Southern support for his railroad by a clever piece of legislation. In the **Kansas-Nebraska Act** (1854), the Illinois senator proposed organizing two territories from the region—the Kansas Territory west of Missouri and the Nebraska Territory west of Iowa. To settle the slavery issue, Douglas returned to the idea of popular sovereignty; each territory would decide the status of slavery for itself. To make popular sovereignty work and to please Southern congressmen, the act repealed the provision of the Missouri Compromise that banned slavery north of 36° 30′ latitude.

Southerners, of course, welcomed this opportunity to expand slavery into an area that had been previously closed to it. Northern resistance, on the other hand, was strong. Due to the large Democratic majority in Congress and the support of nearly all the South, the Kansas-Nebraska Act passed. Afterward, however, a storm of protest broke out across the North and West as people objected to both the expansion of slavery and the scrapping of the Missouri Compromise. Douglas bore much of the fury himself, but his party did not escape. More than two-thirds of the incumbent Northern Democrats in Congress lost their seats in the next election. Only seven of forty-four Northern Democrats in the House who voted for the act were reelected. More important, the Kansas-Nebraska Act resulted in two events that eventually destroyed Democratic dominance of American politics: the rise of the Republican Party and a virtual civil war in Kansas.

Rise of the Republicans

Collapse of the Whigs

The Whigs had never been a party of strong ideas. The party existed primarily as a coalition of various opponents to Democratic policies. The two times the party won a presidential election, for example (1840 and 1848), it had done so in part by refusing to adopt a platform. The poor showing in the presidential election of 1852 weakened the Whigs; the Kansas-Nebraska Act destroyed them. Southern Whigs almost unanimously supported the act; Northern Whigs almost unanimously opposed it. No political party could survive such a traumatic split. Within a few years, the Whigs had disappeared completely, and their demise left a gaping hole in America's two-party system.

The Know-Nothings

For a time it seemed that the Whigs might be replaced by the American Party, better known as the **Know-Nothings**. The Know-Nothings arose in reaction to increasing immigration from Europe in the 1840s and 1850s. The potato famine in Ireland and wars in Germany sent hundreds of thousands of Europeans fleeing to America for refuge. Many Americans feared that the immigrants would take jobs from native-born Americans. The fact that many of the immigrants were Catholic also caused uneasiness among Protestants. Catholicism had been closely linked with tyranny and repression in Europe, and American Protestants feared for the democratic institutions of the United States.

In 1854, the Know-Nothings capitalized on both fear of immigrants and resentment of the Kansas-Nebraska Act to score big gains in Congress and state legislatures. Though the Know-Nothings were stronger in the North, they displayed surprising strength in slave states such as Kentucky and Texas. The movement turned out to be a passing fad, however. Simple negativism was not a strong base on which to build a party, and the Northern and Southern wings of the Know-Nothings had almost as little in common as Northern and Southern Whigs. After the 1856 presidential election, most Southern Know-Nothings eventually joined the Democrats. A number of Northern Know-Nothings joined a new party, the Republicans.

The Republicans

The real successor to the Whigs was the **Republican Party**. Although many cities compete for the title "birthplace of the Republican Party," the honor seems to go to Ripon, Wisconsin. On February 28, 1854, a rally of anti-Nebraska forces in that town called for others of like mind to join under the label of Thomas Jefferson's old party, "Republican." Soon, the Republican movement spread across the North, and the party was able to offer candidates in the 1854 election.

The Republicans began as a generally "antislavery party," but even that description covers a wide range of beliefs. Abolitionists naturally gravitated to the Republicans. Free-Soilers, those who opposed simply the expansion of slavery, also joined. Sadly, the party's opposition to slavery did not necessarily mean that its members had the interests of the slaves at heart. In fact, some Free-Soilers were more interested in preserving the territories for white settlers than in helping blacks. The appeal of the Republicans was by no means built entirely on the slavery issue. The Republicans appropriated many of the pro-business, nationalistic

> ### How the Know-Nothings Got Their Name
>
> The Know-Nothings' curious nickname arose from the secret societies, such as the Order of the Star-Spangled Banner, that gave birth to the movement. When people asked members about their secret order, they were taught to reply that they knew nothing about it. The phrase also aptly describes the party's ideology, for it was rooted in ignorance and fear.

This 1850s cartoon portrays the new Republican Party as an odd assortment of interest groups.

THE GREAT REPUBLICAN REFORM PARTY.
Calling on their Candidate.

ideas of the Whigs, such as a protective tariff and government support of roads, railroads, and other internal improvements. Many Know-Nothings joined as well, if for no other reason than that the Democrats seemed to be the party of the immigrants. Republicans appealed to the small farmer by promising the distribution of inexpensive land to settlers in the western territories. Despite this range of interests, though, the Republicans remained strictly a sectional party; they were nonexistent in the South.

Election of 1856

The election of 1856 revealed both the strengths and the weaknesses of the Republicans and marked the decline of the Know-Nothings. Borrowing from the Whigs' bag of tricks, the Republicans bypassed their most prominent political leaders, such as New York senator William Seward, in favor of a colorful hero. The party nominated explorer-soldier **John C. Frémont**, "Pathfinder of the West" and a hero of the Mexican War. The Republicans also borrowed from the Free-Soil slogan of 1848 as they said that they were for "Free speech, free press, free soil, free men, Frémont and victory." The American Party (Know-Nothings) nominated former president Millard Fillmore, but his devotion to the anti-immigrant, anti-Catholic principles of the party was at best lukewarm. (Fillmore's daughter had, in fact, been educated by nuns.)

The Democrats ignored their colorless incumbent, Pierce, and nominated an accomplished if lackluster legislator and diplomat, **James Buchanan**. As a native Pennsylvanian who was generally sympathetic to the South, Buchanan was the ideal candidate to unite all factions of the party. Also, he had been minister to Great Britain since 1853 and was therefore, unlike prominent Democrats such as Stephen Douglas, not associated with the controversial Kansas-Nebraska Act. Running on a platform defending popular sovereignty, Buchanan offered himself as the safe, sensible alternative to the "extremists," Frémont and Fillmore. Frémont ran well in the North and West, carrying eleven states and winning 114 electoral votes. Fillmore ran surprisingly well in the South but carried only Maryland with its 8 electoral votes. However, Buchanan, as the head of the only party with a truly nationwide following, carried the entire South and enough Northern states to win 174 electoral votes and the election. Again the voters had chosen the moderate, middle course. Signs of trouble were evident, though. Buchanan had won only a plurality, not a majority of the votes, and several Southern leaders had threatened secession during the campaign if Frémont won.

President James Buchanan

"Bleeding Kansas"

One issue that the Republicans had used to good effect in 1856 was the increasingly ugly situation that had developed in Kansas. Douglas's system of popular sovereignty meant that the settlers in the Kansas Territory would decide the fate of slavery there. Because of this fact, hordes of proslavery and antislavery advocates streamed into the territory, each side attempting to win the region for its position. Bloody fighting broke out between the two factions, and the dissension-torn territory became known as **"Bleeding Kansas."**

Lawrence

The situation in Kansas steadily worsened. Proslavery "border ruffians" from Missouri and antislavery "free-staters" clashed in open violence. In May 1856, three events within the span of five days (May 21–25) brought the Kansas conflict to national attention. On May 21, an army of border ruffians sacked the town of Lawrence, Kansas, a center of free-state strength. Because the citizens chose not to resist the attackers, only one man died, a proslavery ruffian who was killed when a collapsing building fell on him. The ruffians freely burned, looted, and destroyed, however, and the **sack of Lawrence** outraged free-staters.

Sumner-Brooks Episode

About the same time, Senator Charles Sumner of Massachusetts, who had a reputation for angry ranting, gave a heated, intemperate speech denouncing "the crime against Kansas." In the process, Sumner heaped vile and abusive scorn on South Carolina senator Andrew Butler, who was not present to defend himself. Two days later, Representative Preston Brooks of South Carolina, a nephew of Butler's, confronted Sumner in the Senate chamber. The harsh language the Massachusetts senator had used (he had called Butler an imbecile) was inexcusable, but Brooks's response was hardly justified. As Sumner sat at his desk, Brooks began to hit him repeatedly with a cane. Brooks continued to beat him mercilessly until the cane snapped and Sumner was bloody and badly injured. Fellow senators stood idly by or kept others from interfering. To the North, Brooks's action confirmed the prejudice that Southern leaders were violent brutes. The Southern reaction did not help matters. Brooks's district overwhelmingly reelected him to the House, and admirers from all over the South sent him new canes. Brooks wrote proudly, "The fragments of the stick are begged for as sacred relics." Sumner did not return to the Senate for nearly two years.

A Northern cartoon reflects the outrage that Northerners felt over Representative Preston Brooks's beating of Senator Charles Sumner in the Senate chamber.

SOUTHERN CHIVALRY — ARGUMENT versus CLUB'S.

Pottawatomie Massacre

The news of the **Sumner-Brooks episode** enraged one Northerner to a murderous fury. **John Brown** was a fanatical abolitionist from Connecticut who had come to Kansas to help win the territory for the antislavery forces. A failure in every business venture he attempted, Brown proved frighteningly successful as a terrorist. The sack of Lawrence infuriated Brown not only because the border ruffians had attacked the town but also because the free-staters had not fought back. When, on top of that, he received news of Brooks's beating of Sumner, Brown, in the words of his son, "went crazy—*crazy.*" Gathering his followers about him on the night of May 24–25, this grim, self-styled "avenging angel" attacked several proslavery families along Pottawatomie (PAHT uh WAHT uh mee) Creek. In the grisly **Pottawatomie Massacre**, Brown's men butchered five proslavery settlers with razor-sharp swords.

The first reaction was almost universal horror among both pro- and antislavery groups. As news of the massacre traveled east, however, antislavery forces changed the story to suit their views. Northern newspapers claimed that the killings had been in self-defense, or that Indians had done it, or even that Brown had not been anywhere near the site of the killings. A congressional investigating committee, thanks to an antislavery majority, suppressed testimony condemning Brown. The "avenging angel" soon found

Dred Scott

Dred Scott was the slave of John Emerson, an army surgeon from Missouri. During the 1830s, Emerson had taken Scott to the free state of Illinois and the unorganized free territory of the Louisiana Purchase. Emerson later returned to Missouri, a slave state, with Scott. After Emerson's death in 1843, Scott sought to gain his freedom on the grounds that he had become free by entering free territory and could not be reenslaved. The Missouri Supreme Court had ruled in 1824 that if a slave owner moved to a free state and lived there, his slaves would be free based on the Northwest Ordinance (1787), which banned slavery north and west of the Ohio. Scott won in a lower court but lost the appeals. The case eventually found its way to the Supreme Court.

The Granger Collection, New York.

himself free to pursue other plans, and in a few years he would burst onto the national scene with even greater impact.

The Dred Scott Decision

On March 6, 1857, only two days after James Buchanan took office, the Supreme Court handed down a decision that further agitated the conflict over slavery. The case ***Dred Scott v. Sandford*** revealed that even the Supreme Court could not provide a solution to the problems that so vexed the nation.

With its pro-Southern majority, the Supreme Court under Chief Justice **Roger Taney** (TAW nee) welcomed the opportunity to settle the slavery question. In a splintered decision (most justices issued separate opinions), the majority ruled in *Dred Scott v. Sandford* that a slave was not a citizen and had no right to sue. Some justices carried the matter further, with Taney's views being the most extreme. According to the chief justice, the Constitution did not recognize slaves or free blacks as citizens. Blacks, in Taney's words, "had no rights which the white man was bound to respect." Taney then went on to examine the Missouri Compromise, which he ruled unconstitutional on the grounds that it had unfairly deprived slave holders of their property in territories north of 36° 30′.

Of course, Taney's decision that Congress could not forbid slavery in the territories was hailed in the South and castigated in the North. It made slavery theoretically legal in all territories until it might be voted out when the territory became a state. Such a decision could not come close to settling the sectional conflict. Proslavery forces claimed that the case forever closed the issue. Antislavery forces argued ingeniously if inaccurately that as soon as the court ruled on Scott's citizenship, the case was decided, and all the rest was merely the opinion of the justices and therefore nonbinding. The two sides remained unreconciled. If anything, the animosity only grew worse.

Lincoln-Douglas Debates

One man caught in the crossfire over the Dred Scott decision was Stephen A. Douglas. Although Douglas personally did not care whether a territory adopted or prohibited slavery, he stoutly maintained under the doctrine of popular sovereignty that the citizens of a territory had the right to decide for themselves. In light of the Dred Scott case, Douglas had to find a way to reconcile popular sovereignty with the Supreme Court's ruling. In what became known as the **Freeport Doctrine** (after one of the cities in which he enunciated the idea), Douglas argued that a territory could still prohibit slavery by refusing to adopt laws establishing and protecting it.

Douglas's Freeport Doctrine, as one would expect, drew the wrath of the proslavery forces. Douglas's political career was further threatened when he broke with President Buchanan over Kansas. Proslavery forces in that territory had, through fraud, elected a convention to draw up a state constitution that established slavery—although the majority of settlers were free-staters. Buchanan, eager to please the South and bring Kansas into the Union as a Democratic state, pushed Congress to accept the slavery constitution and admit Kansas. Douglas led a courageous group of Democrats who resisted the administration's attempts to thwart the will of the majority in Kansas. Under pressure from the Republicans and the Douglas Democrats, Congress put the constitution to a vote in the territory, and the Kansans rejected it overwhelmingly. As Douglas prepared to run for reelection in 1858, he faced opposition from his own Democratic president. In addition, the Republican Party had grown markedly stronger in Illinois and was offering a strong challenger to Douglas—Illinois lawyer **Abraham Lincoln**.

Abraham Lincoln

The story of Abraham Lincoln's life sounds like one of the classic "rags to riches" tales. He was born into the family of a poor farmer living near Hodgenville, Kentucky, in 1809. The family moved to southern Indiana when Abraham was only seven. In both places, the Lincoln family experienced the grinding poverty that oppressed many settlers on the frontier. Young Lincoln spent his youth performing the backbreaking labor of a pioneer farmer—clearing and cultivating the land, splitting rails for fences, and trying to help keep his family from starving.

Lincoln's standard of living improved when the family moved to Illinois in 1830. There Lincoln was able to find work as a store clerk, postmaster, and surveyor. He had always had a hunger for education but was able to attend school only infrequently; his formal education probably totaled about a year. Lacking formal schooling, Lincoln became an avid reader, eagerly consuming the works of Shakespeare, the poems of Robert Burns, and the Bible. He also began to study law on his own, and in 1836 he was licensed to practice.

Lincoln also developed a taste for politics. He joined the Whig Party, headed by his idol, Kentuckian Henry Clay, and became an influential leader in the Illinois party. He served four terms in the Illinois state legislature (1834–42) and one term as a member of the U.S. House of Representatives (1846–48). By 1850, however, Lincoln thought that his political career had gone about as far as it could go, and he left politics to devote himself to his profitable law practice in Springfield, Illinois.

Abraham Lincoln's character was a mixture of genuine kindness, personal ambition, unflinching determination, and political pragmatism. His reputation for honesty earned him the nickname "Honest Abe." Even political opponent Stephen Douglas said that Lincoln "is as honest as he is shrewd." His thoughtfulness and generosity, not to mention his sense of humor and talent for telling amusing stories, charmed those who met him. The driving force behind his political thinking was that slavery was wrong. He often quoted the Declaration of Independence's famous phrase "All men are created equal." As Lincoln said after his election to the presidency, "I have never had a feeling, politically, that did not spring from the sentiments embodied in the Declaration of Independence." Primary among those sentiments, he said, was the "promise that in due time the weights would be lifted from the shoulders of all men, and that all should have an equal chance."

Yet Lincoln was a realist. He knew that slavery could not be easily eliminated, and he believed that the federal government had no right to interfere with slavery in the states where it already existed. Lincoln satisfied himself with the Free-Soil doctrine that slavery should not be allowed to expand any farther than it already had. The territories must be kept free. Perhaps then, Lincoln thought, slavery would die out.

Chief Justice Roger B. Taney

Abraham Lincoln at the time of his famous debates with Stephen Douglas

The Kansas-Nebraska Act brought Lincoln out of his political retirement. "I was losing interest in politics," Lincoln wrote in 1859, "when the repeal of the Missouri Compromise aroused me again." Lincoln denounced the act because it offered the possibility of slavery's expansion into the territories. His eloquence and homey manner pleased listeners and attracted the attention of the anti-Nebraska forces. Conservative by nature, Lincoln tried to work at first through the dying Whig Party. Eventually, however, he realized that the Republicans offered him a better political future. By 1858 he was the leading Republican in Illinois and the natural choice to oppose incumbent Stephen Douglas for the U.S. Senate.

The Debates

Lincoln launched the campaign by giving one of his most famous speeches. Quoting Mark 3:25, Lincoln said,

> "A house divided against itself cannot stand." I believe this government cannot endure, permanently half *slave* and half *free*. I do not expect the Union to be *dissolved*—I do not expect the house to *fall*—but I *do* expect it will cease to be divided. It will become *all* one thing, or *all* the other.

Douglas immediately charged Lincoln with promoting conflict and dissension. After all, Douglas argued, the nation had existed as half slave and half free since its founding. Why should it not continue to do so? Lincoln responded by challenging Douglas to a series of debates. Douglas accepted, and the **Lincoln-Douglas debates** became a platform for not only the Illinois election but also the national debate on slavery.

Lincoln and Douglas met seven times at different sites in Illinois. Douglas continued to promote popular sovereignty as the answer to the slavery question. He also played on the racist prejudices of his listeners by accusing Lincoln of preaching the absolute equality of the races. "I do not believe that the Almighty ever intended the negro to be the equal of the white man," said Douglas. "He belongs to an inferior race, and must always occupy an inferior position."

Put on the defensive, Lincoln—reflecting the prejudices of the day—backed off from the issue of equality. "I am not, nor ever have been in favor of bringing about in any way the social and political equality of the white and black races," he told one audience. Lincoln refused to deny that slavery was immoral, however, and restated his conviction that its expansion must be prohibited. In another town, Lincoln declared,

> Notwithstanding all this, there is no reason in the world why the Negro is not entitled to all the natural rights enumerated in the Declaration of Independence—the right to life, liberty, and the pursuit of happiness. . . . [I]n the right to eat the bread, without the leave of anybody else, which his own hand earns, he is my equal and the equal of Judge Douglas, and the equal of every living man.

The heart of the controversy, Lincoln said, was not black equality but the immorality and expansion of slavery. "The real issue in this controversy . . . is the sentiment on the part of one class that looks upon the institution of slavery as a wrong, and of another class that does not look upon it as a wrong." Douglas, with his indifference to slavery, was in the second group. Lincoln was part of the first group, believing that slavery should "be treated as a wrong, and one of the methods of treating it as a wrong is to make provision that it shall grow no larger."

Douglas won a close election and returned to the Senate. Although Lincoln lost, he had gained a national audience for his views. Two years later, Lincoln would win a greater prize.

Section Quiz

1. Why did Stephen Douglas propose the Kansas-Nebraska Act?
2. What three events during the period of May 21–25, 1856, focused national attention on Kansas?
3. What did the Dred Scott decision do to the Missouri Compromise?
4. Why did Stephen Douglas break with President James Buchanan?
5. How did Abraham Lincoln and Stephen Douglas differ concerning the expansion of slavery?
★ Explain how campaigning as Lincoln and Douglas did in 1858 is actually better for voters than modern techniques of campaigning.

III. Crisis

John Brown's Raid

"Old Man" Brown had more work to do. After his grisly Pottawatomie murders, Brown kept a low profile in the rough Kansas backcountry. Later, he turned up in the plush parlors of Boston's elite. That a man of Brown's sordid credentials could gather such audiences says as much about the temper of the times as about the charisma of the man.

Between 1857 and 1859, Brown raised money and an army for his grand but ill-conceived scheme to incite a general slave revolt in the South and establish a state for the freed slaves in the Allegheny Mountains between Maryland and Virginia. If the far-fetched plan of mass murder and mayhem seemed to confirm Brown's madness, he was not alone. A group of supporters known as the **Secret Six**, which included some of the most prominent clergymen and abolitionists in the Northeast, backed the plan. In addition, dozens of others were aware of Brown's intentions, including prominent Republican leader Senator William Seward. Brown's ties with such well-placed supporters, revealed after the plot unraveled, would further poison sectional relations.

Raid on Harpers Ferry

In the fall of 1859, Brown and several followers moved secretly to a farmhouse near **Harpers Ferry**, Virginia (now West Virginia), to wait for promised supplies to arrive from supporters in New England. In October, Brown was ready to attack the federal arsenal at Harpers Ferry, strategically located at the junction of the Shenandoah and Potomac rivers. Brown expected to capture the arsenal, from which he would supply weapons for a spontaneous slave revolt. He apparently believed that enough slaves and abolitionists would join him to make the liberation possible.

The Secret Six

John Brown's infamous raid on Harpers Ferry was financed by the following Northern abolitionists:

- Gerrit Smith, landowner and reformer; he later suffered a breakdown and was committed to Utica Insane Asylum.
- Samuel G. Howe, physician and husband of Julia Ward Howe, lyricist of the "Battle Hymn of the Republic"; fled to Canada
- Thomas W. Higginson, preacher; raised a regiment of black Massachusetts soldiers
- Theodore Parker, preacher and reformer; died of tuberculosis in Italy
- George Stearns, businessman; fled to Canada
- Franklin Sanborn, teacher

John Brown

During the night of October 16, 1859, Brown and his gang of twenty-one raiders captured the arsenal and cut the telegraph lines. By the next morning, alarmed citizens and militia from Harpers Ferry and nearby towns had surrounded the arsenal. As the day wore on, several people on both sides were mortally wounded, including two of Brown's sons. Ironically, the first person that Brown's raiders killed was a free black working as a baggage man on a train.

Word of the raid spread quickly. Colonel Robert E. Lee of the 2nd United States Cavalry was at home on leave when he received orders to take command of federal troops in the area and recapture the arsenal. Without taking time to put on his uniform, Lee, in civilian clothes, saddled up and headed for Harpers Ferry. On the morning of October 18, Lee ordered a detachment of Marines under the command of Lieutenant James Ewell Brown (J.E.B) Stuart to take Brown's stronghold. After a brief fight, Brown and his remaining raiders were captured and imprisoned.

Aftermath

In trial, Brown was convicted of murder and treason. He spent November in prison awaiting his execution. Southerners were, of course, eager for the man who had such ruthless designs against them to receive his just reward. But a number of Republicans, embarrassed by Brown's ties to their party, were also eager that he be soon silenced. As for the old man himself, he eagerly awaited his execution date. The self-styled martyr saw it as a date with destiny in which he would gain greater glory than he had achieved in life. In a letter to his wife, Brown wrote, "I have been *whiped* as the saying *is*, but am sure I can recover all the lost capital occasioned by that disaster, by only hanging a few moments by the neck; & I feel quite determined to make the utmost possible out of a defeat."

On December 2, 1859, John Brown's body swung from a gallows in Charlestown, Virginia, but this was no routine execution. It was the inauguration of a period of mourning in the North that shocked the South by its excess. Buildings were draped with black bunting, church bells rang their dirges, and poets and pulpiteers poured out their most eloquent words on Brown, so recently convicted for murder and treason. Abolitionists found his death a useful symbol,

This sketch of U.S. Marines storming the engine house at Harpers Ferry to capture John Brown was drawn by an artist who was at the scene when it happened.

and writers such as Emerson, Thoreau, and Louisa May Alcott, in words frankly blasphemous, compared Brown to Christ. Ironically, Thoreau also called Brown "an angel of light," apparently unaware that this is a scriptural name for Satan (2 Cor. 11:14). In that context, most Southerners would have heartily agreed with Thoreau.

The majority of Northerners, however, did not support slave revolts or Brown's methods. Lincoln noted that although Brown "agreed with us in thinking slavery wrong, that cannot excuse violence, bloodshed and treason." Others went even further, denouncing Brown's actions as "among the gravest of crimes."

These voices of moderation, however, were not being heard in the South above the abolitionists' clamor. A siege mentality had developed there. Understandably, unionist sympathies in the South evaporated, and fear of both secret plots and slave revolts multiplied after Harpers Ferry. Across Dixie, Brown's ties with Republican leaders meant guilt by association. If the Republicans came to power, Southerners believed, the South was not safe. Such dark thoughts boded ill for the future as the nation stumbled into the new and fateful year of 1860.

Election of 1860

The election of 1860 was surely the most critical contest in American politics. Perhaps, with the nation at fever pitch following the Harpers Ferry plot, it was not a good time to be choosing a new president. But the Constitution and the calendar required it. The outcome of the campaign would shatter the last truly national institution tying the sections together—the Democratic Party—and serve as a catalyst for the dissolution of the Union.

Democratic Division

The Democratic Party held its convention in Charleston, South Carolina, in April 1860. Going into the convention, Stephen Douglas was generally the preferred nominee over the hapless incumbent, Buchanan. The struggle over the party platform, however, created a serious rift.

Douglas supporters wanted simply to rerun the 1856 platform, which called for congressional noninterference with the slave question in the territories. A number of representatives from the Deep South states called for federal protection of slavery in the territories. Buchanan's supporters, trying to deny Douglas the nomination, advocated this impossible plank in the platform. When the Northern delegates rejected the Southern plank, delegates from Arkansas, Tennessee, Delaware, and the Gulf states bolted the convention.

Eventually, the sectional factions reconvened separately in Baltimore. Northern Democrats nominated Douglas, while Southern Democrats nominated Buchanan's vice president, **John C. Breckinridge** of Kentucky. In addition, between these two wings emerged a coalition of conservative Southerners and Northerners calling themselves the **Constitutional Union Party**. Also meeting in Baltimore, they nominated **John Bell** of Tennessee for the presidency. The Constitutional Union platform was probably the most concise in American history: "The Constitution of the Country, the Union of the States and the Enforcement of the Laws." Bell's party, representing much of the sentiment in the Upper South and border states, offered a pro-Union alternative to those who believed that a Republican victory would bring disunion. Despite the attempts by all the

Democratic factions to keep the Union intact in their own way, the division of their ranks virtually ensured Republican success.

Lincoln's Victory

Republicans met in Chicago for their convention. Although William Seward seemed to be the favorite for the nomination, Abraham Lincoln quickly passed him in the balloting to win the top spot on the ticket. The Republican platform reflected the coalition character of the party. The party opposed the expansion of slavery into the territories and supported a protective tariff for Northern business interests. It also endorsed a transcontinental railroad and opening of western lands to appeal to farmers and immigrants. The Republicans also tried to calm Southern fears by pledging not to interfere with slavery where it already existed.

The presidential campaign was really two sectional races: Lincoln and Douglas competing in the North, Bell and Breckinridge in the South and border states. Douglas became the first presidential candidate to make a nationwide campaign tour, including the South, where he did not expect many votes. With the Democrats hopelessly divided, Lincoln won by a plurality with just under 40 percent of the popular vote. Since his sectional strength was confined to the more populous North, however, he gained a strong majority in the Electoral College.

Secession

The election results triggered disunion. Leaders in the Deep South had promised that if Lincoln won, they would not submit themselves to what they considered a hostile, strictly Northern party. They would **secede** (leave the Union).

South Carolina led the way on December 20, 1860, by unanimously approving an **Ordinance of Secession**. It was South Carolina's Declaration of Independence. By February 1, 1861, Georgia and all the Gulf states from Florida to Texas had joined South Carolina in seceding. On February 7 in Montgomery, Alabama, the seven Southern states drew up a constitutional league to form the Confederate States of America. **Jefferson Davis**, a former senator from Mississippi and the secretary of war under Franklin Pierce, was elected the first president of the Confederacy.

Attempts at Compromise

As the nation unraveled, men frantically searched for a compromise to avert war. Unfortunately there were no Clays, Websters, or Calhouns to be found. Lesser men were in charge now. Buchanan sat in the White House fretting, frustrated, and indecisive. President-elect Lincoln only repeated his campaign promise not to interfere with slavery in the states where it already existed. He refused to commit himself to any course of action until he took office and held the reins of power himself.

As precious time slipped away in the weeks following the election, Senator **John J. Crittenden** of Kentucky proposed a series of amendments that would extend the Missouri Compromise line of 36° 30′ for the western territories and guarantee the protection of slavery where it already existed. Crittenden, who had succeeded Henry Clay upon that statesman's retirement from the Senate, was no "Great Compromiser," yet he made a noble effort to save the Union and preserve the peace. When his compromise ultimately failed in the Republican-controlled Congress, he lost more than a political initiative. His compromise was the last, best hope of avoid-

---

A History of Secession

Talk of secession had occurred at various times for various reasons in both the North and the South since the earliest years of the Republic. The foundational argument was that the individual sovereign states had voluntarily united with other sovereign states to form a union for the purpose of guiding foreign relations and easing relations among the various states. They voluntarily gave up some specified (enumerated) rights and authority to the national union. In so doing, however, they retained all other rights and authority, even if unspecified, and in no way surrendered any of their sovereignty. Having entered the Union, they could at any time leave the Union voluntarily. These were the same foundational principles argued in the Kentucky and Virginia Resolutions (see Chapter 8).

Those taking an opposing view pointed to Article V of the Constitution and noted that it does not recognize the states as independently sovereign in terms of amending the Constitution. An individual state may object to an amendment but is nonetheless bound by it if it meets the stipulations of Article V. This position insisted that ratification of the Constitution entailed the surrender of state sovereignty.

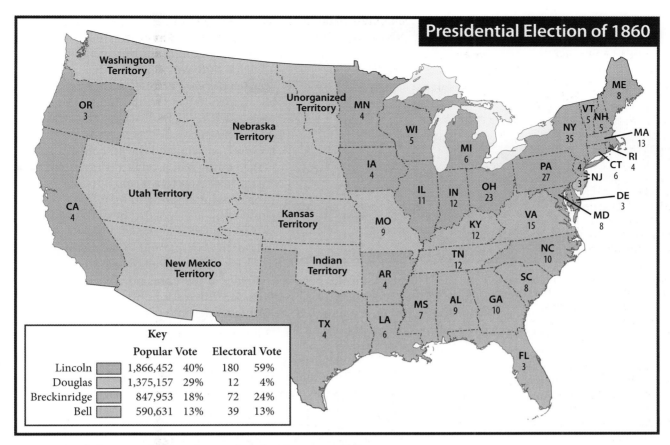

Presidential Election of 1860

Key				
	Popular Vote		**Electoral Vote**	
Lincoln	1,866,452	40%	180	59%
Douglas	1,375,157	29%	12	4%
Breckinridge	847,953	18%	72	24%
Bell	590,631	13%	39	13%

ing war. Its failure would cost Crittenden dearly—one of his sons would become a general in the Union army, the other a general in the Confederate army.

First Fire

Only a spark was needed to bring the country to war. Fear in the South of Northern aggression and frustration and anger in the North over the Southern secession put neither side in the mood for reconciliation. The spark came over the issue of federal forts in the South, particularly **Fort Sumter**, strategically centered in the mouth of Charleston Harbor.

In March the Confederacy sent three peace commissioners to Washington to resolve the problem of federal forts. Both Lincoln and Secretary of State Seward refused to meet the commissioners personally, since to do so would be, in effect, to recognize the Confederate government. Seward, however, sent word that Fort Sumter would be evacuated and on April 7 confirmed his promise in writing—although it is unclear whether Lincoln knew of Seward's actions. On April 9, when the commissioners learned that a squadron of ships had been sent to take supplies to the garrison at Sumter, they could only conclude that they had been deceived. Although Lincoln notified the governor of South Carolina of his intentions, Confederate leaders interpreted his actions as a declaration of war and advised capturing the fort if necessary.

When Lincoln's heavily armed naval expedition neared Charleston, on April 12, 1861, Confederate General Pierre G. T. Beauregard opened fire on Fort Sumter, which was commanded by Major Robert Anderson. Ironically, when Beauregard was a cadet at West Point, his artillery instructor was the same Robert Anderson. Now Beauregard had a chance to show his old teacher just how well

The "Stars and Bars," the first flag of the Confederacy, fly over Fort Sumter.

The North's Declaration of War

Confederate President Jefferson Davis wrote, "The order for the sending of the fleet was a declaration of war. The responsibility is on their shoulders, not on ours. A deadly weapon has been aimed at our heart. Only a fool would wait until the first shot has been fired." Lincoln, on the other hand, believed that he would be recognizing the legitimacy of secession if he did not defend federal property in the South. As he said in his inaugural address, "The power confided to me will be used to hold, occupy, and possess the property, and places belonging to the government."

The Responses of Missouri and Tennessee

When Lincoln called for troops, Missouri's governor replied, "Your requisition is illegal, unconstitutional, revolutionary, inhuman, diabolical, and cannot be complied with." Isham Harris, governor of Tennessee, replied, "Tennessee will not furnish a single man for coercion, but fifty thousand if necessary for the defense of our rights, and those of our Southern Brethren."

he had learned his lessons. After a two-day bombardment Anderson surrendered the garrison; Union troops were permitted to leave for New York on steamships.

Remarkably, no one on either side had been killed in the two-day fight. (Two men were killed accidentally after the battle during the surrender ceremony.) The war, however, was on, and the Lincoln-Seward maneuvering had produced the desired result. In a letter to a friend, Lincoln wrote, "The plan [attempting to reinforce Major Anderson] succeeded. They attacked Sumter—it fell, and thus did more service than it otherwise could." One distinguished historian summarized the Sumter situation thus: "Lincoln, having decided that there was no other way than war for the salvation of his administration, his party, and the Union, maneuvered the Confederates into firing the first shot in order that they, rather than he, should take the blame of beginning bloodshed."

The day after the surrender, Lincoln called for the states still in the Union to supply a total of seventy-five thousand troops to suppress the secessionist states. Many Northern states responded readily with troops. Other states were not so cooperative.

Extremists in both the North and the South welcomed the war as an opportunity to teach the other section a lesson. Their enthusiasm was not shared, however, in the Upper South, where many people had hoped for reconciliation. When Lincoln called up his army to invade the South, Virginia, Arkansas, Tennessee, and North Carolina also seceded, refusing to fight their sister states.

The time for debate and compromise had slipped through the fingers of leaders fumbling with the future. Differences would now be settled by the force of clashing arms rather than with constitutional arguments. The spring of 1861 was the beginning of desolations for the nation. Four bloody, bitter springtimes would pass before Americans had exhausted themselves in killing each other.

Section Quiz

1. Why did John Brown raid the federal arsenal at Harpers Ferry?

2. Name the four presidential candidates and their parties in the election of 1860.

3. Which was the first Southern state to secede from the Union? When did it secede?

4. What event marked the beginning of the Civil War?

✶ Explain the essential positions in favor of and against the principle of secession.

Chapter Review

Making Connections

1. Why did Southerners resist the admission of California to the Union? (Give two reasons.)

2. What did Daniel Webster mean in his "Seventh of March" speech when he said, "I would not take pains to reaffirm an ordinance of nature nor to re-enact the will of God"?

3. What is the difference between an abolitionist and a Free-Soiler?

4. Why did Southerners generally welcome the Kansas-Nebraska Act?

Developing History Skills

1. Why did both abolitionist and nonabolitionist Northerners generally oppose the Fugitive Slave Law that was included in the Compromise of 1850?

2. What was Abraham Lincoln's basic belief concerning the morality of slavery? How did he modify that belief in practice?

Thinking Critically

1. Do you think that the Free-Soilers were right in believing that Americans should tolerate slavery in areas where it already existed? Why or why not?

2. Why did the Compromise of 1850 succeed in avoiding war whereas Senator Crittenden's compromise failed to do so?

Living as a Christian Citizen

1. Many abolitionists condemned the Bible for endorsing slavery, and many on the opposing side rejected abolition because they thought the Bible supported slavery. African-American Christians, however, sought to combine a high regard for the Bible and opposition to slavery. Imagine that you are a nineteenth-century African-American Christian who has the opportunity to write an open letter arguing against slavery from the Bible. What would you say? Consider using Genesis 1:26–27; Exodus 21:16; Deuteronomy 15:7–11; Mark 12:31; Luke 10:30–37; and 1 Timothy 1:10 in your argument.

2. Shared values bind nations together. But when groups within a nation interpret values differently, conflicts arise. Explain how the North and the South interpreted the American values of freedom, equality, individualism, and growth differently.

People, Places, and Things to Remember

Wilmot Proviso
Calhoun Resolutions
popular sovereignty
Zachary Taylor
Free-Soilers
Free-Soil Party
California gold rush
forty-niners
Compromise of 1850
Franklin Pierce
Fugitive Slave Law
Underground Railroad
Fire-Eaters
Uncle Tom's Cabin
Stephen A. Douglas
Kansas-Nebraska Act
Know-Nothings
Republican Party
John C. Frémont
James Buchanan
"Bleeding Kansas"
sack of Lawrence
Sumner-Brooks episode
John Brown
Pottawatomie Massacre
Dred Scott v. Sandford
Roger Taney
Freeport Doctrine
Abraham Lincoln
Lincoln-Douglas debates
Secret Six
Harpers Ferry
John C. Breckinridge
Constitutional Union Party
John Bell
secede
Ordinance of Secession
Jefferson Davis
John J. Crittenden
Fort Sumter

Crobb's and Kershaw's Confederate troops firing from behind a stone wall at Marye's Heights, Fredericksburg

War Between the States (1861–1865)

I. **War of Brothers**

II. **War in the East**

III. **War in the West**

IV. **On the Home Front**

V. **Road to Appomattox**

"Duty is ours; consequences are God's."

Thomas J. "Stonewall" Jackson, 1863

Dogwood blossoms and yellow jasmine danced in the warm spring breeze. Across the country, the boys of '61 gathered on village greens, their knapsacks laden with goodies, their cheeks with kisses, their heads with laurels. Most had seen little or none of the world beyond their horizons, and now they were eager to go teach the Yankees or Rebels—depending upon where those horizons happened to lie—a thing or two.

Shiny brass, scarlet sashes, golden trim, and glistening muzzles all drew the admiration of wives and sweethearts and the envy of little boys with stick guns marching through the milling crowd. The spring of 1861 with its pageantry and patriotism gave little hint of the reality ahead. Four years later those village scenes were, like a tintype, drained of the color and clamor of that first spring. Veterans, pale and disfigured, hobbled past their old parade ground. Black-draped widows shuffled about the square. The little boys so anxious to trade their sticks for swords never made it to the battlefront; many of their fathers never made it back home.

In the fight both sides demonstrated remarkable courage. The Southern soldier heroically fought in the face of insurmountable odds; the Northern soldier tenaciously pursued victory in the face of devastating casualties. The war produced more than courage, however; the bitterness of a war in which countrymen killed each other had far-reaching consequences. The war that swept the land changed forever the face of its people and its politics. Issues that should have been settled with ballots were settled with bullets. As one historian has starkly observed, when the war was over, "Slavery was dead, secession was dead, and six hundred thousand men were dead."

I. War of Brothers

Causes

A number of complex, competing forces converged and clashed to produce the bloodiest chapter in American history.

Union vs. Independence

The central issue that sparked the Civil War concerned the nature of the Union. Could states that voluntarily joined the Union by ratifying the Constitution voluntarily leave the Union? The issue had been hotly debated since the earliest years of the Republic. As early as 1798, Jefferson and Madison proposed secession as a political tool to curb excessive federal power. During the War of 1812, opposition to the war in general and Jeffersonians in particular created strong secessionist sentiment among disgruntled Federalists in New England. After 1830, the growing sense of frustration over the South's minority role in Congress simply renewed what was, in fact, an open constitutional question at the time: Do the states have the right to secede?

The fact that the secession question was a central cause of the war was underscored by the Northern warmakers themselves. The war resolution approved 121 to 2 in the House of Representatives on July 22, 1861, stated plainly that

> in this national emergency, Congress, will recollect only its duty to the whole country; that this war is not waged on their part in any spirit of oppression, or for any purpose of conquest or subjugation, or . . . of overthrowing or interfering

---

The Many Names for the War

Mr. Lincoln's War, Jeff Davis's War, War of the Rebellion, War for Southern Independence, War of Northern Aggression, War Between the States, the Civil War, the Needless War. People neither then nor now can even agree on what to call the war, much less what caused it.

Jefferson Davis's Argument for Secession

In his address to the Confederate Congress in response to Lincoln's call for troops, Jefferson Davis presented a careful constitutional defense of states' rights. He stated that in both the Articles of Confederation and the Tenth Amendment, states had preserved their rights to independence and sovereignty. In addition, Davis asserted that, while secession was constitutional, Lincoln's declaration of war *without congressional approval* was *unconstitutional*. The secessionist states believed that the Confederacy was made in the same mold as the Confederation: sovereign states in league to throw off the shackles of an oppressive, centralized authority. In the South, the war was a Second American Revolution.

with the rights or established institutions of those States, but to defend and maintain the supremacy of the Constitution, and to preserve the Union with all the dignity, equality, and rights of the several States unimpaired; and that as soon as these objects are accomplished the war ought to cease.

Many southern leaders asserted the constitutional right of secession based on state sovereignty. According to the **states' rights** view, each state was largely an independent entity joined in a voluntary compact of union—but a union in which they maintained their identity and were not subservient to a centralized national authority.

Many northern leaders insisted that the right to secede had been abrogated by the signing of the Constitution and the language contained in Article VI of that document. For them, the surrender of state sovereignty was the logical result of the ratification process.

Thus, the war opened with the constitutional questions and countercharges over which statesmen had haggled for decades. The North argued that the Union must be preserved above all else; the South argued that the rights and liberties of the states must be preserved, even at the expense of the Union. Now the issue would be settled in battle.

Economics

Economic differences between the North and the South also played a vital role in bringing about the war. The foundation of the Northern economy was industry and manufacturing whereas the foundation of the Southern economy was agriculture, especially cotton production. But sugar, rice, tobacco, hemp, and other crops were major ingredients of the Southern economy as well. The South produced these raw materials and shipped them both to the Northern factories and to foreign countries. They then bought finished goods from those trading partners but at a higher price than they sold their cotton, which put them in a near colonial relationship to the North. Tied to much of that agricultural economy was the practice of slavery.

Perhaps one of the most often overlooked contributing factors to the war was the tariff. The North favored a high tariff, not as a source of revenue (though it was a good revenue source for the government) but as a means of protecting its industries from foreign imports. The South opposed a high tariff because the South had little industry. Foreign imports and trade supported its economy; a high tariff hurt trade and made foreign products more expensive. A high tariff made foreign countries less likely to buy the South's crops. Southerners believed that they were, in effect, being forced to pay the tariff to support Northern industry.

Slavery

Slavery was an integral part of the southern culture. The Southern states seceded, in part, because they did not believe Lincoln's assurances that he would not interfere in their way of life, which depended on slavery. The Southern agrarian economy relied heavily on slave labor. Thus, while slavery was not the direct issue over which the war was waged, it played an important role in the decisions that led to war.

In the North, abolitionists had made gradual gains in public opinion, at least in opposition to the expansion of slavery. Of course, racial prejudice in the North and fear of the impact of emancipation on the job market made many Northerners indifferent to the plight of blacks in bondage. Nonetheless, the moral high ground of moderate abolitionists—those not associated with the radicalism of Garrison or the terrorism of John Brown—was difficult to ignore. An obvious contradiction existed between "the proposition that all men are created equal" and the institution of slavery.

In the South, opinions on slavery were as varied as its people. However, by the time of the Civil War many Southerners, even those who did not own slaves, argued that slavery was a positive good. Some even insisted that the Southern slave culture cultivated the virtues of honor, courage, duty, and dignity. Slavery also provided educated Southerners time to better themselves intellectually. George McDuffie, governor of South Carolina in the 1840s, called slavery "the cornerstone of our republic edifice." As a result, Northern opposition to slavery was seen as tyrannical interference with the core of Southern society.

Patriotism

Not everyone shared the emotionally charged issues of secession and slavery, union and abolition. Often, people tend to characterize each section as having uniform sympathies and motives. Not so. For example, some proslavery men fought for the Union, and some antislavery, antisecession men fought for the Confederacy. For some Southern nationalists, creation of a Southern nation was more important than states' rights. Extreme states' rights proponents— for example the governors of Georgia and North Carolina—made it hard for the Confederacy to conduct the war. Sometimes one is led to wonder which side they were on.

Perhaps Robert E. Lee best illustrates the dilemma that many Southerners faced at the outset of the war. Lee had a great American heritage as the son of Revolutionary War hero Henry "Light-Horse Harry" Lee, and his wife was the step-granddaughter of George Washington. Lee had already given thirty years of distinguished service to his country as an officer in the army. In April 1861, Lincoln offered him field command of the Union armies. Lee opposed secession and abhorred slavery; yet when Virginia seceded, he refused Lincoln's offer and resigned, declaring, "Save in defence of my native state, I never desire again to draw my sword."

There is an important difference between causing a war and going to war. Most soldiers were indifferent to or even ignorant of the motives with which they are often charged for taking up arms against their countrymen. They answered the call to arms out of a sense of duty, whether as Southern patriots or Northern patriots. Many of them would have instinctively understood the words that characterized Lee's life: "There is a true glory and a true honor, the glory of duty done, the honor of integrity of principle."

Although such men *fought* the war, they did not *cause* it. The war resulted from a leadership failure that permitted extremists to take the terms of debate to their own ends. Historian James Randall summarized the issue thus:

> Let one take all the factors—the Sumter maneuver, the election of Lincoln, abolitionism, slavery in Kansas, cultural and economic differences—and it will be seen that only by a kind of false display could any of these issues, or all of them together, be said to have caused the war if one omits the elements of emotional unreason and overbold leadership. If

---

Lee to His Sister

In a letter to his sister, Robert E. Lee explained his difficult decision: "With all my devotion to the Union, and the feeling of loyalty and duty of an American citizen, I have not been able to . . . raise my hand against my relatives, my children, my home."

one word or phrase were selected to account for the war, that word would not be slavery, or state-rights, or diverse civilizations. It would have to be such a word as fanaticism (on both sides), or misunderstanding, or perhaps politics.

Comparisons

Behind the massing armies of the North and the South were numbers of sectional differences that would prove to be critical factors over the course of the war.

Resources

In terms of the basic resources of population, food production, and industrial output, the North had the advantage in every area. The eighteen Northern states had a population of 18.5 million, twice that of the eleven Confederate states with 9 million people, of which 3.5 million were slaves.

Napoleon once remarked that an army "marches on its stomach." In this regard the Northern army marched farther. The agriculture of the South in terms of volume was geared toward the cash crops of cotton and tobacco, which would do little to sustain hungry troops. The North's Midwest region dominated production of wheat, corn, and oats. The regions, however, were more balanced in the number of livestock.

Sharp differences existed between the sections over manufacturing ability. The North had five times the number of factories and ten times the number of industrial workers. The North also had twice the railroad mileage of the South and the capacity to produce more. In retrospect, it is difficult to see how the South fought on for four years in the face of such odds.

Leaders

One area in which the South surpassed the North, particularly in the early years of the war, was in superior military leadership. The South had a strong military tradition, and many Southerners attended West Point, the national military academy, and military academies in the South. As a result, many of the Confederate officers were better trained than their Union counterparts at the outset of the war. This command difference was particularly pronounced in the eastern campaigns, where Robert E. Lee, "Stonewall" Jackson, and J.E.B. Stuart displayed brilliance and resourcefulness that often mystified their opponents. Lee faced a half dozen different Union commanders over the course of the war, forcing most of them into less strenuous employment.

Other leaders, despite being untrained, proved their worth militarily, especially in the West. Nathan Bedford Forrest, for example, proved to be one of the South's greatest cavalry leaders, and John Hunt Morgan and John Mosby became legendary in their feats of unconventional warfare. The North had its own share of military heroes, but when the war began, the South seemed to have an advantage in military leadership.

Strategy

The two sides also differed in their strategy for winning the war. The North would have to invade the South, thus becoming the belligerent, and defeat the Southern armies in the field. General Winfield Scott, commander of the Union army at the beginning of the war, proposed a blockade of Southern ports to compound the

Confederacy's supply problem. Scott's plan also included the capture of the Mississippi River to split the Confederacy and hamper its ability to move men and supplies from west to east and to trade with the world through New Orleans.

Unlike his more enthusiastic subordinates, Scott—himself a Virginian—believed a quick military victory over the South was unlikely. Rather, his plan involved slowly cutting off the Confederacy's ability to wage war. The Northern press, reflecting the popular view that the war would last only a few weeks, derisively called Scott's scheme the **Anaconda Plan**, after a large South American snake that slowly crushes its prey within its coils. Scott's ideas, though, would eventually prove both realistic and successful.

The Confederate strategy was largely defensive, to outlast the enemy's will to fight. In general, the Southern soldier took up arms for clearer, more compelling reasons than his Northern adversary. The Confederate was fighting to protect home and family from an invading force, which over the long term provided a more compelling motivation in the face of death and deprivation than the Northern soldier's effort to preserve the abstract concept of union.

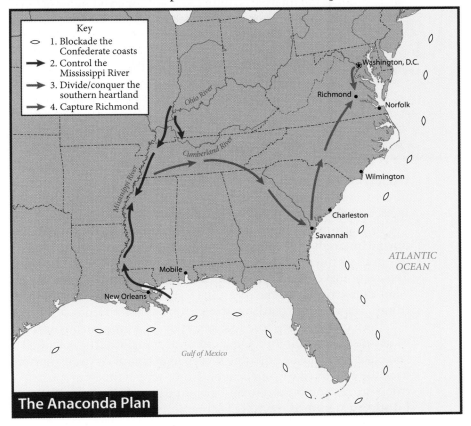

The Anaconda Plan

Section Quiz

1. What was the main issue that sparked the Civil War?

2. Why did some Southerners consider the Civil War to be a Second American Revolution?

3. Which side in the war had the advantage in basic resources (population, food production, and industrial capacity)?

4. Why was Winfield Scott's plan to win the war called the "Anaconda Plan"?

★ What core values were violated by support for slavery?

II. War in the East

The contest in the East, fought largely in Virginia, centered on the North's attempt to rout the Confederate army and capture the new capital at Richmond, Virginia. The Confederate government's move from Montgomery, Alabama, to Richmond linked the success of the Confederacy to the fortunes of the state that would contribute the most to the cause. "On to Richmond" was the battle cry that characterized much of the Union strategy. However, Richmond had capable and courageous defenders who would force the Union army into a long and costly campaign.

In the spring of 1861, in both North and South, most people believed that a quick, decisive battle held somewhere between Washington, D.C., and Richmond would end the war. Lincoln's initial call for troops in April was for an enlistment of three months. These summer soldiers, like their Southern counterparts, were eager for fame and fighting. They would soon get a chance to prove themselves at a little Virginia crossroads called Manassas Junction.

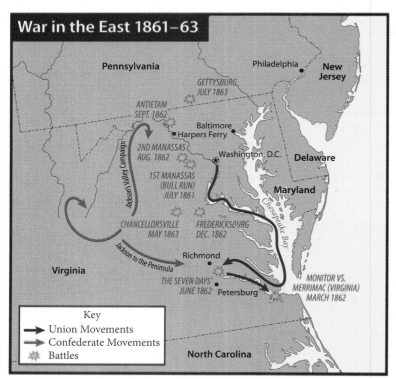

War in the East 1861–63

Pennsylvania

Philadelphia

New Jersey

GETTYSBURG
JULY 1863

ANTIETAM
SEPT. 1862

Baltimore

Harpers Ferry

2ND MANASSAS
AUG. 1862

Washington, D.C.

Delaware

Jackson's Valley Campaign

1ST MANASSAS
(BULL RUN)
JULY 1861

Maryland

CHANCELLORSVILLE
MAY 1863

FREDERICKSBURG
DEC. 1862

Chesapeake Bay

Jackson to the Peninsula

Richmond

Virginia

THE SEVEN DAYS'
JUNE 1862   Petersburg

MONITOR VS.
MERRIMAC (VIRGINIA)
MARCH 1862

Key
→ Union Movements
→ Confederate Movements
✺ Battles

North Carolina

First Manassas (July 1861)

With the Northern press clamoring for something to write about and the three-month enlistments nearing an end for about 80,000 troops, Lincoln felt the pressure to go on the offensive. General Irvin McDowell, field commander of the Union forces, was ordered south to take Richmond. On July 18, McDowell's troops encountered the Confederate troops under General Beauregard near Manassas Junction, a railroad intersection about twenty-five miles southwest of Washington.

In Washington, news of the massing armies was the talk of the town. Hundreds of spectators, from senators to socialites, turned out in their finery with picnic baskets in hand for the gala event. Typical of this curious crowd was Illinois congressman John Logan, who, after arriving for the front-line festivities, decided to join the troops. He went into battle wearing a top hat and tuxedo.

The Confederates chose to take a stand at a little stream near Manassas called Bull Run. On Sunday morning July 21, McDowell launched his attack. At first the raw Federal troops did well, pushing back the equally raw Confederates. However, the timely arrival of troops under South Carolinian Barnard Bee and Virginian **Thomas J. Jackson** stemmed the tide. Facing heavy fire and repeated assaults, Bee's troops were about to buckle. But Bee, galloping among his troops and urging them to hold the line, pointed to Jackson's brigade and shouted, "There stands Jackson like a stone wall! Rally behind the Virginians!" The name stuck; Jackson was thereafter known as "Stonewall." As for Bee, his inspiring words were among his last. Riding at the front of his troops under murderous fire, he was struck down, an early casualty in a long list of war dead.

The Confederate line held, and by mid-afternoon McDowell's troops had been pushed back. The retreat turned into a complete rout as green Union troops and panicky picnickers scrambled toward Washington. The victorious Confederates, however, were too disorganized to follow up their win.

After the Confederate victory at the **First Battle of Manassas** (or Bull Run), the South was relieved and confident, the North demoralized. The next day, Lincoln replaced McDowell with General **George B. McClellan**. The most significant result, however, was that both sides realized that the war would not be over quickly. Many of the congressmen, veterans of the Sunday afternoon picnic near Bull Run, voted for a half million more troops for three-year enlistment. The season for summer soldiers had passed.

Peninsular Campaign (March–July 1862)

In the months following Manassas, McClellan took the shattered remnants of McDowell's army and the flood of raw recruits and organized and drilled them into an impressive force called the **Army of the Potomac**. That, however, was about all McClellan did with his army—organize and drill them. By the spring of 1862, Lincoln, eager for some aggressive action, ordered McClellan south to Richmond. The general, however, offered a better plan. He would move his troops up the peninsula between the James and York rivers and attack Richmond from the east. He could then send a separate force sweeping from the north and crush the capital in a great pincer movement.

The Monitor and the Virginia (March 1862)

McClellan's plan to use the James River as a supply line was nearly upset before the campaign began. The Confederates unveiled a new weapon, an **ironclad** (an iron-plated warship). The ugly but dangerous monster was built on the damaged hull of an abandoned Union warship, the U.S.S. *Merrimac*, which Southerners had renamed the C.S.S. *Virginia*. This vessel with its heavy iron armor, ten guns, and iron ram attached to its bow, sailed out against the Union blockade fleet at Hampton Roads, Virginia, on March 8, 1862. The *Virginia*, virtually impervious to Union cannons, easily sank two large Northern warships. Word quickly spread throughout the panic-stricken North about the South's new weapon.

But when the *Virginia* returned to Hampton Roads the next day, it faced a strange opponent. Described as "a cheese box on a raft" and "a tin can on a shingle," it was the U.S.S. **Monitor**, the Union's own ironclad. It was an unusual craft. Instead of the usual fixed guns on each side of the ship, the Union vessel had only two guns mounted in a revolving turret that could fire in any direction. The *Monitor* battled the *Virginia* for more than four hours without either seriously damaging the other. As the tide began to go out, however, the *Virginia*, with its deeper draft, was forced to retreat to avoid running aground. Although the battle was a draw, the *Monitor* had saved the Union fleet at Hampton Roads. More important, the clash was the first between iron warships, and it spelled the end of the age of wooden ships.

Diversion in the Valley (March–June 1862)

Considering the numerical advantages of the Union forces, McClellan's plan to capture Richmond might have worked if not for Stonewall Jackson and one of the most brilliant campaigns of the war. During the **Valley Campaign** (March 23–June 9, 1862), Jackson, with fewer than 15,000 men, ranged up and down Virginia's Shenandoah Valley, defeating two separate armies. Jackson's forces effectively pinned down 50,000 Federal troops before slipping out of the valley for Richmond to help stop McClellan. Returning from his incredible campaign, "Old Jack" declared, "God has been our shield."

General George B. McClellan

General Robert E. Lee

General J.E.B. Stuart

On to Richmond!

Beginning in April 1862, McClellan, with 100,000 troops, pushed up the neck of land toward Richmond. The outnumbered **Army of Northern Virginia** under General **Joseph E. Johnston** delayed the Union advance, grudgingly giving ground to the overly cautious McClellan. Eventually, however, the Union forces came within sight of the spires of Richmond.

On the last day of May, Johnston struck McClellan hard at Fair Oaks on the outskirts of Richmond. The two-day fight left heavy casualties on both sides. Johnston, severely wounded, would be out of action for months. With the enemy at the gates, Jefferson Davis turned to his military adviser, **Robert E. Lee**, to command the army. Lee, always a man of action, sized up the situation and seized the initiative, launching what would be known as the **Seven Days' Battles**. From June 25 to July 1, at obscure little creeks and cross-roads such as Gaine's Mill, Savage's Station, White Oak Swamp, and Malvern Hill, the Confederates pushed McClellan's grand army back to the James River, with both sides taking heavy losses. Having been outgeneraled by Lee, McClellan abandoned the peninsula and return to Washington, D.C., where he planned to join General John Pope for a new drive on Richmond. Lee, however, had no intention of waiting to be attacked.

Second Manassas (August 1862)

Lee knew that if McClellan's army linked up with Pope's army, they would have an overwhelming advantage in manpower and firepower. He had to neutralize Pope's menacing force. Lee's strategy was as daring as it was successful. He sent his cavalry commander, **J.E.B. Stuart**, to raid Pope from the rear. Stuart swooped down on Pope's headquarters and, while the general was away, took the Federal payroll, battle plans, and—for good measure—Pope's dress coat.

While Stuart was creating havoc at Pope's back door, Lee sent the elusive Jackson around Pope's army. Stonewall's men marched sixty-two miles in forty-eight hours, capturing Federal supplies at Manassas Junction and attacking Pope's lines on the evening of August 28. Just as Pope was preparing to attack Jackson's thin lines the next day, the rest of Lee's army came crashing down on the Federal flank. On the second day of the battle, Southern defenders cut down brave Federal assaults with devastating effect. With a piercing "Rebel yell," the Confederates counterattacked, seeming to one retreating Federal "like demons emerging from the earth." This **Second Battle of Manassas** sent Pope's army reeling back to Washington. Remarkably, after only two months, Lee had cleared practically all of Virginia of Federal forces.

Antietam (September 1862)

After his victory at Manassas, Lee decided to take the war into enemy territory to relieve the pressure on the Confederate capital. In September, he crossed the Potomac into Maryland, hoping to disrupt transportation and communication systems to Washington and gain foreign assistance for the Confederacy. He did not plan to occupy Washington but only to panic the government into terms of peace.

On September 13, Private B. W. Mitchell of the 27th Indiana Volunteers was setting up camp when he found three cigars wrapped in papers that turned out to be Lee's orders to one of his generals, orders that revealed Lee's battle plan. He took the orders to an exuberant McClellan, who waved them and boasted, "Here is a paper with which, if I cannot whip Bobby Lee, I will be willing to go home."

But thanks to J.E.B. Stuart's scouts, Lee knew within a day that McClellan had his battle plan and knew his positions. Lee quickly gathered his army, a force of about 30,000, and drew up a defensive line at **Antietam** Creek near Sharpsburg, Maryland, where they awaited the onslaught of McClellan's 87,000 troops.

At dawn on September 17, Union forces fell upon the Confederate line. At one place between the two armies stood a forty-acre cornfield, ripe and full, ready for harvest. There was, in fact, a grim harvest that day, as the cornfield became a killing field. One survivor wrote that the terrific fire cut down the charging soldiers "like a scythe running through our line."

All along the line, the day was a furious swirl of blood, sweat, and smoke as the armies held each other in a death grip. One Confederate recalled, "The sun seemed almost to go backwards, and it appeared as if night would never come." When night finally did come, 24,000 men had fallen. It was the bloodiest one-day battle in American history. From it came now-famous site names such as the Dunker Church, Bloody Lane, and Burnside's Bridge.

The next morning Lee drew up a line of defense, expecting another attack, but McClellan had no stomach for it. On September 18, Lee slipped his battered army back across the Potomac into Virginia. Technically, Antietam was a Union victory because the Confederates had withdrawn. In reality, however, the battle was a draw. Even so, Lincoln used news of this battle to announce the Emancipation Proclamation.

Fredericksburg (December 1862)

After Antietam, Lincoln gave up on McClellan and replaced him with General Ambrose Burnside. On December 13, 1862, Burnside launched repeated attacks on entrenched Confederate positions on the outskirts of the quaint village of **Fredericksburg**. Before the frigid day was over, 12,000 Union soldiers had fallen before the steady gray line along a slope called Marye's Heights.

As a dismal December closed on 1862—the first full year of the war—Burnside, overwhelmed by his losses, broke off the assault. When Lincoln heard of the defeat, he turned command over to yet another general, "Fighting Joe" Hooker.

Chancellorsville (May 1863)

"Fighting Joe" was a popular, proven general, but he was also a braggart. "May God have mercy on General Lee," the new commander declared, "for I will have none." For three days in May 1863, Lee would give Hooker cause to regret those words.

Dead soldiers lie near the Dunker Church after the Battle of Antietam, the bloodiest one-day battle of the war.

Burnside's Lack of Confidence
The modest Burnside never felt himself capable of high command. At Fredericksburg, Virginia, it was clear that he had good reason for that feeling.

"The Angel of Marye's Heights"
In front of the stone wall where the Confederates took their stand, the dying were strewn among the dead, begging for water. One South Carolina sergeant, nineteen-year-old Richard Kirkland, was overwhelmed by the pitiful cries of the fallen Union troops. With hostile fire raging, Kirkland gathered canteens of water and repeatedly crawled out among the wounded Yankees to quench their thirst—a moving example of Christ's command to "love your enemies." Kirkland's selfless heroism earned him the title "the Angel of Marye's Heights."

General Thomas J. "Stonewall" Jackson

Lee's Reaction to Jackson's Death

Generals Lee and Jackson had a special relationship. Both of them were Virginians and Christians. They worked well together militarily, and it seemed as if each could read the other's mind and predict what the other would do in a given situation. In one concise statement, Lee revealed how much he depended on Jackson. Upon learning of Jackson's death, Lee lamented, "I have lost my right arm."

Hooker, with a huge force of 130,000 men, returned to the Fredericksburg area to crush the Southern army. Lee, with less than half the number of troops, made up with daring what he lacked in numbers. He divided his badly outnumbered army into three parts, half of the troops going with Stonewall Jackson on a march around the Union flank. Jackson's men completely surprised the Federals and rolled up the Union line. Fierce fighting continued for three days in the **Battle of Chancellorsville**, and Hooker never recovered from the shock of Jackson's attack. Baffled and battered, the Union general dragged his huge army northward in retreat.

Lee's triumph, however, was marred by the fatal wounding of Stonewall Jackson. Tragically for the South, on May 2, Confederate troops mistakenly shot Jackson while he rode at the front of his lines at dusk amid the tangled fighting. A surgeon amputated Jackson's left arm, and Stonewall died eight days later of pneumonia. The loss to Lee and the Southern cause was inestimable. Nonetheless, Lee's decisive win at Chancellorsville threw back the Union threat, paving the way for more ambitious plans.

The Confederacy's victories in the East from First Manassas to Chancellorsville were important for more than just military glory. First, these victories succeeded in completely frustrating one of the Union's chief war aims, the capture of Richmond. The only Union "victory" in the campaign was the bloody stalemate at Antietam. Even then, the battle only drove Lee back into Virginia; it did not bring the Northerners any closer to the Confederate capital. Second, the victories raised the morale of the South and lowered that of the North. Despite defeats in the West (discussed in the next section), Confederates took hope from Lee's triumphs that they might yet win the war. Northerners, on the other hand, became weary of defeat. Because all that the South needed to win was for the North to give up, Northern weariness was itself a Southern victory. Third, the longer the South held out and continued to inflict defeats on the Federals, the more likely it was that a European power, such as Britain, would recognize the Confederacy and aid its cause. After Chancellorsville, Southern hopes for independence seemed close to fulfillment.

Gettysburg (July 1863)

Confederate armies in the West had not fared well against Union forces, and growing shortages among Lee's own troops convinced him that the South needed a victory on Northern soil to help turn the tide. In late June, the Confederate army marched through Maryland into Pennsylvania, shielded from view of the Union army by J.E.B. Stuart's cavalry. Lee was careful to order his men not to destroy private property or to molest citizens. The citizens were surprised to see that the lean soldiers who had so often put the Union army to flight were poorly clothed and equipped and that many were barefoot.

A Search for Shoes

On June 30, an advance party of Confederates neared Gettysburg, Pennsylvania, where they believed they would find shoes for their men. Instead, they clashed with an advance unit of Federals under the command of General George Meade, who had replaced Hooker. The two armies had found each other.

On July 1, the vanguard of the Confederate army drove the Federals back, where they entrenched on high ground south of

Stonewall Jackson: Soldier of the Cross

One of the greatest heroes of the South was also one of its most devout Christians. General Thomas Jackson, nicknamed "Stonewall," was converted to Christ shortly after he served in the Mexican War. He started and taught a Sunday school class for blacks in his area. Jackson served brilliantly in the Confederate army, but he combined fervent piety with military genius.

His faith in God carried him through many dangerous battles. An aide asked Jackson how he managed to remain so calm as bullets and shells whistled about him. Jackson replied, "Captain, my religious belief teaches me to feel as safe in battle as in bed. God has fixed the time for my death. I do not concern myself about *that*, but to be always ready no matter when it may overtake me."

Jackson was quick to express his gratitude to God for victory. After the Second Battle of Manassas, an officer on the general's staff said, "We have won this battle by the hardest kind of fighting." Jackson disagreed: "No. No, we have won by the blessing of Almighty God."

Jackson cared for the spiritual needs of his men as well. He ordered regular religious services to be held in camp, and the general himself faithfully attended. He carried saddlebags of religious tracts for his men and welcomed colporteurs (Christian civilians who distributed religious literature among the troops).

Jackson's testimony impressed those who knew him. One evening during the Seven Days' Battles, General Ewell and General William Whiting asked Jackson if they could change their route of march for the next day. Jackson said that he would think it over. After they left, Ewell said to Whiting, "Don't you know why 'Old Jack' would not decide at once? He's going to pray over it first!" Then, realizing he had forgotten his sword, Ewell re-entered the headquarters and found Jackson on his knees beside his bed praying.

After Jackson received his mortal wounds at Chancellorsville, his calm faith and composure deeply impressed those who attended him on his deathbed. When told that he was dying, Jackson took the news calmly. A little later he said, "It is the Lord's Day. . . . My wish is fulfilled. I always wanted to die on Sunday."

On Sunday, May 10, 1863, Jackson said quietly, "Let us cross over the river, and rest under the shade of the trees," and then he died. He left behind the testimony of a man who combined unflinching bravery with unflinching faith. As Jackson's wife said after his death, "The fear of the Lord was the only fear he knew."

Gettysburg. The next day, Lee, who by then had almost his whole army in place, renewed the assault on Meade's position, hitting both flanks, but Union reinforcements held the line.

Pickett's Charge

On July 3, Lee made one final attempt to dislodge Meade's army by ordering an assault on the center of the Union position along Cemetery Ridge. Fresh troops, mostly veteran Virginians under the command of General George Pickett, formed a line nearly a mile long and marched into the face of a murderous artillery barrage. Those who survived **Pickett's Charge** and reached Union lines engaged in fierce hand-to-hand combat.

Fighting on three sides with no reinforcements, Pickett's valiant men were quickly overwhelmed. About 6,750 men of the 12,500 who made the charge were either killed, wounded, or captured. When Pickett returned numbly to the Confederate lines, Lee ordered him to rally his division for the expected Union counterattack. Pickett could only reply, "General, I have no division."

The **Battle of Gettysburg** was over; the two sides had suffered 50,000 casualties between them. It was the single bloodiest engagement of the war. Two days later, the retreating remnants of Lee's army crossed the Potomac into Virginia, and Meade, exhausted by his costly victory, failed to stop him. The South would never again have the strength to launch a major offensive. Yet the war was far from over. Names of sites on the Gettysburg battlefield still evoke images of the savagery of the conflict: Cemetery Ridge, Round Top, Little Round Top, Devil's Den, and the Wheatfield.

Highwater Mark of the Confederacy Described by a Union Soldier

One Massachusetts soldier present described the high-water mark of the battle—and possibly the war—that day on Cemetery Ridge:

Foot to foot, body to body and man to man they struggled, pushed, and strived and killed. . . . The mass of wounded and heaps of dead entangled the feet of the contestants, and, underneath the trampling mass, wounded men who could no longer stand, struggled, fought, shouted and killed—hatless, coatless, drowned in sweat, black with powder, red with blood, . . . with fiendish yells and strange oaths they blindly plied the work of slaughter.

Gettysburg Address Excerpt

Four score and seven years ago, our fathers brought forth, upon this continent, a new nation, conceived in liberty and dedicated to the proposition that all men are created equal.

Now we are engaged in a great civil war, testing whether that nation or any nation so conceived and so dedicated can long endure. . . . In a larger sense, we cannot dedicate—we cannot consecrate—we cannot hallow—this ground. The brave men, living and dead, who struggled here have consecrated it, far above our poor power to add or detract. The world will little note, nor long remember, what we say here, but it can never forget what they did here.

It is for us the living, rather, to be dedicated to the unfinished work which they who fought here have thus far so nobly advanced. . . .

Gettysburg Address

With the human wreckage of war strewn across the Pennsylvania countryside, seventeen acres of the hotly contested ground was set aside to bury the men who had fallen there. Four months after the battle, at the dedication of the cemetery, Lincoln summarized in ten eloquent sentences—his **Gettysburg Address**—the common courage and sacrifice of the soldiers of the North and South.

Section Quiz

1. Why did the Confederates not follow up their victory at the First Battle of Manassas?

2. How did the First Battle of Manassas affect Northern and Southern morale?

3. What is the significance of the clash between the *Monitor* and the *Virginia* (*Merrimac*)?

4. What event marred for the Confederates their victory at Chancellorsville?

5. In what three ways were the series of Confederate victories in the East from First Manassas to Chancellorsville important to the Southern cause?

✳   What core values did Lincoln include in the Gettysburg Address?

III. War in the West

The Civil War in the West differed from the fighting in the East. There were two main campaigns in the West, for example, instead of the prolonged single contest between the Army of Northern Virginia and the Army of the Potomac in the East. In the West, the war from 1861 to 1863 divided between the Mississippi River campaign and the Kentucky-Tennessee campaign. The West also saw a lopsided number of Union victories, in contrast to the Confederate triumphs in the East. In addition, while the South's greatest generals (Lee and Jackson) fought in the East, the North's best commanders (U. S. Grant and William Sherman) rose to fame in the West. In one respect, though, the two theaters of war were identical: the fighting was hard and bloody.

Mississippi River Campaign

One of the most important goals of Winfield Scott's "Anaconda Plan" was the capture of the Mississippi River. Union control of the Mississippi would split the Confederacy in two and provide Northern farmers in the Midwest a needed outlet for their products. Control of the Mississippi was therefore crucial to both sides. The Confederacy sought to maintain its grip through major fortifications on the river, primarily those in Columbus, Kentucky; on Island No. 10 near the Kentucky-Tennessee border; in

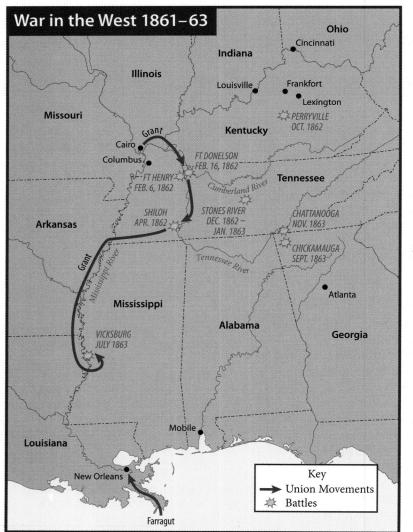

War in the West 1861–63

Key
→ Union Movements
✳ Battles

Vicksburg, Mississippi; and in New Orleans. To win the river, the Union had to break those strongholds.

A Fleet and a General

One major Union advantage was its river fleet of gunboats. These ugly, ungainly ironclad warships were nicknamed "turtles" for their appearance and slow speed. They were not as mighty as the *Virginia*, but they were the most powerful force on the western rivers. Another Union advantage in the West was the presence of one of the North's finest generals, **Ulysses S. Grant**.

Forts Henry and Donelson (February 1862)

The Union high command knew that a frontal attack on heavily fortified Columbus, Kentucky, would be foolhardy. Therefore, Grant was ordered to take his troops and the gunboat fleet and capture two important forts behind Columbus in northwest Tennessee, **Fort Henry** on the Tennessee River and **Fort Donelson** on the Cumberland River. Grant easily captured the poorly designed Fort Henry on February 6, 1862. Even as the fort surrendered, flood waters from the river were slowly submerging it.

Capturing Fort Donelson, only twelve miles to the east, was far more difficult. This fort was well designed and staffed with some 20,000 Confederate troops. The winter fighting for the fort was hard and bitter, and Grant's men outside the fort suffered terribly. Finally, on February 16, the Confederate commander sent a message asking for terms of surrender. Grant replied, "No terms except unconditional and immediate surrender can be accepted." The fort fell, and a jubilant Northern public, playing on the general's initials, honored its new hero with a nickname—"Unconditional Surrender" Grant. With Henry and Donelson in Union hands, the Confederates abandoned Columbus and fell back from western Kentucky. Then Nashville fell to the Union, and Tennessee was open to Union advances.

Shiloh (April 1862)

Grant's popularity lasted only until his next battle. As the Union army moved south along the Tennessee River, Confederate commander General Albert Sidney Johnston decided to strike the enemy a sudden blow. Johnston was helped by the fact that Grant and his men, thinking that the Confederates were on the run, let down their guard. On the morning of April 6, 1862, Johnston's force of 40,000 soldiers attacked a Union force of about equal size near an abandoned Methodist church called "Shiloh." The astonished Federals staggered and reeled under the punishing blows of the Confederates. The screaming hail of shells and bullets was so intense that one Union soldier watched in wonder as a rabbit crawled out of the brush and snuggled next to a soldier for safety. The disorganized Union forces fell back toward the Tennessee River. As darkness fell, the Union army was barely holding on to its positions.

During the night, however, Northern reinforcements arrived. The Confederates had taken heavy losses, including General Johnston, who had suffered a leg wound and bled to death before he realized how serious the wound was. At dawn on April 7, Grant counterattacked and drove the Confederates back. The **Battle of Shiloh** was technically a Union victory, but it was a costly one. Each side suffered more than 10,000 men killed and wounded. Angry

General Ulysses S. Grant

Grant—Unlikely Military Genius

No one who looked at Grant thought of him as a great warrior. He was short and slight and looked rather disheveled. On first meeting Grant's staff, Secretary of War Stanton unknowingly bypassed the general, shook hands with the staff surgeon, and said, "How are you, General Grant? I knew you at sight from your pictures." Nor was Grant particularly accomplished. His record at West Point had been mediocre, and he had resigned from the army in the 1850s under threat of a court-martial for drunkenness. In civilian life, Grant had failed as a farmer and a real-estate salesman, and when the war broke out, he was working in his father's leather shop in Galena, Illinois. After volunteering for the army, Grant was made a brigadier general and entrusted with a command at Cairo, Illinois, the point at which the Ohio and Mississippi rivers join. General Grant soon surprised his superiors with his abilities.

newspapers and politicians called for Grant's dismissal. Lincoln refused, saying, "I can't spare this man. He fights." For his part, Grant learned an important lesson; he would not be caught napping again.

Island No. 10 and New Orleans (April 1862)

April 1862 also brought some good news to the Union. The day after Shiloh, Island No. 10 fell to a combined force of Federal gunboats and troops under General John Pope (before his promotion to the East and his loss at Second Manassas). Then on April 25, Union naval commander **David Farragut** led the fleet up the Mississippi from the Gulf of Mexico and captured New Orleans, the South's largest city and most important seaport. One major obstacle remained for Union control of the river, the city of Vicksburg, Mississippi.

Fall of Vicksburg (July 1863)

Vicksburg was an important river port even before the war. Its high bluffs above the river made it a natural fortress, and the swampy lands near the city made it difficult for an enemy to approach. Jefferson Davis called Vicksburg "the nailhead that held the South's two halves together." As long as the Confederates held the city, they could bring supplies and troops from their western regions. Vicksburg, therefore, became the key to the Mississippi campaign.

Despite the near-disaster at Shiloh, U. S. Grant was the Union's top general, and to him was entrusted the capture of Vicksburg. In the Vicksburg campaign, Grant revealed both a talent for experimentation and a streak of daring. When his first attack on the city in December 1862 failed, Grant decided to gather his forces north of the city and to try to find a way to bypass the guns of the forts. Throughout the winter of 1862–63, Grant tried first digging a canal and then floating his gunboats and troop transports along the bayous, swamps, and streams surrounding the city. All of these attempts failed.

Finally, Grant tried a risky maneuver. First, he marched his men down the swampy western bank of the Mississippi to a point below Vicksburg. Then he floated his fleet of gunboats and transports past the guns on the bluffs under cover of night. This accomplished, Grant ferried his troops across the river below the city. The Union army had outmaneuvered the Confederates, but it had also abandoned its supply line. The army had only what its soldiers carried on their backs. Calmly, Grant wrote that he wanted "to get up what rations of hard bread, coffee and salt we can and make the country furnish the rest."

Grant's bold strategy worked. His move mystified the Confederates and allowed his army to sweep north and surround Vicksburg by May 1863. The defenses of the city were too strong to assault; so Grant laid siege to Vicksburg to starve it into submission. Conditions inside the besieged city worsened. Finally, on July 4, 1863—the same day that Lee began his retreat from Gettysburg—Vicksburg surrendered. The Mississippi River was completely in Union hands.

Hardship in Vicksburg

Life in Vicksburg during the siege was so dangerous that civilians began living in caves they dug into the hillsides around the city. Conditions became so desperate that horses, cats, dogs, and even rats disappeared as the starving populace sought food.

Under cover of night, the Union gunboat fleet runs past the blazing guns on the heights of Vicksburg as part of U. S. Grant's plan for capturing the Mississippi River fortress.

Abraham Lincoln declared with satisfaction, "The Father of Waters again flows unvexed to the sea."

Kentucky-Tennessee Campaign

While Grant was pushing slowly down the Mississippi River, an equally important but less famous campaign was going on—the struggle for control of Kentucky and Tennessee.

Situation in Kentucky

Kentucky was one of the most divided border states. When the war broke out, for example, the governor was pro-Confederate and the state legislature was pro-Union. Faced with this drastic division, the state declared that it would remain neutral. Such neutrality was impossible to maintain, considering Kentucky's location. However, Lincoln and Jefferson Davis—each eager to win the state to his side—promised to respect Kentucky's wishes. Eventually, the need to protect the Mississippi River forced the Confederates to move north to occupy Columbus, Kentucky. The Union responded by sending troops to avenge this violation of Kentucky's neutrality.

At first, the Confederate position looked strong in the state. The Confederates held Columbus in the west, and another force in the east guarded the Cumberland Gap, the gateway to the mountains of East Tennessee and western Virginia. Then in January 1862 the Confederate commander at the Cumberland Gap foolishly pushed north across the Cumberland River. On January 19 a small Union force under General **George Thomas** routed the Southerners at the Battle of Mill Springs. That defeat, coupled with Grant's capture of Forts Henry and Donelson in February, forced the Confederates from Kentucky.

Perryville (October 1862)

After the death of Albert Sidney Johnston at Shiloh, the Confederate government appointed General **Braxton Bragg** to head its armies in the West. Bragg had a distinguished military record, but he tended to anger easily and often refused to listen to suggestions.

Bragg nonetheless came up with a good plan to revive the Confederate cause in the West—an invasion of Kentucky. Such a campaign, Bragg thought, would raise new troops from among the pro-Confederate citizens of Kentucky and might even bring the state into the Confederacy. He also hoped that the attack would force Union forces on the Mississippi River to retreat or at least halt their advance.

In August the great campaign began. A smaller force swept up through eastern Kentucky, capturing the Cumberland Gap, Lexington, and Frankfort, the state capital. Bragg followed with a larger force through the center of the state, about a hundred miles to the west. Soon the Southerners were threatening Louisville and Cincinnati, and the hard-pressed Union commander, Don Carlos Buell, moved his forces between Bragg and the Ohio River.

But the campaign did not work as Bragg had hoped. Although some Kentuckians rallied to the Confederate standard, even more volunteers enlisted in the Union cause to expel the invaders. Pro-Confederate Kentuckians said they would support Bragg—if he could win a great victory. Buell and Bragg finally met in the center of the state in the confused **Battle of Perryville** (October 8, 1862). The outnumbered Southerners, not realizing that Buell's whole force was present, actually attacked and drove back the Federals.

But when Bragg realized the strength of the enemy force, he quickly ordered a retreat into Tennessee. Bragg's great invasion had failed, and the Confederacy never again seriously threatened Kentucky.

Stones River (December 31, 1862–January 2, 1863)

Buell's mixed success at Perryville resulted in his replacement by General William Rosecrans, who set up his headquarters in Nashville. The new commander then pushed his reorganized army southeast to Murfreesboro, Tennessee, where Bragg was gathering his forces to strike Nashville. In the chilling December, the two armies met near Stones River, northwest of Murfreesboro.

The **Battle of Stones River** (also known as the Battle of Murfreesboro) was two days of hard fighting with a day of rest (New Year's Day) between. Although Bragg's troops succeeded in pushing back the Federals at several points, the Confederates could not destroy them. Northern reinforcements poured in from Nashville, forcing Bragg to retreat again.

Chickamauga (September 1863)

Union losses at Stones River forced Rosecrans to pause and rebuild his forces. When the Federals began to move in late June, they steadily pushed back the outnumbered Confederates through Chattanooga and into northern Georgia. Rosecrans pushed his men on what he thought would be the final blow. Bragg's army was not routed, however. Reinforced by James Longstreet's 12,000 veteran troops from Virginia, Bragg took his stand near the banks of a creek named **Chickamauga** (Cherokee for "river of death"). In two days (September 19–20), the Confederates shattered the Union forces. Rosecrans, reacting to rumors that the Confederates were attacking the center, where a hole existed in the Union line, pulled troops from his right to plug the alleged hole. Just as he did so, Longstreet launched an attack where those troops had been, and the rout was on. Rosecrans fled the field with his battered troops.

Complete disaster for the Union was avoided only through the courage of General George Thomas. He calmly held his troops on the field to protect the retreating forces and then slowly withdrew.

Despite the heroics of Thomas and his troops, the Battle of Chickamauga was a major Confederate victory and a disastrous Union defeat. Bragg, however, not realizing the extent of his victory, failed to deliver a knock-out blow. Instead, he trapped the Union army in Chattanooga and threatened to starve it out just as Grant had starved out Vicksburg.

Chattanooga—Climax in the West

Union Reorganization

Rosecrans's disastrous defeat forced the Lincoln administration to make changes. George Thomas replaced Rosecrans as commander of the forces in Chattanooga. Meanwhile, Lincoln rewarded Grant by making him chief of all Union forces in the West. Grant and part of his troops left the Mississippi region for Chattanooga. First, Grant broke the siege that Bragg had laid and got supplies into the hungry city. Then he prepared to drive the Confederates from their strong positions south of the city on Lookout Mountain and Missionary Ridge.

At the same time, Bragg ordered Longstreet to slip northward to destroy Burnside's army in Knoxville, thereby freeing the railroad between Chattanooga and Virginia. Then he was to rush back to rejoin Bragg before Grant arrived in Chattanooga.

But Longstreet's campaign was plagued from the start. He was unable to get enough wagons and rail cars to move his supplies and troops. The rainy weather made the roads almost impassable. He pushed his troops, however, and overtook Burnside's rear guard. Chasing Burnside into Fort Sanders in Knoxville, Longstreet besieged the city and prepared his attack. The fort was surrounded by a ditch, but Longstreet's engineers thought it would present no problem. In a dawn attack on the fort, the soldiers rushed forward only to be tripped by telegraph wires that the Union defenders had stretched ankle high between tree stumps that dotted the landscape in front of the fort. Once they disentangled themselves, the soldiers rushed forward again, leaping into the ditch, which proved to be about ten feet deep, not shallow. The mist of the previous night had frozen the dirt on the parapet of the fort, making the steep slope impossible to climb. Meanwhile, the Union defenders blazed cannon and rifle fire into the ditch, producing carnage. Twenty minutes later, Longstreet recalled the survivors. The Battle of Fort Sanders was over.

Christ in the Camp

Christians served on both sides in the war. The Christian testimonies of Southern generals Robert E. Lee and "Stonewall" Jackson are well known, and several Union officers—such as Admiral Andrew Foote—were also followers of Christ. Lay evangelists, such as Northerner Dwight L. Moody, labored among the soldiers, preaching, witnessing, and ultimately leading many of them to Christ.

The greatest recorded moving of God's Spirit during the war, however, took place in the Southern armies. Revivals in the Confederate ranks of Lee's Army of Northern Virginia occurred throughout the war, but the most sweeping came during the fall and winter of 1862–63 and after the defeat at Gettysburg. During that time, Confederate chaplains and Southern preachers saw a remarkable harvest of souls.

Nearly all Southern denominations joined hands in promoting the revival. One preacher noted of one meeting, "We had a Presbyterian sermon, introduced by Baptist services, under the direction of a Methodist chaplain, in an Episcopal church!"

Estimates of the number of converts vary. Virginia chaplain J. W. Jones, in his book *Christ in the Camp*, estimated conservatively that as many as 15,000 men in Lee's army were converted during the four-year war. The actual number might have been even higher. After the war, Jones tried to follow up on the 410 soldiers he personally had baptized. He found that only three had abandoned their faith and returned to their sinful ways.

During the fall and spring of 1863–64, a similar revival swept through the Army of Tennessee under General Joseph Johnston. One historian estimates that more than 100,000 Confederate soldiers were converted during the course of the war.

Battle for Chattanooga (November 24–25, 1863)

The Yankees rather easily captured Lookout Mountain on November 24 in a mist-enshrouded encounter romantically known as "the Battle Above the Clouds." But the Southerners still held the more formidable position on Missionary Ridge. None of Grant's plans in the **Battle of Missionary Ridge** (November 25) worked as he had envisioned them. When attacks on the flanks of the Confederate line failed, Grant ordered George Thomas's men to create a diversion by capturing enemy rifle pits at the base of Missionary Ridge. The troops not only captured the rifle pits but also spontaneously swept beyond them, swarming up the ridge toward the main Confederate positions. Watching from a distance, an unpleasantly surprised General Grant asked, "Thomas, who ordered those men up the ridge?" "I don't know," replied General Thomas. "I did not." After watching for a few minutes, Grant muttered, "It's all right, if it turns out all right. If not, someone will suffer."

The Union attack, however, surprised the outnumbered Southerners almost as much as it had Grant. Missionary Ridge was soon in Northern hands, and Bragg's troops were again retreating into Georgia. By the time word of the attack got to Knoxville, where Longstreet was besieging the city, it was too late for him to be of any help. After the failed attempt to take Knoxville, Longstreet retreated through upper East Tennessee into Virginia, rejoining Lee. Bragg resigned, and President Davis replaced him with Joe Johnston. President Lincoln promoted Grant, making him commander of all Union forces. Georgia was open to invasion, and the tide in the West was definitely flowing in the Union's favor.

General Grant (left) and his officers on Lookout Mountain after the Union victory there

Section Quiz

1. What were the two main campaigns of the Civil War in the West?

2. For what two reasons did the Union want to control the Mississippi River?

3. How did the South seek to maintain control of the Mississippi River?

4. The capture of what city was the key to the Mississippi River campaign?

5. What were the three goals of Braxton Bragg in his invasion of Kentucky in 1862?

★ What factors might have contributed to the breadth of the revivals in Northern and Southern armies during the war?

IV. On the Home Front

War consists of more than the dramatic clash of arms on the battlefield. In addition to the suffering of the wounded was the quieter but no less real suffering of those at home. Behind the lines of battle lay large civilian populations and their governments, all of which tried to function as effectively as they could in the strained circumstances of war.

Life Behind the Lines

In the South

Because most of the fighting took place on Southern soil, life in the South during the war was far more difficult than life in the North. In addition, the Confederate leaders, having to build a central government almost from scratch, confronted problems that the Lincoln administration never faced. The South, for example, possessed very little gold and silver. The Confederacy, therefore, found itself printing paper money with little to back it up except confidence in the government. As people realized how worthless the money was and as Confederate fortunes on the battlefield declined, prices soared. By late 1864, hams were selling in Richmond for as much as $350 apiece, and by the following January, flour was $425 a barrel. By the end of 1864, Confederate money was worth one-fortieth of its face value. After the war, of course, it was worth nothing. Those who invested most heavily in the Confederate cause often lost everything they had.

Some goods were extremely scarce, and both civilians and soldiers suffered from shortages of food and clothing. People learned to make do with what was on hand. Newspapers in Vicksburg, for example, printed their issues on wallpaper when supplies of newsprint ran out. A Memphis newspaper used shoe polish when it ran out of ink. Sometimes the shortages resulted in anger and violence. In Richmond in April 1863, hungry women started a riot over shortages of bread. Mobs smashed windows, broke into stores, and stole food. Only when Jefferson Davis personally confronted the rioters and persuaded them to disperse did the violence stop.

Confederate currency

The primary cause of the shortages was the Union blockade of the Confederacy. Some daring merchant ships, called **blockade runners**, risked the wrath of the Union navy to bring supplies into Southern ports, where those goods were sold for enormous profits. A phenomenal number of the blockade runners got through. One historian has declared that "no other major effort made by the Confederacy was as well organized and administered," and Southern "defeat might have come much sooner . . . without blockade running." Nonetheless, Southern trade dropped below prewar levels. One of the primary reasons for this drop was the fact that the British—with the mightiest navy in the world—chose to honor the blockade. Had Britain been determined to trade normally with the South, the North could not have stopped the British short of declaring war on them. As the war progressed, the Union built more ships and captured more Confederate seaports. As a result, the effectiveness of the blockade increased, and blockade running became too hazardous to be profitable.

In the North

The situation on the Northern home front was easier, but it was not without its problems. Inflation and shortages also plagued Northern families, but neither became as severe as they did in the South. In fact, after the first shock of secession, the North actually entered a period of prosperity. With most farm hands away fighting, farmers learned to rely more heavily on machinery, such as McCormick's reaper, to do the work. As a result, Northern farms began to produce more foodstuffs during the war than they had before.

Likewise, heavy industries, such as ironworking, profited from the Union army's need for cannons, iron for ships, and other armaments. At the close of the war, an increasingly prosperous North stood in marked contrast to a devastated and war-torn South.

Government in Time of War

Filling the Ranks

The main challenge to both the Union and the Confederacy was putting an army in the field. At first, volunteers were more than enough to fill the ranks. As the war dragged on, however, men became less willing to serve in the army as they saw the casualty lists and realized how their families back home were suffering. Eventually, first the Confederacy and then the Union adopted **conscription**, the "drafting," or compulsory enrollment, of men into military service. Unfortunately, the resulting draft laws were not always fair. Anyone drafted could avoid serving by hiring a substitute or paying an exemption fee. Such provisions led to mutterings in both North and South that it was "a rich man's war and a poor man's fight."

Resistance to the draft arose in both sections. In the South, a surprising amount of the opposition came from state government officials. Having gone to war over the issue of states' rights, many officials resisted giving the central government the power to draft recruits. Especially troublesome were the governors of Georgia and North Carolina. Because the draft law exempted justices of the peace from the draft, for example, the governor of Georgia appointed hundreds of new "justices" to save them from conscription. In all, North Carolina and Georgia accounted for more than 90 percent of the exemptions granted in the Confederate draft.

Although a few Southerners resisted the draft with violence, the North was the scene of the most violent resistance. The most vicious example was the **New York draft riot** in July 1863. The city of New York was home to many recent immigrants, many of whom did not understand the war and few of whom wanted to fight in it. In four days of rioting, mobs attacked not only government officials but also the city's black population. One mob, for example, burned an orphanage for black children, and another seized a crippled black coach driver and hanged him from a lamppost. By the time the riots were suppressed, 119 people had died and 306 had been injured. The results of the draft were scarcely worth the costs of the riot. Only 6 to 7 percent of the Union ranks were filled by conscripts or their hired substitutes. But the New York riots were about more than the draft. Under the surface was racial animosity. New Yorkers, especially Irish and German immigrants, were becoming unwilling to risk death in battle for what they were coming to see as a war to free blacks, thereby creating competitors for their jobs.

Blacks provided a valuable pool of recruits for the ranks. The South used some free blacks behind the lines in noncombatant roles such as wagon drivers and in the construction of fortifications. Some Confederate generals, such as Patrick Cleburne, proposed using blacks in combat roles. At the very end of the war, Robert E. Lee even suggested granting slaves their freedom in return for fighting for the Confederacy, but the idea came too late to be enacted. Most blacks fought in the Union army, where they fought for the freedom of their race. Blacks provided about 10 percent of the

---

East Tennesseans and the Draft

Because East Tennesseans were so badly divided in their sentiments, they suffered drafts from both sides, depending on which side happened to be in control. Many Unionists were drafted into Confederate service, but such men were usually assigned to posts deep inside the South, where they could do less harm and not escape so easily. Men on both sides who were drafted contrary to their beliefs often deserted, hid in the rugged hills and mountains, or became bushwhackers. Many Unionists fled to Kentucky and joined Union armies there.

Union army's fighting men and about a fourth of the navy's enlistees. Their brave performance in battle did much to dispel prejudices that blacks were inferior to whites, and they proved important to the Union cause.

Border States

Of interest to both the Union and the Confederacy were the **border states**, slave states that did not secede from the Union (Missouri, Kentucky, Maryland, and Delaware). Missouri, despite guerrilla warfare among its citizens, remained in the Union. Delaware never seriously considered seceding, and Kentucky, after an initial declaration of neutrality, joined the Union cause.

Maryland was a special case. The loyalty of its citizens was evenly divided, and no one knew for certain which way the state would go. If Maryland seceded, however, Washington, D.C., would be left rather uncomfortably within the Confederacy. To avoid this risk, Lincoln ordered the military occupation of the state. The national government jailed pro-Confederacy leaders without trial and stationed troops in secessionist "hot spots," such as Baltimore. Only in the middle of 1862, after the first crisis had passed, did Lincoln order the release of the political prisoners.

Another "border state" owed its existence to the war. When Virginia seceded from the Union, citizens in the mountainous western portion of the state refused to follow. With the help of the Union army and the federal government, western Virginia set up its own state government. Despite the fact that the Constitution clearly states that "no new state shall be formed or erected within the jurisdiction of any other state . . . without the consent of the legislatures of the states concerned" (Article IV, Section 3), the federal government recognized the pro-Union state, and Congress admitted it to the Union on June 20, 1863, as the state of **West Virginia**. (Pro-Union East Tennesseans tried to form their own state too, but before they could do so, Confederate troops occupied the area and held it for the South.)

Lincoln and the Constitution

As the situations in Maryland and West Virginia indicate, the war strained the North's faithfulness to the Constitution. In fact, Lincoln's Northern opponents complained that the president was making himself a dictator by ignoring the Constitution. Lincoln, for example, suspended writs of *habeas corpus*, meaning that the government could arrest a person without charging him with a crime or bringing him to trial. Such unchecked, sweeping powers led to abuses. A minister in Union-controlled Alexandria, Virginia, for example, was arrested simply for omitting a standard prayer for the president from the service. Lincoln defended his actions by pointing out that the Constitution allowed suspending writs of *habeas corpus* "in cases of rebellion or invasion" (Article I, Section 9). Critics correctly replied that such power belonged only to Congress, for Article I deals with the power of the *legislature*, not the president. As the war progressed and the Union government felt more secure, such violations of the Constitution became less common, and the prisoners already seized were released. In March 1863, to eliminate questions of constitutionality, Congress officially gave the president the power that he had been exercising all along.

Lincoln versus a Copperhead

One particularly worrisome Copperhead got to Lincoln. Democrat Clement Vallandigham of Ohio, who opposed the war and advocated a moderate approach to the South, was outspoken in his condemnation of Lincoln. His continued attacks on President Lincoln resulted in arrest, trial, and imprisonment. Lincoln later commuted his sentence to banishment to the Confederacy. Vallandigham, however, slipped out of the South and into Canada, and then, in disguise, back to Ohio, where he helped in the 1864 presidential campaign of George McClellan.

Copperheads

One reason for Lincoln's actions was his fear of Southern sympathizers in the North. Northerners labeled such men **Copperheads**, after the poisonous snakes of that name. In the border states and the southern parts of Illinois, Indiana, and Ohio, Copperhead sentiment was strong, and Union sympathizers discerned numerous plots—real and imagined—to destroy the war effort. In reality, the Copperheads were not as numerous as the administration feared, and many of them were more interested in securing peace than in directly helping the Southern cause. Their presence, however, was a constant worry for the Lincoln administration.

Diplomatic Maneuvers

The war was fought largely within the borders of the United States, but its impact was international. The main goal of Southern diplomacy was to persuade a European power—preferably Great Britain—to recognize the independence of the Confederacy, just as France had recognized the United States during the War for Independence. The North, obviously, sought to keep Europe out of the affair.

Southern Efforts

Southerners hoped at first that simple economics would force Britain to recognize the Confederacy. The British textile industry depended heavily on Southern cotton to supply its mills. Surely, the South thought, when the British felt the pinch of losing their source of cotton, they would come to the South's aid. Great Britain, however, was not eager to risk war with the United States over what seemed—to the British, at least—a purely internal American matter. The use of inferior cotton from India and Egypt also enabled the British to do without the South's cotton.

The South came closest to receiving British help not because of its diplomacy but because of Union bungling. In November 1861, an incident on the sea nearly brought Britain into the war on the side of the Confederacy. The Confederate government had commissioned two agents, John Slidell and James Mason, to go to Europe to negotiate for aid. They were sailing on a British mail ship, the *Trent*, when Captain Charles Wilkes of the U.S. Navy forced the British ship to surrender the agents.

The ***Trent* affair**, as it was called, outraged the British, who demanded an apology and the release of Mason and Slidell. Secretary of State Seward released the agents and managed to apologize in a way that satisfied the British but did not offend the Northern public. The Union thus narrowly avoided British intervention.

Ultimately, Britain would recognize the Confederacy only if it thought the South could actually win. This fact led many Southerners to hope that a great military victory would bring Britain to their side, much as the Battle of Saratoga had persuaded France to help the United States during the War for Independence. One of the motives for Lee's Maryland campaign, for example, was to win a victory that would impress the British. The uncertain results of the Battle of Antietam, however, dashed those hopes. Despite numerous victories in the early years of the war, the South could never seem to gain the decisive victory that it needed to win British recognition.

President Lincoln meets with General McClellan after the Battle of Antietam.

Emancipation Proclamation

Fear of British intervention was one motive behind Abraham Lincoln's most important diplomatic maneuver of the war. In August 1862 he had expressed a desire to preserve the Union and avoid tackling the slavery issue. Circumstances, however, forced Lincoln to attack slavery as a means of winning the war. In September 1862, after the Battle of Antietam, Lincoln issued the **Emancipation Proclamation**. As of January 1, 1863, Lincoln declared, all slaves in rebel-controlled territory would be freed. The proclamation, therefore, excluded slaves in the Union's border states and in Confederate territories already under Union control, such as New Orleans. In fact, if the Confederacy had surrendered by January 1, 1863 (an unlikely event), no slaves would have been freed at all. It was, to use Lincoln's words, an attempt to save the Union "by freeing some and leaving others alone."

Lincoln achieved his goals. Britain did not recognize the Confederacy, and thousands of blacks joined the Union forces. Although some Northerners initially resisted fighting "to free the slaves," by the end of the war most were describing their fight as a battle for freedom. Lincoln admitted that the Emancipation Proclamation was a war-time emergency act, like his suspension of *habeas corpus*. (Otherwise, of course, the president had no power to make such a sweeping act without the consent of Congress, a fact that his opponents repeatedly emphasized.) The president knew, however, that whatever happened, those who were freed by the act were not likely to be re-enslaved. Regardless of its limitations, the Emancipation Proclamation was an important step toward the elimination of slavery.

Lincoln's Thoughts on the War

Although Lincoln opposed slavery and was happy to strike a blow against it, his motives were primarily practical. As late as August 22, 1862, Lincoln wrote to newspaper editor Horace Greeley, "My paramount object in this struggle is to save the Union, and is not either to save or to destroy slavery. If I could save the Union without freeing any slave I would do it; and if I could save it by freeing all the slaves, I would do it; and if I could do it by freeing some and leaving others alone, I would also do that." Lincoln had three main purposes in issuing the proclamation. He wanted (1) to keep Britain from recognizing the South by appealing to the strong British antislavery feeling, (2) to encourage blacks to join the war effort and fight for the Union, and (3) to revive flagging spirits in the North by giving Northerners another reason for fighting the war in addition to preserving the Union.

Section Quiz

1. How did the fact that so many farm hands went off to fight actually help the growth of agriculture in the North?

2. What were the four border states at the beginning of the war?

3. What was the main goal of Southern diplomacy during the Civil War?

4. What event in 1861 nearly brought Great Britain into the war on the side of the Confederacy?

5. What were Lincoln's three main purposes in issuing the Emancipation Proclamation?

★ Explain how the war adversely affected people on the home front in both the North and the South.

V. Road to Appomattox

War in the Wilderness

After his successes in the West, Lincoln gave Grant field command of Union forces in the East. Grant, however, would learn, according to General Meade, "that Lee and the Army of Northern Virginia are not the same as Bragg and the Army of Tennessee." For Grant's army, it would be an expensive lesson indeed.

Closing Campaigns 1864–65

Ohio

Baltimore

New Jersey

Grant

Maryland

West Virginia

Lee

Washington, D.C.

Delaware

WILDERNESS TO COLD HARBOR MAY–JUNE 1864

Kentucky

APPOMATTOX (LEE SURRENDERS) APRIL 9, 1865

Richmond

PETERSBURG 1864–65

Virginia

Danville

Durham

Tennessee

Greensboro

North Carolina

Sherman 1865

Chattanooga

South Carolina

Wilmington

KENNESAW MT. JUNE 1864

Columbia

ATLANTA SEPT. 1864

Sherman 1864

Charleston

Key
→ Union Movements
→ Confederate Movements
---- Confederate Defenses
✷ Battles and Sieges

Georgia

Savannah

A burial party gathers the grisly remains of the Battle of Cold Harbor.

Wilderness Campaign

With a force of 122,000 troops, Grant marched south toward Richmond. Lee, with half that number, blocked his advance near the scene of his Chancellorsville triumph a year earlier. In the dense woods and tangled underbrush appropriately called "the Wilderness," the two armies began a month-long series of battles. The **Wilderness Campaign** resulted in some of the costliest and most desperate fighting of the war.

In the battles of the Wilderness (May 5–6, 1864), Spotsylvania Court House (May 8–12), and the North Anna River (May 16–23), the Confederates dealt punishing blows to the Union forces. Yet Grant kept up the pressure. Unlike previous Union commanders, such as McClellan, Grant did not retreat after a major setback. At Spotsylvania he wrote, "I propose to fight it out along this line if it takes all summer."

"Grant's Slaughter Pen"

At a dusty crossroads called Cold Harbor, east of Richmond, Grant made his costliest mistake of a campaign that was already being termed a continuous "funeral procession." The **Battle of Cold Harbor** (June 1–3) climaxed on the final day with a massive assault on entrenched Confederate positions that left 7,000 Union soldiers dead or dying before the sun was fully up. When the soldiers were ordered to renew the suicidal assault, they simply refused. Between the two armies lay acres of bodies, what soldiers from both sides dubbed "Grant's Slaughter Pen." A survivor later described it as "not war but murder."

Cold Harbor capped a month of devastation for the bludgeoned Union army. In four weeks of nearly continuous fighting, Grant had lost more men than Lee had in his entire army. The difference, however, was that Grant could replace his numbers; Lee could not. Every assault on the thin gray lines made them thinner yet. In addition, while the Union supply lines were choked with food and clothing, some Southern soldiers were literally starving. In late May, for example, many Confederates received a ration of only one biscuit, with perhaps a slice of bacon, every two days.

War in Georgia

When Grant was made commander of all the Union forces, he left the troops in Chattanooga under the command of his most trusted officer, General **William Tecumseh Sherman**. A tense and excitable man, Sherman had in 1861 been relieved of a major command in Kentucky because of a nervous breakdown. Grant, however, believed in Sherman's talents and helped rebuild Sherman's confidence. At Shiloh, Vicksburg, Chattanooga, and other battles, Sherman justified Grant's faith. Now on his own, Sherman sought to prove that he could lead as well as follow. His task was to destroy Johnston's Southern army and to capture Atlanta, one of the South's most important remaining railroad and manufacturing centers. Sherman approached the job with a grim determination devoid of romanticism and sentiment. "War is cruelty," he said, "and you cannot refine it."

General William T. Sherman

Atlanta Campaign (May–September 1864)

In May 1864, Sherman began his campaign a hundred miles from his goal. Between the Union forces and Atlanta stood a smaller but resolute force under the resourceful General Johnston. A master of defensive tactics, Johnston carefully constructed fortifications of earth, timber, and stone and waited for his adversary to make a mistake. Sherman usually knew better than to attack such strong positions. Instead, he would use his superior numbers to slip around the flanks of the Southerners, forcing them to retreat or be overwhelmed. However, at the Battle of Kennesaw Mountain (June 27), an impatient General Sherman ignored his instincts and launched a frontal attack against entrenched Confederate positions. The bloody results quickly forced Sherman back to his original strategy.

Johnston's slow and skillful retreats frustrated Sherman, but they also frustrated Jefferson Davis, who thought that the Southern general was afraid to fight and was risking the loss of Atlanta. In July when the Union armies forced Johnston back across the Chattahoochee River just north of Atlanta, Davis replaced him with the fiery, energetic John B. Hood. True to his reputation as a fighter, Hood attacked the more numerous Union forces in the **Battle of Atlanta** (July 20–22, 1864). The attack surprised Sherman, but the Federals recovered quickly. The Southerners suffered heavy casualties, more than twice the number of the Northerners. Slowed but not halted, Sherman continued to encircle the city. Faced with destruction if he stayed, Hood abandoned the city on September 2.

The March to the Sea (November–December 1864)

As Sherman sat in Atlanta, he devised an idea to hasten the end of the war. He would wage total war on the South, destroying not only their armies but also their economy and their will. He would march his army across Georgia three hundred miles to Savannah on the coast, waging war against soldiers and civilians alike. Such a march would serve two purposes. First, Sherman's men could destroy food, animals, and other supplies that supported the Confederate army. Second, the march would show Southerners that the Confederacy was rapidly losing the ability to resist. As Sherman himself said, "If the North can march an army right through the South, it is proof positive that the North will prevail." As he prepared what became known as his "**March to the Sea**," Sherman told his superiors in Washington, "I can make the march, and make Georgia howl!"

Before he could march, however, Sherman had to consider Hood's Confederate army, still loose in Georgia and Alabama. Sherman sent a detachment of 30,000 men under General George Thomas back to Nashville, where further reinforcements waited. Thomas was to watch Hood while Sherman made his march. When Sherman began marching toward Savannah on November 15, Hood launched a desperate invasion of Tennessee. Thomas, showing the firmness he had displayed at Chickamauga, repulsed Hood's attacks. Then, at the **Battle of Nashville** (December 15–16, 1864), the Union forces attacked and completely shattered Hood, whose broken army retreated south, no longer a threat to the Northern forces.

Meanwhile, Sherman's men were marching effortlessly through Georgia. They left a trail of destruction fifty to sixty miles wide from Atlanta to Savannah. Anything that could be used to support the Confederate war effort—crops, livestock, railroad lines, personal valuables—was either seized for the Union forces or destroyed. They burned houses and barns by the hundreds. For decades to come, the Georgia countryside was punctuated by lone blackened chimneys, all that remained of once-elegant homes. With only loose control by their officers, some men became little more than vandals, wrecking, looting, and pillaging at will.

When Sherman reached Savannah in December (which he offered as "a Christmas gift" to Lincoln), the general estimated that his army had done $100,000,000 worth of damage to Georgia. The March to the Sea was a deadly blow to the materiel and morale of the Confederate war effort, and it left deep emotional scars on the Southern people.

Election of 1864

Sherman's success almost came too late for Abraham Lincoln. Grant's bloody slugfest with Lee in northern Virginia and Sherman's slow advance in northern Georgia were creating weariness with the war in the North. No end to the fighting seemed to be in sight, and by the summer of 1864, Lincoln's chances for re-election looked slim. On August 23, Lincoln wrote, "This morning, as for some days past, it seems exceedingly probable that this Administration will not be re-elected." Facing Lincoln as the Democratic nominee was none other than George McClellan, former head of the Army of the Potomac. Although McClellan insisted that the Union must be preserved, most members of his party were seeking an end to the war—almost at any price.

The fall of Atlanta in September, however, changed the situation. Suddenly, victory looked probable, even certain. War weariness melted in the warmth of military triumph. On election day, Lincoln won 55 percent of the vote and swamped McClellan 212 to 21 in the Electoral College. The election of 1864 guaranteed that the effort to preserve the Union would go on. Interestingly, Lincoln captured 78 percent of the recorded soldiers' vote against his former general.

Confederate Collapse

Siege of Petersburg (July 1864–March 1865)

After Grant's Cold Harbor disaster, he continued to move southward, slipped across the James River, and laid a twenty-five-mile-long siege line against **Petersburg**, Virginia. Petersburg was the major railroad junction that fed into Richmond from the south.

The "Bummers"

Worse than the regular Union troops were the "bummers," an ugly collection of renegades on the fringes of Sherman's army. Most of the bummers were Union deserters. Under no discipline whatsoever, the bummers committed the worst atrocities of the march—robbery, rape, and murder. Sherman's inability or unwillingness to control his men left a bitter legacy long after the war was over.

If Petersburg fell to the overwhelming Union forces, Richmond would be cut off.

For nine months (July 1864–March 1865), the two armies eyed each other and tested each other's defenses. Battle deaths and disease took their toll on both sides, but the drain was particularly noticeable in the Confederate ranks, for which no replacements were available. The torching of the fertile Shenandoah Valley by Union cavalry under Philip Sheridan and of East Tennessee by George Stoneman's cavalry compounded supply problems for Lee's army. Also, the situation in the Carolinas was quickly sealing the fate of the Confederates. From Savannah, Sherman marched his army north through the Carolinas, wreaking the same havoc there that he had in Georgia. Although Johnston was doing his best to pull together an effective fighting force, he could only harass, not stop, Sherman's army. Union forces pushed north, leaving destruction and bitterness in their wake.

On April 1, 1865, when the fall of Petersburg was imminent, Lee's only hope was to slip out of the siege and link up with Johnston in North Carolina. Davis and his cabinet abandoned Richmond for Danville in southern Virginia. The Confederate army also made a desperate attempt to reach the rail lines first at Danville and then Lynchburg. At every turn, Grant's encircling army cut them off.

Some people urged Lee to scatter his soldiers in small units to conduct guerrilla warfare. But Lee would have no part in creating a legacy of bitterness. He told his men that he was "compelled to yield to overwhelming numbers and resources" and was "determined to avoid the useless sacrifice of those whose past services have endeared them to their countrymen."

Appomattox (April 1865)

On Palm Sunday, April 9, 1865, Lee met Grant at **Appomattox Court House**, Virginia, where they agreed on the terms of surrender for the Army of Northern Virginia. Grant, recalling his impression of their meeting, later wrote that he felt "sad and depressed. I felt anything rather than rejoicing at the downfall of a foe who had fought so long and so valiantly." Grant's generous terms—basically that the Confederates would lay down their weapons and go home—gave an unbowed Lee the opportunity to surrender with honor. Lee appreciatively accepted Grant's offer.

When word of Lee's surrender spread, the noise of celebration and gun salutes erupted throughout the Union lines. But Grant quickly ordered it stopped. "The war is over," he said. "The Rebels are our countrymen again."

Bitter Harvest

Appomattox closed the bloodiest chapter in American history. More Americans died during the War Between the States than in all other wars combined from 1775 to 1975, from the Revolution through Vietnam. More than 650,000 men died in the four-year war. Tens of thousands were maimed for life.

One closing casualty occurred five days after Appomattox. On Good Friday, April 14, an actor named John Wilkes Booth shot

Union troops in the siege lines near Petersburg, Virginia, awaiting the surrender of the Confederates

Furling the Flag

When the proud and sensitive sons of Dixie came to a full realization of the truth that the Confederacy was overthrown and their leader had been compelled to surrender his once invincible army, they could no longer control their emotions, and tears ran like water down their shrunken faces. The flags which they still carried were objects of undisguised affection. These Southern banners had gone down before overwhelming numbers, and torn by shells, riddled by bullets, and laden with the powder and smoke of battle, they aroused intense emotion in the men who had so often followed them to victory. Yielding to overpowering sentiment, these high-mettled men began to tear the flags from the staffs and hide them in their bosoms, as they wet them with burning tears.

(From General John B. Gordon's eyewitness account of the Confederates at Appomattox)

Furling the Flag by Richard N. Brooke, painted in 1872, West Point Museum Art Collection, United States Military Academy, West Point, New York

Oliver O. Howard

Oliver O. Howard had an impressive résumé. He was a Union general in the war, the head of Howard University and West Point, the director of the Freedmen's Bureau in the South after the war, and a peace negotiator with the Indians.

Although Howard had attended church all of his life, he had no inner peace. After graduating from West Point in 1854, he was assigned to a lonely outpost at Tampa, Florida. There, through meditating on the verse "the blood of Jesus Christ . . . cleanseth us from all sin" (1 John 1:7), Howard was converted.

During the war, Howard fought in more major battles than nearly any other Union general. He lost his right arm at the Battle of Fair Oaks. Afterward, General Phil Kearny, who had lost his left arm in the Mexican War, tried to comfort Howard. The wounded Howard replied, "There is one thing that we can do, general; we can buy our gloves together!"

As a commander, Howard was deeply concerned about the spiritual needs of his men. He ensured that services were held each Sunday, and the general himself filled in as speaker when a chaplain was unavailable. General Howard held sessions of prayer and Bible study for his officers, even on the mornings of battles. Howard also went among the wounded after battles to comfort them.

Even those who did not sympathize with Howard's religious views learned to respect him. When the mayor of Columbia, S.C., came to General Sherman to ask for help for his devastated city in 1865, the irreligious Sherman replied, "Go to Howard. Howard runs the religion of this army."

Lincoln in Ford's Theater in Washington. At his last cabinet meeting on the day he was assassinated, Lincoln had extended his hand to the fallen South. According to one cabinet member, the president had warned that "there were men in Congress who . . . possessed feelings of hate and vindictiveness in which he did not sympathize and could not participate."

Casualties			
Union Forces	**Army**	Killed in action/mortally wounded	110,100
		Died of disease	224,580
		Died as prisoners of war	30,192
		Nonbattle deaths	24,881
		Wounded in action	275,175
	Navy	Killed in action/mortally wounded	1,804
		Died of disease/accident	3,000
		Wounded in action	2,226
	Total Union Casualties		671,958
Confederate Armed Forces	**Army**	Killed in action/mortally wounded	94,000
		Died of disease	164,000
		Died as prisoners of war	31,000
		Nonbattle deaths	194,026
	Navy	No figures available	
	Total Confederate Casualties		483,026

In restoring the Confederate states to the Union, Lincoln had wanted "no persecution, no bloody work." Cut down in the hour of his triumph, Lincoln became part martyr, part myth after his death. The new leadership that followed Lincoln, however, little understood Lincoln, the man. With Lincoln gone, the hateful and vindictive men would have their way in the South.

In Davis's last address to his beleaguered citizens, written from his last capital at Danville in the final desperate days in April, he urged, "Let us not then despond, my countrymen, but, relying on the never failing mercies and protecting care of our God, let us meet the foe with fresh defiance, with unconquered and unconquerable hearts." Across the South, that was about all that had not been conquered. It was an impoverished land of widows and orphans where the people nursed the wounds of war in bitterness until the scars became badges of pride. Ahead of the country lay a long and difficult road to national healing.

Dead soldiers at Gettysburg

Section Quiz

1. Why were the casualties in the eastern campaigns of 1864–65 harder on Lee's army than on Grant's even though Grant's losses were greater?

2. Why did Jefferson Davis replace Joseph Johnston as commander of the Confederate forces in Georgia?

3. What were Sherman's two purposes in launching the March to the Sea?

4. What military victory helped Abraham Lincoln win the election of 1864?

⭐ Contrast Grant's attitude toward the human cost of continued warfare with that of Lee.

People, Places, and Things to Remember

states' rights
Anaconda Plan
Thomas J. Jackson
First Battle of Manassas
George B. McClellan
Army of the Potomac
ironclad
Virginia
Monitor
Valley Campaign
Army of Northern Virginia
Joseph E. Johnston
Robert E. Lee
Seven Days' Battles
J.E.B. Stuart
Second Battle of Manassas
Battle of Antietam
Battle of Fredericksburg
Battle of Chancellorsville
Pickett's Charge
Battle of Gettysburg
Gettysburg Address
Ulysses S. Grant
Fort Henry
Fort Donelson
Battle of Shiloh
David G. Farragut
Vicksburg
George Thomas
Braxton Bragg
Battle of Perryville
Battle of Stones River
Battle of Chickamauga
Battle of Missionary Ridge
blockade runners
conscription
New York draft riot
border states
West Virginia
Copperheads
Trent affair
Emancipation Proclamation
Wilderness Campaign
Battle of Cold Harbor
William Tecumseh Sherman
Battle of Atlanta
March to the Sea
Battle of Nashville
siege of Petersburg
Appomattox Court House

Chapter Review

Making Connections

1. Why was life on the home front more difficult in the South than in the North?

2. Why did many state governments in the South oppose conscription?

3. How did the Lincoln administration keep Maryland in the Union?

4. Name one act of the Lincoln administration that opponents considered unconstitutional and explain their reasoning.

5. Why did the South assume at first that Great Britain would come to the aid of the Confederacy?

Developing History Skills

1. Explain briefly why each side in the war thought it was right.

2. Why can one say that slavery was not the only cause of the war?

Thinking Critically

1. Consider William Sherman's statement: "War is cruelty, and you cannot refine it." Is that statement true? What is the potential danger in such an attitude?

2. Why was the Emancipation Proclamation significant even though it only applied to slaves in areas not under Union control?

Living as a Christian Citizen

1. Imagine you are a Southern Christian in 1867 trying to make sense of the war. How will you make sense of your defeat given that your leaders were more faithful Christians than those in the North and your armies enjoyed greater revivals than the Union armies?

2. Imagine that you are a Christian congressional representative from the North. How should your Christian faith influence your response both to the conduct of Sherman and to the treatment of the South after the war?

The ruins that were Richmond

Reconstruction (1865–1877)

I.   Struggle over Reconstruction

II. Reconstruction in the South

III. Years of Corruption

IV. A Reconstructed Nation

"May God forgive, unite and bless us all."

Inscription written on a rocking chair given by a Union veteran to a Confederate acquaintance

On March 4, 1865, Abraham Lincoln closed his Second Inaugural Address with a plea for Americans to put away past hatreds and to unite for the healing of the nation:

> With malice toward none, with charity for all, with firmness in the right as God gives us to see the right, let us strive on to finish the work we are in, to bind up the nation's wounds, to care for him who shall have borne the battle and for his widow and his orphan, to do all which may achieve and cherish a just and lasting peace among ourselves and with all nations.

A little more than a month later, John Wilkes Booth's bullet left Americans wondering whether Lincoln could have achieved these noble goals. Instead, to **Andrew Johnson**, Lincoln's vice president, fell the task of "binding up the nation's wounds."

The period from 1865 to 1877 is usually known as the era of **Reconstruction**. In its narrowest sense, *Reconstruction* refers to the national government's attempts to rebuild the South after the war. Such recovery was not easy, and Southerners, black and white alike, struggled to make their way forward following the terrible devastation. In a broader sense, *Reconstruction* refers to changes in the whole nation. The nation that went into the war in 1861 was not the same nation that emerged from Reconstruction in 1877. The nature of the federal government and its relationship to the states changed dramatically from the relationship intended by the Founding Fathers. Reconstruction shifted the direction of the growth of the American nation.

President Andrew Johnson

I. Struggle over Reconstruction

Plans for Reconstruction

The obvious question facing the national government was how to treat and administer the Southern states after the war was won. Events soon proved that there was little agreement in the North as to what policy should be followed.

Lincoln's Ten Percent Plan

In 1863, Lincoln had formulated his **"ten percent" plan** for restoring the South. As the Union army pushed into the South, Lincoln appointed a military governor for each captured state. These governors were to reestablish civilian government as soon as ten percent of the citizens who had voted in 1860 had taken an oath of allegiance to the Union. Lincoln also intended to grant presidential pardons to many Confederate leaders. This plan was in many ways fairly lenient.

Radicals' View

Opposing Lincoln in Congress was a group known as the **Radical Republicans**. Although they were only a minority within the Republican Party, they were highly influential. They set forth their view of Reconstruction in 1864 in the **Wade-Davis Bill**. It required military governors for each Southern state until a majority of all adult white males, rather than just ten percent of those who had voted in 1860, had signed an oath of allegiance. The bill also demanded several provisions for new state constitutions: it denied to all former Confederate leaders the right of suffrage (the right to vote) and holding political offices, abolished slavery, and repudiated Confederate war debts (that is, the federal government refused to

An Old Warrior's Last Campaign

The fate of Confederate leaders after the war was uncertain. Many Northerners demanded treason trials and hangings. Jefferson Davis, who probably suffered the most of any Confederate leader, was shackled in a cell at Fort Monroe, Virginia. He was never charged with any crime, was denied *habeas corpus*, and was imprisoned until 1867. He was finally granted amnesty in 1868. Northern passions quickly cooled, and most former Confederate leaders quietly began to put their lives back together.

After Appomattox, Robert E. Lee wondered how he would support himself and his family. Tiny Washington College in Lexington, Virginia, invited him to be their president. The school was admittedly in poor shape, had only forty students, and was in physical disrepair. Its presidency was hardly the most prestigious position for the South's greatest hero.

Lee, however, accepted. Rebuilding the school seemed to embody in a small way his desire to see the whole South rebuilt and reestablished. Lee oversaw the repair and restoration of the campus, broadened its curriculum, and made it more flexible to accommodate the changing economic needs of the South. He administered

the school fairly and firmly, always displaying gentlemanly restraint and kindness. Under Lee's guidance, Washington College grew from forty students to four hundred.

Lee's Christian character was plainly evident. Every day, he faithfully took his seat for morning chapel. During the war, Lee had encouraged prayer meetings and preaching among his soldiers, and he continued that emphasis among his students.

Lee also showed his Christian character by laying aside bitterness and hatred after the war. He once told a young lady, "I believe I may say, looking into my own heart, and speaking as in the presence of God, that I have never known one moment of bitterness or resentment."

But that is not to say that he approved of how Reconstruction had gone. In fact, he was disturbed by what he saw. Toward the end of his life (September 1870), he commented to Texas Governor Fletcher Stockdale, "If I had foreseen the use those people designed to make of their victory, there would have been no surrender at Appomattox Courthouse, no Sir, not by me. Had I foreseen those results of subjugation, I would have preferred to die at Appomattox with my brave men, my sword in my right hand."

Five years of toil in behalf of the college wore down Lee's health. He collapsed one evening in 1870 while preparing to say grace before a meal and died a few days later. His last words—an old marching order—were "Strike the tent." His words seemed to both wander back to the gallant war years and commence his final glorious march.

The college trustees honored Lee's memory by changing the name of the school he had rebuilt. Washington and Lee College (now a university) became a memorial to *two* of the noblest sons of Virginia.

pay the debts the Confederate states had incurred during the war). No state was to be readmitted until it had fulfilled those requirements. Lincoln vetoed the bill.

The Wade-Davis Bill clearly showed that the Radical Republicans did not view the South's status as Lincoln did. Lincoln believed that states could not legally secede, so the Southern states were still in the Union. His plan was to restore the rebellious members. The Radicals, on the other hand, viewed the South as a conquered enemy. The leading Radical in the House of Representatives, Pennsylvania's Thaddeus Stevens, viewed the Southern states as "conquered provinces" under the direct authority of Congress. Charles Sumner, the Senate's leading Radical, believed that the Southern states had "committed suicide" and had ceased to exist. Sumner's view, however, was too radical for even the Radicals.

The motives of the Radicals were a mixture of idealistic sentiment, bitter hatred, and crass political opportunism. Some Radicals undeniably believed that only a strict policy of Reconstruction would secure and protect the rights of blacks in the South. Others, as illustrated by Thaddeus Stevens, seemed at times to have no higher motive than simple revenge. Many Republicans thought that a heavy-handed policy would ensure Republican control of the region and, in turn, Republican control of the nation.

Johnson's Plan

After Lincoln's assassination, all eyes turned to Andrew Johnson. What course would he take?

Johnson's plan for Reconstruction was a modification of Lincoln's. Like the latter, it based readmission on the allegiance of ten percent of those who had voted in 1860, but it proposed a stricter policy on qualifications for Southern leadership and on pardons for ex-Confederates. Further, Johnson believed—like Lincoln—that the responsibility for Reconstruction belonged to the president rather than to Congress. As a result, Reconstruction became, in part, a struggle for power between the executive and legislative branches.

President vs. Congress

Division in Washington

Because Congress was not in session when Johnson took office and would not be for several months, the new president decided to proceed with Reconstruction on his own. If he "reconstructed" the South before Congress met, Johnson believed, they would have to go along. When Congress met, however, it rejected Johnson's moves, refused to seat members from the newly "reconstructed" states, and sought to take control of the Reconstruction process.

At this point, Johnson's temper caused him to blunder. Democrats in Congress, along with some conservative and moderate Republicans, were still willing to work with the president. Johnson, however, launched into a speaking tour defending his plan and seeking to unseat his congressional opponents in the midterm elections. In a series of poor performances, he alienated the Northern public. He got into shouting matches with hecklers in the crowds and, in one tasteless display, compared his enemies to Judas Iscariot and himself to Jesus Christ! As Johnson's popularity sank, more Republicans drifted into the Radical camp. Johnson dug in his heels and refused to compromise.

Congress Acts

In the congressional elections of 1866, the Republicans gained more than two-thirds of the seats in both houses of Congress, more than enough to override any vetoes by Johnson. The Radicals acted quickly to limit the power of the president and to seize control of the Reconstruction process. Among the bills passed over Johnson's veto were the Military Reconstruction Act (discussed later) and the **Tenure of Office Act**, which forbade the president from dismissing cabinet members without the consent of the Senate.

The Radicals intended the Tenure of Office Act to protect Secretary of War Edwin Stanton, the most important Radical in the cabinet. Johnson thought that the act was unconstitutional. (The Supreme Court eventually agreed with him.) Furthermore, he disliked the vain, difficult Stanton and viewed him as a Radical spy. Johnson therefore tested the act by dismissing the secretary of war. Stanton responded by literally barricading himself in his office. The president's action delighted the Radicals because it gave them an opportunity to get rid of him.

Summary of Johnson's Life

Like Lincoln, Johnson had been born in poverty and had risen through sheer hard work and dogged determination. He was illiterate until he married a schoolteacher who taught him to read and write. He began his political career by getting elected first as an alderman and then as mayor of Greeneville, Tennessee. Next, he was elected to the Tennessee House of Representatives before being elected to the U.S. House. He was elected governor of Tennessee and then to the U.S. Senate, where he was serving when the war broke out.

Johnson remained loyal to the Union, retaining his Senate seat although Tennessee had seceded. Lincoln named him to be the provisional governor of Tennessee after it was captured by the Northern armies. Lincoln added Johnson to his ticket in 1864 hoping that, as a Southerner and a Democrat, Johnson would broaden the ticket's appeal and help promote unity when the war ended. In addition to his political accomplishments, however, Johnson had a streak of stubbornness and a short temper that hindered him as president.

The Senate committee for President Johnson's impeachment

Impeachment

The Radicals began to agitate for Johnson's **impeachment**, or indictment by the House of Representatives. Impeachment would then be followed by a trial before the Senate. If convicted by the Senate, Johnson would be removed from office, and Benjamin Wade, president pro tempore of the Senate and a leading Radical, would become president. In February 1868, the House of Representatives presented a list of formal charges against Johnson and voted to impeach him. The main charge was violation of the Tenure of Office Act by dismissing Stanton. The case then went to the Senate, which tried Johnson.

Many political leaders questioned the wisdom of removing Johnson for what was in reality no greater "crime" than disagreeing with the Radicals about the best means of Reconstruction. Such an act would reduce the president to a servant of Congress and potentially destroy the balance between the branches of government. When the final vote was tallied, the count stood at 35 to 19 to convict— exactly one vote short of the two-thirds needed to remove Johnson from office. Seven Republicans risked their political careers to follow their consciences and joined twelve Democrats in voting for acquittal. Saved from removal but still at odds with Congress, Johnson rode out the rest of his term quietly and did not again attempt to regain control of the Reconstruction process.

A facsimile of an admission ticket to the impeachment

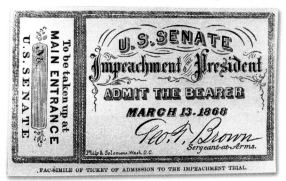

Amending the Constitution

Although Congress passed many important pieces of legislation during the Reconstruction period, the most far-reaching were three amendments to the Constitution.

Thirteenth Amendment

Before the war, Senator Crittenden of Kentucky had tried to avoid the conflict by proposing a thirteenth amendment to the Constitution that would permanently *protect* the institution of slavery. Crittenden's amendment failed to pass. Later, when a thirteenth amendment was adopted, it prohibited slavery. The **Thirteenth Amendment** eliminated the last traces of slavery in the border states and climaxed the work of abolition begun by the Emancipation Proclamation.

The Reconstruction Amendments

The Thirteenth Amendment (ratified 1865), the Fourteenth Amendment (ratified 1868), and the Fifteenth Amendment (ratified 1870) are often known collectively as the "Reconstruction amendments." With the exception of the first ten amendments (the Bill of Rights), no other set of amendments has proved so influential in American life. These three amendments are the most lasting heritage of the Reconstruction period. Their full impact would not be felt, however, until after the middle of the twentieth century.

Fourteenth Amendment

The Thirteenth Amendment freed the slaves, but questions remained about the legal status of freedmen. Congress therefore sought to define the rights of all citizens, including blacks, in the **Fourteenth Amendment**. The amendment contained three important provisions. First, it granted the freedmen full citizenship in both the United States and the states in which they lived. Second, it applied to the states the Constitution's provision that the federal government may not deprive any person "of life, liberty, or property, without due process of law." This provision weakened the original intent of the Tenth Amendment, which reserved to the states all powers not directly delegated to the national government, when courts later interpreted that clause to give the federal government increased authority over the states. Third, the amendment prohibited all former Confederate leaders from holding any office unless first approved by a two-thirds majority of the House and Senate. Because of the way that it increased the power of the national government, the Fourteenth Amendment proved to be the most important and most influential of the three Reconstruction amendments.

Fifteenth Amendment

During Reconstruction, Southerners claimed that the North was being hypocritical in forcing the South to give the vote to African Americans when, as late as 1868, only eleven Northern states (roughly half of them) had legalized black suffrage. Republican leaders agreed with the logic of that complaint and sought vainly to convince other Northern states to give black males the same voting rights as white males. After most of these efforts failed, Congress passed the **Fifteenth Amendment**, which stated clearly, "The right of the citizens of the United States to vote shall not be denied or abridged by the United States or by any state on account of race, color, or previous condition of servitude."

Section Quiz

1. How did Lincoln's ten percent plan differ from the Radicals' Wade-Davis Bill concerning the number of white males taking the oath of allegiance?

2. What is *suffrage*?

3. How did Johnson test the Tenure of Office Act? How did the Radicals respond to his action?

4. Why did seven Republican senators vote for President Johnson's acquittal at his impeachment?

5. What were the three important provisions of the Fourteenth Amendment?

✶ Explain the basic difference in the motivations of Johnson and the Radical Republicans in their respective Reconstruction plans.

II. Reconstruction in the South

At the end of the war, the South lay devastated. Nearly 300,000 Southern men had died in the war in battle, in prison camps, or from disease. The economy of the South was a shambles, devastated by the heavy fighting that had taken place throughout the region.

Charleston at the End of the War

One observer described Charleston, South Carolina, as the scene of "vacant houses, of widowed women, of rotting wharves, of deserted warehouses, of weed-wild gardens, of miles of grass-grown streets, of acres of pitiful and voiceless barrenness."

Some Northern observers touring the region said that morale was so low that Southerners would accept almost any government that the North chose to impose on them. Andrew Johnson's lenient approach, however, encouraged the South. Perhaps, thought Southerners, recovery would not be as painful as they had thought. Then, when the Radicals took control of Reconstruction from the president, the South faced harsher policies. Leniency followed by strictness only further embittered the South and strengthened the region's will to resist. Reconstruction was not off to a good start.

Reconstruction Rule

Military Reconstruction Act

When Congress passed the Tenure of Office Act, it also passed the **Military Reconstruction Act**. This legislation imposed military occupation on the South, like the army of a conquering nation occupying a defeated foe. Tennessee was exempted from the law because it had already ratified the Fourteenth Amendment and had been "reconstructed." The act divided the remaining ten former states of the Confederacy into five military districts, each headed by a presidentially appointed military governor (usually a general in the Union army). Congress instructed the governors to keep peace in the South, by using federal troops and military courts if necessary. The act also required each state to write a new constitution providing for universal male suffrage regardless of race and to pass the Fourteenth Amendment. (Later legislation added passage of the Fifteenth Amendment to the requirements.) Only when a state fulfilled all of these requirements was it considered "reconstructed." Then the army was removed and the state's representatives admitted to Congress.

Freedmen's Bureau

One of the most important agencies in Southern Reconstruction was the **Freedmen's Bureau**, founded in 1865 to provide help to the newly freed slaves. When Congress took control of Reconstruction, the Bureau became a tool for protecting freedmen's legal rights as well. State courts in the South were not being fair to blacks, so Congress set up "Freedman's United States Courts" administered by the Bureau. These Bureau courts protected the rights of the freedmen, but they also offended many Southerners by overriding local courts.

The Bureau also sought to counteract the **Black Codes** passed by President Johnson's "reconstructed" states immediately after the war. Such codes were attempts to regulate the conduct of the former slaves, often unfairly. For example, they allowed blacks to be jailed for vagrancy (lack of self-support) much more easily than whites. When South Carolina and Mississippi, for instance, allowed courts to hire out convicted black vagrants to plantations to work off their fines, Northerners believed that the South was actually trying to re-establish slavery. The codes also prohibited blacks from voting, holding office, suing whites, or serving on juries. Southerners defended the codes by arguing that the uneducated former slaves could be easily manipulated and thus should not have the right to vote. Northerners replied that denial of the right to vote was hardly a long-range solution.

Howard and the Freedmen's Bureau

Headed by Christian general O. O. Howard (Chapter 14), the Bureau originally concerned itself with aiding blacks in the South, distributing food and clothing and building schools for black children. Howard seemed to sincerely seek the good of the freedmen and the country—fighting both the freedmen's poverty and illiteracy and the prejudices of both Northerners and Southerners. Unfortunately, politics kept interfering with his goals.

Former slaves gather in a school run by the Freedmen's Bureau. Education was one of the benefits the Bureau brought to blacks in the postwar South.

Cook Collection, Valentine Richmond History Center

Hiram Revels

When Congress met in January 1870, a new member drew an unusual amount of attention. He was Hiram Revels, senator from Mississippi and the first black to serve in the U.S. Congress.

Revels was born to free black parents in Fayetteville, North Carolina, in 1822. Because higher education was closed to blacks in North Carolina at the time, he moved to the Midwest, where he attended schools in Indiana, Ohio, and Illinois. Revels became a minister in the African Methodist Episcopal Church, the black denomination founded by Richard Allen (see Chapter 11). He preached and taught in the Midwest and the border states and at the outbreak of the war was pastoring in Baltimore.

Revels went to Mississippi in 1864 to preach to the blacks and to care for the needs of the freedmen. He was elected to the state senate in 1868 as a Radical Republican. He was later elected to finish the last year of an unexpired U.S. Senate term.

He served only one year in the Senate, and his legislative role was limited. However, he persuaded the War Department to hire qualified black mechanics in the U.S. Naval Yard and spoke out against segregation in the schools of Washington, D.C., but none of the bills he presented to Congress passed. In fact, some of the Radicals were disappointed by his conservatism. Although he supported the presence of troops in the South (he believed that only the army could protect the rights of blacks in the region), he opposed efforts to deprive former Confederates of the vote. Having seen his own people deprived of the right to vote because of their race, Revels could not see any justice in depriving others of the vote because of their political views.

When his term of office expired, Revels returned to Mississippi, where he served as president of Alcorn College and briefly as Mississippi's secretary of state. He became increasingly disgusted, however, with the corruption of Radical rule. In 1875, he surprised the nation by resigning from the Republican Party and calling for an end to Reconstruction in the South. He complained that Republicans were using blacks as "mere tools" to retain power. After retiring from the presidency of Alcorn because of health problems, Revels returned to the ministry. He spent his last years preaching. He died in 1901 while attending a church conference in Mississippi.

The failure to treat blacks as full-fledged citizens would make it difficult if not impossible for them to become equal members of society.

Carpetbaggers and Scalawags

By denying the vote to many former Confederates, a coalition of blacks and white Radical Republicans was able to elect Radical governments in the South. The majority of white Southerners opposed the Radical Republican governments. They called Northern Radicals who moved to the South "**carpetbaggers,**" after the cheap luggage in which many of them brought all their belongings. Southerners who cooperated with the Radicals were known as "**scalawags.**" Both groups were despised as treasonous, dishonest, and self-serving. However, many of them were far better than Southerners claimed. Some carpetbaggers had come south from idealistic motives, such as aiding in the region's recovery. Likewise, most scalawags had been pro-Union men since before the war, and their behavior was not at all inconsistent with their political beliefs. Many white Southerners were angered that blacks now participated in the writing of the new state constitutions and held elective offices. Bitterness against Northern interference increased when these changes were marred by corruption and electoral fraud.

Evaluation

How good or bad were the Reconstruction governments? Many of them were undeniably corrupt, as men sought to use political power to enrich themselves. The Radical legislature of South Carolina, for example, voted a bonus of $1,000 to its speaker of the house after he had lost that amount betting on a horse race. Corruption, however, was not limited to the "carpetbaggers" in the South during this era. The scandals of the Grant administration and the corruption of Tammany Hall in New York (both discussed in the next section) demonstrate that corruption was fairly widespread. In fact, some of the Southern state governments after Reconstruction were just as bad as those of the Radicals.

The Radical governments in the South could also point with pride to some accomplishments. They enacted universal manhood suffrage; organized public school systems; and rebuilt roads, railroads, and other transportation systems destroyed by the war. Even at their best, however, some of the Radical governments still relied on military might and the **disfranchisement** (denial of the right to vote) of many Southern whites. They were essentially governments imposed against the will of the majority. Over time, Southern whites regained control of their states. When the military departed, the Radical governments collapsed quickly and many black voters were disfranchised.

Southern Reactions

As different people in the South confronted the difficulties of Reconstruction, they reacted in a variety of ways. Some Southerners lashed out in blind violence. Others dedicated themselves to regaining self-rule for the states of the region. Many of them avoided political questions altogether and concentrated simply on surviving.

Violence

Denied participation in the political process, some former Confederates turned to violence. Groups of white vigilantes terrorized parts of the South, directing their wrath against carpetbaggers, scalawags, and particularly blacks. The most important such group was the **Ku Klux Klan**. Dressed in white hoods and robes that supposedly made them look like ghosts, klansmen rode about at night, threatening blacks to keep them from exercising their newly gained political rights. When threats did not work, the klansmen resorted to beatings and even murder. The Klan became so successful at intimidating blacks that Congress passed legislation aimed at curbing the organization. The Ku Klux Klan Act of 1871 broke the power of the Klan. As a result of the act, the government arrested thousands of klansmen and convicted more than twelve hundred. The Klan did not die out completely, however. It went underground for a while and rose to prominence again in the twentieth century. (See Chapter 20.)

Sharecropping

The Southern economy, devastated by the war, did not improve markedly under Radical rule. The freed slaves generally returned to farming, the only occupation they knew, and agriculture remained the leading Southern industry. Land was, in fact, the only Southern resource of consequence. Southern landowners, however, soon found the wage system unsatisfactory. Because little cash was available, they had difficulty paying their workers in cash, and the

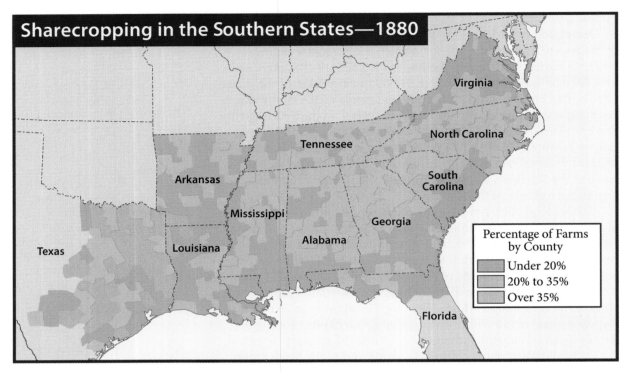

Sharecropping in the Southern States—1880

Percentage of Farms
by County

- Under 20%
- 20% to 35%
- Over 35%

workers became discontent because of low wages. Also, the workers, feeling no particular loyalty to their employers, often left at crucial times, such as during planting, to look for better wages elsewhere.

Sharecropping developed as an answer to the economic deprivations of the South. Several different arrangements existed under the sharecropping system. Some laborers leased the land, provided their own tools and seeds, grew what they wanted, and then paid their rent with cash or crops. Others provided only labor; the landowner provided land, tools, and other supplies. The landowner's share of the crop ranged from one-fourth to one-half of the harvest, depending on how much material he supplied. Because of the need for profits, landowners usually insisted that their tenants grow cash crops such as tobacco or cotton. But those crops quickly depleted the soil of nutrients and obviously provided nothing for the sharecroppers to eat. Low prices for cotton and tobacco after the war only worsened the situation for both sharecroppers and landowners.

Sharecropping was not limited to blacks. About three-fourths of the black farmers in the South and one-third of the white farmers were sharecroppers. In many cases, sharecroppers purchased groceries and supplies on credit and paid for them after harvest. Interest on the credit was so high that most sharecroppers remained constantly in debt. A sharecropper worked as hard as a slave and often received less for his efforts. If he owed money to the landowner or store, the sharecropper could not even leave. As years passed, the debts increased as interest grew and further debts were incurred. Thousands of Southerners—both white and black—were trapped in the endless cycle of annual debt and were unable to save enough money to purchase their own land, even after many years. Sharecropping allowed many Southerners to survive, but it did not enable them to prosper.

Redemption

Most Southerners desired to regain control of their states from the Radicals. Because they wanted "Redemption" from congressional control, men who led the fight for freedom from Radical rule were called **Redeemers**. As in the case of the carpetbaggers and the scalawags, wide generalizations about the Redeemers can sometimes be unfair. Some of them undeniably hoped to strip blacks of the rights and privileges they had gained since the war. Some redeemers reimposed black codes and supported the rise of Jim Crow laws. Most Redeemers, however, sought to achieve what they considered fair play. They wanted to elect their own governments and run their own affairs without outside interference. An example of a fair-minded Redeemer was Democrat Wade Hampton, a former Confederate cavalry general who served two terms as governor of South Carolina after Reconstruction.

Not all Redeemer governors, however, were like Hampton. For example, Ben "Pitchfork" Tillman, who followed Hampton ten years later as South Carolina's governor, was an open racist who sought to use racial turmoil to further his political ambitions. Also, George Houston of Alabama campaigned on a platform of white supremacy. One by one, Southern states turned to the leadership of Redeemers and regained control of their states. By 1876, federal troops remained only in Louisiana, Florida, and South Carolina.

> *Wade Hampton, Redeemer Governor*
>
> During his first campaign for governor, Hampton said, "The only way to bring about prosperity in this state is to bring the two races in friendly relations together. The Democratic Party in South Carolina. . . has promised that every citizen of this state is to be the equal of all; he is to have every right given to him by the Constitution of the United States and of this state. . . . And I pledge my faith, and I pledge it for those gentlemen who are on the ticket with me, that if we are elected, as far as in us lies, we will observe, protect, and defend the rights of the colored man as quickly as [those of] any man in South Carolina."

Section Quiz

1. What requirements did the Military Reconstruction Act set down for the states in order for them to be "reconstructed" and restored to full status?

2. What is the difference between a "carpetbagger" and a "scalawag"?

3. What was the most notorious extremist vigilante group in the South during Reconstruction?

4. What system of farming was the South's main economic response to the devastation caused by the Civil War?

✴ Describe some of the pros and cons of the sharecropping system.

III. Years of Corruption

The North did not undergo Reconstruction as the South did. It had suffered no widespread destruction, it had no need to rebuild the state governments, and certainly it had no military occupation. Nonetheless, the Reconstruction era brought changes to the North just as it did to the South.

The Grant Administration

When the presidential election of 1868 rolled around, the Republicans turned to their leading hero, General **Ulysses S. Grant**, as their candidate. Grant seemed to be the pillar of honesty and strength that the nation needed after the war and the bitter struggle between President Johnson and Congress. Grant captured the mood of the people in his campaign slogan: "Let us have peace."

A Radical President

But Grant proved to be a weak president, and for several reasons he was one of the worst in history. He was a president in the Radical mold, believing that the president should be relatively passive and allow Congress to run the nation. Unlike President Johnson,

President Ulysses S. Grant

he let Congress control the Reconstruction of the South. Another reason for Grant's failure was his lack of political experience. Grant soon learned that leading a nation was far different from leading an army. He had virtually no preparation for the presidency, and the duties of the office seemed to confuse and frustrate him. One visitor to the White House said that Grant looked like "a man with a problem before him of which he does not understand the terms." But the biggest problem with Grant's administration was corruption. Although Grant himself was unquestionably honest, his friends, cabinet members, and other associates seemed to believe that Grant had won the presidency so that they might enrich themselves. A new word, *Grantism*, became a synonym for political corruption.

Scandals

Several scandals rocked the Grant administration. One of them, the **Crédit Mobilier** (CRED-it moh-BEEL-yur) **Scandal**, actually began before Grant took office. The Crédit Mobilier was a railroad construction company controlled by promoters and officers of the Union Pacific Railway. During the construction of the transcontinental railroad (see Chapter 17), the company padded construction expenses and then paid the excesses to the stockholders, most of whom were Union Pacific officers. To discourage congressional investigation, the company sold stock in the Crédit Mobilier to congressmen and other government officials at prices far below the market value. A congressional investigation in 1872 revealed that several prominent Republicans had received shares of the stock, including Vice President Schuyler Colfax.

Perhaps the most notorious scheme that cast shadows on Grant's political reputation was one in which James Fisk and Jay Gould, two unscrupulous financiers, tried to gain control of the gold market. They planned to buy gold on the New York Stock Exchange until the price of gold rose. Then they would sell theirs and make an enormous profit. For their plan to work, however, the federal treasury had to refrain from selling any of its gold reserves, or the price of gold would drop. Fisk and Gould therefore convinced Grant that the nation would be racked with inflation if the secretary of the treasury sold any federal gold. They even bribed Grant's brother-in-law to use his influence to ensure the government's cooperation. Then on September 24, 1869, "Black Friday," Fisk and Gould began to bid up the price of gold. When Grant learned of the scheme, he ordered the treasury to release gold for sale, and the Fisk-Gould plan only partially succeeded. The two schemers did quite well financially, however. "Nothing is lost save honor," said Fisk happily.

Some scandals reached into Grant's inner circle of cabinet members and advisers. Secretary of War William Belknap, Grant's close personal friend, was accused of receiving $24,000 in bribes in return for granting special licenses to sell goods to the Indians. After the House began impeachment proceedings, Belknap resigned in March 1876. One of the worst scandals, revealed in 1875, was the **Whiskey Ring**, a group of whiskey distillers and distributors and federal tax collectors who conspired to cheat the government out of millions of dollars in revenue from excise taxes. Because his private secretary, Orville Babcock, was among the swindlers, Grant was hesitant to demand a thorough investigation; he even testified as a character witness for his secretary. In all, Grant's was probably the most scandal-ridden administration in American history.

William Belknap, Grant's close friend and secretary of war, resigned from office amid charges that he had accepted bribes.

Tammany Hall

The most notorious political corruption in this period was not in the Radical state governments in the South or even in the Grant administration; it was in the city government of New York run by the Democratic **Tammany Hall** under the direction of **William "Boss" Tweed**. Tammany Hall was a political organization founded after the War for Independence that soon grew in influence until it controlled most of New York's political affairs during the last half of the nineteenth century. Under the leadership of Boss Tweed, its corruption in the 1860s and 1870s reached astonishing depths.

New York City's debt increased from $36 million in 1868 to more than $136 million in 1870, largely because Tweed and other Tammany leaders diverted city funds into their own pockets. It has been estimated that fraudulent expenditures from 1865 to 1871 totaled more than $75 million. In only one of his many frauds, Tweed charged New York taxpayers about $11 million to build a courthouse that actually cost about $3 million. (Thermometers for the building, for example, were listed as costing $7,500 each.) Excess funds, entered on the records as fictitious expenditures, were literally stolen by Tweed and others in Tammany Hall. Hospitals, asylums, and other institutions that never existed except on paper received large funds from the city—money which then went into the wallets of Tweed and company.

Boss Tweed and his crooked cohorts managed to stay in power by delivering large blocs of Democratic votes in each election. Needing Tammany's help to win, many Democrats in New York closed their eyes to the corruption in New York City. Tammany politicians used bribes to persuade Republicans to leave them alone.

As a result of reform efforts aimed at destroying Tammany Hall, Tweed was finally arrested in 1871, although Tammany's political influence continued well into the twentieth century. Tweed's arrest and imprisonment were encouraged by the gifted Republican cartoonist **Thomas Nast**, who attacked Tweed and Tammany Hall without mercy. Tweed feared the cartoons more than any other opposition; as Tweed himself said, his uneducated supporters could not read editorials, but they could understand Nast's drawings. Ironically, when Tweed escaped to Spain in 1876, he was identified through one of Nast's cartoons and arrested.

Thomas Nast

The cartoonist who helped bring down Boss Tweed was a short, bespectacled German immigrant who looked more like a bookish professor than a fearless reformer. But Thomas Nast was a man of firm principles with a fierce sense of right, and his political cartoons in *Harper's Weekly* had a sharp edge that made him the leading political cartoonist of the day. A diehard Republican, Nast was not exactly unbiased. Even at the height of the Grant scandals, he defended the president. Yet Nast's opponents could not deny the power of his work. When Tweed died, they learned that he had kept every cartoon Nast had ever drawn of him.

In addition to the Tweed drawings, Nast drew and made popular the symbols of the two parties—the Republicans' elephant and the Democrats' donkey. He also illustrated Clement Moore's poem "A Visit from St. Nicholas," thereby popularizing the modern conception of Santa Claus as a round-bellied, red-cheeked, "jolly old elf" that everyone instantly recognizes today as "Saint Nick."

THE "BRAINS"
That achieved the Tammany Victory at the Rochester Democratic Convention.

Liberal Republicans

The corruption of the Grant administration and the excesses of Radical Reconstruction in the South offended some elements within the Republican Party. As a result, a splinter group calling itself the "**Liberal Republicans**" decided to oppose Grant's reelection in 1872. They called for an end to military occupation of the South and the purging of corruption from the national government. The Democrats, agreeing with these positions and still weakened by the war, decided to join forces with the Liberal Republicans in hopes of defeating Grant.

Unfortunately, this diverse coalition of politicians had trouble finding a candidate acceptable to all factions. Eventually—almost in desperation—they chose New York newspaper editor **Horace Greeley**. Although Greeley was well known and thoroughly honest, he had long been a bitter critic of the South and aroused little excitement among Southern Democrats. (Greeley had once said, "All Democrats may not be rascals, but all rascals are Democrats.") Furthermore, Greeley was an eccentric, advocating such unusual (at least for the time) practices as vegetarianism and spiritualism (communication with the dead). Presidential corruption or not, most voters did not see Greeley as an improvement over Grant. The president crushed Greeley in the election and, in so doing, destroyed the Liberal Republican movement. Exhausted by the campaign, Greeley died three weeks after the election.

Economic Boom and Bust

One of the reasons Grant won reelection so easily was the general prosperity of the nation, particularly in the North. As mentioned in the last chapter, the war had spurred the growth of both agriculture and heavy industry. After the war, business continued to boom as manufacturing quickly shifted from wartime to peacetime goods. A rifle-making plant in Hartford, Connecticut, for example, became a plant for manufacturing sewing machines. For most voters, economic good times covered many of the failures of Grant's administration.

Prosperity came to a devastating halt during Grant's second term, however. A financial collapse called the **Panic of '73** touched off a six-year depression, the worst depression that the United States had endured up to that time. One cause of the panic was a struggle over the nation's currency. At the outset of the war, Congress had issued paper money called "**greenbacks**" (so called because they were printed with green ink) to help pay for the war. Unlike earlier currencies, however, the greenbacks were not backed by gold or silver but simply by the government's promise to honor them. As a result, most Americans viewed greenbacks as less valuable than "hard money" (gold and silver or notes redeemable for gold and silver).

After the war, conservative financiers wanted to get rid of the greenbacks and return to money based entirely on gold. "Easy money" advocates wanted not only to continue using greenbacks but also to print more. Debtors and those on the poorer end of the economic ladder liked the greenbacks because the more money that was in circulation, the more everybody would have. Wages would rise, and it would also be easier to pay off debts. Bankers and other conservative econo-

The Hayes-Wheeler ticket won one of the most hotly disputed presidential elections in American history.

mists quickly pointed out that higher prices on goods and services would also result from an increase in the amount of currency in circulation.

Eventually a compromise of sorts was reached. More than $300 million in greenbacks were left in circulation, but the government pledged to begin redeeming them for their face value in gold. Thus, the greenbacks became "as good as gold." The government's action restricted the amount of money in circulation and thereby made the depression worse. The nation's economic problems began to stir opposition and gave the Democrats a potent political weapon.

Election of 1876

Southern Reconstruction, Republican corruption, and economic hard times were the themes of the presidential election of 1876. Even if there had not been a tradition against electing a president for a third term, the Republicans were not eager to run the scandal-marred Grant again. Nearly all important Republican leaders, however, were tinged with at least a hint of scandal. Finally, the Republicans chose a dark horse, **Rutherford B. Hayes**. Although Hayes had a rather colorless personality, he had served as a Union general in the Civil War, had been a three-time governor of Ohio, and—most important to the Republicans—possessed a reputation for unimpeachable honesty. The Democrats nominated **Samuel J. Tilden**, a brilliant railroad lawyer and former governor of New York. Tilden, who had gained a national reputation by breaking the "Tweed ring" and by reforming the state judiciary system, was an excellent candidate for the Democratic campaign against Republican corruption.

Waving the Bloody Shirt

Since the Democrats had the powerful issues of corruption and economic depression on which to campaign, the Republicans needed an issue to distract voters. Hayes wrote to one Republican leader, "Our strong ground is the dread of a solid South, rebel rule, etc., etc. I hope you will make these topics prominent in your speeches.

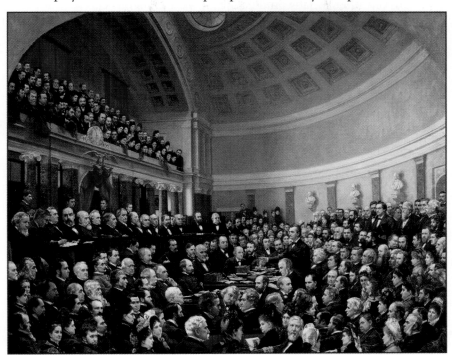

The controversial decision of the electoral commission gave Republican Rutherford B. Hayes the victory over Democrat Samuel Tilden.

The Florida Case Before The Electoral Commission by Cornelia Adèle Strong Fassett, U.S. Senate Collection.

It leads people away from 'hard times,' which is our deadliest foe." Republicans resorted to "waving the bloody shirt," that is, blaming the Democrats for the war and treating them as traitors.

A Disputed Election

When the election returns came in, Tilden seemed to have won. The Democrats won the popular vote by a margin of 250,000, and Tilden had 184 of the 185 electoral votes needed to win. However, three Southern states—Florida, Louisiana, and South Carolina (all states that federal troops still occupied)—sent in conflicting returns. The Republicans claimed that Hayes had won those states; the Democrats, of course, claimed that Tilden had won them. If Tilden could capture at least one of the disputed electoral votes, he would be president. If Hayes captured all nineteen, he would be president.

Congress set up a commission of fifteen men—five each from the Supreme Court, the Senate, and the House—to determine which party should receive the disputed votes. By a vote of eight to seven along strictly party lines, the commission gave all of the disputed votes to the Republicans. The final tally gave Hayes 185 electoral votes to Tilden's 184.

It is difficult to decide who—if anyone—was in the right in the disputed election. Voting corruption marked the efforts of both parties. Southern Democrats, for example, made obvious efforts through threats and fraud to prevent black Republicans from voting. Likewise, the Republican majority on the special congressional election commission was more concerned with electing its candidate than in honestly determining who had won. It might be, as one historian observed, "that the Democrats stole the election first and the Republicans stole it back."

Compromise of 1877

As one might expect, the Democrats contested the commission's decision. The party threatened to hold up the official counting of the electoral votes in Congress so that Hayes could not take office. No one knew what would happen if the Democrats carried out their threat, and a few people even hinted that another war might result. The deadlock was broken, however, when a group of Southern Democrats met secretly with the Republicans to make a deal. The agreement, known as the **Compromise of 1877**, was essentially a tradeoff. Southern Democrats would help Hayes by allowing the electoral votes to be counted. Hayes, in turn, would remove the last federal troops from the South. Each side kept its part of the bargain. Hayes took office on schedule, and within two months he had withdrawn the last troops from the South. Reconstruction was officially over.

Waving the Bloody Shirt

One Republican speaker in 1876 made the following attack on the Democrats:

> Every State that seceded from the Union was a Democratic State.... Every man that shot down Union soldiers was a Democrat.... The man that assassinated Abraham Lincoln was a Democrat.... Soldiers, every scar you have on your heroic bodies was given you by a Democrat. Every scar, every arm that is missing, every limb that is gone, is a souvenir of a Democrat.

Obviously, reason and logic were not strong points of the Republican campaign of 1876.

Section Quiz

1. List three major scandals of the Grant administration.

2. Who was the leader of the corrupt city government of New York during the Reconstruction era? What was his political party?

3. What were the three main campaign themes of the Democrats in 1876?

4. What did Southern Democrats promise in the Compromise of 1877? What did the Republicans promise?

IV. A Reconstructed Nation

As a result of Reconstruction, the United States was a markedly different nation than it had been before the war. Freeing the slaves had been a great triumph, but the impact of that freedom was probably greater than anyone expected. The economy of the South—so long dependent on slavery for its prosperity—was devastated. Furthermore, the struggle over the rights of the newly freed blacks became a heated political issue that has divided and tested the nation up to the present.

The South, bitterly opposed to the Republicans because of the war and Radical Reconstruction, became known as "**the Solid South**" for its commitment to the Democratic Party. With some exceptions, the region elected only Democratic governors, state legislators, and congressmen for nearly a hundred years. Not until 1972 would a Republican candidate for president again carry the South. This unusual political unity gave the region great influence in the Democratic Party and enabled the region to influence the national party's policy and to ensure that the national government left the South alone to run its own affairs for at least seventy-five years.

Perhaps the most important change was the alteration of the nature of the federal government. Before the war, the United States had been a union of states, with the national government limited to a specific defined role with clearly delegated powers. The Founding Fathers tried to balance the powers of the state and national governments and allow them to hold each other in check. The South, of course, believed strongly in the rights of the states and went to war to fight for them. Most Northerners, however, also believed in that principle. Lincoln, for example, opposed secession but did not oppose the idea that many rights are reserved to the states. Lincoln's insistence that he could not constitutionally interfere with slavery in states where it already existed demonstrated his belief in the limited powers of the national government.

But the war altered those attitudes. The association of the idea of "states' rights" with the secessionist South caused many Northerners to suspect the whole concept. Perhaps, they thought, another war might result if they did not repudiate the idea. Also, the abolition of slavery removed one of the main differences between the sections. Abolition at least opened the door for the sections of the nation to draw closer in culture, technology, and economy. Increasingly, Americans began to speak less of "the Union" and more of "the nation." Sentences that had previously begun "The United States *are*. . ." now began "The United States *is*. . . ."

Whatever advantages the United States might have gained from that change, it did produce one great disadvantage: The power of the national government increased significantly. The reduction of the idea of states' rights removed one check on the central government's power. The Fourteenth Amendment, as mentioned earlier, eventually became a wedge that the central government used to enter and eventually control many state and local affairs. One historian noted that before the war virtually the only agency of the national government that touched the lives of the average citizen was the Post Office. Today, the American citizen usually cannot avoid contact—even conflict—with the national bureaucracy as it has steadily grown in power and influence.

> ### *Three Far-Reaching Results*
> Three important, far-reaching events resulted from the Civil War and Reconstruction: the slaves were freed, the South became solidly Democratic, and the powers of the federal government expanded dramatically.

The war and the Reconstruction that followed transformed the "Federal Union" into the "American nation." The goals that motivated this change—preserving the Union and granting the rights of citizenship to blacks—were certainly important. The most important legacy of the Radicals was enactment of the Thirteenth, Fourteenth, and Fifteenth amendments. Could these goals have been achieved without the resulting growth of government power, bitter sectional hatred, and longstanding racial tension? Only after one answers that question can the wisdom of the process of Reconstruction be evaluated. Regardless of the answer, the end of slavery and Reconstruction clearly paved the way for more westward development, including a boom in building new railroads in the 1880s.

Section Quiz

1. What term was applied to the states of the former Confederacy during Reconstruction because of their consistent support of the Democratic Party?

2. Was the South ever really "reconstructed"?

Chapter Review

Making Connections

1. How did Lincoln and Johnson differ with the Radicals concerning the ultimate responsibility for Reconstruction?

2. How did the Fourteenth Amendment provide a way for the central government to extend its power over state and local governments?

3. Why did Southerners resent the Reconstruction governments that the Radicals established over them?

4. Why did the Liberal Republicans' choice of a candidate in 1872 harm their efforts to defeat Grant?

Developing History Skills

1. What is meant by "waving the bloody shirt," and how was it used as an election tactic?

2. Why did one historian say of the presidential election of 1876 "that the Democrats stole the election first and the Republicans stole it back"?

Thinking Critically

1. Why was sharecropping more popular than the wage system in the South during Reconstruction?

2. How were the negative aspects of Reconstruction evident in later history?

Living as a Christian Citizen

1. What would you say if a skeptic pointed out that Southern churches tended to be both more orthodox and more racist while Northern churches, which tended to be more liberal, did more to promote African American freedom?

2. Evaluate the Radical Republicans from a Christian perspective. How could a Christian worldview have improved their strengths and curbed their excesses?

People, Places, and Things to Remember

Andrew Johnson
Reconstruction
ten percent plan
Radical Republicans
Wade-Davis Bill
Tenure of Office Act
impeachment
Thirteenth Amendment
Fourteenth Amendment
Fifteenth Amendment
Military Reconstruction Act
Freedmen's Bureau
Black Codes
carpetbaggers
scalawags
disfranchisement
Ku Klux Klan
sharecropping
Redeemers
Ulysses S. Grant
Grantism
Crédit Mobilier Scandal
Whiskey Ring
Tammany Hall
William "Boss" Tweed
Thomas Nast
Liberal Republicans
Horace Greeley
Panic of '73
greenbacks
Rutherford B. Hayes
Samuel J. Tilden
Compromise of 1877
"the Solid South"

HERSHEY'S

N.º 1

LANCASTER

CHOCOLATE

UNSWEETENED

Superior to all others.

FOR BAKING, COOKING and DRINKING

Warranted Absolutely Pure

HERSHEY CHOCOLATE CO.

LANCASTER, PA. U.S.A.

In 1894, Milton Hershey decided to make a sweet chocolate to use as a coating for his caramel candies. A spinoff was the now-famous milk chocolate bar.

1867 Purchase of Alaska

1869 First transcontinental railroad completed

1870 Rockefeller forms the Standard Oil Company of Ohio

1876 Alexander Graham Bell invents the telephone

1883 Pendleton Act creates Civil Service Commission

1890 Sherman Anti-Trust Act passed

CHAPTERS

16 THE GILDED AGE (1877–1896)

17 AMERICA EXPANDS (1850–1900)

18 THE PROGRESSIVE ERA (1900–1920)

19 THE GREAT WAR (1913–1920)

The waffle cone came as a result of an ice cream salesman's shortage of dishes at the St. Louis World's Fair in 1904. A waffle salesman rolled a waffle to hold the ice cream, and fair visitors loved it.

A Minnesota master mechanic grew tired of having to eat burnt toast. He invented the electric pop-up toaster in 1919 and marketed it to the restaurant industry.

1898 Spanish-American War

1901 U.S. Steel formed

1903 Henry Ford founds Ford Motor Co.; Wright brothers' first flight

1914 Panama Canal opens

1914–18 World War I

1917 U.S. enters World War I

Ellis Island Immigration Station

The Gilded Age (1877–1896)

I.   **Industry and Invention**

II. **Political Reform and Reaction**

III. **Labor, Rural, and Economic Issues**

IV. **Change and Challenge**

> *"Well, well, my boy, things are looking pretty bright now I tell you. Speculation—my! The whole atmosphere's full of money."*
>
> Con man Colonel Beriah Sellers discussing a business venture over a dinner of water and raw turnips in Mark Twain's "The Gilded Age" (1873)

America's horizons were never the same. As the country hurried headlong toward the twentieth century, the skyscraper and the smokestack replaced the steeple as the skyline's most prominent feature. Industrialization put its golden stamp of prosperity on much of society. The period was a time of unprecedented political and economic freedom that enabled a flood of inventions and innovations in almost every industry and area of life and affected everyone. The rich got richer, and even the poor got less poor. Yet behind the glitter of America's growing wealth were contrasts and divisions that would transform national life.

I. Industry and Invention

The Rise of Industrialism

The postwar period witnessed a rapid rise in the importance of industry in the United States. From a few small iron factories and oil wells in the 1850s, American industry grew until the United States was a leader in the world's industrial community.

American industrial growth occurred for several reasons. First, the nation itself grew. A modest postwar baby boom combined with immigration nearly tripled the population from 32 million in 1860 to 92 million in 1910. Increased population led to an increased demand for products and an increased work force to produce them. It also encouraged the movement westward and the accompanying development of farmland and mining in the resource-rich West.

Second, the innovative spirit of the times fostered new machines and methods that enhanced industrial expansion. Communication capabilities improved as entrepreneurs experimented with the telegraph, telephone, and radio.

Third, industry benefited from a sympathetic government. The generally high tariff laws reduced foreign competition, and the nation's liberal immigration laws provided a vast and inexpensive work force for prospective employers.

Fourth, new sources of power sprang up to supplement or supplant the waterpower that had driven America's early industry. Whole new energy industries in oil and electricity spurred greater manufacturing and opened new markets. The success of these industries led to the development of new, more efficient ways of doing and organizing business, especially corporations and trusts. Commercial capitalism made way for industrial capitalism (factories) and then finance capitalism, in which banks and investors played the leading role.

Captains of Industry

At the top of America's growing industrial empire were men whose ideas, energy, and money dominated the age. Their lives often illustrated the best and worst aspects of industrialization. These men were the "captains of industry," and their efforts helped forge America into a prosperous and productive nation. Many historians and journalists, by calling these men "**robber barons**," have tried to make them seem to be personifications of greed and callousness. They were, indeed, aggressive, cost- and efficiency-conscious businessmen, but those characteristics actually accomplished enormous good for the average consumer, lowering prices on consumer goods and making available goods that once had been

> ### *Results of Westward Expansion*
> The development of the West made accessible to the nation an increased supply of raw materials with which to produce goods. It also encouraged the rapid expansion of the railroads, connecting manufacturers with new markets, helping distribute resources and goods throughout the country, and binding East and West with steel rails.

> ### *Why Some People Opposed the "Captains of Industry"*
> Much of the opposition to the Gilded Age "captains of industry" came from people who envied their successes, lacked the power or ability to compete with them, or wanted the government to help them succeed at the expense of taxpayers and successful entrepreneurs. Journalists who attacked successful industrialists for these reasons were known as "muckrakers."

within reach of only the rich. They created jobs by which workers could provide for their families. They made the United States the economic envy of the world and sparked a flood of immigrants seeking "the American dream." They became wealthy by providing efficiently what consumers needed and wanted. Moreover, many of them became great philanthropists, giving to numerous charitable causes, including hospitals and libraries that would benefit the common person.

Historian Burton Folsom groups the captains of industry in two categories: market entrepreneurs and political entrepreneurs. Market entrepreneurs were those who sought success by good business practices—time management, cost-cutting, improved operations, new technology. These practices resulted in more and better products and lower prices for the consumers. Market entrepreneurs made their money from volume, ingenuity, and service to the "little guy," not on the backs of others. The most efficient businesses succeeded; inefficient competitors failed.

Political entrepreneurs, on the other hand, sought success by special privileges or political advantages. They sought high tariffs to price out competitors and asked for government subsidies (taxpayer dollars) to reduce costs to themselves. In fact, some of them found that they could make almost as much money by getting government grants and subsidies as they could by producing products or providing services. They lobbied politicians to influence political decisions that might affect their businesses. Some even resorted to bribery to gain an advantage over competitors.

Entrepreneurs of both types, however, did more to shape America's future than anyone who sat in the White House or Congress at the time. Their lives illustrate a number of important trends during this formative period.

Cornelius Vanderbilt—Shipping

As a young man, **Cornelius Vanderbilt** borrowed one hundred dollars from his mother and started a ferry service. From this humble beginning, Vanderbilt gained control of much of New York's water-borne shipping through hard work and increased cost efficiency. Vanderbilt duplicated his successes throughout the Northeast and into the West. By 1860, he controlled much of the nation's shipping. Besides a fortune, Vanderbilt gained an inflated title—"Commodore."

James J. Hill—Railroads

Another entrepreneur, James J. Hill, gained his fame and fortune in railroads. His climb to fortune began with a job in a grocery store. As a young man, he determined that his future prospects lay in the westward movement. With six hundred dollars he had saved, he traveled to St. Paul, Minnesota, in 1856 to start a shipping business. He got a job as a clerk in a local shipping company and began to learn the business and make plans for his own company. He noted the "puny" railroad systems in the Great Lakes area and determined to find new and better ways of doing things. He became an expert on the economics of the upper Northwest, including the railroad industry.

Edward Collins—Political Entrepreneur

Vanderbilt's success actually began with another entrepreneur, Edward Collins. Collins wanted to compete with the British, who had a virtual monopoly on passenger and freight steamship traffic across the Atlantic. He approached Congress, claiming that he could do so if the government subsidized the building of four steamships. He promised that within a year he would be showing a profit and no longer need government money. Congress voted the appropriation. Collins built the ships and began his service, but he kept coming back year after year for more subsidies, every time offering excuses as to why he could not make a profit.

Vanderbilt approached Congress, saying that he could do what Collins was doing—and actually make a profit—for half the money they were giving Collins. Congress turned him down, so Vanderbilt did it the old-fashioned way—with his own and voluntary investors' money. By the end of his first year, he was turning a profit, and he continued to do so year after year.

James J. Hill, who built the Great Northern Railroad without any special privileges or finances from the government, is an example of a market entrepreneur.

In 1865, he founded James J. Hill Company, providing warehouse facilities for products brought by steamship from the East. He provided railroad tracks directly from the warehouse to the rail line. Successful in that, he shifted his emphasis to railroads, buying up failing rail lines. He also bought land in Dakota Territory in preparation for fulfilling his dream of building a railroad across the northern part of the United States to the Pacific Northwest.

Hill innovated by shifting from wood fuel for his locomotives to coal and soon achieved stunning success in the trading of coal. He sought to get the best prices possible for not only coal but also all other purchases for his companies. For example, he demanded more accurate weighing of carloads of coal, which led to more accurate billing for freight fees, and that in turn translated into savings and greater profits.

In constructing his Great Northern Railroad, Hill applied his core principles: "What we want," he said, "is the best possible line, shortest distance, lowest grades, and least curvature that we can build. We do not care enough for Rocky Mountain scenery to spend a large sum of money developing it." His workers laid rails twice as fast as the Northern Pacific had. He cut costs wherever he could and passed the savings on to customers in the form of lower rates. He adopted as his motto "We have got to prosper with you [the consumers and small businesses] or we have got to be poor with you." He practiced the art of building goodwill by throwing in many extras for those who used his businesses. He taught crop rotation to farmers along his route and provided free seeds and cattle to help farmers recover after a drought. He transported new immigrants to the Great Plains for a low fare if they would settle and farm along his rail lines. He even set up and operated model farms to demonstrate the latest improvements in farming science.

Hill's sharp business eye and his desire to meet the needs of consumers resulted in the Great Northern Railroad, a line that was far superior to any other lines built elsewhere in the world. Most importantly, Hill did all of that without a penny of government money or influence. He prospered immensely—and the population of the northern plains shared in that success.

Andrew Carnegie—Steel

Andrew Carnegie was born in Scotland, but hard times there forced his poor family to immigrate to western Pennsylvania in 1848. His life in America was a classic "rags-to-riches" story. His first job in America was as a bobbin boy in a textile mill, where he earned $1.20 a week. He then worked for a short time as a bookkeeper's clerk before becoming a telegraph delivery boy and then a telegrapher. As he worked hard to advance himself, he developed scorn for those who were lazy, unambitious, and unwilling to work. Because he was diligent, efficient, and quick to learn about everything he undertook, Carnegie advanced rapidly to become superintendent of the Pittsburgh division of the Pennsylvania Railroad (PRR). He saved and invested heavily (eventually doubling his investments) from his PRR salary. By the early 1870s, he was focusing on the steel industry. He invested heavily in anything that involved steel: sleeping-car construction, an iron company, and bridge building. He was always looking for better ways to organize, operate, and capitalize his various business ventures, including a telegraph company (which he eventually sold to Western Union).

Andrew Carnegie was known as both an entrepreneur and a philanthropist.

Carnegie, the Bridge Builder

One of Carnegie's early achievements was construction of the St. Louis Bridge, which his Keystone Bridge Company built. He used pneumatic caissons to sink the piers a decade before the same method was used on the more famous Brooklyn Bridge. He bought all of the iron used in the construction of the bridge from Union Iron Mills, which he owned. He also was the key investment banker for the project. By that time, Carnegie had a net worth of nearly two million dollars, but his cash on hand was only five thousand dollars.

John D. Rockefeller was the victim of muckrakers, who painted him as a callous, uncaring moneygrubber rather than as an entrepreneur who improved the quality of life for millions of common people.

Horizontal Integration

Unlike the vertical integration that Carnegie practiced, in which a company controlled a *part* of *all* segments of the production of a good from raw material to finished product, Rockefeller practiced **horizontal integration**, consolidation of *all* of *one* entire segment of an industry. Rockefeller controlled every aspect of the oil-refining process from barrel making to pipelines and transportation.

Through a method known as **vertical integration**, Carnegie controlled every aspect of steel production from the mine to the market. Such a conglomerate effectively dismantled most of Carnegie's less efficient competitors, most of whom dealt with only one segment of the steel industry. Carnegie Steel soon became the largest steel company in the world, producing about half as much steel as the entire nation of Great Britain and about one-fourth of America's. When financier J. P. Morgan bought out Carnegie in 1901, the former bobbin boy's personal share was nearly $300 million.

Carnegie's companies always provided high-quality products and performance. However, he was more than a financial genius; he was also a philosopher of big business. In 1889, he published *The Gospel of Wealth*, in which he revealed the influence of evolutionist Charles Darwin on his thinking. The accumulation of wealth, Carnegie believed, simply illustrated the survival of the fittest—and he considered himself among "the fittest." Wealth, however, was not an end in itself. Carnegie wrote, "The man who dies rich dies disgraced. . . . Surplus wealth is a sacred trust which its possessor is bound to administer in his lifetime for the good of the community."

John D. Rockefeller—Oil

America's first billionaire was **John D. Rockefeller**, the founder of Standard Oil Company (1870). In 1859, when Rockefeller was still a young businessman, oil was discovered in Titusville, Pennsylvania, and the "black gold" rush began. He saw that his future was in oil, but he thought that drilling for it involved too much risk. He thought that a safer investment and greater profits would be in oil refining, turning raw petroleum into useful products. Others saw the profit potential in refining, too, and competition was stiff and chaotic, but Rockefeller determined that through efficiency and technological improvements he could win out.

Historian Thomas DiLorenzo wrote that Rockefeller, reared as a Baptist, "was religious about working and saving his money. Rockefeller invested $4000 in an oil company and paid meticulous attention to every detail of his business, constantly striving to cut his costs, improve his product, and expand his line of products. He also sometimes joined in with the manual laborers as a means of developing an even more thorough understanding of his business."

Rockefeller also waged a relentless war against waste in his company. When Rockefeller entered the oil industry, only half of the typical barrel of oil was deemed useful in the production of kerosene, the source of lighting for the average person. The rest was thrown away, poured into rivers and lakes, polluting the water and surrounding lands. Through research and development, Rockefeller found ways to use that "useless" half barrel of oil and make money from it. His scientists developed petroleum jelly, paraffin, and other useful products that increased both the quality of consumers' lives and his own profits. He continued to trim costs and improve production until he had cut the cost of refining to three cents per gallon and then to less than a penny by 1885. By 1879, he was so successful that he controlled 90 percent of the American oil market and 65 percent of the world market. Consumers benefited by paying less for those products.

In 1879, Rockefeller organized his oil-refining empire into a **trust**. The trust was a legal device by which a board of trustees was empowered to make decisions and control the operations of a whole

Horizontal Integration

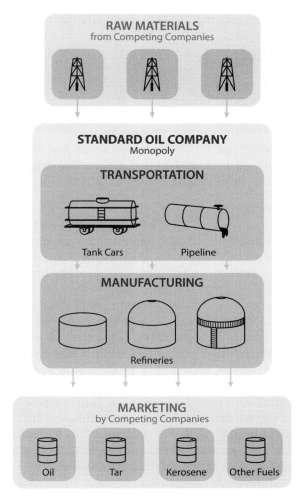

RAW MATERIALS
from Competing Companies

STANDARD OIL COMPANY
Monopoly

TRANSPORTATION

Tank Cars   Pipeline

MANUFACTURING

Refineries

MARKETING
by Competing Companies

Oil   Tar   Kerosene   Other Fuels

Vertical Integration

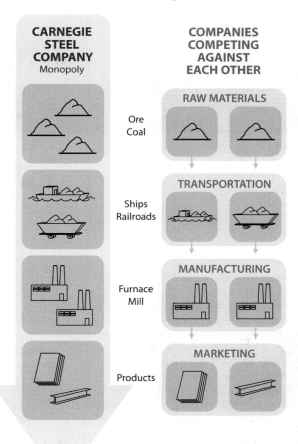

CARNEGIE
STEEL
COMPANY
Monopoly

COMPANIES
COMPETING
AGAINST
EACH OTHER

Ore
Coal

RAW MATERIALS

Ships
Railroads

TRANSPORTATION

Furnace
Mill

MANUFACTURING

Products

MARKETING

group of companies. As a result, the Standard Oil Trust purchased twenty-seven competing oil companies. Rockefeller's trust became the pattern for the formation of other trusts during the 1880s by businessmen who also had the means to buy up competing companies. This led to cries from competitors for the government to break up the giants and to create a so-called fair playing field. The result was the Sherman Antitrust Act of 1890.

The image that many people have today of Rockefeller as a callous, cutthroat competitor was primarily the work of Ida Tarbell, a journalist whose father's company was one that Rockefeller bought out. Tarbell, thinking that Rockefeller had illegally and immorally put her father out of business, produced *The History of the Standard Oil Company*, "a classic of antibusiness propaganda." Unfortunately, the image she painted of Rockefeller has been the most lasting image of the man. As historian Allan Nevins wrote, those stories were repeated and "did [Rockefeller] a gross injustice, and led to the invention of a totally false stereotype of the man."

Furthermore, much of the criticism of Rockefeller overlooks the role that his competitors' unwise business decisions played in their own demise and minimizes Rockefeller's efficiency and honest administration of his business. Whenever Rockefeller bought out a company, he paid the fair market value in cash or stock. Far from being uncaring toward his employees, Rockefeller set up a pension program for them thirty years before any other business did so.

> ### *The Generosity of Rockefeller*
>
> On one occasion, Rockefeller quietly gave one thousand dollars to the American Board of Commissioners for Foreign Missions. When word leaked out, people began to oppose it, saying it was "tainted money." He later gave ten million dollars to the Euclid Avenue Baptist Church General Education Board. According to historian Allan Nevins, Rockefeller "devoutly believed that God had made him a trustee for [his] hundreds of millions, not to be kept but to be given wisely and carefully. . . . [W]e must not forget that Rockefeller began to give as soon as he began to earn."

Standard Oil Company refinery, Whiting, Indiana

During the Panic of 1907, rather than cut wages or lay people off, Standard Oil actually *increased* employment in extensive construction projects.

James Buchanan Duke—Tobacco

After the war, Southerners, as they had done for two centuries, returned to the soil for their livelihood. Nonetheless, many Southerners began to envision a **"New South"** that would match the North in economic and industrial capacity. The economic house of the New South would be built on the twin pillars of the two *T*s—tobacco and textiles. Virginia and Carolina piedmont towns—such as Danville, Virginia, and Greensboro and Charlotte, North Carolina—had largely escaped the ravages of war. Those cities became leaders in the economic revitalization of the postwar New South. By 1900, four hundred cotton mills dotted the old Confederacy, far surpassing the textile production of New England.

Even tobacco, the South's original cash crop, gained a new lease on life during the postwar period. Capitalizing on the popularity of a tobacco known as bright leaf, James Buchanan "Buck" Duke of Durham, North Carolina, used new marketing techniques to create a national and international market for his tobacco products.

Through the skillful use of advertising and promotion, Duke outstripped his competitors. In 1890, Duke founded the American Tobacco Company, which captured 90 percent of the nation's cigarette market. The New South's captain of industry also became a leader in developing hydroelectric power, opening the way for greater economic expansion in the South.

J. P. Morgan—Finance

John Pierpont Morgan was the leading investment banker in America during the Gilded Age. Morgan came to symbolize the power and prestige at the top of America's industrial pyramid.

Morgan's business was not an industrial product but money—buying and selling stocks on a grand scale. Morgan bought up a controlling interest in competing companies to reorganize them into streamlined corporations that could make even more money. His mergers began in the railroad industry, where he reorganized a number of major lines, such as the Northern Pacific, Union Pacific, B & O, and Southern railroads. Morgan's biggest deal, however, was the consolidation of much of the steel industry. Through a series of mergers, culminating in the purchase of the giant Carnegie Steel, Morgan formed the first billion-dollar corporation, **United States Steel Corporation**, in 1901.

Innovations

Behind the rapid industrialization in America were new methods, ideas, and inventions that fueled expansion and created new

---

African Americans in the New South

As influential as Duke was, African Americans also played a major role in developing the New South. Perhaps no black leader encouraged black progress and entrepreneurship during the period more than Tuskegee Institute president Booker T. Washington. On September 18, 1875, he delivered a rousing speech in the Cotton States and International Exposition in Atlanta, during which he encouraged blacks to "put down your bucket where you are," meaning to take advantage of their God-given skills right where they were, develop those skills to their fullest potential, and help the New South succeed by becoming successful themselves. His speech received mixed reviews among other black leaders, some of whom criticized Washington's ideas as kowtowing to southern whites. (You will read more about Washington later in this chapter.)

markets. Thousands of inventions during the Gilded Age completely changed the way Americans lived.

Diet and Dress

The rising standard of living allowed changes in the American diet. Refrigerator cars brought beef and pork from the vast midwestern plains as well as strawberries, tomatoes, and oranges from the South and West to eastern cities and the waiting iceboxes of middle-class homes. By 1880, the mass production of tin cans and new methods of cooking and sealing allowed the preservation of a wider variety of foods.

Americans enjoyed positive changes in their dress as well. The development of the sewing machine and its widespread use during the war of 1861–65 spawned a huge retail market for mass-produced clothing. For the first time, standardized sizes and designs were applied to clothing. Fashion and comfort became important considerations in the American wardrobe. By the turn of the century, suits of lighter weight and color were being produced for men's summer wear. The generous Victorian styles for ladies were gradually being trimmed down. By 1920, a woman's dress required only three yards of material to produce compared with ten yards in the 1890s. Mass production of high-quality, stylish clothing also decreased class

J. P. Morgan was known as America's banker, and he was an organizer of railroads too.

H. J. Heinz

H. J. Heinz was an unbendingly honest food producer in Pittsburgh. A devout Methodist, he wrote in his will, "I desire to set forth, at the very beginning of this Will, as the most important item in it, a confession of my faith in Jesus Christ as my Saviour." Although Heinz pioneered much of modern billboard and newspaper advertising, he refused to allow his products to be advertised in Sunday newspapers; he believed such advertising desecrated the Lord's Day. Heinz gave liberally to Christian works, particularly Sunday school organizations, and he was an officer in various Sunday school associations.

Heinz was a leader in producing bottled and canned foods: horseradish, ketchup, pickles, and dozens of other products. His honesty was a byword in the food industry. Other producers added fillers to their products, such as mixing ground turnips or even wood pulp with their horseradish, and sold their goods in greentinted bottles to hide the impurities. Heinz insisted on 100 percent pure products sold in clear bottles so that everyone could see the purity for themselves.

While other businesses endured strikes and labor unrest, the H. J. Heinz Company never had a single strike during Heinz's life. Heinz ensured that his employees had no reason to strike. He provided them free medical care, gyms, swimming pools, gardens, and educational opportunities, such as libraries and free concerts and lectures. Employees of other companies labored in dark, dirty, noisy factories. Heinz's workers, however, enjoyed clean, well-lit, well-ventilated plants where dining halls provided food at discount prices.

Heinz denied having any "secret" to his success other than honesty and hard work. "To do a common thing uncommonly well brings success," he often said. Another motto was "Do the best you can, where you are, with what you have today."

distinctions. Ordering from a *Sears and Roebuck Catalog*, men and women of even modest means could dress in style.

Communications

Industrialization also created a communications revolution during the Gilded Age. The growth of businesses across the nation resulted in increased correspondence and more sophisticated record keeping. The invention of the typewriter (1867) and an improved system of shorthand (1888) met the new demands of the business world. The development of cheap paper from wood pulp and the invention of continuous action roller presses resulted in the birth of mass media. Inexpensive newspapers, magazines, and books became available for an increasingly literate and sophisticated society.

The crowning communications achievement of the time came in 1876 with the invention of the telephone by **Alexander Graham Bell**. Bell was a Scottish immigrant who arrived in the United States at the age of twenty-four to teach speech to the deaf. An innovative thinker who combined his interest in sound with his propensity for experimentation, Bell struggled for three years with the idea that he could "make iron talk." On March 10, 1876, he transmitted his first message over wire, calling an assistant in another room of his house: "Mr. Watson, come here, I want you." People have been answering phone calls ever since.

The Father of "Ma Bell"

After long and numerous legal battles to defend his patents on the telephone and various long-distance improvements, Bell and his associates formed American Telephone and Telegraph Company in 1885. By 1900, AT&T had a monopoly on the country's phone service.

Thomas Edison in his laboratory, 1888

Electricity

America's most prolific inventor was **Thomas Alva Edison**. Although he had little formal education, Edison had a knack for new ideas and a thirst for discovery. He established an "invention factory" at Menlo Park, New Jersey, that was the forerunner of today's industrial research laboratories.

Edison was responsible for more than a thousand inventions during his lifetime, but the most influential ones were the phonograph, the motion-picture projector, and the incandescent light bulb. On September 4, 1882, after years of experimentation in developing the light bulb and the power system that could make indoor lighting practical, Edison flipped a switch that lit up New York's financial district. A new age was born in the eerie glow on Wall Street.

The contributions of George Westinghouse and Hungarian immigrant Nikola Tesla in devising alternating current generators and

Thought-Provoking Edison Quotations

"If we all did the things we are capable of doing, we would literally astound ourselves."

"Opportunity is missed by most people because it is dressed in overalls and looks like work."

"To invent, you need a good imagination and a pile of junk."

"We don't know a millionth of one percent about anything."

"I find my greatest pleasure, and so my reward, in the work that precedes what the world calls success."

"The three great essentials to achieve anything worthwhile are: Hard work, Stick-to-itiveness, and Common sense."

"Your worth consists in what you are and not in what you have."

"What you are will show in what you do."

"Genius is one percent inspiration and ninety-nine percent perspiration."

transformers gave electrical power long-range practicality. In 1893, for example, power generated at and transmitted from Niagara Falls lit the Columbian Exposition in Chicago. Men rightly marveled at the potential that electricity offered the world. As Harvard President Charles Eliot declared at the turn of the century, electricity is the "carrier of light and power; devourer of time and space; bearer of human speech over land and sea; greatest servant of men."

Section Quiz

1. What were the four causes of American industrial growth in the second half of the nineteenth century?
2. In which industry was each of the following men a leader?
   a. Andrew Carnegie
   b. John D. Rockefeller
   c. J. P. Morgan
   d. James J. Hill
   e. Cornelius Vanderbilt
3. What was unique about the success of James J. Hill?
4. What was the most important invention in communications in the late nineteenth century, and who invented it?
5. Name two of Thomas Edison's most influential inventions.
★ Freedom, individualism, equality, and growth define the values of Americans. Describe how these core values explain the rise of the market entrepreneurs. Which of these values also lies behind the populist characterization of the men as robber barons?

II. Political Reform and Reaction

The rapid and far-reaching changes of the last quarter of the nineteenth century did not occur in a vacuum. They touched the lives of all Americans, from rich industrialists to ragged immigrants. The changes that produced prosperity also caused problems and spawned reform movements in a number of areas.

Four issues dominated American politics from the mid-1870s to the end of the century: government corruption, civil service reform, tariff revision, and regulation of the trusts. Debate over these issues was intensified by some of the most evenly matched party politics in American history.

The "Spoiled" System

During the early part of Rutherford Hayes's administration, reform of the spoils system (see Chapter 10) was the pressing issue. Grant's name especially had become a synonym for government corruption, and the spoils system was associated with corruption and incompetence. Changes were needed to remove the corrupting influence of politics and ensure competent, efficient government workers.

Hayes had been nominated largely because he was a reformer. He courageously attacked political "machines," groups that sought to control voters, although his action cost him political support. He particularly attacked a notorious New York Republican political machine—similar to the Democrats' Tammany Hall—controlled by Senator **Roscoe Conkling**. This machine controlled New York's

The assassination of James Garfield brought Chester Arthur into the presidency.

tariff-collecting agency, the Customs House, where New York politicians manipulated records and siphoned off money belonging to the federal government. Hayes, hoping to check the corrupt practices, removed the Collector of the Port, future president Chester Arthur. The removal angered Conkling and other influential Republicans.

Stalwarts versus Half-breeds

The clash between Hayes and Conkling reflected a growing division within the Republican Party. On one side was Conkling's faction, the **"Stalwarts,"** who favored high tariffs, hard money, and the spoils system. Opposing them were moderate Republicans, called **"Half-breeds,"** who had earlier been dissatisfied with Grant, the Radical Republicans, and Reconstruction and who tended to favor reform. The struggle between Stalwarts and Half-breeds intensified over the Republican presidential nomination in 1880. When the convention deadlocked, the Republican factions eventually compromised by nominating Ohio's **James A. Garfield**, a Half-breed, for president and New York's **Chester A. Arthur**, a Stalwart, for vice president.

In the general election, Garfield faced Democratic nominee Winfield S. Hancock, who had gained fame as a Union general at Gettysburg. Garfield won the electoral vote easily, but the popular vote was extremely close; the Republican candidate won by fewer than ten thousand votes out of nine million cast.

James A. Garfield was a Christian of ability and character, but his efforts at reform were short-lived. On July 2, 1881, just a few months after the inauguration, a distraught office-seeker, Charles J. Guiteau (gih TOH), shot Garfield at a railway station in Washington, D.C., shouting, "I am a Stalwart, and Arthur is now president." After enduring eleven weeks of pain and crude medical care, Garfield died on September 19, and Vice President Arthur became president.

Arthur's past attachment to New York's political machines led Conkling's supporters to rejoice and caused others to feel uneasy. But Arthur, called "the gentleman president," turned out to be a pleasant surprise. He conscientiously assumed his responsibilities as president and refused to use his high office to provide special favors for Conkling's Stalwarts. Arthur also backed civil service reform and favored lowering the tariff.

The Mongrel Tariff

Arthur also tried to revise the tariff. Because general prosperity had led to government surpluses, a commission appointed by Arthur recommended a general tariff reduction of 20 to 25 percent. Congressmen who wanted to protect the trade interests of their constituents, however, added many amendments to the proposed tariff. As a result, when the tariff passed in 1883, it was a mixture of inharmonious policies. Critics soon dubbed it the "Mongrel Tariff." This legislation completely failed to reform the tariff as had been intended. All it did was to clarify party positions on the tariff issue. The Republicans, coming mainly from industrial areas, more com-

Civil Service Reform

Arthur is best known for reforming the civil service (government employee) system. George H. Pendleton, a Democrat from Ohio, introduced what became the **Pendleton Act**, which established an independent **Civil Service Commission** and eliminated much of the spoils system. Garfield's death at the hands of a disappointed office-seeker had spurred interest in such an act, and Pendleton's proposal was enacted in January 1883.

The Pendleton Act authorized the president to appoint three civil service commissioners, who were to be responsible for seeing that only men who scored well on examinations held offices. The intent of the act was to prevent the awarding of political offices for no other reason than party loyalty. To some extent, it succeeded. Although only about 12 percent of the federal offices were filled by the commission during Arthur's term, about 90 percent eventually would be.

monly favored protective tariffs; the Democrats, representing the South and the West, favored low tariffs.

The Election of 1884

In 1884, the Republicans bypassed Arthur, who had offended some Republicans by refusing to grant party members special favors, and chose instead Maine's James G. Blaine, a long-time Republican leader tainted by an earlier railroad corruption scandal. The Democrats nominated New York's former governor **Grover Cleveland**, a courageous opponent of Tammany Hall noted for his honesty. Even many disgusted Republicans supported Cleveland. Stalwarts sneeringly called these party deserters "Mugwumps" (an Indian word meaning "big chief") because the straddling Republicans had their "mugs" on one side of the fence and their "wumps" on the other. The Mugwumps, however, took the name as a badge of honor for their stand for reform.

The 1884 election was a spirited, hard-fought affair better remembered for its mudslinging than for any issues that were debated. Cleveland won a narrow victory. Had Blaine won the extremely close race in New York—he lost there by only 1,149 votes of more than a million cast—he would have won the election. Cleveland's election was the first Democratic victory in twenty-eight years.

Challenging the Trusts

During Cleveland's first term, Congress passed the first comprehensive act to provide for federal regulation of commerce. Some railroad trusts had been engaged in shady activities, such as rate-fixing schemes and discriminatory rates. The railroads were unwilling to police themselves, however, and state railroad commissions had no authority to regulate activities outside the borders of their own states. Nearly all Americans favored federal regulation of the railroads under the interstate commerce clause of the Constitution.

In February 1887, Cleveland signed the **Interstate Commerce Act**, which (1) directed that railroad rates must be "reasonable and just," (2) required that railroad companies publish all rates and make financial reports, and (3) provided for the creation of the Interstate Commerce Commission (ICC), an independent regulatory agency, to investigate and stop alleged abuses.

The Election of 1888

The Democrats renominated the popular Cleveland in 1888. The Republicans, however, abandoned Blaine and nominated Indiana's **Benjamin Harrison**, who, though somewhat colorless, was a capable, honest man. He was also the grandson of ex-president William Henry Harrison, a fact the Republicans loudly proclaimed. Some of Cleveland's aides feared that the president's insistence on lowering the tariffs might cost him the election. Cleveland retorted, "What is the use of being elected unless you stand for something?" Cleveland won more popular votes, but Harrison won more electoral votes and hence the election.

Although personally honest, Harrison was a disappointingly weak president. He appointed Blaine as secretary of state, and Blaine, in turn, dominated both the administration and the Republican Party. The Republicans sought to win favor with the voters and maintain control of the government through liberal spending. The Fifty-first Congress (1889–1891) became known as "the Billion-

Grover Cleveland was a strict constructionist who vetoed over 400 bills, more than twice the number vetoed by all previous presidents.

1884 Election "Mud"

The 1884 campaign produced such memorable political poetry as the Democratic cry "Blaine, Blaine, James G. Blaine, the continental liar from the state of Maine." The Republicans responded with a ditty of their own, alleging that the bachelor Cleveland had fathered an illegitimate child: "Ma, Ma, where's my pa?" they would wail. "Gone to the White House, ha, ha, ha."

Cleveland's Character

Cleveland biographer Henry Graff noted, "He had no 'program' except a commitment to honesty and efficiency and an intention to staff his administration with worthy people. . . . He believed that Divine Providence had made him president, and that fact laid upon him a determination to conduct himself with a devotion to duty that brooked no favors to anyone."

Dollar Congress" because, for the first time in history, the annual budget exceeded a billion dollars. Weak leadership in the White House and Congress combined with free-spending policies only squandered the Treasury surplus that Cleveland had left, without improving Republican popularity.

The Sherman Antitrust Act

One law during the Harrison years, however, was extremely influential. Congress greatly expanded its power to regulate business with the passage of the **Sherman Antitrust Act** in 1890. The public had become increasingly wary of the tendency of big businesses to form monopolies, or "trusts." Companies such as Rockefeller's Standard Oil, after driving all competition out of business or forcing a merger, allegedly took advantage of their monopoly by raising prices to an exorbitant level. If the consumer needed the product and could get it nowhere else, he simply had to pay.

The Sherman Antitrust Act made such monopolizing illegal. It declared, "Every contract, combination in the form of trust or otherwise, or conspiracy, in restraint of trade or commerce . . . is hereby declared to be illegal." The act was difficult to enforce, however, because it offered no specific definitions of *contract*, *combination*, or *restraint of trade*. Therefore, the act was relatively ineffective until the passage of tougher federal regulations in the twentieth century.

Raising the Tariff

A major goal of the Republicans in the Fifty-first Congress was to raise the tariff again. The Republican majority in both houses of Congress was slim but was bolstered by the admission of six new predominantly Republican states: North Dakota, South Dakota, Montana, and Washington in November 1889 and Idaho and Wyoming in July 1890. The addition of Republican representatives and senators from those states enabled the party to pass the **McKinley Tariff** in 1890.

Named for Ohio representative William McKinley, who introduced the bill, the tariff imposed higher duties on manufactured and agricultural imports than had any previous tariff in history, thereby protecting American inefficiency. The high tariff also lowered revenue by radically decreasing trade. This decrease in the government's income, combined with lavish congressional spending, reduced the treasury's reserves alarmingly. The voters demonstrated their anger at the tariff in the congressional election of 1890, reducing the Republican majority in the Senate and giving the Democrats an overwhelming 235–88 advantage in the House. Even Representative McKinley was turned out of office.

The 1890 congressional elections were only a prelude to the 1892 presidential rematch between Benjamin Harrison and Grover Cleveland. Ex-president Cleveland made an ex-president of Harrison by recapturing the White House with a clear victory. Democrats regained control of both the House and the Senate. Unfortunately for the Democrats, a financial collapse called the **Panic of '93** occurred shortly after Cleveland's inauguration, plunging the nation into four years of the worst economic depression it had yet seen. The Democrats watched helplessly as banks and businesses failed and unemployment mounted to a record 20 percent.

Another Viewpoint

During the history of Standard Oil, the tendency was for prices to *fall*, not rise. In spite of the expenditures incurred in improving the quality and availability of kerosene products (the major source of fuel for light and heating at the time), Rockefeller still managed to *reduce* their cost to the public by *nearly 80 percent* over the life of the company. When Rockefeller began in oil in the mid-1860s, the price of a gallon of kerosene was about 60 cents. By 1900, Rockefeller had reduced waste and improved his production techniques so much that the price of kerosene had dropped to less than 6 cents per gallon. This contradicts the idea that Rockefeller was squeezing the consumer or charging exorbitant rates. At the same time, he was creating jobs for hard-working people and enabling them to live a higher quality of life by having access to cheap fuel.

Section Quiz

1. What four issues dominated American politics from the mid-1870s to the end of the nineteenth century?

2. How did Republicans and Democrats differ concerning the tariff in the late nineteenth century?

3. Why was the Fifty-first Congress called "the Billion-Dollar Congress"?

★ Does the civil service system really remove the corrupting influence of politics and ensure better government employees? Defend your answer.

III. Labor, Rural, and Economic Issues

Along with the industrial growth of the Gilded Age came labor problems. The rural areas continued to demand solutions to their unique farm-related problems. And the economy faced unprecedented challenges and unusual suggestions for solving them.

Labor

The demands of industrialization and the flood of immigration swelled the ranks of America's labor force. The rising standard of living that industrialization brought in its wake touched all Americans. Even unskilled immigrants living in difficult circumstances in most cases had better prospects for themselves and their children than they had in the "old country" with its war and poverty.

Yet industrialization had a human cost. Although workers had been accustomed to working long hours on farms, they found that six twelve-hour days or more could be trying when combined with other factors such as unsafe factories and wage cuts. Hard times also brought war widows and children into the factories to make ends meet, further burdening the labor system. Many people opposed child labor, not only because they considered the work inhumane for children but also because it left children no time for formal education.

Child Labor

According to the 1900 census, more than 1,750,000 children ages ten to sixteen worked for wages in the United States, about 20 percent of the children in that age group. An additional 250,000 workers were less than ten years old. Immigrant families who assembled clothing, toys, or other items in their homes used children as young as five years old. Some boys worked on the streets as peddlers, shoeshine boys, and newspaper boys. Children as young as five worked as "breaker boys" in coal mines, picking debris, stones, and sulfur from the coal as it flowed through chutes beneath their feet. At twelve, they went down into the mines. In the seafood industry, children began working at about eight years of age. Even more children worked on their family farms, picking fruit, plowing, weeding, cultivating, caring for animals, and so forth.

During this period, some considered child labor to be acceptable or even necessary for several reasons. One was the extensive loss of male workers in the War Between the States. Another was that children were faster and more agile than adults in doing some tasks. They were also cheaper to hire. For many families, especially newly arrived immigrants, it was an economic necessity for family survival.

Dangers to Child Laborers

Dangers were a constant reality for child workers. Breaker boys could fall into the coal chutes and be crushed by the coal or choked by the dust. They always had a persistent cough from breathing the coal dust. Those who entered the mines faced death or injury from cave-ins, explosions, or asphyxiation from poisonous gases or lack of oxygen. Child workers in canneries, where they shucked oysters or peeled or sliced fruits and vegetables, risked slicing—or even cutting off—fingers or hands.

However, as reformers drew attention to the plight of child workers, state governments began to enact legislation limiting child labor. In 1879, only seven states had laws limiting the age of workers in manufacturing, with the average age being eleven. But by 1909 forty-three of the forty-six states had such laws, with an average age of fourteen. These laws typically limited the age of the child who could work, the number of hours a day, and the number of hours a week. The passage of compulsory school attendance laws also restricted child labor. Overall, as industrialization raised the general standard of living, child labor was becoming less necessary economically.

Labor Unions

After the war, workers occasionally held unorganized strikes in response to wage cuts, and the effectiveness and potential of labor organizations soon became apparent. Responding to the challenge and human cost of industrialization, organized labor became a powerful political and social force during the period.

The earliest significant labor union was the **Knights of Labor**, formed in 1869 as a secret society of skilled and unskilled workers from various occupations. Although weakened by the Panic of 1873, the union emerged as an effective force under the leadership of Terrence V. Powderly, former mayor of Scranton, Pennsylvania.

The Knights advocated an eight-hour workday, laws prohibiting child labor, and equal pay for men and women. However, the Knights, like most early American labor unions, tended to be much more conservative than the radical and even violent unions of Europe. In fact, Powderly favored boycotts and arbitration over strikes to settle wage disputes because strikes often resulted in violence. A number of successful strikes, however, gained the Knights new clout and new members, and the group reached a peak of 700,000 members in 1886.

A more influential labor organization was formed in 1881. The **American Federation of Labor** (AFL), a splinter group from the Knights of Labor, formed craft unions for skilled laborers. Grouping skilled workers together by profession gave union members greater bargaining power with management. Under the leadership of **Samuel Gompers**, the AFL supported higher wages, shorter working hours, safer and cleaner working conditions, and elimination of child labor. The AFL's goals, however, were not entirely humanitarian. Unions in the AFL did not oppose child labor primarily out of sympathy for children but because child labor contributed to low wage rates and made jobs for adults more scarce.

Labor Unrest

During the late 1860s and the 1870s, only scattered, poorly managed strikes occurred over labor grievances. As unions grew, however, strikes—and violence—became more common. Probably the most famous example of labor violence was the **Haymarket Riot** of 1886. Factory workers in Chicago, agitated by anarchists, went on strike, demanding an eight-hour workday. On May 4, 1886, police attempted to disperse a crowd of strikers listening to an anarchist speaker at Haymarket Square in Chicago. (An anarchist is one who stirs up political disorder and confusion but does not offer principles of constructive improvement.) Someone threw a bomb into a group of policemen, touching off a riot. When the unrest ended, seven policemen and four civilians had been killed and many others seriously wounded. The Haymarket Square episode discredited the Knights of Labor and ended the "eight-hour" movement for the time being.

AFL's Most Enduring Achievement

The most enduring achievement of the AFL was the acceptance of the eight-hour workday as a standard. Despite such accomplishments and the rapid growth of its membership, the image of the AFL and other unions was marred by the violence of strikes and infiltration by radical elements.

In 1892, violence erupted during a strike at the Carnegie Steel Company in Homestead, Pennsylvania, a suburb of Pittsburgh. Carnegie's assistant at the company, Henry C. Frick, proposed lowering the workers' wages because of the use of new labor-saving machinery. When the workers threatened to strike, Frick closed the plant, an action that became known as a "lockout." Frick then hired three hundred guards to subdue picketers. The fighting that broke out on July 6, 1892, left nine people dead. The hired guards were beaten back. Despite the temporary victory for the workers, the **Homestead Strike** gained nothing. After five months of striking, the workers agreed to Frick's proposal. The union was broken.

Another violent strike occurred at the Pullman Palace Car Company in Chicago. Although the name *Pullman* is most commonly associated with railroad sleeping cars, the company contracted to carry not only passengers but also the U.S. mail. Therefore, any labor union activity was potentially dangerous and disruptive for both business owners and taxpayers.

The leader of the strike was **Eugene V. Debs**, founder of the American Railway Union and later a presidential candidate on the Socialist ticket. The **Pullman Strike** was precipitated by five successive wage reductions, totaling twenty-five percent, in the spring of 1894. Although these reductions were necessitated by the depression at the time, the company did not simultaneously reduce the rent on the houses it provided its employees or the cost of goods in the company stores. When the workers retaliated by striking, the Pullman Company withdrew the strikers' credit from the company stores. Facing starvation, the Pullman workers appealed to Debs's American Railway Union.

On June 26, Debs ordered union members to cut all Pullman passenger cars out of trains and leave them standing on the sidetracks. The boycott of Pullman cars affected all western railroads. When boycotters were fired, the strike became general, and traffic, including the mail between the West and Chicago, came to a virtual standstill. Strikers and unemployed ruffians destroyed engines, cars, and equipment, causing owners to demand that federal troops be sent to break the strike. They wanted the government to protect their property. President Cleveland complied to keep the U.S. mail moving. He declared, "If it takes every dollar in the Treasury and every soldier in the United States to deliver a postal card in Chicago—that postal card should be delivered."

In addition, the federal courts issued an **injunction**, or court order, forbidding Debs and other strike leaders to further encourage the strike. Debs ignored the order and promoted the general strike; consequently, he spent six months in jail. He claimed that it was while in jail that he became an avowed socialist, but his views actually had been socialistic for all of his adult life. (**Socialism** advocates government regulation or ownership of the means of production.) After Debs's release, he became the leader of the Social Democratic Party of America (later called simply the Socialist Party), a position he was to hold until the 1920s.

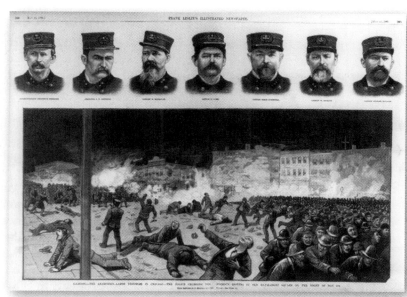

Anarchists helped foment the deadly Haymarket Riot in Chicago.

Jailbird for President!

Eugene V. Debs was a five-time candidate for president on the Socialist Party ticket. He ran in 1900, 1904, 1908, 1912, and 1920. In 1920, he became the first—and to date the only—candidate to campaign from a jail cell.

Legacy of the Unions

The violence and radicalism of the movement discredited unions for nearly half a century. Perhaps in part because of this radicalism, the government tended to side with management by providing court orders to end strikes and even troops to quell violence. Although organized labor made some gains for some workers, most union goals remained unrealized until the twentieth century.

Rural Revolt

Industrialism and innovation caused important changes in American agriculture. Improved farm machinery and methods increased production and made agricultural commodities an important export. Yet, such innovations also created problems for farmers. They could not adjust quickly to supply and demand because of the seasonal nature of farming. They could not know for sure how much of a crop they would have at harvest because of changes in weather. Drought, too much rain, or the right amount of water with a sudden influx of insects or disease could affect output dramatically.

Railroads were the essential link between the farm and the market. High shipping costs siphoned off farm profits into the pockets of railroad owners and left farmers outraged. Abundant production itself became a problem because high yields kept prices low.

High tariffs also affected farmers. Whenever the United States placed a tariff on certain imports, the countries trying to sell those products to U.S. consumers usually retaliated by raising their own tariffs on American exports, often farm products. The American farmers then had a hard time finding buyers. Combining high tariffs with overproduction further complicated the farmers' plight.

The Grange

During the 1870s, protesting farmers organized under the leadership of the Patrons of Husbandry, more commonly called the **Grange**. Oliver H. Kelly founded the organization in 1867 to encourage social contacts and scientific methods of farming. Its growth and influence were negligible until farmers began to use it as a means of confronting railroads. The Granger movement made state regulation of railroads its chief goal, and it gained increasing support during the 1870s.

As a result of Grange influence, several midwestern states passed Granger Laws, legislation regulating railroads. In response, the railroads went to the Supreme Court in the case of *Munn v. Illinois* in 1877. The Court ruled against the railroads, deciding that a state through its "police powers" had the right to regulate a business that was public in nature though privately owned.

Lacking organizational strength, the Grange eventually disappeared but re-emerged in the 1880s as the **Farmers' Alliance**. Taking a lesson from industrial labor, the Farmers' Alliance united farm cooperatives across the country and looked to politics to meet agrarian demands such as railroad regulation, favorable currency policies, and antitrust laws.

Populism

Independent grassroots organizations sprang up throughout the Midwest and eventually merged through the politics of discontent to form the People's or **Populist Party**. The Populist Party seemed to prove the truth of the adage that "misery loves company." The hard times in Middle America between the Great Blizzards of 1886–1887 and the Panic of '93 attracted thousands of farmers and reformers to the party's banner. Although the party officially formed only in 1891, the Populists polled more than a million votes with their presidential candidate, James B. Weaver, in 1892. In fact, the new third party carried four western states and showed remarkable strength in the otherwise solidly Democratic South.

The issue that dominated the Populist movement during the mid-nineties was currency policy. After the failure of the greenback efforts under Grant, easy-money advocates began to view coinage of silver as the answer to their problems. The Populists wanted to make both silver and gold the dual standard for American currency. Money was scarce during the depression of the 1890s, and, for a growing number of Americans who were feeling the squeeze, the solution was the unlimited coinage of silver. Such purposeful inflation would make more money available to the hard-pressed workingman. In the words of the 1894 bestseller *Coin's Financial School*, **free silver** would "make it possible for the debtor to pay his debts; business to start anew, and revivify all the industries of the country, which must remain paralyzed so long as silver as well as all other property is measured by a gold standard." For the farmers, more money in circulation would mean higher prices for crops. What farmers did not consider, however, was that having more money in circulation would also mean that prices for *all* products, including those that farmers had to buy, would go up. In the long run, they would be no better off than before.

> ### Populism and Free Silver
>
> Amid the hard times and the economic complexities of industrialism, silver became a seemingly simple solution for the down-and-out, a kind of patent medicine for all economic ills. In the Midwest, free silver became the battle cry for the Populist legions. Not even the major parties were immune from the growing Populist force. Lacking, however, the organizational, financial, and numerical strength of the major parties, the Populists decided to cast their lot with the more sympathetic Democratic Party in the 1896 presidential election. The result was a colorful, crucial contest—part campaign, part crusade.

Goldbugs versus Silverbugs

The Panic of '93 and the ensuing depression hounded Grover Cleveland throughout his second term and left the Democratic nomination in doubt in 1896. Republicans, however, had a candidate on the first ballot, Ohio's **William McKinley**. A likable though somber figure, McKinley was the friend of industrialists, a fitting candidate for the gold-standard, pro-tariff (having sponsored the highest tariff to that date, the McKinley tariff), big-business platform of the Republicans.

When the Democrats arrived in Chicago for their convention, the place was abuzz with talk of silver and the inevitable question of who would get the nomination and stamp out the "goldbugs." The answer was a thirty-six-year-old Nebraskan named **William Jennings Bryan**.

Bryan, called "the Great Commoner" because of his genuine sympathy for the common man, was both a remarkable political figure and a fervent Christian. His oratory sprang from roots deep in America's heartland. In Chicago, his eloquent appeals for economic deliverance through silver sealed his nomination. Bryan stood before the convention and declared to a sea of rapt faces, "I come to speak to you in defense of a cause as holy as the cause of liberty—the cause of humanity." The government must have a social conscience, he cried. Its voice must be the people's voice, and the people would be heard. He concluded,

> Having behind us the producing masses of this nation and the world, supported by the commercial interests, the laboring interests, and the toilers everywhere, we will answer their [the business interests'] demand for a gold standard by saying to them: You shall not press down upon the brow of labor this crown of thorns, you shall not crucify mankind upon a cross of gold.

William Jennings Bryan electrified free-silver advocates with his "Cross of Gold" speech.

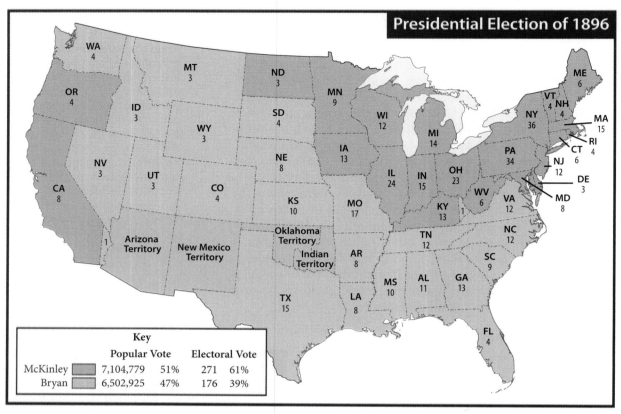

Presidential Election of 1896

	Key			
	Popular Vote		**Electoral Vote**	
McKinley	7,104,779	51%	271	61%
Bryan	6,502,925	47%	176	39%

Bryan's words swept the convention like a prairie fire. The campaign that followed was the first modern campaign and a study in contrasts. Leading a cash-poor campaign (Republicans outspent Democrats as much as twenty to one), Bryan went on a whirlwind tour of the country. He made hundreds of whistle-stops during an 18,000-mile trek and was seen and heard by audiences totaling five million. McKinley, however, stayed home. In a carefully orchestrated effort, McKinley ran a "front porch campaign" from his home in Canton, Ohio. Trainloads of select audiences were given all-expense-paid trips to Canton to hear McKinley read a prepared script, while hundreds of speakers fanned out across the country to promote him.

On election day, Bryan polled six and a half million votes, but McKinley got more than seven million. The Great Commoner, however, was not the only casualty on election day. The Populist Party, in giving up its reform efforts for a single issue and in losing its identity by casting its lot with the Democrats, had betrayed its cause for a few pieces of silver. Other groups would take up many of its reforms, but they would be won under different labels and circumstances in later years.

Importance of the 1896 Election

The 1896 election was a turning point in American political history, the culmination of the struggle between the past and the future, between the farm and the factory—and the factory won. The rural leadership that Populism represented was growing old with the century. For good or bad, America's future lay amid her crowded city streets.

Section Quiz

1. What was the most enduring achievement of the American Federation of Labor?

2. Name the two major labor strikes of the late 1800s.

3. What industry did most farmers blame for their low profits?

4. Describe the difference between the campaigns of the two candidates in the 1896 presidential election, William McKinley and William Jennings Bryan.

IV. Change and Challenge

Growth of Cities

One reason the Populism revolt came up short was that many farmers had moved to the city. The 1890 census revealed that for the first time, the majority of Americans were in nonagricultural occupations. The concentrations of industry with the resulting concentrations of labor made urbanization (movement of population to the cities) the most significant social movement of the period.

Between 1860 and 1910, increases in the urban population were nearly twice the increases in the rural population. The dramatic shift was reflected in the size and number of cities. In 1860, only New York and Philadelphia had populations greater than 500,000. By 1910, Chicago, St. Louis, Boston, Cleveland, Baltimore, and Pittsburgh had joined the ranks of the big cities, with New York City approaching a population of nearly five million. The most phenomenal urban growth, however, was in the small cities with populations of 2,500 or more. There were 400 such cities at the beginning of the Civil War; that number jumped to 2,200 cities in the next fifty years.

What was the attraction of city dwelling? The boom in manufacturing and service industries provided jobs for both the influx of immigrants and down-and-out farm laborers who had been squeezed off the land by hard times or labor-saving machinery. And people found the services and attractions of city living alluring.

To those who lived there, however, the "gilded metropolis" (as one wide-eyed farm boy described Kansas City) became a tinsel town. Urbanization also had an ugly side: slum squalor, high crime, and dangerous diseases. In fact, the infant mortality rate in cities was double that in rural areas. In Chicago in the 1880s, for example, only half the children born lived past their fifth birthday. People also lost their privacy, living in "dumbbell apartments" or, worse yet, living with several people in squalid, one-room apartments.

Industrialization gradually created a substantial, growing middle class. But the path to prosperity was choked with moral and industrial pollutants, and the promises offered by smoke-stacked cities often proved empty.

Immigration

Aggravating the problems of the cities was another wave of immigration. The American continent had been receiving immigrants, of course, since the English settled at Jamestown and Plymouth. After 1865, however, came a wave of immigrants so different from those in the past that it was called the **New Immigration**. As the turn of the twentieth century neared, the percentage of British and German immigrants (who had made up most earlier immigration) shrank in contrast to new immigrants from Southern and Eastern European countries, such as Italy, Greece, and Russia. By 1900, for the first time in American history, immigrants from Southern and Eastern Europe outnumbered those from Northern and Western Europe. Another new element in immigration was the large number of Chinese who began to settle on the West Coast, where they provided labor for the railroads.

> ### Greeley on Urbanization
> Horace Greeley observed, "We cannot all live in cities, yet nearly all seem determined to do so. Hot and cold water, baker's bread, gas, the theatre and the streetcars . . . indicate the tendency of modern taste."

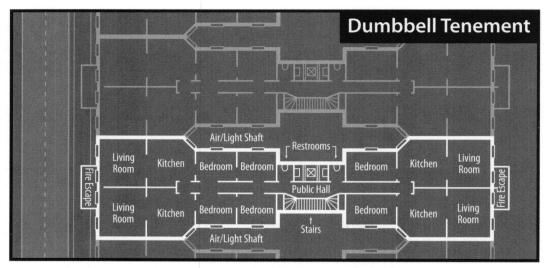

Dumbbell Tenement

For many European immigrants, America provided new hope and opportunity.

Some of the more fortunate immigrants, particularly those from Scandinavia and Germany, were able to move directly to the Midwest and immediately find work in farming or logging. Most of the immigrants, however, had no money or job skills to enable them to move from the cities to which they first came. New York, Chicago, Philadelphia, and other large cities swelled in population. Immigrants tended to band together in the cities so that different neighborhoods often had their own distinct ethnic character—Polish, Italian, Greek, or any one of a number of others. Often illiterate and knowing little English, many of the immigrants had to take low-paying jobs in "sweat shop" factories and live in squalid tenements. American businesses actively recruited immigrant laborers in Europe and even helped them secure passage to the United States. They were willing to work at low-paying jobs to gain the freedom of opportunity that America offered, and they hoped to work their way up financially and socially. Many of them did just that, achieving for themselves and their children the "American dream."

As the New Immigration grew in proportion to the old, so did opposition to immigration. American labor leaders feared—rightly in some cases—that immigrant workers would take jobs from other Americans by agreeing to work longer hours for less pay. The poverty of ethnic slums created fears that immigrants would lower the nation's standard of living and breed crime and disease—although obviously no immigrant wanted to live under such conditions. The large number of Catholic, Jewish, and Eastern Orthodox immigrants raised religious fears among America's predominantly Protestant population. A tiny minority of radicals and revolutionaries among the immigrants caused many of them to be branded as potential enemies of American freedoms and institutions. Racial prejudice, especially in California against the Chinese, also motivated calls for limits to immigration. The simple fact that immigrants tended to form churches and sometimes schools where only their native language was spoken led many Americans to fear that the cultural unity of the nation was being undermined. As a result of these fears, Congress placed an increasing number of quotas and restrictions on immigration. By 1930, such restrictions had reduced immigration from Southern and Eastern Europe to less than a fifth of what it had been in 1910.

Despite the many cultural obstacles, the immigrants continued to come, and many of them prospered. The children of the immigrants, able to learn the language and American customs more easily than their parents, often rose higher economically than their elders. Immigrants provided labor for construction projects and for factories; they built rich and fertile farms in the Midwest; some became prosperous shopkeepers and small businessmen. Immigrants, in short, provided much of the backbone and muscle needed to transform the United States into an industrial giant. Assimilation into the broader American culture was not easy. The immigrants could not transform overnight. But they tried, and eventually they became fully Americanized. As they began to adopt American culture, fears of an ethnically fragmented society began to subside. The aspects of their cultures that the immigrants retained contributed to the growing diversity (especially religious diversity) of the nation. In fact, some people began to speak of the United States as a melting pot in which diverse racial and ethnic cultures would blend to form a new and unified nation.

New Forces

Machines alone were not changing America; new ideas, philosophies, and attitudes were also challenging old systems. Whether these new philosophies were accepted or rejected, they had—and continue to have—a wide influence throughout society.

Darwinism

The book *The Origin of Species* (1859) by **Charles Darwin** found a receptive audience in burgeoning industrial America. Darwin's basic theory involved "natural selection," a process through which all current species, including man, have supposedly struggled and evolved. The survival, development, and improvement of species depend upon their ability to adapt to the changes of a sometimes cruel world. Despite the faulty scientific reasoning and the clear contradiction of the biblical record, a number of Darwin's disciples came to apply his ideas to every area of a rapidly changing society. To them, **Darwinism** was the key to the riddle of life.

The chief proponent of Social Darwinism (the application of the evolutionary theory to social institutions) was Englishman Herbert Spencer, whose only memorable contribution out of eight dense volumes on the new philosophy was the phrase "survival of the fittest." In America, Spencer's Social Darwinism fit well into the progressive and reform movements. Social Darwinism also went hand-in-hand with racism. White supremacy thrived on the concept of racial inferiority of all races other than white.

But not all Darwinists were satisfied with Spencer's conclusions. In the late nineteenth century, a movement known as Reform Darwinism emerged as a result of the work of a Washington bureaucrat named Lester Frank Ward. Ward could view the evolutionary process only from the bottom up. From that perspective, he determined that human progress was best achieved not through competition but through cooperation. Not surprisingly, Ward believed that government was best equipped to promote human progress through cooperation. As a result, government—as an active agent for social change—could remove the two great barriers to a better world: poverty and ignorance. Ward's ideas would have a tremendous impact on social thinking and public policy in the twentieth century.

Liberal theologians and pulpiteers accommodated and incorporated the new philosophy. They used evolution to explain the origin of not only the earth but also the Scriptures. According to these

---

Lady Liberty's Light

As immigrants streamed into the United States, more than a million a year passed through the immigrant reception center on Ellis Island in New York Harbor alone. There in the harbor they saw a gleaming torch-bearer, a bronze lady—the Statue of Liberty. Inscribed in the statue's pedestal were the following words of welcome:

Give me your tired, your poor,

Your huddled masses yearning to breathe free,

The wretched refuse of your teeming shore.

Send these, the homeless, tempest-tossed, to me,

I lift my lamp beside the golden door!

Disappointment for Darwinism

The marvels of the machine age and the miracles of science and invention seemed to offer irrefutable proof of the Darwinist view of human progress. Such millennial optimism, however, would eventually sink in the mud and blood of 1914, as global war brought man's triumphant march to a grinding halt.

Booker T. Washington (above) and W.E.B. Du Bois (below) represented two different views of how blacks could improve their lot in Gilded Age America.

new thinkers, the Bible was not God-inspired (2 Tim. 3:16) but was the result of a process of human aspirations.

In addition, building on a liberal tradition, the Reform Darwinists among the evolutionists believed that man was not, as the Scriptures taught, sinful; rather, man was inherently good. Man could cure the ailments of society by improving the human condition. The social gospel often grew out of a genuine concern to relieve the misery of the slums and was based on the belief that the essence of Christianity was the command "Thou shalt love thy neighbor as thyself." This love, however, was misdirected and inadequate because it embraced only the present life and not the life to come. Love for our neighbor is hardly complete if it gives him food and shelter but leaves his soul in darkness.

Race Relations

Until the 1890s, some hope for improvement in racial relations in the South existed. The Redeemer governments that ruled the South after Reconstruction (see Chapter 15) generally tried to keep their promises to protect black civil rights. Blacks even held elective or appointive office under the Redeemer governments. And in all but one session of Congress from 1869 to 1901, at least one black member served in the House of Representatives.

The situation began to change in the 1890s as southern states began passing **Jim Crow laws**, legislation that required the forced **segregation**, or separation, of the races in trains, restaurants, hotels, schools, and other social settings. (Jim Crow was a black character in a nineteenth-century minstrel song.) In fact, segregation was so extensive that whites and blacks even had separate restrooms and drinking fountains. In addition, southern governments began to deprive blacks of their right to vote by setting up literacy tests for voting (to which whites were often exempt) or requiring special poll taxes that one had to pay before voting. The number of registered black voters in Louisiana, for example, plummeted from more than 130,000 in 1896 to slightly more than 1,300 in 1904.

This change occurred for several reasons. First, the Redeemer politicians were gradually losing ground to overtly racist politicians who played on the fears and prejudices of white voters to rally support to their cause. Second, the alliance of blacks with some reform groups such as the Populists caused many conservative Democrats to disfranchise blacks to dilute Populist political power. Third, the national government and the northern public in general lost interest in the cause of civil rights for blacks. Segregation in the South would not have been possible had not the Supreme Court issued a series of decisions that gutted the enforcement of the Reconstruction civil rights legislation. Perhaps the most infamous of these cases was ***Plessy v. Ferguson***, a ruling that decreed that "separate but equal" facilities for blacks and whites (in that particular case, on trains) were constitutional. Such decisions gave state legislatures the legal justification they needed to pass Jim Crow law codes.

Blacks reacted to the increase in discrimination in differing ways. One approach was represented by **Booker T. Washington**. As described in his famous autobiography *Up from Slavery*, Washington had risen from slavery to the presidency of Tuskegee Institute in Alabama, the nation's leading black industrial school. Washington was basically conservative; in his famous speech in Atlanta in 1895, he urged blacks not to risk strife by agitating politically for their rights. Instead, they should concentrate on bettering themselves economically through vocational education and the establishment of black businesses and trades. In this way, they would make themselves indispensable to the economy. As they became more powerful economically, Washington argued, whites would have to accept them and grant them political equality.

Opposing Washington was another group of blacks led by **W.E.B. Du Bois**. They argued that blacks could not truly improve themselves economically until they enjoyed equal participation in the political process as American citizens. They opposed Washington's exclusive stress on technical and industrial education over liberal arts, fearing that it would force all blacks into an economically inferior laboring class and discourage higher education among blacks. Whereas Washington sought an economic solution to the problem, Du Bois pursued a political solution.

Literature

A number of literary styles emerged during the late nineteenth century, reflecting the changes in society and capturing the spirit of the times. Perhaps the most popular writer of the day was Samuel Langhorne Clemens, who wrote under the pen name **Mark Twain** (*The Adventures of Huckleberry Finn* and *Life on the Mississippi*). Twain's work reflected the literary school of **realism**. In contrast to the emotional, exotic character of romanticism (see Chapter 11), Twain drew a picture of simple, ordinary life colored with his captivating humor. Similarly, realist painters such as Winslow Homer and Thomas Eakins portrayed daily life from the common man's perspective, revealing both its strength and its mundaneness.

By the 1890s, a new literary approach known as **naturalism** developed. In some ways an extreme form of realism that was shaped by Darwinism, naturalism emphasized man's helplessness and struggle with the world. **Stephen Crane** used that style in *Maggie: A Girl of the Streets* (1893) and *The Red Badge of Courage* (1895). **Jack London** (*Call of the Wild*, 1903) also wrote from the naturalist perspective, portraying the triumph of brute force over the cruel world.

Another popular literary form of the time described triumph in the tradition of Benjamin Franklin's *Poor Richard*. It was success literature that emphasized the virtues of hard work, thrift, and honesty. **Horatio Alger** was the premier writer of such rags-to-riches tales. A generation of young readers grew up reading about the heroes of *Luck and Pluck*, *Bound to Rise*, and *Tattered Tom*, who triumphed over adversity, often on the new frontier of America's urban jungle.

Materialism

Jefferson's phrase "the pursuit of happiness" took on a new meaning during the Gilded Age. Mass production and labor-saving machinery provided more people with more things and more time to enjoy them. America was increasingly becoming a consumer society in which people associated with each other based on what they owned. Brand names, advertising, and new mass marketing techniques took on greater importance in the economic choices of daily life. Unfortunately, materialism—the desire for worldly possessions and the belief that they can bring true happiness—became the philosophy of an alarming number of Americans.

Leisure

With the increase of leisure time that mechanization provided, Americans sought a number of new outlets for recreation

You NEED It!

Before industrialization, markets were local, their stock confined to the produce of the region. With the rise of national companies and the mass market, cupboards from Savannah to Seattle held many of the same labels. Nabisco, for example, underscored the national scope of their line of crackers, the Uneeda Biscuit, with this 1904 ad:

When San Francisco folks are eating Uneeda Biscuits for breakfast, New Yorkers are having them for lunch, and the people in between are just getting hungry for more. We were right when we said to the whole country, "Uneeda Biscuit."

Boston played New York in a 1904 American League game at Boston's old Huntington Avenue Park, the predecessor to Fenway Park.

P. T. Barnum advertised the skeleton of his former attraction, the bull elephant named Jumbo, in this 1885 promotional poster.

and amusement. Organized sports took on the broad appeal that other "consumables" had. Baseball became the national pastime beginning in 1869 when the Cincinnati Red Stockings, the first all-professional team, toured the country. In the decades that followed, thousands of fans flocked to city ballparks. In 1903, the first World Series was played; the Boston Pilgrims defeated the Pittsburgh Pirates to become the first "world champions."

Other sports—such as golf, tennis, and particularly croquet—enjoyed an even broader appeal because both men and women could play them. Throughout the entire period, croquet was the sport of choice for upper- and middle-class people. Some enterprising croquet clubs even organized night parties with candles attached to the wickets. The popularity of mixed sports prompted illustrator Charles Dana Gibson to produce the "Gibson girl," the quintessential American woman—athletic yet without the loss of feminine charm.

Other forms of entertainment popular during the period included vaudeville, Wild West shows, and circuses. Vaudeville was a variety stage show that might include such attractions as jugglers, song-and-dance routines, comical skits, and stand-up comics. Vaudevillians had to be able to do it all—sing, dance, speak, and perform physical feats. Several Wild West shows featured marksmen, equine trick riders, buffaloes, cowboys, and even Indians. The most popular shows included those operated by Pawnee Bill and Mexican Joe, but by far the most famous was the Wild West Show of William "Buffalo Bill" Cody. He toured not only the United States but also Europe, featuring his stars Annie Oakley, a crack sharpshooter, and Sitting Bull, the famous Sioux chief.

Traveling circuses were even more plentiful than Wild West shows. The most famous one was begun by hoaxster P. T. Barnum, who had started in the 1840s by featuring such attractions as the midget Tom Thumb, the Fiji mermaid, and Siamese twins. He later merged it with the circus of James Bailey to form the Barnum and Bailey Circus. In the early 1900s, John and Charles Ringling bought them out to form the now-famous (and still active) Ringling Brothers and Barnum and Bailey Circus.

Bicycles were immensely popular during the 1890s, with sales figures showing over a million pedal pushers by 1893. Cycle clubs were so numerous that they even became a political force, lobbying with municipal and state governments for more paved roads. Courting couples in particular found bicycling to be appealing, inspiring turn-of-the-century beaus to croon:

> It won't be a stylish marriage
>
> I can't afford a carriage
>
> But you'll look sweet
>
> Upon the seat
>
> Of a bicycle built for two.

Sadly, consumption of alcoholic beverages also became a growing pastime. Drinking had been an issue since colonial days, but it grew in direct proportion to the huge influx of immigrants. German and Irish immigrants' native cultures were especially accepting of alcohol. Saloons were plentiful. The incidence of actions associated with alcohol—drunkenness, unemployment, child and spousal abuse, and physical assaults, including murder—grew with the increased consumption and led to reform movements.

The material prosperity not only changed social conditions but also influenced spiritual conditions. For many people, financial gain became paramount. In his "Acres of Diamonds" speech, prominent lecturer Russell Conwell told an estimated thirteen million people that it was the Christian's *duty* to be prosperous. The Baptist minister exhorted, "I say, get rich, get rich." Conwell forgot Christ's message of Luke 12:15—life does not consist in the abundance of the things one possesses.

Meeting the Challenge

Christians did not let the challenges of urbanization, materialism, immigration, and class conflict go unanswered. Many Christians sought to deal with those problems scripturally. Some Christians, for example, confronted the squalor of city slums by establishing rescue missions, centers located in the middle of the slums for preaching the gospel and ministering to the physical needs of city dwellers. The most widespread method of meeting those challenges with the gospel, however, was **urban evangelism**, the conducting of large, citywide campaigns in huge auditoriums or large churches in major cities. The leader of the movement during this period was Evangelist **Dwight L. Moody**.

D. L. Moody

Dwight Lyman Moody was born in Northfield, Massachusetts, in 1837. At the age of seventeen, Moody went to seek his fortune in Boston. He worked for his uncle in a shoe store and, at his uncle's insistence, went to church regularly. There Moody sat in the class of a concerned Sunday school teacher, who eventually led the young man to Christ. Despite his salvation, Moody was in some ways still worldly minded. He desired above all to be rich, and to that end he

---

New Sports

Two new sports were introduced during this time: basketball and football. Canadian James Naismith introduced basketball as a YMCA winter sport in 1891. The Ivy League colleges began playing football—without helmets or pads.

Christmas in the Gilded Age

The transformation of the celebration of Christmas perhaps best illustrates the changes that materialism brought. In 1880, F. W. Woolworth, pinching pennies for his Five and Ten Cent Store in Lancaster, Pennsylvania, cautiously ventured to spend $25 for Christmas ornaments. Surprised when eager customers snapped up the decorations, Woolworth began to pour more and more into his Christmas stock to meet the demands of the market. By 1891, Woolworth was reminding the managers of his chain of stores that Christmas "is our harvest time, make it pay." Increasingly, for retailers and consumers alike, Christmas was "good" in proportion to its gain. Somewhere amid the growing materialism, many Americans were trading away spiritual values at bargain prices.

D. L. Moody was America's evangelist to the cities during the Gilded Age.

moved to Chicago in 1856, where he thought lay greater opportunities for wealth.

In Chicago, however, Moody was touched by the Prayer Meeting Revival (see Chapter 11). As a result, he became more involved in Christian work than in the search for wealth. In 1859, he began a Sunday school in the slums of Chicago that grew under his leadership to more than fifteen hundred students. In 1860, Moody completely abandoned his materialistic goals, quit his high-paying job with a shoe company, and devoted himself to working with his Sunday school, the YMCA, and other Christian organizations. He began a church in Chicago, although he was not an ordained minister, and became a popular speaker at conventions and churches on subjects such as Sunday school organization and promotion.

Evangelism

In 1873, Moody began a speaking tour of Great Britain. At first it was small and little-noticed. As the tour continued, however, crowds swelled, and newspapers began to report the success of the "Yankee evangelist." In four months in London alone, Moody conducted 285 meetings attended by two and a half million people. Even the English nobility, including the Princess of Wales, came to hear him.

When Moody returned to the United States in 1875, he was deluged with requests to hold citywide campaigns across the United States. Moody eagerly agreed to as many of those invitations as he could because he believed that reaching the major cities with the gospel would reach the whole nation. "Water runs down hill, and the highest hills in America are the great cities," he said. "If we can stir them we shall stir the whole country." Over the next twenty years, Moody preached to millions in the United States, Canada, the British Isles, and Mexico. Reported conversions numbered in the thousands in each campaign.

Methodology

The reason for the multitudes of people who trusted Christ during the Moody campaigns was, of course, the moving of the Holy Spirit in the hearts of men. In human terms, however, Moody's approach and organization must be given some attention.

Like successful businessmen of his time, Moody was tremendously well organized. One minister noted, "As he stood on the platform, he looked like a businessman, he dressed like a businessman; he took the meeting in hand as a businessman would." Although Moody's services were informal, he demanded order. He carefully planned and organized each element of the massive meetings. Moody rejected the materialism of big business but he insisted on business-like efficiency in his campaigns. The all-important "business" of saving souls, Moody thought, certainly required at least as much care, planning, and forethought as the operation of some secular company.

Effects

Moody launched the urban evangelism movement, and scores of evangelists followed after him. Methodist **Sam Jones**, often called "the Moody of the South," was probably second only to Moody himself in popularity and success. Like Moody, Jones preached in a direct—almost blunt—and colorful manner that spoke to listeners on their own level. Led by evangelists such as Moody and Jones, the period from 1875 to 1915 was the golden age of urban evangelism.

Moody and Sankey

Moody became one of the first evangelists to use music in his campaigns as a means of attracting and winning over a crowd and of presenting "the gospel in song." He recruited baritone **Ira Sankey** to serve as his song leader and soloist. Sankey helped popularize the "gospel song," a sacred tune that is less formal than a hymn and has a more popular, easily sung melody. Sankey composed the tunes for such gospel songs as "A Shelter in the Time of Storm," "Hiding in Thee," and "Faith Is the Victory!" Moody and Sankey also helped establish the gospel song as part of American church life.

How Did He Do It?

Although he was not formally educated, Moody had a gift for communicating. He spoke plainly from the heart and filled his sermons with compelling stories, jokes, and illustrations. His theme was simple but profound: God loves sinners and wants to save them. Moody also avoided denominational ties. He wanted all true Christians of all denominations to join in winning the lost to Christ.

In Moody's campaigns alone, millions of people heard the gospel and tens of thousands professed salvation through Christ. It is difficult to measure what impact those conversions had on American society, but it became clear in the 1890s and 1900s that the urban revivals gave at least a push to reform efforts such as Prohibition. For Moody and the urban evangelists, however, the salvation of the lost was clearly the most important result. Their motto was best summarized in the title of a gospel song—"Rescue the Perishing." As Moody said on one occasion, "I look upon this world as a wrecked vessel. God has given me a lifeboat and said to me, 'Moody, save all you can.'"

At the beginning of the nineteenth century, Methodist circuit riders and frontier camp meetings had been on the leading edge of American Christianity. By Moody's day, however, congregations had moved from brush arbors to big auditoriums. The nation now bridged two oceans, and half the country had moved to the city. As the twentieth century dawned, more change and new challenges lay ahead.

Section Quiz

1. List at least two advantages and two disadvantages of living in the city in the late 1800s.
2. What is the major difference between a traditional hymn and a gospel song?
3. Who was the most prolific hymn writer of the late nineteenth century?
★ Explain the ultimate reason for the success of the Moody campaigns.

Fanny Crosby

The most prolific hymn writer in history was Fanny Crosby. Blinded by an incompetent doctor when she was only six months old, Fanny spent most of her life in darkness. She refused to be bitter, however, and found an outlet for her talents in writing poetry.

Christian musician William Bradbury persuaded Fanny to write the words for songs. Popularized by the Moody-Sankey campaigns, her songs (including "Pass Me Not, O Gentle Saviour," "Jesus Is Calling," "Rescue the Perishing," "Blessed Assurance," "All the Way My Saviour Leads Me," "To God Be the Glory," and "Praise Him! Praise Him!") soon filled the churches of America and Great Britain.

She was so prolific that music publishers asked her to write some songs under pseudonyms so that people would not think that *all* of their songs were by her. (She used at least ninety-four pseudonyms!) Her inspiration might come from a passing thought or an overheard comment. She reportedly wrote "Pass Me Not, O Gentle Saviour," for example, after hearing someone in a rescue mission pray, "Savior, do not pass me by." Crosby's life spanned nearly a century (1820–1915), during which she wrote hundreds of verses, not for wealth or fame but from love and devotion to Christ.

People, Places, and Things to Remember

robber barons
Cornelius Vanderbilt
Andrew Carnegie
vertical integration
John D. Rockefeller
horizontal integration
trust
"New South"
John Pierpont Morgan
United States Steel Corporation
Alexander Graham Bell
Thomas Alva Edison
Roscoe Conkling
"Stalwarts"
"Half-breeds"
James A. Garfield
Chester A. Arthur
Pendleton Act
Civil Service Commission
Grover Cleveland
Interstate Commerce Act
Benjamin Harrison
Sherman Antitrust Act
McKinley Tariff
Panic of '93
Knights of Labor
American Federation of Labor
Samuel Gompers
Haymarket Riot
Homestead Strike
Eugene V. Debs
Pullman Strike
injunction
socialism
Grange
Farmers' Alliance
Populist Party
free silver
William McKinley
William Jennings Bryan
New Immigration
Charles Darwin
Darwinism
Jim Crow laws
segregation
Plessy v. Ferguson
Booker T. Washington
W.E.B. Du Bois
Mark Twain
realism
naturalism
Stephen Crane
Jack London
Horatio Alger
urban evangelism
Dwight L. Moody
Ira Sankey
Sam Jones

Chapter Review

Making Connections

1. With which "captain of industry" do we associate oil refining? steel production? the "New South"?

2. What crime in 1881 helped promote civil service reform by the passage of the Pendleton Act?

3. Give three reasons why many Americans opposed the "New Immigration" of the late nineteenth and early twentieth centuries.

4. What was the most widespread method of meeting the challenges of the city with the gospel?

Developing History Skills

1. Explain the difference between vertical integration and horizontal integration.

2. Review the discussions of the spoils system in Chapter 10 and in this chapter. Then list at least one advantage and one disadvantage of the spoils system. Do you think the system is good or bad?

Thinking Critically

1. Was federal regulation of the railroads, such as the Interstate Commerce Act, necessary? Why or why not?

2. Read Matthew 6:19–21, 24–34. What do those passages teach the Christian concerning his reaction to materialism?

Living as a Christian Citizen

1. Imagine that you are a Christian businessman in the late nineteenth century. Write out a series of biblical principles that will guide you in your business.

2. The opportunity for leisure time has only grown since the nineteenth century. What should a Christian think about leisure time, and how should he use it?

The driving of the Golden Spike at Promontory Point, Utah, marked the completion of the first transcontinental railroad.

America Expands (1850-1900)

    I.   **Western Expansion**

   II.   **Indian Affairs**

  III.   **International Expansion**

"Cuba not contiguous? Puerto Rico not contiguous? The Philippines not contiguous? Our navy will make them contiguous!"

Indiana senator Albert Beveridge, 1899 answering critics of American expansion

Americans were restless and energetic. During the Gilded Age, they not only enlarged their cities and factories but also settled the continent, pushing the frontier to the Pacific and beyond.

With the climax of Manifest Destiny in the Mexican War (1848), the United States faced a new challenge. It now faced the daunting task of developing not only the huge tracts of land won from Mexico but also large segments of the Louisiana Purchase and Oregon territory that were still relatively unsettled. Railroaders, cowboys, miners, and farmers—all pioneers—met this challenge by pushing toward the Pacific in the last great wave of westward expansion in American history.

Yet Manifest Destiny did not really end with victory over Mexico. With the continent in U.S. hands from Atlantic to Pacific, some Americans began to look across the seas to other lands where they could plant the Stars and Stripes. Part of this "overseas Manifest Destiny" was simply economic, the securing of new markets for the products of a growing American economy. Part of the expansion, however, was the same lust for territory that had helped spark the Mexican War. Most of the expansion was peaceful, although before the century closed, the United States found itself involved in its first foreign war in fifty years.

I. Western Expansion

Rails to the West

The history of the American West rode on iron rails. The railroads crisscrossed the country, uniting the eastern and the western halves of the nation. Trains carried settlers into the West, of course, but they also carried to the East the products and resources of the West. Development of the region's resources was not impossible without the railroad; the California gold rush had proved that. But without question, precious metals and rich land for grazing and agriculture became even more valuable when supply sources and markets were as close as the nearest rail junction. Railroads proved to be the main instrument of "civilizing" the American West.

The Transcontinental Idea

The California gold rush created a population explosion on the Pacific coast, and Americans began to dream of the ideal "bridge" over the intervening mountains and prairie—the railroad. But the mammoth cost of building a **transcontinental railroad** frightened potential investors. Congress passed two railroad acts that provided incentives for investors. First, for each mile of track laid, the railroad company would receive land grants of alternating ten-square-mile sections of land along each side of the road. This land grant was doubled in 1864 to twenty-square-mile sections, ultimately giving the participating railroads about twenty million acres—an area nearly as large as the state of Indiana. Second, the government provided loans to the railroads: $16,000 for each mile of track laid in the plains, $32,000 per mile in the foothills, and $48,000 per mile in the mountains.

Two railroads received charters to build the first transcontinental railroad. The **Union Pacific** was to begin in Omaha, Nebraska, and build westward; the **Central Pacific** was to begin in Sacramento, California, and build eastward. Eventually, the two companies raced to see which could lay the most track—and therefore receive the most money. The Union Pacific, with mostly plains to cross, had an easier time than the Central Pacific, which had to cross the steepest part of the Sierra Nevada. Even so, the Union Pacific still had to contend with searing heat, waterless and treeless plains, and Indian attacks. Neither company faced an easy task.

Building the Line

The Union Pacific hired mostly Irish immigrants, many of them former Union army veterans. The Central Pacific Railroad relied mainly on immigrant Chinese workers called "coolies." The Central Pacific faced the major, even potentially fatal, challenge of blasting tunnels through the Sierra Nevada and the Rocky Mountains. Both companies' workers overcame tremendous challenges and astonished their employers with the speed with which they laid track. An English visitor described the process of the Union Pacific track gangs:

> A light car, drawn by a single horse, gallops up to the front with its load of rails. Two men seize the end of a rail and start forward, the rest of the gang taking hold by twos until it is clear of the car. They come forward at a run. At the word of command the rail is dropped in its place, right side up. Less than thirty seconds to a rail for each gang, and so four rails go down to the minute!

Almost poetically, the observer went on to note that there were "three strokes to the spike, . . . ten spikes to the rail, four hundred rails to a mile, eighteen hundred miles to San Francisco."

But the builders soon learned the truth of the adage "Haste makes waste." Because of their rush to lay more track and thereby qualify for more subsidies, the companies often failed to prepare the roadbed properly before laying the track, so over time and under the weight of locomotives and loaded freight cars, the ties sunk or tilted, twisting and misaligning the track. In such cases, the companies had to remove and repair or replace the track. And the companies returned to the government seeking even more financial help.

The climax came on May 10, 1869, when the two lines joined at Promontory (PRAH mun TOHR ee) Point, Utah. Officials drove in four special spikes—two gold, one silver, and one a mixture of gold, silver, and iron. On one of the gold spikes was inscribed, "May God continue the unity of our Country as this Railroad unites the two great Oceans of the world." Within twenty-five years, four more transcontinental lines spanned the country: the Southern Pacific (finished 1883); the Northern Pacific (1883); the Atchison, Topeka, and Santa Fe (1885); and the Great Northern (1893). The Great Northern line was the only one of the four that was completed without a penny of government subsidy. The railroads quickly became the vehicles for tremendous change in the West.

Workin' on the Railroad

The Central Pacific set the single-day record for laying track. At 7:00 a.m. on April 28, 1869, 5,000 men set to work using five trains full of more than 25,000 railroad ties, 3,500 rails, 55,000 spikes, and 14,000 bolts. By the time they stopped at 7:00 p.m., the crews had laid ten miles of track.

Workers for the Union Pacific Railroad lay track westward across the Great Plains.

Resources of the West

Mining

One of the first spurs to the settlement of the West and the building of the transcontinental railroad was the mining of precious metals. The California gold rush in 1849 was but the first of several western scrambles to dig wealth from the earth. One of the earliest gold strikes after California was the **Pikes Peak gold rush** in 1859, which resulted in the settlement of Colorado. Thousands of pioneers seeking to "get rich quick" streamed into Colorado, particularly the wildly expanding "boom town" of Denver. On their wagons, gold hunters boldly advertised, "Pikes Peak or Bust!" When the gold in Colorado gave out, however, many disappointed fortune seekers rode back with a new message: "Busted!"

Miners often found more than gold in the Rockies. Leadville, Colorado, is a splendid example of the diverse resources of the region. After a gold boom in Leadville gave out in the early 1860s, the town shifted its emphasis and became a center for silver and lead mining. After the silver ran out, Leadville also became a center for mining zinc and copper. Towns that could thus diversify thrived; those that could not became ghost towns. The story of Leadville and similar communities often made it seem that the mineral resources of the West were limitless.

With all of his equipment loaded on a single burro, a miner sets out to seek his fortune in the mineral-rich American West.

Farther west, one of the largest and richest mines was the **Comstock Lode** in Nevada. Miners there eagerly dug gold out of the ground, but they were disappointed to find that it was contaminated by some other metal and therefore sold for less. Upon closer examination, the "other metal" turned out to be silver. In fact, more than half of the ore eventually mined from the Comstock Lode was silver; the rest was gold. In all, miners extracted some $400 million worth of gold and silver from the Comstock Lode between 1859 and 1900.

The mining of the Comstock Lode was typical of mining in the latter half of the nineteenth century. No longer was mining a matter of a lone grizzled prospector with his pickaxe and shovel digging for gold in the side of a mountain; mining was big business. Large companies hired dozens of miners, sank shafts hundreds— even thousands—of feet into the earth, and brought in huge drills, pumps, and other heavy machinery to extract the precious ores. Comstock was also typical in spurring the growth of mining towns. Near Comstock was Virginia City, a metropolis of 30,000 at its height, containing only four churches but a hundred saloons. Yet, after the mine gave out, the population plummeted to fewer than a thousand permanent residents.

Other mines throughout the West drew workers and investors to the region. Gold was always the chief attraction, but fortunes could be made in other metals as well. The Anaconda Mine in Montana, for example, began as a rather poor silver mine. But miners soon discovered that the claim included one of the richest veins of copper in the world. Nearby deposits of zinc and lead further enriched the region. Wealth in the West, it seemed, was there for the digging.

Cattle

One romantic element of the American West, celebrated in numerous motion pictures and television programs, was the **cattle drive**. After the war, ranchers in Texas found themselves with herds of cattle too large for nearby markets. In the East, however, there was a large demand for beef. The problem was how to get the meat to market. The answer was simple in concept but enormously difficult in practice: Cattlemen drove the herds overland to northern railroad terminals. Soon, such frontier settlements as Kansas City, Missouri, and Dodge City, Kansas, became thriving "cow towns," centers of the cattle trade. From these towns, the cattle were moved east by rail.

Driving the herds were **cowboys**, men now shrouded by myth but who were actually tough, hard-working ranch hands. The cattle they drove were longhorns—stubborn, ornery, and independent. Their meat was not the best beef, but only the tough longhorns could survive the rigors of the cattle trails. Several of the trails used stretched north from Texas; the Goodnight-Loving Trail and the Chisholm Trail were perhaps the most famous. The cowboys herded the cattle across the "**open ranges**" (so called because the plains were unfenced public lands) and allowed them to feed on the grasses there. For all of the romance later attached to the drives, they were grueling and dangerous work. Stampedes, cattle "rustlers" (thieves), and Indian attacks were the most dramatic threats. A more common and constant danger was simply a lack of water. If the cattle failed to reach the next watering hole in time, the entire herd could perish and leave an owner financially ruined.

The cattle industry owed at least part of its success to the development of a related industry, meat packing. The idea of meat packing had first gained popularity during the Civil War when the Union army used treated meat packed in barrels or tins to feed its soldiers. After the war, city dwellers in particular found the process convenient for purchasing and storing food. Meat-packing plants opened first in Midwestern cities such as Cincinnati, Chicago, Milwaukee, and Minneapolis. At first, cattle were shipped live by train to the packing houses. The invention of the ice-cooled refrigerator railcars by meat-packer Gustavus Swift allowed meat packers to slaughter the beef in the West and ship it to the plants. Eventually, packing houses opened in the West too, shortening the process even further. Meat packers such as Swift and Philip Armour became household names as their canned meat products stocked the shelves of American pantries.

The open-range cattle industry ended in the 1880s. Cattle overgrazed much of the land, ruining it for large herds. In addition, bitterly cold winters in 1886 and 1887 killed thousands of cattle and bankrupted many cattlemen. As railroads expanded in the West, long cattle drives became unnecessary; the chief advantage of the longhorns—their ability to survive long and difficult drives—no longer mattered. Some cattlemen began fencing in their ranches and breeding smaller, meatier stock. Beef remained a profitable product, and related industries such as meat packing continued to thrive, but the era of the cattle drive and the longhorn was over.

Settlers and Sod-busters

The most significant factor in the demise of the open range was farming. The railroads that hauled cattle to meat-packing plants

---

The Life of an American Cowboy on a Cattle Drive

Life on the cattle trails was strenuous. The average herd was about two thousand head of cattle. The trail crew comprised eleven men. The two who led the herd out front were called point men. Two others came behind the point men on the sides. Another two were on the flanks. And two others, called drag men, brought up the rear behind the herds. These two men came in at the end of the day spitting and coughing, covered with dust. The crew was rounded out by a cook, a wrangler to care for the horses, and the trail boss.

Sleep was a luxury. The cowboys' day began when the cook awoke them at 3:00 a.m. and did not end until about 9:00 p.m. when they bedded down the cattle. Everyone except the cook, the wrangler, and the trail boss had to do a two-hour shift of guard duty throughout the night. If everything went well and the weather was nice, cowboys might get a total of five hours of sleep at night, but guard duty often interrupted that. When the weather was bad, they might get an hour of sleep or less. They slept on the ground with only a blanket. They pillowed their heads on their saddles. Much sleep or little, good weather or bad, the wagon rolled the next morning like clockwork.

Cattlemen in Nebraska cut a homesteader's wire fences in 1885 during one of the many farmer-cattleman clashes on the Great Plains.

Solomon D. Butcher Collection, Nebraska State Historical Society, B983-2430, copy and reuse restrictions apply.

Oklahoma Land Rush

Each Oklahoma land rush—three million acres thrown open in 1889 and six million in 1893—began like a race on a set day at a set time. With the sounding of a signal, a massive flood of settlers rushed across the borders to claim the land. In the 1889 rush, more than fifty thousand people entered the territory on the first day. The effects of the rush were dramatic. The town of Guthrie, for example, was founded and immediately grew to a population of six thousand, leading residents to joke, "Rome was not built in a day, but Guthrie was."

also brought back settlers who farmed the land instead of using it for grazing. To help protect their crops from ranging cattle, frontier farmers fenced their properties, breaking up the open ranges and hindering trail drives. Ranchers sent cowboys to drive off the "sod-busters," as farmers were called, and "range wars" often developed between cattlemen and farmers.

The farmers were destined to win the range wars. In the first thirty years after the War Between the States, more new land was settled than in all of America's previous history. By the 1880s, farmers far outnumbered cowboys, and the open ranges began to dwindle as homesteaders fenced in more and more land.

Acquiring Land

Acquiring land was the farmer's first priority. Railroads sold their land grants to settlers, but the location of the lands near the tracks (hence, closer to supply sources and markets) made them much more valuable than other lands. Many settlers could not afford the railroad's prices. The federal government, eager to see the West settled, passed the **Homestead Act** in 1862. This act provided 160 acres of land to any settler who would live on the land for five years and "improve" it by building and farming. The Homestead Act proved to be a tremendous success, and by 1900 nearly a million settlers had filed for homesteads under that law.

Most of the influx of homesteaders was gradual, but the **Oklahoma land rushes** were an exception. When the government decided to open large sections of the Indian Territory (Oklahoma) to white settlement, it decided to do so in five large blows called land runs. Other lands were offered by a lottery and an auction. They were further enlarged by a Supreme Court ruling, *United States v. Texas.* This opening of Indian Territory to white settlement was a violation of treaties made with the Southern Indian tribes and led to renewed conflicts with them. The U.S. government tried to justify the violation by saying that the Cherokees had fought for the Confederacy.

Developing the Land

The **Great Plains** is the region between the Mississippi River Valley and the Rocky Mountains, stretching north to south from Canada to southern Texas. Before the Civil War, Americans often called the region "the Great American Desert," not because it was really a desert but because the grassy plains were nearly treeless and suffered from infrequent rainfall. This treeless, semiarid region provided daunting challenges to settlers.

To make up for the lack of rain, some farmers irrigated their fields from the region's rivers. Others pumped water up from the underground water table using windmills. **Dry farming**, the cultivation of crops by careful conservation of water, was widespread, with farmers using ground covers—such as stubble from previous crops or a top layer of powdery soil—to hold in precious moisture. Because plants use more water while growing than when mature, farmers also planted crops such as winter wheat, which grew to maturity before the heat of summer increased the rate of evaporation. Wheat, in fact, became the main crop of the Great Plains, making that region one of the great "breadbaskets" of the world.

The lack of trees on the plains created a major problem in building construction. Many early pioneers lived in **soddies**, houses built of blocks of earth and sod. Soddies were warm in the winter and cool in the summer, but they were hardly luxurious. Rain, on the rare occasions when it fell, was a particular menace to sod houses. One pioneer wife said,

> Sometimes the water would drip on the stove while I was cooking, and I would have to keep tight lids on the skillets to prevent mud from falling into the food. With my dress pinned up, and rubbers on my feet, I waded around until the clouds rolled by. Life is too short to be spent under a sod roof.

A sod house, such as this one in Nebraska, provided shelter for many early settlers of the Great Plains.
Solomon D. Butcher Collection, Nebraska State Historical Society, B983-1189, copy and reuse restrictions apply.

If rains were heavy or prolonged, the sod house might collapse completely. At best, a soddie lasted only a few years, usually long enough for a settler to build another soddie or to import materials such as lumber by rail and build a more permanent house.

Fencing was likewise a problem in the treeless plains. Obviously, the split-rail fences used in the East were out of the question. Some farmers experimented with hedges, but these took time to grow. The ideal invention for fencing the plains came from Joseph Glidden of Illinois. In the 1870s, he developed **barbed wire**—two twisted strands of wire studded with sharp metal barbs at measured intervals. Pioneers strung the wire along posts, thus fencing their property more easily and quickly than they ever could have done with rail fences. The barbs kept wary livestock away from the fence so that they would not break it down.

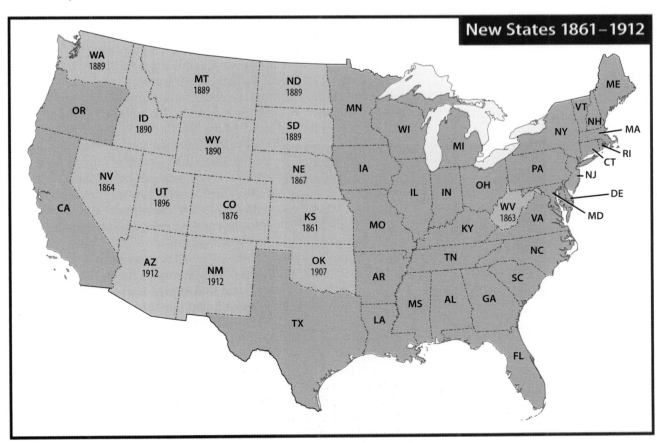

New States 1861–1912

WA 1889
MT 1889
ND 1889
MN
ME
OR
ID 1890
VT
NH
MA
WY 1890
SD 1889
WI
NY
RI
CT
NV 1864
NE 1867
IA
MI
PA
NJ
UT 1896
CO 1876
IL
IN
OH
DE
CA
WV 1863
VA
MD
KS 1861
MO
KY
AZ 1912
NM 1912
OK 1907
AR
TN
NC
SC
MS
AL
GA
TX
LA
FL

The innovations of dry farming and barbed wire—combined with inventions brought from the East, such as the reaper and the steel plow—allowed the plains farmer to transform the grasslands into an agricultural paradise. When traveling on vacation in the West in 1893, Wellesley College teacher Katherine Lee Bates was moved by the sight of the rich and lovely lands. In a notebook she carried, she wrote a poem celebrating that divinely blessed land:

> O beautiful for spacious skies,
>
> For amber waves of grain,
>
> For purple mountain majesties
>
> Above the fruited plain!
>
> America! America!
>
> God shed His grace on thee,
>
> And crown thy good with brotherhood
>
> From sea to shining sea!

Law and Order

The West was big. The law was slow in getting to the West, and even when it got there, the immense distances lawmen had to patrol made enforcement difficult at best. Some of the people who came to the West were tough, independent, and hard to control. Some of them—especially those who had already been notorious criminals back East—had no regard for law and order. Their answer to the difficult life in the West was often to steal to get what they wanted and to kill anyone who got in their way. Crime became a way of life for some of them, and the gun was the tool of their trade. The gun was also the tool used to bring law and order to the "wild West."

Gunfighters of the American West, however, were neither as noble nor as glamorous as their legends suggest. Many "facts" about James Butler "Wild Bill" Hickok, for example, were nothing more than embellished rumors, advertising gimmickry, and outright lies. For instance, Hickok once described to a reporter for *Harper's* magazine how he had handled the "McCanles Gang" in 1861 when they raided a wagon station. Hickok said that he had killed a gang of ten men with his rifle, Colt revolver, and bowie knife, "striking savage blows, following the devils up from one side to the other of the room and into the corners, striking and slashing until everyone was dead."

In reality, McCanles was the former owner of the station, a tough-fisted farmer who had nicknamed Hickok "Duck Bill" for his prominent upper lip. One day, McCanles had come unarmed with his young son and two friends to collect payment on a debt from the station owner. In the argument that ensued, Hickok shot McCanles through the heart. He wounded the other two men and then watched while the wife of the station owner beat one to death with a hoe. Hickok then helped chase down the third man,

This studio shot of western scouts includes two of the most famous: James Butler ("Wild Bill") Hickok (second from left) and William Frederick ("Buffalo Bill") Cody (center).

who was shot in cold blood. Only McCanles's twelve-year-old son escaped.

The author of a 1927 article in the *Nebraska History Magazine* described Wild Bill Hickok's gunfighting reputation, a description that is probably apt for most Western gunfighters: "From all accounts of killings in which Hickok subsequently took part, I have been unable to find one single authentic instance in which he fought a fair fight. . . . He was a cold-blooded killer without heart or conscience. The moment he scented a fight he pulled his gun and shot to kill."

A fierce reputation, however, was no guarantee of safety for a gunfighter. The infamous James Gang, led by the brothers Jesse and Frank James, terrorized Missouri and neighboring states for fifteen years after the war, staging twenty-six raids. They were widely known and even more widely feared. Yet, Jesse was shot in the back of the head by one of his own men while at his home in St. Joseph, Missouri. Frank later turned himself in, lamenting, "I'm tired of running. Tired of waiting for a ball in the back. Tired of looking into the faces of friends and seeing a Judas."

The mild features of Jesse James disguised the heart of a killer. A former Confederate guerrilla in Missouri, he turned to robbery and murder after the war.

The fast draw on the street, one of the standard features of the gunfighter legend, was a myth. Hickok, for instance, was shot in the back of the head as he sat playing cards. The killer refused to risk facing Wild Bill, saying, "I didn't want to commit suicide." No gunfighter would let the other man "go for his gun first" because reaction time would be too slow for him to get off a shot against a quick-draw professional.

The Colt army service revolver became a favorite weapon of gunfighters and outlaws in the West.

Several types of lawmen operated in the Old West. The lowest in prestige was the town marshal. Next up the ladder was the county sheriff, who, like the town marshal, appointed deputies to serve under him. In addition, the U.S. government had an interest in establishing law and order in its territories. The president himself commissioned U.S. marshals and judges to enforce the law in the counties and towns. Finding qualified, honest men was difficult, however, and turnover was high. Furthermore, the lawmen were given unreasonably large territories to cover; one county marshal in Wyoming was responsible for 16,800 square miles of land.

The "Peace Commissioners" of Dodge City, Kansas, pose for a photograph. Included are Wyatt Earp (front row, second from left) and Bat Masterson (back row, on far right).

Most of the U.S. marshal's duties involved politics, tax collection, and paperwork; he usually left the field work to deputies. The town marshal's job was even less glamorous. His duties could include fire and health inspections and even shooting stray dogs. Town marshals, who rarely earned enough to live on, often supplemented their income by running gambling operations. The potential for graft was great.

In the absence of official justice, townspeople sometimes turned to their own brand of justice—lynching. The people of Laramie, Wyoming, once hanged their own town marshal when they found that he was drugging people and taking their

Hanging was the most common form of execution in the Old West. In this photograph, "Black Jack" Ketchum is being prepared for "the final drop" in the New Mexico Territory, 1901.

The city prison in Larned, Kansas, was a typically ugly but reasonably secure jail in the frontier West.

Kansas State Historical Society, Topeka, KS, www.kshs.org/research/collections/documents/photos/webuse.htm

money in the saloon that he managed. Vigilante groups (groups of private citizens who enforced the law without any authority) were another force for "order," although they rarely had the sanction of the law. A few vigilante groups did manage to get tacit approval from the law, even winning legal status as stock growers' associations or homesteaders' associations.

Many businesses on the frontier also wanted to bring law and order to the West. For example, after suffering more than two hundred stagecoach robberies in one month in 1877, the Wells Fargo shipping company hired the Pinkerton National Detective Agency to supplement the work of the government lawmen. The Pinkertons developed America's first extensive "most-wanted" file on criminals, an idea that was later adopted by the Federal Bureau of Investigation. The list of criminals included such men as Black Bart, a well-dressed "gentleman bandit" who robbed twenty-eight stagecoaches but never hurt any passengers. He was finally tracked down after he dropped a handkerchief at the scene of a crime. Pinkerton detectives traced the handkerchief to Black Bart after visiting ninety-one laundries across California all the way from Sonora to San Francisco.

Judges in the early years were often ill trained and not respected. At first, they held court in improvised surroundings, such as a grocery store or a saloon. By their iron will, judges brought a grudging respect for the law. At the local level were the justices of the peace or the police court judges. The territories were divided among district judges, who often traveled great distances to hear a wide variety of cases.

One of the most famous judges of the West was Methodist Isaac Charles Parker, better known as "the Hanging Judge." Parker's jurisdiction was a rough slice of land in western Arkansas bordering Indian Territory (modern Oklahoma). Technically, only Indians were allowed in the vast Indian Territory, but the region had become a hideout for criminals. Although the tribes were self-governing, any case involving a white man was handed over to the single U.S. Court judge in West Arkansas, who had only one federal marshal to support him. As white settlers began to encroach upon the area, the situation became desperate. Legislators in Washington were wringing their hands when the position again became vacant in 1875, until—to everyone's amazement—an honest, qualified man (Parker) volunteered to serve for the $3,500 annual salary. The thirty-six-year-old Parker wanted to do what he could to bring justice to the territory.

Within eight days of bringing his family to the mudhole of Fort Smith, Arkansas, the imposing judge opened his court. The U.S. government granted him final say over any crime committed in Indian Territory, leaving convicted outlaws with no recourse except a presidential pardon. He also hired two hundred deputy marshals to scour the territory. Parker hired a fearsome collection of lawmen. Their instructions were plain: "Bring them in, alive—or dead." During one of his eight-week court sessions, he condemned to death six of the ninety-one people brought before him. A huge oak gallows was erected just for the occasion. Parker kept at his job, despite mounting criticism, for twenty-one years, working six days a week from sunup to sundown and sometimes holding court at night. He said of complaints, "If criticism is due, it should be [for] the system, not the man whose duty lies under it." By the end of his career, he had heard 13,940 cases, found 9,454 men guilty, and had sentenced 88 of them to the gallows. Through his tireless efforts, organizational skills, and firm grasp of the law, Judge Parker brought a measure of peace to a troubled land and won for himself a reputation as the West's greatest judge.

Section Quiz

1. What two incentives did the federal government give the railroads to build a transcontinental line?

2. Name the two railroad companies that were given charters to build the first transcontinental railroad and the city from which each started.

3. What famous judge of the West became known as "the Hanging Judge"?

✯ Describe the opposing sides in the range wars. Explain which side you think was right.

II. Indian Affairs

One could wish that the story of the American West was one of unbroken triumph, of courageous settlers overcoming the obstacles they faced to build a new and better land. Unfortunately, the story has a darker side to it. As white men moved west, they clashed with the Indians, just as they had done since the days of the Jamestown colony in Virginia. This time, however, the conflict would be the final, climactic struggle between white and Indian for control of the rest of the American continent.

Plains Indians

The Great Plains region was already inhabited when the white settlers came. It was home to the **Plains Indians**, tribes such as the Cheyenne, the Comanche, and the **Sioux** (SOO). These tribes came closer to the popular conception of Indians than did the eastern tribes. They lived in tepees, hunted buffalo on swift Indian ponies, and fought American cavalry with bows and arrows. Such superficial stereotypes, however, do not do justice to the surprisingly complex culture of these people.

The key to the survival of the Plains Indians was the buffalo. The men of the tribes, riding on horses descended from those left by the Spanish centuries before, were the ones who usually hunted the buffalo that wandered in herds so huge that they blackened the Great Plains with their numbers. The Indians ate a great deal of buffalo meat, either fresh, in dried strips (jerky), or dried and mixed

The buffalo were essential to the survival of the Plains Indians and their nomadic way of life.

Buffalo Chase, by Seth Eastman, 1868, oil on canvas, Collection of the U.S. House of Representatives

with berries (pemmican). Buffalo hides provided clothing, blankets, curtains, drumheads, tent coverings, and other necessities. Buffalo sinews and tendons provided bowstrings and the thread for sewing coverings together. Some Indians made dice out of buffalo bones for gambling. Even the dung of the buffalo was dried and burned as fuel in the treeless plains. Buffalo were so important to the Indians that during the Indian Wars the U.S. government quietly encouraged the slaughtering of the herds to rob the Indians of their means of livelihood. By 1900, the huge herds of the Great Plains had become nearly extinct. Some historians believe that the destruction of the buffalo was more important in the conquest of the Plains Indians than any military campaign.

White settlers soon learned that the Plains Indians were skilled warriors, dashing about on their horses and firing arrows almost as fast as a man could fire a repeating rifle. The Indians were hardy, independent fighters. One on one, few whites could stand up to them. Only disunity among the tribes and the Indians' tendency to fight as individuals rather than as coordinated units kept them from overwhelming the undersupplied soldiers they often faced.

The Plains Indians were also fiercely proud of their heritage, and they became increasingly protective of their lands as white settlers encroached upon them. The Plains tribes did not intend simply to give their land away, and they soon learned—as other tribes had learned earlier—that the government's word was not always trustworthy. Even when government officials intended to be fair, their lack of understanding of Indian culture sometimes caused them to make fatal errors. And even if one white man intended to abide by an agreement, later white leaders could change the policy if it did not suit their desires. Whites never seemed to understand, for example, that Indian chiefs were more honorary than official and that few chiefs could bind all of their people to a treaty—treaties that, incidentally, the chiefs themselves often did not understand. Misunderstanding fueled by greed resulted in bloody conflict on the Great Plains.

Indian Wars

From the 1850s to the 1870s, the U.S. Army fought a series of campaigns against the Plains Indians. The army demonstrated a remarkable ability to underestimate its opponents. For example, during the First Sioux War in the Wyoming-Montana region (1866–68), Captain William Fetterman bragged that with eighty men, he could ride through the entire Sioux nation. Ironically, Fetterman had exactly eighty men with him when he met a large Sioux war party near Fort Phil Kearny, and he and his troops were slaughtered to the last man. In fact, this war might have the unusual distinction of being the first war that the United States ever lost. The Sioux won every battle and forced the government to give them a treaty granting all of their demands. Unfortunately for the Indians, the government had little intention of honoring that treaty.

The goal of the Indian Wars for the American government was to force the tribes onto **reservations**, special tracts of land set aside for the Indians where they could theoretically live in peace. Some whites undoubtedly thought this policy to be a means of helping and protecting the Indians. Many others, however, viewed it as an opportunity to move the Indians out of the way so that they could seize rich Indian lands. The Indians, for their part, could see no

Brutal, Bloody Affairs

The Indian Wars were brutal, bloody affairs. Both sides committed atrocities and slaughtered without mercy. Whites and Indians did not merely kill each other; they tortured the living and mutilated the dead, including the women and children of both sides. Whites called the Indians "savages" with some reason, but the supposedly civilized white man proved hardly less brutal than his Indian counterpart.

reason for abandoning their tribal lands. Even some Indians who agreed to move to the reservations rebelled when they saw how poor the lands on the reservations were. (The government tended to set up reservations on arid, barren land that was useless to whites.) Perhaps, given the superior numbers and technology of the United States, the result of the Indian Wars was a foregone conclusion. It took long, hard fighting, however, for the American army to emerge victorious.

The Sioux War

The climax of the Indian Wars was what commonly is known as the **Sioux War** (1876–77; also known as the Second Sioux War and the Great Sioux War to distinguish it from the conflict of 1866–68). The fame of this war lies partly in the fact that it was the last great Indian War and partly in the personalities involved: cavalry colonel George Armstrong Custer and Indian leaders Sitting Bull and Crazy Horse.

Ohio-born **George Armstrong Custer** was a rash, dashing, and self-centered army officer. He had risen from the rank of lieutenant to major general during the Civil War as a result of his reckless daring and his constant efforts to impress his superiors. Reduced to the rank of colonel when the army shrank after the war, Custer became a renowned Indian fighter. Typical of his method was the Battle of the Washita (WASH uh TAH) River (1868) in what is today Oklahoma. Coming upon an Indian camp on the banks of the river, Custer divided his force and prepared to attack without any reconnaissance. The attack was a smashing success for the cavalry as they routed the surprised Indians. It turned out that some of the Indians had been raiding white settlements, but Custer had not known that beforehand—nor did he care. To the impetuous Custer, the fact that they were Indians was enough.

Opposing Custer in the Sioux War were **Sitting Bull** and **Crazy Horse**. Although both men were Sioux chiefs, Sitting Bull was more of a political leader of the Sioux forces. He provided moral inspiration to the Indians and led in all negotiations with the whites. Crazy Horse served more as the commander of the Sioux warriors. Under Crazy Horse's leadership, the Sioux warriors fought one of the most unified, best-organized Indian campaigns in history.

The major battle of the Sioux War took place on June 25, 1876. Custer's cavalry regiment came upon a huge Indian camp on the banks of the Little Bighorn River in what is now Montana. Unknown to Custer, Sitting Bull and Crazy Horse had noted his approach and were prepared to meet him. Custer's scouts looked at the size of the camp and warned the colonel that the Sioux had more warriors than the soldiers had bullets. Custer brushed these warnings aside. As he had done at the Washita River eight years before, Custer divided his forces to attack the Indians from two directions. One force, under Major Marcus Reno, attacked the camp head-on and was soon driven back with heavy losses. Even so, Reno's force was the fortunate one. Custer took some two hundred men and swept north of the Indian camp to launch what he thought would be a surprise attack. Instead, the Indians surprised Custer by coming out to meet him in overwhelming numbers. Perhaps two thousand braves attacked the two hundred soldiers. Custer and all of his force lost their lives in the Battle of the Little Bighorn, which is popularly known as **Custer's Last Stand**.

Chief Sitting Bull

Paxson's painting is generally considered one of the most historically accurate portrayals of the Battle of the Little Bighorn.

Custer's Last Stand, by Edgar Samuel Paxson, oil on canvas, Buffalo Bill Historical Center, Cody, Wyoming; Museum purchase, 19.69

This great Indian victory actually worked to the advantage of the U.S. Army. Thinking that they had won the war, many Sioux left Sitting Bull's force. Shocked and sobered by the defeat, the government quickly sent more men and supplies west to defeat the Sioux. Within months of Custer's defeat, the army had forced the Indians to accept peace on the government's terms. Most Sioux went sadly to the reservations. Crazy Horse, after giving himself up, died in a scuffle with soldiers as they attempted to put him in a guardhouse. Sitting Bull fled to Canada for a time. He eventually returned to live on a reservation, only to be killed by Indian police in 1890 during his arrest for allegedly inciting Indians to rebel.

Later Indian Affairs

The fate of the Sioux was typical of what happened to the tribes of the West. Some Indians still resisted the idea of living a dull, impoverished life on the barren reservations. The Apache Geronimo, for example, led a small band of Indians who for several years frus-

Chief Joseph, Man of War and Peace

Of the Indians who fought against the U.S. Army in the nineteenth century, none won more sympathy among the American public than Chief Joseph of the Nez Perce tribe. He conducted a military campaign and march so brilliant that newspapers and even opposing generals called him the "Indian Napoleon."

Joseph and his tribe lived in the Wallowa Valley in what is now Idaho. In 1877, the government tried to force the Nez Perce onto a reservation. Joseph did not want to leave his land, but he hated war. He thought that the tribe must submit or risk destruction at the hands of the army. While he was trying to organize his people for the move, however, a handful of young warriors attacked and killed some white settlers who had mistreated their tribe. With little hope of peace now, Joseph prepared to flee and—if necessary—to fight.

Joseph took his people east, eventually deciding to escape to Canada, where Sitting Bull and his Sioux were already living. In 108 days, Joseph marched more than 700 Indians—most of them women, children, and old men—nearly 1,400 miles. In eight separate battles and skirmishes, the Nez Perce defeated contingents of four separate cavalry units.

Joseph refused to fight a savage war, however. He forbade the killing of women and children and the taking of scalps from the dead. He simply wanted to get his tribe to a place where they could live in peace. Americans followed with interest the newspaper reports describing his trek through the mountains and how he seemed to be outwitting and baffling the army at every turn.

Finally, on September 30, 1877, the U.S. cavalry, led by General O. O. Howard, former head of the Freedmen's Bureau, caught up with Joseph's band just forty miles from the Canadian border. Outnumbered and numbed by a chilling cold, the tribe could go no farther. As he surrendered, Chief Joseph spoke with eloquence: "It is cold and we have no blankets. The little children are freezing to death. . . . Hear me, my chiefs, I am tired; my heart is sick and sad. From where the sun now stands, I will fight no more forever."

Joseph was eventually settled on a reservation in Washington State. He died there on September 21, 1904. A doctor on the reservation said, "Joseph died of a broken heart."

trated the army's attempts to force them onto a reservation. He and his band were finally captured. The Nez Perce (NEHZ PURS) Chief Joseph conducted a masterful campaign to save his tribal lands or at least lead his people to refuge in Canada, but he was forced to surrender in 1877.

The last of the Indian Wars came in 1890 near Wounded Knee Creek in South Dakota when the army tried to disarm and capture a band of Sioux who were resisting removal from their lands. The chief, knowing that he was outnumbered, surrendered. But one brave resisted, firing a wild shot at the soldiers. Fighting quickly broke out. When it was over, 25 soldiers and more than 150 Indians (half of them women and children) were dead. The **Wounded Knee Massacre** was a sad and bloody epilogue to the Indian Wars.

In 1881, Helen Hunt Jackson published *A Century of Dishonor*, a work portraying the government's ruthless and sometimes dishonorable dealings with the Indians. Jackson's book, combined with the decreasing threat of the Plains Indians, inspired some belated sympathy for the Indians' plight. In 1887, Congress tried to undo some of the damage by passing the **Dawes Act**, which allowed Indian lands to be parceled out to individual Indian families to use and develop as they liked. Unfortunately, the act tended to break down the unity of the tribes, and many Indians sold their allotted lands to whites and were soon more impoverished than before.

In the twentieth century, the U.S. government tried to redress some of the wrongs done to the Indians. In 1924, Congress gave Indians full citizenship. In 1934, to preserve the remaining Indian lands, the Indian Reorganization Act halted the allotment program of the Dawes Act and gave the reservations limited self-government. Congress also made it easier for Indians to seek damages for past violations of treaties and other agreements. These acts, however, seem too little in the face of the injustices done to the Indians.

Apache warrior Geronimo, using only small raiding parties, harassed and tied down large numbers of U.S. cavalry before he finally surrendered.

Section Quiz

1. What was the goal of the American government in its campaigns against the Indians?
2. Who was the most famous cavalry officer of the Sioux War of 1876–77? Which two chiefs were his main opponents?
3. Why did the great Indian victory at the Little Bighorn actually work to the advantage of the U.S. Army?
★ How do you think the conflict with the Indians might have been settled peacefully?

III. International Expansion

After reaching the Pacific Ocean at the conclusion of the Mexican War (1848), the United States began to look across the oceans for new lands to annex. The sectional conflict climaxing in the War Between the States postponed most thoughts of overseas expansion, but then a surge of economic and political growth occurred. American foreign policymakers in the last half of the nineteenth century pursued three main goals: (1) to defend the Western Hemisphere from intervention by European powers while maintaining good relations with Europe, (2) to create new economic opportunities for American trade with other countries, and (3) to extend the territory of the United States through purchase, annexation, or conquest.

First Steps Toward Imperialism

While Americans had been defending and expanding at home, the powers of Europe had been building empires. The Germans, Dutch, French, and British—especially the British—had established colonies around the world. The British liked to boast that their empire was so extensive that the sun never set on it. Amid that context, America was poised to take on a relatively minimal involvement in imperialism, but the consequences would be extensive.

Building and Mending Fences

France in Mexico

During the War Between the States, France had mounted one of the most serious challenges to the Monroe Doctrine in American history. Taking advantage of the distractions of the war, Napoleon III (grandnephew of Napoleon Bonaparte and ruler of France) set up a "puppet emperor," the Austrian nobleman **Maximilian I**, in Mexico in 1864. Napoleon III ignored American protests, particularly since the United States government was far too busy to do anything about it. After the war, however, the United States stationed 50,000 veteran troops on the Rio Grande. Secretary of State William Seward then gave Napoleon an ultimatum to withdraw French soldiers from Mexico. The French, worried by the troops and plagued by troubles in Europe, quietly withdrew. Maximilian lost the support of the French, and a Mexican firing squad executed him in 1867. The United States had successfully met one challenge.

Treaty of Washington

After its confrontation with France, the United States sought to settle three longstanding differences with Great Britain. First, the United States sought compensation for the ravages its merchant fleet had suffered from **commerce raiders** during the Civil War. Second, the United States and Britain had been arguing since the 1840s over who owned a group of islands between Vancouver Island and the state of Washington. Third, the United States and Canada had long disagreed over fishing rights off the coasts of North America.

The **Treaty of Washington** (1871) settled these matters by setting up international tribunals to deal with each question. One tribunal awarded the United States more than $15 million in damages from Britain in payment for the destruction caused by the commerce raiders. Another tribunal awarded possession of the islands off Vancouver to the United States. A third required the United States to pay Canada more than $5 million for special fishing privileges. The importance of the treaty was not simply in settling these individual questions; it also paved the way for greater friendship and cooperation between the United States on the one hand and Britain and Canada on the other.

Economic Expansion

Because of improvements in transportation and technology, the United States was able by the mid 1800s to produce more goods—food, raw materials, and manufactured products—than it could use. The nation therefore sought more foreign markets in which to sell its goods.

Perry in Japan (1854)

The California gold rush and the acquisition of Mexican territories after the Mexican War had established America as a potential Pacific power and had made increased trade with Asia a major American goal. However, Japan, one of the main powers in Asia, had isolated itself from the rest of the world for some two hundred years. Hoping to open a door for trade, the United States government commissioned Commodore **Matthew Perry** to take a small squadron of warships to Japan and to negotiate with Japan's rulers. Perry's squadron awed and offended the Japanese. Despite opposition by many in his government, the Japanese ruler agreed to the

---

Commerce Raiders

Commerce raiders were warships owned and commanded by the Confederates but built in British shipyards. The American government believed that Britain was partly responsible for the damage caused by these raiders.

Treaty of Kanagawa (1854), a major victory for American foreign trade. It was also the first step in opening Japan to western influences and molding that island nation into a major economic and military power.

Pan-Americanism

After the Civil War, the United States resumed its push for new markets abroad. One obvious potential market was Latin America. The nations south of the Rio Grande, although rich in raw materials and some foodstuffs, had little industry. The United States hoped to increase inter-American trade and decrease Latin American trade with Europe.

James G. Blaine, secretary of state under Garfield and Harrison, was a major promoter of closer relations with Latin America. He advocated **Pan-Americanism**, a movement favoring greater cooperation and unity among the nations of the Western Hemisphere. Blaine hoped to create economic unity by reducing trade barriers such as tariffs among the nations. Blaine and others even dreamed of creating a loose political confederation of American nations, which the United States would dominate. With some delight, then, Blaine hosted delegates from Latin American countries at the First Pan-American Congress in 1889, but the meeting was not a resounding success. The southern nations feared political and economic domination by the United States, and most could not forget past offenses, such as the Mexican War. Furthermore, the secretary of state's own Republican Party was wary of lowering tariffs. The congress did at least provide a precedent, however, for further discussion and friendlier relations as the years passed.

An Open Door in China

Although the United States pioneered efforts to open Japan for trade, it found itself in the middle of intense competition when attempting to trade with China, the other major nation in Asia. Each European power, along with Japan, was attempting to set up "spheres of influence" in China, regions where one foreign nation could dominate Chinese trade. Some diplomats even talked of carving up China into colonies. The United States, however, was interested only in trading freely in China, not in sending in a military force to establish a colony. Therefore, in 1899 Secretary of State John Hay proposed the **Open Door Policy**. Hay's policy called for all nations trading in China to refrain from interfering with one another and to allow free trade in China. Although the United States could do little to enforce such a policy, the idea fit well with what some European powers—notably Great Britain—already wanted to do in China. Because the policy suited the inclinations of the major powers, it succeeded.

Hay nearly saw his open door close as soon as it had opened, however. The Chinese resented attempts by foreign powers to determine the future of their country. In 1900, an antiforeign movement, the **Boxer Rebellion**, broke out in China. (The name "boxer" comes from a leading organization in the rebellion, "the Righteous and Harmonious Fists.") Chinese rioters destroyed anything foreign. Boxers slaughtered missionaries, diplomats, foreign merchants, and Chinese converts to Christianity (which Boxers considered a "foreign" religion). An international military force, including troops from the United States, intervened to protect foreigners in China. Boxer power was broken.

Uncle Sam (saying, "I'm out for commerce, not conquest!") holds back the great powers of Europe in this *Harper's Weekly* cartoon supporting the idea of free trade in China.

General Research Division, The New York Public Library, Astor, Lenox and Tilden Foundations

The peace terms imposed by the victors were harsh. Secretary Hay, who opposed dividing China among the victors, persuaded the others to accept payments from the Chinese rather than insist on territorial concessions. The nations involved accepted Hay's proposal. The payments totaled $333 million; the United States was promised $25 million, but Congress reduced that amount and sent what it did collect back to China with the understanding that the money would be used to educate Chinese students in America. American efforts to help China, although not free from self-interest, created kind feelings between the two countries.

Territorial Expansion: Imperialism

As the events in China demonstrated, the nineteenth century was the great century of **imperialism**, the extension of power by one people or country over another people or country. An imperialist nation might acquire territory by purchase, annexation, or conquest. Often imperialism meant the conquest and exploitation of weaker nations by the stronger nations. The peoples of conquered lands were often reduced to a servile relation to the representatives of the conquering nations. Despite the sins committed against many peoples in the world, God graciously allowed benefits to flow to the colonized regions as well. Better medical treatment, development of natural resources, and improvements in education and infrastructure often came in the wake of imperial conquest. The greatest side effect of imperialism, however, was the opportunity it presented for missionaries to take the gospel to people who had never heard of Jesus Christ.

Seward's Folly

The largest single American acquisition after the Civil War was the **purchase of Alaska** from Russia in 1867. When Secretary of State William Seward announced the purchase, many Americans—believing Alaska to be only an empty wasteland of snow and ice—called the area "Seward's Folly" or "Seward's Icebox." Still, at a cost of only $7.2 million (less than two cents an acre), Alaska looked like a bargain, and the treaty of purchase passed the Senate easily.

Within a few years, Alaska had proved its value to the United States. First gold and then oil were discovered in the region, making it a source of enormous wealth. Furthermore, the rise of the Soviet Union in the twentieth century and its proximity to Alaska increased Alaska's value as a military base and vindicated the wisdom of those who wanted to take the region out of Russian hands. "Seward's Folly" turned out to be a very shrewd bargain indeed.

Pacific Expansion

Trade with Japan and China was not America's only interest in the Pacific in the last half of the nineteenth century. The United States also began building a Pacific empire. The United States, for example, simply annexed the tiny coral island of Midway in the middle of the Pacific in 1867.

The most important Pacific addition to the United States was **Hawaii** (also known as the Sandwich Islands). The Hawaiian Islands had been an important supply point for whalers, merchant ships, and warships since the 1700s. In the early 1800s, American missionaries had come to the islands and had enjoyed remarkable success in winning many islanders to Christ. Unfortunately, many Americans who followed the missionaries—and, sadly, the sons of

American Samoa

In 1889, the United States joined Britain and Germany in a joint protectorate of the Samoan islands. Disagreements among the three nations, however, led to the division of the islands, the United States forming the eastern islands into the U.S. territory of American Samoa.

the missionaries themselves—proved more interested in profits than in souls. American investors soon built a thriving sugar industry that dominated the economy of the islands and, indeed, helped the islands to prosper.

Until 1891, Hawaii was ruled by native kings who usually went along with the planters' wishes. In that year, however, Queen Liliuokalani (lee LEE oo oh kah LAH nee) took the throne. She tried to reestablish native control of the island and limit the power of the planters. In 1893, the planters revolted against "Queen Lil" and asked to be annexed to the United States. President Grover Cleveland, however, refused to approve the uprising and blocked annexation of the islands. Like Texas after its war for independence, Hawaii was forced to exist for several years as an independent republic. In 1898, however, when McKinley was in office and a war with Spain was making the United States nervous about the security of the Pacific, Congress voted to annex the islands.

Missions

One of the positive elements of imperialism was a growth in Christian missions. Some historians criticize missionaries as "agents of imperialism" who secretly made colonies for their homelands under the cloak of preaching the gospel. Actually, the opposite was often true. For example, Hiram Bingham, one of the first Congregationalist missionaries to go to Hawaii in 1820, clashed with Americans and others who were bent on exploiting the Hawaiians. When Bingham helped end prostitution among the native women, for example, outraged white sailors armed with knives and clubs assaulted him.

Missionaries went to all corners of the globe in the nineteenth century. One nation that attracted many was China, where Methodists took an early lead in establishing American gospel outposts. The most prominent North American leaders in Chinese work in the late nineteenth and early twentieth centuries were not from the United States but from Canada: Jonathan Goforth and his wife, Rosalind. Together, they faithfully preached to the Chinese despite major difficulties, such as the Boxer Rebellion. Another hero of Chinese missions was American Lottie Moon. She bravely traveled into the dangerous interior of China to minister to the Chinese people. She did more to arouse enthusiasm among Baptists for missions than anyone else since Adoniram Judson.

The latter part of the nineteenth century also saw the growth of a new kind of mission board. Up to this time, most mission boards had been tied directly to a major denomination. The denomination collected money from its member churches and, in turn, paid salaries to the missionaries so that they could continue their work. **Faith missions**, on the other hand, are usually independent mission boards that have no guaranteed income. Even today missionaries under "faith boards" go on "deputation" to visit local churches directly and solicit support for their work. One of the first faith mission boards in America was the Christian and Missionary Alliance (C&MA), founded by A. B. Simpson in 1887. The C&MA grew so much that it eventually became an independent denomination. Most faith missions focused on one region of the world. One example was the Central American Mission, founded in 1890 by C. I. Scofield, a Congregationalist pastor in Dallas and later the editor of a famous reference Bible.

Queen Liliuokalani in her later years

The Student Volunteer Movement

One of the most important movements in foreign missions was the **Student Volunteer Movement** (SVM). This organization began in 1886 at a Bible conference in Massachusetts hosted by D. L. Moody. Spurred by an appeal to consider foreign missions, one hundred college students pledged themselves to become missionaries. Taking as its motto "The evangelization of the world in this generation," the SVM grew rapidly. It is credited with ultimately sending twenty thousand missionaries to the mission field.

Whether American missionaries ministered under a denominational or a faith board, they labored loyally and diligently throughout the world. Some suffered martyrdom; thirty-five C&MA missionaries and their children, for example, died in the Boxer Rebellion. Because of the sacrificial labors by so many brave and daring missionaries, many souls came to find Jesus Christ as their Savior.

Climax of Imperialism: The Spanish-American War

The climax of American imperialism came in 1898, when the United States went to war with Spain over that nation's treatment of its colony of Cuba. Although the Cubans had intermittently revolted against the Spanish government for decades, a revolt that broke out in 1895 was unusually serious. A depression with its resulting unemployment—combined with weak, corrupt Spanish rule over the colony—provided ideal conditions for an insurrection. Bands of guerrillas destroyed sugar mills, plantations, and anything else the people loyal to Spain valued. To stop the wanton destruction, Spanish troops arrested rebels and put them in barbed-wire concentration camps, where many of them died of starvation or disease. As American newspapers sensationalized the brutal Spanish suppression of the rebels, American sympathy for the Cubans began to grow.

Causes

Sympathy alone, however, was not enough to push the United States into war. Three other factors fanned American hatred of Spain and hastened the war: (1) yellow journalism, (2) the de Lôme letter, and (3) the sinking of the U.S.S. *Maine.*

"**Yellow journalism**" is sensationalized news reporting aimed more at attracting readers than at reporting the truth. Two of the leading "yellow journals" were William Randolph Hearst's *New York Journal* and Joseph Pulitzer's *New York World.* Each paper attempted to outdo the other in reporting sensational stories that would boost sales. Hearst, for example, paid a famous illustrator, Frederic Remington, to go to Cuba to draw sketches of the revolt. When Remington arrived in Cuba and reported that conditions were not bad enough to warrant U.S. intervention, Hearst reportedly replied, "You furnish the pictures and I'll furnish the war."

American public opinion, inflamed by yellow journalism, began to favor war with Spain to establish Cuba's independence. In spite of journalistic propaganda, however, President McKinley intended to avoid hostilities. The situation was actually improving, and the Spanish government was willing to meet McKinley's demands for better treatment of the Cubans when two incidents gave the prowar party new reason to demand military action.

First, on February 9, 1898, the *New York Journal* published a stolen letter written by the Spanish ambassador in Washington, Enrique Dupuy de Lôme. In the **de Lôme letter**, as it came to be known, the ambassador denounced McKinley as, among other things, "weak and a bidder for the admiration of the crowd." This was hardly strong language. Assistant Secretary of the Navy Theodore Roosevelt, for instance, described McKinley as having "no more backbone than a chocolate eclair." Roosevelt, however, was an American citizen, whereas de Lôme was the representative of a foreign country, and Americans were outraged at the insult to their president. De Lôme resigned, but Spanish-American relations grew still worse.

The cartoon character "The Yellow Kid" symbolized journalism at the time of the Spanish-American War.

A second incident was even more damaging. The battleship **Maine** had been sent to Havana Harbor in Cuba in January 1898 to protect American interests on the island. On February 15, the *Maine* exploded and sank in the harbor, killing 260 Americans. An investigation at that time by the American government claimed that a mine had sunk the *Maine*. Actually, no one knows precisely what happened to the *Maine*. A careful study of the evidence by two American naval engineers in 1975, for example, concluded that the explosion resulted from an accident *inside* the ship, in the ship's coal bunkers. Also, the Spanish had no reason to blow up the battleship. But Americans believed what they *wanted* to believe and what the yellow press told them— that the explosion occurred outside the ship and was an act of Spanish treachery.

The U.S.S. *Maine* enters Havana Harbor, where its mysterious destruction helped spark a war between the United States and Spain.

McKinley caved to political pressure and sent a war message to Congress in April 1898. Congress demanded Spain's withdrawal from Cuba and authorized the president to use force, if necessary, to establish Cuba's independence. Spain refused, and the result was the **Spanish-American War**.

Manila Bay

The United States Navy was a powerful, modern fleet and was reasonably well prepared for war. Ironically, the war over the Caribbean island of Cuba started in the Pacific Ocean, where one of Spain's major fleets was located. America's Pacific fleet, under

Key
- ⬯ U.S. Blockade
- → U.S. Fleet
- → U.S. Army
- → Spanish Navy
- ✯ Battles

Tampa
Florida

BAHAMA ISLANDS

U.S.S. MAINE SUNK FEB. 1898
Havana
CUBA
Santiago

ATLANTIC OCEAN

HAITI **DOMINICAN REPUBLIC**

JAMAICA

PUERTO RICO

✯ EL CANEY
Santiago
SAN JUAN HILL
Siboney   Daiquiri

The Spanish-American War: Caribbean Theater—1898

American Army Not Prepared

The American army was not nearly as well prepared as the navy. The army had done little to prepare for transporting and supplying troops. Many soldiers had to fight in the steaming jungles of Cuba dressed in heavy wool uniforms designed for winter campaigns against the Indians. In fact, the regular army had only 26,000 men at the outbreak of the war, but Congress voted to raise several volunteer regiments. Probably the most famous of the volunteer units was the "**Rough Riders**," a collection of cowboys and adventurers from the West, commanded by Colonel Leonard Wood and Lieutenant Colonel Theodore Roosevelt.

Commodore **George Dewey**, left Hong Kong and on May 1, 1898, engaged the Spanish fleet in Manila Bay, the main harbor of the Spanish-controlled Philippine Islands. The Americans wrecked the antiquated Spanish fleet, sinking eight ships, killing 161 sailors, and wounding 210 others. American losses were slight—one warship damaged, one sailor killed (of heatstroke), and nine others wounded. The **Battle of Manila Bay** destroyed Spanish sea power in the Pacific and left the Philippines in the hands of the United States.

Santiago

On May 19, Spain's Atlantic fleet entered Santiago Harbor in Cuba. The American fleet quickly blockaded the harbor, and the U.S. government decided to send the army into Cuba to capture Santiago and force out the Spanish fleet. In late June, 17,000 American soldiers landed in Cuba. In a series of sharp battles, the Americans pushed back the dispirited Spaniards and encircled the city. The most famous battle was probably the Battle of San Juan Hill in which Roosevelt and his Rough Riders helped storm the Spanish fortifications. (Ironically, the Rough Riders fought on foot because their horses were still in Florida. Besides, it was common practice for American cavalrymen to fight dismounted.) On July 3, the Spanish fleet tried to escape. The resulting **Battle of Santiago Bay** was a repetition of Manila Bay. The American fleet suffered three warships damaged, one sailor killed, and ten others wounded. The Spanish, however, had three ships sunk (one of which they scuttled), three ships run aground, and 474 sailors killed or wounded. The city of Santiago surrendered on July 17. Shortly thereafter, American forces captured the island of Puerto Rico, and the Spanish sued for peace.

Aftermath

An American diplomat called the Spanish-American conflict "a splendid little war." Years later, Theodore Roosevelt said, "It wasn't much of a war, but it was the best war we had."

The Spanish-American War was indeed a "little war" in many ways. It lasted only four months, and only 379 Americans died in battle. (But more than ten times that number died of disease either in Cuba or in unsanitary camps in the United States.) The results of the war, though, were anything but little.

At the beginning of the war, Congress had passed an amendment to a bill proclaiming that the United States wanted no territory in Cuba. That did not stop the U.S., however, from taking Puerto Rico, Guam, and the Philippines during the war, although America paid the Spanish $20 million dollars for the Philippines. Furthermore, the United States virtually ruled Cuba as a protectorate for several years after the war, and the panic caused by the outbreak of the war had hastened American annexation of Hawaii. The United States was now widely recognized as a world power and had an empire of its own.

The nation soon found, however, that empires can be extremely costly. For the first time in its history, the United States had to maintain a large peacetime standing army and navy to protect the newly annexed areas. It also found that not all

"Well, I hardly know which to take first," says Uncle Sam to "waiter" William McKinley as he views the "expansionist menu" in this cartoon from the *Boston Globe*.

WELL, I HARDLY KNOW WHICH TO TAKE FIRST!

of the peoples liberated from Spain were eager to exchange Spanish control for American control. In the Philippines in 1899, **Emilio Aguinaldo** (ay-MEE-lee-oh AH-gee-NAHL-doh), a revolutionary who had aided the United States against the Spanish, led an insurrection to overthrow the Americans and establish Philippine independence. For two years, the United States had to conduct a campaign in the islands that was costlier and far more difficult than the Spanish-American War before finally suppressing the insurrection.

The war and the resulting acquisition of distant islands that many Americans had scarcely heard of before challenged the United States' traditional foreign policy of isolation. When the 1900 presidential election came around, the Democrats, once again headed by William Jennings Bryan, tried to make the election a referendum on American imperialism, which Bryan opposed. The Republicans embraced imperialism, renominating McKinley and running "rough-riding" Roosevelt as vice president. That ticket won an electoral landslide over Bryan and the Democrats. At the dawn of the twentieth century, America—burgeoning, energetic, and continental—was moving irresistibly toward prominent leadership in the world.

Section Quiz

1. What was the most serious challenge to the Monroe Doctrine during this era?

2. What event almost ended John Hay's Open Door Policy for China?

3. What is the difference between a denominational mission board and a faith mission board?

4. What three factors hastened the United States toward war with Spain?

5. What was the central issue of the presidential election of 1900? Who were the two leading candidates, and where did they stand on this issue?

★ Contrast the political aims of imperialism and the religious aims of missions during this time.

People, Places, and Things to Remember

transcontinental railroad
Union Pacific
Central Pacific
Pikes Peak gold rush
Comstock Lode
cattle drive
cowboys
open ranges
Homestead Act
Oklahoma land rushes
Great Plains
dry farming
soddies
barbed wire
Plains Indians
Sioux
reservations
Sioux War (1876–77)
George Armstrong Custer
Sitting Bull
Crazy Horse
Custer's Last Stand
Wounded Knee Massacre
A Century of Dishonor
Dawes Act
Maximilian I
commerce raiders
Treaty of Washington
Matthew Perry
Treaty of Kanagawa
Pan-Americanism
Open Door Policy
Boxer Rebellion
imperialism
purchase of Alaska
Hawaii
Student Volunteer Movement
faith missions
yellow journalism
de Lôme letter
Maine
Spanish-American War (1898)
George Dewey
Battle of Manila Bay
Rough Riders
Battle of Santiago Bay
Emilio Aguinaldo

Chapter Review

Making Connections

1. What method of transportation was most important in the development of the American West in the nineteenth century?

2. Name at least two actions that the United States government took in the twentieth century to alleviate the plight of the American Indians.

3. What were the three major goals of American foreign policy in the last half of the nineteenth century?

4. What event indirectly caused the United States to hasten to annex Hawaii?

Developing History Skills

1. Explain the factors that caused the end of the open-range cattle industry.

2. Describe the three methods by which an imperialist nation might acquire territory, and determine which of them would be the preferred method.

Thinking Critically

1. Do you think that the Spanish-American War was justified? Why or why not?

2. In what ways are the methods of yellow journalism a common tendency of media today?

Living as a Christian Citizen

1. If you were a Christian congressman during this period of American history, what legislation would you propose to govern Indian Affairs?

2. Describe your response to imperialism as if you were a missionary in this period.

A milestone in history captured on film: Wilbur Wright watches as his brother Orville pilots their plane on its historic first flight.

The Progressive Era (1900–1920)

I.   **Progressive Movement**

II. **Progressive Politics**

III. **Progressive Society**

IV. **Progressivism Evaluated**

"The object of government is the welfare of the people."

Theodore Roosevelt,
The New Nationalism (1910)

On September 6, 1901, President William McKinley hosted a public reception at the Pan-American Exposition in Buffalo, New York. In the Exposition's Temple of Music, the president stood in a receiving line greeting the well-wishers who filed past him. McKinley smiled, shook hands, and murmured pleasantries. One tall, thin young man in the line wore what looked like a white bandage on his right hand. Kindheartedly, McKinley stretched out his left hand toward the man's unbandaged hand. The young man, however, pushed the president's outstretched hand aside, and from the "bandage" came the sharp bang of a pistol. Two shots struck the astonished president. As guards and bystanders swarmed over the assailant, the wounded president said pitifully, "Don't let them hurt him."

Doctors could not locate the bullet that was lodged in the president's body, and infection set in. Eight days later, President McKinley died. Unknown to the doctors, in the room next to McKinley was a new invention that might have located the bullet and saved his life—an x-ray machine.

Upon McKinley's death, Vice President Theodore Roosevelt took office as the nation's twenty-sixth president. The change was more than a simple switch in personnel. Two presidents of the same party could hardly have been more different. McKinley was quiet, reserved, and sedate; Roosevelt was energetic, active, and outgoing. More than that, McKinley was a political conservative, a cautious man who favored the tried-and-true Republican policy of supporting "big business" and advocating "little government." Roosevelt was a political progressive, an aggressive man who favored a vigorous, active government. With Roosevelt's presidency, Americans entered what historians call the Progressive Era of United States history.

I. Progressive Movement

Definition

Progressivism was a movement of the early twentieth century that favored achieving political and social reform through education, wider political participation, and direct government action. The progressive movement had its roots in several nineteenth-century movements. Some progressives, such as William Jennings Bryan, had been adherents of Populism. Others were outright Socialists. Still others were from the ranks of pro-reform Republican factions such as the Half-breeds and the Mugwumps. Many people in the movement were members of the middle and upper classes who were shocked by the abuses of some industrialists, by corruption in government, and by the plight of the poor.

The progressives' motives varied. Many of them were simply moral Americans whose sense of justice was outraged. They looked at the abuses and corruption around them and concluded that something had to be done. Some of the progressives, however, were evolutionary in their thinking. In their view, because man supposedly had been evolving and improving from a lower form of life to a higher form, he should continue to improve and progress. To these Reform Darwinists (see Chapter 16), progress was a process of the natural order that could be aided by government intervention. Some Christians strongly opposed the unbiblical evolutionary view of progress but still supported progressive reforms. For these believers, reform was an "opportunity . . . [to] do good unto all men" (Gal. 6:10).

Principles

The progressive movement was a broad coalition of diverse interests. Generally, the progressives favored reform through (1) promoting direct democracy, (2) increasing government efficiency, and (3) advocating government intervention.

Direct Democracy

For progressives, as historian George Tindall noted, "the cure for the ills of democracy was more democracy." Because of their general faith in the basic goodness of man, progressives believed that placing power in the hands of the people would naturally result in better government. William Jennings Bryan said that he favored "anything that makes the government more democratic, more popular in form, anything that gives the people more control over government."

Progressives tried to further the growth of democracy through several specific reforms. They favored the **secret ballot** for elections. Before this time, Americans had to indicate publicly which candidate they preferred as they voted. For example, they would have to request a certain ballot for their candidate or sign their names on a list for the candidate. Such a system allowed unscrupulous political bosses to intimidate voters who favored the "wrong" candidate. The secret ballot reduced the possibility of influencing voters and also frustrated corrupt politicians who now could never be sure whether the votes they "bought" through bribery were actually cast.

Progressives also wanted to replace the nomination of candidates by party conventions and caucuses with **direct primaries**, nominating a party's candidates by popular vote. In theory, the direct primary took power from party bosses and gave it directly to the people. Progressives also called for greater popular participation in legislation through the initiative and the referendum. **Initiative** is a process in which voters initiate legislation by presenting to their legislature petitions that require the legislators to consider some action. A **referendum** allows the people to vote yes or no in a regular election to determine whether a law should be enacted or rejected. Closely related to these two processes is **recall**, in which voters petition to hold a special election to decide whether to remove an elected official from office. Voters can also vote to recall (repeal) specific legislation or even judicial decisions. Although the national government accepted none of these innovations except the secret ballot, many state and city governments embraced them.

America's burgeoning cities, typified by this scene from Mulberry Street on New York's lower East Side, presented numerous challenges to the nation at the turn of the century.

Government Efficiency

Progressives sought to make government more efficient by putting qualified technical experts in positions of responsibility. City governments showed the greatest zeal for such improvements. Some cities abandoned rule by an elected mayor and city council and adopted the city commission form of government, which combined the duties of those offices and vested them in five city commissioners. Other cities adopted the city manager form of government, under which the city council hired a qualified city manager who served as the administrator of the city government.

Government Intervention

The progressives strongly believed that they could best achieve reform by direct government action, although they did not always agree about which action to take. For instance, progressives were united in attacking the alleged abuses and corruptions of trusts, but they differed on how to deal with the problem. Some progressives favored "**trustbusting**," breaking up the monopolies and restoring competition to the marketplace. Others favored leaving the trusts intact but regulating their operations.

For many progressives, government ownership of businesses was the answer. The most extreme progressives—the Socialists—wanted the government to take over nearly all business. (Italian dictator Benito Mussolini would impose just such a system on Italy in the 1920s, but he called his version of it fascism.) Most reformers, however, preferred only limited government ownership. The most widely accepted form of control was "**gas-and-water socialism**," city or state control of utilities such as gas and water companies. The progressives argued that a monopoly was the most efficient way to operate a utility and that the safest monopoly was one owned and operated by the government.

Progressives also promoted government intervention on behalf of labor. They favored legislation to allow labor unions to organize and to force businesses to negotiate fairly with the unions. In this way, unions could provide a check to the power of big business. They favored legislation directly helping the working man. For example, progressives on the city, state, and national levels sponsored laws establishing minimum wage levels, prohibiting child labor, limiting the number of hours in a workday, and mandating safety standards for factories.

Constitutional Progressivism

Four progressive ideas eventually found their way into the U.S. Constitution by the amendment process.

Sixteenth Amendment

The first such amendment was the federal income tax, established by the **Sixteenth Amendment** (ratified 1913). Progressives had two reasons for favoring the tax. First, income taxes would provide the government with funds to initiate reforms and provide the expanded social services that the progressives demanded. Second, the tax rate was *graduated*, that is, the more money one made, the higher percentage of his income he must pay in taxes. Thus, the income tax took money from the very wealthy (ideally the industrialists and monopolists whom the progressives opposed) and used it, theoretically, for the benefit of all Americans. In reality, the taxes ultimately hurt people of *all* classes because they raised prices, discouraged investment in production, and removed monies from other productive endeavors. As overall economic activity declined, the tax gradually reached lower to include even more people in its grip, including many of the very people who were meant to be its beneficiaries.

Progressive Logic

Progressives conceived of government intervention as an extension of the idea of direct democracy. Progressives argued that the people control the government, so government control of business is really popular control of business. Only after time passed did people realize that popular control of government was more difficult to achieve in reality than in theory and that big government could be the ultimate monopoly rather than a solution to monopoly.

Seventeenth Amendment

The second of the "progressive amendments" was the **Seventeenth Amendment** (1913), calling for the direct election of U.S. senators. Under the constitutional procedure before that time (Article I, Section 3, Clause 1), state legislatures elected U.S. senators. Progressives charged that senatorial elections had become corrupt auctions in which the wealthy bribed legislators to elect them. Direct election allegedly would end this abuse and give the decision to the voters of each state. By replacing republicanism with increased democratization, however, the amendment also eliminated one of the safeguards that the Founding Fathers had so painstakingly built into our federal system of government. Whereas the U.S. representatives spoke for the people of their districts at large, U.S. senators were supposed to speak for the state governments. Changing to direct popular vote for senators left the states with no voice in the national government; it removed an important check and balance against demagoguery and centralization of power in the federal government.

Eighteenth Amendment

The third reform was **Prohibition**, banning the manufacture, sale, or transportation of alcoholic beverages. Established by the **Eighteenth Amendment** (1919), Prohibition proved to be the most controversial progressive amendment and was eventually repealed by the Twenty-first Amendment (1933). The progressives saw the amendment as a simple means of solving major social problems. Social workers visiting the slums saw families in which drunken parents neglected or even abused their children and spent money on alcohol that would have been better spent on food and clothing. Prison reformers spoke to inmates who blamed alcohol for leading them into crime. Progressives naturally concluded that eliminating liquor would reduce crime and poverty.

The Eighteenth Amendment also demonstrates the widespread support that reform enjoyed in that period, even beyond the progressive movement. Joining the progressives on behalf of Prohibition was a large group of Christian leaders, who denounced alcohol as sinful. Perhaps the most famous of these Christian crusaders was Evangelist Billy Sunday. Although he did not show a consistent interest in progressivism, Sunday zealously championed the cause of Prohibition. In his huge citywide evangelistic campaigns he vigorously attacked the "damnable, hellish, vile, corrupt, iniquitous liquor business." Also joining the progressives on that issue were businessmen. They saw Prohibition as a means of increasing production by eliminating worker absences and accidents due to drunkenness. When America entered World War I, Americans had another reason to support Prohibition; with shortages of grains and other agricultural products caused by the war, it seemed wasteful to be using those products to manufacture alcoholic beverages.

Capital police arrest two bootleggers who have crashed their car after leading police on a chase through the streets of Washington, D.C.

Nineteenth Amendment

The fourth constitutional reform climaxed a movement much older than the progressive movement. The **Nineteenth Amendment** (1920) granted women *suffrage* (the right to vote). The drive for gaining the vote for women had begun before the War Between the States (see Chapter 11). Throughout the nineteenth century "women suffragettes" had campaigned unceasingly for the right to vote. Led by women such as Elizabeth Cady Stanton and especially **Susan B. Anthony**, the crusade for women's suffrage was part of an overall campaign for equal rights for women.

Personalities

Muckrakers

The literary leaders of progressivism were the **muckrakers**, writers who exposed abuse and corruption. Theodore Roosevelt likened them to the man in John Bunyan's *Pilgrim's Progress* who

> could look no way but downwards with a muck-rake in his hand. There stood also one over his head with a celestial crown in his hand and proffered to give him that crown for his muck-rake; but the man did neither look up, nor regard, but raked to himself the straws, the small sticks, and dust of the floor (*Pilgrim's Progress*, Part II).

The muckrakers served an important purpose in informing the public. The golden age of muckraking began in 1902 when Lincoln Steffens published in *McClure's* magazine an exposé of municipal corruption in St. Louis. His work was soon followed by Ida Tarbell's *History of the Standard Oil Company* (1904), a scathing portrait of allegedly unscrupulous and dishonest methods John D. Rockefeller used to build his oil empire. (As you learned in Chapter 16, however, Tarbell did not tell the whole story and had more than a little bias in her presentation.)

Other muckraking articles and books followed—such as attacks on insurance fraud and on impure and worthless medicines. Unlike proponents of yellow journalism, who reported sensational stories simply to boost sales, muckrakers felt genuine concern for the causes they advanced. For the most part, muckrakers did not call for any specific action; they contented themselves with describing corruption in graphic detail and trusting the revulsion of the American people to motivate reforms. In many cases, their attacks resulted in legislation addressing alleged abuses. In other instances, muckrakers had a political agenda that drove their writing. For example, Upton Sinclair was pushing for political victory for the Socialist Party and tended to write only what supported that goal. (In fact, he was instrumental in starting that party in New Jersey and ran for governor on its ticket.)

Political Progressives

Many politicians embraced the progressive movement. As mentioned earlier, William Jennings Bryan turned from Populism to progressivism and became the leader of the progressive wing of the Democratic Party. One of the major Republican leaders was **Robert La Follette** (LUH FAHL-et) of Wisconsin. As a lawyer, governor, then senator, La Follette pressed for a series of reforms (such as the direct primary and railroad regulation) that made Wisconsin, as Theodore Roosevelt called it, "the laboratory of democracy."

Teddy Bears

A fad developed during Theodore Roosevelt's presidency that shows his popularity with the American public. On a hunting trip in Mississippi, Roosevelt refused to shoot a captured bear. A reporter recounted the story, and an inspired cartoonist drew a caricature of the incident: "Drawing the Line in Mississippi."

The story caught the public fancy. Soon, toy makers were selling stuffed bears in all sorts of garbs, including one in a Rough Rider uniform. Children loved the cuddly toys.

One toy maker, Morris Michtom, wrote to Roosevelt, asking permission to market stuffed toy bears under the name "teddy bear." Roosevelt replied,

"I doubt if my name will mean much in the bear business, but you may use it if you wish." Michtom successfully marketed the teddy bears, and his business eventually became the Ideal Toy Company, a multimillion-dollar corporation today.

By all accounts, Roosevelt was rather embarrassed by the teddy bear boom, but he went along with the fad. Roosevelt had one personal reason for disliking the toy, though—he had always hated the name "Teddy."

Progressive Presidents

Three U.S. presidents governed during the Progressive Era: Theodore Roosevelt (1901–9), William Howard Taft (1909–13), and Woodrow Wilson (1913–21). Each of them reflected to some extent the progressive spirit, but **Theodore Roosevelt** was probably the president most closely associated with progressivism. A member of a moderately wealthy New York family, a Harvard graduate, and an accomplished historian, Roosevelt was in some ways the most "aristocratic" president since John Adams. Yet by living as a cowboy on his cattle ranch in the Dakotas and through his heroics with the Rough Riders in Cuba, Roosevelt shed much of his upper-class image and displayed a great appeal to the common man. As a New York state legislator, member of the U.S. Civil Service Commission, and a New York City police commissioner, Roosevelt had a reputation as a friend of reform. The stage was set for a dramatic change in American government when Roosevelt took office in 1901.

Section Quiz

1. What were the three means proposed by the progressives to further reform?

2. What is the difference between an initiative and a referendum?

3. What were the two popular forms of city government developed during the Progressive Era?

4. What was the most controversial of the four progressive amendments to the Constitution?

5. Who was the leader of the progressive wing of the Democratic Party?

★ Was Prohibition a practical solution to the ills caused by alcoholic drinks? Why or why not?

The boisterous Theodore Roosevelt in many ways personified the energetic, reformist tendencies of the Progressive Era.

II. Progressive Politics

Roosevelt and the Square Deal

Roosevelt approached the presidency as he did life—zealously. He planned to govern actively, to lead instead of follow Congress in setting the political agenda for the nation. By persuasion, intimidation, and sheer force of personality, Roosevelt shaped the policies of the government. Central to his philosophy was his belief that every man and woman should receive fair treatment and equal opportunity, a "**Square Deal**," as he put it.

Trustbusting

Early in his presidency, Roosevelt launched his attack on the abuses of the trusts by reviving the little-used Sherman Antitrust Act. In 1902, the federal government charged the Northern Securities Company with violating the act, and the government filed a lawsuit to break it up. The Northern Securities Company, which controlled the powerful Great Northern and Northern Pacific railroads, fought the suit, but the Supreme Court upheld the government. The **Northern Securities case** was a milestone in vindicating the government's authority to regulate trusts, and it encouraged Roosevelt to proceed against other monopolies. Although it is unclear how much this antitrust activity actually increased competition, it won Roosevelt widespread public acclaim as a "trustbuster."

Regulation

Roosevelt wanted to regulate the conduct of business and industry for what he viewed as the public good. He gave the most attention to railroads, the major means of transportation and shipping in the nation. Consumers often complained that the railroads, which operated as monopolies in some areas, charged excessively high rates and granted special concessions to businesses they favored. The **Hepburn Act** (1906) was Roosevelt's most important railroad-regulating legislation. This act strengthened the Interstate Commerce Commission's (ICC) ability to set rates for railroads and provided a standard bookkeeping system that made it easier to compare and regulate those rates. Most important, the act shifted the burden of proof in rate setting from the ICC to the railroads. Earlier, the ICC had to take a rail company to court to enforce its rate decisions. Under the Hepburn Act, however, the railroads had to take the ICC to court to overturn the commission's decisions. Increasingly, the railroads simply went along with the rates that the ICC set.

Roosevelt also pushed for regulation in the production of food and medicine. The **Pure Food and Drug Act** (1906) outlawed the interstate sale of impure food and drugs and required honest labeling of such products. The **Meat Inspection Act** (1906) required the Department of Agriculture to oversee the preparation and packaging of meat and to inspect the health of animals before they were slaughtered. The supervisory agencies established by those two acts have unquestionably benefited the public, and their powers have not been so extensive that they have seriously hampered private production, as some regulatory agencies have done. In fact, increased public confidence in the quality of food and drugs might actually have helped increase sales.

Growing the Executive Branch

Theodore Roosevelt, though a Republican, was a firm believer in a growing federal government, especially the executive branch. He introduced rule by presidential executive order, which bypassed the congressional legislative process in favor of presidential edict. During his seven years as president, he signed 1,007 executive orders. By contrast, McKinley, whom TR succeeded, had issued only 158. But even with that large number, TR ranks only third in the number of executive orders issued. Learning from TR's example, Woodrow Wilson would issue 1,791, and Franklin Roosevelt would issue 3,723.

A Novel Prompts Novel Regulations

Passage of the Pure Food and Drug Act and the Meat Inspection Act was aided by the public outrage resulting from the publication of *The Jungle* (1906) by muckraker Upton Sinclair. Although supposedly a work of fiction, Sinclair's book was a graphic portrayal of the filthy conditions in Chicago's meatpacking plants.

From *The Jungle*

They were regular alchemists at Durham's [a packing house]; they advertised a mushroom-catsup, and the men who made it did not know what a mushroom looked like. They advertised "potted chicken,"—and it was like the boarding-house soup of the comic papers, through which a chicken had walked with rubbers on. Perhaps they had a secret process for making chickens chemically—who knows? . . . [T]he things that went into the mixture were tripe, and the fat of pork, and beef suet, and hearts of beef, and finally the waste ends of veal, when they had any. They put these up in several grades, and sold them at several prices; but the contents of the cans all came out of the same hopper. And then there was "potted game" and "potted grouse," "potted ham," and "devilled ham"—de-vyled, as the men called it. "De-vyled" ham was made out of the waste ends of smoked beef that were too small to be sliced by the machines; and also tripe, dyed with chemicals so that it would not show white; and trimmings of hams and corned beef; and potatoes, skins and all; and finally the hard cartilaginous gullets of beef, after the tongues had been cut out. All this ingenious mixture was ground up and flavored with spices to make it taste like something. Anybody who could invent a new imitation had been sure of a fortune from old Durham, . . . but it was hard to think of anything new in a place where so many sharp wits had been at work for so long; where men welcomed tuberculosis in the cattle they were feeding, because it made them fatten more quickly; and where they bought up all the old rancid butter left over in the grocery-stores of a continent, and "oxidized" it by a forced-air process, to take away the odor, rechurned it with skim milk, and sold it in bricks in the cities! Up to a year or two ago it had been the custom to kill horses in the yards—ostensibly for fertilizer; but after long agitation the newspapers had been able to make the public realize that the horses were being canned.

Coal Strike

Roosevelt's dedication to a "square deal" for labor and business was severely tested by a coal miners' strike in 1902. Coal was the major source of fuel for steam-operated machinery, including railroad locomotives, and the major source of heat for the entire nation. As winter drew near and the public grew concerned, Roosevelt tried to break the stalemate. He arranged a meeting between the owners and the union leaders at the White House, but the owners refused even to speak to the union men assembled there. Losing his patience, Roosevelt threatened to use federal troops to operate the mines. For the first time, the threat of federal force was used against owners rather than against workers. Reluctantly, the owners consented to a 10 percent pay raise and a nine-hour day. This was the first instance of the federal government's acting as the mediator in a labor dispute, and the success of the effort increased Roosevelt's popularity among labor leaders. His threat against business, however, foreshadowed even greater future government intrusions.

Conservation

Nothing was more important to Roosevelt the rugged outdoorsman than the conservation of natural resources. The Reclamation Act, passed in 1902, set aside nearly 100 million acres of western land to be controlled by the federal government. This was in addition to the millions of acres already set aside for national forests. During his last year in office, Roosevelt established the National Conservation Commission, headed by Gifford Pinchot (PIN shoh), chief of the U.S. Forest Service. The commission was assigned the task of reporting water, timber, soil, land, and mineral resources.

Coal Strike of 1902

How was Roosevelt's threat to use troops to keep the mines running an action against the owners? Wouldn't the owners want the mines kept running? At the time of the strike, there was a surplus of coal, so the price of coal was quite low. As the strike hindered production, the price of coal rose, so the owners were content to let the strike continue. Using troops to keep the mines running would have stopped the increase in the price of coal.

The National Parks President

Colorado's Mesa Verde National Park and Oregon's Crater Lake National Park are two of the five national parks established during Roosevelt's presidency. The others are Wind Cave, South Dakota; Sully's Hill, North Dakota; and Platt National Park in Oklahoma.

Discrimination and Injustice

One of the great failures of progressivism was worsening discrimination. In California, resentment of the growing Asian population resulted in discrimination and even violence. In 1906, the San Francisco school board touched off an international incident when it tried to segregate all Asian students into a separate public school. When the Japanese government strongly protested this treatment, Roosevelt pressured the school board to reverse its decision in return for voluntary Japanese restrictions on immigration.

The situation for black people in the South (where the overwhelming majority of American blacks lived before World War I) worsened during the Progressive Era. Roosevelt stirred up controversy by inviting black educator Booker T. Washington to dine with him at the White House, but progressives on the whole did little to alleviate growing discrimination. Until the 1890s there was some hope for improvement in racial relations in the South. The Redeemer governments that ruled the South after Reconstruction (see Chapter 15) generally tried to keep their promises to protect black civil rights—if for no other reason than to lure black votes into the Democratic column. Blacks even held elective or appointive office under the Redeemer governments. For example, in every session of Congress from 1869 to 1901 except one, there was at least one black member of the House of Representatives.

This situation began to change in the 1890s as states began passing "Jim Crow laws," legislation requiring the forced segregation, or separation, of the races in trains, restaurants, hotels, schools, and other social settings. ("Jim Crow" was a black character in a nineteenth-century minstrel song.) In fact, segregation was so extensive that whites and blacks even had separate restrooms and drinking fountains. In addition, governments began to deprive blacks of their right to vote by setting up literacy tests for voting (to which whites were often exempt) or requiring special poll taxes which one had to pay before voting. The number of registered black voters in Louisiana, for example, plummeted from over 130,000 in 1896 to slightly more than 1,300 in 1904.

There were several reasons for this change. First, the Redeemer politicians were gradually losing ground to overtly racist politicians who played on the fears and prejudices of white voters to rally support to their cause. Second, the alliance of blacks with some reform groups such as the Populists caused many conservative Democrats to disfranchise blacks to dilute Populist political power. Third, the national government and the northern public in general lost interest in the cause of civil rights for blacks. Segregation was strengthened when the Supreme Court issued a series of decisions that gutted the enforcement of the Reconstruction civil rights legislation. Perhaps the most famous of these cases was *Plessy v. Ferguson*, a case which decreed that "separate but equal" facilities for blacks and whites (in this case, on trains) were constitutional. These decisions gave state legislatures the legal justification they needed to pass whole "Jim Crow" law codes.

Blacks reacted to increased discrimination in differing ways. One approach was represented by the outstanding black leader of the era, Booker T. Washington. As described in his famous autobiography, *Up from Slavery*, Washington had risen from slavery to the presidency of Tuskegee Institute in Alabama, the nation's leading black industrial school. Washington was basically conservative;

in a famous speech given in Atlanta in 1895, he urged blacks not to risk strife by agitating politically for their rights. Instead, they should concentrate on bettering themselves economically through vocational education and the establishment of black businesses and trades. As blacks became more powerful economically, Washington argued, whites would be forced to accept them and grant them political equality.

Opposing Washington was a group of black intellectuals led by W.E.B. Du Bois. They argued that blacks could not truly improve themselves economically until they enjoyed equal participation in the political process as American citizens. They opposed Washington's exclusive stress on technical and industrial education over liberal arts, fearing that it would force all blacks into an economically inferior laboring class and discourage higher education among blacks. Where Washington sought an economic solution to the problem, Du Bois pursued a political solution. In 1909 Du Bois and other like-minded leaders—black and white—formed the **National Association for the Advancement of Colored People** (**NAACP**) to fight legal battles on behalf of blacks. During Washington's lifetime, his views dominated relations between black and white people; afterward, however, because many white people refused to recognize the equality of black people, the NAACP's approach gained strength and became the basis of the black civil rights movement of the 1950s and 1960s.

Roosevelt and the "Big Stick"

Theodore Roosevelt's favorite saying was "Speak softly and carry a big stick; you will go far." Just as the phrase "square deal" describes Roosevelt's domestic policy, so the "big stick" describes his foreign policy. His foreign policy was vigorous and expansive and involved the United States more actively in international affairs. His foreign policy was still in line with his reformist impulses; he considered the expansion of a "civilized power" such as the United States into world affairs to be "a victory for law, order and righteousness."

Philippines

One major problem that Roosevelt inherited from McKinley was the situation in the Philippines. Even after the surrender of Emilio Aguinaldo and the end of the insurrection, the Filipinos were not content with American rule; they wanted independence. Roosevelt approached the Philippine problem warily. The governor of the islands, his friend and adviser William Howard Taft, tried to win the affection of the Filipinos. American leaders desired to maintain a foothold in the Pacific and feared that if the islands were granted independence too quickly, they might fall prey to another major power, such as Japan. Therefore, over a period of thirty years, the United States gradually gave the Filipinos increasing amounts of self-rule. After their liberation from Japanese occupation during World War II, the Philippines received their complete independence in 1946.

Theodore Roosevelt stands tall as the Western Hemisphere's "policeman" in this 1905 cartoon. His corollary to the Monroe Doctrine dramatically increased American involvement abroad.

THE WORLD CONSTABLE.

Panama Canal

One of Roosevelt's favorite projects was the building of an American-controlled canal in Central America to link the Atlantic and the Pacific. Members of Congress, however, disagreed about the best route. Some of them favored a route through Nicaragua; others favored a route through Panama (at the time a part of Colombia), where in the 1880s a French company had gone bankrupt trying to dig a canal. The French company, needing the money from the sale of their rights of construction, sent a representative, Philippe Bunau-Varilla (fih-LEEP BOO-noh vuh-REE-yuh), to negotiate with the United States. In 1902, Congress passed an act authorizing purchase of the French rights for $40 million, and in 1903 the Senate passed a treaty with Colombia agreeing to purchase perpetual control of the Canal Zone for $10 million initially, with annual payments of $250,000 thereafter. However, the Colombian senate, hoping to get more money, rejected the treaty.

Infuriated by their action, Roosevelt denounced the Colombians as "foolish and homicidal corruptionists" who were attempting to blackmail the United States. Bunau-Varilla, who was still trying to promote the sale of his company's rights, quickly pointed out to the president that a revolution in Panama was imminent; many Panamanians resented the Colombian government and wanted to break away. Officers of the French company, led by Bunau-Varilla, helped finance and organize the revolt. Roosevelt, for his part, ordered the U.S. Navy to prevent Colombian troops from landing in Panama to crush the rebellion.

Mainly because of that American support, Panama's revolt succeeded on November 3, 1903. Three days later, President Roosevelt recognized Panama's independence, and the Panamanians then appointed Bunau-Varilla as their minister to the United States. He and Secretary of State John Hay signed an agreement on November 18 promising Panama the same payment for the canal that the United States had offered to Colombia.

Construction of the **Panama Canal** took approximately ten years. As many as forty thousand Americans were employed on the project at one time, despite the many hazards. The canal cost about $400 million, but its financial benefits to world shipping outweighed the cost. In August 1914—just days after World War I had broken out in Europe—the canal opened and linked ocean to ocean.

Roosevelt Corollary

Roosevelt's actions in Panama represented his general approach to affairs in Latin America. He envisioned the United States as the leader in the Western Hemisphere, protecting the region and regulating its behavior. Complicating Roosevelt's position was the sometimes irresponsible conduct of some Latin American nations. In 1902, Venezuela ran afoul of Great Britain and Germany when it proved unable to repay loans from those nations. Likewise, a bloody revolution in the Dominican Republic in 1904 worried the European powers that had sizable investments in that nation. Fearing European intervention in the hemisphere, Roosevelt devised an addition to the Monroe Doctrine that became known as the **Roosevelt Corollary**.

To the Monroe Doctrine's assertion that Europe could not intervene in the Americas, Roosevelt's corollary added that the United States would act as a "policeman" to keep Latin American nations in line. Roosevelt's new doctrine placed the United States in

Questionable Means

The circumstances under which the United States acquired the Canal Zone were at least questionable, although the canal clearly benefited most of the nations of the Western Hemisphere. Colombia was understandably resentful, and other Latin American countries expressed their fear of the United States—the "Colossus of the North," as they put it. Some congressmen raised ethical objections, but Roosevelt characteristically commented, "I took the Canal Zone and let Congress debate; and while the debate goes on the Canal does also."

The Roosevelt Corollary

The president told Congress in 1904, "Chronic wrongdoing . . . may in America, as elsewhere, ultimately require intervention by some civilized nation, and in the Western Hemisphere the adherence of the United States to the Monroe Doctrine may force the United States, however reluctantly, in flagrant cases of such wrongdoing or impotence, to the exercise of an international police power."

a position of constantly intervening to prevent European nations from intervening. During the next decade, the United States intervened in Haiti, Honduras, Nicaragua, and the Dominican Republic in attempts to collect debts or maintain order. As a result, European and Latin American resentment toward the United States intensified.

Relations with Japan

American trade with China and its possessions in the Pacific, such as the Philippines and Guam, brought the United States into closer contact with Japan. Throughout the Roosevelt years, relations with the proud and increasingly powerful Japanese were a sensitive issue.

The Japanese were understandably offended at the discriminatory legislation directed at Asians on the West Coast of the United States. Roosevelt finally negotiated what he called the "Gentleman's Agreement" with the Japanese government. Japan agreed to refuse passports to Japanese laborers leaving for the United States; Roosevelt forbade immigration of Japanese traveling by way of other nations. In return for these concessions, Roosevelt was able to win better treatment for Asians in California. The agreement slowed Japanese immigration, and tensions eased.

Great White Fleet

Japanese-American relations also sparked the climax of Roosevelt's foreign policy, a grand display of American naval power. In December 1907, sixteen battleships, referred to as the "Great White Fleet," steamed from Virginia, heading around South America, into the Pacific, and on to Japan. Roosevelt's goal was to impress the Japanese with American strength. Instead of being intimidated or provoked, however, the Japanese welcomed the fleet enthusiastically, and American relations with Japan temporarily improved. In 1908, partly because of that "battleship diplomacy," the two countries signed the **Root-Takahira** (TAH kah HEE rah) **Agreement**, in which both powers pledged to respect each other's territorial claims in the Pacific and to maintain the "open door" for trade in China. The fleet itself imitated Magellan by sailing around the world, symbolizing American power wherever it went.

Roosevelt's foreign policy was not without its critics. Americans were still essentially isolationists, whereas Roosevelt was clearly an internationalist. One of Roosevelt's most vocal critics was William Jennings Bryan. But Roosevelt succeeded in convincing Congress that the nation had to be more involved internationally because of strategic concerns; it needed to expand the market for its exports. Roosevelt set the nation on the road to growing international involvement.

Taft and the Presidency

Roosevelt refused to run for a third term, but he handpicked his successor, **William Howard Taft**. Taft was a huge man (more than three hundred pounds) whose pleasant nature made him almost instantly likable and whose physique gratified political cartoonists. Taft had enjoyed a distinguished public career mostly in appointed positions such as governor of the Philippines and secretary of war. With Roosevelt's support, Taft easily captured the Republican nomination and then comfortably defeated William Jennings Bryan in the 1908 presidential election.

Roosevelt, Nobel Peace Prize Winner

In February 1904, war broke out between Japan and Russia over conflicts of interest in Manchuria (a province of China). The Japanese won a series of quick naval and land victories that worried the other great powers, who feared growing Japanese might in the Pacific. The war, however, strained the finances of both nations, and they invited Roosevelt to mediate. In 1905, at a conference in Portsmouth, New Hampshire, Roosevelt negotiated a settlement that preserved most of Japan's gains but allowed Russia to escape with some of its honor intact. Roosevelt later received the Nobel Peace Prize for his services. Unfortunately, both Russia and Japan were unhappy with the compromises embodied in the **Treaty of Portsmouth** (1905), and American relations with both nations soon cooled.

Loves Me, Loves Me Not

Taft was sympathetic to reform, but he was far more reserved and cautious than Roosevelt. His subdued manner, orderly mind, and legal background actually suited him better for a judicial career than a political one. (He eventually did serve as chief justice of the Supreme Court.) Despite his reformist intentions, Taft's instinctive caution led him into conflict with the progressives of his own party and eventually to a split between him and his former friend, Roosevelt.

Tariff Fiasco

Taft's first effort at reform was a failure. Taft wanted to lower tariff rates—a controversial issue that Roosevelt had not dared to broach during his two terms. The House drafted a bill lowering the tariff moderately, but by the time the Senate was finished with the bill, rates remained virtually unchanged. Progressives urged Taft to veto the bill, but the president accepted it as the best he could get. When Taft tried to defend the new tariff as "on the whole . . . the best [tariff] bill that the Republican party ever passed," progressives became even more dismayed.

Congressional Reform

Many members of the House of Representatives resented the dictatorial powers of the Speaker of the House, **Joseph** ("Czar") **Cannon**. As Speaker, Cannon assigned the members to the various House committees and selected the chairman for each. Furthermore, Cannon himself was chairman of the powerful Rules Committee, which controls when and how bills are debated. In 1910, a coalition of Democrats and Republican "insurgents" joined forces to reduce Cannon's power. They voted to increase the membership of the Rules Committee from five to fifteen members, to remove the Speaker as a member of the committee, and to elect members of the committee by the House. In addition, the insurgents stripped Cannon of his power to appoint members to other committees. Taft, however, did not share in the glory of this reform. Although he had originally supported trimming Cannon's power, Taft relented when other Republican leaders warned him against antagonizing the powerful Speaker. As a result, the progressives thought that Taft had abandoned them, and another wedge was driven between the president and the progressives.

Taft's support of Speaker of the House Joe "Czar" Cannon (second from left) against the wishes of reform-minded representatives in Congress drove a wedge between the president and the progressives.

Split with Roosevelt

Roosevelt, after helping Taft reach the presidency, left in 1909 for an African hunting trip and a tour of Europe. Even overseas, Roosevelt heard complaints about Taft from progressives. One issue that divided the two men was conservation. In reality, Taft was just as concerned with conservation as Roosevelt, and in his four years in office Taft withdrew more public lands to government control than Roosevelt had done in nearly eight years. Taft, however, disliked the way Roosevelt had stretched the law in reserving some lands; the new president preferred to withdraw lands only when the law was clearly and unquestionably on his side. As a result, Taft clashed with the head of the U.S. Forest Service, Gifford Pinchot, who was worried about the future of some of the public lands that Taft was returning to private use. Eventually, Pinchot so publicized his conflicts with the president that Taft dismissed him. This act, combined with Pinchot's denunciations, cast public suspicion on Taft's devotion to conservation. Furthermore, because Pinchot was also a close friend of Roosevelt's, the dismissal chilled the relationship between Taft and Roosevelt.

The final break between Roosevelt and Taft came over antitrust proceedings. Taft had an impressive record in antitrust actions and initiated more antitrust suits in one term than Roosevelt had in two. But one suit in particular upset Roosevelt. In 1907, during

Justice or Law?

The difference in temperament between Roosevelt and Taft has been described as a difference between pursuing justice and preserving law. Roosevelt, in his zealous pursuit of what he considered just causes, extended his presidential powers to their limits and used the widest possible application of existing laws. He favored an active executive branch that used whatever means it could find to achieve just ends.

Taft, with his love for law and order, sought to achieve reform in a restrained, legal manner. He favored an active legislative branch that passed unambiguous laws to accomplish change and remedy injustice.

Roosevelt's second term, U.S. Steel had wanted to purchase the Tennessee Coal and Iron Company, claiming that doing so would help prop up a shaky brokerage house during a financial panic. The businessmen involved in the deal asked whether the government considered such a purchase too monopolistic. Roosevelt agreed that the move seemed necessary and gave his unofficial blessing to the purchase. The Taft administration, however, viewed the transaction as a step in building an illegal monopoly and filed suit against U.S. Steel. Since the charges included the suggestion that Roosevelt had allowed himself to be duped by the corporation, the former president was angry and offended. A formal split was developing, not only between Taft and Roosevelt but also between the conservatives and the progressives within the Republican Party.

Dollar Diplomacy

Taft also adopted a less confrontational foreign policy than the displays of military might that Roosevelt favored. Taft preferred to influence foreign affairs through the investment of American dollars in foreign countries, a policy that was soon nicknamed "**dollar diplomacy**." Concerned by Japan's efforts at expansion in China, he encouraged American companies to build railroads in China and establish themselves as competitors there. Taft also backed similar efforts in Latin America, particularly in Nicaragua. Most businesses, however, feared investing in areas of the world where trouble was brewing. Only as the U.S. government put pressure on American investors did they risk money on such projects.

Election of 1912

Roosevelt finally concluded that Taft was not wholly committed to the progressive cause. Therefore, he "threw his hat into the ring"

Results of Dollar Diplomacy

The results of dollar diplomacy were mixed. It was mildly successful in increasing trade and industry in Latin America, where foreign leaders realized that the United States might intervene militarily to protect American investments. It was less successful in regions such as China where interference was likely to bring little more than formal protests from the United States. Taft's dollar diplomacy was a well-intentioned plan to bring mutual economic benefit and to build better foreign relations between the United States and foreign nations. Its general failure disappointed both Taft and the public and contributed to the perception that Taft was an ineffective president.

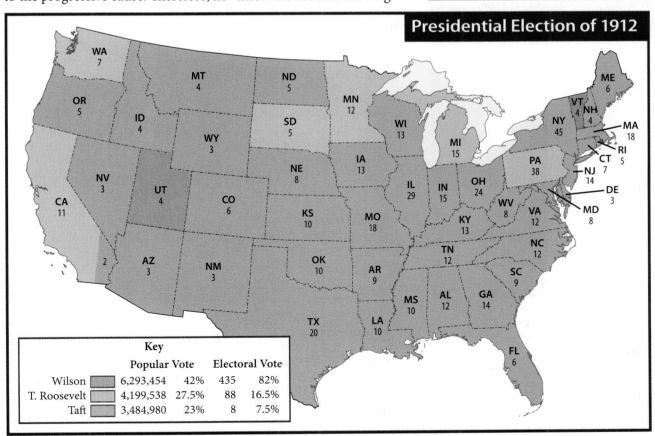

Presidential Election of 1912

Key	Popular Vote		Electoral Vote	
Wilson	6,293,454	42%	435	82%
T. Roosevelt	4,199,538	27.5%	88	16.5%
Taft	3,484,980	23%	8	7.5%

(announced his candidacy) for the Republican nomination in 1912. He was still popular with the voters and won nine of the twelve state primaries that chose delegates for the Republican convention. However, Taft, as the incumbent president, held solid control of the nonprimary states, and he won the hard-fought campaign for the nomination.

Roosevelt declared that Taft had not only betrayed progressivism but also stolen the nomination. He and his followers formed a third party, the **Progressive Party** (popularly known as the Bull Moose Party because Roosevelt had told a reporter that he felt "as strong as a bull moose"). Roosevelt ran on a platform that he called the "**New Nationalism**."

The Democrats also nominated a progressive candidate, Governor **Woodrow Wilson** of New Jersey. As a historian, professor, and president of Princeton University, Wilson had both studied deeply and written intelligently about the American system of government. Elected governor of New Jersey in 1910, Wilson proved to be a zealous progressive. He initiated reforms such as the direct primary, state regulation of utilities, and legislation designed to drive monopolies out of the state. Wilson campaigned under the motto "**New Freedom**." His platform sounded much like the progressive principles of Roosevelt's earlier years in the presidency. For example, Wilson called for increased competition through trustbusting rather than the greater regulation for which Roosevelt was campaigning.

In the election, Roosevelt and the Progressives made the best third-party showing in presidential history. Roosevelt won 4.1 million votes to 3.5 million for Taft, and he won 88 electoral votes to Taft's 8. With the Republicans divided, however, Wilson won 6.3 million votes (43 percent of the total) and 435 electoral votes. Wilson swept into office, and the Democrats captured both houses of Congress. For the first time in nearly twenty years, the Democrats controlled both Congress and the White House.

Wilson and the New Freedom

Most Americans today associate Woodrow Wilson with World War I and the complicated foreign affairs involved in that conflict (discussed in the next chapter). But Wilson's first term was the climax of the progressive movement in America. For example, three of the four "progressive amendments" to the Constitution (17–19) were ratified during Wilson's time in office. His presidency represented the crowning achievements of the Progressive Era.

Revenue Revision

One of the first important reforms of the Wilson administration was the **Underwood Tariff Act** of 1913. Unlike Roosevelt and Taft, Wilson succeeded in achieving the first genuine tariff reform since the Civil War. The new tariff slashed overall rates by about a third from what they had been. Even more important, the act made up for the loss of tariff revenue by adopting the first income tax under the recently ratified Sixteenth Amendment.

Federal Reserve Act

In 1907, the latest in a series of financial panics left American businessmen desiring a better system of regulating currency and banking practices. These businessmen envisioned something similar to the Bank of the United States that Andrew Jackson had destroyed.

The Bull Moose Platform

The Progressive Party called for strong federal regulation of business (instead of breaking up monopolies as Roosevelt had previously favored), a federal securities commission to supervise the sale of stocks and bonds, revision of the tariff, direct primary elections for nomination of candidates, easier amendment of the Constitution, and numerous social reforms, including women's suffrage and labor reforms.

President Woodrow Wilson

The First Income Tax

The first income tax was 1 percent of all annual income over $3,000 ($4,000 for married couples), gradually rising to 6 percent of all income over $500,000. Since the average American income at the time was much less than $3,000, one writer joked, "It will be an exclusive circle, this income-tax class—one which the ordinary . . . man cannot hope to attain." The act nonetheless marked a significant change in American tax policies.

They argued that such a centralized, privately owned national bank could easily set standards for banks and regulate the flow of currency throughout the country. The nation's business interests, therefore, presented this request to the leaders in Washington.

Wilson and the progressives in Congress, however, developed a different system in the **Federal Reserve Act** (1913). This legislation divided the nation into twelve banking districts, each served by a private regional Federal Reserve Bank. Over these district banks was a central, government-run organization, the Federal Reserve Board.

This system represented a compromise between a totally private banking system (as businessmen wanted) and a totally state-controlled system (as many progressives wanted). The Federal Reserve Board, however, represented ultimate government control, if not actual government ownership. In addition to banking regulation, the act created a new currency, the Federal Reserve Note. These bills, issued by the various Federal Reserve Banks, eventually became the main currency of the United States. Today American currency consists of Federal Reserve Notes.

Business and Labor

Wilson's administration passed two important pieces of legislation in 1914 concerning the regulation of business and labor. The **Clayton Antitrust Act** strengthened the Sherman Antitrust Act by expanding the list of practices prohibited to corporations. It also exempted labor unions from antitrust legislation and legalized practices such as strikes, picketing, and boycotts.

Even more sweeping in its effects was the **Federal Trade Commission Act**. That act established the Federal Trade Commission (FTC), a board of five men authorized to help define and halt unfair business practices. The FTC Act marked a growing tendency for government regulation of business practices. Increasingly, the determining of unfair practices, the establishment of regulations, and the enforcement of policies were being left to regulatory agencies such as the FTC instead of to Congress or the courts. This legislation well represented the progressive tendency to view government as the solution to society's problems.

> ### Labor's "Magna Carta"?
> Samuel Gompers, head of the American Federation of Labor, called the Clayton Antitrust Act labor's "Magna Carta." His label was a bit premature, however, because later court rulings weakened or eliminated some of the act's prolabor provisions.

Section Quiz

1. What piece of muckraking literature spurred the passage of the Pure Food and Drug Act and the Meat Inspection Act? Who wrote the work?

2. Why did some Americans fear giving the Philippines their independence too quickly?

3. Why did Colombia reject the canal treaty with the United States in 1903? How did the United States acquire the canal?

4. What method of raising revenue did the Underwood Tariff use in place of reduced tariff rates?

5. What two major pieces of legislation concerning business and labor were passed during Wilson's first term?

★ What effect do third-party candidates typically have on presidential elections? What effect did they have on the election of 1912?

III. Progressive Society

Important changes in other aspects of American life paralleled the dramatic changes in American politics during the Progressive Era. Just as politicians pushed for what they considered inevitable progress, so leaders in other areas called for progress and improvement in their fields—socially, economically, philosophically, and religiously. In some areas, particularly technical fields such as transportation and agriculture, the advances were genuine and remarkable. In education and religion, however, "progressive" proved to be regressive as far as the standards of God's Word are concerned.

Henry Ford, who was once one of Thomas Edison's employees, talks with the genius inventor, who was nearly deaf.

How to Make a Car

"The way to make automobiles," said Ford, "is to make one automobile like another automobile, to make them all alike, to make them come through the factory just alike."

Transportation Transformation

The development of two inventions in the Progressive Era—the automobile and the airplane—transformed American transportation in the twentieth century. They brought greater speed, power, flexibility, and dependability to transportation. The automobile in particular gave the average American a new mobility. Distances that would have daunted an early American pioneer became mere inconveniences in the increasingly hurried life of twentieth-century America.

Automobiles

In 1896, **Henry Ford**, an engineer for the Edison Illuminating Company in Detroit, unveiled in his garage an invention he had been tinkering with in his spare time—a motorized "horseless carriage." Ford did not invent the automobile; other inventors in America and Europe were experimenting with motorcars at the time, and nothing distinguished Ford's car from the others. His vehicle, with its tiny two-cylinder engine, seemed little more than a novelty. However, Ford's grit, determination, and hard work—as well as generous financial support from several backers—enabled him to found the Ford Motor Company in 1903.

In 1908, Ford produced the Model T, a plain but remarkably sturdy car. Although the Model T was well designed, Ford's genius

"Tin Lizzies" ready for the road. Ford's assembly-line process revolutionized American manufacturing and transportation.

lay more in the manufacture of his vehicle than in the car itself. Drawing on the ideas of several other manufacturers, Ford perfected the **assembly line** method of production. Each car moved by stages along the assembly line, where at each stop a worker specializing in one task would attach his part or perform his process. By using standardized, interchangeable parts and the assembly line, Ford achieved a high degree of efficiency and speed in auto manufacturing. When he added the mass production of thousands of identical cars to the increased efficiency, Ford was able to lower costs and make the Model T affordable for nearly everyone. The price of a new Model T dropped steadily from more than $800 when it first came out to $360 by 1916 and to $260 by 1925. By the 1920s, more than half the cars on America's roads were Fords.

Airplanes

Like the development of the automobile, the development of the airplane was the work of little-known, independent, Midwestern inventors. The **Wright brothers**—Orville and Wilbur—were not the only men of the era attempting to fly, but they were the first to succeed. The Wrights had first become interested in flight as boys when their father gave them a toy helicopter powered by rubber bands. Interest in flying, however, was only one aspect of the Wright brothers' mechanical and inventive interests. As young men in Dayton, Ohio, they began a weekly newspaper printed on a press that they had built themselves. Later, the popularity of bicycling led them to open a bicycle sales and repair shop that eventually became a successful bicycle-manufacturing firm.

The profits of their bicycle company enabled the Wrights to pursue their dream of flight. They read all the literature on flying they could lay their hands on, and they experimented with home-built kites and gliders. Needing more room for their work, they set up an experimental proving ground on the treeless, windswept dunes of Kitty Hawk, North Carolina. On December 17, 1903, after years of tiring work, Orville climbed into their flying machine, the *Flyer*. In the damp chill of the morning, the *Flyer* rolled smoothly down its track and rose into the air. The 12-second, 120-foot trip was the first powered, sustained, and controlled flight in history. From this humble beginning at Kitty Hawk, the airplane developed quickly into a faster means of shipping and transportation and a decisive military weapon.

Wilbur and Orville Wright

Agriculture

The era from 1898 to 1914 is often called the "golden age" of American agriculture because the profits of American farmers skyrocketed after years of depressed prices. At least two reasons for this growth stand out. First, America's population was shifting heavily from farms to the cities. This change left increasingly fewer farmers raising food for increasingly larger cities. Farmers were able to sell as much food as they could grow, and the demand naturally drove prices up, giving farmers heftier profits for their goods. Second, technology improved. Probably the most important technical advance was the development of the tractor, which provided more power and speed in sowing, cultivating, and harvesting crops. The greater speed, in turn, allowed farmers to sow and raise even more crops. Improvements in veterinary science also reduced the number of livestock that died from disease; improvements in transportation

George Washington Carver

A leader in Southern agriculture during and after the Progressive Era was **George Washington Carver**, a professor at Booker T. Washington's Tuskegee Institute. Born a slave in Missouri around 1861, he never knew his parents. His father died when George was only two months old. Guerrillas kidnapped George, his mother, and his sister during the war. George's master, Moses Carver, located George and got him back by trading the kidnappers a horse, but he never found George's mother or sister. The Carvers, devout Presbyterians, reared George in a Christian home.

Carver had an insatiable curiosity about nature with particular interest in plants. He taught himself so much about plants and soils that neighbors nicknamed him "the plant doctor." Carver wanted more than anything to get an education. Eventually, he traveled around Missouri, Kansas, and Iowa attending various schools and supporting himself by working as a cook, launderer, and common laborer. In each school, Carver stayed as long as he could learn anything from the often poorly educated teachers and then moved on.

When in his mid-twenties, Carver decided to go to college. One college quickly accepted him—but just as quickly rejected him because he was black. But Carver persevered and was able to attend and graduate from Iowa's State Agricultural College in 1894. He received his master's degree there in 1896.

Booker T. Washington offered him a teaching position at Tuskegee Institute. When Carver got there in 1896, the school had little more than its land and a few ramshackle buildings. Carver stocked his laboratory by rifling through junk piles. He cut down milk bottles to make beakers, made mortars from old coffee cups, and used fruit jars to hold chemicals. To that odd assortment of equipment, he added his own natural genius for research and experimentation.

Cotton growing had depleted the soil of the South. Carver found that certain plants—particularly peanuts—replenished the nitrogen that cotton removed from the soil. Farmers complained, however, that although peanuts might help the soil, they brought little profit to the growers. So Carver set to work to find uses for peanuts to increase their value.

After much experimentation, he developed more than two hundred uses for the peanut, including dyes, a milk substitute, ice cream, livestock feed, fertilizer, and flour.

Carver's gentle spirit disarmed those who met him. Although he sometimes faced racial discrimination, Carver never lashed back at his tormentors. "No man can drag me down so low as to make me hate him," he said. He refused all offers for more prestigious, better-paying jobs. In fact, he refused even to take any raises from Tuskegee. His salary always remained what it had been when he came in 1896—$29 a week. Carver cared only that he could use his knowledge to help others.

Carver also gave his students valuable advice for life.

- "Education is the key to unlock the golden door of freedom."
- "How far you go in life depends on your being tender with the young, compassionate with the aged, sympathetic with the striving, and tolerant of the weak and strong. Because someday in your life you will have been all of these."
- "I love to think of nature as an unlimited broadcasting station, through which God speaks to us every hour, if we will only tune in."
- "Learn to do common things uncommonly well. . . . When you can do the common things in life in an uncommon way, you will command the attention of the world."
- "Ninety-nine percent of the failures come from people who have the habit of making excuses."

made it easier and cheaper to get produce to market. Farmers of the time saw little reason to question the progressives' claim that life for Americans was getting steadily better.

Medicine

Tremendous advances in medicine also occurred in the Progressive Era. Part of these changes involved improvements in medical organization and education. The Mayo Clinic, founded in Rochester,

Minnesota, in 1901, developed the concept of private group medicine (that is, creating a center for medical research and practice that brings together several doctors). That plurality of doctors allowed each physician to contribute to the practice his strengths in medical knowledge and skill, thus providing better treatment for patients. Likewise, the founding of Johns Hopkins Medical School in Baltimore in 1893 created, as one educator described it, "a small but ideal medical school, embodying . . . the best features of medical education in England, France, and Germany."

The medical advance that really captured public attention, however, was the battle against **yellow fever**. The war in Cuba and failed French attempts to build a canal in Panama made Americans aware of the deadliness of this tropical disease. Building on the research of Cuban Carlos Juan Finlay, a commission of army doctors led by Walter Reed proved that mosquitoes transmitted the disease. On the recommendation of Reed's commission, William C. Gorgas, chief sanitary officer of Havana, launched a campaign to destroy the nesting grounds of mosquitoes, and he virtually eliminated yellow fever from the city. In 1904, Gorgas became chief sanitary officer of the Panama Canal project. He improved sanitary conditions in Panama by draining swamps, pouring oil on standing water where mosquitoes bred, and clearing away vermin-infested underbrush. By the time the canal was completed, Gorgas had reduced malaria and yellow fever deaths from about forty per one thousand workers to about seven per one thousand.

Education

What is commonly called **progressive education** actually had its greatest impact in America from the 1920s to the early 1950s. The philosophy of the movement, however, is rooted firmly in the overall progressive movement. In general, progressive educators aimed at improving education by relating learning to the child's interests.

Progressive educators emphasized that they were teaching *students*, not *subjects*. Education, they said, should be based on experience rather than on simple memorization; therefore, activities such as laboratory experiments and field trips became part of the educational process. Progressive educators deemphasized traditional academic subjects, such as history, and emphasized vocational education, which seemed more relevant to the student's needs.

Progressive educators rightly sought to make education interesting and to link understanding to learning. (This is not to say that many traditional educators did *not* want to make learning interesting or that they did *not* emphasize understanding.) The philosophy behind progressive methodology, however, was problematic. **John Dewey**, a professor at Columbia University and the University of Chicago, was the leading representative of progressive education and a major leader in the twentieth-century movement known as **secular humanism**. That philosophy denies the existence of God and affirms the goodness and perfectibility of man.

Ironically, public discontent over progressive education was based on the progressives' own results-oriented standard. Much of the criticism that arose in the 1950s resulted from the realization that progressive education had done a poor job of educating America's children.

Medical Pioneer

Johns Hopkins pioneered the modern medical school in which advanced medical research, laboratory experience, and actual hospital work were essential parts of a physician's education.

Doctors William Mayo (left) and Charles Mayo (right) founded the Mayo Clinic.

Child-Centered Education

Leading progressive educator John Dewey wrote, "The child becomes the sun about which the appliances of education revolve."

Secular Humanism in a Nutshell

Secular humanism replaces absolute standards of truth and morality with relative, pragmatic standards based on human experience (i.e., "whatever works is right"). Obviously, the Christian must reject such a system.

Religion

"Progressive" Religion

Two closely allied religious movements make up what one could call the religious wing of progressivism. One was a theological movement known as **modernism**. Modernism applied Darwinian evolution to Christianity and ended up with a system of belief that was completely anti-Christian. For instance, modernists rejected the idea that Moses wrote the first five books of the Old Testament (Genesis through Deuteronomy). Instead, they contended, the Israelites preserved a series of stories, legends, and myths. The priests and royal scribes, the modernists said, gradually shaped those tales into the biblical books that we know today, an evolutionary process that was completed after the Babylonian captivity of Israel (c. 450 BC). Likewise, modernists did not view Christian doctrine as an expression of God's revealed Word but as the result of an evolution of ideas within the Christian church. Modernists, therefore, denied biblical teachings such as the deity of Christ, His virgin birth, atonement for sin through His blood, and the inspiration of the Bible. Modernists first gained a foothold in American colleges and seminaries and soon began to spread their teachings to American pulpits through graduates who became pastors.

The second progressive religious movement was the **social gospel** movement. Whereas modernism applied the evolutionary aspect of progressivism to religion, the social gospel applied its social reform ethic to religion. The social gospel replaced regeneration of individuals with "regeneration" of society through social reform. Although some of those reforms were worthwhile, advocates of the social gospel joined with the modernists in rejecting the teachings of orthodox Christianity. To proponents of the social gospel, social salvation was the only salvation.

The leader of the social gospel movement was **Walter Rauschenbusch** (ROU shun boosh), a New York Baptist minister and seminary professor. In 1907, he wrote *Christianity and the Social Crisis*, expounding the goals of the social gospel. Rauschenbusch denied that man has a depraved nature as the Bible teaches and believed instead that man's environment corrupts him. Improving a man's environment, therefore, would allow his natural, inherent goodness to develop. Reformers such as Rauschenbusch were sometimes justified in accusing orthodox Protestants of lacking concern for the poor, and they were also correct in saying that Christ was always touched with compassion when He saw hunger, poverty, and suffering. They were wrong, however, when they made Jesus merely a social reformer and lost sight of His more important work in the souls of men. Social reform can never suffice when man's basic need of salvation from his sin is not met.

Orthodox Defense

Orthodox Christians did not ignore these attacks on their faith; many believers responded vigorously. One of the centers for the defense of orthodox Christianity at that time was Princeton Theological Seminary. Theologians at Princeton responded pointedly and intelligently to modernist and evolutionist attacks on the Bible. Perhaps the greatest of those defenders of the Faith in both the extent of his writing and the depth of his thought was **Benjamin B. Warfield**, professor at Princeton from 1887 until his death in 1921.

Dr. Benjamin B. Warfield, a theologian at Princeton Theological Seminary, was one of the great defenders of the Faith against the onslaughts of theological modernism.

Sadly, only a few years after Warfield's death, the modernists found a way to take control of Princeton seminary.

Some Christians opposed unbiblical teachings by thoroughly educating other believers in the truths of Scripture. One method was the **Bible institute**, a school similar to a college but whose curriculum usually consisted almost entirely of courses in Bible or church-related subjects, such as Sunday school work. Bible institutes normally granted certificates or diplomas instead of college degrees.

But not all Christians could attend Bible institutes, so many of them spent their vacations at **Bible conferences**. These sessions featured noted preachers and Bible teachers and were held in resort spots for a week or more during the summer. The two pioneer American Bible conferences were the Niagara Conference, held in Ontario, and Moody's Northfield Conference in Massachusetts. Probably the most important twentieth-century conference in size and longevity was the Winona Lake Bible Conference in Indiana.

One notable orthodox means of defending and furthering the Christian faith was the continuation of the urban revivals popularized by D. L. Moody. After Moody's death in 1899, the most important urban evangelist was William A. **"Billy" Sunday**. Born in Iowa in 1862, the athletic Sunday launched into a successful professional baseball career in 1883.

In 1886, while on a drinking binge in Chicago with his teammates, Sunday heard a group of workers from the Pacific Garden Mission singing in the street. Reminded of the gospel songs his devout mother had sung, Sunday followed the singers back to the mission. After attending several services there, Sunday was converted. He married in 1888 and left baseball altogether in 1891 to work for the YMCA. He then spent two years as an assistant to Evangelist J. Wilbur Chapman. When Chapman temporarily left evangelism to return to the pastorate, Sunday was left without a job. Then three churches in Garner, Iowa, invited Sunday to conduct a campaign in their town, and he entered into a new career as an evangelist. His popular style of preaching soon brought in the crowds.

When church and city auditoriums proved inadequate to hold the growing crowds at Sunday's meetings, he borrowed an idea that Moody had used in his early campaigns—the tabernacle. Tabernacles were wide, low, wooden, barn-like structures built especially for the campaigns. To reduce noise, the floors of the tabernacles were covered with sawdust. When someone came down the aisle in response to one of Sunday's altar calls, he was said to have "hit the sawdust trail."

Billy Sunday's reputation grew throughout the first decade of the twentieth century, and in the 1910s he was at the height of his fame. His most famous campaign was in New York City in 1917. In that ten-week campaign, nearly one and a half *million* people attended his meetings, and almost one hundred thousand responded to his altar calls. That campaign marked the height of Sunday's career and the climax of American urban evangelism.

Gradually, an orthodox alliance was forming in the United States. Orthodox theologians such as Warfield, popular preachers such as Sunday, and other Christians were finding that they had a common interest in defending the Faith against modernism. In the

Evangelist Billy Sunday was noted for his antics in the pulpit and his attacks in support of prohibition.

Early Bible Institutes

One of the earliest major Bible institutes was Nyack Missionary College, founded by A. B. Simpson of the Christian and Missionary Alliance in 1882. Another was D. L. Moody's Chicago Bible Institute (1889; renamed Moody Bible Institute after its founder's death). In 1907, R. A. Torrey founded the Bible Institute of Los Angeles (Biola).

Sunday's Aggressive, Popular Style

To reach the masses, Sunday added dramatic, almost athletic gestures to his sermons and spoke in a slangy vernacular. The following example is from his sermon "The Three Groups":

"I don't expect one of these ossified, petrified, mildewed, dyed-in-the-wool, stamped-on-the-cork, blown-in-the-bottle, horizontal, perpendicular Presbyterians or Episcopalians to shout 'Amen!' but it would do you Methodists good to loosen up. . . . I believe half of the professing Christians amount to nothing as a spiritual force. They go to church, have a kindly regard for religion, but as for having a firm grip on God . . . and [a] willingness to strike hard, staggering blows against the devil, they are almost failures."

1920s, a major battle would occur between orthodox Christianity and liberal religion for control of America's churches.

Section Quiz

1. What two inventions of the Progressive Era transformed American transportation?

2. What was the most important technological advance in agriculture during the Progressive Era?

3. Who was the leading representative of progressive education? In what philosophical movement was he a leader?

4. What two religious movements make up the religious wing of progressivism?

★ Explain the significance of Benjamin B. Warfield to the defence of Christian orthodoxy.

IV. Progressivism Evaluated

The progressive movement was obviously a highly influential force in American history. But were its effects generally beneficial or harmful to the nation? One must conclude, first, that many progressive reforms were worthwhile. Thanks to progressive efforts, Americans enjoyed, for example, purer food and drugs, better service from gas and water utilities, and greater participation in the political process. The value of these reforms is evident; the controversy is whether they were worth the cost.

This controversy leads to a second observation: progressive reform came at the cost of an increase in the powers of government. Only by increasing the government's authority could the progressives achieve the regulation of business and industry that they desired. The Founding Fathers designed a limited government with limited powers; the progressives encouraged a shift to an expanding government with expanding powers. The progressives did not fear the growth of government; after all, they argued, the people control the government, so the government can never get out of hand as private business has done. Experience has shown, however, that the government is not so easily controlled: every expansion of its powers leads only to further expansion and a reduction in individual freedoms. Furthermore, some progressive reforms actually insulated the government from public control. The establishment of an "independent" government bureaucracy to oversee regulation and distribute government benefits created a class of bureaucrats who were immune to political changes and public pressure.

Progressives mistakenly believed in the inevitability of progress, that things continually improve through some natural law. Many progressives based their belief in progress on evolution. The course of world history, evolutionary progressives argued, points to an ever-upward progress toward perfection. Even some progressives who denied evolution still affirmed their faith in unchecked progress. Many Christians of the era, for example, believed that as the gospel spread throughout the world, life on earth would continue to improve until the kingdom of God was established on earth and Christ returned. These sentiments were found in numerous sermons and hymns such as the following:

Progressives' Faulty View of Man

Most progressives had a faulty view of the nature of man. On the whole, they believed that man is basically good and that human nature might be improved. Emphasizing direct democracy (direct primaries, voter initiatives, etc.), they assumed that although some institutions of society might be corrupt, the individual is not. Such a belief, of course, ignored the biblical teaching that man is sinful by nature (Eph. 2:1–3). Progressives also ignored the fact that both the men who built the corrupt institutions and the politicians and staff of the regulatory agencies were fallible men with the same sinful nature.

Rise up, O men of God!

His kingdom tarries long;

Bring in the day of brotherhood

And end the night of wrong.

The problem with this belief, whether evolutionary or Christian, is that progress is *not* inevitable. Improvement in mankind's condition might indeed occur, but that is no guarantee that such improvements will occur as a matter of course.

Finally, progressives proposed false solutions to man's problems. They believed that through education, improved living conditions, and more equal political and economic opportunity, they could solve man's difficulties. Such a position ignores the biblical teaching that man's basic problem is not his ignorance or his environment but his sin—a problem that can be remedied only by forgiveness and cleansing through the death and Resurrection of Christ.

The results of the progressive movement were like the results of many other movements in history—mixed. The progressive movement, however, did establish one major theme of twentieth-century American history—the gradual but almost continuous growth of the power of the federal government.

Section Quiz

1. What major theme of twentieth-century America did the progressives establish?
2. What basic belief about man did progressivism, Darwinism, and religious modernism share, and why is it unbiblical?

People, Places, and Things to Remember

progressivism
secret ballot
direct primaries
initiative
referendum
recall
trustbusting
gas-and-water socialism
Sixteenth Amendment
Seventeenth Amendment
Prohibition
Eighteenth Amendment
Nineteenth Amendment
Susan B. Anthony
muckrakers
Eugene Debs
Robert La Follette
Theodore Roosevelt
"Square Deal"
Northern Securities case
Hepburn Act
Pure Food and Drug Act
Meat Inspection Act
The Jungle
National Association for the Advancement
    of Colored People (NAACP)
Panama Canal
Roosevelt Corollary
Treaty of Portsmouth
Root-Takahira Agreement
William Howard Taft
Joseph Cannon
dollar diplomacy
Progressive Party
"New Nationalism"
Woodrow Wilson
"New Freedom"
Underwood Tariff Act
Federal Reserve Act
Clayton Antitrust Act
Federal Trade Commission Act
Henry Ford
assembly line
Wright brothers
George Washington Carver
yellow fever
progressive education
John Dewey
secular humanism
modernism
social gospel
Walter Rauschenbusch
Benjamin B. Warfield
Bible institute
Bible conferences
Billy Sunday

Chapter Review

Making Connections

1. List at least three specific progressive reforms that expressed progressives' faith in direct democracy.

2. What connection exists between the graduated income tax and government growth?

3. Which of the three presidents of the Progressive Era is most closely identified with the progressive movement?

4. In what way was the progressive view of man's nature unbiblical?

5. List three problems with the ideology of the progressive movement.

Developing History Skills

1. Analyze America's Latin American policy during the early twentieth century.

2. What has been the long-term result of the federal government's setting aside millions of acres of land? (You may need to go beyond this book to provide a complete answer.)

Thinking Critically

1. Which policy—Roosevelt's "Big Stick" or Taft's "dollar diplomacy"—best served U.S. interests in the long term? Support your answer.

2. The power of government grew under Roosevelt, Taft, and Wilson, although the first two presidents came from one party and the third came from another party. Was there really a difference between those two parties? If so, what was it? If not, how were those parties alike?

Living as a Christian Citizen

1. Should Christians have been involved in the various causes of the progressive movement? Explain your answer. Note also the potential dangers in the position you take.

2. Progressives expanded the power of government to deal with social ills. Is there a biblical position on the size and kind of government a nation ought to have?

American soldiers in World War I

The Great War (1913–1920)

    I. **Idealism**

   II. **Intervention**

  III. **Isolation**

"Sometimes people call me an idealist. Well, that is the way I know I am an American . . . America is the only idealistic nation in the world."

Woodrow Wilson, defending his record, 1919

Macy's department store had men's summer suits on sale for $6.95, which shoppers could top off with cool straw hats for a low clearance price of $1.59. For readers of the Sunday edition of the *New York Times* on June 28, 1914, the ads were another reminder that vacation was just around the corner. Elsewhere in the paper, headlines told how the tough fists of boxing champ Jack Johnson had put yet another challenger on the canvas; the Brooklyn Dodgers made easy work of the Philadelphia Phillies in yesterday's double-header; and Kay Laurell was appearing on Broadway with the Ziegfeld Follies. The newspaper's political cartoon that day, celebrating a number of successful diplomatic initiatives, depicted a rusty, scabbarded sword over the caption "Another Business Depression." It was a comforting cartoon for that balmy summer morning in America. Halfway around the world, however, a distant disturbance on that sleepy Sunday was destined to shake an unwary America and the world off its nineteenth-century foundation. In many ways, the twentieth century began on June 28, 1914, in an obscure little city in Central Europe called Sarajevo.

The day in the Austrian provincial capital promised to be festive, a day of parties and parades, for it was the Feast of St. Vitus. In addition, Austrian Archduke Franz Ferdinand, heir to the throne of the Austro-Hungarian Empire, and his wife, Sophie, were coming for a visit. The royal couple had cause for celebration as well because that day was their fourteenth wedding anniversary.

Beneath the flags and bunting, however, a dark scene was quietly shaping. Seven Serbian youths, members of the terrorist group Black Hand, were plotting murder against the Austrians in the name of Serbian nationalism. They positioned themselves along the parade route, awaiting the archduke's motorcade. Then they launched their coordinated attack. After narrowly escaping one assassin's bomb, the chauffeur took a wrong turn into a side street, slowing the car to make the turn and coming within five feet of another of the Serbian assassins, Gavrilo Princip. Princip raised his small Belgian pistol and fired two quick shots. The world would never be the same. Franz Ferdinand was shot in the neck; Sophie, in the abdomen. As the blood ran from her husband's mouth, Sophie cried her last frantic words, "For heaven's sake, what's happened to you?" Slumping over his wife's body, the dying archduke rasped his answer repeatedly: *Es ist nichts, es ist nichts.* ("It is nothing, it is nothing.")

Woodrow Wilson's presidency began with great hope and idealism.

The sun that had risen over a festive city now sank blood-red over Europe. Ironically, what the archduke said was "nothing" sparked a blaze that engulfed the world. Four more summers would come and go before the bitter harvest of war was finally gathered. The body count that followed coldly quantified the death of a generation—ten million killed, another six million crippled for life.

The ominous results of Princip's actions were not readily apparent, however, either in Europe or in faraway America. The next day, the papers duly reported the murder, and President Wilson wired the nation's condolences to the Austrians. In the weeks that followed, though, the European powers, caught in a web of treaties and intrigues, stumbled headlong into war. The **Central Powers**—Germany and Austria—straddled the continent against the **Allies**—France, Britain, and Russia. Despite the broad Atlantic buffer and a long tradition of isolation, not even the United States could avoid the forces of war that pulled the world into Europe's conflict. Much of Woodrow Wilson's two terms would be occupied with avoiding the war, fighting the war, and concluding the war. By the end of the decade, America was shouldered with an ill-fitting mantle of world leadership.

I. Idealism

"It would be an irony of fate if my administration had to deal chiefly with foreign affairs," Woodrow Wilson privately remarked before his inauguration in 1913. Such irony would indeed be his "fate." The bespectacled professor, along with his secretary of state, **William Jennings Bryan**, had little knowledge of international affairs and no experience in diplomacy; yet there was much in Wilson's background and character that would leave an enduring mark on America's foreign policy. He sought to make the United States the moral leader among nations, believing that America's role in the world was to promote democracy and peace by example and persuasion.

Wilson saw America as having a new Manifest Destiny, not of territorial expansion but of sharing political ideals. In a key foreign policy address delivered in Mobile, Alabama, in 1913, Wilson declared,

> We dare not turn from the principle that morality and not expediency is the thing that must guide us and that we will never condone iniquity because it is most convenient to do so. . . . It is a very perilous thing to determine the foreign policy of a nation in the terms of material interest. It not only is unfair to those with whom you are dealing, but it is degrading as regards your own actions.
>
> I want to take this occasion to say that the United States will never again seek one additional foot of territory by conquest. She will devote herself to showing that she knows how to make honorable and fruitful use of the territory she has.

Wilson wanted to expand the United States economically by promoting trade with other nations. In helping American companies make profits, he thought that he could also promote freedom and democracy and raise other countries economically. Despite his noble goals, political realities soon challenged Wilson's ability to practice what he preached. He came to view all opposition to his views as wrong.

The Mexican Muddle

Wilson's idealism was first put to the test in Mexico. From 1876 to 1911 **Porfirio Díaz** (pohr-FEE-ryoh DEE-ahz) ruled Mexico with an iron fist toward his opposition and an open palm toward foreign investors. Dictator Díaz and European and American businessmen all profited from the petroleum and mining resources of Mexico but left the Mexican people impoverished. In 1911, a popular revolt led by Francisco Madero drove Díaz into early retirement, but the rebellion also unleashed violent rivals for power, groups that had previously been suppressed by Díaz's iron rule.

Wilson's Background

Woodrow Wilson grew up in a Presbyterian home. His father, the Reverend Dr. Joseph Ruggles Wilson, instilled in his son sturdy moral convictions and a strong belief in God's sovereign direction in the universe. President Wilson brought that moral vision to his foreign policymaking.

William Jennings Bryan, Wilson's secretary of state, disagreed so much with some of Wilson's foreign policies that he resigned even before the United States entered World War I.

(top) Pancho Villa (center), shown here with General John J. Pershing (right), was a U.S. favorite in the Mexicans' struggle for control of their government.

The Robert Runyon Photograph Collection, 00196, The Dolph Briscoe Center for American History, The University of Texas at Austin

(bottom) Pancho Villa became an enemy of the United States when he led his bandit army in a raid on an American town, killing several Americans. General Pershing was assigned to track him down and bring him to justice. Pershing never found him.

He Couldn't Win

To his credit, Wilson resisted the full-scale war with Mexico that many in Congress urged. Yet in the wake of the American withdrawal, Wilson's heavy-handed idealism gained the president little more than ridicule at home and resentment abroad.

Just weeks before Wilson's inauguration, President Madero was murdered by his own military commander, the ruthless General **Victoriano Huerta** (WEHR tah). Many countries quickly extended diplomatic recognition to the new Mexican government in hopes of reestablishing profitable business relations as in the days of Díaz. Sadly, most countries, including the United States, traditionally extended recognition to a government if it simply *held* power, without concerning themselves with *how* it obtained that power. (Huerta's regime has since been described as "one of the most grotesque tyrannies in Mexican history.")

But this time it was different. Woodrow Wilson refused to recognize "government by murder." "My ideal is an orderly and righteous government in Mexico," he declared. He added, "My passion is for the submerged 85 percent of the people of that Republic who are now struggling toward liberty." The former Presbyterian professor warned, "I am going to teach the South American republics to elect good men!"

Determined to drive, in Wilson's words, the "desperate brute" out of office, the president began supplying arms to Huerta's challengers, Venustiano Carranza (vay-NOOS-tee-AH-noh kah-RAHN-zah) and **Pancho Villa** (PAHN-cho VEE-yah) while also cutting off arms shipments to Huerta. In April 1914, a group of American sailors enforcing the arms embargo at Tampico were arrested. Although they were immediately released and the local commander expressed regret to the American naval commander, the admiral of the American fleet demanded that the Mexicans hoist the U.S. flag and render a twenty-one-gun salute. Huerta, however, refused to grovel. Wilson, citing national honor, went to Congress and requested authority to use punitive force against the insubordinate Huerta. On April 20, 1914, Congress granted the request.

Following a bloody clash between U.S. troops and Mexicans at Vera Cruz, the "ABC powers" (Argentina, Brazil, and Chile) mediated a truce between the United States and Mexico. The accumulated internal and international pressure encouraged by Wilson eventually toppled Huerta, bringing Carranza to power.

Peace, however, did not come with Huerta's exit. Villa, now vying for power against Carranza, sought to raise his popularity by becoming the chief enemy of the American "gringos." He became a legend in Mexico, with people either flocking to his banners or fleeing his bands. He was nicknamed *la cucaracha*, "the cockroach," and a song by that name praised his exploits.

But Villa was a ruthless man. He had eighteen American mining engineers murdered in cold blood, then led a raid into New Mexico, where his band killed seventeen more Americans and burned the border town of Columbus. In response, President Wilson sent General **John J.** ("Black Jack") **Pershing** into Mexico with eleven thousand troops to put the bandit out of business. After months of searching fruitlessly for the elusive Villa, and as problems with the European war loomed ever larger, Wilson ordered Pershing to call off the hunt.

Mexico and the Caribbean During Wilson's Presidency

Caribbean Conflict

At the beginning of his administration, President Wilson denounced both Taft's dollar diplomacy and Roosevelt's "big stick" policies as contrary to the new moral leadership of the United States. But the need to protect the strategic Panama Canal and Wilson's desire to see America's neighbors form orderly democratic governments led to a number of military interventions in the Caribbean.

Virtual anarchy reigned in Haiti from 1914 to 1915. Bloody power struggles left the island strewn with bodies and threatened to catch foreigners in the middle. Fearing both the loss of American lives or property and European intervention, Wilson ordered U.S. Marines to occupy Haiti. American forces were there from July 1915 to 1934, bolstering the new civilian government, building roads and schools, and establishing order.

Next door to Haiti, in the Dominican Republic, civil war erupted in 1916. A U.S. Marine police force occupied that area until 1924. As in Haiti, the Dominican Republic benefited materially during the U.S. occupation, but resentment of the "Colossus of the North" remained high in Latin America.

The Web of War

After Princip's assassination of Archduke Ferdinand on June 28, 1914, fears and friendships among the nations of Europe caused them to slide into war. The Austrian government, assuming that the Serbian government was at least passively responsible for the archduke's assassination, issued an incredible ultimatum on July 23, demanding that Serbia submit to its rule until Serbia was purged of anti-Austrian sentiments. Surprisingly, Serbia replied that it was willing to accept most of Austria's demands. But Austria was not satisfied and declared war on Serbia on July 28.

Russia, fearing that Austria intended to establish control of the Balkans, mobilized its troops on July 30. Germany, Austria's ally, declared war on Russia two days later. Since the Russians had a mutual security pact with the French, Germany demanded to know France's intentions. The French, fearing the German buildup, mobilized their troops, an act that the Germans interpreted as aggressive. Germany consequently declared war on France on August 3.

The Irony of It All

Ironically, Wilson, who set out to mend fences with America's southern neighbors, conducted more peacetime interventions than any of his predecessors. Wilson's idealism often ran afoul of strategic demands and uncontrollable events, sometimes creating sharp differences between rhetoric and reality. Despite Wilson's nagging foreign policy questions over Mexico, Central America, and the Caribbean, a far greater crisis loomed at the same time—the threat of American involvement in a European war.

Alliances Led to War

Over the years since 1873, many of the nations of Europe had aligned themselves into two mutual defense alliances. Germany, under Bismarck, developed the first alliance—made up of Germany, Austria-Hungary, and Russia—called the Three Emperors' League. Later, Bismarck established the Triple Alliance of Germany, Austria-Hungary, and Italy. France, Russia, and Great Britain, responding to the German alliances and fearing the growing German Empire, allied themselves in the Triple Entente (ahn TAHNT). Both alliances pledged that if a member of one alliance was attacked by a member of the other alliance, the signatories would come to the aid of the attacked fellow member. Princip's assassination of Ferdinand lit the powder keg that would blow Europe to pieces and rattle the rest of the world.

The Start of a Long, Bloody War

By the end of 1914, a long, bloody stalemate had settled over the front, as both sides dug into opposing trenches that stretched from Belgium to Switzerland. Between the trenches, in an ironic twist on the Kaiser's words, millions of men fell like autumn leaves.

British Propaganda

After the British seized control of the transatlantic cables, they provided most of the war news available to Americans. After the war, many German "atrocities" that had been reported in the news were exposed as exaggerated products of British propaganda writers. The reality was bad enough. German troops burned Belgian homes and historic monuments, for example, and occasionally shot unarmed civilians whom they had chosen at random.

With France and Russia flanking Germany, the Germans turned to their long-standing plan for waging a two-front war, the Schlieffen (SHLEEF ehn) Plan. According to its directives, the German army had to first crush France quickly by swinging through Belgium and occupying Paris within forty days after declaring war. The troops would then turn east to defeat the Russian hordes, who were not expected to organize quickly.

Neutral Belgium naturally rejected Germany's demand to use its country as an invasion route. At the same time, Britain, having treaty ties guaranteeing the neutrality of Belgium, warned Germany to call off the planned invasion by midnight of August 4 or the two countries would be at war. The German ruler, Kaiser **Wilhelm II**, sneered at Britain's commitment to a "scrap of paper" and ignored the ultimatum. Late that night, after a day of exhausting but vain negotiations, the British foreign minister, Sir Edward Grey, noticed the London streetlamps being extinguished, and sadly—and prophetically—observed, "The lamps are going out all over Europe; we shall not see them lit again in our lifetime." At the stroke of twelve, world war began.

As confident German troops marched into Belgium, the words of their Kaiser rang in their ears: "You will be home before the leaves have fallen from the trees." Brave Belgian and British troops, however, offered tough resistance, buying precious time for the French. By the end of August, the Germans had pushed to the gates of Paris, where their war machine ground to a halt. The French and British made valiant but costly attempts to push back the invasion. In the first month of war, the French alone lost two hundred thousand troops in battle.

The Slippery Slope of Neutrality

When news of the war reached the United States, President Wilson issued a proclamation of neutrality; yet there was anything but neutral sentiment about the war. As the scope of the conflict became evident, the American people were deeply divided.

Melting Pot Problems

The New World could hardly ignore the Old World's war. Many Americans had been born in Germany or were descended from German immigrants. Many Irish immigrants and their descendants also favored Germany, mainly because they opposed Britain. Most Americans, however, had their roots in Great Britain, and Americans generally admired British law, institutions, and culture. They also favored France because of her aid in America's War for Independence. As poet Robert Underwood Johnson glowingly declared:

> Forget us, God, if we forget
> The sacred sword of Lafayette!

Americans who favored the Allies tended to view Germany as an autocratic, militaristic aggressor—a view that British and French propaganda naturally encouraged by portraying Germans ("the Huns") as monsters.

The Trade Trigger

America's strong economic ties with the Allies increased during the war. Because of the British blockade of Germany and the British navy's control of the Atlantic, American trade with the Central Powers all but ceased. When the Allies used up their credit in buying American goods, Wilson allowed American loans to the Allies to avoid a collapse of American trade. In essence, the United States, while proclaiming its neutrality, was actually waging a *pro-Allies* neutrality. This policy would eventually pull the United States into the war. The Germans, suffering the effects of the British blockade, unleashed a deadly weapon on the high seas that made trade with even the Allies all but impossible.

Submarine Warfare

Probably the most significant factor in America's entrance into the war was the violation of American rights on the sea by German submarines. Britain had blockaded Germany, prohibiting even the importation of food. A starving Germany countered by declaring the seas around Britain to be a war zone in which any ship would be liable to submarine attack.

Germany, fearing U.S. intervention, had publicly warned American citizens not to travel into the war zone on British ships. Despite a printed warning in the *New York Times* from the German government, when the British passenger liner **Lusitania** left New York on May 1, 1915, a number of Americans were aboard. When the liner entered the war zone near Ireland on May 7, no British patrol boat gave it the usual escort. The commander of a German submarine spotted the ship and fired a torpedo. Within eighteen minutes, the large liner sank, and 1,198 passengers and crewmen, including 128 Americans, perished.

President Wilson, though deeply moved by the tragedy, resisted the war hawks. With moral idealism, he declared, "There is such a thing as a man being too proud to fight. There is such a thing as a nation being so right that it does not need to convince others by force that it is right."

Although political opponents would skewer Wilson with his own words—"too proud to fight"—the president realized that the country was too divided to fight. One cabinet official remarked after the *Lusitania* incident that Californians were more concerned with their citrus crop than with fighting.

Germany replied to Wilson's demand for apology and reparations with regret for the loss of life but asserted that the sinking was "just self-defense" since the passenger vessel was also carrying

> ## Conflicts with International Rules of Warfare
> According to the rules of international law, warships were to warn and evacuate merchant ships before sinking them. Submarines, however, would not do that because it would require them to surface, making them vulnerable to attacks by deck guns or even ramming by well-directed prows.

The sinking of the *Lusitania* shocked many Americans out of their neutral attitude toward Germany.

> ## Division Within the Cabinet
> Even Wilson's cabinet was divided over how to respond to the German threat. Wilson composed a sharply worded message to Berlin demanding a formal apology and reparation, or payment for losses. Secretary of State Bryan resigned in protest, fearing that Wilson's message was too strong and might lead to war.

munitions. Whatever the Germans' justification, the *Lusitania* incident caused a change in Americans' attitude toward the Germans. As one newspaper said, "The torpedo that sank the *Lusitania* also sank Germany in the opinion of mankind."

The war issue simmered on the back burner in America until the spring of 1916. On March 24, 1916, a German submarine attacked an unarmed French passenger liner, the *Sussex*, in the English Channel. Among those killed and injured were several Americans. The furor over the *Sussex* caused Wilson to warn the Germans that another attack on passenger or merchant vessels would mean a break in diplomatic ties and likely war. Wilson's "***Sussex* pledge**" quieted the seas for a time, but as one historian pointed out, Wilson handed the Germans "a blank check which he could not honorably recall."

Election of 1916

The presidential campaign that geared up in the summer of 1916 naturally could not escape the shadow of the foreign crisis. In St. Louis, Democrats held a thunderous rally to nominate Wilson for a second term, cheering, "He kept us out of war." On the Republican side, Supreme Court justice Charles Evans Hughes left the bench to run for president.

In many ways, the election mirrored the nation's mood. In the East, where war fever was highest, Hughes carried the states handily. However, the "hyphenates," the German-Americans and Irish-Americans of the Midwest, got behind Wilson, and on the Pacific coast, where Europe's war was a distant din, Wilson's neutrality was popular. Wilson's victory over Hughes on the winning slogan "He kept us out of war" seemed to indicate a mandate for his second term. Yet the slogan was in the *past tense*—it was not a pledge at all. The future remained as uncertain as it was threatening.

Section Quiz

1. Why did Wilson refuse to recognize the government of Huerta in Mexico?

2. Name the two countries in the Caribbean in which the United States intervened during Wilson's presidency.

3. The German invasion of what nation brought Great Britain into World War I?

4. The sinking of what ship caused Wilson to declare that further attacks on passenger vessels would break U.S. diplomatic relations with Germany?

★ Why do you think that Wilson's initial policy of neutrality in Europe's war could be considered a "slippery slope"?

II. Intervention

The Great War was going badly for both sides. New technology born of industrialization gave the armies mass-produced weapons for mass-produced death. One tragic illustration of this change is the British offensive at the Somme. On the opening day, July 1, 1916, the British suffered eighty thousand casualties—the bloodiest day in modern history. By the end of the Somme campaign, the British had gained three or four miles of mud, but the price was steep, with half a million British soldiers killed or wounded.

> ### *On the Slaughter at the Somme*
> "Before the war it had seemed incredible that such terrors and slaughters . . . could last more than a few months: After the first two years it was difficult to believe that they would ever end."
> —Winston Churchill

On the other side of the Atlantic, Wilson feared that the war would not end before America was dragged into it. Drawing on the idealism that characterized his foreign policy goals—if not his gains—Wilson appeared before the Senate and issued a historic declaration. He warned the deadlocked nations of Europe that only "peace without victory" could provide a lasting solution. Further, Wilson urged the formation of a League of Nations that would provide a forum for settling international disputes.

In Europe, where millions of men lay in untimely graves, Wilson's "peace without victory" was not even a consideration. A week after Wilson's speech, the Germans, sorely pressed by the British blockade, replied by declaring **unrestricted submarine warfare**. *All* ships in the war zone—passenger or merchant, belligerent or neutral—would be sunk without warning.

Wilson, mindful of his *Sussex* pledge yet knowing that his actions would eventually lead to war, reluctantly severed diplomatic ties with Germany on February 3, 1917. Many Americans, including the president, held out hope that war could yet be avoided. Such thinking, however, would quickly change.

Declaring War

On March 1, tensions heightened with the revelation of a secret, though clumsy, German diplomatic plot. The German foreign minister, Arthur Zimmermann, sought to gain Mexico's support in case the United States joined the Allies. He sent a telegram to Mexico offering Texas, New Mexico, and Arizona in return for Mexican support. He also asked Mexico to influence Japan to join the Central Powers. British intelligence intercepted and decoded the telegram and then enthusiastically forwarded it to the United States. When the details of the **Zimmermann telegram** were first revealed, they seemed so fantastic that some people thought the entire affair was a British hoax. When the truth of Germany's hostility toward the United States finally dawned, however, Americans were outraged. Interestingly, Zimmermann's scheme succeeded in arousing the western United States, an area that had been indifferent to Europe's war. Now, with their lands being "promised" to Mexico, even westerners were on the warpath.

Two weeks later, German submarines made good on their earlier threat by sinking four unarmed American merchant vessels. Wilson had run out of negotiating room. On April 2, the president appeared before a joint session of Congress and requested that the House and Senate formally recognize that Germany had "thrust" a state of war upon the United States. On **April 6, 1917**, Wilson signed the declaration—America had entered World War I.

Over Here

Raising an Army

America found itself ill prepared to answer Wilson's call to war. At the time of the war declaration, the peacetime army and National Guard numbered only 379,000 men. Remarkably, that number increased tenfold to 3.7 million by the end of the war. This rapid recruitment to meet the tremendous manpower demands of modern war was the result of a national draft through the **Selective Service Act**. In 1917, all men ages 21 to 30 were required to register for the draft, and in 1918 the bracket was expanded to include those

Making the World Safe for Democracy

"The world must be made safe for democracy," Wilson declared in his war message. "Its peace must be planted upon the tested foundations of political liberty."

18 to 45 years old. Altogether, 2.8 million men were drafted into the army; half of that number eventually saw action.

When the recruits arrived at hastily constructed boot camps, they quickly learned just how unprepared the United States was for the war to which they were being committed. Theodore Roosevelt, a longtime though often unheeded champion of military preparedness, wrote disappointedly that

> the enormous majority of our men in the encampments were drilling with broomsticks or else with rudely whittled guns. . . . In the camps I saw barrels mounted on sticks on which zealous captains were endeavoring to teach their men how to ride a horse.

The draft could provide the men but not the machinery of war. It took nearly a year for the nation's industry to convert to a full wartime footing. The importance of the industrial mobilization reflected the changing face of modern war. As President Wilson put it, "In the sense in which we have been wont to think of armies, there are no armies in this struggle; there are entire nations armed." All across the home front, Americans enthusiastically met the challenge to war and to win.

Effect of War on the Economy

U.S. entry into the war had several profound effects, some good and some bad. For Americans young and old, the war was "fought" in backyard gardens and factory assembly lines.

But Americans also saw their national government take unprecedented control of the economy. The Wilson administration, already suspicious of the free market, did not think the market could respond quickly or efficiently enough to meet the demands of war. The administration also wanted to prevent profiteering. So Wilson created numerous government agencies to control the economy. Among these were the Fuel Administration, the Railroad Administration, and the War Industries Board.

One of the key needs was an adequate food supply for not only the American forces but also the beleaguered Allies. To address that need, Congress passed the Lever Food and Fuel Control Act of 1917, which instituted the **Food Administration**. Future president **Herbert Hoover** became its administrator and gained international attention for organizing methods of saving and producing food. "Hooverizing" became the byword as citizens joined in "Meatless Mondays" and "Wheatless Wednesdays." Many people, encouraged by the slogan "Food Will Win the War," raised their own food in "Liberty Gardens" so that more of the nation's commercial agricultural production could be sent to alleviate shortages in Europe.

Besides raising food, patriotic Americans raised money. The nationwide effort to invest in war bonds, or "Liberty Loans," reaped $17 billion in revenue. Movie celebrities such as Douglas Fairbanks and Mary Pickford appeared at huge rallies to boost bond sales. Even schoolchildren saved their pennies to fill Liberty Books with 25¢ stamps appropriately captioned "Lick a Stamp and Lick the Kaiser."

The war touched every area of life. Artists used their pens and paints in the war effort, producing posters to recruit men and raise money. And in a day before radio and television, families often

Effects by the Numbers

Industrial production increased by more than a third between 1916 and 1919. The Gross National Product (GNP) increased from $46 billion to $77.2 billion during the same period. The average full-time manufacturing worker saw his annual earnings climb from $751 to $813 in that period.

As head of the Food Administration, Herbert Hoover helped spread Wilson's unprecedented expansion of government into Americans' daily lives.

Purpose of the Wartime Agencies

The main tasks of Wilson's wartime agencies were to control prices and ensure "fair" (by the government's calculations) distribution of resources. The Railroad Administration went further and actually nationalized the rail industry, outlawing all competition and running all railroads. Thankfully for advocates of free enterprise, those agencies lasted only until shortly after the war, when the free market was once again allowed to function unhindered.

gathered around the piano in the evening to sing such sentimental ballads as "I'm Hitting the Trail for Normandy, So Kiss Me Good-bye" or George M. Cohan's rollicking "Over There," the unofficial anthem of the American "**doughboy**," or soldier.

Politics of Patriotism

The national fervor for the war effort understandably led to widespread anti-German sentiment. Many high schools dropped German language courses, and "liberty" replaced virtually every-thing connected with the hated Hun: German measles became "liberty measles," German shepherds were renamed "liberty dogs," and patriotic palates that had lost their taste for sauerkraut were doubtless relieved to discover "liberty cabbage."

The anti-German attitude led to changed laws as well, often at the cost of constitutionally guaranteed liberties. For example, the **Espionage and Sedition Acts** made it a criminal offense to criti-cize the war effort in any way. Yet, such acts must be understood in their wartime context. A number of German spy plots, including the successful sabotage of a New Jersey munitions plant, prompted lawmakers to enact stiff laws to safeguard national security. Un-doubtedly, though, some of the enforcement of the Espionage and Sedition Acts, which resulted in more than a thousand convictions, was the result of unfounded fears and hysteria. Despite examples of excessive enforcement, however, the Supreme Court ruled in the 1919 landmark decision *Schenk v. United States* that Congress *could* limit free speech, particularly during wartime, if such speech presented "a clear and present danger" to national interests. In the ruling, Justice Oliver Wendell Holmes noted, however, "Free speech would not protect a man in falsely shouting fire in a theater, and causing a panic."

For most Americans, support for the war came not from coercion but as a matter of patriotism and idealism. None was better at defining and focusing that idealism than Woodrow Wilson. At the outset he declared,

> We desire no conquest, no dominion, we seek no indemni-ties for ourselves, no material compensation for the sacrifices we shall freely make. We are but one of the champions of the rights of mankind. . . . America is privileged to spend her blood and her might for the principles that gave her birth and happiness and the peace which she has treasured. God help-ing her she can do no other.

"Over There!"

Over there, over there, send the word, send the word, over there,

That the Yanks are coming, the Yanks are coming,

The drums rum-tumming ev'rywhere.

So prepare, say a prayer, send the word, send the word to beware:

We'll be over, we're coming over,

And we won't come back 'til it's over over there!

Women and the War

Women also played an important role in the war effort. For the first time, some industrial jobs became open for women as men went off to Europe. Women also figured promi-nently in propaganda and recruiting posters. While remaining exempt from combat roles, many women still worked near the front lines as nurses or ambulance drivers.

Wartime posters helped rally civilian support for bond drives and voluntary conservation measures for a war that did not directly involve U.S. soil.

Wilson continued his theme of America's moral leadership in formulating a plan that he hoped would produce a lasting peace. His objectives, known as the **Fourteen Points**, proposed freedom of the seas, open diplomacy, and self-determination among the peoples of Central Europe and rejected reparation demands. Wilson's Fourteenth Point renewed his earlier ideas for a **League of Nations**, urging the formation of "a general association of nations . . . for the purpose of affording mutual guarantees of political independence and territorial integrity to great and small states alike." In Wilson's idealist—though unrealistic—thinking, a League of Nations would prevent a recurrence of the events that ignited the 1914 conflagration. Wilson also hoped to turn the war into a crusade for Americans and to use the olive branch of the Fourteen Points as a wedge between the battle-weary German people and their warlords. As such, Wilson's Fourteen Points were widely published in Europe for everyone from kings to common laborers on both sides to consider.

While Wilson was waging war on the diplomatic front, American troops were making a timely entrance and crucial contribution on the *real* front.

Over There

"Lafayette, We Are Here"

On July 4, 1917, the first contingent of U.S. troops of the American Expeditionary Force marched through the streets of Paris. The French were ecstatic. An American colonel, Charles E. Stanton, recalling an old debt and capturing the timeliness of the American arrival, declared simply, "Lafayette, we are here."

The American entry was pivotal for the Allies. On the eastern front the bloody Bolshevik Revolution headed by Vladimir Lenin had swept the Communists to power in Russia in November 1917. Lenin negotiated a separate peace with Germany early in 1918, freeing hundreds of thousands of German troops to join their comrades on the western front. The Germans hoped thereby to deal a final blow to the Allies.

In addition, morale among the beleaguered Allies was miserable. They had suffered seven million casualties in the war. Weary of the face of death, French troops staged mass mutinies in May and June 1917. Some French soldiers even murdered their officers before deserting. As the Allied armies teetered toward collapse, the arrival of the Americans, led by the tough, square-jawed "Black Jack" Pershing, revived Allied spirit. Although the arriving Yanks were green, by the spring of 1918, the doughboys, a million strong, became the critical factor in the Allied recovery and ultimately in the Allied victory.

Holding the Line

The German commander Erich von Ludendorff knew that Germany could not prolong the war when the forces of the United States were added to those of the rest of the Allies. He decided to wage a full offensive against the British and French, forcing them to surrender before the United States could give substantial support. Germany began the British phase of the offensive in northern France and Belgium on March 20, 1918, with the heaviest artillery fire ever used. Some 6,000 German guns, answered by 2,500 British guns, pounded the front with tons of steel and explosive shells for more than four hours. Then the German infantry charged across "no man's land," (the area between the Allied and the German lines). Flamethrowers, poison gas, hand grenades, and machine guns were used by both sides. The Germans, aided by a fog cover, successfully broke through in some places, but the drive slowed and faltered. After several days of intense battle, the British, aided by recently arrived American troops, prevented a general collapse of the line.

Sergeant York

A great American hero of World War I was Alvin C. York, a Christian and a shy man from the mountains of north central Tennessee. He earned several honors and medals, including the Congressional Medal of Honor, for his bravery in the Argonne Forest in France.

York was converted in a revival a few years before the war. When drafted into the army, he underwent a crisis; his church taught that killing was always wrong—even in war. He almost registered as a conscientious objector (one who refuses to fight because of religious belief). But York wanted to serve both God and country. He later wrote, "I prayed and prayed. I prayed for two whole days and a night out on the mountainside. And I received my assurance that it was all right, that I should go."

York, one of the best marksmen in his county, impressed his superiors with his accurate shooting and soon attained the rank of corporal. He was sent to France in May 1918 as part of the 82nd Division, the All-American division.

On October 8, 1918, York's unit was exploring an enemy position in the Argonne Forest when they found themselves behind enemy lines. They surprised a group of encamped Germans and took them prisoner. But a nearby machine gun nest opened fire on the Americans, killing several of York's companions. The others dove for cover.

York began to use his shooting skills to good effect. One by one, as the Germans peered over the embankment to take aim, York shot them dead. Finally, York convinced a German major whom the Americans had captured to order the other Germans to surrender.

When York and his prisoners reached the Allied lines, a lieutenant asked, "York, have you captured the whole German army?"

York answered that he had "a tolerable few." The "tolerable few" turned out to be 132 prisoners. In addition, York had single-handedly killed twenty-five other Germans and silenced thirty-five machine guns.

York was promoted to sergeant. On returning to his native Tennessee, York devoted his life to building schools for the mountain children of his home state. He built a small non-denominational Bible college as a "school for God." When asked about his adventures in France, York replied, "We know there were miracles, don't we? Well, this was one. It's the only way I can figure it."

Having failed to break the British line, the Germans opened an attack on the French line to the south on May 27, 1918. The German assault broke the lines by May 30 and reached the Marne River, only fifty miles from Paris. But on June 2 and 3, jaunty Yanks eager for a fight poured into the gaps, halting the German drive at **Château-Thierry** (SHA-TOH TYEH-REE) **and Belleau** (BEL oh) **Wood**.

Push to Victory

On July 18, the Allies began a counterattack, slowly pushing the Germans back. The doughboys won an impressive victory at Saint-Mihiel (SAHN mee-YEL), but the largest effort was the American **Argonne offensive** that began on September 26. It was one of the costliest military campaigns in American history. One and a quarter million U.S. troops, concentrated on a twenty-five-mile front, fought for six weeks toward the central German rail center at Sedan. The Americans suffered 117,000 casualties, including 26,000

Four Aces

Both sides in World War I glamorized the bravery of a new breed of warrior—the fighter pilot. "Flyboys" seemed to embody the charm, chivalry, and daring of warfare that were lacking in the muddy carnage of trench warfare. Most famous were the "aces," those who scored at least five "kills" (enemy planes shot down). Following are descriptions of the four major powers' top aces.

Manfred von Richthofen. Better known as the Red Baron because of his scarlet red triplane (a three-wing Fokker Dr 1), von Richthofen was the most successful ace in the war, scoring eighty kills. On April 8, 1918, he scored his eightieth kill. The next day, he was mortally wounded, allegedly shot by a Canadian soldier on the ground.

Paul-René Fonck. Fonck was France's premier ace, with seventy-five kills. He embodied the jaunty, cocky, almost arrogant attitude that many people associated with the aces. Fonck twice shot down six enemy planes in one day and once brought down three planes in ten seconds. Fonck survived the war and later, fittingly, became an exhibition pilot.

Edward "Mick" Mannock. The chief British ace (seventy-three kills) was "Mick" Mannock, an altogether different kind of character—moody and restless. He was blind in one eye, but he practiced his gunnery constantly to overcome his handicap. He

was not a carefree "knight of the air." He took a grim delight in shooting down Germans, but he went to his quarters and wept when one of his mates was shot down. Mannock suffered from a fear of fire and was tormented by dreams of being trapped in a burning plane. Sadly, his plane was hit by antiaircraft fire in 1918, and he died in a fiery crash.

Eddie Rickenbacker. America's "ace of aces," Rickenbacker scored twenty-six kills. He was a race-car driver before the war and once held the world land-speed record. He combined his knowledge of engines with his personal bravery to become America's leading pilot. Perhaps his most famous exploit was a solo attack on seven German planes. He downed

two of them and then escaped from the others unharmed. He won the Medal of Honor for his exploits.

During World War II, he was a military consultant. Once, the B-17 in which he was flying with a secret message to General McArthur crashed at sea. He took command of the situation and helped the crewmen survive against amazing odds for twenty-four days. Using Psalm 46, he encouraged them to turn to Christ. He and all but one of the crewmen were rescued. In later years, he was first president and then chairman of Eastern Airlines. He also spoke out against the "creeping socialism" he saw infesting the American government.

American ace Captain Eddie Rickenbacker

Dark Clouds Over the Peace

One of the people who felt betrayed by the truce and was still willing to fight to the death for the fatherland was a twenty-nine-year-old German corporal named Adolf Hitler. His dark mind burned with dreams of revenge. Of course, none of that was apparent on Armistice Day, only jubilation that the fighting was over.

killed in action, but the effort turned the tide. In October, the German leadership began to negotiate for peace along the lines of Wilson's Fourteen Points. By early November, the kaiser fled into exile; the German lines collapsed. On November 11, 1918—at the eleventh hour of the eleventh day of the eleventh month—the **Armistice** was signed. The Great War was over.

The French commander Ferdinand Foch (FAHSH) recalled the surrender signing ceremony: "I saw Erzberger [head of the German delegation] brandish his pen and grind his teeth. I was then glad that I had exerted my will . . . for the business was settled." Hardly. The next generation would add an enlarged second edition to the volume begun in 1914.

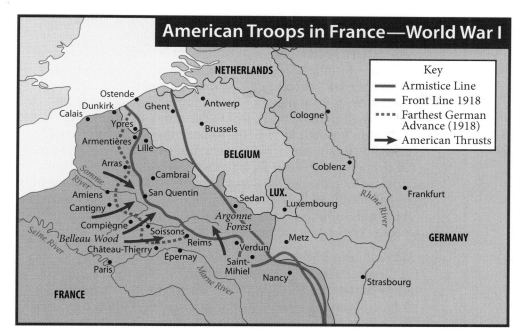

American Troops in France—World War I

Key
— Armistice Line
— Front Line 1918
···· Farthest German Advance (1918)
→ American Thrusts

Section Quiz

1. What German decision caused Wilson to break diplomatic relations with Germany?

2. Name two methods that Americans on the home front used to raise food and money for the war effort.

3. What conditions on the eastern front in early 1918 made the entry of the United States crucial to the Allies?

4. What World War I offensive was the largest and one of the costliest military campaigns in American history up to that time?

✶ How great was the influence of U.S. troops on the outcome of the war?

Prominently waving an American flag, an exuberant crowd in Paris celebrates the Armistice.

III. Isolation

With their lines collapsing, their leadership fleeing, and their people starving, the Germans asked for an armistice, or truce, in hopes of getting the best peace terms possible—peace according to Wilson's Fourteen Points. After the Armistice, though, hopes for a favorable settlement proved empty. The German people would not be the only ones disappointed by the results of what one writer referred to as "The Great War and the Petty Peace."

Treaty of Versailles

No single treaty ended the war, although the Treaty of Versailles generally receives the most attention. For example, the Austrians signed the Treaty of St. Germain, and the Ottomans signed the Treaty of Sèvres.

Wilson as Diplomat

Just one week after the Armistice was signed, Wilson announced that he would personally lead the peace delegation to meet at Versailles near Paris. Wilson's decision drew immediate fire from his critics, who charged that by personally negotiating the treaty the president would be more susceptible to public pressures and

---

Treaty of Sèvres—Sowing the Seeds of Modern Islamic Terrorism?

The Treaty of Sèvres broke up the Muslim Ottoman Empire and founded modern Turkey, perhaps also beginning the Muslim animosity toward the West that rages today.

hasty decisions. But Wilson believed that a personal appearance, given his tremendous prestige in Europe, would best help preserve his Fourteen Points, particularly the establishment of a League of Nations, which he believed would ensure lasting peace. Wilson's critics charged that he had a "messiah complex."

Whatever Wilson's motivation, his peace mission was seriously flawed from the start, for the delegation included not a single prominent Republican from the Senate, where any treaty would have to be submitted for ratification. Just two weeks earlier, in the fall elections of 1918, the Democrats lost their majorities in both houses of Congress to the Republicans. Instead of cooperating with his opponents, Wilson and his partisan band headed for the cheering crowds of Europe without inviting any Republican leaders; his enemies back home became entrenched.

Big Four, Big Differences

The Paris Peace Conference, held from January to June 1919, was dominated by the "**Big Four**"—President Wilson, France's Premier Georges Clemenceau (CLEM MAHN SOH), Italy's Premier Vittorio Orlando, and Britain's Prime Minister David Lloyd George. Each nation had distinct aims. Wilson made clear that the U.S. wanted no territory in return for its participation in the war. What Wilson wanted was acceptance of the Fourteen Points. He was interested in peace, but his Allied colleagues were interested in prey.

Clemenceau, though claiming to support the Fourteen Points, was more interested in revenge for France than in anything else. Conflicts between France and Germany over the mineral-rich coal and iron-mining area west of the Rhine River, including the area known as Alsace-Lorraine, dated to the days of the Franks and the Gauls. Germany had annexed Alsace-Lorraine in 1871, and France wanted it back. France also wanted a buffer zone east of the Rhine to ensure its future security.

The Big Four at Versailles: (left to right) David Lloyd George, Great Britain; Vittorio Orlando, Italy; Georges Clemenceau, France; and Woodrow Wilson, United States

Italy's Orlando represented a nation that had been Germany's ally at the beginning of the war but had then joined the Allies, in part because of British promises of territory in Austria. Orlando came expecting a large share of the spoils of victory to fall Italy's way at the peace table, although Italy had contributed little to the actual victory.

Lloyd George was a master politician, willing to do whatever was necessary to maintain British control of the seas. Although he professed to support the terms of the Armistice, he had campaigned for reelection in December 1918 promising that the Germans would be made to bear the entire cost of the war. "We will squeeze them till the pips squeak," Lloyd George crowed. And for good measure he promised to "hang the Kaiser!" With a strong electoral victory, Lloyd George went to Versailles armed with his mandate of revenge.

Petty Peace

The **Treaty of Versailles** was signed on June 28, 1919—five long years after the Black Hand triggered a war that led to ten million deaths. The treaty drastically changed the map of Europe and had far-reaching consequences.

The Germans were permitted no part in the treaty negotiations. They were, in effect, offered the treaty on a bayonet point and forced to sign a **"war-guilt" clause** stating that the German nation was responsible for the war. The German delegation essentially signed a blank check for the vengeful victors to fill in. If Germany was responsible, then Germany would pay the bill. As a result, Britain and France demanded huge **reparation payments** to cover not just war damages but the entire cost of the war—more than $30 billion. Such an unreasonable demand only deepened poverty and resentment in Germany.

After all the haggling among Allied leaders was over, only two major planks of Wilson's Fourteen Points were incorporated into the Treaty of Versailles: national self-determination for the peoples of Europe and the formation of the League of Nations. Independence and national boundaries for Poland, Czechoslovakia, Yugoslavia, and the Baltic countries of Lithuania, Latvia, and Estonia were all based on treaty provisions. While the new national identities satisfied the political aspirations of millions, they also created problems. Many of the new countries encompassed a number of ethnic groups whose own nationalist desires were further awakened by the changes. For example, Yugoslavia, composed of six major groups, was originally called the Kingdom of the Serbs, Croats, and Slovenes—hardly a name to inspire national unity. In addition, thousands of Germans found themselves living under foreign flags after the mapmakers in Versailles finished drawing the lines. Hitler would use that point of irritation to trigger a second world war twenty years later.

Wilson and others were not unaware of the problems of the Treaty of Versailles. They believed, though, that the League of Nations would fix those flaws. First, however, if the U.S. were to take the lead in the newly formed League, Wilson would have to find enough senators to ratify the treaty. It would be the toughest fight of his life, and, some people said, one that ultimately led to his death.

Rejection and Retreat

When Wilson returned from Europe, his most formidable opponent against the Treaty of Versailles and its most important component, the League of Nations, was Senate majority leader **Henry Cabot Lodge** of Massachusetts. Besides stubbornness, Wilson and Lodge had one other thing in common—they hated each other.

Most Democrats in the Senate naturally sided with their party leader, President Wilson, but the Democrats were in the minority. The focus was on the Republicans, who were divided into two groups: the "irreconcilables" opposed any entanglement in European politics, and the "reservationists," led by Lodge, would ratify the treaty but only with reservations attached that would limit U.S. commitment. The reservationists feared that unqualified support of the League could drag Americans into future European wars by tying the country to unwanted alliances. Making a deliberate jab at Wilson's idealism, the hard-bargaining Lodge described the Versailles Treaty as "the beautiful scheme of making mankind virtuous by a statute or a written constitution." America's security, Lodge believed, was best protected by two oceans and a strong military force.

Senator Henry Cabot Lodge led the Republican reservationists in attacking the Treaty of Versailles, especially the provision for the League of Nations.

As the debate over treaty ratification dragged on, public opinion, which had initially favored the ideas behind the treaty, began to shift in Lodge's direction. Wilson, who opposed compromising on any of the treaty provisions, decided to take the issue to the people. In a marathon mission of eight thousand miles in twenty-two days, the president delivered forty speeches in favor of the treaty and membership in his brainchild, the League of Nations. The president declared, "America does not want to feed upon the rest of the world. She wants to feed it and serve it. America . . . is the only national idealistic force in the world, and idealism is going to save the world."

Wilson's crusade, however, nearly killed him. On September 25, 1919, after an enthusiastic rally in Pueblo, Colorado, the president slumped over with exhaustion. His aides canceled the rest of the tour and took Wilson back to Washington, where he suffered a serious stroke that paralyzed him on one side. Wilson's wife and a few close friends shielded his condition from the public, but his fighting days were over. For seven critical months, Wilson did not meet with his cabinet. Most executive functions were performed on his behalf by his wife and his closest aide, Colonel Edward House. In November, the Senate vote on the treaty fell short of ratification.

When public and administration pressure brought a reconsideration of the treaty in March 1920, it seemed that the amended treaty would finally pass. But Wilson, who had regained some of his strength, bitterly fought any changes. Ironically, Wilson sided with the irreconcilables to defeat his own treaty in the interest of keeping it intact. The stricken president, having lost all contact with political and practical realities, became his own enemy.

The United States never joined the League of Nations nor ratified the Treaty of Versailles. Not until July 2, 1921, after Wilson's term, did Congress quietly pass a joint resolution ending the official state of war between the United States and Germany. By then, Wilson had been replaced by Warren G. Harding, a Republican whose critics said that his only qualification for the job was that he "looked like a president." Harding was no crusader, but he was an avid card player and he enjoyed cutting ribbons. Harding's striking contrast to Wilson illustrated the changing mood of the country. America had helped liberate the Old World, but now it was shifting out of the uncomfortable harness of international leadership and retreating into the 1920s.

Why the League Failed in the Senate

Perhaps Wilson's attorney general, T. W. Gregory, best summarized the nature of the president's lost cause: "The League was defeated in the United States, not because it was a League of Nations, but because it was a Woodrow Wilson league, and because the great leader had fallen and there was no one who could wield his mighty sword."

Section Quiz

1. Name the members of the Big Four and the nation that each represented.

2. What two provisions of the Versailles treaty were most offensive to the Germans?

3. What was the difference between the Republican irreconcilables and reservationists concerning the Versailles treaty?

★ Was the U.S. Senate correct in rejecting the League of Nations, or should the United States have joined the League?

Chapter Review

Making Connections

1. What event sparked World War I? How?

2. How did the British blockade of Germany actually bring the neutral Americans closer to the Allies?

3. How did the *Sussex* pledge almost guarantee that the United States would soon be involved in Europe's war?

4. Who was the main opponent of the League of Nations in the Senate and why?

Developing History Skills

1. Place the following events in chronological order.

   a. Great Britain declares war on Germany.

   b. Germany declares war on France.

   c. Austria declares war on Serbia.

   d. Russia declares war on Austria.

2. Why did William Jennings Bryan resign as secretary of state when Wilson sent a sharp message to Germany after the sinking of the *Lusitania*?

Thinking Critically

1. Wilson said, "I am going to teach the South American republics to elect good men!" What characteristic of Wilson's foreign policy does that statement reflect? Is that characteristic necessarily a benefit in conducting foreign policy? Why or why not?

2. Wilson said, "Idealism will save the world." What truths or fallacies or both are behind that statement?

Living as a Christian Citizen

1. Should Christians try to transform their world? If yes, how do they avoid the problems of Wilsonian idealism? If no, what role should Christians play in broader society?

2. Evaluate the Treaty of Versailles from a Christian perspective.

People, Places, and Things to Remember

Central Powers
Allies
William Jennings Bryan
Porfirio Díaz
Victoriano Huerta
Pancho Villa
John J. Pershing
Wilhelm II
Lusitania
Sussex pledge
unrestricted submarine warfare
Zimmermann telegram
America enters the war (April 1917)
Selective Service Act
Food Administration
Herbert Hoover
doughboy
Espionage and Sedition Acts
Schenk v. United States
Fourteen Points
League of Nations
Château-Thierry and Belleau Wood
Argonne offensive
Armistice (November 11, 1918)
Big Four
Treaty of Versailles
"war-guilt" clause
reparation payments
Henry Cabot Lodge

UNIT 6

LEADERSHIP
★
1919-1945

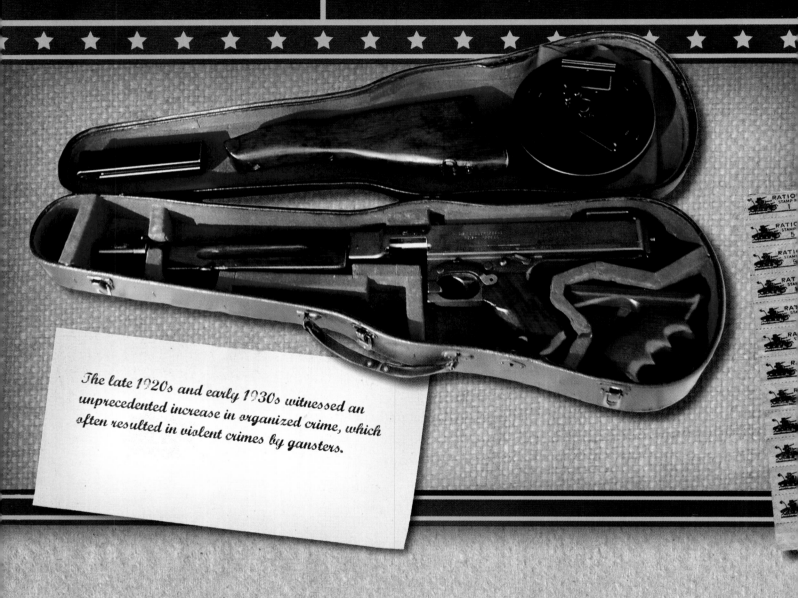

The late 1920s and early 1930s witnessed an unprecedented increase in organized crime, which often resulted in violent crimes by gansters.

1919 "Red Scare"

1925 Scopes Trial

1928 Kellogg-Briand Pact

1929 Stock Market Crash

1931 Japan invades Manchuria

CHAPTERS

20 THE TWENTIES (1920–1929)

21 THE THIRTIES (1929–1939)

22 THE WORLD AT WAR (1939–1945)

UNITED STATES OF AMERICA
OFFICE OF PRICE ADMINISTRATION

Nº 920315 BM

WAR RATION BOOK No. 3 Void if altered

NOT VALID WITHOUT STAMP

Identification of person to whom issued: PRINT IN FULL

(First name) (Middle name) (Last name)

Street number or rural route

City or post office _____ State _____

AGE	SEX	WEIGHT Lbs.	HEIGHT Ft. In.	OCCUPATION

SIGNATURE
(Person to whom book is issued. If such person is unable to sign because of age or incapacity, another may sign in his behalf.)

LOCAL BOARD ACTION

Issued by _____
(Local board number) (Date)

Street address _____

State _____

(Signature of issuing officer)

Two atomic bombs–including "Fat Man,"which was dropped on Nagasaki–ended World War II.

1933 FDR's "Hundred Days"

1939 World War II begins

1941 Attack on Pearl Harbor— U.S. enters World War II

1944 D-day

1945 End of World War II

The "Roaring Twenties" was a period of national frivolity.
Missouri History Museum, St. Louis

The Twenties (1920–1929)

I. Normalcy and Shortsightedness

II. Culture Wars

III. From Roar to Ruin

"The business of America is business."

*President Calvin Coolidge, January 17, 1925,
to the Society of American Newspaper Editors*

It was the age of flappers, foxtrots, Freud, and all that jazz. If the country was growing up, then the 1920s was America's adolescence. "Over There" was strangely out of date; America was singing "Ain't We Got Fun?" The generation coming of age in the 1920s enjoyed postwar prosperity and passive politicians. Moral crusades were out, replaced with a sometimes mindless pursuit of frolic and frivolity. The new heroes were on the silver screen, the athletic field, and the radio waves. The roar of the Twenties seemed to drown out problems both at home and abroad, but by the decade's end the lines at America's movie palaces had turned into bread lines at soup kitchens. The party was over.

I. Normalcy and Shortsightedness

On the campaign trail in 1920, Warren G. Harding preached the political philosophy that carried the United States into the new decade: "America's present need is not heroics but healing; not nostrums but normalcy; not revolution but restoration; . . . not surgery but serenity." **Normalcy** was a new word, and whatever else it was, it became the goal of a people wishing to distance themselves from wartime pressures and problems.

Postwar Problems

In 1920, America was readjusting to the challenges of peacetime. The nation's industries and manpower were no longer demanded by the war effort. The people's energies and emotions were no longer focused on defeating a foreign enemy. The mundane activities of a workaday world replaced the drama of wartime, and the resulting changes in American life brought some unpleasant side effects.

When the war ended and the doughboys returned and the parades down main street were over, the soldiers often found that America held few opportunities for them. War industries closed, but peacetime industries did not resume activities quickly because they had to retool to make consumer goods. With more than two million men returning from the American Expeditionary Force to a dismal job market, unemployment climbed to a staggering 11.9 percent in 1921. Not until after this problematic peak would business activity boom and factory jobs begin to absorb the excess workers.

If a soldier returning from the Great War decided to farm instead of seeking his fortune in the city, his prospects were no less bleak. Agriculture had been a profitable business during the war; American farms were not only feeding the nation and its soldiers but also exporting farm products to war-torn regions. With the war over, however, the agricultural market faced an upheaval.

The bountiful harvest of 1920 brought farmers calamity instead of profit. Exports of farm products declined as Europeans began to farm their own lands again, and the tremendous wartime demand for foodstuffs vanished. All that farmers could do was to sell their abundant produce for the ordinary peacetime needs of the nation. In keeping with the law of supply and demand, the huge surpluses caused food prices to plunge by the end of 1920. The meager returns for their labors devastated farmers, especially since many farmers were heavily in debt for land and equipment purchased during the years of high demand. Continued overproduction and low prices kept the agricultural market depressed, not just for a year or two but for the entire decade. The farm problem remained a major domestic issue throughout the 1920s.

Another change Americans had to face once the war ended was the discarding of emotions raised by newspapers, war posters, rallies, and songs. The kaiser had been defeated, but some Americans feared that other enemies were still at large. They especially feared Communists and anarchists (people who seek to destroy governmental authority), who had talked of overthrowing the U.S. government ever since the Bolshevik Revolution had engulfed Russia in 1917. The violent activities of a few leftists stirred this fear and created a panic called the **Red Scare**.

The scare began in 1919 when a few anarchists mailed small packages containing bombs to various government officials and businessmen who had opposed their actions by breaking strikes and prosecuting suspected leftists. One of the bombs blew up in the hands of a senator's maid, injuring her and the senator's wife. Although the other mail bombs were discovered before they exploded, the violence set off a wave of leftist bombings that resulted in death and great property destruction. Even the house of Wilson's attorney general, A. Mitchell Palmer, was bombed. The terrorism led to an intense government effort to track down foreigners with objectionable political views and either prosecute them for crimes or simply deport them. When a predicted "Red revolution" did not break out on May Day (a Communist holiday) in 1920, the scare subsided, but Americans' widespread suspicions of foreign leftists occasionally resurfaced in following years.

World Relations

The general theme of American foreign policy in the 1920s was **isolationism**. The taste of war had left many Americans disillusioned with idealistic efforts to change the world. Wilson's failure to persuade the United States to join the League of Nations punctuated the prevailing preference to focus on things at home rather than dabble in foreign matters. Nonetheless, America had proved itself to be a world leader, and in that role it could not avoid affecting the history of the 1920s.

The United States faced two basic foreign policy tasks in the twenties: to maintain world peace and to stabilize the world economy. Americans undertook both of those tasks with special attention to how any action would affect the peace and prosperity of the United States. Americans did not want foreign conflicts to draw their sons into battle again, and they did not want foreign economic problems and policies to endanger American business and prosperity.

Pursuit of Peace

Although America sent "unofficial observers" to meetings of the League of Nations, major American activities in pursuit of world peace were independent of that organization. The first such activity was the **Washington Naval Conference** of 1921. The buildup of sea power sparked by the war did not halt abruptly at the Armistice. Japan and Britain continued strengthening their navies to acquire military advantages over potential enemies. France and

Reaction Against Organized Labor

Americans feared the threat of labor violence during the Red Scare. One labor organization, The Industrial Workers of the World—or "Wobblies," as they were commonly known—tried to organize workers to achieve their socialistic goals. But in the wake of the Bolshevik Revolution, Americans did not receive them well. Because Americans were already suspicious of dangerous radicals, organized labor did not prosper during the twenties.

The home of Attorney General A. Mitchell Palmer was bombed by anarchists.

Internationalism Amid Isolationism

Although isolation was the general theme, it was by no means total. The counter theme of internationalism was clearly evident. Examples include several efforts to secure peace among nations through arms limitations and even to outlaw war. A worldwide economic depression also forced nations to work more closely together than they might otherwise have done.

Italy also were determined to enhance their naval strength. To keep these powers in check, the United States had to continue the expansion of its own navy, thereby participating in a necessary (and expensive) armament. The Washington Naval Conference brought foreign diplomats to the nation's capital to negotiate an agreement limiting the growth of naval power. The result was a plan that called for Japan, Britain, and the United States to scrap some of their vessels, curtail battleship construction, and establish a ratio for naval forces of 5 : 5 : 3 : 1.75 : 1.75. For every 5 tons of naval vessels that the United States had, Britain would maintain 5 tons; Japan, 3; and France and Italy, 1.75 each.

Idealists hailed the noble treaties devised at the Washington Naval Conference. But the agreements had some notable flaws that later led to a war in the Pacific. Although they limited the buildup of battleships, they did not restrict the buildup of cruisers, destroyers, or submarines—the vessels that would prove more valuable in future naval warfare. Also, Japan left the conference unsatisfied. Japan resented being given an inferior standing to Britain and the United States, and its militaristic goals necessitated naval expansion. For these reasons, Japan would later abandon any appearance of adhering to the treaties. Other conferences in 1927 and 1930 revived the principles established at the first conference, but cooperation among the nations soon deteriorated.

The second major peace initiative of the 1920s was set forth by President Coolidge's secretary of state, Frank B. Kellogg, and the French foreign minister, Aristide Briand. They proposed an international agreement that would outlaw war by international law. On August 27, 1928, fourteen nations signed the **Kellogg-Briand Pact** in Paris, and most other nations assented later. The pact won great praise, but it had a severe flaw that, in effect, rendered it worthless—it had absolutely no means of enforcement. This feature, however, allowed America to maintain its isolationist stance rather than entangle itself in the web of international politics.

In addition to making these efforts to maintain peace, the United States also modified its relationship with Latin American nations to promote peace with these near neighbors. President Wilson had maintained a forceful protection of American interests in the region. Presidents Harding and Coolidge continued that policy so that in 1925 the United States had marines stationed in several of those lands and controlled the financial policies of half of the twenty countries in the region. Naturally, such interventionism created resentment toward the United States by its Latin neighbors. Eventually, many Americans began to question the wisdom of such dealings with fellow independent nations.

Coolidge's secretary of state, Charles Evans Hughes, began softening the policies of the Roosevelt Corollary to the Monroe Doctrine, which had asserted the police power of the United States in the Western Hemisphere. Hughes also urged the withdrawal of troops from Latin American countries.

Economic Entrapment

World War I had wreaked havoc on the economy of Europe. Not only were its farms and factories devastated by warfare, but also its surviving governments were saddled with an incredible burden of debt. Although the war had depleted the economic resources of Europe, the United States had escaped relatively unscathed with its finances in order and its factories intact. The

Limited Agreement

Although the Washington Naval Conference limited construction of battleships and aircraft carriers, it said nothing about smaller vessels. An arms race continued between the powers as they built up cruisers, destroyers, and submarines. In 1934, Japan withdrew from the treaty. Time revealed that they had been developing the largest fleet in the Pacific realm and had especially focused on building aircraft carriers.

The Failure of Peace and the Cause of War

While the supporters of arms control and peace efforts of the 1920s had laudable goals, their idealism caused them to underestimate the human sinfulness that leads to wars in the first place. Though speaking of interpersonal conflicts, the book of James reveals the source of all conflict: the lusts and desires that people have but cannot fulfill (James 4:1). While Christians should try to avert war whenever possible, they should realize that the sinful urges that lead to war will exist until Christ returns and renovates the world.

Waning Goodwill in Latin America

Attempts to court Latin American goodwill soured in 1927 when the United States sent troops into Nicaragua, but Herbert Hoover revived the effort to improve Latin American relations during his administration. This approach came to be known as the Good Neighbor Policy under President Franklin Roosevelt.

Economic Burdens of the Treaty of Versailles

The Treaty of Versailles demanded that Germany pay $30 billion in reparations to the Allies. Also, in the wake of the war, the United States demanded that the Allies repay $22 billion in war loans—with interest.

Allies were appalled that America would insist on repayment, and the Germans were angered that reparations would be forcefully extracted from their nation. Nevertheless, these conditions dictated the international economic activity of the 1920s.

The Allied debt had been received in the form of war matériel and foodstuffs, yet America required that it be repaid in cash (gold). The war had depleted the Allied coffers, so the logical means for them to acquire the needed sums was by trading European goods for the needed gold. But the United States blocked that method entirely. Intent on protecting America's own reviving industries, Congress passed the **Fordney-McCumber Tariff** in 1922. This high tariff (supplanted by an even higher tariff in 1930) established a nearly insurmountable wall restricting European trade with the United States. Despite its many disagreeable consequences, protectionism remained entrenched in American policy.

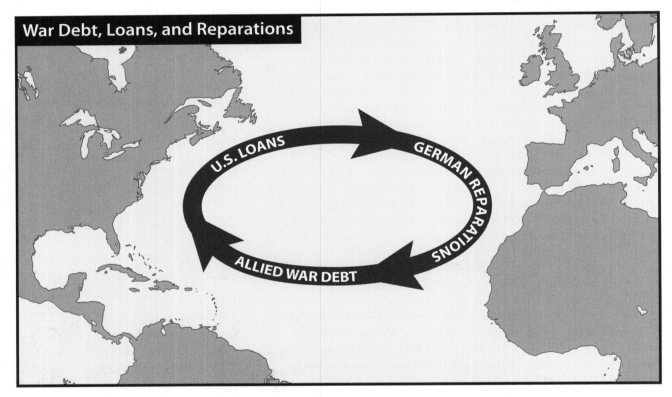

War Debt, Loans, and Reparations

Trade with America being blocked, the Allies had only one other source for the money to pay their debt—the German reparations payments. Those payments, the Allies believed, would cover the Allied debts with extra left over for rebuilding their lands. Germany, however, was in ruins, and its economy was in shambles. The defeated foe had little with which to rebuild its industry, much less to make the colossal reparations payments. Germany had only one means of obtaining the needed cash, and that was through loans. Even so, what country in the postwar era could possibly have money to invest in loans to Germany? The answer was the United States. Thus began a dangerous circular flow of money: money lent by American financial institutions to Germany was passed on by Germany to the other Allies in reparations, which were, in turn, used to repay the United States for war debts. Money repaid to America provided investment capital to spare for more loans to Germany. In the process, Germany fell heavily into debt to the United States without having funds to improve its own economy. As the debts mounted, Germany could not meet its obligations. The Allies, deprived of reparations payments, could not make their loan payments, and American investors were alarmed by unpaid foreign loans.

In 1924, an American banker, Charles Dawes, led a panel of economic experts from the involved countries to resolve the impending crisis. The result was the **Dawes Plan**, which reduced German reparations payments significantly and encouraged private American institutions to continue lending money to help Germany rebuild. The American government also reduced the interest charged on the Allied war debts and offered more generous terms for repayment. Despite these efforts, the financial demands in the absence of free trade continued to sustain the ominous cycle of debt.

Presidents

In an era when Americans generally wanted to mind their own business, have a good time, and make a fortune, they chose political leaders who were in tune with their desires. After Versailles, Wilson's ill health and bitterness over the rejection of his peace plans left America and the Democratic Party without a leader. Republicans easily won the White House in not only 1920 but also 1924 and 1928 as their party received credit for the apparent peace and prosperity of the decade. Those years were politically the most conservative years of the twentieth century. Government regulation and activism were minimal, and laissez-faire capitalism was thriving.

Harding

Warren G. Harding, the first of the Republican presidents of the 1920s, had been a newspaper editor in Marion, Ohio, until a state politician named Harry Daugherty took him under his wing. Daugherty thought Harding *looked* like a president, and as the leader of a group of state politicians called the Ohio Gang, he assisted the unassuming editor up the political ladder. Harding was elected to the Senate in 1914, but he was not particularly well known at the time of the 1920 Republican convention. His old friend Daugherty wanted to change that. Several weeks before the convention, Daugherty predicted a deadlocked convention that would be overcome when, in the middle of the night, "fifteen men in a smoke-filled room" would agree to make Senator Harding the Republican candidate. His prediction came true, and Harding entered a race against the Democratic candidate, Governor James M. Cox of Ohio, and his running mate, Franklin D. Roosevelt of New York. Harding's theme of a **return to** "**normalcy**" pleased the nation, and he won decisively.

The American public generally liked Harding and approved of his policies, but some scandals in his administration brought his name into disrepute soon after his death in 1923. Most historians agree that Harding was personally honest, but he rewarded his friends in the Ohio Gang with high offices and imprudent favors. The improprieties of those friends soon put the president under extreme strain, and this, in addition to a weak heart, possibly hastened his death.

Following his death, the most infamous of the scandals became public knowledge. This incident involved his secretary of the interior, Albert B. Fall. Fall had won Harding's approval to take control of the navy's oil reserves at two locations, Teapot Dome in

Fruit of the Cycle of Debt

The tensions resulting from the postwar cycle of debt plagued international relations throughout the twenties. Eventually, the Great Depression brought down the entire system of repayment as the world economy collapsed.

Ranking the Presidents

Whenever historians rank the best presidents, few of them include on their lists the presidents in this chapter. That is because of the liberal (broad constructionist) assumption that only activist presidents are great whereas passive, "do-nothing" presidents (strict constructionists) are bad. Many historians rank Harding and Coolidge low because they both had a "hands-off" philosophy of government that gave the greatest possible freedom to individuals and the market economy. They rank Hoover low because they blame him for causing the Depression. But they are wrong on all counts.

Harding was a dapper dresser but made poor choices of character when it came to his appointees.

Harding on His Scandalous Friends

"I have no trouble with my enemies. I can take care of my enemies in a fight. But my friends, . . . they're the ones who keep me walking the floor at nights!"

Wyoming and Elk Hills in California. In turn, Fall leased the oil rights on those properties to two friends, who were later found to have returned the favor to Fall in the form of sizable "loans." The **Teapot Dome scandal** also implicated various other members of the administration, but it was not the only scandal of that era. For example, Charles Forbes, head of the Veterans' Bureau, defrauded that agency of more than $200 million. And Harding's old pal, Attorney General Harry Daugherty, was brought to trial after being implicated in bribery schemes. Daugherty managed to have the case dismissed although investigations later revealed that he had burned the records of his account in his brother's bank. Daugherty refused to give his reason for destroying the records but cannily implied that the revelation would further harm the memory of the late President Harding.

Harding was a weak president, but not because he involved the federal government in few intrusive activities. He was weak because his character was weak, and he did not appoint strong officials or deal with officials' misdeeds as soon as they occurred. He was, however, responsible for allowing the free market to adjust without interference and pull America out of the postwar economic downturn.

Coolidge

When **Calvin Coolidge**, Harding's vice president, became president upon Harding's sudden death from a heart attack in 1923, the Harding scandals were just beginning to unfold. Coolidge immediately made clear that thorough investigations into the underhanded dealings would be conducted and that the guilty would be punished. As a result, this man of few words from rural Vermont distanced himself from the corruption and won both the praise of the American people and their votes in 1924. Coolidge had first gained national fame in 1919 as governor of Massachusetts by quelling a Boston police strike. When Samuel Gompers of the American Federation of Labor asked Coolidge to acknowledge the right of the police to express their grievances, the governor declared, "There can be no right to strike against the public safety by anybody, anywhere, anytime." That strong statement elicited the applause of the nation, which was immersed in the Red Scare at that time, and soon brought him the vice presidency.

As president, Coolidge took a hands-off approach to administration. He was content to let the market have free rein, saying, "The business of America is business." His philosophy of hard work, frugality, and simple living struck a chord with many Americans. That was what they had been taught, and Coolidge expressed their inner spirit because that was what they wanted. They did not want an intrusive, activist government.

Encouraged by the president's approval, investors watched the prices on the stock market climb and prosperity in the country boom. In 1924, Coolidge was elected president in his own right. In light of his popularity, Coolidge surprised the nation when he announced in 1927, "I do not choose to run for president in 1928."

Hoover

That announcement opened the door for Coolidge's secretary of commerce, **Herbert Hoover**, to seek the presidential nomination. After gaining a fortune as an engineer, Hoover had headed the Food Administration under Wilson, organized American food

Calvin Coolidge was a man of few words, but he believed strongly in the free market economic system.

The Quotable Coolidge

"I've never been hurt by anything I didn't say."

"Don't expect to build up the weak by pulling down the strong."

"Prosperity is only an instrument to be used, not a deity to be worshipped."

"Nothing in the world can take the place of persistence. Talent will not; nothing is more common than unsuccessful men with talent. Genius will not; unrewarded genius is almost a proverb. Education will not; the world is full of educated derelicts."

Coolidge, Fiscal Conservative

Under Coolidge, although the nation was experiencing unprecedented prosperity, federal spending never was more than $3.3 billion.

"Silent Cal" Coolidge

Calvin Coolidge's views on economic policies and social conversation could be summarized in one word: *economy* (i.e., frugality). He was nicknamed "Silent Cal."

One Sunday Mrs. Coolidge was unable to attend church with him. When he returned, she asked him what the minister's sermon was about.

"Sin," Coolidge replied bluntly.

"Well, what did he have to say about sin?" Grace pressed.

"He's agin it," he deadpanned.

Coolidge could give a public speech that equaled that of any other politician, but when he was elected to his fourth term in the Massachusetts senate, he gave the shortest speech in that body's history:

"My sincere thanks, I offer you. Conserve the firm foundations of our institutions. Do your work with the spirit of a soldier in the public service. Be loyal to the Commonwealth and to yourselves. And be brief, above all things, be brief."

Perhaps to remind himself not to be loquacious, he had the following embroidered quotation over his mantelpiece:

A wise old owl sat on an oak;
The more he saw, the less he spoke;
The less he spoke, the more he heard.
Why can't we be like that old bird?

Even when Coolidge made a joke (and he did have an immense sense of humor, albeit abbreviated), he did so with a straight face. He was infamous for pulling practical jokes on the White House staff. For example, he would push all the buttons on his desk simultaneously and then watch happily as the people came rushing from everywhere in the building to see what he wanted. He sometimes pushed the elevator button and then ran before the doors opened, leaving a baffled operator scratching his head.

He often had groups of congressmen eat breakfast with him. During one such event, the congressmen, none of whom had eaten with the president before, were on their best behavior, observing the president and following his lead to avoid any mistake in etiquette. When coffee was served, the president quietly poured cream into his saucer before sipping his coffee. The congressmen were perplexed, but they did not want to offend the president, so they did the same. Then they watched in embarrassment as Coolidge calmly placed his saucer of cream on the floor for his cat.

Coolidge's silence was often a political asset. He never spoke hastily or acted rashly, preferring to give time a chance to work out ticklish issues—which it usually did, making him look all the wiser.

He believed that political office should seek the man, so he made no effort to promote himself. But he was politically astute, leading Walter Lippman to call Cal's practice "active inactivity." In his campaign speeches, he spoke of honesty and integrity, economy and industry, work and savings, patriotism and love of country. How could opponents contradict those "issues"?

Coolidge was immensely popular in all regions of the country, and he was considered a shoo-in for re-election in 1928. On August 2, 1927, he announced that he would hold a press conference. As the newsmen filed into the room, he handed each a two-by-nine-inch slip of paper that read, "I do not choose to run for president in nineteen twenty-eight." No explanation. No questions. Later, when pressed, Coolidge confided, "It is a pretty good idea to get out when they still want you."

(Adapted from "'Silent Cal' Coolidge" by Dennis L. Peterson, *The Elks Magazine*, Feb. 1999.)

relief for Belgium during World War I, and served with distinction as secretary of commerce in the cabinets of both Harding and Coolidge. After winning the Republican nomination, Hoover faced New York governor **Al Smith** in the 1928 election. There were two reasons that many Americans opposed Smith—he was Roman Catholic and he opposed Prohibition. At that time, Americans were not ready to accept either a Catholic or a "wet" as their chief executive, so Hoover won handily. In the early twentieth century, the mainstream of American culture was Protestant. Catholicism appeared to many Americans to be foreign and contrary to the democratic spirit. In addition, Prohibition became a moral crusade that united all Protestants, conservative and liberal alike.

However, Hoover's reign over American prosperity was brief. Within a year of his inauguration, the stock market crashed, and America began to fall into the most severe economic depression in its history. Hoover is commonly blamed for the depression as an advocate of the free market who did too little too late. However, he

In stark contrast to Harding and Coolidge, Herbert Hoover wanted the federal government to intervene in the nation's economy.

Hoover's Interventionism

Hoover pushed for farm subsidies when he was secretary of commerce. He urged farmers to cut production when foreign countries were increasing theirs. He supported going off the gold standard. He expanded credit the week in which the crash occurred, ensuring that the market was falsely stimulated. He pushed for higher wages, which ensured greater unemployment. His views on public relief were exactly the opposite of Harding and Coolidge's emphasis on individual initiative and local charitable relief. His administration increased the corporate income tax, the personal income tax, the estate tax, and postal rates, all of which suppressed economic growth. He revived wartime excise taxes; imposed sales taxes on gasoline, tires, automobiles, electricity, furs, jewelry, and other consumer items; and increased the gift tax. Hoover was an advocate of higher tariff rates and signed the Smoot-Hawley Tariff, the largest tariff in American history.

These interventionist, socialist measures show that Hoover was no free-market advocate. In fact, many of Roosevelt's New Deal programs had their antecedents in the Hoover presidency.

When presidents follow a free-market philosophy—expanded opportunities for private business initiative and limited government interference—the result has always been the greatest freedom and prosperity of any nation in the world.

Albert Einstein

was just as much an economic interventionist president as his successor, Franklin Roosevelt. Hoover's increasingly intrusive government interventions in the free market had consequences, including the Republican Party's loss of power for the next twenty years and the worst depression in American history.

Section Quiz

1. What temporary panic concerning fears of a leftist revolution beset America in 1919?

2. What two major efforts to maintain world peace did the United States endorse in the 1920s?

3. Describe the circular flow of money between the United States and Europe that developed following World War I.

4. What proposal for resolving the foreign debt crisis was introduced by an American banker?

5. Who were the three Republican presidents that took office in the 1920s?

★ How should a Christian view attempts to ensure peace between nations?

II. Culture Wars

The twenties was the first decade of what is considered modern America and one of the most glamorous periods in the nation's history. "The greatest, gaudiest spree in history," novelist F. Scott Fitzgerald labeled it. Behind the glitter, however, new philosophies ravaged the moral character of a generation—a society that poet T. S. Eliot characterized as a "waste land."

New Ideas

Darwinism and Marxism

Modern ideas brought about many of the changes in American society that were evident in the 1920s. Although the writings of Charles Darwin (evolution) and Karl Marx (communism) had appeared in the nineteenth century, their full impact did not become apparent until after World War I. Darwin's theory contradicted the scriptural account of Creation, and Marx's economic philosophy denied the depravity of man. Although these ideas had been too radical for most nineteenth-century Americans, evolution and socialism found widespread interest and acceptance in the 1920s. A growing disregard of scriptural truth naturally presaged the acceptance of these views. But many people also opposed them. Americans were especially suspicious of communism, which they had seen take over Russia in 1917. They worried that it could take over America too.

Theory of Relativity

As the 1920s dawned, **Albert Einstein**, a German scientist, set forth a scientific theory that many writers and philosophers used to cast additional doubt upon the scriptural and moral standards of Americans. Since the days of Sir Isaac Newton, scientists and philosophers had believed in an orderly world ruled by natural laws discovered by the scientific method. Using reason and common sense, man could comprehend the universe, which was certain and machinelike. This comfortable view was shattered by Einstein's **theory of relativity**—that space, time, and matter are not absolute dimensions but are relative to the location and motion of the observer. By 1929, a Harvard mathematician confessed, "The physicist thus finds himself in a world from which the bottom has dropped clean out." Seemingly, the absolutes of science were no longer absolute.

Freud

The ideas of **Sigmund Freud** became popular in the twenties. This Austrian psychologist believed that sexual disturbances in childhood could explain the development of emotional problems later in life. Sex is pervasive in man's unconscious motivation, Freud believed, and he contributed to the popular sentiment that one has to reject inhibitions to have a healthy emotional life. Thereafter, many Americans argued that self-restraint ("repression") led to emotional disorders and that psychoanalysis was the cure. For some people who had lost their moral bearings, the psychiatrist replaced the minister as counselor.

Literature and Art

Modern literature and art in the early twentieth century revealed the influence of the new ideas. In literature, as in art and music, traditional standards yielded to modern ones. Painting was abstract and depicted inner feelings rather than real images, and atonal music moved beyond normal harmony. Poetry written in free verse and novels in stream-of-consciousness form represented the modern break from the conventions of literature in the nineteenth century.

Both the themes and the techniques used in the literature of the twenties echoed the modern era. T. S. Eliot's poetry spoke of despair and disillusionment and criticized the emptiness of modern society. Novelist William Faulkner—with his awkward syntax, departure from traditional narrative, and emphasis on man's evil—created a meaningless world from which the old values had been removed.

Prohibition

One seeming victory for the forces of civic righteousness was the passage and ratification of the Eighteenth Amendment, or Prohibition. The amendment passed the Senate and the House of Representatives in 1917, and the necessary thirty-five states ratified it by 1919. (Eventually, forty-five states ratified the amendment. Rhode Island was the only state to reject it. Illinois and Indiana did not vote since it was already law.) The amendment prohibited the manufacture, sale, or transportation of intoxicating liquors. Unfortunately, the law resulted in an increase in illegal activity. Illegal liquor created a large and lucrative black market, and violent crime increased as gangsters competed for control of illegal alcohol trade in their territories.

Congress had passed the Volstead Act (over Wilson's veto) in October 1919 to provide for the enforcement of Prohibition; it defined illegal beverages as those that contained more than half

---

Einstein Explains Relativity

"Gravitation cannot be held responsible for people falling in love. How on earth can you explain in terms of chemistry and physics so important a biological phenomenon as first love? Put your hand on a stove for a minute and it seems like an hour. Sit with that special girl for an hour and it seems like a minute. That's relativity."

American Writers of the Twenties

The disillusionment of American writers in the twenties was evident from the number of prominent authors who chose to live and write in Europe (particularly Paris) rather than in the United States. Among them were Ernest Hemingway and F. Scott Fitzgerald.

What the Prohibition Amendment Did NOT Do

Contrary to popular belief, Prohibition did not outlaw the consumption of alcoholic beverages. It merely made obtaining them very difficult.

Revenue agents pose with the largest still confiscated in Washington, D.C., during Prohibition.

of 1 percent alcohol by volume. When enforcement of Prohibition proved to be a problem, President Hoover appointed the Wickersham Commission to investigate the lax enforcement. The commission found that Prohibition was impossible to enforce because a large part of the nation was willing to violate the law. The commission did not recommend repeal, but vocal opposition to Prohibition grew, especially among Democrats. When Franklin Roosevelt, who favored repeal, was elected in 1932, Prohibition's days were numbered. The end of the "noble experiment," as Hoover once called it, came in December 1933 with the ratification of the Twenty-first Amendment.

The Roaring Twenties

The modern ideas that gained acceptance in the 1920s led to a social revolution in America. So obvious was the new disregard for moral standards that the decade has often been called the Jazz Age, the ballyhoo years, the age of excess, or more commonly, the "Roaring Twenties."

The breakdown in morality naturally weakened the family. From the 1870s to the 1920s, the U.S. population increased 300 percent, but divorce increased 2,000 percent. Several factors contributed to this rapid rise in divorce. Women were freed from some household chores by new inventions and new services from local businesses. Also, families were generally smaller than in previous generations. The result was that wives often had time for work and social activities outside the home, and sometimes those interests interfered with family relationships. Also, the newspapers and the silent screen were ablaze with stories of immorality, and that emphasis naturally changed attitudes about purity and fidelity.

In addition to these evidences of moral and family breakdown, the 1920s witnessed the incredible popularity of the frivolous and the sensational. Young Americans rushed to follow the latest fads, such as wearing raccoon coats, working crossword puzzles, playing a game called mahjong, marathon dancing, and flagpole sitting. Tabloids and radio informed a nation craving the details of scandalous love affairs, murders, and dramatic true-life stories. In a world where standards had been broken down, people tended to seek thrills and adventure to fill the void in their lives.

Heroes and Villains

The twenties was certainly a colorful time in American history. The spread of daily newspapers, the advent of radio, and the shift from vaudeville to movies allowed people in every corner of the nation to keep tabs on not only rising stars in sports, entertainment, and politics but also notorious criminals. Movies became the biggest source of entertainment for the working class. Movies were big moneymakers and in many ways reflected the changing values of the culture. They also changed the way the world viewed America.

American Idols

Organized sports became major entertainment in the twenties. In 1921, fans overflowed a sixty-thousand-seat stadium near Jersey City to watch boxer Jack Dempsey knock out the French boxer Georges Carpentier. It was the first "million-dollar gate" for sports in the United States and the first major sports event to be broadcast by radio. Babe Ruth, "the Sultan of Swat," thrilled huge crowds at baseball games in Yankee Stadium, and in the 1927 season he hit

Flappers and "Flaming Youth"

The young people caught up in the moral vacuum of the twenties were known as "flaming youth," and they captured attention by their rebellious behavior. Before World War I, police arrested women in towns and cities for smoking or for dressing immodestly, but during the twenties some young women in the cities flaunted their newfound freedom by drinking and smoking openly and by shortening their hemlines. Bobbed hair and the boyish look were fashionable for these "flappers." Immorality became glamorous, and virtue was too old-fashioned for many of the pleasure-seeking young people of the era. And the dance known as the "Charleston" was all the rage.

Babe Ruth, "the Sultan of Swat"

sixty home runs. Fans filled college football stadiums to thrill in the exploits of athletes such as Red Grange of Illinois and the Four Horsemen of Notre Dame, coached by the legendary Knute Rockne.

By the end of the 1920s, about a hundred million Americans, almost the entire population, were going to the movies weekly to see famous comedians such as Charlie Chaplin and Laurel and Hardy or sensual stars such as Rudolph Valentino, Clara Bow, and Gloria Swanson. Popular "talkies" replaced silent films in 1927, and the more than twenty thousand movie palaces in the nation rivaled churches as the most important downtown buildings. By the twenties, many middle-class Americans had become addicted to Hollywood, not only to the world of luxury and immorality portrayed on the screen but also to the promiscuity and glamour of the stars' offscreen lives, as reported by the nation's tabloids. Concerned about the public image of Hollywood, moviemakers hired Will Hays, Harding's postmaster general and a Presbyterian lay leader, to censor the films.

Other Sports Heroes

Other sports heroes gained wealth, fame, and admiration during the 1920s while popularizing their sports for the enjoyment of millions of Americans. Bobby Jones became the king of the golf links, and William Tilden aspired to the heights of the tennis world. Golf courses and tennis courts multiplied across the land.

America's Air Ambassador

At 7:52 a.m. on May 20, 1927, one man in a small silver airplane named *Spirit of St. Louis* took off from Roosevelt Field on Long Island. The single-engine craft rose into the morning haze and carried its pilot into the headlines and history books.

That man was twenty-five-year-old **Charles A. Lindbergh**. He was trying to become the first person to fly solo nonstop across the Atlantic Ocean, from New York to Paris.

Although he was relatively unknown before his historic flight, Lindbergh captured the attention of both the United States and western Europe as they awaited news of his fate. Then, at last, word came that "the Lone Eagle" had reached his destination on the night of May 21. The next day, the *New York Times* proclaimed

in its headline, "LINDBERGH DOES IT! TO PARIS IN 33½ HOURS; FLIES 1,000 MILES THROUGH SNOW AND SLEET; CHEERING FRENCH CARRY HIM OFF FIELD."

A ticker-tape parade and numerous awards, including the Distinguished Flying Cross from President Calvin Coolidge, awaited Lindbergh in New York City and St. Louis. Lindbergh's flight received more publicity in American newspapers than did the Armistice of 1918 and sparked a great number of commemorative items, including a postage stamp.

Although he modestly claimed to be only a stunt flyer, Lindbergh riveted the world's attention on the potential of air power. America showered him with acclaim and fondly remembered "Lucky Lindy's" heroic flight for years to come.

The Lone Eagle, Charles Lindbergh, poses with his plane, *Spirit of St. Louis*, ten days after his history-making flight.

Pride and Prejudice

Around the turn of the century, American culture became more diverse with the increased "New Immigration" (discussed in Chapter 16). From 1900 to 1910, almost nine million immigrants entered this country, the highest number for any one decade. Most of them were from southern and eastern Europe. These immigrants kept their languages, religions, and cultures and usually lived in crowded neighborhoods of the same nationality in the nation's major cities. Middle-class Protestant Americans, who had long been predominant in the population, perceived the large numbers of Catholics and Jews in this wave of immigration as a threat. Many

The National Origins Act

The suspicion of foreigners combined with the surge in immigration after the war resulted in congressional restrictions. The **National Origins Act** (1924) set quotas to restrict immigration. It limited immigration of a nationality to 2 percent of that nationality living in the United States as of the 1890 census. In addition, it totally prohibited Japanese immigration. Clearly the government wanted to preserve America from a threat to its Anglo-Saxon heritage.

In September 1926, the Ku Klux Klan conducted a march in Washington, D.C., against blacks, Catholics, and Jews.

of the foreigners were poor and uneducated, and some had radical political ideas.

The Red Scare of 1919 encouraged the public to associate crime with immigrants, and this association was evident in the famous **Sacco-Vanzetti case**. In 1920, Nicola Sacco and Bartolomeo Vanzetti allegedly murdered two men during a robbery in South Braintree, Massachusetts. After their case received mounting publicity for several years, the two men were convicted and in 1927 were executed. Their defenders argued that they had been convicted because they were Italian-born aliens and anarchists, not because of the evidence, which many people viewed as doubtful.

During World War I and the 1920s, another trend altered American cities as black Americans migrated from the South to the North. With the reduction in immigrants, northern industries needed workers, and the one million blacks who moved to northern cities between 1910 and 1930 helped fill that need. The northern urban setting offered political opportunities for blacks. Oscar DePriest from Chicago became the first black congressman from the North. **Marcus Garvey** of New York City, with his Universal Negro Improvement Association, organized urban blacks into a potent force. Touting racial pride, he enrolled six million members by 1923. Culturally, blacks gained even greater visibility. With the **Harlem Renaissance**, black intellectuals and writers including James Weldon Johnson, Alain Locke, and Langston Hughes achieved prominence. Entertainers such as trumpeter Louis Armstrong and singer Paul Robeson appealed increasingly to white Americans. Several fashionable night spots in the twenties featured black performers playing popular jazz music. But black people remained excluded from the audiences.

The rapid social changes of the 1920s caused some Americans to react with violence. Fear of immigrants and blacks led in 1915 to the revival of the **Ku Klux Klan**, a secretive, ritualistic group patterned after the organization founded during Reconstruction. It promoted "100% Americanism" and limited membership to native-born white Protestants. Through skillful promotion, the Klan expanded nationally from the South through the early 1920s, becoming a strong social and political force in many northern cities, where immigrant and black populations were rising. In 1924, for example, 40 percent of the Klan's total membership was located in the states of Ohio, Indiana, and Illinois, and a Klan-backed write-in candidate nearly won a three-way race for mayor of Detroit. Feeding on bigotry and racism, the Klan's organizers resorted to intimidation and violence against blacks, Catholics, and Jews.

While the evils of the Klan's aims and methods are now clear to see, Klan members in the 1920s would probably have claimed to be on the side of righteousness, fighting the decline in morality and using the symbol of the cross. In addition to blacks, immigrants, and Catholics, Klan targets included bootleggers, wife-beaters, and immoral movies. In some communities, the Klan achieved a degree of respectability as it worked with politicians. The 1924 Democratic National Convention refused, by a narrow

Scarface

Chicago was headquarters for a man who was probably the most infamous gangster of the twenties—**Al Capone**.

Several gangs entered the bootlegging business in Chicago during the 1920s. Johnny Torrio led one of those gangs with the help of a strong man, barely out of his teens, named Alphonse Capone. Growing up in New York, Capone was slashed in a knife fight, receiving three prominent scars on the left side of his face (hence the nickname "Scarface," which he hated).

Torrio brought Capone to Chicago in 1920 as a bodyguard, but Capone quickly proved to be clever and effective in operating the illegal businesses of the gang. After Torrio was wounded in a gangland attack in 1925, he left town and gave Capone command of his crime ring. Capone soon established himself as the king of Chicago's underworld. People who stood in his way were likely to meet a sudden death. The most famous example of gang violence was probably the "Saint Valentine's Day Massacre" in 1929, when members of Capone's gang, disguised as policemen, gunned down members of a rival gang in a garage.

Despite Capone's opulent lifestyle, which was obviously the result of illegal gain, authorities struggled to find evidence that would put him behind bars. His subordinates were too well paid, too loyal, or too afraid to testify against him. He was careful to leave no written evidence of his ill-gotten gains. Finally, federal investigators uncovered evidence of about $1 million in income on which Capone had paid no taxes. Prosecutors brought Capone to trial for income tax evasion in 1931. The court found him guilty and sentenced him to eleven years in prison, part of which was spent in Alcatraz. While Capone was in prison, venereal disease ravaged his brain. At age forty-eight, the kingpin of 1920s Chicago died in 1947 without his fortune.

margin, to condemn it by name. Because of its secretive nature, precise statistics on membership are elusive, but the Klan's membership reached several million according to some estimates. That number declined after the mid-1920s. The 1924 immigration law reduced the number of immigrants and the fears they generated. Also, the Klan's use of violence alienated mainstream America, and a sex scandal among the Indiana Klan leaders made a mockery of the Klan's moral crusade.

Fighting for the Faith

Rise of Fundamentalism

One religious movement reacted strongly to the modern trends of the 1920s. As was mentioned in Chapter 18, several orthodox movements in the Progressive Era resisted the theological errors of modernism, the social gospel, and the inroads of Darwinian evolution into Christian denominations. Some Christian leaders were willing to make peace with advocates of these ideas in the name

Role of Premillennialism

Another influence on American Christianity at that time was premillennialism. Premillennialists rejected the liberals' unfounded faith in progress, and they contended that the world was actually growing worse. Most importantly, premillennialists emphasized that Christ could return at any time to establish His millennial kingdom. After World War I, various conservative movements (such as premillennialism) from several denominations joined forces to form what became known as Fundamentalism.

The Term Fundamentalist Today

Today the term *Fundamentalist* has become a slur with little specific content. In modern usage, a person can be a Muslim fundamentalist or a Hindu fundamentalist. The term is simply used for someone who radically holds to an extreme form of his or her religion, and usually the implication is that fundamentalists are intellectually backward. Christians who self-identify as Fundamentalists, however, stand in the mainstream of the orthodox Christian tradition with all its rich intellectual heritage. They are distinct from other Christian groups by their insistence that the Bible is verbally inspired and that church discipline (separation) be exercised toward non-Christians who insinuate themselves into the church and toward the indifferentists who tolerate them.

of Christian unity. These leaders were indifferent to the compromise that would result. Another group of Christians argued that theological modernism was a different religion from Christianity and that the social gospel was no gospel at all. There can be no Christian unity with those who promote a false gospel, they said. These Christians fought to remove modernists from their denominations or, if that failed, left and founded denominations, churches, and schools that remained faithful to the gospel. These Christians became known as **Fundamentalists**.

The origin of the term *Fundamentalism* lies in the belief of some Bible-believing Christians that certain "fundamental" doctrines exist that no one can deny and still be a Christian—doctrines such as the authority of Scripture, Christ's deity and vicarious atonement, the Resurrection, and the Second Coming. In 1910, two Christian businessmen sponsored the publication of a series of essays by some of the leading Christian scholars of the day to defend key doctrines. They sent these essays, called *The Fundamentals*, at no cost, to pastors, professors, and laymen all over the country. In 1920, a Christian editor wrote, "We suggest that those who still cling to the great fundamentals and who mean to do battle royal for the fundamentals be called 'Fundamentalists.'"

The Fundamentalist-Modernist Controversy

In the North, Fundamentalism developed into a theological battle with modernists. This battle, called the **Fundamentalist-Modernist controversy**, raged over doctrine and the control of the major denominations' schools, mission boards, and institutions. Such men as William Bell Riley fought for the Faith in the Northern Baptist Convention. J. Gresham Machen and others battled the liberals for the historic Christian Faith in the northern Presbyterian church. Machen's book *Christianity and Liberalism*, written in 1923, forcefully pointed out that modernism was not Christianity but another religion.

Orthodox Christians remained the majority in the denominations. However, those who remained indifferent to the compromise were unwilling to expel modernists from their denominations if such action risked a major split. By siding with the modernists, compromising Christians prevented the Fundamentalists from removing false teachers from key leadership positions within the denominations. The militant Fundamentalists, therefore, began to leave the major denominations and form their own associations. Fundamentalists in the Northern Baptist Convention left to form the General Association of Regular Baptist Churches (GARBC) in 1932. Machen led a group of Presbyterian Fundamentalists to form the Orthodox Presbyterian Church in 1936.

Anti-evolution Crusade

In the South—where the major Baptist, Methodist, and Presbyterian denominations were generally sound in the twenties—one of the Fundamentalist efforts focused on removing the teaching of evolution from the public schools. As these Christians pointed out, evolution was not only irreconcilable with the biblical account of Creation but also directly assaulted the authority of Scripture. With leaders such as former secretary of state and presidential candidate William Jennings Bryan, they pushed for laws banning the teaching of evolution but succeeded in doing so in only a few Southern states, one of them being Tennessee. Wanting to put their town on

Bryan: "He Kept the Faith"

William Jennings Bryan was one of the dominant figures of his era. He was a three-time candidate for president, secretary of state under Wilson, and a political crusader and reformer. Bryan also had a clear Christian testimony. He recalled, "At the age of fourteen, I reached one of the turning points in my life. I attended a revival that was being conducted in a Presbyterian church and was converted." That event, Bryan said, "has had more influence in my life for good than any other experience."

Bryan's reputation as a political progressive sometimes confuses those who associate conservative religious beliefs with conservative political beliefs. Some Christians of Bryan's day supported progressive political reforms as a means of allowing the government to be "the minister of God . . . for good" (Rom. 13:4). Some Christians continue to embrace this use of political reforms.

Bryan devoted himself to Christian causes, especially in the last ten years of his life. The defense of Christianity took him to the Scopes trial in Dayton, Tennessee. He told the court, "I want the Christian world to know that any atheist, agnostic, unbeliever, can question me any time as to my belief in God, and I will answer him." Bryan, therefore, faced "foolish and unlearned questions" (2 Tim. 2:23) from the cynical, scoffing Darrow, questions that Bryan frankly was neither scientist nor theologian enough to answer adequately. But his courage was beyond doubt.

Following his death only days after the Scopes trial, Bryan was buried in Arlington National Cemetery. On his tomb is a simple and powerful epitaph: "He Kept the Faith."

---

the map, some town leaders of Dayton, Tennessee, coaxed a high school teacher, **John T. Scopes**, to challenge the law.

The result was a media event as national attention focused on the town for the summer of 1925. The American Civil Liberties Union hired Clarence Darrow, a famous expert trial lawyer and an agnostic, to defend Scopes. Bryan, who helped the prosecution, also was a witness, called by the defense as an expert on the Bible. Although Bryan showed commendable courage in his defense of the Faith, he was no Bible scholar and did not make the best case for the cause. Scopes was ultimately convicted, but Bryan and the anti-evolutionists lost the publicity battle.

Fundamentalist Successes

In a larger sense, Fundamentalists in the twenties were battling the modern culture that aggressively assaulted the old-time religion. Philosophers, writers, and even liberal ministers dogmatically trusted science as the source of true knowledge and extolled the virtues of Freud and Darwin. American society had become increasingly secular, as revealed in movies, magazines, radio, literature, jazz, and urban lifestyles. Fundamentalists fought the increasingly irreligious mood in America. The failure of World War I to bring peace and the corruption in government and society gave credibility to their message.

Despite the Scopes trial debacle, Fundamentalism flourished in the twenties. By 1930, more than fifty Bible colleges and seminaries offered training for those who could no longer trust their denominational colleges and seminaries. Fundamentalists also took to the airwaves. In 1932, *Sunday School Times* listed more than four hundred evangelical programs on eighty different radio stations in the country.

Premature Obituary for Fundamentalism

Bryan died only a few days after the Scopes trial. For many wishful critics, Fundamentalism died with Bryan in Tennessee. But the movement was still very much alive, as it demonstrated in 1928 when it assisted in defeating the antiprohibition, Roman Catholic, Democratic candidate Al Smith in the presidential election. Ironically, while the mainline denominations that resisted Fundamentalism declined, Fundamentalist institutions prospered.

Section Quiz

1. Name four men whose philosophical and scientific theories helped to reshape the moral attitudes of the 1920s in ways detrimental to Christianity.

2. What term describes the young people of the 1920s who lacked moral values?

3. In what two occupational groups did Americans of the 1920s find many of their heroes?

4. What were two major evidences of American resentment toward immigrants and blacks in the 1920s?

5. What two groups were involved in a major religious controversy during the 1920s?

✶ Does the failure of Prohibition demonstrate that it is impossible to legislate morality?

Hoover's Ill-Fated Prediction

"One of the oldest and perhaps the noblest of human aspirations has been the abolition of poverty. . . . We in America today are nearer to the final triumph over poverty than ever before in the history of any land. The poorhouse is vanishing from among us. We have not yet reached the goal, but, given a chance to go forward with the policies of the last eight years, we shall soon, with the help of God, be in sight of the day when poverty will be banished from this nation."

Mail-order catalogs sold all sorts of merchandise, including several models of Sears, Roebuck and Company homes.

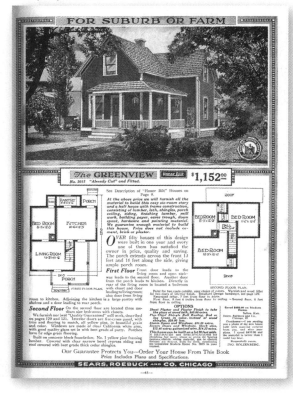

III. From Roar to Ruin

As the 1920s progressed, Americans grew accustomed to the economic prosperity of the era. It was the most prosperous decade in American history to that point. Businesses thrived and living standards improved, making life more comfortable for most Americans. The widespread prosperity created a growing middle class and improved the lives of even the lower class through new jobs, new inventions, and expanding opportunities. A new service industry developed as well as a new classification of workers—the managerial class.

The economy was improving so much that when Herbert Hoover accepted the Republican nomination in 1928, he even predicted a total eradication of poverty in the land. Hoover's rosy prediction must have seemed legitimate at the time, but events would soon prove that material prosperity is fleeting.

We've Got the Goods

If America was on the road to ruin, it was certainly driving there in style. America was fast becoming a consumer society that was spending without counting the cost. In 1920, there had been only about nine million automobiles in the United States. During the decade, that number nearly tripled. Henry Ford had made his black Model T affordable and commonplace, but it was dull and drab in contrast to the sleek styles and colors introduced by other automakers in the twenties. Chevrolet and other competitors attracted buyers who wanted something different, forcing Ford to introduce the Model A in 1927. Chevy and Ford also set up credit corporations—the General Motors Acceptance Corporation and Ford's Universal Credit Corporation—to help consumers who did not have the money for a car to buy one on credit. With advertising to make the product known and **installment plans** (making small monthly payments until the item is paid for) available to finance the price, Americans eagerly stepped into the driver's seat and sped away in debt.

The automobile had social as well as economic influence. Good roads improved transportation and gave rise to the suburbs, as workers no longer had to live within walking distance of their jobs. Rural families could visit the cities often rather than just a few times a year, and tourism boomed as the average family could travel for vacations. Also, with cars, young couples had opportunities for unchaperoned dates.

Radio was another influential item of the 1920s. From the time the first commercial station **KDKA** went on the air in Pittsburgh, Americans began to tune in to the news, music, sports, and other entertainment that it offered. At first, the enthralled listeners built crude crystal sets to receive the radio broadcasts, but during the decade those archaic radios gave way to bigger and better professionally manufactured receivers, many of them in the form of fine pieces of furniture. Rural and urban Americans alike gathered around these prized possessions to listen to the songs of their favorite crooners, to thrill to stories of adventure, to laugh at the jokes of popular comedians, and to hear religious songs and sermons.

In addition to cars and radios, Americans acquired many more new material possessions in the 1920s. With electricity becoming increasingly available in both smaller towns and large cities, electric appliances multiplied. Phonographs, refrigerators, irons,

---

Diving into Debt

Two-thirds of all cars sold in 1927 were sold on the installment plan. By 1929, credit purchases for all sorts of major products, not just cars, made consumer loans the tenth largest industry in the nation.

Technological "Firsts"

Station KDKA in Pittsburgh broadcasted the first election returns over radio on November 2, 1920. Harding's was the first inauguration to use a public address system for amplification. And Harding became the first president to make a speech over radio when he dedicated the Francis Scott Key Memorial at Fort McHenry on June 14, 1922.

The Golden Age of Radio

The 1920s and 1930s have been called "the golden age of radio." During that time, many "firsts" were accomplished. In the process, many radio personalities—musicians, comedians, advertisers, and news reporters—became household names.

Some of the "Firsts"

The first religious broadcast—1921, Calvary Episcopal Church, KDKA, Pittsburgh

The first World Series baseball game—1922 (New York Giants defeated New York Yankees in five games), KDKA

First commercial ad time sold—1922, $9 for a 30-sec. spot, WEAF, Albany, N.Y.

First business-sponsored program—"The Ever-Ready Hour," a variety show, WEAF, 1923

First network broadcast—1923

First government regulation of radio broadcasting—1925, Federal Radio Commission

In the 1920s, radio became the major medium of news and entertainment for the nation, a dominance that radio did not lose until the advent of television after World War II.

Some Popular Radio Shows

"National Barn Dance"—1924, WLS, Chicago

"Grand Ole' Opry"—1925, WSM, Nashville

"Amos 'N' Andy—1928, WMAQ, Chicago

Some Popular Songs Heard on the Radio in the Twenties

"Rhapsody in Blue"

"Yes, We Have No Bananas"

"Barney Google"

"Tea for Two"

"I Found a Million-Dollar Baby in a Five-and-Ten-Cent Store"

"Bye, Bye, Blackbird"

"Ol' Man River"

"Blue Skies"

"You're the Cream in My Coffee"

"Button Up Your Overcoat"

"Stardust"

"Tiptoe Through the Tulips"

Some Popular Crooners of the Twenties

Billy Jones and Ernie Hare, "The Happiness Boys"

Rudy Vallee

Al Jolson

and other devices brought pleasure, comfort, and more leisure time into many homes. Telephone wires spread to many more homes, allowing people to communicate more easily with one another. A seemingly unlimited array of desirable possessions were available to catch the eye of the American consumer and make modern life more enjoyable.

On a Spending Spree

The materialism of the twenties was widely evident, but other elements were corrupting American society in more subtle ways. Advertising began to coax the public to buy things even if they did not need the products or have the money. Mass production was providing greater and greater numbers of products that needed to be sold. Therefore, mass consumption was also necessary. Through increased newspaper, magazine, and radio advertisements, businesses promoted goods ranging from cigarettes to soap and automobiles to mouthwash. Advertising appeals emphasized youth, sex, happiness, luxury, and keeping up with one's neighbors. Celebrity endorsements, or testimonials, began to add glamour to products. Consumers were tempted to spend, not to save; to enjoy the present, not to think about future needs or emergencies; to pamper themselves, not to practice self-denial. Such materialistic values undercut biblical values as advertisers increasingly persuaded Americans to be better consumers of goods than producers of them. Buying on credit through installment plans made that possible.

Ever in debt for their purchases, Americans searched for ways to acquire the money they needed to maintain their comfortable lifestyles. Some resorted to fraud, bootlegging, and other illegal means; others turned to **speculation**, buying something with the hope of selling it later at a profit. One hot item for speculation in the 1920s was land in Florida, especially around Miami. Billed as a

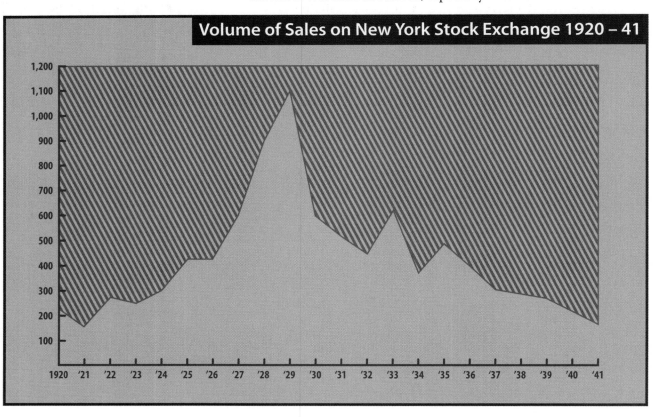

Volume of Sales on New York Stock Exchange 1920 – 41

tropical paradise, acreage there began to sell, and the more buyers expressed interest, the higher land prices went. Speculators bought large tracts of land and subdivided them for sale. As the land boom progressed, they sold and resold the properties for higher and higher amounts. Much of the land was marshland or otherwise undesirable, but promises of future golf courses, shopping areas, and other developments tempted many people to buy a lot nearby for $20,000 or more. Then in 1926 a severe hurricane hit the Miami area, killing four hundred people and destroying thousands of houses. The disaster brought a sudden end to the land boom as people awoke to the hazards of their speculation. The credit that had sustained the boom collapsed as land prices plummeted. Many fortunes made in the boom were lost overnight, and thousands of unwary Americans were left with heavy debts and worthless land deeds.

As a great **bull market** (a stock market characterized by optimism and rising prices) began in 1927, stock became a prime target for American speculation. Wall Street had prospered throughout the decade as public infatuation with business grew and as ordinary people who had gained experience buying war bonds now became aware of the promising securities market.

Easy credit also fueled an interest in owning shares of corporations as investors were allowed to buy stock "**on the margin.**" In this process, investors would purchase stock through a broker but pay only a percentage (30 to 50 percent on average) of the purchase price. The broker would finance the remaining amount for the investor with money he had borrowed from a bank or other sources. As long as the stock's value remained constant or increased, the broker was assured of collateral to cover the loan. However, if the stock price dropped, he would call in the investor's loan and force him to increase his margin or pay for the stock immediately.

From March 1928 to September 1929, prices of many favored stocks doubled, and nearly every stock rose. The possibilities of profits from stock speculation fueled tremendous activity on Wall Street and created even greater admiration and expectations of American business. President Coolidge disapproved of speculation, but he had certainly encouraged American faith in business, and Hoover's election helped to prompt the amazing stock market flourish that followed for several months. Republicans reveled in the prosperity that seemed to abound.

Boom Goes Bust

While Wall Street was booming, Americans naturally focused their attention on the excitement and affluence that it afforded. However, the nation's economic condition was dependent on far more than the price of corporate stock. Besides, most Americans were not even involved in the stock market. Several fundamental problems had been developing through the decade, but optimistic Americans brushed aside the possible dangers until October 1929.

In the middle of that month, stock prices began to sag, and investors began to grow wary. On October 24 ("Black Thursday"), fear began to fuel panic selling. Millions of shares were offered for sale, but virtually no one bought. Prices dropped dramatically until New York's leading financiers pooled their resources to buy stock and halt the devastating decline. The attempt to prop up the market worked for that day, but not before stock prices had taken a significant fall. Banks began to pressure brokers, and brokers began to pressure

The Federal Reserve's Role in Producing an Overheated Stock Market

During the late 1920s, Americans watched stock prices climb dramatically and almost steadily. The Federal Reserve flooded the market with cheap credit that encouraged many people to make unwise investments and to buy on the margin. They hoped to sell at a huge profit, pay off their stockbrokers, and pocket a tidy sum without ever risking a large amount of their own money.

The show biz newspaper *Variety* reported the Black Thursday stock market crash in interesting terms.

The Granger Collection, New York

investors who had bought stock on the margin to pay up. Because most of these speculators did not have the extra cash, they opted to sell the stock, which resulted in a new wave of selling at the stock exchange and an accompanying drop in prices. On **Black Tuesday**, October 29, the bottom fell out of the market. More than sixteen million shares were dumped on the market, and investors lost $30 billion in the process. Americans hoped that the **stock market crash** was only a temporary "readjustment" of the inordinately high stock prices caused by speculation. Those hopes eroded, however, as prices on the market continued to decline gradually for three years.

What Really Caused the Depression?

In reality, the Depression consisted of *four* consecutive depressions that are collectively known as the Great Depression. Many problems caused, contributed to, or aggravated the Depression, leading to business decline, unemployment, and hardship for the people. Economic historians, however, have identified three major factors as causes of the Depression.

First were the cumulative consequences following World War I and the economic problems of European powers. Many of the Allies were heavily in debt from the war—this debt included money owed to the United States. But when Germany could not pay reparations to them, those European countries could not repay the United States. The United States was also in debt, and the Allies' failure to pay their loans only increased economic difficulties for the United States.

Another cause was the government's pursuit of reckless monetary policies. In the early 1920s the Federal Reserve System began to expand credit and to pump more money into the economy. This inflation of the monetary supply initiated a new but artificial economic boom. The Fed did this again in 1927, increasing the volume of farm and personal mortgages dramatically. State and local governments also increased their own indebtedness. Consequently, prices of real estate and stocks rose. The Fed finally abandoned its easy-money policy in mid-1929, and the economy began to readjust itself to match the true economic situation. The resulting collapse of credit devastated America's financial market.

A third cause, which came after the stock market crash but before Hoover's term ended, was the Smoot-Hawley Tariff of 1932. It was the highest tariff in American history, and it practically closed off all American foreign trade. Supposedly designed to protect American domestic manufacturers and farmers, in reality it hurt everyone because foreign nations retaliated with their own tariffs against American goods. In a very real sense, the tariff sowed the seeds of another world war because, as has been said, "When goods don't cross borders, armies will."

Although most histories of the period typically blame unwise stock speculation for the Depression, that was only one of many problems. In fact, most Americans did not even own stock; stock speculation was the opportunity of only a relative few. The cause behind the recklessness on Wall Street was actually the Fed's easy-money policy. Buying stock on credit had resulted in more than $8 million in loans from banks to brokers by October 1929. All that credit was based on the presumed value of stocks in a speculative market, and that value was shaky indeed. The inherent worth of many stocks had not increased during the bull market because

---

How the Federal Reserve Helped Bring about the Depression

The Federal Reserve System raised interest rates four times in 1928–29, thereby slowing and discouraging economic growth.

Unintended Consequences

The Smoot-Hawley tariff is a good illustration of how an action done with perhaps good intentions can have unintended negative consequences. The tariff was intended to protect selected American industries, but it actually hurt other leading industries. Economic historian Burton Folsom Jr. wrote, "The tariff on tungsten, for example, hurt steel; the tariff on linseed oil damaged the paint industry." It also "increased the duty on over eight hundred items used in making cars." Furthermore, foreign manufacturers "slapped retaliatory tariffs on the United States." As a result, American cars became more expensive, and U.S. car sales "plummeted from over 5.3 million in 1929 to 1.8 million in 1932."

[Burton Folsom Jr. in *New Deal or Raw Deal? How FDR's Economic Legacy has Damaged America* (New York: Threshold Editions, 2008), 31–32.]

many American industries became no more prosperous during that era. Neither their profits nor the dividends they paid shareholders had increased significantly. The stock market crash ended the speculative inflation.

Americans, now mired in debt and pessimistic about their future, tightened their belts in an attempt to regain their own economic security. All the causes that have been mentioned were the result of government activism, *not* the free market. Unfortunately, as the Depression deepened, the proposed—and implemented—solutions only made the problem worse, prolonging the Depression and opening the nation to demands for even more government interference in the free market.

Section Quiz

1. What two inventions in particular had a tremendous effect on American life in the 1920s?

2. Name two practices that encouraged Americans to spend money extravagantly during the 1920s.

3. In what year did the stock market crash?

★ What dangers does a consumer culture hold for a Christian?

People, Places, and Things to Remember

"normalcy"
Red Scare
isolationism
Washington Naval Conference
Kellogg-Briand Pact
Fordney-McCumber Tariff
Dawes Plan
Warren G. Harding
return to "normalcy"
Teapot Dome scandal
Calvin Coolidge
Herbert Hoover
Al Smith
Albert Einstein
theory of relativity
Sigmund Freud
Charles A. Lindbergh
Sacco-Vanzetti case
National Origins Act
Marcus Garvey
Harlem Renaissance
Ku Klux Klan
Al Capone
Fundamentalism
Fundamentalist-Modernist controversy
John T. Scopes
installment plans
radio
KDKA
speculation
bull market
"on the margin"
Black Tuesday
stock market crash (1929)

Chapter Review

Making Connections

1. Why was there a "farm problem" in the years following World War I?

2. Why did President Harding's reputation become tarnished after his death?

3. What trends in the ethnic and racial make-up of America's population disturbed many people in the 1920s?

4. What was one of the main focuses of Fundamentalist efforts in the North? in the South?

5. List at least three social effects of the automobile upon American society in the 1920s.

Developing History Skills

1. How did immigration impact the United States in the 1920s?

2. What techniques did businesses use in the 1920s to change Americans' spending habits?

Thinking Critically

1. What are some potential dangers of hero worship? Illustrate your answer with examples from the 1920s and today.

2. What are some biblical principles to guide one's involvement in installment buying or speculation in economic endeavors?

Living as a Christian Citizen

1. Imagine that you are a Fundamentalist pastor in the 1930s. Write a brief paragraph arguing for the removal of modernists from your denomination. Use Galatians 1:8–9; 2 Corinthians 6:14–7:1; Romans 16:17–18; and 2 John 7–10.

2. Immigration was a concern for Americans in the early part of the twentieth century, and it is again a concern for Americans in the early part of the twenty-first century. How should Christians view immigration, especially the immigration of those with other religions?

Out-of-work Americans line up for relief assistance during the Great Depression.

The Thirties (1929–1939)

I. Hoover Gets the Blame

II. FDR and the New Deal

III. Worst of Times, Best of Times

"I can't. This is my sister's day to eat."

A little girl's response to a teacher's suggestion that she go home and eat something (c.1932)

The jobless stood on city street corners, hoping to sell apples for 5¢ each. The homeless rode the rails from freight yard to freight yard, often camping in "hobo jungles." Down-and-out "Okies" left their dust-choked farms on the Great Plains, looking for work in the fruit and vegetable fields of California. Poor teachers in Chicago prepared little meals from their meager resources to feed their hungry students.

The nation that had come to be the wealthiest and most powerful in the world was somehow thrown into a confusing economic quagmire, entrapping millions of its people in poverty and despair. Although most Americans escaped severe deprivations, few of them passed through the 1930s without some hardship and anxiety. All around were unwanted reminders that the prosperity of the 1920s was gone and that the future was doubtful. Franklin Roosevelt, during his 1932 campaign, described the prevalent despondency when he commented, "I have looked into the faces of thousands of Americans. . . . They have the frightened look of lost children." Hard times and great challenges gripped the nation in the decade of the **Great Depression**.

I. Hoover Gets the Blame

During the 1928 election campaign, Herbert Hoover had promised the nation "a chicken in every pot and a car in every garage." The Republicans gladly accepted credit for the prosperity of the 1920s and promised more, a promise that the American people wanted to believe. Americans gave their support to Hoover, expecting him to extend their carefree existence for another four years. But when the stock market crash of 1929 hit, blame for the end of prosperity began to fall on the shoulders of one man: Herbert Hoover.

President Hoover signs the Farm Relief Bill into law, June 15, 1929.

Call It a Depression

Contrary to popular assumptions, America's economic prosperity did not evaporate overnight in October 1929. The conditions that led to the stock market crash had been developing during the twenties, and their impact was compounded in the months of uncertainty that followed the crash. The problems of unemployment, poverty, and despair began to surface but did not become widespread until about a year after the collapse on Wall Street. Even so, the economic decline could not be ignored for long. Because Hoover was intent on keeping Americans' morale high, he avoided the standard historical terms for an economic decline—*panic* or *crisis*—and instead chose to call the downturn by a title that, at the time, evoked less emotion. He called it a "depression." Although that economic term seemed less alarming at the time, the word came to strike fear in the hearts of Americans in the decades that followed and would bring to mind painful memories for the rest of the century.

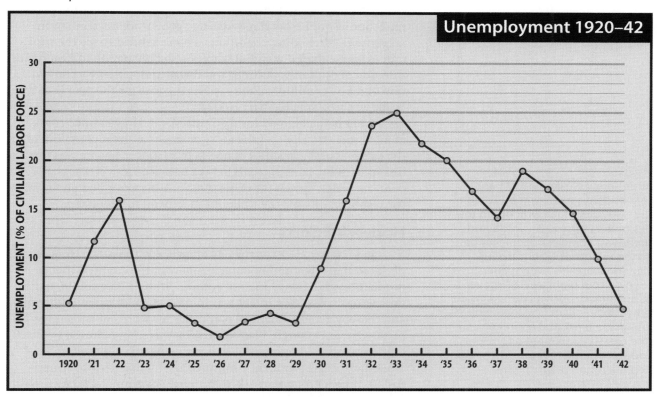

Unemployment 1920–42

Historians, economists, and politicians endlessly analyze the causes of the Great Depression, and although certain factors clearly contributed to the economic demise of the decade, there are no easy answers. It is evident that the growing debts of consumers in the 1920s eventually resulted in a loss of purchasing power by the end of that decade. This loss decreased demand for industrial production, which, in turn, caused businesses to slow production and lay off workers. The increase in unemployment led to further decline in the purchasing power of consumers, and that, in turn, led to further cutbacks in industry. The regressive cycle continued and was worsened by the harsh realities of the stock market crash until the nation was seized with bewilderment and fear over its economic future.

But what caused the dreadful stagnation of the economy? Some people fault America's businessmen, who reaped large profits during the 1920s while they allegedly paid meager wages to their workers. Others

An Oregon "Hooverville"

condemn the federal government for its blatant support of laissez-faire capitalism and its failure to intervene boldly in the nation's economic affairs when problems began to arise. Still others, including President Hoover, blame the international economic situation involving the unpaid debts of the Allies and Germany to the United States. The decline of international trade in response to high tariffs and Hoover's interventionist programs should also be added as contributing factors. Another factor, of course, was the willingness of the American people to incur heavy debts for autos, land, homes, stock, and other purchases before the downturn. One more point that should not be overlooked is the growth of pessimism in response to foreboding conditions. People tended to see the situation as worse than it was. But whatever led the nation to experience a decade of economic decline (and it was undoubtedly a combination of many conditions), the easiest response for the people of the 1930s was to blame Herbert Hoover.

About being blamed for the Depression, Hoover once commented sarcastically that the ascription was a "great compliment to the energies and capacities of one man." Hoover's name was forever linked with the hardships of that era because Hoover was the president "on watch" when the crisis struck. A disappointed public laid the responsibility for their plight squarely on his doorstep.

Hoover's Efforts

On October 25, 1929, the day after Black Thursday, Hoover declared that "the fundamental business of the country, that is production and distribution of commodities, is on a sound and prosperous basis." His intent was to restore American confidence and thereby avoid a financial panic, but his words of encouragement were not enough. Black Thursday was soon followed by Black Tuesday, and the nation went into a downward economic spiral. Nonetheless, the president continued trying to convince Americans, telling a group that asked for more government works projects in June 1930, "Gentlemen, you have come sixty days too late. The Depression is over." It was not so easy, Hoover found, to inspire the same optimism in the nation.

It has often been implied that Hoover made little effort to combat the Depression beyond assuring the nation that everything was going to be all right. This reputation for inaction, however, was not well earned. Hoover was a progressive Republican who was willing to make changes, including getting government involved where it had never been involved. He took steps to deal with the situation almost immediately. By the end of 1929, he got Congress to cut taxes by $140 million, and he encouraged an increase of $420 million on spending for federal **public works** (government-financed construction of public facilities) to create jobs. These were not small steps, but they gained little notice and, unfortunately, provided few immediate substantial results.

Early in 1932, Hoover reversed course and pressed Congress to pass the Revenue Act, which revived many taxes from World War I

Hoover's Legacy

As conditions grew bleaker in 1931 and 1932, the president's name was attached to practically everything that symbolized the adversities of the Depression. Cardboard shacks sheltering homeless people in the parks and vacant lots of American cities were called "Hoovervilles." Newspapers used for covering on cold nights were "Hoover blankets," and empty pockets turned inside out became "Hoover flags." As unemployment, business failures, and apprehension spread, the pressure mounted on the president to "do something" to rescue the nation and hasten the return of prosperity.

The impact of the Great Depression forced many former wage-earners to seek their meals in free "soup kitchens."

and imposed a sales tax on gasoline, tires, cars, electricity, and other items. It taxed stock transfers and phone, telegraph, and radio messages. It raised the personal income tax, the corporate income tax, and the gift tax. Hoover also expanded credit, which artificially stimulated the economy. At a time when he should have cut government spending and taxes, Hoover increased both, making the problems worse.

Voluntary Cooperation

Hoover also launched a major campaign for "voluntary" cooperation in the fight against depression. In December 1929, the president called a meeting of four hundred of the nation's leading business executives. He urged them to voluntarily keep their workers and maintain satisfactory wage levels. He also asked that they continue to invest in new construction and equipment rather than cut back industrial growth. Although the businessmen tried to cooperate, by the end of 1930 economic realities made support impossible. To abide by the agreement would have sent many firms into bankruptcy. So unemployment grew, wages declined, and industrial expansion virtually ceased.

Even before the stock market crash, Hoover had directed Congress to create the Federal Farm Board. This agency, intended to relieve the prolonged hardships of American farmers, instituted public stabilization corporations chartered by the states rather than by the federal government. These corporations were supposed to bolster the prices of farm products by buying surpluses while also trying to persuade farmers to cut back production voluntarily. When the Depression began and needs increased, Hoover hoped that these efforts would ease the farm problems. But the plan quickly fell apart as overproduction continued and funds for propping up farm prices ran out.

Other voluntary efforts initiated by the Hoover administration included the President's Emergency Committee for Employment (PECE), formed in October 1930. This committee tried to coordinate the efforts of public and private charities as they provided assistance to the poor and funneled information about relief conditions back to the government. About a year later, the President's Organization for Unemployment Relief (POUR) superseded PECE, but no matter its name, it never had the resources to deal effectively with the growing crisis. Another program was the National Credit Corporation (NCC). Facing increasing bank failures (from 651 in 1929 to almost 2,300 in 1931), Hoover wanted banks to cooperate to maintain their own stability. He expected the nation's prosperous banks to help establish a credit reserve fund to provide assistance to banks in danger of failing. By helping each other in this way, they might avoid further panic in the banking industry. This idea also met a humiliating end. Years later, Hoover said that the effort quickly "became ultraconservative, then fearful, and finally died."

In only one area did Hoover prefer true voluntary initiative over government intervention. He sincerely believed that it was the duty of private individuals, not the government, to help the needy with voluntary assistance, or relief. Hoover believed that relief and aid to the unemployed was a local matter. Reluctantly, he agreed to give federal relief money to state governments for indirect distribution. Unfortunately, in the face of an uncertain future and an apparently steady economic decline, by the autumn of 1931, the public outcry for government action was mounting rapidly.

> **Farm Prices Adjust to Real Market Conditions**
> The price for wheat fell from $1.05 a bushel in 1929 to 68¢ in 1930 and 39¢ in 1931. Other farm prices dropped similarly, throwing farmers deeper into debt and despair.

> **Commitment to Private Charity**
> The belief in private, voluntary relief or charity was so strong in the country that the Red Cross opposed a bill giving the organization $25 million. As the Red Cross told a congressional committee, taking government money would cause voluntary giving to dry up.

Government Involvement

When voluntary cooperation did not seem to provide the desired results quickly enough, Hoover initiated government measures to hasten recovery. Although he adamantly opposed any form of dole (an unearned government handout) to meet the needs of impoverished Americans, he believed that **work relief** was acceptable. Employment in a government relief job would at least discourage idleness and preserve the self-respect of the needy. Hoover also wanted to keep most of the relief efforts under the control of state and local government rather than creating large federal relief agencies. That way the measures taken could be adapted more easily to the specific needs in each local area.

Hoover also was determined to keep the federal budget in balance, even if it required tax increases. He declared that "the course of unbalanced budgets is the road to ruin." Most Americans shared Hoover's view that deficit spending would jeopardize confidence in the nation's financial stability and further discourage industrial recovery.

Although Hoover rejected many of the relief proposals that Congress scrambled to enact, in 1932 he approved the Emergency Relief and Construction Act, which established the **Reconstruction Finance Corporation** (RFC). This agency was his most important interventionist measure. Patterned after the War Finance Corporation of World War I, the RFC received $500 million to loan to businesses (primarily banks). Although this move helped stabilize the banking industry and a few other economic concerns temporarily, it did not inspire the expansion of credit and return of confidence that Hoover wanted.

In June 1930, Hoover signed the **Smoot-Hawley tariff**, which pushed tariffs on foreign industrial and agricultural prices to their highest level in history, from 33 percent to 40 percent. The high protectionist tariff, though intended to help American producers and stabilize prices, actually shut off foreign trade and thereby reduced the market for American goods. It is impossible to measure the total effect of the tariff revision on the economy, but it certainly did not help bring recovery to the depressed nation.

The increase in the tariff undoubtedly helped to precipitate an economic collapse in Europe in 1931. Hoover was especially concerned about this international crisis because he believed that America's foreign economic ties contributed to the Depression. He soon declared an unpopular but unavoidable moratorium on European debt payments to the United States. He also called for an international economic conference to solve international economic problems. Even so, no action was taken to lower the tariff until 1934.

Although Hoover's efforts to overcome the Depression did not turn the nation's economy back to prosperity—in fact, they actually worsened and prolonged it—his actions set a precedent for a significant increase in federal government involvement in America's economic affairs. In 1930, he asked for a $25 million loan to the Department of Agriculture for the provision of seed and feed to impoverished farmers, an action that was cited to justify future agricultural subsidies that exist to this day. He began the expansion of public works, spending unprecedented amounts of money for "make-work" projects; provided the first (though meager) federal funds for relief; established some pioneer programs in home financing and public housing; and established the Reconstruction Finance

Criticism of the RFC

The RFC was roundly criticized for helping the wealthy—bankers and businessmen—rather than the truly needy. The RFC loaned money to businesses that were about to fail when it should have allowed their failure as the market made its own readjustments.

Effect of Smoot-Hawley on Farmers

The American Farm Bureau Federation concluded that the Smoot-Hawley tariff provided farmers with a $30 million benefit from the agricultural tariffs while also imposing a $330 million loss.

Corporation, a major lending agency that would become an integral part of his successor's relief efforts. The next administration would embrace and greatly expand such federal activity, and, following those examples, government has been expanding ever since.

A Demand for Change

Although Hoover did not neglect the mounting economic crisis, the spread of poverty and despair was beginning to take a toll on the American people, and they began to cry for action to stop their suffering. In 1932, the situation was obviously bleak. The nation's measure of productivity, its GNP (Gross National Product, the annual value of all goods and services that a nation produces) fell to $41 billion, down from $104 billion in 1929. More than five thousand American banks had failed, eighty-six thousand businesses had closed, and a quarter of a million families had been evicted from their homes. In September of that year, *Fortune* magazine estimated that 28 percent of the population—about 34 million men, women, and children—were without any income whatsoever. As the hardships of the Depression spread, many Americans began to clamor for help and change.

The Bonus Army

A major episode in the Hoover administration's struggle with the Depression took place in the summer of 1932. A large group of unemployed World War I veterans made their way to Washington, D.C., to ask for an early payment of the bonus promised to them by the Adjusted Compensation Act of 1924. These veterans of the American Expeditionary Force now called themselves the **Bonus Army**, but this "army" did not win support from Congress. They turned to Hoover for help, but he would not deal with them. Dismayed but unwilling to concede defeat, a large number of the more than twenty thousand veterans, some with their wives and children, settled into a hastily built shantytown on the edge of the city and into some vacant buildings near the Capitol. As weeks passed, Hoover became more and more frustrated by their embarrassing presence in the capital city.

Federal troops burned the Bonus Army camp in Washington, forcing the protesting veterans to leave.

On July 28, the situation came to a head. Government agents informed the Bonus Army that they must move out of the downtown buildings, but they refused. Police with nightsticks in hand were sent to force the illegal occupants from the buildings, but the veterans, reinforced by men from the main camp, met the officers with a volley of bricks. In the melee, some of the policemen began to fire on the veterans, killing two and wounding two others. Hoover learned of the trouble and sent troops under General Douglas MacArthur to quell the disorder and destroy the shantytown. MacArthur, contrary to Hoover's orders, determined to use all necessary force to drive the veterans not only from the condemned buildings but also completely from the capital. After an hour's warning, the general's forces marched in with tear gas, tanks, and bayonets. Once the downtown buildings were cleared, MacArthur moved on to the main camp, driving out the veterans who remained and burning their shacks.

Although the action had been much harsher than he intended, Hoover took full responsibility for the affair. In doing so, he seemed more callous than ever to the needs of struggling Americans. A desire for change was leading many people to look elsewhere for relief. Some began to espouse various socialistic plans, even praising the Communist Soviet Union. Mussolini's Fascist regime in Italy also won admiration for dealing with economic difficulties. Such extreme political views were not the norm, but people without food, income, and other necessities were becoming desperate.

Election of 1932

As the 1932 presidential election approached, Republican prospects for reelection were bleak. Hoover had lost his appeal to the impatient public, but no other bright stars were on the Republican horizon that year. Republican congressmen and governors had generally fallen out of favor along with Hoover as voters held the whole party responsible for the continuing Depression. As a result, Hoover won renomination easily, but the Republicans entered the fall campaign with little confidence.

The Democrats, however, did have a rising star to offer in the 1932 campaign. For some time, **Franklin Delano Roosevelt** had desired the office once held by his Republican cousin Theodore, but that ambition seemed to be shattered in August 1921 when polio struck the young politician, paralyzing him from the waist down for life. Nonetheless, Roosevelt's courageous struggle to overcome his disability added appeal to his public image. In 1928, Roosevelt won the governorship of New York, despite overwhelming public support for Republicans in that year. With the rising public disapproval of the Republicans in 1930, the governor won reelection easily.

Roosevelt entered the Democratic convention in 1932 as the front-runner for the nomination. The governor met some stiff opposition from several factions of the party, including conservatives and Tammany Hall, but he managed to appease the conservatives with his vice-presidential pick, John Nance Garner of Texas. Roosevelt won on the fourth ballot, and, on notification of that fact, he flew from Albany to Chicago to make his acceptance speech in person at the convention. This unprecedented but calculated action helped to portray the candidate as a daring man who was willing to challenge tradition.

That perceived defiance of traditional actions proved to be the central issue of the campaign between Hoover and Roosevelt. Hoover pointed out that theme when he said, "My countrymen! The fundamental issue that will fix the national direction for one hundred years to come is whether we shall go in fidelity to American traditions or whether we shall turn to innovations." Because many needy Americans were critical of Hoover's insistence on tradition, they were ready to turn to innovations. Roosevelt promised them action, and they believed him. Even his campaign song renewed hope in a change for the better:

> Happy days are here again!
>
> The skies above are clear again!
>
> Let's all sing a song of cheer again—
>
> Happy days are here again!

Cautious Governor Roosevelt

The measures Roosevelt took to combat the Depression in New York were not particularly daring or successful. Nevertheless, Roosevelt skillfully increased his popularity and gained an advantageous position as the presidential election approached.

President Hoover and president-elect Roosevelt ride to the inauguration.

Republicans, caught in the crossfire of events, were not in a singing mood.

Roosevelt was in an enviable position throughout the race against Hoover. Because so many Americans wanted something different in their new president, Roosevelt would be an easy winner unless he foolishly antagonized the public. Therefore, he carefully avoided explaining the details of his economic plans. He spread hope and assurance of action to meet the crisis.

In his acceptance speech, Roosevelt stated, "I pledge you, I pledge myself, to a new deal for the American people." That promise of a "**New Deal**" (a name that would soon be permanently attached to his efforts to conquer the Depression) was what the people wanted to hear, regardless of his ambiguity on the particulars. The people were willing to look to a man who had overcome a serious handicap and trust that he would help the nation overcome its serious difficulties. They heard in his speeches what they *wanted* to hear. Conservatives heard "balance the budget"; liberals heard "innovations" and "action now." Surprisingly, even the poor identified with the wealthy and aristocratic Roosevelt because of his physical adversity. Such popularity could only result in a decisive win for the New York governor. Roosevelt won more than 57 percent of the popular vote in November and 472 electoral votes to Hoover's 59.

Final Desperate Days

During the months between the November election and the March 4 inauguration of Roosevelt, the defeated president was left to struggle with the continuing problems of the Depression. Hoover was not only somewhat bitter about his fate but also deeply concerned that Roosevelt would take government intervention too far. A brief upturn in the economy during the latter months of 1932 convinced the outbound president that his policies were working. He blamed Roosevelt, with some legitimacy, for scaring business with vague references to economic planning and deliberate inflation. Hoover feared that such hints of future socialism would destroy his efforts to encourage a business recovery.

Nonetheless, Hoover tried to enlist Roosevelt's help in a cooperative effort to deal with the difficulties arising in the early weeks of 1933. For any new effort to gain acceptance, it must have the approval of the popular president-elect. Roosevelt, however, avoided approving any of Hoover's programs for fear that the people would transfer the blame for failures to him. Roosevelt wanted to start his job without any ties to the unpopular moves of the outgoing administration. This position was politically wise for Roosevelt, but it was disastrous for the nation during those intervening weeks.

Despite the efforts of the Reconstruction Finance Corporation and other Hoover initiatives, a terrible **banking crisis** began to sweep the country. The nation's banking system was on the brink of total collapse. Depositors across the land were rushing to their banks to withdraw their money before it was too late, but panic only hastened the failure of many of these institutions and jeopardized the savings of other depositors. Roosevelt continued to refuse cooperation, leaving Hoover unable to act. As the hours passed before Roosevelt's inauguration, the nation seemed to be slipping into economic chaos.

FDR's Promises
FDR pledged to increase direct federal relief to the poor while promising to cut government expenditures and balance the budget. Is it possible to do all of this at the same time? If so, how? If not, why not?

New Deal?
Although FDR coined the phrase, President Hoover had already moved the country in the direction of government planning and federal intervention. President Roosevelt merely multiplied and greatly expanded what Hoover had begun.

Section Quiz

1. Why did Hoover call the economic decline a "depression"?

2. What two steps did Hoover take almost immediately to combat the oncoming depression with federal action?

3. What kind of assistance to the poor did Hoover favor over a dole?

4. What episode involving World War I veterans in Washington, D.C., became a problem to the Hoover administration?

5. Who were the two major party candidates for the presidency in 1932?

★ How did the Smoot-Hawley tariff affect the U.S. and world economies?

II. FDR and the New Deal

The drama of the banking crisis provided an emotional backdrop to the inauguration of the new president. The sense of imminent danger made Roosevelt look like a knight in shining armor rushing in to save a nation in distress. Radiating confidence, he quickly calmed apprehensions with a terse statement in his inaugural address: "First of all, let me assert my firm belief that the only thing we have to fear is fear itself."

Fighting Fear

Immediately after assuming office, Roosevelt began to set the government in motion once again. His first two actions were to call Congress into special session and to declare a "**bank holiday**." The banking crisis had brought the financial markets of the nation to a virtual standstill. By March 4, the day of his inauguration, thirty-eight states had closed their banks, and elsewhere the institutions were operating on a restricted basis. The collapse would be devastating if order and confidence were not restored. Therefore, Roosevelt called for a four-day closing of all banks to calm the fears of a jittery public. The banks that proved to be basically sound were allowed to reopen (all but 5 percent eventually reopened). This action renewed the people's confidence in banks and greatly reduced panic withdrawals.

During the bank holiday, Roosevelt issued an executive order forbidding the export of gold. Later, when Congress met, he got them to push through the Emergency Banking Act, forcing all Americans to turn in their gold in exchange for paper money. He took America off the gold standard and set the price of gold at $35 an ounce, up from $20.67 an ounce. This made the dollar worth less and allowed Roosevelt to pursue inflationary programs.

The First Hundred Days

Congress convened on March 9 and remained in an emergency session until June 16. In those crucial one hundred days, Congress passed Roosevelt's New Deal programs one after another. The support that the president had won in the election, along with the many newly elected Democratic congressmen, guaranteed smooth passage for most New Deal legislation. Rarely has a president enjoyed such cooperation in accomplishing his agenda. The nation watched in approval of the quick action.

Why a Special Session of Congress Was Necessary

Congress, according to the Constitution, was not due to convene until December. The new president had to call Congress to meet in special session to deal with the emergency and begin the implementation of his proposals.

Just Do Something!

"The whole country is with him," commented the popular humorist Will Rogers of FDR. "Just so he does something. If he burned down the Capitol, we would cheer and say, `Well, we at least got a fire started anyhow.'"

Besides his cabinet members (which included the first female secretary of labor, Frances Perkins), Roosevelt had recruited a group of advisers to help him formulate his plans for combating the Depression. This group, called the "**Brain Trust**," was composed mostly of professors from Columbia and other major universities who could offer ideas, often shaped by socialistic thinking, on economic policies and legislation. Roosevelt used many of their ideas to frame his legislative agenda.

On the first day of the emergency session, Congress approved the Emergency Banking Act, a measure that endorsed Roosevelt's bank holiday and authorized measures to deal with an impending currency shortage due to the bank closures and hoarding. That action was followed by a dozen more significant pieces of New Deal legislation. These laws took the nation off the gold standard, established the Civilian Conservation Corps (CCC), provided nearly $4 billion in federal relief, and created the Agricultural Adjustment Administration (AAA) to deal with farm problems. They also legalized beer (a measure followed shortly by the national repeal of Prohibition), provided insurance for bank deposits, established regulations for the financial activities of Wall Street, provided for the refinancing of home mortgages, attempted to provide some regulation for the nation's industries, and approved the Tennessee Valley Authority (TVA).

Franklin Roosevelt delivered reassurance and confidence in his "fireside chats."

To keep the nation informed and inspired, and to ensure that public support remained behind him, Roosevelt used the radio. He began his frequent "**fireside chats**" on March 7. About half of all American families owned radios in 1933, and many of those who did not made their way to the homes of neighbors or to local businesses to hear the president's messages. His personal charm and fatherly manner carried over the airwaves to persuade Americans that they could trust him to make the government work for their benefit.

Alphabet Agencies

New Deal legislation created a vast array of programs and agencies that came to be known by their initials. The nation's conversations were soon filled with talk of the CCC, the AAA, the NRA, the TVA, and other "alphabet agencies." Former Democratic presidential candidate Al Smith said of those labels, "It looks as if one of the absentminded professors had played anagrams with the alphabet soup."

The goal of Roosevelt's New Deal involved the "three Rs"—*relief*, *recovery*, and *reform*. The major role that the New Deal played in broadening the activities and authority of the federal government warrants a brief survey of some of the most important programs.

Providing work relief to furnish income to the millions of needy unemployed was a responsibility that several new agencies assumed. One was the **Civilian Conservation Corps** (CCC). The CCC put young, unmarried men to work in reforestation and soil conservation projects under the supervision of the army; it proved to be one of the most popular New Deal agencies, lasting until after American entry into World War II.

CCC—Preparation for Military Service?

Some people have said that the CCC's emphasis on rigid discipline, team effort, and military-like uniforms and administration was actually a cover for preparing men for military service. The men marched like soldiers, carrying not rifles but shovels, rakes, and hoes. When World War II erupted, the CCC certainly provided a ready supply of recruits.

Another provider of work relief was the **Public Works Administration (PWA)**, which during its six years of existence built school buildings, courthouses, hospitals, bridges, and other public facilities all over the country. The PWA also built ships and planes for the nation's military. Similarly, the short-lived Civil Works Administration (CWA) put the jobless to work building roads, playgrounds, and airports. It also supported teachers, artists, and writers in public enrichment activities. The Federal Emergency Relief Administration (FERA) carried on some CWA projects and created others.

All of these programs combined, however, were unable to provide enough jobs to eliminate the dole. Therefore, one other major program, the **Works Progress Administration (WPA)**, was created in 1935 in an attempt to eliminate the despised relief doles. The WPA employed almost anyone in almost any kind of job. It built and repaired roads; constructed public buildings and recreational areas; supported actors, directors, writers, and artists in art programs; and manufactured a wide variety of other jobs. Many people considered the WPA "make-work"—unnecessary jobs done with lackluster efforts. This vast effort, costing almost $5 billion, was not enough to eradicate widespread unemployment.

The New Deal launched two major measures to attack the widespread problems in American agriculture and industry, both under the control of Secretary of Agriculture (and later Progressive presidential candidate) Henry A. Wallace. The **Agricultural Adjustment Act (AAA)** and its supplements established a new method of subsidizing farm products and aided debt-ridden farmers in danger of losing their farms to foreclosure. To reduce the huge surpluses expected in the 1933 harvest, the AAA offered benefit payments to farmers who plowed up cotton and slaughtered pigs. That policy, however, was contemptible to a nation in which thousands of children wore rags and remained undernourished, and it brought rampant criticism of the entire program.

Spending Must Lead to Taxation

Economist Henry Hazlitt estimates that the WPA destroyed as many jobs as it created: "Every dollar of government spending must be raised through a dollar of taxation." And the tax money is not being used to create jobs demanded by the free market.

The **National Industrial Recovery Act** (**NIRA**) attempted to organize guidelines for industries to increase employment, maintain wages, and reduce unwanted competition. While these guidelines were described as voluntary, businessmen who did not follow the guidelines faced stiff fines or imprisonment. Businesses that complied with the codes were allowed to display the blue eagle symbol of the **National Recovery Administration** (**NRA**), the agency designed to carry out the activities prescribed by the NIRA.

The NRA established about 540 specific codes, all of which tended to raise prices and wages, reduce hours, and remove both competition and opportunity for innovation. It also included some unusual code provisions, such as the following.

- Lumber companies were required to keep a list of all customers' names.
- Investment securities analysts were fined for sending letters to prospective clients without their prior permission.
- Jewelers could not advertise watch-repair prices.
- Dry cleaners who operated in low-traffic areas could not charge lower prices to compete with cleaners operating in high-traffic areas.
- Businesses could not offer discounts to customers.

This unsuccessful government attempt at industrial planning also met opposition and ultimate elimination. The NIRA—along with the AAA—was declared unconstitutional by the Supreme Court.

One more large group of New Deal programs was intended to provide security, improved conditions, or other benefits for large groups of Americans. A banking act led to the formation of the **Federal Deposit Insurance Corporation** (**FDIC**), an agency devised to insure the bank deposits of millions of Americans against loss. The **Tennessee Valley Authority** (**TVA**) undertook an extensive project to build dams along the Tennessee River that would provide navigation, flood control, and cheap electricity for the valley residents.

Congress passed the **Social Security Act** in 1935, instituting old-age pensions and unemployment insurance for American workers. Social Security was essentially a pay-as-you-go system by which benefits were to be paid to beneficiaries from the taxes paid into the system by younger workers. The designers of this social program assumed that there would always be more workers paying in than retirees withdrawing benefits. But today the worker-to-retiree ratio is narrowing, and Social Security is beginning to pay more out to retirees than workers pay into the system. Another program was the Rural Electrification Administration (REA), which offered funds to farmer cooperatives for extending electricity to the many rural areas still lacking that utility.

A waitress installs the NRA blue eagle emblem in the window of a restaurant.

Who Set the Guidelines?

A group of government officials and representatives of the largest industrial leaders set the NIRA guidelines. Their fixed prices and so-called codes of fair competition ensured NIRA-compliant businesses a large profit. This led to higher costs for the customer and financially burdened many who struggled to survive during the Depression.

Norris Dam, north of Knoxville, Tennessee, was the first dam completed in the TVA system.

"The Four Horsemen of Reaction"

In the early years of the New Deal, the Supreme Court was made up of four conservatives, four progressives, and a "swing" justice. In several rulings against New Deal measures, the Court was unanimous or had only one dissenter. Because the four conservatives frequently ruled against FDR, he began calling them "the Four Horsemen of Reaction." But just who were those four men—and the fifth swing justice—who were able to slow FDR's headlong rush into socialism?

Willis Van Devanter

Willis Van Devanter was a lawyer whose interests lay in cattle and railroads. William McKinley had appointed him assistant attorney general, and Theodore Roosevelt nominated him for the Eighth Circuit U.S. Court of Appeals. William Howard Taft nominated him for the U.S. Supreme Court, where he served for twenty-six years.

James Clark McReynolds, a lifelong Democrat, was a corporate lawyer appointed assistant attorney general by President Theodore Roosevelt, a Republican. Democrat Woodrow Wilson nominated him for the Supreme Court. His opinions emphasized protection of private property and the freedoms of contract and speech. As he saw the New Deal programs unfolding, he concluded that FDR was an "utter incompetent."

James Clark McReynolds

Pierce Butler was a lawyer whom Taft sought to help his administration prosecute antitrust cases, especially those involving the meat-packing and railroad industries. Butler argued several such cases before the Supreme Court. Warren Harding later nominated him for the Supreme Court. Butler seems to have loved individualism and free enterprise.

Pierce Butler

George Sutherland was "the most impressive thinker" among the Four Horsemen. He believed that the most important function of law was to protect individual liberty by restraining government power. He was especially concerned about protecting economic liberties. Although a lawyer, he had more practical political experience than the others, having served in both the U.S. House and the U.S. Senate. As a senator, he had introduced the "Anthony Amend-

George Sutherland

ment," a constitutional amendment to give women the right to vote. He was an adviser to Harding, and Harding nominated him for the Supreme Court shortly after becoming president.

Charles Evans Hughes

The swing justice was Chief Justice Charles Evans Hughes. He could be a flip-flopper. He sometimes voted in favor of New Deal expansions of government power but joined the Four Horsemen in opposing other such programs when he became concerned about FDR's attacks on economic freedoms. He later returned to supporting the New Deal measures. Of the five justices, he was the least consistent in his positions.

Roadblocks and Pitfalls

Roosevelt's extensive New Deal activities sought to meet the nation's demand for change. He had stated during his 1932 campaign that

> the country needs and, unless I mistake its temper, the country demands bold, persistent experimentation. It is common sense to take a method and try it: If it fails, admit it frankly and try another. But above all, try something.

Because he was taking action, he received widespread praise from many Americans, especially the poor, regardless of whether their lives were improved. One woman wrote Roosevelt in 1935 to tell him of the undernourishment of her children, but she did not neglect to add, "you are the best president we ever had." Such praise for FDR was not uncommon, but then neither was criticism.

Opposition from the Right

People to the political right of Roosevelt, including most Republicans and a few Democrats, found much in the New Deal to criticize. First was its great expense. The government was spending billions of dollars to support the various programs, sending the nation heavily into debt in the process. Also, many of the programs were bringing more and greater government regulation of American businesses and a corresponding loss of freedom, a tendency that looked suspiciously socialistic. For instance, the NRA was a significant step toward the nationalization of industry, and the TVA was simply government ownership and control of a large electricity-producing industry. Finally, the New Deal was not bringing recovery. American businesses were still in the doldrums, and millions of people were still unemployed.

Roosevelt's opponents found cause for rejoicing in 1935 when the Supreme Court, still dominated by conservative Republican appointees, began to reject some New Deal legislation. Until that time, the Court had not found occasion to strike down popular measures, especially in light of the "national emergency." But after two years of compliance, it began to question certain New Deal actions and even to strike down some minor pieces of legislation. Then, on May 27, 1935, the court declared unanimously that the National Industrial Recovery Act was unconstitutional. Roosevelt denounced the decision, but his NRA was doomed. Early in 1936, the Supreme Court, in a 6–3 decision, struck down the Agricultural Adjustment Act. Clearly, that phase of the New Deal was losing its momentum.

Opposition from the Left

In addition to those who thought the president was doing too much were others who complained that he was not doing enough. Three different men gained wide followings by advocating bolder governmental moves to combat the Depression. One was Senator **Huey Long**, a flamboyant, loud-mouthed, plain-spoken former governor of Louisiana. His "Share Our Wealth" scheme proposed that the government heavily tax the rich and redistribute that wealth to the poor. The idea was alarming, not to mention impractical, but it became popular among the uneducated poor who thought that they could get rich quick. Long seemed to be stealing some support from Roosevelt in advance of the 1936 election, but the rise of the Louisiana "Kingfish" ended suddenly with his assassination in September 1935.

Louisiana senator and former governor Huey Long attacked FDR and promoted his own "Share Our Wealth" scheme.

(above) Dr. Francis Townsend also thought the New Deal did not go far enough and proposed his own pension scheme. (above right) Father Charles Coughlin used his fiery oratory to promote his own version of "social justice."

A Short-Lived Alliance

Coughlin allied with Townsend briefly in 1936 to help support a third-party candidate for the presidency. The effort died, however, as the radio priest became increasingly caustic in his verbal attacks against President Roosevelt and began to praise fascism.

Another popular plan, especially among older Americans, was espoused by Dr. **Francis Townsend**. He proposed that the government pay a pension of $200 a month to each citizen over sixty, provided that they agreed to hold no job and to spend every penny they received. This pension would be financed, supposedly, by a 2 percent national sales tax. Thousands joined Townsend clubs, and many began to buy merchandise on credit in expectation of receiving the monthly checks. The plan's supporters, however, failed to recognize that it would simply rob younger Americans of their purchasing power to give that power to the elderly.

Another challenger who promoted his own brand of government action during the 1930s was Father **Charles Coughlin**, a Roman Catholic priest from Royal Oak, Michigan. Coughlin turned his weekly radio program of sermons into a national political broadcast. By 1934, the eloquent priest was telling his huge radio audience that the nation needed to abandon the "pagan god of gold" and coin large amounts of silver, thereby inflating the money supply. He also began to propose that capitalism be replaced with his own system of "social justice." (He published a weekly magazine titled *Social Justice*.)

Although the radical opposition to the New Deal was ultimately unsuccessful, the wide popularity evoked by those socialistic schemes posed a threat to America's economic foundations. The New Deal, by contrast, was definitely the lesser of the evils.

"A Switch in Time Saves Nine"

Roosevelt believed that his overwhelming election victory had given him a clear mandate to proceed with his New Deal. The decisions of the Supreme Court in 1935 and 1936 declaring various New Deal measures unconstitutional, however, disturbed the president greatly. At first, he thought about pushing for a constitutional amendment to protect New Deal legislation but dismissed the strategy because it could be defeated easily and would take too long. On February 5, 1937, he announced instead a plan to enlarge the Court. For every justice over seventy who did not retire, he wanted the right to appoint an additional justice up to a maximum of six. Roosevelt argued that the new members would make the Court more efficient.

The president's proposal generated a storm of opposition from many quarters and for many reasons. Many people attacked the

plan because it threatened the American tradition of an independent judiciary. Conservatives argued that efficiency was not the issue; having more justices would actually delay Court proceedings. Rather, they pointed out, Roosevelt wanted to "pack the Court" with liberal New Dealers. Politicians who before had not dared oppose Roosevelt publicly because of his popularity spoke out against the **court-packing plan** because they sensed that the public was on their side.

Because of the extensive opposition to the plan, Court reform failed to win approval even in the Democrat-controlled Congress, but Roosevelt won the "war." One of the justices announced his retirement from the Court, giving the president the opportunity to replace him with a liberal appointee. Meanwhile, another justice left the conservative bloc on the Court and voted with a new majority that approved New Deal programs in several decisions. Newspapers characterized it as a "switch in time saves nine." Roosevelt eventually was able to nominate several members of the Supreme Court. By 1940, five of the nine justices were his appointees. In the end, however, Roosevelt did pay a price. The fight over the Court divided his party and strengthened the enemies of the New Deal.

Elusive Recovery

Despite the criticisms Roosevelt faced during his first term in office, his popularity remained widespread. Millions of Americans had received some form of government aid through the CCC, the WPA, or other federal program, making those people as grateful to Roosevelt as they had been bitter toward Hoover. On the surface, economic conditions seemed to be improving, ensuring the New Deal some credit in the upcoming election.

1936 Election

In 1936, the Republicans had only one viable candidate to offer in the race against Roosevelt—**Alf Landon**. As one of only seven Republican governors at the time and the only one to have won reelection in 1934, Landon was the "most available" man. Being from Kansas, he was free of the image of Wall Street and big

Republican Kansas governor Alf Landon ran a losing campaign against FDR in 1936.

business, an image that had plagued the Republican Party since the Depression began.

Although Landon had a progressive record and supported much of the New Deal, Republicans hoped that he would be "the Kansas Coolidge," bringing a return of business prosperity to the nation. Unfortunately for Landon, the big business interests launched a major effort to elect the Kansas governor, thereby linking him with that unpopular segment of society after all. Roosevelt jumped at the chance to lash out at the forces of "organized money," thereby solidifying his support from the poorer classes.

Nevertheless, Landon maintained hopes of winning the election when a poll conducted by the *Literary Digest* predicted a decisive Republican victory. This straw vote, however, was based on replies from people with telephone listings and automobile registrations, thereby entirely overlooking the preferences of the poor, who lacked those luxuries. On election day, the votes of the poor were not overlooked, and Roosevelt won by a landslide. Landon won only two states—Maine and Vermont—and garnered only 8 electoral votes to Roosevelt's 523. Republicans were able to salvage only a few seats in the Senate and the House of Representatives, and the future of their party was in doubt. The Democrats and their leader, FDR, were clearly in control of the nation's political machinery.

No Way Out

Despite his impressive victory in the 1936 election, Roosevelt still faced major problems. Four years after he took office and initiated his myriad New Deal programs, the nation was still beleaguered by a severe economic depression—despite his having spent more in his first five years than all the presidents before him. When Roosevelt took his oath of office again in 1937, he still saw "one-third of a nation ill-housed, ill-clad, ill-nourished."

What is more, in that year the nation experienced a sharper economic decline than the one that had occurred following the stock market crash. It was a depression within the Depression. Any gains that had been credited to the New Deal were washed away. The government was pumping billions of dollars into the economy and plunging the nation ever deeper into debt only to find that recovery was as elusive as ever and millions of Americans were still in need. In addition, Roosevelt's aura of invincibility would soon be badly damaged by the court-packing episode.

Adding to the other problems of the time, labor unions were gaining strength and using strikes to cripple big industries. **John L. Lewis**, president of the United Mine Workers, recognized that recent legislation had provided the opportunity to organize the workers in large industries. The American Federation of Labor (AFL) had limited its unions to skilled craftsmen, but millions of unskilled industrial workers suffering hardships wanted more from their jobs. As a result, Lewis organized the **Congress of Industrial Organizations (CIO)** to accommodate those workers, and the CIO broke off from the AFL in 1936. The CIO quickly made the headlines when its rubber industry workers at the Firestone, Goodyear, and Goodrich plants in Akron, Ohio, staged a simultaneous sit-down strike. The workers simply sat down on the job, refusing both to work and to leave the factories until their point was made with the management. Two of the companies gave in to the workers' demands, but Goodyear refused until a month-long strike forced it to concede.

Where's the Logic?

While FDR was telling Americans that one-third of the nation was ill-fed, farmers were being paid millions of dollars *not* to grow food, to destroy what did grow, and to kill piglets. But American food imports skyrocketed, as the following table shows:

Commodity	Imports
1934 / 1935	
138,283 / 7,684,637	Beef/veal (lbs.)
626,148 / 2,846,005	Ham/bacon (lbs.)
535,144 / 21,948,458	Butter (lbs.)
816,694 / 34,809,120	Corn (bu.)
3,330,188 / 13,446,009	Wheat (bu.)
7,328,084 / 36,353,324	Raw cotton (lbs.)

[Cited in Folsom, *New Deal or Raw Deal?*]

The success of the CIO in Akron gave new hope to thousands of disgruntled workers and sent a shudder through the nation's employers. Later in 1936, the automobile industry began to feel the pressure of increased CIO membership among its workers. The CIO's ranks soon swelled to 400,000, and, with the increase, sit-down strikes multiplied as well. Violence was inevitable, and it came on Memorial Day 1937 when, in response to a barrage of rocks and sticks, police killed ten striking workers at the Republic Steel mill in South Chicago. Besides their dismay at the violence, middle-class Americans were alarmed by the sit-down tactic, which endangered private property rights. (The strikers frequently abused, destroyed, or pilfered company property during their sit-down strikes.) Finally, the Supreme Court outlawed the sit-down strike in 1939. This decision eliminated the CIO's most effective weapon, but the union remained powerful, eventually reuniting with the AFL to become the AFL-CIO.

Many domestic problems plagued the United States during the later years of the Depression. However, the focus would soon shift to foreign concerns. The unemployment, poverty, and despair of the Depression would ultimately give way to the fear, excitement, and activity of World War II.

Section Quiz

1. What were the first two actions that Roosevelt took to deal with the Depression?
2. What was the name for Roosevelt's radio talks that were used to inspire confidence and approval for New Deal measures?
3. What was the common purpose of the CCC, the PWA, and the WPA?
4. What New Deal program involved the government in ownership and control of a large electricity-producing industry?
5. How did Roosevelt attempt to make the Supreme Court support the New Deal?
* Explain evidences that the early New Deal did not resolve the problems of the Depression but actually made them worse.

III. Worst of Times, Best of Times

The 1930s was a bewildering decade for Americans. They often did not understand the reasons for their plight, and they found it difficult to believe that there was any hope of something better in the future. Too many dreams had been shattered when the crash and Depression hurled financiers, factory workers, and farmers alike into unemployment, bankruptcy, and desperation. Yet in the midst of the Depression, life went on in the nation, and the people found ways to cope and even laugh in the face of difficulty.

Depths of Depression

The Family

Once the Depression struck, almost anything that President Hoover said was used to mock him, especially when he told reporters, "Nobody is starving. The hoboes, for example, are better fed than they have ever been. One hobo in New York got ten meals in one day." Soon a flood of newspaper headlines refuted the

---

The Legacy of the New Deal

The New Deal did not rescue the nation from the Depression. However, it did install the framework for a burgeoning federal bureaucracy that is with us to this day.

Did the War End the Depression?

Many people believe that U.S. entry into World War II ended the Depression. They point to such statistics as unemployment and the GDP.

Granted, unemployment fell dramatically when the war broke out. The war, however, did not give people *productive* jobs; it merely transferred them from unemployment lines in the United States to the front lines in Europe or the Pacific. Also, the GDP is simply the total value of goods produced by a country; it does not distinguish those goods as war goods designed for *destruction* and consumer goods designed for *constructive* purposes to improve citizens' lives. In each year between 1942 and 1945, the vast majority of the GDP was attributable to war spending.

And during the war, although the people who stayed behind had plenty of jobs and made good wages, they also endured rationing of a vast array of consumer goods, from meat to sugar to nylon stockings to automobile tires. What good was more money if needed items were not available?

When the war was over, many of the men who managed to survive were still unemployed for a time. Also, the companies that had produced war goods had to absorb the expenses of and take the time necessary for retooling so they could once again produce consumer goods. Wars do not make countries richer!

Migrant farm workers and their families often lived in makeshift tents while they worked harvesting fruits and vegetables in California.

Begging Directly to the President and Mrs. Roosevelt

Thousands of people wrote letters to President Roosevelt, and even more wrote to his wife, Eleanor, telling them their trials and needs and asking for some help. An uneducated, disabled man wrote, "My family is barfooted and naked and an suferns and we all are a goin to purish if I cannot get some help some way." Some women pleaded with Mrs. Roosevelt to send them clothing for their children or old clothes discarded by the first lady for themselves. Many such petitioners added a final request, asking that their letters be kept private so that no one else would know of their disgrace.

Looking for a Place to Live

As renters were evicted and homes and farms foreclosed, thousands of families were left to scramble for a place to live. Some people moved in with relatives; others built their own shacks in a Hooverville; and still others found other landlords with more patience.

president's point. Ninety-five cases of starvation were reported in New York City during 1931. That report is probably inflated because substantiated reports were few, but some starvation did occur. And malnutrition was commonplace among the poor. In 1932, the New York City Health Department declared that more than 20 percent of the city's public school children were suffering from malnutrition. Jobless men who happened to find work were sometimes too weak from hunger to handle their new responsibilities. As late as May 1939, unemployment again numbered more than 20 percent.

Near the end of FDR's second term, his trusted secretary of the treasury Henry Morgenthau lamented, "We have tried spending money. We are spending more than we have ever spent before, and it does not work. . . . We have never made good on our promises. . . . I say after eight years of this Administration we have just as much unemployment as when we started. . . . And an enormous debt to boot!"

Private charities had maintained rescue missions and soup kitchens for the down and out in the past, but they were not prepared to help the vast numbers now swelling the ranks of the unemployed. The federal funds given to states for relief were partly used to provide needed extra provisions for the hungry. Soon "**bread lines**" formed along city streets as the desperate sought food in the soup kitchens. Local agencies were set up to provide some cash for relief to those who applied and met all the strict guidelines of destitution. Even then, the sums given were hardly enough to feed a family, much less clothe and house them. A FERA representative in North Carolina reported that a good relief payment to help support a family of five totaled $5.25 per week. The amount was $2.39 in New York City. When New Jersey's relief funds ran out, that state decided to issue licenses for begging.

Often it was the parents' concern for their children that finally brought the family to apply for relief, but that concern could not cover the sense of humiliation that the adults felt. Husbands and fathers who had trudged from business to business trying to find work blamed themselves for their inability to gain and hold a job. Wives struggled with their own cares, trying to keep the ragged clothes that their families wore from falling apart and even searching for housecleaning jobs or other employment that might bring in some money.

Homelessness

About two million people were uprooted from their homes in the 1930s. A few of them had deliberately fled from the torment of watching their families suffer, but many were simply young, unmarried men and teenage boys who had given up all hope of finding a job and settling down. They rode in, on, or even under boxcars on freight trains from place to place, eating in soup kitchens, sleeping in city parks, camping in hobo jungles, and perhaps dreaming that the next stop might hold promise for a job.

Countless thousands of families faced the threat of homelessness. Some of them had had mortgages on modest homes, but now, without income, they could not keep up their payments. Banks were seldom quick to foreclose, but many institutions eventually had to repossess the houses. Other people rented houses or apartments for which they now had no money to pay. Rent in those days was typically low (often around $10 to $12 per month), but even that was beyond the means of a family on relief.

Race

The hardships of the Depression fell heavily on black Americans, although hardships were not new to them. In 1932, about half of all African-American workers were unemployed, a rate of joblessness double that of the general population. Farm problems and government policies drove sharecroppers in the South, many of them black, off the land. Many of them moved to cities in the North and West, continuing the migration of African Americans that had begun with World War I. With unemployment wracking America's cities, the North was hardly a promised land for jobless blacks.

Government relief efforts were slow to reach needy black Americans. At first, Roosevelt was reluctant to press for needed steps for fear of angering Southern Democrats, and some aspects of his AAA and NRA were actually harmful to the interests of blacks. However, Eleanor Roosevelt helped to turn attention to problems of discrimination by openly befriending African-American leaders. FDR then began to try to prohibit racial discrimination in some federal programs, beginning in 1935 with the WPA. The PWA also constructed a large share of its public housing projects for black Americans.

The most noticeable effect of Roosevelt's policies was the winning of African-American votes for the Democratic Party. Black Americans had voted strongly Republican ever since they had achieved the right to vote—even voting for Herbert Hoover in 1932. But while Republicans offered no hope for efforts to relieve the problems of blacks, the actions of FDR and the Democrats at least seemed encouraging.

Hispanic families in the Southwest who were not U.S. citizens generally returned to Mexico when the Depression hit, or they were deported. Jobs were not available for Americans, much less foreign immigrants. Those who remained faced the same problems that whites did as farmers and migrant workers, but they also faced prejudice and even violence because they were competing for jobs. Most migrated to urban areas, hoping to get jobs in the lower tier of unskilled workers.

WPA workers

FDR and Civil Rights

Although the immediate benefits of the New Deal were meager for black Americans, subtle changes in governmental attitudes were opening a path for a more potent civil rights movement in the future.

FDR and Black Voters

In 1936, Roosevelt gained 76 percent of the black vote, initiating a long-term political trend of blacks voting for Democrats.

The Good Times

Although the 1930s witnessed a quarter or more of the population in want, 80 million Americans (of a population of about 123 million) did *not* experience great deprivations. They might have experienced some hardships because of the departure of the prosperous Roaring Twenties, but they still had jobs, food on their tables, clothes on their backs, and roofs over their heads. These Americans at least had some good times in the midst of the Depression.

Amusements

Americans often seemed intent on forgetting their troubles during the rough times. Many of them found escape from their cares in reading books such as Margaret Mitchell's epic Civil War novel *Gone with the Wind*, which appeared in 1936 and became a popular movie in 1939. Hollywood produced

Radio was the major source of news and entertainment during the thirties, especially for rural families.

The Dust Bowl

In the opening decades of the twentieth century, farmers poured into the Great Plains region. They plowed the tough prairie sod, sowed wheat, and met with enough success to build a respectable life for themselves and their families. In the process, they converted millions of acres from prairie grassland to fields of fertile, powdery soil. In the late 1920s, abundant rains brought bountiful crops and temporary prosperity to the farmers.

But soon came the Depression with its falling farm prices combined with a ruinous drought that began in 1932. For four years, rainfall was rare, and the region's produce all but vanished. To add to the woes that the farmers were experiencing, the prairie winds began to pick up the powdery dust from the plains and carry it across the land. Billowing black clouds of dust sometimes engulfed the region,

the dirt sifting through every crack in a farmer's house, piling in huge drifts against buildings and fences, obscuring sunlight, and nearly suffocating anyone who ventured outdoors. Even indoors the people often slept with wet cloths over their faces to keep from breathing the dust. This was the "**Dust Bowl**," a term coined by a newspaper reporter in 1935.

The Dust Bowl reached as far north as Colorado and Kansas and as far south as Texas and New Mexico, but its most brutal effects were felt in Oklahoma. Some of the stricken farmers resorted to relief through WPA jobs and various agencies while trying to reclaim their farms.

Others gave up and moved away. Called "Okies," thousands of them loaded their cars or trucks with all their possessions and headed west to California. There they sought jobs as migrant farm workers, harvesting various crops as they came in season. The uprooted farm families generally remained in poverty until the end of the Depression, but at least they had opportunities for work.

Those who remained on the land soon learned to adjust their farming methods to the needs of their arid land. Much acreage was returned to grassland and used as pasture for livestock, and soil conservation techniques prevailed on the remaining fields. Those efforts continue today to keep the dust of the plains settled, thereby averting any recurrence of the Dust Bowl.

Why the War of the Worlds Broadcast Was So Believable

Americans had become enthralled with radio during the twenties. By the thirties, they were used to radio programs being interrupted occasionally to announce items of breaking national or even world news. That is why so many people believed the dramatized news broadcasts reporting invaders from outer space.

more than five thousand feature films of fantasy and drama, providing escape and entertainment for millions of Americans. Walt Disney's first full-length animated presentation, *Snow White*, debuted in 1938, and many new movie stars began to draw wide admiration, among them a little girl named Shirley Temple, who became the darling of the nation.

Radio became the most popular medium of home entertainment in America. Old and young alike laughed at the comedy "Amos and Andy," swooned to the songs of crooner Bing Crosby, and thrilled to the adventures of the Lone Ranger. Children listened devotedly to the tales of Little Orphan Annie and cowboy hero Tom Mix. Clarinetist and band leader Benny Goodman introduced "swing music" in 1935, and soon a host of big bands were broadcasting jazzy orchestra numbers on popular radio programs. Radio created one of the most dramatic and yet comic episodes of the 1930s when Orson Welles presented his radio dramatization of H. G. Wells's *War of the Worlds* on a major network in 1938. So realistic was his version of the story of invasion from Mars that thousands of listeners who tuned in to the program as it was in progress were terrified, unaware that the frightening account of a spaceship landing in New Jersey was only fiction. Radio stations and public officials hastened to quell the growing panic, but several days passed before emotions were entirely calmed.

Other Diversions

Real-life drama also captured the nation's attention during the 1930s. One of the biggest headlines was the 1932 kidnapping of the infant son of aviation hero Charles Lindbergh. All across the nation, people were eager to hear of any developments in the case, and they grieved when word finally came that the child had been found dead. The search for the murderer required more than two years of intense detective work and ended in the conviction and execution of Bruno Hauptmann, a German immigrant.

(left) FBI special agent Melvin Purvis tracked down John Dillinger (right), Public Enemy No. 1.

Other crimes gained wide attention during the Depression, particularly those of bank-robbing gangs. Although those desperate criminals sometimes were lauded as modern-day Robin Hoods, they were brutal. John Dillinger topped the "most wanted list," but he was joined by desperados such as "Pretty Boy" Floyd, "Machine Gun" Kelly, "Baby Face" Nelson, and a couple-in-crime, Bonnie Parker and Clyde Barrow. Most of these criminals died in a hail of gunfire or spent long stints in jail. Lawmen, especially agents of the newly formed Federal Bureau of Investigation, led by director J. Edgar Hoover, became heroes as they tracked down criminals. FBI agent Melvin Purvis gained fame as the top "G-man" when he led the team that cornered and killed Dillinger.

Amelia Earhart became America's flying heroine when, in 1932, she became the first woman to cross the Atlantic. But in 1937, during an adventurous round-the-world flight, the aviatrix disappeared somewhere in the Pacific. Hers was not the only air tragedy of the 1930s, however. Popular humorist Will Rogers perished in an airplane crash while on a tour of Alaska with Wiley Post, the first man to fly solo around the world. The most dramatic of the 1930s air tragedies was the explosion and crash of the zeppelin *Hindenburg*. As the giant, blimp-like craft approached its moorings in Lakehurst, New Jersey, in 1937, it suddenly burst into flames. A radio announcer watching the landing described the catastrophe for the nation with uncontrollable emotion:

Amelia Earhart, heroine of the air, disappeared somewhere in the Pacific Ocean.

Oh, flames four or five hundred feet into the sky, it's a terrific crash, ladies and gentlemen, the smoke and the flames now and the crashing to the ground, not quite to the mooring, oh the humanity, and I told you, I can't even talk, mass of smoking wreckage, I can, I can hardly breathe!

Thirty-six of the airship's ninety-seven passengers perished.

Sports continued to attract many fans, and fads such as miniature golf and Chinese checkers gained momentary popularity. World's fairs also became a big attraction in the decade. Chicago hosted one on its lakeshore in 1934. It featured, among other "Century of Progress" innovations and wonders, an exhibit of premature babies in incubators and the Burlington Route's *Zephyr*, a streamlined diesel locomotive that set the record for a Denver-to-Chicago run. The Chicago fair was surpassed by the spectacular **New York World's Fair** in 1939. From its opening to its closing two years later, the New York fair attracted 45 million visitors to its 1,500 exhibits. People marveled at the technological innovations on display at this

Depression-Era Comic Relief

During the Great Depression, Americans wanted some escape, no matter how brief, from their pressing problems. Some sought relief through destructive means, such as alcohol. Most, however, found harmless diversion through popular entertainment. One source of drama, adventure, and comedy was as near as the daily newspaper—the comic strip.

Comic strips had been appearing in newspapers since the 1890s. The 1930s, however, proved to be a golden age of comics. Whether in the black-and-white strips found in the daily papers or in the four-color "funny papers" found in Sunday editions, comics provided millions of readers (children *and* adults) with an avenue to adventure.

One of the most popular strips was *Little Orphan Annie*. Along with her dog Sandy, Annie, an orphan waif with open, pupilless eyes overcame the challenges of the Depression with pluck and courage. Adopted by a wealthy weapons manufacturer (appropriately named Daddy Warbucks), Annie was a reflection of her creator's philosophy. Harold Gray, who began the strip in 1924, was a conservative Republican and dedi-

cated opponent of FDR's New Deal. Through Annie and her friends, Gray espoused his views in favor of self-help through hard work. As Daddy Warbucks says in one early strip, "Annie doesn't need charity—just give her an even break and she'll do the rest—Charity!!—BAH!"

The lawlessness of the 1920s and 1930s also gave birth to one of the toughest detectives comics have ever seen—Dick Tracy. Created by Chester

Gould in 1931, *Dick Tracy* brought a realism to police comics never before seen. In the best "crime does not pay" tradition, villains in *Dick Tracy* often died realistically (and sometimes gruesomely). The police used the most advanced scientific methods of crime detection, such as "two-way wrist radios" (miniature walkie-talkies). Tracy's grotesque rogues' gallery of such villains as Flattop, Pruneface, the Mole, and Mumbles was an important part of the comic strip's appeal.

Those who wanted to escape the problems of the 1930s could travel by comic strip to exotic, faraway places. *Tarzan* took the readers to "deepest, darkest Africa" with the adventures of Edgar Rice Burroughs. Or readers could follow the Stone Age exploits of *Alley Oop*. Other similar adventure strips were *Captain Easy*, *Terry and the Pirates*, *Joe Palooka*, *Prince Valiant*, and *The Phantom*. But the ultimate superhero was *Superman*.

Two popular science fiction strips were *Flash Gordon* and *Buck Rogers*.

For pure humor, one could read *Popeye*, *Krazy Kat*, *Blondie*, *Li'l Abner*, *Our Boarding House*, or *Nancy*. The "funnies" became one small means of facing the Depression with a smile.

event christened "The World of Tomorrow," and they delighted in the breathtaking carnival rides. One of the most popular attractions, General Motors' "Futurama," carried fairgoers on a fifteen-minute tour of America in 1960. The 1939 prophets provided breathless audiences with a fast-lane future of 100-mph highways traveled by Americans in radio-controlled, raindrop-shaped cars, enjoying their two months of vacation each year. In retrospect, the seers provided a good example of man's inability to predict the future.

New Decade Dawning

For America as it emerged from the Depression, the "world of tomorrow" would be as fast-paced as the fair prophets predicted, but it would be no carnival. Even as the 1939 audiences marveled at future prospects of peace and prosperity, undercurrents of war were roiling the world's already troubled waters. Soon, the tides of war would reach America's shore and shake the nation's lethargic economy in ways FDR had only dreamed, turning bread lines into assembly lines and forging a new role of world leadership in the decade to come.

On May 6, 1937, the hydrogen-filled *Hindenburg* exploded mysteriously as it approached its mooring mast in Lakehurst, N.J., after a transatlantic flight.

Section Quiz

1. In what way did American blacks change their voting patterns during the Depression?

2. What was the most popular means of home entertainment during the Depression?

3. What famous kidnapping case captured national attention in the 1930s?

★ How did Americans try to relieve their minds of worries about economic troubles that were beyond their control?

People, Places, and Things to Remember

Great Depression
public works
work relief
Reconstruction Finance Corporation (RFC)
Smoot-Hawley tariff
Bonus Army
Franklin Delano Roosevelt
New Deal
banking crisis
bank holiday
Brain Trust
fireside chats
Civilian Conservation Corps (CCC)
Public Works Administration (PWA)
Works Progress Administration (WPA)
Agricultural Adjustment Act (AAA)
National Industrial Recovery Act (NIRA)
National Recovery Administration (NRA)
Federal Deposit Insurance Corporation (FDIC)
Tennessee Valley Authority (TVA)
Social Security Act
Huey Long
Francis Townsend
Charles Coughlin
court-packing plan
Alf Landon
John L. Lewis
Congress of Industrial Organizations (CIO)
bread lines
Dust Bowl
New York World's Fair

Chapter Review

Making Connections

1. Why was Hoover blamed for the Depression?

2. What American governmental action in 1930 precipitated a European economic collapse in 1931 by dealing a harmful blow to world trade?

3. What problematic situation arose to heighten economic tensions in the final days before Roosevelt's inauguration?

4. What two major pieces of New Deal legislation were struck down by the Supreme Court?

5. Name three demagogic leaders who denounced Roosevelt's New Deal for not doing enough to combat the Depression's problems, and state their proposals for solving the Depression.

6. What proposal made by President Roosevelt following the 1936 election alarmed many Democrats as well as Republicans?

Developing History Skills

1. Examine Hoover's efforts to end the Depression and compare them with Roosevelt's programs.

2. How did Roosevelt's effort to pack the Supreme Court place the integrity and power of the Supreme Court at risk?

Thinking Critically

1. In what ways was the increased role of government that resulted from the New Deal beneficial to America? In what ways was it harmful?

Living as a Christian Citizen

1. The Bible contains passages such as Deuteronomy 15:7–11 that command generosity to the poor. How should this affect Christian support for government programs to assist the poor? Refer to Deuteronomy 14:28–29 in your answer.

2. In what ways can an individual Christian help the poor today?

U.S. Marines and a Navy medic raise the American flag on Mount Suribachi on
Iwo Jima.

The World at War (1939–1945)

I. A Time of Tyrants

II. Isolation and Infamy

III. The Fight for Fortress Europe

IV. The War in the Pacific

*"'Not in vain' may be the pride of those who
survived and the epitaph of those who fell."*

British Prime Minister Winston Churchill,
September 28, 1944

It's a long one down to around the three yard line. . . .

The radio announcer's voice crackled across the airwaves. The New York Giants, the champs of the National Football League's Eastern Division, were getting a surprise beating from the Brooklyn Dodgers at the Polo Grounds in New York.

Ward Cuff takes it. . . .
Coming up to his left . . . he's over the 10. . . .
Nice block by Leemans! Cuff still going. . . .

Listeners across the country edged up in their seats.

He's up to the 25. . . .
And now he's hit and hit hard about the 27-yard line!
Bruiser Kinard made the tack—
We interrupt this broadcast to bring you this important bulletin from the United Press:
FLASH Washington:
The White House announces Japanese attack on Pearl Harbor. . . .

The announcement on that Sunday afternoon of December 7, 1941, did more than interrupt a football game; it shattered America's uneasy peace. The nation had been plunged into the largest, costliest war in history. Isolation was over; the heroic effort to liberate the Pacific from the Japanese warlords and Europe from the Nazi war machine was under way. The global conflict changed the face of the world for the rest of the century and gave America a superpower role in that new world.

I. A Time of Tyrants

Clouds on the Horizon

In the early 1920s, Americans reveled in their return to normalcy and enjoyed the ease of isolation. Meanwhile, storm clouds were building on the world horizons in both Europe and the Orient. International communism had been born in Russia during World War I and was consolidated under dictator **Joseph Stalin**. Then two forms of nationalistic socialism reared their heads in Italy and Germany. Another militant nationalism grew in Japan.

Dictators Benito Mussolini and Adolf Hitler were in Munich, Germany, for the Munich Conference in 1938. As Shakespeare wrote, "'Tis time to fear when tyrants seem to kiss."

Italy: Benito Mussolini

Fascism, first established as a governing force in Italy in 1922 under **Benito Mussolini**, was a nationalistic, militaristic, totalitarian mass movement that profited from the discontent spawned by hard times. Mussolini promised the masses gathered before him that he would restore the glory of Caesar's empire. His black-shirted followers pronounced him *Il Duce* (DOO chay), the leader, and they crushed all visible opposition.

If Italy were to have power and prestige in the world, Mussolini reasoned, the country would need to acquire foreign territories and markets. In search of easy prey, Mussolini moved against backward but resource-rich Ethiopia in 1935. Sword- and stone-wielding Ethiopian tribesmen bravely but vainly fought machine guns and tanks. Mussolini quickly conquered and annexed Ethiopia. When the League of Nations tried to condemn Italy by voting sanctions and shutting off military supplies, the Italian representatives simply walked out. Later, Italy initiated an alliance with its Fascist friends to the north, the Nazis.

Germany: Adolf Hitler

In 1923, a German war veteran sought to avenge Germany's defeat in World War I by using radical politics. **Adolf Hitler** tried to overthrow the Bavarian government in Munich. The failed coup landed him in jail. While imprisoned, he wrote his personal memoir of hatred, *Mein Kampf* ("My Struggle"), in which he set forth his ideas for a new German order. He advocated scrapping the League of Nations, ridding Germany of the "weakening" influence of democracy, uniting all Germans, and eliminating all Communists

Fascism, Nazism, and Socialism: Striking Similarities

Although fascism, Nazism, and socialism developed in and are associated with different countries, they share many characteristics. There are a few variations, but their similarities far surpass their differences.

The four essential beliefs that those ideologies share are (1) the supremacy of the state over the individual, (2) the desire for a planned economy, (3) government-business partnerships, and (4) mercantilism and protectionism.

Their most important shared characteristic is the supremacy of government over the individual, which they justify by saying that the common good (i.e., the interests of the state) is more important than individual interests. Mussolini said that "the state is an absolute before which individuals and groups are relative." A motto of the Fascists was "everything in the state, nothing outside the state, nothing against the state."

All three systems permit the ownership of private property, but under each the government heavily regulates, controls, and restricts how that property can be used and what the individual can do with any profits of using it. All individual or business activity must fit within the interest of the state. These systems justify such control by claiming to provide economic equality for all, but to deliver on that pledge, they must use force,

taking from the "haves" to give to the "have nots" or to those who have less. Then, when they cannot deliver the equality they promise, they must provide scapegoats on whom to heap the blame, be that another nationality, another race, or another economic class. That, in turn, leads to suppression of and violence against the targeted group. As one economist stated, "Fascism and socialism grow only in the soil of envy and hate."

Fascism was originally called corporatism. Mussolini, who linked Italian nationalism with socialism, organized industries into categories called syndicates. He insisted that the government plan, or coordinate, all economic activity in so-called partnership with the syndicates. The catch was that the government was the "senior partner" in such arrangements and therefore had the final say. This policy was based on the idea that government knows best. One historian described fascism as nationalizing socialism and socializing nationalism.

Nazism did essentially the same thing. In fact, the very name of the party is the National *Socialist* German Workers' Party. But, as economist Ludwig von Mises wrote, "The main difference was that the Fascists were less efficient and even more corrupt than the Nazis."

If an industry that the state considered essential was failing, the government, rather than letting the free market cleanse itself of an unprofitable entity, stepped in to subsidize it, or "bail it out." In that sense, fascism, Nazism, and socialism are all systems of massive corporate welfare. At the height of Mussolini's Fascist state, three-fourths of the Italian economy was being subsidized. Rather than serving the needs of the consumers, businesses had to serve the interests of an elite few who happened to have the favor of the Fascist state. That is the epitome of mercantilism and protectionism.

At the same time that fascism and Nazism were arising in Italy and Germany, forms of socialism were gaining acceptance in the democracies of Europe and in the United States. American socialists, however, recognized that Americans reacted negatively to the term *socialism*, associating it with violent revolution, so they chose instead to call their views "progressivism." As long as socialistic programs and policies were presented as "reforms," they tended to gain public approval. Even when rallying the American people against Hitler and Mussolini, the U.S. government condemned only the evil deeds of the Fascist dictators, not their economic policies.

The Japanese were taught to view Hirohito, their emperor and head of the military, as a god.

Hideki Tojo was eager to use the Japanese military to do his emperor's bidding.

Soviet Collectivization

Basically, the Soviet collectivization program involved the Communist government's seizing all private land and crops and forcing farm workers to labor wherever they were told. Any who resisted the seizure of their property or refused to work where ordered were imprisoned or killed.

and Jews. After his release, he preached his doctrines to growing audiences of all classes. Hitler and his National Socialist German Workers' Party, or Nazi Party, came to power in Germany in 1933 when he was elected chancellor of Germany. Hitler used his new power to crush all opposition and establish himself as the *führer* (FYOOR ur). He called the Nazi regime the "Third Reich," a German empire that would last a thousand years.

Gradually, Hitler forged a police state of blind nationalism, anti-Semitism, and totalitarianism. For years, in violation of the Versailles agreements, he secretly rebuilt the German navy, army, and air force. This war machine used all the latest technological improvements and proved a fearful instrument in Hitler's hands.

Japan: Hirohito and Hideki Tojo

The Japanese, who had come late to the scene of industrialism and world trade, found that the European nations that had carved out Asian "spheres of influence" during the late nineteenth century had established many trade barriers against Japan. With growing militarism, the Japanese sought to carve out their own spheres through direct conquest. Their first show of force was the subjugation of Manchuria, a province of China, in 1931. In 1937, the Japanese launched a full-scale war against China, a war that would not end until 1945. With the permission of Emperor **Hirohito**, Japan became a military dictatorship. The military was led by the cruel **Hideki Tojo**.

With the distraction of the Great Depression at home and an ongoing desire to remain isolated from the rest of the world, the United States took little action to check Japanese aggression. In 1934, Japan canceled the Washington Naval Treaty, and relations with Japan continued to deteriorate during Roosevelt's first term. Encountering no real opposition from America or the other world powers, and desiring to gain resources through military force, Japan continued to lay plans for greater gain. As U.S. trade policies tightened in an effort to halt the Japanese brutalization of China, Japanese leaders developed an animosity toward their chief rival in the Pacific—the United States. In 1940, Japan joined Italy and Germany to form the **Rome-Berlin-Tokyo Axis**, an alliance of dictator states.

Soviet Union: Joseph Stalin

In Russia, the decades of the twenties and thirties were among the bloodiest years in human history. Stalin oversaw systematic terror and bloodshed throughout those years and became one of the bloodiest tyrants of the times.

Stalin crushed all opposition, both in and out of the Communist Party. In 1928, he ordered the destruction of all resistance to his agricultural "reforms," or collectivization, and ordered the murder of at least ten million men, women, and children. Another ten million died in Siberian slave-labor camps. Throughout the 1930s, Stalin continued to push Russia into the industrial age and fortify his own power with a chilling callousness perhaps best summarized by Stalin himself: "A single death is a tragedy; a million deaths is a statistic." Stalin also trampled any perceived threat by organized religion. Many Christians suffered and died in labor camps simply because of their loyalty to Christ.

Meanwhile, Americans watched events unfold. Things were bad, they agreed, but that was not America's business. But the dictators in Italy, Germany, Japan, and the Soviet Union would soon take the world, including the United States, into the maelstrom known as World War II.

The Coming of War

Hitler was neither a skilled diplomat nor, as later blunders would prove, a military genius. But he was a master politician who could size up other leaders, predict their responses, and outmaneuver them. Despite Hitler's open violations of the Treaty of Versailles and the growing threat he represented to Europe, the rest of Europe did nothing. In fact, they allowed Hitler to make numerous territorial gains unopposed. He assured other nations that he was interested only in consolidating German territory, reestablishing German control over areas "stolen" by the victors in World War I through the Treaty of Versailles.

Easy Acquisitions

In March 1936, German troops moved into the **Rhineland**, an industrial region of Germany near Alsace-Lorraine that, under the Versailles Treaty, was to remain demilitarized. The League of Nations protested Hitler's action, but the Nazis were not concerned about world opinion. The Germans then began building the Siegfried Line, a series of fortifications along the German bank of the Rhine River from the Swiss border to the North Sea. Hitler claimed that the Siegfried Line was a response to the Maginot (MAZH eh NOH) Line, a similar French line of fortification on the west side of the river. Except for Winston Churchill's lone voice in the British Parliament, few protests were raised.

Hitler next moved against Austria. He had long dreamed of union, or *Anschluss* (AHN schl*oos*), with Austria, a German-speaking land and Hitler's birthplace. Despite explicit prohibitions against such unification in the World War I peace treaties, Hitler in 1938 incited Austrian Nazis to stage a coup, and then the Austrians "invited" German Nazis to join them. Hitler naturally accepted the invitation, knowing the British and French lacked the will to stop him.

The Munich Conference

Czechoslovakia was next on Hitler's menu. The führer declared that Germany had a right to annex the **Sudetenland** (soo DATE un LAND), a predominantly German area in western Czechoslovakia. Czech leaders appealed to the British and French to protect them from such naked aggression. Unfortunately for the Czechs, the appeasers were in power.

England's prime minister Neville Chamberlain and France's premier Édouard Daladier agreed to meet with Hitler in Munich, Germany, in September 1938. Hitler was determined to get his way at the conference, even if it meant going to war. To "preserve the peace," Chamberlain and Daladier agreed to allow Hitler to take the Sudetenland—but nothing more. Hitler promised, "This is

Appeasement

France, Great Britain, and the other democratic governments of Europe practiced a policy of **appeasement** toward Hitler, trying to satisfy the dictator by giving in to his stated demands. Appeasement, however, was a weak and wishful response that succeeded only in whetting Hitler's appetite for more territory.

German policemen enter Austria upon achievement of *Anschluss*.

Annexation Without Representation

At least a quarter million Sudeten Germans had fled from Germany to the Sudetenland to escape Hitler's tyranny. The Munich agreement put them back under the Nazi regime. The Czechs, whose fate was at stake at the Munich Conference, were not allowed to have a representative at the conference. The representatives of other nations decided their future for them.

the last territorial claim I have to make in Europe." Chamberlain, believing Hitler to be a man of his word, returned to England proclaiming that the Allies had achieved "peace for our time."

Munich became a synonym for appeasement and defeatism. Churchill observed bitterly, "The German dictator, instead of snatching his victuals from the table, has been content to have them served to him course by course." In March 1939, Hitler took another bite—the rest of Czechoslovakia. Public outrage over Hitler's betrayal of his promise forced the British and French leaders to sign security agreements with Romania and Poland in hopes of reining in Hitler.

Tyrants' Prey

If Hitler were to continue his expansion eastward, he would have to calm Soviet fears. Throughout the spring and summer of 1939, Hitler sought a nonaggression treaty with Stalin. He secretly offered Stalin a free hand to take the Baltic countries of Lithuania, Latvia, Estonia, and Finland and a slice of eastern Poland. In exchange, Hitler wanted a free hand to invade Poland from the west. Stalin agreed. The pact was based on no mutual trust, but like vultures feeding on a carcass, the tyrants' mouths were too full of flesh to be concerned with devouring each other.

On August 23, 1939, the surprising announcement of the **Nazi-Soviet nonaggression pact** was published. Hitler lost little time taking advantage of its secret clauses. Munich had emboldened the führer to ignore British and French threats to intervene. The war began on **September 1, 1939**, when sixteen hundred *Luftwaffe* (Nazi air force) aircraft bombed and strafed military and civilian targets while fifty-six German divisions rolled across the Polish border. The swift assault coined a new word: *blitzkrieg*, "lightning war." Forty-eight hours after the assault began, the brave Polish defenders had suffered one hundred thousand casualties, and by the end of September, Hitler's conquest was complete. By war's end, the Germans and Russians would kill six million Poles, half of them Jews.

On September 3, Chamberlain reluctantly acknowledged his commitment to Poland, and Great Britain declared war on Germany. With equal dread and even more foot-dragging, France followed Britain. Those hesitant Allies did little, leaving the initiative with Hitler. Americans watched with growing concern but did nothing. It was not their affair.

More German Victories

Denmark and Norway

In the spring of 1940, Hitler began his biggest push to date. The true meaning of the word *blitzkrieg* became apparent in April, when powerful German armored divisions, or panzers—assisted by fighters, bombers, and paratroopers—occupied neutral Denmark in a matter of hours. That same day, Germany attacked neutral Norway to gain naval bases and access to iron-rich Sweden. Norway, however, resisted fiercely, fighting for sixty-two days before they were betrayed. German destroyers sailed under land-based guns that could have sent them to the bottom. The guns, though, had been rendered useless by sabotage because of a prominent Norwegian political official named Vidkun Quisling. Acquisition of Denmark and Norway secured the northern border of the Third Reich. The securing of the southern border was next.

Birds of a Feather

Politically, Hitler and Stalin were different sides of the same coin. Both tyrants understood power. They were both dictators over socialistic totalitarian regimes that viewed people as mere tools of the state.

Norway's Benedict Arnold

Vidkun Quisling assisted German agents for months before the invasion. As a reward for his treason, the Nazis made him the puppet governor of Norway during the Nazi occupation of his land. Like the name Benedict Arnold, the name Quisling became a loathsome synonym for *traitor*.

The Fall of France

On May 10, Germany launched a coordinated attack on the countries on her western border from southern France to the North Sea. Against the overwhelming German force, resistance in the Low Countries was short-lived. Luxembourg fell after only two days, Holland in five days, and Belgium in eighteen days.

In June 1940, the French army, reinforced by the British, found itself outflanked and penetrated by swift armored units. The *Luftwaffe* destroyed French fortifications far ahead of German armored divisions and infantry. Millions of refugees scattered, trying to escape their doomed cities. German *Stuka* dive-bombers dominated the air. These new weapons and tactics were a total departure from the trench warfare of World War I. For the French, who relied on the old methods of the last war, *blitzkrieg* was disastrous.

The German forces drove the British and French forces northward to the French port of **Dunkirk** on the English Channel and surrounded them. But before the Germans could move to annihilate the Allied army, a dense fog rolled in over the Channel for several days, grounding the *Luftwaffe*. Shortly before, Hitler had ordered his land armies to hold back so that the *Luftwaffe* could receive the glory for destroying the enemy. Communication failed, and the army continued to hold back even though the air force was grounded. The usually efficient Nazi war machine ground to a halt.

The Allies, encouraged by what was apparently divine intervention on their behalf, moved to rescue their men. Using fishing boats, yachts, and almost anything else that would float, British citizens crossed the twenty-two-mile-wide English Channel to rescue some 330,000 men.

With the British gone, the French reserves gone, and Paris abandoned by the government, France accepted the inevitable. In the same railroad car in which the Germans had signed the humiliating armistice terms in 1918, France accepted the German terms of surrender on June 22, 1940.

Britain Alone

Britain faced the Nazi menace alone. Hitler decided to bomb the island into submission, hoping to "soften" it before landing troops. Throughout the late summer and fall of 1940, the great **Battle of Britain** took place in the skies above southern England and the Channel. Bombing during the daylight hours, however, became too expensive for the *Luftwaffe*. The Germans lost three times as many planes as the British and many more pilots; the British pilots who were shot down were usually rescued to fly again. The *Luftwaffe* changed its tactics and began night bombing with incendiaries, or fire bombs.

London, Plymouth, Manchester, Birmingham, Dover, Portsmouth, and Coventry were heavily damaged, and tens of thousands of Britons were killed or injured. Yet British resolve in the face of the enemy was firm. During those fearful days when the fate of Britain hung in the skies above them, the British were steeled and inspired by Churchill, who declared,

Churchill on British Determination

The fall of France stunned the world, especially America, and left Britain on the brink of destruction. At that dark hour, **Winston Churchill** became the new prime minister and inspired the beleaguered Britons with his grand defiance and fighting spirit: "I have nothing to offer but blood, toil, tears, and sweat. . . . You ask, what is our policy? I will say: It is to wage war, by sea, land, and air, with all our might and with all the strength God can give us. . . . You ask, what is our aim? I can answer in one word: It is victory."

London during the Blitz, St. Paul's Cathedral stands in majestic defiance in this famous wartime photograph.

Scorecard for the Battle of Britain

Pilots from thirteen countries opposed the Germans in the Battle of Britain. Of the 2,367 Allied pilots, 1,878 of them were from Great Britain. (Poland provided the second most pilots—141). Between July and October, Allied pilots, all flying for the Royal Air Force, shot down 1,652 *Luftwaffe* planes and lost 1,087 of their own. The Allies lost 446 pilots, 348 of them Brits, but the Germans lost 1,644 pilots and crewmen. As great as the loss in aircraft was, Germany's loss of men was more devastating. Planes could be replaced; trained pilots and crewmen were not so easily replaced.

Hitler knows that he will have to break us on this island or lose the war. If we can stand up to him all Europe may be free and the life of the world may move forward into broad, sunlit uplands. But if we fail, then the whole world, including the United States, including all we have known and cared for, will sink into the abyss of a new Dark Age. . . . Let us therefore brace ourselves to our duty, and so bear ourselves that, if the British Commonwealth and its Empire lasts for a thousand years, men will still say: "This was their finest hour."

Barbarossa

In the wake of the fall of France, continued bombing of Britain, and conquests in the Mediterranean, Hitler again seized the initiative, launching a massive surprise attack on his eastern ally, the Soviet Union. On June 22, 1941, three million troops of the **Wehrmacht** (VEHR MACHT, the German army) rolled deep into Russia, covering five hundred miles of territory within two months on a front that stretched from the Black Sea to the Arctic. In an operation code-named "Barbarossa," the Germans launched attacks at three strategic cities—Leningrad to the north, Moscow in the center, and Stalingrad to the south—engulfing the Soviet heartland in some of the fiercest, costliest fighting of the war.

By September 1941, the Russians were reeling and England was badly battered. Just two years after launching his *blitzkrieg* against Poland, Hitler was virtually master of Europe. Americans watched with growing unease. But still it was not their fight.

The Axis in North Africa

Mussolini invaded Sudan, Kenya, Libya, and Egypt in 1940. But by mid-1941, Italian forces were facing defeat. Hitler sent the *Afrika Korps* (an elite armored division commanded by General Erwin Rommel, the "Desert Fox") and a *Luftwaffe* air wing to support his ally, and they turned things back to the favor of the Axis.

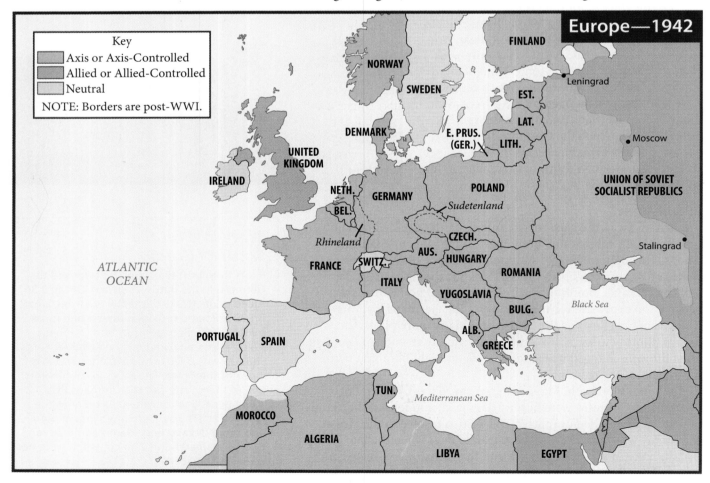

Europe—1942

Key
Axis or Axis-Controlled
Allied or Allied-Controlled
Neutral
NOTE: Borders are post-WWI.

Section Quiz

1. Name the dictators who rose to power in Italy and the Soviet Union in the 1920s and in Germany in the 1930s.

2. What African nation did Italy conquer in the 1930s?

3. What was *Anschluss*?

4. What nation was forced to surrender one region of its land to Germany at the Munich Conference? What was the name of that region?

5. Place the following nations in the proper chronological order in which they fell to Germany: Belgium, Denmark, France, Norway, Poland.

✶ What lessons can one learn about appeasement and totalitarian, expansionist regimes from the events in this section?

II. Isolation and Infamy

While war was tearing Europe apart, America sat safe behind its ocean walls. Three major forces kept the United States on the sidelines as war clouds gathered over Europe and Asia. First, tradition held America to an isolationist foreign policy. Rejection of membership in the League of Nations was indicative of a return to pre–World War I attitudes. Franklin Roosevelt had begun his political career as an outspoken supporter of his mentor's League in 1920. Yet, by 1932, Roosevelt campaigned on his *opposition* to the League.

Second, isolationism was spurred by the war debt problem (see Chapter 20), which created resentment on both sides of the Atlantic. Americans viewed the huge war loans to the Allies during World War I, which totaled $22 billion, as just that—*loans*. Payment from the debtor nations, however, was difficult not only because of the slowness of their postwar recovery but also because trade with the United States, which would have helped pay their bill, was effectively cut off by America's high protective tariffs. In addition, Europeans took a different view of their debts. The old Allies observed that much of the American credit was used to purchase American goods, which fueled the American economy. Europeans viewed settling their American debt with about as much enthusiasm as they would have when making a funeral payment. After bitter losses of millions killed and maimed, the British and French pointed to miles of graves as payment enough. By 1933, most of America's former allies had repudiated their war debts.

Third, the Great Depression kept most Americans focused on domestic rather than international concerns. Leaders in Washington were too occupied with economic recovery to take more than a sideline role in European and Asian politics.

Despite the drift to isolationism, the sympathies of most Americans were with the Allies. As in the days before U.S. entry into World War I, Americans felt their strong cultural ties to Britain. They also felt a natural sympathy for the nations devastated by the vicious Nazi war machine. Yet, Americans wanted no part of the war itself if they could avoid it. They hoped that the Allies would quash the German aggressions without direct U.S. military support. They based those hopes on a number of illusory beliefs. Many

PATH OF APPEASEMENT

LET ME ALONE, IT IS SO PEACEFUL

This 1930s cartoon ridiculed Roosevelt's announced policy of isolation in the face of Nazi aggression.

Preparedness

Despite the isolationist tendencies of most Americans, there was an increasing sense of the need for preparedness. In addition to changes in the neutrality laws, Congress instituted a peacetime draft—the first in American history—in September 1940. The following month, Congress approved a huge $17 billion defense budget.

One Democrat's Assessment of Willkie

Willkie, a former Indiana farm boy who became a wealthy businessman, drew enthusiastic crowds across the country with his down-home charm. One respectful Democrat wryly observed that Willkie was "a simple, barefoot, Wall Street lawyer."

Americans, like the French, believed that France's Maginot Line would stop Hitler's tanks. They believed that the Germans could not sustain their war effort long without oil, rubber, and food—supplies that Germany could not easily acquire in adequate amounts. And many people hoped that the German people themselves would not long support their mad dictator's bloody ambition.

Nervous Neutrality

Changing with the Times

In September 1939, while the Germans were mopping up the remnants of Polish resistance and the Russians were devouring the Baltic states, President Roosevelt called Congress into special session to consider changes in the Neutrality Act of 1937. That law had cut off American military supplies to belligerents—nations engaged in war. Ironically, the Neutrality Act had not greatly affected Germany because Hitler had been rearming for years using German factories and had little need for U.S. arms. It had, however, seriously hurt the democratic nations because they could not purchase military supplies from the United States when they needed them most.

After stiff debate, Congress passed the **Neutrality Act of 1939**, which provided that belligerents could purchase weaponry from the United States but only on a cash basis. It further stipulated that the buyers must transport the weapons in their own ships. This "cash-and-carry" policy was a help to England, which had a large navy. In addition, the act prohibited U.S. ships and passengers from entering the ports of belligerent nations. That unwittingly helped Germany by ensuring that U.S. ships would not be traveling into the ports of Germany's enemies; thus, Hitler could initiate unrestricted submarine warfare with less fear of becoming involved with the United States.

The more vocal isolationists and militant pacifists organized into **America First committees.** Charles Lindbergh was one of their leading spokesmen. These organizations, many of them in the Midwest, were watchdogs to keep Allied sympathy and American involvement in check.

1940 Election

Despite preparedness measures, the American public and leaders vacillated between preparedness and pacifism. During the election of 1940, Roosevelt, running for an unprecedented third term, promised from the stump, "I have said this before, but I shall say it again and again and again: Your boys are not going to be sent into any foreign wars."

FDR's opponent, Republican **Wendell Willkie**, a former New Deal Democrat, had early recognized the Nazi menace and urged preparedness and support of the Allies, but he was careful not to seem to support U.S. intervention. He received twenty-two million votes in the November election, but with Nazis having their way in Europe, most Americans agreed with the Democratic slogan that year: "Don't switch horses in the middle of the stream." The next four years for Roosevelt and the nation would be among the most demanding in American history.

The Arsenal of Democracy

Roosevelt's election in 1940 ensured further aid to England and the other Allies. America had to become the "arsenal of democracy," and the Allies were to use that aid to guarantee what Roosevelt called the "Four Freedoms": freedom of speech and of worship, and freedom from want and from fear.

Lend-Lease

Backed by a growing popular attitude that the United States would have to fight the enemies of free people alone if England were destroyed, FDR asked for and received from Congress "all-out aid" to the Allies. "They do not need manpower," the president stated. "They do need billions of dollars' worth of weapons of defense." On March 11, he signed the **Lend-Lease Act**, and Congress appropriated $7 billion to provide supplies for the embattled nations. Under the provisions of the act, Roosevelt was empowered to supply any Allied nation with war materiel on almost any terms he desired. Eventually, the United States distributed nearly $50 billion worth of military supplies to thirty-eight countries. In addition, U.S. forces were stationed in Iceland and Greenland to protect the vital shipping lanes of the North Atlantic as American supplies were ferried to Britain.

As part of Lend-Lease, the United States sent China one hundred P-40 Tomahawk fighter planes and Claire Chennault, a retired Army Air Force captain, as air advisor. Later, a group of pilots known as the American Volunteer Group, more commonly called the "**Flying Tigers**," joined him in Burma. Although always outnumbered, the Flying Tigers became the scourge of Japanese pilots, downing 286 Japanese planes in seven months.

The Atlantic Charter

The alliance between the United States and Britain was galvanized in August 1941 when Churchill and Roosevelt secretly met at Placentia Bay, Newfoundland. In an exchange of meetings aboard the American cruiser *Augusta* and the British battleship *Prince of Wales*, the two leaders drew up the **Atlantic Charter**, a list of "common principles" such as self-determination, freedom of the seas, and economic cooperation. Increasingly, President Roosevelt's rhetoric against Germany and massive supplies to the Allies were making America, as one newspaper editor observed, "as unneutral as possible without getting into war."

Hitler was not unaware of America's "unneutral" neutrality. In May 1941, a German submarine attacked and sank an American merchant vessel in the waters off Brazil. In September, the U.S. destroyer *Greer* was fired on by a German submarine, after which Roosevelt ordered the fleet to "shoot on sight" German or Italian attack vessels. In October, another U.S. destroyer, the *Kearny*, was torpedoed, and eleven sailors were killed in the attack. Later that same month, the destroyer *Reuben James* was sunk west of Iceland with the loss of more than a hundred Americans. In the waning days of 1941, escalating tensions in the Atlantic brought America to the verge of war. Yet, surprisingly, when the blow finally came, it fell not in the Atlantic, but in the Pacific.

The "Flying Tigers" of the American Volunteer Group helped China fight the Japanese before the United States officially entered the war.

The Atlantic Charter in a Nutshell

The Atlantic Charter was essentially a list of the goals of the anti-Axis nations. It sought to provide "a better future for the world" and expressed America's moral commitment to the Allied cause.

Another Perspective on the Greer and Kearny Incidents

After the war, investigations revealed that the U.S.S. *Greer* had chased the German submarine for three hours before the sub turned and fired two torpedoes. The *Greer* responded with depth charges. The U.S.S. *Kearny* had sighted the German sub with which it was involved and fired on it first. In both cases, the U.S. ships had provoked the attacks, so the U.S. government did not make a public issue of either incident. Hence, the American public did not become enflamed when these incidents occurred or when the *Reuben James*, the first American ship that the Germans actually sunk, was torpedoed.

A day of infamy—the U.S.S. *Shaw* explodes during the Japanese attack on Pearl Harbor.

"Remember Pearl Harbor!"

Japan's insatiable appetite for territory placed increasing strain on U.S.-Japanese relations. The decade-long ravaging of China culminated in the summer of 1941 with the Japanese seizure of the strategic oil fields and rubber plantations of French Indochina in Southeast Asia. Roosevelt responded by placing an oil embargo on the Japanese and freezing Japanese assets. He named General **Douglas MacArthur** commander of all American forces in the Far East.

The Japanese, though, had bigger plans than simply taking French Indochina. With England being pounded by Hitler and the Netherlands under Nazi occupation, the Japanese eyed the resource-rich British and Dutch colonies of the Pacific Rim. First, however, the Japanese warlords would have to deal with the chief naval threat in the Pacific— the United States.

The Attack on Pearl Harbor

At 7:53 a.m. on Sunday, **December 7, 1941**, Japanese warplanes swept across the blue Hawaiian sky over Pearl Harbor. Commander Mitsuo Fuchida signaled, *"Tora! Tora! Tora!"* ("Tiger! Tiger! Tiger!"), and the strike commenced. In fifteen minutes, the Japanese neutralized the main battle line of the U.S. Pacific Fleet. In a series of bomber attacks, the Japanese sank three battleships and seriously damaged sixteen other warships. Within two hours, most American air power in Hawaii had been destroyed as Japanese planes destroyed about 150 aircraft at nearby Hickam Field. The two-hour attack took a heavy toll in American lives as well, with 3,581 killed and 1,200 wounded.

In their broader whirlwind attack, Japanese forces conquered many other U.S. and British bases throughout the South Pacific during the rest of December, including Guam, Hong Kong, Wake Island, and the Gilbert Islands.

Despite the heavy American losses, Pearl Harbor was not a complete success for the Japanese. First, they had missed the American aircraft carriers, which were out on maneuvers at the time. In the war that had begun, the carrier, not the battleship, would be the decisive factor. Second, by not coming back to Hawaii for a third or fourth attack, Japan failed to put the final nail in the coffin of American Pacific naval power. The Americans would rebuild with the facilities that remained. Third, with one stroke, the Japanese had done what Hitler's accumulated atrocities and aggressions had not—united the American nation to war and to win.

The day after the Pearl Harbor attack, President Roosevelt addressed a joint session of Congress, declaring that December 7, 1941, would be a date that would "live in infamy." Congress quickly declared war on Japan, as did Britain that same day. In a flurry of war declarations, China declared war on the Axis on December 9, and on December 11 Germany and Italy declared war on the United States, which responded by declaring war on them. Pearl Harbor had triggered war on a global scale.

Dorie Miller, Hero

Doris "Dorie" Miller was one of many heroes at Pearl Harbor on Sunday, December 7, 1941. He was an African-American mess attendant aboard the battleship U.S.S. *West Virginia* at the time. He was awarded the Navy Cross for his courageous actions that fateful day. The citation reads in part, "While at the side of his Captain on the bridge, Miller, despite enemy strafing and bombing and in the face of a serious fire, assisted in moving his Captain, who had been mortally wounded, to a place of greater safety, and later manned a machine gun directed at enemy Japanese attacking aircraft until ordered to leave the bridge."

Fall of the Philippines

In the Philippines, the Japanese forced the American and Philippine forces to retreat to the Bataan Peninsula by early January 1942. Slowly, the huge Japanese force advanced in the face of stiff American resistance. In March, to prevent the capture of General Douglas MacArthur, Roosevelt ordered him to leave. MacArthur, vowing "I shall return," left for Australia, where he laid plans for thwarting the Japanese advance and reversing Japanese gains in the Pacific. In April, the surviving American defenders on Bataan surrendered to the Japanese. On May 6, the last American troops, holding out on the island fortress of Corregidor, surrendered. The conquest of the Philippines was complete. The Japanese, who had not planned for dealing with so many prisoners, forced the American and Filipino prisoners to make a brutal eighty-mile "death march" to prison camps. They shot or bayoneted anyone who fell behind, paused for water or rest, or tried to help those who did.

First Strike Against Japan

After American forces had suffered one defeat after another, the American people badly needed positive news. They needed to know that U.S. forces were fighting back. Military planners considered a raid over Japan, but the range of typical navy planes was limited, and aircraft carriers could not get close enough to Japan to allow the planes to operate. Army bombers could travel farther but required longer takeoff distances.

The solution to the dilemma was the B-25, a medium bomber that was compact enough to take off at sea. After intense special training, volunteer crews under General Jimmy Doolittle set out with sixteen B-25 bombers from the United States aboard the carrier U.S.S. *Hornet*, which joined Task Force 16 at sea under the command of Vice Admiral "Bull" Halsey.

The original plan was for the B-25s to take off when the task force was 400 miles off Japan's coast. But the force was detected by a Japanese fishing ship, which the cruiser *Vincennes* promptly sank. The possibility that the fishermen had radioed, warning Japan of the task force, required takeoffs at 625 miles instead.

The bombing raid was successful. But bad weather and other circumstances foiled the landings on the Chinese mainland that the American raiders had planned. One plane landed in the Soviet Union, where the crew was imprisoned for thirteen months. Eleven crews had to bail out, and four crash-landed. Three men were killed, seven wounded, and eight captured by the Japanese.

Although the raid did not do a lot of damage to the factories, military installations, and oil storage facilities that the Americans hit, it encouraged Americans and rattled the Japanese, who were mystified as to where the planes had originated. They knew that American forces were within striking range, which forced them to keep some military personnel and equipment on the home islands.

Battle of Midway

With the fall of Corregidor in May 1942, the Japanese controlled a huge Pacific empire stretching from Burma to the Bering Sea. Yet, May 1942 was the high-water mark (greatest extent) of the Japanese advance. A naval and air battle in the Coral Sea that month checked the Japanese advance toward Australia. Japanese expansion was again halted at Midway Island in the northern Pacific in June. The **Battle of Midway** was a critical battle—perhaps

Damages at Pearl Harbor
U.S. Losses:
5 of 8 battleships—sunk
3 battleships—heavily damaged
3 of 6 cruisers—sunk
3 of 29 destroyers—sunk; others damaged
188 of 390 planes—destroyed
155 other planes—damaged
3,581 military and 103 civilians—killed
Japanese Losses:
29 of 441 planes—destroyed
55 airmen—killed
5 midget submarines—sunk

Executive Order 9066

Early in 1942, the U.S. government, fearing that some Japanese-Americans might be spies or saboteurs, rounded up and relocated all Japanese living on the U.S. West Coast. This group of more than 120,000 people, most of whom were American citizens, was moved to inland internment camps. President Reagan formally apologized for that mistreatment in 1988. The United States ended up paying $1.6 million to internees or their families as reparations. The following table shows the names of the major camps, their locations, and the maximum number of internees that were held in each camp.

Manzinar	CA	10,046
Tule Lake	CA	18,789
Poston	AZ	17,814
Gila River	AZ	13,348
Granada	CO	7,318
Heart Mountain	WY	10,767
Minidoka	ID	9,397
Topaz	UT	8,130
Rohwer	AR	8,475
Jerome	AR	8,497

Race and World War II

The Nisei

After the attack on Pearl Harbor, many Americans feared anyone of Japanese ancestry, even other *Americans*. The fear of potential spies and saboteurs was especially great on the West Coast, where most Nisei (nee SAY), or second-generation Japanese-Americans, lived. Early in 1942, the former attorney general of California asked Congress to restrict the freedom of Japanese-Americans because "they are not of an assimilable race and they are strangers to our customs, our way of life. . . . If they are permitted to live at large among us, the possibility of disaster cannot be reckoned."

Responding to that wartime hysteria, President Roosevelt on February 19, 1942, authorized the War Department to restrict Japanese-Americans. Some 120,000 were forced from their homes in California, Oregon, and Washington and placed in highly undesirable detention camps farther inland. None was ever charged with or convicted of treason or espionage.

In 1976, President Gerald Ford marked the thirty-fourth anniversary of Roosevelt's action by issuing a proclamation, which ended with these words: "We have learned from the tragedy of that long-ago experience forever to treasure liberty and justice for each individual American, and resolve that this kind of action shall never be repeated." In 1988, a formal apology and financial redress were offered to the Japanese-Americans who had been interned as a result of what a congressional commission called "race prejudice, war hysteria, and a failure of political leadership."

Despite the gross violations of their civil liberties during internment, 30,000 Nisei demonstrated their patriotism by serving in combat units in Europe. The first all-Nisei unit formed was the 100th Infantry Battalion, which became known as the "Purple Heart Battalion" because so many of its men were wounded in combat. The most famous unit was the 442nd Regimental Combat Team, which became the most decorated combat unit in the war.

The Navajo "Code Talkers"

Another racial group that got little recognition until well after the war was the Navajo Indians. They became famous as the "code talkers" who, by using their native language, frustrated Japanese code breakers throughout the entire war. Japanese intelligence forces were never able to "decode" the language. The idea for using Navajo for code work came from missionary Philip Johnson.

The code talkers became famous for their speed, skill, and accuracy.

About 540 Navajos served in the U.S. Marines, 375–420 of them as code talkers. Other Native Americans served in the U.S. Army, most of them Cherokees, Choctaws, and Comanches. Three Native Americans won the Medal of Honor: one Cherokee, one Choctaw, and one Creek.

Black Americans

More than 2.5 million black Americans registered for the draft in World War II. Although blacks served in every branch of the service, about 909,000 of them served in the U.S. Army. No matter which branch they served in, they were segregated from white soldiers, reflecting the practice in the broader civilian society.

The first black U.S. Marine was Howard Perry. Eventually, 1,200 black enlistees were organized into an all-black unit called the 51st Composite Defense Battalion.

Brigadier General Benjamin Davis was the first black general in the U.S. Army. Also, his son commanded the all-black Tuskegee Airmen of the U.S. Army Air Corps.

No black Americans received the Medal of Honor during World War II, but President Clinton awarded Medals of Honor to seven blacks on January 13, 1997, six of them posthumously.

the turning point of the war in the Pacific. By breaking the Japanese radio codes, the U.S. intercepted war messages and anticipated Japanese moves. U.S. Admiral **Chester W. Nimitz** skillfully directed carrier forces against the Japanese, destroying four Japanese carriers. The outstanding victory at Midway, combined with the Battle of the Coral Sea, turned the tide of Japanese conquest. Despite those victories, Tokyo was far away; the road to victory would be long and bloody.

Home Front

The idea that "each citizen should be a soldier" was born in the French Revolution, but it had its greatest demonstration during the Second World War. The war would not be won, as in olden days, by one army defeating another on the field of battle. Rather, the war would be won both on the field and in the factory. This war would impact everyone. The price for that united mobilization for war was the surrendering of some individual freedoms and an enormous expansion of federal power over the entire economy through regulation.

Through Roosevelt's generous Lend-Lease program, the economic output of the United States had already been critical to sustaining both Britain and the Soviet Union, which was teetering on the brink of defeat by the Nazis. Now America's tremendous production capability would be a crucial factor in bringing victory over the Axis.

Mobilizing the Economy

The new War Powers Act of 1941 authorized President Roosevelt, as commander in chief, to get the nation's economy on a war footing. The **War Production Board** (WPB), which began operation in January 1942, immediately halted nearly all domestic building construction to conserve materials for war production. Production of many consumer goods was discontinued through much of the war because the WPB ordered massive industrial conversion from civilian to military production.

Conserving vital goods such as foodstuffs, rubber, and gasoline for diversion to the war effort required a system of nationwide **rationing** under the direction of the Office of Price Administration. The government issued every man and woman ration books containing stamps needed to purchase various goods such as meat, sugar, and shortening. Even the purchase of shoes was limited to three pairs a year. Ladies' nylon stockings were almost nonexistent; the nylon was needed for parachutes. A new generation of "Victory Gardens" also sprang up in backyards across America to offset the shortages created by the war. By 1943, those gardens produced one-third of the nation's vegetables. Gasoline was rationed; motorists received a monthly allowance in relation to the importance of their vehicle to the war effort. In addition, several states established a "Victory Speed" of 35 mph to conserve fuel.

Besides conservation measures, recycling was an important part of the national war effort. Boy Scouts fanned out through their neighborhoods collecting cooking grease and discarded metal and rubber goods. Farm boys scoured the fields for old plow tips and even junk cars, doing their part to help "scrap" the Axis.

Precedent for Restricted Liberties

You read in Chapter 19 of how the government either took control of or heavily regulated much of the economy during World War I through the Food Administration, the Fuel Administration, the Railroad Administration, and the War Industries Board. Those restrictions set the stage for massive government controls over the economy and reduction of individual freedoms during World War II.

U.S. Government to Consumer Goods Manufacturers: "Stop! Produce War Goods Instead!"

Manufacturers made few goods for consumers during the war; instead, the government told them they had to produce war goods. For example, civilian automobiles were not produced from February 1942 to July 1945. Instead, the government ordered Ford Motor Company to build B-24 bombers, General Motors to produce tanks, and its Cadillac division to build P-51 fighter planes and engines for tanks. Clothing manufacturers turned out uniforms, blankets, and parachutes. Even small manufacturers, such as the maker of Hoover vacuum cleaners, switched to producing helmets and bomb fuses.

(above) Women put the finishing touches on B-25 bomber nose cones, 1942.

(above right) Female pilots ferried bombers for the Army Air Force, including these B-17s.

Women in the Military

Although men generally get the attention in accounts of the war, women made great contributions too. In fact, about 268,000 women joined the various women's auxiliary units of the service branches. The largest such unit was the Women's Army Corps (WAC), which enlisted 150,000 women. The Navy enlisted 86,000 women in its WAVES (Women Accepted for Volunteer Emergency Service) program. The Coast Guard also had a unit called the SPARs, named for the Coast Guard motto, "*Semper Paratus,* Always Ready," which about 10,000 women joined. The 2,000 WASPs (Women Air Service Pilots) flew new warplanes to their frontline bases for the Army Air Corps. About 20,000 women also joined the marines' auxiliary, but their unit did not have any special name or acronym.

Manpower and Womanpower

The war also created massive changes in the labor force and, as a result, dramatic changes in American society. Fifteen million men and women answered the call to arms during the course of the war. The war increased the production needs of industry but at the same time subjected every able-bodied man between the ages of eighteen and forty-five to the draft. Consequently, it created a huge demand for workers. Women filled many of those jobs.

The number of women in the job market jumped from 25 percent in 1941 to 36 percent by 1944. In addition, female workers filled many traditionally male-oriented jobs, particularly in the defense industry. "Rosie the Riveter" came to symbolize the American woman on the assembly line and in the shipyard, filling a vital role in the war on the home front.

The contribution that women made in the work force was not without its cost, however. During the war, married women outnumbered single women for the first time, and working mothers placed new strains on the home and created new concerns over childcare. Women also became more independent, which, in some cases, led to marital tensions when husbands returned after the war.

Axis Taxes

Paying for the war not only became a political football for the duration of the conflict but also had long-term effects on both the taxed and the taxer alike. America's war bill totaled more than $300 billion, a figure that Roosevelt believed should be paid with increased taxes rather than allowing the nation to lapse into debt. Congress, however, was less enthusiastic about raising taxes. With elections looming in 1942, Congress supported only half the tax increase that FDR recommended. Altogether, about 45 percent of the war's cost was paid through taxation, and the national debt increased sixfold. The government not only imposed new taxes but also developed new means of collecting them. Congress introduced payroll deductions for income tax nationally in 1943 to help improve the government's tax flow.

But for most Americans the war was about far more than taxes and ration books. With the mobilization of millions of men, nearly every family had an intense personal interest in the news from the war front. Blue star banners proudly hung in windows across America, representing a son gone to war. "Gold star mothers" replaced the blue banner with a gold one in memory of a fallen son who would not be coming home. The war required the courage, patriotism, sacrifice, and sometimes grief of millions of Americans.

Section Quiz

1. What three forces kept the United States out of the war until late 1941?
2. Who was one of the leading spokesmen for the isolationist America First committees?
3. What three actions did FDR take in response to Japan's seizure of French Indochina?
4. What was the turning point of the Pacific war?
5. What action did several states take during World War II to conserve gasoline?
* Was complete national isolation a realistic position for the United States before the bombing of Pearl Harbor? Why or why not? Is it realistic today? Why or why not?

III. The Fight for Fortress Europe

Hitler's occupied Europe was imposing and seemingly invincible. Yet by 1942 faint cracks in his empire could be detected. The eastern "wall" of "Fortress Europe," deep within Russia, was locked in bitter cold and bitter fighting. German casualties mounted to a million since the invasion was launched. Westward, Hitler's defenses, which ranged from the Aegean Sea to the Arctic Ocean, did not invite attack. Yet the führer underestimated his enemy. The British, led by Churchill, had much fight left in them, and Hitler's latest enemy, the United States, loomed beyond the Atlantic. Hitler's air chief, Hermann Goering, dismissed the now-awakened industrial giant: "All the Americans can make are razor blades and refrigerators," he said. But Americans turned their plowshares into swords and soon showed their eagerness to fight against Hitler's Fortress Europe.

Desert War

Mussolini, seeking to expand his African empire by building on his Ethiopian conquest, moved to conquer more territory in North Africa. The British, to protect their interests in the Middle East, sent troops to halt the Italian advance. In February 1941, the British cornered the Italians in Libya and forced them to surrender.

The British triumph was short-lived, however: the British had exhausted their resources, and German panzers led by the famed **Erwin Rommel** arrived by the end of February. Rommel took command of the Axis forces in North Africa at Tripoli. With the superb military strategy that earned him the nickname "the Desert Fox," Rommel moved his *Afrika Korps* eastward toward the Suez Canal, hoping to force Britain into a desert showdown. For months, the tank war in the desert moved back and forth from Egypt to Libya. At times, the fall of Egypt seemed imminent. After a string of stinging British defeats at the hands of Rommel, Churchill ordered Field Marshall **Bernard Montgomery** to take command.

This desert war was the first in which U.S. forces took part. On November 8, 1942, **Operation Torch**, commanded by General **Dwight D. Eisenhower**, used 850 ships to land troops on the west coast of Africa at Casablanca, Oran, and Algiers. In a three-day advance, the American tanks raced eastward toward Tunisia. With the feisty Montgomery coming west, the German and Italian tank corps were caught in the middle. After suffering repeated defeats and numerous shortages, the last German outpost at Tunis fell on May 13, 1943.

Italian Campaign

Casablanca Conference

In January 1943, while the desert war was raging far to the east in Tunisia, Franklin Roosevelt, Winston Churchill, and Charles de Gaulle of the Free French met in **Casablanca** to forge an Allied strategy for the assault on Hitler's Europe. Stalin, who had been invited but was not present because of the ongoing Nazi siege of Stalingrad, had been urging a second front in France to relieve German pressure on the Russian front. Both Roosevelt and Churchill refused to commit themselves to such an invasion, citing a lack of troops and preparedness for such a grand assault. They did agree, however, to open a front in southern Europe against Mussolini's Italy, which Churchill described as Europe's "soft underbelly." A successful invasion there would not only thrust into the heart of Europe but also reopen Mediterranean sea lanes.

Up the Boot

The invasion of Italy began with the capture of Sicily, an island off the toe of the Italian boot. In **Operation Husky**, three thousand ships and landing craft carried troops and equipment to Sicily. Although suffering heavy casualties, the Allied forces defeated the Italian army and forced the German army off the island. By the end of the summer, Sicily was an Allied base. From there, the Allies, led by General Mark Clark, landed at Salerno and Anzio, Italy. After fighting bitter battles with the German forces there, American troops began fighting their way slowly north toward Rome, facing stiff German resistance, especially around the city of Casino. They finally marched into Rome on June 4, 1944. The cheering Romans viewed the conquest of their city as a deliverance. An American GI, viewing the ancient ruins of the Forum for the first time, whistled and said with amazement, "I didn't know our bombers had done *that* much damage in Rome."

Despite the successful capture of Rome, the Italian campaign was far from over. The push into northern Italy continued to be costly as the "soft underbelly" turned out to be rock-ribbed with tough Nazi resistance. Not until the closing days of the war did the Allies finally cross the Po River at the foot of the Alps.

D-day

On June 4, 1944, the German legend Rommel looked at his impressive coastal defenses on the French side of the English Channel and glanced at the threatening skies. (After the Nazi loss of North Africa, Hitler had assigned Rommel to defend France from the expected Allied invasion across the English Channel.) Based on the weather forecasts, no Allied invasion was imminent, he decided. He would have time to surprise his wife in Berlin with a

---

A Threat and a Snub at Casablanca

At first, Charles de Gaulle refused to attend the Casablanca Conference, but he changed his mind when Churchill threatened to support recognition of Henri Giraud as head of the Free French forces. Chiang Kai-shek of China wanted to attend the conference to discuss plans for defending China against both Japan and, after the war, the Chinese Communists, but he was not even invited.

visit on her birthday in two days. As it turned out, Mrs. Rommel was not the only one surprised on June 6.

In January 1944, General Eisenhower had been appointed Supreme Allied Commander and tasked with coordinating a cross-channel invasion into occupied France. Eisenhower (or "Ike," as his men called him) was not only a strategist but also an organizer who had demonstrated in Africa and Italy his ability to work with the multinational Allied army. The fifty-three-year-old Midwesterner now faced his greatest challenge ever—an amphibious assault on the "Atlantic Wall of Fortress Europe." Three million Allied soldiers, sailors, and airmen—half of them Americans—were readied in southern England for the grand invasion.

The invasion, code-named Operation Overlord, began on the morning of "**D-day**," **June 6, 1944**. In spite of the bad weather and deadly opposition, the Allied Expeditionary Force (AEF) established a beachhead along a sixty-mile stretch of the Normandy coast of France, taking beaches code-named Gold, Sword, Juno, Utah, and Omaha in fierce fighting. The invaders encountered mines and pilings along the beaches and under the water level. On the shore, the Germans had set up miles of barbed wire, machine guns, and heavy artillery. Before the beach assault began, paratroopers and soldiers in gliders landed behind German lines in the darkness. They cut vital transportation and communication lines and captured key bridges and roads for miles around the invasion site. Allied bombers pounded the Nazi defenses while battleships, cruisers, and destroyers hurled tons of high explosives onto the same areas. Then 175,000 troops in landing crafts raced through the surf and landed on the beaches under intense enemy fire.

The Nazis resisted fiercely but could not stop the surprise invasion. They were outplanned, out-equipped, and outnumbered. The Allies controlled the skies, bombing roads, bridges, and supply depots to prevent German reinforcements from reaching the front. This invasion, the greatest in history, was a crucial success.

After intense fighting among hedgerows inland and street fighting at **St. Lô**, the Allied forces broke out into the French countryside for the push to Paris. The hard-fighting American general George Patton led the rapid advance to Paris, which Allied soldiers liberated on August 25, 1944. Another invading army landed in southern France, opening new ports and supply bases. The troops pushed quickly up the Rhone Valley to join the forces in northern

(above left) General Dwight Eisenhower, the Supreme Allied Commander, exhorts the troops involved in the D-day landings.

(above) Allied troops wade ashore under heavy enemy fire during the Normandy landings.

A German Soldier's Impression of the D-day Invasion

A German soldier manning the beach defenses at Normandy recalled his impression of the scene at first light on June 6, 1944. "When it started to get light, I saw ships through the haze. When the fog lifted, it looked like a city out there. Between the ships you couldn't see any water. It was unbelievable—terrifying to behold."

General Taylor's "Crickets"

American general Maxwell Taylor, commander of the 101st Airborne Division, inspired *esprit de corps* in his soldiers. He combined integrity, courage, duty, and creativity with practical concern for his men. He did not command from the rear but fought alongside his men on the front lines. As he and his command prepared to parachute into Normandy on D-day, he grew concerned about scattered paratroopers' ability to distinguish between friend and foe in the darkness. His solution was both simple and original: he ordered thousands of toy "crickets." Each man received one of the clicking tin noisemakers as a signaling device. Whenever a soldier heard an approaching person, he would click his cricket. If the unknown person responded with a similar click, he knew it was a friend. If he got no click in return, it was an enemy. During that tough Normandy night, many lives were spared and the operation expedited by General Taylor's "crickets."

France. By the end of 1944, France, Holland, and much of Luxembourg and Belgium had been freed of German armies. The three-million-man Allied force was at Germany's borders, ready to break the famous Siegfried Line and move on to Berlin.

Battle of the Bulge

As snow fell in early December, mounting victories and thoughts of home had many Allied soldiers believing that the war would be over by Christmas. But Hitler had other plans. At 5:00 a.m. on December 16, 1944, Hitler unleashed a terrific counteroffensive out of Belgium's Ardennes Forest in a bold drive to cut the Allied forces in two.

The massive Nazi spearhead against the weakest point in the Allied line sent green American troops reeling. The thrust created a "bulge" fifty miles deep into the Allied lines, giving the battle its name—the **Battle of the Bulge**. By Christmas Day, the Germans had captured thousands of troops and had surrounded American forces in the city of Bastogne. When the German commander ordered the American commander, General Anthony McAuliffe, to surrender his outnumbered army, the defiant American sent a one-word reply—"Nuts!"

Americans fought desperately in snow, cold, and the dense woods of the Ardennes Forest during the Battle of the Bulge.

Elsewhere along the Allied lines, the same fighting spirit prevailed. Eisenhower ordered Montgomery to go against the northern face of the Bulge while he sent the irrepressible Patton against the southern face to free Bastogne. Together, they squeezed the Bulge back by the middle of January 1945. Hitler's last gamble had cost him one hundred thousand casualties, one thousand aircraft, and eight hundred tanks. American troops, who had borne the brunt of the attack, suffered heavy losses too, but they had stood the test and were ready to cross the Rhine for the final push into the German heartland.

Section Quiz

1. What was the first military operation of World War II in which the United States took part?

2. At their conference at Casablanca, where did FDR and Churchill agree to open another front against the Axis?

3. In what region of France did the landings in Operation Overlord take place?

4. What battle resulted from Hitler's last gamble to win the war in the West?

★ What dangers do you think Churchill foresaw that encouraged him to support a second front against Europe's "soft underbelly" rather than solely an invasion of France as the initial relief for Soviet troops?

IV. The War in the Pacific

While war raged in Europe against Hitler's *Wehrmacht*, the United States also had the necessary task of defeating the Japanese

---

Strategy Overview of the Pacific War

In broad terms, the Pacific war consisted of a two-pronged drive, with General Douglas MacArthur of the U.S. Army heading the southern force from New Guinea and Admiral Chester Nimitz of the U.S. Navy commanding the Central Pacific force. These two separate campaigns would converge to reclaim the Philippines and then make the final assault on the Japanese home islands.

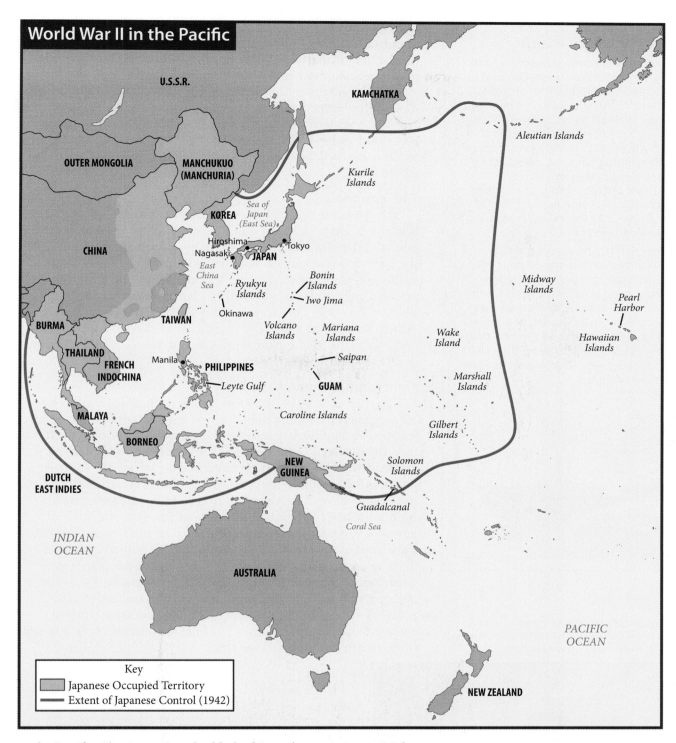

World War II in the Pacific

U.S.S.R.

KAMCHATKA

Aleutian Islands

OUTER MONGOLIA

MANCHUKUO
(MANCHURIA)

Kurile
Islands

KOREA

*Sea of
Japan
(East Sea)*

CHINA

Hiroshima
Nagasaki · Tokyo
JAPAN

*East
China
Sea*

*Ryukyu
Islands*

*Bonin
Islands*

Midway
Islands

Pearl
Harbor

*Volcano
Islands*

Iwo Jima

BURMA

Okinawa

TAIWAN

*Mariana
Islands*

*Wake
Island*

*Hawaiian
Islands*

THAILAND

FRENCH
INDOCHINA

Manila

PHILIPPINES

Saipan

GUAM

*Marshall
Islands*

Leyte Gulf

MALAYA

Caroline Islands

BORNEO

*Gilbert
Islands*

DUTCH
EAST INDIES

NEW
GUINEA

*Solomon
Islands*

Guadalcanal

*INDIAN
OCEAN*

Coral Sea

AUSTRALIA

*PACIFIC
OCEAN*

Key
Japanese Occupied Territory
Extent of Japanese Control (1942)

NEW ZEALAND

in the Pacific. The Americans had halted Japan's expansion at Midway in June 1942, but victory for America came only after many costly battles at sea on tiny islands known only because they were the scenes of some of the most desperate fighting of the entire war.

"Island Hopping"

In August 1942, the drive to defeat Japan began when U.S. Marines landed on **Guadalcanal** (GWAD ul kuh NAL), a jungle island in the Solomon Islands, three thousand miles from Tokyo. After several desperate sea battles and months of bloody jungle fighting, Japanese troops abandoned the island in February 1943. American forces then began "**island hopping**" toward Tokyo, bypassing the

PT Boats in World War II

Small, motorized torpedo boats were used extensively in World War II, especially in the Pacific theater. Called PT (patrol torpedo) or "mosquito" boats, they usually operated in squadrons called "mosquito fleets." They were built mainly of mahogany plywood and ranged from 70 to 80 feet long, depending on the manufacturer, and about 20 feet abeam. They were amazingly sturdy, and many of them withstood major damage but remained afloat. Powered by three Packard twelve-cylinder, 1500 horsepower engines, they were sleek and built for speed.

Armament on PT boats varied, but they typically had two to four one-ton torpedoes; two to four depth charges, which rolled off racks mounted astern; two twin .30- or .50-caliber machine guns; and sometimes a 40 mm cannon aft. By the end of the war, PT boats had more "firepower per ton" than any other vessel in the U.S. Navy. They also boasted smoke-generating machines aft for laying smoke screens.

This Japanese plane, which attempted to attack the escort carrier *Kitkun Bay*, was among many shot down during "the Great Marianas Turkey Shoot."

heavily fortified islands and securing air bases on less-fortified islands. Launching from runways on these islands, bombers such as the B-17 Flying Fortress and the B-29 Superfortress bombed Japanese fortifications on other islands and cut supply lines.

For the next year, U.S. forces slowly reduced the area of Japanese control in the South and Central Pacific. The United States retook the western Aleutian Islands that the Japanese had occupied. Early in 1944, U.S. troops captured the Marshall Islands and in April attacked New Guinea, cutting off fifty thousand Japanese troops there.

The Marianas

The Japanese resistance became desperate and bitter during the summer of 1944. The most significant fight of the summer was the taking of the Mariana Islands, including Saipan and Guam. While the amphibious assault on Saipan was under way, a massive air battle took place between carrier-based fighters. The F6-F Hellcats, new U.S. fighter planes, knocked 346 Japanese warplanes from the sky, a victory that Americans quickly dubbed "the Great Marianas Turkey Shoot." The capture of the Marianas enabled Allied bombers to fly to the Japanese home islands and the occupied Philippines to deliver their destructive cargoes.

Fight for the Philippines

By the fall of 1944, the lower prong of the Pacific strategy converged on the Philippines. The first major assault on the heavily fortified Philippines began around the central island of Leyte (LAY tee). The **Battle of Leyte Gulf** was the largest sea battle in history and a critical blow to Japanese naval and air forces. The Japanese lost three battleships, nine cruisers, ten destroyers, and one hundred eighty aircraft to American firepower, opening the gate to Manila and the liberation of the Philippines. After the Battle of Leyte Gulf, the Japanese, in desperation over their losses, organized squadrons of suicide pilots, or **kamikazes** (KAH mih KAH zeez). Their mission was simply to crash their bomb-laden planes into American warships. Although American gunners, by concentrated antiaircraft fire, stopped many of the fanatical missions, many others got through. The emperor's kamikazes sank or crippled three hundred U.S. warships in the final ten months of the war and inflicted fifteen thousand casualties.

Iwo Jima

While MacArthur's forces pushed toward Manila, American strategists looked ahead to the next target— Okinawa (OH kih NAH wah)—and eventually the assault on Japan itself. The planners also determined that they needed a secondary foothold, a place where damaged B-29s could land as they returned from bombing raids over Japan. Scanning the map, they chose a little speck of volcanic ash called **Iwo Jima** (EE-woh JEE-muh).

U.S. Marines landed on Iwo Jima on February 19, 1945, beginning what would become the toughest, costliest battle of their illustrious history. On the cave-riddled volcanic island, the marines fought against 21,000 Japanese defenders for every foot of black sand. More than 6,800 American soldiers were killed, and 20,000 were wounded before they crushed Japanese resistance.

Okinawa

The grim victory at Iwo Jima opened the way to **Okinawa**, the bloodiest single campaign in the Pacific. Both sides, knowing the importance of Okinawa to the final stages of the war, fought fiercely. For the Americans, a victory on Okinawa would pierce the Japanese defense perimeter and provide a base for intensive bombing raids and a launch site for an amphibious assault on the Japanese home islands. For the Japanese, the loss of Okinawa would mean the next-to-last step in their death struggle.

The Americans launched the invasion of Okinawa on Easter Sunday, April 1, 1945, beginning a fierce two-and-a-half-month battle. While the infantry fought for the island, the U.S. Navy found itself locked in combat with an equally determined aerial foe. Nearly two thousand kamikazes attacked the American fleet, killing five thousand American sailors and sinking thirty-eight U.S. ships. But by mid-June, Okinawa had been conquered.

Even more sad than the military losses were the mass suicides by Okinawan civilians. Survivors testified that before the invasion began, Japanese soldiers distributed grenades to civilians, ordering them to throw all but one at the American soldiers and to use the last one to commit suicide. Other Okinawan civilians (more than 140,000 according to U.S. Army estimates) jumped from cliffs onto jagged rocks or into the sea to escape the Americans.

The grim tale of Okinawa cast a pall over plans for the invasion of the Japanese home islands. As the war neared an end in Europe, fear of "an Okinawa from one end of Japan to the other" that would leave a million Americans dead raised thorny questions about how to end the conflict. Those problems weighed heavily on the mind of President Roosevelt as he met with fellow Allied chiefs Churchill and Stalin to discuss the future of war and peace.

Planning for Victory

A week before the assault on Iwo Jima in February 1945, the Big Three—Roosevelt, Churchill, and Stalin—had met at the Soviet Union's Black Sea resort of **Yalta**. Much had happened since their first meeting at Teheran in November 1943, when they discussed plans for the opening of a second front. Now, with Allied forces pushing Hitler's crumbling army from both the east and the west, the Big Three laid plans for postwar Europe.

Roosevelt came to Yalta enjoying the wide support of the American people. The previous November, he had won an unprecedented fourth term, defeating New York governor Thomas Dewey. In fact, one of the biggest fights for FDR during the 1944 election was not with the Republicans but with his own party over his vice president, Henry Wallace. Southern conservatives did not like Wallace's ties to the left, and political bosses in the North did not like his ties to labor. As a result, Roosevelt tapped a little-known senator from Missouri named **Harry Truman** for vice president. Just as he had handled a split in his own party, Roosevelt came to Yalta expecting to handle the growing rift between the Western nations and their at-arm's-length ally, the Soviet Union.

> ### "Uncommon Valor Was a Common Virtue."
> That is how Admiral Chester Nimitz eulogized the marines' conduct on Iwo Jima. The marines earned on Iwo Jima 30 percent of the Medals of Honor they earned during the entire war.

In this rare event, a Japanese soldier emerges from a cave on Okinawa to surrender to an American soldier.

> ### The Price of Victory on Okinawa
> The victory on Okinawa came at a high price: 12,000 American servicemen killed and 50,000 wounded. The Japanese casualty figures underscored their suicidal resistance. Of their 117,000 casualties, 110,000 were killed. Committed to fighting to the death, most of the Japanese captives were those so seriously wounded as to be unable to kill themselves.

The Big Three at Yalta

But Roosevelt came to Yalta with two misconceptions. First was the idea that if the United States simply corrected the mistake, as FDR saw it, of not joining the League of Nations, then the postwar world would be secure. As a result, formation of an international organization for peace was at the top of his Yalta agenda. Getting the Soviet Union to join the United Nations, however, would not be a panacea.

The Holocaust

As Allied forces freed Europe from Nazi tyranny, they came across unexpected horrors. In Nazi prison camps they found evidence of mass murder and racial and ethnic cleansing. That astounding massacre of millions of people became known as the **Holocaust**.

Nazis believed in the doctrine of "Aryan" (German) superiority over all other "lesser" peoples. Hitler used his ruthless Gestapo (secret police) and SS (*Schutzstaffel*, special security) forces to control, isolate, and exterminate "undesirable" elements in Germany and the countries that Nazi forces conquered. "Undesirables" included political opponents, Jews, prisoners of war, Poles, Romanies, the disabled, and Jehovah's Witnesses, but Jews had Hitler's special attention.

The first concentration camp was opened at Dachau on March 23, 1933, less than two months after Hitler was appointed chancellor of Germany. Two weeks later, the *Reichstag* began passing laws against Jews: forcing Jewish government workers to retire, excluding Jews from the army, defining "Jew" as anyone with two Jewish grandparents, revoking citizenship rights for Jews, and requiring Jews to wear yellow triangles or stars of David.

The Nazis encouraged Germans to boycott all Jewish businesses. On November 9, 1938, the Nazis vandalized thousands of Jewish businesses, burned scores of synagogues, and robbed, shamed, and arrested thousands of Jews all across Germany.

That night became known as *Kristallnacht*, "the night of broken glass."

Next, Hitler ordered that all Jews be segregated in **ghettos**. There they lived in crowded, unsanitary conditions, often with several families in one apartment. They had little food or fuel for warmth. The Warsaw ghetto was the most infamous.

In April 1940, the Nazis opened a concentration camp at Auschwitz, Poland, and began to transport thousands of Polish Jews there by train in filthy, unheated, and overcrowded cattle cars. Hundreds died en route. As the war progressed and began going against the Nazis, Hitler ordered the "final solution" implemented—the mass extermination of all Jews by gassing.

The guards expelled the gas with ventilators and then removed the bodies. Other prisoners shaved the heads of the corpses and removed any gold fillings from their teeth be-

fore shoving the bodies into ovens for cremation.

Also part of the Holocaust was the mass murder of thousands of Soviet Jews and captured Soviet prisoners of war.

Concentration camps and extermination camps existed all across Germany, Poland, and Austria. Auschwitz, Bergen-Belsen, Ravensbrück, Buchenwald, Dachau, Treblinka, Sobibor, Belzec, Chelmno, Mauthausen, and other such camps revealed their own gruesome secrets. One American soldier related that as U.S. troops neared Dachau, they "could smell the camp from at least five miles away."

An estimated 6 million Jews alone were killed in Hitler's program of state-supported mass murder. Combining this number with the number of non-Jews killed, an estimated 11 to 17 million people died at the hands of the Nazis.

Roosevelt's second misconception was his perceived ability to deal with Stalin. FDR thought that he could deal with Stalin as one party boss to another. But Stalin was no politician; he was a tyrant. The Big Three agreed to support democratic elections and government in all the liberated nations of Europe. Stalin gave the appropriate nods and smiles that FDR wanted on the issue while the Soviet army destroyed democratic forces in Eastern Europe and set up puppet governments. Wherever the Red Army advanced, Nazi control was simply replaced with Communist control. Roosevelt was aware of the gulf between Soviet promises and practices, but, because of Stalin's agreement to join the war against Japan after Germany was defeated, FDR did not press the issue.

At the time, that concession was paramount in Roosevelt's thinking. With Americans bogged down in costly fights in the South Pacific and the atomic bomb still in development, Roosevelt wanted Russia's help in defeating the Japanese. Stalin agreed to join the fight, but he wanted additional Asian territory for his trouble. Roosevelt agreed.

Franklin Roosevelt's disappointing performance at Yalta reflected political realities, wishful thinking, and the president's declining health. Just eight weeks after Yalta, on April 12, Roosevelt died of a cerebral hemorrhage at Warm Springs, Georgia. After less than three months as vice president, Harry Truman was the new commander in chief.

Victory Achieved!

Victory in Europe

On April 20, 1945, Hitler celebrated his fifty-sixth birthday in his command bunker deep in the heart of Berlin. He could hear the sound of Soviet artillery shells exploding in his capital. Allied forces to the west under Eisenhower had pushed as far as the Elbe River in central Germany, where he ordered them to halt while the Soviets devoured eastern Germany.

By April 30, the Battle of Berlin raged less than a quarter mile from Hitler's underground headquarters. That morning, the führer fed cyanide, a poison, to his favorite dog, Blondi, and her pups,

FDR's Health at Yalta— Did It Affect His Ability to Deal with Stalin?

Comparing photos of the participants at Casablanca, Teheran, and Yalta reveals the deterioration of Roosevelt's physical condition. Some historians suggest that FDR's apparent unwillingness to deal firmly with Stalin may have been the result of FDR's declining health.

Little Cost but a Great Return

The problem with Stalin's promise to fight against Japan was that the Russians did not declare war on Japan until early August 1945. That was just days before Japan surrendered, so the Russians had little, if any, impact on the outcome of the war. Yet they insisted on receiving what had been promised to them.

American infantry march through the rubbled streets of Bensheim, Germany, in March 1945 as a resident gazes in anguish at the destruction.

killing them. That afternoon, he and his new bride, Eva Braun, committed suicide. (Accounts vary, but the most widely accepted account states that Eva took cyanide and Hitler shot himself in the right temple with his pistol.) The Reich was no more. On May 7 and 8, the Nazis surrendered on both fronts. News of victory in Europe triggered joyous celebrations from Times Square to Red Square.

In his victory address to the nation, President Truman pointed to the unfinished task.

> We must work to bind up the wounds of a suffering world—
> to build an abiding peace, a peace rooted in justice and law.
> We can build such a peace only by hard, toilsome, painstak-
> ing work—by understanding and working with our Allies in
> peace as we have in war.

Truman would soon learn that "working with our Allies," particularly the Soviet Union, would be the hardest work of all.

Potsdam

Truman traveled to Berlin in July 1945 to meet with Churchill and Stalin to plan the conclusion of the war in the Pacific. Truman was not the only new face among the Big Three at **Potsdam**. Elections in Britain during the conference had swept Churchill's party out of power, replacing the great war leader with a new prime minister, Clement Attlee.

In other ways, the Potsdam Conference underscored changes in the alliance. Stalin had installed puppet governments throughout much of the area his armies occupied. Truman could do little more than remind Stalin of his promises to support free elections in Eastern Europe. But Stalin's problem was not memory loss. The previous spring, shortly after Yalta, the dictator had boasted, "This war is unlike all past wars. Whoever occupies a territory imposes his own social system . . . as far as his army can advance."

One item on which the Big Three at Potsdam could agree was the demand for Japan's unconditional surrender. Behind that declaration was perhaps the biggest event to occur during the conference. Shortly after arriving at Potsdam, Truman received the following message:

TOP SECRET

PRIORITY WAR 33556

TO SECRETARY OF WAR FROM HARRISON. DOCTOR HAS JUST RETURNED MOST ENTHUSIASTIC AND CONFIDENT THAT THE LITTLE BOY IS AS HUSKY AS HIS BIG BROTHER. THE LIGHT IN HIS EYES DISCERNIBLE FROM HERE TO HIGHHOLD AND I COULD HAVE HEARD HIS SCREAMS FROM HERE TO MY FARM.

The coded words meant that the test of the **atomic bomb** had been successful; the noise of the blast could be heard for forty miles. The secret weapon awaited the president's orders for its use against Japan.

"These Proceedings Are Closed"

The Allies issued to Japan an ultimatum—surrender or face destruction. The Japanese premier pronounced the Allied ultimatum "absurd." Truman's warning, however, was no empty threat. On the morning of August 6, Colonel Paul Tibbets piloted a B-29 (christened the *Enola Gay* after his mother) over the sun-drenched city of **Hiroshima** (HIR uh SHEE muh) and dropped the first

The aftermath of the atomic bomb—Nagasaki is reduced to a wasteland, prompting Japanese surrender.

atomic bomb. The extraordinary weapon destroyed half the city in a single blast. Three days later, Charles Sweeney, piloting a B-29 named *Bocks Car*, dropped the second bomb on **Nagasaki** (NAH guh SAH kee), and Japanese emperor Hirohito accepted the inevitable. On September 2, 1945, the Japanese surrendered aboard the U.S.S. *Missouri* anchored in Tokyo Bay. General MacArthur stood on deck and addressed victor and vanquished alike:

> We are gathered here, representatives of the major warring powers, to conclude a solemn agreement whereby peace may be restored. The issues, involving divergent ideals and ideologies, have been determined on the battlefields of the world and hence are not for our discussion or debate. Nor is it for us here to meet, representing as we do a majority of the people of the earth, in a spirit of distrust, malice, or hatred. But rather it is for us, both victors and vanquished, to serve, committing all our people unreservedly to faithful compliance with the understanding they are here formally to assume. It is my earnest hope . . . that from this solemn occasion a better world shall emerge . . . a world dedicated to the dignity of man. . . . Let us pray that peace be now restored to the world, and that God will preserve it always. These proceedings are closed.

Silent Guns

While victory celebrations erupted around the world, in lands where the victory occurred, survivors in search of food picked through the rubble of what had once been their homes. For the millions of destitute refugees in Europe, peace did not follow victory. Perhaps a million civilians died in 1945 from exposure or from the vengeful guns of Russian soldiers. Throughout the world the wounds of war ran deep. The grim tally was simply overwhelming: fifty million men, women, and children killed, with millions more maimed for life.

Japan's representative signs the terms of surrender aboard the U.S.S. *Missouri* anchored in Tokyo Bay.

The United States, insulated by oceans, suffered no direct civilian loss, but 292,000 American soldiers, sailors, and airmen gave their lives for the cause of freedom. Victory placed the heavy mantle of world leadership on the shoulders of the United States. As the specter of communism hung over the ruined cities of Europe and the wasted fields of Asia, America would soon learn that vigilance in peace is as important as vigilance in war.

Section Quiz

1. Who was the military commander of each of the two prongs of the Allied attack in the Pacific war?

2. What was the largest sea battle in history?

3. What island did American forces capture as a launching point for the final assault on Japan?

4. What two cities were the sites of the first uses of the atomic bomb in warfare?

★ What was the wisdom in MacArthur's strategy of island hopping?

Chapter Review

Making Connections

1. Place the following events in their correct chronological order.
   a. Battle of Britain
   b. invasion of the Low Countries
   c. Operation Barbarossa
   d. invasion of Denmark and Norway
   e. invasion of Poland
   f. evacuation of Dunkirk
2. Why was the United States called "the arsenal of democracy"?
3. What nations made up the Big Three? Who represented each nation at Yalta? at Potsdam?

Developing History Skills

1. Could President Roosevelt have made the outcome of the Yalta Conference more beneficial to the United States? Why or why not?
2. Did the American government have valid arguments for its internment of Japanese-Americans during World War II? Why or why not?

Thinking Critically

1. Was President Truman right to use the atomic bomb against Japan? Defend your answer.

Living as a Christian Citizen

1. How should a Christian in one of the occupied countries obey Christ's command to "love your enemies" and "do good to them which hate you" (Luke 6:27)? Could a Christian obey that command and participate in armed resistance?

People, Places, and Things to Remember

Joseph Stalin
fascism
Benito Mussolini
Adolf Hitler
Hirohito
Hideki Tojo
Rome-Berlin-Tokyo Axis
appeasement
Rhineland
Sudetenland
Nazi-Soviet nonaggression pact
beginning of World War II (Sept. 1, 1939)
blitzkrieg
Dunkirk
Winston Churchill
Battle of Britain
Wehrmacht
Neutrality Act of 1939
America First committees
Wendell Willkie
Lend-Lease Act
Flying Tigers
Atlantic Charter
Douglas MacArthur
Japanese attack on Pearl Harbor (Dec. 7, 1941)
Battle of Midway
Chester W. Nimitz
War Production Board
rationing
Erwin Rommel
Bernard Montgomery
Operation Torch
Dwight D. Eisenhower
Casablanca
Operation Husky
D-day (June 6, 1944)
St. Lô
Battle of the Bulge
Guadalcanal
island hopping
Battle of Leyte Gulf
kamikazes
Iwo Jima
Okinawa
Yalta
Harry Truman
Holocaust
ghettos
Potsdam
atomic bomb
Hiroshima
Nagasaki

UNIT 7

CHALLENGE

★

1945–2010

The 1950s witnessed the introduction of many long, sleek, gadget-filled automobile designs.

1948 European Recovery Program (Marshall Plan)

1949 NATO formed

1950–53 Korean War

1954 Brown v. Board of Education

1961 First American space flight

1964 Civil Rights Act of 1964

1964–73 American involvement in Vietnam War

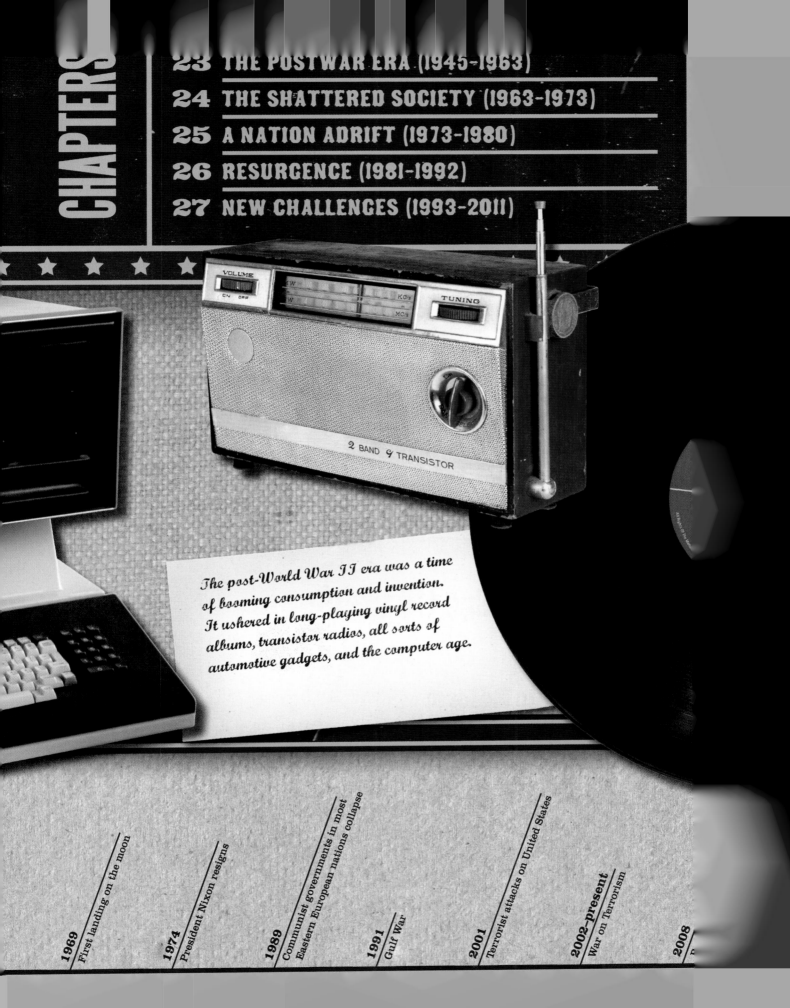

CHAPTERS

23 THE POSTWAR ERA (1945-1963)

24 THE SHATTERED SOCIETY (1963-1973)

25 A NATION ADRIFT (1973-1980)

26 RESURGENCE (1981-1992)

27 NEW CHALLENGES (1993-2011)

VOLUME

ON OFF

TUNING

2 BAND 9 TRANSISTOR

The post-World War II era was a time of booming consumption and invention. It ushered in long-playing vinyl record albums, transistor radios, all sorts of automotive gadgets, and the computer age.

1969 First landing on the moon

1974 President Nixon resigns

1989 Communist governments in most Eastern European nations collapse

1991 Gulf War

2001 Terrorist attacks on United States

2002-present War on Terrorism

2008

America enters the ominous atomic age: a test explosion of the atomic bomb in the South Pacific, 1946.

The Postwar Era (1945–1963)

I. Cold War

II. Domestic Reform

III. Life in Postwar America

"...Let every nation know, whether it wishes us well or ill, that we shall pay any price, bear any burden, meet any hardship, support any friend, oppose any foe, in order to assure the survival and success of liberty."

President John F. Kennedy,
Inaugural Address, January 20, 1961

On April 12, 1945, the day Franklin Roosevelt died, **Harry Truman** took the presidential oath of office. "Boys, if you ever pray, pray for me now," the overwhelmed Truman confided to reporters the next day. "I don't know whether you fellows ever had a load of hay fall on you, but when they told me yesterday what had happened, I felt like the moon, the stars, and all the planets had fallen on me." Truman indeed seemed unprepared for the White House. Taking office after serving less than three months as vice president, Truman had little experience in foreign policy. Left out of briefings by FDR, he did not even know about the project to develop the atomic bomb until he became president. Little in his background foreshadowed greatness. Only a high school graduate, Truman failed in the clothing business; then, working with a local political machine in Missouri, he was elected county judge. In 1934, he won a U.S. Senate seat and there gained praise for his work as chairman of a committee to investigate war mobilization. In 1944, President Roosevelt—seeking a moderate vice-presidential candidate to replace the radically liberal Henry Wallace—had turned to Truman as an alternative.

Prepared or not, Truman proceeded to make his mark on American policy at home and in the world. Aided by his own toughness and common sense and the best advice he could get, the president charted a course unknown to America for peacetime. After involvement in wars, past presidents typically had resumed an isolationist position. Truman, however, led the United States into membership in, and even sponsorship of, international organizations such as the United Nations and the North Atlantic Treaty Organization (NATO). Furthermore, in a departure from tradition, he pushed for a peacetime buildup of America's armed forces, a buildup anchored by atomic weapons.

Truman was followed as president by Dwight Eisenhower and John Kennedy, two men who exhibited a different style from the peppery Truman. Eisenhower was a former commanding general and grandfather-like figure; Kennedy was a handsome young senator and war hero. Both Eisenhower and Kennedy, however, pursued Truman's goal of American leadership in international affairs. They even followed Truman to a lesser extent in domestic affairs, particularly in the gradual increase in the size and power of government. These three presidents reflected the burgeoning military, political, and economic growth of postwar America.

I. Cold War

United Nations

One idealistic effort to maintain peace was the **United Nations** (UN). Born out of wartime cooperation among the Allies, the UN began on April 25, 1945, in San Francisco with delegates from fifty nations writing a charter for the organization. The United States Senate ratified the UN charter in 1945 by an overwhelming margin, and eventually the UN made its permanent home in New York City.

The UN includes three major agencies. The General Assembly includes delegates from all member nations and meets annually, providing a forum in which all member nations may express their views. The Security Council currently includes five permanent members—the United States, Russia, Britain, France, and China—

Harry S. or Harry S?

When Harry Truman was born, his parents wanted to avoid offending either of his grandfathers, Anderson Shippe Truman and Solomon Young. The parents compromised by giving young Harry the middle initial *S* but no middle name, so each grandfather could claim that Harry was named for him. (Truman personally preferred the name *Shippe* and occasionally used it.)

But when Truman was sworn in as president, Chief Justice Harlan Stone administered the oath of office by saying, "I, Harry Shippe Truman. . . ." Truman responded, "I, Harry S. Truman. . . ." Since the president's middle name was really simply *S*, shouldn't the period be omitted? Many newspapers, deciding that it should, referred to him as "Harry S Truman." Although the omission was sensible, it looked too much like a mistake, so one style manual devised a special rule: "For convenience and consistency, . . . it is recommended that all initials given with a name be followed by a period." The president, incidentally, agreed.

The United Nations was yet another attempt to bring about world peace through discussion rather than war.

and ten members elected by the General Assembly for two-year terms. Permanent members have veto power over UN proposals. The Secretariat is the bureaucracy and center of administration.

Proponents of the United Nations hoped that the body would provide a forum for rational discussion and a means of furthering world peace. Good intentions lay behind the founding of the United Nations, but its record as a mediator and preserver of the peace has been uneven.

Containing Communism

The Cold War

The failures of the United Nations in the postwar era are highlighted by the struggle of the free world against the aggressive policies of the Soviet Union. Presidential adviser Bernard Baruch dubbed this hostility between the two superpowers—the United States and the Soviet Union—and their allies the "**Cold War.**" The United States and the Soviet Union entered a period of tension and intense competition which occasionally flared into actual military conflict (i.e., a "hot war"). The relationship between the two countries had never been cordial. The United States government did not grant diplomatic recognition to the Soviet Union until 1933. Even when fighting their common enemy, Hitler, during World War II, Roosevelt and Stalin disagreed about the location and timing of the opening of a second front. What really launched the Cold War, however, was the realization that the USSR intended to spread its dominion throughout the world. The Cold War was waged around the world as the forces of democracy and communism squared off in nation after nation.

Eastern Europe

The first campaign of the Cold War took place in Eastern Europe as the Soviets imposed pro-Soviet governments there. Before World War II ended, the Soviet Union had installed "puppet" governments in Poland and Rumania. After 1945, East Germany, Hungary, Bulgaria, Albania, and Yugoslavia fell under Communist control. In 1948, Czechoslovakia was the last Eastern European country to succumb to Soviet conquest. All of this was contrary to Soviet guarantees at Yalta of free democratic elections in those nations. Winston Churchill described the unfolding events in Europe as the descent of an "**iron curtain**" separating the Communist East from the free West.

President Truman responded to the Soviet presence in Eastern Europe with the policy of **containment**. Unwilling to dislodge the Red Army through military action, the West conceded the area to the Soviets. Truman declared, however, that further Communist aggression would be resisted. In 1945, for example, the combative Truman confronted Soviet foreign minister Molotov about Poland. "I have never been talked to like that in my life," Molotov said. "Carry out your agreements and you won't get talked to like that," Truman shot back. Faced with the growing Communist menace, Truman was intent on pursuing the policy of containment by providing military and economic support to halt Soviet expansion.

Middle East and Mediterranean

The policy of containment achieved some success. In 1946, the Soviets withdrew their forces from Iran. More critically, that same year civil war erupted in Greece, where Communists tried to take over the country. The Soviet Union also pressured Turkey for territory and the right to establish naval bases on the Bosporus, the strategic waterway providing access between the Black Sea and the Aegean Sea. To prevent the spread of Soviet influence in the Mediterranean, Truman asked Congress for $400 million in economic aid for Greece and Turkey. This policy of aiding countries in fighting Communist takeovers became known as the **Truman Doctrine**. Both Greece and Turkey successfully warded off Communist threats.

Western Europe

After 1945, American attention focused on Western Europe, where economic ruin from the war created an opportunity for Communist advances. France and Italy, for example, already had strong left-wing parties that could pave the way for Communist takeover. To blunt the appeal of the Soviets, Secretary of State George C. Marshall in 1947 offered a plan for massive economic aid to all European countries. The Soviet Union and its puppet governments in Eastern Europe refused the aid, but Western Europe welcomed it. In 1948, Congress passed this European Recovery Program, better known as the **Marshall Plan**. By 1951, the United States had spent $13 billion on restoring the economy of Western Europe. The Marshall Plan not only further immunized the region against communism but also restored those European countries as trading partners with the United States.

Reacting to the Soviet military threat to the West, the Western nations forged a military alliance to defend themselves. In April 1949, representatives from ten Western European countries, the United States, and Canada formed the **North Atlantic Treaty Organization** (**NATO**). The U.S. Senate overwhelmingly ratified the North Atlantic Treaty. In 1955, the Communist countries of Eastern Europe reacted by creating the **Warsaw Pact** to counter NATO.

The division of Germany after the war into Communist East Germany and Allied-controlled West Germany also created tensions between the United States and the USSR. In 1948, the Americans, the British, and the French consolidated their occupied zones in western Germany and began the process of forming a government. Threatened by the prospect of a unified West Germany, the Soviets blockaded West Berlin. That city, located deep in East Germany, had also been divided into Communist East Berlin and free West Berlin after the war. Surrounded by the Communist East, West Berlin was especially vulnerable. By cutting off all access to West Berlin, Stalin hoped to take over all of Berlin or force the West to stop the unification of West Germany. Truman responded quickly with a massive airlift of food and supplies to West Berlin, and by May 1949 the **Berlin airlift** had forced the Soviet Union to end the blockade. Afterward, the Soviets reacted to the formation of the Federal Republic of Germany (West Germany) by fashioning East Germany into a Communist state, the German Democratic Republic. Germany remained divided until 1990.

"Year of Shocks"

For the free world, 1949 was a "year of shocks." Since the 1920s, China had endured civil war between the Nationalists led by **Chiang Kai-shek** (CHANG KYE-SHEK) and the Communists led by **Mao Zedong** (MOU DZUH-DONG). World War II interrupted their fighting as they both battled the Japanese, but after 1945 civil war resumed. The United States supported the Nationalists with

$2 billion in aid from 1945 to 1949, but it was not enough. In 1949, Communist forces gained control of mainland China. Nationalist forces fled to the island of Taiwan (Formosa) off the coast of China, and there they set up their government. The United States continued to recognize the Nationalists in Taiwan as the "real" China in the UN. Only in the 1970s did the U.S. officially recognize the government of Mao on the mainland.

The existence of nuclear weapons heightened Cold War tensions. In 1949, the Soviet Union detonated its first atomic bomb and forced Truman to reevaluate America's defense policy. He called first for building up conventional military forces since the Soviets possessed "the bomb" and America's nuclear threat now carried less punch. Truman also escalated the arms race by ordering development of a more powerful weapon, the hydrogen bomb. When the "H-bomb," as it was popularly known, was finally developed in 1952, it had an explosive power hundreds of times greater than the bomb dropped on Hiroshima. Within a year, the Soviet Union revealed that it, too, had developed a hydrogen bomb.

The Korean War

The most serious military conflict of the early Cold War occurred in Asia on the Korean peninsula. Freed from Japanese control after World War II, Korea had been divided along the **38th parallel** of latitude into Communist North Korea and non-Communist South Korea. The Communists, however, reneged on promises to conduct free elections that would unite the country. Then on June 25, 1950, the North invaded the South in an attempt to unite the peninsula under Communist rule. President Truman, rather than ask Congress for a declaration of war, worked through the Security Council of the United Nations in responding to this act of aggression. The USSR, which could have vetoed the action, was temporarily absent in protest of America's refusal to recognize the government of Communist China. Although fourteen other nations sent troops, the United States contributed the most men, and General **Douglas MacArthur**, America's hero of the Pacific in World War II, was in charge of the UN military forces.

General Douglas MacArthur

American troops advance on Communist forces in the Korean conflict, June 1951.

Initially, the North Koreans penetrated deeply into the South, easily brushing aside both disorganized South Korean resistance and the first American units sent to Korea. MacArthur, however, reversed the situation by taking advantage of his superior air and naval power to launch an amphibious invasion behind North Korean lines at **Inchon**, a seaport halfway up the western coast of Korea. In one magnificent stroke, MacArthur cut the North Korean supply lines and began destroying the North Korean forces. Soon, the UN forces had pushed the Communists back across the 38th parallel and into the North, hoping to unify the peninsula under a non-Communist government.

But MacArthur's success had an unexpected effect. Communist China sent thousands of troops into North Korea to rescue the North's Communist government. The Chinese sent the UN forces reeling back down the peninsula. MacArthur, who had downplayed the possibility of Chinese intervention, now admitted, "We face an entirely new war." Communist forces pushed the UN troops back to the 38th parallel. Soon, a replay of the trench warfare of World War I was in effect, with the two well-entrenched sides fighting each other desperately for a few square miles of worthless land. The Korean conflict had become a stalemate.

MacArthur—declaring, "There is no substitute for victory"— argued for breaking the stalemate by expanding the war into China. Truman, however, held to the principle of **limited war**, a war with a limited objective short of total victory over the enemy. Calling war with China a "gigantic booby trap," Truman refused to expand the conflict and risk what he thought would be a third world war.

Frozen Chosin

The influx of Red Chinese forces into the Korean War caught MacArthur's army off guard. U.S. Marines 1st Division, holding a position by the Chosin Reservoir not far from the Yalu River, was nearly surrounded by the oncoming Chinese. The division's only hope of escape was to break out to the south toward the seaport of Hungnam.

One colonel told his men, "The enemy is in front of us, behind us, to the left of us, and the right of us. They won't escape *this* time." The commanding general of the division, Oliver P. Smith, denied that the action was a retreat. "We are simply attacking in another direction," he said. The marines' escape involved combat just as fierce as any offensive operation.

Bitterly cold weather complicated the situation. Marines joked that *Chosin* rhymed with *frozen*, but the subzero temperatures were no laughing matter. Something as simple as tossing a grenade meant removing a glove and risking frostbite. Weapons froze. (One ingenious soldier found that lubricating his gun with Wild Root hair cream kept it in operation.)

The breakout produced countless individual acts of bravery. One sergeant, his legs paralyzed from a bullet wound, died holding off the enemy on a hilltop for ten minutes while his comrades escaped. Others used shovels like baseball bats to return grenades that the enemy tossed at them. A private was being treated for severely frost-bitten feet when he found out his unit was in danger. Without hesitation, he took off toward his buddies, his feet leaving bloody footprints in the snow. A sergeant holding off the Chinese in one gap was hit twice but refused medical attention. "There isn't time," he said. "They're only small holes anyway." The sergeant died of blood loss, but his unit held the line.

Fox Company deserved special commendation. The company had to hold the heights of Toktong Pass south of Chosin Reservoir against overwhelming odds or the enemy would cut off the withdrawal. The unit would have to fight to the last man if necessary; there could be no retreat.

For five days, Fox Company hung on grimly against waves of attacking Chinese soldiers. Of the company's 240 men, 115 of them were killed or wounded, including all but one of its officers. Even when relief arrived, the rest of the unit stayed until the last truck was safely through Toktong Pass. The peak they defended was thereafter known as Fox Hill.

The withdrawal took fourteen days, and the Chinese contested almost every foot of the more than fifty miles from the reservoir to Hungnam. The marines suffered nearly 13,000 casualties from both battle and the bitter cold; the Chinese took even heavier losses—37,500 casualties. The Marine Corps added the men of "Frozen Chosin" to its roll call of valor.

MacArthur disagreed publicly with the president's decision, and Truman relieved him of his command. Truce talks began in July 1951. Fighting continued for two years until a truce was reached on July 27, 1953. More than 33,000 Americans died in a war that left the boundary between North and South Korea about where it was before the war began.

Accommodating Communism

In part because of the unpopularity of the Korean War, Truman did not seek re-election in 1952. **Dwight Eisenhower** was elected president and served two terms. He was followed by **John Kennedy**. Eisenhower and Kennedy gave containment a twist, mixing it with more of a willingness to accommodate communism. **"Peaceful coexistence"** was the phrase coined to describe the goal of U.S.-USSR relations. The United States was changing its goal from pursuit of total victory over communism to achieving some sort of agreeable accommodation.

Indochina

Another Cold War trouble spot was Indochina. France had controlled Indochina from the middle of the nineteenth century until Japan captured it during World War II. After the war, France attempted to reclaim its former colony. Communists in Vietnam, the largest part of Indochina, played on the anti-French sentiment of the people to foment a revolution. The Communist leader, **Ho Chi Minh** (HOE CHEE MIN), successfully conducted a guerrilla war against the French which climaxed in 1954 with the defeat of the French at the Battle of Dien Bien Phu.

In 1954, an international conference at Geneva divided Vietnam between the Communist North and the French-controlled South. The United States did not sign the Geneva agreement, but the U.S. continued to aid South Vietnam under its anti-Communist president **Ngo Dinh Diem** (dee EM) after the French withdrew. In short, the United States was willing to tolerate the existence of the Communist North while helping to check the threat of Communist influence in South Vietnam. Eisenhower sent 2,000 military advisers to aid Diem in training and organizing his forces. Eisenhower's rationale for helping anticommunism in Vietnam was what became known as the **domino theory**—if one non-Communist nation in Southeast Asia fell to communism, then other nations would fall like a row of dominoes.

President Kennedy boosted the American commitment to 16,000 advisers, but the situation in Vietnam did not improve. A coup in 1963 overthrew and murdered Diem, and the Communists' guerrilla war intensified. The stage was set for massive American military intervention in South Vietnam under Kennedy's successor, Lyndon Johnson. Vietnam soon replaced Korea as the Cold War's hottest conflict.

Cuba

In Cuba, as in Vietnam, America accommodated the further spread of communism in violation of the spirit of containment. In 1959, **Fidel Castro** overthrew the Cuban dictator Fulgencio Batista y Zaldívar. But instead of installing a democracy, he created a Communist state only ninety miles from Florida. He nationalized foreign-owned property and signed a trade agreement with the Soviet Union. President Eisenhower responded with trade sanc-

Cuban dictator Fidel Castro brought communism to the Western Hemisphere.

tions, broke diplomatic relations, and authorized the CIA to plan a counterattack to topple Castro. That CIA project culminated during the Kennedy administration when Cuban exiles, assisted by the CIA, invaded their homeland on April 19, 1961. The **Bay of Pigs** operation ended in total failure after only three days of struggle because U.S. aid was withdrawn at the last minute. An embarrassed John Kennedy was philosophical: "Victory has a thousand fathers, but defeat is an orphan."

The most dramatic confrontation over Cuba did not come until October 1962. The Soviets apparently interpreted Kennedy's refusal to use enough military force to overthrow Castro as a sign of weakness, and they challenged the president by attempting to install in Cuba missiles capable of carrying nuclear warheads. American intelligence confirmed the existence of missile sites under construction, and Kennedy demanded their removal. In what became known as the **Cuban missile crisis**, he ordered a blockade of Cuba, and fortunately the Soviets honored it. Shortly thereafter, Soviet premier Khrushchev agreed to remove the missiles in return for a pledge by the United States not to invade Cuba. Kennedy accepted the proposal, and a very tense week ended.

When he learned that the Soviets had chosen to honor the blockade of Cuba, Secretary of State Dean Rusk said, "We're eyeball to eyeball, and I think the other fellow just blinked." Indeed, most Americans viewed the crisis as a clear-cut American triumph. What the public did not know was that Kennedy had secretly agreed to remove a number of missiles in Turkey in exchange for the Soviet concession. That secret deal and Kennedy's pledge not to invade Castro's Cuba showed the president's willingness to accommodate the Communists and even to tolerate a Communist foothold in the Western Hemisphere.

Berlin Wall

Just as Cuba was an insult to American pride, West Berlin remained an embarrassment to the Communists because it was a "showcase of democracy" and a haven for refugees fleeing from East Germany. In 1961, Khrushchev met with Kennedy in Vienna and threatened to restrict western access to Berlin. In response, Kennedy asked Congress for increased defense spending, but he did not respond with force when the East German government began

These photos show how three East Germans escaped into West Germany: (top) their route through the barriers, (bottom) how they hid in the car, and (left) how the driver, having removed the windshield, got under the bars of the gates.

building the **Berlin Wall** in August 1961. The wall solved the East German refugee problem but demonstrated the failure of communism as the second Berlin crisis of the Cold War ended.

Section Quiz

1. What was the last Eastern European nation to fall to Soviet domination after World War II?

2. Name the two countries whose resistance to communism caused Truman to announce the Truman Doctrine.

3. What action by the Allies caused Stalin to blockade West Berlin?

4. In addition to calling for stronger conventional forces, what did Truman do in reaction to the Soviet development of the atomic bomb?

5. Why were the Soviets unable to veto the UN's decision to intervene in Korea?

6. What country became a Communist foothold in the Western Hemisphere in the late 1950s?

★ Who do you think was right in the disagreement between MacArthur and Truman and why?

II. Domestic Reform

Each U.S. president during this period not only dealt with Cold War affairs but also pursued a policy of domestic reform. The "Fair Deal" (Truman), "Dynamic Conservatism" (Eisenhower), and the "New Frontier" (Kennedy) were the slogans that America's postwar presidents used to describe their policies.

Truman and the Fair Deal

Shortly after the war, President Truman sent Congress a list of proposals signaling that his domestic program would be an expansion of the New Deal. By 1949, he was calling his legislative goals the **Fair Deal**. Truman sought a government commitment to full employment (federal spending designed to ensure jobs for the unemployed), but conservative opposition killed it. Truman settled instead for the Employment Act of 1946, which created the Council of Economic Advisers to advise the president on the economy. That year Congress also created the Atomic Energy Commission, which gave control over atomic energy to civilian rather than military authorities.

With economic problems, foreign policy setbacks, and charges of Communists in government, Truman's approval ratings sank and Democrats lost public support. The wife of a leading Republican senator captured the mood when she quipped, "To err is Truman." "Had enough?" was an effective Republican slogan. In the 1946 elections, Republicans captured both Houses of Congress for the first time since 1928. With control of Congress, Republicans pushed through the **Taft-Hartley Act** of 1947. This antiunion measure, passed over Truman's veto, permitted states to pass "right-to-work" laws banning the union shop, which required union membership as a condition for hiring. The act also required an eighty-day cooling-off period for strikes in businesses involving national interests, and union officials had to swear that they were not Communists. In another matter of national security in 1949, Congress changed the American military establishment with the **National Security Act**. World War II, especially the Pearl Harbor disaster, had revealed the need for greater coordination among the armed forces. This act created the post of secretary of defense, a civilian cabinet position set over the army, navy, and air force. The National Security Council and Central Intelligence Agency (CIA) were also created to assist the president in foreign policy matters.

Election of 1948

When Truman faced the voters in the 1948 election, prospects for victory looked dim. The left wing of the Democratic Party was enraged over the president's firing of Secretary of Commerce **Henry A. Wallace** for his pro-Soviet positions. These extreme liberals bolted the party and supported Wallace on the Progressive ticket. (This was a far different Progressive Party from the one Theodore Roosevelt had run under in 1912.) Conservative southern Democrats, upset over Truman's support of civil rights for black Americans, walked out of the Democratic National Convention and eventually nominated Governor **Strom Thurmond** of South Carolina on a States' Rights Party ticket, more commonly known as "**Dixiecrats**." Confident because of the disarray among Democrats, Republicans chose **Thomas Dewey**, the popular governor of New York, as their candidate.

Displaying the *Chicago Daily Tribune*'s premature headline, an elated Harry Truman celebrates his upset victory over Thomas Dewey.

Undaunted, Truman campaigned vigorously against the odds. He called the Republican-controlled Congress back into a special session. When it refused to act on several of his proposals, he dubbed it the "do-nothing" Eightieth Congress and used it as a campaign issue. Truman targeted his appeals to labor and blacks in the cities as well as to farmers in the Midwest and West in hopes of keeping the old New Deal coalition alive. On a 31,000-mile "whistle-stop" train tour, Truman continued his attacks on the Republicans. On election day he made good on his promise that "I will win this election and make the Republicans like it." Although many Americans went to bed on election night thinking that Dewey had won, the ballot count the next morning revealed that Truman had beaten Dewey easily in one of the biggest upsets in the history of presidential elections. After his election, Congress passed many of the president's Fair Deal proposals, which basically updated the New Deal. Congress raised the minimum wage, extended Social Security coverage, and gave more aid to farmers. Congress, however, rejected civil rights bills, federal aid to education, and national health insurance. Like most presidents, Truman got only part of what he wanted from Congress.

Anticommunism in America

One important domestic issue throughout the postwar era was a growing anti-Communist crusade in the United States. Just as a "Red Scare" (widespread fear of communism) followed World War I in the United States, so a second **Red Scare** followed World War II. Many Americans blamed subversives in their own government for Soviet advances, and several events in the postwar era gave credibility to the charge. The most sensational case involved **Alger Hiss**, a former State Department official. In 1948, Whittaker Chambers, a former Communist, went before Congress and accused Hiss of passing secret documents to him ten years before when Chambers was a Soviet agent. Hiss could not be tried for espionage since the statute of limitations had expired, but he was convicted of perjury when he denied the accusations under oath. The Hiss case also launched the political career of Congressman **Richard Nixon**, whose aggressive work eventually sent Hiss to jail. In addition to the charges against Hiss, the government in 1950 revealed the existence of a British-American spy ring. Two members of that ring, Julius and Ethel Rosenberg, were convicted of passing atomic secrets to the Soviets during World War II. They were executed in 1953 for their treason.

Nixon used his meeting with Khrushchev to tout the superiority of a capitalist economy over communism.

The government reacted quickly to these threats. In 1947, President Truman instituted a loyalty program to check federal employees. The House Un-American Activities Committee (HUAC) in Congress conducted extensive investigations, such as that for the Hiss case and an in-depth study of Communist activity in the entertainment industry. With fears heightened by revelations of subversion, Congress in 1950 passed, over Truman's veto, the McCarran Internal Security Act, which made it easier for the government to combat espionage. One provision of this act required Communists and their organizations to register with the Justice Department.

A Couple of Spies

No incident better illustrates the reality of the Communist threat to America during and after World War II than the theft of the secret of the atomic bomb.

Julius Rosenberg had been reared in a Jewish home and had even considered becoming a rabbi. In college, however, Rosenberg became a Communist. He later married a Communist, Ethel Greenglass. A talented engineer, Rosenberg secured a civilian job with the U.S. Army during World War II.

Keeping his Communist ties secret, Rosenberg became the center of a Soviet spy ring. His recruits included David Greenglass, his brother-in-law, who worked at the top-secret atomic bomb research center in Los Alamos, New Mexico. In 1944 and 1945, Rosenberg, with his wife's knowledge and complicity, helped funnel classified information concerning the atomic bomb to the Soviets, helping to speed Russia's development of atomic weapons.

In 1950, British investigators uncovered a major figure in the spy ring, scientist Klaus Fuchs (FYOOKS), who had been one of the most important developers of the atomic bomb. Fuchs confessed. Using information gained from him, the FBI tracked down other Soviet agents, including David Greenglass. To save himself, Greenglass became a witness for the government and turned in his sister and brother-in-law, Ethel and Julius Rosenberg.

The Rosenbergs were arrested and tried. Convicted of espionage, the Rosenbergs were sentenced to death in the electric chair and were executed in 1953. Many left-wing writers have tried to make the Rosenbergs "martyrs" of the Red Scare, victims of paranoid hysteria. The facts,

though, reveal that the Rosenbergs were guilty of one of the greatest acts of treason in American history—they had given a totalitarian nation the most destructive weapon in history.

The man most closely associated with the Red Scare in the 1950s was Senator **Joseph McCarthy** of Wisconsin. In a 1951 speech at Wheeling, West Virginia, McCarthy declared boldly that the State Department harbored Communists; in fact, he said, he had a list of their names. A Senate committee investigated the charges and concluded that the charges were "a fraud and a hoax." McCarthy continued his attacks, however, and he even headed a Senate subcommittee that looked into the presence of Communists in government. His political power was greatest during the Korean War, when no one dared attack him for fear of being suspected of Communist sympathies. Republicans encouraged McCarthy, some because they believed him but others simply because fighting Communists was a winning political issue. Despite his well-publicized investigations, the senator never found a single Communist in the government. (His failure was due in part to Truman's previous success in rooting security risks out of the government.) By the end of 1954, McCarthy's charges had become increasingly irresponsible, and his Senate colleagues censured him for his conduct. His opponents coined a new word, "**McCarthyism**," to describe his alleged use of lies, distortion, and innuendo. What was often ignored in the outrage over McCarthy's methods was the reality of the Communist threat in America.

Senator Joseph McCarthy points to a map during televised hearings on alleged Communist subversion in the U.S. Army. On the left sits an emotionally drained Boston attorney, Joseph Welch. Only shortly before, Welch—in response to McCarthy's reckless charge that a member of Welch's staff was a Communist—had demanded in anger, "Have you no sense of decency, sir, at long last?"

Eisenhower and "Dynamic Conservatism"

With his popularity at a low ebb, due mainly to the Korean War, Truman declined to run for re-election in 1952. Republicans, frustrated by their defeat in 1948, looked for victory with Dwight Eisenhower, former Allied commander in World War II and commander of NATO, as their standard bearer. The popular war hero balanced the Republican ticket by choosing thirty-nine-year-old Senator Richard Nixon, a conservative, as his vice-presidential running mate. The Democrats nominated the governor of Illinois, **Adlai Stevenson**, for president. Pompously intellectual, Stevenson could not match the popularity and charm of Eisenhower, captured in the slogan "I like Ike." Eisenhower promised to end corruption in Washington and the war in Korea. Elected in a landslide, Eisenhower was the first Republican president since Herbert Hoover. The new president described his philosophy as "**Dynamic Conservatism**," calling himself "conservative when it comes to money and liberal when it comes to human beings." In 1954, his new budget cut expenditures by nearly 10 percent. Eisenhower abolished the Reconstruction Finance Corporation, a holdover from the Depression, and reduced farm price subsidies. Furthermore, the presence of millionaire businessmen in the cabinet gave the administration a strong conservative image. Because several cabinet members were from the auto industry, Adlai Stevenson quipped that the New Dealers had been replaced by the "car dealers."

The ticket of Eisenhower and Nixon brought the Republicans two lopsided presidential election victories in the 1950s.

Summary Statement of the Eisenhower Years

"On the level of norms—or, what people profess—the Age of Eisenhower was, indeed, a conservative period. However, on the level of values—or what people practice—the 1950s was a time of wide-ranging and significant change."

—Alan Petigny, "Two Great Myths about the 1950s," *Historically Speaking* (April 2010)

Like the Truman administration, however, Eisenhower expanded the New Deal in many ways, much to the frustration of conservatives. Congress broadened Social Security to cover professionals, domestics, farm workers, armed services personnel, and other groups that had previously been excluded. In 1955, Congress increased the minimum wage from 75¢ to $1 an hour. The federal bureaucracy grew as the government created a new cabinet department in 1953—Health, Education, and Welfare (renamed Health and Human Services in 1979)—to coordinate federal social programs. Eisenhower supported the National Defense Education Act, which poured unprecedented amounts of federal funds into education. One of his most enduring projects was a new federal highway act that committed the national government to pay for 90 percent of an extensive **interstate highway system**. These limited-access "interstates," as they are commonly known, have become the main arteries of highway transportation in the United States.

Kennedy and the New Frontier

In the election of 1960, two World War II veterans competed for the leadership of a new generation of Americans. John F. Kennedy—youthful, handsome, and witty—skillfully promoted himself as an author and war hero. As a result of eight years of service in the Senate (and a lot of money from his millionaire father), Kennedy won a close election over Vice President Richard Nixon, the Republican nominee. Despite a lackluster record in the Senate, where he had avoided controversies such as McCarthyism and civil rights, Kennedy impressed the voters with a vigorous campaign. His apparent grasp of the issues overcame doubts about his age. (At forty-three Kennedy was the youngest elected president.) He also eased doubts about his religion as he became the first Catholic to serve as president. Kennedy deftly used television as a new political weapon. Poised and charismatic, Kennedy bested Nixon—at least in image—in four televised presidential debates.

Because of his youth and vigor, Kennedy seemed to embody a dramatic change in government. People admired the handsome, glib Kennedy; his lovely young wife, Jacqueline, became a model and trendsetter for women's fashion. The sight of the young president romping with his children in the White House presented a

The televised debate between Nixon and Kennedy did not show Nixon in a good light, although voters who had only heard but not seen the debate thought Nixon had won it.

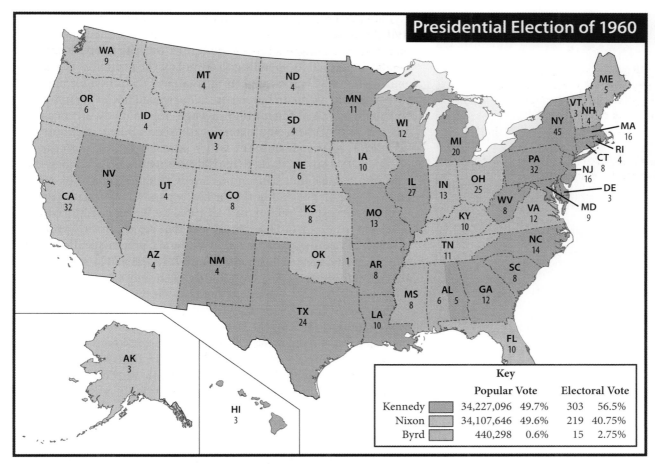

Presidential Election of 1960

	Popular Vote		Electoral Vote	
Kennedy	34,227,096	49.7%	303	56.5%
Nixon	34,107,646	49.6%	219	40.75%
Byrd	440,298	0.6%	15	2.75%

pleasing picture to most Americans. Kennedy himself proclaimed a change in emphasis. In his inaugural speech the president said,

> Let the word go forth from this time and place, to friend and foe alike, that the torch has been passed to a new generation of Americans—born in this century, tempered by war, disciplined by a hard and bitter peace, proud of our ancient heritage—and unwilling to witness or permit the slow undoing of those human rights to which this Nation has always been committed, and to which we are committed today at home and around the world.

Kennedy appealed to American idealism, as demonstrated by the famous line from his inaugural address: "And so, my fellow Americans, ask not what your country can do for you: Ask what you can do for your country." He gave his legislative program the inspiring name the **New Frontier**. An example of this idealism was one of Kennedy's most popular programs, the **Peace Corps**, a government project designed to send skilled volunteers overseas to help underdeveloped nations. To deal with the threat of a Communist economic foothold in Latin America, Kennedy initiated the **Alliance for Progress** in 1961. Through it, the United States granted economic aid in the hope of strengthening economic cooperation between North and South America. The program aimed at increasing Latin America's per capita income, decreasing its illiteracy, establishing democratic governments, and avoiding extremes of inflation and deflation. Although some of the economic goals were reached in some countries, politically the Alliance was a failure. During the 1960s, thirteen constitutional governments fell to military coups and became dictatorships.

The John F. Kennedy family

Adventure in Magnificence

ROADMASTER

Automobile ads like this appealed to Americans' desires for new things, stylish cars, and travel for leisure.

Kennedy's administration differed from previous ones more in style than in substance. Entering office in 1961, Kennedy faced one of the worst recessions in the postwar period. The government sharply increased its spending to stimulate the economy; Congress expanded public works, appropriated almost $5 billion for housing, gave financial aid to distressed areas, increased Social Security benefits, and raised the minimum wage. Yet Kennedy's record in office sometimes reflected a conservative bent. Business endorsed his 1962 Trade Expansion Act, which stimulated trade with the European Common Market. The Telstar satellite system aided the communications industry, and Kennedy's challenge to put a man on the moon by the end of the decade expanded the space program, a boon to aerospace companies. In 1962, the Revenue Act gave $1 billion in tax credits to business. Later that year, Kennedy proposed a drastic tax cut in an address that a liberal economist called "the most Republican speech since William McKinley." Congress enacted it, however, a few months after Kennedy's death.

Liberals criticized Kennedy not only for pro-business policies but also for a lack of leadership in federal aid to education, medical care for the elderly, and civil rights. Kennedy's defenders argued that his narrow victory over Nixon dictated caution in the White House. Following Kennedy's assassination in Dallas, Texas, in November 1963, liberals gained a staunch ally in President Lyndon Johnson.

Section Quiz

1. What is a "right-to-work" law?

2. Name the four major candidates and their parties in the 1948 presidential election.

3. Give at least one example each of how Truman and Eisenhower expanded the New Deal.

4. What new political weapon was important in helping Kennedy defeat Nixon in 1960?

★ How was Kennedy's idealism evident in his New Frontier?

III. Life in Postwar America

The Affluent Society

After World War II, many Americans feared another economic decline because the war demand had stimulated the economy. They need not have worried, however, for the postwar era brought unprecedented economic prosperity. Between 1945 and 1960 the Gross National Product (GNP) almost doubled. The biggest reason for the economic improvement was defense spending, a necessary expense given the challenges of the Cold War, especially in Korea. With Europe and Japan devastated by the war, America had little competition as a major supplier of industrial goods to the world. With new industries such as aerospace, electronics, and chemicals and technological improvement in automation, productivity jumped dramatically. Also, American consumers, after sacrificing and saving during the war, went on an unrestrained buying spree. They bought automobiles, homes, washing machines, televisions, refrigerators, and numerous other items for their new homes. The number of homeowners in the United States increased by 50 percent between 1945 and 1960. By 1955, about twice as many people belonged to the middle class as did in 1929, before the Great Depression. Americans were making money and spending it to improve their standard of living. They had become the **Affluent Society**. Never before had Americans been so well off.

The economic growth altered American culture as well. Less attuned to "producing," that is, working hard, Americans turned their attention to consuming, buying the latest goods in the marketplace. Business carefully orchestrated the "consumer culture." Borrowing from the 1920s, advertisers taught the public to forget the frugality of the Depression and war years and to spend. Manufacturers continually offered different models and styles so that earlier models were out-dated or out of style. Such "planned obsolescence" fueled the urge to buy. Marketing specialists appealed to self-gratification, social status, and materialism. With televisions in 90 percent of American homes by 1960, almost no one was immune to such appeals.

In 1950, Diner's Club inaugurated the credit card, and by 1965 more than a million people had one. Other cards, such as American Express, soon equaled the success of Diner's Club. Soon, consumers, less thrifty and less concerned about debt, readily used their credit cards when they did not have the money. Retail activity in the postwar period shifted from the downtown to the suburban malls, and the number of malls mushroomed from eight in 1945 to almost four thousand by 1960. Shopping—drudgery for previous generations of housewives—became a significant leisure activity for millions.

Young people also became avid consumers. When rock music exploded on the scene in the 1950s, businessmen capitalized on the craze by marketing transistor radios, phonographs, and "forty-fives" (small records played at forty-five revolutions per minute). The pop culture also included magazines and movies that featured all of the teen idols. Many, such as actor James Dean and singer Elvis Presley, came to symbolize rebellion against traditional values.

Family

Baby Boom

Postwar America witnessed enormous changes in the family. Young adults had postponed marriage and children during the war; after 1945, they married and started families. Americans had one of the highest marriage rates in the world for the period 1944 to 1948. Some fifteen million returning soldiers became new fathers, contributing to the "**baby boom**," a massive rise in the birth rate lasting until 1964. Between 1945 and 1960, America's population increased by almost 30 percent. With the prosperity of the 1940s and 1950s, more couples were having more children.

Television, which replaced movies as the chief source of entertainment, celebrated the American middle-class family. The Andersons of *Father Knows Best*, the Cleavers of *Leave It to Beaver*, and the Nelsons of *Ozzie and Harriet* were models of the perfect family, presided over by a patient and dutiful father who had all the answers. Jackie Gleason's *The Honeymooners* carried the theme of a bickering but devoted working-class husband and wife. Lucille Ball's *I Love Lucy* program gave a comic dimension to the ideal family.

The Nelsons—Ozzie, Harriett, David, and Ricky—were a real-life family who portrayed a family in a comedy program during the early days of television.

But the ideal family faced some daunting threats in the real world. Divorce rates climbed in 1946, leveled off for several years, and then increased again after 1958. The 1950s also produced national concern over juvenile delinquency. Some people blamed television, movies, and crime comic books; others cited the breakdown of discipline in the home and the school. Dr. Benjamin Spock's book *Baby and Child Care* might have contributed to underlying permissiveness, according to his conservative critics, by advocating less structured methods of child-rearing. Spock, popularizing theories of psychologist Sigmund Freud and philosopher John Dewey, wanted children eventually to become well-adjusted, guilt-free adults. His child-care book sold 23 million copies between 1946 and 1976. Only the Bible, a much better answer to the problem of human guilt, outsold it during that same period.

Women at Work

The role of women changed after World War II. According to the popular ideal, women married, had children, and reigned over the middle-class suburban household as "queens of domesticity." Mothers, wives, and family managers, they juggled numerous tasks—ranging from cooking, gardening, and club meetings to Little League for the sons and piano lessons for the girls—all with a self-sacrificing spirit. The family was still important to society in the 1950s, and being a housewife was considered a rewarding career for a woman.

Much in the postwar society, however, contradicted the image of the ideal housewife. More women than ever worked outside the home. Government policy had encouraged it during the war because of the shortage of workers in the defense industries. When "Rosie the Riveter" came marching home, she was accustomed to the income and independence and often continued to work, not just in traditional female jobs but in male ones as well. By 1970, 41 percent of married women were in the work force. The increase in divorce posed another problem for women; the number of single-parent heads of household rose dramatically. Such trends did not bode well for the family.

Emergence of Minority Rights

The push for equality of the races gained momentum after the war with the rise of the **civil rights movement**. A *civil right* is a basic right that is granted by virtue of one's citizenship and that the government is responsible for actively protecting from both government and individual encroachment. In modern American history, the phrase *civil rights movement* refers primarily to attempts by blacks to secure the exercise and protection of their basic civil rights as citizens.

Truman was the first president to accept civil rights for blacks as an issue. He appointed black judges and territorial governors and ordered the end of discrimination in the armed forces.

The first great victory of the modern civil rights movement was the Supreme Court decision **Brown v. Board of Education** of *Topeka Kansas* (1954), the climax of years of legal action by the NAACP. Citing sociological evidence, the Court concluded that segregated public schools stamped blacks as inferior and that such institutions had no place in American society. *Brown* overturned an earlier court ruling, *Plessy v. Ferguson* (1869), which approved the

Jackie Robinson

Professional sports, like most areas of American life before the 1950s, were racially-segregated. Baseball, America's national pastime, was no exception. The best white players joined the major league teams of the National and American Leagues. Black players participated in leagues composed of all-black teams. But a brave and talented ballplayer, Jackie Robinson, broke that color barrier.

Robinson was born in Georgia but moved with his family to California while still a child. A gifted athlete, Robinson won a scholarship to UCLA, where he starred in football, basketball, track, and baseball. After serving in the army during World War II, Robinson joined the Kansas City Monarchs, a team in one of the black leagues. There he came to the attention of Branch Rickey, president of the Brooklyn Dodgers.

Rickey was determined to break the color barrier in the major leagues. But the player who would break it would have to be special. He not only had to be a talented player but also had to have the strength of character to withstand intense public scrutiny and even open bigotry. Rickey observed Robinson and became convinced that Robinson had the necessary talent and character to become baseball's black pioneer.

Robinson joined the Dodgers in 1947 as their second baseman. Rickey had not overestimated the challenge Robinson faced. He heard racial slurs and insults from not only hecklers in the crowd from his first time at bat but also from opposing players. Some players tried to start fights with him or, when sliding into second, purposely tried to spike him. In many cities, Robinson had to stay in a separate hotel from his white teammates.

Aware that the nation's eyes were on him, Robinson curbed both his natural competitiveness and his resentment of the treatment he received. He knew that—fairly or not—many Americans would judge black Americans by his behavior. For Robinson, Branch Rickey later wrote, "There could be but one direction of dedication—the doctrine of turning the other cheek. There came in the greatness of Jackie Robinson."

In his first season, Robinson won Rookie of the Year. In 1949, his .342 batting average and 37 stolen bases helped him win the league's Most Valuable Player Award. In Robinson's ten seasons with Brooklyn, the Dodgers won six pennants and one World Series. After his retirement, he was elected to baseball's Hall of Fame. In 1997, as a permanent acknowledgement of Robinson's achievements, Major League Baseball retired his uniform number, 42, across all major league teams.

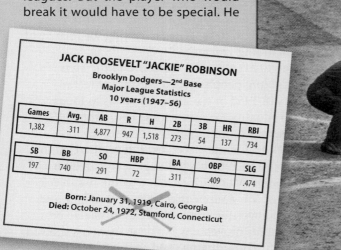

JACK ROOSEVELT "JACKIE" ROBINSON
Brooklyn Dodgers—2nd Base
Major League Statistics
10 years (1947–56)

Games	Avg.	AB	R	H	2B	3B	HR	RBI
1,382	.311	4,877	947	1,518	273	54	137	734

SB	BB	SO	HBP	BA	OBP	SLG
197	740	291	72	.311	.409	.474

Born: January 31, 1919, Cairo, Georgia
Died: October 24, 1972, Stamford, Connecticut

doctrine of "separate but equal" schools. The Court then ordered an end to segregated schools. Compliance came slowly, however, because some states resisted. The most dramatic stand-off occurred in 1957 in Little Rock, Arkansas, when Governor Orval Faubus used the National Guard to block nine black students from entering a high school. He later withdrew the force under court order, and Eisenhower used troops to protect the black students, to keep order in the school, and to enforce obedience to the *Brown* decision.

In 1955, the civil rights struggle shifted from legal to mass action with a **bus boycott** in Montgomery, Alabama. At that time, blacks sat in the back of all city buses in Montgomery and had to give up their seats to whites and stand if the buses became crowded. On December 1, 1955, a black seamstress named Rosa Parks refused to give up her seat to a white male. She was arrested and fined for refusing the bus driver's order to stand. Her small act of defiance energized the black community of Montgomery. More than 90 percent of the city's blacks joined a boycott of the city's bus system. The boycott financially devastated the Montgomery city bus system, but the fight did not end until a Supreme Court decision forbade discrimination in public transportation.

The boycott also launched a popular and charismatic figure in the civil rights movement, Baptist pastor **Martin Luther King Jr.**, leader of the fight against Montgomery's bus system. King was convinced that black churches could become the vehicles of such reform in the United States, and the Montgomery effort seemed to vindicate his ideas. In 1957, King and his associates organized the Southern Christian Leadership Conference to further the cause of black rights. King and the SCLC encouraged nonviolent marches and protests against laws that violated the rights of black Americans.

King's appeal was not limited to the black population; many middle-class whites also found his oratory compelling. He was a pastor and employed biblical terminology and the cadence of a preacher. They also liked his efforts to achieve equal rights without resorting to violence when many equal rights activists were calling for the use of any necessary means, including violence.

Martin Luther King Jr. addresses the crowd at the march on Washington in 1963.

The early 1960s brought even greater exposure to the civil rights movement. Black young people staged "sit-ins" at restaurants and lunch counters in 1960 in six southern states to focus more attention on social equality for minorities. Testing the effect of Supreme Court decisions prohibiting discrimination in interstate transportation, black and white "freedom riders" traveled in buses across the Deep South in 1961 to challenge segregated buses and terminals. In 1962, James Meredith enrolled as the first black student at the University of Mississippi after federal marshals and troops overcame a defiant governor and mob. Television also became an ally of the civil rights movement. As news cameras showed police dogs, tear gas, and fire hoses being used against demonstrators in their protests, middle-class Americans began to realize the need to protect the rights of black Americans.

In August 1963, more than two hundred thousand people—both black and white—gathered in the nation's capital for the **march on Washington**, the largest civil rights protest in United States history. The highlight for the protestors was Martin Luther King's speech in front of the Lincoln Memorial. King said,

I have a dream that one day this nation will rise up and live out the true meaning of its creed: "We hold these truths to be self-evident: that all men are created equal." I have a dream that one day on the red hills of Georgia sons of former slaves and the sons of former slave-owners will be able to sit down together at the table of brotherhood. . . . I have a dream that my four children will one day live in a nation where they will not be judged by the color of their skin but by the content of their character.

The events of 1963 pushed the previously cautious John Kennedy to publicly support a major civil rights bill. The legislation was not passed, however, until after his assassination.

Religion

Americans displayed a renewed interest in religion in the postwar era, and membership in religious groups rose from 50 to more than 60 percent in the decade after the war. However, this renewed interest proved to be more a bland public piety than a genuine spiritual revival. In 1953, President Eisenhower joined a church for the first time in his public life and began to promote religion in general with comments such as "Our government makes no sense, unless it is founded in a deeply felt religious faith—and I don't care what it is." Congress in 1954 added "one nation under God" to the Pledge of Allegiance and the next year required that "In God We Trust" be placed on U.S. currency.

The Power of Positive Thinking (1952) by Norman Vincent Peale, a leading liberal Protestant minister, was a bestseller for years. His emphasis on how to be happy was more psychological therapy than biblical faith, but he touched a chord in a generation anxious about life and seeking material success. The message from the liberal religious establishment was soothing but ultimately unsatisfying.

The **ecumenical movement** promoted unity among nominal Christians merely for the sake of unity. Advocates of this movement often quoted Christ's words from John 17:20–21:

Neither pray I for these alone, but for them also which shall believe on me through their word; that they all may be one; as thou, Father, art in me, and I in thee, that they also may be one in us: that the world may believe that thou hast sent me.

The ultimate goal of the ecumenical movement was to form one great church to which all Christians would belong. One aspect of this movement was the uniting of different bodies with similar denominational backgrounds. American Methodists, for example, had healed their 1844 North-South split in 1939, and in 1968 they merged with the Evangelical United Brethren to form the United Methodist Church. Another feature of the ecumenical movement was uniting dissimilar bodies in cooperative organizations, sort of religious versions of the UN. The World Council of Churches, founded in 1948, was the main international ecumenical body, and the National Council of Churches, founded in 1950, was the primary ecumenical body in the United States. The great shortcoming of the ecumenical movement, however, was that it compromised the truths of Scripture to achieve outward unity. Significant differences in doctrine and even modernistic unbelief were tolerated in the interest of unity. Proponents of the movement did not seem to realize that true Christian unity is based on God's truth.

Conservative Christian groups also grew in the 1940s and 1950s. Generally ignored by the media and the religious establishment, fundamentalist Protestants expanded through large local

The ecumenically oriented evangelistic campaigns of Billy Graham became a major point of division among conservative Christians in the late 1950s.

churches and evangelistic ministries. Charles E. Fuller on his very popular "Old Fashioned Revival Hour" radio program preached to millions the simple gospel message of saving faith in Christ. His audience was huge, despite the fact that the major networks would not carry his broadcasts. Youth rallies during the war led to the creation in 1945 of a large evangelistic outreach called Youth for Christ. Many Christians who had served in the military felt a burden for missions in the foreign nations they had visited and returned to those lands as soldiers for the Lord.

The first full-time evangelist for Youth for Christ was **Billy Graham**, who, after receiving positive attention by the press during his 1949 Los Angeles crusade, gained national fame. Graham also became the center of the major postwar dispute in fundamentalist Christianity. In 1957, Graham accepted the sponsorship of liberal Protestants in a New York City crusade. Graham and his supporters claimed that such a move would help bring fundamentalism into the mainstream of public life and allow it to build bridges to liberal Christianity. However, some Christian leaders broke with Graham over this issue. Having come through the fierce struggles with modernism in the 1920s, staunch fundamentalist Christians would not compromise their faith by joining with religious liberals. Protestants who accepted Graham's cooperation with liberal churches adopted the label "new evangelicals." Those who rejected Graham's movement kept the name "fundamentalist."

There were other divisions in American society that would deepen into wounds in the coming decade. Divisions during the turbulent decade that followed Kennedy's assassination—divisions over war and peace, over poverty and plenty, over rights and rioting—would tear at America's social fabric and produce fundamental changes in the nation's politics and moral direction.

Section Quiz

1. During the postwar era, what replaced the downtown area in most cities as the center of retail business activity?

2. What became the nation's chief source of entertainment in the 1950s?

3. Technically, what is a "civil right"?

4. What action sparked the Montgomery bus boycott? Who emerged as the leader of the boycott?

5. What is the major international ecumenical body? What is the major national ecumenical body in the United States?

★ Explain a major argument against being involved in the ecumenical movement.

Chapter Review

Making Connections

1. What are the three major agencies of the United Nations? Which agency has veto power over the UN's actions?

2. Name three nations that were split into Communist and non-Communist divisions after World War II.

3. Which of the two Chinese governments did the United States recognize as the "real" China after 1949?

4. What event caused MacArthur to say that the Korean conflict had become "an entirely new war"?

5. How did the Communists respond to the flight of refugees to West Berlin?

6. Under which president was the interstate highway system begun?

Developing History Skills

1. How does the career of Joseph McCarthy illustrate the danger of pursuing a worthy cause in an unworthy manner?

2. What lessons can one learn from the history of the Berlin Wall?

Thinking Critically

1. Was the Korean War a success or a failure for the United States? Why?

2. Study the map of the presidential election of 1960 and offer some reasons why the states in certain sections of the nation voted for Kennedy rather than Nixon.

Living as a Christian Citizen

1. During the postwar era, many Christians were reluctant to support the civil rights movement, in part, because it was supported by theological and political liberals. Evaluate this stance from Scripture.

2. How should a Christian view the rise of consumerism?

People, Places, and Things to Remember

Harry Truman
United Nations
Cold War
iron curtain
containment
Truman Doctrine
Marshall Plan
North Atlantic Treaty Organization (NATO)
Warsaw Pact
Berlin airlift
Chiang Kai-shek
Mao Zedong
38th parallel
Douglas MacArthur
Inchon
limited war
Dwight Eisenhower
John Kennedy
"peaceful coexistence"
Ho Chi Minh
Ngo Dinh Diem
domino theory
Fidel Castro
Bay of Pigs
Cuban missile crisis
Berlin Wall
Fair Deal
Taft-Hartley Act
National Security Act
Henry A. Wallace
Strom Thurmond
"Dixiecrats"
Thomas Dewey
Red Scare
Alger Hiss
Richard Nixon
Joseph McCarthy
"McCarthyism"
Adlai Stevenson
"Dynamic Conservatism"
interstate highway system
New Frontier
Peace Corps
Alliance for Progress
Affluent Society
"baby boom"
civil rights movement
Brown v. Board of Education
Montgomery bus boycott
Martin Luther King Jr.
march on Washington
ecumenical movement
Billy Graham

The Vietnam War was the defining event of the presidencies of both Johnson and Nixon.

The Shattered Society (1963–1973)

I. Johnson and the Great Society

II. Upheaval

III. 1968

IV. Nixon and the Silent Majority

"The Great Society has become the sick society."

Senator William Fulbright, 1968

On the afternoon of November 22, 1963, millions of Americans were watching the afternoon soap operas when, suddenly, an announcer interrupted with a shocking news bulletin: "In Dallas, Texas, three shots were fired at President Kennedy's motorcade in downtown Dallas. The first reports say that President Kennedy has been seriously wounded by the shooting." Soon came the horrifying news—President Kennedy was dead. Only two days later, Kennedy's alleged assassin, Lee Harvey Oswald, was gunned down by a Dallas nightclub owner in front of seventy policemen and a national television audience.

Over the next ten years, Americans endured a series of similar news bulletins flashing over their TVs and radios. Civil rights leader Martin Luther King Jr. was slain on the balcony of a motel in Memphis by a sniper's bullet. Senator Robert Kennedy was assassinated in a California hotel during his presidential campaign. Democratic presidential hopeful Governor George Wallace of Alabama was shot and paralyzed in a mall parking lot in Maryland.

These acts of violence were but the individual highlights of a decade of massive civil unrest. The nation witnessed urban riots punctuated by looting and killing, student protests often climaxing in bloody clashes between protesters and police, and, above all, scenes of the frustrating carnage of the seemingly endless war in Vietnam. The war in Southeast Asia might have been far away in miles, but every night television brought it into the living rooms of America.

In the midst of apparent chaos, many Americans looked to their political leaders for guidance—and deliverance. The presidents during the era were two of the shrewdest, most experienced politicians in America—Democrat Lyndon B. Johnson and Republican Richard M. Nixon. Yet both men found that America's problems defied their best efforts to solve them. Johnson's presidency was wrecked by his inability to deal with violence at home and the quagmire of American involvement in Vietnam. Nixon finally ended the war, and domestic violence at last subsided, but serious divisions remained. From 1963 to 1973, the United States was shattered by hatred and conflict. More than a few people wondered whether the social fabric could stand the strain.

> ### Headed for Collapse
> "We just seem to be headed toward a collapse of everything."
> —A California newspaper editor reviewing the unrest in the United States during the 1960s

I. Johnson and the Great Society

Although he lacked Kennedy's charisma, **Lyndon Johnson** of Texas was well prepared for political leadership. He was one of the country's most experienced, energetic, and crafty politicians. He had spent twelve years in the Senate, including five years as majority leader. Few other presidents have known how to work as well with Congress as Johnson did. He also came to the presidency with a clear vision of what he thought the United States must accomplish. Johnson believed that the government had the power and resources to eliminate poverty and inequality, to create a "**Great Society**" in which government would help all citizens gain the opportunity to better themselves politically, socially, and economically.

Building the Great Society

Civil Rights

By dedicating legislation to the slain Kennedy and using his considerable political skill, Johnson won from Congress the legislation he

> ### The Civil Rights Act of 1964
> This act established fairer procedures for voter registration, forbade racial discrimination in public buildings such as restaurants and stores, promoted the desegregation of public schools, authorized withholding federal funds from projects or institutions that discriminated against minorities, and created the Equal Opportunity Commission to ensure that job seekers did not encounter discrimination.

An assembly of politicians and civil rights leaders, including Martin Luther King Jr., watches as Lyndon Johnson signs the Voting Rights Act of 1965.

Senator Barry Goldwater, Republican candidate in the 1964 presidential election

Philosophical Differences Between the Candidates

Goldwater advocated a philosophy of government almost diametrically opposite that of Johnson. The Arizona senator believed that less government activity and regulation would benefit the nation. Goldwater opposed anything that gave the federal government more power to interfere in the private lives of citizens. Johnson, on the other hand, was committed to more government and more regulation.

needed to build his Great Society. A major part of his agenda was civil rights legislation, the first and most important of which was the **Civil Rights Act of 1964**.

The following year, Johnson encouraged Congress to pass the **Voting Rights Act of 1965**, which sent federal officials into states to help register blacks to vote and outlawed literacy tests for voters. Such tests were often administered only to black Americans to prevent their voting. This measure augmented the provisions of the **Twenty-fourth Amendment**, ratified in January 1964, which outlawed the use of poll taxes, similarly used to prevent black suffrage. The intent of both the amendment and the Voting Rights Act was to help blacks acquire more nearly equal treatment by giving them a greater political voice.

War on Poverty

In his first State of the Union message, Johnson also declared a "**War on Poverty**." Through the newly formed Office of Economic Opportunity (OEO), the government attacked poverty through job-training and job-placement programs; Head Start (a preschool program for children in poor families); and Volunteers in Service to America (VISTA), a sort of domestic Peace Corps in which thousands of enthusiastic young people volunteered to work in government programs helping the poor. The programs of the War on Poverty did succeed in raising thousands of people above the poverty level (although the general economic prosperity of the Johnson years might have had much to do with that success).

1964 Election

A factor that further helped Johnson push his program through Congress was his landslide victory in the 1964 presidential election. Even before Kennedy's assassination, most political observers had predicted a Democratic victory in 1964. The shock of the president's death made Americans even less likely to change leaders again in less than a year. Johnson was further helped by the Republican nomination of Senator **Barry Goldwater** of Arizona. Goldwater was an honest, unbending conservative, and he rejected the usual political practice of tailoring his message to please his audience. He denounced the Social Security system in front of senior citizens in Florida, for example, and suggested in a speech in Knoxville, Tennessee, that the government sell the Tennessee Valley Authority.

Goldwater fought a losing battle from the beginning. Black Americans objected to Goldwater's vote against the civil rights bill, and liberal Republicans refused to support him. Besides representing a minority party, Goldwater frightened many voters by his indiscreet statements about how he would conduct the war in Vietnam, including possible use of nuclear weapons. Johnson, on the other hand, soberly committed himself to "no wider war" in Vietnam. He tried to scare voters by running a TV ad showing a little girl in a field plucking petals from a daisy, a voice-over giving a countdown, which was followed by a photo of a nuclear explosion. On election day, Johnson scored an overwhelming victory with 61 percent of the vote. He garnered 486 electoral votes to only 52 for Goldwater, who won only his home state and five states of the Deep South. Johnson believed that he had an unquestioned mandate for the Great Society.

A Flood of Legislation

The 1964 elections also gave the Democrats huge majorities in Congress, 68–32 in the Senate and 295–140 in the House. In the first session of Congress, Johnson used his tremendous victory and lopsided majorities to push no fewer than eighty-nine bills through the legislature, including a bill increasing federal aid to education ($1.5 billion).

The program having the widest impact, perhaps, was **Medicare**, a government health insurance program established in 1965 to help elderly people pay for medical care. Medicare was designed to ensure that the nation's elderly would be able to afford proper medical treatment. The federal government paid for this program by taxing the wages of all Americans.

The Warren Court

Even before the Johnson years, the Supreme Court had followed the same approach that Johnson advocated. Led by Chief Justice **Earl Warren**, the Warren Court (1953–1969) pursued a policy of **judicial activism**, interpreting the law and the Constitution broadly to address what the judges perceived as major social problems.

The Warren Court is probably best known for its civil rights decisions, beginning with *Brown v. Board of Education of Topeka, Kansas* (1954). The Court also handed down decisions touching *all* areas of American life. The Court placed tighter restrictions on law enforcement officials and gave greater protection to accused criminals in cases such as *Gideon v. Wainwright* (1963), which required the state to provide an attorney for defendants who could not afford one, and *Miranda v. Arizona* (1966), which required that criminal suspects be informed of their constitutional rights before they could be questioned.

In *Engel v. Vitale* (1962), the Court banned state-sponsored prayers in public schools as an alleged violation of the First Amendment. In *Roth v. United States* (1957) the Supreme Court ruled that obscenity was not protected by the First Amendment's guarantee of freedom of speech, but it defined *obscenity* so narrowly that the decision actually struck down many obscenity laws. As a result, a flourishing pornography industry continued to grow in the United States in the 1960s.

In another decision, the Court ordered the redrawing of legislative districts in a series of "**one man, one vote**" **decisions**. In these cases, the justices ruled that districts that were unequal in population violated the guarantees for "equal protection of the law" in the Fourteenth Amendment. The Court eventually extended the "one man, one vote" principle all the way to city councils and local school boards.

Not all of the justices agreed with the Court's policy. In a dissenting opinion in 1964, Justice John Harlan warned,

> The Constitution is not a panacea for every blot upon the public welfare, nor should this Court, ordained as a judicial body, be thought of as a general haven for reform movements. . . . This Court . . . does not serve its high purpose, when it

---

What Is the Difference Between Medicare and Medicaid?

Medicare: Everyone over age 65 (younger if disabled) qualifies, regardless of income. A monthly premium is required, as is a co-pay. It is federally administered.

Medicaid: All ages qualify. It is income based. No monthly premiums or co-pays are required. It is state administered with federal regulation.

Does the Constitution Mention a "Wall of Separation Between Church and State"?

Contrary to what many people have been led to believe, the Constitution—including the First Amendment—does *not* mention a "wall of separation between church and state." That phrase originated in a letter from Thomas Jefferson to Virginia Baptists who opposed a state church. To calm their fears and win their support for ratification of the Constitution, the Founders included the First Amendment, which states that the federal government shall "make no law respecting an establishment of religion, or prohibiting the free exercise thereof."

exceeds its authority even to satisfy justified impatience with the slow workings of the political process.

However, a majority of Harlan's associates did not heed his warning.

Evaluating the Great Society

The Great Society was, on the whole, a failure. Individual programs alleviated some effects of poverty and inequality, and part of the legislation aimed at eliminating discrimination (such as civil rights legislation) did, in Johnson's words, "replace . . . despair with opportunity." However, Johnson's utopian goal ("to use [our] wealth to enrich and elevate our national life—and to advance the quality of American civilization . . . upward to the Great Society") remained an unrealized dream. Poverty, inequality, and unrest remained; in fact, the nation seemed to be even more divided at the end of Johnson's presidency than it had been at the beginning.

Liberal critics claimed that the president did not do enough; they said that he should have spent much more on his antipoverty programs. Yet the cost of the War on Poverty, combined with the cost of the war in Vietnam, was already creating a huge deficit in the federal budget. Conservative critics said that the failure proved what they had maintained all along: government legislation and regulation are not sufficient to solve society's problems. Ultimately, the individual is responsible for helping himself, conservatives argued, and only such self-help will produce lasting results.

Johnson and Vietnam

America's commitment to maintaining the non-Communist government in South Vietnam had begun under Eisenhower (see Chap. 23). From the 2,000 military advisers that Eisenhower had sent to the 16,000 that Kennedy had sent, that commitment had increased. Ostensibly, the troops were there to train and advise the South Vietnamese army and to protect American personnel. However, the situation in Asia, as one historian noted, proved to be like a "tar baby": the more the United States tried to free itself, the more entangled it became. Under Johnson, the "advisers" became combatants, and the United States became engaged in a full-fledged war.

Escalation

During his campaign against Goldwater, Johnson had said, "We are not about to send American boys nine or ten thousand miles away from home to do what Asian boys ought to be doing for themselves." Yet an incident occurred off the coast of Vietnam during the campaign that changed the complexion of the war. In the summer of 1964, the American destroyer *Maddox* repulsed an attack by North Vietnamese patrol boats in the Gulf of Tonkin. Although the affair was relatively minor, Johnson denounced the attack and asked Congress to pass a joint resolution giving him authority to respond to Communist aggression in Vietnam.

The Vietnam War 1961–1973

CHINA

NORTH VIETNAM

Hanoi

Haiphong

LAOS

Gulf of Tonkin

HAINAN

Vinh

Mekong River

Dong Hoi

DMZ (Demilitarized Zone)

17th Parallel

Hue

THAILAND

Da Nang

South China Sea

CAMBODIA

SOUTH VIETNAM

Mekong River

Nha Trang

Gulf of Siam

Phnom Penh

Saigon

Mekong Delta

Key
- Countries Allied with U.S.
- Communist Countries
- Neutral Countries
- → Ho Chi Minh Trail

Congress overwhelmingly approved the **Gulf of Tonkin resolution**, approving "the determination of the President . . . to take all necessary measures to repel any armed attack against the forces of the United States and to prevent further aggression."

Armed with this resolution, Johnson began to *escalate* the war in Vietnam, increasing the number and expanding the role of American troops. Americans began to take over a large part of the fighting from the South Vietnamese army. By 1968, U.S. forces there numbered more than 500,000. Johnson also ordered American bombers to extend the war to North Vietnam by bombing supply lines and military sites in that nation.

Several factors made the war far more difficult to win than American politicians and generals had imagined. First, the war was not a clear-cut conflict between two separate nations, as the Korean War had been. Americans were fighting both the North Vietnamese and pro-Communist South Vietnamese guerrillas called the **Viet Cong**. It was fought mainly within South Vietnam between the cities (held by the government of South Vietnam) and the countryside (controlled by the Viet Cong). At the same time, both China and the Soviet Union supplied North Vietnam and the Viet Cong.

Second, supplies for the Communist forces from North Vietnam flowed not only across the North-South border but also through the neighboring and supposedly neutral countries of Laos and Cambodia on the west. Such supply lines would be impossible to cut without attacking those nations, and American political leaders were hesitant to do so.

Third, the government of South Vietnam—although non-Communist—was corrupt, undemocratic, and unstable. The only advantage it offered to Americans was that it was "better than the Communists."

Fourth, the civilian leadership in both the executive and legislative branches wanted to micromanage the war rather than to set broad strategy and let the military professionals determine the tactics appropriate for executing the strategy. The civilian leaders tended to let politics and how their decisions might affect the next election determine how the war was conducted.

Fifth, and most importantly, Johnson was committed to the idea of a limited, defensive war. He did not want to risk an outright war against North Vietnam—a war that might draw in the Soviet Union or Communist China, divert dollars from the Great Society at home, and prove politically damaging. He wanted to "have both guns and butter," to conduct a war but not allow it to affect economic prosperity or his social agenda.

For many soldiers, the war took on an unreal, nightmarish hue. The Viet Cong looked, dressed, and acted just like the South Vietnamese civilians—until they opened fire. There were no clear fronts or lines of battle; enemy forces emerged suddenly from the jungle, attacked, and then faded out of sight, into the thick forests or even into networks of tunnels that honeycombed some areas. Americans

U.S. soldiers carry a wounded comrade through a swamp in Vietnam.

Tunnel Rats

Whenever American soldiers found a Viet Cong tunnel, they sent one man into the tunnel to flush out the enemy. Such "tunnel rats," as they were called, were armed only with a .45-caliber pistol and a flashlight. The work was dirty and dangerous; the tunnels often were booby trapped. After the "rat" killed or captured any Viet Cong in the tunnel, he brought in explosives and destroyed the tunnel.

Protests against the Vietnam War were one of the major expressions of the rebellion of the counterculture in the late 1960s and early 1970s.

tried to cope by using their superior technology. Huge helicopters armed with machine guns and carrying troops swooped like war birds over the jungles; napalm, Agent Orange, and other chemical defoliants burned away the jungle cover; American fighter planes and bombers pounded enemy positions. Yet the enemy kept coming back. The American military at times seemed to be trying to win the war by sheer firepower. In an extreme case, one major said after a fierce battle for one town, "It became necessary to destroy the town to save it."

Tet Offensive

Grumblings about the war began to arise among the American people, and a student protest movement was growing. The large majority of Americans, however, tended to support the war. Unfortunately, that support was partially the result of misrepresentation and outright deception by the government. President Johnson feared that if Americans knew how deeply committed the United States was to the war and how the war was actually going, they would stop supporting the programs of the Great Society. Therefore, he disguised the number of U.S. troops involved in the conflict and covered setbacks. All that the American people generally heard from the government were optimistic reports of how well the war was going. However, the media began to tell a different story.

Support for the war changed dramatically after the Communists launched the **Tet Offensive** in January 1968. During the South Vietnamese celebration of Tet, the lunar new year (January 30), the Viet Cong infiltrated the major cities in the South. They smuggled in arms, for example, by carrying them into the cities in coffins during funeral processions. On the first day of the new year, 60,000 Viet Cong troops launched attacks on nearly every major city and strategic point in South Vietnam. One force even captured part of the U.S. Embassy for a time. In the weeks that followed the attacks, American and South Vietnamese forces drove back the enemy, recapturing what had been lost and inflicting massive casualties on the enemy.

Militarily, the Tet Offensive was a major failure for the Communists, but it had a dramatic effect on the American public. Television newscasts emphasized only the negative aspects—the suddenness of the attack and the heavy losses—leading many Americans to believe that Tet was a Communist victory. The U.S. government, to some extent, reaped what it had sown. Having misled the American people and media about the course of the war, the government now faced the wrath of a public who wanted to know how things could come so close to disaster so suddenly. After Tet, many Americans were seemingly no longer looking to win the war; they only wanted a way out.

Paris Peace Talks

In May 1968, the North Vietnamese offered to hold peace negotiations, and the United States accepted. The **Paris Peace Talks** began with a heated discussion over a critical topic: what shape of table to use. After that unpromising start, the peace talks dragged on for nearly five years while the fighting continued. The United States wanted out but also wanted to preserve South Vietnam as a non-Communist nation. North Vietnam wanted the reunion of the two nations under Communist rule. The talks droned on while casualties mounted.

Section Quiz

1. What method of keeping blacks from voting was outlawed by the Twenty-fourth Amendment? by the Voting Rights Act of 1965?

2. Why did *Roth v. United States* spur a pornography industry in the U.S. even though the decision said that obscenity is not protected by the First Amendment?

3. List at least three factors that made the Vietnam War harder to win than American politicians and military leaders expected.

4. What event caused the American people to begin to doubt government reports of progress in the Vietnam War?

✭ Should the United States have escalated its involvement in the Vietnam War under Lyndon Johnson? Why or why not?

II. Upheaval

Violence at home paralleled the fighting in Vietnam as the United States endured some of the worst civil disturbances in its history. Even Americans who lived nowhere near the unrest often saw it in graphic detail on their television sets. As the violence and bloodshed increased, many citizens felt a sense of despair and helplessness. One Democratic senator moaned, "The Great Society has become the sick society."

Ethnic Conflict

Ethnic tensions over unequal treatment had been increasing since the late nineteenth century. During the 1960s, more and more Americans supported the legitimate demand for equal rights for all. Black Americans often led the way, and a growing number of white Americans stood with them in their effort to secure these rights. While many, including Martin Luther King Jr. (Chap. 23), restricted their protests to nonviolent activities, others grew impatient and resorted to violent behavior on both sides of the struggle for individual rights.

Opponents of the civil rights movement often used violence against nonviolent protestors. Early protest marches and demonstrations sometimes ended with assaults on the demonstrators by mobs of angry whites or even by policemen using tear gas and police dogs. The violence unleashed on the demonstrators intensified during the Johnson years. In 1964 in Mississippi, members of the Ku Klux Klan brutally murdered three civil rights workers who were trying to help black Americans register to vote. Likewise, during a voting rights protest in Selma, Alabama, three white civil rights advocates died in separate incidents at the hands of Klansmen and other extremists. Violence only increased as the civil rights movement moved north. Many northerners who had approved the implementing of desegregation in the South suddenly found it a far different matter when black Americans in the North began to call for desegregated schools and neighborhoods.

The civil rights movement raised hopes among black Americans that they would soon enjoy equal opportunity for success with white Americans. However, they were disappointed when change did not come as quickly as they had hoped. The combination of this

> ### Spur for Passage of the Voting Rights Act
> President Johnson used the murder of three voting rights advocates in Selma, Alabama, to spur Congress to approve the Voting Rights Act.

Watts became a symbol of urban violence in the late 1960s.

disappointment and increasing violence among the counterculture of the 1960s in general led to **urban riots** during the summers of 1965, 1966, and 1967. The first of these riots began in a predominantly black section of Los Angeles known as Watts. Only days after Congress passed the Voting Rights Act, a white policeman in Watts tried to arrest a young black man for drunk driving. Angry crowds began to gather in the summer heat, and wild tales of police brutality began to circulate. Finally, the tension exploded as mobs roamed Watts, burning and looting. Police, and eventually the National Guard, tried to restore order. In six days of violence, rioters killed thirty-four people, wounded nearly nine hundred others, and destroyed $45 million in property. More than thirty other riots occurred across the nation after the Watts riot. The worst riot was in Detroit in 1967. Forty-three people died there while looters ransacked shops and arsonists set hundreds of fires. Again the National Guard was called in. Detroit took on the appearance of Vietnam as tanks rolled through streets that were filled with smoke from smoldering ruins of buildings. Troops exchanged fire with snipers on buildings.

The riots contributed to the rise of **"black power"** groups such as the misnamed Student Nonviolent Coordinating Committee (SNCC). Instead of simply working to secure black rights, they proclaimed black supremacy over whites, and they were determined to gain supremacy "by any means necessary," including violence.

The effect of the violence was traumatic. Tragically, black Americans felt the brunt of the destruction; their homes and businesses suffered most of the damage, and most of the casualties were black. When the televisions showed nonviolent demonstrators being brutally treated by police, most Americans realized the need for black Americans to receive justice and equal rights with all other Americans. But the violence caused white Americans to become increasingly suspicious of, rather than sympathetic to, civil rights. Even Martin Luther King began to lose ground among white Americans.

By the end of the 1960s, ethnic tensions had reached a new high. As a result, progress on civil rights issues slowed considerably.

Radical Youth

The radicalization of many young blacks was but one aspect of a general radicalization of youth. By the late 1960s, fully half of the population of the United States was under the age of twenty-five. Many of these young people had grown up in the midst of prosperity and affluence, but some began to question and then rebel against the materialistic values of the day—the constant striving after material possessions and luxuries. They became dissatisfied and disillusioned when they found that materialism did not satisfy spiritually. Unfortunately, they often turned for satisfaction to things that were even more destructive than their parents' materialism.

Antiwar Movement

The rallying point for disaffected youth was opposition to the Vietnam War. Antiwar demonstrations grew in proportion to the number of troops Johnson was sending overseas. Demonstrators held rallies to protest the war; antiwar radicals seized control of college buildings, barricaded themselves inside, and dared police to come after them; a number of young men fled to Canada to avoid being drafted into the army.

One force behind the antiwar movement was the "**New Left**," radical groups that hoped to use resentment of the war as a means of overthrowing established American institutions. The Students for a Democratic Society (SDS) was the largest New Left group, with more than five thousand members on more than two hundred campuses. An even more radical group, the Weathermen, actually engaged in terrorist bombings of buildings to "bring the war home." Some demonstrators went beyond protesting U.S. involvement in the war and actually supported the enemy. The North Vietnamese and Viet Cong flags became common symbols at antiwar demonstrations even as protestors burned the American flag. Others waved Mao's "little red book" of Communist maxims. Many men burned their draft cards.

Left-wing sympathies, however, were not sufficiently powerful to motivate the whole antiwar movement. Much of the energy for the movement came from the resistance to authority that is always present in unregenerate humans. The New Left merely harnessed that discontent. Antiwar sentiment began to spread to older age groups, and the number of protesters multiplied. By the end of Johnson's term, military bases were the only places the president could speak without being heckled.

Counterculture

The antiwar movement was itself only a part of an overall youth movement known as the **counterculture**. More an attitude than an ideology, the counterculture of the 1960s and early 1970s had its roots in rebellion, specifically a rejection of the materialism, morals, and values of the previous generation. Proponents of the counterculture believed that the solution to society's problems included self-expression and espousing a philosophy of love and sharing. "Do your own thing" and "All you need is love" were simplistic expressions of the counterculture creed. The counterculture also praised youth as having the answers to society's problems, as illustrated by the popular saying "Don't trust anyone over thirty."

The popular expression of the counterculture was the "hippie" movement (derived from the slang term *hip*, "approving of current tastes and attitudes"). Hippies made a virtue of nonconformity. In place of the neat clothing and appearance of their parents, they wore jeans and t-shirts that were dirty, patched, and garishly colored. Young men grew their hair and beards long as a sign of protest. Rejecting traditional standards, hippies repudiated marriage and advocated unrestricted sexual activity. They embraced rock music, which, with its provocative lyrics and heavy beat, symbolized their rebellion. Hippies were also leaders in the drug culture. They experimented with numerous illegal hallucinogenic drugs, notably LSD (lysergic acid diethylamide). The most popular drug was marijuana, a product of the hemp plant. The American Medical Association estimated that by the late 1960s eight million people had experimented with marijuana.

Much within the counterculture was ungodly—the illicit sex, drug use, and other immoral behavior. Indeed, many hippies embraced the counterculture lifestyle simply so that they could live a carefree life without assuming any responsibility for their actions.

"Aid and Comfort" to the Enemy?

Jane Fonda, a popular actress of the sixties, traveled to North Vietnam and had her picture taken on an antiaircraft gun used to down American planes, thereby encouraging the Communists there and demoralizing American POWs housed in the nearby prison known as the "Hanoi Hilton." Even today, more than forty years later, many Americans still resent Fonda's actions.

Disrespect for Authority

The antiwar movement directed its rage at the president, the ultimate symbol of authority. Johnson became the object of verbal attacks, such as when thousands of demonstrators in Washington chanted, "Hey! Hey! LBJ! How many kids did you kill today?"

Robert Indiana's "pop art" painting *Love*, commemorated on an 8-cent U.S. postage stamp, aptly captures the emphases of the counterculture. Its theme of "love" represents the counterculture's professed faith in love as a remedy for society's problems—a faith that ultimately proved vain as it left the nature of that love undefined.

Countering the Counterculture

The Bible teaches that man is born corrupt (Ps. 58:3; Rom. 5:12), and forsaking possessions or breaking restrictions does nothing to free man from the power of sin. Curing man's ills requires changing his sinful nature through the power of God in salvation.

Theirs was a philosophy that provided a license to sin. Even when they were sincere, however, the hippies were wrong. Their belief that expressing "love" was the answer to man's problems was naive and simplistic; they did not realize that genuine love requires sacrifice and discipline. Furthermore, they believed that material possessions and moral restrictions corrupted man.

Radicalism in Perspective

One can make too much of the radicalism and domestic violence of the 1960s. Even among young people, the radicals were a decided minority, and the United States came nowhere near equaling the death and destruction through civil disorder that occurred in other nations in the decade. (In Nigeria in the late 1960s, for example, a full-blown civil war resulted in the deaths of tens of thousands of people.) The violence shocked Americans, however, especially after the relative calm of the Eisenhower and Kennedy years. They wondered how a nation so advanced and so wealthy could suddenly be convulsed with such disorder. As 1968 neared— a presidential election year—Americans began looking for a leader who could cure the country's ills.

Section Quiz

1. What incident did Johnson use to motivate Congress to pass the Voting Rights Act of 1965?

2. What city was the site of the worst urban riot in the United States in the 1960s?

3. What was the rallying point for disaffected young people in the 1960s and early 1970s?

4. What was the popular expression of the counterculture?

5. What was the most widely used illegal drug of the 1960s?

★ What were some of the factors that tended to encourage heavy involvement of college-aged young people in the civil disruptions of the 1960s?

III. 1968

The violence and conflicting ideologies of the decade of 1963 to 1973 are encapsulated in one year: 1968. Against the background of presidential politics and in a campaign marred by bloodshed, American leaders offered their respective answers to the nation's problems.

Johnson Bows Out

Johnson bemoaned the failure of his Great Society to solve America's problems. Despite his unpopularity, he was favored to win renomination by the Democrats. His only challenger was an antiwar Democrat, Minnesota senator **Eugene McCarthy**, but Johnson's staff did not take McCarthy's threat seriously. Then the Tet Offensive in January reinvigorated the Vietnam issue. In the New Hampshire primary in March, the underdog McCarthy nearly upset the president. New York senator **Robert Kennedy**, a younger brother of the slain president, suddenly announced that he, too, would challenge Johnson. After Johnson's advisers warned him that he could lose badly to McCarthy in the upcoming Wisconsin primary, Johnson stunned the nation by withdrawing from the race.

The burdens and controversy of the Vietnam War forced Johnson to decide not to run for reelection in 1968.

Johnson's withdrawal created a scramble among the Democrats, creating a wide-open race for the nomination. Kennedy and McCarthy competed for the antiwar vote. Vice President **Hubert H. Humphrey** also joined the race, more or less representing Johnson's positions. Humphrey ignored the primaries, depending instead on Johnson's still formidable power and prestige within the Democratic Party organization to win delegates in nonprimary states. McCarthy and Kennedy battled it out in the primaries to win the right to challenge Humphrey at the convention in Chicago.

Death Times Two

In April 1968, while the candidates fought over the nomination, Martin Luther King Jr. went to Memphis to support a strike by garbage workers. A sniper shot and killed King while he stood on the balcony of his hotel. His death sparked a new wave of urban violence. Sadly, the death of King, who had advocated nonviolence, led to fighting, looting, and bloodshed.

As the campaign continued, Kennedy pulled ahead of McCarthy, threatening to wrest the nomination from Humphrey. After Kennedy won a major victory in the California primary, he was greeting scores of supporters in a Los Angeles hotel corridor as he made his way to speak to the press. Suddenly, a young Arab nationalist who opposed Kennedy's support of Israel thrust forward a revolver and fired. Kennedy fell, mortally wounded. Within a period of two months, two major American leaders had died violently.

Nixon Takes the Center

The Republican race narrowed to one question: Could anyone stop **Richard Nixon**? In spite of his losses to John Kennedy in 1960 and in the California governor's race in 1962, the former vice president remained heavily involved in politics. In 1968, he won a series of primaries that made him front-runner for the Republican nomination.

Nixon tried to take the "middle of the road" on political issues. Only that way, he thought, could he appeal to the general public and win the fall election. At the Republican convention in Miami, he beat back challenges by both liberal Nelson Rockefeller and conservative Ronald Reagan to win the nomination.

Nixon sensed the dismay of the American electorate with the violence that racked the country and their sense of helplessness in the face of apparently uncontrollable unrest. So he hit a sympathetic nerve when he called for "law and order" and a firm response to the anarchy. One of the biggest boosts to Nixon's "law and order" message was the contrast provided by the Democratic convention.

Civil rights leader Andrew Young and other colleagues of Martin Luther King Jr., on the motel balcony where an assassin felled King, point in the direction from which the bullet came.

Nixon, a Master Political Strategist

Nixon's main opponents in 1968 were New York governor Nelson Rockefeller, a staunch liberal, and California governor Ronald Reagan, Goldwater's replacement as the hero of Republican conservatives. (Unlike most moderate Republicans, Nixon had campaigned for Goldwater in 1964 and thereby won the respect of Republican conservatives.) Nixon placed himself solidly in the political center between Reagan and Rockefeller.

Richard Nixon and Spiro Agnew were nominated to carry the Republican banner in 1968.

AGIP-Rue des Archives/The Granger Collection, New York

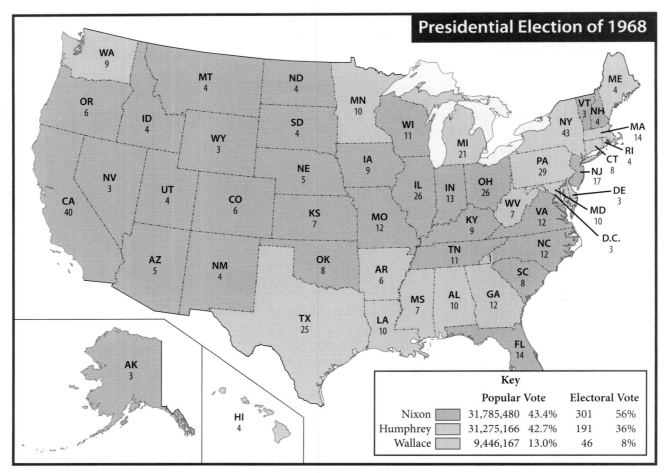

Presidential Election of 1968

Key				
	Popular Vote		**Electoral Vote**	
Nixon	31,785,480	43.4%	301	56%
Humphrey	31,275,166	42.7%	191	36%
Wallace	9,446,167	13.0%	46	8%

The third-party candidacy of Alabama governor George Wallace further complicated the election. He told voters that there was "not a dime's worth of difference" between Humphrey and Nixon.

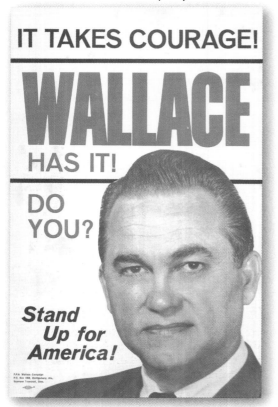

IT TAKES COURAGE!

WALLACE HAS IT!

DO YOU?

Stand Up for America!

Democratic Disarray

With the death of Robert Kennedy, Humphrey easily captured the nomination at the party's Chicago convention. But some Democrats wondered if the nomination would be worth anything. As Americans watched on television, police and radical demonstrators battled outside the convention hall. Inside the hall the Democratic mayor of Chicago shouted obscenities at a Democratic senator who was denouncing what he called the "Gestapo tactics" of Chicago's police. Another weight on Humphrey's candidacy was Johnson's unpopular Vietnam policy, which Humphrey, as vice president, was virtually bound to defend.

The Wallace Factor

Another element in the confusion-filled campaign was the third-party candidacy of Alabama governor **George Wallace**, who ran as the candidate of the newly formed American Independent party. The fiery Wallace had risen to fame as a prosegregation governor during the civil rights struggles of the early 1960s. He sought to draw on popular discontent with the civil rights movement, urban violence, rampant immorality, rising crime rates, and the seemingly endless war in Vietnam. Wallace's political pronouncements were generally conservative but couched in tough, pugnacious language.

Wallace did not really believe that he could win the election, but he hoped that in the three-way contest he could win enough electoral votes to throw the election into the House of Representatives. He believed that a strong showing would "send a message" to

Washington that a bloc of conservative Americans existed that the politicians could not afford to ignore, thereby forcing them to take more conservative positions.

Election: Nixon's the One

The election reflected the fragmented state of American society. Nixon got 31,785,480 votes (43.4 percent) to Humphrey's 31,275,166 (42.7 percent). Nixon's lead in the Electoral College, however, was more substantial, 301–191. Wallace won nearly ten million votes (13.0 percent) and 46 electoral votes. The voters repudiated Johnson's policies but did not give Nixon an overwhelming mandate.

Section Quiz

1. Who was the first antiwar Democrat to challenge the renomination of Lyndon Johnson?
2. After the withdrawal of Johnson in the 1968 campaign, which Democratic candidate best represented the incumbent president's policies?
3. What two major American leaders died violently in 1968?
4. Name the Republican nominee, the Democratic nominee, and the major third-party candidate in the presidential election of 1968.
* Explain the factors in the 1968 presidential election that ensured the election of Richard Nixon.

IV. Nixon and the Silent Majority

In a speech during his first year in office, Richard Nixon appealed to "the great silent majority of . . . Americans" for support. With the term *silent majority*, the president affirmed the belief that most Americans were not violent radicals wholly discontent with the status quo. The bulk of the population, he believed, were quiet, decent, respectable, and hard-working citizens who wanted only peace and order. Nixon claimed that he represented the interests of that silent majority and that his administration would represent their values. Many writers called Nixon's statement an appeal to "Middle America," the views of the dominant middle class.

Domestic Problems

Busing

Nixon confronted a highly emotional issue early in his presidency, one that outraged many Americans. Despite Supreme Court orders for the desegregation of schools since the 1950s, the integration of schools had proceeded slowly. One of the main obstacles to integration was that nearly all schools drew their students from surrounding neighborhoods. Most neighborhoods, however, tended to be segregated by race. As a result, blacks went to predominantly black schools in their own neighborhoods, and whites went to predominantly white schools in their own neighborhoods. To overcome this fact, the courts ordered the **busing** of students out of their neighborhoods to other schools until all schools reflected the overall racial makeup of the city or community as a whole.

Forced-busing was controversial. Some parents opposed busing simply because they opposed racial integration. Other parents

Wallace's Popular Message in the Popular Language

Wallace attacked the "pointy-headed intellectuals" who ran the government bureaucracy. "When I get to Washington," he said, "I'll throw all these phonies and their briefcases into the Potomac." He told cheering audiences, "If any demonstrator ever lays down in front of my car, it'll be the last car he'll ever lay down in front of."

Divided Government for a Divided Country

Nixon was the first president since Zachary Taylor to begin his first term with both houses of Congress in the hands of the opposing party.

The President versus the Courts

Nixon tried to placate antibusing forces by slowing the process of integration. The courts, however, pressed the issue, and busing continued.

thought that it was senseless to bus children to a school miles away when they had a perfectly good one right in their own neighborhood. Angry protesters—mostly blue-collar and middle-class whites—demonstrated against court-ordered busing. Sometimes violence resulted, as in Pontiac, Michigan, where protesters firebombed empty school buses. In time, many neighborhoods became more integrated and the practice of forced busing declined.

Economic Problems

Nixon inherited a deteriorating economic situation. Johnson had tried to pay for both the Great Society and the Vietnam War without raising taxes. The result was a growing budget deficit, which, in turn, led to inflation. When Nixon tried to control inflation by trimming the federal budget and raising interest rates, inflation remained unchanged but unemployment rose and a recession set in. Nixon then responded with what he called his **New Economic Policy** (NEP). First, he imposed a ninety-day freeze in 1971 on all wages and prices. Then he established a board to regulate all wage and price increases. Finally, in 1973, he replaced the mandatory guidelines with voluntary ones.

Diplomatic Successes

China

Nixon scored his most notable triumphs in foreign affairs. Probably his biggest breakthrough was establishing relations with the Communist People's Republic of China. Since the flight of Chiang Kai-shek's Nationalist government to the island of Taiwan in 1949 (Chap. 23), the United States had recognized the Nationalist government as the legitimate government of China rather than that of the Communists on the mainland. Nixon hoped to exploit dissension between Communist China and the Soviet Union by currying favor with the Chinese. In 1971, the president announced that he would visit the People's Republic the following year, and he endorsed the admission of Communist China to the United Nations as an equal of Taiwan.

Nixon's visit was an enormous public relations success. Television cameras followed the president as he toured the Great Wall and other sites long closed to foreigners. He banqueted with Commu-

---

Results and Consequences

Nixon's freeze and mandatory regulations seemed to slow inflation, but they did not reduce unemployment. Also, once the guidelines became voluntary, prices rose again. All of his actions in the NEP were departures from the free market economics supported by his "Silent Majority." They resembled more the policies of his liberal opponents than those of a fiscal conservative.

Nixon's Plan Backfired

Contrary to Nixon's wishes, the United Nations expelled Taiwan when it admitted Communist China in 1971.

President and Mrs. Nixon visit the Great Wall during their historic trip to Communist China in 1972.

nist leaders and exchanged messages of good will with them. The visit portrayed Nixon as an astute diplomat and able statesman. He laid the groundwork for resuming trade with mainland China and for the possible reunification of the mainland with Taiwan. He did not actually abandon Nationalist China, however, by granting full diplomatic recognition to the Communist government. President Carter did that in 1978 when he formally recognized the People's Republic and severed official ties with Nationalist China.

Soviet Union

At least in part because of his overtures to China, Nixon was able to win some concessions from the Soviet Union. Through the influence of Nixon and **Henry Kissinger**, his secretary of state, the United States entered a period of **detente** (day TAHNT), a relaxation of the tension that had existed between the two nations since World War II. In the Strategic Arms Limitations Talks (SALT), the United States and the USSR agreed to limit the number of missiles and warheads each nation had. Nixon also arranged the sale of large amounts of grain to the Soviets. Americans watched in surprise as Nixon, the former anti-Communist "cold warrior," did more to improve relations between the United States and Communist nations than any other president. Under Nixon, the United States government actively sought to develop friendly relationships with repressive Communist regimes.

Nixon and Vietnam

De-escalation and Expansion

In a reversal of Johnson's Vietnam policy, Nixon de-escalated the war by bringing American troops home and leaving the bulk of the fighting to the South Vietnamese. Nixon called his policy of reducing American forces and increasing the role of the South Vietnamese the **Vietnamization** (VYET nah muh ZAY shun) of the war.

While he was reducing the number of American soldiers, however, Nixon took other steps that expanded the war. In an effort to force the North Vietnamese to make peace, the president authorized raids into neutral Cambodia in 1970 and Laos in 1971 to destroy enemy bases. In 1972, he approved massive bombing of North Vietnam, the mining of Haiphong Harbor, and the blockading of North Vietnam.

Dissent at Home

The antiwar movement entered a lull when Nixon took office; protesters waited to see what the new president would do. The bombing of North Vietnam and the expansion of the war into Cambodia and Laos, however, revitalized the movement. At least three traumatic events at home further divided the country over the war.

The first such event was the court-martial of Lieutenant **William Calley**. In March 1968, Calley led C Company into the South Vietnamese village of **My Lai** (MEE LYE). The company had suffered many casualties from Viet Cong in the area, and they were angry and on edge. In My Lai, they killed more than three hundred apparently unarmed civilians whom they suspected of aiding the Viet Cong. When news of the massacre leaked out, the army launched an investigation and a series of courts-martial lasting from 1969 to 1971. Only Calley was convicted of murder; he received a sentence of life in prison. Nixon first reduced Calley's

Vietnamization by the Numbers

Nixon gradually reduced American forces in Vietnam from more than 500,000 when he took office to fewer than 140,000 by the beginning of 1972.

Limited Success of the Expansion

Although Nixon's raids into Laos and Cambodia destroyed some enemy bases and strained the resources of North Vietnam, they did not end the war. In fact, with those two nations drawn directly into the conflict, the fighting was even more widespread.

Public Perception of My Lai

Americans were appalled that American troops could commit such a slaughter, but a large segment of the nation sympathized with Calley. They believed that either the army was making him a scapegoat to cover for other officers or the antiwar movement was persecuting him in anger over the whole war effort.

A girl screams in horror as she kneels by the body of a student killed by a stray bullet fired by National Guardsmen at Kent State University.

A New Perspective on Kent State

A recent technical analysis of a video of the shooting incident suggests that someone shouted a command for the Guardsmen to shoot, which might explain why the shooting was orderly and simultaneous, not spontaneous and sporadic. Apparently, the Guardsmen fired as many as sixty-four shots.

sentence to twenty years and then, in 1974, placed him under a mild form of house arrest.

The second event took place in May 1970 at **Kent State** University near Cleveland, Ohio. Demonstrators protesting the invasion of Cambodia rioted on and near the campus and even burned an ROTC building at the university. The governor of Ohio called out the National Guard. On May 4, a group of protesters taunted the Guardsmen and hurled rocks at them. A few of the soldiers panicked and fired. Four students, two of whom were simply walking to class and had nothing to do with the protest, were killed.

The Kent State incident revealed the deep divisions in the nation over the war. One faction considered the slain students martyrs for peace. Another faction, angered at what they considered a lack of patriotism by the antiwar movement, claimed that the students "had it coming to them." Peace seemed no closer at home than it did in Vietnam.

The third event was the publication of the **Pentagon Papers** in 1971. Pentagon staff analyst Daniel Ellsberg stole a number of confidential documents concerning the progress of American involvement in Vietnam and released them to the *New York Times*. The Nixon administration tried vainly to block publication in the interest of "national security." But the documents were more embarrassing to the government than they were dangerous to the nation. They revealed the blunders and deceptions of primarily the Kennedy and Johnson administrations in the conduct of the war. Readers learned, for example, that Johnson had drafted what became the Gulf of Tonkin resolution months before the actual incident in the Gulf of Tonkin took place. These revelations of government deceit prompted even more antiwar sentiment.

"Peace"

Although Nixon's Vietnam policy was unpopular at home, it was wearing down North Vietnam. The North Vietnamese were not near defeat, but the constant casualties and bombings were draining the Communists' resources. After an extremely heavy "Christmas bombing" late in 1972, the war-weary Americans and North Vietnamese reached an agreement at the Paris Peace Talks early in 1973. The United States recalled its troops, and North Vietnam released most U.S. prisoners of war. The United States gave South Vietnam huge amounts of arms to protect itself, but North Vietnam still maintained troops and guerrillas in the South. Nixon hoped that the supply of arms and the threat of future American intervention would protect South Vietnam. Secretary of State Kissinger hinted, however, that all the United States wanted was a "decent interval" between the removal of American forces and the fall of South Vietnam.

Aftermath

In spring 1975, North Vietnam launched a massive offensive, and South Vietnamese resistance collapsed with astonishing speed. Nixon was no longer in office, and President Ford was unable to persuade Congress to help South Vietnam. With no outside help and torn by internal dissension and corruption, the South fell. Vietnam was finally united and at "peace"—under Communist rule.

The results of the war at least partially proved Eisenhower's "domino theory" (Chap. 23). One after the other, South Vietnam, Laos, and Cambodia fell to the Communists. Fears of Communist atrocities in the fallen nations also proved justified. The worst example was the cruel Communist regime in Cambodia called the Khmer Rouge. Led by dictator Pol Pot, the Khmer Rouge slaughtered 1.2 million Cambodians—one-fifth of the nation's population. "Relief" came to the Cambodians in 1979 when Vietnam invaded the nation, toppled the murderous Khmer Rouge government, and installed its own "milder" totalitarian rule.

In America, the result was a wave of isolationism. Citizens wanted "no more Vietnams," which usually meant almost no commitment of any U.S. troops to fight anywhere for any reason. Upset at how American presidents—particularly Johnson and Nixon—had run the war on their own authority, Congress passed a series of acts, including the War Powers Act of 1973, limiting the president's power to use American troops abroad.

Why did America lose in Vietnam? Liberal critics argued that, given the unpopularity and corruption of the South Vietnamese government, the war was unwinnable; Communist domination was inevitable. Conservative critics, however, charged that an earlier commitment of larger forces, or even an invasion of North Vietnam, would have won the war; only the halfhearted concept of "limited war" prevented victory. Conservatives also accused the American media of sapping American support for the war by unsympathetic and even distorted reporting. Such questions are, of course, ultimately unanswerable. What was certain was that the American people were deeply wounded by the trauma of the Vietnam experience and would not soon recover.

> ### The War Powers Act of 1973
> The War Powers Act requires that the president notify Congress within forty-eight hours of his committing U.S. troops to military action and withdraw such troops after sixty days unless Congress specifically approves continued use of those forces.

> ### LeMay's Plan for Victory
> General Curtis LeMay proposed a plan to guarantee U.S. victory in Vietnam. LeMay, who had led the American bombing of Japan, advocated bombing the North Vietnamese "back to the Stone Age." Because it had worked in defeating the Japanese, he thought it would work again when used against the North Vietnamese. He was even willing to use atomic weapons again.

1972 Election

In the 1972 presidential election, Nixon's chances of re-election, strengthened by his trip to China and the de-escalation of the Vietnam War, looked good. His opposition for the Republican nomination was minor: a liberal congressman who accused the president of being too conservative and a conservative congressman who accused him of being too liberal. The Democrats, furthermore, were again divided. George Wallace campaigned for the Democratic nomination and, by crusading against busing, was able to win primaries not only in the South but also in northern industrial states such as Massachusetts and Michigan. A would-be assassin shot him in Maryland, cutting short his campaign and leaving him paralyzed and in pain for life.

The Democratic nomination eventually went to a candidate who was almost the exact opposite of Wallace, the zealously liberal South Dakota senator **George McGovern**. His campaign, though, was almost hopeless. He was far to the left of most American voters, and he managed to botch his best issue—discontent with the war in Vietnam—by saying that he would "crawl" to

The Democrats' nominee in 1972 was the very liberal senator from South Dakota, George McGovern.

North Vietnam if necessary for peace. Then word leaked that his running mate, Thomas Eagleton, had twice undergone electroshock treatments for a nervous disorder. At first, McGovern announced that he was "1000 percent" behind Eagleton, but a week later he forced him off the ticket. Five leading Democrats turned McGovern down before he could find someone else to run with him.

The election was much like that of 1964: the incumbent president crushed an unpopular challenger. Nixon won 61 percent of the popular vote and captured every state except Massachusetts and the District of Columbia for a 520–17 edge in the Electoral College. It proved to be like 1964 in another respect: the winner would be discredited—even hated—before the next presidential election. Within two years of his triumph, Nixon would be disgraced and out of office.

McGovern's Eventual Running Mate

The man who finally agreed to be his running mate was Sargent Shriver, John F. Kennedy's brother-in-law.

Section Quiz

1. What method did the courts order to speed the integration of public schools?

2. What were the three components of Nixon's New Economic Policy?

3. What was Nixon's greatest triumph in foreign affairs?

4. What three actions did Nixon take in 1970, 1971, and 1972 to force the North Vietnamese to make peace?

5. What two other Southeast Asian nations fell to communism after the fall of South Vietnam?

★ Although Nixon had positioned himself as a conservative and an anti-Communist in 1968, which economic policies of his administration contradicted his claims?

Chapter Review

Making Connections

1. Give at least three reasons for Barry Goldwater's unpopularity with most American voters in 1964.

2. Match each of the following slogans with the tenet of counter-culture philosophy that it describes.

   a. "Do your own thing."

   b. "All you need is love."

   c. "Don't trust anyone over thirty."

   (1) the ability of man to work out his problems in a spirit of cooperation

   (2) the belief that youth alone has the answer to society's problems

   (3) the importance of nonconformity

Developing History Skills

1. Why were the results of the 1968 election a repudiation of Johnson but not a mandate for Nixon?

2. What is the danger of the isolationist philosophy illustrated by the postwar phrase "no more Vietnams"?

Thinking Critically

1. Why is a policy of judicial activism such as that pursued by the Warren Court dangerous?

2. Why is a philosophy inadequate that simply espouses "love" as the solution to man's problems?

Living as a Christian Citizen

1. Leviticus 19:9–10 instructed the Israelites to leave behind produce so that the poor could come and glean it. This law does not directly apply in the New Testament era, and the United States is no longer primarily a nation based on agriculture. But the principle of helping the poor remains (Luke 14:13–14). What are ways that Christians can help the poor today? What are some dangers to avoid?

2. Select a current or proposed legislation and evaluate it in terms of how its goals, methods, and likely outcome align with Scripture principles. In areas in which it falls short, offer alternatives.

People, Places, and Things to Remember

Lyndon Johnson
"Great Society"
Civil Rights Act of 1964
Voting Rights Act of 1965
Twenty-fourth Amendment
"War on Poverty"
Barry Goldwater
Medicare
Earl Warren
judicial activism
"one man, one vote" decisions
Gulf of Tonkin resolution
Viet Cong
Tet Offensive
Paris Peace Talks
urban riots
"black power"
"New Left"
counterculture
Eugene McCarthy
Robert Kennedy
Hubert H. Humphrey
Richard Nixon
George Wallace
silent majority
busing
New Economic Policy
Henry Kissinger
detente
Vietnamization
William Calley
My Lai
Kent State
Pentagon Papers
George McGovern

President Gerald Ford, the only unelected president

A Nation Adrift (1973-1980)

I. The Embattled Presidency

II. Domestic Difficulties

III. The Ineffectual Presidency

IV. The Rising Conservative Tide

"I did not take the sacred oath of office to preside over the decline and fall of the United States of America."

President Gerald Ford, September 1975

An average American watching the evening news on December 1, 1979, would have noticed a difference from broadcasts that aired a few weeks earlier. Each night, Walter Cronkite, anchor of the *CBS Evening News*, closed his program with his trademark line "And that's the way it is. . . ." But that night—shortly after Muslim extremists seized fifty-three American hostages in the American embassy in Teheran, Iran—viewers heard Cronkite add a final phrase: ". . . on the twenty-seventh day of captivity for the American hostages in Iran." Each night thereafter, Cronkite added another day to the total—thirty, forty, fifty, one hundred, two hundred, and still more with no end in sight. The nightly broadcasts were like drumbeats to Americans, each beat echoing the helplessness of the United States, its decline as a world power, and the inability of its president to deal with the world situation. Cronkite continued the demoralizing count until the 444th day, the day on which the hostages were freed and Americans inaugurated a new president that their frustration, in part, had led them to elect.

The repudiated president in 1980 was Jimmy Carter, but he was only the latest in a series of presidents that American voters had rejected. For much of the 1970s, the United States suffered a "leadership crisis." It began when one president (Nixon), hounded by scandal, was forced to resign. It continued as his successor, Gerald Ford, tried vainly to unite the nation. Ford had been named, but not elected, vice president, and he had never even won an election outside his own congressional district in Grand Rapids, Michigan. It ended with Carter, a man elected in part because of the failures of his predecessors, being voted from office by a disillusioned American electorate. For much of the 1970s, the United States was a nation adrift.

I. The Embattled Presidency

The Fall of Richard Nixon

Watergate Affair

In the summer of 1972, during the heat of the presidential campaign, police arrested five burglars who, carrying electronic listening devices, were trying to break into the headquarters of the Democratic National Committee at the Watergate Office Complex in Washington. The event caused little stir at the time. The White House vigorously denied any connection with that "third-rate burglary," and George McGovern's campaign was already in such deep trouble that few listened to his charges of criminality and corruption against Nixon.

After the election, however, more about the **Watergate affair** began to leak out. One of the convicted burglars alleged to the trial judge that authorities "higher up" were behind the break-in and were trying to cover up the fact. Further investigation revealed a pattern of questionable and illegal activities organized by Nixon's Committee to Re-elect the President (CREEP).

Resignation of Agnew

Another problem that plagued Nixon's administration was the allegation that Vice President **Spiro Agnew** had taken bribes from building contractors as the governor of Maryland and as vice president. By striking a bargain with prosecutors, Agnew was allowed to

> ### More Political Shenanigans
> Some Nixon aides sent libelous letters to newspapers, accusing Democratic candidates of racism and sexual immorality. Others burglarized the office of Daniel Ellsberg's psychiatrist (Ellsberg had stolen the Pentagon Papers), trying to find material with which to discredit Ellsberg. In 1973, investigations by both Congress and a federal court resulted in the firing or resignation of several members of Nixon's staff and cabinet. The controversy did not go away with those dismissals, however; people wondered whether the president himself was involved and, if so, how deeply.

plead *nolo contendere* (no contest; in substance but not technically guilty), and he received only a fine and probation. He also resigned as vice president in October 1973, becoming the first vice president to resign from office since John C. Calhoun resigned for political (not criminal) reasons in 1832 (see Chapter 10). Although Agnew's crimes were unrelated to Watergate, they increased the perception that the Nixon administration was thoroughly corrupt. Using the procedure outlined by the Twenty-fifth Amendment (ratified 1967), President Nixon nominated House minority leader **Gerald Ford** of Michigan to succeed Agnew; both houses of Congress confirmed the nomination by overwhelming margins. Nixon hoped that Ford's popularity in Congress and reputation for honesty would help deflect criticism from his administration.

Senator Howard Baker (R-TN; left) and Bible-quoting Senator Sam Ervin (D-NC; center) directed the nationally televised Senate Watergate hearings.

Resignation of Nixon

Despite all the charges and investigations, no evidence had come to light that implicated Nixon himself in the Watergate scandal. That situation changed in the middle of 1973 when a White House aide revealed that Nixon had installed a secret recording system in the Oval Office that taped every conversation there. Immediately, both the courts and Congress pressed Nixon to release the tapes. The president refused, claiming that national security and the separation of powers were at stake. His refusal began a long struggle over control of the tapes. Nixon tried to placate investigators by first releasing edited transcripts of the tapes and then by releasing some of the tapes. Meanwhile, he maintained his complete innocence of wrongdoing. The president's approval rating plummeted. The tapes and wrenching judicial and congressional inquiries exposed the seamy side of the Nixon administration—the political "dirty tricks," subtle lies, and outright deceit that Nixon and his aides had practiced. They also revealed that Nixon had a foul mouth.

The Watergate affair became a national trauma. For months, the government seemed paralyzed by the accusations and rumors that flew about. Televised congressional hearings kept the scandal constantly before the public eye. Finally, in July 1974, the Supreme Court ruled unanimously that Nixon must release all the tapes. Those tapes showed that although the president had not known about the Watergate break-in beforehand, he participated in attempts to cover up the involvement of his White House subordinates. With impeachment by the House and conviction by the Senate a virtual certainty in the Democrat-controlled Congress, Nixon resigned on August 9. Gerald Ford, in his first speech as president, said, "My fellow Americans, our long national nightmare is over."

The Unelected President

Gerald Ford enjoyed a flood of goodwill when he took office. The American people indeed wanted to put the "long national nightmare" behind them. Furthermore, Ford's reputation as a decent, honest man was a welcome contrast to Nixon and his bitter struggle with Capitol Hill. But after only a month in office, Ford dashed his popularity with one stroke: he granted Nixon a full **pardon** for any crimes he might have committed while in office. The president maintained that his action would put the Watergate affair behind the nation and that it would save the United States the agony of enduring the trial of a former president.

Ford's act was brave but politically damaging. Many critics thought it unfair that Nixon should escape punishment while his subordinates suffered. As a result, Ford's popularity fell dramatically.

Ford also faced several other obstacles that hampered his effectiveness. For instance, he was the nation's first unelected president. He owed his elevation to the nation's highest office not to a national election but to an appointment and a resignation. As Ford himself said, "I am acutely aware that I have received the votes of none of you." Complicating the situation for the Ford administration, the man whom Ford nominated to be vice president, Nelson Rockefeller, also had not been elected by the people. For the first time in history, neither of the nation's top two officials had been elected.

A second obstacle was the public's increasingly critical perception of Ford. Despite Ford's athletic ability (which included a stint as a star center for the University of Michigan's football team), a series of public accidents gave people the impression that he was clumsy. For example, he stumbled as he descended the ramp of the presidential jet, and he accidentally hit spectators with balls when he played golf.

Ford's greatest obstacle, however, was a hostile Congress. The Democrats held comfortable majorities in both houses, and they were determined to control the government after the excesses of the Nixon administration. Ford's main weapon against them was the veto; he vetoed sixty-one bills in less than three years in office in an attempt to hold down government spending and protect the powers of the presidency. Congress, however, overrode twelve of his vetoes, one of the highest number of overrides since the beleaguered presidency of Andrew Johnson. The standoff between Ford and Congress created a legislative deadlock.

Factors beyond the president's control also damaged his reputation. In 1975, America tasted final defeat in Southeast Asia as South Vietnam, Cambodia, and Laos fell to the Communists. A sluggish national economy also worried voters. Under Nixon and Ford, the paralyzed presidency had sunk to its lowest level of prestige since the era of Warren G. Harding.

Gerald Ford became president during a time of great uncertainty following President Nixon's resignation.

Section Quiz

1. Why did the release of the presidential tapes cause President Nixon to resign?

2. What event early in Ford's administration drastically lowered his popularity with the American people?

3. What was Ford's greatest obstacle to effectiveness in his presidency?

✶ Was Gerald Ford an ineffective president as his critics claimed, or was he merely the victim of circumstances?

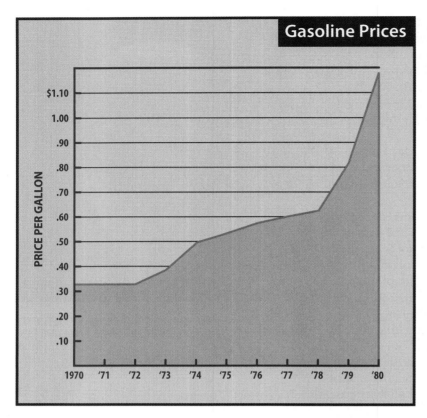

II. Domestic Difficulties

The problems of the 1960s—urban violence, student unrest, and racial conflict—gave way to problems in the 1970s that were less dramatic but no less important. Despite all its problems, the 1960s had been economically prosperous; in the 1970s, however, economic conditions became the nation's primary concern. Also, the success of the civil rights movement in the 1960s spurred other groups to agitate for their "rights"—some legitimate, some not—in the 1970s.

Economic Woes

Energy Crisis

In October 1973 the Arab nations of Egypt and Syria attacked the neighboring Jewish state of Israel. The United States, as it had done since Israel became a nation in 1948, supported the Israelis against the Arabs. In retaliation, the oil-producing Arab nations—all members of the Organization of Petroleum Exporting Countries (OPEC)—announced an **oil embargo** against the United States, prohibiting the sale of any oil to America. When the embargo started, the United States was still under President Nixon's wage and price controls. With a shrinking supply of gasoline held at an artificially low price, supplies became scarce. Gas stations were open fewer hours and limited the amount of gas each customer could buy. Motorists often had to wait in long lines to buy the gas that was available. When price controls were finally lifted, the price of gasoline shot from about 35¢ a gallon at the beginning of 1973 to well over a dollar a gallon by 1980.

The gasoline shortages were only part of an overall **energy crisis**, a combination of higher prices for and shortages of American energy resources. Until the 1970s, Americans had always assumed that there would be enough cheap fuel resources to power any project that American industry undertook. They began to realize, however, that America's energy sources were not

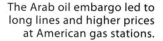

The Arab oil embargo led to long lines and higher prices at American gas stations.

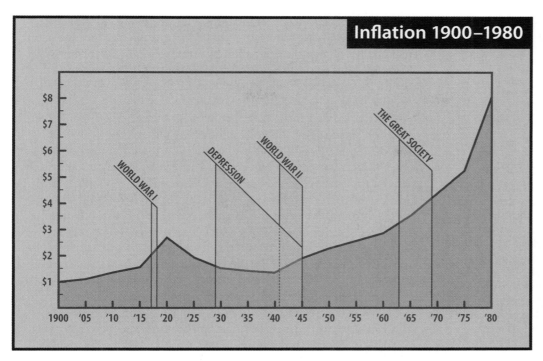

Inflation 1900–1980

WORLD WAR I

DEPRESSION

WORLD WAR II

THE GREAT SOCIETY

inexhaustible and would not always be inexpensive. Petroleum production had already begun to drop before the embargo, and the embargo itself simply heightened the shortages and drove up prices more quickly. Even when the Arabs lifted the oil embargo, they increased their prices for crude oil fourfold, nudging prices even higher. The prices for all petroleum products—from heating oil and fuels for power plants to phonograph records and asphalt —went up.

During this time, a growing number of people voiced concern about the effects of industrial development on the environment. Beginning in the 1960s, the so-called **environmental movement**— composed of disparate groups including pantheists, Communists, and antihuman organizations—began to sound warnings about industrial pollution of the water and air, particularly that caused by automobiles. Under pressure from these groups, Congress passed a number of laws regulating pollution. In 1970, Congress established the Environmental Protection Agency to oversee and coordinate environmental regulations. The main acts to combat pollution were the Clean Air Act (1970; amended 1977) and the Clean Water Act (1977).

Those actions helped reduce pollution of the environment, but they also increased demands on the nation's energy resources. Many industries, for example, began to switch from highly pollutant coal to oil as a power source, further straining American oil resources. Likewise, regulations to reduce air pollution by cars required adding emission-control devices, which reduced pollution but also lowered fuel efficiency. Additional costs led many industries to plead for delays in implementing the environmental regulations to give them time to make the adjustments.

Stagflation

Normally, when inflation is high, unemployment is low; and when unemployment is high, inflation is low. In the 1970s, however, the United States experienced high inflation and high unemployment at the same time, a condition that economists called **stagflation**.

Christians and Pollution

While Christians should not ally themselves with the pantheistic and antihuman attitudes often found in the environmental movement, there is a role for Christians in controlling or preventing pollution. The Creation Mandate in Genesis 1:26–28 requires Christians to exercise dominion over God's creation. Proper stewardship would include dealing with pollution. Because pollution harms humans, Christians should combat it to obey Christ's command to love one's neighbor.

Three factors caused the stagflation. First, the energy crisis created a scarcity of many products and pushed prices up. Second, Johnson had created a large budget deficit by attempting to pay for both the Vietnam War and the Great Society without raising taxes. As a result, the government had to print more money to cover the deficit, further fueling inflation.

The third and most complicated cause was the United States' decision to abandon the gold standard. From World War II to 1971, the United States had promised foreign nations that anyone outside the United States could redeem any American currency he held for American gold at a price of $35 an ounce. (The U.S. had not allowed American citizens, however, to redeem currency for gold since 1933.) While the United States was exporting more goods than it imported, this policy was not a problem because few foreign investors held sizable amounts of American currency. In 1971, however, the United States suffered its first **trade deficit** since the 1890s; it imported more goods than it exported. Foreign investors, primarily in Europe, now had abundant amounts of American currency and began to exchange them for gold.

Faced with the possible depletion of America's gold reserves, Nixon stopped the redeeming of currency for gold. As a result, nothing backed U.S. currency except the government's promise. Without being fixed to a standard, the value of the dollar dropped in relation to foreign currencies, and the costs of buying foreign goods rose.

Rights Movements

Since black Americans had made dramatic gains in securing their civil rights, many other minorities attempted, with varying degrees of success, to broaden their legal rights. American Indians, for example, protested to dramatize their plight: a high rate of unemployment and lower life expectancy. One of the most publicized protests was at Wounded Knee, South Dakota, in 1973, on the hundredth anniversary of the Wounded Knee Massacre (see Chapter 17). Some Indian groups sued the government for violating numerous treaties with the Indians, and the courts often granted the Indians generous financial compensation. Some rights movements of the era agitated for the recognition of unbiblical practices. The "gay rights" movement tried to remove legal prohibitions to the homosexual lifestyle. It also sought to gain legal recognition of homosexual "marriages" for financial purposes such as insurance benefits and for the purpose of normalizing homosexual behavior. The push for homosexual rights has gained ground because it is presented as a struggle for freedom. But opponents to homosexual practice argue that it is immoral. The issue of morality places homosexual practice in a different category from ethnicity, a point that Christians will often argue from Scripture. Others, even some Christians, will argue this on the basis of nature—how the human body is formed—and indicate the negative effects of homosexuality on society. These arguments have lost ground, however, under a steady rejection of scriptural authority in a culture that values freedom above all else.

One of the largest and most influential movements in the 1970s was the **women's rights movement**. Although not a numerical minority, women as a group suffered from various forms of discrimination. For instance, women often received less pay than men working at the same job. In some states, a married woman could

Economy—The Number One Issue

The energy crisis, the budget deficit, and abandonment of the gold standard fueled inflation without providing a means of reducing unemployment. Stagflation left Congress in a dilemma. Attacking inflation by cutting government spending added to the already high unemployment, because many jobs depended on federal funds. On the other hand, attacking unemployment through government spending added to the already alarming inflation rate. By 1980, most Americans listed economic issues—primarily inflation—as their main concern.

Women's Lib

A radical element that generally preferred the name **women's liberation movement** complicated the feminist movement. These extreme feminists portrayed modern American marriage as a form of slavery in which wives labored in the "demeaning" roles of mother and homemaker. They wanted to "liberate" women from such "slavery" and looked down on women who preferred the traditional role of housewife—being a wife and mother in the home. To achieve their vision of equality, some women's liberationists advocated a platform of bold immorality: "free love" (premarital and extramarital sex), easier divorce laws, recognition of lesbian "marriages," and, above all, a woman's unquestioned "right" to abortion on demand. State laws had long restricted or even prohibited abortion. In the landmark case **Roe v. Wade** (1973), however, the Supreme Court struck down most state abortion laws. Consequently, the slaughter of unborn children by abortion rose to more than one million a year by 1978. Women's liberationists celebrated the decision.

The Woman Who Stopped the ERA

The leader of the fight against the Equal Rights Amendment was a determined woman named Phyllis Schlafly, who was used to competing against long odds. She worked her way through college during World War II, test-firing bullets in an ammunition plant. She earned her master's degree from Radcliffe College, a prestigious women's school. After marrying, she was a homemaker, rearing six children. She also ran for Congress twice, served as a delegate to the Republican National Convention four times, and wrote nine books.

Schlafly first made headlines in 1964 when she published *A Choice Not an Echo*, an examination of Republican national politics that is often credited with helping Barry Goldwater win the 1964 presidential nomination. After Congress sent the ERA to the states for ratification in 1972, Schlafly tirelessly and relentlessly visited the states that had not ratified the ERA to stress the dangers of the amendment to the traditional rights of women.

She took abuse from reporters, radical feminists, and other opponents, often being insulted and spat upon. Through it all, she remained calm, even, and courteous. She stated her arguments in crisp tones and supported them with a wealth of carefully researched facts. When opponents ridiculed her for speaking out on legal and constitutional issues without being a lawyer, she entered law school and earned her law degree—in her "spare time."

"The claim that American women are downtrodden and unfairly treated is the fraud of the century," Schlafly said. She pointed to her own success. "I've achieved my goals in life and I did it without sex-neutral laws."

not own property in her own name. In addition, widows sometimes discovered after the death of a spouse that the excellent credit rating they had built with their husbands no longer existed; a widower's credit rating, however, continued unimpaired. With such injustices as illustrations, **feminists** (advocates of women's rights) successfully appealed to the public's sense of fairness to address these problems.

Although radical feminists seized much of the public's attention, the real strength of the women's movement lay in the basic justice of its demands in the marketplace. Many women who were uninterested in or even opposed to the demands of the liberationists (see side margin note) were very interested in economic equality. Both higher inflation and rising divorce rates were forcing more women out of the home and into the workplace simply to survive. Those women desired only the opportunity to make a living and support their families. Therefore, Congress and the states corrected economic inequality by passing legislation to give women equal access to employment and equal pay for performing the same jobs as men.

The most controversial and divisive piece of pro-feminist legislation was the **Equal Rights Amendment** (ERA) passed by Congress in 1972. Section 1 of that proposed amendment said briefly, "Equality of rights under the law shall not be denied or abridged by the United States or by any state on account of sex." Proponents of the amendment claimed that it would reinforce the basic rights as citizens that women held under the Constitution. Opponents claimed that sufficient laws were already in effect to guarantee those rights. Opponents also feared that the amendment would break down the traditional protections that women enjoyed, such as exemption from the military draft, and would increase government intrusions into individual privacy, such as matters of adoption and child custody. A bitter fight over ratification of the ERA ended in 1982 when the amendment failed to garner the necessary approval of three-fourths of the state legislatures before its deadline for ratification passed. Its failure was a blow to the radicals but did not diminish the genuine gains that women had made.

Section Quiz

1. Why did Arab nations place an oil embargo on the United States in 1973?
2. Name the agency and the two major acts which were Congress's main attempts to protect the environment from pollution.
3. What were the three causes of stagflation in the 1970s?
4. What is the name for the radical wing of the women's rights movement?
✭ Why do you think the Equal Rights Amendment failed to achieve sufficient support to become part of the Constitution?

III. The Ineffectual Presidency

Rise of Jimmy Carter

1976 Election

Gerald Ford entered the 1976 presidential race encumbered by numerous weights. Although he was the incumbent, he was an unelected incumbent. The high unemployment rate, the Nixon pardon, and the public perception of Ford as a good-natured bumbler all hampered the president's reelection efforts. Furthermore, Ford was not even the preferred choice of many members of his own party. Former California governor **Ronald Reagan**, the hero of the Republican conservatives who dominated the party, mounted a strong challenge to Ford in the primaries. The president won renomination but only by a narrow margin after a bruising fight.

The Democrats' candidate proved unusual. **Jimmy Carter** was a well-to-do peanut farmer whose political experience consisted of one term in the Georgia state senate and one term as governor of Georgia. But he surprised the experts by winning the Democratic nomination. Carter's strategy was clever. He placed himself in the political center where he could attract the most voters—to the right of a host of liberal Democratic candidates but to the left of Democratic firebrand George Wallace. He also ran as an "outsider," a candidate untainted by the corruption in Washington and therefore supposedly better able to clean it up.

The 1976 election looked at first as though it would be a landslide for Carter. Ford, however, fought back. The incumbent hammered away at Carter's vagueness on the issues. "Jimmy Carter will say anything anywhere to be president of the United States," Ford said. "He wavers, he wanders, he wiggles, and he waffles." But Ford hurt himself by proclaiming in a televised debate that he did not believe Eastern Europe was under Soviet domination, despite the presence of Soviet-imposed governments and thousands of Soviet troops in those nations. This gaffe merely reinforced the perception of some people that Ford was a bungler. In the end, Carter won

---

An Assessment of the 1976 Presidential Race

One Democrat, noting Ford's plight, said gleefully, "We could run an aardvark this year and win."

Using "Born-Again" as a Campaign Strategy

As a further contrast to the dishonesty of the Nixon years, Carter claimed to be a "born-again" Christian who wanted a government "as filled with love as the American people." After the trauma of Watergate, Americans were attracted to a candidate who said plainly, "I'll never tell a lie."

narrowly—50.1 percent to 48 percent in the popular vote. The vote in the Electoral College, 297 to 240, was the closest since Woodrow Wilson defeated Charles Evans Hughes in 1916.

The Carter Style

Carter entered office professing his desire to be a "people's president" with an open, honest, and compassionate administration. He appointed record numbers of women and minorities to government positions. But not all his "healing" gestures were appreciated. When he granted amnesty (a general pardon) to draft dodgers who fled the country to avoid fighting in Vietnam, Carter felt the wrath of veterans who had loyally fulfilled their obligation and fought in the war.

Carter also had some negative characteristics. Like James Polk, he was a compulsive worker who tried to micromanage every aspect of the government; as a result, he was often bogged down by details that could have been delegated to subordinates. Carter's "outsider" status in Washington and his aloof, humorless personality made it hard for him to work with Congress, despite large Democratic majorities in both houses. These flaws eventually damaged Carter, causing Americans to become disenchanted with his policies and adding to his public perception as a colorless, ineffective leader.

Foreign Affairs

Carter tried to pursue a foreign policy based on fairness and morality, much as Woodrow Wilson had tried to do. The cornerstone of Carter's foreign policy was the defense of **human rights**, protecting people from government oppression. While Carter's goals were laudable, the United States could influence only friendly nations concerning human rights. Communist nations, among the worst violators of human rights, were impervious to Carter's pressures and continued to brutally oppress their people.

Panama Canal Treaty

Carter's first great challenge in foreign affairs concerned the Panama Canal. Panamanians had resented American control of the canal for many years. The United States had helped Panama win its independence and paid Panama for control of the Canal Zone, according to the original treaty, "in perpetuity" (i.e., essentially forever). The Nixon and Ford administrations had begun negotiations to return the canal to Panama; Carter merely completed the process. He signed the **Panama Canal Treaty** in 1977, and the Senate narrowly ratified it the following year. The new treaty allowed Panama and the United States to operate the canal jointly until 2000, when Panama would take over the operation completely.

The treaty created controversy in the United States. Administration officials, numerous leading Democrats, and even some Republicans, such as Gerald Ford and Senator Howard Baker, defended the treaty. They claimed that the canal's narrow width and the growth of air power made the canal neither militarily nor economically important to the United States. (They pointed out, for example, that aircraft carriers and oil tankers were too wide to use the canal.) Supporters also hoped that the U.S. action would improve relations with Latin America.

Opponents of the treaty claimed that the waterway was still vital to American interests and should not be handed over to the

Presidential Informality

Carter surprised and delighted the American people by walking down Pennsylvania Avenue after his inauguration instead of riding in the usual armored limousine. He made some televised addresses wearing a sweater instead of a suit, and many photographs showed him relaxing in blue jeans. He calculated that all of these "down-home" images would endear him to the public as "one of them."

President and Mrs. Carter walk down Pennsylvania Avenue after his inauguration.

Carter's Policies in Practice

An example of the shortcomings of Carter's foreign policy was Nicaragua. The Carter administration pressured the friendly but dictatorial regime there to improve its human rights record. Eventually, revolutionaries, with the American government's quiet approval, overthrew the Nicaraguan dictator. Afterward, however, a Marxist government took power; it was just as repressive as the previous government but far more hostile to the United States.

Panama Canal Treaty Senate Vote

The treaty (actually, there were two treaties collectively known as the Torrijos-Carter Treaty) by which the United States ceded the Panama Canal to Panama was ratified in the Senate by a vote of 68–32. (Both treaties received the same number of votes.) Fifty-two Democrats and 16 Republicans voted to ratify; 10 Democrats and 22 Republicans voted against it.

authoritarian and sometimes unstable government of Panama. As for its narrowness, it could be widened to accommodate larger ships. (It currently is being widened.) Despite passage of the treaty, U.S.–Latin American relations did not improve perceptibly. Furthermore, surrender of the canal increased the perception at home and abroad that the United States was declining in power and influence.

Camp David Accords

President Carter's greatest triumph came in diplomacy in the Middle East. After becoming a nation in 1948, Israel was in constant conflict with its Arab neighbors. The nation fought four brief wars, and the region suffered from constant unrest and violence. But Egypt, one of Israel's most powerful opponents, was tired of the fighting, which had brought it no gain but much loss. In 1978 Carter invited the president of Egypt, Anwar Sadat (AHN-wahr sah-DAHT), and the prime minister of Israel, Menachem Begin (mehn-AH-kehm BAY-gihn), to meet with him at Camp David, the presidential retreat in Maryland.

After thirteen days of arduous negotiations, the three men reached an uneasy agreement known as the **Camp David Accords**. In return for Egypt's recognition of Israel's sovereignty (which no other Arab nation had done) and a guarantee of peace, Israel returned to Egypt the Sinai Peninsula, which it had taken in the Six-Day War (1967). Although some parts of the accords eventually broke down, the agreement marked one of the greatest advances for peace in the Middle East since World War II. Egypt and Israel have yet to go to war since that agreement.

President Carter (center) enjoyed his greatest foreign affairs triumph in negotiating the Camp David Accords between Egypt's president, Anwar Sadat (right), and Israel's prime minister, Menachem Begin (left).

Soviet Union

Carter's success with the Camp David Accords, however, was overshadowed by several setbacks in foreign policy. His dealings with the Soviet Union are one example. Like Nixon and Ford before him, Carter pursued a policy of *detente* with the Soviet Union. The key to good relations, Carter decided, would be passage of the **SALT II Treaty**. This treaty was the result of Strategic Arms Limitation Talks (SALT) between the Soviets and the Americans to limit the number and kinds of nuclear weapons of each superpower. The president signed the treaty in June 1979, but he faced a stiff challenge getting it ratified by the Senate. Conservatives charged that the treaty would put the Soviet Union ahead of the United States in nuclear weaponry and that, given the Communists' consistent treaty violations, the United States could not be sure that the Soviets would maintain the agreement.

Two days after Christmas in 1979, all chance of passing the treaty vanished when the Soviet Union invaded the neighboring nation of Afghanistan. The Soviets claimed that they were going to "help" the pro-Communist ruler of Afghanistan, but he was quickly assassinated and replaced by a more pliable Soviet puppet. Furious, Carter announced an embargo on all sales of grain to the Soviets and an American boycott of the 1980 summer Olympic Games in Moscow. He also withdrew the SALT II Treaty from the

Senate's consideration and called for a new registration of young men for the discontinued draft (although he did not revive the draft itself). In his State of the Union address for 1980, he enunciated the "Carter Doctrine," that the United States would resist by military force if necessary any Soviet attempt to push farther south to the Persian Gulf.

Yet even that relatively mild reaction brought a storm of criticism of Carter. Liberals described the Carter Doctrine, draft registration, and withdrawal of the SALT II Treaty as harsh, provocative overreactions that threatened world peace. Farmers complained about their financial losses from the grain embargo. Conservatives claimed that Carter was all talk and that his few concrete actions—such as boycotting the Olympics—were pitifully weak. Whether he tried firmness or conciliation, Carter seemed unable to please anyone.

Iran

The Camp David Accords gave Carter his greatest triumph, but the Middle East also gave him his most damaging defeat when revolution convulsed Iran. The shah (king) of that nation, **Mohammed Reza Pahlavi** (known as the Shah of Iran), was long known to be pro-West in his outlook but repressive in his rule. In January 1979, after months of violent disorder, the Shah fled the country, and a fanatical Islamic extremist, the **Ayatollah Ruhollah Khomeini** (koh MAY nee) took power. Khomeini denounced everyone who was not as zealous as he and his followers were—the Shah, other Arab nations, the Soviet Union, and especially "the great Satan" who had supported the Shah, the United States. In November, when the exiled Shah went to the United States to receive medical treatment for terminal cancer, enraged Muslims stormed the American embassy in Teheran, Iran, and took fifty-three Americans hostage.

The **Iranian hostage crisis** became Carter's foreign policy nightmare. American citizens raged helplessly as television networks almost daily broadcast footage of Iranians burning American flags and chanting anti-American slogans. The Iranians toyed with the United States for months, raising hopes that they would release the hostages and then dashing those hopes with an almost sadistic glee. Carter, with few options open to him short of military invasion, tried vainly to use economic sanctions, negotiations, and world opinion to move the Iranians to release the hostages.

As the weeks dragged on, the American public's frustration and anger partially turned from Iran to the president himself. The whole nation seemed to be asking, "Why doesn't the president do something?" Carter's inaction—which was perhaps not entirely his fault, considering his limited choices—made him seem weak, indecisive, even spineless.

Domestic Disaster

Carter's foreign problems were matched by his domestic difficulties. The economy was the primary problem. Ford had managed to get the rate of inflation down to 5 percent, but the

The rise of Islamic extremist groups and Arab terrorism in the late 1970s and 1980s presented Carter (and later presidents Reagan and Bush) with some of their thorniest issues in foreign affairs.

Tragic Abortive Rescue Attempt

In April 1980 an attempted military rescue of the hostages turned into a fiasco. An American helicopter collided with a transport plane in the desert of Iran, and eight American soldiers died without ever getting near the hostages.

A Timely Release

The hostages were finally released after 444 days of captivity on January 20, 1981—the day Americans inaugurated President Ronald Reagan, who promised to bring the United States back to world leadership.

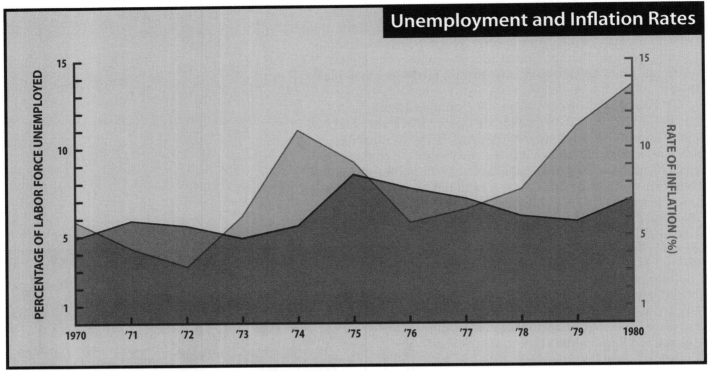

Unemployment and Inflation Rates

PERCENTAGE OF LABOR FORCE UNEMPLOYED

RATE OF INFLATION (%)

1970 '71 '72 '73 '74 '75 '76 '77 '78 '79 1980

More Frustrations

Carter's inability to get along with Congress continued to aggravate matters. His reserved personality and Congress's determination to be independent after the excesses of Watergate paralyzed legislation. A growing number of Americans became frustrated when President Carter and a Democrat majority in Congress could not agree on how to help the nation. Plus, the Iranian revolution in 1979 diminished oil supplies in the United States again, reviving the long lines and high prices at gas stations that had characterized the early 1970s.

result was a recession and an unemployment rate of 8 percent by the time he left office. In four years in office, Carter was able to lower unemployment only slightly, to 7.5 percent. Inflation, however, soared. By 1980, the annual inflation rate rose to over 13 percent. Depositors and investors worried about how inflation was ravaging their hard-earned savings. Consumers complained loudly about rising prices for food, clothing, fuel, and other necessities. The American economy was careening out of control, and Carter seemed helpless to do anything.

As American anger rose, Carter's popularity dropped. By December 1979 only 19 percent of the American people approved of Carter's performance—a rating lower than that of Richard Nixon during the depths of the Watergate affair. The American people—fed up with the failures of Nixon, Ford, and Carter—were looking for bold, new leadership.

Section Quiz

1. Name at least two difficulties President Ford faced in his campaign for reelection.

2. What act did Carter perform at his inauguration to symbolize his desire to be a "people's president"?

3. Why was the narrow width of the Panama Canal an argument against its value to the United States?

4. What was President Carter's greatest diplomatic triumph?

5. What event virtually eliminated all chance of the Senate's ratifying the SALT II Treaty?

✫ Knowing what we do now, how was the hostage crisis in Iran near the end of Carter's term a warning to the United States of further dangers to come?

IV. The Rising Conservative Tide

Thunder on the Right

Among the people who were unhappy with the course that America was taking in the 1960s and 1970s were political conservatives, typified by Republicans Barry Goldwater and Ronald Reagan. Traditional conservatives held to a firm ideology of limited powers for the national government and staunch opposition to the growth of communism. They opposed increased government spending, especially since the nation's budget deficit was growing at an alarming rate. Such conservatives feared particularly that the United States was falling behind the Soviet Union in military power and therefore opposed initiatives such as President Carter's SALT II Treaty. They also denounced Carter's decision to break relations with Nationalist China on Taiwan to establish relations with Communist China. Such an action was to them a cowardly betrayal of a long-time friend and anti-Communist force to accommodate a totalitarian Communist regime. Likewise, most political conservatives opposed the Panama Canal Treaty as symbolic of America's declining power and prestige. Those events energized conservatives as a political force.

New Right

Joining the old-line conservatives was a faction called the **New Right**. Those conservatives shared many beliefs of the traditionalists, notably opposition to communism and belief in limited government. But the New Right was also motivated by numerous social and moral issues, and many New Right groups focused on a single overriding issue. The *Roe v. Wade* decision legalizing abortion, for example, spurred a Right-to-Life movement that opposed abortion and sought to use such means as a constitutional amendment to overturn the *Roe* decision. Other New Right activists called for reduction of the increasingly heavy burden of taxation by national, state, and local governments.

Religious Right

An important component of the New Right was the **Religious Right**, various conservative Christian leaders and organizations that were concerned primarily with moral issues. The Religious Right grew in reaction to immoral trends in the United States, such as widespread drug abuse, the legalization of abortion, and increased toleration and even advocacy of homosexuality. The Religious Right hoped to stem the tide of immorality through political action that would reestablish America's traditional standards of morality, standards that reflected the unique contribution of the Christian faith to American history.

Many of the most prominent leaders of the Religious Right were adherents of the **Charismatic movement**. Using television extensively, the Charismatics managed to motivate many Christians to become active politically. The most influential of the Charismatic television evangelists was **Pat Robertson**, who founded the first Christian television station in the United States

> ### Lower My Taxes!
> The most publicized event in the "taxpayers' revolt" was the passage of **Proposition 13** in California in 1978. This initiative, overwhelmingly approved by California voters, forced the state to roll back property taxes drastically.

The Supreme Court decision legalizing abortion sparked a groundswell of opposition and launched a Right-to-Life movement dedicated to finding legal means to overturn the decision.

Jerry Falwell with President George H. W. Bush

in 1961. From that start, he built the Christian Broadcasting Network (CBN) and became host of a prominent Christian talk show, *The 700 Club.*

Not all the leaders of the Religious Right were Charismatics. Catholics, Mormons, and numerous non-Charismatic Protestants joined the vaguely religious crusade for morality. One such leader was Baptist pastor **Jerry Falwell** of Virginia, who, like Robertson, used television to promote his cause. Falwell founded a religious political action group called the Moral Majority to help elect conservative candidates and to further conservative causes.

Falwell drew heated criticism from liberals, who attacked him for supposedly breaking down the alleged wall of separation between church and state. They accused him of attempting to force his religious views on the general public and also criticized him for using a religious organization to achieve political ends. (Many of those liberals were silent, however, when liberal politicians and civil rights leaders used liberal churches to register voters and advance liberal causes.)

The Religious Right also benefited because more Americans were turning from theologically liberal churches to more doctrinally conservative ones. In a 1977 survey, seventy million Americans described themselves as "born-again" Christians. Although definitions of "born again" did not always agree with the scriptural doctrine of regeneration, those numbers meant that a large portion of the American population was at least sympathetic to conservative religious views.

The Religious Right greatly feared that the government was undercutting the nation's traditional religious freedoms. The 1963 Supreme Court decisions against prayer and Bible reading in public schools are major examples of government interference. Another fear was government control of Christian schools. Since the 1960s, many Christians had placed their children in private Christian day schools or had even begun to educate them at home to protect them from secular influences and declining public school educational standards. Some state and federal authorities began to call for regulation or even closing of Christian schools. Religious conservatives, realizing that growing governmental power could threaten all constitutional religious freedoms, began to fight back with their dollars and their ballots.

Election of 1980

Nomination of Reagan

Riding the surge of conservatism to the Republican nomination was Ronald Reagan. A polished speaker whose tone conveyed a sense of absolute sincerity, Reagan had been a leading and persuasive advocate of conservative causes since the 1950s. Trained by his experience in radio broadcasting and acting, Reagan used his vocal skills to rouse conservatives by his defense of free enterprise. He called for shrinking the federal government and steadfastly opposed Communist expansion.

Reagan brushed aside his competition in the 1980 primaries and won the nomination easily. To unify the party, he chose one of his politically moderate opponents, George Bush, to be his running mate. With Reagan at the head of the ticket and the nation in a conservative mood, Republicans believed that they could win back the presidency that they had lost four years earlier.

Reagan's Road to National Fame

Ronald Reagan rose to fame politically by giving a persuasive television address on behalf of Barry Goldwater in 1964. In 1966, he was elected governor of California by a huge margin and was reelected in 1970. Reagan had made two previous runs at the Republican presidential nomination—a brief attempt to halt Richard Nixon in 1968 and a nearly successful bid to wrest the nomination from Gerald Ford in 1976. By 1980, Reagan was certainly the best-known and most popular Republican in the nation.

Carter's Problems

Carter had more than Reagan to worry about. Despite his moderately liberal social policies, Carter's more conservative economic policies did not please the liberal wing of the Democratic Party. Liberals rallied behind Massachusetts senator **Edward Kennedy**, the younger brother of John and Robert. Kennedy soon realized that he had almost no chance to beat Carter, but he stubbornly remained in the campaign to force the president to pursue more liberal policies. This divisive candidacy hampered Carter's attempts to unify the party behind him.

Carter also faced a second liberal opponent. Liberal Republican **John Anderson** of Illinois, proclaiming that both Reagan and Carter were too conservative, announced that he would run as an independent third-party candidate. Anderson had no chance to win, of course, but he was more likely to draw votes from the moderately liberal Carter than from the staunchly conservative Reagan.

The Campaign

Conservative zeal alone was not enough to win a national election. The Republicans were banking on popular discontent with Carter and the Democrats to help them. The hostages in Iran were like a cancer eating at the Carter candidacy, reminding voters of Carter's foreign policy failures. Even more immediate was the state of the economy, mainly the dangerously high inflation rate. Reagan shrewdly perceived the public sentiment. In his closing statement during a televised debate with Carter only a week before the election, Reagan turned to the camera and asked the American people,

The Misery Index

Republican economists combined the unemployment rate with the inflation rate to create the "misery index." Whereas the index had been 2.9 percent in 1953, in June 1980 it was 21.98 percent.

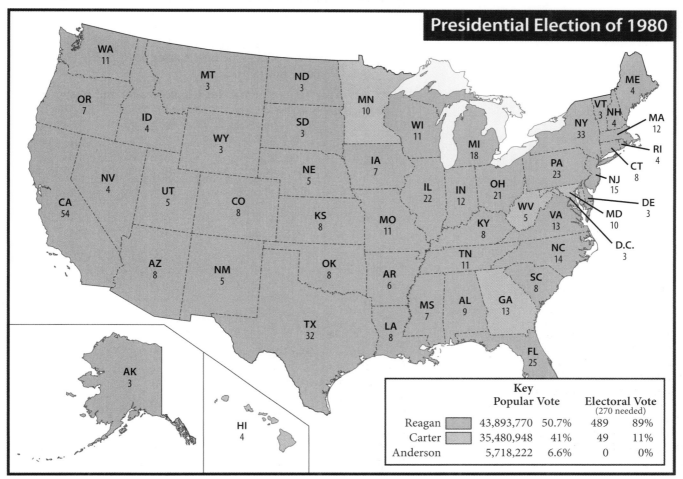

Ronald Reagan won the presidency by a landslide and restored confidence to America.

Are you better off than you were four years ago? Is it easier for you to go and buy things in the stores than it was four years ago? . . . Is America as respected throughout the world as it was? . . . I would like to lead that crusade to take government off the backs of the great people of this country and turn you loose again to do those things that I know you can do so well, because you did them and made this country great.

Until the last days of the campaign, the polls predicted a close race. It was not. On election day, Reagan won 50.7 percent of the popular vote to Carter's 41 percent and John Anderson's 6.6 percent. In the Electoral College, Reagan carried forty-four states for a massive 489–49 landslide victory. In addition, the Republicans picked up twelve seats in the Senate, capturing control of that body for the first time since Eisenhower's first term. The nation had decisively rejected not only Jimmy Carter but also his party. Now it was up to Ronald Reagan and the Republicans to demonstrate their ability to do a better job.

Section Quiz

1. What was the goal of the Right-to-Life movement?
2. Name the most important Charismatic and non-Charismatic political leaders of the Religious Right.
3. Who was the major third-party candidate of the 1980 presidential election? Why did he run?
4. What foreign policy issue hurt Carter most in the 1980 election? What domestic issue?
★ Why was Reagan such a charismatic leader and so successful with the people?

Chapter Review

Making Connections

1. Under the provisions of what amendment did Gerald Ford become vice president? Whom did he replace?

2. Why did attempts to make automobiles produce less pollution actually heighten the energy crisis?

3. What was the most controversial piece of pro-feminist legislation? Why did it not become law?

Developing History Skills

1. How can some extreme "rights movements," such as the homosexuals' gay rights movement, undermine genuine civil liberties?

Thinking Critically

1. Why did conservatives oppose the SALT II Treaty?

2. Some political observers in the late 1970s claimed that the presidency had grown too large for one man to handle. Why would they think so? Do you agree or disagree with their claim? Why?

Living as a Christian Citizen

1. Is political activity by Christians, such as that of the Religious Right, legitimate in light of the alleged separation of church and state? Why or why not?

People, Places, and Things to Remember

Watergate affair
Spiro Agnew
Gerald Ford
Nixon pardon
oil embargo
energy crisis
environmental movement
stagflation
trade deficit
women's liberation movement
Roe v. Wade
women's rights movement
feminists
Equal Rights Amendment
Ronald Reagan
Jimmy Carter
human rights
Panama Canal Treaty
Camp David Accords
SALT II Treaty
Mohammed Reza Pahlavi (Shah of Iran)
Ayatollah Ruhollah Khomeini
Iranian hostage crisis
New Right
Proposition 13
Religious Right
Charismatic movement
Pat Robertson
Jerry Falwell
Edward Kennedy
John Anderson

President Reagan and Soviet Premier Mikhail Gorbachev converse at the White House.

Resurgence (1981–1992)

I. The Reagan Revolution

II. The Bush Presidency

"It's morning again in America."

Ronald Reagan on the campaign trail in 1984

The bullet had stopped an inch from his heart. For the man and the times, it was one critical, providential inch. **Ronald Reagan**, looking up from the gurney into the worried faces of the physicians, smiled weakly and said, "Please tell me you're Republicans." Their faces brightened. "Mr. President, today we're all Republicans," they replied.

Reagan survived the March 1981 assassination attempt. His resilience and pluck symbolized much of the national spirit that reawakened during the succeeding decade.

The Reagan Magic

After a decade of Vietnam, Watergate, Iran, and national malaise, Ronald Reagan revived hope, restored pride, and put new polish on patriotism. During his years in office, Reagan was a kind of commander in chief of the American spirit, marshaling national emotion with a skill that few leaders have been able to master. When Reagan came to Washington, many critics dismissed him as a has-been, B-grade actor clearly out of his element in the rough-and-tumble national scene and the world of politics. But the critics underestimated both Reagan and the American people. Someone said that Reagan was "simply saturated in the American identity." His talents were not those of an administrator or of an economist; they were that unquantifiable quality called leadership. When Reagan left office in 1989, Americans were once again proud to be Americans, and they once again believed that America could—and would—achieve great things.

I. The Reagan Revolution

The Reagan years marked a clear shift in the nation's leadership, policies, and attitudes. Ronald Reagan projected an image of confident leadership, restoring public faith in the White House. Many Americans, tired of Carter's failures, welcomed the new president's strong presence and inspiring rhetoric.

Yet Reagan brought more than a polished image to the White House; he also brought new and substantive policy changes. As Reagan himself observed near the end of his tenure, "A revolution of ideas became a revolution of governance on January 20, 1981."

Reagan believed that with Communist threats from Central America to Central Asia, the United States had no choice but to maintain a firm grip on the reins of free-world leadership. He also believed that America's economic strength must be unleashed by breaking the shackles of big government and heavy taxes that hindered growth and opportunity. According to his ideal, Reagan wanted to restore and strengthen America's moral fiber by curbing government intrusion into the home, the church, and the school.

Those simple yet ambitious goals of strength and freedom answered a need that many Americans keenly felt in the wake of humiliations abroad and hardships at home. That those goals were never quite achieved and that Reagan's

Confusion reigns as police and Secret Service agents respond to the attempt on Reagan's life. A Secret Service agent has just shoved Reagan to safety inside the limousine, which is about to race to the hospital.

Reagan went directly to the people to sell his tax cuts.

rhetoric often fell short of reality did not diminish the revolution of spirit that America experienced at the dawn of its third century.

Reaganomics

First on Reagan's agenda was tackling the nation's economic woes. Frustration over the economic recession, with its double-digit inflation and high unemployment, had helped elect him, and Reagan determined to address the problem quickly. In his inaugural address, he declared an end to a "tax system which penalizes successful achievement and keeps us from maintaining full productivity." The days of big government spending sprees were also numbered, Reagan declared.

> For decades, we have piled deficit upon deficit, mortgaging our future and our children's future for the temporary convenience of the present. To continue this long trend is to guarantee tremendous social, cultural, political, and economic upheavals. . . . We must act today in order to preserve tomorrow. And let there be no misunderstanding—we are going to begin to act beginning today.

Reagan's prescription for America's inflation ills was **supply-side economics** (or **Reaganomics**, as it was called by his opponents). The supply-side approach seeks to lower inflated prices by enhancing productivity and increasing the supply of goods. Higher productivity and a larger supply of goods help lower prices and energize the economy by providing fuller employment. The supply-side way of increasing productivity fit nicely into Reagan's conservative, limited-government agenda: cut taxes so that citizens will have incentive to earn, save, and invest; and encourage economic expansion by reducing government regulations on business and by providing corporate tax breaks.

The Tax Axe

Central to Reagan's economic policy was tax cuts. Using his skills of persuasion, Reagan took his cause both to Congress and directly to the taxpayers. Congress, fearful of a popular backlash, mustered majorities in both houses to pass the **Economic Recovery Tax Act of 1981**. It cut income taxes by 25 percent over two and a half years, reduced maximum tax rates for upper incomes from 70 to 50 percent, and lowered business taxes.

Budget Battles

Another important part of Reagan's economic plan was budget cuts. In 1981 Congress approved budget cuts of $35 billion, reducing funding for some highway programs and education, welfare, and arts assistance. But critics who feared that the conservative Reagan would have a "take no prisoners" approach to the huge federal budget had little to fear. Ninety cents of every federal budget dollar went for programs that Congress considered untouchable, since cutting them would be politically damaging. It soon became clear that much of the budget was simply a collection of special-interest entitlements. As a result, Congress took no big budget bites; they only gnawed at the edges.

Despite promises of a "safety net" for the needy, the budget cuts were neither without effect on the poor nor without drawbacks for the economy as a whole. Budget restraints, for example, forced cutbacks in Aid to Families with Dependent Children (AFDC), stopping payment to those who had worked for only a four-month period. With more than one-fourth of all children in America living in single-parent homes, the effect was extensive. AFDC payments ended for four hundred thousand homes. Many single mothers, without job skills to bridge the gap from the welfare rolls to the work force, found it necessary to remain on welfare. The growing problems and inadequacies of the welfare system, however, often had more to do with the mounting social problems of drug addiction and illegitimacy than with the budget.

One budget area that did receive a boost by the Reagan administration was defense. The administration added $12 billion to defense programs in 1982, and the buildup continued through the end of the decade. Critics of the defense buildup, altering a famous remark of humorist Will Rogers, charged that President Reagan had never met a weapons system he did not like. In the post-Vietnam era of the 1970s, however, America's military had lost ground in both morale and materiel. Given Communist expansion in Asia, Africa, and Central America and the need to protect vital oil interests in the Middle East, Reagan continued throughout his term to push for superior military forces. (The results became clear during his successor's term.)

Deficit Debacle

Tax cuts, defense hikes, and particularly the unwillingness of Congress and the White House to make serious budget cuts produced a huge deficit problem, drastically increasing the national debt. At the end of the 1970s, the debt had been $834 billion. By 1990, the figure soared to $2.3 trillion. By then, interest payments alone on the debt reached more than $150 billion, effectively wiping out any ground gained by budget cuts. The huge debt presented a continuing threat to America's strength.

By late 1985, with public outcries over dozen-digit deficits, Congress attempted self-discipline by passing the **Gramm-Rudman Act**. The law, largely the work of Senator Phil Gramm of Texas, imposed automatic deficit reduction through across-the-board spending cuts if Congress would not curb the budget on its own. In addition, it mandated a balanced budget by 1991. The president and Congress were not the only ones lacking the will to deal with the debt, however. Many Americans representing many interests supported the *idea* of budget cuts as long as *someone else's* budget was cut. The idea of government services on an easy credit plan soon sank in a sea of red ink.

Recession and Recovery

During the 1980 campaign, while the country was experiencing a deep recession, Carter had quibbled with candidate Reagan over the challenger's assertion that the country was in an actual depression. Reagan responded, "I'm talking in human terms and he is hiding behind a dictionary. If he wants a definition, I'll give him one. A recession is when your neighbor loses his job. A depression is when you lose yours. A recovery is when Jimmy Carter loses his."

Politics 101: Defining Budget "Cuts"

Many people mistakenly think that when politicians talk of budget "cuts" they mean spending *less* money. That is seldom the case. What they actually mean by a "cut" is *a reduction in the amount of increase* in spending. For example, if the budget for a program is $100 billion in fiscal year (FY) 2014 and the proposed budget for that program in FY 2015 is $125 billion, a budget "cut" of $5 billion does not mean that the budget will be $95 billion but that it will be $120 billion. Politicians almost never explain this fact because it is much more popular for them to give the impression that they are attacking wasteful spending. In reality, they are continuing to increase it. This is especially troublesome when the programs are entitlements.

Reagan had a personal charm that made even his political enemies, such as Speaker of the House Tip O'Neill, tend to move in his direction on legislation.

Weakness of Gramm-Rudman

As sweeping as the Gramm-Rudman Act seemed, it was weakened when Congress exempted many programs from being subject to the measure. Spending continued out of control.

Candidate Reagan's punch line drew a good laugh in 1980, but by 1982 President Reagan found that a recession was no laughing matter. That year, the economy slumped along with the president's approval rating, and unemployment grew to more than 10 percent. The president's response was mixed. Abandoning his antitax policies, Reagan pushed through a huge tax increase aimed mainly at business, hoping to calm jitters over the deficit. At the same time, Reagan urged Americans to "stay the course" while the Reaganomics tax cuts and pro-business policies turned the employment problem around.

By 1983 America's economy experienced an upturn. The prosperity that followed—for which Reagan could take only partial credit, but credit nonetheless—began, as one economist observed, "the longest and strongest noninflationary expansion in our history." The result was a boom time of lower unemployment, lower interest rates, and lower oil prices. Nineteen million new jobs were created during the 1980s, and unemployment dropped to below 5 percent. With some regional unemployment figures down to 2 percent, some areas of the country actually had a *labor* shortage rather than a job shortage. The housing market, an important indication of American economic strength, mushroomed. Twenty percent of all homes standing in 1990 were built during the 1980s. In addition, per capita income during Reagan's term grew by an unprecedented 17 percent. Reminiscent of the prosperity of an earlier decade, the Reagan years could well be called the "Roaring 80s."

Section Quiz

1. In addition to cutting taxes for all citizens, what two actions did supply-side economics propose for business in order to promote economic expansion?

2. What element of "Reaganomics" was central to Reagan's economic policies?

3. Which of the two parts of Reagan's program for economic recovery (tax cuts or budget cuts) was less successful?

4. What three factors helped to dramatically increase the budget deficit in the 1980s?

★ Why do voters eagerly vote for someone who pledges to cut wasteful government spending but then, after that candidate wins, oppose him when he tries to keep his promise?

Reagan Doctrine

America faced challenges abroad and at home. For years, American foreign policy had been paralyzed by post-Vietnam trauma. But when Soviet troops invaded Afghanistan and Communists renewed exporting revolution around the world, the debate over containment resurfaced. From the beginning, Reagan demonstrated his determination to confront such aggression. During his first month in office, Reagan characterized the Communist leaders as those who "reserved unto themselves the right to commit any crime, to lie, to cheat" and were still bent on "world domination." Critics groaned that Reagan's harsh words were putting the Cold War into a deep freeze.

In keeping with America's tough stance toward the Soviets, one of the key aspects of Reagan's foreign policy was the **Reagan**

The "Evil Empire"

Reagan's characterization of the Soviet Union as an "evil empire" was rooted in facts. The Soviets invaded Afghanistan. They shot down a Korean airliner in September 1983 (killing all 269 passengers, including conservative Georgia congressman Larry McDonald). And in 1985, an American army major, Arthur Nicholson, was murdered in Communist East Germany.

Doctrine, which pledged America's support to insurgent groups battling Communist governments in the third world. As a result, military and economic aid flowed to anti-Communist fighters on three continents, pressuring both regional Communists and their backers in Moscow. The Reagan Doctrine also sparked battles on the home front as Congress struggled with the White House over the new direction in foreign policy.

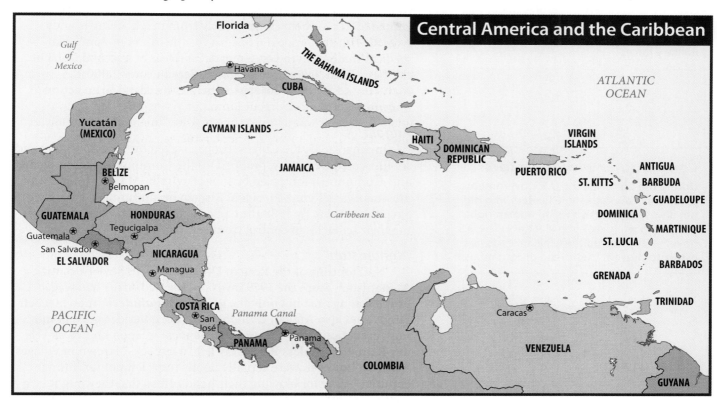

Central America and the Caribbean

Central America

Early in 1981, fighting between Communist rebels and the democratic government of El Salvador flared. True to his doctrine, Reagan responded to the aggression of the Soviet- and Cuban-backed guerrillas by supplying arms, military advisors, and economic aid to the beleaguered Salvadoran government under President José Napoleon Duarte.

American assistance in propping up democracy in El Salvador led to further U.S. involvement in Central America when intelligence revealed that the Salvadoran insurgents were being supplied with arms by the Communist Sandinista government of neighboring Nicaragua. Under the direction of the Central Intelligence Agency (CIA), groups of anti-Sandinista guerrillas known as **Contras** were organized.

Reagan's support for anti-Communist forces in Nicaragua ignited fierce debates in Congress. Critics warned that reviving "big-stick" policies would renew anti-Americanism throughout the region. They urged compromising with the Sandinistas and increasing economic aid to the region. Reagan, however, believed that the Sandinistas posed a threat to not only the democratic elements within Nicaragua but also to the security of all of Central America. With the Soviets supporting Nicaragua's Communist government, particularly through its satellite state of Cuba, U.S. support of the Contras also represented a vital test of American commitment to the

Who Were the Contras?

Many of the Contra fighters had been ousted from power when the Communists seized control of the government in 1979. Others came from groups actively repressed by the Sandinistas, such as the fiercely independent Miskito Indians of northeastern Nicaragua.

Operation Urgent Fury

Although Operation Urgent Fury was a relatively small military operation, Grenada had huge symbolic importance. It sent a clear signal of American resolve to Communist leaders and ended much of the post-Vietnam paranoia over the use of American military force.

Cooperating with Dictators

During the Cold War, the U.S. government made alliances with some leaders who did not always share its views on human rights or the importance of free elections. The U.S. government viewed these alliances as necessary to prevent the spread of communism.

Background of the Lebanon Problem

The Lebanese war was among the Druse (DROOZ), Sunnis, Shiites, Syrians, Yasir Arafat's Palestine Liberation Organization (PLO), and Arab Christians. In June 1982 Israel sent troops into Lebanon to destroy PLO terrorists on its northern border. These troops forced the PLO into Beirut, where they inflicted heavy shelling on the terrorists. Israel's presence, though, complicated an already complex situation.

Monroe Doctrine. Reagan, however, would soon have an opportunity to deal Cuban dictator Fidel Castro a blow.

Grenada, a tiny island in the Caribbean, was being transformed into a fueling station for Cuban troops sailing for Africa and Soviet advisors heading for Nicaragua. In October 1983 the Communist government of Grenada under Maurice Bishop was overthrown by an even more radical Communist faction led by General Hudson Austin. Bishop was murdered, and calls to the United States for help came quickly from neighboring islands. Armed with that appeal, concern for the safety of American medical students living on Grenada, and fear of a second Cuba in the Caribbean, President Reagan ordered nearly 2,000 U.S. Marines and airborne troops to liberate the island in an action known as Operation Urgent Fury.

Angola

In Angola, 35,000 Cuban troops, backed by Soviet advisors and sophisticated weaponry, propped up the Communist regime against anti-Communist forces led by Jonas Savimbi. At the urging of Congressman Jack Kemp, President Reagan began funneling supplies to Savimbi in 1986. By 1988 the Cubans and Soviets began withdrawing their tentacles of control from central Africa.

Afghanistan

The frontline of the Reagan Doctrine was in Soviet-occupied Afghanistan. Since the 1979 invasion, the Red Army had waged a brutal war against not only the guerilla *mujahideen* (moo JAH heh DEEN) but also Afghan civilians of all ages. Besides mass bombings, executions, and the use of a chemical weapon known as Yellow Rain, the ruthless Red Army left "toy trucks" strewn in villages. The toys, however, were actually booby traps left not for killing children—only for blowing their hands off so that they might be a continuing burden on a society already suffering under Soviet oppression.

Reagan supplied military advisors and state-of-the-art weapons, including surface-to-air Stinger missiles, to the mujahideen insurgents. American support, combined with determined rebel resistance, dealt a stunning blow to Moscow's troops. After ten years of fighting, the Soviet army withdrew in the spring of 1989, leaving Afghanistan bloodied and battered. The humiliating Soviet defeat was the first in a generation, and it marked a great triumph for the Reagan Doctrine.

Sadly, the United States did not commit resources to rebuild Afghanistan and form strong alliances in this region following the defeat of the Soviets. Instead, radical elements filled the power vacuum. Future U.S. administrations would expend immense human and financial resources to overcome this rise of Muslim radicalism in Afghanistan.

Terrorism

In contrast to Reagan's successes in Afghanistan, terrorism dogged his administration and produced many setbacks, mainly in Lebanon, which had been in a state of war since the 1970s. Eventually, Reagan ordered American troops into Lebanon to join a multinational "peacekeeping" force to oversee the withdrawal of the PLO from Lebanon. There was, however, little peace to keep; fighting continued to boil over into the streets of Beirut. The Arab factions viewed U.S. soldiers not as peacekeepers but as allies of Israel and thus targets. After repeated Arab attacks on American positions, the U.S. Navy began shelling terrorist bases. On October 23, 1983, a terrorist driving a bomb-laden truck crashed through barricades and into the U.S. Marines barracks at Beirut airport, killing 241 Americans. The ill-defined U.S. peacekeeping mission soon ended with troops returning to offshore warships and leaving battered Beirut to its own bloody fate.

Unfortunately, not all Americans escaped the terror of Lebanon. Several U.S. citizens, some working in Beirut as teachers and journalists, were taken hostage during the 1980s. Efforts by the Reagan administration to gain their release were largely futile. The American public watched in helpless anger.

U.S. Marines clear rubble and remove victims of the bombing of the barracks in Beirut.

Reagan had somewhat more success against terrorism outside the Middle East. In 1985 Arab terrorists hijacked the Italian cruise ship *Achille Lauro*; brutally murdered a wheelchair-bound American, Leon Klinghoffer; and dumped his body overboard. The terrorists returned to safety in Egypt in high spirits, but when they flew to Tunis the happy hijackers themselves were hijacked. In a skillful operation engineered by Lt. Col. Oliver North, the Egyptian airliner was forced by U.S. fighter planes to land at the American air base in Sicily. The jailed terrorists soon had a visitor; Klinghoffer's widow stopped by to identify her husband's murderers and to spit in their faces. Elsewhere in the Mediterranean, Libya's ruler Muammar al-Qaddafi ordered terrorist acts against Americans in 1986. Reagan answered with a successful surprise air strike on Tripoli.

Four More Years

Forty-Nine-State Landslide

In 1984 Democrats renewed some of their old themes against Ronald Reagan: the president's trigger-happy foreign policy, as the Democrats characterized it, was an embarrassment in the international community; and his social policies isolated the poor, ignored the working classes, and insulted women. Even though Reagan had appointed the first woman Supreme Court justice, Sandra Day O'Connor, in 1981 and had named a number of women to important government posts, feminists in the Democratic Party charged that he had ignored the female half of the electorate.

Walter Mondale, former vice president under Jimmy Carter, outlasted all other candidates in the Democratic field to win the nomination. Mondale quickly came under criticism that he was controlled by liberal special-interest groups such as labor unions and feminists. The charges seemed confirmed when Mondale chose New York congresswoman **Geraldine Ferraro** as his running mate. Although Ferraro was the first female vice-presidential candidate for a major party, her narrow, liberal record provided no counterbalance to Mondale's liberal position. On election day, Reagan won by one of the greatest landslides in history, losing only Mondale's home state of Minnesota and the District of Columbia.

Democrats Mondale and Ferraro lost to Reagan in a landslide in 1984.

Reagan's second term was plagued by few of the domestic economic issues that confronted his first term. Despite mounting deficits, the continuing slide in oil prices helped keep the economy strong. Much of the focus of Reagan's second term was on foreign policy: improving relations with the Soviet Union and, after 1986, dealing with the political fallout from the Iran-Contra affair.

Cold War Thaw

The Soviet Union went through a succession of dictators during the Reagan years as death took its toll on the old guard. Leonid Brezhnev died in 1982; his successor, Yuri Andropov, died in 1984; and Andropov's successor, Konstantin Chernenko, died in 1985. But a younger **Mikhail Gorbachev** (mik-HEL GOR-buh-CHOF) took the Kremlin reins in 1985, and he presented a new, polished style in contrast to that of his recent predecessors.

When Gorbachev came to power, the Russian economy was on the verge of collapse and the Red Army was stuck in the quagmire of Afghanistan. In confronting those problems, throughout the late 1980s Gorbachev called for *perestroika* (PEHR ih STROY kuh), or "restructuring," of the stagnant Communist economy, shifting to more free-market policies and private ownership. To make the transition to the Western economic mainstream, Gorbachev urged *glasnost* (GLASS nost), or "openness," in Soviet society.

Gorbachev spoke of new ideas, but he clung to old, failed ideas. Perestroika turned out to be a series of half-measures that raised Soviet expectations rather than the standard of living. Yet in contrast to the slow progress of perestroika, glasnost was perhaps *too* successful from Gorbachev's point of view. Giving the Russian people a taste of freedom only awakened their thirst for more; nationalism replaced Marxism. The diverse ethnic groups of the Soviet Empire, bound together by only military force and a failed Marxist philosophy, called for greater freedom from Kremlin control. Gorbachev and the Red Army responded to those stirrings of independence and nationalism with tear gas and bullets. Glasnost was even more successful on the fringes of the iron curtain as, one by one, Central European countries ousted their Communist governments in 1989, and Germany—divided since World War II—reunited in 1990.

During his second term, Ronald Reagan made a dramatic shift in Soviet relations. In his last three years in office, Reagan met with Gorbachev five times to improve diplomatic ties. The summit meetings between the two leaders were **Strategic Arms Reduction Talks (START)** aimed primarily at reaching an agreement to halve the size of long-range nuclear arsenals, rather than simply slow their growth as earlier agreements had done. Although the Soviets had consistently cheated on earlier arms agreements, Reagan placed a newfound faith in the power of treaties to correct Soviet behavior.

At the Washington Summit in 1987, Reagan and Gorbachev signed the **Intermediate Nuclear Forces (INF) Treaty**, which eliminated most medium-range missiles from Europe. Events in Eastern Europe, though, soon lessened the importance of the INF Treaty. Nonetheless, with both leaders eager to show progress, the superpowers' agreement was heralded as a symbol of friendlier relations.

While Reagan worked the summit circuit, he also kept pressure on the Soviets in two areas: supplying weapons to anti-Communist

Reagan's Dilemma

When a reporter criticized Reagan for not making progress with the Soviet leaders, Reagan quipped in frustration, "Well, they keep dying on me!"

The Start of Something Big

Gorbachev believed that loosening some shackles of Communist control and allowing greater freedom and self-expression would help motivate the masses to move from a passive to a more active economic role. The result was more than he bargained for.

Vice President Bush, President Reagan, and Soviet Premier Gorbachev meet in New York City, marking a thaw in the Cold War.

Commonsense Treaty Making

Having called the Soviet Union an "evil empire," Reagan was not about to make treaties with it under the naive assumption that it would keep its word on its own initiative. Rather, he based his treaty making on the principle of "trust—but verify." His means of working for peace was not unilateral disarmament but "peace through strength."

forces in Asia and Africa and developing the **Strategic Defense Initiative (SDI)**. First announced by Reagan in 1983, SDI—or "Star Wars," as opponents scornfully called it—was a proposed space-based defense shield of satellites, missiles, and lasers designed to safeguard the country from nuclear attack. Although SDI was many years, many billions of dollars, and many technological hurdles away from reality, the program seriously affected the nuclear arms equation. Gorbachev knew that SDI would force the Soviet Union to develop its own defense shield—a long and costly endeavor. With the Soviet economy on the verge of collapse, SDI development strengthened Reagan's bargaining position, and, by the early 1990s, more mundane problems such as empty store shelves would further weaken Gorbachev's position.

Iran-Contra

On election day 1986, Reagan received two strikes against his second-term success. First, he lost his Republican majority in the Senate. The Republican Senate had been a key factor in getting Reagan's programs through Congress during his first term. With Democrats in firm control of both houses of Congress, Democrats could now take more control over domestic and foreign policymaking. And they soon got the opportunity to do just that.

The second strike came from an underground newspaper in faraway Beirut that reported that the Reagan administration had traded arms to Iran in exchange for the release of American hostages in Lebanon. As the story unfolded, it revealed that members of the White House National Security Council (NSC)—principally NSC chief John Poindexter, his aide U.S. Marine Lt. Col. Oliver North, and CIA director William Casey—had set up secret arms sales to Iran. At the time, Iran was locked in a costly war with neighboring Iraq and needed missiles and military spare parts. Because of strategic interests in Iran, the covert operation was aimed at cultivating a moderate successor to the aging Ayatollah Khomeini. In addition, it was hoped that the arms deal would encourage Iran to help gain the release of American hostages in Lebanon who were held by terrorists loyal to Khomeini.

Investigations into what happened to the money from the arms sales to Iran thickened the plot. The money, funneled through Swiss banks, was used to supply the Nicaraguan Contras battling the Communist Sandinistas, giving the whole matter the name **Iran-Contra affair**.

The support to the Contras came at a time when Congress, under the provisions of a law known as the Boland Amendment, had cut off military aid to the Contras. The Reagan White House was already embarrassed over the disclosures of the Iranian arms sales, essentially an attempt to pay ransom to kidnappers, contrary to long-stated policy. The administration faced a Democrat-controlled Congress that was eager to pin criminal charges on the president's men for supplying funds to the Contras. Reagan initially distanced himself from his subordinates, but the whole matter raised questions about Reagan's management of the White House. Then on March 4, 1987, in a speech to the nation, the President took responsibility for the actions of those who served in his administration. Reagan also repudiated the methods used to accomplish what many had viewed as laudable goals of freeing hostages in Iran and supporting anti-Communist forces in Nicaragua.

Reagan's Challenge to Gorbachev

Anticipating what could be, Reagan visited Berlin and delivered a speech in which he looked across the Berlin Wall and issued a public challenge to Gorbachev: "General Secretary Gorbachev, if you seek peace, if you seek prosperity for the Soviet Union and Eastern Europe, if you seek liberalization: Come here to this gate! Mr. Gorbachev, open this gate! Mr. Gorbachev, tear down this wall!" This would soon happen, although Gorbachev didn't welcome it.

The "Teflon President"

During the Iran-Contra controversy, Reagan became known as the "Teflon president" because no charges or accusations of wrongdoing would stick to him.

Bush and Quayle celebrate their nomination at the 1988 Republican National Convention.

Throughout 1987, investigations and congressional hearings continued to bring to light details of the Iran-Contra affair. The White House insisted that the Boland Amendment did not apply to the NSC; congressional investigators disagreed. Eventually, North and Poindexter were tried and convicted on lesser criminal charges. When the dust of dispute settled, however, North's indictments were overturned on a technicality in 1990.

One More for the Gipper

Despite the shadow of Iran-Contra over Reagan's last two years in office, the president remained strong and popular. As the election of 1988 approached, Democrats and Republicans alike were jockeying for a chance at Reagan's job.

Several Republicans claimed the right to Reagan's mantle, from **Jack Kemp**, one of the architects of Reaganomics, to newcomer Pat Robertson of the Religious Right. The nominee who emerged, however, was Reagan's vice president, **George H. W. Bush**. Having been in the shadow of a strong president for nearly eight years, Bush struggled to establish his own identity. Also surviving a crowded field of contenders, Governor **Michael Dukakis** of Massachusetts emerged to win the Democratic nomination. The Democrats held a euphoric convention in Atlanta buoyed by polls that showed Dukakis with a substantial lead over Bush.

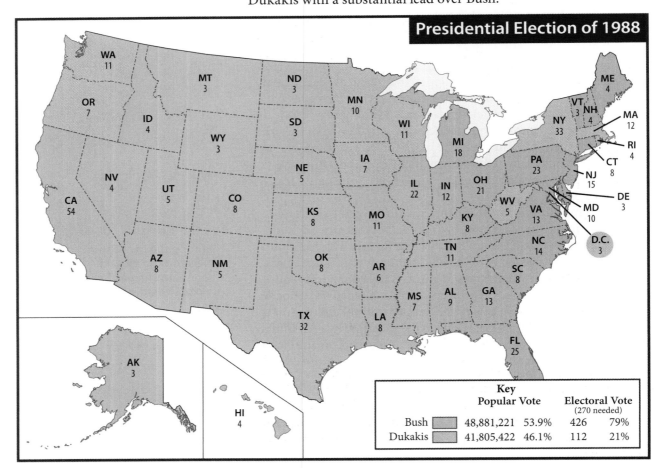

Presidential Election of 1988

	Key			
	Popular Vote		**Electoral Vote** (270 needed)	
Bush	48,881,221	53.9%	426	79%
Dukakis	41,805,422	46.1%	112	21%

Republicans gathered in New Orleans for their national convention, where they gave a last hail to their chief. Reagan, in an emotional farewell to his party faithful, urged them again to "go out there and win one for the Gipper." After a shaky start, Bush rallied support largely under the mantle of the Gipper's popularity and positions: strength at home and abroad and no new taxes. The election provided a decisive win for Bush and his running mate **Dan Quayle**. Bush's victory was in many ways a final vote of approval of Reagan. Reagan's handpicked understudy won forty states, becoming the first vice president since Martin Van Buren in 1836 to be elected president from the second spot.

> ### "The Gipper"
> The nickname "The Gipper" recalled a character and a familiar line from an old movie in which Reagan played George Gipp of Notre Dame, a dying football hero whose name became a rallying cry when his team was down. Reagan—as Gipp—told his boys from his hospital bed, "Just go out there and win one for the Gipper." In the 1988 election opinion polls, the Republican team was down, and they resurrected the saying: "Win one for the Gipper"—Reagan.

Section Quiz

1. What Central Asian country's resistance to a ten-year Soviet occupation marked a great triumph for the Reagan Doctrine?

2. What Caribbean nation was liberated by American forces in 1983, symbolizing America's willingness to use military force in the post-Vietnam era?

3. Terrorism in what Middle Eastern nation gave the Reagan administration its greatest setbacks in foreign policy?

4. Who was the first female Supreme Court justice?

5. What was the official name for the "Star Wars" project?

✶ Explain the Reagan Doctrine and describe when that doctrine was first tested and where it led next.

II. The Bush Presidency

Unfortunately for Bush, he also followed in the footsteps of Van Buren in other ways. After eight years under a popular boss, Bush inherited problems of economic decline and foreign challenge that demanded immediate attention. He proved astonishingly successful in his greatest foreign policy challenge, but domestic difficulties doomed his presidency.

Triumph Abroad

The Bush administration saw the final collapse of the iron curtain and the end of the Cold War. By the time Bush left office, the Soviet Union no longer existed, and Eastern Europe was free of Communist domination. Despite the decline of communism, however, tyranny did not vanish. The United States soon faced a new challenge in an old hot spot, the Middle East.

Confrontation

On August 2, 1990, Iraq, led by dictator Saddam Hussein (sah-DAHM hoo-SANE), launched a military blitzkrieg that overwhelmed its tiny neighbor Kuwait. With Kuwait crushed beneath its war machine, Iraq stood poised for potential further conquest as Hussein massed his forces on the border of Saudi Arabia. Opposing this naked aggression and fearing that much of the world's oil supply was about to fall under the control of Hussein, Bush vowed, "This shall not stand." Working through the Security Council of the United Nations, the United States coordinated a defensive operation. Code-named **Operation Desert Shield**, the plan deployed allied forces (chiefly American) in Saudi Arabia to forestall further Iraqi aggression.

Reagan on the Fall of Communism

Ronald Reagan gave a speech on May 18, 1990, in which he described the collapse of communism and the moral high ground that America occupies in the struggle between free and totalitarian states.

Let me tell you the basis of my optimism for our future. What has made the United States great is that ours has been an empire of ideals. The ideals of freedom, democracy, and a belief in the remarkable potential of the individual. Power isn't simply wealth or troops. Power is also spirit and ideas. And these we have in abundance.

The attitude of wanting to be the biggest and to go the farthest and to get there first and to do the most good when we arrived is part of our national character. Americans have always been larger than life. We wanted to establish the best government on Earth. We wanted to put a man on the moon. This is the spirit we set loose. This is the passion that invented revolutionary technologies and a culture young people everywhere envy.

And this is the attitude that has defeated communism. At some dark, lonely moment during the last decade, a terrible realization set in upon the leaders of the Soviet Union. They realized that their system could not take them where the United States and the rest of the free world was going.

The West's economics and technologies were a powerful booster blasting us into orbits the Communist world could not hope to reach. Our communications technology sailed over the barbed wire and concrete walls, letting their citizens know what democracy could offer, what free markets could provide. Our computer technology left them bewildered and behind, paper societies in an electronic age. . . .

Communist dominoes are falling all over the world. We must continue to give Communist dominoes a good push whenever and wherever we can. There are still those that must fall—China, North Korea, North Vietnam, North Yemen, and of course, Cuba. Cuba is next in democracy's sweep. And let me say directly to Fidel Castro—like Honecker in East Germany, like Ceausescu in Romania, like Noriega in Panama, like all the other has-been dictators of despair, you cannot fight democracy's destiny. Fidel, you're finished! . . .

We should not be timid in our embrace of democracy. We should be as bold and brash in our democratic ideals as ever in our history. The Golden Age of Freedom is near because America has remained true to her ideals. This is not the time to let our support for democracy wane.

Children rest on a fallen statue of Stalin in Monument Park, Moscow.

Storm in the Desert

The United Nations overwhelmingly passed a resolution authorizing the use of military force to push the Iraqis out of Kuwait if they did not withdraw voluntarily by January 15, 1991. It did not, however, authorize the removal of Hussein from power or the invasion of Iraq itself. The allies (the United States, Kuwait, Saudi Arabia, Egypt, Great Britain, France, and several other nations) gathered a force of 700,000 in Saudi Arabia. Before launching a military attack, the allies exhausted every possible diplomatic effort to get the Iraqis to withdraw. Finally, on January 12, 1991, Congress voted to authorize Bush to use force if necessary to get Iraq out of Kuwait. America had declared war for the first time since World War II.

The January deadline became a line in the sand as the Iraqi forces defiantly dug in. On January 16, Bush ordered a massive military assault on Iraqi military targets. Code-named **Operation Desert Storm**, the liberation of Kuwait began. The allied commander,

When the Walls Came Tumbling Down

Although Reagan had issued a challenge to Gorbachev, no Joshua signaled for the walls of communism to come tumbling down. But fall they did in Europe in a few remarkable months in 1989. More than forty years of Soviet domination came to an end as, one by one, the iron curtain countries cast off communism and opened their borders to Western influence. The amazing developments that year not only captured the attention of sympathetic Americans but also presented the United States with new foreign policy questions to be answered in the decades to come. The following simplified chronicle recounts some of the many startling events of those memorable days.

April 18—Poland legalized the Solidarity union and opened the way for the first free elections in Poland in forty years.

May 2—Hungarians began to tear down the fences along their Austrian border.

June 4—Solidarity candidates won stunning victories over Communists in Poland's parliamentary elections.

August 25—Poland's new non-Communist government took power.

September 10—Hungary opened its western borders. Many East Germans and Romanians began to use Hungary as an escape route to the West.

October 11—Hungary's Communist Party abandoned communism and changed its name to compete better in free elections.

October 18—East German Communist leader Erich Honecker resigned under pressure, later to be arrested and charged with criminal acts.

October 24—Hungary declared itself an independent republic.

October 25—Soviet leader Gorbachev told the West that his nation would no longer use force to keep the governments of Eastern Europe under Communist control, thereby opening the way for greater change in the region.

November 9—East Germany opened its borders. The Berlin Wall was no longer a barrier for East Germans as the gates swung open. The Wall, the symbol of Cold War division, began to come down three days later, and East Germany and West Germany were on the road to reunification.

November 24—The Communist politburo in Czechoslovakia resigned, leaving the nation to hold free elections. Bulgaria's Communist leader was ousted, and thousands of demonstrators in Sofia chanted for democracy and free elections.

December 22—A popular uprising led to the capture, trial, and execution of Romania's oppressive Communist dictator, Nicolae Ceausescu, and his wife. The once-solid walls of Communist control had fallen in the last of the Soviet-bloc nations of Eastern Europe.

American general Norman Schwarzkopf, told his forces, "Now you must be the thunder and lightning of Desert Storm."

The war began with more than five weeks of massive, around-the-clock bombing and air strikes on military targets in Iraq and Kuwait. Allied cruise missiles, bombers, and fighters, including the new Stealth fighters, pounded enemy installations. Enjoying almost complete air superiority, the U.S.-led forces destroyed much of Iraq's military capability—communications networks, airfields, bridges, roads, chemical-weapons plants, and missile launch sites. Then the attacks targeted Iraq's ground forces, demolishing tanks and artillery and relentlessly pounding Hussein's entrenched legions.

The 100-Hour War

The second stage of the war was a ground attack on the Iraqis. On February 24, a coalition of American, Arab, and British troops assaulted enemy positions in southern Kuwait, pinning down the Iraqis, who thought this attack was the main thrust. But while the attack was raging, American and British forces, supported by French units, moved into southern Iraq west of Kuwait. With amazing speed, armored and infantry forces flanked the Iraqi lines, encircling and entrapping the main Iraqi force in Kuwait and southern Iraq. Dispirited by the weeks of bombing

Allied bombs rain down on Baghdad during the air phase of the Gulf War.

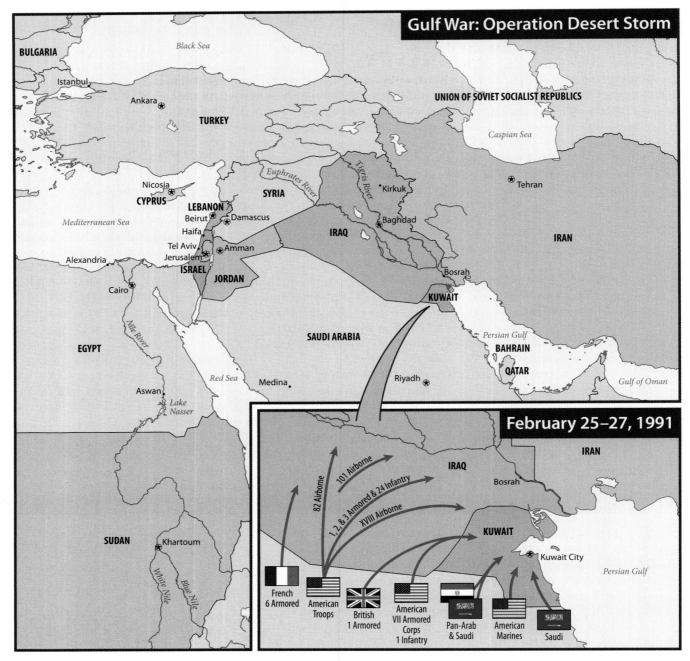

Gulf War: Operation Desert Storm

February 25–27, 1991

and virtually surrounded, thousands of Iraqi soldiers deserted and surrendered to the coalition army. Some Iraqi units fought fiercely but, with lines of communication severed, ineffectively. The allies destroyed them piecemeal. On February 27—just one hundred hours after the ground war began—Bush addressed a television audience:

> Kuwait is liberated. Iraq's army is defeated. Our military objectives are met. . . . No one country can claim this victory as its own. It was not only a victory for Kuwait, but a victory for all the coalition partners. This is a victory for the United Nations, for all mankind, for the rule of law, and for what is right.

Aftermath

The **Gulf War** was the most intensive American military effort since World War II. Allied planes flew more than 100,000 missions during the six-week war, losing fewer than 50 aircraft. The American-led coalition wrecked nearly 4,000 enemy tanks and captured more than 50,000 prisoners as it destroyed the effectiveness of an enemy force numbering more than 500,000 soldiers.

Long-term, however, the results were not so positive. Although defeated, Saddam Hussein still ruled Iraq and threatened the stability of the Middle East. He resisted all efforts by UN officials to inspect his military sites and defied an embargo the victors imposed on him. Among the allies, differences forgotten in war were soon remembered in peace. Trouble continued to simmer in the Middle East long after Desert Storm had blown over. The presence of U.S. troops in Saudi Arabia also fueled Islamic terrorism. For George Bush personally, great military victory was a prelude to bitter political defeat.

Problems at Home

Bush's experience was different on the home front. One sign of economic trouble was the failure of a number of the nation's savings and loan (S&L) banks. Unsound investments and declining oil prices drove several of the S&Ls into bankruptcy. Because government guarantees underwrote the deposits in the banks, the government spent some $300 billion ($3,000 per adult taxpayer) to cover the debts of the defaulting banks. Voters and federal prosecutors wanted to know why so many troubled S&Ls were allowed to stay afloat for so long. Some people suspected that political favors, more than financial soundness, kept the S&Ls open.

President Bush lost some public support by first opposing and then finally signing the **Americans with Disabilities Act**. This legislation prohibited job discrimination based on disabilities. It also required local governments and businesses to improve and alter their accommodations (e.g., provide special parking places for the disabled and install ramps for wheelchairs) for the disabled. When Bush opposed the legislation as an intrusion by the federal government on local governments and private citizens, the bill's supporters labeled him as uncompassionate. When he finally gave in and signed the bill, he angered those who opposed the new costs and invited a potential flood of lawsuits (which did not materialize).

A War of Precision

Allied forces had lost fewer than 200 men and women in the Gulf War. Because of the technological advances in weaponry, military and civilian casualties and "collateral damage" were less than in any other war on that scale. The United States used precision-guided missiles and "smart bombs" that pinpointed targets to within a few feet. Numerous videos released by the Defense Department show pilots placing such camera-carrying bombs right into air ducts of targeted military installations. General Schwarzkopf said, "The loss of one human life is intolerable to any of us who are in the military. But . . . casualties of that order of magnitude, considering the job that's been done and the number of forces that are involved, is almost miraculous."

Looking Into the S&L Crisis

Investigators in several states delved into the murky transactions behind the S&Ls. Among those investigated in the scandals was the then little-known governor of Arkansas, future president Bill Clinton.

The Twenty-seventh Amendment

The Bush administration saw the adoption of a new amendment to the Constitution—one drafted by James Madison more than two hundred years before! When he originally proposed the Bill of Rights, Madison offered twelve amendments, not just the ten that we are familiar with today. One of the two that were not adopted by the states reads, "No law, varying the compensation for the services of the Senators and Representatives, shall take effect, until an election of Representatives shall have intervened." Because it was not adopted along with the other ten, the proposed amendment remained in legal limbo. Only six states had ratified it by 1792. Ohio joined them by ratifying it in 1873.

The old amendment gained new life in the 1980s. Taxpayers were outraged when Congress tried to vote itself pay raises, even when the national economy was in a downturn. In 1989, Congress voted itself not only a hefty pay raise but also automatic adjustments for inflation. The resulting furor gave a fresh push to the old Madison amendment. On May 7, 1992, Michigan became the thirty-eighth state to ratify the amendment. Now when Congress passes pay raises, they do not take effect until after the next election, giving voters a chance to register their opinion with their ballots for or against sitting senators and representatives.

Probably the most damaging mistake George Bush made, however, was breaking a campaign promise. During the 1988 presidential election campaign, he had undercut the Democrats by declaring, "The Congress will push me to raise taxes, and I'll say no, and they'll push, and I'll say no, and they'll push again, and I'll say to them, 'Read my lips, no new taxes.'" Americans took him at his word and elected him. But budget deficits and pressure from Democrats in Congress made him rethink his vow. Persuaded by Democrats in Congress, the president agreed to a budget deal that sought to tame the federal deficit by increasing taxes. Although both the president and Congress worked on the legislation, Bush took the blame for the tax hike. Disappointed voters did not forget; when the election rolled around, they made him pay for breaking his vow.

The 1992 Election

In the glow of the triumph immediately following the Gulf War, George Bush looked unbeatable as he prepared to run for reelection. His approval rating was 87 percent. As a result, major Democratic candidates hesitated to enter the presidential race and endure what looked to be certain failure. Their hesitancy opened the door for a political unknown to capture the nomination.

Bill Clinton, the governor of Arkansas, surprised the experts by winning the Democratic nomination. A shrewd politician with a strong popular appeal, Clinton sidestepped and deflected charges concerning his past behavior. First his Democratic opponents and then the Republicans leveled charges concerning Clinton's alleged sexual immorality, marijuana use, draft dodging during

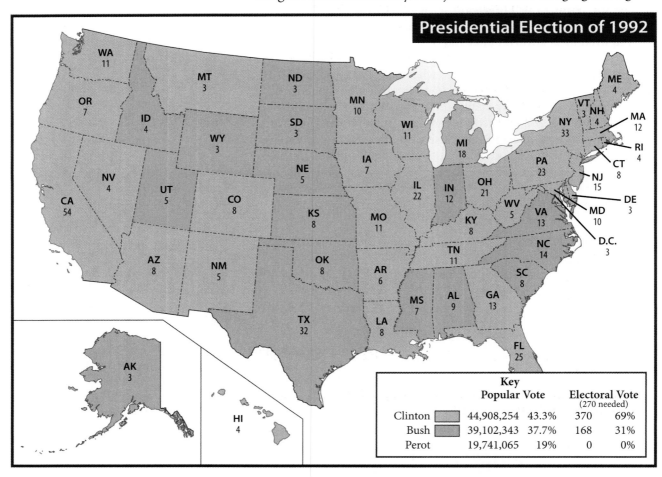

Presidential Election of 1992

Key	Popular Vote		Electoral Vote (270 needed)	
Clinton	44,908,254	43.3%	370	69%
Bush	39,102,343	37.7%	168	31%
Perot	19,741,065	19%	0	0%

the Vietnam War, and shady financial transactions as governor of Arkansas. Clinton shrugged off these attacks and marketed himself as a "**New Democrat**." He claimed that he would not promote big government and would end the tax-and-spend policies that the Democrats had followed in the past.

Complicating the campaign was an unusual third-party candidate. Billionaire **Ross Perot** financed his own campaign for the presidency. A small, folksy man with the spirit and blunt speaking of a Texas maverick, Perot promised to put an end to "politics as usual" and to trim the budget deficit. He made a virtue of the fact that he was no politician. Many Americans—put off by the candidates of the major parties and what they saw as dirty Washington politics—warmed to a candidate who was a true outsider. Even his wealth, which might have offended some voters, made Perot seem independent and self-sufficient. No special interests could "buy" him in return for their financial support.

The campaign was confusing. Perot first dropped out of the race and then returned. Bush focused on Clinton's moral failings and tried, unsuccessfully, to label him as just another "tax-and-spend" liberal like those Reagan vanquished. Responding to the recession that followed the Gulf War, Clinton shrewdly made the economy his central issue. With the Cold War won and no immediate foreign threats facing the country, Americans worried about domestic issues such as education, health care, and especially the economy. Clinton's campaign gurus placed signs in their offices reminding themselves, "It's the economy, Stupid!"

By election day 1992, Bush's approval rating had dropped to less than 40 percent. American voters decidedly rejected Bush and slightly endorsed Clinton. Democrats lost some ground in Congress but retained control of both chambers. In the presidential race, Perot won 19 percent of the popular vote, the largest total for a third-party candidate since Theodore Roosevelt in 1912, but he won no electoral votes. Clinton defeated Bush by only a plurality, 43 to 37 percent, but in the Electoral College, he won by a landslide of 370 to 168. Although he did not have a majority of the voters behind him, Clinton became the new president and brought an end to the Reagan era.

Bill Clinton

Section Quiz

1. The invasion of what country sparked a Middle Eastern war in the early 1990s? What country invaded it?

2. Through what organization did the United States coordinate its efforts in the Gulf War?

3. What amendment was added to the Constitution during the Bush administration? What issue did it address?

4. How did George Bush offend many voters so badly that it cost him the 1992 election?

5. Who was the significant third-party candidate in the election of 1992?

★ Why did the Bush administration not push for a total victory over Iraq in the Persian Gulf War?

<table>
<tr><td>

People, Places, and Things to Remember

Ronald Reagan
"Reagan Revolution"
supply-side economics (Reaganomics)
Economic Recovery Tax Act of 1981
Gramm-Rudman Act
Reagan Doctrine
Contras
Grenada
mujahideen
Walter Mondale
Geraldine Ferraro
Mikhail Gorbachev
perestroika
glasnost
Strategic Arms Reduction Talks (START)
Intermediate Nuclear Forces (INF) Treaty
Strategic Defense Initiative (SDI)
Iran-Contra affair
Jack Kemp
George H. W. Bush
Michael Dukakis
Dan Quayle
Operation Desert Shield
Operation Desert Storm
Gulf War
Americans with Disabilities Act
Bill Clinton
"New Democrat"
Ross Perot

</td></tr>
</table>

Chapter Review

Making Connections

1. How did the results of the congressional elections of 1986 hamper President Reagan in the final two years of his second term?

2. What was the difference between Operation Desert Shield and Operation Desert Storm?

3. What financial crisis during the Bush administration required $300 billion in "bail-out" funds from the federal government?

Developing History Skills

1. How does the unwillingness of the federal government to control spending reflect on the American public?

2. The Reagan Doctrine, as well as the defense buildup of the 1980s, was said to exhibit "peace through strength." What does this slogan mean?

Thinking Critically

1. Review the Twenty-seventh Amendment. Why would such an idea be popular with voters?

2. Is the United States right to involve itself in military efforts such as the Gulf War in which its own territory is not threatened? Why or why not?

3. Do you agree or disagree with the Americans with Disabilities Act? Why?

Living as a Christian Citizen

1. The Reagan Revolution also saw the rise of the Religious Right. What are the benefits and the dangers of organized Christian involvement in politics?

2. Many people, including professed Christians, argued that the military buildup of the 1980s was immoral, especially because it included nuclear armaments. Was Ronald Reagan wrong for his policy of peace through strength? Why or why not?

Bill Clinton takes the oath of office as the forty-second president of the United States.

New Challenges (1993-2011)

I. **The Clinton Administration**

II. **Election of 2000**

III. **The Bush Administration**

IV. **Election of 2008**

V. **The Obama Administration**

"There is a religious war going on in our country for the soul of America. It is a cultural war, as critical to the kind of nation we will one day be as was the Cold War itself."

Pat Buchanan, August 17, 1992,
at the Republican National Convention

In honor of Presidents' Day (February 21, 2000), a cable television network invited a team of historians to rank America's presidents from best to worst. The results, for the most part, were not too surprising. Abraham Lincoln ranked first, just ahead of Franklin Roosevelt and George Washington. Lincoln's predecessor, James Buchanan, came in last, just behind Lincoln's successor, Andrew Johnson. The president in office at that time, Bill Clinton, finished in the middle of the pack. He was twenty-first, behind George H. W. Bush (the man he had defeated for the presidency) and just ahead of Jimmy Carter.

A Siena poll conducted in 2010 showed a significant difference from the previous poll. FDR, Teddy Roosevelt, and Abraham Lincoln ranked first, second, and third respectively. Bill Clinton had advanced to thirteenth, and President Obama ranked fifteenth. James Buchanan had advanced one position, and Andrew Johnson had slipped to last place.

I. The Clinton Administration

Bill Clinton had been overcoming obstacles even before he was born. Three months before his birth, his father died in a car accident. He was raised by an alcoholic and sometimes abusive stepfather. Yet he graduated from Yale Law School, went on to become attorney general of Arkansas, and in 1978, at age 32, became governor of that state. After a single two-year term as governor, however, Clinton lost a reelection bid when the people began to view him as arrogant and too liberal. This event caused him to revamp his political philosophy. Clinton pursued more moderate policies and kept a close ear tuned to public opinion. He recaptured the governor's office in 1982 and won successive reelection until he assumed the presidency. He became a major leader in the Democratic Party's moderate faction, which opposed the liberal extremes that had led to so many Republican victories.

First Term

Defeats and Victories

On assuming the presidency, however, Clinton seemed to forget the lessons he had learned in Arkansas. He proposed, for example, to permit open homosexuals to serve in the armed forces. The plan roused an uproar of opposition from the military, Congress, and the public at large. Quickly, Clinton backed down and adopted a policy of "don't ask, don't tell" for homosexuals in the military: they were not to declare their homosexuality, and no one was to ask them about it. It was an uneasy compromise.

Past controversies also dogged Clinton. A series of women from the president's past accused him of sexual immorality. The most significant scandal, however, was the **"Whitewater" scandal**. It took its name from the president's earlier investment in the failed Whitewater Development Corporation, a resort in northeastern Arkansas. Rumors surfaced that Governor Clinton had unethically used his influence to promote the Whitewater scheme for his private benefit. Eventually, the federal justice department hired an independent counsel (an attorney not under the control of the executive branch) to investigate the Whitewater affair. This investigation continued throughout the Clinton administration and eventually led to the president's greatest humiliation late in his second term.

Despite these distractions and with a Democratic majority in Congress, Clinton was able to push through some significant legislation. The **Family and Medical Leave Act** required businesses to give employees up to twelve weeks of unpaid leave to care for newborn children or seriously ill family members. The **Brady Bill** (named for a top Reagan administration staffer wounded in the assassination attempt on President Reagan) mandated that before a gun shop could sell an individual a gun, the buyer had to wait five days and undergo a background check. The **National Voter Registration Act**, commonly called the "motor voter act," required states to allow voters to register to vote when they applied for or renewed a driver's license. Also, with the help of Republicans and over the objections of his own party, the president herded through the North American Free Trade Act (**NAFTA**), which opened free trade with Mexico.

The Brady Bill initially required a five-day waiting period and a background check for all buyers. Subsequently, an instant background check replaced this waiting period.

Many of those bills were further extensions of the federal government's power over state and local governments, businesses, and individuals. But another piece of legislation, a sweeping attempt at reform, led to Clinton's first major defeat in Congress.

Health-Care Fumble

When he undertook to reform American health care, Clinton found that even a Democratic Congress was no guarantee of legislative victory. Joining the president in that effort (and in the blame for its defeat) was the First Lady, **Hillary Rodham Clinton**. Like her husband, she was an attorney, but she was more openly liberal than he was. During the presidential election, she had quickly taken a back seat when the Clinton staff realized that her views were unpopular with moderate voters. But with the election won, she again took an open role in shaping the health-care plan.

She took charge of a task force to plan the best way to implement health-care reform. In late 1993, she presented a massive 1,342-page plan addressing what her husband had called a health-care "crisis" during his presidential campaign. The plan promised to care for those who had insufficient (or no) medical insurance and to hold down rising costs.

At first, the promises of universal insurance coverage and low costs for medical care attracted many Americans. Then, as details of the plan emerged, the public realized that someone would have to pay for the benefits given to the uninsured. The First Lady suggested raising taxes to pay for the plan. She added further controversy by insisting that the plan provide tax money to pay for abortions. The sheer size of the plan also gave many people pause. The Clinton health-care plan would create a new government bureaucracy and bring one-seventh of American business under government regulation. Soon, an outcry arose from those who saw the plan as too expensive and too intrusive.

Conservative Backlash

The Clinton health-care plan fell before an alliance of Republicans, medical professionals, and even some Democrats who were lukewarm to the plan. The battle over health care also revealed the

Conservative Talk Radio

The most important conservative talk radio host was Rush Limbaugh. He built a nationwide network of listeners energized to speak out on political issues. He was quickly followed by other conservative hosts, both local and national, with their own following of conservatives. Liberals tried to enter the fray with their version of talk radio called Air America, but it was a failure with both listeners and advertisers.

(top) The Christian Coalition, founded by Pat Robertson, was a leading voice of religious political conservatives. (bottom) Newt Gingrich orchestrated the "Contract with America" that returned Republicans to power in Congress.

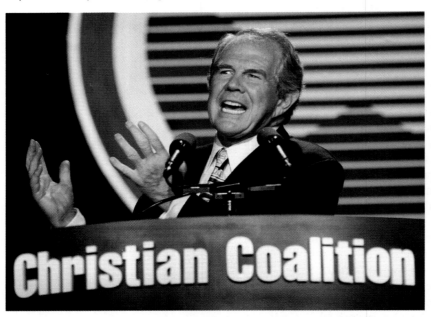

power of a new and surprising force in America: "**talk radio**." Radio had not been a great political force since the 1950s, when television displaced it as America's favorite source of entertainment and information. Radio became mostly a medium for music and brief news reports. In talk radio, speech replaced music. Aggressive and impassioned radio hosts expressed their usually conservative views and took phone calls on the air; listeners earnestly and heatedly voiced their protests about conditions in America.

Also displaying new political muscle was the Religious Right. The Moral Majority (see Chapter 25) had gradually weakened and dissolved in the late 1980s, and new conservative religious organizations took its place. Probably the most important one was the **Christian Coalition**. Religious broadcaster Pat Robertson had begun this organization after his failed attempt to win the Republican presidential nomination in 1988. Robertson revitalized the Religious Right by putting together a grassroots network of Roman Catholics, Charismatics, and evangelicals who were united on moral issues such as abortion and homosexuality. The Coalition mailed and distributed voter guides in churches, showing how candidates had voted on ethical issues. The organization also focused on electing conservative candidates on the local level, such as in school board races.

Another conservative force, combining the appeal of radio and religion, was the broadcast *Focus on the Family* hosted by James Dobson. Although it was less directly involved than the Christian Coalition in specific election campaigns, the program took a conservative stand on issues such as abortion and homosexuality. The program encouraged Christians to get involved politically.

As the 1994 congressional elections approached, Republicans in the House of Representatives issued what they called a "**Contract with America**." House Republicans laid out ten popular bills they promised to bring up for a vote—if they were elected—in their first hundred days in office. This legislation included such issues as term limits and a balanced federal budget. Displeasure with the Clinton health-care plan; the opposition to Democratic policies, amplified by talk radio; the efforts of the Religious Right; and the Contract with America all contributed to a stunning repudiation of the president in the fall elections. The Republicans captured control of both houses of Congress for the first time since Eisenhower's first term. Some Republicans confidently predicted that Clinton would be a one-term president like George H. W. Bush. But as those opponents would soon learn, the president was only down, not out.

Section Quiz

1. Why was the National Voter Registration Act commonly called the "motor voter act"?

2. What ambitious legislative effort by the Clinton administration sparked a backlash in public opinion?

3. Name the two organizations and their founders that represented the resurgence of the Religious Right in the 1990s.

4. What was the result of the congressional elections of 1994?

★ What role do you think conservative talk radio played in the defeat or scale-down of many of Clinton's early proposals?

"The Comeback Kid"

Throughout his career, Bill Clinton was often called "the comeback kid." After his defeat in the 1980 Arkansas governor's race, he came back to recapture that office two years later. After allegations of sexual immorality led to his defeat in the 1992 New Hampshire presidential primary, he rebounded to capture the Democratic nomination. Faced with embarrassing defeats involving his healthcare plan and the congressional elections, Clinton began another comeback.

Battling with Congress

The Republican Congress began with a rush. Under the aggressive leadership of House Speaker **Newt Gingrich**, House Republicans kept their "Contract with America" by pushing through votes on the promised legislation. But only two of the bills actually made it past the House and through the Senate to be signed into law by the president. One of those two bills—the **line-item veto** (which allowed the president to eliminate individual spending items in the federal budget)—was later struck down by the Supreme Court. The "Contract" had attracted voters, but Republicans had trouble getting its agenda through, particularly with the president ready to veto their efforts.

Meanwhile, Clinton picked his battles with Congress shrewdly. Despite the defeat of his party in the 1994 congressional elections, he still retained his popularity with the public. He also proved to be more skilled than the Republicans in shaping public opinion. He showed these strengths in a battle over the federal budget. The new Republican Congress insisted on real spending cuts that addressed the government's budget deficit. Clinton and the Democrats opposed cuts that they alleged would hurt the poor and needy. A core of determined Republicans refused to pass any budget if it did not deal with the deficit. As a result, twice (in November 1995 and in December/January 1995–96) the government technically ran out of money and shut down "nonessential" federal agencies, such as national parks. Unfortunately for Republicans, the Democrats and some in the media shaped these events to convince the public that Republicans were irresponsible and coldhearted. Under public pressure, Congress passed a budget more to the president's liking.

Move to the Middle

In addition to outmaneuvering Republicans by swaying public opinion, the president also made a sharp shift toward the middle of the political spectrum. Aware that many voters had begun to view him as liberal, Clinton moved to the centrist, middle-of-the-road stance that had gotten him elected. In his 1996 State of the Union address, Clinton presented himself again as a New Democrat—tough on crime, supportive of family values, and ready to reform welfare. He declared, "The era of big government is over."

But the president did more than talk. Despite his endorsement of the drive for homosexual rights, he signed the **Defense of Marriage Act**, which secured federal benefits, such as health insurance, for spouses in traditional marriages only, denying any status to homosexual "unions." Then he signed the Republicans' welfare reform bill. The **Welfare Reform Act of 1996** rolled back federal guarantees for the poor for the first time since FDR's New Deal. These shifts bothered many Democrats.

Election of 1996

The success of Clinton's comeback became evident in the 1996 presidential election. The Republicans nominated Senate Majority Leader **Bob Dole** of Kansas. Dole was a decorated World War II veteran with a conservative voting record. He was also an experienced legislator with a thorough knowledge of Washington politics. Ross Perot was on the ballot again with his Reform Party, splitting the votes of Clinton opponents.

Clinton cruised to reelection. Although he failed again to get a majority of the popular vote, he had 49 percent to Dole's 41 percent and Perot's 8 percent. In the Electoral College, the president swamped Dole 379–159. But the Republicans retained control of Congress and maintained their hold on the majority of governors' chairs. Bill Clinton "came back," but his party remained in the minority in Congress.

Section Quiz

1. During Congress's showdown with President Clinton over the federal budget, what events caused the public to view Republicans as irresponsible?

2. What were the provisions of the Welfare Reform Act passed during the Clinton administration?

3. Who was the Republican candidate in the 1996 presidential election? Who was the significant third-party candidate? What was his political party?

✷ What lessons can be learned from the Republicans' "Contract with America"?

Second Term

Economic Prosperity

One of the reasons for Clinton's sweeping reelection was the nation's booming economy. In 1992, the motto "It's the economy, Stupid!" reminded candidate Clinton to hammer Bush on economic issues, which were the greatest concern of American voters. By the dawn of Clinton's second term, the slogan had taken on a new twist. The United States was enjoying unparalleled economic growth, and citizens generally credited the president for their prosperity. A strong economy bolstered the president's popularity as most Americans remained generally satisfied, even optimistic, about the nation's financial status. The president's popularity surged with the growing economy.

Welfare Reform Act of 1996

The new law required welfare recipients to go back to work within two years and set a lifetime cap of five years for assistance. It also gave blocks of federal funds to the states to address welfare reform as they saw fit, without federal strings attached. It was an attempt, as Clinton said, to "end welfare as we know it."

Dole's Weaknesses

Bob Dole's greatest weakness was that he was a lackluster campaigner. He avoided social issues, such as abortion, leaving Republican activists apathetic about his campaign. Even his considerable political experience turned off voters who blamed "politics in Washington" for many of the nation's problems. He tried unsuccessfully to rouse Americans by calling for tax cuts and accusing Clinton of double-dealing. These weaknesses combined to cost Dole the election.

Economic Conditions Under Clinton

Inflation remained low. Unemployment fell steadily to its lowest level in thirty years. Businesses had to offer higher salaries and benefits not only to attract but also to retain skilled employees. The stock market soared to record levels, fueled especially by growth in "e-technology," computer-related businesses. The Internet opened new markets as people began to make more purchases online. By Clinton's second term, the government was actually showing a budget surplus instead of the deficits that had characterized the federal budget since the Vietnam War.

Foreign Affairs

As the governor of a small state, Bill Clinton came to the presidency with little experience in foreign affairs. Early in his first term, he displayed that lack of experience when he encountered disaster in the famine-stricken country of Somalia. Bush had sent American soldiers to that country in 1992 to aid United Nations peacekeeping forces. But the military factions in Somalia resisted all attempts to control or disarm them. Clinton eventually sent Army Rangers to track down the most brutal of the Somali warlords. But the Somalis shot down a military helicopter, and Americans watched their televisions in horror as the victorious Somalis dragged the body of an American soldier through the streets. Baffled by his administration's inability to deal with the warlords, Clinton withdrew all American forces from the country.

Following this humiliating experience, Clinton suspended the American policy of committing U.S. troops to warring regions where casualties might result. He limited the use of American forces to peacekeeping missions after fighting had already ceased. Muslim terrorists noticed that American leaders quickly removed forces upon sustaining casualties and began to plan accordingly.

Clinton was somewhat more successful in Haiti. A brutal military junta in that country had overthrown a democratically elected president in 1991. When he took office, Clinton began to pressure the Haitian regime to allow the ousted president to return to office. When Clinton gathered a military force off the island and threatened armed intervention, the Haitian military backed down. The United States succeeded in putting the former president back in office but could provide little help for Haiti's serious long-term problems of poverty and political corruption.

Probably the most significant American involvement overseas in the Clinton years was in the Balkans. The United States became involved first in Bosnia, located in the center of the former Yugoslavia. Bosnia embodied all the conflicts in the region. While other countries were predominantly Croat or Serb, Bosnia's population had both Croats and Serbs. In addition, Bosnia had one of the largest Muslim populations in the Balkans. In 1992, civil war broke out—a war furthered by Croatia in the west and what was left of Yugoslavia in the east.

At first, Clinton did not send soldiers to Bosnia, but he did provide air support for the United Nations' efforts to keep the peace.

Background of the Balkan Conflict

The fierce ethnic and religious divisions of the Balkans had long been an explosion waiting to happen. Catholics, Muslims, and Orthodox Christians there competed fiercely with each other. The Serbs and the Croats were (and still are) the dominant ethnic groups, with several other smaller groups. Some fifty years of cruel Communist oppression after World War II enforced a relative peace in the region. When communism fell in most of the area in the 1980s and 1990s, however, conflict broke out again. The nation of Yugoslavia became the focus of the trouble as it splintered into several different nations.

Evaluating Clinton's Foreign Policy

On the whole, the foreign policy of the Clinton administration showed a willingness to use military force. In most cases (Somalia was an exception), these efforts achieved the government's immediate goals. But tactical military victories were not long-term solutions. In particular, the intervention in Kosovo raised questions about whether and how the United States or any other country should intervene in another country's internal affairs.

Clinton's Response

When the story broke, the president declared, "I did not have sexual relations with that woman. . . . I never told anybody to lie." He had, in fact, said the same thing about Lewinsky under oath in an earlier investigation. Evidence soon confirmed, however, that he had been involved sexually with her.

Headlines proclaimed the impeachment of President Bill Clinton.

Furthermore, American diplomats took a leading role in trying to negotiate a peaceful settlement in the area. Finally, all the parties met together at Wright Patterson Air Force Base in Dayton, Ohio, and hammered out the **Dayton Accords**. That fragile agreement fashioned Bosnia into a confederation in which the Serbs, Croats, and Muslims shared power. To enact the agreement, the United Nations worked with NATO (see Chapter 23). The UN was responsible for the civil duties; NATO took on the burden of the military duties. As part of the peacekeeping efforts, Clinton sent American troops to Bosnia. An uneasy peace settled over the bitterly divided nation.

The creation of new nations in the Balkans reduced Yugoslavia to a federal union of two small states, Serbia and Montenegro. Even in the shrunken Yugoslavia, the province of Kosovo became the scene of ethnic clashes. Most of the people in the province were Albanian Muslims, but a large minority were Serbs, who were nominally Christian.

In the mid-1990s, an Albanian Muslim group, the Kosovo Liberation Army, began armed resistance to the Serb government. In response, Yugoslavia cracked down on any sign of Kosovar independence. Violence flared, with both sides committing massacres and atrocities. Eventually, the conflict forced thousands of Albanians caught between the revolutionaries and the government to flee the province. The Yugoslav government encouraged the flight as its armed forces sought ruthlessly to bring order to the province.

The plight of the Kosovar refugees and the brutal policies of the Serb government caught the world's attention. Clinton committed American troops to join UN and NATO forces in stopping the oppression. When negotiations with the Yugoslav government failed, the military stepped in. In March 1999, NATO forces, including Americans, launched massive air strikes against Yugoslavia. The strikes hit military and government targets, along with accidental attacks on civilians. Casualties mounted, and finally, in July, the Yugoslavs gave in. NATO and Russian forces moved in and restored peace in Kosovo.

Impeachment

No other event dominated Clinton's second term as did the **Lewinsky scandal** and the history-making impeachment trial that followed. The investigation of the Whitewater affair continued into the president's second term, and although it led to the trial and convictions of several friends of the president, including the governor of Arkansas who succeeded Clinton, the evidence never touched the president himself. Then in January 1998, while digging deeper into Whitewater, Kenneth Starr, the independent counsel, found evidence that the president had been having an adulterous relationship with a young White House intern named Monica Lewinsky and that Clinton and his staff were trying to cover it up. Moreover, there was strong indication that the White House staff had tried to hinder the investigation of the matter.

There was little question that the president committed perjury (lying under oath) about the relationship. He was likely guilty of obstruction of justice in not only the Lewinsky matter but also a separate investigation in which a woman had accused him of sexual impropriety. As a result, the House of Representatives conducted an investigation marked by bitter conflict between Republicans and Democrats. Finally, in December 1998, the House voted to impeach (to formally charge) the president. For the second time in American history, the president would be tried. If convicted, Clinton would be removed from office.

In contrast to Andrew Johnson, Clinton was in little danger. Two-thirds of the senators would have to vote against him before he could be removed from office. The support of the Democratic minority for the president almost guaranteed that Clinton would be acquitted. Furthermore, polls indicated that the American public did not want him removed from office. Many Americans apparently did not consider his behavior anything more than a private matter. Other Americans were disgusted with what the president had done, but they did not think that "lying about sex" was sufficient grounds for removing him from office.

The trial before the Senate took place in January and February 1999. Members of the House of Representatives served as prosecutors while Chief Justice William Rehnquist presided. The Senate weighed two charges against the president: perjury and obstruction of justice. By a vote of 45–55, the Senate declared him not guilty of perjury. The vote was tied 50–50 on the charge of obstruction of justice. Not a single Democrat voted against him. On neither charge was there anything close to the 67 votes needed to remove him from office. Bill Clinton, "the comeback kid," had survived again, and he claimed that the vote vindicated him. His reputation, however, suffered serious damage, even among his supporters and members of his own party.

> ### *Historical Impeachments*
> The only other president to be impeached was Andrew Johnson in 1868. Nixon was never formally impeached. Andrew Johnson barely avoided removal from office during his Senate trial in 1868; he was acquitted by a single vote.

Section Quiz

1. What African country was the scene of a disastrous military effort early in the Clinton administration?

2. What are the two major ethnic groups in the Balkans?

3. The splintering of what nation in the Balkans led to deep unrest in the region? In what nation did the United States first become involved?

4. What were the two charges against President Clinton in his trial before the Senate?

5. How many Democrats voted to convict the president?

★ Why were the votes on the articles of impeachment so partisan?

II. Election of 2000

The presidential election of 2000 developed into a referendum on the Clinton presidency. On the one hand, the Democrats nominated Clinton's vice president, **Al Gore**, as their candidate. As a leading member of the Clinton administration, Gore represented the Clinton policies and approach. The vice president was not involved in the Lewinsky scandal, but he had loyally stood by the president during the impeachment. More than any other candidate, he represented the Clinton heritage.

The Republicans turned to the son of the man whom Clinton had defeated in 1992. Texas governor **George W. Bush** ran on a theme of "compassionate conservatism." He promised educational reforms and swore that he would restore honor and dignity to the White House.

The Candidates Compared

Bush and Gore differed significantly on some issues. Governor Bush was pro-life, for example, and Vice President Gore was pro-abortion. But both candidates tried to appeal to the undecided, middle-of-the-road voters. Both wanted tax cuts, for example, but of a different nature. Gore wanted tax cuts for selected groups whereas Bush favored cuts for all taxpayers. Many of the dominant issues focused more on personality. The Gore team tried to portray Bush as an "intellectual lightweight" who was incapable of handling the job of president. The Bush forces responded by highlighting the vice president's numerous exaggerations, including his remarks suggesting that he had played a role in inventing the Internet.

The two sides ran the closest presidential campaign in a generation. Each man chose a running mate who buttressed his apparent weaknesses. Since Bush had little experience in Washington politics, he selected **Richard Cheney**, a former congressman from Wyoming who had served both as an assistant and chief of staff for President Gerald Ford and as secretary of defense under the elder Bush during the Gulf War. Gore, needing to distance himself from the scandals of the Clinton presidency, chose Connecticut senator **Joseph Lieberman**. The first practicing Jew ever to run on a major ticket, Lieberman had criticized Clinton's behavior in the Lewinsky scandal (though he did not vote to impeach the president). Lieberman also had severely criticized the entertainment industry for the deplorable morals portrayed in film and on television. He added a moral tone to the Democratic ticket.

The election turned out to be the most unusual since the disputed 1876 election in which Rutherford B. Hayes defeated Samuel Tilden (see Chapter 15). It was, in fact, about as close to being a tie as a national election could be. Gore narrowly won the popular vote by a little more than five hundred thousand votes out of more than one hundred million cast, a margin of about one-half of 1 percent of the vote. In the twentieth century, only John F. Kennedy's margin over Richard Nixon in 1960 was smaller.

The Electoral College, however, not the popular vote, decides the presidency. The candidate who could win enough states to garner 270 electoral votes would be president. After the dust from

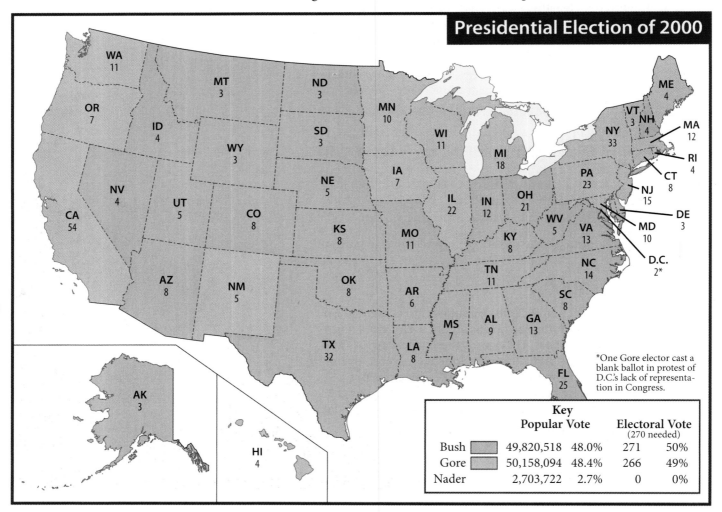

Presidential Election of 2000

*One Gore elector cast a blank ballot in protest of D.C.'s lack of representation in Congress.

Key	Popular Vote		Electoral Vote (270 needed)	
Bush	49,820,518	48.0%	271	50%
Gore	50,158,094	48.4%	266	49%
Nader	2,703,722	2.7%	0	0%

The Florida Recount

The recount of Florida votes led to confusion, anger, and even some laughter.

election day settled, the count showed Gore ahead of Bush, but the crucial state of Florida (with 25 electoral votes) was too close to call. Bush led after the initial count in that state by only about eighteen hundred votes out of some six million cast. A recount of the votes in Florida (required by Florida law because the result was so close) cut Bush's lead to just under one thousand votes.

With the presidency at stake, both sides began to plead their case before the American people and especially before the courts. The Democrats claimed that many of the computer-read ballots should be recounted by hand, but they asked for those recounts only in heavily Democratic counties where the results would favor Gore. Republicans replied that such hand-counting was done by arbitrary standards and therefore was unfair.

More recounting occurred, and Bush's lead shrank again to about five hundred votes. A flood of sometimes contradictory court decisions from Florida state courts, federal courts, and the U.S. Supreme Court interrupted the recount. Weeks dragged by as some court decisions favored Bush and others favored Gore. Finally, on December 12—exactly five weeks after election day—the Supreme Court ruled for Bush, halting all recounts and, by default, making him the winner of Florida's votes and therefore the winner of the presidency.

This dramatic contest illustrated divisions within the government. The two candidates had almost equal support in the nation. Republicans controlled both houses of Congress, but only by narrow margins. During his campaign, Bush had promised to bring a spirit of cooperation to Washington, saying, "I'm a uniter, not a divider." A divided Congress and a slender electoral mandate would give Bush the opportunity to prove his claim.

Popular Vote Vs. Electoral College

Gore became the first candidate since Grover Cleveland in 1888 to win the popular vote but lose in the Electoral College.

George W. Bush takes the oath of office as the forty-third president of the United States.

1. Who were the presidential candidates of the Democratic and Republican parties in the presidential election of 2000? How did they differ on the issues of abortion and tax cuts?

2. Which candidate won the most popular votes? Which won the majority of votes in the Electoral College?

3. The electoral votes of which state ultimately decided the presidential election?

✶ The disputed election of 2000 renewed efforts to ditch the Electoral College in favor of the direct popular election of the president. Do you think that is a good or a bad idea and why?

The war with Islamic radicalism began with the terrorist attacks on the World Trade Center and the Pentagon.

III. The Bush Administration

When Bush took office in 2001, the Republicans controlled the House of Representatives, but in the Senate each party had fifty members. The vice president, as president of the Senate, would have to break any tie votes. Then, liberal Republican James Jeffords of Vermont became an independent, shifting control of the Senate to the Democrats by one seat.

Unfazed, Bush called for a major tax cut of $1.6 trillion to stimulate the economy. Democrats opposed it, claiming that the plan favored the wealthy and would reduce the budget surplus. Compromising, Bush and Congress agreed on a $1.35 trillion tax cut over eleven years.

September 11, 2001

On the morning of **September 11, 2001**, terrorists hijacked several airliners and flew two of them into the twin towers of the World Trade Center. Shortly, both towers collapsed. Thousands of people were killed and several blocks of the city were inundated with dust and smoke. Terrorists flew a third plane into the Pentagon. Heroic passengers in a fourth plane learned about the other attacks on their cell phones and fought with the terrorists who had hijacked their plane. It crashed in rural Pennsylvania, killing everyone on board. Some people speculated that the terrorists in the fourth plane had wanted to crash it into the Capitol or the White House. The hijackers were all Muslims.

In response, Americans generously poured forth money and gave of their time to help the victims, especially those at the World Trade Center. American flags suddenly appeared on front porches and on cars. Members of both political parties attended public ceremonies all across the country in demonstrations of unity. Baseball fans sang "God Bless America" during the seventh-inning stretch. Bush pledged to achieve victory over the terrorists when he visited "Ground Zero" at the World Trade Center crash site. People around the world publicly sympathized with America. But many Palestinians and Muslims rejoiced, dancing in the streets. The *jihad* against "the Great Satan," the United States, had begun in earnest.

Attack on Innocent People and American Symbols

The 9/11 attack was the worst terrorist attack in the nation's history, killing or injuring more than three thousand people. The terrorists purposely targeted innocent civilians; military personnel, policemen, and firefighters; and Americans and foreigners from about eighty countries who worked in the World Trade Center. They struck at symbols of the heart of America—its wealth in New York City and its government in the nation's capital.

Intelligence experts learned that the nineteen hijackers were members of an international terrorist network called **al-Qaeda**, led by **Osama bin Laden**, a wealthy Saudi. The organization was linked to several other terrorist attacks. Such Muslim extremists hated the Jews, Israel, and America, considering them obstacles to the expansion of Islam. Al-Qaeda members trained for terrorist activities at bases in Afghanistan, where the Taliban government protected them. Osama bin Laden financed and commanded al-Qaeda's worldwide network.

The War on Terror

Thus began the U.S. war against terrorism, both at home and in foreign countries. Bush warned that the war would be neither short nor conventional. Some of the warfare would be publicly visible; other parts would be clandestine.

(left) President Bush rallied the nation and encouraged rescuers on a pile of rubble at what had been the World Trade Center. (right) Americans drove the Taliban from power in Afghanistan.

Bush's first task was to assemble a multinational coalition to oust the Taliban from Afghanistan. On October 7, those allied forces invaded Afghanistan, using "smart" weapons to minimize military and civilian casualties. The coalition got help from the anti-Taliban Northern Alliance in Afghanistan and from Pakistani volunteers. In only two months, Taliban forces fled into the mountains on the Afghan-Pakistani border. Afghan leaders of several anti-Taliban factions met in Germany in December and signed a peace agreement. They established a temporary government and began working to rebuild their country.

To protect Americans at home, Bush created the **Office of Homeland Security**. It later became a cabinet-level department. Congress also overwhelmingly passed the **Patriot Act**, making it easier for law enforcement officials and the courts to catch, convict, and imprison terrorists. Most Americans agreed with Bush's practical, common-sense approach. But critics complained that the government, in its zeal to protect citizens from terrorism, had gone too far and was infringing on the rights of Americans. The Supreme Court later declared some provisions of the Patriot Act unconstitutional.

The War with Iraq

Rather than wait for another terrorist attack, Bush used the U.S. military to attack the terrorists before they could strike again. One target was the regime of Iraqi dictator Saddam Hussein, who

The Rise of Muslim Terrorist Groups

After the Cold War, the United States was the world's only superpower. For a growing minority of Muslims, hatred of the West, especially America, fueled a network of terrorist groups in some sixty countries, most of them in the Middle East, Africa, and Asia. They operated secretly. No tactic—even the slaughter of civilians—was deemed too violent if it helped achieve their goals. Sometimes rogue nations protected such terrorists, but the terrorists were not officially part of those governments, so fighting the terrorist groups proved difficult.

The Work of the Office of Homeland Security

Bureaucrats covered security issues related to U.S. borders, transportation (especially at airports), chemical and biological attacks, and preparations for emergencies. To screen for potential terrorists, Americans accepted longer delays and lines for check-in at airports.

A New Type of Enemy

In the Cold War, potential enemies had been restricted by the very threat of nuclear force. Muslim extremists, however, had no such restraints in their thinking. They followed no conventional rules of war. They resorted to suicide bombings, targeted innocent civilians, and even threatened to use weapons of mass destruction (such as biological or chemical weapons), a special fear of Americans and Europeans.

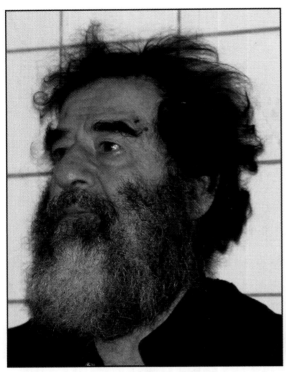

Saddam Hussein was tracked down and captured by the Americans and tried and executed by an Iraqi court.

continued to threaten peace in the Middle East. Rumors abounded of his development of chemical and biological weapons of mass destruction (WMDs). After all, he had used chemical weapons against the Kurds, citizens of his own country.

After 9/11, Bush and other world leaders feared that Saddam also had links to terrorists. Bush asked the UN to support his actions against Iraq, and the Security Council threatened Saddam with "serious consequences" if he did not destroy his WMDs. Congress supported Bush, passing a resolution calling for the use of force if necessary.

But Saddam refused to cooperate with the UN, and American, British, and Spanish officials pushed for a UN resolution authorizing force against Iraq. Germany, France, Russia, China, and other countries opposed military action.

On March 19, 2003, the United States and a **"coalition of the willing"** invaded Iraq, defeating that country's military forces in only two weeks. But Iraqi terrorists, aided by terrorists from other Muslim countries, continued the fight as guerillas, launching terrorist attacks, encouraging suicide bombings, and setting improvised explosive devices (IEDs) beside roads.

As the war dragged on, Muslim factions began fighting each other. Sunnis attacked Shiites and bombed their mosques. The Shiites launched revenge attacks. Sunnis and Shiites attacked Kurds. Amid the chaos, some Iraqis, desiring freedom, held elections and approved a constitution.

Americans were deeply divided over the Iraq War. Many were upset when the military found no evidence of the much-discussed WMDs. The invasion only made Muslims hate America more. Supporters of the war argued that the war in Iraq was part of the war on terror. Terrorists in Iraq had to be defeated. Fighting them in Iraq made more sense than fighting them in the United States.

The Election of 2004

In the 2004 elections, Republicans gained two Senate seats, regaining control of the Senate. They also gained four seats in the House. The Democratic nominee for president was liberal Massachusetts senator **John Kerry**. He tried to present himself to the public as being in the mold of Bill Clinton, but he could not escape his liberal record. He supported the traditional liberal line—pro-homosexual rights, pro-feminism, and pro-labor union.

Bush's reelection campaign was influenced by mixed economic news, violence and mounting casualties in Iraq, and a scandal over mistreatment of prisoners of war at Abu Ghraib prison in Iraq. His approval ratings plummeted. When the votes were counted, however, Bush won by 3.3 million votes. His support came from southern and central states and evangelical voters. He also picked up more female and Hispanic votes than he had received in 2000.

The role of evangelicals in the Bush administration was reflected in the number of Christians Bush named to prominent positions. For example, **John Ashcroft**, Bush's attorney general, was a Pentecostal minister. **Condoleeza Rice** was Bush's national security advisor; he later named her his secretary of state. Other Christians included Don Evans (secretary of commerce), Michael Gerson (speechwriter), Andrew Card (chief of staff), and Karen Hughes (undersecretary of state for public diplomacy).

An Antiwar Veteran

Although John Kerry was a decorated Vietnam veteran, he returned home to oppose the war, and that opposition to the Vietnam War hurt him among veterans in the 2004 election. Kerry also seemed indecisive. After voting for the Iraq War, he later opposed measures necessary for fighting it. His effort to defend his actions—"I actually voted for the war before I voted against it"—only cemented his image as a "flip-flopper."

First Hispanic Attorney General

In 2005, Bush named the first Hispanic attorney general in American history. **Alberto Gonzales** became the nation's top law-enforcement and legal authority; he displayed an urgency to protect Americans from terrorists while protecting citizens' liberties from government interference. But a controversy involving the firing of several attorneys in the Justice Department forced him to resign in 2007.

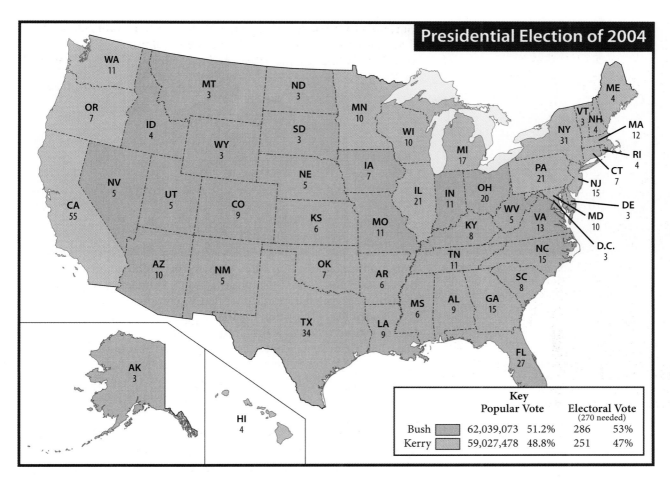

Presidential Election of 2004

WA 11
MT 3
ND 3
MN 10
ME 4
OR 7
ID 4
WY 3
SD 3
WI 10
VT 3
NH 4
MA 12
NY 31
NV 5
UT 5
CO 9
NE 5
IA 7
MI 17
RI 4
CT 7
CA 55
KS 6
MO 11
IL 21
IN 11
OH 20
PA 21
NJ 15
DE 3
AZ 10
NM 5
OK 7
AR 6
KY 8
WV 5
VA 13
MD 10
D.C. 3
TN 11
NC 15
MS 6
AL 9
GA 15
SC 8
TX 34
LA 9
FL 27
AK 3
HI 4

	Key Popular Vote		Electoral Vote (270 needed)	
Bush	62,039,073	51.2%	286	53%
Kerry	59,027,478	48.8%	251	47%

Economic Developments

When Bush took office in 2001, the economy was sluggish, but his tax cut that year—and two other cuts over the next two years—and the abolition of the "marriage penalty" spurred economic activity. Congress, however, did not cut spending; rather, it increased spending. As a result, the deficit hit record levels. Unemployment rose from 4.7 percent to 6.2 percent in June 2003, but then it dropped back to 4.8 percent in February 2006. Inflation was low, unemployment was low, wages were higher, and output was greater. Trade with China also increased.

But the global economy did not help all Americans. Red ink continued to rise as the budget deficit for 2004 reached $639 billion, the highest since 1983 and the second highest since World War II. Trade deficits increased. Some people complained that free trade was unfair because foreign competitors paid their workers less. Many foreigners also were unhappy, seeing globalization as Americanization. They resented American culture as a threat to their traditional way of life.

The business boom also brought with it several instances of corporate corruption. Certain executives and companies came to symbolize corporate greed and corruption. Ken Lay of Enron and Martha Stewart are two people who became synonymous with corporate misdeeds.

Judicial Happenings

For decades, the Supreme Court had issued a flood of liberal rulings. For example, the Court removed prayer and Bible reading

Personal Faith Expressed Publicly in the White House

Bush personally made religion a more prominent issue. He was unashamed to share his faith in Christ, and he embraced a greater role for evangelical Christians, enlisting pastors, both whites and minorities, to help administer government social programs that put into practice his "compassionate conservatism." Such **faith-based initiatives** became an important part of his domestic program to combat problems in the inner cities. But some conservative Christians questioned the wisdom of those initiatives. They worried about government involvement in their programs.

(left) John Roberts, a Bush nominee, became chief justice of the U.S. Supreme Court following the death of William Rehnquist. (right) Samuel Alito joined Roberts on the Court, giving it a slight right turn in judicial philosophy.

Toward More Strict Construction

Justice Alito was a member of the Federalist Society, which seeks a return to traditional legal views, including a strict constructionist view of the U.S. Constitution.

Ahmadinejad's Anti-Semitism

Ahmadinejad is an uncompromising anti-Semite. He has repeatedly and publicly denied that the Holocaust ever happened. He also blatantly declared that Israel should be "wiped off the map."

from public schools. It granted women the "right" to an abortion. But in 2005 and 2006, Bush nominated two conservative justices to the Court, giving it a more conservative composition.

Sandra Day O'Connor, the first woman to serve on the Supreme Court, retired in 2005. **John G. Roberts Jr.** was nominated to replace her. Before the Senate could vote on the nomination, however, Chief Justice William Rehnquist died. Bush chose Roberts to replace Rehnquist, and Roberts was confirmed. He was sworn in as the seventeenth chief justice of the United States on September 29, 2005.

Bush then chose **Samuel Alito Jr.** to replace O'Connor. The Senate confirmed Alito in January 2006. Alito and Roberts were both Catholics. For the first time, the Supreme Court had a Catholic majority, represented in Justices Alito, Roberts, Scalia, Kennedy, and Thomas.

Diplomatic Successes and Problems

Bush's diplomatic successes included convincing Libya to abandon terrorism and weapons of mass destruction and to seek closer ties with the West. He also succeeded in toppling Saddam Hussein and convincing Pakistan to cooperate in the war on terror. He forged closer economic and diplomatic ties with China and negotiated with China, Japan, and the Koreas to ensure stability in East Asia.

But Bush also faced problems with North Korea and Iran as they both sought to develop nuclear weapons. Mahmoud Ahmadinejad, the leader of Iran, seemed to thrive on baiting the United States and making outlandish statements about Israel. Like every other president from Truman forward, Bush was bedeviled by problems between Israel and the Arab nations. Progress toward peace was hindered by several events. Yasir Arafat, leader of the Palestine Liberation Organization, died. Israeli prime minister Ariel Sharon was incapacitated when he went into a coma. Hamas, a Palestinian terrorist group, won control of the parliament of the Palestinian Authority. Although hopes for peace were improved in 2005 when Israel withdrew from the Gaza Strip and surrendered it to the Palestinians, peace in the Middle East is still elusive.

Problems of Nature

Hurricane Katrina, a category 3 storm, hit the Gulf Coast of Louisiana, Mississippi, and Alabama on August 29, 2005. Floodwaters broke the levees in New Orleans, putting 80 percent of the city under water. Gulf residents suffered greatly from Hurricane Katrina. More than eighteen hundred people were killed and about

$75 billion in damages occurred, making it the costliest hurricane in American history.

Bush got much of the blame for the disaster. The **Federal Emergency Management Administration** (FEMA) was criticized severely for its slowness to respond. But faulty decisions by local officials and local residents and the crime wave that swept the area in the aftermath of the hurricane were also to blame for much of the loss. Misplaced priorities during the cleanup played a role as well. For example, in Biloxi, Mississippi, another hard-hit area, Katrina had destroyed the "floating casinos." These casinos were the first businesses to be rebuilt and were rebuilt before most homes. The legislature even passed a special law allowing them to be built on land. Within four months, gambling revenues were approaching pre-Katrina levels.

But Hurricane Katrina also brought out the best in some people. Aid workers risked their lives to help victims, other Americans gave generous financial support, and cities throughout the nation offered to house refugees in shelters. Schools, church groups, and other nonprofit organizations went to the Gulf region to help rescue and rebuild. Christians had the opportunity to show love to fellow citizens and live the truth that Paul described in 1 Corinthians 13—the greatness of love.

IV. Election of 2008

The 2008 presidential election campaign began earlier than any other race in recent history, and more money was raised and spent during that campaign than in any other presidential campaign in U.S. history.

The Democrats narrowed their field of candidates to former First Lady Hillary Clinton and Illinois senator Barack Obama. Clinton seemed to have the nomination sewn up, but Obama won in the last few primaries, capturing the nomination.

With Bush out of the picture, the Republicans had a large number of contestants. They included Arkansas governor Mike Huckabee, New York mayor Rudy Guiliani, and former Massachusetts governor Mitt Romney. But Arizona senator John McCain won. He chose Alaska governor Sarah Palin as his running mate.

Human Contributions to the Disaster

Residents were warned to evacuate New Orleans well before the hurricane hit, but thousands of them failed to do so. Dozens of school buses could have been used to evacuate people who had no other means of transport. But city officials ignored this option, and the buses sat unused until they were stranded in floodwaters. Some rescuers were driven away from the very people they wanted to save when criminals shot at their helicopters, boats, and other rescue vehicles. Many New Orleans police officers simply walked away from their jobs, leaving the city undefended.

Change?

Despite having campaigned on the theme of change, Obama chose as his vice presidential running mate a career politician, Delaware senator Joe Biden.

The Bidens and Obamas on inauguration day

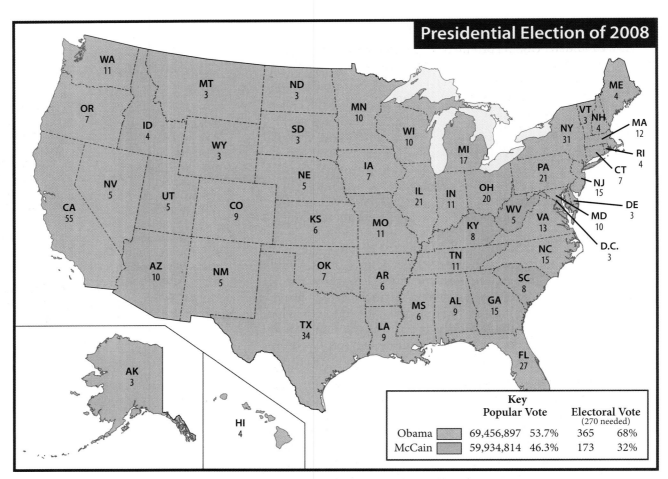

Presidential Election of 2008

		Key			
		Popular Vote		Electoral Vote (270 needed)	
Obama		69,456,897	53.7%	365	68%
McCain		59,934,814	46.3%	173	32%

The Republican campaign focused on Obama's lack of administrative experience or accomplishment. McCain, however, was an uninspiring speaker, and he could not connect with the voters, many of whom did not trust him because of his willingness to compromise. On the other hand, voters greeted Palin enthusiastically.

Obama was a tough campaigner. He was able to create an image of himself as powerful, authoritative, and hopeful. Although critics repeatedly argued that his speeches lacked substance, his charisma, the support of the media, and the support of the black electorate launched him to the presidency. He became the nation's first African-American president when on November 4, 2008, he defeated McCain by several million popular votes and by 365–173 in the Electoral College vote. He was sworn in on January 20, 2009.

Democrat candidates for the U.S. House and Senate benefited from Obama's popularity as they added to Democrat majorities in both chambers. In the Senate, however, the party had trouble keeping some Southern "blue dog" Democrats in line.

Section Quiz

1. What event became the defining moment of the Bush presidency?

2. What effect did Bush's Supreme Court nominations have on the direction of the Court?

3. What action of the Bush presidency deeply divided Americans?

★ What action (or inaction) by Bush might have angered or frustrated fiscal conservatives and why?

V. The Obama Administration

As a candidate, Obama promised hope, change, and transparency. As president, however, he nominated insiders, many of them from the Clinton presidency, to important positions. In fact, Obama chose Hillary Clinton as his secretary of state. Similarly, he named lobbyists to positions in the administration, including the cabinet. He did, however, name two Republicans to the positions of secretary of defense (Robert Gates) and secretary of commerce (Judd Gregg).

The First Two Years

Two of Obama's first actions as president were executive orders to close the POW prison at Guantánamo Bay, Cuba, and to resume federal funding for abortions performed overseas. But his top priority was the economy. Stating that the economic situation was too bad for the free market to solve (in fact, he said that the free market had caused the problems), he called for the government to take unprecedented measures.

Building on the example that Bush had set at the end of his own presidency, Obama got Congress to vote massive **bailouts** of businesses and industries that he deemed "**too big to fail**," including many of the American automakers. (Of the "Big Three," only Ford refused to take the government money.) In addition, Congress added to each of the bailout packages billions of dollars of "pork" that would do nothing to improve the economy. In return for the government money, Obama basically nationalized those businesses, requiring the executives to do business his way. He even fired the chief executive officer of General Motors and replaced him with his own man.

As critics had predicted, such extreme measures did nothing to improve the economy. It remained depressed, businesses downsized or closed, unemployment increased, and consumers saved rather than spent. Perhaps most alarming, the deficit shot to the largest in the nation's history. The critics warned that hyperinflation would soon hit the country.

Next, Obama tackled the nation's health-care system. He proposed a confusingly complicated system whereby the federal government would run health care—set prices, determine levels of care, and essentially ration health care. It would also mandate health-care insurance for every person in the country and fine those who did not get it. Critics warned of future problems similar to those being experienced by Canada and Great Britain, both of which have socialized health-care systems. They also raised the specter of "death panels" made up of government bureaucrats who would determine who qualified to receive care based on age and potential for benefiting society. Nonetheless, both houses of Congress voted to approve the massive plan.

Other controversies arose over ACORN, a group of "community organizers" that had orchestrated Obama's "Get Out the Vote" efforts, and over Obama's desire to run the census. ACORN was already under federal investigation for voter fraud because people wearing hidden cameras captured its workers advising voters on how to file fraudulent information on mortgage applications and tax returns. Another flap resulted over the White House's alleged tracking of information from people who e-mailed the White House to criticize or complain about the Obama administration. A still greater outcry resulted when Obama officials hinted at renewing the ill-named Fairness Doctrine and initiating government control of the Internet.

Judd Gregg, Short-Lived Commerce Secretary

Judd Gregg (R-NH) accepted appointment as Obama's secretary of commerce but soon resigned as he became uncomfortable with the unfolding details of the Obama administration. Obama's plan to take an active roll in directing the 2010 census proved to be the last straw for Gregg because he thought that the administration would seek to use the census for political gain.

First-Year Spending

Obama spent $3.5 trillion in his first year as president, far surpassing any other president in history for first-year spending.

Massive Legislation with a Hefty Price Tag

The final health-care bill, which was more than twenty-five hundred pages long, passed Congress in 2010 despite opposition from Republicans, a quickly growing number of concerned voters, and a handful of moderate Democrats. Most legislators admitted that they never read the entire bill before voting to support it.

Obama's Supreme Court Nominees

Obama quickly got a chance to influence the direction of the U.S. Supreme Court when Justice David Souter and then Justice John Paul Stevens resigned. Obama nominated **Sonia Sotomayor** to replace Souter. Taking office on August 8, 2009, Sotomayor became the first Hispanic justice. In April 2010, Stevens, the Court's longest-serving justice, retired. Obama named **Elena Kagan** to succeed Stevens. Both Sotomayor and Kagan are considered liberals who believe in a broad interpretation of the Constitution and that the race, ethnicity, and financial condition of the defendants and plaintiffs should be considered in court rulings. Conservatives and strict constructionists opposed both nominees, stating that justice should be blind and that rulings should be based on the founders' original intent. Despite opposition, both appointees were confirmed by the Senate.

Al-Qaeda Decapitated

In the dark hours of Sunday, May 1, 2011, two combat helicopters bearing a special squad of U.S. Navy SEALS descended upon a military compound in Abbottabad, Pakistan. They were acting on highly credible intelligence that Osama bin Laden, head of the al-Qaeda terrorist network, was hiding there. One helicopter had mechanical problems and landed hard inside the compound. The other chopper also landed, and SEALS sped from both in a well-rehearsed operation to capture or kill bin Laden. A fierce firefight erupted as bin Laden and his lieutenants and bodyguards tried to avoid capture. Although he used a woman as a human shield, bin Laden fell victim to a SEAL bullet. The SEALS grabbed bin Laden's body as well as extensive documentation found in the compound and departed into the night aboard the functioning helicopter, but not before destroying the damaged chopper. The entire operation had taken only about forty minutes. Safely back at their base, the SEALS obtained DNA and conducted facial recognition tests to confirm bin Laden's identity. They then washed the body according to Islamic practice and flew it to an American naval vessel. Then, because no country was willing to accept the body, they buried it at sea. Only time would tell what would result from this decapitation of al-Qaeda, but one thing was sure: the war against terrorism was not over; al-Qaeda remained committed to the destruction of Americans.

The 2010 off-year elections promised to be a referendum on Obama and the Democrat-controlled Congress as citizens resisted the increasing encroachments of government in massive "tea party" rallies. They called for a return to constitutionalism and limited government. The record of the Obama administration, they said, indicated that the era of big government was *not* over. Although government had continued to grow under both Clinton and Bush, it had expanded at an even more alarming pace during Obama's administration. Perhaps more alarming than the growth of government and its effect on the economy was the government's apparent disregard for the U.S. Constitution and the myriad effects that such growth has on individual liberty.

The 2010 Elections

On November 2, 2010, American voters sent a strong message to elected officials all across the nation, from state legislatures to the U.S. Congress. In Obama's words, the Democrats "took a shellacking" as Republicans, many of them backed by the "tea party" movement, made greater gains than they had in their victory in 1994. Republicans regained control of the House of Representatives, picking up more than sixty seats, and fell just short of winning control in the Senate.

The sweep was even more dramatic on the state level as the Republicans won most of the governorships that were up for grabs, bringing the tally to 29–18 in favor of Republicans (with two elections pending). Of eighty-eight legislative chambers in play, Republicans won fifty-five. Republican wins on the state level gave Republicans enormous power over the process of congressional redistricting based on the 2010 census.

As the Republicans basked in their victory, they also laid plans for the Congress that would commence in January 2011. High on the agenda of many congressmen was the repeal of Obama's national health-care program and the extension of the Bush-era tax cuts. They also wanted to get the lagging economy back on track by reducing interference of government in private business and funding the ballooning budget deficit. And they wanted to reinvigorate the war on terrorism, ensuring an acceptable end to the war in Afghanistan and securing U.S. borders.

But before the Republicans could pursue those goals, they had to await the conclusion of the "lame duck" Congress. Led by Senate Majority Leader Harry Reid and Speaker of the House Nancy Pelosi, the Democrats insisted on trying to push through more of Obama's big government agenda. Republicans, however, were just as adamant about preventing that. Only the future would show whether the president would continue pushing his agenda or move toward the center to reach compromises with Republican lawmakers.

Section Quiz

1. How did Obama and the Democrat-controlled Congress address the economic downturn during Obama's first days in office?

2. Which domestic industry did the Obama administration try to take over? Which company in that industry refused to take government money?

3. How much did the Obama administration spend in Obama's first year in office?

Chapter Review

Making Connections

1. What was President Clinton's "don't ask, don't tell" policy for homosexuals in the military?

2. List two indications of the strength of the economy during the Clinton administration.

3. How did the Whitewater investigation lead to the impeachment of President Clinton?

4. Compare the Japanese attack on Pearl Harbor with the terrorists' attack on the United States on 9/11.

Developing History Skills

1. In light of the circumstances facing Bush, evaluate his presidency. Rank him in relation to the other presidents before him. Support your assessments.

2. List at least three events that have occurred since the beginning of the school year that you think will be included in future history books. Support your answers.

Critical Thinking

1. Is it right for the United States to intervene militarily in other nations' internal affairs, as it did in Kosovo? Why or why not?

2. Do you think the Senate was right to acquit President Clinton? Explain your answer.

Living as a Christian Citizen

1. When Christians vote or otherwise participate in the political process, they should consider the Bible's direction regarding specific areas of life. Evaluate the following policies from a biblical perspective: the Welfare Reform Act of 1996, recognition of homosexual marriage, and government health care.

People, Places, and Things to Remember

"Whitewater" scandal
Family and Medical Leave Act
Brady Bill
National Voter Registration Act
NAFTA
Hillary Rodham Clinton
"talk radio"
Christian Coalition
"Contract with America"
Newt Gingrich
line-item veto
Defense of Marriage Act
Welfare Reform Act of 1996
Bob Dole
Dayton Accords
Kosovo
Lewinsky scandal
Al Gore
George W. Bush
Richard Cheney
Joseph Lieberman
September 11, 2001
al-Qaeda
Osama bin Laden
Office of Homeland Security
Patriot Act
"coalition of the willing"
John Kerry
Alberto Gonzales
John Ashcroft
Condoleeza Rice
faith-based initiatives
John G. Roberts Jr.
Samuel Alito Jr.
Hurricane Katrina
Federal Emergency Management Administration
bailout
"too big to fail"
Sonia Sotomayor
Elena Kagan

Order of Admission	State	Admitted	Capital	Nickname
1	Delaware	1787	Dover	Diamond State, First State
2	Pennsylvania	1787	Harrisburg	Keystone State
3	New Jersey	1787	Trenton	Garden State
4	Georgia	1788	Atlanta	Empire State of the South, Peach State
5	Connecticut	1788	Hartford	Constitution State, Nutmeg State
6	Massachusetts	1788	Boston	Bay State, Old Colony
7	Maryland	1788	Annapolis	Old Line State, Free State
8	South Carolina	1788	Columbia	Palmetto State
9	New Hampshire	1788	Concord	Granite State
10	Virginia	1788	Richmond	Old Dominion State
11	New York	1788	Albany	Empire State
12	North Carolina	1789	Raleigh	Tar Heel State, Old North State
13	Rhode Island	1790	Providence	Little Rhody, Ocean State
14	Vermont	1791	Montpelier	Green Mountain State
15	Kentucky	1792	Frankfort	Bluegrass State
16	Tennessee	1796	Nashville	Volunteer State
17	Ohio	1803	Columbus	Buckeye State
18	Louisiana	1812	Baton Rouge	Pelican State
19	Indiana	1816	Indianapolis	Hoosier State
20	Mississippi	1817	Jackson	Magnolia State
21	Illinois	1818	Springfield	Land of Lincoln, Prairie State
22	Alabama	1819	Montgomery	Heart of Dixie, Camellia State
23	Maine	1820	Augusta	Pine Tree State
24	Missouri	1821	Jefferson City	"Show Me" State
25	Arkansas	1836	Little Rock	Natural State, Razorback State
26	Michigan	1837	Lansing	Wolverine State, Great Lakes State
27	Florida	1845	Tallahassee	Sunshine State
28	Texas	1845	Austin	Lone Star State
29	Iowa	1846	Des Moines	Hawkeye State
30	Wisconsin	1848	Madison	Badger State
31	California	1850	Sacramento	Golden State
32	Minnesota	1858	St. Paul	North Star State, Gopher State
33	Oregon	1859	Salem	Beaver State
34	Kansas	1861	Topeka	Sunflower State
35	West Virginia	1863	Charleston	Mountain State
36	Nevada	1864	Carson City	Sagebrush State, Silver State, Battle Born State
37	Nebraska	1867	Lincoln	Cornhusker State
38	Colorado	1876	Denver	Centennial State
39	North Dakota	1889	Bismarck	Peace Garden State
40	South Dakota	1889	Pierre	Coyote State, Mt. Rushmore State
41	Montana	1889	Helena	Treasure State
42	Washington	1889	Olympia	Evergreen State
43	Idaho	1890	Boise	Gem State
44	Wyoming	1890	Cheyenne	Equality State, Cowboy State
45	Utah	1896	Salt Lake City	Beehive State
46	Oklahoma	1907	Oklahoma City	Sooner State
47	New Mexico	1912	Santa Fe	Land of Enchantment
48	Arizona	1912	Phoenix	Grand Canyon State
49	Alaska	1959	Juneau	The Last Frontier
50	Hawaii	1959	Honolulu	Aloha State
District of Columbia		1791	Washington	

President	Term(s)	Political Party	Home State	Vice President(s)
George Washington	1789-1797	None	Virginia	John Adams
John Adams	1797-1801	Federalist	Massachusetts	Thomas Jefferson
Thomas Jefferson	1801-1809	Republican	Virginia	Aaron Burr George Clinton
James Madison	1809-1817	Republican	Virginia	George Clinton Elbridge Gerry
James Monroe	1817-1825	Republican	Virginia	Daniel D. Tompkins
John Quincy Adams	1825-1829	Republican	Massachusetts	John C. Calhoun
Andrew Jackson	1829-1837	Democrat	Tennessee	John C. Calhoun Martin Van Buren
Martin Van Buren	1837-1841	Democrat	New York	Richard M. Johnson
William H. Harrison	1841	Whig	Ohio	John Tyler
John Tyler	1841-1845	Whig	Virginia	
James K. Polk	1845-1849	Democrat	Tennessee	George M. Dallas
Zachary Taylor	1849-1850	Whig	Louisiana	Millard Fillmore
Millard Fillmore	1850-1853	Whig	New York	
Franklin Pierce	1853-1857	Democrat	New Hampshire	William R. King
James Buchanan	1857-1861	Democrat	Pennsylvania	John C. Breckinridge
Abraham Lincoln	1861-1865	Republican	Illinois	Hannibal Hamlin Andrew Johnson
Andrew Johnson	1865-1869	Republican	Tennessee	
Ulysses S. Grant	1869-1877	Republican	Illinois	Schuyler Colfax Henry Wilson
Rutherford B. Hayes	1877-1881	Republican	Ohio	William A. Wheeler
James A. Garfield	1881	Republican	Ohio	Chester A. Arthur
Chester A. Arthur	1881-1885	Republican	New York	
Grover Cleveland	1885-1889	Democrat	New York	Thomas A. Hendricks
Benjamin Harrison	1889-1893	Republican	Indiana	Levi P. Morton
Grover Cleveland	1893-1897	Democrat	New York	Adlai E. Stevenson
William McKinley	1897-1901	Republican	Ohio	Garret A. Hobart Theodore Roosevelt
Theodore Roosevelt	1901-1909	Republican	New York	Charles W. Fairbanks
William H. Taft	1909-1913	Republican	Ohio	James S. Sherman
Woodrow Wilson	1913-1921	Democrat	New Jersey	Thomas R. Marshall
Warren G. Harding	1921-1923	Republican	Ohio	Calvin Coolidge
Calvin Coolidge	1923-1929	Republican	Massachusetts	Charles G. Dawes
Herbert Hoover	1929-1933	Republican	California	Charles Curtis
Franklin D. Roosevelt	1933-1945	Democrat	New York	John Garner John Garner Henry A. Wallace Harry S. Truman
Harry S. Truman	1945-1953	Democrat	Missouri	Alben W. Barkley
Dwight D. Eisenhower	1953-1961	Republican	Pennsylvania	Richard M. Nixon
John F. Kennedy	1961-1963	Democrat	Massachusetts	Lyndon B. Johnson
Lyndon B. Johnson	1963-1969	Democrat	Texas	Hubert H. Humphrey
Richard M. Nixon	1969-1974	Republican	California	Spiro T. Agnew Gerald R. Ford
Gerald R. Ford	1974-1977	Republican	Michigan	Nelson A. Rockefeller
Jimmy Carter	1977-1981	Democrat	Georgia	Walter F. Mondale
Ronald Reagan	1981-1989	Republican	California	George Bush
George Bush	1989-1993	Republican	Texas	Dan Quayle
Bill Clinton	1993-2001	Democrat	Arkansas	Al Gore
George W. Bush	2001-2009	Republican	Texas	Richard Cheney
Barack Obama	2009–	Democrat	Illinois	Joe Biden

WASHINGTON
Olympia •
▲ Mt. Rainier
▲ Mt. St. Helens
• Salem

OREGON

MONTANA
• Helena

NORTH DAKOTA
• Bismarck

Badlands

SOUTH DAKOTA
• Pierre

IDAHO
• Boise

WYOMING

Black Hills

NEBRASKA

Rocky Mountains

Platte River

Salt Lake City •
• Cheyenne

Sacramento •
• Carson City

Sierra Nevada

NEVADA

UTAH

• Denver
▲ Pikes Peak

Lincoln •

KANSAS

Top

CALIFORNIA

Colorado River

Grand Canyon

COLORADO

Arkansas

PACIFIC
OCEAN

ARIZONA

• Santa Fe

NEW MEXICO

OKLAHOMA

Oklahoma City •

• Phoenix

Red River

TEXAS

Rio Grande

Austin •

• Honolulu

HAWAII

same scale as large map

Yukon River

ALASKA

• Juneau

0 100 200 300 400 500

scale in miles

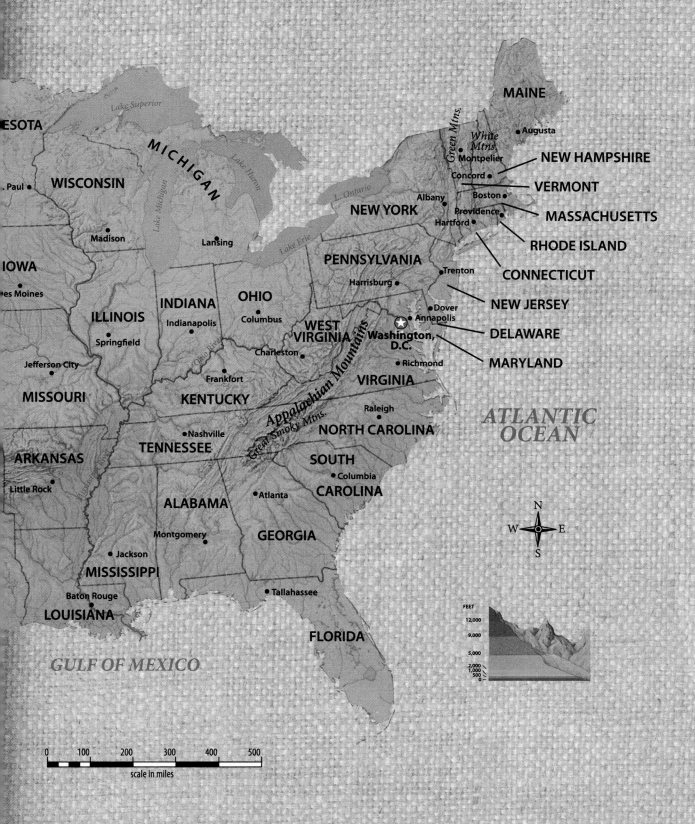

Lake Superior

ESOTA

MICHIGAN

WISCONSIN

Lake Huron

Lake Michigan

MAINE

Green Mtns.

White Mtns.

• Augusta

Montpelier

NEW HAMPSHIRE

Concord •

VERMONT

Albany •

Boston •

MASSACHUSETTS

. Paul •

Madison •

Lansing •

L. Ontario

NEW YORK

Providence •

Hartford •

RHODE ISLAND

CONNECTICUT

Lake Erie

PENNSYLVANIA

IOWA

es Moines •

INDIANA

OHIO

Harrisburg •

Trenton •

NEW JERSEY

ILLINOIS

Springfield •

Indianapolis •

Columbus •

WEST
VIRGINIA

Dover •

Annapolis •

DELAWARE

Ohio River

Washington,
D.C.

MARYLAND

Jefferson City •

Frankfort •

Charleston •

Richmond •

MISSOURI

KENTUCKY

VIRGINIA

Appalachian Mountains

Nashville •

Great Smoky Mtns.

Raleigh •

ATLANTIC
OCEAN

ARKANSAS

TENNESSEE

NORTH CAROLINA

Little Rock •

SOUTH

ALABAMA

Atlanta •

Columbia •

CAROLINA

Montgomery •

GEORGIA

N

Jackson •

W   E

MISSISSIPPI

S

Baton Rouge •

Tallahassee •

LOUISIANA

FLORIDA

FEET

12,000

GULF OF MEXICO

9,000

5,000

2,000
1,000
500
0

0   100   200   300   400   500

scale in miles

In CONGRESS, July 4, 1776.

The unanimous Declaration of the thirteen united States of America.

When in the Course of human events, it becomes necessary for one people to dissolve the political bands which have connected them with another, and to assume among the powers of the earth, the separate and equal station to which the Laws of Nature and of Nature's God entitle them, a decent respect to the opinions of mankind requires that they should declare the causes which impel them to the separation.

We hold these truths to be self-evident, that all men are created equal, that they are endowed by their Creator with certain unalienable Rights, that among these are Life, Liberty and the pursuit of Happiness. That to secure these rights, Governments are instituted among Men, deriving their just powers from the consent of the governed. That whenever any Form of Government becomes destructive of these ends, it is the Right of the People to alter or to abolish it, and to institute new Government, laying its foundation on such principles and organizing its powers in such form, as to them shall seem most likely to effect their Safety and Happiness. Prudence, indeed, will dictate that Governments long established should not be changed for light and transient causes, and accordingly, all experience hath shewn, that mankind are more disposed to suffer, while evils are sufferable, than to right themselves by abolishing the forms to which they are accustomed. But when a long train of abuses and usurpations, pursuing invariably the same Object, evinces a design to reduce them under absolute Despotism, it is their right, it is their duty, to throw off such Government, and to provide new Guards for their future security. Such has been the patient sufferance of the Colonies; and such is now the necessity which constrains them to expunge their former systems of government. The history of the present King of Great Britain is a history of the unremitting injuries and usurpations, all having in direct object the establishment of an absolute tyranny over these states. To prove this let facts be submitted to a candid world.

He has refused to pass other laws for the accommodation of large districts of people, unless those people would relinquish the right of representation in the legislature, a right inestimable to them, and formidable to tyrants only.

He has called together legislative bodies at places unusual, uncomfortable, and distant from the depository of the public records, for the sole purpose of fatiguing them into compliance with his measures.

He has dissolved representative houses repeatedly and continually for opposing with manly firmness his invasions on the right of the people.

He has refused for a long time after such dissolutions to cause others to be elected whereby the legislative powers incapable of annihilation have returned to the people at large for their exercise, the state remaining in the meantime exposed to all the dangers of invasion from without and convulsions within.

He has endeavored to prevent the population of these states, for that purpose obstructing the laws for naturalization of foreigners, refusing to pass others to encourage their migrations hither, and raising the conditions of new appropriations of lands.

He has suffered the administration of justice totally to cease in some of these states, refusing his assent to laws for establishing judiciary powers.

He has made judges dependent on his will alone, for the tenure of their offices and the amount and payment of their salaries.

He has erected a multitude of new offices, and sent hither swarms of officers to harass our people and eat out their substance.

He has kept among us, in times of peace, standing armies without the consent of our legislatures.

He has affected to render the military independent of and superior to the civil power.

He has combined with others to subject us to a jurisdiction foreign to our constitutions and unacknowledged by our laws, giving his assent to their acts of pretended legislation, for quartering large bodies of armed troops among us; for protecting them, by a mock trial, from punishment for any murders which they should commit on the inhabitants of these states; for cutting off our trade with all parts of the world; for imposing taxes on us without our consent; for depriving us in many cases of the benefits of trial by jury; for transporting us beyond seas to be tried for pretended offenses; for abolishing the free system of English laws in a neighboring province, establishing therein an arbitrary government, and enlarging its boundaries so as to render it at once an example and fit instrument for introducing the same absolute rule into these colonies; for taking away our charters, abolishing our most valuable laws, and altering fundamentally the forms of our governments; for suspending our own legislatures and declaring themselves invested with power to legislate for us in cases whatsoever.

He has abdicated government here by declaring us out of his protection, and waging war against us.

He has plundered our seas, ravaged our coasts, burnt our towns, and destroyed the lives of our people.

He is at this time transporting large armies of foreign mercenaries to complete the works of death, desolation, and tyranny, already begun with circumstances of cruelty and perfidy scarcely parallel in the most barbarous ages, and totally unworthy the head of a civilized nation.

He has excited domestic insurrection amongst us, and has endeavoured to bring on the inhabitants of our frontiers, the merciless Indian savages, whose known rules of warfare is an undistinguished destruction of all ages, sexes and conditions.

He has constrained our fellow citizens, taken captive on the high seas, to bear arms against their country, to become the executioners of their friends and brethren, or to fall themselves by their hands.

In every stage of these oppressions we have petitioned for redress in the most humble terms; our repeated petitions have been answered only by repeated injuries. A prince whose character is thus marked by every act which may define a tyrant is unfit to be the ruler of a people.

Nor have we been wanting in attentions to our British brethren. We have warned them from time to time of attempts by their legislature to extend an unwarrantable jurisdiction over us. We have reminded them of the circumstances of our emigration and settlement here. We have appealed to their native justice and magnanimity and have conjured them by the ties of our common kindred to disavow these usurpations which would inevitably interrupt our connection and correspondence. They too have been deaf to the voice of justice and of consanguinity. We must therefore acquiesce in the necessity which denounces our separation and hold them, as we hold the rest of mankind, enemies in war, in peace, friends.

We, therefore, the Representatives of the United States of America, in General Congress assembled, appealing to the Supreme Judge of the world for the rectitude of our intentions, do, in the name, and by authority of the good People of these Colonies, solemnly publish and declare, that these United Colonies are, and of right ought to be, free and independent states; that they are absolved from all allegiance to the British Crown, and that all political connection between them and the state of Great Britain is, and ought to be, totally dissolved; and that as free and independent states, they have full power to levy war, conclude peace, contract alliances, establish commerce, and to do all other acts and things which independent states may of right do.

And for the support of this Declaration, with a firm reliance on the protection of divine Providence, we mutually pledge to each other our lives, our fortunes, and our sacred honor.

The Constitution of the United States

We the People of the United States, in order to form a more perfect union, establish justice, insure domestic tranquility, provide for the common defense, promote the general welfare, and secure the blessings of liberty to ourselves and our posterity, do ordain and establish this Constitution for the United States of America.

Article I: The Legislative Branch

Section 1

All legislative powers herein granted shall be vested in a Congress of the United States, which shall consist of a Senate and House of Representatives.

Section 2

1. The House of Representatives shall be composed of members chosen every second year by the people of the several states, and the electors in each state shall have the qualifications requisite for electors of the most numerous branch of the state legislature.

2. No person shall be a representative who shall not have attained to the age of twenty-five years, and been seven years a citizen of the United States, and who shall not, when elected, be an inhabitant of that state in which he shall be chosen.

3. Representatives and direct taxes shall be apportioned among the several states which may be included within this Union, according to their respective numbers, *which shall be determined by adding to the whole number of free persons, including those bound to service for a term of years, and excluding Indians not taxed, three-fifths of all other persons.* The actual enumeration shall be made within three years after the first meeting of the Congress of the United States, and within every subsequent term of ten years, in such manners as they shall by law direct. The number of representatives shall not exceed one for every thirty thousand, but each state shall have at least one representative; *and until such enumeration shall be made, the state of New Hampshire shall be entitled to choose three, Massachusetts eight, Rhode Island and Providence Plantations one, Connecticut five, New York six, New Jersey four, Pennsylvania eight, Delaware one, Maryland six, Virginia ten, North Carolina five, South Carolina five, and Georgia three.*

4. When vacancies happen in the representation from any state, the executive authority thereof shall issue writs of election to fill such vacancies.

5. The House of Representatives shall choose their speaker and other officers; and shall have the sole power of impeachment.

Section 3

1. The Senate of the United States shall be composed of two senators from each state, chosen by the legislature thereof for six years; and each senator shall have one vote.

2. Immediately after they shall be assembled in consequence of the first election, they shall be divided as equally as may be into three classes. *The seats of the senators of the first class shall be vacated at the expiration of the second year of the second class at the expiration of the fourth year and of the third class at the expiration of the sixth year* so that one-third may be chosen every second year; *and if vacancies happen by resignation, or otherwise, during the recess of the legislature of any state, the executive thereof may make temporary appointments until the next meeting of the legislature, which shall then fill such vacancies.*

3. No person shall be a senator who shall not have attained to the age of thirty years, and been nine years a citizen of the United States, and who shall not, when elected, be an inhabitant of that state for which he shall be chosen.

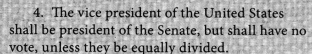

4. The vice president of the United States shall be president of the Senate, but shall have no vote, unless they be equally divided.

5. The Senate shall choose their other officers, and also a president pro tempore, in the absence of the vice president, or when he shall exercise the office of president of the United States.

6. The Senate shall have the sole power to try all impeachments. When sitting for that purpose, they shall be on oath or affirmation. When the president of the United States is tried, the chief justice shall preside: And no person shall be convicted without the concurrence of two-thirds of the members present.

7. Judgment in cases of impeachment shall not extend further than to removal from office, and disqualification to hold and enjoy any office of honor, trust or profit under the United States; but the party convicted shall nevertheless be liable and subject to indictment, trial, judgment and punishment, according to law.

Section 4

1. The times, places and manner of holding elections, for senators and representatives, shall be prescribed in each state by the legislature thereof, but the Congress may at any time by law make or alter such regulations, except as to the places of choosing senators.

2. The Congress shall assemble at least once in every year, *and such meeting shall be on the first Monday in December, unless they shall by law appoint a different day.*

Section 5

1. Each house shall be the judge of the elections, returns and qualifications of its own members, and a majority of each shall constitute a quorum to do business; but a smaller number may adjourn from day to day, and may be authorized to compel the attendance of absent members, in such manner, and under such penalties as each house may provide.

2. Each house may determine the rules of its proceedings, punish its members for disorderly behavior, and, with the concurrence of two-thirds, expel a member.

3. Each house shall keep a journal of its proceedings, and from time to time publish the same, excepting such parts as may, in their judgment, require secrecy; and the yeas and nays of the members of either house on any question, shall, at the desire of one-fifth of those present, be entered on the journal.

4. Neither house, during the session of Congress, shall, without the consent of the other, adjourn for more than three days, nor to any other place than that in which the two houses shall be sitting.

Section 6

1. The senators and representatives shall receive a compensation for their services, to be ascertained by law, and paid out of the treasury of the United States. They shall in all cases, except treason, felony, and breach of the peace, be privileged from arrest during their attendance at the session of their respective houses, and in going to and returning from the same; and for any speech or debate in either house, they shall not be questioned in any other place.

2. No senator or representative shall, during the time for which he was elected, be appointed to any civil office under the authority of the United States, which shall have been created, or the emoluments whereof shall have been increased during such time; and no person holding any office under the United States, shall be a member of either house during his continuance in office.

Section 7

1. All bills for raising revenue shall originate in the House of Representatives; but the Senate may propose or concur with amendments as on other bills.

2. Every bill which shall have passed the House of Representatives and the Senate, shall, before it becomes a law, be presented to the president of the United States; if he approves, he shall sign it, but if not, he shall return it, with his

objections, to that house in which it shall have originated, who shall enter the objections at large on their journal, and proceed to reconsider it. If after such reconsideration, two-thirds of that house shall agree to pass the bill, it shall be sent, together with the objections, to the other house, by which it shall likewise be reconsidered, and if approved by two-thirds of that house, it shall become a law. But in all such cases the votes of both houses shall be determined by yeas and nays, and the names of the persons voting for and against the bill shall be entered on the journal of each house respectively. If any bill shall not be returned by the president within ten days (Sundays excepted) after it shall have been presented to him, the same shall be a law, in like manner as if he had signed it, unless the Congress by their adjournment prevent its return, in which case it shall not be a law.

3. Every order, resolution, or vote to which the concurrence of the Senate and House of Representatives may be necessary (except on a question of adjournment) shall be presented to the president of the United States; and before the same shall take effect, shall be approved by him, or, being disapproved by him, shall be passed by two-thirds of the Senate and House of Representatives, according to the rules and limitations prescribed in the case of a bill.

Section 8

The Congress shall have power

1. To lay and collect taxes, duties, imposts and excises, to pay the debts and provide for the common defense and general welfare of the United States; but all duties, imposts, and excises shall be uniform throughout the United States.

2. To borrow money on the credit of the United States;

3. To regulate commerce with foreign nations, and among the several states, and with the Indian tribes;

4. To establish a uniform rule of naturalization, and uniform laws on the subject of bankruptcies throughout the United States;

5. To coin money, regulate the value thereof, and of foreign coin, and fix the standard of weights and measures;

6. To provide for the punishment of counterfeiting the securities and current coin of the United States;

7. To establish post-offices and post-roads;

8. To promote the progress of science and useful arts, by securing for limited times to authors and inventors the exclusive right to their respective writings and discoveries;

9. To constitute tribunals inferior to the Supreme Court;

10. To define and punish piracies and felonies committed on the high seas, and offenses against the law of nations;

11. To declare war, grant letters of marque and reprisal, and make rules concerning captures on land and water;

12. To raise and support armies, but no appropriation of money to that use shall be for a longer term than two years;

13. To provide and maintain a navy;

14. To make rules for the government and regulation of the land and naval forces;

15. To provide for calling forth the militia to execute the laws of the Union, suppress insurrections and repel invasions;

16. To provide for organizing, arming and disciplining the militia, and for governing such part of them as may be employed in the service of the United States, reserving to the states respectively, the appointment of the officers, and the authority of training the militia according to the discipline prescribed by Congress;

17. To exercise exclusive legislation in all cases whatsoever, over such district (not exceeding ten miles square) as may, by cession of particular states, and the acceptance of Congress, become the seat of the government of the United States, and to exercise like authority over all places purchased by the consent of the legislature of the state in which the same shall be, for

the erection of forts, magazines, arsenals, dock-yards, and other needful buildings; and

18. To make all laws which shall be necessary and proper for carrying into execution the foregoing powers, and all other powers vested by this Constitution in the government of the United States, or in any department or officer thereof.

Section 9

1. The migration or importation of such persons as any of the states now existing shall think proper to admit, shall not be prohibited by the Congress prior to the year 1808, but a tax or duty may be imposed on such importations, not exceeding ten dollars for each person.

2. The privilege of the writ of habeas corpus shall not be suspended, unless when in cases of rebellion or invasion the public safety may require it.

3. No bill of attainder or ex post facto law shall be passed.

4. No capitation, or other direct tax shall be laid unless in proportion to the census or enumeration herein before directed to be taken.

5. No tax or duty shall be laid on articles exported from any state.

6. No preference shall be given by any regulation of commerce or revenue to the ports of one state over those of another: nor shall vessels bound to, or from one state, be obliged to enter, clear, or pay duties in another.

7. No money shall be drawn from the treasury but in consequence of appropriations made by law; and a regular statement and account of the receipts and expenditures of all public money shall be published from time to time.

8. No title of nobility shall be granted by the United States: and no person holding any office of profit or trust under them, shall, without the consent of the Congress, accept of any present, emolument, office, or title, of any kind whatever, from any king, prince or foreign state.

Section 10

1. No state shall enter into any treaty, alliance, or confederation; grant letters of marque and reprisal; coin money; emit bills of credit; make any thing but gold and silver coin a tender in payment of debts; pass any bill of attainder, ex post facto law, or law impairing the obligation of contracts, or grant any title of nobility.

2. No state shall, without the consent of the Congress, lay any imposts or duties on imports or exports, except what may be absolutely necessary for executing its inspection laws; and the net produce of all duties and imposts, laid by any state on imports or exports, shall be for the use of the treasury of the United States; and all such laws shall be subject to the revision and control of the Congress.

3. No state shall, without the consent of Congress, lay any duty of tonnage, keep troops, or ships of war in time of peace, enter into any agreement or compact with another state, or with a foreign power, or engage in war, unless actually invaded, or in such imminent danger as will not admit of delay.

Article II: The Executive Branch

Section 1

1. The executive power shall be vested in a president of the United States of America. He shall hold his office during the term of four years, and, together with the vice president, chosen for the same term, be elected as follows.

2. Each state shall appoint, in such manner as the legislature thereof may direct, a number of electors, equal to the whole number of senators and representatives to which the state may be entitled in the Congress; but no senator or representative, or person holding an office of trust or profit under the United States, shall be appointed an elector.

The electors shall meet in their respective states, and vote by ballot for two persons, of whom one at least shall not be an inhabitant of the same state with themselves. And they shall make a list of all the persons voted for and of the number of votes for each; which list they shall sign and certify, and transmit sealed to the seat of the government of the United States, directed to the president of the Senate. The president of the Senate shall, in the presence of the Senate and House of Representatives, open all the certificates and the votes shall then be counted. The person having the greatest number of votes shall be the president, if such number be a majority of the whole number of electors appointed; and if there be more than one who have such majority, and have an equal number of votes, then the House of Representatives shall immediately choose by ballot one of them for president; and if no person have a majority, then from the five highest on the list, the said House shall, in like manner, choose the president. But in choosing the president, the votes shall be taken by states, the representation from each state having one vote; a quorum for this purpose shall consist of a member or members from two-thirds of the states, and a majority of all the states shall be necessary to a choice. In every case, after the choice of the president, the person having the greatest number of votes of the electors shall be the vice president. But if there should remain two or more who have equal votes, the Senate shall choose from them by ballot the vice president.

3. The Congress may determine the time of choosing the electors, and the day on which they shall give their votes; which day shall be the same throughout the United States.

4. No person except a natural born citizen, or a citizen of the United States, at the time of the adoption of this Constitution, shall be eligible to the office, who shall not have attained to the age of thirty-five years, and been fourteen years a resident within the United States.

5. In case of the removal of the president from office, or of his death, resignation, or inability to discharge the powers and duties of the said office, the same shall devolve on the vice president, and the Congress may by law provide for the case of removal, death, resignation, or inability, both of the president and vice president, declaring what officer shall then act as president,

and such officer shall act accordingly, until the disability be removed, or a president shall be elected.

6. The president shall, at stated times, receive for his services, a compensation, which shall neither be increased nor diminished during the period for which he shall have been elected, and he shall not receive within that period any other emolument from the United States, or any of them.

7. Before he enter on the execution of his office, he shall take the following oath or affirmation:—"I do solemnly swear (or affirm) that I will faithfully execute the office of president of the United States, and will to the best of my ability, preserve, protect and defend the Constitution of the United States."

Section 2

1. The president shall be commander in chief of the army and navy of the United States, and of the militia of the several states, when called into the actual service of the United States; he may require the opinion, in writing, of the principal officer in each of the executive departments, upon any subject relating to the duties of their respective offices, and he shall have power to grant reprieves and pardons for offenses against the United States, except in cases of impeachment.

2. He shall have power, by and with the advice and consent of the Senate, to make treaties, provided two-thirds of the senators present concur; and he shall nominate, and by and with the advice and consent of the Senate, shall appoint ambassadors, other public ministers and consuls, judges of the Supreme Court, and all other officers of the United States, whose appointments are not herein otherwise provided for, and which shall be established by law. But the Congress may by law vest the appointment of such inferior officers, as they think proper in the president alone, in the courts of law, or in the heads of departments.

3. The president shall have power to fill up all vacancies that may happen during the recess

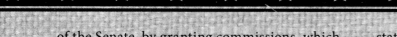

of the Senate, by granting commissions, which shall expire at the end of their next session.

Section 3

He shall; from time to time, give to the Congress information of the state of the Union, and recommend to their consideration, such measures as he shall judge necessary and expedient; he may, on extraordinary occasions, convene both houses, or either of them, and in case of disagreement between them, with respect to the time of adjournment, he may adjourn them to such time as he shall think proper; he shall receive ambassadors and other public ministers; he shall take care that the laws be faithfully executed, and shall commission all the officers of the United States.

Section 4

The president, vice president, and all civil officers of the United States shall be removed from office on impeachment for, and conviction of, treason, bribery, or other high crimes and misdemeanors.

Article III: The Judicial Branch

Section 1

The judicial power of the United States shall be vested in one Supreme Court, and in such court and in such inferior courts as the Congress may from time to time, ordain and establish. The judges, both of the Supreme and inferior courts, shall hold their offices during good behavior, and shall, at stated times, receive for their services a compensation, which shall not be diminished during their continuance in office.

Section 2

1. The judicial powers shall extend to all cases, in law and equity, arising under this Constitution, the laws of the United States, and treaties made, or which shall be made under their authority; to all cases affecting ambassadors, other public ministers and consuls; to all cases of admiralty and maritime jurisdiction; to controversies to which the United States shall be a party; to controversies between two or more

states; *between a state and citizens of another state*; between citizens of different states, between citizens of the same state claiming lands under grants of different states, and between a state, or the citizens thereof, and foreign states, citizens or subjects.

2. In all cases affecting ambassadors, other public ministers and consuls, and those in which a state shall be party, the Supreme Court shall have original jurisdiction. In all the other cases before mentioned, the Supreme Court shall have appellate jurisdiction, both as to law and fact, with such exceptions, and under such regulations as the Congress shall make.

3. The trial of all crimes, except in cases of impeachment, shall be by jury; and such trial shall be held in the state where the said crimes shall have been committed; but when not committed within any state, the trial shall be at such place or places as the Congress may by law have directed.

Section 3

1. Treason against the United States shall consist only in levying war against them, or in adhering to their enemies, giving them aid and comfort. No person shall be convicted of treason unless on the testimony of two witnesses to the same overt act, or on confession in open court.

2. The Congress shall have power to declare the punishment of treason, but no attainder of treason shall work corruption of blood, or forfeiture, except during the life of the person attained.

Article IV: Interstate Relations

Section 1

Full faith and credit shall be given each state to the public acts, records and judicial proceedings of every other state. And the Congress may by general laws prescribe the manner in which such acts, records and proceedings shall be proved, and the effect thereof.

Section 2

1. The citizens of each state shall be entitled to all privileges and immunities of citizens in the several states.

2. A person charged in any state with treason, felony, or other crime, who, shall flee from justice, and be found in another state, shall, on demand of the executive authority of the state from which he fled, be delivered up, to be removed to the state having jurisdiction of the crime.

3. *No person held to service or labor in one state, under the laws thereof escaping into another shall, in consequence of any law or regulation therein, be discharged from such service or labor but shall be delivered up on claim of the party to whom such service or labor may be due.*

Section 3

1. New states may be admitted by the Congress into this Union; but no new state shall be formed or erected within the jurisdiction of any other state, nor any state be formed by the junction of two or more states, or parts of states, without the consent of the legislatures of the states concerned as well as of the Congress.

2. The Congress shall have power to dispose of and make all needful rules and regulations respecting the territory or other property belonging to the United States; and nothing in this Constitution shall be so construed as to prejudice any claims of the United States, or any particular state.

Section 4

The United States shall guarantee to every state in this Union a republican form of government, and shall protect each of them against invasion; and on application of the legislature, or of the executive (when the legislature cannot be convened), against domestic violence.

Article V: Amending the Constitution

The Congress, whenever two-thirds of both houses shall deem it necessary, shall propose amendments to this Constitution, or on the application of the legislatures of two-thirds of the several states, shall call a convention for proposing amendments, which, in either case, shall be valid to all intents and purposes, as part of this Constitution, which ratified by the legislatures of three-fourths of the several states, or by conventions in three-fourths thereof, as the one or the other mode of ratification may be proposed by the Congress; Provided that *no amendment which may be made prior to the year 1808 shall in any manner affect the first and fourth clauses in the ninth section of the first article; and that* no state, without its consent, shall be deprived of its equal suffrage in the Senate.

Article VI: Constitutional and National Supremacy

1. All debts contracted and engagements entered into, before the adoption of this Constitution, shall be as valid against the United States under this Constitution, as under the confederation.

2. This Constitution, and the laws of the United States which shall be made in pursuance thereof; and all treaties made, or which shall be made, under the authority of the United States, shall be the supreme law of the land; and the judges in every state shall be bound thereby, anything in the constitution or laws of any state to the contrary notwithstanding.

3. The senators and representatives before mentioned, and the members of the several state legislatures, and all executive and judicial officers, both of the United States and of the several states, shall be bound by oath or affirmation, to support this Constitution; but no religious test shall ever be required as a qualification to any office or public trust under the United States.

Article VII: Ratifying the Constitution

The ratification of the conventions of nine states shall be sufficient for the establishment of this Constitution between the states so ratifying the same. Done in convention by the unanimous consent of the states present, the seventeenth

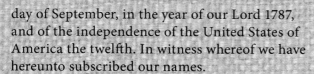

day of September, in the year of our Lord 1787, and of the independence of the United States of America the twelfth. In witness whereof we have hereunto subscribed our names.

George Washington, President and Deputy from Virginia

New Hampshire: John Langdon, Nicholas Gilman

Massachusetts: Nathaniel Gorham, Rufus King

Connecticut: William Samuel Johnson, Roger Sherman

New York: Alexander Hamilton

New Jersey: William Livingston, David Brearley, William Paterson, Jonathan Dayton

Pennsylvania: Benjamin Franklin, Thomas Mifflin, Robert Morris, George Clymer, Thomas Fitzsimons, Jared Ingersoll, James Wilson, Gouverneur Morris

Delaware: George Read, Gunning Bedford Jr., John Dickinson, Richard Bassett, Jacob Broom

Maryland: James McHenry, Daniel of St. Thomas Jenifer, Daniel Carroll

Virginia: John Blair, James Madison Jr.

North Carolina: William Blount, Richard Dobbs Spaight, Hugh Williamson

South Carolina: John Rutledge, Charles Cotesworth Pinckney, Charles Pinckney, Pierce Butler

Georgia: William Few, Abraham Baldwin

Amendments to the Constitution

Amendment I: Foundational Freedoms

Congress shall make no law respecting an establishment of religion, or prohibiting the free exercise thereof, or abridging the freedom of speech or of the press; or the right of the people peaceably to assemble, and to petition the government for a redress of grievances.

Amendment II: The Right to Bear Arms

A well-regulated militia being necessary to the security of a free state, the right of the people to keep and bear arms shall not be infringed.

Amendment III: No Quartering of Troops

No soldier shall, in time of peace, be quartered in any house without the consent of the owner, nor in time of war but in a manner to be prescribed by law.

Amendment IV: No Unreasonable Searches

The right of the people to be secure in their persons, houses, papers, and effects, against unreasonable searches and seizures, shall not be violated, and no warrants shall issue but upon probable cause, supported by oath or affirmation, and particularly describing the place to be searched, and the persons or things to be seized.

Amendment V: Rights of the Accused

No person shall be held to answer for a capital or other infamous crime unless on a presentment or indictment of a grand jury, except in cases arising in the land or naval forces, or in the militia, when in actual service, in time of war or public danger; nor shall any person be subject for the same offense to be twice put in jeopardy of life or limb; nor shall be compelled in any criminal case to be a witness against himself, nor be deprived of life, liberty, or property, without due process of law; nor shall private property be taken for public use without just compensation.

Amendment VI: Rights of the Accused in Criminal Trials

In all criminal prosecutions, the accused shall enjoy the right to a speedy and public trial, by an impartial jury of the state and district wherein the crime shall have been committed, which district shall have been previously ascertained by law, and to be informed of the nature and cause of the accusation; to be confronted with the witnesses against him; to have compulsory process for obtaining witnesses in his favor,

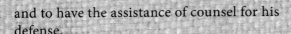

and to have the assistance of counsel for his defense.

Amendment VII: Rights of Citizens in Civil Trials

In suits at common law, where the value in controversy shall exceed twenty dollars, the right of trial by jury shall be preserved, and no fact tried by a jury shall be otherwise re-examined in any court of the United States than according to the rules of the common law.

Amendment VIII: Cruel, Unusual, and Unjust Punishments

Excessive bail shall not be required, nor excessive fines imposed, nor cruel and unusual punishments inflicted.

Amendment IX: Unspecified Rights

The enumeration in the Constitution of certain rights shall not be construed to deny or disparage others retained by the people.

Amendment X: Unlisted Rights Go to States or to the People

The powers not delegated to the United States by the Constitution, nor prohibited by it to the states, are reserved to the states respectively, or to the people.

Amendment XI: Suing States

(Proposed March 4, 1794; ratified January 8, 1798)

The judicial power of the United States shall not be construed to extend to any suit in law or equity, commenced or prosecuted against one of the United States, by citizens of another state, or by citizens or subjects of any foreign state.

Amendment XII: Separate Ballots for President and Vice President

(Proposed December 9, 1803; ratified September 25, 1804)

The electors shall meet in their respective states, and vote by ballot for president and vice president, one of whom, at least, shall not be an inhabitant of the same state with themselves; they shall name in their ballots the person voted for as president, and in distinct ballots, the person voted for as vice president, and they shall make distinct lists of all persons voted for as president and of all persons voted for as vice president, and of the number of votes for each, which lists they shall sign and certify, and transmit sealed to the seat of the government of the United States, directed to the president of the Senate; the president of the Senate shall, in the presence of the Senate and House of Representatives, open all the certificates and the votes shall then be counted; the person having the greatest number of votes for president, shall be the president, if such number be a majority of the whole number of electors appointed; and if no person have such majority, then from the persons having the highest numbers not exceeding three on the list of those voted for as president, the House of Representatives shall choose immediately, by ballot, the president. But in choosing the president, the votes shall be taken by states, the representation from each state having one vote; a quorum for this purpose shall consist of a member or members from two-thirds of the states, and a majority of all the states shall be necessary to a choice. And if the House of Representatives shall not choose a president whenever the right of choice shall devolve upon them, *before the fourth day of March next following,* then the vice president shall act as president, as in the case of the death or other constitutional disability of the president. The person having the greatest number of votes as vice president shall be the vice president, if such number be a majority of the whole number of electors appointed, and if no person have a majority, then from the two highest numbers on the list, the Senate shall choose the vice president; a quorum for the purpose shall consist of two-thirds of the whole number of senators, and a majority of the whole number shall be necessary to a choice. But no person constitutionally ineligible to the office of president shall be eligible to that of vice president of the United States.

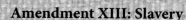

Amendment XIII: Slavery

(Proposed January 31, 1865; ratified December 18, 1865)

Section 1. Neither slavery nor involuntary servitude, except as a punishment for crime whereof the party shall have been duly convicted, shall exist within the United States, or any place subject to their jurisdiction.

Section 2. Congress shall have power to enforce this article by appropriate legislation.

Amendment XIV: Citizenship

(Proposed June 13, 1866; ratified July 28, 1868)

Section 1. All persons born or naturalized in the United States, and subject to the jurisdiction thereof, are citizens of the United States and of the state wherein they reside. No state shall make or enforce any law which shall abridge the privileges or immunities of citizens of the United States; nor shall any state deprive any person of life, liberty, or property without due process of law; nor deny to any person within its jurisdiction the equal protection of the law.

Section 2. Representatives shall be apportioned among the several states according to their respective numbers, counting the whole number of persons in each state, *excluding Indians not taxed.* But when the right to vote at any election for the choice of electors for president and vice president of the United States, representatives in Congress, the executive and judicial officers of a state, or the members of the legislature thereof, is denied to any of the male inhabitants of such state being of twentyone years of age, and citizens of the United States, or in any way abridged, except for participation in rebellion or other crime, the basis of representation therein shall be reduced in the proportion which the number of such male citizens shall bear to the whole number of male citizens twenty-one years of age in such state.

Section 3. No person shall be a senator or representative in Congress, or elector of president and vice president, or hold any office, civil or military, under the United States, or under any state, who having previously taken an oath, as a member of Congress, or as an officer of the United States, or as a member of any state legislature, or as an executive or judicial officer of any state, to support the Constitution of the United States, shall have engaged in insurrection or rebellion against the same, or given aid and comfort to the enemies thereof. But Congress may, by a vote of two-thirds of each house, remove such disability.

Section 4. The validity of the public debt of the United States, authorized by law, including debts incurred for payment of pensions and bounties for services in suppressing insurrection or rebellion, shall not be questioned. But neither the United States nor any state shall assume or pay any debt or obligation incurred in aid of insurrection or rebellion against the United States, or any claim for the loss or emancipation of any slave; but all such debts, obligations, and claims shall be held illegal and void.

Section 5. The Congress shall have power to enforce, by appropriate legislation, the provisions of this article.

Amendment XV: Black Voting Rights

(Proposed February 26, 1869; ratified March 30, 1870)

Section 1. The right of the citizens of the United States to vote shall not be denied or abridged by the United States or by any state, on account of race, color, or previous condition of servitude.

Section 2. The Congress shall have power to enforce this article by appropriate legislation.

Amendment XVI: Income Tax

(Proposed July 12, 1909; ratified February 25, 1913)

The Congress shall have power to lay and collect taxes on incomes, from whatever source derived, without apportionment among the several states, and without regard to any census or enumeration.

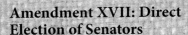

Amendment XVII: Direct Election of Senators

(Proposed May 13, 1912; ratified May 31, 1913)

The Senate of the United States shall be composed of two senators from each state, elected by the people thereof for six years; and each senator shall have one vote. The electors in each state shall have the qualifications requisite for electors of the most numerous branch of the state legislatures.

When vacancies happen in the representation of any state in the Senate, the executive authority of such state shall issue writs of election to fill such vacancies; provided, that the legislature of any state may empower the executive thereof to make temporary appointments until the people fill the vacancies by election as the legislature may direct.

This amendment shall not be so construed as to affect the election or term of any senator chosen before it becomes valid as part of the Constitution.

Amendment XVIII: Prohibition

(Proposed December 18, 1917; ratified January 29, 1919)

Section 1. *After one year from the ratification of this article the manufacture, sale, or transportation of intoxicating liquors within, the importation thereof into, or exportation thereof from the United States and all territory subject to the jurisdiction thereof for beverage purposes is hereby prohibited.*

Section 2. *The Congress and the several states shall have concurrent power to enforce this article by appropriate legislation.*

Section 3. *This article shall be inoperative unless it shall have been ratified as an amendment to the Constitution by the legislatures of the several states, as provided in the Constitution, within seven years from the date of submission hereof to the states by the Congress.*

Amendment XIX: Women's Suffrage

(Proposed June 4, 1919; ratified August 26, 1920)

Section 1. The right of the citizens of the United States to vote shall not be denied or abridged by the United States or by any state on account of sex.

Section 2. The Congress shall have power to enforce this article by appropriate legislation.

Amendment XX: Lame Duck Amendment

(Proposed March 2, 1932; ratified February 6, 1933)

Section 1. The terms of the president and the vice president shall end at noon on the 20th day of January, and the terms of senators and representatives at noon on the 3rd day of January, of the years in which such terms would have ended if this article had not been ratified; and the terms of their successors shall then begin.

Section 2. The Congress shall assemble at least once in every year, and such meeting shall begin at noon on the 3rd day of January, unless they shall by law appoint a different day.

Section 3. If, at the time fixed for the beginning of the term of president, the president-elect shall have died, the vice president-elect shall become president. If a president shall not have been chosen before the time fixed for the beginning of his term, or if the president-elect shall have failed to qualify, then the vice president-elect shall act as president until a president shall have qualified; and the Congress may by law provide for the case wherein neither a president-elect nor a vice president-elect shall have qualified, declaring who shall then act as president, or the manner in which one who is to act shall be selected, and such person shall act accordingly until a president or vice president shall have qualified.

Section 4. The Congress may by law provide for the case of the death of any of the persons from whom the House of Representatives may choose a president, whenever the right of choice shall have devolved upon them, and for the case of the death of any of the persons from whom the Senate may choose a vice president, whenever the right of choice shall have devolved upon them.

Section 5. Sections 1 and 2 shall take effect on the 15th day of October following the ratification of this article.

Section 6. *This article shall be inoperative unless it shall have been ratified as an amendment to the Constitution by the legislatures of three-fourths of the several states within seven years from the date of its submission.*

Amendment XXI: Repeal of Prohibition

(Proposed February 20, 1933; ratified December 5, 1933)

Section 1. The eighteenth article of amendment to the Constitution of the United States is hereby repealed.

Section 2. The transportation or importation into any state, territory, or possession of the United States, for delivery or use therein of intoxicating liquors, in violation of the laws thereof, is hereby prohibited.

Section 3. *This article shall be inoperative unless it shall have been ratified as an amendment to the Constitution by conventions in the several states, as provided in the Constitution, within seven years from the date of the submission thereof to the states by the Congress.*

Amendment XXII: Presidential Terms

(Proposed March 24, 1947; ratified February 27, 1951)

Section 1. No person shall be elected to the office of the president more than twice, and no person who has held the office of president, or acted as president, for more than two years of a term to which some other person who was elected president shall be elected to the office of the president more than once. *But this article shall not apply to any person holding the office of president when this article was proposed by the Congress, and shall not prevent any person who may be holding the office of president, or acting as president, during the term within which this article becomes operative from holding the office of president, or acting as president during the remainder of such term.*

Section 2. *This article shall be inoperative unless it shall have been ratified as an amendment to the Constitution by the legislatures of three-fourths of the several states within seven years*

from the date of its submission to the states by the Congress.

Amendment XXIII: Voting for Washington, D.C.

(Proposed June 16, 1960; ratified April 3, 1961)

Section 1. The District constituting the seat of government of the United States shall appoint in such manner as Congress may direct:

A number of electors of president and vice president equal to the whole number of senators and representatives in Congress to which the District would be entitled if it were a state, but in no event more than the least populous state; they shall be in addition to those appointed by the states, but they shall be considered, for the purposes of the election of president and vice president, to be electors appointed by a state; and they shall meet in the District and perform such duties as provided by the twelfth article of amendment.

Section 2. The Congress shall have power to enforce this article by appropriate legislation.

Amendment XXIV: No Poll Tax

(Proposed August 27, 1962; ratified February 4, 1964)

Section 1. The right of citizens of the United States to vote in any primary or other election for president or vice president, for electors for president or vice president, or for senator or representative in Congress, shall not be denied or abridged by the United States or any state by reason of failure to pay any poll tax or other tax.

Section 2. The Congress shall have the power to enforce this article by appropriate legislation.

Amendment XXV: Presidential Succession

(Proposed July 6, 1965; ratified February 23, 1967)

Section 1. In case of the removal of the president from office or of his death or resignation, the vice president shall become president.

Section 2. Whenever there is a vacancy in the office of the vice president, the president shall nominate a vice president who shall take office

upon confirmation by a majority vote of both houses of Congress.

Section 3. Whenever the president transmits to the president pro tempore of the Senate and the Speaker of the House of Representatives his written declaration that he is unable to discharge the powers and duties of his office, and until he transmits to them written declaration to the contrary, such powers and duties shall be discharged by the vice president as acting president.

Section 4. Whenever the vice president and a majority of either the principal officers of the executive departments or of such other body as Congress may by law provide, transmit to the president pro tempore of the Senate and the Speaker of the House of Representatives their written declaration that the president is unable to discharge the powers and duties of his office, the vice president shall immediately assume the powers and duties of the office as acting president.

Thereafter, when the president transmits to the president pro tempore of the Senate and the Speaker of the House of Representatives his written declaration that no inability exists, he shall resume the powers and duties of his office unless the vice president and a majority of either the principal officers of the executive department or of such other body as Congress may by law provide, transmit within four days to the president pro tempore of the Senate and the Speaker of the

House of Representatives their written declaration that the president is unable to discharge the powers and duties of his office. Thereupon Congress shall decide the issue, assembling within forty-eight hours for that purpose if not in session. If the Congress, within twenty-one days after receipt of the latter written declaration, or, if Congress is not in session, within twenty-one days after Congress is required to assemble, determines by two-thirds vote of both houses that the president is unable to discharge the powers and duties of his office, the vice president shall continue to discharge the same as acting president; otherwise, the president shall resume the powers and duties of his office.

Amendment XXVI: Eighteen-Year-Old Vote
(Proposed March 23, 1971; ratified July 5, 1971)

Section 1. The right of citizens of the United States, who are eighteen years of age or older, to vote shall not be denied or abridged by the United States or by any state on account of age.

Section 2. The Congress shall have power to enforce this article by appropriate legislation.

Amendment XXVII: Congressional Pay Raises
(Proposed June 8, 1789; ratified May 7, 1992)

No law, varying the compensation for the services of the senators and representatives, shall take effect until an election of representatives shall have intervened.

Federalist No. 10
Securing the Public Good and Private Rights
Against the Dangers of Faction
by James Madison

10.1 Among the numerous advantages promised by a well-constructed Union, none deserves to be more accurately developed than its tendency to break and control the violence of faction. The friend of popular governments never finds himself so much alarmed for their character and fate, as when he contemplates their propensity to the dangerous vice. He will not fail, therefore, to set a due value on any plan which, without violating the principles to which he is attached, provides a proper cure for it.

The Public Good Is Disregarded in the Conflicts of Rival Parties

10.2 The instability, injustice, and confusion introduced into the public councils, have, in truth, been the mortal diseases under which popular governments have everywhere perished; as they continue to be the favorite and fruitful topics from which the adversaries to liberty derive their most specious declamations. The valuable improvements made by the American constitutions on the popular models, both ancient and modem, cannot certainly be too much admired; but it would be an unwarrantable partiality, to contend that they have as effectually obviated the danger on this side, as was wished and expected. Complaints are everywhere heard from our most considerate and virtuous citizens, equally the friends of public and private faith, and of public and personal liberty, that our governments are too unstable, that the public good is disregarded in the conflicts of rival parties, and that measures are too often decided, not according to the rules of justice and the rights of the minor party, but by the superior force of an interested and overbearing majority.

10.3 However anxiously we may wish that these complaints had no foundation, the evidence of known facts will not permit us to deny that they are in some degree true. It will be found, indeed, on a candid review of our situation, that some of the distresses under which we labor have been erroneously charged on the operations of our governments; but it will be found, at the same time, that other causes will not alone account for many of our heaviest misfortunes; and, particularly, for that prevailing and increasing distrust of public engagement, and alarm for private rights, which are echoed from one end of the continent to the other. These must be chiefly, if not wholly, effects of the unsteadiness and injustice with which a factious spirit has tainted our public administrations.

A Faction Is Defined as a Group of People Adverse to the Rights of Other Citizens

10.4 By a faction, I understand a number of citizens, whether amounting to a majority or minority of the whole, who are united and actuated by some common impulse of passion, or of interest, adverse to the rights of other citizens, or to the permanent and aggregate interest of the community.

There Are Two Methods of Curing the Mischiefs of Faction

10.5 There are two methods of curing the mischiefs of faction: the one, by removing its causes; the other, by controlling its effects.

There are Two Methods of Removing the Causes of Faction

10.6 There are again two methods of removing the causes of faction: the one, by destroying the liberty which is essential to its existence; the other, by giving to every citizen the same opinions, the same passions, and the same interests.

The First Remedy Is Worse Than the Disease

10.7 It could never be more truly said than of the first remedy, that it was worse than the disease. Liberty is to faction what air is to fire, an aliment without which it instantly expires. But it could not be less folly to abolish liberty, which is essential to political life, because it nourishes faction, than it would be to wish the annihilation of air, which is essential to animal life, because it imparts to fire its destructive agency.

The Second Remedy Is Impracticable

10.8 The second expedient is as impracticable as the first would be unwise. As long as the reason of man continues fallible, and he is at liberty to exercise it, different opinions will be formed. As long as the connection subsists between his reason and his self-love, his opinions and his passions will have a reciprocal influence on each other; and the former will be objects to which the latter will attach themselves.

Protection of the Rights of Property Is the First Object of Government

10.9 The diversity in the faculties of men, from which the rights of property originate, is not less an insuperable obstacle to a uniformity of interests. The protection of these faculties is the first object of government. From the protection of different and unequal faculties of acquiring property, the possession of different degrees and kinds of property immediately results; and from the influence of these on the sentiments and views of the respective proprietors, ensues a division of the society into different interests and parties.

The Latent Causes of Faction Are Sown into the Nature of Man

10.10 The latent causes of faction are thus sown in the nature of man; and we see them everywhere brought into different degrees of activity, according to the different circumstances of civil society. A zeal for different opinions concerning religion, concerning government, and many other points, as well of speculation as of practice; an attachment to different leaders ambitiously contending for pre-eminence and power; or to persons of other descriptions whose fortunes have been interesting to the human passions, have, in turn, divided mankind into parties, inflamed them with mutual animosity, and rendered them much more disposed to vex and oppress each other than to cooperate for their common good. So strong is this propensity of mankind to fall into mutual animosities, that where no substantial occasion presents itself, the most frivolous distinctions have been sufficient to kindle their unfriendly passions and excite their most violent conflicts.

The Most Common Source of Factions Has Been over the Unequal Distribution of Property

10.11 But the most common and durable source of factions has been the various and unequal distribution of property. Those who hold and those who are without property have ever formed distinct interests in society. Those who are creditors, and those who are debtors, fall under a like discrimination. A landed interest, a manufacturing interest, a mercantile interest, a moneyed interest, with many lesser interests, grow up of necessity in civilized nations, and divide them into different classes, actuated by different sentiments and views.

The Principal Task of Modern Legislation Is to Regulate Various Interfering Interests

10.12 The regulation of these various and interfering interests forms the principal task of modern legislation, and involves the spirit of party and faction in the necessary and ordinary operations of government.

10.13 No man is allowed to be a judge in his own cause, because his interest would certainly bias his judgment, and, not improbably, corrupt his integrity. With equal, nay with greater reason, a body of men are unfit to be both judges

and parties at the same time; yet what are many of the most important acts of legislation, but so many judicial determinations, not indeed concerning the rights of single persons, but concerning the rights of large bodies of citizens? And what are the different classes of legislators but advocates and parties to the causes which they determine? Is a law proposed concerning private debts? It is a question to which the creditors are parties on one side and the debtors on the other. Justice ought to hold the balance between them. Yet the parties are, and must be, themselves the judges; and the most numerous party, or, in other words, the most powerful faction must be expected to prevail. Shall domestic manufactures be encouraged, and in what degree, by restrictions on foreign manufactures? are questions which would be differently decided by the landed and the manufacturing classes, and probably by neither with a sole regard to justice and the public good.

Property Taxes Provide a Great Opportunity and Temptation to Trample the Rules of Justice

10.14 The apportionment of taxes on the various descriptions of property is an act which seems to require the most exact impartiality; yet there is, perhaps, no legislative act in which greater opportunity and temptation are given to a predominant party to trample on the rules of justice. Every shilling with which they overburden the inferior number, is a shilling saved to their own pockets.

Enlightened Statesmen Will Not Always Be at the Helm

10.15 It is vain to say that enlightened statesmen will be able to adjust these clashing interests, and render them all subservient to the public good. Enlightened statesmen will not always be at the helm. Nor, in many cases, can such an adjustment be made at all without taking into view indirect and remote considerations, which will rarely prevail over the immediate interest which one party may find in

disregarding the rights of another or the good of the whole.

It Is Necessary to Control the Effects of Faction

10.16 The inference to which we are brought is, that the causes of faction cannot be removed, and that relief is only to be sought in the means of controlling its effects.

The Constitution Protects the Majority of the People from a Faction of the Minority

10.17 If a faction consists of less than a majority, relief is supplied by the republican principle, which enables the majority to defeat its sinister views by regular vote. It may clog the administration, it may convulse the society; but it will be unable to execute and mask its violence under the forms of the Constitution.

10.18 When a majority is included in a faction, the form of popular government, on the other hand, enables it to sacrifice to its ruling passion or interest both the public good and the rights of other citizens.

Securing the Public Good and Private Rights Against the Dangers of Faction Is the Great Object

10.19 To secure the public good and private rights against the danger of such a faction, and at the same time to preserve the spirit and the form of popular government, is then the great object to which our inquiries are directed. Let me add that it is the great desideratum by which this form of government can be rescued from the opprobrium under which it has so long labored, and be recommended to the esteem and adoption of mankind.

10.20 By what means is this object attainable? Evidently by one of two only. Either the existence of the same passion or interest in a majority at the same time must be prevented, or the majority, having such coexistent passion or interest, must be rendered, by the number and local situation, unable to concert and carry into effect schemes of oppression. If the impulse and the opportunity be suffered to coincide, we well know that neither moral nor religious motives

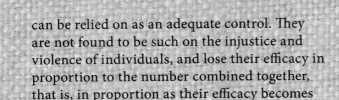

can be relied on as an adequate control. They are not found to be such on the injustice and violence of individuals, and lose their efficacy in proportion to the number combined together, that is, in proportion as their efficacy becomes needful.

A Pure Democracy Can Admit of No Cure for the Mischiefs of Faction

10.21 From this view of the subject it may be concluded that a pure democracy, by which I mean a society of a small number of citizens, who assemble and administer the government in person, can admit of no cure for the mischiefs of faction. A common passion or interest will, in almost every case, be felt by a majority of the whole; a communication and concert result from the form of government itself; and there is nothing to check the inducements to sacrifice the weaker party or an obnoxious individual.

Democracies Have Ever Been Found Incompatible with Personal Security and the Rights of Property

10.22 Hence it is that such democracies have ever been spectacles of turbulence and contention; have ever been found incompatible with personal security or the rights of property; and have in general been as short in their lives as they have been violent in their deaths.

Politicians Have Made Erroneous Assumptions Regarding Political Rights

10.23 Theoretic politicians, who have patronized this species of government, have erroneously supposed that by reducing mankind to a perfect equality in their political rights, they would, at the same time, be perfectly equalized and assimilated in their possessions, their opinions, and their passions.

Republican Government Promises to Secure the Public Good and Private Rights against the Danger of Faction

10.24 A republic, by which I mean a government in which the scheme of representation takes place, opens a different prospect, and promises the cure for which we are seeking. Let us examine the points in which it varies from pure democracy and we shall comprehend both the nature of the cure and the efficacy which it must derive from the Union.

There Are Two Main Differences between a Democracy and a Republic

10.25 The two great points of difference between a democracy and a republic are: first, the delegation of the government, in the latter, to a small number of citizens elected by the rest; secondly, the greater number of citizens, and greater sphere of country, over which the latter may be extended.

The Virtues of Patriotic and Just Representatives Are Founded in Their Desire for Public Good

10.26 The effect of the first difference is, on the one hand, to refine and enlarge the public views, by passing them through the medium of a chosen body of citizens, whose wisdom may best discern the true interest of their country, and whose patriotism and love of justice will be least likely to sacrifice it to temporary or partial considerations. Under such a regulation, it may well happen that the public voice, pronounced by the representatives of the people, will be more consonant to the public good than if pronounced by the people themselves, convened for the purpose.

Sinister Representatives May Betray the Interests of the People

10.27 On the other hand, the effect maybe inverted. Men of factious tempers, of local prejudices, or of sinister designs, may, by intrigue, by corruption, or by other means, first obtain the suffrages, and then betray the interests, of the people.

Large Republics Are More Favorable to the Election of Proper Representatives

10.28 The question resulting is, whether small or extensive republics are more favorable to the election of proper guardians of the public weal; and it is clearly decided in favor of the latter by two obvious considerations:

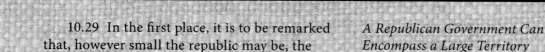

10.29 In the first place, it is to be remarked that, however small the republic may be, the representatives must be raised to a certain number, in order to guard against the cabals of a few; and that, however large it may be, they must be limited to a certain number, in order to guard against the confusion of a multitude. Hence, the number of representatives in the two cases not being in proportion to that of the two constituents, and being proportionally greater in the small republic, it follows that, if the proportion of fit characters be not less in the large than in the small republic, the former will present a greater option, and consequently a greater probability of a fit choice.

The Constitution Provides for the Public to Be Protected from Unworthy Candidates

10.30 In the next place, as each representative will be chosen by a greater number of citizens in the large than in the small republic, it will be more difficult for unworthy candidates to practice with success the vicious arts by which elections are too often carried; and the suffrages of the people being more free, will be more likely to center in men who possess the most attractive merit and the most diffusive and established characters.

The Federal Constitution Provides a Proper Combination for Best Representation

10.31 It must be confessed that in this, as in most other cases, there is a mean, on both sides of which inconveniences will be found to lie. By enlarging too much the number of electors, you render the representative too little acquainted with all their local circumstances and lesser interests; as by reducing it too much, you render him unduly attached to these, and too little fit to comprehend and pursue great and national objects. The federal Constitution forms a happy combination in this respect; the great and aggregate interest being referred to the national, the local and particularly the State legislatures.

A Republican Government Can Encompass a Large Territory

10.32 The other point of difference is, the greater number of citizens and extent of territory which may be brought within the compass of republican than of democratic government; and it is this circumstance principally which renders factious combinations less to be dreaded in the former than in the latter. The smaller the society, the fewer probably will be the distinct parties and interests composing it; the fewer the distinct parties and interests, the more frequently will a majority be found of the same party; and the smaller the number of individuals composing a majority, and the smaller the compass within which they are placed, the more easily will they concert and execute their plans of oppression. Extend the sphere and you take in a greater variety of parties and interests; you make it less probable that a majority of the whole will have a common motive to invade the rights of other citizens; or if such a common motive exists, it will be more difficult for all who feel it to discover their own strength, and to act in unison with each other. Besides the other impediments, it may be remarked that, where there is a consciousness of unjust or dishonorable purposes, communication is always checked by distrust in proportion to the number whose concurrence is necessary.

A Large Republic Has the Advantage over a Small Republic in Controlling the Effects of Faction

10.33 Hence, it clearly appears, that the same advantage which a republic has over a democracy, in controlling the effects of faction, is enjoyed by a large over a small republic—is enjoyed by the Union over the States composing it. Does the advantage consist in the substitution of the representatives whose enlightened views and virtuous sentiments render them superior to local prejudices and to schemes of injustice? It will not be denied that the representation of the Union will be most likely to possess these requisite endowments. Does it consist in the greater security afforded by a greater variety of parties,

against the event of any one party being able to outnumber and oppress the rest? In an equal degree does the increased variety of parties comprised within the Union, increase this security. Does it, in fine, consist in the greater obstacles opposed to the concert and accomplishment of the secret wishes of an unjust and interested majority? Here, again, the extent of the Union gives it the most palpable advantage.

Numerous States Provide a Bulwark Against Factious Leaders

10.34 The influence of factious leaders may kindle a flame within their particular States, but will be unable to spread a general conflagration through the other States. A religious sect may degenerate into a political faction in a part of the Confederacy; but the variety of sects dispersed over the entire face of it must secure the national councils against any danger from that source.

Equal Division of Property Is Considered Wicked

10.35 A rage for paper money, for an abolition of debts, for an equal division of property, or for any other improper or wicked project, will be less apt to pervade the whole body of the Union than a particular member of it; in the same proportion as such a malady is more likely to taint a particular county or district, than an entire State.

10.36 In the extent and proper structure of the Union, therefore, we behold a republican remedy for the disease most incident to republican government. And according to the degree of pleasure and pride we feel in being republicans, ought to be our zeal in cherishing the spirit and supporting the character of Federalists.

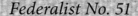

Federalist No. 51

The Federal Republic of America

by James Madison

51.1 To WHAT expedient, then, shall we finally resort, for maintaining in practice the necessary partition of power among the several departments, as laid down in the Constitution? The only answer that can be given is, that as all these exterior provisions are found to be inadequate, the defect must be supplied, by so contriving the interior structure of the government as that its several constituent parts may, by their mutual relations, be the means of keeping each other in their proper places. Without presuming to undertake a full development of this important idea, I will hazard a few general observations, which may perhaps place it in a clearer light, and enable us to form a more correct judgment of the principles and structure of government planned by the convention.

Separation of Power Is Essential to the Preservation of Liberty

51.2 In order to lay a foundation for that separate and distinct exercise of the different powers of government, which to a certain extent is admitted on all hands to be essential to the preservation of liberty, it is evident that each department should have a will of its own; and consequently should be so constituted that the members of each should have as little agency as possible in the appointment of the members of the others.

The Fountain of All Authority Is the People

51.3 Were this principle rigorously adhered to, it would require that all the appointments for the supreme executive, legislative, and judiciary magistracies should be drawn from the same fountain of authority, the people, through channels having no communication whatever with one another. Perhaps such a plan of constructing the several departments would be less difficult in practice than it may in contemplation appear. Some difficulties, however, and some additional expense would attend the execution of it. Some deviations, therefore, from the principle must be admitted. In the constitution of the judiciary department in particular, it might be inexpedient to insist rigorously on the principle: first, because peculiar qualifications being essential in the members, the primary consideration ought to be to select that mode of choice which best secures these qualifications; secondly, because the permanent tenure by which the appointments are held in that department must soon destroy all sense of dependence on the authority conferring them.

The Three Branches of Government Should Be as Independent as Possible

51.4 It is equally evident, that the members of each department should be as little dependent as possible on those of the others, for the emoluments annexed to their offices. Were the executive magistrate, or the judges, not independent of the legislature in this particular, their independence in every other would be merely nominal.

We Need to Guard Against a Gradual Concentration of Power in One Department of Government

51.5 But the great security against a gradual concentration of the several powers in the same department consists in giving to those who administer each department the necessary constitutional means and personal motives to resist encroachment of the others. The provision for defense must in this, as in all other cases, be made commensurate to the danger of attack.

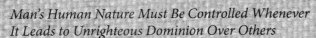

Man's Human Nature Must Be Controlled Whenever It Leads to Unrighteous Dominion Over Others

51.6 Ambition must be made to counteract ambition. The interest of the man must be connected with the constitutional rights of the place. It may be a reflection on human nature, that such devices should be necessary to control the abuses of government. But what is government itself, but the greatest of all reflections on human nature? If men were angels, no government would be necessary. If angels were to govern men, neither external nor internal controls on government would be necessary. In framing a government which is to be administered by men over men, the great difficulty lies in this: you must first enable the government to control the governed; and in the next place oblige it to control itself.

The Primary Control on the Government Is Its Total Dependence on the People

51.7 A dependence on the people is, no doubt the primary control on the government; but experience has taught mankind the necessity of auxiliary precautions.

The Constant Aim Is to Divide and Arrange the Different Government Offices so that They Check Each Other

51.8 This policy of supplying, by opposite and rival interests, the defect of better motives, might be traced through the whole system of human affairs, private as well as public. We see it particularly displayed in all the subordinate distribution of powers, where the constant aim is to divide and arrange the several offices in such a manner as that each may be a check on the other—that the private interest of every individual may be a sentinel over the public rights. These inventions of every prudence cannot be less requisite in the distribution of the supreme powers of the State.

In Republican Government the Legislative Authority Is Predominant

51.9 But it is not possible to give each department an equal power of self-defence. In republican government, the legislative authority necessarily predominates. The remedy for this inconveniency is to divide the legislature into different branches; and to render them, by different modes of election and different principles of action, as little connected with each other as the nature of their common functions and their common dependence on the society will admit.

It May Be Necessary to Guard Against Encroachments of Power by the Legislative Branch

51.10 It may even be necessary to guard against dangerous encroachments by still further precautions. As the weight of the legislative authority requires that it should be thus divided, the weakness of the executive may require on the other hand, that it should be fortified. An absolute negative on the legislative appears, at first view, to be the natural defence with which the executive magistrate should be armed. But perhaps it would be neither altogether safe nor alone sufficient. On ordinary occasions it might not be exerted with the requisite firmness, and on extraordinary occasions it might be perfidiously abused. May not this defect of an absolute negative be supplied by some qualified connection between this weaker department and the weaker branch of the stronger department, by which the latter may be led to support the constitutional rights of the former, without being too much detached from the rights of its own department?

Two Considerations Are Applicable to the Federal System of America

51.11 If the principles on which these observations are founded be just, as I persuade myself they are, and they be applied as a criterion to the several State constitutions, and to the federal Constitution, it will be found that if the latter does not perfectly correspond with them, the former are infinitely less able to bear such a test.

51.12 There are, moreover, two considerations particularly applicable to the federal system of America, which place that system in a very interesting point of view.

In the Compound Republic of America the Power Surrendered by the People Is Divided Between Two Distinct Governments

51.13 *First.* In a single republic, all the power surrendered by the people is submitted to the administration of a single government; and the usurpations are guarded against by a division of the government into distinct and separate departments. In the compound republic of America, the power surrendered by the people is first divided between two distinct governments, and then the

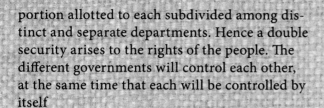

portion allotted to each subdivided among distinct and separate departments. Hence a double security arises to the rights of the people. The different governments will control each other, at the same time that each will be controlled by itself

It Is Very Important that a Republic Guard the Rights of the Minority

51.14 *Second.* It is of great importance in a republic not only to guard the society against the oppression of its rulers, but to guard one part of the society against the injustice of the other part. Different interests necessarily exist in different classes of citizens. If a majority be united by a common interest, the rights of the minority will be insecure. There are but two methods of providing against this evil: the one by creating a will in the community independent of the majority—that is, of the society itself, the other, by comprehending in the society so many separate descriptions of citizens as will render an unjust combination of a majority of the whole very improbable, if not impracticable. The first method prevails in all governments possessing an hereditary or self-appointed authority. This, at best, is but a precarious security; because a power independent of the society may as well espouse the unjust views of the major, as the rightful interests of the minor party, and may possibly be turned against both parties. The second method will be exemplified in the federal republic of the United States. Whilst all authority in it will be derived from and dependent on the society, the society itself will be broken into so many parts, interests and classes of citizens, that the rights of individuals, or of the minority, will be in little danger from interested combinations of the majority.

The Security of Civil and Religious Rights Must Be the Same

51.15 In a free government the security for civil rights must be the same as that for religious rights. It consists in the one case in the multiplicity of interests, and in the other in the mul-

tiplicity of sects. The degree of security in both cases will depend on the number of interests and sects; and this may be presumed to depend on the extent of country and number of people comprehended under the same government.

Justice Is the End of Government

51.16 This view of the subject must particularly recommend a proper federal system to all the sincere and considerate friends of republican government, since it shows that in exact proportion as the territory of the Union may be formed into more circumscribed Confederacies, or States, oppressive combinations of a majority will be facilitated: the best security, under the republican forms, for the rights of every class of citizens, will be diminished; and consequently the stability and independence of some member of the government, the only other security, must be proportionally increased. Justice is the end of government. It is the end of civil society. It ever has been and ever will be pursued until it is obtained, or until liberty be lost in the pursuit.

In a Society Where the Weaker Faction Is Not Protected from the Stronger Faction, Anarchy Reigns

51.17 In a society under the forms of which the stronger faction can readily unite and oppress the weaker, anarchy may as truly be said to reign as in a state of nature, where the weaker individual is not secured against the violence of the stronger; and as, in the latter state, even the stronger individuals are prompted, by the uncertainty of their condition, to submit to a government which may protect the weak as well as themselves; so, in the former state, will the more powerful factions or parties be gradually induced, by a like motive, to wish for a government which will protect all parties, the weaker as well as the more powerful. It can be little doubted that if the State of Rhode Island was separated from the Confederacy and left to itself, the insecurity of rights under the popular form of government within such narrow limits would be displayed by such reiterated oppres-

sions of factious majorities that some power altogether independent of the people would soon be called for by the voice of the very factions whose misrule had proved the necessity of it.

The Principles of Justice and Common Good Are to Reign in America

51.18 In the extended republic of the United States, and among the great variety of interests, parties, and sects which it embraces, a coalition of a majority of the whole society could seldom take place on any other principles than those of justice and the general good; whilst there being thus less danger to a minor from the will of a major party, there must be less pretext, also, to provide for the security of the former, by introducing into the government a will not dependent on the latter, or, in other words, a will independent of the society itself.

The Larger the Society the More Capable It Will Be of Self-Government

51.19 It is no less certain than it is important, notwithstanding the contrary opinions which have been entertained, that the larger the society, provided it lie within a practical sphere, the more duly capable it will be of self-government. And happily for the republican cause, the practicable sphere may be carried to a very great extent, by a judicious modification and mixture of the federal principle.

Index

A

abolition/abolitionists, 79, 221–23, 264, 265, 273, 282–83, 327

abortion, 560, 567, 593, 594, 600

Acadians, 91

Adams, John, 59, 105, 109, 115, 130, 134, 148 presidency of, 162–66

Adams, John Quincy, 188, 192, 196–98, 202

Adams, Samuel, 99, 100, 101, 105, 107, 109, 147

Adams-Onis Treaty, 188

Affluent Society, 526–27

Afghanistan, 564, 576, 578, 603

AFL-CIO, 473

African Methodist Episcopal (AME) Church, 230, 318, 531

Agnew, Spiro, 555–56

Agricultural Adjustment Act (AAA), 466, 467, 469, 475

Agricultural Adjustment Administration (AAA), 465

Agriculture, Department of, 392, 460

Aguinaldo, Emilio, 383

Aid to Families with Dependent Children (AFDC), 575

Aix-la-Chapelle, Peace of, 88

Alabama, 192

Alamo, the, 242–43

Alaska, 378 purchase of, 378

Albania, 514

Albany Congress, 91

Albemarle, 40

Alcatraz, 445

alcoholic beverages, 50, 160, 224, 357, 389, 441–42, 465, 478

Alcott, Louisa May, 275

Alger, Horatio, 355

Algonquin Indians, 74, 85

Alien and Sedition Acts, 163–65, 173

Alito, Samuel, 606

Allen, Ethan, 113, 120, 229

Allen, Richard, 230, 318

Alliance for Progress, 525

Allies (WWI), 413, 435, 436, 452

Allies (WWII), 486, 487, 489, 490–91, 495, 498–500, 503, 506, 513, 515

al-Qaeda, 603, 610

Amendment I, 154, 164, 537, 625

Amendment II, 154, 625

Amendment III, 154, 625

Amendment IV, 154, 625

Amendment V, 154, 625

Amendment VI, 154, 625

Amendment VII, 154, 626

Amendment VIII, 154, 626

Amendment IX, 154, 626

Amendment X, 154, 626

Amendment XI, 626

Amendment XII, 157, 165, 173, 197, 626

Amendment XIII, 315, 627

Amendment XIV, 316, 327, 537, 627

Amendment XV, 315, 316, 627

Amendment XVI, 388, 400, 627

Amendment XVII, 389, 628

Amendment XVIII, 224, 389, 441, 628

Amendment XIX, 390, 628

Amendment XX, 628

Amendment XXI, 389, 442, 629

Amendment XXII, 629

Amendment XXIII, 629

Amendment XXIV, 536, 629

Amendment XXV, 556, 629

Amendment XXVI, 630

Amendment XXVII, 587, 630

America First committees, 490

American Board of Commissioners for Foreign Missions (ABCFM), 231, 240, 337

American Expeditionary Force, 433, 461

American Federation of Labor (AFL), 346, 472

American Independent party, 546

American Samoa, 378

American System, 192–93, 206

American Telephone and Telegraph Company, 340

Americans with Disabilities Act, 587

Amish, 70

Anabaptists, 70

Anaconda Plan, 285, 292

anarchists, 346, 434

Anderson, John, 569, 570

Anderson, Robert, 277–78

André, John, 120

Andropov, Yuri, 580

Anglican Church. *See* Anglicanism

Anglicanism, 64, 73, 108, 109 elements of Roman Catholicism in, 25, 30, 63 forming of, 62–63 in America, 66–67, 69, 80, 222

Annapolis Convention, 139

Anschluss, 485

Anthony, Susan B., 390

Antietam, Battle of, 288–89, 302, 303

Anti-Federalist Papers, The, 146

Anti-Federalists, 146, 153

Anti-Masonic Party, 203

antinomianism, 35–36

Anzio, 498

Apache Indians, 11, 12, 374

Appalachian Mountains, 97, 177

appeasement, 485–86

Appomattox Court House, 307

Arafat, Yasir, 578, 606

architecture colonial style (Williamsburg style), 49 Greek revival, 226

Argonne offensive, 423–24

Arkansas, 278, 529, 592

armistice, 424

Armour, Philip, 365

Armstrong, Louis, 444

Army of Northern Virginia, 288, 307

Army of the Potomac, 287

Arnold, Benedict, 113, 120, 121

art Federalist style, 225–26 modern, 441

Arthur, Chester A., 342–43

Articles of Confederation, 133–38

Asbury, Francis, 229, 230

Ashburton, Lord, 246

Ashcroft, John, 604

Ashley-Cooper, Sir Anthony, 40

assembly line, 403

assumption, 155

astrolabe, 3

astronauts. *See* space program

Atlanta, Battle of, 305

Atlantic Charter, 491

atomic bomb, 505, 506–7, 513, 516, 522. *See also* nuclear weapons

Attlee, Clement, 506

attorney general, 152, 604

Austin, Stephen F., 241

Australia, 493

Austria, 412, 415, 426, 485, 504

automobiles, 402–3, 448–49, 495

Axis powers, 488

Aztec Indians, 8, 15

B

Babcock, Orville, 322

baby boom, 527

bailout, 609

Baker, Howard, 563

Balkans, 597–98

Baltimore, Lord. *See* Calvert, Cecilius

Baltimore & Ohio (B & O) Railroad, 219–20, 338

bank holiday, 464, 465

banking crisis, 463

Bank of the U.S. *See* National Bank

Baptists, 63, 147, 222, 231, 537; General Association of Regular Baptist Churches (GARBC), 446

in the colonial era, 45, 68, 79
    polity of, 64, 68
Barbados, 40
Barbary pirates, 137, 175
Barbary states, 175
barbed wire, 367
Barnum, P.T., 356–57
Barré, Isaac, 97–98, 100
Barrow, Clyde, 477
Baruch, Bernard, 514
Bataan, 493
Bates, Katherine Lee, 368
Batista y Zaldívar, Fulgencio, 518
Bay of Pigs, 519
Bay Psalm Book, 73
Bear Flag Republic, 252
Beauregard, Pierre G.T., 277–78, 286
Bee, Barnard, 286
Begin, Menachem, 564
Belgium, 416, 487, 500
Belknap, William, 322
Bell, Alexander Graham, 340
Bell, John, 275
Belleau Wood, 423
Beringia, 8
Berlin airlift, 515
Berlin Wall, 519–20, 581, 585
Bible conferences, 379, 407
Bible institutes, 407
Biddle, Nicholas, 203
Biden, Joe, 607
Big Four, 426
big stick policy, 395–97
Big Three, 503–5, 506
Bill of Rights, 145, 147, 153–54
Bingham, George Caleb, 226
Bingham, Hiram, 379
bin Laden, Osama, 603, 610
Birney, James, 246
Black Bart, 370
Blackbeard. *See* Teach, Edward
Black Codes, 317
Black Hawk War, 204
black power, 542
blacks, 282–83, 316–19, 354–55, 394–95, 444,
    475, 492, 494, 521, 528–31, 536, 541–42.
    See also slavery/slaves
Black Thursday, 451, 458
Black Tuesday, 452, 458
Bladensburg, Battle of, 185
Blaine, James G., 343, 377
Blair, James, 67
blitzkrieg, 486, 487, 488
blockade (of Southern ports), 284–85, 299
blockade runners, 299
Boland Amendment, 581–82
Bolívar, Simón, 188
Bolshevik Revolution, 110, 422, 434, 484
Bonhomme Richard, 124
Bonus Army, 461–62
Boone, Daniel, 97, 161, 217
Booth, John Wilkes, 307–8, 312
border states, 301, 315

Bosnia, 597–98
Boston, Massachusetts, 33, 34, 74, 99, 100,
    105, 108, 109, 112, 114, 351
Boston Massacre, 101–2
Boston Tea Party, 106–7
Bow, Clara, 443
Bowie, Jim, 242–43
Boxer Rebellion, 377, 379, 380
boycotts, 100, 346, 347, 504, 530
Bradbury, William, 359
Braddock, Edward, 91
Braddock's Road, 217
Bradford, William, 31
Brady Bill, 593
Bragg, Braxton, 295–96, 298
Brainerd, David, 75
Brain Trust, 465
Brandywine, Battle of, 119, 122
Bray, Thomas, 67
bread lines, 474, 479
Breckinridge, John C., 275
Brezhnev, Leonid, 580
Briand, Aristide, 435
Britain, 302, 376. *See also specific wars with
    America*
    colonial wars with France, 85–88, 90–94,
        121, 122, 123, 129, 130
    colonization, 19, 25–40
    during the Reformation, 62–63
    exploration, 5, 18, 21–22
    in World War II, 416, 418, 426, 486,
        487–88, 489, 490–91, 492, 495, 497
Britain, Battle of, 487–88
Brock, Isaac, 184
Brooks, Preston, 269
Brown, John, 269–70, 273–75
Brown University, 79
Brown v. Board of Education, 528, 529, 537
Bryan, William Jennings, 349–50, 383, 386,
    387, 390, 397, 413, 417, 446–47
Buchanan, James, 268, 270, 275
Buell, Don Carlos, 295, 296
Buena Vista, Battle of, 251
buffalo, 371–72
Buffalo Bill Cody's Wild West Show, 356
Bulfinch, Charles, 226
Bulge, Battle of the, 500
bull market, 451, 452
Bull Moose Party, 400
Bull Run. *See* Manassas
Bunau-Varilla, Philippe, 396
Bunker Hill, Battle of, 114
Burgoyne, John, 118, 120–21
Burke, Edmund, 113
Burnside, Ambrose, 289, 296–97
Burr, Aaron, 162, 178
Burroughs, Edgar Rice, 478
bus boycott, 530
Bush, George H. W., 568, 582–89
Bush, George W., 599–607
busing, 547–48
Butler, Andrew, 269

C

Cabinet—first, 152–53. *See also separate
    departments*
Cabot, John, 5
Cajuns, 91
Calhoun, John C., 183, 192, 198, 200, 201,
    202, 249, 262, 263
Calhoun Resolutions, 259
California, 248, 251, 252, 253, 261–62, 394,
    476, 567
California gold rush, 261–62, 362
Calley, William, 549–50
Calvert, Cecilius (Lord Baltimore), 39
Calvin, John, 7, 108
Cambodia, 539, 549, 550, 551, 557
Camden, Battle of, 122, 126
campaigns, presidential. *See* elections
Campanius, John, 74
Camp David Accords, 564, 565
camp meetings, 230, 359
Canada, 19–20, 85, 86–87, 108, 120, 183, 184,
    376, 515, 543
    border with America, 187–88, 245–46,
    248
canals, 193, 219, 396
Canal Zone, 396, 563
Cane Ridge, 230
Cannon, Joseph, 398
Capone, Al, 445
caravel, 3
Caribbean, 415
Carnegie, Andrew, 335–36
Carolina colonies, 40. *See also* North
    Carolina; South Carolina
carpetbaggers, 318
Carranza, Venustiano, 414
Carter, Jimmy, 549, 555, 562–66, 569–70
Carter Doctrine, 565
Cartwright, Peter, 200
Carver, George Washington, 404
Carver, John, 32
Casablanca, 498
Casey, William, 581
Cass, Lewis, 260–61
Castro, Fidel, 518–19, 578
catechism, 72
Cato, 146
cattle drive, 365
caucus, 196, 387
Cayuse Indians, 240–41
Central America, 396, 573, 577–78
    Spanish colonization in, 15
Central Intelligence Agency (CIA), 519, 521,
    577
Central Pacific Railroad, 362–63
Central Powers, 412
Century of Dishonor, A, 375
Chamberlain, Neville, 485–86
Chambers, Whittaker, 522
Chancellorsville, Battle of, 289–90
Chaplin, Charlie, 443

Charismatic movement, 567–68. *See also* religion: Cold War era

Charles I, 25, 29, 39, 40

Charles II, 37, 38

Charleston (Charles Town), S.C., 40, 51, 58, 107, 125, 159, 275, 277, 316
Siege of, 126

charter colony, 29

Château-Thierry, 423

Chattanooga, 296–97
Battle for, 298

checks and balances, 143

Cheney, Richard, 600

Chernenko, Konstantin, 580

Cherokee Indians, 13, 74, 205, 366, 494

Chesapeake affair, 173, 182

Chesapeake Bay, 12, 17, 26, 40, 118, 129, 185

Chesapeake, U.S.S., 173, 185

Cheyenne Indians, 371

Chiang Kai-shek, 498, 515, 548

Chicago, 214, 220, 276, 346, 347, 349, 351, 352, 358, 445, 478

Chickamauga, Battle of, 296

Chickasaw Indians, 13, 205

child labor, 345–46, 388

China, 377–78, 399, 484, 491, 492
Communist, 498, 515–17, 539, 548–49, 567
missions in, 379
Nationalist. *See* Taiwan

Chisholm Trail, 365

Choctaw Indians, 13, 205, 494

Chosin, 517

Christian and Missionary Alliance, 379, 407

Christian Coalition, 594

Christian Science, 233–34

Christian Science Monitor, 234

Christmas, 117–18, 357

church buildings, colonial, 71–72

Churchill, Winston, 485, 486, 487–88, 497, 498, 503, 506, 514

Church of England. *See* Anglicanism

Church of Jesus Christ of Latter-Day Saints, 233

Cincinnati, 178, 295

circuit riding, 229, 359

city commission, 387–88

city manager, 388

Civilian Conservation Corps (CCC), 465, 471

Civilized Tribes, Five, 13, 205

civil liberties, 145

civil rights, 327, 354, 394, 475, 521, 524, 528–31, 535–36, 537, 538, 542, 560

Civil Rights Act of 1964, 535, 536

civil rights movement, 475, 528–31, 541–42, 558

Civil Service Commission, 342

civil service reform, 342

Civil War, 281–309. *See also* War Between the States
casualties, 307, 308

causes, 281–84
Northern/Southern advantages, 284–85

Civil Works Administration (CWA), 466

Clark, George Rogers, 124–25

Clark, Mark, 498

Clark, William, 176–77, 179

Clay, Henry, 183, 192, 194, 196–97, 202, 203, 245, 246, 262–63

Clayton Antitrust Act, 401

Clemenceau, Georges, 426

Clemens, Samuel Langhorne. *See* Twain, Mark

Cleveland, Grover, 343–44, 347, 349, 379

Clinton, Bill, 587, 588–89, 592–99

Clinton, DeWitt, 187, 219

Clinton, George, 146

Clinton, Henry, 123, 125, 126, 129, 130

Clinton, Hillary Rodham, 593, 607, 609

clipper ships, 220

coalition of the willing, 604

Cody, William "Buffalo Bill," 356

Coercive Acts. *See* Intolerable Acts

Colbert, Jean, 85

Cold Harbor, Battle of, 304

Cold War, 513–20, 526, 580–81, 583

Colfax, Schuyler, 322

Colombia, 396

Colonies, Thirteen. *See also individual colonies*
colonial administration, 22, 28, 29, 31, 34, 37, 40, 96, 97, 108–9
French threat to, 85–88, 90–95
growing rift with Britain, 93–102
plan for union, 91
settlement, 25–42
social culture, 45–59

Colorado, 364

Colt, Samuel, 213

Columbia River, 177, 248

Columbia University, 154, 465

Columbus, Christopher, 5

Comanche Indians, 11, 371, 494

commerce raiders, 376

Committees of Correspondence, 105, 106, 108

Common Market, 526

Common Sense, 115, 116, 146

communications, 220–21, 333, 340

Communism/Communists, 422, 434, 440, 482, 559
during the Cold War, 514–23, 538–40, 548–51, 567, 573, 575–78, 584, 597
during World War II, 483, 484, 505

compass, 3

Compromise of 1850, 262–63

Compromise of 1877, 326

Compromise Tariff of 1833, 202

Comstock Lode, 364

Concord, Battle of, 111–12

Confederacy, 276, 281–309

Confederate army/forces, 284, 286–88, 290, 297, 300, 304, 307

Confederate States of America. *See* Confederacy

Confederation. *See* government: Confederation

Congregationalists, 64, 76, 77, 222, 231, 232
evangelism of Indians, 74–75
See also Congregational polity

Congregational polity, 64, 68

Congress of Industrial Organizations (CIO), 472, 473

Congress. *See* government: Federal

Conkling, Roscoe, 341–42

Connecticut, 147, 217
colonization, 34

Connecticut Compromise. *See* Great Compromise

conquistadores, 12, 15–17

conscription. *See* draft

conservation, 393, 398

Constitution, 110, 133, 142–45, 301
amendments, 144, 154, 315–16, 388–90.
See also individual amendments
flexibility, 156
ratification, 145–49. *See also* government, Federal

Constitutional Convention, 139–45

Constitutional Union Party, 275

Constitution, U.S.S., 184

containment, 514–18, 576

Continental Congress
First, 108–9
Second, 113–15, 120, 121, 133

Continental dollars, 121, 137

Contract with America, 594, 595

Contras, 577, 581

Conwell, Russell, 357

Coolidge, Calvin, 435, 437, 438, 439, 443, 451

Cooper, James Fenimore, 227

Cooper, Peter, 219

Copperheads, 302

Coral Sea, Battle of, 493, 495

corduroy roads, 218

Cornstalk, Chief, 97

Cornwallis, Charles, 118, 119, 122, 126–29

Coronado, Francisco de, 16

Corregidor, 493

Cortés, Hernando, 15

cotton, 201, 214–16, 282, 284, 302, 320, 338, 404

Cotton, John, 35

cotton gin, 216

Coughlin, Charles, 470

Council for New England, 30, 31

counterculture, 542–44

covenant, 33, 63–66

cowboys, 365–66, 391

Cowpens, Battle of, 128

Cox, James M., 437

Crane, Stephen, 355

Crater Lake National Park, 393

Crawford, William H., 196–97

Crazy Horse, 373, 374

Crédit Mobilier Scandal, 322

Creek Indians, 13, 185, 186, 205, 494
Crittenden, John J., 276–77, 315
Crockett, Davy, 243
Cronkite, Walter, 555
Crosby, Bing, 476
Crosby, Fanny, 359
Cuba, 15, 380–82, 518–19
Cuban missile crisis, 519
Cumberland Gap, 161, 295
Cumberland Road. *See* National Road
Custer, George Armstrong, 373
Custer's Last Stand, 373
Czechoslovakia, 427, 485–86, 514, 585

D

da Gama, Vasco, 4
Daladier, Édouard, 485
dame schools, 51
Dan River, 128
    race to the, 128
Dare, Virginia, 19
dark horse, 246, 325
Darrow, Clarence, 447
Dartmouth College, 75, 79
Darwin, Charles, 336, 353, 440, 447
Darwinism, 336, 353–54, 355, 406, 408, 440,
    445–47
    Reform Darwinism, 353–54, 386
    Social Darwinism, 353
Daugherty, Harry, 437, 438
Davies, Samuel, 78, 99
Davis, Jefferson, 276, 278, 281, 299, 309, 313
Dawes, Billy, 111
Dawes, Charles, 437
Dawes, William, 111
Dawes Act, 375
Dawes Plan, 437
Dayton Accords, 598
D-day, 498–99
Debs, Eugene V., 347, 390
Decatur, Stephen, 186
Declaration of American Rights, 109
Declaration of Independence, 108, 115–16,
    139
Deere, John, 214
Deerfield Massacre, 89
Defense of Marriage Act, 596
de Gaulle, Charles, 498
de Grasse, Admiral, 129
deism, 66, 229
de Kalb, Baron, 122, 126
Delaware, 147, 301
    colonization, 21, 39
    religion in, 69
    Revolutionary era, 119
Delaware, Lord, 27, 28
Delaware Indians, 21, 74
delegated powers, 174
De Lôme, Enrique Dupuy, 380
De Lôme letter, 380
democracy, 142–43

Democratic Party/Democrats, 198, 200, 206,
    207, 208, 260–61, 268, 275–76, 325–26,
    343, 344, 349, 350, 354, 462, 475, 537,
    546, 557, 593, 579, 589, 607–8, 610
    progressivism in, 390, 400
Democratic-Republicans, 157–58, 163–66,
    172, 187
Democratization. *See* Government, Federal
Dempsey, Jack, 442
Denmark, 486
Denver, 364
Depression, Great. *See* Great Depression
depressions. *See* economic conditions
DePriest, Oscar, 444
desegregation. *See* segregation
de Soto, Hernando, 17
detente, 549, 564
Detroit, 124, 184, 542
Dewey, George, 382
Dewey, John, 405, 528
Dewey, Thomas, 503, 521
Dias, Bartholomeu, 4
Díaz, Porfirio, 413
Dickinson, John, 100, 109, 133
Diem, Ngo Dinh, 518
Dien Bien Phu, Battle of, 518
Dillinger, John, 477
Dinwiddie, Governor Robert, 90
direct primaries, 387
discrimination, 394–95, 535, 560–61
    in colonial era, 28, 42, 72
    See also racial discrimination
diseases. *See* epidemics
disfranchisement, 319
Disney, Walt, 476
District of Columbia–slave trade, 262–63
Dix, Dorothea, 224
Dixiecrats, 521
Doak, Samuel, 79
Dobson, James, 594
Dole, Bob, 596
dollar diplomacy, 399
Dominican Republic, 396, 397, 415
domino theory, 518, 551
Donner, George, 244
Doolittle, Jimmy, 493
doughboys, 421, 422, 423
Douglass, Frederick, 223
Douglas, Stephen A., 260, 266, 270–73, 275
draft, 565
    Civil War, 300
    World War I, 419–20
    World War II, 496
Drake, Francis, 18
Dred Scott decision, 270
drug abuse, 543
dry farming, 366
Duarte, José Napoleon, 577
Du Bois, W.E.B., 355, 395
Duché, Jacob, 109
Dukakis, Michael, 582
Duke, James Buchanan, 338
Dunkers, 45

Dunkirk, 487
Dust Bowl, 476
Dutch. *See* Netherlands
Dutch West India Company, 20
Dutch Reformed, 69, 79
Dwight, Timothy, 230
Dynamic Conservatism, 520, 523

E

Eagleton, Thomas, 552
Eakins, Thomas, 355
Earhart, Amelia, 477
Earp, Wyatt, 369
Eastern Europe, 505, 506, 514, 515, 583, 585
Eastern Woodlands Indians, 13
East India Company, 106
economic conditions, 204, 207, 324–25, 349,
    596, 605
    after World War I, 433–34, 435–37, 438,
    448–51
    Cold War era, 526–27, 548, 558–60,
    565–66, 574–76
    Great Depression, 439, 440, 451–53,
    456–79, 484, 489
Economic Recovery Tax Act of 1981, 574
ecumenical movement, 531
Eddy, Mary Baker, 233–34
Edison, Thomas Alva, 340
education, 223–24, 229–30, 231, 524, 537,
    568
    among blacks, 394–95, 528–29
    in the colonies, 33, 50–51, 75, 78–79
    in Northwest Territory, 135–36
    progressive education, 405, 446–47
Edward VI, 62
Edwards, Jonathan, 62, 73, 74, 77, 178, 230
Egypt, 488, 497, 558, 564
Einstein, Albert, 440–41
Eisenhower, Dwight D., 498, 499, 500, 505,
    513, 518, 523–24, 531
elections, of 1796, 162; of 1800, 165; of 1824,
    196–97; of 1828, 198; of 1832, 203; of
    1836, 206; of 1840, 208–9; of 1844, 246; of
    1848, 260–61; of 1852, 264; of 1856, 268;
    of 1860, 275–76; of 1864, 306; of 1868,
    321; of 1872, 324; of 1876, 325–26; of
    1880; of 1884, 343; of 1888, 343; of 1892,
    344, 348; of 1896, 349, 350; of 1900, 383;
    of 1908, 397; of 1912, 399–400; of 1916,
    418; of 1920; of 1928, 439, 448, 456; of
    1932, 456, 462–63; of 1936, 471–72; of
    1940, 490; of 1944, 503; of 1946, 520; of
    1948, 521; of 1952, 518, 523; of 1960, 524;
    of 1964, 536–37; of 1968, 544–47; of 1972,
    551–52; of 1976, 562–63; of 1980, 568–70;
    of 1984, 579; of 1988, 582; of 1992,
    588–89; of 1996, 596; of 2000, 599–601; of
    2004, 604; of 2008, 607–8; of 2010, 610
    progressive changes, 387, 389
Electoral College, 143, 144, 195–96, 600–01
electricity, 220, 340–41, 449–50, 467
Eliot, Charles, 341

Eliot, John, 74
Eliot, T. S., 440, 441
Elizabeth I, 18, 19, 21, 62–63
Elizabethan settlement, 63
Ellis Island, 353
Ellsberg, Daniel, 550, 555
El Salvador, 577
Emancipation Proclamation, 289, 303, 315
Embargo Act, 173, 182, 192
Emerson, John, 270
Emerson, Ralph Waldo, 111, 225, 227, 259, 264, 275
energy crisis, 558
Engel v. Vitale, 537
England. *See* Britain
Enlightenment, 108, 110, 116, 142, 172
entertainment,
    colonial era, 57–59;
    Gilded Age, 355–57
    motion pictures, 443, 475–76
    radio, 449, 476
    sports: 442–43, 478; baseball, 356,
        442–43, 529; basketball, 357;
        bicycling, 357, 403; croquet, 356;
        football, 357, 443; golf, 356, 443;
        tennis, 356, 443;
    television, 527, 594, 600
environmental movement, 559
Environmental Protection Agency, 559
epidemics, 47
Episcopal polity, 64
Equal Rights Amendment, 561–62
Era of Good Feelings, 187–89
Erie Canal, 219
Espionage and Sedition Acts, 421
Ethiopia, 482–83
evangelism. *See* missions
evolution. *See* Darwinism
Ewell, Richard, 291

F

Fair Deal, 520, 521
Fair Oaks, Battle of, 288
faith-based initiatives, 605
faith missions, 379
Fall, Albert B., 437–38
Fallen Timbers, Battle of, 178–79
Falwell, Jerry, 568
Family and Medical Leave Act, 593
Farmers' Alliance, 348
Farragut, David G., 294
fascism, 388, 462, 482–84
Faubus, Orval, 529
Faulkner, William, 441
Federal Bureau of Investigation (FBI), 370,
    477, 522
Federal Deposit Insurance Corporation
    (FDIC), 467
Federal Emergency Management
    Administration, 607
Federal Emergency Relief Administration
    (FERA), 466

Federal Farm Board, 459
Federalism, 143–44, 152
Federalist, The, 146
Federalist Party/Federalists, 154–58, 163–66,
    172, 173–74, 187
Federalists (constitutional), 146–47
Federal Reserve Act, 401
Federal Reserve System, 401, 451, 452
Federal Trade Commission Act, 401
feminists, 560, 561, 579
Ferdinand, Archduke Franz, 412
Ferguson, Patrick, 127
Ferraro, Geraldine, 579
Fillmore, Millard, 263, 268
Finlay, Carlos Juan, 405
Finney, Charles, 221, 231–32
Fire-Eaters, 265
fireside chats, 465
Fisk, James, 322
Fitzgerald, F. Scott, 440, 441
Five Civilized Tribes. *See* Civilized Tribes,
    Five
Florida, 204–5, 450–51, 601
    purchased from Spain, 188
    Spanish rule, 16–17, 130
Floyd, "Pretty Boy", 477
Flying Tigers, 491
Foch, Ferdinand, 424
Fonck, Paul-René, 424
Food Administration, 420, 438
Force Bill, 202
Ford, Gerald, 494, 550, 555, 556–57, 562
Ford, Henry, 402–3, 448
Fordney-McCumber Tariff, 436
Forest Service, U.S., 393, 398
Forrest, Nathan Bedford, 284
Fort Donelson, 293
Fort Duquesne, 90, 91, 92. *See also* Pittsburgh
Fort Greenville, Treaty of, 179
Fort Henry, 293
Fort McHenry, 185, 186
Fort Necessity, 90
Fort Sumter, 277–78
Fort Ticonderoga, 92, 113, 114, 120
Fort William Henry, 91–92
forty-niners, 261, 262
Foster, Stephen, 227
Fourteen Points, 422, 424, 425, 426, 427
Fox Indians, 204
Fox, George, 68
France, 182, 422, 426, 515
    colonial wars with Britain, 85–88, 90–94,
        121, 122, 123, 129, 130;
    during French Revolution, 110, 122,
        158–59, 163, 176
    Indochina, 492, 518
    Mexico, 376
    New World, 19–20, 85, 124
    Reformation era, 69
    World War I era, 422–26
    World War II era, 486, 487, 498–500
Franklin, Benjamin, 46, 54, 58, 78, 91, 107,
    113, 115, 130, 145, 148, 149, 229

Fredericksburg, Battle of, 289
Freedmen's Bureau, 308, 317
freedom of assembly, 80, 153
freedom of petition, 154
freedom of the press, 153
freedom of religion, 25, 30–32, 46, 69, 78, 80,
    94, 109, 147, 153, 537, 568
freedom of speech, 80, 153, 537
Freeport Doctrine, 270
Free-Soilers, 260, 267
Free-Soil Party, 260
Frelinghuysen, Theodore, 76
Frémont, John C., 252, 268
French and Indian War, 75, 85, 90–94
French Reformed. *See* Huguenots
French Revolution, 110, 158–59
Freud, Sigmund, 441, 447, 528
Frontenac, Comte de, 86
Fuchs, Klaus, 522
Fugitive Slave Law, 264
Fuller, Charles E., 532
Fulton, Robert, 217
Fundamentalism, 445–47
Fundamentalist-Modernist controversy, 446
Fundamentalists, 445–46, 531–32
Fundamental Orders of Connecticut, 34
funding, 155, 203

G

Gadsden Purchase, 254, 266
Gage, Thomas, 108, 111, 114
Gallatin, Albert, 173
Garfield, James A., 296, 342
Garner, John Nance, 462
Garrison, William Lloyd, 222, 265
Garvey, Marcus, 444
gas-and-water socialism, 388
Gaspee, 105
Gates, Horatio, 121, 126
Gates, Thomas, 27, 28
gay rights, 560
General Motors, 479, 495, 609
Genêt, Citizen Edmond Charles, 159
George II, 88
George III, 93, 101, 107, 115, 127, 130
Georgia, 147, 298, 305–6
    colonization, 40–41
    Revolutionary era, 125, 126
German Reformed Church, 69
German settlers/immigrants, 45–46, 267,
    300, 357, 416
Germantown, Battle of, 119
Germany, 267
    in World War I, 415–18, 422, 423, 426–27
    in World War II, 483–91, 492, 497–500,
        504
    war reparations, 435, 436–37, 452
    See also German settlers/immigrants
Germany, East, 514, 515, 519–20, 585
Germany, West, 515, 585
Geronimo, 374
Gerry, Elbridge, 145

Gettysburg Address, 292
Gettysburg, Battle of, 290–91
Ghent, Treaty of, 186, 187
ghettos, 504
Gibbons v. Ogden, 174
Gideon v. Wainwright, 537
Gilbert Islands, 492
Gilded Age, 333–59
Gingrich, Newt, 595
glasnost, 580
Glidden, Joseph, 367
Gnadenhütten, 75
Goforth, Jonathan and Rosalind, 379
gold, 4, 27, 322, 324–25, 364, 464
    in Alaska, 378
    in California, 261–62
    in New World, 15, 18
gold standard, 349, 440, 464, 465, 560
Goldwater, Barry, 536–37, 561, 567, 568
Gompers, Samuel, 346, 401, 438
Gonzales, Alberto, 604
Goodman, Benny, 476
Good Neighbor Policy, 435
Goodnight-Loving Trail, 365
Gorbachev, Mikhail, 110, 580, 585
Gore, Al, 599–601
Gorgas, William C., 405
Gould, Jay, 322
government, 160
    bicameral, 140
    bureaucracy/regulation, 347, 392, 401,
        437, 440, 451, 452–53, 469, 483, 524,
        568, 574, 593, 609–10
    centralization/decentralization of, 91,
        133–34, 140, 144, 152, 154, 156, 158,
        172, 300
    Colonial, 22, 28, 29, 34, 40, 96, 97, 105,
        108–9, 113–16
    Confederation, 133–38
    democratization, 192, 195–98
    Federal, 142–44, 192, 195–98
    Federal authority increased during the
        Cold War era, 513, 524, 526, 535–38,
        547–48, 561–62; increased during
        Great Depression/FDR's Presidency,
        458–59, 460–61, 463–71; increased
        by Progressivism, 154, 388, 389, 392,
        408, 409, 420, 483; increased during
        Reconstruction, 316, 327; increased
        during World War II, 495
    unicameral, 133, 140
Graham, Billy, 532
Graham, Sylvester, 224
Gramm, Phil, 575
Gramm-Rudman Act, 575
Grand Canyon, 16
Grange, the, 348
Grant, Ulysses S., 253, 293–94, 296, 298, 304,
    306, 307, 341
    presidency of, 319, 321–22
Grantism, 322

Great Awakening,
    First, 76–80, 96, 110
    Second, 221–22, 228–31
Great Britain. *See* Britain
Great Compromise, 141
Great Depression, 437, 439, 440, 451–53,
    456–79, 484, 489
Great Lakes, 88, 134, 178, 187
Great Migration, 32
Great Philadelphia Wagon Road, 45, 217
Great Plains, 177, 366–68, 476
Great Society, 535–38, 540, 541, 544, 560
Great War. *See* World War I
Great White Fleet, 397
Greece, 226, 514–15
Greeley, Horace, 206, 228, 324
Green Mountain Boys, 113
greenbacks, 324–25, 349
Greene, Nathanael, 128
Greenland, 491
Grenada, 578
Grenville, George, 97, 98
Grimké sisters, 222
Guadalcanal, 501
Guadalupe Hidalgo, Treaty of, 253
Guam, 382, 492, 502
guerilla warfare, 90, 518
Guilford Court House, 128
Guiteau, Charles J., 342
Gulf of Tonkin resolution, 538–39, 550
Gulf War, 584–87

H

Haiti, 397, 415, 597
Hakluyt, Richard, the Younger, 19
Half-breeds, 342
Half-Way Covenant, 66, 76, 79
Hamilton, Alexander, 110, 139, 146, 147, 152,
    154–55, 157–58, 162, 178
Hamilton, Henry, 124–25
Hampton, Wade, 321
Hancock, John, 100, 147
Harding, Warren G., 428, 433, 435, 437–38,
    449
hard money, 137, 204, 324
Harlem Renaissance, 444
Harmony Society, 224
Harpers Ferry, 273–74
Harrison, Benjamin, 179, 343, 344
Harrison, William Henry, 179–81, 184–85,
    206, 208–9, 343
Hartford Convention, 187, 201–2
Harvard College, 33, 66, 79, 162, 225, 232
Hauptmann, Bruno, 477
Hawaii, 378–79, 382, 492
Hawthorne, Nathaniel, 227
Hay, John, 377–78, 396
Hayes, Rutherford B., 325–26, 341–42
Haymarket Riot, 346
Hayne, Robert Y., 201, 202
Hays, Mary. *See* Molly Pitcher
headrights, 25

Health, Education, and Welfare, Department
    of, 524
Health and Human Services, Department of,
    524
Hearst, William Randolph, 380
Heath, Sir Robert, 40
Heinz, H. J., 339
Henry, Patrick, 71, 98–99, 109, 146, 147
Henry VIII, 62
Hepburn Act, 392
Hessians, 113, 115, 117–18, 121, 125
Hickok, James Butler "Wild Bill," 368–69
High-church Anglicans, 63
Hill, James J., 334–35
Hindenburg, 477–78
hippies, 543–44
Hirohito, 484, 507
Hiroshima, 506–7
Hispaniola, 15
Hiss, Alger, 522
Hitler, Adolf, 424, 483–88, 490, 500, 504,
    505–6
hoboes, 456, 473, 474
Ho Chi Minh, 518
Holmes, Oliver Wendell, 421
Holocaust, 504
Homeland Security, Office of, 603
Homestead Act, 366
Homestead Strike, 347
Honduras, 397
Honecker, Erich, 585
Hong Kong, 492
Hood, John B., 305–6
Hooker, Joseph "Fighting Joe," 289–90
Hooker, Thomas, 34
Hoover, Herbert, 420, 435, 437, 438–40, 448,
    451, 456–63, 471, 473
Hoover, J. Edgar, 477
Hooverizing, 420
horizontal integration, 336
hornbook, 51
Horseshoe Bend, Battle of, 186
House of Burgesses, 22, 28, 98
House of Representatives, 140, 141
House Un-American Activities Committee,
    522
Houston, Sam, 242, 243, 247
Howard, Oliver, 308, 317, 374
Howard University, 308
Howe, Elias, 213
Howe, William, 116, 118–20
Hudson, Henry, 20, 36
Hudson River school, 226
Huerta, Victoriano, 414
Hughes, Charles Evans, 418, 435, 468
Huguenots, 16–17, 69
Humanism, secular, 110, 172
human rights, 105, 154, 563
Humphrey, Hubert H., 545–47
Hungary, 412, 514, 585
Hunt, Robert, 66
Hurricane Katrina, 606–7
Huss, John, 70

Hussein, Saddam, 583–84, 587, 603–4
Hutchinson, Anne, 35–36
Hutchinson, Thomas, 105, 106
hymns and gospel songs, 73, 227, 358, 359

I

Idaho, 344
idealism, 435, 525;
 under Wilson, 413–18, 419, 421, 422,
  425–28, 434
Illinois, 192, 200, 271, 272
immigrants/immigration, 241, 333, 335, 345,
  363, 394
 German, 45–46, 267, 300, 357, 416
 Irish, 45–46, 267, 300, 357, 416
 New, 351–53, 443–45
 restrictions, 164, 203, 352, 397, 444, 445
impeachment, 315, 556, 598–99
imperialism, 375–79, 380–83
implied powers, 174
impressment, 159, 182, 183
Inca Indians, 8, 17
Inchon, 516
income taxes. *See* taxes
indenture, 25
indentured servants, 28
Independence Hall, 139
independent treasury, 208
India, 4
Indiana, 192
Indian removal, 34, 372–75
 Policy, 204–5
Indian Reorganization Act, 375
Indians. *See also individual tribal names*
 and the conquistadores, 15–17
 culture/history, 8–14
 and diseases, 14, 15, 107, 241
 in the East, 13
 and English colonists, 21, 27, 29, 32, 34,
  38
 French alliances with, 85, 90–94, 178
 at Horseshoe Bend, 186
 Jackson's policies toward, 204–5
 in Kentucky, 161
 missionary efforts to, 73–75, 205, 240–41
 named by Columbus, 5
 in Northwest Territory, 178–81, 184–85
 removal of. *See* Indian removal
 during Revolution, 124, 125
 rights movement, 560
 sale of Manhattan, 36
 in the Southeast, 13, 14, 186, 205
 and Thanksgiving, 32
 in the West, 12, 14, 177
Indian Territory, 21, 29, 35, 86, 178, 180, 181,
  204–5, 366, 372, 375
Indian Wars, 74, 86–88, 90–95, 178–79,
  180–81, 183, 185, 186, 188, 204–5, 372–75
Indochina. *See* Southeast Asia
industrialism, 333–41, 348, 484. *See also*
  economic conditions

industry/industrial development, 212–14,
  345, 351. *See also* industrialism
infant mortality, 47, 351
inflation, 204, 525, 548, 559–60, 561, 566,
  569, 574, 596
initiative, 387
injunctions, 347
installment plans, 448, 449, 450
interchangeable parts, 213, 403
Intermediate Nuclear Forces (INF) Treaty,
  580
internal improvements, 193, 206
Interstate Commerce Act, 343
Interstate Commerce Commission (ICC),
  343, 392
interstate highway system, 524
Intolerable Acts, 108
Iran, 514, 565, 566, 581
Iran-Contra affair, 581–82
Iranian hostage crisis, 565, 569
Iraq, 581, 583–87, 603–4
Ireland, 267
 Northern, 45
ironclads, 287, 293
iron curtain, 514, 583
Iroquois Indians, 11, 85
Irving, Washington, 227
Isabella, queen of Spain, 5
island hopping, 501–2
Island No. 10, 294
isolationism, 186, 189, 383, 397, 413, 434,
  435, 482, 484, 489–90, 513, 551
Israel, 545, 558, 564
Italy, 482–83, 488, 492, 497–98, 515
Iwo Jima, 502, 503

J

Jackson, Andrew, 185–86, 188, 192, 196–206
Jackson, Thomas J. "Stonewall," 253, 284,
  286, 287, 288, 290, 291
Jacksonian democracy, 195–98
James I, 25, 26, 28
James II (duke of York), 37
James, Frank, 369
James, Jesse, 369
Jamestown, 26–28, 66
Japan, 376–77, 397, 435, 444
 called Cipango, 3
 in World War II, 484, 492–95, 500–03,
  505, 506–7
Japanese-Nisei, 493, 494
Jarratt, Devereaux, 51
Jay, John, 130, 146, 152, 159–60, 173
Jay Treaty, 159–60
Jefferson, Thomas, 108, 115, 135, 152, 155,
  157–58, 159, 162, 164–66, 171–77, 178,
  180, 182
 religious views, 172, 229
Jeffersonian Republicanism, 157–58, 171–72,
  187, 189
Jews, 443–44, 484, 486, 504, 600
Jim Crow laws, 354, 394

Johns Hopkins Medical School, 405
Johnson, Andrew, 312, 314–15, 599
Johnson, Lyndon B., 518, 526, 535–41, 543,
  544–45, 550, 551, 560
Johnston, Albert Sidney, 293
Johnston, Joseph E., 288, 298, 305, 307
joint resolution, 247
joint-stock companies, 26
Joliet, Louis, 85
Jones, John Paul, 124
Jones, Sam, 358
Joseph, Chief (Nez Perce), 374, 375
judicial activism, 537
judicial review, 174
Judiciary Act of 1789, 152
Judiciary Act of 1801, 166, 172, 174
Judson, Adoniram, 231
Jungle, The, 392, 393
Justice, Department of, 592, 604

K

Kagan, Elena, 610
kamikazes, 502, 503
Kanagawa, Treaty of, 376–77
Kansas,
 Bleeding Kansas, 268–71
Kansas City, 365
Kansas-Nebraska Act, 266
Kaskaskia, Illinois, 124–25
KDKA, 449
Kearny, Phil, 308
Kearny, Stephen, 251, 252
Kellogg, Frank B., 435
Kellogg-Briand Pact, 435
Kelly, "Machine Gun," 477
Kelly, Oliver H., 348
Kemp, Jack, 578, 582
Kennedy, Edward, 569
Kennedy, Jacqueline, 524
Kennedy, John F., 513, 518, 519, 524–26, 531,
  532, 535
Kennedy, Robert, 535, 544, 545
Kent State, 550
Kentucky, 124, 125, 160, 161, 293, 295–96,
  301
Kentucky Resolutions, 164, 276
Kerry, John, 604
Key, Francis Scott, 186
Khomeini, Ayatollah Ruhollah, 565, 581
Khrushchev, Nikita, 519
King George's War, 86, 88
King, Martin Luther, Jr., 530–31, 535, 541,
  542, 545
Kings Mountain, Battle of, 127
King William's War, 86–87
Kissinger, Henry, 549, 550
Kitchen Cabinet, 200
Kitty Hawk, N.C., 403
Knights of Labor, 346
Know-Nothings, 267, 268
Knox, Henry, 114, 152

Korea,
    North, 516–18
    South, 516–18
Korean War, 516–18, 523
Kosovo, 598
Ku Klux Klan, 319, 444–45, 541
Kuwait, 583–84

L

labor unions, 346–47, 388, 401, 472–73, 520
Lafayette, Marquis de, 122, 129
La Follette, Robert, 390
Lake Champlain, 113, 118, 120, 185
Lake Erie, 184, 219
Lake Erie, Battle of, 184
Lake Michigan, 219
Lake Ontario, 120
Landon, Alf, 471–72
Land Ordinance of 1785, 135
Laos, 539, 549, 551, 557
La Salle, Robert Cavelier, sieur de, 85
Latin America, 188, 377, 396, 399, 435, 525, 563
Latrobe, Benjamin, 226
Lawrence (Kansas), sack of, 269
League of Nations, 419, 422, 426–28, 434, 489
    during World War II, 483, 485, 504
Lebanon, 578, 581
Lee, Henry "Light-Horse Harry," 128, 283
Lee, Mother Ann, 233
Lee, Richard Henry, 115, 133
Lee, Robert E., 253, 274, 283, 284, 288–91, 307, 313
Leland, John, 147
Lend-Lease Act, 491
Lenin, Vladimir, 110, 422
Leo X, Pope,
Letters from a Farmer in Pennsylvania, 100
Lewinsky scandal, 598, 599, 600
Lewis and Clark Expedition, 176–77
Lewis, John L., 472
Lewis, Meriwether, 176–77, 179
Lexington, Battle of, 111–12
Leyte Gulf, Battle of, 502
Liberal Republicans, 324
Liberator, 222, 265
Liberty Party, 246
Libya, 488, 497
Lieberman, Joseph, 600
Liliuokalani, Queen, 379
Limbaugh, Rush, 594
limited government, 143, 144, 152, 164–65, 172, 440, 567, 568, 573, 574, 610
limited war, 517, 539, 551
Lincoln, Abraham, 200, 206, 249, 271–73, 276, 277, 278, 301–3, 306, 307–9, 312, 592
Lincoln-Douglas debates, 270–73
Lindbergh, Charles A., 443, 477, 490
line-item veto, 595
literature, 226–27, 265, 392, 441, 475
Little Bighorn, Battle of, 373

Livingstone, Robert, 115, 176
Lloyd George, David, 426
Locke, John, 108
Lodge, Henry Cabot, 427–28
Logan, John, 286
log cabin, 39, 49–50
    campaign, 208–9
Log College, 78
London, Jack, 355
London Company, 26
Long, Huey, 469
Long Island, Battle of, 117
Longstreet, James, 296–97
loose constructionists, 156, 174, 437
Los Angeles, 252, 542
Lost Colony. *See* Roanoke Colony
Louis XIV, 46, 69, 85, 86, 88
Louis XVI, 158
Louisiana, 192
    French, 85, 91
Louisiana Purchase, 175–76
Low-church Anglicans, 63, 67
Loyalists, 107, 109, 113, 123–28, 134
Luftwaffe, 486, 487, 488
Lusitania, 417–18
Luther, Martin, 7, 69
Lutherans, 69–70, 74
Luxembourg, 487, 500

M

MacArthur, Douglas, 461–62, 492, 493, 500, 507, 516–18
Machen, J. Gresham, 446
Macon's Bill Number Two, 182
Madison, James, 139, 140, 146, 147, 153, 154, 155, 156, 157, 164–65, 171, 173, 174, 587
    presidency of, 181, 183
Magellan, Ferdinand, 6
Maginot Line, 485, 490
Maine, 120, 194, 224, 246
Maine, U.S.S., 381
Makemie, Francis, 69
Manassas, First Battle of, 286–87
Manassas, Second Battle of, 288
Manchuria, 397, 484
Manhattan Island, 117
Manifest Destiny, 239–54, 327, 362, 413
Manila Bay, Battle of, 381–82
Mann, Horace, 223
Mannock, Edward "Mick", 424
Mao Zedong, 515
Marbury, William, 174
Marbury v. Madison, 174
March to the Sea, 305–6
Mariana Islands, 502
Marion, Francis, 127
market entrepreneurs, 334
Marquette, Jacques, 85
Marshall, George C., 515
Marshall, John, 165, 173–74, 178, 205
Marshall Plan, 515

Marx, Karl, 440
Mary (Queen of England), 62
Maryland, 134, 147, 174, 185, 288–89, 301
    colonization, 39–40
    Revolutionary era, 118–19
Mason, George, 141, 145, 146, 147
Mason, James, 302
Mason, Lowell, 227
Massachusetts, 147, 154, 217
    Bay Colony, 32–34, 51, 74
    colonization, 30–34
    Revolutionary era, 99–100, 105–8, 109, 111–12
Massachusetts Bay Company, 33, 34
Masterson, Bat, 369
materialism, 33, 64, 66, 355, 357, 450, 527, 531, 542–43
Mather, Cotton, 48, 65
Maximilian I, 376
Mayflower, 30, 31
Mayflower Compact, 31
Mayo Clinic, 404–5
McAuliffe, Anthony, 500
McCain, John, 607–8
McCarthy, Eugene, 544, 545
McCarthy, Joseph, 523
McCarthyism, 523, 524
McClellan, George B., 287–88, 289, 306
McCormick, Cyrus, 214
McCulloch v. Maryland, 174
McDowell, Irvin, 286–87
McGovern, George, 551–52, 555
McGuffey, William H., 224
McKinley, William, 344, 349–50, 380, 383, 386
McKinley Tariff, 344
Meade, George, 290–91
Meat Inspection Act, 392
meat-packing industry, 365, 392
Medicare, 537
medicine, 404–5
melting pot, 353
Mencken, H. L., 209
Mennonites, 70
mercantilism, 4, 483
Meredith, James, 530
Merrimac. See *Virginia*
Methodists, 200, 222, 229, 231, 531
Mexican War (1846–48), 248–54, 377
Mexico, 241–43, 376, 413–14, 419
    conquered by Cortés, 15
    held by the Spanish, 177
Miami, 450–51
Michigan, 587
middle colonies,
    founding of, 36–39. *See also individual colonies*
    Great Awakening in, 76
    Revolutionary era, 116–23
Middle East, 497, 514–15, 564, 575, 583–87, 604, 606
midnight appointments, 165–66, 174
Midway, 378, 493, 501

Midway, Battle of, 493, 495
Military Reconstruction Act, 314, 317
militia, 109
Miller, William, 232–33
Millerites, 232–33
miners/mining, 364
Minuit, Peter, 21, 36
Minutemen, 109
Miranda v. Arizona, 537
Missionary Ridge, Battle of, 296, 298
missions, 67, 70, 73–75, 231, 240–41, 357–59, 378, 379–80, 532
Mississippi, 192, 318
Mississippi River, 85, 130, 134, 175, 177, 183, 219, 285
    Civil War Campaign, 292–95
Missouri, 192, 194–95, 301
Missouri Compromise, 194–95, 263, 266
Missouri River, 85, 177
Model T, 402–3, 448
modernism, 406–8, 445–46, 531–32
Molotov, Vyacheslav, 514
Mondale, Walter, 579
Mongrel Tariff, 342–43
Monitor, U.S.S., 287
Monmouth, Battle of, 123
Monroe, James, 146, 171, 176, 187
Monroe Doctrine, 188–89, 396, 435
Montana, 177, 344
Montcalm, Marquis de, 91–92, 93
Monterrey, Battle of, 250
Montezuma, 15
Montgomery, Bernard, 497–98, 500
Monticello, 226
Moody, Dwight L., 214, 297, 357–59, 379, 407
Moody Bible Institute, 407
Moral Majority, 568, 594
Moravians, 70–71, 75
Morgan, Daniel, 121, 128
Morgan, John Pierpont, 336, 338
Mormonism/Mormons, 233, 244, 568
Mormon Trail, 244
Morse, Samuel F. B., 220–21, 225
motion pictures, 443, 475–76, 600
Mound Builders, 12
Mount Vernon, 139, 158
muckrakers, 333, 390
Mugwumps, 343
Muhlenberg, Henry, 69–70
mujahideen, 578
Munich Conference, 485–86
Munn v. Illinois, 348
music, 73, 441. *See also* hymns and gospel songs
    modern, 476
    rock, 527, 543
Muslims, 175, 597–98, 602, 603, 604
    merchants to China, 4
Mussolini, Benito, 388, 462, 482–83, 497
My Lai Massacre, 549

N

NAFTA, 593
Nagasaki, 507
Napoleon III, 376
Napoleon Bonaparte, 163, 176, 182, 188, 376
Narragansett Indians, 35
Nashville, 293, 296, 306
Nashville, Battle of, 306
Nast, Thomas, 323
National Association for the Advancement of Colored People (NAACP), 395, 528
National Bank, 203–4, 400–401
    first, 154, 155–56, 173
    second, 193
National Council of Churches, 531
National Guard, 529, 542, 550
National Industrial Recovery Act (NIRA), 467, 469
nationalism, 95–96, 101, 192–93, 198, 482–84
National Origins Act, 444
National Recovery Administration (NRA), 465, 467, 469, 475
National Republicans, 198
National Road, 193, 219
National Security Act, 521
National Security Council, 521
National Socialist German Workers' Party. *See* Nazism
National Voter Registration Act, 593
Naturalism, 355
Navajo code talkers, 494
Navy, U.S., 124, 160, 163, 175, 183, 184, 185, 435
    in Progressivism, 396, 397
    in Spanish-American War, 381–82
    in World War II, 492, 502, 503
Nazism/Nazis, 483–84, 485, 487, 489, 498–500, 504, 505–6
Nazi-Soviet nonaggression pact, 486
Nelson, "Baby Face," 477
Netherlands, 487, 492, 500
Neutrality Act of 1939, 490
New Amsterdam. *See* New Netherland
Newburgh Conspiracy, 137–38
New Deal, 440, 463–73, 524
New Democrat, 589, 596
New Economic Policy, 548
New England, 86, 155, 187, 201–2, 217, 232
    Great Awakening in, 77
    Puritans in, 32–34, 63, 65, 66
    Revolutionary era, 105–9, 111–12, 114
    settlement of, 29–36; *See also individual colonies*
New England Primer, 51
New Evangelicals, 532
New France. *See* Canada
New Freedom, 400–01
New Frontier, 520, 525
New Guinea, 500, 502
New Hampshire, 147
    colonization, 36

New Harmony, 225
New Jersey, 147;
    College of. *See* Princeton
    colonization, 37
    Great Awakening in, 76
    Revolutionary era, 117–23
New Jersey Plan, 140
New Left, 543
New Lights, 76–77
New Measures, 232
New Mexico, 248, 251, 253, 262
New Nationalism, 400
New Netherland, 20, 36–37, 69
New Orleans, 175, 176, 185, 285, 294, 606–7
    Battle of, 186
New Right, 567
New South, 338
newspapers, 58, 205, 222, 227–28, 340, 442, 478
    inciting the Spanish-American War, 380
New Sweden, 21, 39
Newton, Sir Isaac, 440
New World colonization, 20–21
    Separatists in, 30, 31
New York, 134, 147, 174
    colonization, 36–37
    Revolutionary era, 106, 107, 113, 116–17, 118, 121, 123, 130
New York City, 37, 116, 118, 148, 217, 234, 323, 351, 352, 474, 513, 602
New York draft riot, 300
New York World's Fair, 478–79
Nez Perce Indians, 240, 374, 375
Niagara Falls, 184, 341
Nicaragua, 396, 397, 399, 435, 563, 577, 581
Nimitz, Chester W., 495, 500, 503
Nine-eleven. *See* September 11, 2001
Nixon, Richard M., 522, 523, 524, 535, 545, 547–52, 555–56, 599
    pardon of, 557, 562
Non-Intercourse Act, 182
Noriega, Manuel,
Normalcy, 433, 437
Normandy invasion, 498–99
North, Lord, 101, 106, 107
North, Oliver, 579, 581–82
North American Free Trade Act (NAFTA), 593
North Atlantic Treaty Organization (NATO), 513, 515
North Carolina, 40, 107, 147, 278, 338
    Revolutionary era, 127, 128–29
North Dakota, 177, 344
Northern Baptist Convention, 446
Northern Securities case, 392
Northwest Ordinance of 1787, 136, 263
Northwest Ordinances, 135–36
Northwest Territory, 123–25, 134–36, 178–81, 184–85, 186
Norway, 486
Notre Dame, 443
nuclear weapons, 513, 516, 519, 536, 551, 564

nullification, 200–203
    Virginia and Kentucky Resolutions, 164–65, 201

O

Oakley, Annie, 356
Obama, Barak, 607–10
Oberlin College, 221, 232
O'Connor, Sandra Day, 579
Office of Price Administration, 495
Oglethorpe, James, 40
Ohio, 178, 179
Ohio River, 90, 108, 123–25, 135, 178, 219
oil embargo, 492, 558–59
Okies, 456, 476
Okinawa, 502, 503
Oklahoma, 205
    land rushes, 366
Old Deluder Satan Law, 51
Old Ironsides, 184
Old Lights, 76–77
Olive Branch Petition, 115
one man, one vote decisions, 537
Open Door Policy, 377, 397
open ranges, 365
Operation Barbarossa, 488
Operation Desert Shield, 583
Operation Desert Storm, 584–87
Operation Husky, 498
Operation Overlord, 499
Operation Torch, 498
Ordinance of 1784, 135
Ordinance of Secession, 276
Oregon, 239–41
Oregon Territory, 188, 239–41, 247–48
Oregon Trail, 244
Organization of Petroleum Exporting Countries (OPEC), 558
organized labor, 434
Origin of Species, The, 353
Orlando, Vittorio, 426
Orthodox Presbyterian Church, 446
Osceola, 204
Oswald, Lee Harvey, 535
Owen, Robert, 225

P

Pacific Garden Mission, 407
Pahlavi, Mohammed Reza, 565
Paine, Thomas, 115, 229
Palestine Liberation Organization (PLO), 578
Palin, Sarah, 607–8
Panama, 396, 563–64
Panama Canal, 396, 405, 415, 563
Panama Canal Treaty, 563–64, 567
Pan-Americanism, 377
Panic of 1819, 194
Panic of 1837, 207
Panic of '73 (1873), 324, 346
Panic of '93 (1893), 344, 349
Paris, Treaty of (War for Independence), 130, 134, 160, 178

Paris, Treaty of (1763), 93
Paris Peace Talks, 540, 550
Parks, Rosa, 530
Parliament, 97–101, 106, 108, 113, 115
patents, 213
Paterson, William, 140
Patriot Act, 603
Patriots, 100, 101, 102, 106, 108–15, 117, 125, 127
    in the Civil War, 283–84
patroon system, 37
Patton, George, 499, 500
Paxton Boys, 107
Peace Corps, 525
peaceful coexistence, 518
Peale, Norman Vincent, 531
Pearl Harbor, 492
Pelosi, Nancy, 610
Pendleton Act, 342
Peninsular Campaign, 287–88
Penn, William, 37–38, 68
Pennsylvania, 147, 160, 290
    colonization, 37–39
    colony, 46, 107
    religion in, 68, 69, 70
    Revolutionary era, 118–19
Pennsylvania Dutch, 46
penny newspaper, 228
Pentagon, 602
Pentagon Papers, 550
People's Republic of China. *See* China, Communist
Pequot Indians, 34
perestroika, 580
Perkins, Frances, 465
Perot, Ross, 589, 596
Perry, Matthew, 376
Perry, Oliver Hazard, 184, 185
Perryville, Battle of, 295–96
Pershing, John J. "Black Jack", 414, 422
Persian Gulf, 565
pet banks, 203
Petersburg, siege of, 306–7
Petition of Right, 98
Philadelphia, 38, 106, 107, 108, 113, 118–20, 121, 123, 139, 155, 351, 352
Philip II, 18
Philippines, 382, 383, 395, 493, 500, 502
Pickett, George, 291
Pickett's Charge, 291
Pierce, Franklin, 264
Pietism, 70, 76
Pike, Zebulon, 177, 179
Pikes Peak gold rush, 364
Pilgrims, 30–32, 63
Pinchot, Gifford, 393, 398
Pinckney, Charles Cotesworth, 165, 181
Pinckney, Thomas, 162
Pinkertons, 370
pirates, 40
    Barbary, 175
Pitcher, Molly, 123
Pitt, William, 92, 113

Pittsburgh, 90, 92, 97, 351
Plains Indians, 371–75
Plains of Abraham, Battle of the, 93
plank roads, 217–18
platform, party, 203
Plessy v. Ferguson, 394, 528–29
Plymouth Colony, 31–32
Plymouth Company, 26
Pocahontas, 27, 29, 74
Poe, Edgar Allan, 227
Poindexter, John, 581–82
Poland, 122, 427, 486, 504, 514, 585
political entrepreneurs, 334
political parties, 206–9
    emergence of, 156–58, 162
    national conventions, 203
    nominating conventions, 203
Polk, James K., 246, 247–48
poll taxes, 354, 394, 536
Polo, Marco, 3
Ponce de León, 16
Pontiac/Pontiac's War, 94–95, 107
Pony express, 221
Poor Richard's Almanac, 54, 124
Pope, John, 288, 294
popular sovereignty, 144–45, 260, 266, 268, 270, 272
Populism/Populists, 348–50, 351, 354
Populist Party, 348, 350
Portsmouth, Treaty of, 397
Portugal, 4
Portuguese explorers, 4
Potomac River, 155
Potsdam, 506
Pottawatomie Massacre, 269–70
Poverty, War on, 536
Powderly, Terrence V., 346
Power of the purse, 96, 100, 105
Powhatan, 27
Prayer Meeting Revival, 234, 358. *See also* Religion, Revivals/Evangelism
Preamble, 144
Premillennialism, 232, 233, 446
Presbyterian polity, 64, 69
Presbyterians, 178, 199, 446
    in the colonial era, 45, 69, 76–78, 79
Princeton, Battle of, 118
Princeton Theological Seminary, 406–7
Princeton University, 78, 79, 178
Princip, Gavrilo, 412
Proclamation Line, 97
Proclamation of Neutrality, 159, 416, 417
Progressive Era, 386–409
Progressive Party, 400–01
Progressive Party (1948), 521
Progressivism/Progressives, 386, 398, 483. *See also* Progressive Era
Prohibition, 13, 224, 359, 389, 439, 441–42, 465
Promontory Point, 363
Prophet, the, 180–81
Proposition 13, 567
proprietary colony, 29

protective tariff, 192–93, 282, 344, 348, 460, 489

Protestant Reformation, 7–8, 25, 30, 50–51, 110
 doctrines of, 63
 in England, 62–63

Protestants, 108, 110, 568. *See also individual denominations*

Providence, 19, 50, 117

Prussia, 90, 92, 122

public works, 458, 460, 526

Public Works Administration (PWA), 466, 475

Publius, 146

Pueblo Indians, 12

Puerto Rico, 382

Pulaski, Count Casimir, 122

Pulitzer, Joseph, 380

Pullman Strike, 347

Pure Food and Drug Act, 392

Puritans, 30, 63–66
 and education, 51, 75
 and founding of Massachusetts Bay Colony, 32–34
 beliefs of, 63–64
 sermons of, 73

Q

Qaddafi, Muammar al-, 579

Quakers, 37–38, 63, 68, 222

Quartering Act, 98

Quasi War, 162–63

Quayle, Dan, 583

Quebec, 88, 92–93, 108, 120

Quebec Act, 108

Queen Anne's War, 86, 88

Quisling, Vidkun, 486

R

racial discrimination, 222, 272, 300, 352, 353, 354
 during the 1920s, 443–45
 during the Cold War era, 528, 530, 535, 538
 during the Great Depression, 475
 during World War II, 484, 493, 494, 504
 in the Progressive Era, 394–95, 404
 in Reconstruction, 317–18, 321

racism. *See* racial discrimination

Radical Republicans, 312–14, 318, 319

radio, 442, 465, 476, 527
 talk, 594

railroads, 213, 219–20, 334–35, 338, 343, 348, 420
 regulation of, 392
 transcontinental, 254, 266, 362–63

Raleigh, Sir Walter, 19

Randolph, Edmund, 140, 145, 146, 147, 152

range wars, 366

rationing, 495

Rauschenbusch, Walter, 406

Reagan, Ronald, 545, 562, 565, 567, 568–70, 573–83

Reagan Doctrine, 576–77, 578

Reaganomics, 574, 576

Reagan Revolution, 573–83

Realism, 355

recall, 387

Reclamation Act, 393

Reconstruction, 312–28

Reconstruction amendments, 315–16

Reconstruction Finance Corporation, 460–61, 463, 523

Redeemers, 320–21, 354, 394

Red Scare, 434, 438, 444, 521–23

Reed, Walter, 405

referendum, 387

Reform Darwinism. *See* Darwinism

reform movements, 221–28, 341–44
 Progressivism, 386–409, 483

regulars, 109

Regulators, 107

Rehnquist, William, 599

Reid, Harry, 610

relativity, theory of, 440–41

religion. *See also individual denominations, groups, and movements*
 American churches and slavery, 79, 221–22, 265
 church and State, 17, 33, 35, 62, 109, 154
 church polity, 64
 church services, 58, 68, 72–73
 Cold War era, 531–32, 567–68
 colonial history, 30–36, 62–80, 96
 conversion/salvation, 73–77, 79, 178, 205, 220, 223, 229, 230, 231, 291, 357–59, 423
 freedom of. *See* freedom of religion
 Gilded Age, 357–59
 Jacksonian Era, 195, 196
 persecution, 484
 Progressive Era, 406–8
 revivals, 76–80, 110, 228–31, 234, 297
 Twenties, 445–47
 unorthodox, 231–34;

Religious Right, 567–68, 582, 594

reparation payments. *See* reparations

reparations, 417, 422, 426, 427, 435, 436–37, 452

Republic, 142–43, 146

Republican Party/Republicans, 267–68, 276, 314, 325–26, 342, 343–44, 349, 350, 440, 462, 475, 520, 523, 562, 568, 570, 583, 594, 596, 607–8, 610

Republicans (Jeffersonians). *See* Democratic-Republicans

rescue missions, 357

reservations, Indian, 372–73, 375

Revels, Hiram, 318

Revere, Paul, 96, 111

Revolution/Revolutionary War, 105–30
 compared to French and Russian revolutions, 110, 158–59.
 See also War for Independence

Rhineland, 46, 426, 485

Rhode Island, 147, 212, 441
 colonization, 35–36
 colony, 68
 Revolutionary era, 105

Rice, Condoleeza, 604

Richmond, Virginia, 286, 287, 288, 290, 299, 306–7

Richthofen, Manfred von, 424

Rickenbacker, Eddie, 424

Rickey, Branch, 529

rights movements, 528–31, 560–62

Right-to-Life movement, 567

Rio Grande, 249, 253, 376

riots, 299, 300, 346, 535, 542, 550

road building, 193, 217–19

Roanoke Colony, 19

Roanoke Island, 19

robber barons, 333–34

Roberts, John G., 606

Robertson, Pat, 567–68, 582, 594

Robinson, Jackie, 529

Rockefeller, John D., 336–38, 344, 390

Rockefeller, Nelson, 545, 557

Rocky Mountains, 177, 364, 366

Roe v. Wade, 560, 567

Rogers, Will, 464, 477, 575

Rolfe, John, 27, 29

Roman Catholicism, 108, 439, 443–44, 524, 568
 elements in Anglican Church, 2, 30, 63
 Henry VIII's break from, 62
 in Maryland, 39–40, 71
 in Spanish America, 17

Romania, 486, 514, 585

Romanticism, 226–27

Romanticism (literature), 226–27, 355

Rome-Berlin-Tokyo Axis, 484

Rommel, Erwin, 488, 497, 498

Roosevelt, Eleanor, 474, 475

Roosevelt, Franklin Delano, 435, 437, 440, 456, 462–75, 489, 490–91, 492, 494, 495, 498, 503–5

Roosevelt, Theodore, 380, 382, 383, 386, 391–97, 398–400

Roosevelt Corollary, 396–97, 435

Root-Takahira Agreement, 397

Rosecrans, William, 296

Rosenberg, Julius and Ethel, 522

Roth v. United States, 537

Rough Riders, 382, 391

royal colony, 29

rubber, 472

Rural Electrification Administration (REA), 467

Rush-Bagot Treaty, 187

Rusk, Dean, 519

Russell, James Lowell, 249

Russia, 110, 397, 415, 484, 488, 505, 522. *See also* Soviet Union

Russian Revolution. *See* Bolshevik Revolution

Rutgers, 79

Ruth, Babe, 442–43

S

Sacajawea, 177
Sacco, Nicola, 444
Sacco-Vanzetti case, 444
Sadat, Anwar, 564
Saipan, 502
Salem witch trials, 65, 66
Salerno, 498
Salt II Treaty, 564–65, 567
Salt Lake City, 233, 244
Sandinistas, 577
San Francisco, 394
San Jacinto, Battle of, 242, 243
Sankey, Ira, 358
San Martín, José de, 188
Santa Anna, Antonio López de, 242, 243, 247, 250–51, 252–53, 254
Santa Fe Trail, 244, 251
Santiago Bay, Battle of, 382
Sarajevo, 412
Saratoga, Battle of, 120–21
Saratoga campaign, 121
Saudi Arabia, 583, 587
Sauk Indians, 204
Savannah, Georgia, 41, 126, 306
Scalawags, 318
Schenk v. United States. See Supreme Court decisions
Schlafly, Phyllis, 561
Schlieffen Plan, 416
Schwarzkopf, Norman, 587
Scopes, John T., 447
Scopes trial, 447
Scots-Irish, 45–46, 107
Scott, Dred, 270
Scott, Winfield, 250, 252, 264, 284–85
Scripture. *See* religion
Sea Dogs, 18
secede. *See* secession
secession, 164–65, 201–2, 276, 281–82
secret ballot, 387
Secret Six, 273
Sectionalism, North/South, 155, 192, 193–95, 200–203, 259, 262, 264–65, 284–85
secular humanism, 110, 405
segregation/desegregation, 354, 318, 394, 494, 528–29, 535, 541, 547
Selective Service Act, 419
Seminole Indians, 13, 204–5
Seminole War, 204–5
Senate, 141
Seneca Falls Convention, 224
separation of powers, 142, 143
Separatists, 30–32, 63. *See also* Pilgrims
September 11, 2001, 602–3
Sequoyah, 205
Seven Days' Battles, 288
Seventh-day Adventists, 233
Seven Years' War. *See* French and Indian War
Sevier, John, 127

Sewall, Samuel, 65
Seward, William, 206, 268, 273, 276, 277, 278, 302, 376, 378
Shakers, 233
sharecropping, 319–20, 475
Shawnee Indians, 97, 180
Shays, Daniel, 138
Shays's Rebellion, 138
Shelby, Isaac, 127
Shenandoah Valley, 45, 46, 287, 307
Sherman, Roger, 115, 141
Sherman, William Tecumseh, 253, 305–6, 307, 308
Sherman Antitrust Act, 337, 344, 392
Shiloh, Battle of, 293–94
Shoshone Indians, 177
Siegfried Line, 485, 500
Sierra Nevada, 244
silent majority, 547
silver, 4, 18, 324, 364, 470
   free silver, 349
Simons, Menno, 70
Sinclair, Upton, 390, 392
"Sinners in the Hands of an Angry God," 62, 73, 77
Sioux Indians, 371, 373–74, 375
Sioux War, 373–74
Sitting Bull, 356, 373, 374
Slater, Samuel, 212
slaves/slavery, 135, 136, 189, 194–95, 216, 217, 246, 247, 259, 263, 264–65, 266, 282–83, 303
   abolishing of, 221–23, 315, 327
   in England's colonies, 28
   issue at Constitutional Convention, 141
   Lincoln's position on, 272–73
   Spanish and Portuguese trade, 17–18
Slidell, John, 302
smallpox, 14, 15, 47, 48, 107
Smith, Al, 439, 447, 465
Smith, Captain John, 27, 31
Smith, Joseph, 233
Smoky Mountains, 205
Smoot-Hawley tariff, 440, 452, 460
Social Darwinism. *See* Darwinism
social gospel, 354, 406, 445–46
Socialism/Socialists, 347, 388, 390, 440, 463, 468, 469
   World War II era, 482, 483, 486
Socialist Party, 347, 390
Social Security Act, 467
Society for the Promotion of Christian Knowledge (SPCK), 67
Society for the Propagation of the Gospel in Foreign Parts (SPG), 67
Society for the Propagation of the Gospel in New England, 74
Society of Friends. *See* Quakers
sod houses. *See* soddies
soddies, 367
Solid South, 327
Sons of Liberty, 98, 99, 101, 107, 113
Sotomayor, Sonia, 610

soup kitchens, 474
South, the, 142, 155, 200–03, 214–16
   during Civil War, 282–83, 290, 299, 305–6. *See also* individual battles
   during Reconstruction, 309, 316–21, 327
   during War of 1812, 185–86
   Great Awakening in, 78–79, 80
   Revolutionary era, 123, 125–29
   solid, 327
South Carolina, 147, 201–3, 217, 220, 276–77
   colonization, 40
   colony, 69
   Revolutionary era, 107, 113, 125–28
South Dakota, 177, 344
Southeast Asia, 492, 518
Southern Christian Leadership Conference, 530
Southern colonies, 39–41. *See also individual colonies*
Soviet Union, 110, 378, 462, 583
   Cold War era, 514–16, 518–19, 522, 539, 549, 564–65, 576–78, 580
   World War II era, 484–85, 486, 488, 495, 503–5
space program, 526
Spain, 130, 380–83
   exploration, 5, 6, 15–19
Spanish-American War, 186, 380–83
Spanish Armada, 18–19
Specie Circular of 1836, 204
speculation, 450–51, 452–53
Spirit of St. Louis, 443
Spock, Benjamin, 528
spoils system, 200, 341
Squanto, 32
Square Deal, 392–93
stagflation, 559–60
Stalin, Joseph, 110, 482, 484, 486, 498, 503, 505, 506
Stalwarts, 342
Stamp Act, 97, 98, 100
Stamp Act Congress, 99
Standard Oil Company, 336–38, 344, 390
Stanton, Edwin, 314, 315
Stanton, Elizabeth Cady, 390
Star-Spangled Banner, The, 186
starving time, 28
State, Department of, 152
Statehood, process for, 136
States' rights, 133, 134, 137, 144, 153, 154, 164–65, 172, 276, 281–82, 300, 327, 389
Statue of Liberty, 353
St. Augustine, 17
steamships, 216–17, 220
Stearns, Shubal, 79
steel, 213, 335–36, 338
Steffens, Lincoln, 390
Steuben, Baron von, 122, 123
Stevens, Thaddeus, 313, 314
Stevenson, Adlai, 523
St. Lawrence River, 85, 92
St. Lô, 499
St. Louis, 177, 351

stock market, 438, 451, 596
stock market crash, 439, 451–53, 456, 457
Stone, Harlan Fiske, 513
Stones River, Battle of, 296
Stowe, Harriet Beecher, 265
Strategic Arms Limitations Talks (SALT)
    treaties, 549, 564
Strategic Arms Reduction Talks (START),
    580
Strategic Defense Initiative (SDI), 581
Strict constructionists, 156, 437
strikes, 346–47, 393, 434, 438, 472–73, 520
Stuart, Gilbert, 226
Stuart, James Ewell Brown, "Jeb," 274, 284,
    288, 289, 290
Student Nonviolent Coordinating Committee
    (SNCC), 542
Students for a Democratic Society (SDS), 543
Student Volunteer Movement (SVM), 379
Stuyvesant, Peter, 20
submarine warfare, 417–18
    unrestricted, 419, 490, 491
Sudetenland, 485
suffrage, 312, 319
    blacks, 354, 316, 317, 536, 541
    women's, 224, 390, 468
    See also Voting rights
Sugar Act, 97
Sumner, Charles, 269, 313
Sumner-Brooks Episode, 269
Sunday, Billy, 389, 407
supply-side economics (Reaganomics), 574
Supreme Court, 143, 153, 556, 601, 605, 610
    court-packing plan, 470–71
    during FDR's presidency, 467, 468, 469,
        473
    Marshall court, 173–74
    Warren Court, 537
Supreme Court decisions
    Brown v. Board of Education, 528, 529,
        537
    Dred Scott v. Sandford, 270
    Engel v. Vitale, 537
    Gibbons v. Ogden, 174
    Gideon v. Wainwright, 537
    Marbury v. Madison, 174
    McCulloch v. Maryland, 174
    Miranda v. Arizona, 537
    Munn v. Illinois, 348
    Northern Securities case, 392
    Plessy v. Ferguson, 354, 394, 528–29
    Roe v. Wade, 560, 567
    Roth v. United States, 537
    Schenk v. United States, 421
Sussex pledge, 418, 419
Sutter, John, 261, 262
Sweden/Swedes, 486
Swift, Gustavus, 365

T

Taft, Robert,
Taft, William Howard, 391, 395, 397–400

Taft-Hartley Act, 520
Taiwan, 515–16, 548–49, 567
Tallmadge, James, 194
Tammany Hall, 319, 323, 341, 343
Taney, Roger B., 203, 270
Tarbell, Ida, 337, 390
tariffs, 97, 160, 192, 333, 342–43, 344, 398,
    400, 440, 452, 460
    of Abominations, 200–02
    of 1816, 192
Tarleton, Banastre, 126, 128
taxes, 440, 458–59, 466, 526, 567, 573,
    574–75
    colonial, 96–100, 106–7
    Confederation era, 134
    federal income tax, 388, 400, 459, 574
    internal, 97, 160
    World War II era, 496
Taylor, Maxwell, 499
Taylor, Zachary, 249, 250–51, 260–61, 262,
    263
Tea Act of 1773, 106
Teach, Edward "Blackbeard," 40
Tea Party. *See* Boston Tea Party
Teapot Dome scandal, 437–38
Tecumseh, 178, 179, 180–81, 183, 185
teddy bears, 391
Teheran, 503, 555
telegraph, 220–21
telephones, 340, 450
television, 524, 527, 528, 530, 535, 567, 568,
    594
Tennent, Gilbert, 76, 77, 78
Tennent, William, Sr., 78
Tennessee, 79, 127, 160, 199, 278, 293, 300,
    314, 317, 446–47
Tennessee Valley Authority (TVA), 465, 467,
    469
Ten percent plan, 312, 314
Tenure of Office Act, 314, 315
terrorism, 412, 434, 578–79, 587, 602–3, 604,
    610
Tet Offensive, 540, 544
Texan War for Independence, 241–43
Texas, 241–43
    annexation of, 247
    Republic of, 243
textile industry, 212, 338
Thames, Battle of the, 185
Thanksgiving, 32
Third party, 203, 348, 400
38th parallel, 516–17
Thomas, George, 295, 296, 298, 306
Thoreau, Henry David, 225, 227, 275
Three-Fifths Compromise, 141
Thumb, General Tom, 356
Thurmond, Strom, 521
Tibbets, Paul, 506
Tilden, Samuel J., 325–26
Tippecanoe, Battle of, 181
tobacco, 12, 28, 29, 40, 201, 214, 284, 320,
    338
Tojo, Hideki, 484

Toleration Act of 1649, 39
toll roads, 218
Tom Thumb, 219–20
Tories. *See* Loyalists
Townsend, Francis, 470
Townshend, Charles, 100
Townshend Acts, 100
trade deficit, 560
Trail of Tears, 205
Transcendentalism, 225
transportation, 216–20, 402–4
    highway, 219
Treasury, Department of, 152
Trent affair, 302
Trenton, Battle of, 117–18
Tripoli, 175, 497, 579
Truman, Harry, 503, 505, 506, 513–18,
    520–22, 523, 528
Truman Doctrine, 515
Trumbull, John, 226
trustbusting, 388, 392
trusts, 336–37, 343, 344, 388, 392
Tubman, Harriet, 223
Turner, Nat, 222
turnpikes, 218
Tuskegee Institute, 338, 354, 394, 404
Twain, Mark, 355
Tweed, William "Boss," 323
Two-Penny Act, 99
Tyler, John, 208, 209, 245, 246, 247

U

Uncle Tom's Cabin, 265
Underground Railroad, 265
Underwood Tariff Act, 400
unemployment, 207, 344, 433, 440, 520, 548,
    559–60, 562, 566, 569, 574, 576, 596
    during the Great Depression, 452, 456,
        457, 458, 459, 465, 466, 469, 473, 474,
        475
Union army/forces, 286–87, 289, 290, 300,
    304, 307
Union Pacific Railroad, 338, 362–63
Unitarianism, 66, 223, 225, 232
United Kingdom. *See* Britain
United Nations, 504, 513–14, 516–17, 548,
    584, 597
United States Steel Corporation, 338
Urban evangelism, 357–59, 407
Urbanization, 351, 357
urban riots, 542, 545
Utah, 233
Utopian reformers, 224–25
Utrecht, Treaty of, 88

V

Valley Campaign, 287
Valley Forge, 121–22
Van Buren, Martin, 198, 200, 203, 206–8,
    209, 246, 260
Vanderbilt, Cornelius, 334
Vanzetti, Bartolomeo, 444

Vera Cruz, Battle of, 252
Vermont, 113, 121, 160
Versailles,
    peace conference, 425–27
    Treaty of, 425–28, 435, 485
vertical integration, 336
Vespucci, Amerigo, 5
Veterans' Bureau, 438
Vicksburg, 293
    siege of, 294
Victoria, Queen,
Viet Cong, 539, 549
Vietnam, 518, 538–40, 551, 557
Vietnamization, 549
Vietnam War, 518, 535, 536, 538–40, 549,
    550–52
    antiwar movement, 540, 542–43, 549–50
Villa, Pancho, 414
Vincennes, Indiana, 124–25, 181
Virginia, 134, 147, 217, 278, 286–88, 289–90,
    338
    colonization, 26–29
    religion in, 66–67, 78, 79, 109;
    Revolutionary era, 98–99, 106, 108, 109,
      122, 128, 129
Virginia Company. *See* London Company
Virginia, C.S.S., 287
Virginia Plan, 140
Virginia Resolutions, 164, 276
voting rights, 34, 42, 195, 224, 354, 312, 316,
    318, 390, 394, 468, 535, 536, 541
Voting Rights Act of 1965, 536, 541

W

Wade, Benjamin, 315
Wade-Davis Bill, 312–13
Wake Island, 492
Wallace, George, 535, 546–47, 551, 562
Wallace, Henry A., 466, 503, 513, 521
War, Department of, 152
War Between the States. *See* Civil War
Warfield, Benjamin B., 406–7
War for Independence, 105–30
war-guilt clause, 427
War Hawks, 183, 188
War of 1812, 181–86
War of Austrian Succession. *See* King George's
    War
War of Jenkins' Ear. *See* King George's War
War of the League of Augsburg. *See* King
    William's War
War of the Spanish Succession. *See* Queen
    Anne's War
War on Terror, 603
War Powers Act, 551
War Production Board, 495
Warren, Earl, 537
Warsaw Pact, 515
Washington (state), 344
Washington and Lee University, 79, 313
Washington, Booker T., 338, 354–55, 394–95
Washington, D.C., 153, 165, 171, 185, 286, 301

Washington, George, 148–49, 226, 283
    Farewell Address, 160–61
    in Constitutional Convention, 139–40
    in French and Indian War, 90, 91
    in Newburgh Conspiracy, 137–38
    in War for Independence, 108–9, 114–23,
      129
    presidency of, 152–53, 156–61
Washington, march on, 530–31
Washington, Treaty of, 376
Washington Naval Conference/Treaty, 434–35,
    484
Watergate affair, 555–56, 557
Watts, Isaac, 227
Watts riot, 542
waving the bloody shirt, 325–26
Wayne, "Mad Anthony," 178
weapons, 154, 213, 549, 603, 604. *See also*
    nuclear weapons
Weathermen, 543
Weaver, James B., 348
Webster, Daniel, 136, 192, 201–2, 206, 245,
    262, 263
Webster, Noah, 223
Webster-Ashburton Treaty, 245–46
Wehrmacht, 488, 500
Welfare Reform Act of 1996, 596
Welles, Orson, 476
Wells, H.G., 476
Wesley, Charles, 74
Wesley, John, 70, 71, 74, 229
West, American, 262, 362–83
West, Benjamin, 220, 226
western lands, 123–25
    confederation era, 134–36
    conservation, 393
    homesteading, 366–67
    sale of, 366
Westinghouse, George, 340
West Point, 120, 253, 284, 308
West Virginia, 301
westward movement, 97, 239–54, 261–62, 333
    trails, 243–44
Wheelock, Eleazar, 75
Whig Party/Whigs, 206, 207, 208–9, 260,
    266–67
Whiskey Rebellion, 160
Whiskey Ring, 322
Whitefield, George, 77–78, 79, 109
Whitewater scandal, 592, 598
Whitman, Marcus and Narcissa, 240–41
Whitman, Walt, 225, 227
Whitney, Eli, 213, 215–16
Wilderness campaign, 304
Wilderness Road, 161, 217
Wilhelm II, Kaiser, 416
William III, 86
William and Mary College, 67
Williams, Roger, 35, 68, 74
Williamsburg, Virginia, 108
Willkie, Wendell, 490
Wilmot, David, 259
Wilmot Proviso, 259, 260

Wilson, Woodrow, 391, 400–01, 413–20, 422,
    425–28, 434, 435
Winona Lake Bible Conference, 407
Winthrop, John, 33
Winthrop, John, Jr., 34
Wolfe, James, 92, 93
women
    in World War II, 496
    post-World War II, 528
women's liberation movement, 560
women's rights movement, 224, 390, 560–62
Wood, Leonard, 382
Woodmason, Charles, 58
Woolworth, F.W., 357
work relief, 460
Works Progress Administration (WPA), 466,
    471, 475
World Council of Churches, 531
World Trade Center, 602
World War I, 412–13, 415–24
    posters, 421
World War II, 473, 482–88, 500
    in North Africa, 488, 497–98
    in the Pacific, 492–95, 500–03
    Italian Campaign, 498
    Normandy Invasion, 498–99
Wounded Knee Massacre, 375, 560
Wright Brothers (Wilbur and Orville), 403
Wyoming, 344

X

XYZ Affair, 163

Y

Yale, 77, 79, 229–30
Yalta, 503–5, 514
yellow fever, 405
yellow journalism, 380, 390
Yellowstone National Park, 161, 177
York, Alvin C., 423
Yorktown, 122, 129–30
Young, Brigham, 233
Young Men's Christian Association (YMCA),
    234, 358
Youth for Christ, 532
Yugoslavia, 427, 514, 597–98

Z

Zeisberger, David, 75
Zimmermann telegram, 419
Zinzendorf, Nicholas von, 70

Photograph Credits

The following agencies and individuals have furnished materials to meet the photographic needs of this textbook. We wish to express our gratitude to them for their important contribution.

Alamy
Suzanne R. Altizer
American Philosophical Society
Architect of the Capitol
Associated Press
BigStockPhoto.com
BJU Photo Services
Bob Jones University Museum & Gallery
James Brooks
Buffalo Bill Historical Center
Chessie System Railroads
Chicago History Museum
Colt Industries Firearms Division
Jeff Danziger
Denver Public Library
Department of Defense
The Dolph Briscoe Center for American History
Dover Publications, Inc.
Dwight D. Eisenhower Library
Federal Bureau of Investigation
ScottFinley www.flickr.com/photos/sfinley
Fotolia
Franklin D. Roosevelt Library
Frank H. McClung Museum
Gerald R. Ford Library
Getty Images
George R. Collins
The Granger Collection, New York
Hargrett Rare Book and Manuscript Library
Hemera Technologies
Historical Center of the Presbyterian Church
Hudson Library & Historical Society
Idaho Travel Council
Indiana Historical Bureau
Iowa State University
iStockphoto.com
Jamestown-Yorktown Foundation
Jimmy Carter Library
John F. Kennedy Library
JupiterImages Corporation
Kansas State Historical Society
Landis Valley Village & Farm Museum
Library of Congress
Lyndon Baines Johnson Library
Mayo Foundation
Missouri History Museum, St. Louis
National Archives

National Baseball Library, Cooperstown
National Guard
National Museum of American History
National Park Service
Naval Historical Foundation
Nebraska State Historical Society
The New York Public Library
Northwestern University Library
Ohio Historical Society
Poor Richard, 1733: Almanack
Ronald Reagan Library
Rosenbach Museum & Library
Phyllis Schlafly
The Senate Historical Office
R.T. Smith
Smithsonian Institution
The State Preservation Board, Texas
SuperStock
Syracuse University
Tennessee State Library and Archives
Thinkstock
Tim Keesee
Tuskegee University
Union Pacific Railroad Museum Collection
University of Tennessee
The University of Texas at Arlington Library
The University of Texas at Austin
United States Air Force Museum
U.S. Army
U.S. Army Military History Institute
U.S. Army, Signal Corps
USDA
U.S. Department of State
U.S. Energy Department and Resources Administration
U.S. House of Representatives
U.S. Marine Corps
U.S. Naval Historical Center
U.S. Naval Academy Museum
U.S. Navy
U.S. Senate Collection
Valentine Richmond History Center
Westinghouse Broadcasting and Cable, Inc.
West Point Museum Art Collection
Western History Collection
The White House
The White House Historical Association
Wikimedia Commons

Perry Wright
Woolaroc Museum
Yale University Manuscripts & Archives

Front Matter

Library of Congress xi (top left, top right); Nativestock.com/Marilyn Angel Wynn/Collection Mix: Subjects/Getty Images xi (center left); U.S. Naval Historical Center Photograph. Courtesy of the Navy Art Collection, Washington, DC xi (center right); © iStockphoto.com/ray roper xi (center); DOD/U.S. Army photo taken by Spc. Eric E. Hughes xi (bottom left); © Greg Martin / SuperStock xi (bottom right)

Unit 1

Library of Congress xii (left); © 2010 JupiterImages Corporation xii (right); Hemera Technologies/PhotoObjects.net/Thinkstock 1 (left); Jennie A. Brownscombe/Wikimedia Commons/Public Domain 1 (right)

Chapter 1

Architect of the Capitol/Wikimedia Commons/Public Domain 2; Library of Congress 10 (top left, center left, bottom left, bottom center); Northwestern University Library, Edward S. Curtis's The North American Indian: the Photographic Images, 2001/Library of Congress 10 (bottom right); Library of Congress/Wikimedia Commons/Public Domain 11 (top right); Jim Henderson/Wikimedia Commons/Public Domain 11 (bottom); Scott Finley www.flickr.com/photos/sfinley 12 (both); ©2010 JupiterImages.com 13 (top); Ohio Historical Society 13 (bottom); Frank H. McClung Museum. The University of Tennessee, Knoxville. Carlyle Urello 14; © Ken Kohn. Image from BigStockPhoto.com 17 (top); J. Cipriani/ National Park Service 17 (bottom); © Fotolia/Sharpshot 18; Stock Montage/Getty Images 19; Collection of the U.S. House of Representatives. Discovery of the Hudson River, by Albert Bierstadt, oil on canvas, 1874. Detail. 20

(top); Hulton Archive/Getty Images 20 (bottom)

Chapter 2

MPI/Getty Images 24; Jamestown-Yorktown Foundation 26; Library of Congress 27, 31 (both), 33, 35 (bottom), 38; Architect of the Capitol/Wikimedia Commons/Public Domain 30; BJU Photo Services 34; The Granger Collection, New York 35 (top); A Brief Description of the Province of Carolina on the Coasts of Floreda, Tracy W. McGregor Library of American History, Special Collections, University of Virginia Library 40 (bottom); Courtesy of Hargrett Rare Book and Manuscript Library 41

Chapter 3

John Singleton Copley/Wikimedia Commons/Public Domain, from The Yorck Project. Compilation by Zenodot Verlagsgesellschaft mbH and licensed under the GNU Free Documentation License 44; Library of Congress 46, 47 (bottom), 48, 51; Poor Richard, 1733: An Almanack For the Year of Christ 1733, Richard Saunders (Benjamin Franklin), Rosenbach Museum & Library, Philadelphia, Photo by Peter Harholdt 54

Chapter 4

Library of Congress 61, 65, 66, 74, 77; BJU Press Files/James Brooks, artist 69; David Bjorgen/Wikimedia Commons/ Creative Commons Attribution-Share Alike 3.0 Unported license, GNU Free Documentation License, Version 1.2. 70; 1640 Bay Psalm Book/Rosenbach Museum/Public domain 73

Unit 2

Library of Congress 82 (left); © iStock-photo.com/Thinkstock 82 (right); National Archives 83 (left); SSPL/Getty Images 83 (right)

Chapter 5

Benjamin West/Wikimedia Commons/ Public Domain 84; Wilhelm Lamprecht/ Wikimedia Commons/Public Domain 85; The Granger Collection, New York 88, 90, 95; Library of Congress 91, 92, 94, 97, 98 (both), 100 (both), 102; Library of Congress/Wikimedia Commons/Public Domain 101

Chapter 6

The Granger Collection, New York 104; Library of Congress 106 (both), 113 (top), 114 (bottom), 115, 121 (both), 123, 124; National Archives 111; Emory Kristof/ National Geographic/Getty Images 113 (bottom); Charles Willson Peale/ Wikimedia Commons/Public Domain 114 (top); Copyright © 2008 by Dover Publications, Inc. 117; Americasroof/ Wikimedia Commons/Creative Commons Attribution-Share Alike 2.5 Generic License 120; Courtesy Indiana Historical Bureau, State of Indiana 125; U.S. Senate Collection 126; North Wind Picture Archives / Alamy 127; MPI/Getty Images 128; Architect of the Capitol 130

Chapter 7

Architect of the Capitol 132; The Granger Collection, New York 134; Courtesy of Tim Keesee 137; Wikimedia Commons/ Public Domain 138; Library of Congress 139, 141 (both), 146 (both), 147 (both); Gilbert Stuart/Wikimedia Commons/ Public Domain 148

Chapter 8

Donna Neary/National Guard 151; Library of Congress 152, 159, 164; National Archives 153; ScottyBoy900Q/Wikimedia Commons/GNU Free Documentation License, Version 1.2, Creative Commons Attribution ShareAlike 3.0 License 155; Tennessee State Library and Archives 161; U.S. Navy/Wikimedia Commons/Public Domain 162

Unit 3

Yale University Manuscripts & Archives Digital Images Database/Wikimedia Commons/Public Domain 168 (left); Morse-Vail telegraph key, Division of Work & Industry, National Museum of American History, Behring Center, Smithsonian Institution 168 (right); Library of Congress 169 (left); Haragayato/ Wikimedia Commons/GNU Free Documentation License, Version 1.2 and Creative Commons Attribution-Share Alike 3.0 Unported License 169 (right)

Chapter 9

Library of Congress 170, 171 (bottom), 176 (both), 185, 186, 187; Rembrandt Peale/ Wikimedia Commons/Public Domain 171 (top), 180 (top); Wikimedia Commons/ Public Domain 173 (top); U.S. Department of State/Wikimedia Commons/Public

Domain 173 (bottom); Idaho Travel Council 177 (top); Courtesy American Philosophical Society 177 (bottom); John Vanderlyn/Wikimedia Commons/Public Domain 178; Chicago History Museum 179; MPI/Getty Images 180 (bottom)

Chapter 10

Library of Congress 191, 200, 201 (left, right), 206 (both); Wikimedia Commons/ Public Domain 192, 196; © iStockphoto .com/HultonArchive 201 (center), 202; BJU Photo Services 203; National Portrait Gallery, Smithsonian Institution 204; Woolaroc Museum, Bartlesville, Oklahoma 205

Chapter 11

Library of Congress 211, 217, 222, 223, 224, 226, 227, 229, 233 (both); Colt Industries Firearms Division 213 (top); Chessie System Railroads 220; From the Bob Jones University Museum & Gallery 225; Hulton Archive/Getty Images 230; Wikimedia Commons/Public Domain 231

Chapter 12

Courtesy, Special Collections, The University of Texas at Arlington Library, Arlington, Texas 238; © iStockphoto. com/HultonArchive 240; The State Preservation Board, Austin, Texas 241; Library of Congress 242 (top), 243 (right), 245, 246, 252, 253 (center top); MPI/Getty Images 242 (bottom); Wikimedia Commons/Public Domain 243 (left), 253 (far left, left, center bottom, right); Yale Collection of Western Americana, Beinecke Rare Book and Manuscript Library, Yale University 249; James Reid Lambdin/ Wikimedia Commons/Public Domain 250; © iStockphoto.com/Steven Wynn 253 (far right)

Unit 4

Ricce/Wikimedia Commons/Public domain 256; Hulton Archive/Getty Images 257 (left); Wikimedia Commons/Public domain 257 (right)

Chapter 13

Kansas State Historical Society, Topeka, Kansas, www.kshs.org/research/collec-tions/documents/photos/webuse.htm 258; Wikimedia Commons/Public Domain 259, 263 (top), 266, 269; Library of Congress 261, 263 (bottom), 264, 265, 267, 268, 271, 272, 274 (both); Photographic History

Collection, National Museum of American History, Smithsonian Institution (negative number: 38416C) 262; The Granger Collection, New York 270; National Archives 278

Chapter 14

Library of Congress 280, 289, 293, 304, 305, 308, 309; Wikimedia Commons/ Public Domain 287, 288 (both), 307 (top); Library of Congress/Wikimedia Commons/Public Domain 290; United States Naval Academy Museum 294; National Archives 298; BJU Photo Services 299; National Archives/Wikimedia Commons/Public Domain 303; West Point Museum Art Collection, United States Military Academy, West Point, New York 307 (bottom)

Chapter 15

Copyright © 2008 by Dover Publications, Inc. 311; Wikimedia Commons/Public Domain 312; Library of Congress 313, 315 (both); 322, 323 (center), 324; Cook Collection, Valentine Richmond History Center 317; Library of Congress/ Wikimedia Commons/Public Domain 318, 321, 323 (left, right); U.S. Senate Collection 325

Unit 5

From the collection of Landis Valley Village & Farm Museum, Lancaster, Pa., Pennsylvania Historical & Museum Commission 330; © iStockphoto.com/ christopherconrad 331 (left); Getty Images/Creatas/Thinkstock 331 (right)

Chapter 16

Library of Congress 332, 334, 335, 336, 338, 339 (top, center right), 340, 342, 343, 347, 349, 352, 354 (both), 356 (both), 357; BJUP files 359

Chapter 17

Union Pacific Railroad Museum Collection 361, 363; Library of Congress 364, 369 (top), 375, 379; Solomon D. Butcher Collection, Nebraska State Historical Society, B983-2430, copy and reuse restrictions apply 366, 367; Denver Public Library, Western History Collection, Z-6084 368; BJU Photo Services/Courtesy of Terry Rude 369 (center); National Archives 369 (bottom), 370 (top), 374 (bottom), 381; Kansas State Historical Society, Topeka, Kansas, www.kshs.org/research/collections/documents/

photos/webuse.htm 370 (bottom); Buffalo Chase, by Seth Eastman, 1868, oil on canvas, Collection of the U.S. House of Representatives 371; Library of Congress/ Wikimedia Commons/Public domain 373, 382; Custer's Last Stand, by Edgar Samuel Paxson, oil on canvas, Buffalo Bill Historical Center, Cody, Wyoming; Museum purchase, 19.69 374 (top); General Research Division, The New York Public Library, Astor, Lenox and Tilden Foundations 377; Special Collections Research Center, Syracuse University 380

Chapter 18

Library of Congress 385, 387, 389, 391 (bottom), 395, 398, 400, 402 (bottom), 403; National Archives 391 (top), 402 (top); Tuskegee University/Polk, Courtesy Iowa State University Library/ Special Collections Department 404; By permission of Mayo Foundation for Medical Education and Research. All rights reserved. 405; Historical Center of the Presbyterian Church in America, Photo Collection-http://www.pcahistory .org 406; Courtesy of Bob Jones University 407

Chapter 19

The U.S. Army Military History Institute 411; Library of Congress 412, 413, 414 (bottom), 420, 421 (left), 426, 427; The Robert Runyon Photograph Collection, 00196, The Dolph Briscoe Center for American History, The University of Texas at Austin 414 (top); BJUP Files/Public Domain 417; Courtesy of Tim Keesee/ Public Domain 421 (center left, center right, right); Signal Corps, U.S. Army 423; National Archives 424, 425

Unit 6

C. Corleis/Wikimedia Commons/ Creative Commons Attribution-Share Alike 3.0 Unported license 430; Bill Faulk/ Wikimedia Commons/Public Domain 431 (left, center); National Archives/ Wikimedia Commons/Public Domain 431 (right)

Chapter 20

Missouri History Museum, St. Louis 432; Library of Congress 434, 437, 438, 439, 440, 441, 444, 447; National Baseball Library, Cooperstown, NY 442; National Archives 443; US Department of Justice/ Wikimedia Commons/Public Domain 445 (left); Chicago History Museum/Getty

Images 445 (right); Sears Roebuck Catalog (1919)/Wikimedia Commons/Public Domain 448; Westinghouse Broadcasting and Cable, Inc. 449 (left); © iStockphoto .com/Erick Jones 449 (center); The Granger Collection, New York 451

Chapter 21

Library of Congress 455, 456, 457, 462, 467 (bottom), 468 (all), 470 (left), 471 (both); National Archives 458, 479; Signal Corps Photographer/Wikimedia Commons/ Public Domain 461; Franklin D. Roosevelt Library 465, 466, 467 (top), 474, 476; Library of Congress/Wikimedia Commons/ Public Domain 469; Lewis W. Hine/ George Eastman House/Getty Images 475 (top); USDA photo/National Archives 475 (bottom); Federal Bureau of Investigation 477 (top left, top right); SSPL/Getty Images 477 (bottom); Petrified Collection/The Image Bank/Getty Images 478

Chapter 22

Joe Rosenthal, Associated Press 481; National Archives 482, 485, 487, 492 (top), 494 (top, bottom left), 503 (bottom), 504, 505; Wikimedia Commons/Public Domain 484 (both), 500, 502 (bottom); Library of Congress 490, 494 (bottom right), 496 (left), 499 (left); © R.T. Smith used by permission of Brad Smith 491; Naval Historical Foundation 492 (bottom), 502 (top), 507 (bottom); United States Air Force Museum 496 (right); Franklin D. Roosevelt Library 499 (right); Keystone/Getty Images 503 (top); U.S. Energy Department and Resources Administration 507 (top)

Unit 7

Fletcher6/Wikimedia Commons/Creative Commons Attribution-Share Alike 3.0 Unported License 510 (left); © iStockphoto .com/ranplett 510 (right); © iStockphoto .com/hadi djunaedi 511 (center); © iStock-photo.com/Sven Hoppe 511 (right)

Chapter 23

National Archives 512, 516 (top), 519 (all), 521; Steve Cadman/Wikimedia Commons/ Creative Commons Attribution-Share Alike 2.0 Generic license 513; Library of Congress 516 (bottom), 518; United States Marine Corps photo by Corporal Peter McDonald/ Wikimedia Commons/Public Domain 517; Howard Sochurek//Time Life Pictures/ Getty Images 522 (top); NY Daily News Archive via Getty Images 522 (bottom);

The Senate Historical Office 523 (top); Courtesy Dwight D. Eisenhower Library 523 (bottom); MPI/Getty Images 524; The White House Historical Association/John F. Kennedy Library 526 (top); ©APIC/Getty Images 526 (bottom); Michael Ochs Archives/Getty Images 527; Hulton Archive/Getty Images 529; Central Press/Getty Images 530; BJU Photo Services 532

Chapter 24

U.S. Air Force photo/Wikimedia Commons/Public Domain 534; Lyndon Baines Johnson Library 536 (top), 544; The Lyndon Baines Johnson Library and Museum 536 (bottom); National Archives 539 (top), 548; George R. Collins 539 (bottom); New York World-Telegram/Wikimedia Commons/Public Domain 542; © iStockphoto.com/Denise Roup 543; Joseph Louw/Time & Life Pictures/Getty Images 545 (top); AGIP - Rue des Archives / The Granger Collection, New York 545 (bottom); Hudson Library & Historical Society 546; John Filo/Getty Images 550; Library of Congress 551

Chapter 25

White House Photograph Courtesy Gerald R. Ford Library 554; Senate Historical Office 556; Library of Congress 557; Ted Thai//Time Life Pictures/Getty Images 558; Courtesy of Phyllis Schlafly 561; Ron Galella/WireImage/Getty Images 563; Jimmy Carter Library, National Archives 564; Perry Wright 565; Suzanne R. Altizer 567; Terry Ashe/Time & Life Pictures/Getty Images 568; Courtesy Ronald Reagan Library 570

Chapter 26

Courtesy Ronald Reagan Library 572, 573 (bottom), 574, 575, 580; National Archives/Wikimedia Commons/Public Domain 573

(top); Associated Press 579 (both); The White House/Pete Souza 582; AP Photo/Dieter Endlicher 584; AP Photo/Dominique Mollard 585; The White House 589

Chapter 27

The White House 591; Rob Nelson/Time Life Pictures/Getty Images 593; James A. Parcell/The Washington Post/Getty Images 594 (top); RICHARD ELLIS/AFP/Getty Images 594 (bottom); AP Photo/Wilfredo Lee 598; Courtesy of Jeff Danziger 601 (top); The White House/John Ficaro 601 (bottom); Spencer Platt/Getty Images 602; AP Photo/Doug Mills 603 (left); Official USMC photo by Lance Cpl. James Patrick Douglas 603 (right); Department of Defense 604; AP Photo/Susan Walsh 606 (left); Mark Wilson/Getty Images 606 (right); JIM WATSON/AFP/Getty Images 607